W9-BPN-394

Organization Theory and Design

FIRST CANADIAN EDITION

Organization Theory and Design

FIRST CANADIAN EDITION

Richard L. Daft

VANDERBILT UNIVERSITY

Ann Armstrong

ROTMAN SCHOOL OF MANAGEMENT,
UNIVERSITY OF TORONTO

NELSON EDUCATION

NELSON EDUCATION

Organization Theory and Design, First Canadian Edition

by Richard L. Daft and Ann Armstrong

Associate Vice President, Editorial Director:
Evelyn Veitch

Editor-in-Chief, Higher Education:
Anne Williams

Acquisitions Editor:
Amie Plourde

Marketing Manager:
Kathaleen McCormick

Managing Developmental Editor:
Lesley Mann

Photo Researcher:
Beth Yarzab

Permissions Coordinator:
Beth Yarzab

Production Service:
Macmillan Publishing Solutions

Copy Editor:
Karen Rolfe

Proofreader:
Dianne Fowlie

Indexer:
Maura Brown

Manufacturing Manager:
Joanne McNeil

Design Director:
Ken Phipps

Managing Designer:
Katherine Strain

Interior Design:
ArtPlus Limited

Cover Design:
Dianna Little

Cover Image:
Freeman Patterson/Masterfile

Compositor:
Macmillan Publishing Solutions

Printer:
Edwards Brothers

Printed and bound in the United States
1 2 3 4 11 10 09 08

For more information contact Nelson Education Ltd., 1120 Birchmount Road, Toronto, Ontario, M1K 5G4. Or you can visit our Internet site at http://www.nelson.com

Library and Archives Canada Cataloguing in Publication

Daft, Richard L
Organization theory and design / Richard L. Daft, Ann Armstrong.—1st Canadian ed.

Includes bibliographical references and index.

ISBN 978-0-17-644102-9

1. Organization. 2. Organizational sociology—Case studies. I. Armstrong, Ann, 1951- II. Title.

HD58.8.D33 2008 658.4

C2008-906272-8

ISBN-13: 978-0-17-644102-9
ISBN-10: 0-17-644102-6

Brief Contents

Contents

Preface

When I was approached to prepare a Canadian version of the ninth edition of Dr. Daft's *Organization Theory and Design*, I was excited to build on his wonderful book. In the process, I have learned so much about Canada and, particularly, the variety of organizations that span sea to sea to sea. I hope that I have been able to capture the richness of the Canadian experience for both the students and faculty who will use this book.

I chose the book's cover to symbolize Canadian organizations as I was struck by the overwhelming presence of silver birch trees in Canada when I took a VIA train tour across the country. Freeman Patterson, who took the photograph, is one of our most talented photographers. I have come to appreciate that Canada is a splendid country whose organizations are interesting to analyze. I hope that you will also come to a renewed appreciation!

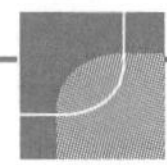

Distinguishing Features of the First Canadian Edition

The Canadianization of Dr. Daft's book has been extensive. However, a number of U.S. and international examples were retained or updated to accurately represent Canada's role in the world. Each chapter has a cartoon to highlight the chapter's concepts in a light-hearted way.

Leading by Design The Leading by Design features describe organizations that have undergone a major shift in organizational design, strategic direction, values, or culture as they strive to be more competitive in today's turbulent global environment. Many of these organizations are applying new design ideas, such as network organizing, e-business, or temporary systems for flexibility and innovation. Examples of Leading by Design organizations include Four Seasons, Médecins sans Frontières (MSF), Manitoba Telecom Services, GE Bromont, and WestJet Airlines.

Book Marks Book Marks, a special feature of this text, are book reviews that reflect current issues of concern for managers working in real-life organizations. These reviews describe the varied ways organizations are meeting the challenges of today's changing environment. New Book Marks in the first Canadian edition include a review of Andrea Mandel-Campbell's *Why Mexicans Don't Drink Molson,* Don Tapscott and Anthony D. Williams's *Wikinomics: How Mass Collaboration Changes Everything,* and Joel Bakan's *The Corporation: The Pathological Pursuit of Profit and Power.*

New Case Examples This edition contains many new examples to illustrate theoretical concepts. Many examples are Canadian, and all are based on real organizations. They include iStockphoto.com: Turning Community into Commerce, Jones Soda, The Print Shop at Eva's Phoenix, Apple, Ivanhoe Mines, and eBay Canada.

In Practice There are many cases used within chapters to illustrate specific concepts. They include Mackenzie Valley Natural Gas Pipeline Project, Garrison Guitars, Aravind Eye Hospital, Joe Fresh Style, Apotex, McCain Foods, and Doepker Industries, to name only a few.

A Look Inside This feature introduces each chapter with a relevant and interesting organizational example. Many examples are Canadian, and all are based on real organizations. New examples include Air Canada, Alcan, InnoCentive.com, and Anishinabek Nation, to name a few.

PDA Located in the chapter margins, this feature tells students how to use concepts to analyze cases and manage organizations.

Text Exhibits Frequent exhibits are used to help students visualize organizational relationships, and the artwork has been redone to communicate concepts more clearly.

Summary and Interpretation The summary and interpretation section tells students how the chapter points are important in the broader context of organizational theory.

Cases for Analysis These cases are tailored to chapter concepts and provide a vehicle for student analysis and discussion.

Integrative Cases The integrative cases at the end of the text are designed to encourage in-depth discussion and involvement. These cases include Tim Horton's, the Hospital for Sick Children, Rogers' Chocolates, CIBC, Solomon Business School, and Workbrain. The first two cases were written for the first Canadian edition.

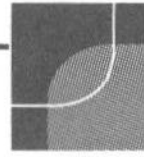

New Concepts

Many concepts have been added or expanded in this edition. New material has been added on culture, learning, and performance; virtual network organization structures; applying ethics to create socially responsible organizations; outsourcing; lean manufacturing; customer relationship management; political tactics for increasing and using managerial power; applying business intelligence; and the use of global coordination mechanisms for transferring knowledge and innovation. Many ideas are aimed at helping students learn to design organizations for an environment characterized by uncertainty, a renewed emphasis on ethics and social responsibility, and the need for a speedy response to change, crises, or shifting customer expectations. In addition, coping with the complexity of today's global environment is explored thoroughly. To help students see the relationships among the concepts, I have designed a Framework for the Organization of This Book, which can be used both as a course and a concept map. The Framework appears in Chapter 1 on page 33.

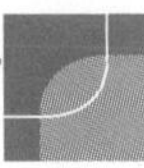

Chapter Organization

Each chapter is highly focused and is organized into a logical framework. Many organization theory textbooks treat material in sequential fashion, such as "Here's View A, Here's View B, Here's View C," and so on. *Organization Theory and Design* shows how they apply in organizations. Moreover, each chapter sticks to the essential point. Students are not introduced to extraneous material or confusing methodological squabbles that occur among organizational researchers. The body of research in most areas points to a major trend, which is reported here. Several chapters develop a framework that organizes major ideas into an overall scheme.

As I was working on the book, I often solicited ideas from my undergraduate and graduate students. I am sure that they will see their impact! The combination of organizational theory concepts, book reviews, examples of organizations recommended by the students, case illustrations, experiential exercises, and other teaching devices is designed to effectively meet students' learning needs.

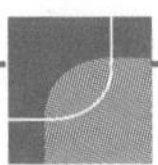

Chapter Changes in the Canadian Edition

Specific changes for the Canadian edition include the following:

Chapter 1: Organizations and Organizational Theory

- The section on diversity has been revised with Canadian demographics.
- The section on types of organizations includes more material on nonprofits.
- The new In Practice box looks at the Mackenzie Valley Natural Gas Pipeline Project.
- The new Exhibit 1.8 outlines the Framework for the Organization of This Book.

Chapter 2: Strategy, Organizational Design, and Effectiveness

- The section on employee development examines the success of Winnipeg-based Wellington West Capital in recruiting and developing employees.
- The discussion of other factors affecting organization design includes new material on issues unique to Canada, from the challenges of structuring an organization in both Quebec and English Canada to the threats and opportunities posed when foreign organizations take over iconic Canadian companies.
- A new section on new directions sets out the big questions strategy seeks to answer, including how new perspectives and lines of research are emerging as a result of shifting dynamics in the global economy and the environment.

Chapter 3: Fundamentals of Organizational Structure

- A new In Practice box discusses the organizational changes at Ford that led to the development of the Escape Hybrid.
- "The Print Shop at Eva's Phoenix" is a new case that examines how a socially and environmentally responsible commercial printer helps homeless and at-risk youth in Toronto achieve self-sufficiency.

Chapter 4: The External Environment

- The Task Environment section examines the implications of Canada's lag in training and skills development.
- The section on general environment looks at the organizational implications of Canada's growing foreign-born population.
- Recent trends in mergers and acquisitions rates of Canadian organizations are discussed in the section on organization.

Chapter 5: Interorganizational Relationships

- The section on the changing role of management discusses how various organizations came together to form the Global Business Coalition on HIV/AIDS, Tuberculosis and Malaria (GBC).
- The section on resource dependence shows how various Canadian sports organizations developed strategies to use their power differences and reduce their dependence on the environment.
- Vancouver-based Angiotech, Leave No Trace Canada, and Ontario Craft Brewers are discussed as examples of organizations that achieved higher levels of innovation and performance through the development of interorganizational relationships.

Chapter 6: Designing Organizations for the International Environment

- Vancouver-based biopharmaceutical company QLT is discussed as an example of global expansion through international strategic alliances.
- Wal-Mart's difficulties applying its North American format to the German market are contrasted with the successes enjoyed by Bombardier and Tim's Canadian Deli in the section on models for global versus local opportunities.
- Gesteland's four major cultural value patterns that characterize countries around the world are examined in the section on national value systems.

Chapter 7: Manufacturing and Service Technologies

- The section on service firms describes how Rosenort, Manitoba–based Lo-Pel Manufacturing provides service support for customers of its earthmoving scrapers.
- Organizational redesign at Celestica is examined in the section on structural priority.
- The 11 core principles that underlie sociotechnical systems thinking and design are listed and explained in the section on the impact of technology on job design.

Chapter 8: Information Technology and Control

- The section on organizational decision-making systems profiles information systems of various sizes, from CN's SmartYard to Longo Brothers Fruit Markets' Market PO.
- Trillium Health Centre's THINK dashboard system is highlighted in the section on management control systems.

Chapter 9: Organization Size, Life Cycle, and Decline

- Corel founder Michael Cowpland's takeover of ZIM Technologies International Inc. is discussed as an example of the entrepreneurial stage of an organization's life cycle.
- The section on other approaches to reducing bureaucracy looks at how changes in the value of the Canadian dollar have prompted Canadian manufacturers to streamline their processes.
- The new In Practice box on Dofasco looks at measures the steel company took to assist employees through downsizing and layoffs.

Chapter 10: Organizational Culture and Ethical Values

- Key factors in the discipline culture, as identified by Jim Collins, are discussed in this chapter.
- In the section on sources of ethical values in organizations, Roger Martin's article "The Virtue Matrix: Calculating the Return on Corporate Responsibility" is described as a tool that provides guidance to CEOs, and a related group exercise appears in the end-of-chapter Workshop.
- Green initiatives for the 2010 winter Olympics are included in the discussion of values-based leadership.
- Me to We is a Canadian social enterprise that provides ethically manufactured apparel, with 50 percent of the profit going to Free The Children; the organization is discussed in the section on corporate culture and ethics in a global environment.

Chapter 11: Innovation and Change

- New material on the history of innovation in Canada has been added at the beginning of this chapter.
- The section on new products and services looks at the stories behind famous flops such as the Bricklin car and Avro Arrow.
- The discussion of techniques for implementation introduces ExperiencePoint, a Toronto-based company that develops web-based simulations to help organizations predict outcomes before proceeding with change.

Chapter 12: Decision-Making Processes

- The opening vignette features the Anishinabek Nation's co-management approach to water management of the Great Lakes.
- The discussion of constraint and tradeoffs in individual decision making looks at the kinds of complex decisions that had to be made during the 2003 SARS crisis in Toronto.
- The new In Practice box Algorithms Rule! describes efforts by Canadian researchers to apply principles of management science to various problems—from reducing waiting times to finding the optimal level of radiation that can be used in cancer treatment.

Chapter 13: Conflict, Power, and Politics

- The section on intergroup conflict in organizations discusses conflict in the history of the Canadian Autoworkers' Union.
- The approach to formal power exhibited by Sylvia Vogel, founder and CEO of Québec's Canderm Pharmacal, is examined in the section on sources of vertical power.
- A new In Practice box looks at the case of Dr. Nancy Olivieri and Apotex Inc. as an example of how financial power sources can bring pressure to influence organizations.

Supplements for Instructors

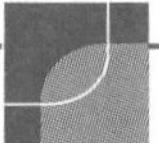

Instructor's Resource CD-ROM (ISBN 13: 978-0-17-644110-4/ISBN 10: 0-17-644110-7) Key instructor ancillaries are provided on CD-ROM, giving instructors the ultimate tool for customizing lectures and presentations. The ancillaries have all been revised by Ann Armstrong, the Canadian author, to ensure they reflect the contents of the text. These ancillaries include:

Instructor's Manual. The Instructor's Manual contains chapter overviews, chapter outlines, lecture enhancements, discussion questions, discussion of workbook activities, discussion of chapter cases, Internet activities, and teaching notes and case notes for integrative cases.

Test Materials—Introducing NETA. In most college and university courses, a large percentage of student assessment is based on multiple-choice testing. Many instructors use multiple-choice questions reluctantly, believing that it is a methodology best used for teaching what a student *remembers* rather than what she or he has *learned*. Furthermore, the quality of publisher-supplied test banks can vary.

Nelson Education Ltd. believes that a good quality multiple-choice test bank can test not just what students remember, but ***higher-level thinking*** skills as well. Recognizing the importance of multiple-choice testing in today's classroom, Nelson has created the Nelson Education Testing Advantage program (NETA) to ensure the high quality of our test banks.

The test bank for *Organization Theory and Design* was developed under the Nelson Education Testing Advantage. NETA was created in partnership with David DiBattista of Brock University, a specialist in the psychology of testing. NETA ensures that test bank authors have had training in two areas: developing clear multiple-choice test questions while avoiding common errors in construction and creating multiple-choice test questions that "get beyond remembering" to assess higher-level thinking.

The outcome of NETA development is that as you select multiple-choice questions from your Nelson test bank for inclusion in tests, you can easily identify whether items are memory-based or require your students to engage in higher-level thinking. By making your selections appropriately, you can construct tests that contain the proportion of recall and higher-level questions that reflects your personal instructional goals.

All NETA test banks include David DiBattista's guide for instructors, "Multiple Choice Tests: Getting Beyond Remembering." This guide has been designed to assist you in using Nelson test banks to achieve your desired outcomes in the classroom.

The NETA test materials for *Organization Theory and Design* are provided in two formats:

- **Test Bank.** The Test Bank consists of multiple-choice, true/false, and short-answer questions. Files are provided in rich text format for easy editing and printing with all common word-processing formats.
- **ExamView.** All Test Bank questions are included in the ExamView computerized version. The easy-to-use software is compatible with Microsoft Windows and Mac. Instructors can create tests by selecting questions from the question bank, modifying these questions as desired, and adding new questions they write themselves. Instructors can administer quizzes online and export tests to WebCT, Blackboard, and other formats.

PowerPoint® Lecture Presentation. The PowerPoint® Lecture Presentation enables instructors to customize their own multimedia classroom presentations. The package contains approximately 150 slides, including figures and tables from the text, as well as outside materials to supplement chapter concepts. Material is organized by chapter and can be modified or expanded for individual classroom use. PowerPoints are also easily printed to create customized transparency masters.

Image Bank. Many of the figures and illustrations from the book are provided in jpeg format so instructors can incorporate them into PowerPoint® presentations they create. (Note: Some graphics may not be available due to copyright restrictions.)

Day One. Day One—Prof InClass is a PowerPoint® presentation that instructors can customize to orient students to the class and their text at the beginning of the course.

Website (http://www.orgtheory.nelson.com). The Daft website is a comprehensive, resource-rich location for both instructors and students to find pertinent information. The Instructor Resources section contains an Instructor's Manual download, PowerPoint® download, Day One—ProfInClass presentation, and case material.

Turning Point®: JoinIn™ on TurningPoint®. Now instructors can author, deliver, show, access, and grade, all in PowerPoint®—with no toggling back and forth between screens! JoinIn™ on Turning Point® is the only classroom response software tool that provides true PowerPoint® integration. With JoinIn™, instructors are no longer tied to their computer. They can walk about their classroom while lecturing, showing slides, and collecting and displaying responses with ease. There is simply no easier or more effective way to turn a lecture hall into a personal, fully interactive experience for students. Using JoinIn™ on TurningPoint® is as easy as using PowerPoint®!

***Experiential Exercises in Organization Theory and Design,* Second Edition (ISBN 13: 978-0324-36010-3/ISBN 10: 0-324-36010-X).** Written by H. Eugene Baker III and Steven K. Paulson of the University of North Florida, this book is tailored to the Table of Contents in Daft's *Organization Theory and Design*. The core purpose of *Experiential Exercises in Organization Theory and Design* is to provide courses in organizational theory with a set of classroom exercises that will help students better understand and internalize the basic principles of the course. The chapters of the book cover the most basic and widely covered concepts in the field. Each chapter focuses on a central topic, such as organizational power, production technology, or organizational culture, and provides all necessary materials to fully participate in three different exercises. Some exercises are intended to be completed by individuals, others in groups, and still others can be used either way. The exercises range from instrumentation-based and assessment questionnaires to actual creative production activities.

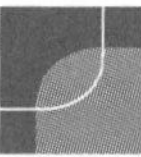

Supplements for Students

Website (http://www.orgtheory.nelson.com) The Student section of the website includes self-quizzes so students can test their knowledge of each chapter. Multiple-choice and true/false questions are included, as well as an online glossary and other materials.

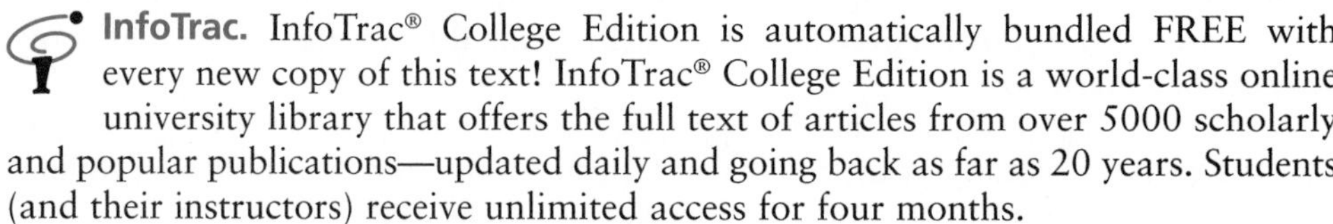

InfoTrac. InfoTrac® College Edition is automatically bundled FREE with every new copy of this text! InfoTrac® College Edition is a world-class online university library that offers the full text of articles from over 5000 scholarly and popular publications—updated daily and going back as far as 20 years. Students (and their instructors) receive unlimited access for four months.

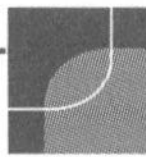

Acknowledgements for the First Canadian Edition

First, I would like to thank Dick Daft. Not only did he write a wonderful book, but also sent me useful material for the first Canadian edition. Among my Rotman School of Management colleagues, I would like to thank Vice-Dean Peter Pauly, who has been so enthusiastic about the project. I thank my colleagues Alan Saks and Uli Menzefricke, both seasoned textbook writers, for orienting me to the realities of writing a textbook! I thank Alison Kemper for her work on Chapter 2, which she did right after she finished her comprehensive exam in the School's strategy Ph.D. program. As well, I would like to thank Dean Roger Martin for providing the special opportunity to direct the School's social enterprise initiative.

The reviewers made an especially important contribution. They praised many features, were critical of things that didn't work well, and offered valuable suggestions. I was impressed by the constructive nature of their feedback. Thanks to

Don Ausman
Concordia University College of Alberta

Tom Cooper
Memorial University

Gudrun Curri
Dalhousie University

Gerald Hunt
Ryerson University

The team at Nelson are amazing! Amie Plourde, Acquisitions Editor, was always open to my off-the-wall suggestions. Karen Rolfe, freelance copyeditor, found my errors and made valuable suggestions. Beth Yarzab, permissions and photo researcher, worked so diligently to ensure that the permissions were received in a timely way. Joanne McNeil, Manufacturing Manager; Kathaleen McCormick, Marketing Manager; and Susan Calvert, Director of Content and Media Production, worked hard to ensure that the book would be well received by students and faculty alike. I would like to thank Charu Khanna and Gunjan Chandola for their patience as we worked on the last stages of book production. The first Canadian edition would not have been completed if it were not for Lesley Mann, Managing Developmental Editor! I really enjoyed working with Lesley—particularly her intellect and her wit. Lesley kept me on track and was a gentle and firm taskmaster.

Finally, I want to thank my friends and family who heard more about the book than they wanted to hear, and listened so patiently! I dedicate this book in loving memory of my Mother, whose advice and kindness I miss.

Ann Armstrong

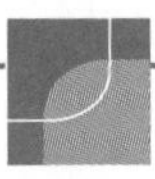

Postscript from the Publisher

Nelson Education Ltd. and Dr. Armstrong have made a donation to one of Canada's social enterprises, The Print Shop of Eva's Phoenix, in recognition of its innovative design, which marries social and economic outcomes. See page 126 for the case that describes this exciting company!

PART 1

Introduction to Organizations

1. Organizations and Organizational Theory

1

Organizations and Organizational Theory

The Canadian Press/Winnipeg Free Press/MARC GALLANT

A Look Inside

Air Canada

Air Canada filed for bankruptcy protection on April 1, 2003. Robert Milton, CEO and chair (see photo), was ridiculed for managing a monopoly into bankruptcy! However, under his leadership, Air Canada emerged from bankruptcy on September 30, 2004. Air Canada cut thousands of jobs, renegotiated contracts with its 30,000 unionized employees, slashed fares, and eliminated free drinks and meals on many of its flights. In November 2005, Robert Milton was named CEO of the year by *Report on Business Magazine,* which lauded Milton for managing the massive restructuring of Air Canada and for repositioning the airline to offer smaller, more cost-efficient planes for regional routes. "While Air Canada spilled almost five billion dollars in red ink between 2000 and 2004 and wiped out billions more in shareholder value, . . . [it] is poised to post a healthy profit [in 2005 and 2006]."[1]

Background

Air Canada has had a bumpy history since it was founded as Trans-Canada Airlines in 1937. As Canada's national airline, it started with three planes and $5 million. Forty years later, it had revenues of more than $500 million and 90 planes. In 1977, Air Canada was reorganized under the *Air Canada Act*. In 1988, Air Canada was privatized and 43 percent of its shares sold to the public. The privatization was designed to level the competitive environment between Air Canada and its chief competitor, Canadian Airlines International, (CAI). In 1989, the privatization was complete. By 1991, CAI was suffering financially and the two airlines began merger talks.

The 1992 recession in North America hit both airlines hard. Both were losing a million dollars a day as passenger volumes dropped dramatically. Air Canada suspended its freight operations and laid off more than 2,000 employees. Air Canada then suggested a merger with CAI, which the latter accepted. However, Air Canada had second thoughts about managing the $7.7 billion dollar debt and the deal did not proceed.

The federal government deregulated flights between Canada and the United States and, in 1999, suspended the *Competition Act* to let the two airlines discuss restructuring. At that time, the Onex Corporation attempted, unsuccessfully, to buy Air Canada. By year's end, Air Canada won its bid for CAI after it received more than 50 percent of CAI's shares and struck a deal with American Airlines for its 25 percent stake in CAI.

Soon after September 11, 2001, as Air Canada's losses continued to mount, it asked the federal government for $4 billion dollars in aid, cut 5,000 jobs, and grounded 84 planes. In early 2002, Air Canada announced its biggest loss—$1.25 billion! In late 2002, it announced that it would no longer issue paper tickets for domestic flights. Job cuts continued and, in 2003, Air Canada filed for bankruptcy protection. After difficult and often acrimonious negotiations, both with potential investors and the unions representing Air Canada's staff, Air Canada took flight again.

Air Canada was restructured; Robert Milton became CEO and chair of a new parent company, ACE Aviation Holdings. The company also got an American investor, Cerbrus Capital Management, which invested $250 million. ACE Aviation Holdings debuted on the Toronto Stock Exchange on October 1, 2004. Its shares traded at $20 and have traded in the range of $16 to $32 since. In the summer of 2005, Air Canada had a profit of $168 million in the preceding quarter and had an average plane capacity of 80 percent.

Competition Heats Up

As Air Canada was recovering from its near-death experience, two new airlines entered the Canadian industry—WestJet Airlines (WestJet) and Jetsgo. They offered cheap, no-frills flights and were able to take one-third of Air Canada's domestic business. Although Jetsgo went out of business, WestJet continues to thrive.

WestJet was founded in 1996 by four Calgary entrepreneurs. They modelled their low-fare airline on Southwest Airlines in the United States. WestJet took off with 220 employees and three planes that flew between five cities. Since then, WestJet has grown dramatically and flies throughout Canada and into the United States. In 2000, the four founders received the Ernst & Young Entrepreneur of the Year Award and, in 2003, WestJet was named Canada's second most respected corporation in an Ipsos Reid survey of 255 of Canada's leading CEOs.[2]

Soon after, WestJet found itself caught in an industrial espionage scandal. Air Canada accused WestJet executives of spying by tapping into its website and of stealing confidential information. Air Canada filed a $220 million lawsuit against WestJet. WestJet did not deny the accusations; the vice-president of strategic planning for WestJet resigned. Clive Beddoe, president of WestJet, apologized and WestJet paid $15.5 million to settle the suit. "WestJet, which typically casts itself as the David to Air Canada's Goliath, admitted in a joint statement . . . that its campaign of online snooping 'was both unethical and unacceptable' and offered a rare apology to Air Canada and Robert Milton . . ."[3]

The Survivor

Robert Milton survived the turbulence at Air Canada. When asked what he had learned about himself as he was vilified throughout the restructuring proess, he commented

> When you know your game—and I believe I do know the airline industry—and you know where you've got to take them, sometimes you just have to put your head down and just drive through the walls and just stop listening to all the people who tell you that it can't be done. Because a lot of those people that said it couldn't be done are now awfully quiet. And so it really was about knowing the business and knowing how we had to change and now I think even those that weren't too happy recognize they're a lot better off.[4]

Welcome to the exciting and complex world of organizational theory. The shifting fortunes of Air Canada illustrate organizational theory in action. Everyone at Air Canada was deeply involved in organizational theory every day at work. Managers did not fully understand how the organization related to the environment or how it should function internally. Familiarity with organizational theory helped Robert Milton and his management team analyze and diagnose what was happening and the changes needed to keep the company competitive. Organizational theory gives us the tools to explain Air Canada's birth, decline, and rebirth and to understand Air Canada's turnaround. It helps us explain what happened in the past, as well as what may happen in the future, so that we can manage organizations more effectively.

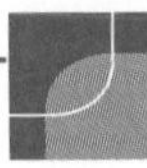

Organizational Theory in Action

Topics

The Air Canada case illustrates many of the topics in the book. We can see the importance of choosing the right **change strategy** and then designing the right structure. We see the importance of the changing environment and its impact on Air Canada's effectiveness. We see the move to electronic technology. We learn that organizations go through life cycles and face crises along the way. We also see that organizations face ethical challenges and tough decisions must be made and conflict addressed. These are some of the topics that organizational theory examines.

Of course, the concepts of organizational theory are not limited to Air Canada. The Ganong family has an acute understanding of the impact of changing environmental conditions on their 134-year-old New Brunswick chocolate business. Mr. Ganong notes that "[you've] got four moving parts underneath this business . . . exchange rates, corn syrup, sugar and cocoa."[5] Global organizations such as IBM, Hewlett-Packard, and Ford Motor Company have all undergone major structural transformations using concepts based in organizational theory. Organizational theory also applies to nonprofit organizations such as Free the Children, Heart and Stroke Foundation, local arts organizations, colleges and universities, and the Make-a-Wish Foundation. Rock groups such as the Rolling Stones benefit from an appreciation of organizational theory (see this chapter's Leading by Design box).

Organizational theory draws lessons from organizations such as the Rolling Stones, IBM, and Air Canada and makes those lessons available to students and managers. The story of Air Canada's rebirth is important because it demonstrates that even large, successful organizations are vulnerable, that lessons are not learned automatically, and that organizations are only as strong as their decision makers. Organizations are not static; they continuously adapt to shifts in the external environment. Today, many companies are facing the need to transform themselves into dramatically different organizations because of new challenges in the environment.

PDA

Remember...

Do not ignore the external environment or protect the organization from it. Because the environment is unpredictable, do not expect to achieve complete order and rationality within the organization. Strive for a balance between order and flexibility.

Current Challenges

Research into hundreds of organizations provides the knowledge base to make Air Canada and other organizations more effective. For example, challenges facing organizations today are quite different from those of the past, and thus the concept of organizations and organizational theory is evolving. For one thing, the world is changing more rapidly than ever before. Surveys of top executives indicate that coping with rapid change is the most common problem facing managers and organizations.[6] Some specific challenges are dealing with globalization, maintaining high standards of ethics and social responsibility, responding rapidly to environmental changes and customer needs, managing the digital workplace, and supporting diversity.

Globalization. The cliché that the world is getting smaller is dramatically true for today's organizations. With rapid advances in technology and communications, the time it takes to exert influence around the world from even the most remote locations has been reduced from years to only seconds. Markets, technologies, and organizations are increasingly interconnected.[7] Today's organizations have to feel "at home" anywhere in the world. Companies can locate different parts of the organization wherever it makes the most business sense: top leadership in one country, technical brainpower and production in other locales. A related trend is to contract out some functions to organizations in other countries or to partner with foreign organizations to gain global advantage. India's Wipro used to sell cooking oils; today, its 15,000 employees develop sophisticated software applications, design semiconductors, and manage back-office solutions for giant companies from all over the world, including Nortel, Home Depot, and Sony. Korea's Samsung Electronics, which has manufacturing plants in 14 countries, has long supplied components for U.S. computer firms, and it recently designed a new laptop that it will manufacture for Texas-based Dell Computer. Many of Intel's new chip circuits are designed by companies in India and China. These organizations can do the job for 50 to 60 percent less than organizations based in the United States, creating new advantages as well as greater competition for North American organizations.[8]

This growing interdependence means that the environment for companies is becoming extremely complex and extremely competitive. Organizations have to learn to cross lines of time, culture, and geography in order to survive. Companies large and small are searching for the right structures and processes that can

Leading *by Design*

The Rolling Stones

They may be old, but they keep on rocking and rolling after more than 40 years in the music business! The Rolling Stones have enjoyed phenomenal commercial success in recent decades, generating billions of dollars in revenue from record sales, song rights, concert tickets, sponsorships, and merchandising.

The Rolling Stones group was recently cited as one of the world's ten most enduring organizations, according to a study commissioned by consulting firm Booz Allen Hamilton. One reason for the Stones' success is that the band operates like an effective global business organization. The Stones have set up a solid organizational structure, with different divisions to run different aspects of the business, such as touring or merchandising. At the top of the organization is a core top management team made up of the four band members: Mick Jagger, who acts as a sort of CEO, Keith Richards, Charlie Watts, and Ronnie Wood. This core team manages a group of somewhat autonomous yet interlocking companies that include Promotour, Promopub, Promotone, and Musidor, each dedicated to a particular part of the overall business. At times, depending on what's happening in the organization, each company might employ only a few dozen people. When the band is touring, on the other hand, head count goes way up and the organization resembles a flourishing start-up company. Jagger himself keeps a close eye on the market-price range for concert tickets so that the band can keep their prices competitive. That sometimes means cutting costs and increasing efficiency to make sure the organization turns a profit.

The Stones also recognize the importance of interorganizational partnerships, cutting sponsorship deals with big companies such as Sprint, Anheuser-Busch, and Microsoft, which reportedly paid $4 million for the rights to "Start Me Up" for the launch of Windows 95. And they hire lawyers, accountants, managers, and consultants to keep in touch with changes in the environment and manage relationships with customers (fans), partners, employees, record companies, promoters, and tour sites. Jagger learned from the early days that creativity and talent aren't enough to ensure success—in the mid-1960s, the band was selling millions of records but still living hand to mouth. Today, effective control systems and widespread information sharing make sure that doesn't happen.

"You don't start to play your guitar thinking you're going to be running an organization that will maybe generate millions," Jagger says. Yet by understanding and applying organizational theory, the Rolling Stones have become one of the most successful organizations ever in the music industry—and the wealthiest rock 'n' roll band on the planet.[9]

help them reap the advantages of global interdependence and minimize the disadvantages.

Ethics and Social Responsibility. Ethics and social responsibility have become some of the hottest topics in organizations today. The list of executives and major corporations involved in financial and ethical scandals continues to grow. The sordid story of high-flying Enron Corporation, where managers admitted they inflated earnings and hid debt through a series of complex partnerships, was just the beginning. Executives profited handsomely from the fraud at Enron, but when the company collapsed, employees and average investors lost billions. Arthur Andersen LLP, the company's auditor, was found guilty of obstruction of justice for improperly shredding documents related to the Enron investigation. Martha Stewart, who built a multimillion-dollar style empire, has served time in jail, convicted of lying about why she unloaded shares of ImClone Systems stock just before the price plunged. And Yale University's School of Management is forcing out the head of its corporate governance institute over alleged expense-account abuse.[10] Pick up any major newspaper on almost any day, and the front page will contain news about some organization embroiled in an ethical scandal. This is corporate corruption on a scale never before seen, and the effects within organizations and society will be felt for years to come.

Although some executives and officials continue to insist that it is a few bad apples involved in all the wrongdoing, the public is quickly forming the opinion that all corporate executives are crooks.[11] It is disgusted with the whole mess, and leaders face tremendous pressure from the government and the public to hold their organizations and employees to high ethical and professional standards.

Speed of Responsiveness. A third significant challenge for organizations is to respond quickly and decisively to environmental changes, organizational crises, or shifting customer expectations. For much of the twentieth century, organizations operated in a relatively stable environment, so managers could focus on designing structures and systems that kept the organization running smoothly and efficiently. There was little need to search for new ways to cope with increased competition, volatile environmental shifts, or changing customer demands. Today, globalization and advancing technology have accelerated the pace at which organizations in all industries must roll out new products and services to stay competitive.

Today's customers also want products and services tailored to their exact needs. Companies that relied on mass production and distribution techniques must be prepared with new computer-aided systems that can produce one-of-a-kind variations and streamlined distribution systems that deliver products directly from the manufacturer to the consumer. Another shift brought about by technology is that the financial basis of today's economy is increasingly *information*, not machines and factories. Of concern to organizational leaders is that the primary factor of production becomes knowledge, to which managers must respond by increasing the power of employees. Employees, not production machinery, have the power and knowledge needed to keep the company competitive.

Considering the turmoil and flux inherent in today's world, the mindset needed by organizational leaders is to expect the unexpected and be ready for rapid change and potential crises through nimble organizational designs. Crisis management has moved to the forefront in light of terrorist attacks; a tough economy, rocky stock market, and weakening consumer confidence; widespread ethical scandals; and, in general, an environment that may shift dramatically at a moment's notice.

The Digital Workplace. Many traditional managers feel particularly awkward in today's technology-driven workplace. Organizations have been engulfed by information technology that affects how organizations are designed and managed. In today's workplace, many employees perform much of their work on computers and may work in virtual teams, connected electronically to colleagues around the world. In addition, organizations are becoming enmeshed in electronic networks. The world of e-business is booming as more and more business takes place by digital processes over a computer network rather than in physical space. Some companies have taken e-business to very high levels to achieve amazing performance. Dell Computer pioneered the use of end-to-end digital supply-chain networks to keep in touch with customers, take orders, buy components from suppliers, coordinate with manufacturing partners, and ship customized products directly to consumers. This trend toward *disintermediation*—eliminating the middleperson—is affecting every industry, prompting a group of consultants at a Harvard University conference to conclude that businesses today must either "Dell or Be Delled."[12] These advances mean that organizational leaders not only need to be technologically savvy but are also responsible for managing a web of relationships that reaches far beyond the boundaries of the physical organization, building flexible e-links between a company and its employees, suppliers, contract partners, and customers.[13]

Diversity. Diversity is a fact of life that no organization can afford to ignore. As organizations increasingly operate on a global playing field, the workforce—as well as the customer base—is changing dramatically. Many of today's leading organizations have an international face. Look at the makeup of the international consulting firm McKinsey & Co. In the 1970s, most consultants were American, but by the turn of the century, McKinsey's chief partner was a foreign national (Rajat Gupta from India), only 40 percent of consultants were American, and the firm's foreign-born consultants came from 40 different countries.[14]

The demographics of the Canadian population and workforce are also shifting. In 2005, Statistics Canada developed a demographic projection of the Canadian population in 2017. The study projects that (1) Canada will have a population of 33 to 36 million, of whom 6.4 to 8.5 million will be members of visible minorities; and (2) half the members of visible minorities will be South Asian or Chinese, followed by Blacks at one to 1.2 million.[15] Population growth will be from immigration. Today's average worker is older, and many more women, visible minorities, and immigrants are seeking job and advancement opportunities. A 2005 report by RBC Financial Group argues that "immigrants, women, and baby boomers approaching retirement will need to play more significant roles in the country's workforce, as Canada needs to capitalize on the broader economic benefits that a more diverse population has to offer."[16] This growing diversity brings a variety of challenges, such as maintaining a strong organizational culture while supporting diversity, balancing work and family concerns, and coping with the conflict brought about by varying cultural styles.

Managing diversity may be one of the most rewarding challenges for organizations competing on a global basis. For example, research has indicated that women's style of doing business may hold important lessons for success in the emerging global world of the twenty-first century. Yet the glass (or plastic) ceiling persists, keeping women from reaching positions of top leadership.[17]

Purpose of This Chapter

This chapter explore the nature of organizations and organizational theory today. Organizational theory has developed from the systematic study of organizations by scholars. Concepts are obtained from living, ongoing organizations. Organizational theory can be practical, as illustrated in the Air Canada case. It helps us understand, diagnose, and respond to emerging organizational needs and problems.

The next section begins with a formal definition of organization and then explores introductory concepts for describing and analyzing organizations. Next, the scope and nature of organizational theory are discussed more fully. Succeeding sections examine the history of organizational theory and design, the development of new organizational forms in response to changes in the environment, and how organizational theory can help people manage complex organizations in a rapidly changing world. The chapter closes with a brief overview of the themes to be covered in this book.

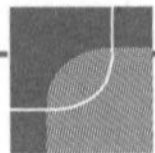

What Is an Organization?

Organizations are ubiquitous but are hard to see. We see outcroppings, such as a tall building, a computer workstation, or a friendly employee; but the whole organization is vague and abstract and may be scattered among several locations, even around the world. We know organizations are there because they touch us every day. Indeed, they are so common that we take them for granted. We hardly notice that we are born in a hospital, have our birth records registered in a government agency, are educated in schools and universities, are raised on food produced by agribusinesses, are treated by doctors engaged in a joint practice, buy a house built by a construction company and sold by a real estate agency, borrow money from a bank, turn to police and fire departments when trouble erupts, use moving companies to change residences, receive an array of benefits from government, spend 40 (or more) hours a week working in an organization, and are even laid to rest by a funeral home.[18]

Definition

Organizations as diverse as a prison, a hospital, and Air Canada have characteristics in common. The definition used in this book to describe organizations is as follows: **organizations** are (1) social entities that are (2) goal-directed, (3) designed as deliberately structured and coordinated activity systems, and (4) linked to the external environment.

The key element of an organization is not, of course, a building or a set of policies and procedures; organizations comprise people and their relationships with one another. An organization exists when people interact with one another to perform essential functions that help attain goals. Recent trends in management recognize the importance of human resources, with most new approaches designed to empower employees with greater opportunities to learn and contribute as they work together toward common goals.

Managers deliberately structure and coordinate organizational resources to achieve the organization's purpose. However, even though work may be structured into separate departments or sets of activities, most organizations today are striving for greater horizontal coordination of work activities, often using teams of employees from different functional areas to work together on projects. Boundaries between departments, as well as those between organizations, are becoming more flexible and diffuse as companies face the need to respond to changes in the external environment more rapidly. An organization cannot exist without interacting with customers, suppliers, competitors, and other elements of the external environment. Today, some companies are even cooperating with their competitors, sharing information and technology to their mutual advantage.

Types of Organizations

Some organizations are large, multinational corporations. Others are small, family-owned shops. Some manufacture products such as automobiles or computers, whereas others provide services such as legal representation, banking, or medical services. Later in this text, Chapter 7 will look at the distinctions between manufacturing and service technologies. Chapter 9 discusses size and life cycle and describes some differences between small and large organizations.

Another important distinction is between for-profit businesses and nonprofit organizations. All of the topics in this text apply to nonprofit organizations such as the Salvation Army, the World Wildlife Fund, the Heart and Stroke Foundation, and Toronto's Hospital for Sick Children, just as they do to such businesses as Timothy's World Coffee, eBay, or Holiday Inn. However, there are some important differences to keep in mind. The primary difference is that managers in businesses direct their activities toward earning money for the company, whereas managers in nonprofits direct their efforts toward generating some kind of social impact. The unique characteristics and needs of nonprofit organizations created by this distinction present difficult challenges for organizational leaders.[19]

Financial resources for nonprofits typically come from government grants, and individual and corporate donations rather than from the sale of products or services to customers. In businesses, managers focus on improving the organization's products and services to increase sales revenues. In nonprofits, however, services are typically provided to non-paying clients, and a major problem for many organizations is securing a steady stream of funds to continue operating. Nonprofit managers, committed to serving clients with limited funds, must focus on keeping organizational costs as low as possible and demonstrating a highly efficient use of resources.[20] Another problem is that, since nonprofit organizations do not have a conventional "bottom line," managers often struggle with the question of what constitutes organizational effectiveness. It is easy to measure dollars and cents, but nonprofits have to measure intangible goals such as "improve public health" or "make a difference in the lives of the disenfranchised."

Managers in nonprofit organizations also deal with many diverse stakeholders and must market their services to attract not only clients (customers) but also volunteers and donors. Some nonprofits have responded to such challenges by developing new organizations. In 2001, Big Brothers and Sisters of Canada and Big

Sisters Association of Ontario merged so that each organization could better serve more clients. The merger was also designed to reduce confusion in the eyes of the funders and the public that having two organizations with similar names and mandates had created. As well, it was an opportunity to pool the resources and expertise of the two organizations.[21] However, not all members of the Big Sisters Association of Ontario supported the merger as they believed that girls' interests would not be as well served by the new organization. They formed new organizations that continue the original social mandate.

Thus, the organizational design concepts discussed throughout this book, such as setting goals and measuring effectiveness, coping with environmental uncertainty, implementing effective control mechanisms, satisfying multiple stakeholders, and addressing issues of power and conflict, apply to nonprofit organizations such as the Big Brothers and Big Sisters just as they do to Microsoft, Purolator Courier, or Air Canada, as described in the chapter opening. These concepts and theories are adapted and revised as needed to fit unique needs and problems.

Book Mark 1.0 (HAVE YOU READ THIS BOOK?)

The Company: A Short History of a Revolutionary Idea
By John Micklethwait and Adrian Wooldridge

"The limited liability corporation is the greatest single discovery of modern times," is one conclusion of the concise and readable book, *The Company: A Short History of a Revolutionary Idea* by John Micklethwait and Adrian Wooldridge. Companies are so ubiquitous today that we take them for granted, so it may come as a surprise that the company as we know it is a relatively recent innovation. Although people have joined together in groups for commercial purposes since ancient Greek and Roman times, the modern company has its roots in the late nineteenth century. The idea of a *limited liability company* that was legally an "artificial person" began with the *Joint Stock Companies Act*, enacted by the London Board of Trade in 1856. Today the company is seen as "the most important organization in the world." Here are a few reasons that is the case:

- The corporation was the first autonomous legal and social institution that was within society yet independent of the central government.
- The concept of a limited liability company unleashed entrepreneurs to raise money because investors could lose only what they invested. Increasing the pool of entrepreneurial capital spurred innovation and generally enriched the societies in which companies operated.
- The company is the most efficient creator of goods and services that the world has ever known. Without a company to harness resources and organize activities, the cost to consumers for almost any product we know today would be impossible to afford.
- Historically, the corporation has been a force for civilized behaviour and provided people with worthwhile activities, identity, and community, as well as a paycheque.
- The Virginia Company, a forerunner of the limited liability corporation, helped introduce the revolutionary concept of democracy to the American colonies.
- The modern multinational corporation began in Britain in the third quarter of the 1800s with the railroads, which built rail networks throughout Europe by shipping into each country the managers, materials, equipment, and labour needed.

During the past few years, it seems that large corporations have been increasingly in conflict with societies' interests. Yet large companies have been reviled throughout modern history—consider the robber barons at the beginning of the twentieth century—and the authors suggest that recent abuses are relatively mild compared to some historical incidents. Everyone knows that corporations can be scoundrels, but overall, Micklethwait and Wooldridge argue, their force has been overwhelmingly for the cumulative social and economic good.

The Company: A Short History of a Revolutionary Idea, by John Micklethwait and Adrian Wooldridge, is published by The Modern Library.

Importance of Organizations

It may seem hard to believe today, but organizations as we know them are relatively recent in the history of humankind. Even in the late nineteenth century there were few organizations of any size or importance—no labour unions, no trade associations, and few large businesses, nonprofit organizations, or governmental departments. What a change has occurred since then! The development of large organizations transformed all of society, and, indeed, the modern corporation may be the most significant innovation of the past 100 years.[22] This chapter's Book Mark examined the rise of the corporation and its significance in our society. Organizations are central to people's lives and exert a tremendous influence.

Organizations are all around us and shape our lives in many ways. But what contributions do organizations make? Why are they important? Exhibit 1.1 lists seven reasons organizations are important to you and to society. First, organizations bring together resources to accomplish specific goals. Consider Bombardier, which designs and builds planes, for the business, regional, and amphibious markets, as well as trains. Putting together an airplane is an incredibly complex and labour-intensive job involving many different kinds of components built to the highest standards of quality.

Organizations also produce goods and services that customers want at competitive prices. Bill Gates, who built Microsoft into a global powerhouse, asserts that the modern organization "is one of the most effective means to allocate resources we've ever seen. It transforms great ideas into customer benefits on an unimaginably large scale."[23]

Companies look for innovative ways to produce and distribute desirable goods and services more efficiently. Two ways are through e-business and through the use of computer-based manufacturing technologies. Redesigning organizational structures and management practices can also contribute to increased efficiency. Organizations create a drive for innovation rather than a reliance on standard products and outmoded ways of doing things.

EXHIBIT 1.1
Importance of Organizations

Organizations exist to do the following:

1. *Bring together resources to achieve desired goals and outcomes*
2. *Produce goods and services efficiently*
3. *Facilitate innovation*
4. *Use modern manufacturing and information technologies*
5. *Adapt to and influence a changing environment*
6. *Create value for owners, customers, and employees*
7. *Accommodate ongoing challenges of diversity, ethics, and the motivation and coordination of employees*

Organizations adapt to and influence a rapidly changing environment. Consider Google, provider of the Internet's most popular search engine, which continues to adapt and evolve along with the evolving Internet. Rather than being a rigid service, Google is continually adding technological features that create a better service by accretion. At any time, Google's site features several technologies in development so that engineers can get ideas and feedback from users.[24] Some large businesses have entire departments charged with monitoring the external environment and finding ways to adapt to or influence that environment. One of the most significant changes in the external environment today is globalization. Organizations such as Coca-Cola, Alcan, Labatt Breweries of Canada, and IBM are involved in strategic alliances and partnerships with companies around the world in an effort to influence the environment and compete on a global scale.

Through all of these activities, organizations create value for their owners, customers, and employees. Managers analyze which parts of the operation create value and which parts do not; a company can be profitable only when the value it creates is greater than the cost of resources. Air Canada Jazz, a subsidiary of ACE Aviation Holdings, offers flights to 68 destinations, offering competitive pricing choices.

Finally, organizations have to cope with and accommodate today's challenges of workforce diversity and growing concerns over ethics and social responsibility, as well as find effective ways to motivate employees to work together to accomplish organizational goals.

Organizations shape our lives, and well-informed managers can shape organizations. An understanding of organizational theory enables managers to design organizations to function more effectively.

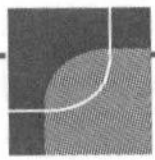

Perspectives on Organizations

There are various ways to look at and think about organizations and how they function. Two important perspectives are the open-systems approach and the organizational-configuration framework.

Open Systems

One significant development in the study of organizations was the distinction between closed and open systems.[25] A **closed system** would not depend on its environment; it would be autonomous, enclosed, and sealed off from the outside world. Although a true closed system cannot exist, early organizational studies focused on internal systems. Early management concepts, including scientific management, leadership style, and industrial engineering, were closed-system approaches because they took the environment for granted and assumed the organization could be made more effective through internal design. The management of a closed system would be quite easy. The environment would be stable and predictable and would not intervene to cause problems. The primary management issue would be to run things efficiently.

An **open system** must interact with the environment to survive; it both consumes resources and exports resources to the environment. It cannot seal itself off. It must continuously adapt to the environment. Open systems can be enormously complex. Internal efficiency is just one issue—and sometimes a minor one. The organization has to find and obtain needed resources, interpret and act on environmental changes, dispose of outputs, and control and coordinate internal activities in the face of environmental disturbances and uncertainty. Every system that must interact with the environment to survive is an open system. The human being is an open system. So is the planet Earth, Iqaluit, the capital of Nunavut, and Air Canada. Indeed, one problem at Air Canada was that top managers seemed to forget they were part of an open system. They isolated themselves within the bureaucratic culture and failed to pay close attention to what was going on with their customers, suppliers, and competitors. The rapid changes over the past few decades, including globalization and increased competition, the explosion of the Internet and e-business, and the growing diversity of the population and workforce, have forced many managers to reorient toward an open-systems mindset and recognize their business as part of a complex, interconnected whole.

To understand the whole organization, we must view it as a system. A **system** is a set of interacting elements that acquires inputs from the environment, transforms them, and discharges outputs to the external environment. The need for inputs and outputs reflects dependency on the environment. Interacting elements mean that people and departments depend on one another and must work together.

Exhibit 1.2 illustrates an open system. Inputs to an organizational system include raw materials and other physical resources, employees, information, and financial resources. The transformation process changes these inputs into something of value that can be exported back to the environment. Outputs include specific products and services for customers and clients. Outputs may also include employee satisfaction, pollution, and other byproducts of the transformation process.

PDA Remember...

Design the organization so that the five basic parts—technical core, technical support, administrative support, top management, and middle management—adequately perform the subsystem functions of production, maintenance, adaptation, management, and boundary spanning. Try to maintain a balance among the five parts so that they work together for organizational effectiveness.

A system comprises several **subsystems**, as illustrated at the bottom of Exhibit 1.2. These subsystems perform the specific functions required for organizational survival, such as production, boundary spanning, maintenance, adaptation, and management. The production subsystem produces the product and service outputs of the organization. Boundary subsystems are responsible for exchanges with the external environment. They include activities such as purchasing supplies or marketing products. The maintenance subsystem maintains the smooth operation and upkeep of the organization's physical and human elements. The adaptive subsystems are responsible for organizational change and adaptation. Management is a distinct subsystem, responsible for coordinating and directing the other subsystems of the organization.

EXHIBIT 1.2
An Open System and Its Subsystems

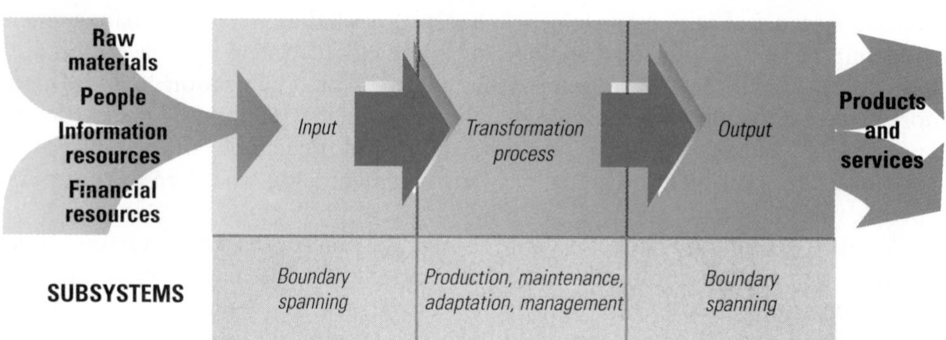

Organizational Configuration

Various parts of the organization are designed to perform the key subsystem functions illustrated in Exhibit 1.2. One framework proposed by the esteemed Canadian scholar, Henry Mintzberg, suggests that every organization has five parts.[26] These parts, illustrated in Exhibit 1.3, include the technical core, top management, middle management, technical support, and administrative support. The five parts of the organization may vary in size and importance depending on the organization's environment, technology, and other factors.

Technical Core. The technical core includes people who do the basic work of the organization. It performs the production subsystem function and actually produces the product and service outputs of the organization. This is where the primary transformation from inputs to outputs takes place. The technical core is the production department in a manufacturing firm, the teachers and classes in a university, and the medical activities in a hospital. At Air Canada, the technical core includes pilots, flight attendants, and baggage handlers.

Technical Support. The technical support function helps the organization adapt to the environment. Technical support employees such as engineers and researchers scan the environment for problems, opportunities, and technological developments. Technical support is responsible for creating innovations in the technical core, helping the organization change and adapt. Technical support at Air Canada is provided by Air Canada Technical Services.

Administrative Support. The administrative support function is responsible for the smooth operation and upkeep of the organization, including its physical and human elements. This includes human resource activities such as recruiting and hiring, establishing compensation and benefits, and employee training and development, as well as maintenance activities such as cleaning of buildings and service and repair of machines. Administrative support functions in a corporation such as Air Canada might include the human resource department, organizational development, the employee cafeteria, and the maintenance staff.

Management. Management is a distinct subsystem, responsible for directing and coordinating other parts of the organization. Top management provides direction,

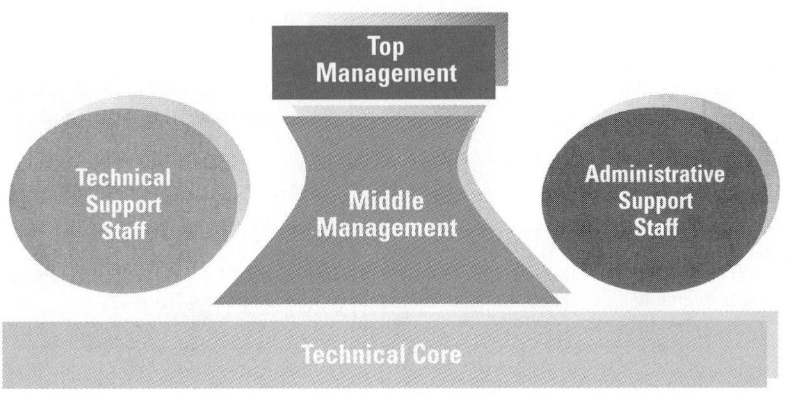

EXHIBIT 1.3A
Five Basic Parts of an Organization
Source: Based on Henry Mintzberg, *The Structuring of Organizations* (Englewood Cliffs, N.J.: Prentice-Hall, 1979), 215–297; and Henry Mintzberg, "Organization Design: Fashion or Fit?" *Harvard Business Review* 59 (January–February 1981), 103–116.

EXHIBIT 1.3B

Organizational Types and Their Basic Components

	SIMPLE STRUCTURE	MACHINE BUREAUCRACY	PROFESSIONAL BUREAUCRACY	DIVISIONALIZED FORM	ADHOCRACY
Key Means of Coordination	Direct supervision	Standardization of work	Standardization of skills	Standardization of outputs	Mutual Adjustment
Key Part of Organization	Strategic apex	Technostructure	Operating core	Middle line	Support staff (with operating core in operating adhocracy)
STRUCTURAL ELEMENTS					
Specialization of Jobs	Little specialization	*Much horizontal and vertical specialization*	*Much horizontal specialization*	Some horizontal and vertical specialization (between divisions and headquarters)	*Much horizontal specialization*
Training and Indoctrination	Little training and indoctrination	Little training and indoctrination	*Much training and indoctrination*	Some training and indoctrination (of division managers)	Much training
Formalization of Behavior—Bureaucratic/ Organic	*Little formalization—organic*	*Much formalization —bureaucratic*	*Little formalization —bureaucratic*	Much formalization (within divisions)—bureaucratic	*Little formalization —organic*
Grouping	Usually functional	*Usually functional*	Functional and market	*Market*	Functional and market
Unit Size	Wide	Wide at bottom, narrow elsewhere	Wide at bottom, narrow elsewhere	Wide at top	Narrow throughout
Planning and Control Systems	Little planning and control	Action planning	Little planning and control	*Much performance control*	Limited action planning (esp. in administrative adhocracy)
Liaison Devices	Few liaison devices	Few liaison devices	Liaison devices in administration	Few liaison devices	*Many liaison devices throughout*
Decentralization	*Centralization*	*Limited horizontal decentralization*	*Horizontal and vertical decentralization*	Limited vertical decentralization	*Selective decentralization*
SITUATIONAL ELEMENTS					
Age and Size	Typically young and small	Typically old and large	Varies	Typically old and very large	Typically young (operating adhocracy)
Technical System	Simple, not regulating	Regulating but not automated, not very complex	Not regulating or complex	Divisible, otherwise like machine bureaucracy	Very complex, often automated (in administrative adhocracy), not regulating or complex (in operating adhocracy)
Environment	Simple and dynamic; sometimes hostile	Simple and stable	Complex and stable	Relatively simple and stable; diversified markets (esp. products and services)	Complex and dynamic; sometimes disparate (in administrative adhocracy)
Power	Chief executive control; often owner managed; not fashionable	Technocratic and external control; not fashionable	Professional operator control; fashionable	Middle-line control; fashionable (esp. in industry)	Expert control; very fashionable

Note: *Italic* type in columns 2–6 indicates key design parameters.

Source: Henry Mintzberg, "Organization Design: Fashion or Fit?" *Harvard Business Review* 59 (January–February 1981), 6–7.

strategy, goals, and policies for the entire organization or major divisions. Middle management is responsible for implementation and coordination at the departmental level. In traditional organizations, middle managers are responsible for mediating between top management and the technical core, such as implementing rules and passing information up and down the hierarchy.

In practice, the five parts are interrelated and often serve more than one subsystem function. For example, managers coordinate and direct other parts of the system, but they may also be involved in administrative and technical support. In addition, several of the parts serve the *boundary spanning* function mentioned in the previous section. For example, in the administrative support realm, human resource departments are responsible for working with the external environment to find quality employees. Purchasing departments acquire needed materials and supplies. In the technical support area, research and development (R&D) departments work directly with the external environment to learn about new technological developments. Managers perform boundary spanning as well. The important boundary-spanning subsystem is embraced by several areas, rather than being confined to one part of the organization.

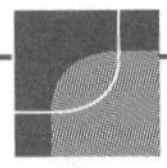

Dimensions of Organizational Design

The systems view pertains to dynamic, ongoing activities within organizations. The next step for understanding organizations is to look at dimensions that describe specific organizational design traits. These dimensions describe organizations in much the same way that personality and physical traits describe people.

Organizational dimensions fall into two types: structural and contextual, illustrated in Exhibit 1.4. **Structural dimensions** provide labels to describe the internal characteristics of an organization. They create a basis for measuring and comparing organizations. **Contextual dimensions** characterize the whole organization, including its size, technology, environment, and goals. They describe the organizational setting that influences and shapes the structural dimensions. Contextual dimensions can be confusing because they represent both the organization and the environment. Contextual dimensions can be envisioned as a set of overlapping elements that underlie an organization's structure and work processes. To understand and evaluate organizations, one must examine both structural and contextual dimensions.[27] These dimensions of organizational design interact with one another and can be adjusted to accomplish the purposes listed earlier in Exhibit 1.1.

Structural Dimensions

1. *Formalization* pertains to the amount of written documentation in the organization. Documentation includes procedures, job descriptions, regulations, and policy manuals. These written documents describe behaviour and activities. Formalization is often measured by simply counting the number of pages of documentation within the organization. Large universities, for example, tend to be high on formalization because they have several volumes of written rules for such things as registration, dropping and adding classes, student associations,

EXHIBIT 1.4
Interacting Contextual and Structural Dimensions of Organizational Design

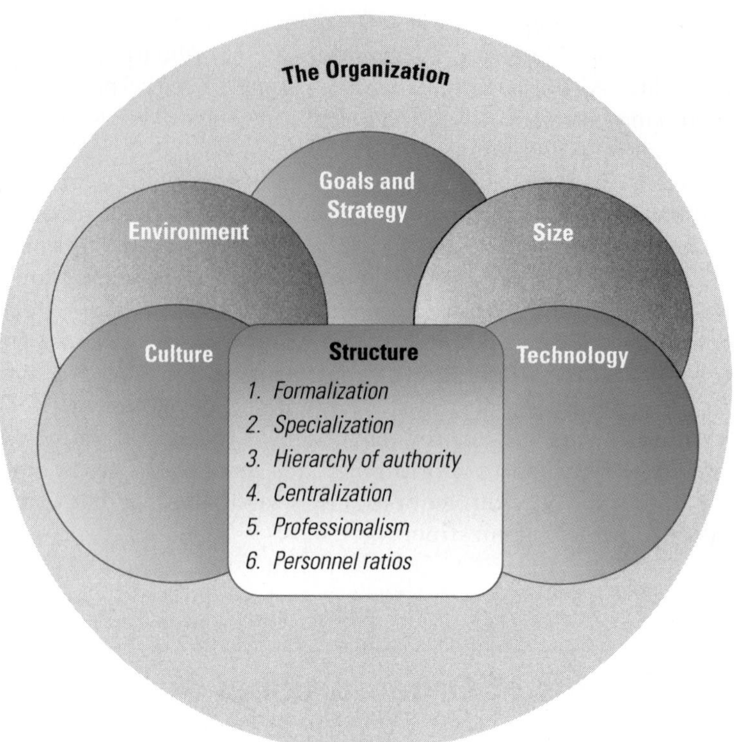

dormitory governance, and financial assistance. A small, family-owned business, in contrast, may have almost no written rules and would be considered informal.

2. *Specialization* is the degree to which organizational tasks are subdivided into separate jobs. If specialization is extensive, each employee performs only a narrow range of tasks. If specialization is low, employees perform a wide range of tasks in their jobs. Specialization is sometimes referred to as the division of labour.
3. *Hierarchy of authority* describes who reports to whom and the span of control for each manager. The hierarchy is depicted by the vertical lines on an organizational chart. See Exhibit 1.5 for a lighthearted depiction of an organizational chart! The hierarchy is related to span of control (the number of employees reporting to a supervisor). When *spans of control* are narrow, the hierarchy tends to be tall. When spans of control are wide, the hierarchy of authority will be shorter.
4. *Centralization* refers to the hierarchical level that has authority to make a decision. When decision making is kept at the top level, the organization is centralized. When decisions are delegated to lower organizational levels, it is decentralized. Organizational decisions that might be centralized or decentralized include purchasing equipment, establishing goals, choosing suppliers, setting prices, hiring employees, and deciding marketing territories.
5. *Professionalism* is the level of formal education and training of employees. Professionalism is considered high when employees require long periods of training to hold jobs in the organization. Professionalism is generally measured as the

EXHIBIT 1.5
An Unusual Hierarchy

"Just how long has there been a maraschino cherry at the top of the organizational chart?"

average number of years of education of employees, which could be as high as twenty in a medical practice and less than ten in a catering company.

6. *Personnel ratios* refer to the deployment of people to various functions and departments. Personnel ratios include the administrative ratio, the clerical ratio, the professional staff ratio, and the ratio of indirect to direct labour employees. A personnel ratio is measured by dividing the number of employees in a classification by the total number of organizational employees.

PDA
Remember...

Think of the organization as an entity distinct from the individuals who work in it. Describe the organization according to its size, formalization, decentralization, specialization, professionalism, and personnel ratios.

Use these characteristics to describe and analyze the organization and to compare it with other organizations.

Contextual Dimensions

1. *Size* is the organization's magnitude as reflected in the number of people in the organization. It can be measured for the organization as a whole or for specific components, such as a plant or division. Because organizations are social systems, size is typically measured by the number of employees. Other measures such as total sales or total assets also reflect magnitude, but they do not indicate the size of the human part of the system.
2. *Organizational technology* refers to the tools, techniques, and actions used to transform inputs into outputs. It concerns how the organization actually produces the products and services it provides for customers and includes such things as flexible manufacturing, advanced information systems, and the Internet. An automobile assembly line, a college classroom, and an overnight package delivery system are technologies, although they differ from one another.
3. The *environment* includes all elements outside the boundary of the organization. Key elements include the industry, government, customers, suppliers, and the financial community. The environmental elements that affect an organization the most are often other organizations.

4. The organization's *goals and strategy* define the purpose and competitive techniques that set it apart from other organizations. Goals are often written down as an enduring statement of company intent. A strategy is the plan of action that describes resource allocation and activities for dealing with the environment and for reaching the organization's goals. Goals and strategies define the scope of operations and the relationship with employees, customers, and competitors.
5. An organization's *culture* is the underlying set of key values, beliefs, understandings, and norms shared by employees. These underlying values may pertain to ethical behaviour, commitment to employees, efficiency, or customer service, and they provide the glue to hold organization members together. An organization's culture is unwritten but can be observed in its stories, slogans, ceremonies, dress, and office layout.

The 11 contextual and structural dimensions discussed here are interdependent. For example, large organizational size, a routine technology, and a stable environment all tend to create an organization that has greater formalization, specialization, and centralization. More detailed relationships among the dimensions are explored in later chapters of this book.

These dimensions provide a basis for the measurement and analysis of characteristics that cannot be seen by the casual observer, and they reveal significant information about an organization. Consider, for example, the dimensions of EllisDon Construction and the Museum of Contemporary Canadian Art (MOCCA) compared with those of Wal-Mart.

In Practice

EllisDon, MOCCA, Wal-Mart

EllisDon

EllisDon, founded in 1951 by two brothers in London, Ontario, has become a leading international construction company. It has undertaken projects in Europe, the Middle East, the Caribbean, and the United States. The projects range in size from several thousand to several hundred million dollars. It sees itself as a "construction services" company, offering such services as construction and project management, design and build services, and health and safety consulting. EllisDon has 1,200 employees and has offices across Canada and in the United States, Greece, Dubai, U.A.E., and St. Lucia. One of its best-known projects is the building of the world's first sports stadium with a retractable roof, the Toronto SkyDome, now known as the Rogers Centre.

Donald Smith, EllisDon's founder, recruited individuals with a sense of adventure and entrepreneurial drive. "The company's defining characteristic emerged very early on: EllisDon was prepared to assume risk. We were seen as innovative and dynamic in our approach to a construction challenge. Above all, we were seen as builders."

EllisDon employees have recognized EllisDon as one of Canada's Fifty Best Employers for five consecutive years and, in 2006, it ranked third. EllisDon's President and CEO, Geoff Smith, believes that the "key to industry leadership is creating a culture of independent thought, of individual confidence, openness, initiative and enjoyment. We believe that success doesn't necessarily lie in the larger innovations, but in the smaller daily breakthroughs that occur on the sites, in the hard work, and in finding ways to say yes when a client asks. That is the way great companies, and great places to work, are built."[28]

MOCCA

MOCCA, founded in 1999, has a mandate to exhibit, research, collect and promote innovative art by Canadian artists "whose works engage and reflect the relevant stories of our times." MOCCA is a nonprofit arms-length agency of the city of Toronto's Culture Division. Its permanent collection numbers 400 works of art by 150 artists. MOCCA has presented more than 40 exhibitions of contemporary Canadian and international works in eight countries. "It is MOCCA's belief that this local-to-global investment in Canadian arts and culture will strengthen our ability to serve the artistic, cultural and general public communities of Toronto, Canada and beyond." MOCCA has a staff of seven and is supported, in part, by memberships.[29]

Wal-Mart

Wal-Mart achieves its competitive edge through human resource efficiency and internal cost efficiency. A standard formula is used to build each store, with uniform displays and merchandise. Wal-Mart operates about 1,600 discount stores, 1,100 Supercentres, and 500 Sam's Clubs in the United States, and more than 1,000 international stores. Its administrative expenses are the lowest of any chain. The distribution system is a marvel of efficiency. Goods can be delivered to any store in less than two days after an order is placed. Stores are controlled from the top, but store managers have also been given some freedom to adapt to local conditions.

EllisDon is a medium-sized construction services organization that ranks quite low on formalization, specialization, and centralization. Employees work on different projects. Wal-Mart is much more formalized, specialized, and centralized. Efficiency is more important than innovation, so most activities are guided by standard regulations. The percentage of non-workflow personnel is kept to a minimum. In contrast, MOCCA is small and ranks low on formalization, specialization, and centralization. MOCCA needs to be flexible in design so that it can achieve its creative goals.

Structural and contextual dimensions can thus tell a lot about an organization and about differences among organizations. Organizational design dimensions are examined in more detail in later chapters to determine the appropriate level of each dimension needed to perform effectively in each organizational setting.

PDA Remember...

Consider the needs and interests of all stakeholders when setting goals and designing the organization to achieve effectiveness.

Performance and Effectiveness Outcomes

The whole point of understanding varying perspectives and the structural and contextual dimensions of organizations is to design the organization in such a way as to achieve high performance and effectiveness. Managers adjust structural and contextual dimensions and organizational subsystems to most efficiently and effectively transform inputs into outputs and provide value. **Efficiency** refers to the amount of resources used to achieve the organization's goals. It is based on the quantity of raw materials, money, and employees necessary to produce a given level of output. **Effectiveness** is a broader term, meaning the degree to which an organization achieves its goals. Simply put, efficiency is "doing things right" while effectiveness is "doing the right thing."

To be effective, organizations need clear, focused goals and appropriate strategies for achieving them. Strategy, goals, and approaches to measuring effectiveness will be discussed in detail in Chapter 2. Many organizations are using new technology to improve efficiency and effectiveness. For example, Air Canada became the first airline to introduce self-service express check-in kiosks in Canada. Purolator Courier uses technologically sophisticated package-handling equipment and computerized logistics systems to reduce delivery time for cross-border shipping.

However, achieving effectiveness is not always a simple matter because different people want different things from the organization. For customers, the primary concern is high-quality products and services at a reasonable price, whereas employees

EXHIBIT 1.6
Major Stakeholder Groups and What They Expect

are mostly concerned with adequate pay, good working conditions, and job satisfaction. Managers carefully balance the needs and interests of various stakeholders in setting goals and striving for effectiveness. This is referred to as the **stakeholder approach**, which integrates diverse organizational activities by looking at various organizational stakeholders and what they want from the organization. A **stakeholder** is any group within or outside the organization that has a stake in the organization's performance. The satisfaction level of each group can be assessed as an indication of the organization's performance and effectiveness.[30]

Exhibit 1.6 illustrates various stakeholders and what each group wants from the organization. Organizations often find it difficult to simultaneously satisfy the demands of all groups. A business might have high customer satisfaction, but the organization might have difficulties with creditors or supplier relationships might be poor. Consider Wal-Mart. Customers love its efficiency and low prices, but the low-cost emphasis the company uses with suppliers has caused friction. Some activist groups argue that Wal-Mart's tactics are unethical because they force suppliers to lay off workers, close factories, and outsource to manufacturers from low-wage countries. One supplier said clothing is being sold at Wal-Mart so cheaply that many North American companies couldn't compete even if they paid their workers nothing. The challenges of managing such a huge organization have also led to strains in relationships with employees and other stakeholder groups, as evidenced by recent gender discrimination suits and complaints about low wages.[31]

Stakeholder interests sometimes conflict, such as when unions demand wage increases that might hurt shareholders' financial returns or require a switch to lower-cost suppliers. In nonprofit organizations, the needs and interests of clients sometimes conflict with restrictions on use of government funds or contributions from donors. In reality, it is unreasonable to assume that all stakeholders can be equally satisfied. However, if an organization fails to meet the needs of several stakeholder groups, it is probably not meeting its effectiveness goals. Recall from the opening case Air Canada's problems with satisfying employees, customers, creditors, unions, stockholders, and government regulators.

Research has shown that the assessment of multiple stakeholder groups is an accurate reflection of organizational effectiveness, especially with respect to organizational adaptability.[32] Moreover, both profit and nonprofit organizations care deeply about their reputations and attempt to shape stakeholders' perceptions of their performance.[33]

Managers strive to at least minimally satisfy the interests of all stakeholders. When any one group becomes seriously dissatisfied, it may withdraw its support and hurt future organizational performance. Satisfying multiple stakeholders can be challenging, particularly as goals and priorities change, as illustrated by the following example.

In Practice

Mackenzie Valley Natural Gas Pipeline Project

The proposed Mackenzie Pipeline Project is enormous; it proposes to develop natural gas fields in the Mackenzie Delta of the Northwest Territories and deliver the gas to market through a 1,300 kilometre pipeline built along the Mackenzie Valley. It is a multi–billion dollar project that is expected to create 2,600 jobs. There are five business partners in the proposed venture: Imperial Oil, Shell Canada, Exxon Mobile Canada , Conoco Phillips Canada, and the Aboriginal Peoples' Group (APG). The APG was formed in 2000 to represent the interests of the First Nations peoples of Northwest Territories and consists of members of the Dehcho Dene, Sahtu, Gwich'in, and Inuvialuit First Nations.

The Project makes two commitments: (1) "[the] Mackenzie Gas Project respects the peoples of Canada's North and the land, wildlife and environment that sustains them. Our priorities include maintaining worker and public safety at all times and caring for the environment before, during and after construction . . . and (2) [we] are also committed to working with Aboriginal and non-Aboriginal northern residents to ensure northern individuals, communities and businesses have an opportunity to benefit from the Project."[34]

Even though the 30 First Nations stakeholder groups signed a memorandum of agreement under the aegis of the APG, the project has been controversial from its outset. Mr. Justice Thomas Berger, in his 1977 report to assess the impact of a pipeline wrote "[we] are at our last frontier. It is a frontier that all of us have read about, but few of us have seen. Profound issues, touching our deepest concerns as a nation, await us there."[35] In 2004, there was renewed momentum for building the pipeline but negotiations between governments, the project partners, and the First Nations groups stalled. In July 2005, the federal government pledged $500 million to address the socioeconomic concerns of the First Nations. The Dehcho Dene First Nation has not signed on to the project as it has concerns about the impact of the pipeline on caribou and moose habitats and traplines. The APG has stated that the Dehcho's 34 percent share will be held for them. Production is estimated to start in 2014 and the costs of the project are estimated to be $16 billion. In November 2007, the joint review panel, comprising the project's stakeholders, concluded its public hearings and planned to report its findings to the federal government.[36]

This example provides a glimpse of how difficult it can be for managers to satisfy multiple stakeholders. In all organizations, managers have to evaluate stakeholder concerns and establish goals that can achieve at least minimal satisfaction for major stakeholder groups.

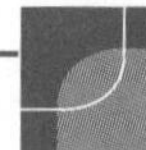

The Evolution of Organizational Theory and Design

Organizational theory is not a collection of facts; it is a way of thinking about organizations. Organizational theory is a way to see and analyze organizations more accurately and deeply than one otherwise could. The way to see and think about organizations is based on patterns and regularities in organizational design and behaviour. Organization scholars search for these regularities, define them, measure them, and make them available to the rest of us. The facts from the research are not as important as the general patterns and insights into organizational functioning.

Historical Perspectives

Organizational design and management practices have varied over time in response to changes in the larger society.

The modern era of management theory began with the classical management perspective in the late nineteenth and early twentieth century. The emergence of the factory system during the Industrial Revolution posed problems that earlier organizations had not encountered. As work was performed on a much larger scale by a larger number of workers, people began thinking about how to design and manage work in order to increase productivity and help organizations attain maximum efficiency. The classical perspective, which sought to make organizations run like efficient, well-oiled machines, is associated with the development of hierarchy and bureaucratic organizations and remains the basis of much of modern management theory and practice. In this section, we will examine the classical perspective, with its emphasis on efficiency and organization, as well as other perspectives that emerged to address new concerns, such as employee needs and the role of the environment. Elements of each perspective are still used in organizational design, although they have been adapted and revised to meet changing needs.

Efficiency Is Everything. Pioneered by Frederick Winslow Taylor, **scientific management** postulates that decisions about organizations and job design should be based on precise, scientific study of individual situations.[37] To use this approach, managers develop precise, standard procedures for doing each job; select workers with appropriate abilities; train workers in the standard procedures; carefully plan work; and provide wage incentives to increase output. Taylor's approach is illustrated by the unloading of iron from railcars and reloading finished steel for the Bethlehem Steel plant in 1898. Taylor calculated that with correct movements, tools, and sequencing, each man was capable of loading 47.5 tons per day instead of the typical 12.5 tons. He also worked out an incentive system that paid each man $1.85 per day for meeting the new standard, an increase from the previous rate of $1.15. Productivity at Bethlehem Steel shot up overnight. These insights helped to establish organizational assumptions that the role of management is to maintain stability and efficiency, with top managers doing the thinking and workers doing what they are told.

How to Get Organized. Another subfield of the classical perspective took a broader look at the organization. Whereas scientific management focused primarily on the technical core—on work performed on the shop floor—**administrative principles** looked at the design and functioning of the organization as a whole. For example, Henri Fayol proposed 14 principles of management, such as "each subordinate receives orders from only one superior" (unity of command) and "similar activities in an organization should be grouped together under one manager" (unity of direction). These principles formed the foundation for modern management practice and organizational design.

The scientific management and administrative principles approaches were powerful and gave organizations fundamental new ideas for establishing high productivity and increasing prosperity. Administrative principles in particular contributed to the development of **bureaucratic organizations**, which emphasized designing and managing organizations on an impersonal, rational basis through such elements as clearly defined authority and responsibility, formal record keeping, and uniform application of standard rules. Although the term *bureaucracy* has taken on negative connotations in today's organizations, bureaucratic characteristics worked extremely well for the needs of the Industrial Age. One problem with the classical perspective, however, is that it failed to consider the social context and human needs.

What about People? Early work on industrial psychology and human relations received little attention because of the prominence of scientific management. However, a major breakthrough occurred with a series of experiments at a Chicago electric company, which came to be known as the **Hawthorne Studies**. Interpretations of these studies concluded that positive treatment of employees improved their motivation and productivity. The publication of these findings led to a revolution in worker treatment and laid the groundwork for subsequent work examining treatment of workers, leadership, motivation, and human resource management. These human relations and behavioural approaches added new and important contributions to the study of management and organizations.

However, the hierarchical system and bureaucratic approaches that developed during the Industrial Revolution remained the primary approach to organizational design and functioning well into the 1970s and 1980s. In general, this approach worked well for most organizations until the past few decades. However, during the 1980s, it began to lead to problems. Increased competition, especially on a global scale, changed the playing field.[38] North American companies had to find a better way.

The 1980s produced new organizational cultures that valued lean staff, flexibility, rapid response to the customer, motivated employees, caring for customers, and quality products.

Over the past two decades, the world of organizations has undergone even more profound and far-reaching changes. The Internet and other advances in information technology, globalization, rapid social and economic changes, and other challenges from the environment call for new management perspectives and more flexible approaches to organizational design.

PDA Remember...

Be cautious when applying something that works in one situation to another situation. All organizational systems are not the same. Use organizational theory to identify the correct structure, goals, strategy, and management systems for each organization.

Don't Forget the Environment. Many problems occur when all organizations are treated as similar, which was the case with scientific management and administrative principles approaches that attempted to design all organizations alike. The structures and systems that work in the retail division of a conglomerate will not be appropriate for the manufacturing division. The organizational charts and financial procedures that are best for an entrepreneurial Internet firm like eBay or Google will not work for a large food processing plant.

Contingency means that one thing depends on other things, and for organizations to be effective, there must be a "goodness of fit" between their structure and the conditions in their external environment.[39] What works in one setting may not work in another setting; there is not one best way. Contingency theory means "it depends." For example, some organizations experience a certain environment, use a routine technology, and desire efficiency. In this situation, a management approach that uses bureaucratic control procedures, a hierarchical structure, and formal communication would be appropriate. Likewise, free-flowing management processes work best in an uncertain environment with a nonroutine technology. The correct management approach is *contingent* on—depends on—the organization's situation.

Today, almost all organizations operate in highly uncertain environments. Thus, we are involved in a significant period of transition, in which concepts of organizational theory and design are changing as dramatically as they did with the dawning of the Industrial Revolution.

■ Contemporary Organizational Design

To a great extent, managers and organizations are still imprinted with the hierarchical, bureaucratic approach that arose more than a century ago. Yet the challenges presented by today's environment—globalization, diversity, ethical concerns, rapid advances in technology, the rise of e-business, a shift to knowledge and information as organizations' most important form of capital, and the growing expectations of workers for meaningful work and opportunities for personal and professional growth—call for dramatically different responses from people and organizations. The perspectives of the past do not provide a road map for steering today's organizations. Managers can design and orchestrate new responses for a dramatically new world.

Today's organizations and managers may be seen as shifting from a mindset based on mechanical systems to one based on natural and biological systems. These changing beliefs and perceptions affect how we think about organizations and the patterns of behaviour within organizations.

For most of the twentieth century, eighteenth-century Newtonian science, which suggests that the world functions as a well-behaved machine, continued to guide managers' thinking about organizations.[40] The environment was perceived as orderly and predictable, and the role of managers was to maintain stability. This mindset worked quite well for the Industrial Age.[41] Growth was a primary criterion for organizational success.

Organizations became large and complex, and boundaries between functional departments and between organizations were distinct. Internal structures grew more complex, vertical, and bureaucratic. Leadership was based on solid management principles and tended to be autocratic; communication was primarily through formal memos, letters, and reports. Managers did all the planning and "thought work," while employees did the manual labour in exchange for wages and other compensation.

The environment for today's companies, however, is anything but stable. With the turbulence of recent years, managers can no longer maintain an illusion of order and predictability. The science of **chaos theory** suggests that relationships in complex, adaptive systems—including organizations—are nonlinear and made up of numerous interconnections and divergent choices that create unintended effects and render the universe unpredictable.[42] The world is full of uncertainty, characterized by surprise, rapid change, and confusion. Managers can't measure, predict, or control in traditional ways the unfolding drama inside or outside the organization. However, chaos theory also recognizes that this randomness and disorder occurs within certain larger patterns of order. The ideas of chaos theory suggest that organizations should be viewed more as natural systems than as well-oiled, predictable machines.

Many organizations are shifting from strict vertical hierarchies to flexible, decentralized structures that emphasize horizontal collaboration, widespread information sharing, and adaptability. According to Christopher White, a minister in the United Church of Canada, "adaptability, tenacity, courage, endurance, humour, tolerance for ambiguity, and the capacity to live in paradox are all needed as we move together into the ever-shifting present. We have to find a way to sprint the marathon, while at the same time rooting ourselves in the values that have withstood the tests of centuries."[43] As the ministry of the United Church changes, the organization needs to design more adaptable structures. The United Church of Canada, the largest Protestant denomination in Canada, continues to increase its social justice work while ministering to its membership of three million in 3,500 congregations. One of its social justice activities is a partnership in KAIROS, a "coalition of Canadian churches, church based agencies and religious organizations dedicated to promoting human rights, justice and peace, viable human development and universal solidarity among the peoples of the Earth."[44] The Church's organizational chart shows the changing nature of its work; for example, there are executive ministers for "ethnic ministries, faith formation and education, justice, global and ecumenical relations, ministries in French, support to local ministries, financial services and stewardship, information technology services, ministry employment policies and services, and resource production and distribution."[45]

Businesses and other nonprofit organizations today also need greater fluidity and adaptability. Many managers are redesigning their companies toward something called the **learning organization.** The learning organization promotes communication and collaboration so that everyone is engaged in identifying and solving problems, enabling the organization to continuously experiment, improve, and increase its capability. The learning organization is based on equality, open information, little hierarchy, and a culture that encourages adaptability and participation, enabling ideas to bubble up from anywhere to help the organization seize opportunities and handle crises. In a learning organization, the essential value is problem solving, as opposed to the traditional organizational designed for efficient performance.

PDA

Remember...

When designing an organization for learning and adaptation in a turbulent environment, include elements such as horizontal structure, shared information, empowered roles, collaborative strategy, and adaptive culture. In stable environments, organizations can achieve efficient performance with a vertical structure, formal information and control systems, routine tasks, competitive strategy, and a stable culture.

■ Efficient Performance versus the Learning Organization

As managers struggle toward the learning organization, they are finding that specific dimensions of the organization—the interconnected elements of structure, tasks, systems, culture, and strategy—have to change.

From Vertical to Horizontal Structure. Traditionally, the most common organizational structure has been one in which activities are grouped together by common work from the bottom to the top of the organization. Generally, little collaboration occurs across functional departments, and the whole organization is coordinated and controlled through the vertical hierarchy, with decision-making authority residing with upper-level managers. This structure can be quite effective. It promotes efficient production and in-depth skill development, and the hierarchy of authority provides a sensible mechanism for supervision and control in large organizations. However, in a rapidly changing environment, the hierarchy becomes overloaded. Top executives are not able to respond rapidly enough to problems or opportunities.

In the learning organization, the vertical structure that creates distance between managers at the top of the organization and workers in the technical core is disbanded. Structure is created around horizontal workflows or processes rather than departmental functions. The vertical hierarchy is dramatically flattened, with perhaps only a few senior executives in traditional support functions such as finance or human resources. Self-directed teams are the fundamental work unit in the learning organization. Boundaries between functions are practically eliminated because teams include members from several functional areas. In some cases, organizations do away with departments altogether. For example, at Oticon Holding A/S, a Danish company that introduced the world's first digital hearing aid, there are no organizational charts, no departments, no functions, and no titles. Employees are continuously forming and re-forming into self-directed teams that work on specific projects.[46]

From Routine Tasks to Empowered Roles. Another shift in thinking relates to the degree of formal structure and control placed on employees in the performance of their work. Recall that scientific management advocated precisely defining each job and how it should be performed. A **task** is a narrowly defined piece of work assigned to a person. In traditional organizations, tasks are broken down into specialized, separate parts, as in a machine. Knowledge and control of tasks are centralized at the top of the organization, and employees are expected to do as they are told. A **role**, in contrast, is a part in a dynamic social system. A role has discretion and responsibility, allowing the person to use his or her discretion and ability to achieve an outcome or meet a goal. In learning organizations, employees play a role in the team or department, and roles may be continually redefined or adjusted. There are few rules or procedures, and knowledge and control of tasks are located with workers rather than with supervisors or top executives. Employees are encouraged to take care of problems by working with one another and with customers. Delta Hotels, founded in British Columbia, emphasizes the importance of creating a healthy and engaged workplace through two programs—"Response-Ability and Power to Please." The programs are designed to give employees both the responsibility and authority to deal with workplace issues. Employees are also part of planning groups for improving processes; the housekeeping staff, for example, is involved in recommending cleaning supplies, designing effective cleaning processes, and creating amenity packages. According to Bill Pallett, Senior Vice President, People, Resources and Quality, "[if] you have an engaged workforce, you have a loyal customer and if you have a loyal customer base, you're going to increase share value."[47]

From Formal Control Systems to Shared Information. In young, small organizations, communication is generally informal and face-to-face. There are few formal control and information systems because the top leaders of the company usually work directly with employees in the day-to-day operation of the business. However, when organizations grow large and complex, the distance between top leaders and workers in the technical core increases. Formal systems are often implemented to manage the growing amount of complex information and to detect deviations from established standards and goals.[48]

In learning organizations, information serves a very different purpose. The widespread sharing of information keeps the organization functioning at an optimum level. The learning organization strives to return to the condition of a small, entrepreneurial firm in which all employees have complete information about the company so they can act quickly. Ideas and information are shared throughout the organization. Rather than using information to control employees, a significant part of a manager's job is to find ways to open channels of communication so that ideas flow in all directions. In addition, learning organizations maintain open lines of communication with customers, suppliers, and even competitors to enhance learning capability. Magna International, the giant auto parts manufacturer, for example, has set up MIND (Managing Innovative New Developments). It is a web-based program designed to encourage employees to submit new product and process ideas across the organization. Employees are rewarded appropriately for successful ideas.[49] Information technology also plays a key role in keeping people across the organization connected.

From Competitive to Collaborative Strategy. In traditional organizations designed for efficient performance, strategy is formulated by top managers and imposed on the organization. Top executives think about how the organization can best respond to competition, efficiently use resources, and cope with environmental changes. In the learning organization, in contrast, the accumulated actions of an informed and empowered workforce contribute to strategy development. Since all employees are in touch with customers, suppliers, and new technology, they help identify needs and solutions and participate in strategy making. In addition, strategy emerges from partnerships with suppliers, customers, and even competitors. Organizations become collaborators as well as competitors, experimenting to find the best way to learn and adapt. Boundaries between organizations are becoming diffuse, with companies often forming partnerships to compete globally, sometimes joining in nodes or virtual network organizations that are connected electronically.

From Rigid to Adaptive Culture. For an organization to remain healthy, its culture should encourage adaptation to the external environment. A danger for many organizations is that the culture becomes ossified, as if set in concrete. Organizations that were highly successful in stable environments often become victims of their own success when the environment begins to change dramatically. One of the reasons for the demise of Eatons, whose mail-order catalogue achieved near biblical status, was that "Eaton's management failed at numerous stages to understand the strategic contours involved in the terrain of successfully turning around a company . . ."[50] The cultural values, ideas, and practices that helped attain success were detrimental to effective performance in a rapidly changing environment.

In a learning organization, the culture encourages openness, equality, continuous improvement, and change. People in the organization are aware of the whole system, how everything fits together, and how the various parts of the organization interact with one another and with the environment. This whole-system mindset minimizes boundaries within the organization and with other organizations. In addition, activities and symbols that create status differences, such as executive dining rooms or reserved parking spaces, are discarded. Each person is a valued contributor and the organization becomes a place for creating a web of relationships that allows people to develop and apply their full potential. Consider the Boston Pizza franchise's emphasis on the importance of training its employees, which it articulates in its mission statement. Its mission is "to be a world class franchisor through selecting and training people to profitably manage an outstanding foodservice business."[51] The emphasis on treating everyone with care and respect creates a climate in which people feel safe to experiment, take risks, and make mistakes, all of which encourage learning.

No company represents a perfect example of a learning organization, although many of today's most competitive organizations have shifted toward ideas and forms based on the concept of a living, dynamic system. Some of these organizations are spotlighted throughout this book in the Leading by Design boxes.

Managers today are involved in a struggle as they attempt to change their companies into learning organizations. The critical challenge for managers is to maintain some level of stability as they actively promote change toward the new way of thinking, to navigate between order and chaos. One organization that is transforming into a learning organization is Mexico's Cementos Mexicanos (Cemex).

In Practice

Cementos Mexicanos

Cementos Mexicanos (Cemex), based in Monterrey, Mexico, has been making and delivering concrete for nearly a century. But the organization is on the cutting edge of organizational design, a model of what it takes to succeed in the complex environment of the twenty-first century.

Cemex specializes in delivering concrete to developing areas of the world, places where anything can, and usually does, go wrong. Even in Monterrey, Cemex copes with unpredictable weather and traffic conditions, spontaneous labour disruptions, building permit snafus, and arbitrary government inspections of construction sites. In addition, more than half of all orders are changed or cancelled by customers, usually at the last minute. Considering that a load of concrete is never more than ninety minutes from spoiling, those chaotic conditions mean high costs, complex scheduling, and frustration for employees, managers, and customers.

To help the organization compete in this environment, managers looked for both technological and organizational innovations. Leaders call their new approach "living with chaos." Rather than trying to change the customers, Cemex resolved to do business on the customers' own terms and design a system in which last-minute changes and unexpected problems are routine.

A core element of this approach is a complex information technology system, including a global positioning satellite system and onboard computers in all delivery trucks, which is fed with streams of day-to-day data on customer orders, production schedules, traffic problems, weather conditions, and so forth. Now Cemex trucks head out every morning to cruise the streets. When a customer order comes in, an employee checks the customer's credit status, locates a nearby truck, and relays directions for delivery. If the order is cancelled, computers automatically direct the plant to scale back production.

Cemex also made managerial and organizational changes to support the new approach. The company enrolled all its drivers, who had an average of six years of formal schooling, in weekly secondary-education classes and began training them in delivering not just cement but quality service. In addition, many strict and demanding work rules were abolished so that workers had more discretion and responsibility for identifying and rapidly responding to problems and customer needs. As a result, Cemex trucks now operate as self-organizing business units, run by well-trained employees who think like businesspeople. According to Francisco Perez, operations manager at Cemex in Guadalajara, "They used to think of themselves as drivers. But anyone can deliver concrete. Now our people know that they're delivering a service that the competition cannot deliver."

Cemex has transformed the industry by combining extensive networking technology with a new management approach that taps into the mindpower of everyone in the company. People at Cemex are constantly learning—on the job, in training classes, and through visits to other organizations. As a result, the company has a startling capacity to anticipate customer needs, solve problems, and innovate quickly. In addition, Cemex freely shares what it knows with other organizations, even competitors, believing the widespread sharing of knowledge and information is the best way to keep the organization thriving in a world of complexity. This philosophy has helped transform a once-sleepy cement company into a global powerhouse, with 2,200 operating units in 22 countries.[52]

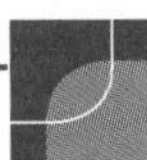

Framework for the Book

What topic areas are relevant to organizational theory and design? How does a course in management or organizational behaviour differ from a course in organizational theory? The answer is related to the concept called level of analysis.

PDA Remember...

Make yourself a competent, influential manager by using the frameworks that organizational theory provides to interpret and understand the organization around you.

Levels of Analysis

Four **levels of analysis** normally characterize organizations, as illustrated in Exhibit 1.7. The individual human being is the basic building block of organizations. The human being is to the organization what a cell is to a biological system. The next higher system level is the group or department. These are collections of individuals who work together to perform group tasks. The next level of analysis is the organization itself. An organization is a collection of groups or departments that combine into the total organization.

Organizations themselves can be grouped together into the next higher level of analysis, which is the interorganizational set and community. The interorganizational set is the group of organizations with which a single organization interacts. Other organizations in the community also make up an important part of an organization's environment.

Organizational theory focuses on the organizational level of analysis but with concern for groups and the environment. To explain the organization, one should look at not only its characteristics but also the characteristics of the environment and of the departments and groups that make up the organization. The focus of this

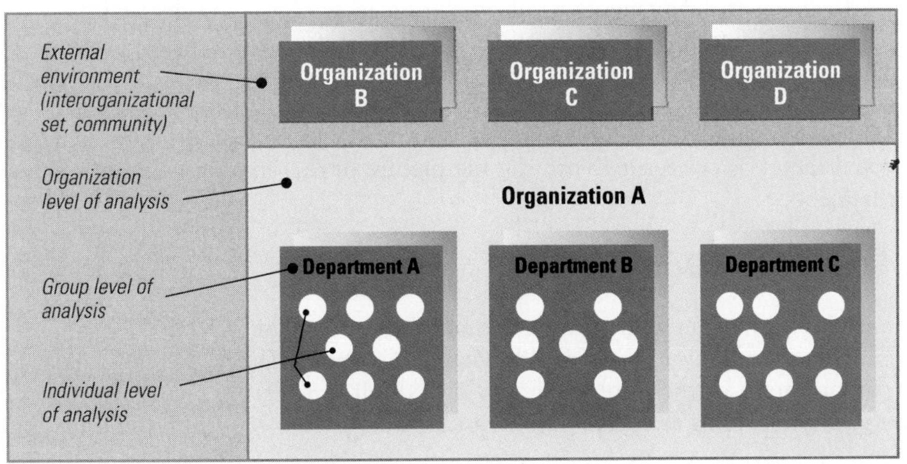

EXHIBIT 1.7
Levels of Analysis in Organizations
Source: Based on Andrew H. Van De Ven and Diane L. Ferry, *Measuring and Assessing Performance* (New York: Wiley, 1980), 8; and Richard L. Daft and Richard M. Steers, *Organizations: A Micro/Macro Approach* (Glenview, Ill.: Scott, Foresman, 1986), 8.

book is to help you understand organizations by examining their specific characteristics, the nature of and relationships among groups and departments that make up the organization, and the collection of organizations that make up the environment.

Are individuals included in organizational theory? Organizational theory does consider the behaviour of individuals, but in the aggregate. People are important, but they are not the primary focus of analysis. Organizational theory is distinct from organizational behaviour.

Organizational behaviour is the micro approach to organizations because it focuses on the individuals within organizations as the relevant units of analysis. Organizational behaviour examines concepts such as motivation, leadership style, and personality, and is concerned with cognitive and emotional differences among people within organizations.

Organizational theory is a macro examination of organizations because it analyzes the whole organization as a unit. Organizational theory is concerned with people aggregated into departments and organizations, and with the differences in structure and behaviour at the organization level of analysis. Organizational theory is the sociology of organizations, while organizational behaviour is the psychology of organizations.

A new approach to organization studies is called *meso theory*. Most organizational research and many management courses specialize in either organizational behaviour or organizational theory. **Meso theory** (*meso* means "in between") concerns the integration of both micro and macro levels of analysis. Individuals and groups affect the organization, and the organization in return influences individuals and groups. To thrive in organizations, managers and employees need to understand multiple levels simultaneously. For example, research may show that employee diversity enhances innovation. To facilitate innovation, managers need to understand how structure and context (organizational theory) are related to interactions among diverse employees (organizational behaviour) to foster innovation, because both macro and micro variables account for innovation.[53]

Organizational theory is directly relevant to top- and middle-management concerns and partly relevant to lower management. Top managers are responsible for the entire organization and must set goals, develop strategy, interpret the external environment, and decide organizational structure and design. Middle management is concerned with major departments, such as marketing or research, and must decide how the department relates to the rest of the organization. Middle managers must design their departments to fit work-unit technology and deal with issues of power and politics, intergroup conflict, and information and control systems, each of which is part of organizational theory. Organizational theory is only partly concerned with lower management because this level of supervision is concerned with employees who operate machines, input data, teach classes, and sell goods. Organizational theory is concerned with the big picture of the organization and its major departments.

Plan of the Book

The topics within the field of organizational theory are interrelated. Chapters are presented so that major ideas unfold in logical sequence. The framework that guides the organization of the book is shown in Exhibit 1.8. Part 1 introduces the basic idea of organizations as social systems and the nature of organizational theory. This

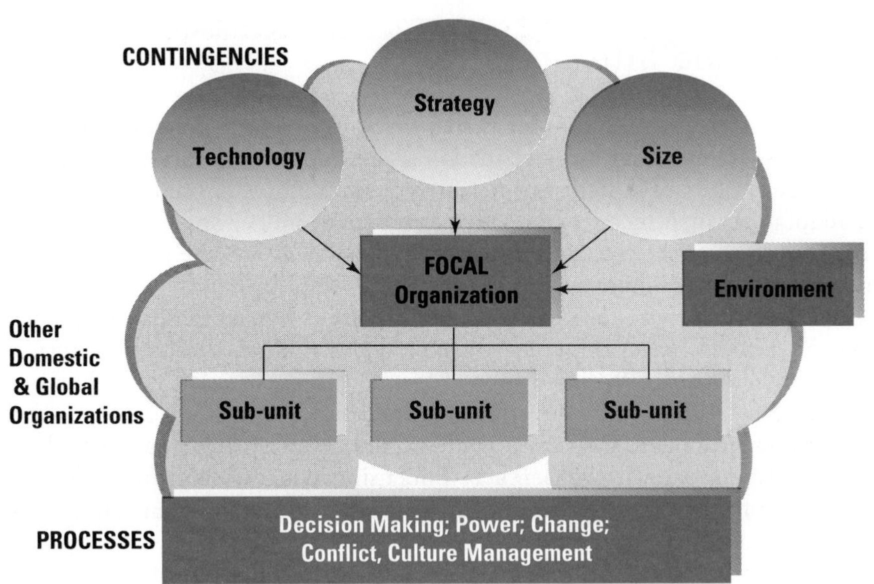

EXHIBIT 1.8
Framework for the Organization of This Book
Source: Copyright © 2008 by Ann Armstrong.

discussion provides the groundwork for Part 2, which is about strategic management, goals and effectiveness, and the fundamentals of organizational structure. Organizations are open systems that exist for a purpose. This part examines how managers help the organization achieve its purpose, including the design of an appropriate structure, such as a functional, divisional, matrix, or horizontal structure. Part 3 looks at the various open-system elements that influence organizational structure and design, including the external environment, interorganizational relationships, and the international environment.

Parts 4 and 5 look at processes inside the organization. Part 4 describes how organizational design is related to such factors as manufacturing and service technology; information and control systems; and organizational size, life cycle, and decline. Part 5 shifts to dynamic processes that exist within and between major organizational departments and includes topics such as culture and ethical values; innovation and change; decision-making processes; and conflict, power, and politics.

■ Plan of Each Chapter

Each chapter begins with an organizational case to illustrate the topic to be covered. Theoretical concepts are introduced and explained in the body of the chapter. Several *In Practice* segments are included in each chapter to illustrate the concepts and show how they apply to real organizations. *Book Marks* are included in most chapters to present organizational issues that managers face right now. These book reviews discuss current concepts and applications to deepen and enrich your understanding of organizations. The *Leading by Design* examples illustrate the dramatic changes taking place in management thinking and practice. Key points for designing and managing organizations are highlighted in the *PDA* items throughout the chapter. Each chapter closes with a "Summary and Interpretation" section that reviews and explains important theoretical concepts.

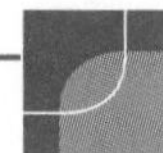

Summary and Interpretation

One important idea in this chapter is that organizations are systems. In particular, they are open systems that must adapt to the environment to survive. Various parts of the organization are designed to perform the key subsystem functions of production, adaptation, maintenance, management, and boundary spanning. Five parts of the organization are the technical core, top management, middle management, technical support, and administrative support.

The focus of analysis for organizational theory is not individual people but the organization itself. Relevant concepts include the dimensions of organizational structure and context. The dimensions of formalization, specialization, hierarchy of authority, centralization, professionalism, personnel ratios, size, organizational technology, environment, goals and strategy, and culture provide labels for measuring and analyzing organizations. These dimensions vary widely from organization to organization. Subsequent chapters provide frameworks for analyzing organizations with these concepts.

Many types of organizations exist. One important distinction is between for-profit businesses, in which managers direct their activities toward earning money for the company, and nonprofit organizations, in which managers direct their efforts toward generating some kind of social impact. Managers strive to design organizations to achieve high performance and effectiveness. Effectiveness is complex because different stakeholders have different interests and needs that they want satisfied by the organization.

Turbulence and complexity have replaced stability and predictability as defining traits for today's organizations. Some of the specific challenges managers and organizations face include coping with globalization; maintaining high standards of ethics and social responsibility; achieving rapid response to environmental changes, organizational crises, or new customer expectations; shifting to a technology-based workplace; and supporting diversity.

These challenges are leading to changes in organizational design and management practices. The trend is away from highly structured systems based on a mechanical model toward looser, more flexible systems based on a natural, biological model. Many managers are redesigning companies toward the learning organization, which is characterized by a horizontal structure, empowered employees, shared information, collaborative strategy, and an adaptive culture.

Finally, most concepts in organizational theory pertain to the top- and middle-management levels of the organization. This book is concerned more with the topics of those levels than with the operational-level topics of supervision and motivation of employees, which are discussed in courses on organizational behaviour.

Key Concepts

administrative principles, p. 25
bureaucratic organizations, p. 25
change strategy, p. 5
chaos theory, p. 26
closed system, p. 13
contextual dimensions, p. 17
contingency, p. 26
effectiveness, p. 21
efficiency, p. 21
Hawthorne Studies, p. 25
learning organization, p. 27
level of analysis, p. 31

meso theory, p. 32
open system, p. 13
organization, p. 9
organizational behaviour, p. 32
organizational theory, p. 32
role, p. 28
scientific management, p. 24
stakeholder, p. 22
stakeholder approach, p. 22
structural dimensions, p. 17
subsystems, p. 14
system, p. 14
task, p. 28

Discussion Questions

1. What is the definition of *organization*? Briefly explain each part of the definition.
2. What is the difference between an open system and a closed system? Can you give an example of a closed system? How is the stakeholder approach related to this concept?
3. Explain how Mintzberg's five basic parts of the organization perform the subsystem functions shown at the bottom of Exhibit 1.2. If an organization had to give up one of these five parts, which one could it survive the longest without? Discuss.
4. A handful of companies on the Fortune 500 list are more than 100 years old, which is rare. What organizational characteristics do you think might explain 100-year longevity?
5. What is the difference between formalization and specialization? Do you think an organization high on one dimension would also be high on the other? Discuss.
6. What does *contingency* mean? What are the implications of contingency theories for managers?
7. What are the primary differences between an organization designed for efficiency and one designed for flexibility? Discuss the pros and cons of each approach for today's organizations.

Chapter 1 Workbook: Measuring Dimensions of Organizations*

Analyze two organizations along the dimensions shown below. Indicate where you think each organization would fall on each of the scales. Use an X to indicate the first organization and an * to show the second.

You may choose any two organizations you are familiar with, such as your place of work; the university; a student organization; your church, mosque, or synagogue; or your family.

Formalization

Many written rules 1 2 3 4 5 6 7 8 9 10 Few rules

Specialization

Separate tasks and roles 1 2 3 4 5 6 7 8 9 10 Overlapping tasks

Hierarchy

Tall hierarchy of authority 1 2 3 4 5 6 7 8 9 10 Flat hierarchy of authority

Technology

Product 1 2 3 4 5 6 7 8 9 10 Service

External Environment

Stable 1 2 3 4 5 6 7 8 9 10 Unstable

Culture

Clear norms and values 1 2 3 4 5 6 7 8 9 10 Ambiguous norms and values

Professionalism

High professional training	1	2	3	4	5	6	7	8	9	10	Low professional training

Goals

Well-defined goals	1	2	3	4	5	6	7	8	9	10	Goals not defined

Size

Small	1	2	3	4	5	6	7	8	9	10	Large

Organizational Mindset

Mechanical system	1	2	3	4	5	6	7	8	9	10	Biological system

Questions

1. What are the main differences between the two organizations you evaluated?
2. Would you recommend that one or both of the organizations have different ratings on any of the scales? Why?

Case for Analysis: iStockphoto.com: Turning Community into Commerce*

The clash of cultures was bound to happen one day. When Bruce Livingstone started iStockphoto.com in 2000, his objective was to share his vast collection of stock photography with graphic designers worldwide and, in the process, help others do the same. By 2001, however, monthly bandwidth charges had reached $10,000. It was clear that iStockphoto could no longer survive strictly as a free exchange service. With regret, Livingstone and his partners instituted a minimal charge for downloads to cover the cost of bandwidth.

A year later, it seemed that the very philosophy of the company might be challenged. Patrick Lor, iStockphoto's first full-time employee, had tabled a business plan that proposed new fees and a profit objective for the company. Under Lor's plan, fees would increase from $0.25 to $1.00 per photo credit; contributing photographers would continue to receive 20 per cent commission on the sale of their images. Livingstone and his partners had always known there was revenue potential in their vast inventory of stock photography. But this was an enterprise founded on the notion of community and collaboration—not commerce. Should the model change and, even if it should, what would it take to make a significant culture change work?

The Evolution of iStockphoto

It was impossible to point to the precise birth date of iStockphoto. However, it certainly began to germinate in 2000, when Bruce Livingstone floated a business plan to various Canadian funding agencies. He proposed creating royalty-free collections of stock photography on CD-ROMs and selling them for $149 per disk. The concept was attractive enough to get him $50,000 in start-up funding, and he was on the road to becoming a stock photo provider.

Livingstone had three partners in this start-up effort: Brad Ralph, Ian Russell and Paul Harris. The four set up a small office over a sewing shop, providing corporate website services to such clients as Fiberlink, Digital Music Express, Shaw Cable and MTV Canada, as a way to jumpstart revenues. When they realized that their website work was occupying all of their time, and they were no closer to delivering on the promise of the stock photo

IVEY
Richard Ivey School of Business
The University of Western Ontario

*Meghan Stothers wrote this case under the supervision of Rebecca Grant solely to provide material for class discussion. The authors do not intend to illustrate either effective or ineffective handling of a managerial situation. The authors may have disguised certain names and other identifying information to protect confidentiality.

CD-ROM, Livingstone took six months and concentrated on shooting stock images. He also scanned all the photos and negatives his mother had lying around. At the end of the six months, he had four CD-ROMs that could be brought to market.

After spending significant amounts of money to produce the CD-ROMs in volume, it became clear that the idea was not going to fly. Advertising was too expensive, mass direct mail was impossible and acquiring a clean mailing list of a high-quality target market was no easier. But the death of the CD-ROM plan proved to be just the start of a better idea. As Livingstone explained:

It was the dot-com heyday and everyone was watching the i-this and e-this. I think the iPod had just come out, and we were riffing on the name. We said, "Let's buy iStockphoto [as a domain name]. Let's give all this stuff away. We worked so hard on it, let's give back to the community and share our photos and see what happens." It wasn't meant to be some huge business. It was just meant to give away the photos. . . . We wanted to see them used.

Within months, the community that would become the heart of the business had emerged. The founders were swamped with e-mail from people who had downloaded the images from iStockphoto and wanted to share their own work. Livingstone designed a simple system that let members upload images. He also added all-important communication features and forums. As news spread through word of mouth, the site attracted a loyal cadre of contributors who posted pictures, frequented the site's message boards and gave each other advice and feedback on their photography.

As the collection of images expanded, Livingstone wanted to create an alternative to traditional subscription models used by companies such as arttoday.com. Taking the ideas he'd generated while working at Image Club Graphics in the 1990s, he designed an exchange-based model. A member of the community could upload an image to iStockphoto at any time. If someone subsequently downloaded the image, the photographer received one credit. That credit could then be used to download an image from the site. This original system didn't distinguish among sizes or types of image; every download cost the downloader one credit, and earned the uploader one credit.

The iStockphoto approach to building its collection was unique. Every image submitted was scrutinized by an iStockphoto inspector before being posted to the member-accessible portion of the site. The inspectors, respected members of the iStockphoto contributor community, reviewed the images to ensure they met the company's standards of content and quality. They approved photos for posting, provided advice on improving images that weren't accepted and generally mentored contributors new to the stock photo business. The inspection process also confirmed, based on the best available information, that the image was the original work of the contributor and didn't violate any known copyrights or digital rights restrictions.

The iStockphoto business was built on the concept of royalty-free use. Whereas traditional stock photography houses generally attached specific or limited rights to the use of images they sold, iStockphoto images came with a blanket use agreement that provided at least 500,000 reproductions of the image without additional per-use charges (see Exhibit 1).

The iStockphoto Community

Community-based models are almost as old as the World Wide Web itself.

The Well (www.well.com), launched in 1985, is widely considered the birthplace of the online community movement. The emotional and intellectual bonds formed online prompted an early Well participant, Howard Rheingold, to coin the phrase "virtual community." Other early online community models included TheGlobe, Tripod, Xoom.com and GeoCities.

An online community site is not a one-way street. Its strength and success depends on its members' involvement beyond buying and selling. Members understand that the growth of the community site depends directly on their willingness to contribute to the site on a regular basis. The community often decides for itself what it does and does not like.

The members of the iStockphoto community were primarily graphic designers, illustrators and amateur photographers. Like Livingstone and his partners, they had been producing images for their own use, largely as a cost-effective alternative to expensive stock houses and as a way to meet client requirements. Thus, many had large personal collections of images that would be of interest to others, if there were only a simple way to promote and distribute them. Members shared their experience as well as their images. Member Andrzej Burbak, half of the Polish husband-and-wife team known as Bubitim, expressed the essence of iStockphoto: "It's a great community from all over the world, many wonderful people full of passion. The management never sleeps, and they treat people with respect."

The iStockphoto online community of some 200,000 members participated in forums to communicate ideas to other members, to gain a better understanding of the site and to improve their specific skills. They could browse through forums on design and photography, as well as link to related blogs and articles from industry gurus. Members used the site to make comments, offer advice and network with other photographers and designers. People could connect both socially and professionally, as

EXHIBIT 1
Details of License Agreement

Use of iStockphoto.com Digital Files (Plain English)

First off, a "digital file" is any file on iStockphoto.com whether a photograph, illustration, movie, audio file or code snippet.

You may (providing the digital file is marked as "Royalty Free"):

- Download an iStockphoto.com digital file to one computer.
- Make one (1) backup of iStockphoto.com digital files.
- Move or Copy the digital file to another computer.
- Use iStockphoto digital files in web sites (commercial or otherwise), advertising, promotional material, presentations, broadcast television and multimedia content such as Flash® files, Director® and movies. File use includes commercial items such as product packaging, product brochures and any type of promotional material.
- Provide an iStockphoto.com digital file to your printer or other 3rd party for the purposes of printing or production of materials.
- Reproduce (copy, modify or incorporate) iStockphoto.com digital files, royalty-free, in print and digital publications, presentations and multimedia content.
- Create derivative works from iStockphoto.com digital files.

You may not:

- Redistribute a copy or backup of iStockphoto.com digital file.
- Allow anyone else to distribute or copy an iStockphoto.com digital file.
- Make more than one (1) copy of an iStockphoto.com digital file.
- Use a member uploaded digital file (or file) in your final designs that is marked "Personal Use Only". If you want to use a member uploaded digital file in your final designs, iStockphoto.com suggests you contact the member directly. iStockphoto.com is not responsible for copyrights or misuse of member uploaded files (see the section on this page called "Use of Member Uploaded digital files" for more information).
- Sell or charge a client or 3rd party for an iStockphoto.com digital file.
- Generate revenue directly from the use or sale of iStockphoto.com digital files in "for sale" items. This means digital files downloaded from iStockphoto.com cannot be used to create a "for sale" item where the digital file is the primary feature or the compelling reason for the sale of the product. You can't print an iStockphoto.com digital file on a greeting card, t-shirt, poster, etc. and sell it, unless the digital file is part of an overall design. If there is ever a discrepancy around this issue, iStockphoto.com reserves the right to decide if acceptable use is being followed.
- Repackage and/or resell digital files in the form of clip art, digital stock photography or print photography archives, or any other inclusion of recordable media.
- Duplicate (or allow anyone else to duplicate) in any form, whether printed, digital, photographic or otherwise, any of the digital files on this iStockphoto.com archive, except when iStockphoto.com digital files are incorporated by you into printed material or on-screen material. (This means you have to "design" something with the digital files).
- Upload (or allow anyone else to upload) any of the digital files from iStockphoto.com on an electronic bulletin board or any other form of on-line service such as Hotline servers.

Use (or allow anyone else to use) any of the digital files from iStockphoto.com in any form of fraudulent, pornographic, defamatory, immoral, infringing or illegal material, the determination of which is left to the sole discretion of iStockphoto.com.

Contractual Information

Failure to comply with the license agreement is a material breach. This license is not a sale. Title and copyrights in and to the digital files, accompanying documentation and any copy made by us remain with iStockphoto.com or its suppliers or licensors. Unauthorized copying of the iStockphoto.com digital files or otherwise failing to comply with terms and conditions of this Agreement will result in automatic termination of this license and you will make available to iStockphoto.com any legal remedies deemed necessary by iStockphoto.com. Upon termination of this Agreement, the licenses granted herein will terminate and you must immediately return all licensed material and all backup copies thereof, to iStockphoto.com Copyright infringers will be prosecuted to the fullest extent of the law.

EXHIBIT 1 CONTINUED . . .

Use of Member Uploaded digital files
Member Uploaded digital files are digital files supplied and uploaded by members of iStockphoto.com. iStockphoto.com makes no guarantee that digital files provided by its members are Royalty Free Content. Use of Member Uploaded digital files in your designs and artwork is done so at your own risk. Digital files are provided "as is". Neither iStockphoto.com nor any of its directors, officers, employees, partners, or agents shall be liable for any damages, whether direct, indirect, consequential or incidental, arising out of the use of, or the inability to use, any Royalty Free digital files downloaded from this web site. Full rights and ownership of member uploaded digital files is provided as a reference and questions regarding the usability for any purpose or proposed use should be directed to the member who uploaded the file.

Warranties
iStockphoto.com warrants that it has the right to grant this license to you. iStockphoto.com makes no other warranty, expressed or implied, including any implied warranties of merchantability or fitness for a particular purpose. Some states or provinces may not permit the exclusion of implied warranties and you may have other rights that may vary from state to state or province to province. Digital files and digital files are provided "as is". iStockphoto.com makes no warranty, either expressed or implied, of merchantability, fitness for any particular use, type or quality of digital file, or compatibility with any computer or other kind of equipment. Neither iStockphoto.com nor any of its directors, officers, employees, partners, or agents shall be liable for any damages, whether direct, indirect, consequential or incidental, arising out of the use of, or the inability to use, any Royalty Free digital files downloaded from this web site. The international copyright laws of the United States and Canada will govern this Agreement. If any provision of this Agreement is held invalid, the remainder of this Agreement shall continue in full force effect. If you have any questions regarding this Agreement, please contact us in writing.

©2001 iStockphoto.com All Rights Reserved. All other brands or product names are trademarks or registered trademarks of their respective holders. WARNING: If you are in doubt of the validity of a proposed use, don't risk it. Instead, please contact us at info@iStockphoto.com to discuss obtaining permission.

Source: Company files.

when mmroberts posted, "I am really looking for good people & architecture shots. Please contact me with any photos that you would like me to consider adding."

Members organized photo galleries based on specific themes or topics. The themes were based strictly on the interests of the members who launched the galleries and ran the gamut from "I Love New York" and "Around the Office" to "Light Sources" and "Great Pics that Have Had Few Downloads." In another feature, staff at iStockphoto chose an "Image of the Week," which was posted on the home page and frequently triggered dialogue and new collaborations among members. An image chosen late in May, 2001, for example, prompted this posting by member machnewmedia:

Nice Picture of South Side of Pittsburgh: I know that place as well. That's an old one, but a good choice for picture of the week. Let's make a Pburgh gallery dude! I think we have about 30 shots or so between the two of us.

Livingstone was never far from the community he created. He worked relentlessly to build a vibrant iStockphoto community, structuring the site with forums and blogs in order to share members' comments and experiences. These activities inspired a level of communication and openness between members previously unheard of in the stock photo industry. Under the online name of Bitter, he regularly posted comments on the home page promoting members and their work, such as when he noted, "Great new stuff from Delirium, also a tasty food series from izusek (to name a couple). We'll be back at it tomorrow."

The company had a reputation for regular interaction with its membership, seeking and welcoming discussion of new business ideas or changes to the site before and after implementation. The site was refreshed regularly, and Livingstone constantly looked ahead to keep members entertained and inspired, thinking of ways to help members profile their creations and provide a forum in which photographers could mentor and help one another. He and his colleagues continuously invented new search functions, inviting members to decide on keywords and color. Receiving both criticism and advice from members was essential to the growth of the online community.

The website, relaunched in February of 2002, conveyed a playful tone and invited participation from its members (see Exhibit 2). Online contests such as Images of Fall and the iStockphoto T-shirt Contest fostered a fun and competitive spirit. The site profiled an eclectic selection of images on the home page; each image included a link to the photographer's profile. Public liteboxes let community members "play curator" and organize their images for other members to enjoy. The site also included dedicated areas for its members, such as "my uploads," "my mailbox" and "my profile," encouraging them to create personal and permanent spaces on the iStockphoto site (see Exhibit 3). Last but not least, iStockphoto provided contributors with referrals, training, business cards and other marketing tools, as well as recognition for sales and artistic successes.

In further commitment to the community, Livingstone refused to run commercial advertising on the site. As he explained:

It's a visual interruption to a designer . . . people come to the site to work and I've always thought iStockphoto should be part of the design process. You don't want to interrupt people with advertising when they're working.

However, that commitment meant that the company had to look for other sources of revenue. The collection of high-quality images had grown quickly and dramatically—and the bandwidth charges grew right along with them. It had become clear in 2001 that the company could no longer carry the cost of bandwidth as a service to its member[s], so Livingstone had solicited members for their comments about fees and invited them to vote on a variety of payment models, including a subscription and a pay-per-use model.

The online community had come out solidly in favor of the pay-per-use approach. As a result, iStockphoto moved away from granting free credits to anyone who contributed to the micropayment model. Under its new micropayment model, anyone (contributor or not) could buy bundles of non-expiring credits. The basic cost of a credit was $0.25, with small discounts for large bundles. A single download cost one credit, and contributors received a commission of five cents each time one of their images was downloaded.[1] Because the money was collected up front (when the credits were sold) and stored until an image was purchased, photographers could be paid soon after their image was downloaded.

This move to micropayments was widely considered to be the step that pioneered the microstock industry. Traditional stock photography from large companies, such as Corbis and Getty, was known as macrostock. Stock images from macrostock firms typically cost upwards of $500 per image; custom photo shoots would be considerably more expensive. The macrostock fee would generally come with significant restrictions as to the type of use and the number of times the image could be used without additional fees. Microstock images, on the other hand, were royalty-free and sold at a very low price, or even given away free. Instead of a low-volume, high-price industry, microstock used high volume at low prices to drive revenue. The revolutionary principle was simple: anyone with a great image could sell it overnight throughout the world, and make some money from it.

Many professional photographers felt that low pricing and royalty-free models undervalued their work, cost them significant income and would ultimately destroy the commercial viability of their livelihood. The management of iStockphoto argued, as did many others, that quantity would prevail and photographers would end up making as much from many microstock sales as they would from a few large macrostock sales. Indeed, many iStockphoto members described the fun of "watching the nickels roll in"—repeatedly refreshing their online account screens to watch the immediate effect of downloads from customers around the world.

In 2002, iStockphoto customers downloaded more than 405,000 images. With a purchase happening roughly every 80 seconds, the nickels added up quickly and gave many semi-pros the confidence to launch themselves as full-time photographers. One such contributor was Lise Gagne. Lise began her relationship with iStockphoto when she was buying photos for her employer, a small company with a low promotion budget. She explained her transition from downloader to uploader:

We needed a particular picture but could not find it; that's how I became involved as a photographer . . . There weren't a lot of people shots [at that time]. So after trying to find something for many hours, I decided to do the picture by myself, with my little A40 Canon "point and shoot" and the people working with me as models. I uploaded it on iStock [see Exhibit 4]. The image was a great success; from then on, I became involved as a full-time contributor.

Eventually, Gagne left her "regular" job behind and became a full-time stock photographer. Her loyalty is typical of a large segment of the company's contributors:

What I like most about iStock is the total freedom that I have. There's something special about iStock. They have good marketing strategies, the team works nonstop for us, they believe in their photographers, and they like them. We are important for them, and they take care of us.

[1] The commission was thus approximately 20 per cent. In some cases, it was higher: bundled credits cost something less than $0.25 but iStockphoto did not discount the commission, even if the image was bought with "cheaper" credits.

EXHIBIT 2
iStockphoto.com Home Page

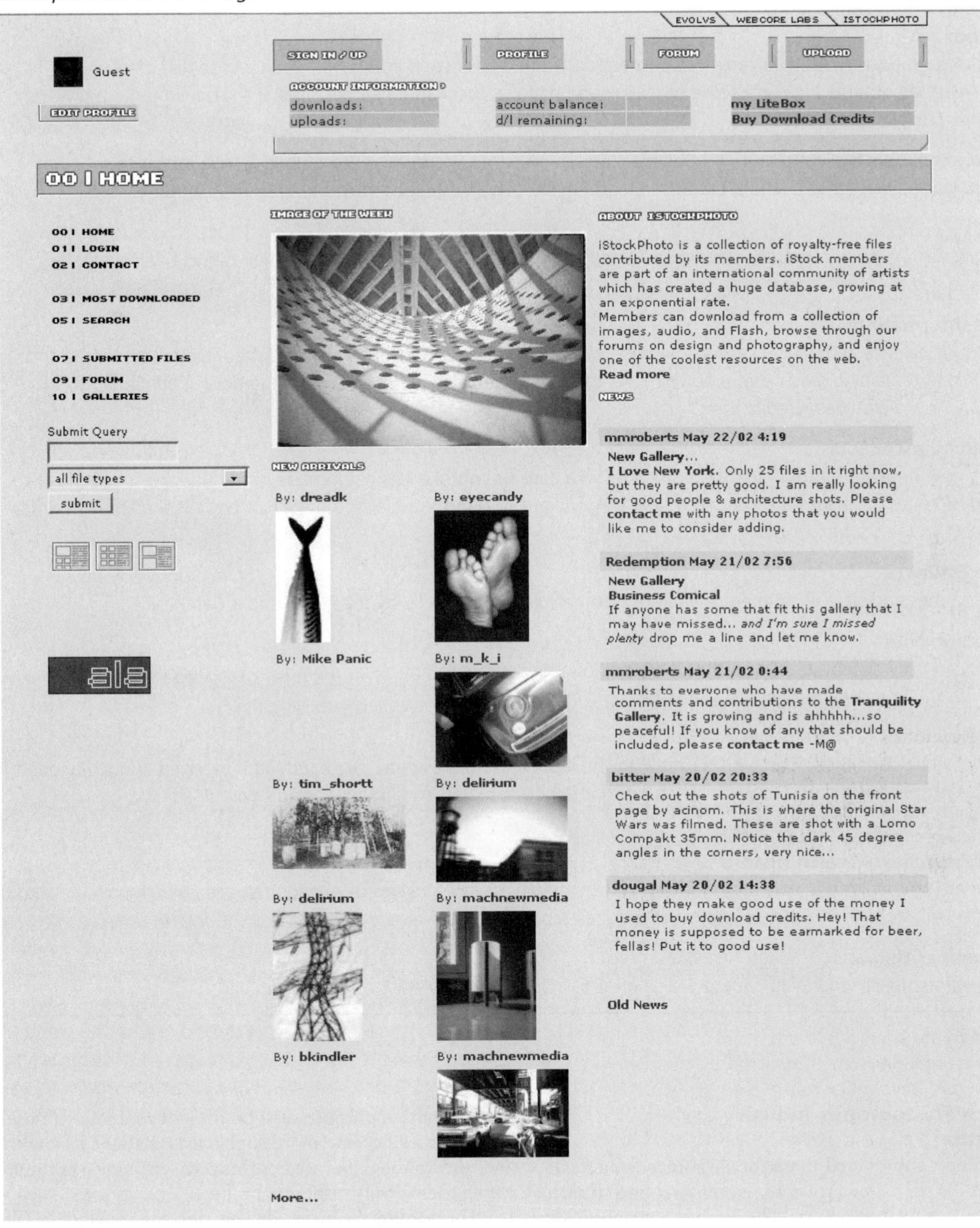

Source: Company files.

EXHIBIT 3
iStockphoto.com Features

My Litebox
The Litebox is a space where you can store photos for future reference. If you have to suggest some comp photos to someone else, or want to show off some of your own portfolio, you can email the Litebox to someone.

Avatars
Avatars are the icons that represent your member profile on iStock. If you want to upload a new Avatar to the collection, go to "Edit Profile" and click on "Upload Avatar". Avatar images must be a 25x25 pixel GIF or JPG.

Site Mail
iStock now has member-to-member mailboxes. Send site mail to anyone by clicking on their name and "Send Site Mail".

Account Information
Your account balance and activity is always visible to you in the upper part of the screen. When your account balance and download remaining reach zero, you will have to buy more credits in order to continue downloading. Do this by clicking on "Buy Download Credits".

Improved Member Tools
Members now have full control over their own files. If a spelling mistake has been made in the title, keywords need to be added, updates to images are needed or you simply want to remove a file from iStock, members are able to control every aspect of their submissions.

File Size Estimate
Download times and sizes at different scales are now calculated on the fly by the super-duper database.

Deactivating Files
Members can now deactivate files so that they are no longer visible to any other members. The deactivate button is available on the image page.

Faster Downloads
Previously, iStock had limited bandwidth, but with the launch of the new site, the bandwidth received a much needed increase. With the burst rate, iStock is able to reach a full 10 megabit, so file uploads and downloads will greatly increase.

Detailed Searches + Search History
Members are now able to search titles, file number, by member name, keywords, categories, search within results and soon iStock will store your searches and other features too.

View Member Uploads
If you like a member's work, you can now click on their name and view a list of all their uploads.

Source: Company files.

The Stock Photography Industry and Competition

Stock photography offered those looking for commercial grade photos an alternative to expensive and time-consuming custom photo shoots. The product first appeared in the early 1900s and, for decades, consisted largely of outtakes or "seconds" from commercial magazine assignments. By the 1980s, however, it had become a specialty in its own right, with photographers creating new material for the express purpose of submitting it to a stock house. Stock houses became more sophisticated about following and anticipating the needs of advertisers, and communicating these needs to photographers.

The leading agencies during this time included The Image Bank, SuperStock, Comstock Images, FPG, Index Stock Imagery and Masterfile. However, the 1990s proved to be a period of consolidation through acquisition, with Getty Images and Corbis emerging as the two dominant

EXHIBIT 4
Lise Gagne's First Contribution

Source: Photo © Lise Gagne, www.istockphoto.com, accessed September 1, 2006.

forces in the industry. By 2002, stock photography companies had largely moved online. JupiterMedia Corporation bought smaller players in the market, aggregating them under the banner of their JupiterImages division. Jupiter soon became the third largest player in the market.

By 2002, Getty Images owned more than 70 million images; the average licenced stock photo cost $500. On a typical business day, the company's website served up more than 35 million thumbnail images in response to customer searches, managed 150,000 visitor sessions and processed more than five million page views and more than 3,000 purchase transactions.[2] At the time, approximately 85 per cent of the company's business came from "creative" work, meaning work that was arranged, such as fashion shoots.[3]

That same year, Corbis added another 60,000 commercial images to its stock collection. The company also beefed up its site with a new layout, increased speed and enhanced search functionalities. For the first time, the site could accommodate French and German users. In addition to rights-managed images, the company sold royalty-free images for US$29.95. Corbis also launched a set of specialty image catalogues that also profiled a select group of photographers—an unusual move in the stock photo industry, but one Corbis felt would demonstrate its support for the company's talent.[4]

[2]GettyImages.com, Getty Images 2002 Annual Report, Letter to Shareholders, available at http://corporate.gettyimages.com/source/investors/index.aspx?pageID=annualReports&shPage=annual.cfm, accessed July 2006.

[3]Steve Hoare, "A Pretty Picture," Lawyer, June 16, 2003, p. 14.

[4]"Baby Boomers Redefine the Image of Aging," Press Release, April 22, 2002, http://www.creativepro.com/story/news/16557.html, accessed July 2006.

The use of stock photography began migrating into new and unexpected areas. The explosion of home personal computers (PCs) and the growing sophistication of small and home businesses meant the potential market was growing beyond traditional stock photo users to small businesses, students and individuals. Enhanced download speeds, increased availability of broadband services and the sheer breadth of stock photo collections made global expansion a real prospect. These factors accompanied a waning interest in traditional chromes and slides, in favor of digital images. Stock photography, illustration and video were maturing into a first-choice solution for a wide range of graphic arts, advertising, publishing and Internet work.

Despite consolidation among the major players, stock photography remained a highly fragmented industry. More than 53 medium-sized, professional stock photo services were available online to North American customers, and a host of sites offering images of varying quality for free.

The majority of the smaller commercial firms offered limited collections on CDs or by subscriptions, though there were also single-image purchase options. Firms selling royalty-free single images for US$19 to US$99 marketed themselves as a low-price option to the large commercial houses. Ablestock.com, for example, offered royalty-free images based on file size (25 MB images at $99.99, 10 MB images and 1.5 MB images for $49.99 and $19.99, respectively). PhotoSpin's annual subscription service ($149 for a basic subscription and $249 for a professional subscription) tried to appeal to the time-conscious designer by offering access to images, illustrations, fonts, film clips and sound files. Like their larger competitors, many smaller firms were selling images produced internally or by a small group of professional photographers working exclusively for the company. After dropping its prices significantly in 2002, Dreamstime sold themed CD collections (2,178 royalty-free images on four CDs for $65, 945 royalty-free images on two CDs for $40 and 450 royalty-free images on two CDs for $35.)

Boutique agencies, such Colorado-based Desert Dolphin, aimed at keeping image collections lean and focused on the works from a select group of photographers. Cofounder Paul Ambrose said: "We offer photographers something that's becoming quite rare, respect. As the larger agencies group together under Getty and Corbis, some photographers are feeling left out. There are literally millions of photographs in those collections. It's hard for the individual to get noticed."[5] Fees for the company's rights-protected images depended on the intended usage; they ranged from $75 for low-resolution Web use to $1,000 for a one-year advertising use.

The most notable industry trend in 2002 was the shift toward royalty-free images over royalty-based, negotiated-use images. Royalty-free imagery was not without its controversies, particularly among photographers, but many designers and production firms increasingly preferred the ease and lower expense of royalty-free imagery.[6] In addition, the popularity of and competition in microstock was growing. When iStockphoto launched its micropayment model early in the year, there were no other firms with a comparable model. As the end of 2002 approached, that situation was changing, and competition was sure to grow.

The Decision

Despite the growing commerce on his site, Livingstone was adamant about keeping the concept of community alive. His idea was to continue to grow an online community that nurtured, educated and mentored photographers, providing them with the opportunity to earn a living doing what they loved.

There was no doubt that iStockphoto was a hit with its existing model. By November 2002, the site had hosted more than 23,000 images and was adding more than 1,000 new images each week. (See Exhibits 5 and 6 for iStockphoto's financial statements for 2002.) At the same time, having proven the feasibility of the micropayment model, iStockphoto could well be left behind as the competition evolved. What kind of organization would it take to turn the community into commerce, and could that organization support photographers and buyers alike?

[5]Photographers Flocking to New Stock Agency, CreativePro.com Press Release, January 22, 2002, http:// www.reativepro.com:80/story/news/15473.html, accessed July, 2006.

[6]"Creatives Increasingly Prefer Royalty-Free to Negotiated-Use Fee Images," TrendWatch, November 12, 2002, http://www.creativepro.com/story/news/18196.html, accessed July, 2006.

EXHIBIT 5
Balance Sheet as of December 31, 2002

Assets		Liabilities & Equity	
Current Assets		Liabilities	
Chequing/Savings		Current Liabilities	
CAD Checking	$2,106	A/P	
USD Checking-OUT	−$29,615	CAD A/P	$23,245
Total Chequing/Savings	−$27,509	USD A/P	$4,209
Accounts Receivable		Total A/P	$27,454
USD Accounts Receivable	$55,601	Other	
Total Accounts Receivable	$55,601	Accrued Liabilities	$20,327
Other Current Assets		Tax Payable	−$2,487
Inventory Assets	$1,712	Holding Account	$164
Total Other Current Assets	$1,712	Total Other	$18,004
Total Current Assets	$29,804	Total Current Liabilities	$45,458
Fixed Assets		Long Term Liabilities	
Computer Equipment		Due to/(from) Shareholders	$7,304
Original Cost	$10,275	Total Long Term Liabilities	$7,304
Depreciation	−$857	Total Liabilities	$52,762
Total Computer Equipment	$9,418	Equity	
Photography Equip		Share Capital	$400
Original Cost	$336	Net Income	−$13,523
Accum Deprec	−$19	Total Equity	−$13,123
Total Photography Equip	$317	Total Liabilities & Equity	$39,639
Total Fixed Assets	$9,735		
Other Assets	$100		
Total Assets	$39,639		

Source: Company files.

EXHIBIT 6
Statement of Profit and Loss, January to December, 2002

Ordinary Income/Expense		Expenses	
Income		Marketing	
iStockphoto Revenue	$73,839	Advertising (print)	$1,449
iStockphoto Store Revenue	$180	Other	$1,569
Total Income	$74,019	Total Marketing	$3,018
Cost of Goods Sold		Systems Admin/hosting	$20,205
Direct Costs		Development	$34,493
Royalties	$20,259	General & Admin	
E-commerce Fees		Telephone	$227
Merchant Acct-Moneris	$3,707	Postage and Delivery (Office)	$192
Merchant Acct-Paypal	$111	Professional Fees	$1,800
Other	$54	Rent	$1,417
Total E-commerce Fees	$3,872	Bank Service Charges	$117
Total Direct Costs	$24,130	Depreciation	$876
Total COGS	$24,130	Exchange Gain/Loss	$367
Gross Profit	$49,889	Building Repairs & Maint	$676
		Total General & Admin	$5,672
		Total Expense	$63,388
		Net Ordinary Income	−$13,499
		Other Income/Expense	
		Other Expense	$24
		Net Other Income	−$24
		Net Income	−$13,523

Source: Company files.

PART 2

Organizational Purpose and Structural Design

2 Strategy, Organizational Design, and Effectiveness

The Canadian Press/BILL GRAVELAND

A Look Inside

Tim Hortons

Which company has taken hold in the everyday lives of Canadians? Many would argue that it is Tim Hortons, which has created its own slang ("double double"),[1] made its stores part of every busy Canadian street corner,[2] spawned a phenomenon in which people arrive at work or at school with a "Tims," and consistently promoted Canadian culture and sports in its advertising and sponsorships. In a hugely popular move, it opened a store on July 1, 2006, for Canadian troops stationed in Kandahar, Afghanistan (see photo).[3]

NHL hockey star Tim Horton opened a coffee and doughnut shop in Hamilton, Ontario, in 1964 in order to earn income in the off-season. Soon afterward, he met Ron Joyce, a local police officer, who joined the business. By 1967, Joyce was a partner, and in 1974, he bought out the Horton family after Tim's death to become its sole owner. The chain has grown rapidly between 1964 and 2006—in 1964, there was only one store in Hamilton, Ontario, but by December 2006, there were 3,000 in Canada and the United States.[4]

In Canada, Tim Hortons is synonymous less with doughnuts than with coffee. It has been able to break out of the narrowly defined market typical of Krispy Kreme to anchor its brand in coffee. "While doughnuts play an important role in our product mix, they aren't the key to our growth or our success," said Patti Jameson, a spokeswoman for Tim Hortons, noting the company's restaurants also sell bagels, sandwiches, soups and coffee, with coffee providing close to 50 percent of sales. The company sees room for 3,000 stores in Canada.[5]

By centring its brand on coffee, Tim Hortons has gained enormous success. It has a 62 percent market share in the Canadian coffee segment. The second largest share is that of Starbucks, at 7 percent.[6] The anchoring effect of coffee allows the company to explore other products and revise its mix as necessary. At the end of the day, however, the products are all branded as Tim Hortons. The company topped *Canadian Business*'s annual survey of best-managed brands in 2004, 2005, and 2006.[7]

Tim Hortons has had a remarkable history of ownership and governance. At first, Tim Horton both owned and managed it. Then Ron Joyce became a partner in the ownership and management. Upon Horton's death, Joyce became the sole owner. When Ron Joyce needed funds to expand, he didn't issue stock to the public, but instead borrowed money, retaining his sole ownership. (Canadian companies with publicly listed shares of stock are subject to extensive regulation. Their executives must report annually to the shareholders and regularly to a board of directors.) In 1995, as Joyce approached retirement age, he sold Tim Hortons to the American fast food chain Wendy's. In spite of its place in Canadian society, it had its head office in Dublin, Ohio, and was no longer under Canadian ownership. The latest shift in the company's structure happened in 2006, when investors demanded that the company be spun off from Wendy's. Today, the company's head office is in Oakville, Ontario, and the stock is listed on the New York and Toronto exchanges.

Tim Hortons has achieved success only through attention to its brand. Unlike Starbucks, which sells its enticing aroma, sophisticated music, comfortable seats, attractive staff, and welcoming atmosphere, Tim Hortons has been able to sell itself not only as a destination, but also as part of typically Canadian experiences outside its doors. Tim Hortons has driven the high level of Canadian out-of-the-home coffee drinking. Due in part to the high number of drive-through outlets, "Timmies" are seen in workplaces, at meetings, in rinks, and anywhere Canadians gather. They sponsor activities that enhance their image as a deeply Canadian company: Timbits Minor Sports Program, free swimming at community pools and holiday skating at local arenas, and summer camp for underprivileged children.

However, the company's ability to sell coffee to people on their way to work has not compromised its ability to attract Canadians to its stores. In recognizing Tim Hortons as the best-managed Canadian restaurant brand in 2006, Interbrand focuses on this capacity: "Canada's beloved Tim Hortons sells coffee but truly produces loyalty and ranks number six. With market penetration in Canada that makes even global giant Starbucks roast with envy, Tim Hortons is the country's fourth place after home, work, and the hockey rink."[8] Company research indicates that approximately 46 percent of customers visit four or more times per week, a marker of the company's success at making a visit to Tim's part of daily routines in Canada.[9] The Tim Hortons' story is described in detail in the integrated case at the back of the book.

Top managers such as Ron Joyce and his successor, Paul House, are responsible for positioning their organizations for success by establishing goals and strategies that can help the company be competitive. An **organizational goal** is a desired state of affairs that the organization attempts to reach.[10] A goal represents a result or end point toward which organizational efforts are directed. It specifies where energy and resources are to be used. The goals for Tim Hortons in 2007 included adding no new franchises in English Canada, but many in the northern United States and Québec. The goals fit with the company's overall strategy of gradual expansion into adjacent areas, retaining Canadian identity, and maintaining consistency. The choice of goals and strategy affects organizational design, as we will discuss in this chapter.

Purpose of This Chapter

Top managers give direction to organizations. They set goals and develop the plans for their organization to attain those goals. The purpose of this chapter is to help you understand the types of goals that organizations pursue and some of the competitive strategies managers use to reach those goals. We will examine two significant frameworks for determining strategic action and look at how strategies affect organizational design. The chapter also describes the most popular approaches to measuring the effectiveness of organizational efforts. To manage organizations well, managers need a clear sense of how to measure effectiveness.

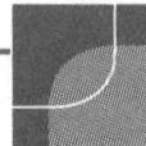

The Role of Strategic Direction in Organizational Design

An organization is created to achieve some purpose, which is decided by the chief executive officer (CEO) and the top management team. Top executives decide on the end purpose the organization will strive for and determine the direction it will take to accomplish it. It is this purpose and direction that shapes how the organization is designed and managed. Indeed, *the primary responsibility of top management is to determine an organization's goals, strategy, and design, therein adapting the organization to a changing environment.*[11] Middle managers do much the same thing for major departments within the guidelines provided by top management. On the other hand, many nonprofits see these issues as the board's responsibility.[12] The relationships through which top managers provide direction and then design are illustrated in Exhibit 2.1.

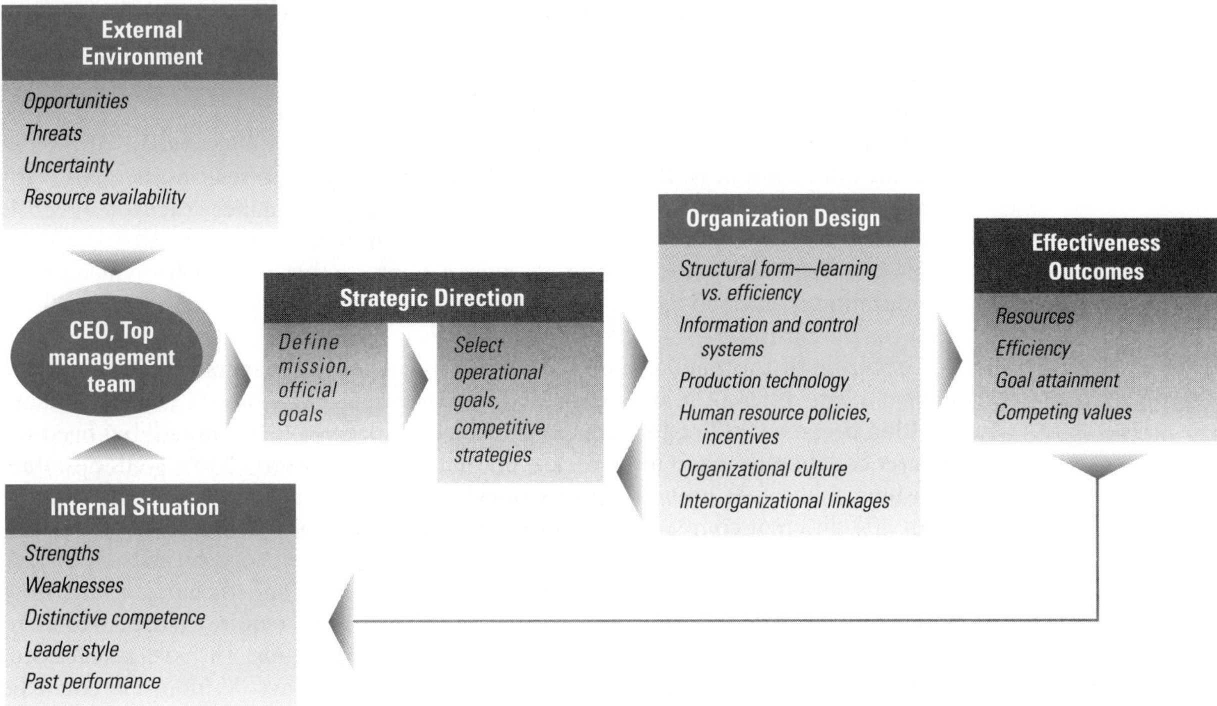

EXHIBIT 2.1
Top Management Role in Organization Direction, Design, and Effectiveness
Source: Adapted from Arie Y. Lewin and Carroll U. Stephens, "Individual Properties of the CEO as Determinants of Organization Design," unpublished manuscript, Duke University, 1990; and Arie Y. Lewin and Carroll U. Stephens, "CEO Attributes as Determinants of Organization Design: An Integrated Model," *Organization Studies* 15, no. 2 (1994): 183–212.

The direction-setting process typically begins with an assessment of the opportunities and threats in the external environment, including the amount of change, uncertainty, and resource availability, which we discuss in more detail in Chapter 4. Top managers also assess internal strengths and weaknesses to define the company's distinctive competence compared with other firms in the industry.[13] The assessment of internal environment often includes an evaluation of each department and is shaped by past performance and the leadership style of the CEO and top management team. The next step is to define overall mission and official goals based on the correct fit between external opportunities and internal strengths. Specific operational goals or strategies can then be formulated to define how the organization is to accomplish its overall mission.

In Exhibit 2.1, organizational design reflects the way goals and strategies are implemented. Organizational design is the administration and execution of the strategic plan. Organization direction is implemented through decisions about structural form, including whether the organization will be designed for a learning or an efficiency orientation, as discussed in Chapter 1, as well as choices about information and control systems, the type of production technology, human resource policies, culture, and linkages to other organizations. Changes in **structure**, technology, human resource policies, culture, and interorganizational linkages will be discussed in subsequent chapters. Also note the arrow in Exhibit 2.1 running from organizational design back to strategic direction. This means that strategies are often made within the current structure of the organization, so that current design constrains or puts limits on goals and strategy. More often than not, however, the new goals and strategy are selected based on environmental needs, and then top management attempts to redesign the organization to achieve those ends.

Finally, Exhibit 2.1 illustrates how managers evaluate the effectiveness of organizational efforts—that is, the extent to which the organization realizes its goals. This chart reflects the most popular ways of measuring performance, each of which is discussed later in this chapter. It is important to note here that performance measurements feed back into the internal environment, so that past performance of the organization is assessed by top management in setting new goals and strategic direction for the future.

The role of top management is important because managers can interpret the environment differently and develop different goals. For example, when William Weldon became CEO of Johnson & Johnson, he recognized an underlying need for greater collaboration and information sharing among Johnson & Johnson's disparate divisions. Johnson & Johnson is an extremely complex organization, made up of more than 200 different companies organized into three divisions: drugs, medical devices, and diagnostics. The company has thrived by giving its various businesses almost complete autonomy. However, Weldon believes the system has to change to thrive in today's shifting environment. Weldon has set new goals that require managers to build alliances across the three major divisions.[14] "If you are going to have a successful corporate program, it has to be directed from the top," says Weldon. He could be talking about cost-cutting initiatives or a new talent-management protocol.[15]

The choices top managers make about goals, strategies, and organizational design have a tremendous impact on organizational effectiveness. Remember that goals and strategy are not fixed or taken for granted. Top managers and middle managers must select goals for their respective units, and the ability to make these choices largely determines firm success. Organizational design is used to implement goals and strategy and also determines organization success. We will now discuss further the concept of organizational goals and strategy, and in the latter part of this chapter we will discuss various ways to evaluate organizational effectiveness.

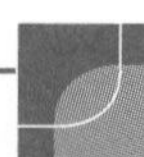

Organizational Purpose

PDA Remember...

Establish and communicate organizational mission and goals. Communicate official goals to provide a statement of the organization's mission to external constituents. Communicate operational goals to provide internal direction, guidelines, and standards of performance for employees.

Organizations are created and continued in order to accomplish something. All organizations, including Johnson & Johnson, Dalhousie University, Cineplex Odeon, the United Church of Canada, the local dry cleaner, the Assembly of First Nations, and the neighbourhood milk store, exist for a purpose. This purpose may be referred to as the overall goal, or mission. Different parts of the organization establish their own goals and objectives to help meet the overall goal, mission, or purpose of the organization.

Many types of goals exist in an organization, and each performs a different function. One major distinction is between the officially stated goals, or mission, of the organization and the operative goals the organization actually pursues.

Mission

The overall goal for an organization is often called the **mission**—the organization's reason for existence. The mission describes the organization's vision, its shared

EXHIBIT 2.2
London Police Service (London, Ontario) Mission Statement

Mission

The London Police Service is committed to providing a safe and secure community through community partnerships and by striving to attain the highest level of professionalism and accountability.

Vision

Recognizing that our strength stems from our partnerships with all sectors of the community, we envision an organization structured to meet the changing needs of citizens and our profession. Our success in accomplishing this goal depends on our ability to:

- Provide optimum public safety and security to enhance the quality of life in the community;
- Foster trusting, caring partnerships with the community in all its diversity;
- Develop effective communications within our organization and with those we serve;
- Promote a safe and equitable workplace, allowing for the professional development of employees to their fullest potential;
- Promote training and life long learning; and
- Acquire and use resources efficiently and responsibly.

Statement of Values

The London Police Service, in pursuit of its mission, believes in providing quality service with the highest possible degree of excellence, based upon the principles of fairness, integrity, honesty, and respect for human dignity.

Employees are reminded to familiarize themselves with the Mission Statement, Statement of Values, and Vision of Success, and to embrace these goals as we collectively strive to provide the most effective police service for our citizens.

Source: London Police Service, "Mission Statement," at http://www.police.london.ca/AboutLPS/MissionStatement.htm (accessed June 2, 2008).

values and beliefs, and its reason for being. It can have a powerful impact on an organization.[16] The mission is sometimes called the **official goals**, which refers to the formally stated definition of business scope and outcomes the organization is trying to achieve. Official goal statements typically define business operations and may focus on values, markets, and customers that distinguish the organization. Whether called a mission statement or official goals, the organization's general statement of its purpose and philosophy is often written down in a policy manual or the annual report. The mission statement for the London Police Service (London, Ontario) is shown in Exhibit 2.2. Note how the overall mission, values, and goals are all defined.

One of the primary purposes of a mission statement is to serve as a communication tool.[17] The *mission statement* communicates to current and prospective employees, customers, investors, suppliers, and competitors what the organization stands for and what it is trying to achieve. A mission statement communicates legitimacy to internal and external stakeholders, who may join and be committed to the organization because they identify with its stated purpose. Most top leaders want employees, customers, competitors, suppliers, investors, and the local community to look on them in a favourable light, and the concept of legitimacy plays a critical role.[18] The corporate concern for legitimacy is real and pertinent. Consider the accounting firm Arthur Andersen, which was accused of obstructing justice by shredding accounting documents related to the Enron investigation. Once the previously respected global firm lost legitimacy with clients, investors, and the public, it was all but dead. In the post-Enron environment of weakened trust and increasing regulation, many organizations face the need to redefine their purpose and mission to emphasize the firm's purpose in more than financial terms.[19] Companies where managers are sincerely guided by mission statements that focus on their social purpose, such as LifeLabs' "At every step in the testing process, from collection to reporting, our goal is to deliver caring, compassionate, quality service that contributes to enhanced patient care" or Dofasco's "Our product is steel. Our strength is people" typically attract better employees, have better relationships with external parties, and perform better in the marketplace over the long term.[20]

Operative Goals

Operative goals designate the ends sought through the actual operating procedures of the organization and explain what the organization is actually trying to do.[21] Operative goals describe specific measurable outcomes and are often concerned with the short run. Operative versus official goals represent actual versus stated goals. Operative goals typically pertain to the primary tasks an organization must perform, similar to the subsystem activities identified in Chapter 1.[22] These goals concern overall performance, boundary spanning, maintenance, adaptation, and production activities. Specific goals for each primary task provide direction for the day-to-day decisions and activities within departments.

Overall Performance. Profitability reflects the overall performance of for-profit organizations. Profitability may be expressed in terms of net income, earnings per share, or return on investment. Other overall performance goals are growth and output volume. Growth pertains to increases in sales or profits over time. Volume pertains to total sales or the amount of products or services delivered. For example, Volkswagen's Audi division has a 2007–2008 growth goal of increasing sales by 10 percent, to one million vehicles a year.[23]

Government and nonprofit organizations such as social service agencies or labour unions do not have goals of profitability, but they do have goals that attempt to specify the delivery of services to clients or members within specified expense levels. The Government of British Columbia has set specific numerical targets for a wide variety of services. For instance, it has committed to adding nearly 30,000 child care spaces and 15,000 subsidies to the child care system in the period from 2003/2004 to 2007/2008.[24] Growth and volume goals also may be indicators of overall performance in nonprofit organizations. Treasury Board of Canada encourages the government to manage its contracts with nonprofits and charities through service-level agreements.[25]

Resources. Resource goals pertain to the acquisition of needed material and financial resources from the environment. They may involve obtaining financing for the construction of new plants, finding less-expensive sources for raw materials, or hiring top-quality technology graduates. Resource goals for York University include attracting top-notch professors and students. Honda Motor Company has resource goals of obtaining high-quality auto parts at low cost. United Way of Greater Toronto sets annual fundraising targets, which it frequently exceeds, in order to help maintain social programs in the Toronto area. In 2007, it set a goal of $108 million and raised $108.1 million.[26]

Market. Market goals relate to the market share or market standing desired by the organization. Market goals are the responsibility of marketing, sales, and advertising departments. An example of a market goal is Honda's desire to overtake Toyota Motor Company as the number-one seller of cars in Japan. Honda recently surpassed Nissan to become number two in Japan, and the recently introduced Fit subcompact has eclipsed the Toyota Corolla as the best-selling car in that market. In the toy industry, Canada's Mega Bloks achieved its goal of doubling its share of the toy building block market to 30 percent. The giant of the industry, Denmark's Lego, is re-evaluating strategies to try to regain the market share it has lost.[27]

Employee Development. Employee development pertains to the training, promotion, safety, and growth of employees. It includes both managers and workers. Strong employee development goals are one of the characteristics common to organizations that regularly show up on *Report on Business*'s list of "50 Best Employers in Canada." For example, Wellington West Capital, a financial services firm in Winnipeg, has garnered two successive awards as number-two-rated and then number-one-rated employer in Canada in 2006 and 2007. Two of its seven principles centre on people: the company identifies and recruits the best, and is confident in the quality of its staff. *The Globe and Mail* notes that "[companies] fare better when managers coach workers up the corporate rungs."[28]

Innovation and Change. Innovation goals pertain to internal flexibility and readiness to adapt to unexpected changes in the environment. Innovation goals are often defined with respect to the development of specific new services, products, or production processes. The 3M Company has a goal that 30 percent of sales come from products that are less than four years old.[29]

Productivity. Productivity goals concern the amount of output achieved from available resources. They typically describe the amount of resource inputs required to reach desired outputs and are thus stated in terms of "cost for a unit of production," "units produced per employee," or "resource cost per employee." Managers at Akamai Technologies, which sells Web content delivery services, keep a close eye on sales per employee to see if the company is meeting productivity goals. Akamai's chief financial officer, Timothy Weller, sees this statistic as "the single easiest measure of employee productivity." Boeing Company installed a new moving assembly line for the 737 aircraft to increase productivity. Once the wings and landing gear are attached, each plane is dragged toward the door at two inches a minute, with workers moving along with it on a floatlike apparatus. Boeing's productivity goal is to push a 737 out the door in five days, down from the eleven it currently takes.[30]

Successful organizations use a carefully balanced set of operative goals. Although profitability goals are important, some of today's best companies recognize that a single-minded focus on bottom-line profits may not be the best way to achieve high performance. Increasing numbers of companies are using triple-bottom-line accounting, a system in which companies assess their environmental and social performance as well as their profits.[31] Innovation and change goals are increasingly important, even though they may initially cause a *decrease* in profits. Employee development goals are critical for helping to maintain a motivated, committed workforce.

Leading *by Design*

Four Seasons

Hotels are often terrible workplaces. The nonmanagement jobs are often physically tough. Housekeepers have to wrestle large mattresses and heavy linens. Cleaners work with hazardous chemicals. The jobs are often low paying, and the workers seldom achieve any recognition or status. A 2002 study of San Francisco workers found that

> In addition to physical job demands, 83% of the room cleaners reported constant time pressure. Other job stressors often reported include lack of respect from supervisors (40%), poor job security (52%), and poor job promotion prospects (61%). On average, 30% of the room cleaners experienced an imbalance between their work efforts and the material and nonmaterial rewards they receive. This imbalance is an indicator for job stress. In addition, 38% of the room cleaners experienced high levels of job strain, measured as the combination of high job demands and little job control. Both these findings suggest that more than a third of the room cleaners experience high levels of job stress.[32]

Since the mid-1990s, Unite Here has been fighting difficult but successful organizing campaigns among hotel workers, fuelled by dissatisfaction over wages and working conditions.[33] "Turnover rates throughout the industry, according to the American Hotel & Motel Association, are 158 percent for front-line employees and 129 percent for managers."[34]

Four Seasons, the Canadian-based luxury hotelier, believes in doing things differently from the rest of the industry. Its employee turnover rates are 25 percent for all Four Seasons employees, and 19 percent for managers.[35] The company has never missed being listed as one of the "100 Best Companies to Work for in America." Until Four Seasons restructured the company in 2007, its stock traded at 40 to 50 times earnings, far higher than most others in the industry. Why is this hotel considered much more valuable than its competitors? Does part of the answer lie in the relationships it builds with its staff?

Izzy Sharpe thinks so. The celebrated founder of the company believes that the experience of luxury must be based in exemplary service. He believes that the employees providing that service cannot do it well if they are not supported, encouraged, and led by managers committed to them.

Take the time Mercedes Simon applied for a job cleaning the public bathrooms in the Westlake Village hotel. "People were very polite, but I didn't really get it at first," she says of the four successive rounds of interviews she was asked to undergo.

But then, as she sat down for a break in the cafeteria on her first day, the hotel's manager walked up to her. "May I bring you something, Mercedes?" he asked with a smile.

Stunned by his graciousness—let alone by the fact that he remembered her name, "I said, 'Oh, no, thanks,'" she recalls sheepishly. "But that's when I realized this place really is different. It made me want to work here."[36]

This attention to service, which results in enormous brand equity, is no accident: Sharpe has been building it into every management decision for decades. The Four Seasons' human resource policies are not about emulating best practices; they are designed to be an integral part of the company's strategy to make profits.

■ The Importance of Goals

Both official goals and operative goals are important for the organization, but they serve very different purposes. Official goals and mission statements describe a value system for the organization; operative goals represent the primary tasks of the organization. Official goals legitimize the organization; operative goals are more explicit and well defined.

Operative goals can provide employees with a sense of direction, so that they know what they are working toward. This can help to motivate employees toward goal accomplishment, especially if employees are involved in setting the targets. The events at Walkerton, Ontario's water plant provide a negative illustration of the motivating power of goals: "In May 2000, Walkerton's drinking water system became contaminated with deadly bacteria, primarily Escherichia coli O157:H7.1 Seven people died, and more than 2,300 became ill. The community was devastated. The losses were enormous. There were widespread feelings of frustration, anger, and insecurity." Justice Dennis O'Connor's report concludes that cuts to the inspections budget of the Ministry of the Environment were part of the chain of events that led to the disaster. "In February 1996, the Cabinet approved the budget reductions in the face of the warnings of increased risk to the environment and human health." The Conservative provincial government of the mid-1990s did not intend to reduce the quality of drinking water, but its goal of reducing expenditures was paramount. With many fewer provincial inspections, public utilities commissioners and staff were neither accountable for nor motivated to do their work.[37] Managers need to understand the power of goals and use care when setting and implementing them. Another important purpose of goals is to act as guidelines for employee behaviour and decision making. Appropriate goals can act as a set of constraints on individual behaviour and actions so that employees behave within boundaries that are acceptable to the organization and larger society.[38] They help to define the appropriate decisions concerning organizational structure, innovation, employee welfare, or growth. Finally, goals provide a standard for assessment. The level of organizational performance, whether in terms of profits, units produced, degree of employee satisfaction, level of innovation, or number of customer complaints, needs a basis for evaluation. Operative goals provide this standard for measurement.

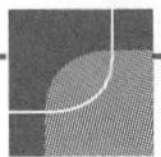

A Framework for Selecting Strategy and Design

To support and accomplish the direction determined by organizational mission and operative goals, managers have to select specific strategy and design options that will help the organization achieve its purpose and goals within its competitive environment. In this section, we examine a couple of practical approaches to selecting strategy and design.

A **strategy** is a plan for interacting with the competitive environment to achieve organizational goals. Some managers think of goals and strategies as interchangeable, but for our purposes, *goals* define where the organization wants to go and *strategies* define how it will get there. For example, a goal might be to achieve 15 percent annual sales growth; strategies to reach that goal might include aggressive advertising to attract new customers, motivating salespeople to increase the average size of customer purchases, and acquiring other businesses that produce similar products. Strategies can include any number of techniques to achieve the goal. The essence of formulating strategies is choosing whether the organization will perform different activities than its competitors or will execute similar activities more efficiently than its competitors do.[39]

PDA Remember...

After goals have been defined, select strategies for achieving those goals. Define specific strategies based on Porter's competitive strategies or Miles and Snow's strategy typology.

Two models for formulating strategies are the Porter model of competitive strategies and Miles and Snow's strategy typology. Each provides a framework for competitive action. After describing the two models, we will discuss how the choice of strategies affects organizational design.

Porter's Competitive Strategies

Michael E. Porter studied a number of businesses and introduced a framework describing three competitive strategies: low-cost leadership, differentiation, and focus.[40] The focus strategy, in which the organization concentrates on a specific market or buyer group, is further divided into *focused low cost* and *focused differentiation*. This yields four basic strategies, as illustrated in Exhibit 2.3. To use this model, managers evaluate two factors, competitive advantage and competitive scope.

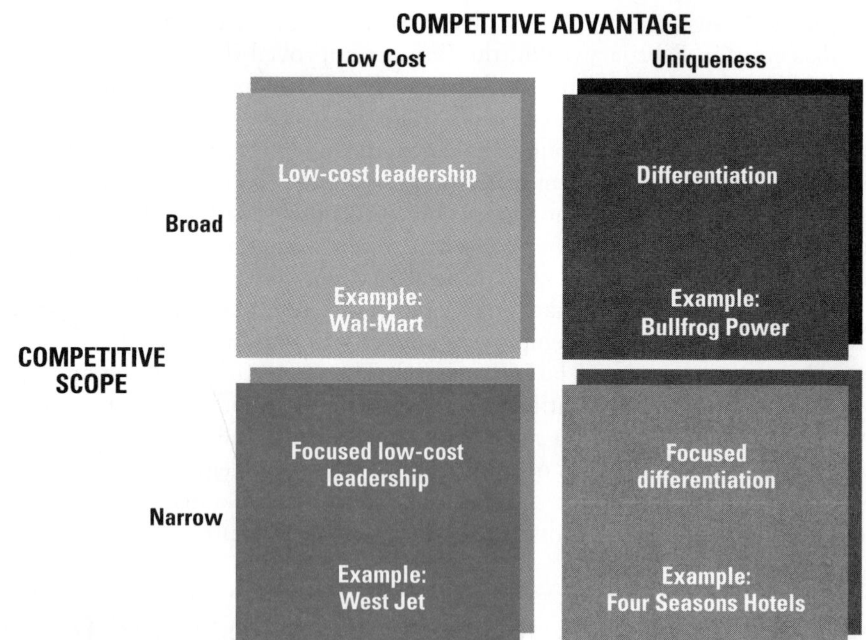

EXHIBIT 2.3
Porter's Competitive Strategies
Source: Adapted with the permission of The Free Press, a Division of Simon & Schuster Adult Publishing Group, from *Competitive Advantage: Creating and Sustaining Superior Performance* by Michael E. Porter, Copyright © 1985, 1988 by Michael E. Porter; and from Stonehouse, G. and B. Snowden (2007) "Competitive Advantage Revisited, Michael Porter on Strategy and Competitiveness," *Journal of Management Inquiry,* 16, 3: 256–273.

With respect to advantage, managers determine whether to compete through lower cost or through the ability to offer unique or distinctive products and services that can command a premium price. Managers then determine whether the organization will compete on a broad scope (competing in many customer segments) or a narrow scope (competing in a selected customer segment or group of segments). These choices determine the selection of strategies, as illustrated in Exhibit 2.3.

Differentiation. In a differentiation strategy, organizations attempt to distinguish their products or services from others in the industry. An organization may use advertising, distinctive product features, exceptional service, or new technology to achieve a product perceived as unique. This strategy usually targets customers who are not particularly concerned with price, so it can be quite profitable. Toronto-based Cervélo bicycles,[41] Roots clothing, and Jaguar automobiles are examples of products from companies using a differentiation strategy. Service firms such as Four Seasons Hotels and utilities such as Bullfrog Power can use a differentiation strategy as well.

A differentiation strategy can reduce rivalry with competitors and fight off the threat of substitute products because customers are loyal to the company's brand. However, companies must remember that successful differentiation strategies require a number of costly activities, such as product research and design and extensive advertising. Companies that pursue a differentiation strategy need strong marketing abilities and creative employees who are given the time and resources to seek innovations.

Low-Cost Leadership. The **low-cost leadership** strategy tries to increase market share by emphasizing low cost compared to competitors. With a low-cost leadership strategy, the organization aggressively seeks efficient facilities, pursues cost reductions, and uses tight controls to produce products or services more efficiently than its competitors. One good example of a low-cost leadership strategy is WestJet.

In Practice
WestJet

For decades, new airlines have fought to end Air Canada's domination of the Canadian market. Canadian, WardAir, Caledonia, and others have started with a base in the west and worked to compete with Air Canada's long-established routes and reputation. In 1996, Clive Beddoe, Mark Hill, Tim Morgan, and Donald Bell founded WestJet to serve the country from Winnipeg to Vancouver. It grew quickly and generated profits like Southwest, the low-cost airline it wished to emulate.

Westjet has succeeded through constant, planned, incremental growth. In contrast to more established carriers, it quickly identifies and abandons strategies, markets, and technologies that are unprofitable. (It no longer flies to Gander, San Francisco, San Diego, or LaGuardia; moved its eastern hub from Hamilton to Toronto; and abandoned plans to buy Boeing 737-600s.) Like Ryanair and Southwest, its counterparts in Europe and the United States, WestJet uses new, high-efficiency aircraft. Westjet staff are compensated in part through profit sharing, thereby reducing pressure to unionize and minimizing labour costs. Westjet watches its costs closely, allowing every point in market share to be realized as profits.[42]

The low-cost leadership strategy is concerned primarily with stability rather than taking risks or seeking new opportunities for innovation and growth. A low-cost position means a company can undercut competitors' prices and still offer comparable quality and earn a reasonable profit.

A low-cost strategy can help a company defend against current competitors because customers cannot find lower prices elsewhere. In addition, if substitute products or potential new competitors enter the picture, the low-cost producer is in a better position to prevent loss of market share.

Focus. With Porter's third strategy, the **focus strategy,** the organization concentrates on a specific regional market or buyer group. The company will try to achieve either a low-cost advantage or a differentiation advantage within a narrowly defined market. One good example of a focused strategy is Edward Jones, a St. Louis–based brokerage house. The firm has succeeded by building its business in rural and small-town North America and providing investors with conservative, long-term investments.[43] An example of a focused differentiation strategy is Puma, the German athletic-wear manufacturer. Ten years ago, Puma was on the brink of bankruptcy. CEO Jochen Zeitz, then only 30 years old, revived the brand by targeting selected customer groups, especially armchair athletes, and creating stylish shoes and clothes that are setting design trends. Puma is "going out of its way to be different," says analyst Roland Könen, and sales and profits reflect the change. Puma has been profitable every year since 1994, and its sales are growing faster than those of competitors.[44]

When managers fail to adopt a competitive strategy, the organization is left with no strategic advantage and performance suffers. Porter found that companies that did not consciously adopt a low-cost, differentiation, or focus strategy, for example, achieved below-average profits compared to those that used one of the three strategies. Many Internet companies have failed because they did not develop competitive strategies that would distinguish them in the marketplace.[45] On the other hand, eBay and Google have been highly successful with coherent differentiation strategies. The ability of managers to devise and maintain a clear competitive strategy is one of the defining factors in an organization's success, as further discussed in this chapter's Book Mark.

Miles and Snow's Strategy Typology

Another business strategy typology was developed from the study of business strategies by Raymond Miles and Charles Snow.[46] The Miles and Snow typology is based on the idea that managers seek to formulate strategies that will be congruent with the external environment. Organizations strive for a fit among internal organization characteristics, strategy, and the external environment. The four strategies that can be developed are the prospector, the defender, the analyzer, and the reactor.

Prospector. The **prospector** strategy is to innovate, take risks, seek out new opportunities, and grow. This strategy is suited to a dynamic, growing environment, where creativity is more important than efficiency. Research In Motion Limited (RIM), which innovates in both wireless communication devices and the software that powers them, exemplifies the prospector strategy, as do other leading high-tech companies, such as Microsoft.

Defender. The **defender** strategy is almost the opposite of the prospector. Rather than taking risks and seeking out new opportunities, the defender strategy is concerned with stability or even retrenchment. This strategy seeks to hold onto current customers, but it neither innovates nor seeks to grow. The defender is concerned primarily with internal efficiency and control to produce reliable, high-quality products for steady customers. This strategy can be successful when the organization exists in a declining industry or a stable environment. As the market for department stores has declined over the last 30 years, Canadians have seen the Hudson's Bay Company and Eaton's adopt different approaches to the defender strategy. Eaton's tried every possible innovation in its last years, but none were successful enough to save the company. HBC, on the other hand, has carefully monitored its margins and spending, maintained its discount brand (Zellers) in order to successfully compete with Wal-Mart, and survived as Canada's only national department store. Like many Canadian companies, its recent purchase by United States–based Target signals its success rather than failure.

Analyzer. The **analyzer** tries to maintain a stable business while innovating on the periphery. It seems to lie midway between the prospector and the defender. Some products will be targeted toward stable environments in which an efficiency strategy designed to keep current customers is used. Others will be targeted toward new, more dynamic environments, where growth is possible. The analyzer attempts to balance efficient production for current product lines with the creative development of new product lines.[47] We can see this strategy in use at Rogers Communications. Rogers works within mature markets such as cable TV, where it has a significant but stable revenue base and few opportunities for new customers. However, the company explores growth strategies in areas like wireless data transfer.

Reactor. The **reactor** strategy is not really a strategy at all. Rather, reactors respond to environmental threats and opportunities in an ad hoc fashion. In a reactor strategy, top management has not defined a long-range plan or given the organization an explicit mission or goal, so the organization takes whatever actions seem to meet immediate needs. Although the reactor strategy can sometimes be successful, it can also lead to failed companies. Some large, once highly successful companies, such as Xerox and Kodak, are struggling because managers failed to adopt a strategy

Book Mark 2.0 (HAVE YOU READ THIS BOOK?)

What Really Works: The 4 + 2 Formula for Sustained Business Success
By William F. Joyce, Nitin Nohria, and Bruce Roberson

In *What Really Works: The 4 + 2 Formula for Sustained Business Success,* William Joyce, Nitin Nohria, and Bruce Roberson contend that there are certain reliable indicators of enduring organizational success. The book is based on a large-scale, rigorous research project that involved 5 years of analyzing data collected over a decade from 160 companies representing 40 different industries. The findings indicate that there is a direct connection between high financial performance and sustained excellence in six key practices.

WHAT IS THE 4 + 2 FORMULA?

The authors say there are four key practices at which *all* outstanding companies excel, no matter what their size or industry:

- *Stay clear on strategy.* First and foremost is the ability to devise and maintain a clearly stated, focused strategy. Compare Target and Kmart. During the years of the study, Target rose to become America's second-largest discounter, behind Wal-Mart, by focusing on providing unique and higher-end merchandise at value prices. During the same time, Kmart floundered time and time again as managers shifted from one strategy to another—for example, shifting to pursue a more affluent fashion-conscious consumer, then shifting back to compete with Wal-Mart on price.
- *Maintain flawless operational execution.* Winning companies implement and maintain operational changes that increase their productivity at about twice the industry average. They don't try to outperform competitors on every facet of operations, but focus their energies on core competencies, such as Wal-Mart's use of sophisticated information technology to scrupulously manage inventory.
- *Build a performance-driven culture.* Outstanding companies encourage both individual and team contributions, and hold everyone accountable for results. One example is Home Depot, which gives everyone from the janitor to the top executive a sense of ownership over the stores.
- *Maintain a fast, flexible structure.* The most successful companies keep bureaucracy to a minimum, trimming unnecessary layers of management, cutting out excessive rules and regulations, and doing away with boundaries that inhibit communication and collaboration. Nucor, a steel company, confines its management structure to four layers—foreman, department head, plant manager, and CEO.

In addition to these four primary practices, the authors found that winning companies embrace two out of four secondary practices: *talent of employees, leadership and governance, innovation,* or *mergers and partnerships.*

DOES IT REALLY WORK?

Over the 10-year period, investors in the 4 + 2 companies saw their money multiply nearly tenfold, with a total return to shareholders of 945 percent. The losing companies produced only 62 percent in total returns over the same decade. Anecdotes from the companies are interesting and instructive for general readers and managers alike.

What Really Works: The 4 + 2 Formula for Sustained Business Success, by William Joyce, Nitin Nohria, and Bruce Roberson, is published by Harper Business.

consistent with consumer trends. In recent years, managers at McDonald's, long one of the most successful fast-food franchises in the world, have been attempting to find the appropriate strategy. McDonald's had a string of disappointing quarterly profits as competitors continued to steal market share. Franchisees grew aggravated and discouraged by the uncertainty and lack of clear strategic direction for the future. Recent innovations such as healthier food options have revived sales and profits, but managers still are struggling to implement a coherent strategy.[48] The last few years of the now defunct Eaton's, as mentioned above, can be seen as an example of a reactive company.

The Miles and Snow typology has been widely used, and researchers have tested its validity in a variety of organizations, including hospitals, colleges, banking institutions, industrial products companies, and life insurance firms. In general, researchers have found strong support for the effectiveness of this typology for organization managers in real-world situations.[49]

PDA
Remember...

Design the organization to support the firm's competitive strategy. With a low-cost leadership or defender strategy, select design characteristics associated with an efficiency orientation. For a differentiation or prospector strategy, on the other hand, choose characteristics that encourage learning, innovation, and adaptation. Use a balanced mixture of characteristics for an analyzer strategy.

How Strategies Affect Organizational Design

Choice of strategy affects internal organization characteristics. Organizational design characteristics need to support the firm's competitive approach. For example, a company wanting to grow and invent new products looks and "feels" different from a company that is focused on maintaining market share for long-established products in a stable industry. Exhibit 2.4 summarizes organizational design characteristics associated with the Porter and Miles and Snow strategies.

With a low-cost leadership strategy, managers take an efficiency approach to organizational design, whereas a differentiation strategy calls for a learning approach. Recall from Chapter 1 that organizations designed for efficiency have different characteristics from those designed for learning. A low-cost leadership strategy (efficiency) is associated with strong, centralized authority; tight control; standard

EXHIBIT 2.4
Organizational Design Outcomes of Strategy

Porter's Competitive Strategies	Miles and Snow's Strategy Typology
Strategy: Differentiation **Organizational Design:** • Learning orientation; acts in a flexible, loosely knit way, with strong horizontal coordination • Strong capability in research • Values and builds in mechanisms for customer intimacy • Rewards employee creativity, risk taking, and innovation **Strategy:** Low-Cost Leadership **Organizational Design:** • Efficiency orientation; strong central authority; tight cost control, with frequent, detailed control reports • Standard operating procedures • Highly efficient procurement and distribution systems • Close supervision; routine tasks; limited employee empowerment	**Strategy:** Prospector **Organizational Design:** • Learning orientation; flexible, fluid, decentralized structure • Strong capability in research **Strategy:** Defender **Organizational Design:** • Efficiency orientation; centralized authority and tight cost control • Emphasis on production efficiency; low overhead • Close supervision; little employee empowerment **Strategy:** Analyzer **Organizational Design:** • Balances efficiency and learning; tight cost control with flexibility and adaptability • Efficient production for stable product lines; emphasis on creativity, research, risk taking for innovation **Strategy:** Reactor **Organizational Design:** • No clear organizational approach; design characteristics may shift abruptly, depending on current needs

Source: Based on Michael E. Porter, *Competitive Strategy: Techniques for Analyzing Industries and Competitors* (New York: The Free Press, 1980); Michael Treacy and Fred Wiersema, "How Market Leaders Keep Their Edge," *Fortune* (February 6, 1995), 88–98; Michael Hitt, R. Duane Ireland, and Robert E. Hoskisson, *Strategic Management* (St. Paul, Minn.: West, 1995), 100–113; and Raymond E. Miles, Charles C. Snow, Alan D. Meyer, and Henry J. Coleman, Jr., "Organizational Strategy, Structure, and Process," *Academy of Management Review* 3 (1978): 546–562.

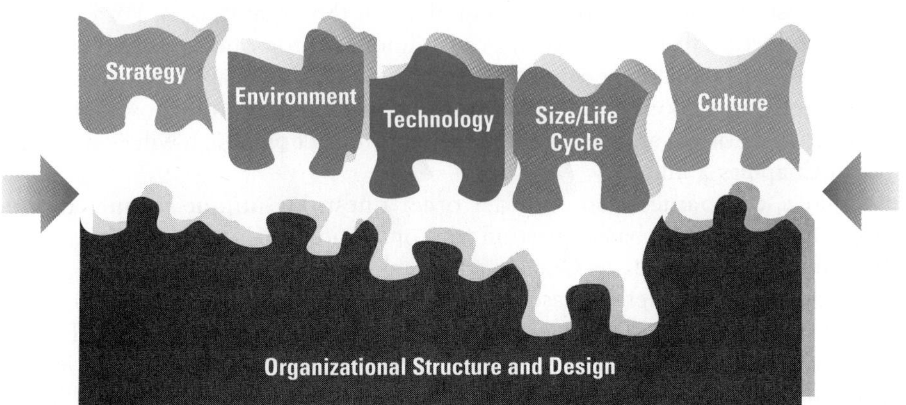

The Right Mix of Design Characteristics Fits the Contingency Factors

EXHIBIT 2.5
Contingency Factors Affecting Organizational Design

operating procedures; and emphasis on efficient procurement and distribution systems. Employees generally perform routine tasks under close supervision and control and are not empowered to make decisions or take action on their own. A differentiation strategy, on the other hand, requires that employees be constantly experimenting and learning. Structure is fluid and flexible, with strong horizontal coordination. Empowered employees work directly with customers and are rewarded for creativity and risk taking. The organization values research, creativity, and innovativeness over efficiency and standard procedures.

The prospector strategy requires characteristics similar to a differentiation strategy, and the defender strategy takes an efficiency approach similar to low-cost leadership. Because the analyzer strategy attempts to balance efficiency for stable product lines with flexibility and learning for new products, it is associated with a mix of characteristics, as listed in Exhibit 2.5. With a reactor strategy, managers have left the organization with no direction and no clear approach to design.

Other Factors Affecting Organizational Design

Strategy is one important factor that affects organizational design. Ultimately, however, organization design is a result of numerous contingencies, which will be discussed throughout this book. The emphasis placed on efficiency and control versus learning and flexibility is determined by the contingencies of strategy, environment, size and life cycle, technology, and organizational culture. The organization is designed to "fit" the contingency factors, as illustrated in Exhibit 2.5.

For example, in a stable environment, the organization can have a traditional structure that emphasizes vertical control, efficiency, specialization, standard procedures, and centralized decision making. However, a rapidly changing environment may call for a more flexible structure, with strong horizontal coordination and collaboration through teams or other mechanisms. Environment will be discussed in detail in Chapter 4. In terms of size and life cycle, young, small organizations are generally informal and have little division of labour, few rules and regulations, and ad hoc budgeting and performance systems. Large organizations such as Coca-Cola, Sony, or General Electric, on the other hand, have an extensive division of labour, numerous rules and regulations, and standard procedures and systems for budgeting, control, rewards, and innovation. Size and stages of the life cycle will be discussed in Chapter 9.

Design must also fit the workflow technology of the organization. For example, with mass production technology, such as a traditional automobile assembly line, the organization functions best by emphasizing efficiency, formalization, specialization, centralized decision making, and tight control. An e-business, on the other hand, might need to be informal and flexible. Technology's impact on design will be discussed in detail in Chapters 7 and 8.

In Canada, companies also consider other questions unique to our culture, geography, and history. A basic question for companies that operate nationwide is how to structure themselves in Québec and English Canada. Neither a functional scheme (production, marketing, research and development, etc.) nor product divisions reflect the differences in language, culture, and law between Québec and English Canada. As well, companies financed and governed as publicly held entities are subject to foreign takeover. Such iconic Canadian companies as the Hudson's Bay Company (the oldest continuously operated incorporated company in the world), Alcan, and virtually all companies in Alberta's oil patch are owned by non-Canadians. Nortel and Thomson have both moved their head offices out of Canada; Canadian markets, know-how, and resources are valuable to the entire world. Business managers in Canada are obligated to ensure their companies become as valuable as possible: the strategy and structure of Canadian companies is devoted to gaining value, not retaining Canadian ownership or control. It is an issue that has attracted the interest of Canadians within and outside the business community. Will future business leaders be constrained in their search for value? Will they be able to use foreign ownership and financing as a means to survive and thrive, as did Tim Hortons, which later returned to Canadian-based autonomy, larger and stronger? Or will we see the continuing "hollowing out" of Canadian head offices as foreign takeovers dominate the news? Will the structure of our companies help to determine the future?

A final contingency that affects organization design is organizational culture. An organizational culture that values teamwork, collaboration, creativity, and open communication among all employees and managers, for example, would not function well with a tight, vertical structure and strict rules and regulations. The role of culture is discussed in Chapter 10.

One responsibility of managers is to design organizations that fit the contingency factors of strategy, environment, size and life cycle, technology, and culture. Finding the right fit leads to organizational effectiveness, whereas a poor fit can lead to decline or even the demise of the organization.

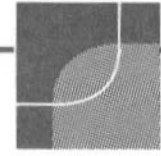

Assessing Organizational Effectiveness

Understanding organizational goals and strategies, as well as the concept of fitting design to various contingencies, is a first step toward understanding organizational effectiveness. Organizational goals represent the reason for an organization's existence and the outcomes it seeks to achieve. The next few sections of the chapter explore the topic of effectiveness and how effectiveness is measured in organizations.

Recall from Chapter 1 that organizational effectiveness is the degree to which an organization realizes its goals.[50] *Effectiveness* is a broad concept. It implicitly takes into consideration a range of variables at both the organizational and departmental levels. Effectiveness evaluates the extent to which multiple goals—whether official or operative—are attained.

Efficiency is a more limited concept that pertains to the internal workings of the organization. Organizational efficiency is the amount of resources used to produce a unit of output.[51] It can be measured as the ratio of inputs to outputs. If one organization can achieve a given production level with fewer resources than another organization, it would be described as more efficient.[52]

Sometimes efficiency leads to effectiveness. In other organizations, efficiency and effectiveness are not related. An organization may be highly efficient but fail to achieve its goals because it makes a product for which there is no demand. Likewise, an organization may achieve its strategic goals but be inefficient.

Overall effectiveness is difficult to measure in organizations. Organizations are large, diverse, and fragmented. They perform many activities simultaneously, pursue multiple goals, and generate many outcomes, some intended and some unintended.[53] Managers determine what indicators to measure in order to gauge the effectiveness of their organizations. One study found that many managers have a difficult time with the concept of evaluating effectiveness based on characteristics that are not subject to hard, quantitative measurement.[54] However, top executives at some of today's leading companies are finding new ways to measure effectiveness, including the use of such "soft" indications as "customer delight" and employee satisfaction. A number of approaches to measuring effectiveness look at which measurements managers choose to track. These *contingency effectiveness approaches*, discussed in the next section, are based on looking at which part of the organization managers consider most important to measure. Later, we will examine an approach that integrates concern for various parts of the organization.

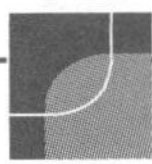

Contingency Effectiveness Approaches

Contingency approaches to measuring effectiveness focus on different parts of the organization. Organizations bring resources in from the environment, and those resources are transformed into outputs delivered back into the environment, as shown in Exhibit 2.6. The **goal approach** to organizational effectiveness is concerned with the output side and whether the organization achieves its goals in terms of desired

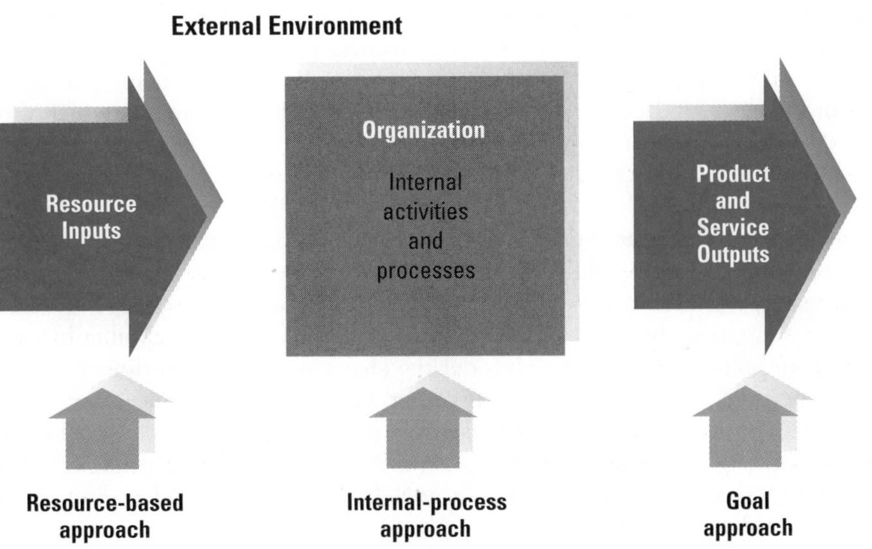

EXHIBIT 2.6
Contingency Approaches to the Measurement of Organizational Effectiveness

levels of output.[55] The **resource-based approach** assesses effectiveness by observing the beginning of the process and evaluating whether the organization effectively obtains resources necessary for high performance. The **internal-process approach** looks at internal activities and assesses effectiveness by indicators of internal health and efficiency. Each has its strengths but each is limited in its scope.

Resource-Based Approach

The resource-based approach looks at the input side of the transformation process shown in Exhibit 2.6. It assumes organizations must be successful in obtaining and managing valued resources in order to be effective. From a resource-based perspective, organizational effectiveness is defined as the ability of the organization, in either absolute or relative terms, to obtain scarce and valued resources and successfully integrate and manage them.[56]

Indicators. Obtaining and successfully managing resources is the criterion by which organizational effectiveness is assessed. In a broad sense, indicators of effectiveness according to the resource-based approach encompass the following dimensions:

- Bargaining position—the ability of the organization to obtain from its environment scarce and valued resources, including financial resources, raw materials, human resources, knowledge, and technology
- The abilities of the organization's decision makers to perceive and correctly interpret the real properties of the external environment
- The abilities of managers to use tangible (e.g., supplies, people) and intangible (e.g., knowledge, organizational culture) resources in day-to-day organizational activities to achieve superior performance
- The ability of the organization to respond to changes in the environment.

Usefulness. The resource-based approach is valuable when other indicators of performance are difficult to obtain. In many not-for-profit and social welfare organizations, for example, it is hard to measure output goals or internal efficiency. Some for-profit organizations also use a resource-based approach. For example, Mathsoft, which provides a broad range of technical-calculation and analytical software for business and academia, evaluates its effectiveness partly by looking at how many top-rate PhDs it can recruit. CEO Charles Digate believes Mathsoft has a higher ratio of PhDs to total employees than any other software company, which directly affects product quality and the company's image.[57]

Although the resource-based approach is valuable when other measures of effectiveness are not available, it does have shortcomings. For one thing, the approach only vaguely considers the organization's link to the needs of customers in the external environment. A superior ability to acquire and use resources is important only if resources and capabilities are used to achieve something that meets a need in the environment. Critics have challenged that the approach assumes stability in the marketplace and fails to adequately consider the changing value of various resources as the competitive environment and customer needs change.[58] The resource-based approach is most valuable when measures of goal attainment cannot be readily obtained. The Government of British Columbia can easily see if it has reached the number of child care spaces it set as a goal for 2007–2008 and use its results to adapt its strategy to ensure success.

Internal-Process Approach

In the internal-process approach, effectiveness is measured as internal organizational health and efficiency. An effective organization has a smooth, well-oiled internal process; employees are happy and satisfied; and department activities mesh with one another to ensure high productivity. This approach does not consider the external environment. The important element in effectiveness is what the organization does with the resources it has, as reflected in internal health and efficiency.

Indicators. One indicator of internal-process effectiveness is the organization's economic efficiency. However, the best-known proponents of a process model are from the human relations approach to organizations. Such writers as Chris Argyris, Warren G. Bennis, Rensis Likert, and Richard Beckhard have all worked extensively with human resources in organizations and emphasize the connection between human resources and effectiveness.[59] Writers on organizational culture and organizational excellence have stressed the importance of internal processes. Results from a study of nearly 200 secondary schools showed that both human resources and employee-oriented processes were important in explaining and promoting effectiveness in those organizations.[60]

There are seven indicators of an effective organization as seen from an internal-process approach:

1. Strong organizational culture and positive work climate
2. Team spirit, group loyalty, and teamwork
3. Confidence, trust, and communication between workers and management
4. Decision making near sources of information, regardless of where those sources are on the organizational chart
5. Undistorted horizontal and vertical communication; sharing of relevant facts and feelings
6. Rewards to managers for performance, growth, and development of subordinates and for creating an effective work group
7. Interaction between the organization and its parts, with conflict that occurs over projects resolved in the interest of the organization.[61]

PDA

Remember...

Use the goal approach, internal-process approach, and resource-based approach to obtain specific pictures of organizational effectiveness. Assess competing values to obtain a broader, more-balanced picture of effectiveness.

Usefulness. The internal-process approach is important because the efficient use of resources and harmonious internal functioning are ways to assess organizational effectiveness. Today, most managers believe that happy, committed, actively involved employees and a positive organizational culture are important measures of effectiveness. Innovative and highly successful clothing company American Apparel is having problems because CEO and founder Dov Charney feels free to engage in consensual sexual relationships with his staff. "I've had relationships, loving relationships, that I'm proud of," he says. "I think it's a [U.S.] First Amendment right to pursue one's affection for another human being."[62] This departure from contemporary corporate norms may be reducing the impact of the company's achievements in creating a locally made, constantly evolving line of casual clothing for young, urban North Americans. Although its business model is extremely promising, its human relations and organizational culture are under fire. In May 2007, three former employees sued Charney for sexual harassment at work. In contrast, Four Seasons Hotels, a luxury chain of hotels with headquarters in Toronto, reflects smooth internal processes. Treating employees well is considered key to the organization's success.

Workers at each hotel select a peer to receive the Employee of the Year award, which includes an expenses-paid vacation and a $1,000 shopping spree.[63]

The internal-process approach also has shortcomings. Total output and the organization's relationship with the external environment are not evaluated. Another problem is that evaluations of internal health and functioning are often subjective, because many aspects of inputs and internal processes are not quantifiable.

Goal Approach

The goal approach to effectiveness consists of identifying an organization's output goals and assessing how well the organization has attained those goals.[64] This is a logical approach because organizations do try to attain certain levels of output, profit, or client satisfaction. The goal approach measures progress toward attainment of those goals. For example, the Toronto Transit Commission centres its business plan around the number of riders per year. Its authoritative planning document is the Ridership Growth Strategy.[65] Although the TTC forecast 454 million riders in 2007, it is likely to hit 462 million.[66] The TTC has become a victim of its own success: because of the city's capital budget constraints,[67] it is unable to keep up with the demand for service.[68]

Indicators. The important goals to consider are operative goals. Efforts to measure effectiveness have been more productive using operative goals than using official goals.[69] Official goals tend to be abstract and difficult to measure. Operative goals reflect activities the organization is actually performing. Organizations often have multiple (and conflicting) operative goals.

Usefulness. The goal approach is used in business organizations because output goals can be readily measured. Business firms typically evaluate performance in terms of profitability, growth, market share, and return on investment. However, identifying operative goals and measuring performance of an organization are not always easy. Two problems that must be resolved are the issues of multiple goals and subjective indicators of goal attainment.

Since organizations have multiple and conflicting goals, effectiveness often cannot be assessed by a single indicator. High achievement on one goal might mean low achievement on another. Moreover, there are department goals as well as overall performance goals. The full assessment of effectiveness consider several goals simultaneously. Most organizations use a balanced approach to measuring goals. For instance, the vision of Diavik Diamond Mines does not mention creation of profits for the shareholders of Rio Tinto, but states "Our vision is to be Canada's premier diamond producer, creating a legacy of responsible safety, environmental, and employee development practice and enduring community benefit."[70] Senior managers cannot ignore the mandate to create profits for the parent company, but the organization's stated goal is to be Canada's premier diamond producer. Can it reach this goal, fulfill its obligations to the parent, and still build an exemplary legacy in the other three areas? How will the company know the areas are balanced? How will it know that its work is optimal? Operational goals are difficult to measure and achieve because of their diversity.

The other issue to resolve with the goal approach is how to identify operative goals for an organization and how to measure goal attainment. Business organizations often have objective indicators for certain goals, such as profit or growth. However, subjective assessment is needed for other goals, such as employee welfare or social responsibility. Someone has to go into the organization and learn what the actual goals are by talking with the top management team. Once goals are identified, subjective perceptions of goal attainment have to be used when quantitative indicators are not available. Managers rely on information from customers, competitors, suppliers, and employees, as well as their own intuition, when considering these goals. Consider the case of Canadian grocery giant, Loblaw.

In Practice
Loblaw

Loblaw was the dominant grocer of Canada throughout the 1980s and 90s. President Dave Nichol pioneered the use of private-label groceries as high-margin items uniquely available at Weston's own stores. On the strength of the President's Choice products, Loblaw could brand itself as the highest-quality grocer and charge correspondingly high prices. Such items as "Decadent" chocolate chip cookies and "Memories of Szechuan" peanut sauce attracted customers who were unable to find these products elsewhere. Selling private-label products with premium prices directly drove the company's margins up from the 2 to 4 percent margins normal in the industry to a staggeringly high 6 percent.

However, in 2005, the company's margins had fallen to 4.7 percent. Management discovered that customers were not happy to purchase a bag of milk in a 3000 m^2 superstore in which the dairy section could be more than 100 m from the car. Loblaw bought Maple Leaf Gardens, intending to convert it to a superstore, but was unable to finance the conversion and fulfill its promise of a new kind of icing in this location.

When Galen G. Weston, the new 34-year-old head of the company took over in late 2006, he was faced with unhappy customers, heavily financed real estate, and investors who wanted returns commensurate with other Canadian grocers. The company had lost $6 billion in value over the last two years. What could Weston, the heir to his parents' vast holdings, do to ensure that the company would return to its prior position as Canada's leader?

In February 2007, he announced the new plan. Profits would go up 10 percent a year. Loblaw would cut prices, increase marketing, improve staffing, and become more innovative. "In other words, the plan involves taking a hit to revenue while increasing expenses, yet profit margins are supposed to go up."[71]

Is this a recipe for success? Can the company achieve these goals simultaneously? What are the indicators Loblaw management should measure to ensure their strategy is on track? Can they measure the improvement in their staffing? How? What about innovation? Which indicators should be most likely to point to or "lead" profits?

See Exhibit 2.7 for an illustration of a strategic mistake that organizations will want to avoid!

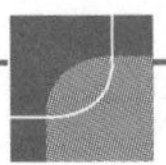

An Integrated Effectiveness Model

The three approaches—goal, resource-based, internal process—to organizational effectiveness described earlier all have something to offer, but each one tells only part of the story. The **competing-values model** tries to balance a concern with various parts of the organization rather than focusing on one part. This approach to effectiveness acknowledges that organizations do many things and have many outcomes.[72] It combines several indicators of effectiveness into a single framework.

EXHIBIT 2.7
When a Strategy Goes Wrong . . .

"We made a miscalculation, but it's consistent with our over-all strategy."

The model is based on the assumption that there are disagreements and competing viewpoints about what constitutes effectiveness. Managers sometimes disagree over which are the most important goals to pursue and measure. In addition, stakeholders have competing claims on what they want from the organization, as described in Chapter 1. One tragic example of conflicting viewpoints and competing interests comes from NASA. After seven astronauts died in the explosion of the space shuttle *Columbia* in February 2003, an investigative committee found deep organizational flaws at NASA, including ineffective mechanisms for incorporating dissenting opinions between scheduling managers and safety managers. External pressures to launch on time overrode safety concerns with the *Columbia* launch. As Wayne Hale, the NASA executive charged with giving the go-ahead for the next shuttle launch, puts it, "We dropped the torch through our own complacency, our arrogance, self-assurance, sheer stupidity, and through continuing attempt[s] to please everyone."[73] NASA is an extremely complex organization that operates not only with different viewpoints internally but also from the U.S. Congress, the U.S. president, and the expectations of the American public.

The competing-values model takes into account these complexities. The model was originally developed by Robert Quinn and John Rohrbaugh to combine the diverse indicators of performance used by managers and researchers.[74] Using a comprehensive list of performance indicators, a panel of experts in organizational effectiveness rated the indicators for similarity. The analysis produced underlying dimensions of effectiveness criteria that represented competing management values in organizations.

Indicators. The first value dimension pertains to organizational **focus**, which is whether dominant values concern issues that are *internal* or *external* to the firm. Internal focus reflects a management concern for the well-being and efficiency of employees, and external focus represents an emphasis on the well-being of the organization itself with respect to the environment. The second value dimension pertains to organizational structure, and whether *stability* versus *flexibility* is the dominant structural

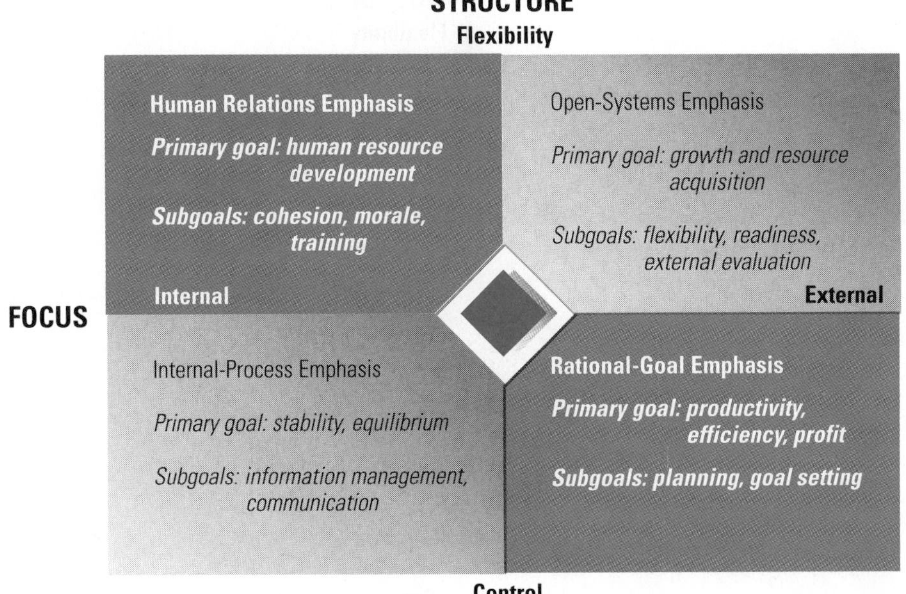

EXHIBIT 2.8
Four Approaches to Effectiveness Values
Source: Adapted from Robert E. Quinn and John Rohrbaugh, "A Spatial Model of Effectiveness Criteria: Toward a Competing Values Approach to Organizational Analysis," *Management Science* 29 (1983): 363–377; and Robert E. Quinn and Kim Cameron, "Organizational Life Cycles and Shifting Criteria of Effectiveness: Some Preliminary Evidence," *Management Science* 29 (1983): 33–51.

consideration. Stability reflects a management value for efficiency and top-down control, whereas flexibility represents a value for learning and change.

The value dimensions of structure and focus are illustrated in Exhibit 2.8. The combination of dimensions provides four approaches to organizational effectiveness, which, though seemingly different, are closely related. In real organizations, these competing values can and often do exist together. Each approach reflects a different management emphasis with respect to structure and focus.[75]

A combination of external focus and flexible structure leads to an **open-systems emphasis.** Management's primary goals are growth and resource acquisition. The organization accomplishes these goals through the subgoals of flexibility, readiness, and a positive external evaluation. The dominant value is establishing a good relationship with the environment to acquire resources and grow. This emphasis is similar in some ways to the resource-based approach described earlier.

The **rational-goal emphasis** represents management values of structural control and external focus. The primary goals are productivity, efficiency, and profit. The organization wants to achieve output goals in a controlled way. Subgoals that facilitate these outcomes are internal planning and goal setting, which are rational management tools. The rational-goal emphasis is similar to the goal approach described earlier.

The **internal-process emphasis** is in the lower-left section of Exhibit 2.8; it reflects the values of internal focus and structural control. The primary outcome is a stable organizational setting that maintains itself in an orderly way. Organizations that are well established in the environment and simply want to maintain their current position reflect this emphasis. Subgoals include mechanisms for efficient communication, information management, and subsequent decision making. Although this part of the competing-values model is similar in some ways to the internal-process approach described earlier, it is less concerned with human resources than with other internal processes that lead to efficiency.

The **human relations emphasis** incorporates the values of an internal focus and a flexible structure. Here, management concern is for the development of human

EXHIBIT 2.9
Effectiveness Values for Two Organizations

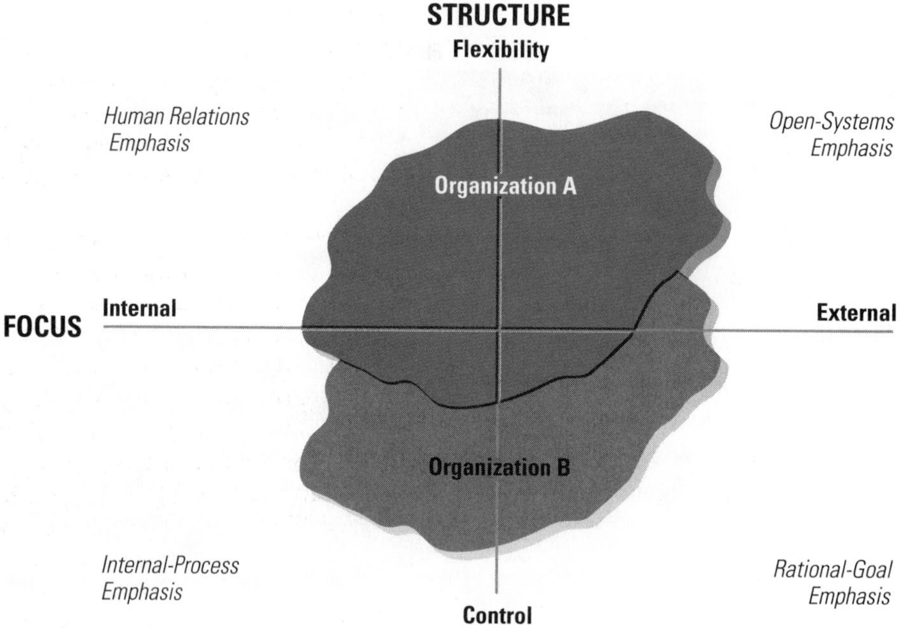

resources. Employees are given opportunities for autonomy and development. Management works toward the subgoals of cohesion, morale, and training opportunities. Organizations adopting this emphasis are more concerned with employees than with the environment.

The four cells in Exhibit 2.8 represent opposing organizational values. Managers decide which goal values will take priority in the organization. The way two organizations are mapped onto the four approaches is shown in Exhibit 2.9.[76] Organization A is a young organization concerned with finding a niche and becoming established in the external environment. Primary emphasis is given to flexibility, innovation, the acquisition of resources from the environment, and the satisfaction of external constituencies. This organization gives moderate emphasis to human relations and even less emphasis to current productivity and profits. Satisfying and adapting to the environment are more important. The attention given to open-systems values means that the internal-process emphasis is practically nonexistent. Stability and equilibrium are of little concern.

Organization B, in contrast, is an established business in which the dominant value is productivity and profits. This organization is characterized by planning and goal setting. Organization B is a large company that is well established in the environment and is primarily concerned with successful production and profits. Flexibility and human resources are not major concerns. This organization prefers stability and equilibrium to learning and innovation because it wants to take advantage of its established customers.

Usefulness. The competing-values model makes two contributions. First, it integrates diverse concepts of effectiveness into a single perspective. It incorporates the ideas of output goals, resource acquisition, and human resource development as goals the organization tries to accomplish. Second, the model calls attention to effectiveness criteria as management values and shows how opposing values exist at the same time. Managers must decide which values they wish to pursue and which values will receive less emphasis. The four competing values exist simultaneously, but not all will receive equal priority. For example, a new, small organization that concentrates on establishing itself within a competitive environment will give less emphasis to developing employees than to the external environment.

The dominant values in an organization often change over time as organizations experience new environmental demands or new top leadership.

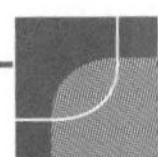

New Directions

Strategic management scholars are really social scientists who employ statistical tools to understand the way organizations, particularly companies, change and function in our society and around the world. Most researchers use large data sets that encompass many companies, numerous variables, and multiple years. At the same time, a few careful scholars have used field work and case studies of small groups of organizations to develop deeper and narrower veins of material. What are the big questions that strategy tries to answer?

- Why do so many firms look alike and why are there differences? How do these differences shape different performance?
- How do firms gain, store, and use knowledge? What makes a company innovative?
- When do companies chose to make an alliance with another company rather than buy their products? What are the costs and gains? What are the conditions that make this a good choice?
- What kind of oversight do corporate boards provide? What kids of relationships between investors, board and managers exist, and what influences their structures?
- What is the function of contracts? Of trust? Of monitoring? Under which conditions does a company use one or another to protect its interests?
- How do companies change with the increasing globalization of trade?
- Why do particular industries cluster in some cities and not in others?
- What are the effects of social and political institutions on the performance of firms?
- What is the role of the company in society? In what ways are companies constrained by ethical expectations?

Some strategy scholars are now asking whether they are working on the right problems and asking the right questions; for instance, few scholars have brought their skills to bear on highly controversial questions, like the future of the oil patch in Canada in the midst of global warming, or the increasing impact of income inequality in a globalized economy. The quickly shifting dynamics of a global economy and a disintegrating environment invites new perspectives and creates new lines of research into corporate roles, characteristics, and behaviours.

Even the blogosphere has discovered strategy. Two blogs cover the field, http://www.orgtheory.net and http://www.organizationsandmarkets.com, reflecting its sociological and economic roots. They gather the reflections of many different scholars from various academic traditions. Posts include "The network of Inuit languages" and "Three frontiers of science that sociologists should really care about" on orgtheory.net, and "9-11, Strategic Management, and Public Policy" and "Economic Darwinism during recessions" on organizationsandmarkets.com. Each lists its own blogroll with sites of interest to commerce, business, and management students.

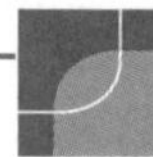

Summary and Interpretation

This chapter discussed organizational goals and the strategies that top managers use to help organizations achieve those goals. Goals specify the mission or purpose of an organization and its desired future state; strategies define how the organization will reach its goals. The chapter also discussed the impact of strategy on organization design and how designing the organization to fit strategy and other contingencies can lead to organizational effectiveness. The chapter closed with an examination of the most popular approaches to measuring effectiveness; that is, how well the organization realizes its purpose and attains its desired future state.

Organizations exist for a purpose; top managers define a specific mission or task to be accomplished. The mission statement, or official goals, makes explicit the purpose and direction of an organization. Official and operative goals are a key element in organizations because they meet these needs—establishing legitimacy with external groups and setting standards of performance for participants.

Managers must develop strategies that describe the actions required to achieve goals. Strategies may include any number of techniques to achieve the stated goals. Two models for formulating strategies are Porter's competitive strategies and the Miles and Snow strategy typology. Organization design needs to fit the firm's competitive approach to contribute to organizational effectiveness.

Assessing organizational effectiveness reflects the complexity of organizations as a topic of study. No one measure will guarantee an unequivocal assessment of performance. Organizations must perform diverse activities well—from obtaining resource inputs to delivering outputs—to be successful. Contingency approaches use output goals, resource acquisition, or internal health and efficiency as the criteria of effectiveness. The competing-values model is a balanced approach that considers multiple criteria simultaneously. No approach is suitable for every organization, but each offers some advantages that the others may lack.

From the point of view of managers, the goal approach to effectiveness and measures of internal efficiency are useful when measures are available. The attainment of output and profit goals reflects the purpose of the organization, and efficiency reflects the cost of attaining those goals. Other factors such as top-management preferences, the extent to which goals are measurable, and the scarcity of environmental resources may influence the use of effectiveness criteria. In nonprofit organizations, where internal processes and output criteria are often not quantifiable, resource acquisition may be the best available indicator of effectiveness.

From the point of view of people outside the organization, such as academic investigators or government researchers, the competing-values model of organizational effectiveness may be preferable. This model acknowledges different areas of focus (internal, external) and structure (flexibility, stability), and allows managers to choose among approaches—human relations, open systems, rational goal, or internal process—in order to emphasize the values they wish to pursue.

Key Concepts

analyzer, p. 60
competing-values model, p. 69
defender, p. 60
focus, p. 70
focus strategy, p. 59
goal approach, p. 65
human relations emphasis, p. 71
internal-process approach, p. 66

Discussion Questions

1. Discuss the role of top management in setting organizational direction.
2. How might a company's goals for employee development be related to its goals for innovation and change? to goals for productivity? Can you discuss ways these types of goals might conflict in an organization?
3. What is a goal for the class for which you are reading this text? Who established this goal? Discuss how the goal affects your direction and motivation.
4. What is the difference between a goal and a strategy as defined in the text? Identify both a goal and a strategy for a campus or community organization with which you are involved.
5. Discuss the similarities and differences in the strategies described in Porter's competitive strategies and Miles and Snow's typology.
6. Do you believe mission statements and official goal statements provide an organization with genuine legitimacy in the external environment? Discuss.
7. Suppose you have been asked to evaluate the effectiveness of the police department in a medium-sized community. Where would you begin, and how would you proceed? What effectiveness approach would you prefer?
8. What are the advantages and disadvantages of the resource-based approach versus the goal approach for measuring organizational effectiveness?
9. What are the similarities and differences between assessing effectiveness on the basis of competing values versus the stakeholder approach described in Chapter 1? Explain.
10. A noted organization theorist once said, "Organizational effectiveness can be whatever top management defines it to be." Discuss.

Chapter 2 Workbook: Identifying Company Goals and Strategies*

Choose three companies, either in the same industry or in three different industries. Search the Internet for information on the companies, including annual reports. For each company, look particularly at the goals expressed.

	Articulated Goals	Strategies from Porter Used
Organization 1		
Organization 2		
Organization 3		

Questions

1. Which goals seem most important?
2. Look for differences in the goals and strategies of the three companies and develop an explanation for those differences.
3. Which of the goals or strategies should be changed? Why?
4. Compare your table with those of other students and look for common themes. Which companies seem to articulate and communicate their goals and strategies best?

Case for Analysis: Jones Soda*

In an energetic, enormously candid interview, Jones Soda's founder shares some stories about the building blocks of his business.

Juice Guise

I was thrown into the beverage industry without any aspirations to be in the beverage industry. I didn't wake up one morning and say I want to be in the beverage industry. What happened was, I was in the *ski industry*. I was fairly young at the time. My father was a psychiatrist and he was, like, "You've got to go to school." And 'I'm, like, "Dude, I get paid to go to ski right now. I've got a sweet car. You're on drugs if you think I'm giving this up. I've got my own credit card. I'm paid to ski. What are you thinking?" This was in Edmonton, Alberta.

I basically blew him off, and when I realized that I wasn't good enough [at skiing], and that school was probably the right option, I was so stubborn that I couldn't do it. I couldn't go to school because I told him I didn't need it. But I also realized I wasn't good enough to be a professional skier of any great magnitude. I was 22, 23 at the time. I had traveled Europe and done all the things you do after high school. To make a long story short, I started a fruit stand. The ski industry pays you for 12 months, but you only work nine, so you have these paid summer vacations.

The guy I was buying my fruit from said, "You've got to look at this orange juice from Florida." I did the due diligence on the OJ market in Canada. And it's 55% of a $365-millon industry. There's no premium fresh-squeezed frozen OJ, yadda, yadda, yadda. So I sold my car and brought this OJ up from Florida to Canada. And that's how I got into the beverage industry.

I got US $14,400 for my car. It was a Chiraco. It was a sweet Chiraco. But it wasn't too gooey. Just the right amount of goo on it. It was a beautiful car. I sold the car to buy the OJ. It was a product called Just Picked. The guy who sold it to me was from New York and the company was from Florida. And the first batch he sold to me was the extra-thick stuff. So I had 1,440 cases. And this stuff was so thick you could stick a spoon in. So I was going to restaurants to sell it with champagne. The solids would separate. So you'd have a clump of crap. And I'm, like, "Oh my god, I've got all this OJ. What am I going to do?" So I'm walking up and down the street, telling people it'll lower their cholesterol, it's got fibre, you can eat it with a spoon. It was horrible. It tasted really good, but it was absolutely horrible in quality. It actually caught on. The next year the sales were $12,500 for the entire company. I was able to fight through that.

The Jones Soda story is really one of determination and fighting through challenges that most companies would never have to. No one's given us anything. Everything we've done, we've had to fight for, probably harder than we should have. The fighting is getting less and less now.

After the OJ started to take off, I started to import other beverages and built a distribution company, a beverage distribution company, in Vancouver. We sold Snapple, Arizona Ice Tea, Pepsi, Coke, we were selling tons of different beverages. We were the largest independent beverage distributor in Western Canada.

That was by 1994, 1995. We built the business to about $6.9 million in sales. One of the problems was, I didn't like dealing with the suppliers and I wanted to create my own brand. Because I had seen all these companies come to me and say, hey sell my crap in Canada.

If someone asked me at 18, is this what you dreamt to do? I would say no. The reality is that it's been a weird game to get to where I'm at now. But at the age of 41, I'm very qualified to do what I do. I understand the consumers better than a lot of people do.

Not Necessarily Needed

Around this time, we started to import concentrated root beer. We were bottling a root beer. So I started to understand how to make soda. So we started Urban Juice and Soda and by 1994, we were flying. Sales were going through the roof. Snapple sold to Gatorade for $1.6 billion, 432 new ice teas are coming out.

I'm saying, this is crazy. I'm seeing this stuff come flying at me. People are knocking on the door everyday trying to get me to sell their stuff. Then I said, I don't want to sell other people's stuff anymore. That's horrible. It's not fun. It's not yours.

But the world doesn't need any more of this stuff. Because nobody cares when this stuff goes off the market. If Jones Soda fell off the face of the earth today—or if I got hit by a bus and the company got closed down, nobody would lose any sleep over it. And that's the attitude you have to take today. That's the attitude we took in 1995–96. It's more relevant today because of consolidation in the biz world. It's more relevant today because of the Internet and the number of channels. But it's still relevant and was relevant in 1995. The reality is that consumers don't need our stuff. I don't mean to say that. But when you start thinking that way—a lot of time, business people, marketers convince themselves that people need their stuff. They're passionate about how you need my new widget. You need it!

The fact is, you *don't* need it! And as soon as you get off the fact that you don't need it you become, in my opinion, you become a better marketer, you get a better understanding of your customer. You're not listening to your customer when you tell them, "You need me." You listen to [your] customers when you say, "You really don't need me." Coca-Cola sold 500 million cans of soda yesterday. I think a consumer can find a cold beverage somewhere if they really need to. Let's just get this stuff clear. Clearly, let's call an ace an ace. Nobody's going to lose any sleep, no one's going to get dehydrated. That's a fundamental difference, I believe, between marketers and brand builders. Brand builders realize that brands need to be accepted by the consumer and that it's a privilege and honour for someone to pay $1.70 for a bottle of Jones Soda. I'm very honoured by that.

The Rules

I came to that insight pretty early on in the game because when you're selling so many widgets—here I had a distribution warehouse, where I have 600 different beverages and I realized that all I'm doing is moving one to the other and nobody really gives a rat's ass. But I wasn't inundated with the culture of a big company. I didn't have the three or four years of big-time corporation. And by not going to business school—and I wish I had gone to biz school in order to learn the game—but I'm so glad I didn't learn to believe in the rules. That's a key component of what I do: I'm not convinced that I don't have to play by anybody's rules. Well, that's not true. We have three. A. The world doesn't need another soda. B. We don't believe people need our soda. C. We can't play by anybody's rules. If we adhere to those three things, then we're going to create an emotional connection with our consumers, we're going to be bigger than a lot of companies think we can get because we're doing the right thing, and we're going to have a lot of fun doing it.

Passionate Brands

Great brands are built because people are passionate about them. The very first case of Jones Soda went to the founder of Nike, Phil Knight. He got the first case of Jones Soda. I don't know if he ever saw it. But he sent a letter—I don't know if he signed it or if his secretary signed it. I don't care; it's framed in the boardroom. I just really like what he was doing. One of the things about Jones Soda, I always viewed Jones as an accessory. So when we looked at companies to emulate, we never looked at beverage companies. It doesn't make any sense. If I'm trying to be a leader in a category, why look at the big guys because I'm just going to try and follow what they're doing. So the approach has always been to say I don't care what anybody does in the beverage industry. I really don't. They're going to do what they're going to do, so who gives a rat's ass. We've got to do what we've got to do. You have to know what they're doing, but you don't have to follow what they're doing.

If you don't like Jones Soda, if you're not into it, I don't give a rat's ass. I'm not going to change my formula to please you. That's a very profound statement because if you talk to companies today, they say the customer's always right. Well, no. Forget that. The customer's not always right. If you are always trying to cater to all of the customers you have, you have no soul. You have to define yourself.

You're always going to piss people off. We had people pissed off that we had a salt and pepper shaker on our label, because they said it was promoting "racial commingling." You are an idiot. It's a salt and pepper shaker. There was a cue ball, and that was promoting cocaine. There was a Zippo lighter and that was promoting "smoking and weed." The point is, fine, have a nice day. But I'm not going to pull those off. Now do I have a kid being beaten? No. I had a salt and pepper shaker.

A great brand is going to evoke passion. You're going to love it or hate it. And I'm good with that. I'm good with people loving us. And I'm good with people hating us.

On Health and Humour

My daughter drinks one Jones a week. And I'm good with that. We don't sell two litres. It's a treat. And everybody wigs out on it, saying it causes obesity. It's the fact that you drink 44 fluid ounces of this stuff. Ten years ago the average size of a soda was 12 ounces. Now, the average size is 43 ounces. Well, you don't have to be a rocket scientist to do the math, you morons. So we sell in 12-ounce. That's it. Have a nice soda. If you're going to drink a gallon of soda, you better figure out that that's a lot of sugar. The reality is that Jones can be a powerful brand. We can be a powerful brand by—we're selling 12-packs in Target now. That's going to show me how we stack up against Coke and Pepsi. And so far, we're doing better than they thought we would do. And we're doing better than I thought we would do. And the reality is that we haven't advertised it. Nobody knows about it. But then, you're going to see our turkey and gravy holiday pack. That stuff is outrageous. No one's going to come up with mashed potato flavour, green bean, and fried onions. Fruitcake, which is disgusting, and cranberry sauce.

I can't drink a case of the stuff. No, it's more about having fun. What I really wanted to do with the turkey and gravy, I wanted to say we're not afraid to do it. And now what we're making fun of is the whole carb thing. Now you can have a carb-free turkey and gravy dinner. We're just going to hammer away and make it a big, big parody.

One year on April Fool's Day we sent a press release saying we were acquired by John Deere. That was hilarious. You sold out man! It was a joke, dude. We spelled Deere wrong. It was one of the funniest things we've ever done. We said they wanted their own weed-flavoured soda. We came up with that stuff and people went ballistic. We were getting phone calls: "I can't believe you sold out. You sold out to the big guy." Dude, it was a tractor company. It's really very harmless. I mean we live in a society today where there's a lot of stuff going on. We've got wars, we've got terrorism, we've got fuel prices, we've got elections, we've got a very divided country right now. And if Jones can throw some realistic humour, that's harmless.

Patently Personalized

I don't want to be a soda company. I have no desire to say Jones is just a soda company. I have a desire to say Jones is a lifestyle company. Look at what we did with myjonesmusic.com.

In 1997, Ernest von Rosen [developer of Jones' Web site] and I were in Vancouver, he was saying, Dude we're getting a ton of baby photos. I'm like, yeah, we are. He's like how many baby photos do you really want to see on a bottle of Jones soda? But these people love their baby photos—of course they do, and we're fired up about it. So he said I've got this guy by the name of Vaclav—and Vaclav is from Eastern Europe. He doesn't speak any English. He speaks in white board. You know these guys, they just have a white board and they talk in white board? So this is 1997, we're now thinking about people emailing photos. In 2004, this is no big deal. Photos are flying across email. But in 1997, nobody's talking about this stuff. So we're talking about it. So Vaclav creates myjones and myjones, we get the patent for. So we own the patent for customizing branded merchandising over a computer network. Our value is not so much as a soda company. Our value is as a company that can create ideas like myjones, myjonesmusic, and create the stuff that's truly in tune with our consumers in a positive way.

Getting Real

Look at somebody like Jon Stewart. Why is he so funny and so in synch with people? Because he's real. And Coke says it's real. But saying it and being it are two different things. So if you say it, you better be it. My daughter, she couldn't give a rat's ass about Coke. And her friends—she's 10, they're 10—they don't care because it's *everywhere*. It's nothing new, it's nothing special. That's what big companies have forgotten. The most important thing is not about money.

If somebody said to me, Peter I want to give you $100 million, and I want you to launch a successful brand tomorrow, I'd say take your money and walk away. You want to give me $10 million and five years to do it, I'll knock the ball out of the park. It's not about money, it's about time.

We have people who come up to our door—they've traveled from, say, Utah—to go to the Jones mecca.

And they cry when they're here. It's soda, dude. But I totally get it. People get fired up about Jones because it's theirs. It's not my soda. When you buy a bottle of Jones Soda there is a person's name on the bottle who took the photo. That is their soda. And when you go to a Target and buy a 12-pack of Jones, there are seven people's names on this. Seven people are saying, "This is my stuff." The most important thing is that whenever you do something with real people, it gets real. And that's the difference between saying you're real and being real.

Now I'm scamming. Companies are paying me to give talks. I think it's a pretty good gig. They'll pay me 10 grand to come talk to them. Maybe if I write a book, I get can that up there more. I do a good job and all the money goes to charity—so it's not a total scam. So far we've built two schools.

Our customers, they can spot BS. And that's totally kosher. If you don't live up to what you say you're going to do, like being real, they throw you under the bus. You just feed their existing perception of companies. Right or wrong, that's the way it is.

And a Child Shall Lead Them

We're going to invoke an advisory board of kids. We're going to do it online. It's going to be like a reality TV show. One is actually going to be a board member. Somebody, 16–17 years old, is actually going to be a director of the company. Now that's absolutely insane. But it's not. It's totally sane. You know, I'm reading *Barrons* about having directors approve their advertising. These guys are 70 years old! How the heck can he approve anything about anything? How can they approve it? I'm just saying, I couldn't approve advertising for golfing or something. And I shouldn't approve it.

The way marketing has taught us to talk about demographics is BS. Let's look at the 35–40 year olds. That's where their income is. But if you're going to be their aspirational brand, then you really have to look lower than the 35 year old. There's not a 35-year-old woman looking to a 45-year-old woman to see how she dresses. They're looking at a 25 year old. And they're finding the balance between a 25 year old and a 35 year old. So the aspiration always goes down. Everybody knocks Jones, says you're a kid's soda. Sweet, if I'm a 12- to 24-year-old brand. It's not the actual demographic you're aiming for, it's the aspirational demographic.

I'd like for people to talk about Jones the same way they talk about brands such as Diesel Jeans. Puma, Diesel, Nike. I want to be in that category. I don't want to be Coke or Pepsi. I like Puma because they created a category in a category. Diesel because they're always relevant, always fresh, always on target.

Listen and Learn

If you're able to give your customers the ability to give you info and you listen to them from their perspective, not everything they say will make sense. Not everything they do will be right. But you will know more about what you have to do based on the info you have. Because it's one component, but very critical component.

Focus groups are toilet paper: They're only used to cover your ass. You can get a focus group to tell you anything you want. When we do focus groups, tastings really, we have two choices: Does it taste good, or does it taste like crap? Yummy or crappy? Good or bad? It's not rocket science. And you get really good information. You have to be careful to make a distinction between getting the answers you want and honest answers.

People get cash-itis—meaning they have cash and they think they have to spend it to drive revenues, etc. You've got cash, and you've got to do the right thing with it. Corporations think they can buy these kids and the kids are saying, screw you, you're a loser. That's the simple math. You have to have time to allow kids to discover you.

Built to Spill (Over)

Execution is where we need to improve. That's where we can get better. If you judge our company, for the last seven years we've been playing in the minors. And then last year, we got called up to the majors with Panera, Barnes and Noble. And we were sitting on the bench. This year we got to the plate once. With Target. In 2004 we got called up to the plate. From a baseball analogy, we've been in the minors for a long time. Now we've got something to prove. So obviously execution is something we have to improve. And if we're hitting in all aspects, this thing is going to go.

First thing is you change the rules. The Target deal is rule-breaker that is unbelievable [sic]. For the beverage industry, we took their game and shoved it up their ass. I watched Richard Branson try to do it by playing by the rules. He couldn't do it. It's so easy to scale this up by not playing by the rules. It's so hard to scale by playing by rules.

To steal a line from Sam Cook from Boston Beer, we don't sell as much as Coke or Pepsi spill in a day. There's so much room to grow—Coke and Pepsi are so big—we've got a long way to go before anyone notices. I'm more interested in growing geographically—both domestic and international—than by volume, to boost brand equity.

*R. Underwood, "Jonesing for Soda" *Fast Company* (March 2005).

Case for Analysis: The University Art Museum*

Visitors to the campus were always shown the University Art Museum, of which the large and distinguished university was very proud. A photograph of the handsome neoclassical building that housed the museum had long been used by the university for the cover of its brochures and catalogs.

The building, together with a substantial endowment, was given to the university around 1912 by an alumnus, the son of the university's first president, who had become very wealthy as an investment banker. He also gave the university his own small, but high-quality, collections—one of Etruscan figurines, and one, unique in America, of English pre-Raphaelite paintings. He then served as the museum's unpaid director until his death. During his tenure he brought a few additional collections to the museum, largely from other alumni of the university. Only rarely did the museum purchase anything. As a result, the museum housed several small collections of uneven quality. As long as the founder ran the museum, none of the collections were ever shown to anybody except a few members of the university's art history faculty, who were admitted as the founder's private guests.

After the founder's death, in the late 1920s, the university intended to bring in a professional museum director. Indeed, this had been part of the agreement under which the founder had given the museum. A search committee was to be appointed; but in the meantime a graduate student in art history, who had shown interest in the museum and who had spent a good many hours in it, took over temporarily. At first, Miss Kirkoff did not even have a title, let alone a salary. But she stayed on acting as the museum's director and over the next 30 years was promoted in stages to that title. But from the first day, whatever her title, she was in charge. She immediately set about changing the museum altogether. She cataloged the collections. She pursued new gifts, again primarily small collections from alumni and other friends of the university. She organized fund raising for the museum. But, above all, she began to integrate the museum into the work of the university.

When a space problem arose in the years immediately following World War II, Miss Kirkoff offered the third floor of the museum to the art history faculty, which moved its offices there. She remodeled the building to include classrooms and a modern and well-appointed auditorium. She raised funds to build one of the best research and reference libraries in art history in the country. She also began to organize a series of special exhibitions built around one of the museum's own collections, complemented by loans from outside collections. For each of these exhibitions, she had a distinguished member of the university's art faculty write a catalog. These catalogs speedily became the leading scholarly texts in the fields.

Miss Kirkoff ran the University Art Museum for almost half a century. But at the age of 68, after suffering a severe stroke, she had to retire. In her letter of resignation she proudly pointed to the museum's growth and accomplishment under her stewardship. "Our endowment," she wrote, "now compares favorably with museums several times our size. We never have had to ask the university for any money other than our share of the university's insurance policies. Our collections in the areas of our strength, while small, are of first-rate quality and importance. Above all, we are being used by more people than any museum of our size. Our lecture series, in which members of the university's art history faculty present a major subject to a university audience of students and faculty, attracts regularly three hundred to five hundred people; and if we had the seating capacity, we could easily have a larger audience. Our exhibitions are seen and studied by more visitors, most of them members of the university community, than all but the most highly publicized exhibitions in the very big museums ever draw. Above all, the courses and seminars offered in the museum have become one of the most popular and most rapidly growing educational features of the university. No other museum in this country or anywhere else," concluded Miss Kirkoff, "has so successfully integrated art into the life of a major university and a major university into the work of a museum."

Miss Kirkoff strongly recommended that the university bring in a professional museum director as her successor. "The museum is much too big and much too important to be entrusted to another amateur such as I was forty-five years ago," she wrote. "And it needs careful thinking regarding its direction, its basis of support, and its future relationship with the university."

The university took Miss Kirkoff's advice. A search committee was duly appointed and, after one year's work, it produced a candidate whom everybody approved. The candidate was himself a graduate of the university who had then obtained his Ph.D. in art history and in museum work from the university. Both his teaching and his administrative record were sound, leading to his current museum directorship in a medium-sized city. There he converted an old, well-known, but rather sleepy museum to a lively, community-oriented museum whose exhibitions were well publicized and attracted large crowds.

The new museum director took over with great fanfare in September 1981. Less than 3 years later he left—with less fanfare, but still with considerable noise. Whether he resigned or was fired was not quite clear. But that there was bitterness on both sides was only too obvious.

The new director, upon his arrival, had announced that he looked upon the museum as a "major community resource" and intended to "make the tremendous artistic and scholarly resources of the museum fully available to the academic community as well as to the public." When he said these things in an interview with the college newspaper, everybody nodded in approval. It soon became clear that what he meant by "community resource" and what the faculty and students understood by these words were not the same. The museum had always been "open to the public" but, in practice, it was members of the college community who used the museum and attended its lectures, its exhibitions, and its frequent seminars.

The first thing the new director did, however, was to promote visits from the public schools in the area. He soon began to change the exhibition policy. Instead of organizing small shows, focused on a major collection of the museum and built around a scholarly catalog, he began to organize "popular exhibitions" around "topics of general interest" such as "Women Artists through the Ages." He promoted these exhibitions vigorously in the newspapers, in radio and television interviews, and, above all, in the local schools. As a result, what had been a busy but quiet place was soon knee-deep with schoolchildren, taken to the museum in special buses that cluttered the access roads around the museum and throughout the campus. The faculty, which was not particularly happy with the resulting noise and confusion, became thoroughly upset when the scholarly old chairman of the art history department was mobbed by fourth-graders who sprayed him with their water pistols as he tried to push his way through the main hall to his office.

Increasingly, the new director did not design his own shows, but brought in traveling exhibitions from major museums, importing their catalog as well rather than have his own faculty produce one.

The students, too, were apparently unenthusiastic after the first 6 or 8 months, during which the new director had been somewhat of a campus hero. Attendance at the classes and seminars held at the art museum fell off sharply, as did attendance at the evening lectures. When the editor of the campus newspaper interviewed students for a story on the museum, he was told again and again that the museum had become too noisy and too "sensational" for students to enjoy the classes and to have a chance to learn.

What brought all this to a head was an Islamic art exhibit in late 1983. Since the museum had little Islamic art, nobody criticized the showing of a traveling exhibit, offered on very advantageous terms with generous financial assistance from some of the Arab governments. But then, instead of inviting one of the university's own faculty members to deliver the customary talk at the opening of the exhibit, the director brought in a cultural attaché of one of the Arab embassies in Washington. The speaker, it was reported, used the occasion to deliver a violent attack on Israel and on the American policy of supporting Israel against the Arabs. A week later, the university senate decided to appoint an advisory committee, drawn mostly from members of the art history faculty, which, in the future, would have to approve all plans for exhibits and lectures. The director thereupon, in an interview with the campus newspaper, sharply attacked the faculty as "elitist" and "snobbish" and as believing that "art belongs to the rich." Six months later, in June 1984, his resignation was announced.

Under the bylaws of the university, the academic senate appoints a search committee. Normally, this is pure formality. The chairperson of the appropriate department submits the department's nominees for the committee who are approved and appointed, usually without debate. But when the academic senate early the following semester was asked to appoint the search committee, things were far from "normal." The dean who presided, sensing the tempers in the room, tried to smooth over things by saying, "Clearly, we picked the wrong person the last time. We will have to try very hard to find the right one this time."

He was immediately interrupted by an economist, known for his populism, who broke in and said, "I admit that the late director was probably not the right personality. But I strongly believe that his personality was not at the root of the problem. He tried to do what needs doing, and this got him in trouble with the faculty. He tried to make our museum a community resource, to bring in the community and to make art accessible to broad masses of people, to the blacks and the Puerto Ricans, to the kids from the ghetto schools and to a lay public. And this is what we really resented. Maybe his methods were not the most tactful ones—I admit I could have done without those interviews he gave. But what he tried to do was right. We had better commit ourselves to the policy he wanted to put into effect, or else we will have deserved his attacks on us as 'elitist' and 'snobbish.'"

"This is nonsense," cut in the usually silent and polite senate member from the art history faculty. "It makes absolutely no sense for our museum to become the kind of community resource our late director and my distinguished colleague want it to be. First, there is no need. The city has one of the world's finest and biggest museums, and it does exactly that and does it very well. Secondly, we have neither the artistic resources nor the financial resources to serve the community at large. We can do something different but equally important and indeed unique. Ours is the only museum in the country, and perhaps in the world, that is fully integrated with an academic community and truly a teaching institution. We are using it, or at least we used to until the last few unfortunate years, as a major educational resource for all our students. No other museum in the country, and as far as I know in the world, is bringing undergraduates into art the way we do. All of us, in addition to our scholarly and graduate work, teach undergraduate courses for people who are not going to be art majors or art historians. We work with the engineering students and show them what we do in our conservation and restoration work. We work with architecture students and show them the development of architecture through the ages. Above all, we work with liberal arts students, who often have had no exposure to art before they came here and who enjoy our courses all the more because they are scholarly and not just 'art appreciation.' This is unique and this is what our museum can do and should do."

"I doubt that this is really what we should be doing," commented the chairman of the mathematics department. "The museum, as far as I know, is part of the graduate faculty. It should concentrate on training art historians in its Ph.D. program, on its scholarly work, and on its research. I would strongly urge that the museum be considered an adjunct to graduate and especially to Ph.D. education, confine itself to this work, and stay out of all attempts to be 'popular,' both on campus and outside of it. The glory of the museum is the scholarly catalogs produced by our faculty, and our Ph.D. graduates who are sought after by art history faculties throughout the country. This is the museum's mission, which can only be impaired by the attempts to be 'popular,' whether with students or with the public."

"These are very interesting and important comments," said the dean, still trying to pacify. "But I think this can wait until we know who the new director is going to be. Then we should raise these questions with him."

"I beg to differ, Mr. Dean," said one of the elder statesmen of the faculty. "During the summer months, I discussed this question with an old friend and neighbor of mine in the country, the director of one of the nation's great museums. He said to me: 'You do not have a personality problem; you have a management problem. You have not, as a university, taken responsibility for the mission, the direction, and the objectives of your museum. Until you do this, no director can succeed. And this is your decision. In fact, you cannot hope to get a good director until you can tell that person what your basic objectives are. If your late director is to blame—I know him and I know that he is abrasive—it is for being willing to take on a job when you, the university, had not faced up to the basic management decisions. There is no point talking about who should manage until it is clear what it is that has to be managed and for what.'"

At this point the dean realized that he had to adjourn the discussion unless he wanted the meeting to degenerate into a brawl. But he also realized that he had to identify the issues and possible decisions before the next senate meeting a month later.

*Case #3, "The University Art Museum: Defining Purpose and Mission" (pp. 28–35), from *Management Cases* by Peter F. Drucker.

Chapter 2 Workshop: Competing Values and Organizational Effectiveness*

1. Divide into groups of four to six members.
2. Select an organization to "study" for this exercise. It should be an organization about which you can easily and quickly gather extensive information.
3. Using the exhibit "Four Approaches to Effectiveness Values" (Exhibit 2.8), your group should list eight potential measures that show a balanced view of performance. These should relate not only to work activities, but also to goal values for the company. Use the table below.
4. How will achieving these goal values help the organization to become more effective? Which values could be given more weight than others? Why?
5. Present your competing values chart to the rest of the class. Each group should explain why it chose those particular values and which are more important. Be prepared to defend your position to the other groups, which are encouraged to question your choices.

Goal or Subgoal		Performance Gauge	How to Measure	Source of Data	What Do You Consider Effective?
(Example) Equilibrium		Turnover rates	Compare percentages of workers who left	HRM files	25% reduction in first year
Open system	1.				
	2.				
Human relations	3.				
	4.				
Internal process	5.				
	6.				
Rational goal	7.				
	8.				

*Adapted by Dorothy Marcic from general ideas in Jennifer Howard and Larry Miller, *Team Management*, The Miller Consulting Group, 1994, p. 92.

3 Fundamentals of Organizational Structure

The Canadian Press/PAUL CHIASSON

A Look Inside

Cooperatives (Co-ops) and Credit Unions

Canada has a large and vibrant cooperative sector. There are over 10,000 cooperatives with approximately 12 million members from sea to sea to sea. There are three types of cooperative structure: (1) primary co-ops do business or provide services directly to individual members, (2) second-tier co-ops are federated or central organizations designed to provide goods and services that benefit members of multiple organizations, and (3) third-tier co-ops are associations of second-tier co-ops designed to provide sector-wide services locally and globally.

The fundamental organizational design principle of co-ops is democratic control by the membership. Members are elected to a board of directors, which, in turn, hires management. The board of directors creates several committees to take on the various functions of the co-op such as membership, finance, and communications. Some co-ops are structured as nonprofits while other are structured as for-profits. Nonprofit co-ops do not distribute investment shares while for-profit co-ops can distribute dividends among members and staff.[1] There are many different types of co-ops—beer, childcare, coffee, computer graphics, dairy, forestry, health care, housing, kayaking and finance.

Desjardins is one of the best-known credit unions in the country (see photo). It was founded more than 100 years ago by Alphonse Desjardins in Lévis, Québec. Desjardins' mission is

> To contribute to the economic and social well-being of people and their communities within the compatible limits of our field of activity by:
>
> - developing an integrated cooperative network of secure and profitable financial services on a permanent basis, owned by the members and administered by them, and a network of complementary financial companies with a competitive return, also controlled by the members; and
> - educating the public, and in particular our members, officers and employees, about democracy, the economy, solidarity, and individual and collective responsibility.[2]

The number-one financial institution in Québec, Desjardins upholds its unique presence through its caisses, business centres, subsidiary distribution networks, and virtual networks. Desjardins is present in Ontario, Manitoba, and New Brunswick through its components and its affiliated cooperative caisse networks, and through Desjardins Credit Union. Several subsidiary businesses are also active in all Canadian provinces.

When in the United States, members and clients can count on the services offered by Desjardins Bank and Caisse centrale Desjardins to support them in their business development or to help make their lives easier when they travel. On the international stage, Desjardins is actively involved in international cooperation, supporting four million people in some 20 developing and emerging countries.

Every caisse and credit union is a financial services cooperative that serves and protects the interests of its members. Desjardins Business Centres are owned by the caisses in the area and, together, they meet the needs of the members in their community.

Together, subsidiaries, caisses, credit unions, and business centres offer their 5.8 million members and clients a full range of financial products and services.

As Exhibit 3.1 illustrates, Desjardins is a complex organization designed according to the principle of democratic control by the members. As of December 2007, Desjardins had total assets of $144 billion, 536 caisses, 919 service centres, 5,796,312 members, 6,545 elected officers, 40,345 employees and 2,769 automated-teller machines.[3]

EXHIBIT 3.1
Desjardins' Organization Structure—as of January 1, 2008

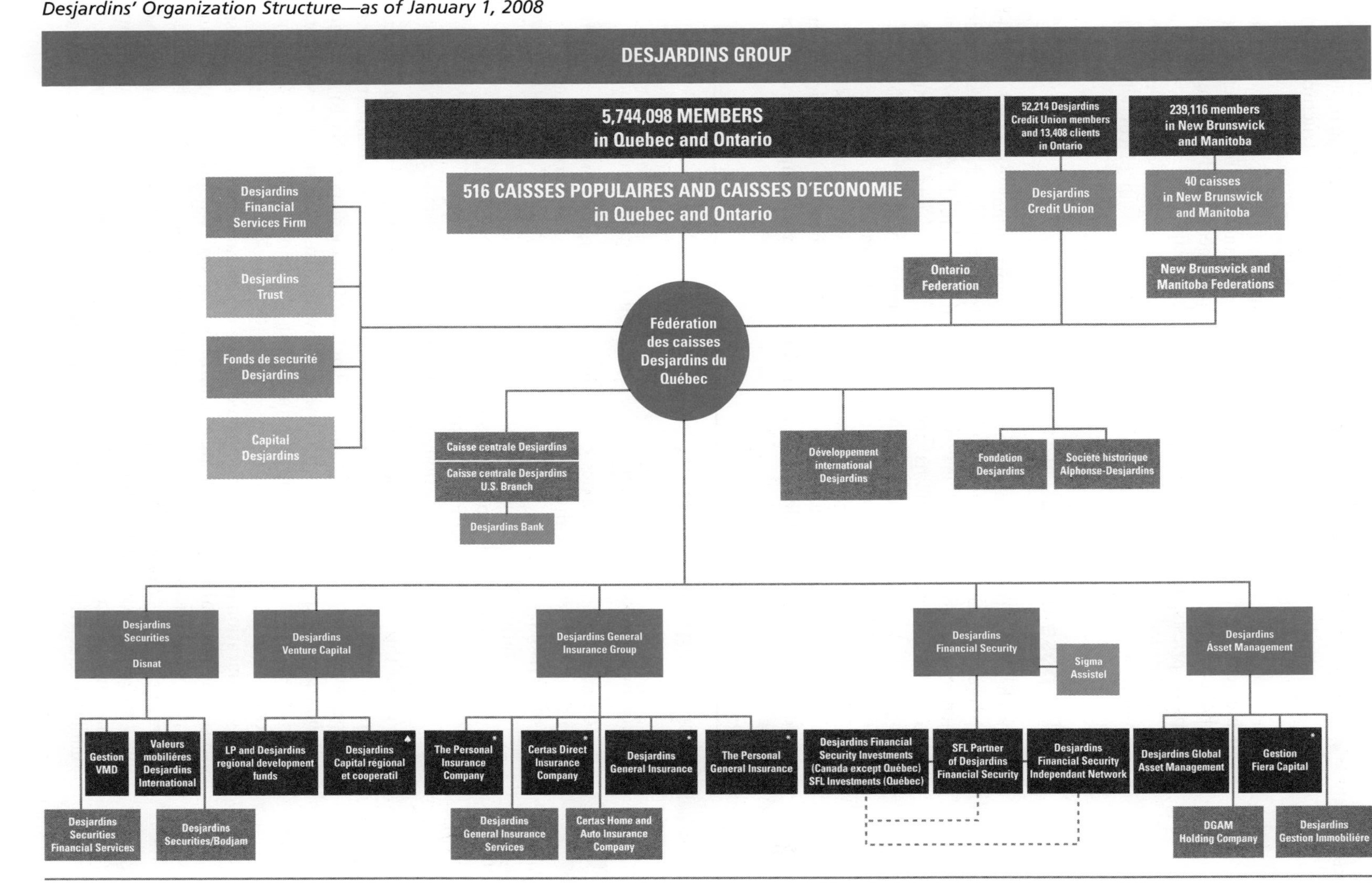

Source: "About Desjardins," (January 1, 2008) at http://www.desjardins.com/en/a_propos/qui-nous-sommes/organigramme (accessed June 3, 2008).

Organizations use various structural alternatives to help them achieve their purpose and goals. Nearly every firm needs to undergo structural reorganization at some point to help meet new challenges. Structural changes are needed to reflect new strategies or respond to changes in other contingency factors such as environment, technology, size and life cycle, and culture. For example, the Catholic Church is reorganizing to meet the challenges of a dwindling and aging corps of priests, financial pressures, shifting demographics, and ethical scandals. The traditional top-down, authoritarian management style is being re-evaluated in an effort to improve decision making and put resources in places where they're needed most.[4]

Purpose of This Chapter

This chapter introduces basic concepts of organizational structure and shows how to design structure as it appears on the organizational chart. First we define structure and provide an overview of structural design. Then, an information-processing perspective explains how to design vertical and horizontal linkages to provide needed information flow. The chapter next presents basic design options, followed by strategies for grouping organizational activities into functional, divisional, geographical, matrix, horizontal, virtual network, or hybrid structures. The final section examines how the application of basic structures depends on the organization's situation and outlines the symptoms of structural misalignment.

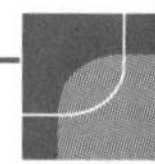

Organizational Structure

PDA Remember...

Develop organizational charts that describe task responsibilities, reporting relationships, and the grouping of individuals into departments. Provide sufficient documentation so that all people within the organization know to whom they report and how they fit into the total organization picture.

There are three key components in the definition of **organizational structure**:

1. Organizational structure designates formal reporting relationships, including the number of levels in the hierarchy and the span of control of managers and supervisors.
2. Organizational structure identifies the grouping together of individuals into departments and of departments into the total organization.
3. Organizational structure includes the design of systems to ensure effective communication, coordination, and integration of efforts across departments.[5]

These three elements of structure pertain to both vertical and horizontal aspects of organizing. For example, the first two elements are the structural *framework*, which is the vertical hierarchy.[6] The third element pertains to the pattern of *interactions* among organizational employees. An ideal structure encourages employees to provide horizontal information and coordination where and when needed.

Organizational structure is reflected in the organizational chart. It isn't possible to see the internal structure of an organization the way we might see its manufacturing tools, offices, or products. Although we might see employees going about their duties, performing different tasks, and working in different locations, the only way to actually see the structure underlying all this activity is through an organizational chart. An organizational chart is the visual representation of a whole set of underlying activities and processes in an organization at a particular point in time.

The organizational chart can be quite useful in understanding how a company works. It shows the various parts of an organization, how they are interrelated, and how each position and department fits into the whole.

The concept of an organizational chart, showing what positions exist, how they are grouped, and who reports to whom, has been around for centuries.[7] For example, diagrams outlining church hierarchy can be found in medieval churches in Spain. However, the use of the organizational chart for business stems largely from the Industrial Revolution. As we discussed in Chapter 1, as work grew more complex and was performed by greater and greater numbers of workers, there was a pressing need to develop ways of managing and controlling organizations. The type of organizational structure that grew out of these efforts in the late-19th and early-20th centuries was one in which the CEO was placed at the top and everyone else was arranged in layers down below. The thinking and decision making are done by those at the top, and the physical work is performed by employees who are organized into distinct, functional departments. This structure was quite effective and became entrenched in business, nonprofit, and military organizations for much of the 20th century. However, this type of vertical structure is not always effective, particularly in rapidly changing environments. Over the years, organizations have developed other structural designs, many of them aimed at increasing horizontal coordination and communication and encouraging adaptation to external changes. This chapter's Book Mark argues that business is on the verge of a tremendous historic transformation, in which centralized hierarchical forms of organizing will give way to decentralized structures based on horizontal processes. In this chapter, we will examine five basic structural designs and show how they are reflected in the organizational chart.

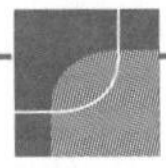

Information-Processing Perspective on Structure

The organization should be designed to provide both vertical and horizontal information flow as necessary to accomplish the organization's overall goals. If the structure does not fit the information requirements of the organization, people either will have too little information or will spend time processing information that is not vital to their tasks, thus reducing effectiveness.[8] However, there is an inherent tension between vertical and horizontal mechanisms in an organization. While vertical linkages are designed primarily for control, horizontal linkages are designed for coordination and collaboration, which usually means reducing control.

Organizations can choose whether to orient toward a traditional organization designed for efficiency, which emphasizes vertical communication and control, or toward a contemporary learning organization, which emphasizes horizontal communication and coordination. Exhibit 3.2 compares organizations designed for efficiency with those designed for learning. An emphasis on efficiency and control is associated with specialized tasks, a strict hierarchy of authority and rules, vertical reporting systems, few teams or task forces, and **centralized** decision making, which means problems and decisions are funnelled to top levels of the hierarchy for resolution. Emphasis on learning is associated with shared tasks, a horizontal hierarchy, few rules, face-to-face communication, many teams and task forces, and informal, **decentralized** decision making. Decentralized decision making means decision-making authority is pushed down to lower organizational levels. Organizations may have to

Book Mark 3.0 (HAVE YOU READ THIS BOOK?)

The Future of Work: How the New Order of Business Will Shape Your Organization, Your Management Style, and Your Life

By Thomas W. Malone

Organizations are experiencing tremendous change, and Thomas W. Malone suggests in his book *The Future of Work* that they are on the verge of a fundamental, transformational paradigm shift. Rigid, highly centralized vertical hierarchies, he says, will essentially be a thing of the past as organizations move to flexible decentralized forms of organizing based on horizontal work processes. Command-and-control management and top-down decision making will give way to empowered teams of employees focused on specific workflows and processes, working across organizational boundaries and making their own decisions based on up-to-the-minute information.

THE BRAVE NEW WORLD OF WORK

Malone describes several decentralized management structures and provides numerous examples of organizations that are experimenting with new forms of organizing and innovative management techniques. Here are some of Malone's key points about the future of work.

- *Information technology is the key driver of the transformation.* The falling cost of communication is making the distribution of power away from the corporate suite both inevitable and desirable. Outsourcing information work to India, for example, is possible because digital communication with India is so cheap. In the same way, accessible information makes it possible for any lower-level employee to plan his or her work more effectively, network and get advice from people anywhere, and make good decisions based on accurate information.
- *Managers will move from command-and-control to coordinate-and-cultivate.* To coordinate is to organize work so that good things happen, whether managers are "in control" or not. To cultivate means to bring out the best in employees with the right combination of control and freedom. W. L. Gore, the maker of Gore-Tex fabric, lets people decide what they want to do. Leaders emerge based on who has a good idea and can recruit people to work on it. AES, one of the world's largest electric power producers, coordinates and cultivates so well that it lets low-level workers make critical multimillion-dollar decisions about such things as acquiring new subsidiaries.
- *Every organization needs standards.* Many people think clear standards are incompatible with flexibility and decentralization. Malone points out, though, that when employees have guidelines and standards within which to make decisions and take action, they can do their jobs with greater freedom and authority. Consider eBay, which has more than 430,000 people who make their primary living as sellers on the site. eBay managers have no direct control over those 430,000 people, yet they've established clear standards and guidelines for trading that maintain order and accountability.

THE TRANSITION YEARS

Malone acknowledges that hierarchy and centralization continue to provide tremendous advantages for some companies in today's economy. In addition, for most organizations, centralized and decentralized structures and management systems will coexist well into the future. Yet, he is convinced that, ultimately, rigid hierarchical centralized structures will be consigned to the dustbin of history.

The Future of Work: How the New Order of Business Will Shape Your Organization, Your Management Style, and Your Life, by Thomas W. Malone, is published by Harvard Business School Press.

experiment to find the correct degree of centralization or decentralization to meet their needs. For example, a recent study found that three large school districts that shifted to a more flexible, decentralized structure performed better and more efficiently than large districts that were highly centralized.[9] On the other hand, decentralized companies such as Nortel and Procter & Gamble have found a need in recent years to build in more centralized communication and control systems to keep these huge, global corporations functioning efficiently. Thus, managers are always searching for the best combination of vertical control and horizontal collaboration, centralization and decentralization, for their own situations.[10]

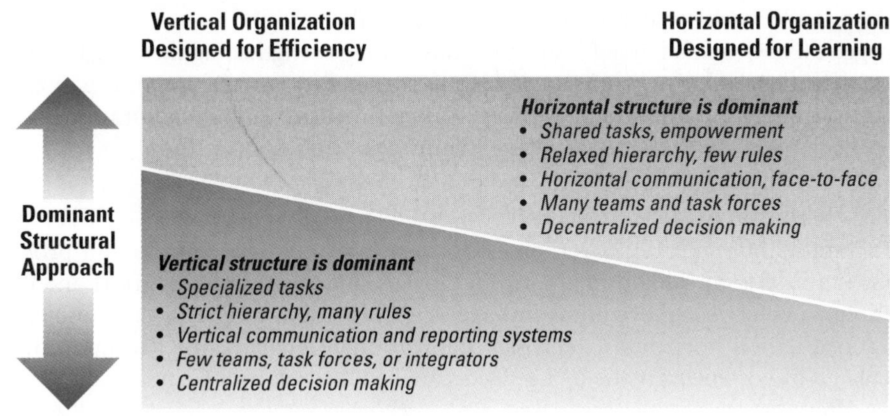

EXHIBIT 3.2
The Relationship of Organizational Design to Efficiency versus Learning Outcomes

Vertical Information Linkages

Organizational design should facilitate the communication among employees and departments that is necessary to accomplish the organization's overall task. *Linkage* is defined as the extent of communication and coordination among organizational elements. **Vertical linkages** are used to coordinate activities between the top and bottom of an organization, and are designed primarily for control of the organization. Employees at lower levels should carry out activities consistent with top-level goals, and top executives must be informed of activities and accomplishments at the lower levels. Organizations may use any of a variety of structural devices to achieve vertical linkage, including hierarchical referral, rules, plans, and formal management information systems.[11]

Hierarchical Referral. The first vertical device is the hierarchy, or chain of command, which is illustrated by the vertical lines in Exhibit 3.1. If a problem arises that employees don't know how to solve, it can be referred up to the next level in the hierarchy. When the problem is solved, the answer is passed back down to lower levels. The lines of the organizational chart act as communication channels.

Rules and Plans. The next linkage device is the use of rules and plans. To the extent that problems and decisions are repetitious, a rule or procedure can be established so employees know how to respond without communicating directly with their manager. Rules provide a standard information source enabling employees to be coordinated without actually communicating about every task. A plan also provides standing information for employees. The most widely used plan is the budget. With carefully designed budget plans, employees at lower levels can be left on their own to perform activities within their resource allotment.

Vertical Information Systems. A **vertical information system** is another strategy for increasing vertical information capacity. Vertical information systems include the periodic reports, written information, and computer-based communications distributed to managers. Information systems make communication up and down the hierarchy more efficient. Vertical information systems are an important component of vertical control at software-maker Oracle.[12]

PDA Remember...

Provide vertical and horizontal information linkages to integrate diverse departments into a coherent whole. Achieve vertical linkage through hierarchy referral, rules and plans, and vertical information systems. Achieve horizontal linkage through cross-functional information systems, direct contact, task forces, full-time integrators, and teams.

In today's world of corporate financial scandals and ethical concerns, many top managers, like Oracle's Larry Ellison, are considering strengthening their organization's linkages for vertical information and control. The other major issue in organizing is to provide adequate horizontal linkages for coordination and collaboration.

Horizontal Information Linkages

Horizontal communication overcomes barriers between departments and provides opportunities for coordination among employees to achieve unity of effort and organizational objectives. **Horizontal linkage** refers to the amount of communication and coordination horizontally across organizational departments. Its importance is articulated by comments made by Lee Iacocca when he took over Chrysler Corporation in the 1980s.

What I found at Chrysler were thirty-five vice presidents, each with his own turf . . . I couldn't believe, for example, that the guy running engineering departments wasn't in constant touch with his counterpart in manufacturing. But that's how it was. Everybody worked independently. I took one look at that system and I almost threw up. That's when I knew I was in really deep trouble . . . Nobody at Chrysler seemed to understand that interaction among the different functions in a company is absolutely critical. People in engineering and manufacturing almost have to be sleeping together. These guys weren't even flirting![13]

During his tenure at Chrysler, Iacocca pushed horizontal coordination to a high level. Everyone working on a specific vehicle project—designers, engineers, and manufacturers, as well as representatives from marketing, finance, purchasing, and even outside suppliers—worked together on a single floor so they could constantly communicate.

Horizontal linkage mechanisms often are not drawn on the organizational chart, but nevertheless are part of organizational structure. The following devices are structural alternatives that can improve horizontal coordination and information flow.[14] Each device enables people to exchange information.

Information Systems. A significant method of providing horizontal linkage in today's organizations is the use of cross-functional information systems. Computerized information systems can enable managers or frontline workers throughout the organization to routinely exchange information about problems, opportunities, activities, or decisions. For example, Siemens, a large international conglomerate headquartered in Germany, uses an organization-wide information system that enables 450,000 employees around the world to share knowledge and collaborate on projects to provide better solutions to customers. The information and communications division recently collaborated with the medical division to develop new products for the health care market.[15]

Some organizations also encourage employees to use the company's information systems to build relationships all across the organization, aiming to support and enhance ongoing horizontal coordination across projects and geographical boundaries. CARE International, one of the world's largest private international relief organizations, enhanced its personnel database to make it easy for people to find others with congruent interests, concerns, or needs. Each person in the database has listed past and current responsibilities, experience, language abilities, knowledge of foreign countries, emergency experiences, skills and competencies, and outside interests. The database makes it easy for employees working across borders to seek out each other, share ideas and information, and build enduring horizontal connections.[16]

Direct Contact. A higher level of horizontal linkage is direct contact between managers or employees affected by a problem. One way to promote direct contact is to create a special **liaison role.** A liaison person is located in one department but has the responsibility for communicating and achieving coordination with another department. Liaison roles often exist between engineering and manufacturing departments because engineering has to develop and test products to fit the limitations of manufacturing facilities. At Johnson & Johnson, CEO William C. Weldon has set up a committee comprising managers from R&D and sales and marketing. The direct contact between managers in these two departments enables the company to set priorities for which new drugs to pursue and market. Weldon also created a new position to oversee R&D, with an express charge to increase coordination with sales and marketing executives.[17] Another approach is to locate people close together so they will have direct contact on a regular basis.

Task Forces. Liaison roles usually link only two departments. When linkage involves several departments, a more complex device such as a task force is required. A **task force** is a temporary committee composed of representatives from each organizational unit affected by a problem.[18] Each member represents the interest of a department or division and can carry information from the meeting back to that department.

Task forces are an effective horizontal linkage device for temporary issues. They solve problems by direct horizontal coordination and reduce the information load on the vertical hierarchy. Typically, they are disbanded after their tasks are accomplished.

Organizations have used task forces for everything from organizing the annual company picnic to solving expensive and complex manufacturing problems. One example was the executive automotive committee formed by DaimlerChrysler CEO Jürgen Schrempp. This task force was set up specifically to identify ideas for increasing cooperation and component sharing among Chrysler, Mercedes, and Mitsubishi (in which DaimlerChrysler owns a 37 percent stake). The task force started with a product road map, showing all Mercedes, Chrysler, Dodge, Jeep, and Mitsubishi vehicles to be launched over a 10-year period, along with an analysis of the components they would use, so task force members could identify overlap and find ways to share parts, and cut time and costs.[19] (However, the much-hyped 1998 merger between equals was a failure for two reasons: (1) it was really a takeover of Chrysler by Daimler and (2) the savings and marketing clout the two expected from the merger did not materialize. In less than 10 years, the companies were again separate entities.[20])

Full-Time Integrator. A stronger horizontal linkage device is to create a full-time position or department solely for the purpose of coordination. A full-time **integrator** frequently has a title such as product manager, project manager, program manager, or brand manager. Unlike the liaison person described earlier, the integrator does not report to one of the functional departments being coordinated. He or she is located outside the departments and has the responsibility for coordinating several departments. For example, General Motors has brand managers who are responsible for marketing and sales strategies for each of GM's new models.[21]

EXHIBIT 3.3
Project Manager Location in the Structure

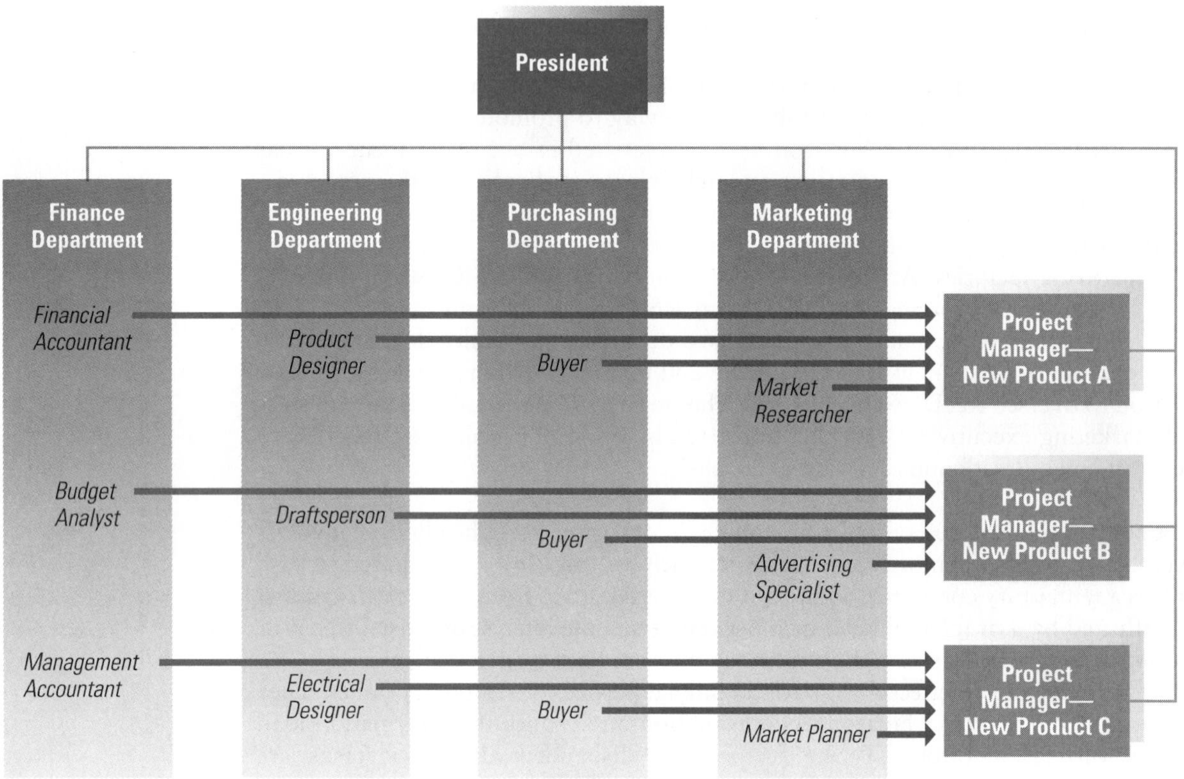

The integrator can also be responsible for an innovation or change project, such as coordinating the design, financing, and marketing of a new product. An organizational chart that illustrates the location of project managers for new product development is shown in Exhibit 3.3. The project managers are drawn to the side to indicate their separation from other departments. The arrows indicate project members assigned to the new product development. New Product A, for example, has a financial accountant assigned to keep track of costs and budgets. The engineering member provides design advice, and purchasing and manufacturing members represent their areas. The project manager is responsible for the entire project. He or she sees that the new product is completed on time, is introduced to the market, and achieves other project goals. The horizontal lines in Exhibit 3.3 indicate that project managers do not have formal authority over team members with respect to giving pay raises, hiring, or firing. Formal authority rests with the managers of the functional departments, who have formal authority over subordinates.

PDA Remember...

Recognize that the strongest horizontal linkage mechanisms are more costly in terms of time and human resources but are necessary when the organization needs a high degree of horizontal coordination to achieve its goals.

Integrators need excellent people skills. Integrators in most companies have a lot of responsibility but little authority. The integrator has to use expertise and persuasion to achieve coordination. He or she spans the boundary between departments and must be able to get people together, maintain their trust, confront problems, and resolve conflicts and disputes in the interest of the organization.[22]

Teams. Project teams tend to be the strongest horizontal linkage mechanism. **Teams** are permanent task forces and are often used in conjunction with a full-time integrator. When activities among departments require strong coordination over a long period of time, a cross-functional team is often the solution. Special project teams may be used when organizations have a large-scale project, a major innovation, or a new product line.

In Practice
Imagination Limited (Imagination)

Imagination has 10 offices in Europe, the Americas, and Asia. Its mission is communication: "[no] matter the channel or the audience, we conceive, develop and deliver communication that has relevance, immediacy and clarity, to connect client with consumer."[23] Its clients include Virgin Mobile for which Imagination created a 16-city global road show for Virgin Mobile's 2007 listing on the New York Stock Exchange. Imagination has received many accolades for its work. Founded in 1978, Imagination is Britain's largest design firm, whose structure is based entirely on teamwork. At the beginning of each project, Imagination puts together a team of designers, writers, artists, marketing experts, information specialists, and representatives of other functional areas to carry out the entire project from beginning to end.

One of its most interesting projects was to make waiting in a 700-person lineup to get into Skyscape, an attraction inside Britain's Millennium Dome, a fun experience. According to Imagination's director of marketing and strategic planning, "[the] work was quite mad, really . . . We wanted to push the queue experience to a new place."[24] Imagination started with a team of in-house employees—an architect, a lighting designer, a graphic designer, and a film director. Later, a choreographer joined the team. Together they designed the Journey Zone and the TalkZone so that the wait would be part of the experience.

Imagination understands the value and the power of teamwork. The organization is nonhierarchical by design—only four individuals have formal titles—and everyone therefore is responsible for the success of a project. As one of the graphic designers, Martin Brown, puts it, "[we've] got a lot of performers and a few clowns. Enough to make it funny."

Hewlett-Packard's Medical Products Group uses **virtual cross-functional teams,** made up of members from various countries, to develop and market medical products and services such as electrocardiograph systems, ultrasound imaging technologies, and patient monitoring systems.[25] A **virtual team** is one that is made up of organizationally or geographically dispersed members who are linked primarily through advanced information and communications technologies. Members frequently use the Internet and collaborative software to work together, rather than meeting face to face.

Ford Motor Company provides another good illustration of the use of teams for horizontal coordination.

In Practice
Ford Motor Company (Ford)

The demand for hybrid vehicles is growing quickly, but many people want more than the small cars from Toyota and Honda that were first on the market. Ford Motor Company vowed to be the first auto manufacturer to come out with a hybrid SUV. CEO Bill Ford raved for years about plans for a new model that would handle like a muscular V6 but sip tiny amounts of gas and produce minuscule emissions. The Escape Hybrid SUV would be the most technologically advanced vehicle Ford had ever made, and perhaps its most important since the Model T.

The problem was, the Escape Hybrid was a dramatically different product for Ford and involved nine new major technologies, which Ford wanted to develop in-house rather than licensing patents from Toyota's hybrid system. Introducing even one major technological breakthrough was a challenge for Ford's traditional design and engineering process. Typically, researchers and product engineers haven't worked closely together at Ford—in fact, they were located in different buildings a half-mile apart. To meet the demanding schedule for getting the Escape Hybrid on the market, Ford created a sort of hybrid team, made up of scientists and product engineers from far-flung departments, now working side by side, creating and building software and hardware together, then working with production personnel to bring their creation to life. The team's leader, Prabhaker Patil, was himself a hybrid, a PhD scientist who had started out working in Ford's lab and then crossed over to hands-on product development. Patil was careful to select team members he knew would be open to collaboration. Whereas in the past problems were "tossed over the wall," they would now be ironed out collaboratively. The approach was revolutionary for Ford, and it led to amazing breakthroughs.

The Escape Hybrid team was given nearly complete autonomy, another rarity for Ford. Because the team was allowed to be entrepreneurial, their productivity zoomed. Decisions that once would have taken days were made on the spot. As a result, the team met the demanding schedule, and the Ford Escape Hybrid was introduced right on time—and to amazing success. It was named the best truck of the year at the 2005 North American International Auto Show, and Ford will use the technologies the team developed to introduce four more hybrid vehicles over the next three years.[26] For example, in late 2007, Ford delivered the first 20 Escape plug-in hybrid vehicles for road testing.[27]

Just as Ford Motor Company first made the automobile accessible to the everyday consumer, it has taken a bold step by introducing a team-based structure to bring the hybrid to a mass market. A study by the Freedonia Group estimates that the hybrid car and light truck market will rise to 7.8 million units by 2020.[28] Most automakers outside Japan have been shortsighted by failing to invest in hybrid technology.[29] Therefore, Ford has an early lead, thanks largely to the communication and collaboration made possible by the team approach. Many of today's organizations are using teams as a way to increase horizontal collaboration, spur innovation, and speed new products and services to market.

Exhibit 3.4 summarizes the mechanisms for achieving horizontal linkages. These devices represent alternatives that managers can select to increase horizontal

EXHIBIT 3.4
Ladder of Mechanisms for Horizontal Linkage and Coordination

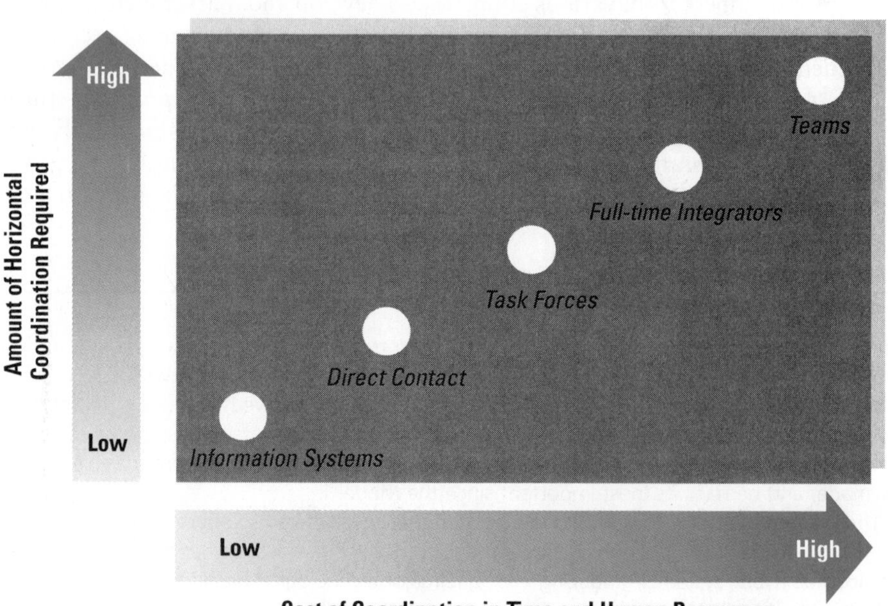

coordination in any organization. The higher-level devices provide more horizontal information capacity, although the cost to the organization in terms of time and human resources is greater. If horizontal communication is insufficient, departments will find themselves out of synchronization and will not contribute to the overall goals of the organization. When the amount of horizontal coordination required is high, managers should select higher-level mechanisms.

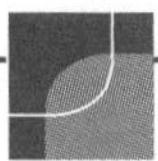

Organizational Design Alternatives

The overall design of organizational structure indicates three things—required work activities, reporting relationships, and departmental groupings.

Required Work Activities

Departments are created to perform tasks considered strategically important to the company. For example, in a typical manufacturing company, work activities fall into a range of functions that help the organization accomplish its goals, such as a human resource department to recruit and train employees, a purchasing department to obtain supplies and raw materials, a production department to build products, a sales department to sell products, and so forth. As organizations grow larger and more complex, more and more functions need to be performed. Organizations typically define new departments or divisions as a way to accomplish tasks deemed valuable by the organization. Today, many companies are finding it important to establish departments such as information technology or e-business to take advantage of new technology and new business opportunities.

Reporting Relationships

Once required work activities and departments are defined, the next question is how these activities and departments should fit together in the organizational hierarchy. Reporting relationships, often called the **chain of command**, are represented by vertical lines on an organizational chart. The chain of command should be an unbroken line of authority that links all persons in an organization and shows who reports to whom. In a large organization like Motorola or Ford Motor Company, 100 or more charts are required to identify reporting relationships among thousands of employees. The definition of departments and the drawing of reporting relationships define how employees are to be grouped into departments.

Departmental Grouping Options

Options for departmental grouping, including functional grouping, divisional grouping, multifocused grouping, horizontal grouping, and virtual network grouping, are illustrated in Exhibit 3.5. **Departmental grouping** affects employees because they share a common supervisor and common resources, are jointly responsible for performance, and tend to identify and collaborate with one another.[30] For example, if a credit manager were shifted from the finance department to the marketing department, he or she would work with salespeople to increase sales, thus becoming more liberal with credit than when he or she was located in the finance department.

EXHIBIT 3.5
Structural Design Options for Grouping Employees into Departments
Source: Adapted from David Nadler and Michael Tushman, *Strategic* Organization Design (Glenview, Ill.: Scott Foresman, 1988), 68.

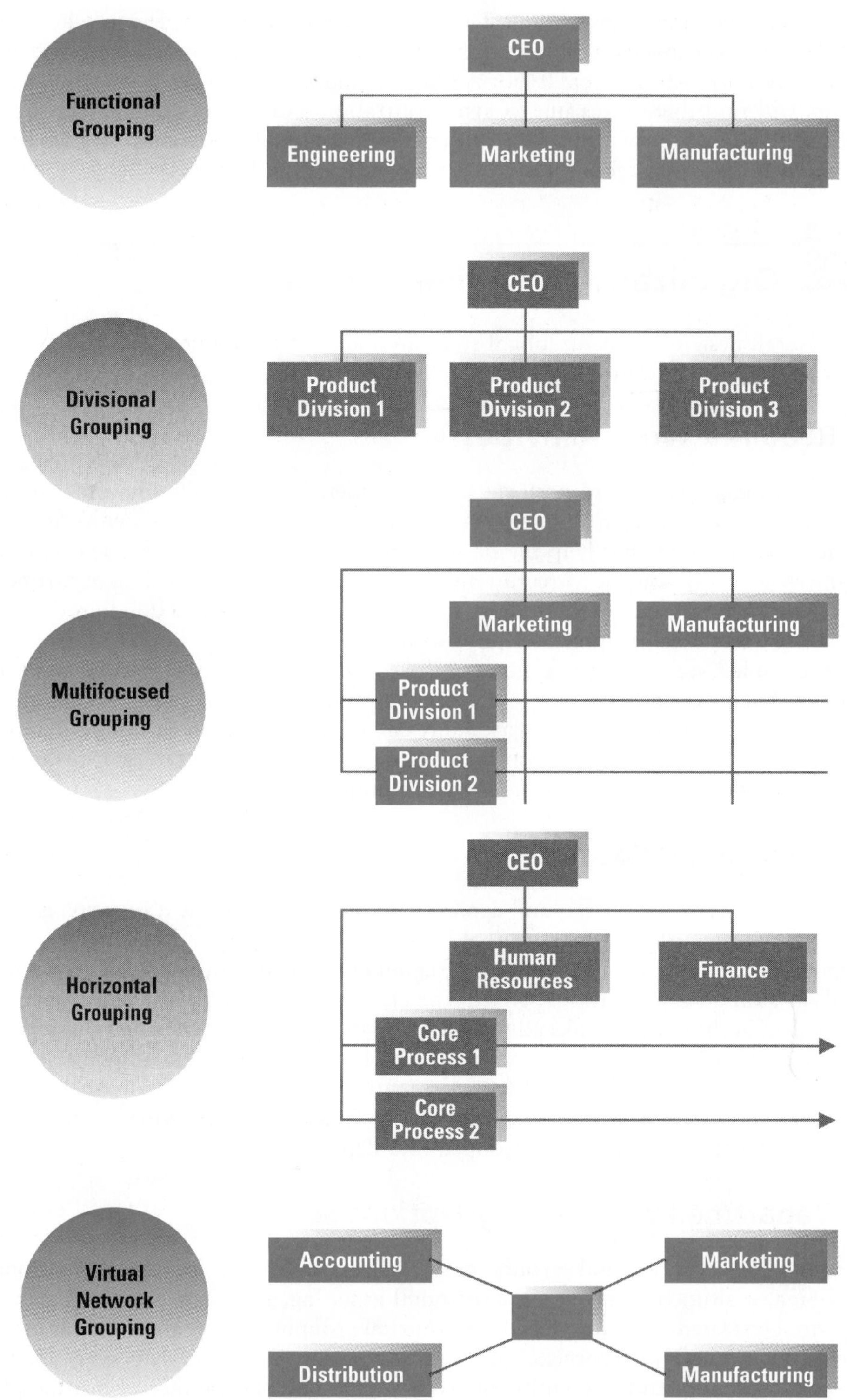

Functional grouping places together employees who perform similar functions or work processes or who bring similar knowledge and skills to bear. For example, all marketing people work together under the same supervisor, as do manufacturing and engineering people. All people associated with the assembly process for generators are grouped together in one department. All chemists may be grouped in a department different from biologists because they represent different disciplines.

Divisional grouping means people are organized according to what the organization produces. All people required to produce toothpaste—including personnel in marketing, manufacturing, and sales—are grouped together under one executive. In huge corporations such as EDS, some product or service lines may represent independent businesses, such as A. T. Kearney, a management consulting firm, and Wendover Financial Services.

Multifocused grouping means an organization embraces two structural grouping alternatives simultaneously. These structural forms are often called *matrix* or *hybrid*. They will be discussed in more detail later in this chapter. An organization may need to group by function and product division simultaneously or perhaps by product division and geography.

Horizontal grouping means employees are organized around core work processes, the end-to-end work, information, and material flows that provide value directly to customers. All the people who work on a core process are brought together in a group rather than being separated into functional departments.

Virtual network grouping is the most recent approach to departmental grouping. With this grouping, the organization is a loosely connected cluster of separate components. In essence, departments are separate organizations that are electronically connected for the sharing of information and completion of tasks. Departments can be spread all over the world rather than located together in one geographical location.

The organizational forms described in Exhibit 3.5 provide the overall options within which the organizational chart is drawn and the detailed structure is designed. Each structural design alternative has significant strengths and weaknesses, to which we now turn.

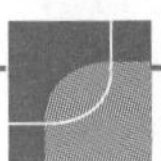

Functional, Divisional, and Geographical Designs

Functional grouping and divisional grouping are the two most common approaches to structural design.

Functional Structure

In a **functional structure**, activities are grouped together by common function from the bottom to the top of the organization. All engineers are located in the engineering department, and the vice president of engineering is responsible for all engineering activities. The same is true in marketing, R&D, and manufacturing.

With a functional structure, all human knowledge and skills with respect to specific activities are consolidated, providing a valuable depth of knowledge for the organization. This structure is most effective when in-depth expertise is critical to meeting organizational goals, when the organization needs to be controlled and coordinated through the vertical hierarchy, and when efficiency is important. The structure can be quite effective if there is little need for horizontal coordination. Exhibit 3.6 summarizes the strengths and weaknesses of the functional structure.

EXHIBIT 3.6
Strengths and Weaknesses of the Functional Organizational Structure

Strengths	Weaknesses
1. Allows economies of scale within functional departments 2. Enables in-depth knowledge and skill development 3. Enables organization to accomplish functional goals 4. Is best with only one or a few products	1. Slow response time to environmental changes 2. May cause decisions to pile up, hierarchy overload 3. Leads to poor horizontal coordination among departments 4. Results in less innovation 5. Involves restricted view of organizational goals

Source: Adapted from Robert Duncan, "What Is the Right Organization Structure? Decision Tree Analysis Provides the Answer," *Organizational Dynamics* (Winter 1979), 429.

One strength of the functional structure is that it promotes economy of scale within functions. Economy of scale results when all employees are located in the same place and can share facilities. Producing all products in a single plant, for example, enables the plant to acquire the latest machinery. Constructing only one facility instead of separate facilities for each product line reduces duplication and waste. The functional structure also promotes in-depth skill development of employees. Employees are exposed to a range of functional activities within their own department.[31] The functional structure allows the organization to accomplish functional goals.

The main weakness of the functional structure is a slow response to environmental changes that require coordination across departments. Decisions may pile up, so the vertical hierarchy becomes overloaded. There may be poor horizontal coordination among departments. Other disadvantages of the functional structure are that innovation is slow because of poor coordination, and each employee has a restricted view of overall goals.

Some organizations perform very effectively with a functional structure. However, as the organization expands, it may have problems coordinating across departments, requiring stronger horizontal linkage mechanisms.

Functional Structure with Horizontal Linkages

Today, there is a shift toward flatter, more horizontal structures because of the challenges described in Chapter 1. Very few of today's successful companies can maintain a strictly functional structure. Organizations compensate for the vertical functional hierarchy by installing horizontal linkages, as described earlier in this chapter. Managers improve horizontal coordination by using information systems, direct contact between departments, full-time integrators or project managers, task forces, or teams. One interesting use of horizontal linkages occurred at Karolinska Hospital in Stockholm, Sweden, which had 47 functional departments. Even after top executives cut that down to 11, coordination was still woefully inadequate. The team set about reorganizing workflow at the hospital around patient care. Instead of bouncing a patient from department to department, Karolinska now envisions the illness to recovery period as a process with "pit stops" in admissions, X-ray, surgery, and so forth. The most interesting aspect of the approach is the new position of nurse coordinator. Nurse coordinators serve as full-time integrators, troubleshooting transitions within or between departments. The improved horizontal coordination dramatically improved productivity and patient care at Karolinska.[32] Karolinska is effectively using horizontal linkages to overcome some of the disadvantages of the functional structure.

PDA Remember...

When designing overall organizational structure, choose a functional structure when efficiency is important, when in-depth knowledge and expertise are critical to meeting organizational goals, and when the organization needs to be controlled and coordinated through the vertical hierarchy. Use a divisional structure in a large organization with multiple product lines and when you wish to give priority to product goals and coordination across functions.

Divisional Structure

The term **divisional structure** is used here as the generic term for what is sometimes called a *product structure* or *strategic business units*. With this structure, divisions can be organized according to individual products, services, product groups, major projects or programs, divisions, businesses, or profit centres. The distinctive feature of a divisional structure is that grouping is based on organizational outputs.

The difference between a divisional structure and a functional structure is illustrated in Exhibit 3.7. The functional structure can be redesigned into separate product groups, and each group contains the functional departments of R&D, manufacturing, accounting, and marketing. Coordination across functional departments within each product group is maximized. The divisional structure promotes flexibility and change because each unit is smaller and can adapt to the needs of its environment.

EXHIBIT 3.7
Reorganization from Functional Structure to Divisional Structure at Info-Tech

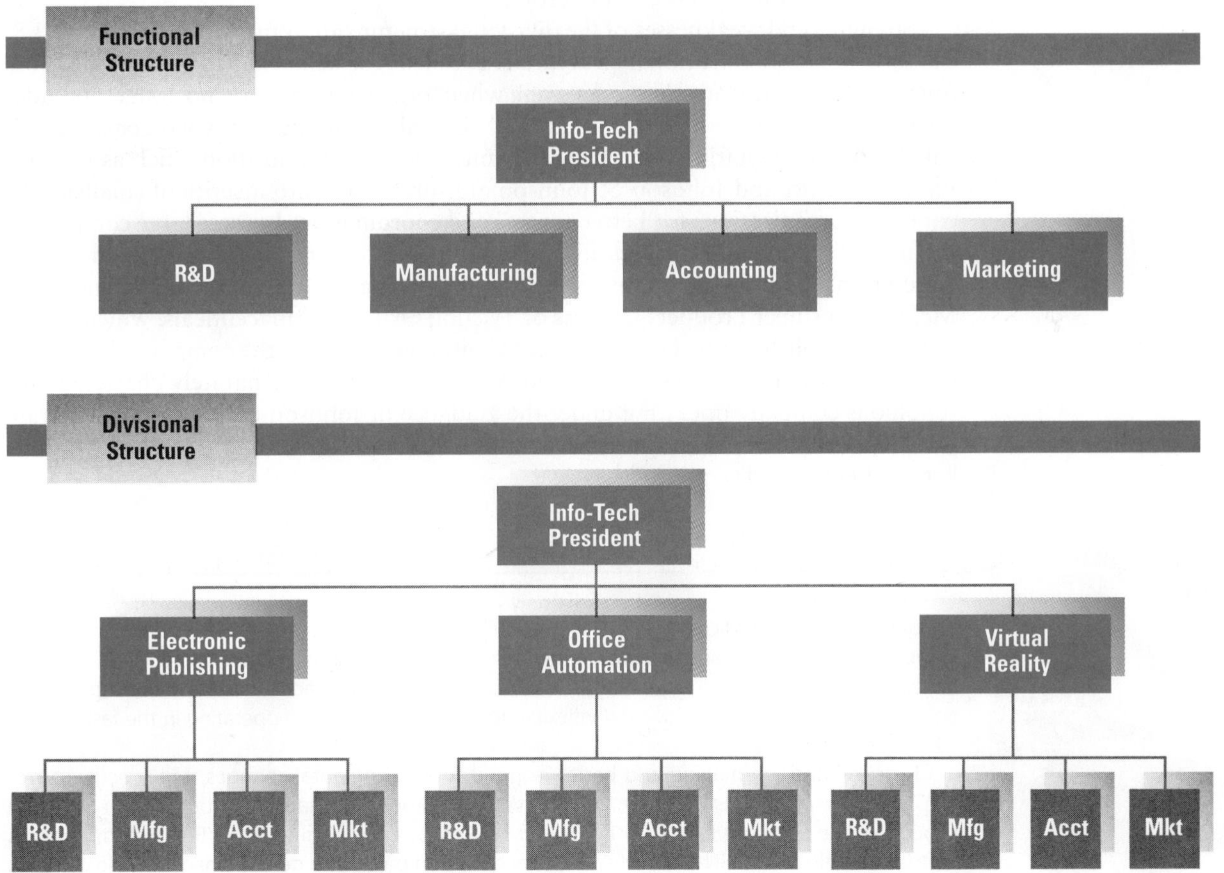

EXHIBIT 3.8
Strengths and Weaknesses of the Divisional Organizational Structure

Strengths	Weaknesses
1. Suited to fast change in unstable environment 2. Leads to customer satisfaction because product responsibility and contact points are clear 3. Involves high coordination across functions 4. Allows units to adapt to differences in products, regions, customers 5. Best in large organizations with several products 6. Decentralizes decision making	1. Eliminates economies of scale in functional departments 2. Leads to poor coordination across product lines 3. Eliminates in-depth competence and technical specialization 4. Makes integration and standardization across product lines difficult

Source: Adapted from Robert Duncan, "What Is the Right Organization Structure? Decision Tree Analysis Provides the Answer," *Organization Dynamics* (Winter 1979), 431.

Moreover, the divisional structure *decentralizes* decision making, because the lines of authority converge at a lower level in the hierarchy. The functional structure, by contrast, is *centralized,* because it forces decisions all the way to the top before a problem affecting several functions can be resolved.

Strengths and weaknesses of the divisional structure are summarized in Exhibit 3.8. The divisional organizational structure is excellent for achieving coordination across functional departments. It works well when organizations can no longer be adequately controlled through the traditional vertical hierarchy, and when goals are oriented toward adaptation and change. Giant, complex organizations such as General Electric, Nestlé, and Johnson & Johnson are subdivided into a series of smaller, self-contained organizations for better control and coordination. In these large companies, the units are sometimes called divisions, businesses, or strategic business units. The structure at Johnson & Johnson includes 204 separate operating units, including McNeil Consumer Products, makers of Tylenol; Ortho Pharmaceuticals, which makes Retin-A and birth-control pills; and J&J Consumer Products, the company that brings us Johnson's Baby Shampoo and Band-Aids. Each unit is a separately chartered, autonomous company operating under the guidance of Johnson & Johnson's corporate headquarters.[33] Microsoft Corporation uses a divisional structure to develop and market different software products.

In Practice

Microsoft

Bill Gates co-founded Microsoft in 1975 and built it into the most profitable technology company in the world. But as the company grew larger, the functional structure became ineffective. Employees began complaining about the growing bureaucracy and the snail's pace for decision making. A functional structure was just too slow and inflexible for a large organization operating in the fast-moving technology industry.

To speed decision making and better respond to environmental changes, top executives created seven business units based on Microsoft's major products: Windows Group; Server Software Group; Mobile Software Group; Office Software Group; Video Games and XBox Group; Business Software Group; and MSN-Internet Group. Each division is run by a general manager and contains most of the functions of a stand-alone company, including product development, sales, marketing, and finance.

What really makes the new structure revolutionary for Microsoft is that the heads of the seven divisions are given the freedom and authority to run the businesses and spend their budgets as they see fit to meet goals. The general managers and chief financial officers for each division set their own budgets and manage their own profit and loss statements. Previously, the two top executives, Bill Gates and Steven Ballmer, were involved in practically every decision, large and small. Managers of the divisions are charged up by the new authority and responsibility. One manager said he feels "like I am running my own little company."[34]

The divisional structure has several strengths that are of benefit to Microsoft.[35] This structure is suited to fast change in an unstable environment and provides high product or service visibility. Since each product line has its own separate division, customers are able to contact the correct division and achieve satisfaction. Coordination across functions is excellent. Each product can adapt to requirements of individual customers or regions. The divisional structure typically works best in organizations that have multiple products or services and enough personnel to staff separate functional units. At corporations like Johnson & Johnson and Microsoft, decision making is pushed down to the lowest levels. Each division is small enough to be quick on its feet, responding rapidly to changes in the market.

One disadvantage of using divisional structures is that the organization loses economies of scale. Instead of 50 research engineers sharing a common facility in a functional structure, ten engineers may be assigned to each of five product divisions. The critical mass required for in-depth research is lost, and physical facilities have to be duplicated for each product line. Another problem is that product lines become separate from each other, and coordination across product lines can be difficult. As one Johnson & Johnson executive said, "We have to keep reminding ourselves that we work for the same corporation."[36] There is some concern at Microsoft that the newly independent divisions might start offering products and services that conflict with one another.

Companies such as Xerox, Hewlett-Packard, and Sony have a large number of divisions and have had real problems with horizontal coordination. Sony is far behind in the business of digital media products partly because of poor coordination. Apple's iPod quickly captured 60 percent of the American market versus 10 percent for Sony. The digital music business depends on seamless coordination. Currently, Sony's Walkman doesn't even recognize some of the music sets that can be made with the company's SonicStage software, and thus doesn't mesh well with the division selling music downloads. Sony has set up a new company, called Connect Co., specifically to coordinate among the different units for the development of digital media businesses.[37] Unless effective horizontal mechanisms are in place, a divisional structure can cause real problems. One division may produce products or programs that are incompatible or compete with products sold by another division. Customers are frustrated when a sales representative from one division is unaware of developments in other divisions. Task forces and other linkage devices are needed to coordinate across divisions. A lack of technical specialization is also a problem in a divisional structure because employees identify with the product line rather than with a functional specialty. R&D personnel, for example, tend to do applied research to benefit the product line rather than basic research to benefit the entire organization.

Geographical Structure

Another basis for structural grouping is the organization's users or customers. The most common structure in this category is geography since each region of the country may have distinct tastes and needs. Each geographic unit includes all functions required to produce and market products or services in that region. Large nonprofit organizations such as Habitat for Humanity, Make-a-Wish Foundation, and United Way frequently use a type of geographical structure, with a central headquarters and semi-autonomous local units. The national organization provides brand recognition, coordinates fundraising services, and handles some shared administrative functions, while day-to-day control and decision making is decentralized to local or regional units.[38] The Leading by Design describes the design for Médecins sans Frontières, the world's leading international medical relief organization, which has five centres in Europe and 14 national sections around the world.

For multinational corporations, self-contained units are created for different countries and parts of the world. Some years ago, Apple Computer reorganized from a functional to a geographical structure to facilitate manufacture and delivery of Apple computers to customers around the world. Apple used the structure to focus managers and employees on specific geographical customers and sales targets. (See Exhibit 3.9 for an example of a geographical structure.)

The strengths and weaknesses of a geographic divisional structure are similar to the divisional organization characteristics listed in Exhibit 3.8. The organization can adapt to specific needs of its own region, and employees identify with regional goals rather than with national goals. Horizontal coordination within a region is emphasized rather than linkages across regions or to the national office.

EXHIBIT 3.9
An Example of Geographical Structure

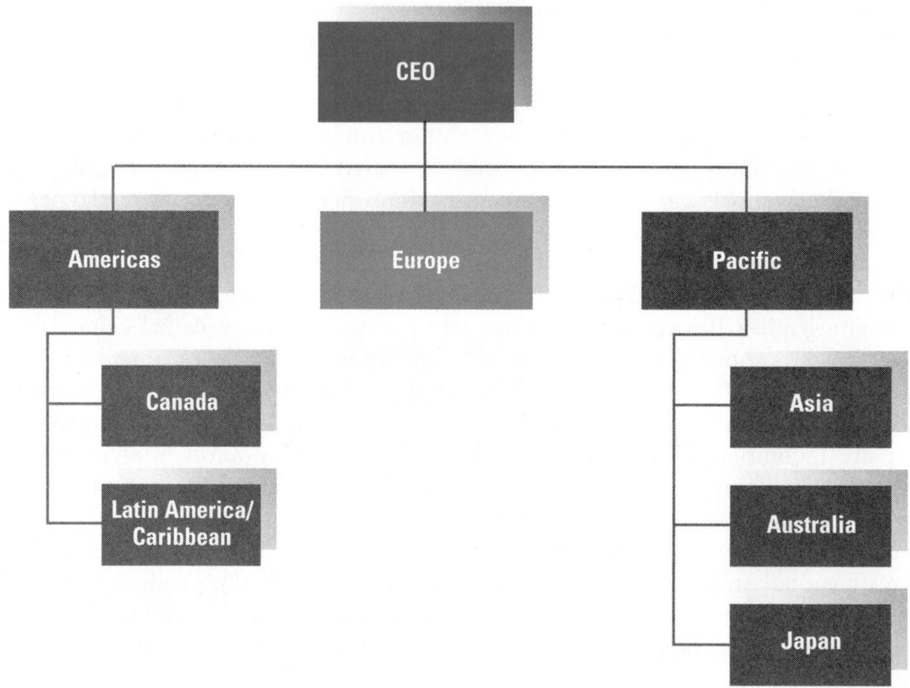

Leading *by Design*

Médecins sans Frontières (MSF)

MSF was started in 1971 by a small group of French doctors and journalists who had worked in Biafra, a short-lived independent state in Nigeria. The founders wanted to create an autonomous way to respond to public health crises, free of economic, religious or political influence. MSF's Charter states that

- Médecins Sans Frontières offers assistance to populations in distress, to victims of natural or man-made disasters and to victims of armed conflict, without discrimination and irrespective of race, religion, creed or political affiliation.
- Médecins Sans Frontières observes neutrality and impartiality in the name of universal medical ethics and the right to humanitarian assistance and demands full and unhindered freedom in the exercise of its functions.
- Médecins Sans Frontières' volunteers promise to honour their professional code of ethics and to maintain complete independence from all political, economic and religious powers.
- As volunteers, members are aware of the risks and dangers of the missions they undertake and have no right to compensation for themselves or their beneficiaries other than that which Médecins Sans Frontières is able to afford them.[39]

MSF starts a project when it identifies a humanitarian crisis: first a medical team is sent to assess the situation and report its findings and recommendations to the operations department in one of its five operational offices. The operations department makes the decision to proceed and determines the medical priorities. The work can involve massive vaccination campaigns, training and supervision of local medical staff, water and sanitation improvement, data collection, feeding, physical and mental health care, maternal and paediatric care, medical and drug supplies distribution, rehabilitation of hospitals and clinics, and HIV/AIDS care and prevention.[40] In 1999, MSF received the Nobel Peace prize in recognition of its pioneering humanitarian work—MSF relief workers had brought medical assistance to more than 80 countries, 20 of which were in conflict.

Michael White, a Canadian aid worker and award-winning film director and producer, blogs evocatively about his work as a Logistician Administrator in charge of supply logistics for the Pieri project [in Sudan]—one of the most isolated projects that MSF runs.

08:00 Road trip to Yuai cancelled.

08:15 Learn that our beloved Sudanese nurse/midwife Hellen needs to return to Khartoum for an undisclosed amount of time for personal reasons (a solid blow to the team—we just lost our African Mom).

. . .

09:20 Hear screams of life-halting horror coming from our medical clinic more than 200 metres away.

09:30 Learn that a middle-aged man has passed away from unknown causes in our Inpatient Department (IPD).

10:00 The deceased is from a village over a day's walk away, and his wife, daughter and son have no way to remove or dispose of the corpse.

10:01 It's Sunday and we're short staff, which in this case is the same thing as a short straw.

10:30 Nothing in my life has prepared me for this. Flies and fecal fluids have filled the middle-aged man's *tukul*. He's naked and dead and I'm breathing and confused by the simplicity of it all. I can taste the smell of death in the back of my mouth. I keep thinking the middle-aged man is going to move and it scares me a lot.

10:35 Thankfully John Yany (pronounced Yang) and a guard crawl into the *tukul* ahead of me and roll the middle-aged man onto a stretcher. To be honest I don't think I could have done it.

. . .

11:01 We start digging beside a couple of the week's other tragedies. No cemetery, no markers ... just mounds of death in the middle of a field.

11:10 Maina and six men from Pieri including Stephen Mai, our logistical supervisor, come and relieve me of my duties. (Which for the record are not my duties.)

. . .

12:50 Our amazing 29-year-old Dutch doctor Ortillia and super-star Canadian nurse Sue know that I've never witnessed a birth and want to. Sue suggests that in Hellen's absence they could use an extra set of hands. My first thought is that 1 in 6 babies die during childbirth in Sudan, the highest toll anywhere in the world. My second thought is that I should man up and do it!

. . .

1:35 Without the aid of any drugs this woman has withstood a barrage of contractions, and an episiotomy and has barely made a sound.

1:40 The mood suddenly shifts when Ortillia calmly mentions to Sue that the umbilical cord is wrapped around the baby's neck. With only basic medical tools at their disposal, the girls continue their inspired work, while for the first time since arriving I'm grateful that the woman in labour doesn't speak English.

1:41 I can't stop watching Sue and Ortillia do their thing. They are so calm and never once let on that there may a problem. But there is a problem, a huge one.

1:42 Ortillia performs some orchestrated moment of magic with her arms and like that the baby appears untangled in front of Sue and its Mom.

1:42 Silence surrounds us.

1:42 Everyone and everything is soundless. It feels like we somehow stepped into a vacuum. In my mind I start chanting . . . Cry . . . Cry . . . Cry . . . Time passes with a glacial sense of speed. Please cry!

1:43 For those of you who have heard the first cry of a newborn, you know that there is no sweeter sound on earth. It's a boy and I'm never having sex again!

. . .

I don't know how to reconcile the divergent nature of that Sunday. I've learned that the Sudanese circle of life is the same as anywhere else [; its] circumference is just a lot smaller. I have always had a very difficult time with the concept of life and death. Ever since I was old enough to understand death it has frightened me more than I believe is either normal or healthy. Notorious B.I.G. summed it up best, when talking about Tupac's demise. "Death, there ain't no comin' back from that shit." While I don't pretend to know if that's true, I do understand that although death is inevitable, sickness and suffering doesn't always have to be. To that end MSF's work in Sudan and around the world is a tribute to human compassion, and inspired action.[41]

As you can see from Exhibit 3.10, MSF is structured geographically. The structure of MSF fits well with its purpose and its strategy.

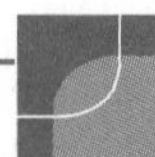

Matrix Structure

Sometimes an organization's structure needs to be multifocused in that both product and function or product and geography are emphasized at the same time. One way to achieve this is through the **matrix structure**. The matrix can be used when both technical expertise and product innovation and change are important for meeting organizational goals. The matrix structure often is the answer when organizations find that the functional, divisional, and geographical structures combined with horizontal linkage mechanisms will not work.

The matrix is a strong form of horizontal linkage. The unique characteristic of the matrix organization is that both product division and functional structures (horizontal and vertical) are implemented simultaneously, as shown in Exhibit 3.11. The product managers and functional managers have equal authority within the organization, and employees report to both of them. The matrix structure is similar to the use of full-time integrators or product managers described earlier in this chapter (Exhibit 3.3), except that in the matrix structure the product managers (horizontal) are given formal authority equal to that of the functional managers (vertical).

Conditions for the Matrix

A dual hierarchy may seem an unusual way to design an organization, but the matrix is the correct structure when the following conditions are met:[42]

- *Condition 1*. Pressure exists to share scarce resources across product lines. The organization is typically medium sized and has a moderate number of product lines. It feels pressure for the shared and flexible use of people and equipment across those products. For example, the organization is not large enough to assign engineers full-time to each product line, so engineers are assigned part-time to several products or projects.

EXHIBIT 3.10
Unofficial MSF Organizational Chart

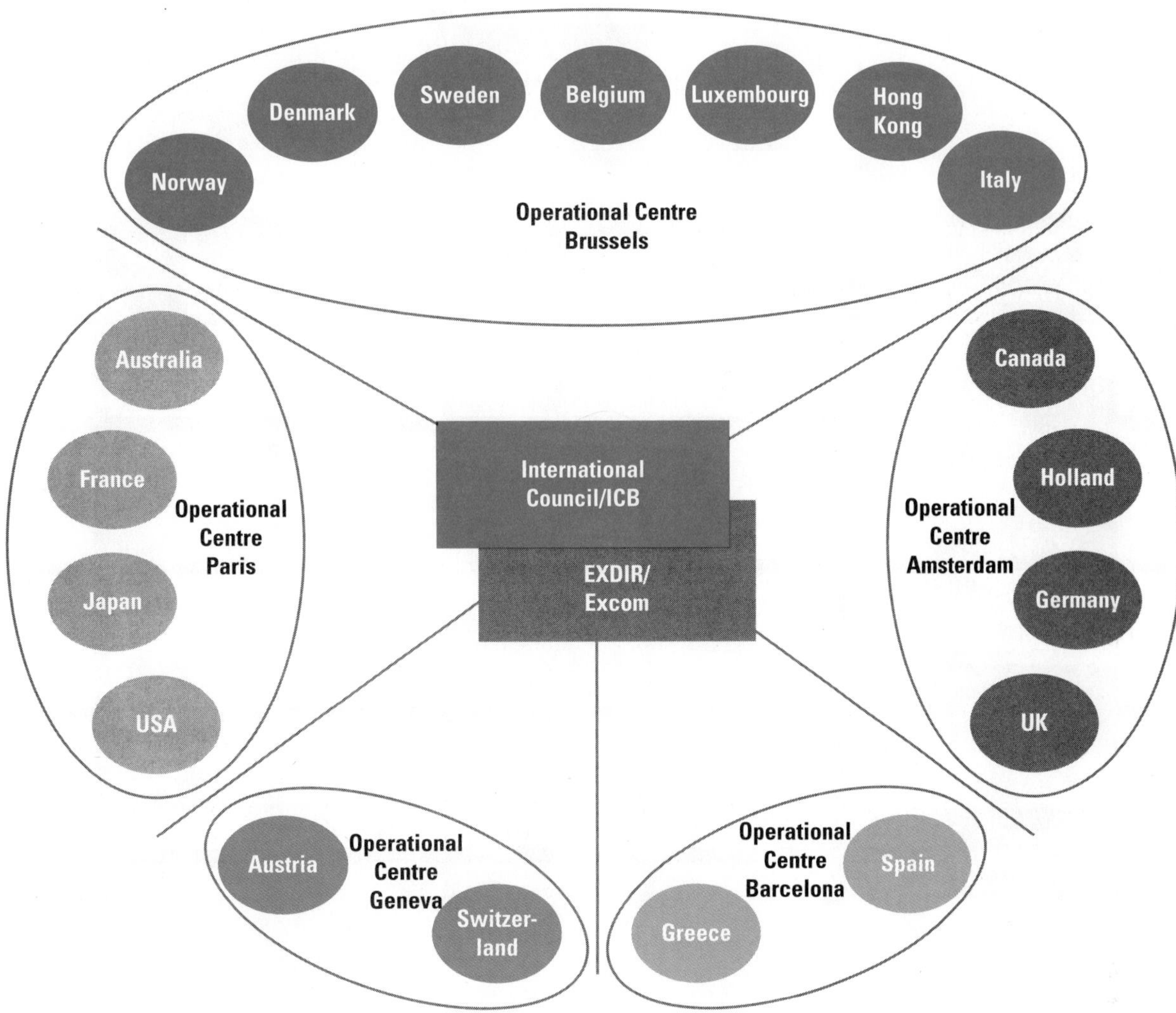

Note: At the time of printing in 2008, the organizational chart of Médecins Sans Frontières (Doctors Without Borders) featuring 19 national sections did not include 11 so-called "new entities" in places such as Brazil, India, Ireland, South Africa, and the United Arab Emirates. Affiliated organizations such as the Campaign for Access to Essential Medicines, Epicentre, and the Drugs for Neglected Diseases initiative were also not included in this chart. Please consult http://www.msf.org for current information about MSF and links to national websites.
Source: Ann Armstrong in consultation with MSF Canada, 2008.

- *Condition 2.* Environmental pressure exists for two or more critical outputs, such as for in-depth technical knowledge (functional structure) and frequent new products (divisional structure). This dual pressure means a balance of power is needed between the functional and product sides of the organization, and a dual-authority structure is needed to maintain that balance.
- *Condition 3.* The environmental domain of the organization is both complex and unstable. Frequent external changes and high interdependence between departments require a large amount of coordination and information processing in both vertical and horizontal directions.

EXHIBIT 3.11
Dual-Authority Structure in a Matrix Organization

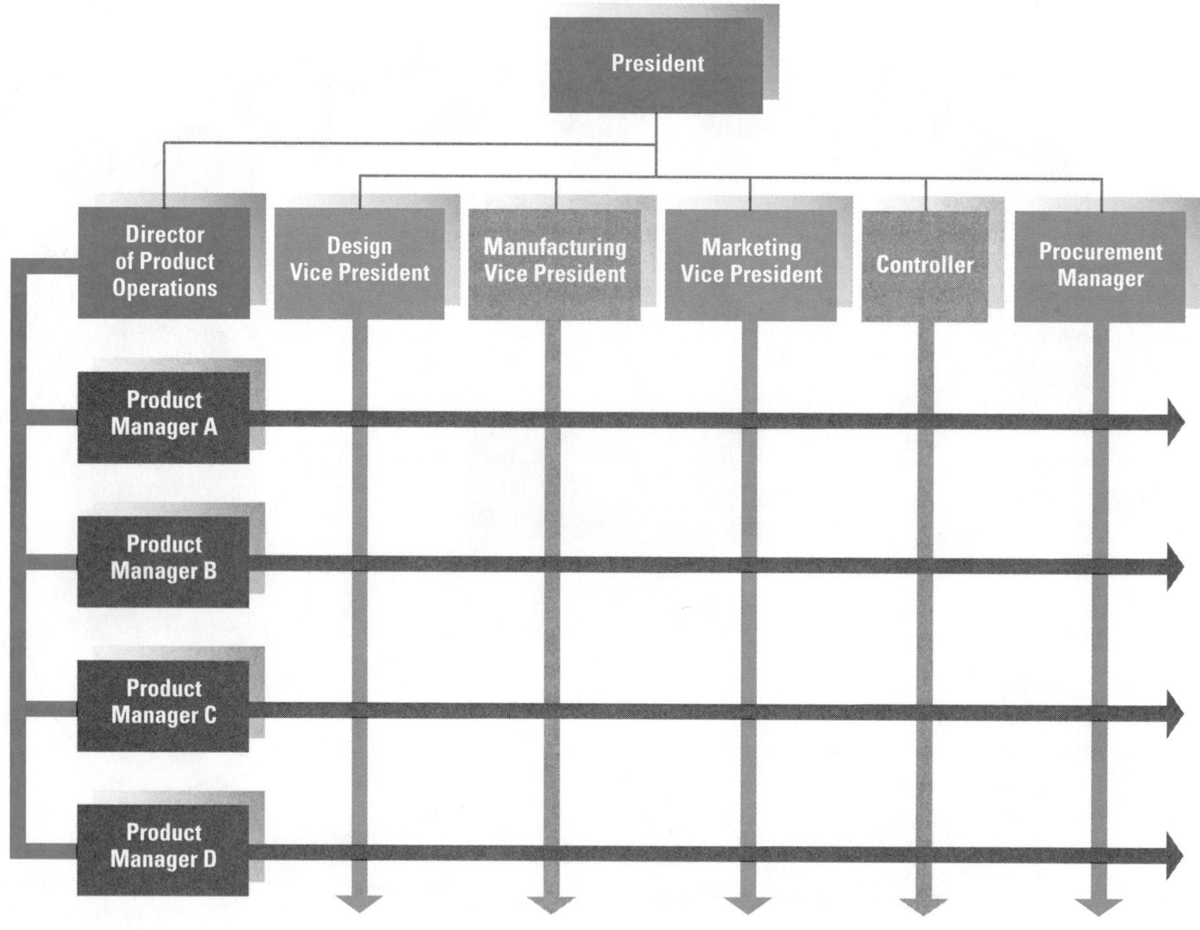

Under these three conditions, the vertical and horizontal lines of authority must be given equal recognition. A dual-authority structure is thereby created so the balance of power between them is equal.

Referring again to Exhibit 3.11, assume the matrix structure is for a clothing manufacturer. Product A is footwear, product B is outerwear, product C is sleepwear, and so on. Each product line serves a different market and customers. As a medium-sized organization, the company must effectively use people from manufacturing, design, and marketing to work on each product line. There are not enough designers to warrant a separate design department for each product line, so the designers are shared across product lines. Moreover, by keeping the manufacturing, design, and marketing functions intact, employees can develop the in-depth expertise to serve all product lines efficiently.

The matrix formalizes horizontal teams along with the traditional vertical hierarchy and tries to give equal balance to both. However, the matrix may shift one way or the other. Many companies have found a balanced matrix hard to implement and maintain because one side of the authority structure often dominates. As a consequence, two variations of matrix structure have evolved—the **functional matrix** and the **product matrix.** In a functional matrix, the functional bosses have primary authority and the project or product managers simply coordinate product activities. In a product matrix, by contrast, the project or product managers have primary authority and functional managers simply assign technical personnel to projects and provide advisory expertise as needed. For many organizations, one of these approaches works better than the balanced matrix with dual lines of authority.[43]

All kinds of organizations have experimented with the matrix, including hospitals, consulting firms, banks, insurance companies, government agencies, and many types of industrial firms.[44] This structure has been used successfully by large global organizations such as Procter & Gamble and Unilever, and in local plants such as the Cummins Engine plant in Jamestown, New York, which fine-tuned the matrix to suit its own particular goals and culture. Project-based organizations often use the matrix structure. For example, Defence Research and Development Canada, whose purpose is to inform, enable, and respond to Canada's defence and security priorities, is structured as a matrix to connect the people and departments that direct, deliver, and exploit knowledge about national and international innovations in military operations.[45]

PDA Remember...

Consider a matrix structure when the organization needs to give equal priority to both products and functions because of dual pressures from customers in the environment. Use either a functional matrix or a product matrix if the balanced matrix with dual lines of authority is not appropriate for your organization.

Strengths and Weaknesses

The matrix structure is best when environmental change is high and when goals reflect a dual requirement, such as for both product and functional goals. The dual-authority structure facilitates communication and coordination to cope with rapid environmental change and enables an equal balance between product and functional bosses. The matrix facilitates discussion and adaptation to unexpected problems. It tends to work best in organizations of moderate size with a few product lines. The matrix is not needed for only a single product line, and too many product lines make it difficult to coordinate both directions at once. Exhibit 3.12 summarizes the strengths and weaknesses of the matrix structure based on what we know of organizations that use it.[46]

EXHIBIT 3.12
Strengths and Weaknesses of the Matrix Organizational Structure

Strengths	Weaknesses
1. Achieves coordination necessary to meet dual demands from customers 2. Flexible sharing of human resources across products 3. Suited to complex decisions and frequent changes in unstable environment 4. Provides opportunity for both functional and product skill development 5. Best in medium-sized organizations with multiple products	1. Causes participants to experience dual authority, which can be frustrating and confusing 2. Means participants need good interpersonal skills and extensive training 3. Is time consuming; involves frequent meetings and conflict-resolution sessions 4. Will not work unless participants understand it and adopt collegial rather than vertical-type relationships 5. Requires great effort to maintain power balance

Source: Adapted from Robert Duncan, "What Is the Right Organization Structure? Decision Tree Analysis Provides the Answer," *Organizational Dynamics* (Winter 1979), 429.

The strength of the matrix is that it enables an organization to meet dual demands from customers in the environment. Resources (people, equipment) can be flexibly allocated across different products, and the organization can adapt to changing external requirements.[47] This structure also provides an opportunity for employees to acquire either functional or general management skills, depending on their interests.

One disadvantage of the matrix is that employees experience dual authority, reporting to two bosses and sometimes juggling conflicting demands. This can be frustrating and confusing, especially if roles and responsibilities are not clearly defined by top managers.[48] Employees working in a matrix need excellent interpersonal and conflict-resolution skills, which may require special training in human relations. The matrix also forces managers to spend a great deal of time in meetings.[49] If managers do not adapt to the information and power sharing required by the matrix, the system will not work. Managers must collaborate with one another rather than rely on vertical authority in decision making. As well, managers must work hard at maintaining the power balance between the members of the matrix. The successful implementation of one matrix structure occurred at a steel company in Great Britain.

In Practice
Englander Steel

As far back as anyone could remember, the steel industry in England was stable and certain. Then in the 1980s and 1990s, excess European steel capacity, an economic downturn, the emergence of the mini mill electric arc furnace, and competition from steelmakers in Germany and Japan forever changed the English steel industry. By the turn of the century, traditional steel mills in the United States, such as Bethlehem Steel and LTV, were facing bankruptcy. Mittal Steel in Asia and Europe's leading steelmaker, Arcelor, started acquiring steel companies to become world steel titans. The survival hope of small traditional steel manufacturers was to sell specialized products. A small company could market specialty products aggressively and quickly adapt to customer needs. Complex process settings and operating conditions had to be rapidly changed for each customer's order—a difficult feat for the titans.

Englander Steel employed 2,900 people, made 400,000 tonnes of steel a year (about 1 percent of Arcelor's output), and was 180 years old. For 160 of those years, a functional structure worked fine. As the environment became more turbulent and competitive, however, Englander Steel managers realized they were not keeping up. Fifty percent of Englander's orders were behind schedule. Profits were eroded by labour, material, and energy cost increases. Market share declined.

In consultation with outside experts, the president of Englander Steel saw that the company had to walk a tightrope. It had to specialize in a few high-value-added products tailored for separate markets, while maintaining economies of scale and sophisticated technology within functional departments. The dual pressure led to an unusual solution for a steel company: a matrix structure.

Englander Steel had four product lines: open-die forgings, ring-mill products, wheels and axles, and sheet steel. A business manager was given responsibility for and authority over each line, which included preparing a business plan and developing targets for production costs, product inventory, shipping dates, and gross profit. The managers were given authority to meet those targets and to make their lines profitable. Functional vice presidents were responsible for technical decisions. Functional managers were expected to stay abreast of the latest techniques in their areas and to keep personnel trained in new technologies that could apply to product lines. With 20,000 recipes for specialty steels and several hundred new recipes ordered each month, functional personnel had to stay current. Two functional departments—field sales and industrial relations—were not included in the matrix because they worked independently. The final design was a hybrid matrix structure with both matrix and functional relationships, as illustrated in Exhibit 3.13.

Implementation of the matrix was slow. Middle managers were confused. Meetings to coordinate orders across functional departments seemed to be held every day. However, after about a year of training by external consultants, Englander Steel was on track. Ninety percent of the orders were now delivered on time, and market share recovered. Both productivity and profitability increased steadily. The managers thrived on matrix involvement. Meetings to coordinate product and functional decisions provided a growth experience. Middle managers began including younger managers in the matrix discussions as training for future management responsibility.[50]

This example illustrates the appropriate use of a matrix structure. The dual pressure to maintain economies of scale and to market four product lines gave equal emphasis to the functional and product hierarchies. Through continuous meetings for coordination, Englander Steel achieved both economies of scale and flexibility.

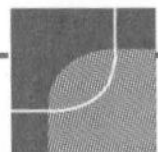

Horizontal Structure

A recent approach to organizing is the **horizontal structure**, which organizes employees around core processes. Organizations typically shift toward a horizontal structure during a procedure called re-engineering. **Re-engineering**, or *business process re-engineering*, basically means the redesign of a vertical organization along its horizontal workflows and processes. A **process** refers to an organized group of related tasks and activities that work together to transform inputs into outputs that create value for customers.[51] Re-engineering changes the way managers think about how work is done; rather than focusing on narrow jobs structured into distinct functional departments, they emphasize core processes that cut horizontally across the organization and involve teams of employees working together to serve customers. Examples of processes include order fulfillment, new product development, and customer service.

A good illustration of process is provided by claims handling at Progressive Casualty Insurance Company, headquartered in Cleveland, Ohio. In the past, a customer would report an accident to an agent, who would pass the information to a customer service representative, who, in turn, would pass it to a claims manager. The claims manager would batch the claim with others from the same territory and assign it to an adjuster, who would schedule a time to inspect the vehicle damage. Today, adjusters are organized into teams that handle the entire claims process from beginning to end. One member handles claimant calls to the office while others are stationed in the field. When an adjuster takes a call, he or she does whatever is possible over the phone. If an inspection is needed, the adjuster contacts a team member in the field and schedules an appointment immediately. Progressive now measures the time from call to inspection in hours rather than the seven to ten days it once took.[52]

When a company is re-engineered to a horizontal structure, all the people throughout the organization who work on a particular process (such as claims handling or order fulfillment) have easy access to one another so they can communicate

EXHIBIT 3.13
Matrix Structure for Englander Steel

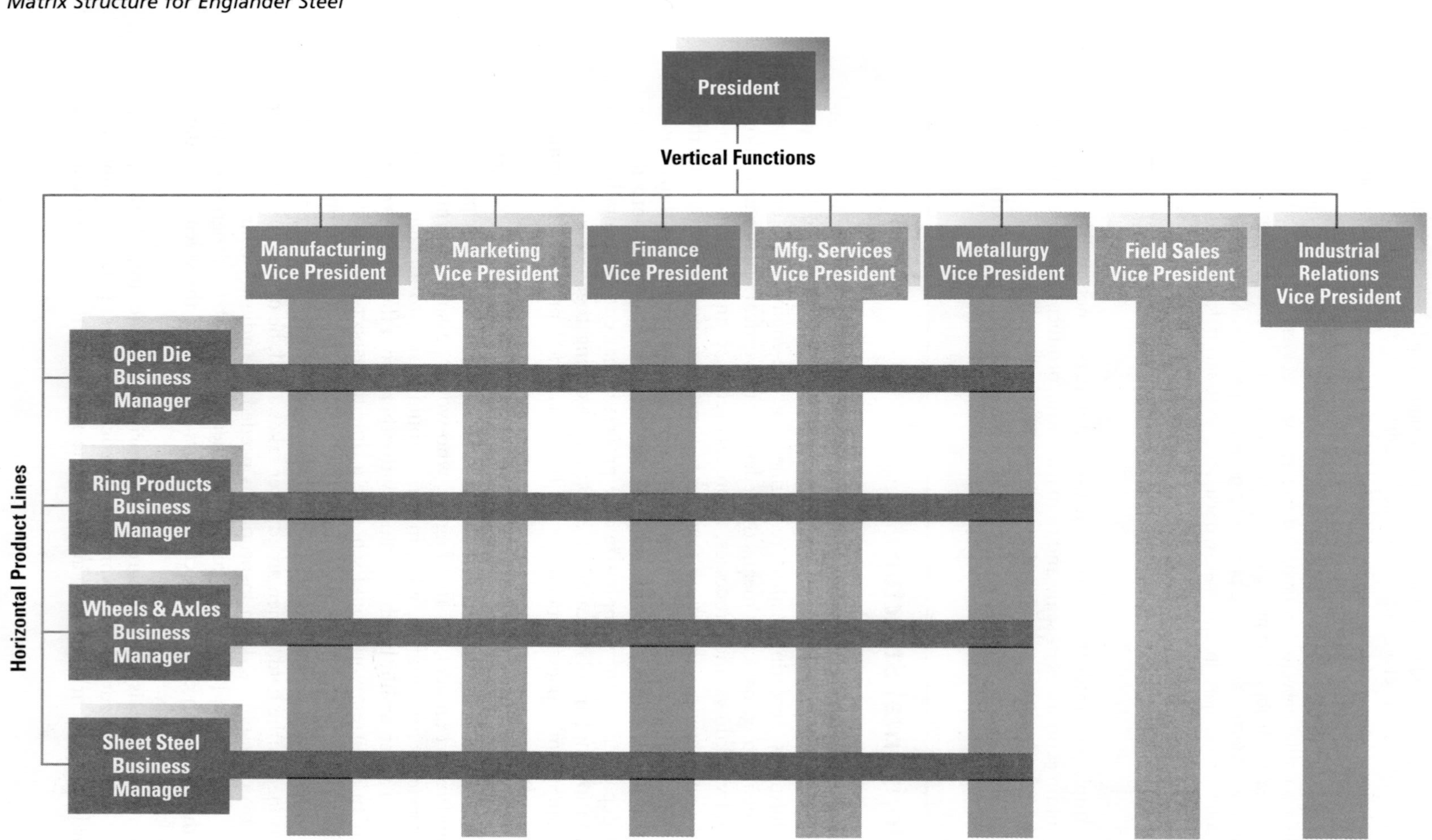

and coordinate their efforts. The horizontal structure virtually eliminates both the vertical hierarchy and old departmental boundaries. This structural approach is largely a response to the profound changes that have occurred in the workplace and the business environment over the past 15 to 20 years. Technological progress emphasizes computer- and Internet-based integration and coordination. Customers expect faster and better service, and employees want opportunities to use their minds, learn new skills, and assume greater responsibility. Organizations mired in a vertical mindset have a hard time meeting these challenges. Thus, numerous organizations have experimented with horizontal mechanisms such as cross-functional teams to achieve coordination across departments or task forces to accomplish temporary projects. Increasingly, organizations are shifting away from hierarchical, function-based structures to structures based on horizontal processes.

PDA Remember...

Consider a horizontal structure when customer needs and demands change rapidly and when learning and innovation are critical to organizational success. Carefully determine core processes and train managers and employees to work within the horizontal structure.

Characteristics

An illustration of a company re-engineered into a horizontal structure appears in Exhibit 3.14. Such an organization has the following characteristics:[53]

- Structure is created around cross-functional core processes rather than tasks, functions, or geography. Thus, boundaries between departments are obliterated. Ford Motor Company's Customer Service Division, for example, has core process groups for business development, parts supply and logistics, vehicle service and programs, and technical support.
- Self-directed teams, not individuals, are the basis of organizational design and performance.
- Process owners have responsibility for each core process in its entirety. For Ford's procurement and logistics process, for example, a number of teams may work on jobs such as parts analysis, purchasing, material flow, and distribution, but a process owner is responsible for coordinating the entire process.
- People on the team are given the skills, tools, motivation, and authority to make decisions central to the team's performance. Team members are cross-trained to perform one another's jobs, and the combined skills are sufficient to complete a major organizational task.
- Teams have the freedom to think creatively and respond flexibly to new challenges that arise.
- Customers drive the horizontal corporation. Effectiveness is measured by end-of-process performance objectives (based on the goal of bringing value to the customer), as well as customer satisfaction, employee satisfaction, and financial contribution.
- The culture is one of openness, trust, and collaboration, focused on continuous improvement. The culture values employee empowerment, responsibility, and well-being.

The Chemainus Sawmill, described below, re-engineered a traditional sawmill into a team-based structure supported by multiskilling training and pay-for-skills compensation systems.

EXHIBIT 3.14
A Horizontal Structure
Source: Based on Frank Ostroff, *The Horizontal Organization* (New York: Oxford University Press, 1999); John A. Byrne, "The Horizontal Corporation," *BusinessWeek* (December 20, 1993), 76–81; and Thomas A. Stewart, "The Search for the Organization of Tomorrow," *Fortune* (May 18, 1992), 92–98.

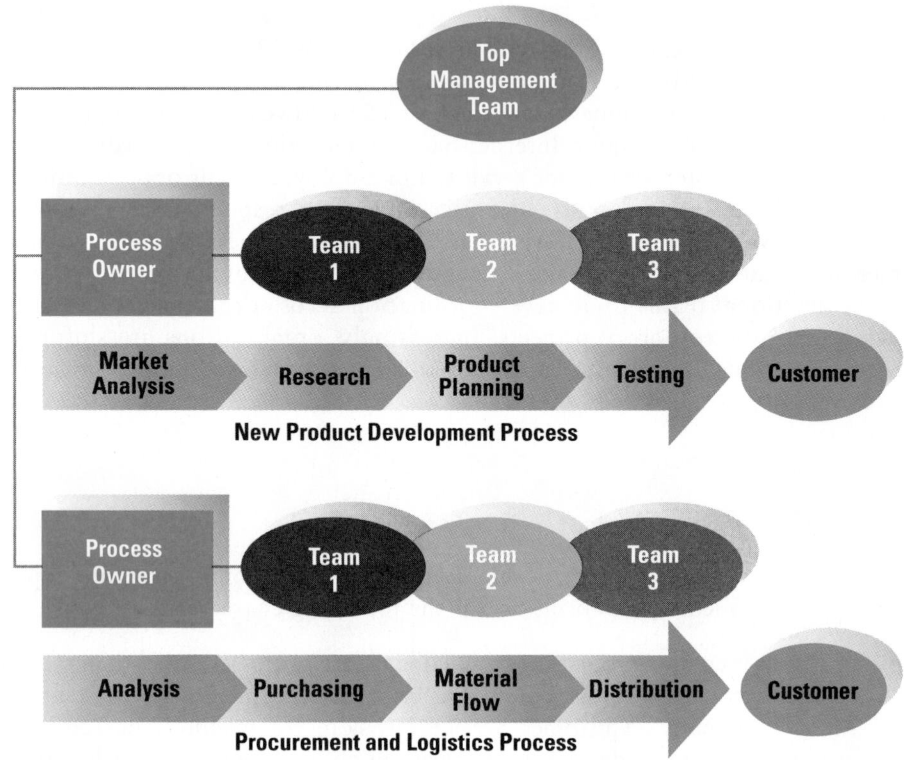

In Practice

Weyerhaeuser Company's Chemainus Sawmill (Sawmill)

The Chemainus Sawmill, which re-opened in 1985, is the fifth in the 150-year history of sawmilling in the small town of Chemainus on Vancouver Island. The town is known also for its large murals on the exterior walls of many of its buildings. The outdoor art gallery received international recognition in 1985 when Chemainus won first prize in the global Downtown Revitalizations Awards competition.

When the Sawmill re-opened, its mission was "to be first choice with customers and with the community."[54] It was structured to meet seven goals: (1) to provide a high value product in terms of size, grade, and presentation; (2) to provide dependable delivery; (3) to respond proactively to market demands through organizational flexibility; (4) to respond to feedback; (5) to provide rewarding work; (6) to provide a safe and healthy workplace; and (7) to develop and to maintain trust within the Sawmill and the community.

The Sawmill has several teams. There are six production teams with varying numbers of work stations for log prep, log breakdown, trim, grading, merchandising, and yard. There is also a team of shippers. The operators and the shippers are expected to rotate through all the work stations in their teams to become multiskilled and to train others in the skills they have mastered. The operators report to a shift foreperson who, in turn, reports to a department foreperson. The shippers report to a yard foreperson. The maintenance team consists of several millwrights, filers, electricians, oilers, and mechanics. They report to charge hands who, in turn, report to the maintenance supervisor. Lastly, there is the management team, headed by the mill manager, which consists of the operations superintendent, the personnel supervisor, the accountant, the sales superintendent, and other managerial staff.

Central to nurturing the team concept at the Sawmill is its communications network, a series of production team, crew, and other meetings for employee input. As well, each production team has an official team representative. The workers are also represented by Local 1-80 of the International Woodworkers of America. As noted in Chapter 7, the plant has been successful and recently received its ISO certification.

Strengths and Weaknesses

As with all structures, the horizontal structure has weaknesses as well as strengths. The strengths and weaknesses of the horizontal structure are listed in Exhibit 3.15.

The most significant strength of the horizontal structure is that it can dramatically increase the company's flexibility and response to changes in customer needs because of the enhanced coordination. The structure directs everyone's attention toward the customer, which leads to greater customer satisfaction as well as improvements in productivity, speed, and efficiency. In addition, because there are no boundaries between functional departments, employees take a broader view of organizational goals rather than being focused on the goals of a single department. The horizontal structure promotes an emphasis on teamwork and cooperation, so that team members share a commitment to meeting common objectives. Finally, the horizontal structure can improve the quality of life for employees by giving them opportunities to share responsibility, make decisions, and contribute significantly to the organization.

A weakness of the horizontal structure is that it can harm rather than help organizational performance unless managers carefully determine which core processes are critical for bringing value to customers. Simply defining the processes around which to organize can be difficult. In addition, shifting to a horizontal structure is complicated and time consuming because it requires significant changes in culture, job design, management philosophy, and information and reward systems. Traditional managers may balk when they have to give up power and authority to serve instead as coaches and facilitators of teams. Employees have to be trained to work effectively in a team environment. Finally, because of the cross-functional nature of work, a horizontal structure can limit in-depth knowledge and skill development unless measures are taken to give employees opportunities to maintain and build technical expertise.

EXHIBIT 3.15
Strengths and Weaknesses of the Horizontal Structure

Strengths	Weaknesses
1. Promotes flexibility and rapid response to changes in customer needs 2. Directs the attention of everyone toward the production and delivery of value to the customer 3. Each employee has a broader view of organizational goals 4. Promotes a focus on teamwork and collaboration 5. Improves quality of life for employees by offering them the opportunity to share responsibility, make decisions, and be accountable for outcomes	1. Determining core processes is difficult and time consuming 2. Requires changes in culture, job design, management philosophy, and information and reward systems 3. Traditional managers may balk when they have to give up power and authority 4. Requires significant training of employees to work effectively in a horizontal team environment 5. Can limit in-depth skill development

Source: Based on Frank Ostroff, *The Horizontal Organization: What the Organization of the Future Looks Like and How It Delivers Value to Customers* (New York: Oxford University Press, 1999); and Richard L. Daft, Organization *Theory and Design,* 6th ed. (Cincinnati, Ohio: South-Western, 1998), 253.

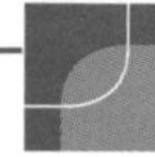

Virtual Network Structure

The virtual network structure extends the concept of horizontal coordination and collaboration beyond the boundaries of the traditional organization. Many of today's organizations farm out some of their activities to other companies that can do it more efficiently. **Outsourcing** means to contract out certain corporate functions, such as manufacturing, information technology, or credit processing, to other companies. This is a significant trend in all industries that is affecting organizational structure.[55] Accenture, for example, handles all aspects of information technology for the British food retailer J. Sainsbury's. Companies in India, Malaysia, and Scotland manage call centre and technical support for North American computer and cell phone companies. Entire chunks of General Motors' and BMW's automobiles are engineered and built by outside contractors such as Magna International. Fiat Auto is involved in multiple complex outsourcing relationships, with other companies handling logistics, maintenance, and the manufacturing of some parts.[56]

PDA Remember...

Use a virtual network structure for extreme flexibility and rapid response to changing market conditions. Focus on key activities that give the organization its competitive advantage and outsource other activities to carefully selected partners.

These interorganizational relationships reflect a significant shift in organizational design. A few organizations carry outsourcing to the extreme and create a virtual network structure. With a **virtual network structure,** sometimes called a *modular structure*, the firm subcontracts many or most of its major processes to separate companies and coordinates their activities from a small headquarters organization.[57]

How the Structure Works

The virtual network organization may be viewed as a central hub surrounded by a network of outside specialists. Rather than being housed under one roof or located within one organization, services such as accounting, design, manufacturing, marketing, and distribution are outsourced to separate companies that are connected electronically to a central office. Organizational partners located in different parts of the world may use networked computers or the Internet to exchange data and information so rapidly and smoothly that a loosely connected network of suppliers, manufacturers, and distributors can look and act like one seamless company. The virtual network form incorporates a free-market style to replace the traditional vertical hierarchy. Subcontractors may flow into and out of the system as needed to meet changing needs.

With a network structure, the hub maintains control over processes in which it has world-class or difficult-to-imitate capabilities and then transfers other activities—along with the decision making and control over them—to other organizations. These partner organizations organize and accomplish their work using their own ideas, assets, and tools.[58] The idea is that a firm can concentrate on what it does best and contract out everything else to companies with distinctive competence in those specific areas, enabling the organization to do more with less.[59] The network structure is often advantageous for start-up companies.

Strengths and Weaknesses

Exhibit 3.16 summarizes the strengths and weaknesses of the virtual network structure. One of the major strengths is that the organization, no matter how small, can

Strengths	Weaknesses
1. Enables even small organizations to obtain talent and resources worldwide 2. Gives a company immediate scale and reach without huge investments in factories, equipment, or distribution facilities 3. Enables the organization to be highly flexible and responsive to changing needs 4. Reduces administrative overhead costs	1. Managers do not have hands-on control over many activities and employees 2. Requires a great deal of time to manage relationships and potential conflicts with contract partners 3. There is a risk of organizational failure if a partner fails to deliver or goes out of business 4. Employee loyalty and organizational culture might be weak because employees feel they can be replaced by contract services

EXHIBIT 3.16
Strengths and Weaknesses of Virtual Network Structure

Source: Based on Linda S. Ackerman, "Transition Management: An In-Depth Look at Managing Complex Change," *Organizational Dynamics* (Summer 1982), 46–66; and Frank Ostroff, *The Horizontal Organization* (New York: Oxford University Press, 1999), Fig 2.1, 34.

be truly global, drawing on resources worldwide to achieve the best quality and price, and then selling products or services worldwide just as easily through subcontractors. The network structure also enables new or small organizations to develop products or services and get them to market rapidly without huge investments in factories, equipment, warehouses, or distribution facilities. The ability to arrange and rearrange resources to meet changing needs and best serve customers gives the network structure flexibility and rapid response. New technologies can be developed quickly by tapping into a worldwide network of experts. The organization can continually redefine itself to meet changing product or market opportunities. A final strength is reduced administrative overhead. Large teams of staff specialists and administrators are not needed. Managerial and technical talent can be focused on key activities that provide competitive advantage while other activities are outsourced.[60]

The virtual network structure also has a number of weaknesses.[61] The primary weakness is a lack of control. The network structure takes decentralization to the extreme. Managers do not have all operations under their jurisdiction and must rely on contracts, coordination, and negotiation to hold things together. This also means increased time spent managing relationships with partners and resolving conflicts.

A problem of equal importance is the risk of failure if one organizational partner fails to deliver, has a plant burn down, or goes out of business. Managers in the headquarters organization have to act quickly to spot problems and find new arrangements. Finally, from a human resource perspective, employee loyalty can be weak in a network organization because of concerns over job security. Employees may feel that they can be replaced by contract services. In addition, it is more difficult to develop a cohesive organizational culture. Turnover may be higher because emotional commitment between the organization and employees is low. With changing products, markets, and partners, the organization may need to reshuffle employees at any time to get the correct mix of skills and capabilities.

PDA
Remember...

Implement hybrid structures, when needed, to combine characteristics of functional, divisional, and horizontal structures. Use a hybrid structure in complex environments to take advantage of the strengths of various structural characteristics and avoid some of the weaknesses.

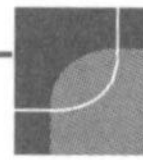

Hybrid Structure

As a practical matter, many structures in the real world do not exist in the pure forms we have outlined in this chapter. Organizations often use a **hybrid structure** that combines characteristics of various approaches tailored to specific strategic needs. Most companies combine characteristics of functional, divisional, geographical, horizontal, or network structures to take advantage of the strengths of various structures and to avoid some of the weaknesses. Hybrid structures tend to be used in rapidly changing environments because they offer the organization greater flexibility.

One type of hybrid that is often used combines characteristics of the functional and divisional structures. When a corporation grows large and has several products or markets, it typically is organized into self-contained divisions of some type. Functions that are important to each product or market are decentralized to the self-contained units. However, some functions that are relatively stable and require economies of scale and in-depth specialization are also centralized at headquarters. The departments provide services for the entire organization. For example, Rogers Communications Inc, has three business units—wireless, cable and telecom, and media—as well as functional support across the organization.

Exhibit 3.17 illustrates another hybrid structure. Ford Motor Company's Customer Service Division, a global operation made up of 12,000 employees serving

EXHIBIT 3.17
Hybrid Structure at Ford Motor Company's Customer Service Division

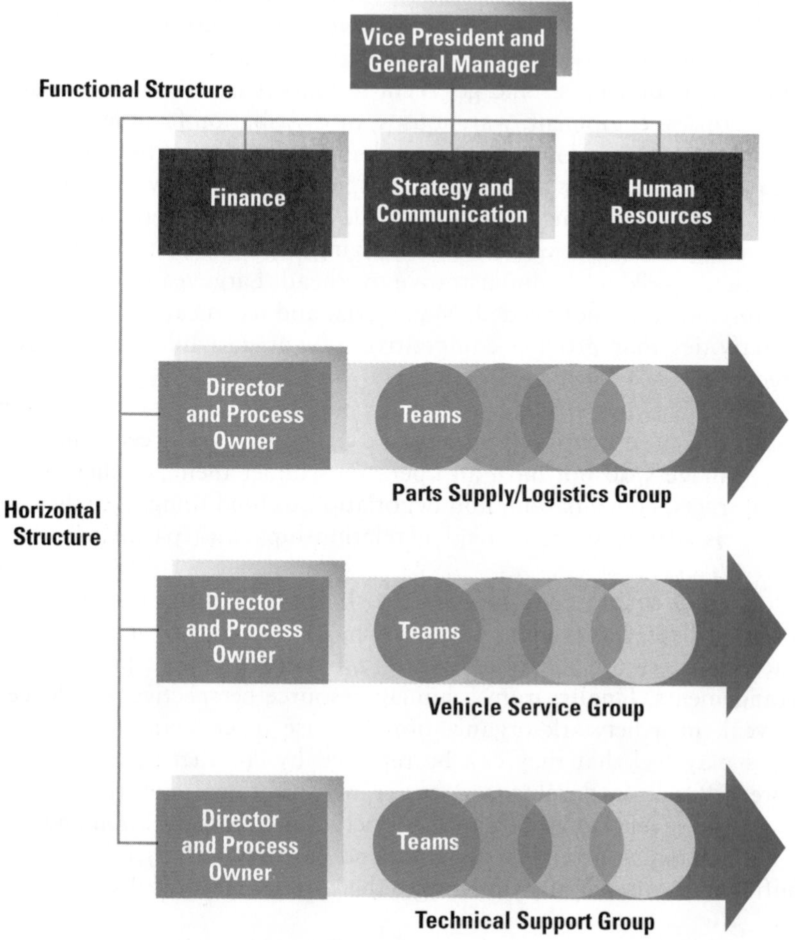

nearly 15,000 dealers, provides an example of this type of hybrid. Beginning in 1995, when Ford launched its "Ford 2000" initiative to become the world's leading automotive firm in the 21st century, top executives grew increasingly concerned about complaints regarding customer service. They decided that the horizontal model offered the best chance to gain a faster, more efficient, integrated approach to customer service. Several horizontally aligned groups, made up of multiskilled teams, focus on core processes such as parts supply and logistics (acquiring parts and getting them to dealers quickly and efficiently), vehicle service and programs (collecting and disseminating information about repair problems), and technical support (ensuring that every service department receives updated technical information). Each group has a process owner who is responsible for seeing that the teams meet overall objectives. Ford's Customer Service Division retained a functional structure for finance, strategy and communication, and human resources departments. Each of these departments provides services for the entire division.[62]

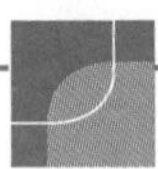

Applications of Structural Design

Each type of structure is applied in different situations and meets different needs. In short, design follows purpose. In describing the various structures, we touched briefly on conditions such as environmental stability or change and organizational size that are related to structure. Each form of structure—functional, divisional, matrix, horizontal, network, hybrid—represents a tool that can help managers make an organization more effective, depending on the demands of its situation.

PDA Remember...

Find the correct balance between vertical control and horizontal coordination to meet the needs of the organization. Consider a structural reorganization when symptoms of structural deficiency are observed.

Structural Alignment

Ultimately, the most important decision that managers make about structural design is to find the right balance between vertical control and horizontal coordination, depending on the needs of the organization. Vertical control is associated with goals of efficiency and stability, while horizontal coordination is associated with learning, innovation, and flexibility. Exhibit 3.18 shows a simplified continuum that illustrates how structural approaches are associated with vertical control versus horizontal coordination. The functional structure is appropriate when the organization needs to be coordinated through the vertical hierarchy and when efficiency is important for meeting organizational goals. The functional structure uses task specialization and a strict chain of command to gain efficient use of scarce resources, but it does not enable the organization to be flexible or innovative. At the opposite end of the scale, the horizontal structure is appropriate when the organization has a high need for coordination among functions to achieve innovation and promote learning. The horizontal structure enables organizations to differentiate themselves and respond quickly to changes, but at the expense of efficient resource use. The virtual network structure offers even greater flexibility and potential for rapid response by allowing the organization to add or subtract pieces as needed to adapt and meet changing needs from the environment and marketplace. Exhibit 3.18 also shows how other types of structure defined in this chapter—functional with cross-functional linkages, divisional, and matrix—represent intermediate steps on the organization's path to efficiency or innovation and learning. The exhibit does not include all

EXHIBIT 3.18
Relationship of Structure to Organization's Need for Efficiency versus Learning

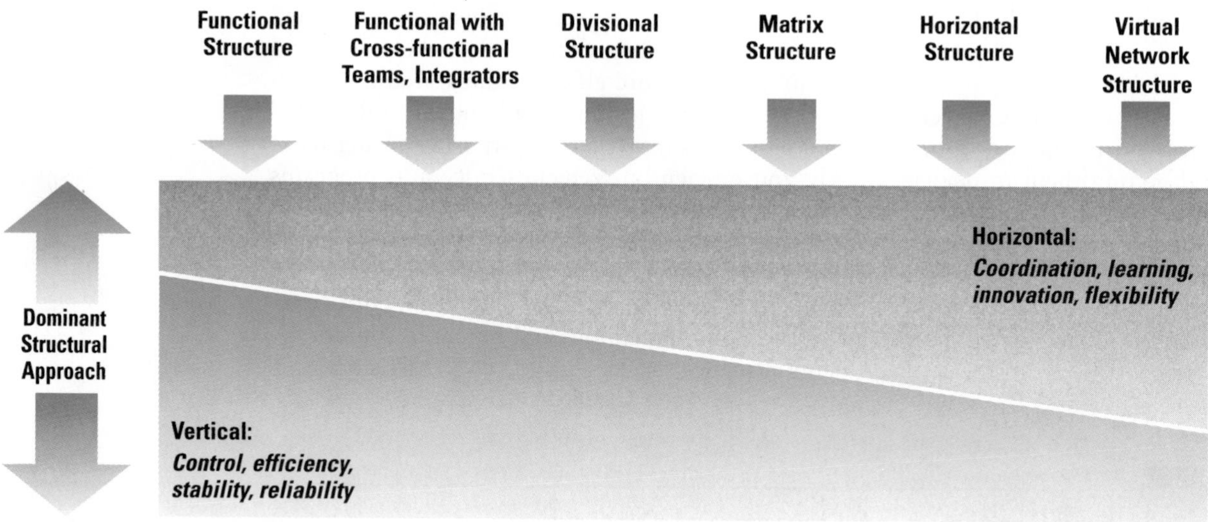

possible structures, but it illustrates how organizations attempt to balance the needs for efficiency and vertical control with innovation and horizontal coordination. In addition, as described in the chapter, many organizations use a hybrid structure to combine characteristics of these structural types. There are many structural choices and, as The Canadian Inquisition shows, one possibility is a web of inclusion.[63]

In Practice

The Canadian Inquisition (The Inquisition)

The Inquisition is a trivia league formed in 1986 in Toronto. The participants call it a cooperative pub trivia league as there is no formal organizational structure. There are 15 to 16 teams with five players per team in a game. There are about 130 players in the league, included the quiz masters, who ask the questions. Games take place at various Toronto pubs on Monday nights; there are three seasons per year and a final competition for a total of 33 games per year. Players include teachers, programmers, reporters, editors, cab drivers, and real estate agents. Each team has a captain who is responsible to ensure that the players know where game is being played and to line up substitute players, if necessary. The captain meets the team at the start of the season to discuss any rule changes and to review the finances. Players pay three dollars per game to cover costs such as photocopying and buying trophies. A volunteer treasurer for the Inquisition manages the league's bank account. Another volunteer compiles the statistics, and prizes are awarded every season for winning teams, individual scores, and team performance in the Canadiana and stinker rounds. The website is maintained, as well, by a volunteer.

The Inquisition is a loose, self-sustaining organization that has survived on trust, co-operation and commitment.[64]

The Rules

"One team sits out each season and takes care of writing the questions, organizing the schedule, and running the games. A game consists of 10 rounds with 10 questions in each round. Each question is first posed to an individual player: if he or she gives the correct answer, the team gets two points. If the individual player doesn't get the answer, the whole team can discuss the question, and if they get the right answer, the team gets one point. You have 60 seconds to answer, individually or as a group. The next question in the round is posed to a player on the opposite team, and so forth.

Except on round 10, one team can't 'steal' from another team that misses the answer; there is no penalty for guessing a wrong answer. . . . The challenge round is always the tenth round and works differently from the others. First of all, there are six categories of questions, with two questions per category. Each player gets to pick the category they want (unless that category is used up). You have 30 seconds to answer (for two points) but if you don't get the answer the question goes to the person opposite you on the other team. He or she then has 20 seconds to answer for one point. . . . The league final (championship) game has three teams, not two. A wildcard team, the team that scored the greatest number of "question" points gets to play, plus the teams with the best win-loss records in each division (ignoring the wildcard team). There are still ten rounds of questions, but normally each round is divided into triplets with a common theme under a more general theme such as "science" or "geography". There is usually a video round, and sometimes there are more imaginative question formats such as identifying objects or substances, or interpreting a hand gesture".[65]

Symptoms of Structural Deficiency

Top executives periodically evaluate organizational structure to determine whether it is appropriate to changing organization needs. Many organizations try one organizational structure and then reorganize to another structure in an effort to find the right fit between internal reporting relationships and the needs of the external environment. As Exhibit 3.19 shows, it is critical to know and to design to the organization's purpose!

As a general rule, when organizational structure is out of alignment with organization needs, one or more of the following **symptoms of structural deficiency** appear.[66]

- *Decision making is delayed or lacking in quality.* Decision makers may be overloaded because the hierarchy funnels too many problems and decisions to them. Delegation to lower levels may be insufficient. Another cause of poor-quality

EXHIBIT 3.19
Core Business!

"Can anyone remember what our core business is?"

decisions is that information may not reach the correct people. Information linkages in either the vertical or horizontal direction may be inadequate to ensure decision quality.

- *The organization does not respond innovatively to a changing environment.* One reason for lack of innovation is that departments are not coordinated horizontally. The identification of customer needs by the marketing department and the identification of technological developments in the research department must be coordinated. Organizational structure also has to specify departmental responsibilities that include environmental scanning and innovation.
- *Employee performance declines and goals are not being met.* Employee performance may decline because the structure doesn't provide clear goals, responsibilities, and mechanisms for coordination. The structure should reflect the complexity of the market environment and be straightforward enough for employees to effectively work within.
- *Too much conflict is evident.* Organizational structure should allow conflicting departmental goals to combine into a single set of goals for the entire organization. When departments act at cross-purposes or are under pressure to achieve departmental goals at the expense of organizational goals, the structure is often at fault. Horizontal linkage mechanisms are not adequate.

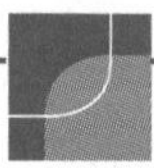

New Directions

Some organizational theorists use images to help us understand different kinds of organizational designs. One of the most influential is Gareth Morgan at York University. He argues that "[all] theories of organization and management are based on implicit images or metaphors that lead us to see, understand, and manage organizations in distinctive yet partial ways."[67] Morgan provides eight metaphors through which we can understand organizations: organizations as (1) machines, (2) organisms, (3) brains, (4) cultures, (5) political systems, (6) psychic prisons, (7) flux and transformation, and (8) instruments of domination. Morgan argues that managers need to look at organizations through all the images so that they can get a rich and accurate understanding of their organizations so that they can make more informed decisions. He notes that "[the] concept of organization is a product of the mechanical age. Now that we are living in an electronic age, new organizing principles [or images] are necessary."[68]

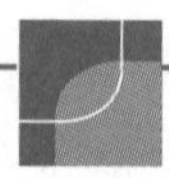

Summary and Interpretation

Organizational structure must accomplish two things for the organization. It must provide a framework of responsibilities, reporting relationships, and groupings, and it must provide mechanisms for linking and coordinating organizational elements into a coherent whole. The structure is reflected on the organizational chart. Linking the organization into a coherent whole requires the use of information systems and linkage devices in addition to the organizational chart.

It is important to understand the information-processing perspective on structure. Organizational structure can be designed to provide vertical and horizontal information linkages based on the information processing required to meet the organization's overall goal. Managers can choose whether to orient toward a traditional organization designed for efficiency, which emphasizes vertical linkages such as hierarchy, rules and plans, and formal information systems, or toward a contemporary learning organization, which emphasizes horizontal communication and coordination. Vertical linkages are not sufficient for most organizations today. Organizations provide horizontal linkages through cross-functional information systems, direct contact between managers across department lines, temporary task forces, full-time integrators, and teams.

Alternatives for grouping employees and departments into overall structural design include functional grouping, divisional grouping, multifocused grouping, horizontal grouping, and network grouping. The choice among functional, divisional, and horizontal structures determines where coordination and integration will be greatest. With functional and divisional structures, managers also use horizontal linkage mechanisms to complement the vertical dimension and achieve integration of departments and levels into an organizational whole. With a horizontal structure, activities are organized horizontally around core work processes. A virtual network structure extends the concept of horizontal coordination and collaboration beyond the boundaries of the organization. Core activities are performed by a central hub while other functions and activities are outsourced to contract partners. The matrix structure attempts to achieve an equal balance between the vertical and horizontal dimensions of structure. Most organizations do not exist in these pure forms, using instead a hybrid structure that incorporates characteristics of two or more types of structure. Ultimately, managers attempt to find the correct balance between vertical control and horizontal coordination.

Finally, an organizational chart is only so many lines and boxes on a piece of paper. The purpose of the organizational chart is to encourage and direct employees into activities and communications that enable the organization to achieve its goals. The organizational chart provides the structure, but employees provide the behaviour. The chart is a guideline to encourage people to work together, but management must implement the structure and carry it out.

Key Concepts

centralized, p. 87
chain of command, p. 95
decentralized, p. 87
departmental grouping, p. 95
divisional grouping, p. 97
divisional structure, p. 99
functional grouping, p. 97
functional matrix, p. 107
functional structure, p. 97
horizontal grouping, p. 97
horizontal linkage, p. 90
horizontal structure, p. 109
hybrid structure, p. 116
integrator, p. 91
liaison role, p. 91
matrix structure, p. 104
multifocused grouping, p. 97
organizational structure, p. 86

Discussion Questions

1. What is the definition of *organizational structure*? Does organizational structure appear on the organizational chart? Explain.
2. How do rules and plans help an organization achieve vertical integration?
3. When is a functional structure preferable to a divisional structure?
4. Large corporations tend to use hybrid structures. Why?
5. What are the primary differences between a traditional organization designed for efficiency and a more contemporary organization designed for learning?
6. What is the difference between a task force and a team? between a liaison role and an integrating role? Which of the four provides the greatest amount of horizontal coordination?
7. What conditions usually have to be present before an organization should adopt a matrix structure?
8. The manager of a consumer products firm said, "We use the brand manager position to train future executives." Do you think the brand manager position is a good training ground? Discuss.
9. Why do companies using a horizontal structure have cultures that emphasize openness, employee empowerment, and responsibility? What do you think a manager's job would be like in a horizontally organized company?
10. How is structure related to the organization's need for efficiency versus its need for learning and innovation? How can managers tell if structure is out of alignment with the organization's needs?
11. Describe the virtual network structure. Why do you think this is becoming a good structural alternative for some of today's organizations?

Chapter 3 Workbook: You and Organizational Structure*

To better understand the importance of organizational structure in your life, do the following assignment.

Select one of the following organizations to design:

- A copy and printing shop
- A travel agency
- A sports rental (such as snowmobiles) in a resort area
- A bakery

Background

Organization is a way of gaining some power against an unreliable environment. The environment provides the organization with inputs, which include raw materials, human resources, and financial resources. There is a service or product to produce that involves technology. The output goes to clients, a group that must be nurtured. The complexities of the environment and the technology determine the complexity of the organization.

Planning Your Organization

1. Write down the mission or purpose of the organization in a few sentences.
2. What are the specific tasks to be completed to accomplish the mission?
3. Based on the specifics in number 2, develop an organizational chart. Each position in the chart will perform a specific task or is responsible for a certain outcome.
4. You are into your third year of operation, and your business has been very successful. You want to add a second location a few miles away. What issues will you face running the business at two locations? Draw an

organizational chart that includes the two business locations.

5. Five more years go by and the business has grown to five locations in two cities. How do you keep in touch with it all? What issues of control and coordination have arisen? Draw an up-to-date organizational chart and explain your rationale for it.
6. Twenty years later you have seventy-five business locations in five provinces. What are the issues and problems that have to be dealt with through organizational structure? Draw an organizational chart for this organization showing how information will flow within the organization.

*Adapted by Dorothy Marcic from "Organizing," in Donald D. White and H. William Vroman, Action in Organizations, 2nd ed. (Boston: Allyn and Bacon, 1982), 154, and Cheryl Harvey and Kim Morouney, "Organization Structure and Design: The Club Ed Exercise," *Journal of Management Education* (June 1985), 425–429.

Case for Analysis: Aquarius Advertising Agency*

The Aquarius Advertising Agency is a middle-sized firm that offered two basic services to its clients: (1) customized plans for the content of an advertising campaign (for example, slogans and layouts) and (2) complete plans for media (such as radio, TV, newspapers, billboards, and Internet). Additional services included aid in marketing and distribution of products and marketing research to test advertising effectiveness.

Its activities were organized in a traditional manner. The organizational chart is shown in Exhibit 3.20. Each department included similar functions.

Each client account was coordinated by an account executive who acted as a liaison between the client and the various specialists on the professional staff of the operations and marketing divisions. The number of direct communications and contacts between clients and Aquarius specialists, clients and account executives, and Aquarius specialists and account executives is indicated in Exhibit 3.21. These sociometric data were gathered by a consultant who conducted a study of the patterns of formal and informal communication. Each intersecting cell of Aquarius personnel and the clients contains an index of the direct contacts between them.

Although an account executive was designated to be the liaison between the client and specialists within the agency, communications frequently occurred directly between clients and account managers and executives and bypassed the specialists. These direct contacts involved a wide range of interactions, such as meetings, telephone calls, e-mail messages, and so on. A large number of direct communications occurred between agency specialists and their counterparts in the client organization. For example, an art specialist working as one member of a team on a particular client account would be occasionally contacted directly by the client's in-house art specialist, and agency research personnel had direct communication with research people of the client firm. Also, some of the unstructured contacts often led to more formal meetings with clients in which agency personnel made presentations, interpreted and defended agency policy, and committed the agency to certain courses of action.

Both hierarchical and professional systems operated within the departments of the operations and marketing divisions. Each department was organized hierarchically with a director, an assistant director, and several levels of authority. Professional communications were widespread and mainly concerned with sharing knowledge and techniques, technical evaluation of work, and development of professional interests. Control in each department was exercised mainly through control of promotions and supervision of work done by subordinates. Many account executives, however, felt the need for more influence, and one commented:

Creativity and art. That's all I hear around here. It is hard as hell to effectively manage six or seven hotshots who claim they have to do their own thing. Each of them tries to sell his or her idea to the client, and most of the time I don't know what has happened until a week later. If I were a despot, I would make all of them check with me first to get approval. Things would sure change around here.

The need for reorganization was made more acute by changes in the environment. Within a short period of time, there was a rapid turnover in the major accounts handled by the agency. It was typical for advertising agencies to gain or lose clients quickly, often with no advance warning as consumer behaviour and lifestyle changes emerged and product innovations occurred.

An agency reorganization was one solution proposed by top management to increase flexibility in this

EXHIBIT 3.20
Aquarius Advertising Agency Organization Chart

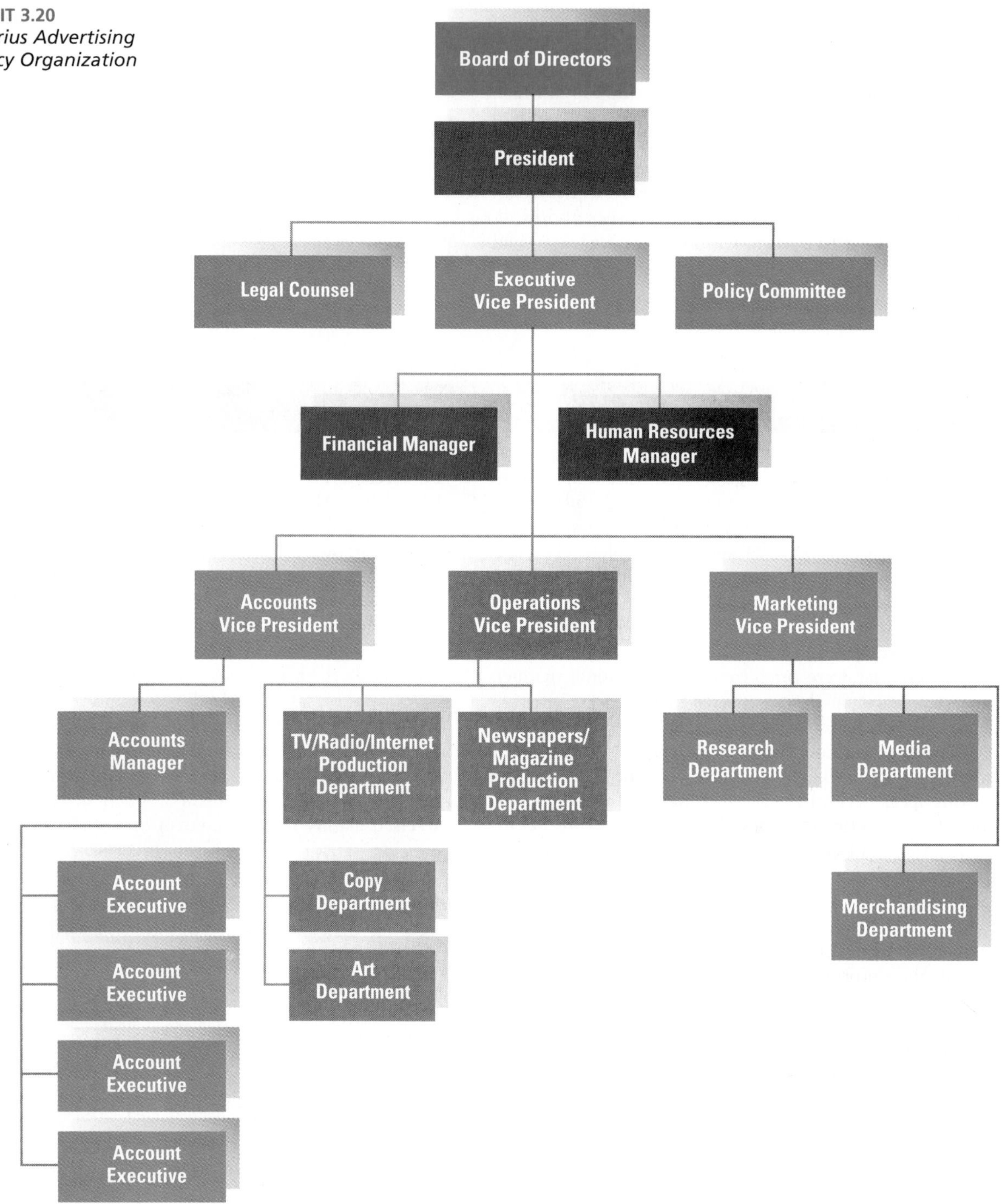

EXHIBIT 3.21
Sociometric Index of Aquarius Personnel and Clients
F = Frequent—daily
O = Occasional—once or twice per project
N = None

	Clients	Account Manager	Account Executives	TV/Radio Specialists	Newspaper/Magazine Specialists	Copy Specialists	Art Specialists	Merchandising Specialists	Media Specialists	Research Specialists
Clients	X	F	F	N	N	O	O	O	O	O
Account Manager		X	F	N	N	N	N	N	N	N
Account Executives			X	F	F	F	F	F	F	F
TV/Radio Specialists				X	N	O	O	N	N	O
Newspaper/Magazine Specialists					X	O	O	N	O	O
Copy Specialists						X	N	O	O	O
Art Specialists							X	O	O	O
Merchandising Specialists								X	F	F
Media Specialists									X	F
Research Specialists										X

unpredictable environment. The reorganization would be aimed at reducing the agency's response time to environmental changes and at increasing cooperation and communication among specialists from different departments. The top managers are not sure what type of reorganization is appropriate. They would like your help analyzing their context and current structure and welcome your advice on proposing a new structure.

*Adapted from John F. Veiga and John N. Yanouzas, "Aquarius Advertising Agency," *The Dynamics of Organization Theory* (St. Paul, Minn.: West, 1984), 212–217, with permission.

Case for Analysis: The Print Shop at Eva's Phoenix

I just wanted to keep you posted that I'm still with Astley-Gilbert and I'm no longer a receiver but now I'm working in the Offset Bindery Department as a helper. I'm learning how to use the folder machine and the stitcher as well. I get a lot of overtime plus my situation in life seems to be getting a little better. I want to thank you for all your help, I couldn't have done it without your support. (2006 graduate)

Introduction

Described in 2007 by Print Action Magazine as 'Canada's leading social program with printing ties', Toronto's Eva's Phoenix Print Shop is a socially and environmentally responsible commercial printer that helps homeless and at-risk youth achieve self-sufficiency. The enterprise is an initiative of Eva's Initiatives, an award-winning charity for homeless youth.

Operating since 2002, it is the only print based social enterprise working with youth in Toronto, and virtually the only location where one can gain significant mechanical skills training in print. The Print Shop is guided by an Advisory Board comprised of senior corporate and graphic industry professionals as well as three youth graduates each of whom works in graphics.

Organization Design

Critical to the enterprise's success is 'careful integration': both between social and commercial elements of the enterprise, and between the enterprise and the Eva's Phoenix housing and employment facility. The current extent to which the social and commercial elements are integrated within the enterprise itself delivers useful synergy. Examples include effective use of shared physical plant, as well as cross-fertilization of staff skills and knowledge. In terms of integration with the 'host' Eva's Phoenix, there are positives, but a further degree of separation will be beneficial for both elements. The plan to shift the print shop to an adjacent site would preserve the benefit of, for example, immediate access for Eva's Phoenix youth, and create greater commercial workflow efficiency with larger and dedicated space. Expansion will require a review of what legal structure best suits the enterprise's long-term objectives in relation to those of its parent, Eva's Initiatives. See Exhibit 3.22 for the current organizational chart.

Social Operations

The print training department of Eva's Phoenix Print Shop is called Foundations of Print. Every quarter up to eight youth receive hands-on print training. They are not paid, but receive supports such as a transit pass, access to housing at Eva's Phoenix, math tutoring and honoraria for completed assignments and good attendance. Youth who complete training are supported to apply for full-time work in the graphics industry.

Foundations of Print currently costs approximately $190,000 per year, and is paid for by the United Way's Toronto Enterprise Fund as well as corporate, foundation and individual contributions.

Commercial Operations

Print Services:

- Design, offset/digital print, finishing (cut, fold, stitch, collate, shrink-wrap, drill)
- MAC and PC: Quark, Photoshop, Illustrator, InDesign
- Current customers include PricewaterhouseCoopers LLP, TD Bank, Toronto Hydro, Scotia Capital, United Way, Salvation Army, Bombardier.

Current operating costs are approximately $180,000. The 2007 objective is to sell approximately $300,000 of print for a gross profit of $120,000 and a net loss of $55,000. The goal is to break-even in fiscal 2009, with a stretch goal of 2008. Longer term (three to five years) the Print Shop wants the commercial department to generate a profit to help pay for Foundations of Print. As the business grows, the Print Shop also envisions hiring some graduates to join the team on a permanent basis.

Pivotal Point in Enterprise Development

The enterprise started in 2002. At that time funding came from several sources, including the Rotary Club, the United Way, a corporate donor and the federal government. The federal government contract required that youth be paid for on-the job training. At any given time, four to six youth with little or no graphics experience were working on live customer jobs and training at the same time. Despite frequent contract changes and disruptions, the enterprise achieved strong social results, but the business achieved little growth and suffered with ongoing quality control issues. The business challenges were exacerbated by not having the 'right people on the bus'.

A 2005 strategic review, led by an MBA research intern, led to pivotal change. First, the enterprise withdrew from participation in the federal government contract, electing to increase revenues from corporate, foundation, and individual sources. This decision allowed the leadership team to draw on four years of experience

EXHIBIT 3.22
Eva's Phoenix Print Shop

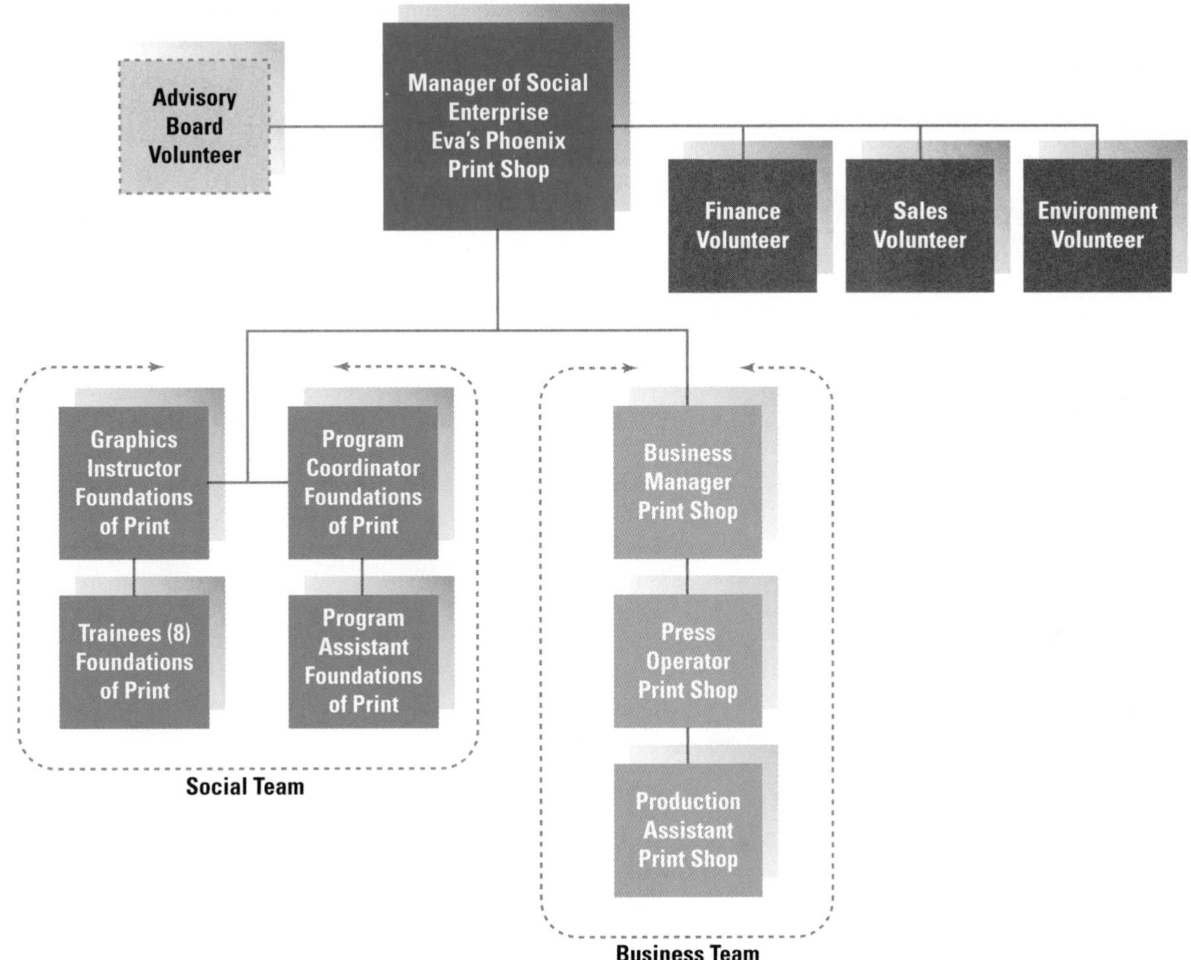

and implement changes that would benefit both the social and business bottom-lines. The new structure required a clearer separation between training and production, without losing the synergy created by their interaction. The key move was a redefinition of roles, which, fortuitously, led to the right people joining the bus, and in the right seats!

Under the government regulated structure concurrent teaching and production created ongoing conflicting priorities. Learning at such a beginner level is better with a dedicated instructor because youth build a foundation of knowledge in a logical sequence. On the business side, having an experienced business manager and press operator led to immediate improvements in quality and productivity. Overall shop infrastructure is used more effectively—stretching use over a 12-hour, rather than an 8-hour, time frame. In one year the enterprise doubled the number of youth participants and increased sales by 250%.

The Print Shop is a 2007 Toronto Community Foundation Vital Ideas Award Winner, recognizing 'leading edge programs that combine experience, expertise and ingenuity to create practical solutions that strengthen Toronto's vital signs'. In addition, it was selected by Vancouver's Vancity Foundation as one of eight Canadian social enterprises to contribute to an 18-month initiative to develop common tools for Demonstrating Value.

Through its Vital Ideas Award, the Print Shop is working with Resiliency Canada to implement a "strength-based model". This model, instead of focusing on the negative risks and barriers associated with the homeless youth, directly involves youth in identifying both strengths and challenges, and tracking their progress over time with our support. Elements of this tracking model are comprised of youth intake assessment, service plan development, evaluation protocol, and database system. From an organizational point of view this model will ensure consistency in our data evaluation and articulation of long-term outcomes.

The Manager of Social Enterprise at Eva's Phoenix, Andrew Macdonald, was chosen by *Print Action Magazine* as one of Canada's 50 most influential people in graphic communications, noting that: "Eva's Phoenix Print Shop provides opportunities for at-risk youth with much needed press and pre-press skills for the heart of Canada's printing community.

Source: A. Macdonald (2007) *Eva's Phoenix Print Shop*. Used with permission.

PART 3

Open-System Design Elements

4 The External Environment

© John Robertson/Alamy

A Look Inside

Nokia

Nokia (see photo) became the world's leading maker of cell phone handsets in 1998, and the giant Finnish company looked poised to run rivals out of the handset business for good. But by 2004, products that didn't match consumer needs and strained relationships with major customers had cost Nokia nearly a fifth of its 35 percent global market share. Revenue growth shifted into reverse and the stock took a nosedive.

What went wrong? For one thing, Nokia missed the hottest growth sector in cell phones, the market for mid-range models with cameras and high-resolution colour screens. Nokia's leaders chose instead to pump hundreds of millions of dollars into the development of "smart phones" that allow consumers to get on the Internet, play video games, listen to music, and watch movies or television shows. The problem was, the new phones proved too bulky and expensive for many consumers, who began turning instead to cheaper, stylish models from Motorola, Samsung, and Siemens. The clamshell design, in particular, which allowed users to fold the phone in half when it wasn't in use, fuelled a new cell phone boom in Europe and North America. Nokia had stuck to the "candy bar" handset and was caught without a competitor in the battle. Nokia also neglected some of its biggest customers. Mobile operators such as Orange SA, France Telecom SA's wireless unit, pushed for customized phones with special features that their customers wanted, but Nokia was slow to respond.

These missteps allowed rivals to gobble up market share. To get Nokia back on track, leaders have cranked up the introduction of new mid-range phones, slashed costs on low-end models for developing countries, and promised mobile operators to tailor phones to their specifications. Nokia also continues to invest heavily in gadgets that feature advanced software and run programs just like a computer. The key question is: Will customers want the gadgets Nokia is developing?[1]

Many companies, like Nokia, face tremendous uncertainty in dealing with the external environment. The only way a high-tech company like Nokia can continue to grow is through innovation, yet unless the company makes products that people want to buy, the huge investments in research and development will not pay off. Nokia is getting its strongest sales in China due to a growing demand for less expensive phones in rural areas. It remains to be seen if the company's new, technologically advanced products will catch on in the marketplace. Nokia still holds the largest share of the mobile phone market, but its sales and profits are stagnant while those of rival Samsung Electronics of Korea are zooming.[2] In the third quarter of 2007, Nokia reported a 39 percent of global market share.[3]

Some companies are surprised by shifts in the environment and are unable to quickly adapt to new competition, changing consumer interests, or innovative technologies. Music World and Sam the Record Man have gone out of business in the wake of Apple's iPod and other new channels that allow music lovers to download just what they want. Traditional music retailers are surviving only by diversifying into new areas or forming partnerships to create their own downloading services. Exhibit 4.1 shows the profound impact of the iPod! Similarly, in the airline industry, major carriers that use the traditional hub-and-spoke system, invented by American Airlines, have been pummelled by smaller, nimbler competitors like Ryanair and Southwest Airlines, which can prosper in today's difficult environment by keeping operations costs ultra-low.[4]

EXHIBIT 4.1
The Success of the iPod

The external environment, referred to throughout this chapter as "the environment," including international competition and events, is the source of turbulence, uncertainty, and major threats confronting today's organizations. The environment often imposes significant constraints on the choices that managers make for an organization.

Purpose of This Chapter

The purpose of this chapter is to develop a framework for assessing environments and how organizations respond to them. First, we will identify the environmental domain and the sectors that influence the organization. Then, we will explore two major environmental forces on the organization—the need for information and the need for resources. Organizations respond to these forces through structural design, planning systems, and attempts to change and control elements in the environment.

The Environmental Domain

In a broad sense the environment is infinite and includes everything outside the organization. However, the analysis presented here considers only those aspects of the environment to which the organization is sensitive and must respond to survive. Thus, **organizational environment** is defined as all elements that exist outside the boundary of the organization that have the potential to affect all or part of the organization.

The concept of environment in the discipline of organizational theory and design looks at the **green environment** only indirectly. In a thought-provoking article, Shrivastava argues that organization studies uses "denatured, narrow and parochial concepts of organizational environment" and goes on to argue that "[at] the present time, when environmental crises proliferate around the world, nature-centred organizational theories are particularly important."[5] This is particularly important as it is organizations, and their managers, that are responsible for much of the damage to the natural environment. In recognition of the environmental costs of its work, the National Hockey League Players Association (NHLPA) and the David Suzuki Foundation in late 2007 created a partnership that includes the NHLPA Carbon

Neutral Challenge and a program promoting action on climate change and environmental responsibility. ". . . NHLPA members are doing their part to reduce global warming through the NHLPA Carbon Neutral Challenge. This initiative, researched and designed specifically for the players by the David Suzuki Foundation, involves individual NHL players purchasing carbon credits to offset the carbon footprint produced by their extensive travel schedule. Over 350 players have already taken the challenge, with hundreds more expected to jump aboard in the coming weeks."[6]

The environment of an organization can be understood by analyzing its domain within external sectors. An organization's **domain** is the chosen field of action. It is the territory an organization stakes out for itself for its products, services, and markets served. Domain defines the organization's niche and defines those external sectors with which the organization will interact to accomplish its goals.

The environment comprises several **sectors** or subdivisions of the external environment that contain similar elements. Ten sectors can be analyzed for each organization: industry, raw materials, human resources, financial resources, market, technology, economic conditions, government, socio-cultural, and international. The sectors and a hypothetical organizational domain are illustrated in Exhibit 4.2; the sectors can be further subdivided into the task environment and general environment.

PDA Remember...

Classify elements in the external environment into ten sectors for analysis: industry, raw materials, human resources, financial resources, market, technology, economic conditions, government, socio-cultural, and international. Focus on sectors that may experience significant change at any time.

Task Environment

The **task environment** includes sectors with which the organization interacts directly and that have a direct impact on the organization's ability to achieve its goals. The task environment typically includes the industry, raw materials, and market sectors, and perhaps the human resources and international sectors.

The following examples illustrate how each of these sectors can affect organizations:

- In the *industry* sector, Wal-Mart has become the United States' largest food retailer, and nontraditional outlets such as club stores and discounters now account for more than 30 percent of the grocery market. This shift is forcing traditional supermarkets to find new ways to compete.
- An interesting example in the *raw materials sector* concerns the beverage can industry. Steelmakers owned the beverage can market until the mid-1960s, when Reynolds Aluminum Company launched a huge recycling program to gain a cheaper source of raw materials and make aluminium cans price competitive with steel.[7]
- In the *market sector*, keeping up with consumers' rapidly changing tastes is a real headache for big food companies such as Kraft and Nestlé SA. A few years ago, Kraft was at the top of the food chain, with a portfolio of brands including Philadelphia, Jell-O, Oreo, and Ritz. But growing consumer concerns over obesity and food-related health issues have taken a huge toll on Kraft's earnings. The company is now looking for growth primarily by expanding its organic and gourmet product offerings rather than pushing macaroni and cheese or cookies and crackers.[8]
- The *human resources sector* is of significant concern to every organization. Research shows that while secondary and post-secondary systems of education are producing graduates with good literacy and numeracy skills, there remains a gap between the demand for workers with strong literacy and numeracy skills and the supply of Canadians who possess them. "Many of Canada's competitors have recognized the need to increase the level and equitable distribution of

EXHIBIT 4.2
An Organization's Environment

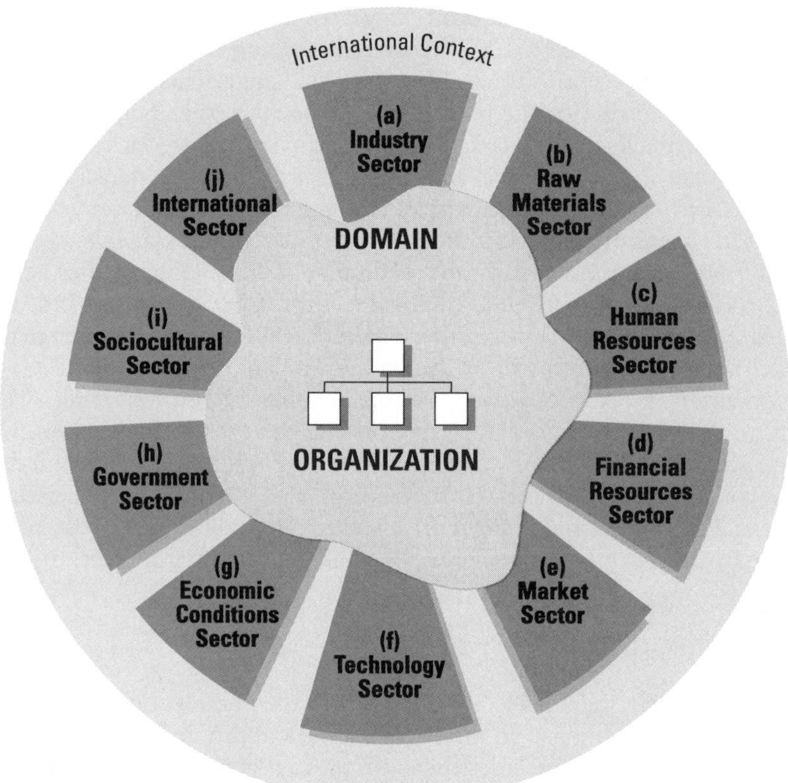

(a) Competitors, industry size and competitiveness, related industries
(b) Suppliers, manufacturers, real estate, services
(c) Labour market, employment agencies, universities, training schools, employees in other companies, unionization
(d) Stock markets, banks, credit unions, private investors
(e) Customers, clients, potential users of products and services
(f) Techniques of production, science, computers, information technology, e-commerce
(g) Recession, unemployment rate, inflation rate, rate of investment, economics, growth
(h) City, provincial, federal laws and regulations, taxes, services, court system, political processes
(i) Age, values, beliefs, education, religion, work ethic, consumer and green movements
(j) Competition from and acquisition by foreign firms, entry into overseas markets, foreign customs, regulations, exchange rate

adult literacy and numeracy skills. The [United Kingdom], Sweden, Ireland and the Netherlands have all increased their level of investment in adult skills, including literacy and numeracy."[9] However, Canada has not increased its investment in talent development and training for the last ten years.[10]

- For many companies today, the *international sector* is also a part of the task environment because of globalization and intense competition. Outsourcing has become a hot-button issue, with companies in industries from toy manufacturing to information technology sending work to lower-wage countries to become more competitive. Biotechnology and life sciences firms once seemed immune to the trend, but that too is changing. Large drug manufacturers are facing pressures as smaller firms gain cost advantages by outsourcing to companies such as WuXi Pharmatech in Shanghai or Biocon in India.[11]

General Environment

The **general environment** includes those sectors that might not have a direct impact on the daily operations of a firm but will indirectly influence it. The general environment often includes the government, socio-cultural, economic conditions, technology, and financial resources sectors. These sectors affect all organizations eventually. Consider the following examples.

- In the *government sector*, new European Union (EU) environmental and consumer protection legislation could cause challenges for some North American firms. For example, one new rule requires chemical makers that do business in EU countries to run safety and environmental impact tests on more than 30,000 chemicals, a process that could cost these companies more than $7 billion. Other new regulations require companies to pick up the tab for recycling the products they sell in the EU.[12]
- Shifting demographics is a significant element in the *socio-cultural sector*. A 2007 study by Statistics Canada found that foreign-born people make up almost 20 percent of Canada's population. As the birth rate declines, immigration is expected to be the primary source of labour. ProMation Engineering, located in Mississauga, Ontario, produces robotics for the automotive industry, and has 77 employees who speak a total of 27 languages![13]
- General *economic conditions* often affect the way a company does business. Germany's two most celebrated daily newspapers, the *Frankfurter Allgemeine Zeitung* and the *Süddeutsche Zeitung*, expanded pell-mell during the economic boom of the late 1990s. When the economy crashed, both papers found themselves in dire financial circumstances and have had to cut jobs, close regional offices, scrap special sections, and cut out customized inserts.[14]
- The *technology sector* is an area in which massive changes have occurred in recent years, from digital music and video recorders to advances in cloning technology and stem-cell research. One technology having a tremendous impact on organizations is online software that allows people to easily create and maintain blogs. One estimate is that, in early 2005, 23,000 new blogs were being created each day, with everyday people widely publishing information on everything from bad customer service to poor product performance.[15] By early 2006, there were 100 million blogs around the world, and they continue to proliferate.[16]
- All organizations have to be concerned with *financial resources*, but this sector is often first and foremost in the minds of entrepreneurs starting a new business. Ken Vaughan started a gas-mask business to take advantage of a boom in the asbestos-removal business. When the boom ended, it looked like Neoterik Health Technologies would end too. But after the terrorist attacks of September 11, 2001, Vaughan attracted the attention of venture capitalists, who were eager to invest financial resources in a company that could profit from concerns over U.S. security.[17]

International Context

The international sector can directly affect many organizations, and it has become extremely important in the last few years. In addition, all domestic sectors can be affected by international events. Despite the significance of international events for today's organizations, many students fail to appreciate the importance of international events and still think domestically. Think again. Even if you stay in your hometown, your company may be purchased tomorrow by the English, Americans, Japanese, or Germans. The Japanese alone own thousands of North American companies, including steel mills, rubber and tire factories, automobile assembly plants, and auto parts suppliers.[18] For example, Sleeman Breweries, Canada's third-largest beer producer, was taken over by Japan's Sapporo Breweries in 2006.[19]

The distinctions between foreign and domestic operations have become increasingly irrelevant. For example, in the auto industry, Ford owns Sweden's Volvo, while Chrysler, still considered one of America's Big Three automakers, was owned by Germany's DaimlerChrysler and builds its PT Cruiser in Mexico. Toyota is a Japanese company but it has built more than 10 million vehicles in North American factories. In addition, Canadian organizations are involved in thousands of partnerships and alliances with firms all around the world. For example, Sea Breeze Power Corporation, headquartered in Vancouver, is a member of the Methane to Markets Partnerships, which is "an international initiative that advances cost-effective, near-term methane recovery and use as a clean energy source. The goal of the Partnership is to reduce global methane emissions in order to enhance economic growth, strengthen energy security, improve air quality, improve industrial safety, and reduce emissions of greenhouse gases."[20] These increasing global interconnections have both positive and negative implications for organizations. Because of the significance of the international sector and its tremendous impact on organizational design, this topic will be covered in detail in Chapter 6.

The growing importance of the international sector means that the environment for all organizations is becoming extremely complex and extremely competitive. However, every organization faces uncertainty domestically as well as globally. Consider how changing elements in the various environmental sectors have created uncertainty for advertising agencies such as Ogilvy & Mather.

In Practice
Ogilvy & Mather

On November 9, 2007, Ogilvy & Mather received the Grand Prix at the Cassies Awards for its work on Dove's campaign for the Dove Self-Esteem Fund. According to Nancy Vonk, co-chief creative officer, "[it's] been the best year ever in many, many ways . . . "[We] really turned a corner from the traditional ad agency perch . . . to approaching the task in a much more holistic way and in a media-neutral way."[21]

However, it was not too long ago that Ogilvy & Mather, one of the most respected advertising agencies on Madison Avenue and beyond, was reduced to competing for business in a live online auction. The agency won the account, but that eased the pain only slightly. The world has changed dramatically since Ogilvy & Mather's founders made deals with corporate CEOs over golf games and could reach 90 percent of the North American public with a prime-time commercial on network television. Today, agency executives frequently have to dicker with people from their client's procurement department, who are used to beating down suppliers on the price of cardboard boxes or paper bags. Clients want to get the best deal, and they want to see a whole lot more than a couple of television spots.

The economic decline that followed the crash of the dot-coms and the September 11, 2001 attacks in the United States led to the worst advertising recession in more than half a century. Marketing budgets were often the first to be cut, and worldwide ad spending declined 7 percent in 2001. The agencies laid off 40,000 employees, nearly 20 percent of their workforce. The weak economic climate also led to a major change in how corporations pay for advertising. Up until that time, most clients paid their agencies a 15 percent commission on media purchases rather than paying them directly for their work. Today, though, many companies have cut out commissions altogether. Corporate procurement departments are demanding that the agencies clearly spell out their labour costs and how they are billing the client. The agencies are having a hard time making the shift.

And that's not even the biggest problem the ad agencies are having. Traditionally, agencies have relied on television and print media, but that's just not working anymore. New forms of media such as the Internet, video on demand, cellular phones, and video games are taking up a larger and larger percentage of people's time. Corporations are clamouring for more innovative low-key approaches, such as product placements in video games or products integrated into television shows and music events, as well as lower-cost options such as direct mail and Internet advertising. Yet the agencies have been slow to adapt, still clinging to the notion that making good half-million-dollar 30-second television commercials will pay off.

The combination of weak economic conditions, media fragmentation, new technologies, and changing habits has the advertising industry reeling. Although many of these developments have been predicted for some time, the big agencies were caught unaware when they actually came to pass. As Ogilvy & Mather's CEO, Shelly Lazurus, says of the recent past, "These have not been the best years."[22]

Advertising agencies aren't the only organizations that have had a hard time adapting to massive shifts in the environment. In the following sections, we will discuss in greater detail how organizations can cope with and respond to environmental uncertainty and instability.

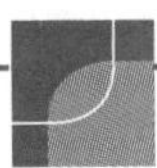

Environmental Uncertainty

How does the environment influence an organization? The patterns and events occurring in the environment can be described along several dimensions, such as whether the environment is stable or unstable, homogeneous or heterogeneous, simple or complex; the *munificence*, or amount of resources available to support the organization's growth; whether those resources are concentrated or dispersed; and the degree of consensus in the environment regarding the organization's intended domain.[23] These dimensions boil down to two essential ways the environment influences organizations: (1) the need for information about the environment and (2) the need for resources from the environment. The environmental conditions of complexity and change create a greater need to gather information and to respond based on that information. The organization also is concerned with scarce material and financial resources, and with the need to ensure availability of resources.

Environmental uncertainty applies primarily to those sectors that an organization deals with on a regular, day-to-day basis. Recall the earlier discussion of the general environment and the task environment. Although sectors of the general environment—such as economic conditions, social trends, or technological changes—can create uncertainty for organizations, determining an organization's environmental uncertainty generally means focusing on sectors of the *task environment*, such as how many elements the organization deals with regularly, how rapidly these elements change, and so forth. To assess uncertainty, each sector of the organization's task environment can be analyzed along dimensions such as stability or instability and degree of complexity.[24] The total amount of uncertainty felt by an organization is the uncertainty accumulated across environmental sectors.

Organizations must cope with and manage uncertainty to be effective. **Uncertainty** means that decision makers do not have sufficient information about environmental factors, and they have a difficult time predicting external changes. Uncertainty increases the risk of failure for organizational responses and makes it difficult to compute costs and probabilities associated with decision alternatives.[25] The remainder of this section will focus on the information perspective, which is concerned with uncertainty created by the extent to which the environment is simple or complex and the extent to which events are stable or unstable. Later in the chapter, we discuss how organizations control the environment to acquire needed resources.

Simple–Complex Dimension

The **simple–complex dimension** concerns environmental complexity, which refers to heterogeneity, or the number and dissimilarity of external elements relevant to an organization's operations. The more external factors that regularly influence the organization and the greater number of other organizations in an organization's domain, the greater the complexity. A complex environment is one in which the organization interacts with and is influenced by numerous diverse and different external elements. In a simple environment, the organization interacts with and is influenced by only a few similar external elements.

Aerospace firms such as Boeing Company and Europe's Airbus operate in a complex environment, as do universities. Universities span a large number of technologies and are continually buffeted by social, cultural, and value changes. Universities also must cope with numerous ever-changing government regulations, competition for quality students and highly educated employees, and scarce financial resources for many programs. They deal with granting agencies, professional and scientific associations, alumni, parents, foundations, legislators, community residents, international agencies, donors, corporations, and athletic teams. This large number of external elements makes up the organization's domain, creating a complex environment. On the other hand, a family-owned hardware store operating in the suburbs competes in a simple environment. The store does not have to deal with complex technologies or extensive government regulations, and cultural and social changes have little impact. Human resources are not a problem because the store is run by family members and part-time help. The only external elements of real importance are a few competitors, suppliers, and customers.

Stable–Unstable Dimension

The **stable–unstable dimension** refers to whether elements in the environment are dynamic. An environmental domain is stable if it remains the same over a period of months or years, or experiences readily predictable change. Under unstable conditions, environmental elements shift abruptly and unexpectedly. Environmental domains seem to be increasingly unstable for most organizations. This chapter's Book Mark examines the volatile nature of today's business world and gives some tips for managing in a fast-shifting environment.

Book Mark 4.0 (HAVE YOU READ THIS BOOK?)

Confronting Reality: Doing What Matters to Get Things Right

By Lawrence A. Bossidy and Ram Charan

The business world has changed in recent years and will continue to change at an increasingly rapid pace. That's the reality that spurred Larry Bossidy, retired chairman and CEO of Honeywell International, and Ram Charan, a noted author, speaker, and business consultant, to write *Confronting Reality: Doing What Matters to Get Things Right*. Too many managers, they believe, are tempted to hide their heads in the sand of financial issues rather than face the confusion and complexity of the organization's environment.

LESSONS FOR FACING REALITY

For many companies, today's environment is characterized by global hyper-competition, declining prices, and the growing power of consumers. Bossidy and Charan offer some lessons to leaders for navigating a fast-changing world.

- *Understand the environment as it is now and is likely to be in the future, rather than as it was in the past.* Relying on the past and conventional wisdom can lead to disaster. Kmart, for example, stuck to its old formula as Wal-Mart gobbled its customers and carved out a new business model.
- *Seek out and welcome diverse and unorthodox ideas.* Managers need to be proactive and open-minded toward conversing with employees, suppliers, customers, colleagues, and anyone else they come in contact with. What are people thinking about? What changes and opportunities do they see? What worries them about the future?
- *Avoid the common causes of manager failure to confront reality: filtered information, selective hearing, wishful thinking, fear, emotional overinvestment in a failing course of action, and unrealistic expectations.* For example, when sales and profits fell off a cliff at data-storage giant EMC Corporation in early 2001, managers displayed a bias toward hearing good news and believed the company was experiencing only a blip in the growth curve. When Joe Tucci was named CEO, however, he was determined to find out if the slump was temporary. By talking directly with top leaders at his customers' organizations, Tucci was able to face the reality that EMC's existing business model based on high-cost technology was dead. Tucci implemented a new business model to fit that reality.
- *Ruthlessly assess your organization.* Understanding the internal environment is just as important. Managers need to evaluate whether their company has the talent, commitment, and attitude needed to drive the important changes. At EMC, Tucci realized his sales force needed an attitude shift to sell software, services, and business solutions rather than just expensive hardware. The arrogant, hard-driving sales tactics of the past had to be replaced with a softer, more customer-oriented approach.

STAYING ALIVE

Staying alive in today's business environment requires that managers stay alert. Managers should always be looking at their competitors, broad industry trends, technological changes, shifting government policies, changing market forces, and economic developments. At the same time, they work hard to stay in touch with what their customers really think and really want. By doing so, leaders can confront reality and be poised for change.

Confronting Reality: Doing What Matters to Get Things Right, by Lawrence A. Bossidy and Ram Charan, is published by Crown Business Publishing.

Instability may occur when competitors react with aggressive moves and countermoves regarding advertising and new products, as happened with Nokia, described in the chapter opening. Sometimes specific, unpredictable events—such as Janet Jackson's so-called wardrobe malfunction at the 2004 Super Bowl halftime show, accounts of anthrax-laced letters being sent through the U.S. Postal Service, or the discovery of heart problems related to pain drugs such as Vioxx and Celebrex—create unstable conditions. Today, "hate sites" on the World Wide Web, such as *Ihatemcdonalds.com* and *Walmartsucks.com*, are an important source of instability for scores of companies. In addition, freewheeling bloggers can destroy a company's reputation virtually overnight. Kryptonite's reputation in bicycle locks plummeted after a Web log posted that the locks could be opened with a Bic pen. Within 10 days, Kryptonite announced a free product exchange that would cost it about $10 million.[26]

Although environments are more unstable for most organizations today, an example of a traditionally stable environment is a public utility.[27] A gradual increase in demand may occur, which is easily predicted over time. Toy companies, by contrast, have an unstable environment. Hot new toys are difficult to predict, a problem compounded by the fact that children are losing interest in toys at a younger age, their interest captured by video games, cable TV, and the Internet. Adding to the instability for toymakers such as Mattel and Hasbro is the shrinking retail market, with big toy retailers going out of business trying to compete with discounters such as Wal-Mart. Toy manufacturers often find their biggest products languishing on shelves as shoppers turn to less-expensive knock-offs produced for Wal-Mart by low-cost manufacturers in China.[28] As well, the major toy makers have had to make massive recalls because of concerns about the lead content of many of the toys made in China.[29]

Framework

The simple–complex and stable–unstable dimensions are combined into a framework for assessing environmental uncertainty in Exhibit 4.3. In the *simple, stable* environment, uncertainty is low. There are only a few external elements to contend with, and they tend to remain stable. The *complex, stable* environment represents somewhat greater uncertainty. A large number of elements have to be scanned, analyzed, and acted upon for the organization to perform well. External elements do not change rapidly or unexpectedly in this environment.

Even greater uncertainty is felt in the *simple, unstable* environment.[30] Rapid change creates uncertainty for managers. Even though the organization has few external elements, those elements are hard to predict, and they react unexpectedly to organizational initiatives. The greatest uncertainty for an organization occurs in the *complex, unstable* environment. A large number of elements impinge upon the organization, and they shift frequently or react strongly to organizational initiatives. When several sectors change simultaneously, the environment becomes turbulent.[31]

A beer distributor functions in a simple, stable environment. Demand for beer changes only gradually; for example, there was little change in demand for domestic beer between 2005 and 2006.[32] The distributor has an established delivery route, and supplies of beer arrive on schedule. Appliance manufacturers and insurance companies are in somewhat stable, complex environments. A large number of external elements are present, but although they change, changes are gradual and predictable.

Toy manufacturers are in simple, unstable environments. Organizations that design, make, and sell toys, as well as those that are involved in the clothing or music industry, face shifting supply and demand. Most e-commerce companies focus on a specific competitive niche and, hence, operate in simple but unstable environments as well. Although there may be few elements to contend with, such as technology and competitors, they are difficult to predict and change abruptly and unexpectedly.

The telecommunications industry and the airline industry face complex, unstable environments. Many external sectors are changing simultaneously. In the case of airlines, in just a few years they were confronted with an air-traffic controller shortage, price cuts from low-cost carriers such as WestJet Airlines, soaring fuel prices, the entry of new competitors, a series of major air-traffic disasters, and a drastic decline in customer demand following the September 11, 2001 attacks. WestJet Airlines itself faces possible competition from NewAir & Tours, a Calgary-based carrier that will fly travellers in smaller cities to larger ones. NewAir & Tours was

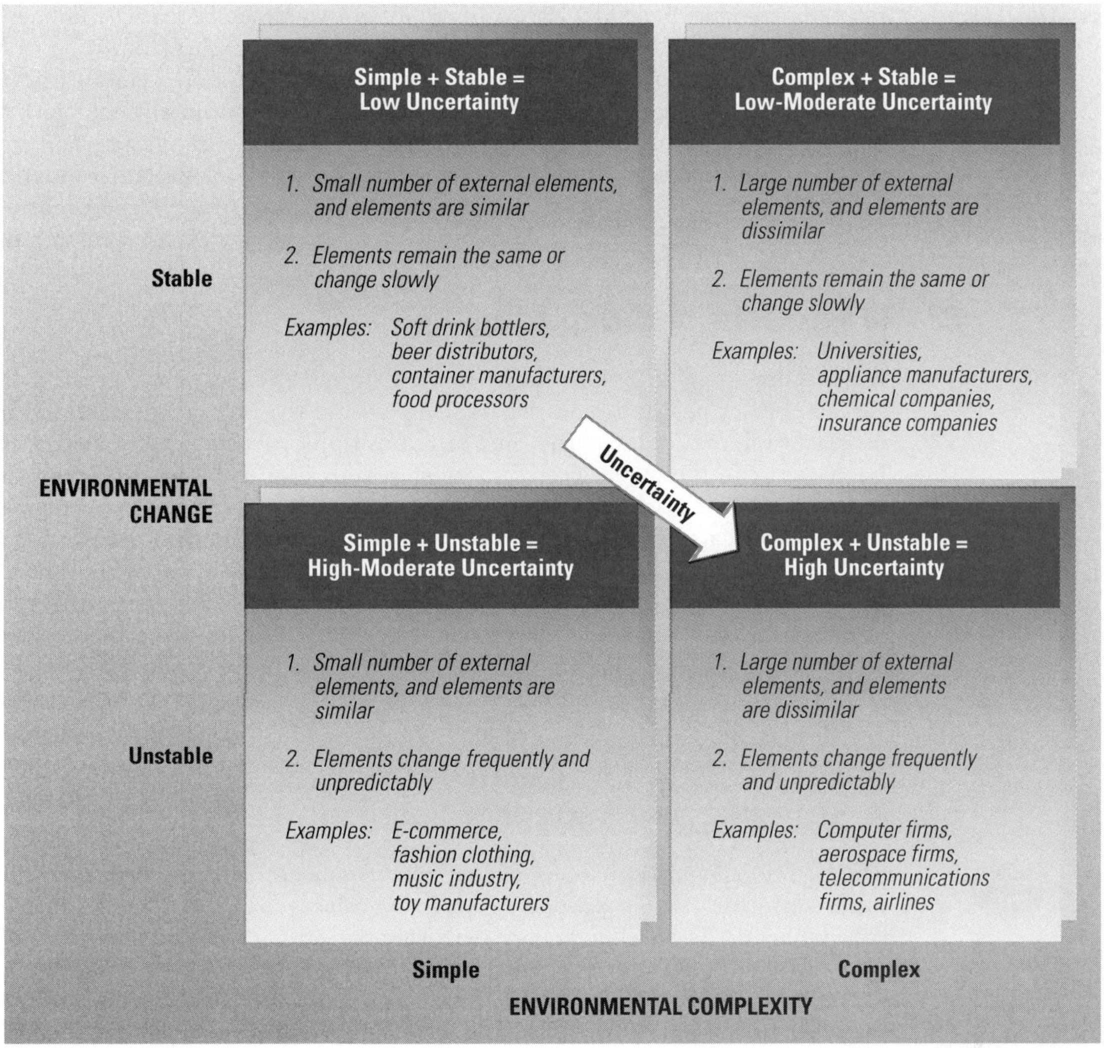

ENVIRONMENTAL CHANGE	Simple	Complex
Stable	**Simple + Stable = Low Uncertainty** 1. *Small number of external elements, and elements are similar* 2. *Elements remain the same or change slowly* *Examples: Soft drink bottlers, beer distributors, container manufacturers, food processors*	**Complex + Stable = Low-Moderate Uncertainty** 1. *Large number of external elements, and elements are dissimilar* 2. *Elements remain the same or change slowly* *Examples: Universities, appliance manufacturers, chemical companies, insurance companies*
Unstable	**Simple + Unstable = High-Moderate Uncertainty** 1. *Small number of external elements, and elements are similar* 2. *Elements change frequently and unpredictably* *Examples: E-commerce, fashion clothing, music industry, toy manufacturers*	**Complex + Unstable = High Uncertainty** 1. *Large number of external elements, and elements are dissimilar* 2. *Elements change frequently and unpredictably* *Examples: Computer firms, aerospace firms, telecommunications firms, airlines*

Uncertainty

ENVIRONMENTAL COMPLEXITY

EXHIBIT 4.3
Framework for Assessing Environmental Uncertainty
Source: Adapted and reprinted from "Characteristics of Perceived Environments and Perceived Environmental Uncertainty," by Robert B. Duncan, published in *Administrative Science Quarterly* 17 (1972), 313–327, by permission of *The Administrative Science Quarterly*. Copyright © 1972 by Cornell University.

started by four former WestJet Airlines executives and is expected to be in operation in 2008–2009.[33]

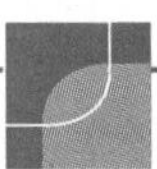

Adapting to Environmental Uncertainty

Once you see how environments differ with respect to change and complexity, the next question is, "How do organizations adapt to each level of environmental uncertainty?" Environmental uncertainty represents an important contingency for organizational structure and internal behaviours. Recall from Chapter 3 that organizations facing uncertainty generally have a more horizontal structure that encourages cross-functional communication and collaboration to help the organization adapt to changes in the environment. In this section we discuss in more detail how the environment affects organizations. An organization in a certain environment will be managed and controlled differently from an organization in an uncertain environment with respect to positions and departments, organizational differentiation and integration, control processes, and future planning and forecasting. Organizations need to have the right fit between internal structure and the external environment.

Positions and Departments

As the complexity and uncertainty in the external environment increases, so does the number of positions and departments within the organization, which in turn increases internal complexity. This relationship is part of being an open system. Each sector in the external environment requires an employee or department to deal with it. The human resource department deals with unemployed people who want to work for the company. The marketing department finds customers. Procurement employees obtain raw materials from hundreds of suppliers. The finance group deals with bankers. The legal department works with the courts and government agencies. Many companies have added e-business departments to handle electronic commerce and information technology departments to deal with the increasing complexity of computerized information and knowledge management systems.

Buffering and Boundary Spanning

The traditional approach to coping with environmental uncertainty was to establish buffer departments. The purpose of **buffering roles** is to absorb uncertainty from the environment.[34] The technical core performs the primary production activity of an organization. Buffer departments surround the technical core and exchange materials, resources, and money between the environment and the organization. They help the technical core function efficiently. The purchasing department buffers the technical core by stockpiling supplies and raw materials. The human resource department buffers the technical core by handling the uncertainty associated with finding, hiring, and training production employees.

PDA Remember...

Scan the external environment for threats, changes, and opportunities. Use boundary-spanning roles, such as market research and competitive-intelligence departments, to bring into the organization information about changes in the environment. Enhance boundary-spanning capabilities when the environment is uncertain.

A newer approach some organizations are trying is to drop the buffers and expose the technical core to the uncertain environment. These organizations no longer create buffers because they believe being well connected to customers and suppliers is more important than internal efficiency. For example, John Deere has assembly-line workers visiting local farms to determine and respond to customer concerns. Whirlpool Corporation pays hundreds of customers to test computer-simulated products and features.[35] Opening up the organization to the environment makes it more fluid and adaptable.

Boundary-spanning roles link and coordinate an organization with key elements in the external environment. Boundary spanning is primarily concerned with the exchange of information to (1) detect and bring into the organization information about changes in the environment and (2) send information into the environment that presents the organization in a favourable light.[36]

Organizations have to keep in touch with what is going on in the environment so that managers can respond to market changes and other developments. A study of high-tech firms found that 97 percent of competitive failures resulted from lack of attention to market changes or the failure to act on vital information.[37] To detect and bring important information into the organization, boundary personnel scan the environment. For example, a market-research department scans and monitors trends in consumer tastes. Boundary spanners in engineering and R&D departments scan new technological developments, innovations, and raw materials. Boundary spanners prevent the organization from stagnating by keeping top managers informed about environmental changes. Often, the greater the uncertainty in the environment, the greater the importance of boundary spanners.[38]

One new approach to boundary spanning is business intelligence, which refers to the high-tech analysis of large amounts of internal and external data to spot patterns and relationships that might be significant. For example, the federal government provides business intelligence through its Innovation in Canada branch.[39] However, according to a 2005 Ipsos Reid poll, the use of business intelligence is not extensive or sophisticated, and focuses only on knowledge management, data mining, environmental scanning and competitive intelligence.[40]

Business intelligence is related to another important area of boundary spanning, known as *competitive intelligence* (CI). Membership in the Society of Competitive Intelligence Professionals has more than doubled since 1997, and colleges are setting up master's degree programs in CI to respond to the growing demand for these professionals in organizations.[41] Competitive intelligence gives top executives a systematic way to collect and analyze public information about rivals and use it to make better decisions.[42] Using techniques that range from Internet surfing to digging through trash cans, intelligence professionals dig up information on competitors' new products, manufacturing costs, or training methods, and share it with top leaders.

In today's turbulent environment, many successful companies involve everyone in boundary-spanning activities. People at the grass-roots level are often able to see and interpret changes or problems sooner than managers, who are typically more removed from the day-to-day work.[43] At Ottawa-based and IBM-owned Cognos, which sells planning and budgeting programs to large corporations, any of the company's 3,000 employees can submit scoops about competitors through an internal website called Street Fighter. Each day, R&D and sales managers pore over the dozens of entries. Good tips are rewarded with prizes.[44]

The boundary task of sending information into the environment to represent the organization is used to influence other people's perception of the organization. In the marketing department, advertising and salespeople represent the organization to customers. Purchasers may call on suppliers and describe purchasing needs. The legal department informs lobbyists and elected officials about the organization's needs or views on political matters. Many companies set up their own web pages to present the organization in a favourable light. For example, to counteract hate sites that criticize its labour practices in developing countries, Nike has created websites specifically to tell its side of the story.[45]

All organizations have to keep in touch with the environment. Here's how Joe Fresh Style, a growing fashion retailer that markets high-quality inexpensive apparel, spans the boundary in the shifting environment of the fashion industry.

In Practice
Joe Fresh Style

Joe Mimran has been creating fashion trends for many years. Mimran is a chartered accountant by training and practised his profession for a couple of years before joining his mother and his brother in their small clothing company. The family eventually hired designer Alfred Sung and soon the Alfred Sung brand was a success here and in the United States. In 1983, Alfred Sung was described as the King of Fashion by *Maclean's*.

Then Mimran realized that he was missing out on the casual apparel business, so "[he] started to play around with a bunch of concepts and came up with the notion of being vertically integrated with one thumbprint from beginning to end, so nobody would tamper with the vision."[46] Mimran decided to start Club Monaco on Queen Street West in Toronto; the company grew rapidly. In 48 months, 50 new stores opened in Canada and around the world. According to Mimran, "[the] brand was very urban-driven . . . because of this, growth in Canada was limited."[47] He also ventured into home furnishings through his Caban stores. In 1999, he sold both Club Monaco and Caban to the Ralph Lauren Corporation and did well on the sale.

After the sale, Mimran started Joseph Mimran and Associates and worked with a few clients. He was approached by Loblaw Companies to develop an apparel line—the Joe Fresh Style line. Now available in many Loblaw stores, the line consists of classic but stylish casuals with an average price of $15. The line has been well received and is continuing to grow in its range of apparel. According to Mimran, he is able to keep the prices low by "[being] really smart with your fabric and color choices. It's that simple. You have to understand the production process, . . . Of a hundred [fabric] swatches, you have to pick the right one." He goes on to note that "Canadian customers are very much value-driven, . . . They prefer classics that run to the core. And they really love fashion."[48]

Differentiation and Integration

Another response to environmental uncertainty is the amount of differentiation and integration among departments. Organizational **differentiation** is "the differences in cognitive and emotional orientations among managers in different functional departments, and the difference in formal structure among these departments."[49] When the external environment is complex and rapidly changing, organizational departments become highly specialized to handle the uncertainty in their external sector. Success in each sector requires special expertise and behaviour. Employees in an R&D department thus have unique attitudes, values, goals, and education that distinguish them from employees in manufacturing or sales departments.

A study by Paul Lawrence and Jay Lorsch examined three organizational departments—manufacturing, research, and sales—in ten corporations.[50] This study found that each department evolved toward a different orientation and structure to deal with specialized parts of the external environment. The market, scientific, and manufacturing subenvironments identified by Lawrence and Lorsch are illustrated in Exhibit 4.4. Each department interacted with different external groups. The differences that evolved among departments within the organizations are shown in Exhibit 4.5. To work effectively with the scientific subenvironment, R&D had a goal of quality work, a long time horizon (up to five years), an informal structure, and task-oriented employees. Sales was at the opposite extreme. It had a goal of customer satisfaction, was oriented toward the short term (two weeks or so), had a very formal structure, and was socially oriented.

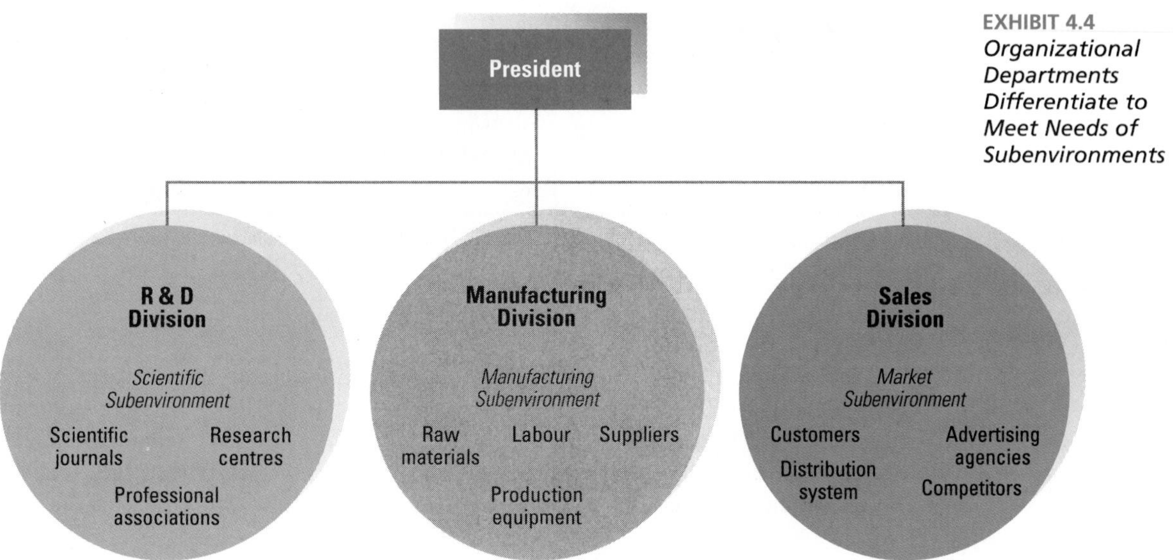

EXHIBIT 4.4
Organizational Departments Differentiate to Meet Needs of Subenvironments

One outcome of high differentiation is that coordination among departments becomes difficult. More time and resources must be devoted to achieving coordination when attitudes, goals, and work orientation differ so widely. **Integration** is the quality of collaboration among departments.[51] Formal integrators are often required to coordinate departments. When the environment is highly uncertain, frequent changes require more information processing to achieve horizontal coordination, so integrators become a necessary addition to the organizational structure. Sometimes integrators are called liaison personnel, project managers, brand managers, or coordinators. As illustrated in Exhibit 4.6, organizations with highly uncertain environments and a highly differentiated structure assign about 22 percent of management personnel to integration activities, such as serving on committees, on task forces, or in liaison roles.[52] In organizations characterized by very simple, stable environments, almost no managers are assigned to integration roles. Exhibit 4.6 shows that, as environmental uncertainty increases, so does differentiation among departments; hence, the organization must assign a larger percentage of managers to coordinating roles.

EXHIBIT 4.5
Differences in Goals and Orientations Among Organizational Departments

Characteristic	R&D Department	Manufacturing Department	Sales Department
Goals	New developments, quality	Efficient production	Customer satisfaction
Time horizon	Long	Short	Short
Interpersonal orientation	Mostly task	Task	Social
Formality of structure	Low	High	High

Source: Based on Paul R. Lawrence and Jay W. Lorsch, *Organization and Environment* (Homewood, Ill.: Irwin, 1969), 23–29.

EXHIBIT 4.6
Environmental Uncertainty and Organizational Integrators

Industry	Plastics	Foods	Container
Environmental uncertainty	High	Moderate	Low
Departmental differentiation	High	Moderate	Low
Percentage of management in integrating roles	22%	17%	0%

Source: Based on Jay W. Lorsch and Paul R. Lawrence, "Environmental Factors and Organizational Integration," *Organizational Planning: Cases and Concepts* (Homewood, Ill.: Irwin and Dorsey, 1972), 45.

Lawrence and Lorsch's research concluded that organizations perform better when the levels of differentiation and integration match the level of uncertainty in the environment. Organizations that performed well in uncertain environments had high levels of both differentiation and integration, while those performing well in less-uncertain environments had lower levels of differentiation and integration.

Organic versus Mechanistic Management Processes

PDA Remember...

Match internal organizational structure to the external environment. If the external environment is complex, make the organizational structure complex. Associate a stable environment with a mechanistic structure and an unstable environment with an organic structure. If the external environment is both complex and changing, make the organization highly differentiated and organic, and use mechanisms to achieve coordination across departments.

Another response to environmental uncertainty is the amount of formal structure and control imposed on employees. Tom Burns and G. M. Stalker observed 20 industrial firms in England and discovered that external environment was related to internal management structure.[53] When the external environment was stable, the internal organization was characterized by rules, procedures, and a clear hierarchy of authority. Organizations were formalized. They were also centralized, with most decisions made at the top. Burns and Stalker called this a **mechanistic** organizational system.

In rapidly changing environments, the internal organization was much looser, free-flowing, and adaptive. Rules and regulations often were not written down or, if written down, were ignored. People had to find their own way through the system to figure out what to do. The hierarchy of authority was not clear. Decision-making authority was decentralized. Burns and Stalker used the term **organic** to characterize this type of management structure.

Exhibit 4.7 summarizes the differences in organic and mechanistic systems. As environmental uncertainty increases, organizations tend to become more organic, which means decentralizing authority and responsibility to lower levels, encouraging employees to take care of problems by working directly with one another, encouraging teamwork, and taking an informal approach to assigning tasks and responsibility. Thus, the organization is more fluid and is able to adapt continually to changes in the external environment.[54]

The learning organization, described in Chapter 1, and the horizontal and virtual network structures, described in Chapter 3, are organic organizational forms used by companies to compete in rapidly changing environments. Guiltless Gourmet, headquartered in New Jersey, sells low-fat tortilla chips and other high-quality snack foods. The company shifted to a flexible network structure to remain competitive when large companies like Frito Lay entered the low-fat snack-food market. The company redesigned itself to become basically a full-time marketing organization, while production and other activities were outsourced. An 18,000-square-foot plant in Austin, Texas, was closed and the workforce cut from 125 to about 10 core people who handle marketing and sales promotions. The flexible structure allows Guiltless Gourmet to adapt quickly to changing market conditions.[55]

EXHIBIT 4.7
Mechanistic and Organic Forms

Mechanistic	Organic
1. Tasks are broken down into specialized, separate parts. 2. Tasks are rigidly defined. 3. There is a strict hierarchy of authority and control, and there are many rules. 4. Knowledge and control of tasks are centralized at the top of the organization. 5. Communication is vertical.	1. Employees contribute to the common tasks of the department. 2. Tasks are adjusted and redefined through employee teamwork. 3. There is less hierarchy of authority and control, and there are few rules. 4. Knowledge and control of tasks are located anywhere in the organization. 5. Communication is horizontal.

Source: Adapted from Gerald Zaltman, Robert Duncan, and Jonny Holbek, *Innovations and Organizations* (New York: Wiley, 1973), 131.

Planning, Forecasting, and Responsiveness

The whole point of increasing internal integration and shifting to more organic processes is to enhance the organization's ability to quickly respond to sudden changes in an uncertain environment. It might seem that in an environment where everything is changing all the time, planning is useless. However, in uncertain environments, planning and environmental forecasting actually become *more* important as a way to keep the organization geared for a coordinated, speedy response. Japanese electronic giants such as Toshiba and Fujitsu, for example, were caught off guard by a combination of nimble new competitors, rapid technological change, deregulation, the declining stability of Japan's banking system, and the sudden end of the 1990s, technology boom. Lulled into complacency by years of success, Japan's industrial electronics companies were unprepared to respond to these dramatic changes and lost billions.[56]

When the environment is stable, the organization can concentrate on current operational problems and day-to-day efficiency. Long-range planning and forecasting are not needed because environmental demands in the future will be the same as they are today.

With increasing environmental uncertainty, planning and forecasting become necessary.[57] Planning can soften the adverse impact of external shifts. Organizations that have unstable environments often establish a separate planning department. In an unpredictable environment, planners scan environmental elements and analyze potential moves and countermoves by other organizations. Planning can be extensive and may forecast various scenarios for environmental contingencies. With scenario building, managers mentally rehearse different scenarios based on anticipating various changes that could affect the organization. Scenarios are like stories that offer alternative, vivid pictures of what the future will look like and how managers will respond. Royal Dutch/Shell Oil has long used scenario building and has been a leader in speedy response to massive changes that other organizations failed to perceive until it was too late.[58]

Planning, however, cannot substitute for other actions, such as effective boundary spanning and adequate internal integration and coordination. The organizations that are most successful in uncertain environments are those that keep everyone in close touch with the environment so they can spot threats and opportunities, enabling the organization to respond immediately.

Leading *by Design*

Manitoba Telecom Services (MTS)

Manitoba Telecom Services (MTS) is the leading telecommunications company in Manitoba. The company handles local telephone service throughout Manitoba, and also offers cellular communication, paging, and group communication networks. The company also offers long-distance service throughout the province. The company's MTS Media subsidiary produces advertising and information directories, especially through the Internet. Another subsidiary, Qunara, provides consulting services on information security, web management, and information management. MTS also owns a 40 percent share in Bell West, a local and long-distance communications carrier. MTS was formerly known as the Manitoba Telephone System, a public utility owned and managed by the province of Manitoba. The utility became a public for-profit company in 1996. MTS also owns MTS Allstream whose national broadband fibre network spans more than 24,300 kilometres.[59] MTS has had a rocky history but, by 2003, it was being described as the belle of the telco ball by *Canadian Business*. It has most of the local and long-distance phone service and 60 percent of the Internet service in the province. Its principal competitors are Shaw Communications and Rogers Wireless Communication.[60]

In 1993, MTS and its union, the Communication, Energy & Paperworkers Union, engaged in a joint work redesign of its operator services. The redesign project was named M-POWER (i.e., Professional Operators with Enhanced Responsibilities). The catalyst for the redesign was a power surge in MTS's Winnipeg office after which operators began to experience shocks. A work stoppage was ordered; however, a technical analysis found no problems with the equipment. A joint committee of management and union representatives was created to understand and remedy the situation. It was at the urging of Gareth Morgan, one of Canada's pre-eminent theorists in organization theory and design, that the joint committee was created. The committee identified and canvassed all the key stakeholders.

The redesign committee developed an action statement to guide its work: "To trial organizational and managerial systems and processes that will improve the working environment by reorganizing work, improving communication, empowering employees and managers to be more directly involved in decisions while maintaining and improving the level of customer service."[61] The redesign committee made nine recommendations: (1) the creation of small teams of operators, (2) the immediate removal of remote monitoring of the operators, (3) the implementation of extensive cross-training, (4) personalizing customer service, (5) removing restrictions on operators' trades, (6) increasing scheduling and work flexibility, (7) increasing training for the operators, (8) increasing the product knowledge of the operators, and (9) dedicating training space. Most of the recommendations were followed and both management and union were pleased with the process and the outcome.[62]

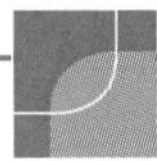

Framework for Organizational Responses to Uncertainty

The ways environmental uncertainty influences organizational characteristics are summarized in Exhibit 4.8. The change and complexity dimensions are combined and illustrate four levels of uncertainty. The low-uncertainty environment is simple and stable. Organizations in this environment have few departments and a mechanistic structure. In a low-moderate uncertainty environment, more departments are needed, along with more integrating roles to coordinate the departments. Some planning may occur. Environments that are high-moderate uncertainty are unstable but simple. Organizational structure is organic and decentralized. Planning is emphasized and managers are quick to make internal changes as needed. The high-uncertainty environment is both complex and unstable and is the most difficult environment from a management perspective. Organizations are large and have many departments, but they are also organic. A large number of management personnel are assigned to coordination and integration, and the organization uses boundary spanning, planning, and forecasting to enable a high-speed response to environmental changes.

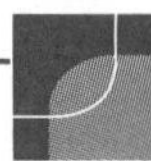

Resource Dependence

Thus far, this chapter has described several ways in which organizations adapt to the lack of information and to the uncertainty caused by environmental change and complexity. We turn now to the third characteristic of the organization–environment relationship that affects organizations, which is the need for material and financial resources. The environment is the source of scarce and valued resources essential to organizational survival. Research in this area is called the resource-dependence perspective. **Resource dependence** means that organizations depend on the environment but strive to acquire control over resources to minimize their dependence.[63] Organizations are vulnerable if vital resources are controlled by other organizations, so they try to be as independent as possible. Organizations do not want to become too vulnerable to other organizations because of negative effects on performance.

Although companies like to minimize their dependence, when costs and risks are high they also team up to share scarce resources and be more competitive on a global basis. Formal relationships with other organizations present a dilemma to managers. Organizational linkages require coordination,[64] and they reduce the freedom of each organization to make decisions without concern for the needs and goals of other organizations. Interorganizational relationships thus represent a trade-off between resources and autonomy. To maintain autonomy, organizations that already have abundant resources will tend not to establish new linkages. Organizations that need resources will give up independence to acquire those resources.

Dependence on shared resources gives power to other organizations. Once an organization relies on others for valued resources, those other organizations can influence managerial decision making. When a large company like IBM, Motorola, or BMW forges a partnership with a supplier for parts, both sides benefit, but each loses a small amount of autonomy. For example, some of these large companies are now putting strong pressure on vendors to lower costs, and the vendors have few alternatives but to go along.[65] In much the same way, dependence on shared resources gives advertisers power over print and electronic media companies. For example, as newspapers face increasingly tough financial times, they are less likely to run stories critical of advertisers. Though newspapers insist advertisers do not get special treatment, some editors admit there is growing talk of the need for advertiser-friendly newspapers.[66]

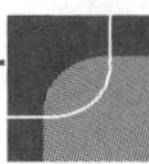

Controlling Environmental Resources

Organizations maintain this balance between linkages with other organizations and their own independence through attempts to modify, manipulate, or control other organizations.[67] To survive, the focal organization often tries to reach out and change or control elements in the environment. Two strategies can be adopted to manage resources in the external environment: (1) establish favourable linkages with key elements in the environment and (2) shape the environmental domain.[68] As

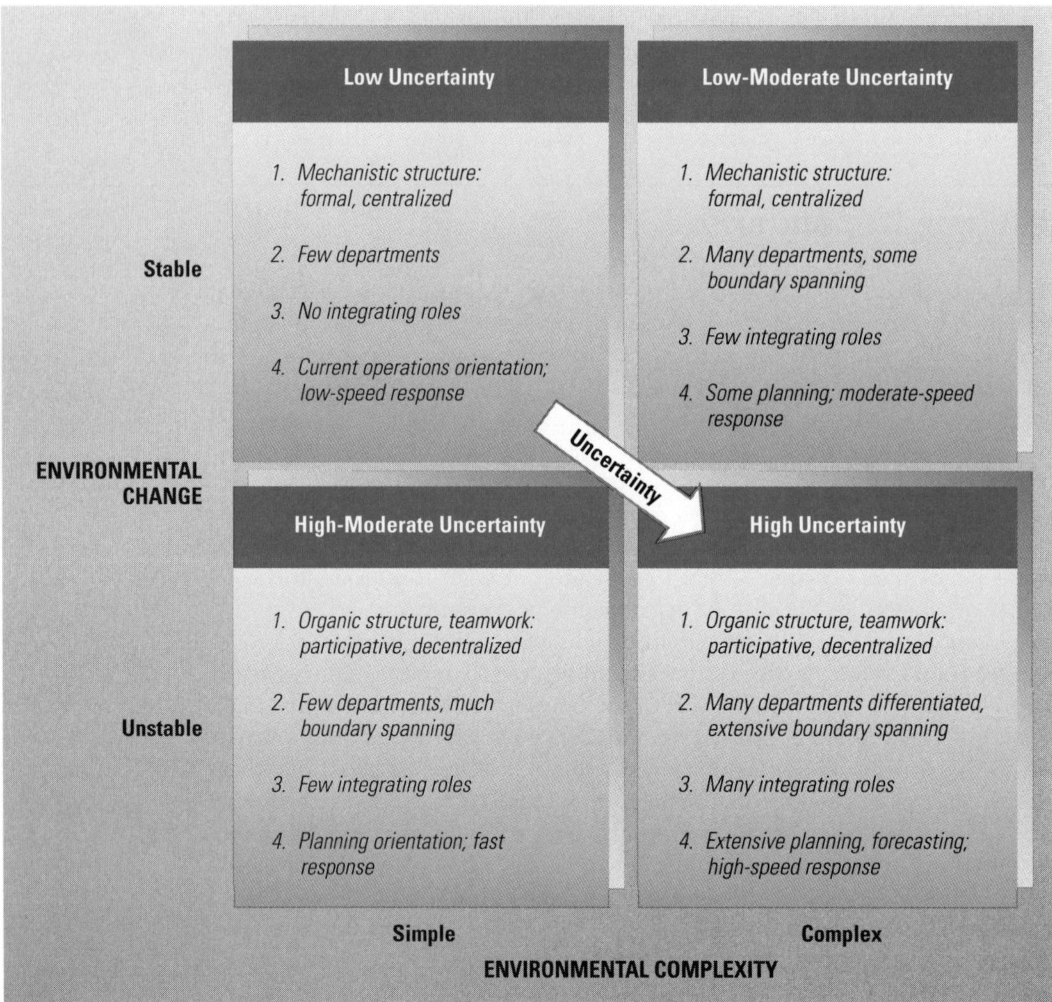

EXHIBIT 4.8
Contingency Framework for Environmental Uncertainty and Organizational Responses

PDA Remember...

Reach out and control external sectors that threaten needed resources. Influence the domain by engaging in political activity, joining trade associations, and establishing favourable linkages. Establish linkages through ownership, strategic alliances, cooptation, interlocking directorates, and executive recruitment. Reduce the amount of change or threat from the external environment so the organization will not have to change internally.

a general rule, when organizations sense that valued resources are scarce, they will use such strategies rather than go it alone. Notice how dissimilar these strategies are from the responses to environmental change and complexity described in Exhibit 4.8. The dissimilarity reflects the difference between responding to the need for resources and responding to the need for information.

Establishing Interorganizational Linkages

Ownership. Companies use ownership to establish linkages when they buy a part of or a controlling interest in another company. This gives the company access to technology, products, or other resources it doesn't currently have.

A greater degree of ownership and control is obtained through acquisition or merger. An acquisition involves the purchase of one organization by another so that the buyer assumes control. A merger is the unification of two or more organizations into a single unit.[69] These forms of ownership reduce uncertainty in an area important to the acquiring company. In the past few years, there has been a huge wave of acquisition and merger activity in the telecommunications industry, reflecting the tremendous uncertainty these organizations face. According to the law firm McMillan Binch Mendelsohn, "Canadian M&A activity in 2006 was higher than any year since the technology boom of 2000, buoyed by a strong economy, low interest rates, high energy and commodity prices and continued cross-border activity. Continuing trends include: increased involvement by private equity funds (particularly U.S.-based funds), Chinese participation, large cross-border transactions, increased income trust activity (particularly after the October 31, 2006, announcement by the federal government that the favourable tax treatment accorded to income trusts will come to an end), increased willingness to launch hostile and competing bids, increased institutional shareholder activism and growing recognition of national security interests in the context of M&A transactions. In addition, cash continues to be king in competitive auctions (e.g., Falconbridge and Inco transactions)."[70]

In Practice

TSX Group and Montréal Exchange

After some sparring between the Toronto and Montréal exchanges, "Canada's largest stock and derivatives exchanges have made it official, striking a $1.3 billion marriage pact."[71] The federal finance minister had urged the two organizations to put aside their differences and join forces for the national interest. Both the New York Mercantile Exchange and the Intercontinental Exchange had expressed interest in acquiring the Montréal Exchange. The new organization is named the TMX Group and is managed from Toronto. However, derivatives trading stayed in Montréal at the same location and with the same management. Montréal exchange shareholders received a half Toronto exchange share and $13.95 for each of the shares in the Montréal derivatives exchange. When the merger was approved, Montréal exchange shareholders owned 18 percent of the new exchange and Toronto exchange shareholders owned the remainder.

The merger created an organization that has the size to compete and to expand globally. The Montréal exchange has a stake in the Boston Options Exchange, and the newly created organization plans to expand further in the United States. According to Richard Nesbitt, CEO of the Toronto Exchange, "[this] combination grows out of a common vision for the future of the Canadian capital markets. . . . . Customers in Canada and internationally will benefit from increased liquidity levels, accelerated product development, a fully diversified product suite, and superior technology."[72] Cost savings from the merger are estimated to be $25 million per year. One analyst referred to the proposed merger as a "not-so-stunning [but positive] move"[73] in the long run.

Formal Strategic Alliances. When there is a high level of complementarity between the business lines, geographical positions, or skills of two companies, the firms often go the route of a strategic alliance rather than ownership through merger or acquisition.[74] Such alliances are formed through contracts and joint ventures.

Contracts and joint ventures reduce uncertainty through a legal and binding relationship with another firm. Contracts come in the form of *license agreements* that involve the purchase of the right to use an asset (such as a new technology) for a specific time and *supplier arrangements* that contract for the sale of one firm's output to another. Contracts can provide long-term security by tying customers and suppliers to specific amounts and prices. For example, Italian fashion house Versace has forged a deal to license its primary asset—its name—for a line of designer eyeglasses. McCain's contracts for an entire crop of russet potatoes to be certain of its supply of French-fries. It also gains influence over suppliers through these contracts and has changed the way farmers grow potatoes and the profit margins they earn, which is consistent with the resource-dependence perspective.[75] Large retailers such as Wal-Mart and Home Depot are gaining so much clout that they can almost dictate contracts, telling manufacturers what to make, how to make it, and how much to charge for it. Many music companies edit songs and visual covers of their CDs to cut out "offensive material" in order to get their products on the shelves of Wal-Mart, which sells more than 50 million CDs annually.[76]

Joint ventures result in the creation of a new organization that is formally independent of the parents, although the parents will have some control.[77] In a joint venture, organizations share the risk and cost associated with large projects or innovations. AOL created a joint venture with Venezuela's Cisneros Group to smooth its entry into the Latin American online market. In 2006, CUBANIQUEL Corporation and Sherritt International developed a joint venture to increase productive capacity of nickel and cobalt mining in Cuba and Canada with capital from both partners.[78]

Cooptation, Interlocking Directorates. **Cooptation** occurs when leaders from important sectors in the environment are made part of an organization. It takes place, for example, when influential customers or suppliers are appointed to the board of directors, such as when the senior executive of a bank sits on the board of a manufacturing company. As a board member, the banker may become psychologically coopted into the interests of the manufacturing firm. Community leaders also can be appointed to a company's board of directors or to other organizational committees or task forces. These influential people are thus introduced to the needs of the company and are more likely to include the company's interests in their decision making.

An **interlocking directorate** is a formal linkage that occurs when a member of the board of directors of one company sits on the board of directors of another company. The individual is a communications link between companies and can influence policies and decisions. When one individual is the link between two companies, this is typically referred to as a **direct interlock**. An **indirect interlock** occurs when a director of company A and a director of company B are both directors of company C. They have access to one another but do not have direct influence over their respective companies.[79] Recent research shows that, as a firm's financial fortunes decline, direct interlocks with financial institutions increase. Financial uncertainty facing an industry also has been associated with greater indirect interlocks between competing companies.[80]

Executive Recruitment. Transferring or exchanging executives also offers a method of establishing favourable linkages with external organizations. For example, each year the aerospace industry hires retired generals and executives from the Department of Defence. These generals have personal friends in the department, so the aerospace companies obtain better information about technical specifications, prices, and dates for new weapons systems. They can learn the needs of the defence department and are able to present their case for defence contracts in a more effective way. Companies without personal contacts find it nearly impossible to get a defence contract.

Having channels of influence and communication between organizations serves to reduce financial uncertainty and dependence for an organization.

Advertising and Public Relations. A traditional way of establishing favourable relationships is through advertising. Organizations spend large amounts of money to influence the taste of consumers. Advertising is especially important in highly competitive consumer industries and in industries that experience variable demand. Advertising is a major part of Apple's strategy to increase its market share for its computer line; its advertisements focus on Apple's innovations with such taglines as "Think Different."

Public relations is similar to advertising, except that stories often are free and aimed at public opinion. Public relations people cast an organization in a favourable light in speeches, in press reports, and on television. Public relations attempts to shape the company's image in the minds of customers, suppliers, and government officials. For example, in an effort to survive in this antismoking era, tobacco companies have launched an aggressive public relations campaign touting smokers' rights and freedom of choice.

Controlling the Environmental Domain

In addition to establishing favourable linkages to obtain resources, organizations often try to change the environment. There are four techniques for influencing or changing a firm's environmental domain.

Change of Domain. The ten sectors described earlier in this chapter are not fixed. The organization decides which business it is in; the market to enter; and the suppliers, banks, employees, and location to use—and this domain can be changed.[81]An organization can seek new environmental relationships and drop old ones. An organization may try to find a domain where there is little competition, no government regulation, abundant suppliers, affluent customers, and barriers to keep competitors out.

Acquisition and divestment are two techniques for altering the domain. Bombardier, maker of Ski-Doo snowmobiles, began a series of acquisitions to alter its domain when the snowmobile industry declined. CEO Laurent Beaudoin gradually moved the company into the aerospace industry by negotiating deals to purchase Canadair, Boeing's de Havilland unit, business-jet pioneer Learjet, and Short Brothers of Northern Ireland.[82]

Political Activity, Regulation. Political activity includes techniques to influence government legislation and regulation. Political strategy can be used to erect regulatory barriers against new competitors or to quash unfavourable legislation. Corporations also try to influence the appointment to agencies of people who are sympathetic to their needs. Canadian defence contractors, for example, have lobbied the American military to get work on the U.S. missile shield system. Ron Kane, vice president of the Aerospace Industries Association of Canada, notes that "it's an area where Canadian industry has been very successful in the past, supporting U.S. military programs . . ."[83]

In Practice
Wal-Mart

In the late 1990s, Wal-Mart discovered a problem that could hamper its ambitious international expansion plans—U.S. negotiators for China's entry into the World Trade Organization had agreed to a 30-store limit on foreign retailers doing business there. Worse still, executives for the giant retailer realized they didn't know the right people in Washington to talk to about the situation.

Until 1998, Wal-Mart didn't even have a lobbyist on the payroll and spent virtually nothing on political activity. The issue of China's entry into the WTO was a wake-up call, and Wal-Mart began transforming itself from a company that shunned politics to one that works hard to bend public policy to suit its business needs. Hiring in-house lobbyists and working with lobbying organizations favourable to its goals has enabled Wal-Mart to gain significant wins on global trade issues.

In addition to concerns over global trade, Wal-Mart has found other reasons it needs government support. In recent years, the company has been fighting off legal challenges from labour unions, employees' lawyers, and federal investigators. For example, the United Food and Commercial Workers International Union helped Wal-Mart employees file a series of complaints about the company's overtime, health care, and other policies with the National Labor Relations Board, leading to dozens of class-action lawsuits. Wal-Mart in turn poured millions of dollars into a campaign that presses for limits on awards in class-action suits and began lobbying for legislation that bars unions from soliciting outside retail stores. Although that legislation failed, top executives are pleased with their lobbyists' progress. Yet they admit they still have a lot to learn about the best way to influence government legislation and regulation in Wal-Mart's favour.[84]

In Canada, Wal-Mart has fought attempts to unionize its stores. The United Food and Commercial Workers were successful in organizing the Jonquière, Québec, Wal-Mart store; it was the first North American Wal-Mart store to have a union. However, Wal-Mart closed the Jonquière store soon after and fired the store's 200 workers. The workers tried to launch a class action suit against Wal-Mart but the Québec Court of Appeal declined to hear the case. The Court's decision upheld a November 2005 decision by the Québec Superior Court that the firing of the unionized workers was best decided by the province's labour relations board.[85]

In addition to hiring lobbyists and working with other organizations, many CEOs believe they should do their own lobbying. CEOs have easier access than lobbyists and can be especially effective when they do the politicking. Political activity is so important that "informal lobbyist" is an unwritten part of almost any CEO's job description.[86]

Trade Associations. Much of the work to influence the external environment is accomplished jointly with other organizations that have similar interests. For example, most large pharmaceutical companies belong to Pharmaceutical Research and Manufacturers of America. Manufacturing companies are part of the Canadian Manufacturers and Exporters, and retailers are part of the Retail Council of Canada. Microsoft and other software companies join the Initiative for Software Choice (ISC). By pooling resources, these organizations can pay people to carry out activities such as lobbying legislators, influencing new regulations, developing public relations campaigns, and making campaign contributions. There are more specialized trade associations like the Hellenic Canadian Board of Trade, the Confectionery Manufacturers Association of Canada, the Music Industries Association of Canada, and Trade Team PEI.

Illegitimate Activities. Illegitimate activities represent the final technique companies sometimes use to control their environmental domain. Certain conditions, such as low profits, pressure from senior managers, or scarce environmental resources, may lead managers to adopt behaviours not considered legitimate.[87] Many well-known companies have been found guilty of unlawful or unethical activities. Examples include payoffs to foreign governments, illegal political contributions, promotional gifts, and wiretapping. At formerly high-flying companies such as Enron and WorldCom, pressure for financial performance encouraged managers to disguise financial problems through complex partnerships or questionable accounting practices. In the Canadian airlines industry, for example, intense competition between Air Canada and WestJet resulted in an industrial espionage case. "In the spring of 2004, Air Canada sued WestJet for $220 million for logging on more than 240,000 times to an internal website that contained passenger-load data. WestJet, a discount carrier, then sued Air Canada for, among other things, hiring private investigators who dressed as garbage collectors to retrieve documents from the home of a former executive." WestJet apologized and took responsibility for the unethical act.[88]

One study found that companies in industries with low demand, shortages, and strikes were more likely to be convicted for illegal activities, implying that illegal acts are an attempt to cope with resource scarcity. Some nonprofit organizations have been found to use illegitimate or illegal actions to bolster their visibility and reputation as they compete with other organizations for scarce grants and donations.[89] A recent series of *Toronto Star* articles highlighted questionable practices of a few charities. One charity, International Charity Association Network (ICAN), has been suspended by the Charities Directorate. ICAN is not allowed to issue tax receipts and must warn potential donors that it is under suspension.[90]

Organization–Environment Integrative Framework

The relationships illustrated in Exhibit 4.9 summarize the two major themes about organization–environment relationships discussed in this chapter. One theme is that the amount of complexity and change in an organization's domain influences the need for information and hence the uncertainty felt within an organization. Greater information uncertainty is resolved through greater structural flexibility and the assignment of additional departments and boundary roles. When uncertainty is low, management structures can be more mechanistic, and the number of departments and boundary roles can be fewer. The second theme pertains to the scarcity of material and financial resources. The more dependent an organization is on other organizations for those resources, the more important it is to either establish favourable linkages with those organizations or control entry into the domain. If dependence on external resources is low, the organization can maintain autonomy and does not need to establish linkages or control the external domain.

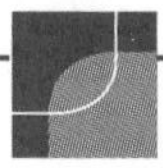

Summary and Interpretation

The external environment has an overwhelming impact on management uncertainty and organization functioning. Organizations are open social systems. Most are involved with hundreds of external elements. The change and complexity in environmental domains have major implications for organizational design and action. Most organizational decisions, activities, and outcomes can be traced to stimuli in the external environment.

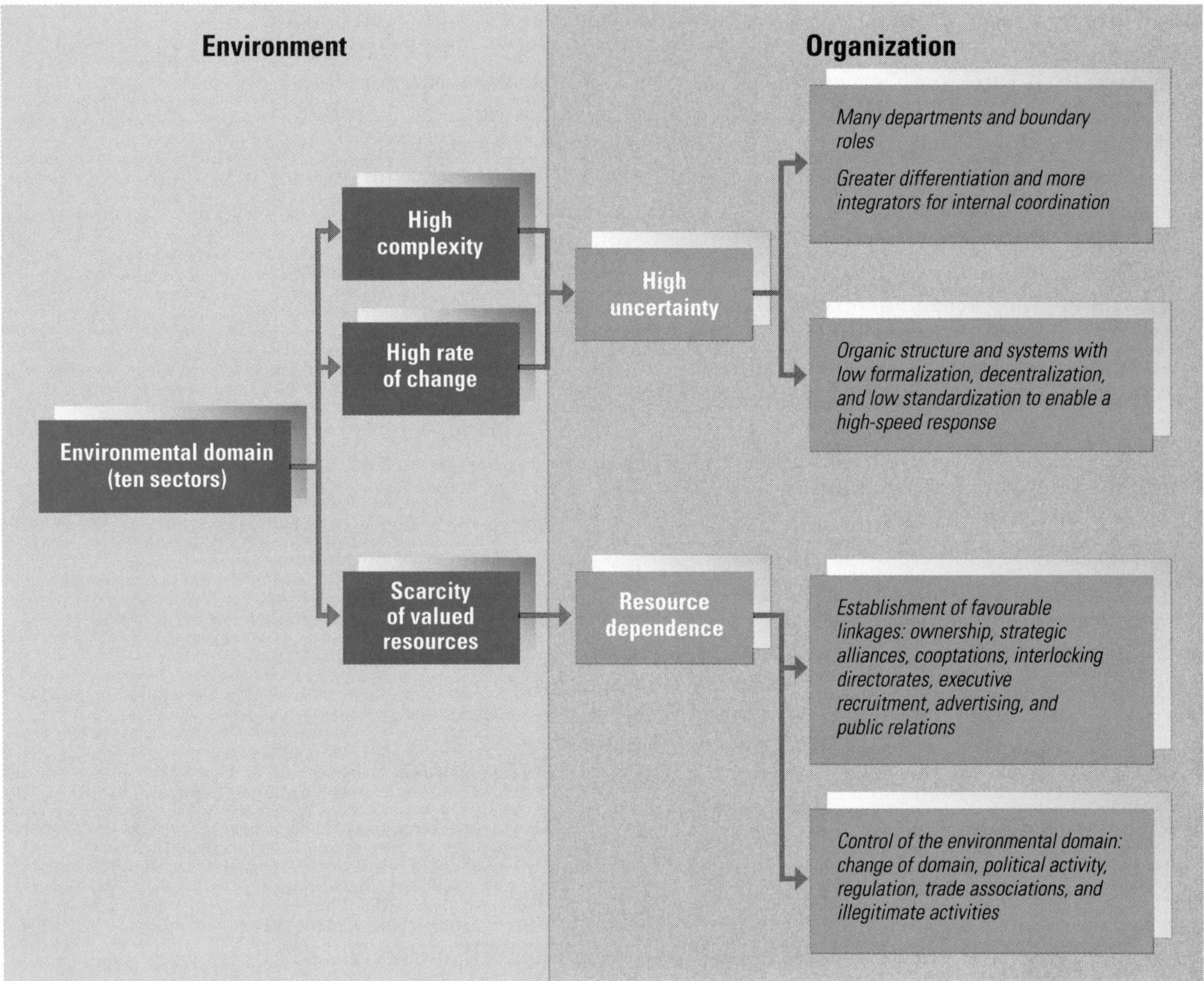

EXHIBIT 4.9
Relationship between Environmental Characteristics and Organizational Actions

Organizational environments differ in terms of uncertainty and resource dependence. Organizational uncertainty is the result of the stable–unstable and simple–complex dimensions of the environment. Resource dependence is the result of scarcity of the material and financial resources needed by the organization.

Organizational design takes on a logical perspective when the environment is considered. Organizations try to survive and achieve efficiencies in a world characterized by uncertainty and scarcity. Specific departments and functions are created to deal with uncertainties. The organization can be conceptualized as a technical core and departments that buffer environmental uncertainty. Boundary-spanning roles provide information about the environment.

The concepts in this chapter provide specific frameworks for understanding how the environment influences the structure and functioning of an organization. Environmental complexity and change, for example, have specific impact on internal complexity and adaptability. Under great uncertainty, more resources are allocated to departments that will plan, deal with specific environmental elements, and integrate diverse internal activities. Moreover, when risk is great or resources are scarce, the organization can establish linkages through the acquisition of ownership and through strategic alliances, interlocking directorates, executive recruitment, or advertising and public relations that will minimize risk and maintain a supply of scarce resources. Other techniques for controlling the environment include a change of the domain in which the organization operates, political activity, participation in trade associations, and perhaps illegitimate activities.

Two important themes in this chapter are that organizations can learn and adapt to the environment and that organizations can change and control the environment. These strategies are especially true for large organizations that command many resources. Such organizations can adapt when necessary but can also neutralize or change problematic areas in the environment.

Key Concepts

boundary-spanning roles, p. 142
buffering roles, p. 142
cooptation, p. 152
differentiation, p. 144
direct interlock, p. 152
domain, p. 133
general environment, p. 135
green environment, p. 132
indirect interlock, p. 152
integration, p. 145
interlocking directorate, p. 152
mechanistic, p. 146
organic, p. 146
organizational environment, p. 132
resource dependence, p. 149
sectors, p. 133
simple–complex dimension, p. 138
stable–unstable dimension, p. 138
task environment, p. 133
uncertainty, p. 138

Discussion Questions

1. Define *organizational environment.* Would the task environment of a new Internet-based company be the same as that of a government welfare agency? Discuss.
2. What are some forces that influence environmental uncertainty? Which typically has the greatest impact on uncertainty—environmental complexity or environmental change? Why?
3. Why does environmental complexity lead to organizational complexity? Explain.
4. Discuss the importance of the international, compared to domestic sectors, for today's organizations. What are some ways in which the international sector affects organizations in your city or community?
5. Describe differentiation and integration. In what type of environmental uncertainty will differentiation and integration be greatest? Least?
6. Under what environmental conditions is organizational planning emphasized? Is planning an appropriate response to a turbulent environment?
7. What is an organic organization? What is a mechanistic organization? How does the environment influence organic and mechanistic structures?
8. Why do organizations become involved in interorganizational relationships? Do these relationships affect an organization's dependency? Performance?
9. Assume you have been asked to calculate the ratio of staff employees to production employees in two organizations—one in a simple, stable environment and one in a complex, shifting environment. How would you expect these ratios to differ? Why?
10. Is changing the organization's domain a feasible strategy for coping with a threatening environment? Explain.

Chapter 4 Workbook: Organizations You Rely On*

Below, list eight organizations you somehow rely on in your daily life. Examples might be a restaurant, a clothing store, a university, your family, the post office, the telephone company, an airline, a pizzeria that delivers, your place of work, and so on. In the first column, list those eight organizations. Then, in Column 2, choose another organization you could use if the ones in Column 1 were not available. In Column 3, evaluate your level of dependence on the organizations listed in column 1 as Strong, Medium, or Weak. Finally, in Column 4, rate the certainty of that organization being able to meet your needs as High (certainty), Medium, or Low.

Organization	Backup Organization	Level of Dependence	Level of Certainty
1.			
2.			
3.			
4.			
5.			
6.			
7.			
8.			

*Adapted by Dorothy Marcic from "Organizational Dependencies," in Ricky W. Griffin and Thomas C. Head, *Practicing Management,* 2nd ed. (Dallas: Houghton Mifflin), 2–3.

Questions

1. Do you have adequate backup organizations for those of high dependence? How might you create even more backups?
2. What would you do if an organization you rated high for dependence and high for certainty suddenly became high-dependence and low-certainty? How would your behaviour relate to the concept of resource dependence?

Case for Analysis: The Paradoxical Twins: Acme and Omega Electronics

Part I

In 1986, Technological Products of Fort Erie was bought out by a Cleveland, Ohio, manufacturer. The Cleveland firm had no interest in the electronics division of Technological Products and subsequently sold two plants that manufactured computer chips and printed circuit boards to different investors. Integrated circuits, or chips, were the first step into microminiaturization in the electronics industry, and both plants had developed some expertise in the technology, along with their superior capabilities in manufacturing printed circuit boards. One of the plants, located in nearby Walden, was renamed Acme Electronics; the other plant, within the city limits of Fort Erie, was renamed Omega Electronics, Inc.

Acme retained its original management and upgraded its general manager to president. Omega hired a new president who had been a director of a large electronic research laboratory and upgraded several of the existing personnel within the plant. Acme and Omega often competed for the same contracts. As subcontractors, both firms benefited from the electronics boom and both looked forward to future growth and expansion. The world was going digital, and both companies began producing digital microprocessors along with the production of circuit boards. Acme had annual sales of $100 million and employed 550 people. Omega had annual sales of $80 million and employed 480 people. Acme regularly achieved greater net profits, much to the chagrin of Omega's management.

Inside Acme

The president of Acme, John Tyler, was confident that, had the demand not been so great, Acme's competitor would not have survived. "In fact," he said, "we have been able to beat Omega regularly for the most profitable contracts, thereby increasing our profit." Tyler credited his firm's greater effectiveness to his managers' abilities to run a "tight ship." He explained that he had retained the basic structure developed by Technological Products because it was most efficient for high-volume manufacturing. Acme had detailed organization charts and job descriptions. Tyler believed everyone should have clear responsibilities and narrowly defined jobs, which would lead to efficient performance and high company profits. People were generally satisfied with their work at Acme; however, some of the managers voiced the desire to have a little more latitude in their jobs.

Inside Omega

Omega's president, Jim Rawls, did not believe in organization charts. He felt his organization had departments similar to Acme's, but he thought Omega's plant was small enough that things such as organization charts just put artificial barriers between specialists who should be working together. Written memos were not allowed since, as Rawls expressed it, "the plant is small enough that if people want to communicate, they can just drop by and talk things over."

The head of the mechanical engineering department said, "Jim spends too much of his time and mine making sure everyone understands what we're doing and listening to suggestions." Rawls was concerned with employee satisfaction and wanted everyone to feel part of the organization. The top management team reflected Rawls's attitudes. They also believed that employees should be familiar with activities throughout the organization so that cooperation between departments would be increased. A newer member of the industrial engineering department said, "When I first got here, I wasn't sure what I was supposed to do. One day I worked with some mechanical engineers and the next day I helped the shipping department design some packing cartons. The first months on the job were hectic, but at least I got a real feel for what makes Omega tick."

Part II

In the 1990s, mixed analog and digital devices began threatening the demand for the complex circuit boards manufactured by Acme and Omega. This "system-on-a-chip" technology combined analog functions, such as sound, graphics, and power management, together with digital circuitry, such as logic and memory, making it highly useful for new products such as cellular phones and wireless computers. Both Acme and Omega realized the threat to their futures and began aggressively to seek new customers.

In July 1992, a major photocopier manufacturer was looking for a subcontractor to assemble the digital memory units of its new experimental copier. The projected contract for the job was estimated to be $7 million to $9 million in annual sales.

Both Acme and Omega were geographically close to this manufacturer, and both submitted highly competitive bids for the production of 100 prototypes. Acme's bid was slightly lower than Omega's; however, both firms were asked to produce 100 units. The photocopier manufacturer told both firms that speed was critical because its president had boasted to other manufacturers that the firm would have a finished copier available by Christmas. This boast, much to the designer's dismay, required pressure on all subcontractors to begin prototype production before the final design of the copier was complete. This meant Acme and Omega would have at most two weeks to produce the prototypes or would delay the final copier production.

Part III

Inside Acme

As soon as John Tyler was given the blueprints (Monday, July 13, 1992), he sent a memo to the purchasing department asking to move forward on the purchase of all necessary materials. At the same time, he sent the blueprints to the drafting department and asked that it prepare manufacturing prints. The industrial engineering department was told to begin methods design work for use by the production department supervisors. Tyler also sent a memo to all department heads and executives indicating the critical time constraints of this job and how he expected that all employees would perform as efficiently as they had in the past.

The departments had little contact with one another for several days, and each seemed to work at its own speed. Each department also encountered problems. Purchasing could not acquire all the parts on time. Industrial engineering had difficulty arranging an efficient assembly sequence. Mechanical engineering did not take the deadline seriously and parceled its work to vendors so the engineers could work on other jobs scheduled previously. Tyler made it a point to stay in touch with the photocopier manufacturer to let it know things were progressing and to learn of any new developments. He traditionally worked to keep important clients happy. Tyler telephoned someone at the photocopier company at least twice a week and got to know the head designer quite well.

On July 17, Tyler learned that mechanical engineering was far behind in its development work, and he "hit the roof." To make matters worse, purchasing had not obtained all the parts, so the industrial engineers decided to assemble the product without one part, which would be inserted at the last minute. On Thursday, July 23, the final units were being assembled, although the process was delayed several times. On Friday, July 24, the last units were finished while Tyler paced around the plant. Late that afternoon, Tyler received a phone call from the head designer of the photocopier manufacturer, who told Tyler that he had received a call on Wednesday from Jim Rawls of Omega. He explained that Rawls's workers had found an error in the design of the connector cable and taken corrective action on their prototypes. He told Tyler that he had checked out the design error and that Omega was right. Tyler, a bit overwhelmed by this information, told the designer that he had all the memory units ready for shipment and that, as soon as they received the missing component on Monday or Tuesday, they would be able to deliver the final units. The designer explained that the design error would be rectified in a new blueprint he was sending over by messenger and that he would hold Acme to the Tuesday delivery date.

When the blueprint arrived, Tyler called in the production supervisor to assess the damage. The alterations in the design would call for total disassembly and the unsoldering of several connections. Tyler told the supervisor to put extra people on the alterations first thing Monday morning and to try to finish the job by Tuesday. Late Tuesday afternoon, the alterations were finished and the missing components were delivered. Wednesday morning, the production supervisor discovered that the units would have to be torn apart again to install the missing component. When John Tyler received the news, he again "hit the roof." He called industrial engineering and asked if it could help out. The production supervisor and the methods engineer couldn't agree on how to install the component. John Tyler settled the argument by ordering that all units be taken apart again and the missing component installed. He told shipping to prepare cartons for delivery on Friday afternoon.

On Friday, July 31, fifty prototypes were shipped from Acme without final inspection. John Tyler was concerned about his firm's reputation, so he waived the final inspection after he personally tested one unit and found it operational. On Tuesday, August 4, Acme shipped the last fifty units.

Inside Omega

On Friday, July 10, Jim Rawls called a meeting that included department heads to tell them about the potential contract they were to receive. He told them that as soon as he received the blueprints, work could begin. On Monday, July 13, the prints arrived and again the department heads met to discuss the project. At the end of the meeting, drafting had agreed to prepare manufacturing prints, while industrial engineering and production would begin methods design.

Two problems arose within Omega that were similar to those at Acme. Certain ordered parts could not be delivered on time, and the assembly sequence was difficult to engineer. The departments proposed ideas to help one another, however, and department heads and key employees had daily meetings to discuss progress. The head of electrical engineering knew of a Japanese source for the components that could not be purchased from normal suppliers. Most problems were solved by Saturday, July 18.

On Monday, July 20, a methods engineer and the production supervisor formulated the assembly plans, and production was set to begin on Tuesday morning. On Monday afternoon, people from mechanical engineering, electrical engineering, production, and industrial engineering got together to produce a prototype just to ensure that there would be no snags in production. While they were building the unit, they discovered an error in the connector cable design. All the engineers agreed, after checking and rechecking the blueprints, that the cable was erroneously designed. People from mechanical engineering and electrical engineering spent Monday night redesigning the cable, and on Tuesday morning, the drafting department finalized the changes in the manufacturing prints. On Tuesday morning, Rawls was a bit apprehensive about the design changes and decided to get formal approval. Rawls received word on Wednesday from the head designer at the photocopier firm that they could proceed with the design changes as discussed on the phone. On Friday, July 24, the final units were inspected by quality control and were then shipped.

Part IV

Ten of Acme's final memory units were defective, whereas all of Omega's units passed the photocopier firm's tests. The photocopier firm was disappointed with Acme's delivery delay and incurred further delays in repairing the defective Acme units. However, rather than give the entire contract to one firm, the final contract was split between Acme and Omega with two directives added: (1) maintain zero defects and (2) reduce final cost. In 1993, through extensive cost-cutting efforts, Acme reduced its unit cost by 20 per cent and was ultimately awarded the total contract.

5 Interorganizational Relationships

GARY TRAMONTINA/Bloomberg News/Landov

A Look Inside

Toyota Motor Corporation (Toyota)

Toyota (see photo) is considered the standard setter in developing, managing, and sustaining relationships with its network of nearly 200 suppliers. The Toyota Group, as the network is called, creates a strong identity of co-existence and co-prosperity, reciprocity and knowledge transfer. Toyota is governed by 14 management principles. They include a focus on the long term in decision making, a commitment to getting quality right from the outset, a culture of relentless reflection, continuous learning and improvement, and developing deep relationships with its suppliers. Principle 11 states "Respect your extended network of partners and suppliers by challenging them and helping them to improve."[1]

Toyota's underlying strategy for its supplier relationships is *keiretsu*, a tight network of suppliers that learns and prospers alongside the parent organization. Toyota sources about 80 percent of its manufacturing costs from its outside suppliers and works to ensure that the relationships are mutually advantageous. To that end, Toyota conducts joint improvement activities, shares information intensively but selectively develops its suppliers' technical capabilities, supervises its suppliers, turns supplier rivalry into opportunity, and understands how suppliers work. For example, Toyota has a guest engineer program whereby its suppliers send their engineers to Toyota's facilities for two or three years to work with Toyota's engineers to learn about and to contribute to the Toyota Way.

According to Toyota's management, its tight relationships with its suppliers has resulted in faster production times so that it can design a new car in 12 to 18 months, compared to the industry norm of 24 to 36 months. As well, Toyota reduced its manufacturing costs on the Camry by 25 percent in the 1990s while scoring top spot on the J.D. Powers customer satisfaction surveys. When compared to the top three North American manufacturers, Toyota is the most productive; Toyota requires 27.9 hours per vehicle for assembly while Ford and Chrysler require 37 and 35.9 hours, respectively.[2]

Organizations of all sizes in all industries are rethinking how they do business in response to today's chaotic environment. One of the most widespread trends is to reduce boundaries and increase collaboration between companies, sometimes even between competitors. Today's aerospace companies, for example, depend on strategic partnerships with other organizations. Bombardier and Boeing, a U.S. aerospace company, are both involved in multiple relationships with suppliers, competitors, and other organizations. Global semiconductor makers have been collaborating while competing for years because of the high costs and risks associated with creating and marketing a new generation of semiconductors.

Global competition and rapid advances in technology, communications, and transportation have created amazing new opportunities for organizations, but they have also raised the cost of doing business and made it increasingly difficult for any company to take advantage of those opportunities on its own. In this new economy, webs of organizations are emerging. A large company like General Electric develops a special relationship with a supplier that eliminates intermediaries by sharing complete information and reducing the costs of salespeople and distributors. Several small companies may join together to produce and market non-competing products. You can see the results of interorganizational collaboration when movies such as the *Harry Potter* series are launched. Before seeing the movie, you might read a cover story in entertainment magazines, see a preview clip or chat live with the stars at an online site, find action toys being promoted through a fast-food franchise, and notice retail stores loaded with movie-related merchandise. For some blockbuster movies, coordinated action among companies can yield millions in addition to box-office and DVD profits. In the new economy, organizations think of themselves as teams that create value *jointly* rather than as autonomous companies that are in competition with all others.

Purpose of This Chapter

This chapter explores the most recent trend in organizing, which is the increasingly dense web of relationships among organizations. Companies have always been dependent on other organizations for supplies, materials, and information. The question is how these relationships are managed. At one time it was a matter of a large, powerful company like General Electric or Johnson & Johnson tightening the screws on small suppliers. Today a company can choose to develop positive, trusting relationships. Or a large company like General Motors might find it difficult to adapt to the environment and hence create a new organizational form, such as Saturn, to operate with a different structure and culture. The notion of horizontal relationships described in Chapter 3 and the understanding of environmental uncertainty in Chapter 4 lead to the next stage of organizational evolution, which is horizontal relationships *across* organizations. Organizations can choose to build relationships in many ways, such as appointing preferred suppliers, establishing agreements, business partnering, joint ventures, or even mergers and acquisitions.

Interorganizational research has yielded perspectives such as resource-dependence, collaborative networks, population ecology, and institutionalism. The sum total of these ideas can be daunting, because it means managers no longer can rest in the safety of managing a single organization. They have to understand how to manage a whole set of interorganizational relationships, which is a great deal more challenging and complex. The cartoon in Exhibit 5.1 illustrates the possibilities!

EXHIBIT 5.1
The Challenge of Interorganizational Relationships

"It's agreed then: dogs, cats, gerbils and parakeets will merge, forming an entity which will be called Unipet."

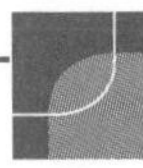

Organizational Ecosystems

Interorganizational relationships are the relatively enduring resource transactions, flows, and linkages that occur among two or more organizations.[3] Traditionally, these transactions and relationships have been seen as a necessary evil to obtain what an organization needs. The presumption has been that the world is composed of distinct businesses that thrive on autonomy and compete for supremacy. A company may be forced into interorganizational relationships depending on its needs and the instability and complexity of the environment.

One current view argues that organizations are now evolving into business ecosystems. An **organizational ecosystem** is a system formed by the interaction of a community of organizations and their environment. An ecosystem cuts across traditional industry lines. A company can create its own ecosystem. Microsoft travels in four major industries: consumer electronics, information, communications, and personal computers. Its ecosystem also includes hundreds of suppliers, including Hewlett-Packard and Intel, and millions of customers across many markets. Cable companies like Rogers Communications are offering home phone service as well as wireless, television, and Internet services, and telephone companies like Bell Canada are now in the satellite television business.

Apple Computer is arguably having greater success as an entertainment company with its iPod and iTunes Music Store than it ever had as a computer manufacturer. Apple's success grows out of close partnerships with other organizations, including music companies, consumer electronics firms, cell phone makers, other computer companies, and even car manufacturers.[4] Samsung of South Korea is the major supplier of parts in Apple's iPhone—its components account for more that $80 in each iPhone. A key component also comes from a subsidiary of the automotive parts manufacturer, Magna International.[5] Apple and Microsoft, like other business ecosystems, develop relationships with hundreds of organizations cutting across traditional business boundaries. The first Case for Analysis details the ecosystem that Apple has spawned.

PDA
Remember...

Look for and develop relationships with other organizations. Don't limit your thinking to a single industry or business type. Build an ecosystem of which your organization is a part.

Is Competition Dead?

No company can go it alone under a constant onslaught of international competitors, changing technology, and new regulations. Organizations around the world are embedded in complex networks of confusing relationships—collaborating in some markets, competing fiercely in others. Indeed, research indicates that a large percentage of new alliances in recent years have been between competitors. These alliances influence organizations' competitive behaviour in varied ways.[6]

Traditional competition, which assumes a distinct company competing for survival and supremacy with other stand-alone businesses, no longer exists because each organization both supports and depends on the others for success, and perhaps for survival. However, most managers recognize that the competitive stakes are higher than ever in a world where market share can crumble overnight and no industry is immune from almost instant obsolescence.[7] In today's world, a new form of competition is in fact intensifying.[8]

Organizations now need to coevolve with others in the ecosystem so that everyone gets stronger. Consider the wolf and the caribou. Wolves cull weaker caribou, which strengthens the herd. A strong herd means that wolves must become stronger themselves. With coevolution, the whole system becomes stronger. In the same way, companies coevolve through discussion with each other, shared visions, alliances, and managing complex relationships. Chapters.Indigo.ca and its retail partners illustrate this approach.

In Practice

chapters.indigo.ca (Indigo.ca)

Indigo Books and Music started as a small bricks-and-mortar store; it expanded by buying Chapters and Coles to become the largest book retailer in Canada. Indigo.ca was one of the earliest players in online retailing in Canada. Indigo.ca has continued to evolve from an online bookseller to an online retailer of books, DVDs, CDs, gift items, iPods and accessories, toys, and diamonds. Indigo.ca deals with 160 suppliers.

Blue Nile, a U.S.–based online jeweller, launched its Canadian website in 2005, www.bluenile.ca, while simultaneously entering a partnership with Indigo.ca. Blue Nile sells loose diamonds, engagement rings, earrings, pendants, and wedding bands. Customers are able to design their own jewellery thorough its Build Your Own application. Indigo.ca used to sell Blue Nile's high-end diamonds and fine jewellery through its main site. Now, Indigo links directly to http://www.bluenile.ca, which is described as a "trusted partner" selling diamonds and fine jewellery. In 2006, Indigo.ca partnered with iUniverse, which supports self-publishing, to offer authors prominent placement of their self-published books in an Indigo, Chapters, or Coles store.[9]

Indigo.ca and its partners represent a virtual ecosystem, in which each company depends to some extent on the others and each has the opportunity to grow stronger. Ecosystems constantly change and evolve, with some relationships growing stronger while others weaken or are terminated. The changing pattern of relationships and interactions in an ecosystem contributes to the health and vitality of the system as an integrated whole.[10]

In an organizational ecosystem, conflict and cooperation frequently exist at the same time. Mutual dependencies and partnerships have become a fact of life in business ecosystems, so is competition dead? Companies today may use their strength to win conflicts and negotiations, but ultimately cooperation carries the day. For example, Intel reversed itself and became involved in supporting the One Laptop Per Child Foundation even though the head of the Foundation and Intel's chair had feuded publicly. As William Swope, Intel's Director of Corporate Affairs put it, "By aligning here we are going to help more kids."[11]

Similarly, as part of the Toronto port lands area redevelopment, two rivals have united to build the largest studio complex in Toronto. Although movie mogul Paul Bronfman had lost a bid to build a major film studio in the area to Sam Reisman, a developer, the two are now partnering to build the Filmport studio complex. As Bronfman put it, "Sam won the deal fair and square, but we've always had a great relationship and I'm glad that I could get involved. . . . Toronto is losing out to other cities and this studio will help put Toronto back on the map [as Hollywood North]."[12] The first phase of the Filmport project will create the largest sound stage in North America and, once completed, Filmport is expected to be more than three million square feet. It expects to have competition from another studio, Pinewood Studios, which has access to the expertise of the largest European studio. But, according to Reisman, "I think it will help in attracting more production to the city.

No different than having more stores in a plaza, it gives people options and at this point we can't be accused of overcapacity."[13]

The Changing Role of Management

Within business, ecosystems managers learn to move beyond traditional responsibilities of corporate strategy and designing hierarchical structures and control systems. If a top manager looks down to enforce order and uniformity, the company is missing opportunities for new and evolving external relationships.[14] In this new world, managers think about horizontal processes rather than vertical structures. Important initiatives are not just top down but also cut across the boundaries separating organizational units. Moreover, horizontal relationships, as described in Chapter 3, now include linkages with suppliers and customers, who become part of the team. Business leaders can learn to lead economic coevolution. Managers learn to see and appreciate the rich environment of opportunities that grows from cooperative relationships with other contributors to the ecosystem. Rather than trying to force suppliers into low prices or customers into high prices, managers strive to strengthen the larger system evolving around them, finding ways to understand this big picture and to contribute.

This is a broader leadership role than ever before. For example, the Global Business Coalition on HIV/AIDS, Tuberculosis and Malaria (GBC) has spent the past five years developing an alliance of over 200 international companies dedicated to combating the AIDS epidemic through the business sector's unique skills and expertise. Headquartered in New York, GBC maintains regional offices in Beijing, Geneva, Johannesburg, Nairobi, and Paris; "it harnesses the individual and collective power of the world's top corporations to fight AIDS at the local, national, and international levels."[15] GBC is also in the process of merging with the Transatlantic Partners Against AIDS. Its Canadian members include Alcan, Bank of Nova Scotia, Barrick Gold, BMO Financial Group, Indigo Books and Music, Power Corporation of Canada, Royal Bank of Canada, Sun Life Financial, and TD Financial Group.

Interorganizational Framework

Understanding this larger organizational ecosystem is one of the most exciting areas of organizational theory. The models and perspectives for understanding interorganizational relationships ultimately help managers change their role from top-down management to horizontal management across organizations. A framework for analyzing the different views of interorganizational relationships is in Exhibit 5.2. Relationships among organizations can be characterized by whether the organizations are dissimilar or similar and whether relationships are competitive or cooperative. By understanding these perspectives, managers can assess their environment and adopt strategies to suit their needs. The first perspective is called resource-dependence theory, which was briefly described in Chapter 4. It describes rational ways organizations deal with each other to reduce dependence on the environment. The second perspective is about collaborative networks, wherein organizations allow themselves to become dependent on other organizations to increase value and productivity for both. The third perspective is population ecology, which examines how new organizations fill niches left open by established organizations, and how a rich variety of new organizational forms benefits society. The final approach is called

PDA
Remember...

Reach out and control external sectors that threaten needed resources. Adopt strategies to control resources, especially when your organization is dependent and has little power. Assert your organization's influence when you have power and control over resources.

EXHIBIT 5.2
*A Framework of Interorganizational Relationships**

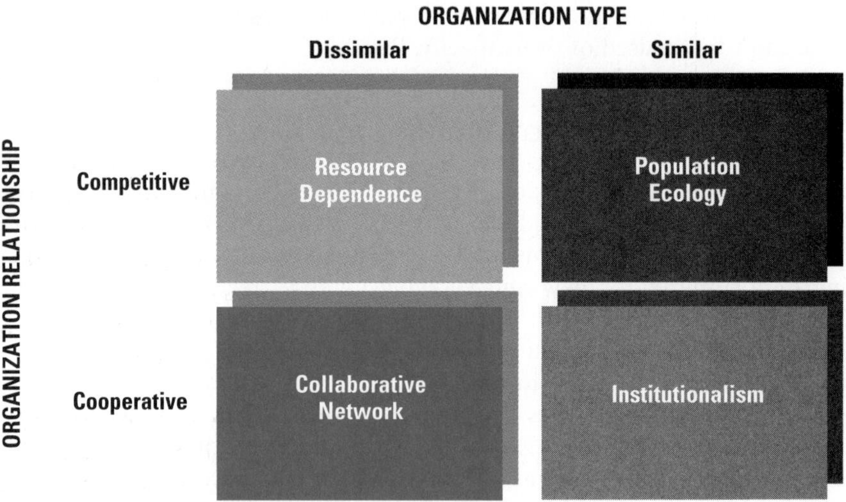

*Thanks to Anand Narasimhan for suggesting this framework.

institutionalism and explains why and how organizations legitimate themselves in the larger environment and design structures by borrowing ideas from each other. These four approaches to the study of interorganizational relationships are described in the remainder of this chapter.

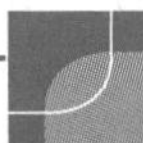

Resource Dependence

Resource dependence represents the traditional view of relationships among organizations. As described in Chapter 4, resource-dependence theory argues that organizations try to minimize their dependence on other organizations for the supply of important resources and try to influence the environment to make resources available.[16] Organizations succeed by striving for independence and autonomy. When threatened by greater dependence, organizations will assert control over external resources to minimize that dependence. Resource-dependence theory argues that organizations do not want to become vulnerable to other organizations because of negative effects on performance.

The amount of dependence on a resource is based on two factors. First is the importance of the resource to the organization, and second is how much discretion or monopoly power those who control a resource have over its allocation and use.[17] Organizations aware of resource dependence tend to develop strategies to reduce their dependence on the environment and learn how to use their power differences. For example, one study of Canadian university athletics departments found that they perceived that the central administration of universities had considerable control over them.[18] Another study of Canadian sports organizations reports that linkages are increasing between nonprofit sports organizations, governments, and corporations. The linkages are designed to help the organizations to share resources and to coordinate their work.[19] In 2006, Swimming Canada and the Red Cross of Canada become partners: Swimming Canada will promote the Red Cross's safety messages and the Red Cross will identify potential competitive swimmers.[20]

Resource Strategies

When organizations feel resource or supply constraints, the resource-dependence perspective says they manoeuvre to maintain their autonomy through a variety of strategies, several of which were described in Chapter 4. One strategy is to adapt to or alter the interdependent relationships. This could mean purchasing ownership in suppliers, developing long-term contracts or joint ventures to lock in necessary resources, or building relationships in other ways. Another technique is to use interlocking directorships, which means boards of directors include members of the boards of supplier companies. Organizations may also join trade associations to coordinate their needs, sign trade agreements, or merge with another firm to guarantee resources and material supplies. Some organizations may take political action, such as lobbying for new regulations or deregulation, favourable taxation, tariffs, or subsidies, or push for new standards that make resource acquisition easier. Organizations operating under the resource-dependence philosophy will do whatever is needed to avoid excessive dependence on the environment to maintain control of resources and hence reduce uncertainty.

Power Strategies

In resource-dependence theory, large, independent companies have power over small suppliers.[21] For example, power in consumer products has shifted from vendors such as Rubbermaid and Procter & Gamble to the big discount retail chains, which can demand—and receive—special pricing deals. Wal-Mart has grown so large and powerful that it can dictate the terms with virtually any supplier. Consider Levi Strauss, which for much of its 150-year history was a powerful supplier, with a jeans brand that millions of people wanted and retailers were eager to stock. "When I first started in this business, retailers were a waystation to the consumer," says Levi's CEO Philip Marineau. "Manufacturers had a tendency to tell retailers how to do business." But the balance of power has shifted dramatically. In order to sell to Wal-Mart, Levi Strauss had to overhaul its entire operation, from design and production to pricing and distribution. For example, Levi jeans used to go from factories to a company-owned distribution centre where they were labelled, packed, and sent on to retailers. Now, to meet Wal-Mart's need to get products quickly, jeans are shipped already tagged from contract factories direct to Wal-Mart distribution centres, where Wal-Mart trucks pick them up and deliver them to individual stores.[22] When one company has power over another, it can ask suppliers to absorb more costs, ship more efficiently, and provide more services than ever before, often without a price increase. Often the suppliers have no choice but to go along, and those who fail to do so may go out of business.

Power is also shifting in other industries. For decades, technology vendors have been putting out incompatible products and expecting their corporate customers to assume the burden and expense of making everything work together. Those days are coming to an end. When the economy began declining, big corporations cut back their spending on technology, which led to stiffer competition among vendors and gave corporate customers greater power to make demands. Microsoft and Sun Microsystems, which have been waging war for 15 years, recently buried the hatchet and negotiated a collaboration agreement that will smooth the way for providing compatible software products.[23]

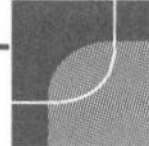

Collaborative Networks

Traditionally, the relationship between organizations and their suppliers has been an adversarial one. Indeed, North American companies typically have worked alone, competing with each other and believing in the tradition of individualism and self-reliance. Today, however, thanks to an uncertain global environment, a realignment in corporate relationships is taking place. The **collaborative-network** perspective is an emerging alternative to resource-dependence theory. Companies join together to become more competitive and to share scarce resources. Technology companies join together to produce next-generation products. Large aerospace firms partner with one another and with smaller companies and suppliers to design next-generation jets. Large pharmaceutical companies join with small biotechnology firms to share resources and knowledge and spur innovation. Nonprofit organizations often build bridges or bond to deal with the impact to their survival that environmental changes in the social sector bring.[24] Consulting firms, investment companies, and accounting firms may join in an alliance to meet customer demands for expanded services.[25] As companies move into their own uncharted territory, they are also racing into alliances.

Why Collaboration?

Why all this interest in interorganizational collaboration? Major reasons are sharing risks when entering new markets, mounting expensive new programs and reducing costs, and enhancing organizational profile in selected industries or technologies. Cooperation is a prerequisite for greater innovation, problem solving, and performance.[26] In addition, partnerships are a major avenue for entering global markets, with both large and small firms developing partnerships overseas and in North America.

North Americans have learned from their international experience just how effective interorganizational relationships can be. Both Japan and Korea have long traditions of corporate clans or industrial groups that collaborate and assist each other. North Americans typically have considered interdependence a bad thing, believing it would reduce competition. However, the experience of collaboration in other countries has shown that competition among companies can be fierce in some areas even as they collaborate in others. It is as if the brothers and sisters of a single family went into separate businesses and want to outdo one another, but they still love one another and will help each other when needed.

Interorganizational linkages provide a kind of safety net that encourages long-term investment and risk taking. Companies can achieve higher levels of innovation and performance as they learn to shift from an adversarial to a partnership mindset.[27] In many cases companies are learning to work closely together. Consider the following examples:

- Angiotech, a pharmaceutical and medical device company headquartered in Vancouver, has partnered with Boston Scientific Corporation to market coronary stent systems in Japan.[28]
- International pharmaceuticals giant Pfizer collaborates with more than 400 companies on research and development projects and co-marketing campaigns. For example, Pfizer has earned billions from co-promotion of Warner-Lambert's Lipitor, a drug for treating elevated cholesterol.[29]

- Leave No Trace Canada is a nonprofit organization whose mission is to promote and to inspire responsible outdoor recreation through education, research, and partnerships. To fulfill its mission, it has partnerships with co-operatives, governments, and business associations.[30]
- Small companies are banding together to compete against much larger firms. The Ontario Craft Brewers was formed in 2005 to increase awareness about members' beers with the goal of increasing their market share from 4 percent in 2005 to 12 percent by 2014. The Government of Ontario provided money to support the brewers' marketing campaign.[31]

PDA Remember...

Seek collaborative partnerships that enable mutual dependence and enhance value and gain for both sides. Get deeply involved in your partner's business, and vice versa, to benefit both.

From Adversaries to Partners

Fresh flowers are blooming on the battle-scarred landscape where once-bitter rivalries among suppliers, customers, and competitors took place. In North America, collaboration among organizations initially occurred in not-for-profit social service and mental health organizations where public interest was involved. Community organizations collaborated to achieve greater effectiveness and better use scarce resources.[32] With the push from international competitors and international examples, hard-nosed business managers began shifting to a new partnership paradigm on which to base their relationships.

A summary of this change in mindset is in Exhibit 5.3. More companies are changing from a traditional adversarial mindset to a partnership orientation. Evidence from studies of such companies as General Electric, Toyota, Whirlpool, Harley-Davidson, and Microsoft indicate that partnering allows reduced cost and increased value for both parties in a predatory world economy.[33] Rather than organizations

EXHIBIT 5.3 *Changing Characteristics of Interorganizational Relationships*

Traditional Orientation: Adversarial	New Orientation: Partnership
Low dependence	High dependence
Suspicion, competition, arm's length	Trust, addition of value to both sides, high commitment
Detailed performance measures, closely monitored	Loose performance measures, problems discussed
Price, efficacy, own profits	Equity, fair dealing, both profit
Limited information and feedback	Electronic linkages to share key information, problem feedback, and discussion
Legal resolution of conflict	Mechanisms for close coordination, people on site
Minimal involvement and up-front investment, separate resources	Involvement in partner's product design and production, shared resources
Short-term contracts	Long-term contracts
Contract limiting the relationship	Business assistance beyond the contract

Source: Based on Mick Marchington and Steven Vincent, "Analysing the Influence of Institutional, Organizational, and Interpersonal Forces in Shaping Inter-Organizational Relations," *Journal of Management Studies* 41, no. 6 (September 2004), 1029–1056; Jeffrey H. Dyer, "How Chrysler Created an American Keiretsu," *Harvard Business Review* (July–August 1996), 42–56; Myron Magnet, "The New Golden Rule of Business," *Fortune* (February 21, 1994), 60–64; and Peter Grittner, "Four Elements of Successful Sourcing Strategies," *Management Review* (October 1995), 41–45.

maintaining independence, the new model is based on interdependence and trust. Performance measures for the partnership are loosely defined, and problems are resolved through discussion and dialogue. Managing strategic relationships with other firms has become a critical management skill, as discussed in this chapter's Book Mark. In the new orientation, people try to add value to both sides and believe in high commitment rather than suspicion and competition. Companies work toward equitable profits for both sides rather than just for their own benefit. The new model is characterized by lots of shared information, including electronic linkages for automatic ordering and face-to-face discussions to provide corrective feedback and solve problems. Sometimes people from other companies are on site to enable very close coordination, as we saw in the chapter-opening example. Partners are involved in each other's product design and production, and they invest for the long term, with an assumption of continuing relations. Partners develop equitable solutions to conflicts rather than relying on legal contractual relationships. Contracts may be loosely specified, and it is not unusual for business partners to help each other outside whatever is specified in the contract.[34]

Book Mark 5.0 (HAVE YOU READ THIS BOOK?)

Managing Strategic Relationships: The Key to Business Success
By Leonard Greenhalgh

What determines organizational success in the 21st century? According to Leonard Greenhalgh, author of *Managing Strategic Relationships: The Key to Business Success*, it's how successfully managers support, foster, and protect collaborative relationships both inside and outside the firm. The book offers strategies for managing relationships between people and groups within the company and with other organizations. Effectively managing relationships generates a sense of commonwealth and consensus, which ultimately results in competitive advantage.

MANAGING RELATIONSHIPS IN A NEW ERA

Greenhalgh says managers need a new way of thinking to fit the realities of the new era. Here are a few guidelines:

- *Recognize that detailed legal contracts can undermine trust and goodwill.* Greenhalgh stresses the need to build relationships that are based on honesty, trust, understanding, and common goals instead of on narrowly defined legal contracts that concentrate on what one business can give to the other.
- *Treat partners like members of your own organization.* Members of partner organizations need to be active participants in the learning experience by becoming involved in training, team meetings, and other activities. Giving a partner organization's employees a chance to make genuine contributions promotes deeper bonds and a sense of unity.
- *Top managers must be champions for the alliance.* Managers from both organizations have to act in ways that signal to everyone inside and outside the organization a new emphasis on partnership and collaboration. Using ceremony and symbols can help instill a commitment to partnership in the company culture.

CONCLUSION

To succeed in today's environment, old-paradigm management practices based on power, hierarchy, and adversarial relationships must be traded for new-era commonwealth practices that emphasize collaboration and communal forms of organization. The companies that will thrive, Greenhalgh believes, "are those that really have their act together—those that can successfully integrate strategy, processes, business arrangements, resources, systems, and empowered workforces." That can be accomplished, he argues, only by effectively creating, shaping, and sustaining strategic relationships.

Managing Strategic Relationships: The Key to Business Success, by Leonard Greenhalgh, is published by The Free Press.

This new partnership mindset can be seen in a number of industries. Microsoft hired contract manufacturer Flextronics to not only build but also help design Xbox, its electronic game console.[35] Many supermarkets and other retailers rely on key suppliers to help them determine what goes on the store shelves. A large vendor such as Procter & Gamble, for example, analyzes national data and makes recommendations for what products the store should offer, including not just P&G's brands, but products from its competitors as well.[36] A large company in England that supplies pigments to the automobile, plastics, and printing industries has a long-standing interdependent relationship with a key chemicals supplier, with the two organizations sharing information about their long-term business needs so that any changes in products or processes can benefit both sides.[37]

In this new view of partnerships, dependence on another company is seen to reduce rather than increase risks. Greater value can be achieved by both parties. By being embedded in a system of interorganizational relationships, everyone does better by helping each other. This is a far cry from the belief that organizations do best by being autonomous and independent. Sales representatives may have a desk on the customer's factory floor, and they have access to information systems and the research lab.[38] Coordination is so intimate that it's sometimes hard to tell one organization from another. Consider how Bombardier and its suppliers are linked together almost like one organization in building the Continental, a "super-midsize" business jet that can comfortably fly eight passengers nonstop from coast to coast.

In Practice
Bombardier

In an assembly plant on the edge of Mid-Continent Airport in Wichita, Kansas, a new plane is taking shape as great chunks of it are rolled in and joined together. Not counting rivets, it takes just a dozen big parts—all manufactured elsewhere—to put Bombardier's Continental together. Those big subassemblies come from all over the world—the engines from Phoenix in the United States; the nose and cockpit from Montréal; the mid-fuselage from Belfast, Northern Ireland; the tail from Taichung, Taiwan; the wings from Nagoya, Japan; and other parts from Australia, France, Germany, and Austria. When production is up to full speed, it will take just four days to put a plane together and get it in the air.

In the past, most executive-jet companies have made major parts in-house. Bombardier, instead, relies heavily on suppliers for design support and the sharing of development costs and market risks. The company is intertwined with about 30 suppliers, a dozen or so of which have been involved since the design stage. At one point, about 250 team members from Bombardier and 250 from outsider suppliers worked together in Montréal to make sure the design would be good for everyone involved. Bombardier has so far invested about $250 million in the Continental, but suppliers have equalled that amount in development costs. In addition to sharing costs, the supplier companies also share the risks. "They haven't got a contract that says, 'You're going to sell us twenty-five wings a year for the next 10 years.' If the market's there, it's there, and if it's not, it's not," says John Holding, who is in charge of Bombardier's engineering and product development.[39]

Integrating partners so that everyone benefits from and depends on the others—and managing this multinational, multi-company endeavour—is no easy task, but with development costs for a new plane reaching more than $1 billion, the partnership approach just makes sense.[40]

By breaking down boundaries and becoming involved in partnerships with an attitude of fair dealing and adding value to both sides, today's companies are changing the concept of what makes an organization. The type of collaborative network illustrated by Bombardier is also being used by a growing number of automotive companies, including Volkswagen and General Motors. These companies are pushing the idea of partnership further than ever before, moving somewhat toward a network approach to organizational design.

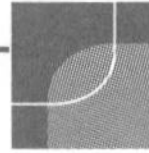

Population Ecology

This section introduces a different perspective on relationships among organizations. The **population-ecology perspective** differs from the other perspectives because it focuses on organizational diversity and adaptation within a population of organizations.[41] A **population** is a set of organizations engaged in similar activities with similar patterns of resource utilization and outcomes. Organizations within a population compete for similar resources or similar customers, such as financial institutions in the Edmonton area would do.

Within a population, the question asked by ecology researchers is about the large number and variation of organizations in society. Why are new organizational forms that create such diversity constantly appearing? The answer is that individual organizational adaptation is severely limited compared to the changes demanded by the environment. Innovation and change in a population of organizations take place through the birth of new forms and kinds of organizations more so than by the reform and change of existing organizations. Indeed, organizational forms are considered relatively stable, and the good of a whole society is served by the development of new forms of organization through entrepreneurial initiatives. New organizations meet the new needs of society more than established organizations that are slow to change.[42]

What does this theory mean in practical terms? It means that large, established organizations often become dinosaurs. As discussed in the previous chapter, large airlines that rely on a hub-and-spoke system have had tremendous difficulty adapting to a rapidly changing environment. Hence, new organizational forms are emerging that fit the current environment, fill a new niche, and, over time, take away business from established companies. Bullfrog Power, for example, provides 100 percent green electricity to Ontario and Alberta residents and businesses, and is changing the landscape of electricity generation.[43]

PDA Remember...

Adapt your organization to new variations being selected and retained in the external environment. If you are starting a new organization, find a niche that contains a strong environmental need for your product or service, and be prepared for a competitive struggle over scarce resources.

Why do established organizations have such a hard time adapting to a rapidly changing environment? Michael Hannan and John Freeman, originators of the population-ecology model of organization, argue that there are many limitations on the ability of organizations to change. The limitations come from heavy investment in plants, equipment, and specialized personnel; limited information; established viewpoints of decision makers; the organization's own successful history that justifies current procedures; and the difficulty of changing organizational culture. True transformation is a rare and unlikely event in the face of all these barriers

For example, large equipment makers such as Cisco, Nortel Networks, and Sun Microsystems are feeling the pinch as they lose million-dollar deals to used-equipment brokers. Another recent change is the development of corporate universities within large companies like Motorola and FedEx. There are more than 2,000 corporate universities, compared to just 200 a few years ago. One reason they've developed so quickly is that companies can't get desired services from established universities, which are too stuck in traditional ways of thinking and teaching.[44]

According to the population-ecology view, when looking at an organizational population as a whole, the changing environment determines which organizations survive or fail. The assumption is that individual organizations suffer from structural inertia and find it difficult to adapt to environmental changes. Thus, when rapid change occurs, old organizations are likely to decline or fail, and new organizations emerge that are better suited to the needs of the environment.

The population-ecology model is developed from theories of natural selection in biology, and the terms *evolution* and *selection* are used to refer to the underlying behavioural processes. Theories of biological evolution try to explain why certain life forms appear and survive whereas others perish. Some theories suggest the forms that survive are typically best fitted to the immediate environment.

Some years ago, *Forbes* magazine reported a study of American businesses over 70 years, from 1917 to 1987. Of the 22 that remained in the top 100, only 11 did so under their original names. The environment of the 1940s and 1950s was suitable to Woolworth, but new organizational forms like Wal-Mart became dominant in the 1980s. In 1917, most of the top 100 companies were huge steel and mining industrial organizations, which were replaced by high-technology companies such as IBM and Merck.[45] Two companies that seemed to prosper over a long period were Ford and General Motors, but they are now being threatened by world changes in the automobile industry. Meanwhile, technology continues to change the environment. The expansion of the Internet into the many consumers' households has brought a proliferation of new organizations such as Facebook, Google, Skype, and eBay.

No company is immune to the processes of social change. More and more Canadian firms are being bought by international companies and there is concern that the Canadian economy is being hollowed out. In response to the concern, a federal panel was set up in 2007 to review foreign ownership and to examine the *Investment Canada Act*.[46] On the other hand, Canadian National Railway has been buying up American railways; in 2007, it bought the major portion of the Elgin, Joliet, and Eastern Railway (EJ&E) for US$300 million.[47]

Organizational Form and Niche

The population-ecology model is concerned with organizational form. **Organizational form** is an organization's specific technology, structure, products, goals, and personnel, which can be selected or rejected by the environment. Each new organization tries to find a **niche** (a domain of unique environmental resources and needs) sufficient to support it. The niche is usually small in the early stages of an organization but may increase in size over time if the organization is successful. If a niche is not available, the organization will decline and may perish.

From the viewpoint of a single firm, luck, chance, and randomness play important parts in survival. New products and ideas are continually being proposed by both entrepreneurs and large organizations. Whether these ideas and organizational forms survive or fail is often a matter of chance—whether external circumstances happen to support them. Success or failure of a single firm is predicted by the characteristics of the environment as much as by the skills or strategies used by the organization.

EXHIBIT 5.4
Elements in the Population-Ecology Model of Organizations

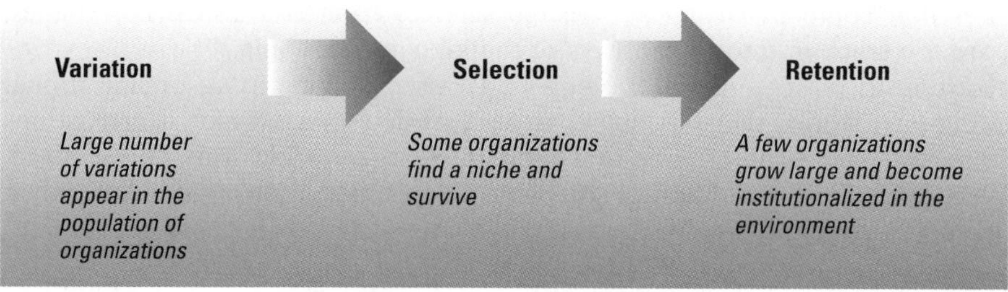

Process of Ecological Change

The population-ecology model assumes that new organizations are always appearing in the population. Thus, organization populations are continually undergoing change. The process of change in the population is defined by three principles that occur in stages: variation, selection, and retention. These stages are summarized in Exhibit 5.4.

- **Variation** means the appearance of new, diverse forms in a population of organizations. These new organizational forms are initiated by entrepreneurs, established with venture capital by large corporations, or set up by a government seeking to provide new services. Some forms may be conceived to cope with a perceived need in the external environment. In recent years, a large number of new firms have been initiated to develop computer software, to provide consulting and other services to large corporations, and to develop products and technologies for Internet commerce. Other new organizations produce a traditional product such as steel, but do it using minimal technology and new management techniques that make the new companies, such as the steel company Nucor, far more able to survive. Organizational variations are analogous to mutations in biology, and they add to the scope and complexity of organizational forms in the environment. This chapter's Leading by Design box describes a new organizational form conceived by a British entrepreneur to capitalize on advances in information technology and wireless text messaging.
- **Selection** refers to whether a new organizational form is suited to the environment and can survive. Only a few variations are "selected in" by the environment and survive over the long term. Some variations will suit the external environment better than others. Some prove beneficial and thus are able to find a niche and acquire the resources from the environment necessary to survive. Other variations fail to meet the needs of the environment and perish. When there is insufficient demand for a firm's product and when insufficient resources are available to the organization, that organization will be "selected out." For example, Shazam, described in the Leading by Design box, was launched in mid-2002. If demand for the new service does not continue to grow, or if the company cannot obtain needed resources, the company will be selected out and cease to exist. (In 2008, Shazam had become established and, for example, was on Facebook.)
- **Retention** is the preservation and institutionalization of selected organizational forms. Certain technologies, products, and services are highly valued by the

environment, and the retained organizational form may become a dominant part of the environment. Many forms of organization have been institutionalized, such as government, schools, churches, and automobile manufacturers. McDonald's, which owns 43 percent of the fast-food market and provides the first job for many teenagers, has become institutionalized in North American life.

Institutionalized organizations like McDonald's seem to be relatively permanent features in the population of organizations, but they are not permanent in the long run. The environment is always changing, and, if the dominant organizational forms do not adapt to external change, they will gradually diminish and be replaced by other organizations. McDonald's is struggling because customers think rivals Burger King and Wendy's provide fresher, higher-quality food at better prices. In addition, chains such as Subway and Quizno's are offering today's health-conscious customer an alternative to fast-food burgers and fries. In an annual consumer satisfaction survey, McDonald's has scored dead last among fast-food restaurants every year since 1992.[48] In response, McDonald's has launched the "latest evolution of the

Leading *by Design*

Shazam—It's Magic!

Many people have had the experience of hearing a song they like on the radio or in a dance club and waiting in vain for the DJ to identify it. Shazam, a mobile-phone music service launched in the United Kingdom in August 2002, has come to the rescue. The next time a cell phone user hears that mystery tune, he or she simply dials a four-digit number on the cell phone, lets the music play into the handset, and moments later receives a text message with the artist and song title. The user can forward a 30-second clip of the track to friends, or even download the song directly to his or her phone. The song can then be legally copied from the mobile phone to a computer and shared between multiple devices.

Shazam's magic happens through the use of a pattern-recognition software algorithm developed by the company's chief scientist. The algorithm picks out the salient characteristics of a tune and matches them against a massive music database. The company, founded by Californian entrepreneur Chris Barton, calls the process "tagging," and users in the United Kingdom alone have already tagged more than 5.5 million music tracks. Users can go online and see a list of all the songs they've tagged.

Shazam's success depends on collaborative partnerships with mobile-phone companies, major record labels, software companies, and others. A recent partnership with Swiss-based SDC (Secure Digital Container) AG provides the technology that enables a complete "tag to download" in three simple steps, allowing users to purchase music on the move. A strategic alliance with MTV Japan helped Shazam expand to about 40 million mobile-phone subscribers in Japan. Deals with international mobile operators and media companies throughout the United States, Europe, and Asia make Shazam's service available to more than 1 billion mobile-phone users worldwide.

The mobile-phone companies offer tagging as a premium service to their customers and pay Shazam a cut of the profits. Since tagging promises to drive up call times, most mobile-phone companies are interested. And the record labels' interests are served by getting new music in front of consumers. Word-of-mouth recommendations are a powerful means of driving music sales, so the idea of people all over the world forwarding 30-second clips of their new songs has music companies paying attention. The service has proven to be a good predictor of future hits in Britain, so the music industry closely watches Shazam's weekly chart of tagged pre-release tracks.

Shazam is the world's first in music recognition and one of the brightest new ideas in the world of technology. With multiple deals and a presence in 12 countries, it is clear that Shazam is suited to the environment and has found a solid niche. However, managing the complex network of global relationships will be a challenge for managers of the small company, and it remains to be seen if they can take a good idea and build a lasting organization.[49]

Canadian Balanced Lifestyles program, [promoted by] Canadian hockey legend Wayne Gretzky."[50] Unless it adapts effectively, McDonald's may no longer be competitive in the fast-food market.

From the population-ecology perspective, the environment is the important determinant of organizational success or failure. The organization must meet an environmental need, or it will be selected out. The process of variation, selection, and retention leads to the establishment of new organizational forms in a population of organizations.

Strategies for Survival

Another principle that underlies the population-ecology model is the **struggle for existence**, or competition. Organizations and populations of organizations are engaged in a competitive struggle over resources, and each organizational form is fighting to survive. For example, since coming out from under the protection of the *Companies' Creditors Arrangement Act* in April 2006, Stelco has lost $240 million as it overestimated demand from the automotive sector and underestimated the role steel imports play in Canada. CEO Rodney Mott is now "holding a garage sale of . . . non-core assets that were somehow core enough to survive the restructure attempt under [the Act]"[51] so that Stelco might survive.

The struggle is most intense among new organizations, and both the birth and survival frequencies of new organizations are related to factors in the larger environment. Factors such as size of urban area, percentage of immigrants, political turbulence, industry growth rate, and environmental variability have influenced the launching and survival of newspapers, telecommunication firms, railroads, government agencies, labour unions, and even voluntary organizations.[52]

In the population-ecology perspective, **generalist** and **specialist** strategies distinguish organizational forms in the struggle for survival. Organizations with a wide niche or domain, that is, those that offer a broad range of products or services or that serve a broad market, are generalists. Organizations that provide a narrower range of goods or services or that serve a narrower market are specialists. In the business world, Indigo.ca started with a specialist strategy, selling books over the Internet, but evolved to a generalist strategy with the addition of music, DVDs, greeting cards, and other products, plus partnering with other organizations to sell a wide range of products online. An organization such as inuitart.ca, whose product line includes traditional Holman packing dolls of the Northwest Territories, would be considered a specialist, whereas Mattel is a generalist, marketing a broad range of toys for children of all ages.[53]

Specialists are generally more competitive than generalists in the narrow area in which their domains overlap. However, the breadth of the generalist's domain serves to protect it somewhat from environmental changes. Though demand may decrease for some of the generalist's products or services, it usually increases for others at the same time. In addition, because of the diversity of products, services, and customers, generalists are able to reallocate resources internally to adapt to a changing environment, whereas specialists are not. However, because specialists are often smaller companies, they can sometimes move faster and be more flexible in adapting to changes.[54]

Managerial impact on company success often comes from selecting a strategy that steers a company into an open niche. Consider how Apotex has thrived in the generic drug sector.

In Practice

Apotex

Barry Sherman, using his mother's life savings as collateral, founded Apotex in 1974. "Notoriously litigious (and persistent), [CEO] Sherman has filed hundreds of lawsuits against manufacturers that have blocked Apotex from making cheap clones of their products."[55] He has also sued researchers and, in 2007, sued his cousin for $8 million.[56] On the other hand, he gives away 20 percent of his income every year and drives a modest car.

Apotex has grown to become the nation's largest pharmaceutical company with 5,000 employees in research, development, manufacturing, and distribution facilities around the world. It specializes in the production and distribution of generic drugs. Apotex produces more than 250 generic drugs in approximately 4,000 dosages and formats that fill 60 million prescriptions annually in Canada alone.

Apotex exports its drugs to 115 countries and has subsidiaries, joint ventures, or licensing agreements in the Czech Republic, Mexico, China, Poland, New Zealand, France, Italy, and other countries. Apotex also researches, develops, and manufactures fine chemicals, non-prescription and private-label medicines, and disposable plastics for medical use. It controls several health-related companies, including Winnipeg-based Cangene and U.S.–based Barr Laboratories , the pharmacist to Wal-Mart. Apotex's annual worldwide sales in 2006 were $900 million. In 2005, Apotex spent $153 million in research and development.[57]

Apotex manufactures an anti–AIDS drug that the Rwandan government plans to buy. Rwanda is the first country in the world to use global trade rules to override pharmaceutical patents and import generic drugs. Rwanda plans to buy 260,000 packs of Apotex's TriAvir, which combines three patented brand-name drugs: zidovudine, lamivudine, and nevirapine. The announcement by Rwanda is the first step for Apotex to get a licence that will allow it to produce and export the drug. As well, Apotex has an agreement with Médecins sans Frontières and has stockpiled its anti–AIDS drug for distribution in Africa.[58]

Apotex isn't immune from the volatility and uncertainty inherent in the industry, but it found a niche that put the company on a solid foundation for survival over the long term. CEO Sherman chose a specialist strategy, focusing on generic drugs.

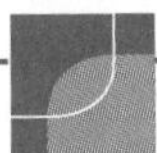

Institutionalism

The institutional perspective provides yet another view of interorganizational relationships.[59] Organizations are highly interconnected. Just as companies need efficient production to survive, the institutional view argues that organizations need legitimacy from their stakeholders. Companies perform well when they are perceived by the larger environment to have a legitimate right to exist. Thus, the **institutional perspective** describes how organizations survive and succeed through congruence between an organization and the expectations from its environment. The **institutional environment** is composed of norms and values from stakeholders (customers, investors, associations, boards, government, and collaborating organizations). Thus the institutional view believes that organizations adopt structures and processes to please outsiders, and these activities come to take on rule-like status in organizations. The institutional environment reflects what the greater society views as correct ways of organizing and behaving.[60]

Legitimacy is defined as the general perspective that an organization's actions are desirable, proper, and appropriate within the environment's system of norms, values, and beliefs.[61] Institutional theory thus is concerned with the set of intangible norms and values that shape behaviour, as opposed to the tangible elements of technology and structure. Organizations must fit within the cognitive and emotional expectations of their audience. For example, people will not deposit money in a bank unless it sends signals of compliance with norms of wise financial management. Consider also your municipal government and whether it could raise property taxes for increased police services if community residents did not approve.

Most organizations are concerned with legitimacy. Corporations are paying attention to their social responsibility rankings. In 2007, the Royal Bank of Canada was ranked first in Corporate Knights' annual listing of Best 50 Corporate Citizens. Alcan, VanCity Savings Credit Union, Dofasco, and Hydro-Quebec round out the top five.[62] Many corporations actively shape and manage their reputations to increase their competitive advantage, and managers are searching for new ways to bolster legitimacy in the wake of ethical and financial scandals at such well-known companies as Boeing, Enron, and WorldCom. One American company that has built a reputation as a highly ethical and socially responsible company is Johnson & Johnson, where managers stress the company's commitment to customers, employees, and the broader community. Johnson & Johnson has ranked in first place for six years in a row on the Reputation Quotient, which surveys more than 20,000 people in telephone and online interviews.

In Practice

Wal-Mart

Wal-Mart has been pilloried in the film, *Walmart, The High Cost of Low Price*. For the first time in its history, Wal-Mart is facing a serious legitimacy problem. A combination of factors has led to a decline in the company's reputation and a growing criticism of its practices.

People naturally begin to distrust corporations that grow so large and dominant as Wal-Mart. It is the world's largest corporation and has substantial bargaining power with its suppliers to cut costs. "Wal-Mart is so big and so centralized that it can all at once hook Chinese and other suppliers into its digital system. So—wham—you have a large switch to overseas sourcing in a period quicker than in the old rules of retailing."[63] In addition, the company's size has brought a host of new management challenges. Publicity about cleaning contractors using illegal immigrants in American Wal-Mart stores tarnished the company's pristine image. Wal-Mart's early-1990s' claim to "Buy American" has quietly been shelved as the company has more than doubled its imports from China since then. And some critics charge that manufacturers of everything from bras to bicycles have had to close plants, lay off workers, and outsource to low-wage countries in order to survive in the face of Wal-Mart's cost-cutting demands. Employee complaints about low pay, and a damaging gender-discrimination suit, have compounded the company's image problems.

Wal-Mart's 1998 foray into the German market was unsuccessful, and the company shut down its German outlets in 2006. "Wal-Mart's attempt to apply the company's proven U.S. success formula in an unmodified manner to the German market turned out to be nothing short of a fiasco."[64] Wal-Mart's approach ran afoul of German labour laws and traditions. As well, Wal-Mart underestimated the extent of the differences between the U.S. and German markets; for example, it provided pillow cases that fit North American pillows but did not fit German pillows! Wal-Mart's exit from Germany cost the company $1 billion.[65]

Consumers are still captivated by Wal-Mart's low prices, but there is growing concern and criticism about the high social and economic costs of the company's low-cost approach. "Shoppers could start feeling guilty about shopping with us," says Wal-Mart spokeswoman, Mona Williams. "Communities could make it harder to build our stores."[66] According to a McKinsey study, between 2 and 8 percent of consumers are no longer shopping at Wal-Mart because of its practices. "Wal-Mart operates on such razor thin margins, and [the market] demands such strong quarter-over-quarter sales, that the total impact of the public relations swirl could be devastating in the short and long term."[67]

Wal-Mart has not been seriously damaged by these criticisms, but managers know that how the company is perceived by customers and the public plays a big role in long-term success. Wal-Mart is extremely powerful today, but its power could decline if the company's actions are not considered legitimate and appropriate. Wal-Mart's recent green commitments may help the company to combat its image problems. In 2007, for example, Wal-Mart Canada announced that it was buying green electricity from Bullfrog Power for the next three years and, as a result, it became the nation's largest commercial purchaser of green power.

The fact that there is a payoff for having a good reputation is verified by a study of organizations in the airline industry. Having a good reputation was significantly related to higher levels of performance measures such as return on assets and net profit margin.[68]

The notion of legitimacy answers an important question for institutional theorists. Why is there so much homogeneity in the forms and practices of established organizations? For example, visit banks, high schools, hospitals, government departments, or business firms in a similar industry, in any part of the country, and they will look strikingly similar. When an organizational field is just getting started, such as in e-commerce, diversity is the norm. New organizations fill emerging niches. However, once an industry becomes established, there is an invisible push toward similarity.

The Institutional View and Organizational Design

The institutional view also sees organizations as having two essential dimensions—technical and institutional. The technical dimension is the day-to-day work, technology, and operating requirements. The institutional structure is that part of the organization most visible to the outside public. Moreover, the technical dimension is governed by norms of rationality and efficiency, but the institutional dimension is governed by expectations from the external environment. As a result, the formal structures of some organizations reflect the expectations and values of the environment rather than the demand of work activities. This means that an organization may incorporate positions or activities (equal employment officer, e-commerce division, chief ethics officer) perceived as important by the larger society to increase its legitimacy and survival prospects, even though these elements may decrease efficiency. For example, many small companies set up websites, even though the benefits gained from the site are sometimes outweighed by the costs of maintaining it. Having a website is perceived as essential today. The formal structure and design of an organization may not be rational with respect to workflow and products or services, but it may ensure survival in the larger environment.

Organizations adapt to the environment by signalling their congruence with the demands and expectations stemming from cultural norms, standards set by professional bodies, funding agencies, and customers. Structure is something of a facade disconnected from technical work through which the organization obtains approval, legitimacy, and continuing support. The adoption of structures thus might not be linked to actual production needs, and might occur regardless of whether specific internal problems are solved.[69]

Institutional Similarity

Organizations have a strong need to appear legitimate. In so doing, many aspects of structure and behaviour may be targeted toward environmental acceptance rather

PDA Remember...

Pursue legitimacy with your organization's major stakeholders in the external environment. Adopt strategies, structures, and new management techniques that meet the expectations of significant parties, thereby ensuring their cooperation and access to resources.

than toward internal technical efficiency. Interorganizational relationships thus are characterized by forces that cause organizations in a similar population to look like one another. **Institutional similarity**, called *institutional isomorphism* in the academic literature, is the emergence of a common structure and approach among organizations in the same field. Isomorphism is the process that causes one unit in a population to resemble other units that face the same set of environmental conditions.[70]

Exactly how does increasing similarity occur? How are these forces realized? These three core mechanisms are *mimetic forces,* which result from responses to uncertainty; *coercive forces,* which stem from political influence; and *normative forces,* which result from common training and professionalism.[71]

Mimetic Forces. Most organizations, especially business organizations, face great uncertainty. It is not clear to senior executives exactly what products, services, or technologies will achieve desired goals, and sometimes the goals themselves are not clear. In the face of this uncertainty, **mimetic forces**, the pressure to copy or model other organizations, occur.

Executives observe an innovation in a firm generally regarded as successful, so the management practice is quickly copied. An example is the proliferation of Wi-Fi hotspots in cafes, hotels, and airports. Starbucks was one of the first companies to adopt Wi-Fi, enabling customers to use laptops and handheld computers at Starbucks stores. The practice has rapidly been copied by both large and small companies, from Holiday Inns to the local deli. Many times, this modelling is done without any clear proof that performance will be improved. Mimetic processes explain why fads and fashions occur in the business world. Once a new idea starts, many organizations grab onto it, only to learn that the application is difficult and may cause more problems than it solves. This was the case with the recent merger wave that swept many industries. The past two decades have seen the largest merger and acquisition wave in history, but evidence shows that many of these mergers did not produce the expected financial gains and other benefits. The sheer momentum of the trend was so powerful that many companies chose to merge not because of potential increases in efficiency or profitability but simply because it seemed like the right thing to do.[72] Downsizing of the workforce is another trend that can be attributed partly to mimetic forces. Despite some evidence that massive downsizing actually hurts organizations, managers perceive it as a legitimate and effective means of improving performance.[73]

Techniques such as outsourcing, reengineering, Six Sigma quality programs, and the balanced scorecard have all been adopted without clear evidence that they will improve efficiency or effectiveness. The one certain benefit is that management's feelings of uncertainty will be reduced, and the company's image will be enhanced because the firm is seen as using the latest management techniques. A recent study of 100 organizations confirmed that those companies associated with using popular management techniques were more admired and rated higher in quality of management, even though these organizations often did not reflect higher economic performance.[74] Perhaps the clearest example of official copying is the technique of benchmarking that occurs as part of the total quality movement. *Benchmarking* means identifying who's best at something in an industry and then duplicating the technique for creating excellence, perhaps even improving it in the process.

The mimetic process works because organizations face continuous high uncertainty, they are aware of innovations occurring in the environment, and the innovations are culturally supported, thereby giving legitimacy to adopters. This is a strong mechanism by which a group of banks, or high schools, or manufacturing firms begin to look and act like one another.

Coercive Forces. All organizations are subject to pressure, both formal and informal, from government, regulatory agencies, and other important organizations in the environment, especially those on which a company is dependent. **Coercive forces** are the external pressures exerted on an organization to adopt structures, techniques, or behaviours similar to other organizations. As with other changes, those brought about because of coercive forces may not make the organization more effective, but it will look more effective and will be accepted as legitimate in the environment. Some pressures may have the force of law, such as government mandates to adopt new pollution-control equipment. Health and safety regulations may demand that a safety officer be appointed. New regulations and government oversight boards have been set up for the accounting industry following widespread accounting scandals.[75]

Coercive pressures may also occur between organizations where there is a power difference, as described in the resource-dependence section earlier in this chapter. Large retailers and manufacturers often insist that certain policies, procedures, and techniques be used by their suppliers. When Honda picked Donnelly Corporation of the United States to make all the mirrors for its U.S.–manufactured cars, Honda insisted that Donnelly implement an employee-empowerment program. Honda managers believed the partnership could work only if Donnelly learned how to foster collaborative internal relationships.

Organizational changes that result from coercive forces occur when an organization is dependent on another, when there are political factors such as rules, laws, and sanctions involved, or when some other contractual or legal basis defines the relationship. Organizations operating under those constraints will adopt changes and relate to one another in a way that increases homogeneity and limits diversity.

Normative Forces. According to the institutional view, the third reason organizations change is normative forces. **Normative forces** are pressures to change to achieve standards of professionalism, and to adopt techniques that are considered by the professional community to be up to date and effective. Changes may be in any area, such as information technology, accounting requirements, marketing techniques, or collaborative relationships with other organizations.

Professionals share a body of formal education based on university degrees and professional networks through which ideas are exchanged by consultants and professional leaders. Universities, consulting firms, trade associations, and professional training institutions develop norms among professional managers. People are exposed to similar training and standards and adopt shared values, which are implemented in organizations with which they work. Business schools teach finance, marketing, and human resource students that certain techniques are better than others, so using those techniques becomes a standard in the field. In one study, for example, a radio station changed from a functional to a multidivisional structure because a consultant recommended it as a "higher standard" of doing business. There was no proof that this structure was better, but the radio station wanted legitimacy and to be perceived as fully professional and up to date in its management techniques.

Companies accept normative pressures to become like one another through a sense of obligation or duty to high standards of performance based on professional norms shared by managers and specialists in their respective organizations. These

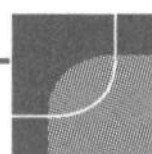

PDA Remember...

Enhance legitimacy by borrowing good ideas from other firms, complying with laws and regulations, and following procedures considered best for your organization.

norms are conveyed through professional education and certification and have almost a moral or ethical requirement based on the highest standards accepted by the profession at that time. In some cases, though, normative forces that maintain legitimacy break down, as they recently did in the accounting industry, and coercive forces are needed to shift organizations back toward acceptable standards.

An organization may use any or all of the mechanisms of mimetic, coercive, or normative forces to change itself for greater legitimacy in the institutional environment. Firms tend to use these mechanisms when they are acting under conditions of dependence, uncertainty, ambiguous goals, and reliance on professional credentials. The outcome of these processes is that organizations become far more homogeneous than would be expected from the natural diversity among managers and environments.

Summary and Interpretation

This chapter has been about the important evolution in interorganizational relationships. At one time organizations considered themselves autonomous and separate, trying to outdo one another. Today more organizations see themselves as part of an ecosystem. The organization may span several industries and will be anchored in a dense web of relationships with other companies. In this ecosystem, collaboration is as important as competition. Indeed, organizations may compete and collaborate at the same time depending on the location and issue. In this business ecosystem, the role of management is changing to include the development of horizontal relationships with other organizations.

Four perspectives have been developed to explain relationships among organizations. The resource-dependence perspective is the most traditional, arguing that organizations try to avoid excessive dependence on other organizations. In this view, organizations devote considerable effort to controlling the environment to ensure ample resources while maintaining independence. Moreover, powerful organizations will exploit the dependence of small ones. The collaborative-network perspective is an emerging alternative. Organizations welcome collaboration and interdependence with other organizations to enhance value for both. Many executives are changing mindsets away from autonomy toward collaboration, often with former corporate enemies. The new mindset emphasizes trust, fair dealing, and achieving profits for all parties in a relationship.

The population-ecology perspective explains why organizational diversity continuously increases with the appearance of new organizations filling niches left open by established companies. This perspective says that large companies usually cannot adapt to meet a changing environment; hence, new companies emerge with the appropriate form and skills to serve new needs. Through the process of variation, selection, and retention, some organizations will survive and grow while others perish. Companies may adopt a generalist or specialist strategy to survive in the population of organizations.

The institutional perspective argues that interorganizational relationships are shaped as much by a company's need for legitimacy as by the need for providing products and services. The need for legitimacy means that the organization will adopt structures and activities that are perceived as valid, proper, and up to date by external stakeholders. In this way, established organizations copy techniques from one another and begin to look very similar. The emergence of common structures and approaches in the same field is called institutional similarity or institutional isomorphism. There are three core mechanisms that explain increasing organizational homogeneity: mimetic forces, which result from responses to uncertainty; coercive forces, which stem from power differences and political influences; and normative forces, which result from common training and professionalism.

Each of the four perspectives is valid. They represent different lenses through which the world of interorganizational relationships can be viewed: organizations experience a competitive struggle for autonomy; they can thrive through collaborative relationships with others; the slowness to adapt provides openings for new organizations to flourish; and organizations seek legitimacy as well as profits from the external environment. The important thing is for managers to be aware of interorganizational relationships and to consciously manage them.

Key Concepts

coercive forces, p. 183
collaborative network, p. 170
generalist, p. 178
institutional environment, p. 179
institutional perspective, p. 179
institutional similarity, p. 182
interorganizational relationships, p. 165
legitimacy, p. 179
mimetic forces, p. 182
niche, p. 175
normative forces, p. 183
organizational ecosystem, p. 165
organizational form, p. 175
population, p. 174
population-ecology perspective, p. 174
retention, p. 176
selection, p. 176
specialist, p. 178
struggle for existence, p. 178
variation, p. 176

Discussion Questions

1. The concept of business ecosystems implies that organizations are more interdependent than ever before. From personal experience, do you agree? Explain.
2. How do you feel about the prospect of becoming a manager and having to manage a set of relationships with other companies rather than just managing your own company? Discuss.
3. Assume you are the manager of a small firm that is dependent on a large computer manufacturing customer that uses the resource-dependence perspective. Put yourself in the position of the small firm, and describe what actions you would take to survive and succeed. From the perspective of the large firm, what actions would you take?
4. Many managers today were trained under assumptions of adversarial relationships with other companies. Do you think operating as adversaries is easier or more difficult than operating as partners with other companies? Discuss.
5. Discuss how the adversarial versus partnership orientations work among students in class. Is there a sense of competition for grades? Is it possible to develop true partnerships in which your work depends on others?
6. The population-ecology perspective argues that it is healthy for society to have new organizations emerging and old organizations dying as the environment changes. Do you agree? Why might European countries pass laws to sustain traditional organizations and inhibit the emergence of new ones?
7. Explain how the process of variation, selection, and retention might explain innovations that take place within an organization.

8. Do you believe that legitimacy really motivates a large, powerful organization such as Wal-Mart? Is acceptance by other people a motivation for individuals as well? Explain.
9. How does the desire for legitimacy result in organizations becoming more similar over time?
10. How do mimetic forces differ from normative forces? Give an example of each.

Chapter 5 Workbook: Management Fads*

Look up one or two articles on current trends or fads in management. Then, find one or two articles on a management fad from several years ago. Finally, surf the Internet for information on both the current and previous fads.

Questions

1. How were these fads used in organizations? Use real examples from your readings.
2. Why do you think the fads were adopted? To what extent were the fads adopted to truly improve productivity and morale versus the company's desire to appear current in its management techniques compared to the competition?
3. Give an example in which a fad did not work as expected. Explain why it did not work.

Case for Analysis: Apple

JULY 9, 2007

Steve Jobs had plenty of problems to contend with as he sauntered onstage for his first speech after returning to the top of Apple in 1997. He faced a shrinking market for his Mac computers, bloated costs, and a severe shortage of cash. But on that day, Jobs chose to talk to the Mac faithful mostly about another problem: Apple's growing isolation. Despite the company's reputation for making the world's finest PCs, very little software or add-on gear worked with the Mac. "Apple lives in an ecosystem, and it needs help from other partners," said Jobs. "And it needs to help other partners."

Jobs then did the unthinkable, inviting arch-nemesis Bill Gates to join him on stage via videoconference to announce details of a deal to forget any patent claims in exchange for $150 million, and a promise by Microsoft Corp. (**MSFT**) to continue making a Mac-compatible version of its ubiquitous Office software.

Today, that Apple Inc. (**AAPL**) ecosystem has morphed from a sad little high-tech shtetl into a global empire. Once known for defining the digital future but never fully capitalizing on it, Apple has been transformed into tech's most influential hit-maker. More than 200,000 companies have signed on in the past year to create Apple-compatible products, a 26% increase from the year before. That includes software makers such as gamemaker Electronic Arts Inc. and corporate supplier VMware, drawn by Mac sales that are growing three times faster than the overall PC market. A cottage industry of iPod accessories continues to blossom into something far more substantial. Consider that this year, some 70% of new U.S.–model cars have iPod connectors built in, and about 100,000 airline seats will have the same. And Apple's online iTunes Music Store has become the world's third-largest music retailer after Wal-Mart Stores Inc. (**WMT**) and Best Buy Co. (**BBY**)

Joining The Jobs Club

With the June 29 debut of the iPhone, Apple seems poised to extend its reach even further. A new flock of partners, from AT&T Corp. to Salesforce.com Inc. (**CRM**), is set to jump on the bandwagon for the slick phone/Web browser/music player/camera. Sure, the hype prior to iPhone's launch bordered on ridiculous; (Comedy Central (**VIA**) Stephen Colbert joked that the iPhone launch is the second most important event in human history, after the birth of Christ). But phonemakers such as Nokia (**NOK**) and Motorola (**MOT**), and carriers like Verizon (**VZ**), are waiting nervously to see if Apple can remake the U.S. cellular business by determining what services consumers get and leaving the carriers out of the loop.

As long as Apple stays on its game, leading providers of everything from silicon chips to Hollywood flicks will feel pressure to strike deals to Jobs' liking. Apple can confer brand hipness on its partners. And its ascendence in markets like cell phones and who knows what else in the future may impose a new focus on more consumer-friendly parts, software, and services. But to be part of the Jobs club, you give up a certain amount of independence on everything from design to identity to pricing.

Jobs is upending two decades of conventional wisdom about the nature of competition in digital markets. Since the rise of Microsoft and Intel's "Wintel" PC standard in the 1980s, the assumption has been that markets would be dominated by those that could set technical standards—say, Microsoft in operating systems or Intel in microprocessors—and then benefit as thousands of others competed to build products on top of these "platforms."

But Apple's strategy is far simpler: Focus on making the best product, and rewards will follow. In fact, Apple's new partners are signing up in spite of, rather than because of, Jobs' rules of engagement. Apple makes little pretense of building a level playing field, but routinely picks favorites—such as Google for building mapping and video applications for the iPhone. And rather than aim for the most partners, Apple focuses on attracting the best ones. As a result, the Mac and iPod feel more like a gated, elitist community, with Apple keeping close watch over who gets in. "The notion of a platform is a very PC-oriented way of looking at the world," says Silicon Valley financier Roger McNamee. "Consumers just want a great experience. They don't buy platforms."

Consider how Apple changed expectations about portable music devices. There were plenty of MP3 players around before the iPod arrived in 2001. Now, if the iPhone works as advertised, it could similarly redefine the mobile-phone experience. As any BlackBerry or Treo owner knows, all of the 25 million smartphones sold last year offer similar capabilities, such as Web browsing and e-mail. But none has captured the heart of the mainstream consumer. And on paper, at least, the iPhone erases myriad frustrations faced by hundreds of millions of phone users—from maddeningly complex menus, to the inability to find a contact while on a call.

Spin it out a few years, and it's not hard to see why many companies want to be on Apple's side. iPhone buyers now sign up for an AT&T cellular package via iTunes. In the future, maybe they'll also be able to sign up for all the broadband and data services needed to power their Macs, iPods, and future Apple products (can you say: "I want my Apple iHomeTheater"?) and make them work together. That would play to Apple's strength—making the complex simple. "What you end up with is a kind of Apple archipelago—this cluster of islands in this big digital sea that are great places to hang out," says Silicon Valley futurist and consultant Paul Saffo.

Of course, Apple's products have to continue to delight—a real question for the iPhone, which doesn't even have a physical keyboard. But if Apple succeeds, it could raise itself and its ecosystem above the cacophony of industry giants now battling to "own" the digital consumer. The telephone and cable companies try to take advantage of their control of customers' access to video, data, and voice content. Google Inc. (GOOG) and Yahoo! Inc. (YHOO) want to leverage their power as online concierge for millions of consumers. Apple comes at it from the device perspective: If it can control the gadget you use to connect with all those other platforms, it increases its control over what you do, and how much you pay (99 cents a song, for example).

There are lots of phone carriers and cable companies, each with fairly similar offerings. Google and Yahoo are powerful in their own right, but they can't totally control their destiny since Web users are a click away from using another search engine or portal. For now, though, Apple is head and shoulders above others in making the actual machines you use to pull up Web pages, music, TV shows, movies, and soon, perhaps, phone conversations. Says David Sanderson, head of Bain & Co.'s global media practice: "We're moving from a distributor-driven paradigm to a consumer-driven paradigm—and Apple gets consumers."

And not just any consumers, but those who will pay a premium. The Mac is gaining share despite an average price tag of $1,400, nearly twice that of the typical PC. iPod shoppers still paid an average price of $181 in May, 15% above other music players. The iPhone is even more audaciously priced. The $499 base price compares with an average $66 for a regular phone, or $160 for a smartphone such as a BlackBerry or Treo, says NPD Group Inc. analyst Stephen Baker.

The Compatibility Factor

None of this would have come about if Jobs hadn't had his epiphany about reaching out beyond the insular world of the Mac. The Office deal was a symbolic first step, but the real wake-up call came with the 2003 decision to do a Windows-compatible version of iTunes. Rather than hurt Mac sales, as some feared, this opened the floodgates on iPod sales by making the device usable by the 98% of computer users who ran Windows. Another milestone came when the company switched from PowerPC processors made by IBM (IBM) to Intel's far more popular chips. This made it possible for Macs to run Windows (an important insurance policy to many Mac newbies) and made it far easier for software developers to adapt their programs for Apple's products.

Consider the perspective of one big video-game producer, Electronic Arts. In the early 1980s, about half of the people working at EA's Redwood City (Calif.) campus were Apple alumni. Yet EA stopped making Mac-compatible games later in the decade, when Apple turned its attention to corporate markets. EA co-founder Bing Gordon recalls his shock when Apple's then-CEO John Sculley said in 1987 that "there is no home-computer market." Says Gordon: "They were working so hard to get respect, the last thing they wanted was for people who wore suits to think of the Mac as a toy." Predictably, game sales on the Mac plummeted, making it even less worthwhile for EA to make the big investments to adapt its PC games to run on the Mac's unique innards.

But because today's Intel-based Macs don't look much different from any Windows PC from EA's perspective, Gordon says it should be cheaper to churn out Mac games than, say, adapting them to game consoles like the Sony (**SNE**) PlayStation or Nintendo (**NTDOY**) Wii. With the Mac rapidly gaining share with younger shoppers, EA has announced plans to release its new *Harry Potter* game and three other titles on the Mac this summer.

Another rarely mentioned advantage is Apple's so-called developer program. Once iPod sales began skyrocketing in 2003, the company worked with makers of portable speakers, music-player cases, and other add-on gadgets. And Apple is working on the most mobile platform of all. Since BMW first added an optional iPod connector in the glove compartment of many of its 2004 models, carmakers including Chrysler (**DCX**), Ford (**F**), and Honda (**HMC**) have followed suit. General Motors Corp.'s (**GM**) 2008 Cadillac CTS will come with a center console that features the iPod's "rotate and click" interface, not only for pulling music off an iPod but also for playing the radio or listening to CDs or satellite radio. "It's about getting to your music, not having to learn a new set of tricks for each service," says James Grace, the 27-year-old GM manager who leads the project.

With the iPhone, Apple seems ready to open up opportunities for software developers who were mostly shut out from the iPod. On June 11, it announced that any Web 2.0 program designed to work with Apple's Safari browser would work on the iPhone. That means such popular sites as MySpace, Digg, or Amazon.com will be able to adapt their services to take advantage of the device—say, by adding a virtual button on their sites so that iPhone users could actually place a phone call with a fellow Netizen, rather than just trade e-mails or post messages.

To be sure, many developers gripe that this approach is a far cry from letting them create applications designed from the ground up to work directly with the iPhone. That's a privilege Apple has conferred on only a few partners, such as Google. But "it's a good first step," says Digg Chairman Jay Adelson, who expects Apple to become more inclusive as time goes by. "For now, it's a very strange kind of controlled system—because they have these insanely high bars [for reliability and user experience] that they want to hit."

Many partners won't wait for a formal invite. Despite doubts about the iPhone's usefulness to serious businesspeople, Salesforce.com is working on an iPhone version of its sales management software. "It's not just about market share, it's about showing what is possible and what is cool," says CEO Marc Benioff. And more than 150 developers have registered to attend an ad hoc "iPhone Developers Camp" in San Francisco on July 6, to trade ideas and create new applications.

But if the Apple orchard is growing, it is still no Eden. For those partners that make the cut, Apple enforces a brutal perfectionism. "The stereotype is that they're this loosey-goosey California company, but nothing could be further from the truth," says Gary Johnson, the former CEO of chipmaker PortalPlayer Inc., which roared to prosperity by providing the electronic brains of the first generations of iPods. Johnson says that whenever a project fell off track or a part fell short of Apple's needs, its engineers were demanding "root cause analysis" and explanations within 12 hours. "You could pacify other customers by putting 10 engineers on a plane to see them. Not Apple."

'An Unreasonableness'

Working with Apple can be exhausting. Johnson says the company almost never issued documents outlining its technical requirements, preferring to keep things oral to avoid a paper trail that might be leaked. And no supplier was given a full picture of what exactly Apple was working on: Everything was on a "need to know" basis. "There's an unreasonableness," says Johnson. "It's as though your entire reason for being is to serve them." Yet he adds he has no hard feelings: "It wasn't a malicious thing. It's almost machine-like. You may have friendships or business relationships, but they don't really count." Johnson found that out on an April morning in 2006, when he learned Apple had decided not to use a chip that had been under development for more than a year and was expected to bring in half of PortalPlayer's sales. The company's stock crashed 50% when Johnson told Wall Street a few days later. Seven months later, it was purchased by Nvidia Corp. (**NVDA**) for $357 million—half of its peak market cap.

Suppliers of TV shows, movies, and other video content have their own reasons for being wary of joining the Apple ecosystem. They know what happened in the music industry. Jobs created a kind of reverse razor-and-blades model with the iPod, where Apple sells lucrative razors (music players) and the studios are stuck selling cheapo blades (music). Hollywood has resisted Jobs' vision for placing movies on the iPod and iPhone. Only movies from Walt Disney Co. (**DIS**) (where Jobs is the largest individual shareholder) and Paramount Pictures (**VIA**) have licensed movies to iTunes. The 52 million TV shows and movies sold so far by Apple amounts to fewer than two videos per iPod.

This makes Apple's newest partnership with AT&T (**T**) for iPhone service all the more intriguing. Since the iPhone was announced in January, many observers have wondered if Jobs pulled another fast one, using his consumer cred to win unprecedented influence over the $140 billion cellular-phone business. Normally, carriers in the U.S. control how cell-phones are priced and marketed, right down to deciding whether they will turn on capabilities built into the phones, such as wireless music downloading. But that's not how Apple rolls. Apple defined the 16 services that are highlighted on the iPhone homepage, and users sign up for them via iTunes, not on AT&T's homepage or in its stores.

Has AT&T set itself up to be marginalized? The carrier stands to steal subscribers from its rivals; CEO Randall L. Stephenson said on June 19 that of the 1.1 million people who had inquired about the iPhone, 40% were not currently signed up with AT&T. But analysts say Apple will earn a luxurious 35% gross margin on each of the $500 devices. AT&T is offering a $59 base plan for phone and data services—roughly $20 less than the cost for corporate e-mail devices like Treo. Besides potentially taking a bite out of AT&T's margins, this could cause its other handset makers to demand sweeter deals, too.

But the real test will be whether Jobs can change the way consumers think about a phone. This is Apple's first entry into a preexisting mass market, and those other phone manufacturers can't afford to let Jobs rewire things to suit Apple's strengths. Some already have rolled out cheaper products that, if not exactly as capable as the iPhone, may be close enough. Will most consumers eventually choose to save money, even at the expense of a bit of elegance? History says they will, according to Harvard Business School professor Clayton M. Christensen: "The world always ends up thanking innovators for their cool products—but won't pay for them. There are forces of gravity at work."

Now there's a matchup worth watching: Steve Jobs vs. gravity.

Source: P. Burrows, "Welcome to Planet Apple," (July 9, 2007) at http://www.businessweek.com/magazine/content/07_28/b4042058.htm?chan=search (accessed July 2, 2008).

Case for Analysis: Hugh Russel, Inc.

The following story is a personal recollection by David Hurst of the experience of a group of managers in a mature organization undergoing profound change. . . . The precipitating event in this change was a serious business crisis. . . .

When I joined Hugh Russel Inc. in 1979, it was a medium-sized Canadian distributor of steel and industrial products. With sales of $535 million and 3,000 employees, the business was controlled by the chairman, Archie Russel, who owned 16 percent of the common shares. The business consisted of four groups—the core steel distribution activities (called "Russelsteel"), industrial bearings and valves distribution, a chain of wholesalers of hardware and sporting goods, and a small manufacturing business. . . .

The company was structured for performance. . . . The management was professional, with each of the divisional hierarchies headed by a group president reporting to Peter Foster in his capacity as president of the corporation. Jobs were described in job descriptions, and their mode of execution was specified in detailed standard operating procedures. Three volumes of the corporate manual spelled out policy on everything from accounting to vacation pay. Extensive accounting and data processing systems allowed managers to track the progress of individual operations against budgets and plans. Compensation was performance-based, with return on net assets (RONA) as the primary measure and large bonuses (up to 100 percent of base) for managers who made their targets.

At the senior management level, the culture was polite but formal. The board of directors consisted of Archie's friends and associates together with management insiders. Archie and Peter ran the organization as if they were majority owners. Their interaction with management outside of the head office was restricted to the occasional field trip. . . .

Crisis

Nine months after I joined the company as a financial planner, we were put "in play" by a raider and, after a fierce bidding war, were acquired in a hostile takeover. Our acquirer was a private company controlled by the eldest son of an entrepreneur of legendary wealth and ability, so we had no inkling at the time of the roller-coaster ride that lay ahead of us. We were unaware that not only did the son not have the support of his father in this venture but also he had neglected to consult his two brothers, who were joint owners of the acquiring company! As he had taken on $300 million of debt to do the deal, this left each of the brothers on the hook for a personal guarantee of $100 million. They were not amused, and it showed!

Within days of the deal, we were inundated by waves of consultants, lawyers, and accountants: each shareholder seemed to have his or her own panel of advisers. After 6 weeks of intensive analysis, it was clear that far too much had been paid for us and that the transaction was vastly overleveraged. At the start of the deal, the acquirer had approached our bankers and asked them if they wanted a piece of the "action." Concerned at the possible loss of our banking business and eager to be associated with such a prominent family, our bankers had agreed to provide the initial financing on a handshake. Now, as they saw the detailed numbers for the first time and became aware of the dissent among the shareholders, they withdrew their support and demanded their money back. We needed to refinance $300 million of debt—fast. . . .

Change

The takeover and the subsequent merger of our new owner's moribund steel-fabricating operations into Hugh Russel changed our agenda completely. We had new shareholders (who fought with each other constantly), new bankers, and new businesses in an environment of soaring interest rates and plummeting demand for our products and services. Almost overnight, the corporation went from a growth-oriented, acquisitive, earnings-driven operation to a broken, cash-starved company, desperate to survive. Closures, layoffs, downsizing, delayering, asset sales, and "rationalization" became our new priorities. . . . At the head office, the clarity of jobs vanished. For example, I had been hired to do financial forecasting and raise capital in the equity markets, but with the company a financial mess, this clearly could not be done. For all of us, the future looked dangerous and frightening as bankruptcy, both personal and corporate, loomed ahead.

And so it was in an atmosphere of crisis that Wayne Mang, the new president (Archie Russel and Peter Foster left the organization soon after the deal), gathered the first group of managers together to discuss the situation. Wayne Mang had been in the steel business for many years and was trusted and respected by the Hugh Russel people. An accountant by training, he used to call himself the "personnel manager" to underscore his belief in both the ability of people to make the difference in the organization and the responsibility of line management to make this happen. The hastily called first meeting consisted of people whom Wayne respected and trusted from all over the organization. They had been selected without regard for their position in the old hierarchy.

The content and style of that first meeting were a revelation to many! Few of them had ever been summoned to the head office for anything but a haranguing over their budgets. Now they were being told the complete gory details of the company's situation and, for the first time, being treated as if they had something to contribute. Wayne asked for their help.

During that first meeting, we counted nineteen major issues confronting the corporation. None of them fell under a single functional area. We arranged ourselves into task forces to deal with them. I say "arranged ourselves" because that was the way it seemed to happen. Individuals volunteered without coercion to work on issues in which they were interested or for which their skills were relevant. They also volunteered others who were not at the meeting but, it was thought, could help. There was some guidance—each task force had one person from the head office whose function it was to report what was happening back to the "center"—and some members found themselves on too many task forces, which required that substitutes be found. But that was the extent of the conscious management of the process.

The meeting broke up at 2:00 a.m., when we all went home to tell our incredulous spouses what had happened. . . .

The cross-functional project team rapidly became our preferred method of organizing new initiatives, and at the head office, the old formal structure virtually disappeared. The teams could be formed at a moment's notice to handle a fast-breaking issue and dissolved just as quickly. We found, for example, that even when we weren't having formal meetings, we seemed to spend most of our time talking to each other informally. Two people would start a conversation in someone's office, and almost before you knew it, others had wandered in and a small group session was going. Later on, we called these events "bubbles;" they became our equivalent of campfire meetings. . . .

Later, when I became executive vice president, Wayne and I deliberately shared an office so we could each hear what the other was doing in real time and create an environment in which "bubbles" might form spontaneously. As people wandered past our open door, we would wave them in to talk; others would wander in after them. The content of these sessions always had to do with our predicament, both corporate and personal. It was serious stuff, but the atmosphere was light and open. Our fate was potentially a bad one, but at least it would be shared. All of us who were involved then cannot remember ever having laughed so much. We laughed at ourselves and at the desperate situation. We laughed at the foolishness of the bankers in having financed such a mess, and we laughed at the antics of the feuding shareholders, whose outrageous manners and language we learned to mimic to perfection.

I think it was the atmosphere from these informal sessions that gradually permeated all our interactions—with employees, bankers, suppliers, everyone with whom we came into contact. Certainly, we often had tough meetings, filled with tension and threat, but we were always able to "bootstrap" ourselves back up emotionally at the informal debriefings afterward. . . .

Perhaps the best example of both the change in structure and the blurring of the boundaries of the organization was our changing relationships with our bankers. In the beginning, at least for the brief time that the loan was in good standing, the association was polite and at arm's length. Communication was formal. As the bank realized the full horror of what it had financed (a process that took about 18 months), the relationship steadily grew more hostile. Senior executives of the bank became threatening, spelling out what actions they might take if we did not solve our problem. This hostility culminated in an investigation by the bank for possible fraud (a standard procedure in many banks when faced with a significant loss).

Throughout this period, we had seen a succession of different bankers, each of whom had been assigned to our account for a few months. As a result of our efforts to brief every new face that appeared, we had built a significant network of contacts within the bank with whom we had openly shared a good deal of information and opinion. When no fraud was found, the bank polled its own people on what to do. Our views, presented so coherently by our people (because everyone knew what was going on), and shared so widely with so many bankers, had an enormous influence on the outcome of this process. The result was the formation of a joint company-bank team to address a shared problem that together we could solve. The boundary between the corporation and the bank was now blurred: to an outside observer, it would have been unclear where the corporation ended and the bank began. . . .

Our corporation had extensive formal reporting systems to allow the monitoring of operations on a regular basis. After the takeover, these systems required substantial modifications. For example . . . we had to report our results to the public every quarter at a time when we were losing nearly 2 million dollars a week! We knew that unless we got to our suppliers ahead of time, they could easily panic and refuse us credit. Hasty moves on their part could have had fatal consequences for the business.

In addition, our closure plans for plants all over Canada and the United States brought us into contact with unions and governments in an entirely different way. We realized that we had no option but to deal with these audiences in advance of events.

I have already described how our relationship with the bankers changed as a result of our open communication. We found exactly the same effect with these new audiences. Initially, our major suppliers could not understand why we had told them we were in trouble before we had to. We succeeded, however, in framing the situation in a way that enlisted their cooperation in our survival, and by the time the "war story" was news, we had their full support. Similarly, most government and union organizations were so pleased to be involved in the process before announcements were made that they bent over backward to be of assistance. Just as had been the case with the bank, we set up joint task forces with these "outside" agencies to resolve what had become shared problems. A significant contributor to our ability to pull this off was the high quality of our internal communication. Everyone on the teams knew the complete, up-to-date picture of what was happening. An outside agency could talk to anyone on a team and get the same story. In this way, we constructed a formidable network of contacts, many of whom had special skills and experience in areas that would turn out to be of great help to us in the future.

The addition of multiple networks to our information systems enhanced our ability both to gather and to disseminate information. The informality and openness of the networks, together with the high volume of face-to-face dialogues, gave us an early-warning system with which to detect hurt feelings and possible hostile moves on the part of shareholders, suppliers, nervous bankers, and even customers. This information helped us head off trouble before it happened. The networks also acted as a broadcast system through which we could test plans and actions before announcing them formally. In this way, not only did we get excellent suggestions for improvement, but everyone felt that he or she had been consulted before action was taken. . . .

We had a similar experience with a group of people outside the company during the hectic last 6 months of 1983, when we were trying to finalize a deal for the shareholders and bankers to sell the steel distribution business to new owners. The group of people in question comprised the secretaries of the numerous lawyers and accountants involved in the deal. . . .

We made these secretaries part of the network, briefing them in advance on the situation, explaining why things were needed, and keeping them updated on the progress of the deal. We were astounded at the cooperation we received: our calls were put through, our messages received prompt responses, and drafts and opinions were produced on time. In the final event, a complex deal that should have taken nine months to complete was done in three. All of this was accomplished by ordinary people going far beyond what might have been expected of them. . . .

We had been thrust into crisis without warning, and our initial activities were almost entirely reactions to issues that imposed themselves upon us. But as we muddled along in the task forces, we began to find that we had unexpected sources of influence over what was happening. The changing relationship with the bank illustrates this neatly. Although we had no formal power in that situation, we found that by framing a confusing predicament in a coherent way, we could, via our network, influence the outcomes of the bank's decisions. The same applied to suppliers: by briefing them ahead of time and presenting a reasonable scenario for the recovery of their advances, we could influence the decisions they would make.

Slowly we began to realize that, although we were powerless in a formal sense, our networks, together with our own internal coherence, gave us an ability to get things done invisibly. As we discussed the situation with all the parties involved, a strategy began to emerge. A complicated financial/tax structure would allow the bank to "manage" its loss and give it an incentive not to call on the shareholders' personal guarantees. The core steel distribution business could be refinanced in the process and sold to new owners. The wrangle between the shareholders could be resolved, and each could go his or her own way. All that had to be done was to bring all the parties together, including a buyer for the steel business, and have them agree that this was the best course to follow. Using our newfound skills, we managed to pull it off.

It was not without excitement: at the last minute, the shareholders raised further objections to the deal. Only the bank could make them sell, and they were reluctant to do so, fearful that they might attract a lawsuit. Discreet calls to the major suppliers, several of whose executives were on the board of the bank, did the trick. "This business needs to be sold and recapitalized," the suppliers were told. "If the deal does not go through, you should probably reduce your credit exposure." The deal went through. By the end of 1983, we had new owners, just in time to benefit from the general business recovery. The ordeal was over.

Source: Reprinted by permission of Harvard Business School Press. From *Crisis and Renewal: Meeting the Challenge of Organizational Change,* by David K. Hurst (Boston: Harvard Business School Press, 1995), pp. 53–73.

Chapter 5 Workshop: Ugli Orange Case*

1. Form groups of three members. One person will be Dr. Roland, one person will be Dr. Jones, and the third person will be an observer.
2. Roland and Jones will read only their own roles, but the observer will read both.
3. Role-play: Instructor announces, "I am Mr./Ms. Cardoza, the owner of the remaining Ugli oranges. My fruit export firm is based in South America. My country does not have diplomatic relations with your country, although we do have strong trade relations."

   The groups will spend about 10 minutes meeting with the other firm's representative and will decide on a course of action. Be prepared to answer the following questions:
   a. What do you plan to do?
   b. If you want to buy the oranges, what price will you offer?
   c. To whom and how will the oranges be delivered?
4. The observers will report the solutions reached. The groups will describe the decision-making process used.
5. The instructor will lead a discussion on the exercise addressing the following questions:
   a. Which groups had the most trust? How did that influence behaviour?
   b. Which groups shared more information? Why?
   c. How are trust and disclosure important in negotiations?

Role of "Dr. Jones"

You are Dr. John W. Jones, a biological research scientist employed by a pharmaceutical firm. You have recently developed a synthetic chemical useful for curing and preventing Rudosen. Rudosen is a disease contracted by pregnant women. If not caught in the first four weeks of pregnancy, the disease causes serious brain, eye, and ear damage to the unborn child. Recently there has been an outbreak of Rudosen in your state, and several thousand women have contracted the disease. You have found, with volunteer patients, that your recently developed synthetic serum cures Rudosen in its early stages. Unfortunately, the serum is made from the juice of the Ugli orange, which is a very rare fruit. Only a small quantity (approximately 4,000) of these oranges were produced last season. No additional Ugli oranges will be available until next season, which will be too late to cure the present Rudosen victims.

You've demonstrated that your synthetic serum is in no way harmful to pregnant women. Consequently, there are no side effects. The production and distribution of the serum as a cure for Rudosen has received regulatory approval. Unfortunately, the current outbreak was unexpected, and your firm had not planned on having the compound serum available for six months. Your firm holds the patent on the synthetic serum, and it is expected to be a highly profitable product when it is generally available to the public.

You have recently been informed on good evidence that R. H. Cardoza, a South American fruit exporter, is in possession of 3,000 Ugli oranges in good condition. If you could obtain the juice of all 3,000 you would be able to both cure present victims and provide sufficient inoculation for the remaining pregnant women in the state. No other state currently has a Rudosen threat.

You have recently been informed that Dr. P. W. Roland is also urgently seeking Ugli oranges and is also aware of Cardoza's possession of the 3,000 available. Dr. Roland is employed by a competing pharmaceutical firm and has been working on biological warfare research for the past several years. There is a great deal of industrial espionage in the pharmaceutical industry. Over the past several years, Dr. Roland's firm and yours have sued each other for infringement of patent rights and espionage law violations several times.

You've been authorized by your firm to approach Cardoza to purchase the 3,000 Ugli oranges. You have been told he will sell them to the highest bidder. Your firm has authorized you to bid as high as $250,000 to obtain the juice of the 3,000 available oranges.

Role of "Dr. Roland"

You are Dr. P. W. Roland. You work as a research biologist for a pharmaceutical firm. The firm is under contract with the U.S. government to do research on methods to combat enemy uses of biological warfare.

Recently several World War II experimental nerve gas bombs were moved from the United States to a small island just off the U.S. coast in the Pacific. In the process of transporting them, two of the bombs developed a leak. The leak is currently controlled by government scientists, who believe that the gas will permeate the bomb chambers within two weeks. They know of no method of preventing the gas from getting into the atmosphere and spreading to other islands and very likely to the West Coast as well. If this occurs, it is likely that several thousand people will incur serious brain damage or die.

You've developed a synthetic vapor that will neutralize the nerve gas if it is injected into the bomb chamber before the gas leaks out. The vapor is made with a chemical taken from the rind of the Ugli orange, a very rare fruit. Unfortunately, only 4,000 of these oranges were produced this season.

You've been informed on good evidence that R. H. Cardoza, a fruit exporter in South America, is in possession of 3,000 Ugli oranges. The chemicals from the rinds of all 3,000 oranges would be sufficient to neutralize the gas if the vapor is developed and injected efficiently. You have been informed that the rinds of these oranges are in good condition.

You have learned that Dr. J. W. Jones is also urgently seeking to purchase Ugli oranges and that he is aware of Cardoza's possession of the 3,000 available. Dr. Jones works for a firm with which your firm is highly competitive. There is a great deal of industrial espionage in the pharmaceutical industry. Over the years, your firm and Dr. Jones's have sued one another for violations of industrial espionage laws and infringement of patent rights several times. Litigation on two suits is still in process.

The U.S. government has asked your firm for assistance. You've been authorized by your firm to approach Cardoza to purchase 3,000 Ugli oranges. You have been told he will sell them to the highest bidder. Your firm has authorized you to bid as high as $250,000 to obtain the rinds of the oranges.

Before approaching Cardoza, you have decided to talk to Dr. Jones to influence him so that he will not prevent you from purchasing the oranges.

*By Robert House, Joseph Frank Bernstein Professor of Organizational Studies; Professor of Management, Wharton University of Pennsylvania. Used with permission.

6 Designing Organizations for the International Environment

FirstLight/NordicPhotos

A Look Inside

Alcan

Alcan planned to invest $1.5 billion to expand an aluminium smelter in Hafnarfjordur, Iceland (see photo). The ISAL smelter is the oldest in Iceland and has been operating since 1969. Hafnarfjordur is a small port suburb of Iceland's capital, Reykjavik. Hafnarfjordur has been a commercial port since the 1300s. Myth claims that the port is full of elves and mystical creatures, the Hidden Folk, who live on rocks near the town's centre.

Alcan had an agreement with the Icelandic government for access to cheap hydroelectricity to run the smelter and was planning to increase output from 180,000 to 460,000 tonnes annually. However, Alcan misjudged the reaction of the 25,000 citizens of Hafnarfjordur. In a referendum held in the spring of 2007, 50.3 percent voted against allowing the government to move a highway and rezone land as part of the proposed expansion of the ISAL smelter. Many citizens opposed the expansion because of environmental concerns. Alcan lost the referendum by 88 votes! Michel Jacques, President and CEO of Alcan's primary metal group, says that the company will review the results carefully—"[we] will consider our options—if we can improve our project to make it more in line with people's expectations, we will do that."[1]

Other aluminium producers have gone to Iceland as its natural terrain—rivers from its glaciers along with the geothermal energy beneath its volcanic rocks—creates the potential for the massive amounts of energy that smelters need to produce aluminium. The smelters are facing opposition from Iceland's environmental and citizens' groups as they are concerned about their impact on Iceland's wilderness.[2]

When an organization decides to do business in another country, managers face a whole new set of challenges. Despite the challenges of doing business internationally, most companies today think the potential rewards outweigh the risks. Canadian companies have long been involved in international business, but interest in global trade is greater now than ever before. Companies have set up foreign operations to produce goods and services needed by consumers in other countries, as well as to obtain lower costs for producing products to sell at home. In return, companies from Japan, Germany, and the United Kingdom compete with Canadian companies on their own turf as well as abroad. Domestic markets for many companies are becoming saturated, and the only potential for growth lies overseas. In 2005, Magna International recognized the importance of becoming a global organization and hired Mark Hogan "to prepare the world's most diversified Tier 1 supplier of automotive systems for the new global order." "The best way to characterize Magna," he says, "is as a Canadian company that grew its North American business in the '70s and '80s. In the '90s, it then focused its attention on growth in Europe, which it did quite successfully. This decade is devoted to making sure we stay competitive in North America and Europe, but to also grow our base of business in Asia—both from a manufacturing standpoint and a customer standpoint."[3]

For e-commerce companies, expanding internationally is becoming a priority. Google, for example, entered the Chinese market but is considered "another imported also-ran"[4] as it competes with Baidu, which does 60 percent of Chinese Internet searches. Succeeding on a global scale isn't easy. Organizations have to make decisions about strategic approach, how best to get involved in international markets, policies, and laws, and how to design the organization to reap the benefits of international expansion.

Purpose of This Chapter

This chapter will explore how managers design organizations for the international environment. We begin by looking at some of the primary motivations for organizations to expand internationally, the typical stages of international development, and the use of strategic alliances as a means for international expansion. Then the chapter examines global strategic approaches and the application of various structural designs for global advantage. Next, we discuss some of the specific challenges global organizations face, mechanisms for addressing them, and cultural differences that influence the organization's approach to designing and managing a global firm. Finally, the chapter takes a look at an emerging type of global organization, the *transnational model,* that achieves high levels of the varied capabilities needed to succeed in a complex and volatile international environment.

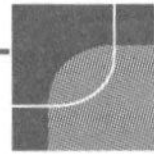

Entering the Global Arena

As recently as 25 years ago, many companies could afford to ignore the international environment. However, the world is becoming a unified global field; today's companies must think globally or get left behind. Extraordinary advancements in communications, technology, and transportation have created a new, highly competitive landscape. Products can be made and sold anywhere in the world, communications are instant, and product-development and life cycles are growing shorter. No company is isolated from global influence. Some large so-called American companies such as Coca-Cola and Procter & Gamble rely on international sales for a substantial portion of their sales and profits. On the other hand, organizations in other countries search for customers in North America. Sony of Japan gets much of its game business sales from North America and European consumers. In 2006, sales in its games business rose 31.4 percent overall, and much of the increase came from North American and European sales of the PlayStation Portable.[5] And even small companies can be actively involved in international business through exports and online business. Lavinia Parrish-Zwicker, founder of Lavinia's Olde English Delights, located in the Annapolis Valley town of Hantsport, sold her hand-crafted specialty food items locally, and globally through her online business.[6]

Motivations for Global Expansion

Economic, technological, and competitive forces have combined to push many companies from a domestic to a global focus. In some industries, being successful now means succeeding on a global scale. The importance of the global environment for today's organizations is reflected in the shifting global economy. As one indication, *Fortune*'s list of the Global 500, the world's 500 largest companies, indicates that economic clout is being diffused across a broad global scale. Although the United States accounts for the majority of the Global 500 revenues, a number of smaller and less-developed countries are growing stronger. China, for example, had 15 companies on the Global 500 in 2003, compared to only 3 companies on the list 10 years earlier. Japan, on the other hand, has declined in importance, dropping from 149 companies to 82.[7] According to the 2007 Global 500, the United States has the most global giants, followed by Japan and France.[8] In general, three primary factors motivate companies to expand internationally: economies of scale, economies of scope, and low-cost production factors.[9]

PDA Remember...

Consider building an international presence to realize economies of scale, exploit economies of scope, or obtain scarce or low-cost production factors such as labour and raw materials.

Economies of Scale. Building a global presence expands an organization's scale of operations, enabling it to realize **economies of scale**. The trend toward large organizations was initially sparked by the Industrial Revolution, which created pressure in many industries for larger factories that could seize the benefits of economies of scale offered by new technologies and production methods. Through large-volume production, these industrial giants were able to achieve the lowest possible cost per unit of production. However, for many companies, domestic markets no longer provide the high level of sales needed to maintain enough volume to achieve scale economies. The Running Room, for example, entered the U.S. market in 2007 as the domestic market was saturated. It started its expansion in the Minneapolis, Minnesota area, but growth has been slow.[10] Entering American markets has not been easy for Canadian companies—retailers especially as "[they] have grossly underestimated the competitiveness of the American market. . . . Americans are take-no-prisoners type retailers."[11]

In an industry such as automobile manufacturing, for example, a company would need a tremendous share of the domestic market to achieve scale economies. Thus, an organization such as Chrysler was forced to become international in order to survive. Economies of scale also enable companies to obtain volume discounts from suppliers, lowering the organization's cost of production.

Economies of Scope. A second factor is the enhanced potential for exploiting **economies of scope**. *Scope* refers to the number and variety of products and services a company offers, as well as the number and variety of regions, countries, and markets it serves. Having a presence in multiple countries provides marketing power and synergy compared to the same size firm that has presence in fewer countries. For example, an advertising agency with a presence in several global markets gains a competitive edge serving large companies that span the globe. Cossette Communication Group, an advertising company best known for its Bell Canada campaign featuring beavers Frank and Gordon, bought Dare Digital Ltd. of London, U.K. as an entry point into European markets. Its foray into the U.S. market had not been particularly successful but Cossette continues to build its American business. As Claude Lessard, CEO, chair and president notes, "[we'll] never be in the top five in the U.S. (Cossette ranks 15th in North America and 25th internationally) . . . [but] we want to be much more aggressive winning new clients and making acquisitions."[12] Economies of scope can also increase a company's market power as compared to competitors, because the company develops broad knowledge of the cultural, social, economic, and other factors that affect its customers in varied locations and can provide specialized products and services to meet those needs.

Low-Cost Production Factors. The third major force motivating global expansion relates to **factors of production**. One of the earliest, and still one of the most powerful, motivations for North American companies to invest abroad is the opportunity to obtain raw materials and other resources at the lowest possible cost. Organizations have long turned overseas to secure raw materials that were scarce or unavailable in their home country. In the early 20th century, tire companies went abroad to develop rubber plantations to supply tires for North America's growing automobile industry. Today, American paper manufacturers such as Weyerhaeuser and U.S. Paper, forced by environmental concerns to look overseas for new timberlands, are managing millions of acres of tree farms in New Zealand.[13]

Many companies also turn to other countries as a source of cheap labour. Textile manufacturing in the United States is now practically nonexistent as companies have shifted most production to Asia, Mexico, Latin America, and the Caribbean, where the costs of labour and supplies are much lower. Between 1997 and 2002, the percentage of clothing sold in the United States but manufactured elsewhere rose to around 75 percent, an increase of nearly 20 percent in five years. A check of the "Made in" tags at one Gap store found clothing made in 24 countries, in addition to the United States.[14] Gildan Activewear, which makes casual apparel such as T-shirts, sports shirts, and fleeces, has been shifting its production to low-cost factories in Central America and the Caribbean. It has done so to boost profits.[15] It shut down its two remaining Montréal factories and laid off 1,365 Mexican workers in early 2007. According to Laurence Sellyn, Gildan Activewear's chief financial and administrative officer, "[we] regret that these closures are necessary in order to be globally competitive . . . [but] the economic case for consolidating offshore is compelling."[16]

Other organizations have gone international in search of lower costs of capital, sources of cheap energy, reduced government restrictions, or other factors that lower the company's total production costs. Companies can locate facilities wherever it makes the most economic sense in terms of needed employee education and skill levels, labour and raw materials costs, and other production factors. Automobile manufacturers such as Toyota, BMW, General Motors, and Ford have built plants in South Africa, Brazil, and Thailand, where they can pay workers less than one-tenth of what workers earn in higher-wage, developed countries. In addition, these countries typically offer dramatically lower costs for factors such as land, water, and electricity.[17] However, they also have lower environmental and health and safety standards. Foreign companies also come to the United States to obtain favourable circumstances. Japan's Honda and Toyota and Switzerland's Novartis, for example, have built plants or research centres in North America to take advantage of incentives, to find skilled workers, and to be closer to major customers and suppliers.[18]

Stages of International Development

No company can become a global giant overnight. Managers have to consciously adopt a strategy for global development and growth. Organizations enter foreign markets in a variety of ways and follow diverse paths. However, the shift from domestic to global typically occurs through stages of development, as illustrated in Exhibit 6.1.[19] In stage one, the **domestic stage**, the company is domestically oriented, but managers are aware of the global environment and may want to consider initial foreign involvement to expand production volume and realize economies of scale. Market potential is limited and is primarily in the home country. The structure of the company is domestic, typically functional or divisional, and initial foreign sales are handled through an export department. The details of freight forwarding, customs problems, and foreign exchange are handled by outsiders.

In stage two, the **international stage**, the company takes exports seriously and begins to think multidomestically. **Multidomestic** means competitive issues in each country are independent of other countries; the company deals with each country individually. The concern is with international competitive positioning compared with other firms in the industry. At this point, an international division has replaced the

EXHIBIT 6.1
Four Stages of International Evolution

	I. Domestic	II. International	III. Multinational	IV. Global
Strategic Orientation	Domestically oriented	Export-oriented multidomestic	Multinational	Global
Stage of Development	Initial foreign involvement	Competitive positioning	Explosion	Global
Structure	Domestic structure, plus export department	Domestic structure, plus international division	Worldwide geographical, product	Matrix, transnational
Market Potential	Moderate, mostly domestic	Large, multidomestic	Very large, multinational	Whole world

Source: Based on Nancy J. Adler, *International Dimensions of Organizational Behavior,* 4th ed. (Cincinnati, Ohio: South-Western, 2002), 8–9; and Theodore T. Herbert, "Strategy and Multinational Organization Structure: An Interorganizational Relationships Perspective," *Academy of Management Review* 9 (1984), 259–271.

export department, and specialists are hired to handle sales, service, and warehousing abroad. Multiple countries are identified as a potential market. Artisan bread maker Ace Bakery, once a ten-seat Toronto bakery, has expanded internationally. It now sells its par-baked bread, which accounts for 60 percent of its sales, across Canada, and in New York, Michigan, and the Bahamas. The Bahamas operations began in 2005 when a chef at a five-star hotel couldn't find high-quality bread locally. Ace Bakery has grown considerably in its 15 years of operation—it has 300 employees and annual sales under $50 million. It commits 10 percent of pre-tax profit in the regions where it does business by investing in organic farming, culinary scholarships, and food and nutrition programs for the poor. [20]

In stage three, the **multinational stage**, the company has extensive experience in a number of international markets and has established marketing, manufacturing, or research and development facilities in several foreign countries. The organization obtains a large percentage of revenues from sales outside the home country. Explosion occurs as international operations take off, and the company has business units scattered around the world along with suppliers, manufacturers, and distributors. Examples of companies in the multinational stage include Sony of Japan, and Coca-Cola of the United States. Wal-Mart, although it is the world's biggest company, is just moving into the multinational stage, with only 18.5 percent of sales and 15.8 percent of profits from international business in 2003.

The fourth and ultimate stage is the **global stage**, which means the company transcends any single country. The business is not merely a collection of domestic industries; rather, subsidiaries are interlinked to the point where competitive position in one country significantly influences activities in other countries.[21] Truly **global companies** no longer think of themselves as having a single home country, and, indeed, have been called *stateless corporations*.[22] This represents a new and dramatic evolution from the multinational company of the 1960s and 1970s.

Global companies operate in truly global fashion, and the entire world is their marketplace. Organizational structure at this stage can be extremely complex and often evolves into an international matrix or transnational model, which will be discussed later in this chapter.

Global companies such as Nestlé, Royal Dutch/Shell, Unilever, and Matsushita Electric may operate in more than a hundred countries. The structural problem of holding together this huge complex of subsidiaries scattered thousands of miles apart is immense.

Global Expansion through International Strategic Alliances

PDA Remember...

Develop international strategic alliances, such as licensing, joint ventures, partnerships, and consortia, as fast and inexpensive ways to become involved in international sales and operations.

One of the most popular ways companies get involved in international operations is through international strategic alliances. Companies in rapidly changing industries such as media and entertainment, pharmaceuticals, biotechnology, and software might have hundreds of these relationships.[23] QLT , for example, a Vancouver-based biopharmaceutical company specializing in the fields of ophthalmology and dermatology, has co-development agreements with Novartis Ophthalmics, and, through QLT USA, has agreements with Pfizer, Sanofi-Synthelabo, Astellas Pharma, MediGene AG, and Mayne Pharma PTY Ltd.[24]

Typical alliances include licensing, joint ventures, and consortia.[25] For example, pharmaceutical companies such as Merck, Eli Lilly, Pfizer, and Warner-Lambert cross-license their newest drugs to one another to support industry-wide innovation and marketing and offset the high fixed costs of research and distribution.[26] A **joint venture** is a separate entity created with two or more active firms as sponsors. This is a popular approach to sharing development and production costs, and penetrating new markets. Joint ventures may be with either customers or competitors.[27] Competing Chinese firms Shanghai Automotive Industries and Nanjing Automobile Corporation have partnered to develop new models so that they can compete globally; in 2007, they signed a "comprehensive co-operation agreement on design, production and sales."[28] Swiss food company Nestlé and French cosmetics giant L'Oréal engaged in a joint venture to develop Inneov, a nutritional supplement intended to improve the health of skin.[29] MTV Networks has joint ventures with companies in Brazil, Australia, and other countries to expand its global media presence.[30]

Companies often seek joint ventures to take advantage of a partner's knowledge of local markets, to achieve production cost savings through economies of scale, to share complementary technological strengths, or to distribute new products and services through another country's distribution channels. Nortel Networks, for example, has developed joint ventures with China Putian and LG Electronics to get access to the Asian markets.[31] Robex Resources,[32] a gold exploration and development company, and Geo Services International, an international company operating in Mali, have an agreement that enables the two to combine their technological power and increase the success of gold exploration and drilling projects in certain areas. ICICI Bank, one of India's largest financial services providers, entered into a joint venture with Lombard, one of Canada's oldest property and casualty insurance companies, to launch general insurance business in India.[33]

Another increasingly popular approach is for companies to become involved in **consortia**, groups of independent companies—including suppliers, customers, and even competitors—that join together to share skills, resources, costs, and access to one another's markets. Airbus Industrie, for example, is a consortium comprising French, British, and German aerospace companies that has been successfully battering U.S. giant Boeing.[34] Consortia are often used in other parts of the world, such as the *keiretsu* family of corporations in Japan. In Korea, these interlocking company arrangements are called *chaebol.*

A type of consortium, the global virtual organization, is increasingly being used and offers a promising approach to meeting worldwide competition. The virtual organization refers to a continually evolving set of company relationships that exist temporarily to exploit unique opportunities or attain specific strategic advantages. A company may be involved in multiple alliances at any one time. Oracle, a software company, is involved in as many as 15,000 short-term organizational partnerships at any time.[35] Some executives believe shifting to a virtual approach is the best way for companies to be competitive in the global marketplace.[36]

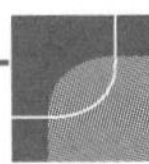

Designing Structure to Fit Global Strategy

As we discussed in Chapter 3, an organization's structure must fit its situation by providing sufficient information processing for coordination and control while focusing employees on specific functions, products, or geographical regions. Organizational design for international firms follows a similar logic, with special interest in global versus local strategic opportunities.

Model for Global versus Local Opportunities

When organizations venture into the international domain, managers strive to formulate a coherent global strategy that will provide synergy among worldwide operations for the purpose of achieving common organizational goals. One dilemma they face is choosing whether to emphasize global **standardization** versus national responsiveness. Managers must decide whether they want each global affiliate to act autonomously or whether activities should be standardized across countries. These decisions are reflected in the choice between a globalization versus a multidomestic global strategy.

The **globalization strategy** means that product design, manufacturing, and marketing strategy are standardized throughout the world.[37] For example, the Japanese took away business from Canadian and American companies by developing similar high-quality, low-cost products for all countries. The Canadian and American companies incurred higher costs by tailoring products to specific countries. Black & Decker became much more competitive internationally when it standardized its line of power hand tools. Other products, such as Coca-Cola, are naturals for globalization, because only advertising and marketing need to be tailored for different regions. In general, services are less suitable for globalization because different customs and habits often require a different approach to providing service. Wal-Mart has had trouble transplanting its successful North American formula without adjustment. In Indonesia, for example, Wal-Mart closed its stores after only a year. Customers didn't like the brightly lit, highly organized stores, and, because no haggling was permitted, they thought the goods were overpriced.[38] On the other hand, Bombardier has enjoyed success in Germany and employs 7,000 people at its seven production facilities. Tim's Canadian Deli has enjoyed success too—it has 75 employees who run three restaurants and a wholesale bakery supplying cafés and supermarkets with Canadian baked goods such as blueberry and chocolate muffins.[39]

Other companies in recent years have also begun shifting away from a strict globalization strategy. Economic and social changes, including a backlash against huge global corporations, have prompted consumers to be less interested in global brands and more in favour of products that have a local feel.[40] However, a globalization strategy can help a manufacturing organization reap economy-of-scale efficiencies by standardizing product design and manufacturing, using common suppliers, introducing products around the world faster, coordinating prices, and eliminating overlapping facilities. By sharing technology, design, suppliers, and manufacturing standards worldwide in a coordinated global automotive operation, Ford saved $5 billion during the first three years.[41] As well, Ford and Toyota have been in discussions about some sort of relationship.[42]

A **multidomestic strategy** means that competition in each country is handled independently of competition in other countries. Thus, a multidomestic strategy would encourage product design, assembly, and marketing tailored to the specific needs of each country. Some companies have found that their products do not thrive in a single global market. For example, people in different countries have very different expectations for personal-care products such as deodorant or toothpaste. The French do not drink orange juice for breakfast, and laundry detergent is used to wash dishes, not clothes, in parts of Mexico. As another example of a multidomestic strategy, Procter & Gamble tried to standardize diaper design, but discovered that cultural values in different parts of the world required style adjustments to make the product acceptable to many mothers. In Italy, for example, designing diapers to cover the baby's navel was critical to successful sales.[43]

Different global organizational designs, as well, are better suited to the need for either global standardization or national responsiveness. Recent research on more than 100 international firms based in Spain has provided further support for the connection between international structure and strategic focus.[44] The model in Exhibit 6.2 illustrates how organizational design and international strategy fit the needs of the environment.[45]

EXHIBIT 6.2
Model to Fit Organization Structure to International Advantages
Source: Roderick E. White and Thomas A. Poynter, "Organizing for Worldwide Advantage," *Business Quarterly* (Summer 1989), 84–89. Adapted by permission of Business Quarterly, published by the Western Business School, the University of Western Ontario, London, Ontario, Canada.

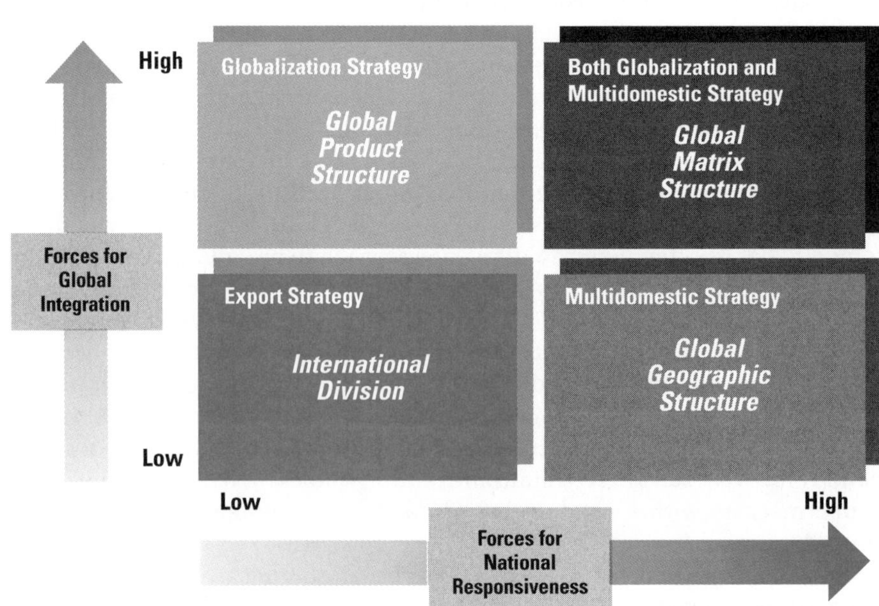

Companies can be characterized by whether their product and service lines have potential for globalization, which means advantages through worldwide standardization. Companies that sell diverse products or services across many countries have a globalization strategy. On the other hand, some companies have products and services appropriate for a multidomestic strategy, which means local-country advantages through differentiation and customization to meet local needs.

As indicated in Exhibit 6.2, when forces for both global standardization and national responsiveness in many countries are low, simply using an international division with the domestic structure is an appropriate way to handle international business. For some industries, however, technological, social, or economic forces may create a situation in which selling standardized products worldwide provides a basis for competitive advantage. In these cases, a global product structure is appropriate. This structure provides product managers with authority to handle their product lines on a global basis and enables the company to take advantage of a unified global marketplace. In other cases, companies can gain competitive advantages through national responsiveness—by responding to unique needs in the various countries in which they do business. For these companies, a global geographical structure is appropriate so that each country or region will have subsidiaries modifying products and services to fit that locale. A good illustration is the advertising firm of Ogilvy & Mather, which divides its operations into four primary geographical regions because advertising approaches need to be modified to fit the tastes, preferences, cultural values, and government regulations in different parts of the world.[46] Children are frequently used to advertise products in Canada, but in France this approach is against the law. The competitive claims of rival products regularly seen on North American television would violate government regulations in Germany.[47]

In many instances, companies will need to respond to both global and local opportunities simultaneously, in which case the global matrix structure can be used. Part of the product line may need to be standardized globally, and other parts tailored to the needs of local countries. Let's discuss each of the structures in Exhibit 6.2 in more detail.

International Division

As companies begin to explore international opportunities, they typically start with an export department that grows into an **international division**. The international division has a status equal to the other major departments or divisions within the company and is illustrated in Exhibit 6.3. Whereas the domestic divisions are typically organized along functional or product lines, the international division is organized according to geographical interests, as illustrated in the exhibit. The international division has its own hierarchy to handle business (licensing, joint ventures) in various countries, selling the products and services created by the domestic divisions, opening subsidiary plants, and in general moving the organization into more sophisticated international operations.

Although functional structures are often used domestically, they are less frequently used to manage a worldwide business.[48] Lines of functional hierarchy running around the world would extend too long, so some form of product or geographical structure is used to subdivide the organization into smaller units. Firms typically start with an international department and, depending on their strategy, later use product or geographical division structures.

EXHIBIT 6.3
Domestic Hybrid Structure with International Division

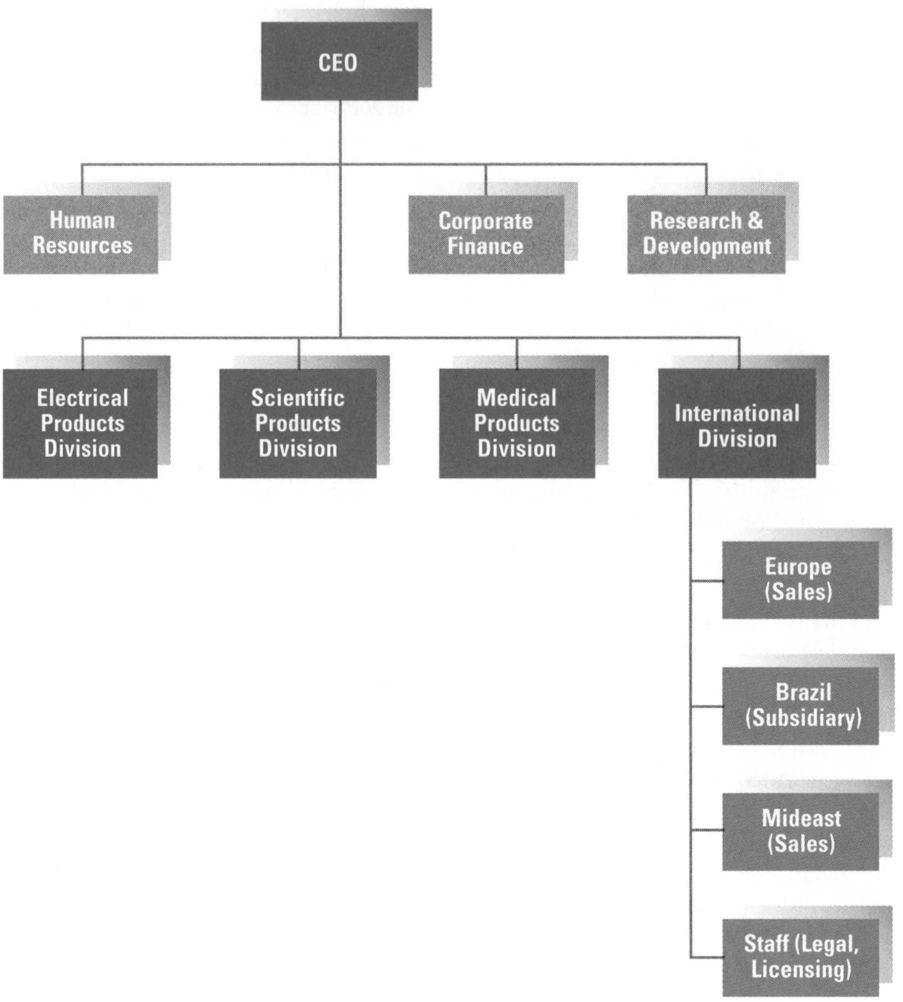

Global Product Structure

In a **global product structure**, the product divisions take responsibility for global operations in their specific product area. This is one of the most commonly used structures through which managers attempt to achieve global goals because it provides a fairly straightforward way to effectively manage a variety of businesses and products around the world. Managers in each product division can focus on organizing international operations as they see fit and directing employees' energy toward their own division's unique set of global problems or opportunities.[49] In addition, the structure provides top managers at headquarters with a broad perspective on competition, enabling the entire corporation to respond more rapidly to a changing global environment.[50]

With a global product structure, each division's manager is responsible for planning, organizing, and controlling all functions for the production and distribution of its products for any market around the world. The product-based structure works best when a division handles products that are technologically similar and can be standardized for marketing worldwide. The global product structure works best

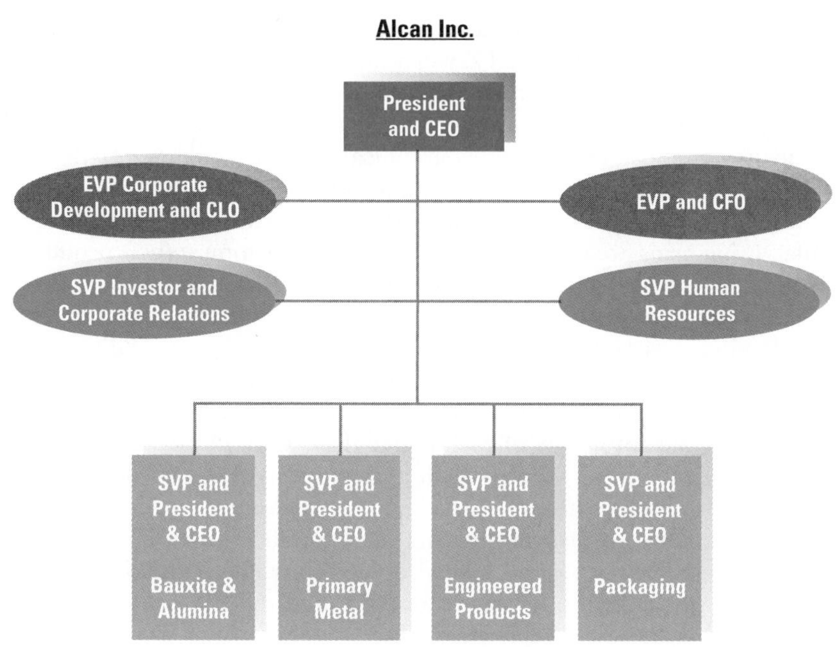

EXHIBIT 6.4
Alcan's Organizational Chart—as of April 2007
Source: "Alcan Inc." (April 2007) at http://www.alcan.com/web/publishing.nsf/content/About+Alcan++Company+Structure/$file/Alcan_Inc_April2007.pdf (accessed July 2, 2008).

PDA Remember...

Choose a global product structure when the organization can gain competitive advantages through a globalization strategy (global integration). Choose a global geographical structure when the company has advantages with a multidomestic strategy (national responsiveness). Use an international division when the company is primarily domestic and has only a few international operations.

when the company has opportunities for worldwide production and sale of standard products for all markets, thus providing economies of scale and standardization of production, marketing, and advertising.

Alcan has used a form of worldwide product structure, as illustrated in Exhibit 6.4. In this structure, Bauxite & Alumina, Primary Metal, Engineered Products and Packaging groupings are responsible for manufacture and/or sale of products worldwide. The product structure is great for standardizing production and sales around the globe, but it also has problems. Often the product divisions do not work well together, competing instead of cooperating in some countries; and some countries may be ignored by product managers.

Global Geographical Structure

A regionally based organization is well suited to companies that want to emphasize adaptation to regional or local market needs through a multidomestic strategy, as noted in Exhibit 6.2. The **global geographical structure** divides the world into geographical regions, with each geographical division reporting to the CEO. Each division has full control of functional activities within its geographical area. For example, Nestlé, with headquarters in Switzerland, puts great emphasis on the autonomy of regional managers who know the local culture. The largest branded food company in the world, Nestlé rejects the idea of a single global market and uses a geographical structure to focus on the local needs and competition in each country. Local managers have the authority to tinker with a product's flavouring, packaging, portion size, or other elements as they see fit. Many of the company's 8,000 brands are registered in only one country.[51]

Companies that use this type of structure have typically been those with mature product lines and stable technologies. They can find low-cost manufacturing within countries, as well as meeting different needs across countries for marketing and sales. However, several business and organizational trends have led to a broadening of the kinds of companies that use the global geographical structure.[52] The growth of service organizations has outpaced manufacturing for several years, and many, but not all, services must occur on a local level. In addition, to meet new competitive threats, many manufacturing firms are emphasizing the ability to customize their products to meet specific needs, which requires a greater emphasis on local and regional responsiveness. All organizations are compelled by current environmental and competitive challenges to develop closer relationships with customers, which may lead companies to shift from product-based to geographical-based structures.

The problems encountered by senior management using a global geographical structure result from the autonomy of each regional division. For example, it is difficult to do planning on a global scale—such as new-product R&D—because each division acts to meet only the needs of its region. New domestic technologies and products can be difficult to transfer to international markets because each division thinks it will develop what it needs. Likewise, it is difficult to rapidly introduce products developed offshore into domestic markets, and there is often duplication of line and staff managers across regions.

Nestlé is currently struggling to adapt its global geographical structure in an effort to cut costs and boost efficiency. Because regional divisions act to meet specific needs in their own areas, tracking, and maintaining control of costs has been a real problem. One analyst referred to Nestlé as "a holding company, with hundreds of companies reporting in."[53] Nestlé needs to find ways to increase efficiency and coordination without losing the benefits of the global geographical structure.

In Practice

McCain Foods Limited (McCain)

McCain Foods, a privately owned multinational family business, is the world's largest producer of frozen French fries (and other foods). It processes nearly one-third of the world's French fries. Its plants around the world have a total production capacity of more than one million pounds of potato products an hour! Its products are sold in 110 countries, and McCain has factories on five continents. In 2005, it opened an $18 million potato processing plant in Ahmedabad, India. In 40 years, McCain morphed from a small Florenceville, New Brunswick, company to one that has 55 production facilities that employ 20,000 people worldwide.

McCain's statement of purpose and values notes that "we will "drink the local wine": we are multicultural and care about our people, our families, and our local communities."[54] In addition to its many plants, McCain has licensing agreements in some countries, such as Switzerland, for the manufacture and distribution of its products. McCain did not enter the American market until 1997 when it bought Ore-Ida from Heinz for $500 million. In 2001, it acquired a frozen appetizer manufacturer, Anchor Food Products.[55] The company's expansion has been guided by the corporate cornerstone of drinking the local wine. According to Howard Mann, president and CEO until 2003, "[we] never march in and say [do] it this way"[56] as tastes can differ significantly. North Americans prefer a thin, crispy French fry while the British prefer a thicker, fatter French fry.

While McCain has succeeded globally as it recognized the need to accommodate global differences, it has been marred by familial conflicts. In the mid-1990s, the two brothers who co-founded McCain, Harrison and Wallace, fought bitterly about who should succeed them. Wallace wanted his son, Michael, to take over while Harrison wanted outside management to run McCain. A New Brunswick court found in favour of Harrison McCain. Howard Mann, a non-family member, became

CEO of McCain in 1995, and Wallace McCain was removed from the company he had co-founded. (Even so, the two brothers reconciled before Harrison McCain's death.) Wallace McCain and his two sons, Michael and Scott, then took over Maple Leaf Foods.[57]

Global Matrix Structure

A **global matrix structure** is similar to the matrix described in Chapter 3, except that for multinational corporations the geographical distances for communication are greater and coordination is more complex. The matrix works best when pressure for decision making balances the interests of both product standardization and geographical localization, and when coordination to share resources is important. For many years, Asea Brown Boveri (ABB), an electrical equipment corporation headquartered in Zurich, used a global matrix structure that worked extremely well to coordinate a 200,000-employee company operating in more than 140 countries.

In Practice

Asea Brown Boveri Ltd. (ABB)

ABB has given new meaning to the notion of "being local worldwide." ABB owns 1,300 subsidiary companies, divided into 5,000 profit centres located in 140 countries. ABB's average plant has fewer than 200 workers and most of the company's 5,000 profit centres contain only 40 to 50 people, meaning almost everyone stays close to the customer. For many years, ABB used a complex global matrix structure similar to Exhibit 6.5 to achieve worldwide economies of scale combined with local flexibility and responsiveness.

At the top are the chief executive officer and an international committee of eight top managers, who hold frequent meetings around the world. Along one side of the matrix are 65 or so business areas located worldwide, into which ABB's products and services are grouped. Each business area leader is responsible for handling business on a global scale, allocating export markets, establishing cost and quality standards, and creating mixed-nationality teams to solve problems. For example, the leader for power transformers is responsible for 25 factories in 16 countries.

Along the other side of the matrix is a country structure; ABB has more than 100 country managers, most of them citizens of the country in which they work. They run national companies and are responsible for local balance sheets, income statements, and career ladders. The German president, for example, is responsible for 36,000 people across several business areas that generate annual revenues in Germany of more than $4 billion.

The matrix structure converges at the level of the 1,300 local companies. The presidents of local companies report to two bosses—the business area leader, who is usually located outside the country, and the country president, who runs the company of which the local organization is a subsidiary.

ABB's philosophy is to decentralize things to the lowest levels. Global managers are open, patient, and multilingual. They must work with teams made up of different nationalities and be culturally sensitive. They craft strategy and evaluate performance for people and subsidiaries around the world. Country managers, by contrast, are regional line managers responsible for several country subsidiaries. They must cooperate with business area managers to achieve worldwide efficiencies and the introduction of new products. Finally, the presidents of local companies have both a global boss—the business area manager—and a country boss, and they learn to coordinate the needs of both.[58]

ABB is a large, successful company that achieved the benefits of both product and geographical organizations through this matrix structure. However, over the past several years, as ABB has faced increasingly complex competitive issues, leaders have

EXHIBIT 6.5
Global Matrix Structure

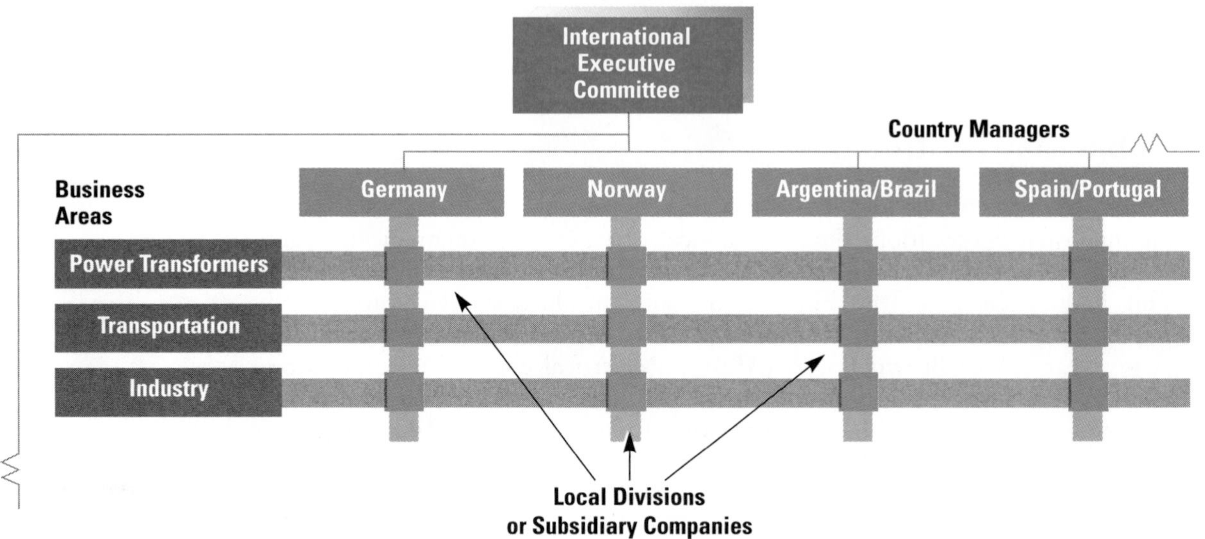

transformed the company toward a complex structure called the transnational model, which will be discussed later in this chapter.

Many international firms apply a global hybrid or mixed structure, in which two or more different structures or elements of different structures are used. Hybrid structures are typical in highly volatile environments. Siemens AG of Germany, for example, combines elements of functional, geographical, and product divisions to respond to dynamic market conditions in the multiple countries where it operates.[59]

Organizations like McCain and Nestlé that operate on a global scale frequently have to make adjustments to their structures to overcome the challenges of doing business in a global environment. In the following sections, we will look at some of the specific challenges organizations face in the global arena and mechanisms for successfully confronting them.

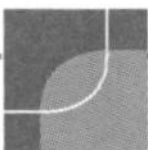

Building Global Capabilities

There are many instances of well-known companies that have trouble transferring successful ideas, products, and services from their home country to the international domain. We talked earlier about the struggles Wal-Mart is facing internationally, but Wal-Mart isn't alone. In the early 1990s, PepsiCo. set a five-year goal to triple its international soft-drink revenues and boldly expanded its presence in international markets. Yet by 1997, the company had withdrawn from some of those markets and had to take a nearly $1 billion loss from international beverage operations.[60] Hundreds of North American companies that saw Vietnam as a tremendous international opportunity in the mid-1990s are now calling it quits amid heavy losses. Political and cultural differences sidetracked most of the ventures. Only a few large companies, such as Citigroup's Citibank unit and Caterpillar's heavy-equipment business, have found success in that country.[61] However, smaller companies such as InoWeb Global, a merger of InoWeb Canada and A.D.K.T. located in Hanoi have enjoyed some success.[62] Managers taking their companies international face a tremendous challenge in how to capitalize on the incredible opportunities that global expansion presents.

The Global Organizational Challenge

There are three primary segments of the global organizational challenge: greater complexity and differentiation, the need for integration, and the problem of transferring knowledge and innovation across a global firm. Organizations have to accept an extremely high level of environmental complexity in the international domain and address the many differences that occur among countries. Environmental complexity and country variations require greater organizational differentiation, as described in Chapter 4.

At the same time, organizations must find ways to effectively achieve coordination and collaboration among far-flung units and facilitate the development and transfer of organizational knowledge and innovation for global learning.[63] Although many small companies are involved in international business, most international companies grow very large, creating a huge coordination problem. For example, Toyota's value added (i.e., the sum of total wages, pretax profits, depreciation, and amortization) was $US30.4 billion while Vietnam's gross domestic product was nearly the same at $US31.3 billion![64]

Increased Complexity and Differentiation. When organizations enter the international arena, they encounter a greater level of internal and external complexity than anything experienced on the domestic front. Companies have to create a structure to operate in numerous countries that differ in economic development, language, political systems and government regulations, cultural norms and values, and infrastructure such as transportation and communication facilities. For example, although most international firms have their headquarters in wealthier, economically advanced countries, smart managers are investing heavily in less-developed countries in Asia, Eastern Europe, and Latin America, which offer huge new markets for their goods and services. In the area of e-commerce, the number of Internet users and the amount of online sales are booming in Latin America, so companies such as Dell and America Online quickly set up online stores and services for customers in that region.[65] Over the past few years, China has become a major centre for international business, including burgeoning local companies as well as big foreign corporations such as Nokia, IBM, Volkswagen, and BMW. Yet doing business in China, with its poor roads and developing infrastructure, is not easy, even for big firms.[66]

Another factor increasing the complexity for organizations is that a growing number of global consumers are rejecting the notion of homogenized products and services, calling for greater response to local preferences. Even McDonald's, perhaps the ultimate example of standardization for a world market, has felt the need to be more responsive to local and national differences. In France, where consumers have been resentful of the fast-food chain's incursion, McDonald's boosted sales even as its North American restaurants stalled by remodelling stores to include features such as hardwood floors, wood-beam ceilings, and comfortable armchairs, and by adding menu items such as espresso, brioche, and more upscale sandwiches.[67]

All this complexity in the international environment is mirrored in a greater internal organizational complexity. Recall from Chapter 4 that, as environments become more complex and uncertain, organizations grow more highly differentiated, with many specialized positions and departments to cope with specific sectors in the environment. Top management might need to set up specialized departments to deal with the diverse government, legal, and accounting regulations in various countries, for example. More boundary-spanning departments are needed to sense and respond to the external environment. In addition, organizations might implement a variety of strategies, a broader array of activities, and a much larger number of products and services on an international level in order to meet the needs of a diverse market.

Need for Integration. As organizations become more differentiated, with multiple products, divisions, departments, and positions scattered across numerous countries, managers face a tremendous integration challenge. As described in Chapter 4, integration refers to the quality of collaboration across organizational units. The question is how to achieve the coordination and collaboration that is necessary for a global organization to reap the benefits of economies of scale, economies of scope, and labour and production cost efficiencies that international expansion offers. Even in a domestic firm, high differentiation among departments requires that more time and resources be devoted to achieving coordination because employees' attitudes, goals, and work orientations differ widely. Imagine what it must be like for an international organization, whose operating units are divided not only by goals and work attitudes but also by geographical distance, time differences, cultural values, and perhaps even language as well. Companies must find ways to share information, ideas, new products, and technologies across the organization. Consider how Sony got blasted by Apple's iPod largely because of integration problems.

In Practice

Sony Corporation (Sony)

Sony once owned the market for mobile music players. With 50 years in the business of providing music on the go—beginning with the transistor radio in the 1950s and continuing with the Walkman, which has sold more than 340 million machines—the consumer electronics giant seemed well positioned to be the front-runner in the world of digital music. But Sony got blindsided by, of all things, a computer company. With the introduction of Apple's iPod, which Steve Jobs referred to as "the twenty-first-century Walkman," and the iTunes music store, Sony no longer even seemed in the game.

A huge problem for Sony was that its digital music businesses were scattered in many different parts of the vast Sony empire, and cooperation among the parts was woefully inadequate. In addition, Sony's insistence on using only its own technology meant that, until recently, customers couldn't use the Walkman to play MP3s. Sony's Connect music store used its own clunky compression technology, which turned users off. In early 2005, Connect ranked number 23 in music sites visited by Internet users, with Yahoo's Launch, AOL Music, and Apple's iTunes the top three sites. Estimates are that Connect lags some 300 million song sales behind iTunes.

In the world of digital music, everything depends on seamless integration, and Apple has gotten it just right. Flawless coordination among hardware, software, and content make buying and playing music ridiculously easy compared to Sony's system. Recently, Sony top executives set up a new division, also called Sony Connect, aimed specifically at getting the Tokyo-centred electronics businesses and the U.S. media businesses to work together. In addition, a new CEO, Sir Howard Stringer, the first non-Japanese native to head Sony, is emphasizing cross-company collaboration over technological prowess to get things back on track.

Linking all the scattered pieces together is not an easy job with a company the size of Sony. "The service side and the electronics side have different opinions and priorities," says Koichiro Tsujino, who serves as co-president (with American Phil Wiser) of Sony Connect. "And when you think of Japan and America, the languages are different, the work styles and time zones are different, and they're physically far away from each other." The new CEO's toughest, yet most important, job might be developing effective mechanisms for getting managers around the world from games, music, movies, and hardware to collaborate, share ideas, and set joint priorities.[68]

This example illustrates the tremendous complexity of large global organizations and the difficulties of getting all the pieces working together. Apple had an advantage in creating the iPod and iTunes because the company is smaller and less scattered, meaning coordination is easier. Sony might never be able to catch up with Apple's iPod, which had 78 percent of the digital music player market in the United States, 45 percent in Canada, 54 percent in Japan, 58 percent in Australia, and 40 percent in the United Kingdom in 2006.[69] However, new structural mechanisms and a new emphasis on integration should enable the disparate parts of the organization to better coordinate their efforts and help Sony regain some of its lost stature.

Transfer of Knowledge and Innovation. The third piece of the international challenge is for organizations to learn from their international experiences by sharing knowledge and innovations across the enterprise. The diversity of the international environment offers extraordinary opportunities for learning and the development of diverse capabilities.

Organizational units in each location acquire the skills and knowledge to meet environmental challenges that arise in that particular locale. Much of that knowledge, which may be related to product improvements, operational efficiencies, technological advancements, or myriad other competencies, is relevant across multiple countries, so organizations need systems that promote the transfer of knowledge and innovation across the global enterprise. One good example comes from Procter & Gamble. Liquid Tide was one of P&G's most successful American product launches in the 1980s, but the product came about from the sharing of innovations developed in diverse parts of the firm. Liquid Tide incorporated a technology for helping to suspend dirt in wash water from P&G headquarters in the United States, the formula for its cleaning agents from P&G technicians in Japan, and special ingredients for fighting mineral salts present in hard water from company scientists in Brussels.[70]

Most organizations tap only a fraction of the potential that is available from the cross-border transfer of knowledge and innovation.[71] There are several reasons for this:

- Knowledge often remains hidden in various units because language, cultural, and geographical distances prevent top managers from recognizing it exists.
- Divisions sometimes view knowledge and innovation as power and want to hold onto it as a way to gain an influential position within the global firm.
- The "not-invented-here" syndrome makes some managers reluctant to tap into the know-how and expertise of other units.
- Much of an organization's knowledge is in the minds of employees and cannot easily be written down and shared with other units.

Organizations have to find ways to encourage both the development and sharing of knowledge, implement systems for tapping into knowledge wherever it exists, and share innovations to meet global challenges.

Global Coordination Mechanisms

Managers meet the global challenge of coordination and transferring knowledge and innovation across highly differentiated units in a variety of ways. Some of the most common are the use of global teams, stronger headquarters planning and control, and specific coordination roles.

Global Teams. The popularity and success of teams on the domestic front allowed managers to see firsthand how this mechanism can achieve strong horizontal coordination, as described in Chapter 3, and thus recognize the promise teams held for coordination across a global firm as well. **Global teams**, also called *transnational teams*, are cross-border work groups made up of multiskilled, multinational members whose activities span multiple countries.[72] Typically, teams are of two types: intercultural teams, whose members come from different countries and meet face to face, and virtual global teams, whose members remain in separate locations around the world and conduct their work electronically.[73] Heineken formed the European Production Task Force, a 13-member team comprising multinational members, to meet regularly and come up with ideas for optimizing the company's production facilities across Europe.[74] The research unit of BT Labs has 660 researchers spread across the United Kingdom and several other countries who work in global virtual teams to investigate virtual reality, artificial intelligence, and other advanced information technologies.[75] The team approach enables technologies, ideas, and learning in one country to rapidly spread across the firm via the constant sharing of information among team members.

The most advanced and competitive use of global teams involves simultaneous contributions in three strategic areas.[76] First, global teams help companies address the differentiation challenge, enabling them to be more locally responsive by providing knowledge to meet the needs of different regional markets, consumer preferences, and political and legal systems. At the same time, teams provide integration benefits, helping organizations achieve global efficiencies by developing regional or worldwide cost advantages and standardizing designs and operations across countries. Finally, these teams contribute to continuous organizational learning, knowledge transfer, and adaptation on a global level.

Stronger Headquarters Planning. A second approach to achieving stronger global coordination is for headquarters to take an active role in planning, scheduling, and control to keep the widely distributed pieces of the global organization working together and moving in the same direction. In one survey, 70 percent of global companies reported that the most important function of corporate headquarters was to "provide enterprise leadership."[77] Without strong leadership, highly autonomous divisions can begin to act like independent companies rather than coordinated parts of a global whole. To counteract this, top management may delegate responsibility and decision-making authority in some areas, such as adapting products or services to meet local needs, while maintaining strong control through centralized management and information systems that enable headquarters to keep track of what's going on and coordinate activities across divisions and countries. Plans, schedules, and formal rules and procedures can help ensure greater communication among divisions and with headquarters, and foster cooperation and synergy among far-flung units to achieve the organization's goals in a cost-efficient way.

Top managers can provide clear strategic direction, guide far-flung operations, and resolve competing demands from various units. This is one of the primary goals of Sir Howard Stringer at Sony, discussed in the previous section. In his first news conference, Sir Howard emphasized his resolve to promote collaboration and creativity to produce "new products, new ideas, new strategies, new alliances, and a shared vision."[78]

PDA Remember...

Use mechanisms such as global teams, headquarters planning, and specific coordination roles to provide needed coordination and integration among far-flung international units. Emphasize information and knowledge sharing to help the organization learn and improve on a global scale.

Specific Coordination Roles. Organizations may also implement structural solutions to achieve stronger coordination and collaboration.[79] Creating specific organizational roles or positions for coordination is a way to integrate all the pieces of the enterprise to achieve a strong competitive position. In successful international firms, the role of top functional managers, for example, is expanded to include responsibility for coordinating across countries, identifying and linking the organization's expertise and resources worldwide. In an international organization, the manufacturing manager has to be aware of and coordinate with manufacturing operations of the company in various other parts of the world so that the company achieves manufacturing efficiency and shares technology and ideas across units. A new manufacturing technology developed to improve efficiency in Ford's Brazilian operations may be valuable for European and North American plants as well. Manufacturing managers are responsible for being aware of new developments wherever they occur and for using their knowledge to improve the organization. Similarly, marketing managers, HR managers, and other functional managers at an international company are involved in not only activities for their particular location but also coordinating with their sister units in other countries.

Whereas functional managers coordinate across countries, country managers coordinate across functions. A country manager for an international firm has to coordinate all the various functional activities to meet the problems, opportunities, needs, and trends in the local market, enabling the organization to achieve multinational flexibility and rapid response. The country manager in Venezuela for a global consumer products firm such as McCain would coordinate everything that goes on in that country, from manufacturing to HR to marketing, to ensure that activities meet the language, cultural, government, and legal requirements of South America. The country manager in India or France would do the same for those countries. Country managers also help with the transfer of ideas, trends, products, and technologies that arise in one country and might have significance on a broader scale.

Some organizations create formal network coordinator positions to coordinate information and activities related to key customer accounts. These coordinators would enable a manufacturing organization, for example, to provide knowledge and integrated solutions across multiple businesses, divisions, and countries for a large customer such as Wal-Mart.[80] Top managers in successful global firms also encourage and support informal networks and relationships to keep information flowing in all directions. Much of an organization's information exchange occurs not through formal systems or structures but through informal channels and relationships. By supporting these informal networks, giving people across boundaries opportunities to get together and develop relationships and then ways to keep in close touch, executives enhance organizational coordination.

International companies today have a hard time staying competitive without strong interunit coordination and collaboration. Those firms that stimulate and support collaboration are typically better able to leverage dispersed resources and capabilities to reap operational and economic benefits.[81] Benefits that result from interunit collaboration include the following:

- *Cost savings*. Collaboration can produce real, measurable results in cost savings from the sharing of best practices across global divisions.
- *Better decision making*. By sharing information and advice across divisions, managers can make better business decisions that support their own unit as well as the organization as a whole.
- *Greater revenues*. By sharing expertise and products among various divisions, organizations can reap increased revenues. For example, more than 75 people from BP's various units around the world flew to China to assist the team developing an acetic acid plant there. As a result, BP finished the project and began realizing revenues sooner than project planners had expected.
- *Increased innovation*. The sharing of ideas and technological innovations across units stimulates creativity and the development of new products and services. Recall the example of Procter & Gamble mentioned earlier, in which P&G developed Liquid Tide based on ideas and innovations that arose in a number of different divisions around the world.

Cultural Differences in Coordination and Control

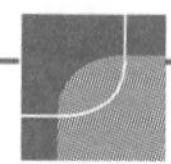

PDA Remember...

Appreciate cultural value differences and strive to use coordination mechanisms that are in tune with local values. When broader coordination mechanisms are needed, focus on education and organizational culture as ways to gain understanding and acceptance.

Just as social and cultural values differ from country to country, management values and organizational norms of international companies tend to vary depending on the organization's home country. Organizational norms and values are influenced by the values in the larger national culture, and these in turn influence the organization's structural approach and the ways managers coordinate and control an international firm.

National Value Systems

Studies have attempted to determine how national value systems influence management and organizations. One of the most influential was conducted by Geert Hofstede, who identified five dimensions of national value systems that vary widely across countries.[82] According to Hofstede, "[culture] is more often a source of conflict than of synergy. Cultural differences are a nuisance at best and often a disaster."[83] For example, two of his five dimensions that seem to have a strong impact within organizations are power distance and uncertainty avoidance. High **power distance** means that people accept inequality in power among institutions, organizations, and people. Low power distance means that people expect equality in power. High **uncertainty avoidance** means that members of a society feel uncomfortable with uncertainty and ambiguity, and thus support beliefs that promise certainty and conformity. Low uncertainty avoidance means that people have a high tolerance for the unstructured, the unclear, and the unpredictable. More recent research by Project GLOBE (Global Leadership and Organizational Behavior Effectiveness) has supported and extended Hofstede's assessment. Project GLOBE used data collected from 18,000 managers in 62 countries to identify nine dimensions that explain cultural differences, including those identified by Hofstede.[84]

The value dimensions of power distance and uncertainty avoidance are reflected within organizations in beliefs regarding the need for hierarchy, centralized decision making and control, formal rules and procedures, and specialized jobs.[85] In countries that value high power distance, for example, organizations tend to be more hierarchical and centralized, with greater control and coordination from the top levels of the organization. On the other hand, organizations in countries that value low power distance are more likely to be decentralized. A low tolerance for uncertainty tends to be reflected in a preference for coordination through rules and procedures. Organizations in countries where people have a high tolerance for uncertainty typically have fewer rules and formal systems, relying more on informal networks and personal communication for coordination. This chapter's Workbook lets you delve further into the five dimensions and their impact.

Although organizations do not always reflect the dominant cultural values, studies have found rather clear patterns of different management structures when comparing countries in Europe, North America, and Asia. For example, Gesteland outlines four major cultural value patterns, which he calls logical patterns, that characterize countries around the world.[86]

- *Deal-focused versus relationship-focused.* Deal-focused cultures, such as those in North America, Australia, and Northern Europe, are task-oriented, while relationship-focused cultures, including those in Arabia, Africa, Latin America, and Asia, are typically people-oriented. Deal-focused individuals approach business in an objective and impersonal way. Relationship-focused individuals believe in building close personal relationships as the appropriate way to conduct business.
- *Informal versus formal.* Informal cultures place a low value on status and power differences, whereas formal cultures are typically hierarchical and status conscious. The unconstrained values of informal cultures, such as those in the United States and Australia, may insult people from formal, hierarchical societies, just as the class-consciousness of formal groups, such as cultures in most of Europe and Latin America, may offend the egalitarian ideals of people in informal cultures.
- *Rigid time versus fluid time.* One part of the world's societies is flexible about time and scheduling, while the other group is more rigid and dedicated to clock time. Conflicts may occur because rigid-time types often consider fluid-time people undisciplined and irresponsible, while fluid-time people regard rigid-time folks as arrogant, demanding, and enslaved by meaningless deadlines.
- *Expressive versus reserved.* Expressive cultures include those in Latin America and the Mediterranean. Reserved cultures are those in East and Southeast Asia as well as Germanic Europe. This distinction can create a major communication gap. People from expressive cultures tend to talk louder and use more hand gestures and facial expressions. Reserved cultures may interpret raised voices and gesturing as signals of anger or instability.

Three National Approaches to Coordination and Control

Let's look at three primary approaches to coordination and control as represented by Japanese, European and North American companies.[87] It should be noted that companies in each country use tools and techniques from each of the three coordination methods. However, there are broad, general patterns that illustrate cultural differences.

Centralized Coordination in Japanese Companies. When expanding internationally, Japanese companies have typically developed coordination mechanisms that rely on centralization. Top managers at headquarters actively direct and control overseas operations, whose primary focus is to implement strategies handed down from headquarters. A recent study of R&D activities in high-tech firms in Japan and Germany supports the idea that Japanese organizations tend to be more centralized. While German firms leaned toward dispersing R&D groups out into different regions, Japanese companies tended to keep these activities centralized in the home country.[88] This centralized approach enables Japanese companies to leverage the knowledge and resources located at the corporate centre, attain global efficiencies, and coordinate across units to obtain synergies and avoid turf battles. Top managers use strong structural linkages to ensure that managers at headquarters remain up to date and fully involved in all strategic decisions. However, centralization has its limits. As the organization expands and divisions grow larger, headquarters can become overloaded and decision making slows. The quality of decisions may also suffer as greater diversity and complexity make it difficult for headquarters to understand and respond to local needs in each region.

Book Mark 6.0 (HAVE YOU READ THIS BOOK?)

Why Mexicans Don't Drink Molson: Rescuing Canadian Business from the Suds of Global Obscurity
By Andrea Mandel-Campbell

In her incisive analysis, Mandel-Campbell argues that Canadian companies do not have the gumption to become global brand leaders. She argues that we need, as a country, to get over our inferiority complex if we are to project ourselves internationally,

Her account of Molson's inability to become a global brand is illuminating. In the 1970s, Molson was about the same size as the Netherlands's Heineken. In 30 years, Heineken has become the world's fourth-largest brewery with 115 breweries in more than 65 countries. In contrast, Molson does not have a single brand in the world's top 20! Rather than expanding into emerging markets such as Russia and China, Molson sold half its breweries to Australian and American brewers and diversified into hardware. Molson had an opportunity to enter the Chinese market in the 1980s when China's Tsingtao Brewery was insolvent and searching for a $20 million investment. Molson did not invest in China but did invest in Brazil. Molson did not provide its own brand to the large South American market but did bring Brazilian beer to the Canadian market! Molson had once been a powerful organization; founded in 1786, it once had steamships, a bank and even its own currency, but it is not the global player it could have been.

Mandel-Campbell provides many other vivid examples of Canadian companies that ignored or failed to see the importance of investing globally. In her last chapter, aptly titled "A New Approach to Parenting," she offers some useful prescriptions. She argues that the Government of Canada has a critical role in fostering global competitiveness—it must have a clear strategy and goal. "The fundamental question that government policy-makers should ask themselves is, how can Canadians graduate from being telemarketers, middle managers and commodity producers to not only running, but *leading*, globally oriented enterprises? (p. 287) She goes on to recommend that industrial policy should be used to promote successful organizations and not to protect failing ones. Mandel-Campbell's other prescriptions are a strong call for Canada, its companies, and its people to become much more entrepreneurial and ambitious and, in short, "to grow up." (p. 311) As she notes in her penultimate sentence, "Canada has all the makings of a global leader. The question is whether it wants to be one." (p. 312)

Why Mexicans Don't Drink Molson: Rescuing Canadian Business from the Suds of Global Obscurity, by Andrea Mandel-Campbell, is published by Douglas & McIntyre.

China is a rapidly growing part of the international business environment, and limited research has been done into management structures of Chinese firms. Many Chinese-based firms are still relatively small and run in a traditional family-like manner. However, similar to Japan, organizations typically reflect a distinct hierarchy of authority and relatively strong centralization. Obligation plays an important role in Chinese culture and management, so employees feel obligated to follow orders directed from above.[89] Interestingly, though, one study found that Chinese employees are loyal not just to the boss, but also to company policies.[90] As Chinese organizations grow larger, more insight will be gained into how these firms handle the balance of coordination and control.

European Firms' Decentralized Approach. A different approach has typically been taken by European companies. Rather than relying on strong, centrally directed coordination and control as in the Japanese firms, international units tend to have a high level of independence and decision-making autonomy. Companies rely on a strong mission, shared values, and informal personal relationships for coordination. Thus, great emphasis is placed on careful selection, training, and development of key managers throughout the international organization. Formal management and control systems are used primarily for financial rather than technical or operational control. With this approach, each international unit focuses on its local markets, enabling the company to excel in meeting diverse needs. One disadvantage is the cost of ensuring, through training and development programs, that managers throughout a huge, global firm share goals, values, and priorities. Decision making can also be slow and complex, and disagreements and conflicts among divisions are more difficult to resolve.

North America: Coordination and Control through Formalization. Many North American companies that have expanded into the international arena have taken a third direction. Typically, these organizations have delegated responsibility to international divisions, yet retained overall control of the enterprise through the use of sophisticated management control systems and the development of specialist headquarters staff. Formal systems, policies, standards of performance, and a regular flow of information from divisions to headquarters are the primary means of coordination and control. Decision making is based on objective data, policies, and procedures, which provides for many operating efficiencies and reduces conflict among divisions and between divisions and headquarters. However, the cost of setting up complex systems, policies, and rules for an international organization may be quite high. This approach also requires a larger headquarters staff for reviewing, interpreting, and sharing information, thus increasing overhead costs. Finally, standard routines and procedures don't always fit the needs of new problems and situations. Flexibility is limited if managers pay so much attention to systems that they fail to recognize opportunities and threats in the environment.

Clearly, each of these approaches has advantages. But as international organizations grow larger and more complex, the disadvantages of each tend to become more pronounced. Because traditional approaches have been inadequate to meet the demands of a rapidly changing, complex international environment, many large international companies are moving toward a new kind of organization form, the *transnational model*, which is highly differentiated to address environmental complexity, yet offers very high levels of coordination, learning, and transfer of organizational knowledge and innovations.

PDA

Remember...

Strive toward a transnational model of organization when the company has to respond to multiple global forces simultaneously and needs to promote worldwide integration, learning, and knowledge sharing.

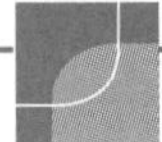

The Transnational Model of Organization

The **transnational model** represents the most advanced kind of international organization. It reflects the ultimate in both organizational complexity, with many diverse units, and organizational coordination, with mechanisms for integrating the varied parts. The transnational model is useful for large, multinational companies with subsidiaries in many countries that try to exploit both global and local advantages as well as technological advancements, rapid innovation, and global learning and knowledge sharing. Rather than building capabilities primarily in one area, such as global efficiency, national responsiveness, or global learning, the transnational model seeks to achieve all three simultaneously. Dealing with multiple, interrelated, complex issues requires a complex form of organization and structure.

The transnational model represents the most current thinking about the kind of structure needed by complex global organizations such as Philips NV, illustrated in Exhibit 6.6. Headquartered in the Netherlands, Philips has hundreds of operating units all over the world and is typical of global companies such as Unilever, Matsushita, or Procter & Gamble.[91]

Achieving coordination, a sense of participation and involvement by subsidiaries, and a sharing of information, knowledge, new technology, and customers is a tremendous challenge. For example, a global corporation like Philips is so large that size alone is a huge problem in coordinating global operations. In addition, some subsidiaries become so large that they no longer fit a narrow strategic role defined by headquarters. While being part of a larger organization, individual units need some autonomy for themselves and the ability to have an impact on other parts of the organization.

The transnational model addresses these challenges by creating an integrated network of individual operations that are linked together to achieve the multidimensional goals of the overall organization.[92] The management philosophy is based on *interdependence* rather than either full divisional independence or total dependence of these units on headquarters for decision making and control. The transnational model is more than just an organizational chart. It is a managerial state of mind, a set of values, a shared desire to make a worldwide learning system work, and an idealized structure for effectively managing such a system. Several characteristics distinguish the transnational organization from other global organization forms such as the matrix, described earlier.

1. *Assets and resources are dispersed worldwide into highly specialized operations that are linked together through interdependent relationships.* Resources and capabilities are widely distributed to help the organization sense and respond to diverse stimuli such as market needs, technological developments, or consumer trends that emerge in different parts of the world. However, managers forge interdependent relationships among the various product, functional, or geographical units. Mechanisms such as cross-subsidiary teams, for example, compel units to work together for the good of their own unit as well as the overall organization. Rather than being completely self-sufficient, each group has to cooperate to achieve its own goals. Such interdependencies encourage the collaborative sharing of information and resources, cross-unit problem solving, and collective implementation demanded by today's competitive international environment. Materials, people, products, ideas, resources, and information are continually flowing

EXHIBIT 6.6

International Organizational Units and Interlinkages within Philips NV

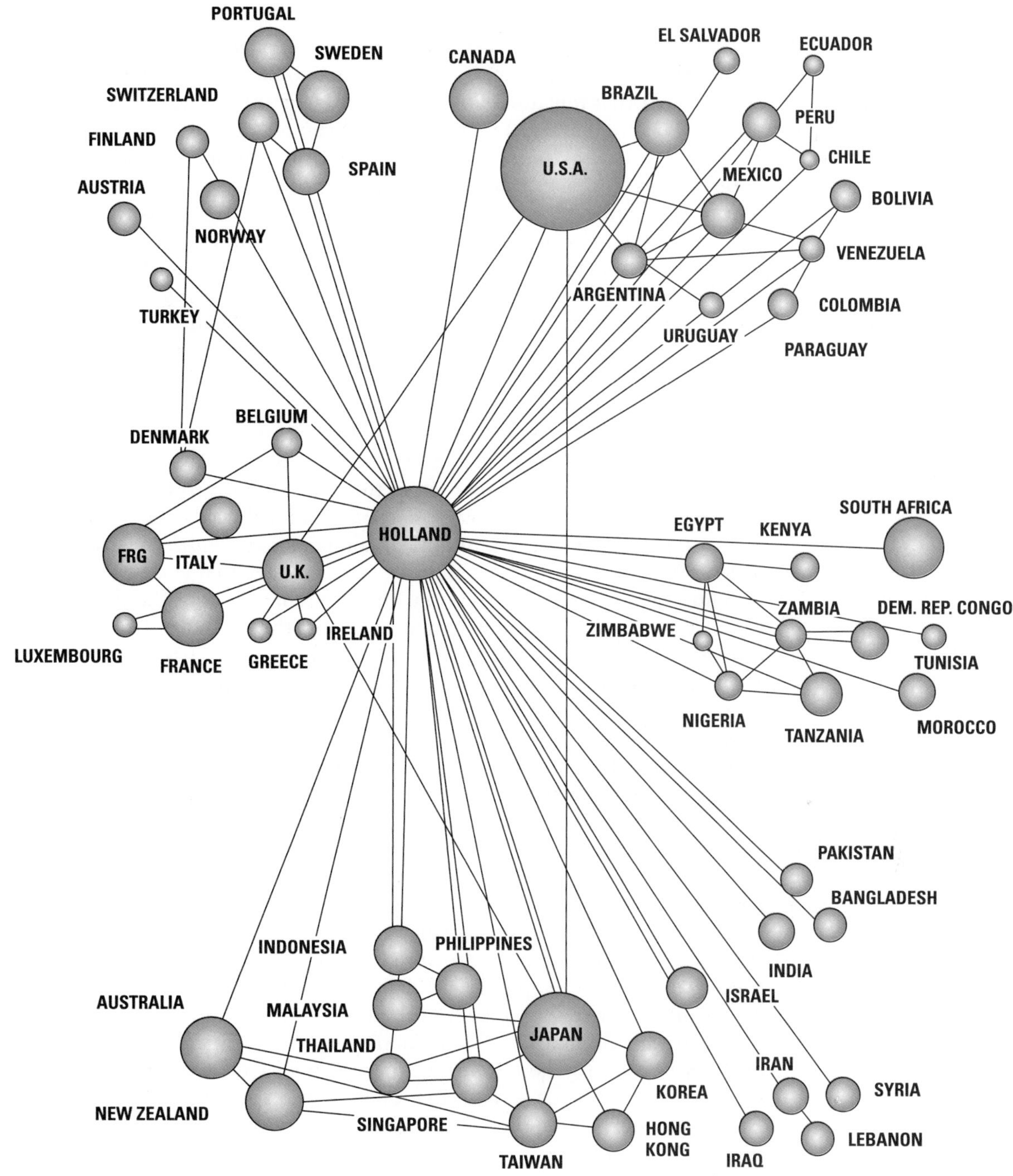

Source: Sumantra Ghoshal and Christopher A. Bartlett, "The Multinational Corporation as an Interorganizational Network," *Academy of Management Review* 15 (1990): 605. Used by permission.

among the dispersed parts of the integrated network. In addition, managers actively shape, manage, and reinforce informal information networks that cross functions, products, divisions, and countries.

2. *Structures are flexible and ever-changing.* The transnational operates on a principle of flexible centralization. It may centralize some functions in one country yet decentralize other functions among its many geographically dispersed operations. An R&D centre may be centralized in Holland and a purchasing centre may be located in Sweden, while financial accounting responsibilities are decentralized to operations in many countries. A unit in Hong Kong may be responsible for coordinating activities across Asia, while activities for all other countries are coordinated by a large division headquarters in London. The transnational model requires that managers be flexible in determining structural needs based on the benefits to be gained. Some functions, products, and geographical regions by their nature may need more central control and coordination than others. In addition, coordination and control mechanisms will change over time to meet new needs or competitive threats.
3. *Subsidiary managers initiate strategy and innovations that become strategy for the corporation as a whole.* In traditional structures, managers have a strategic role only for their division. In a transnational structure, various centres and subsidiaries can shape the company from the bottom up by developing creative responses and initiating programs in response to local needs and dispersing those innovations worldwide. Transnational companies recognize each of the worldwide units as a source of capabilities and knowledge that can be used to benefit the entire organization. In addition, environmental demands and opportunities vary from country to country, and exposing the whole organization to this broader range of environmental stimuli triggers greater learning and innovation.
4. *Unification and coordination are achieved primarily through organizational culture, shared vision and values, and management style, rather than through formal structures and systems.* The transnational structure is essentially a horizontal structure. It is diverse and extended, and it exists in a fluctuating environment so that hierarchy, standard rules, procedures, and close supervision are not appropriate. Achieving unity and coordination in an organization in which employees come from a variety of different national backgrounds, are separated by time and geographical distance, and have different cultural norms is more easily accomplished through shared understanding than through formal systems. Top leaders build a context of shared vision, values, and perspectives among managers who in turn cascade these elements through all parts of the organization. Selection and training of managers emphasize flexibility and open-mindedness. In addition, people are often rotated through different jobs, divisions, and countries to gain broad experience and become socialized into the organizational culture. Achieving coordination in a transnational organization is a much more complex process than simple centralization or decentralization of decision making, and requires shaping and adapting beliefs, culture, and values so that everyone participates in information sharing and learning.

Taken together, these characteristics facilitate strong coordination, organizational learning, and knowledge sharing on a broad global scale. As you can see from Exhibit 6.6, the transnational model is truly a complex and messy way to conceptualize organizational structure, but it is becoming increasingly relevant for large, global firms that treat the whole world as their playing field and do not have a single

EXHIBIT 6.7
Going Global

"Who can we talk to about global investing?"

country base. The autonomy of organizational parts gives strength to smaller units and allows the firm to be flexible in responding to rapid change and competitive opportunities on a local level, while the emphasis on interdependency enables global efficiencies and organizational learning. Each part of the transnational company is aware of and closely integrated with the organization as a whole so local actions complement and enhance other company parts. See Exhibit 6.7, which captures nicely the expanding universe of organizations today!

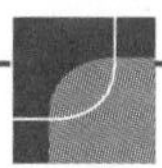

Summary and Interpretation

This chapter has examined how managers design organizations for a complex international environment. Almost every company today is affected by significant global forces, and many are developing overseas operations to take advantage of global markets. Three primary motivations for global expansion are to realize economies of scale, exploit economies of scope, and achieve scarce or low-cost factors of production such as labour, raw materials, or land. One popular way to become involved in international operations is through strategic alliances with international firms. Alliances include licensing, joint ventures, and consortia.

Organizations typically evolve through four stages, beginning with a domestic orientation, shifting to an international orientation, then changing to a multinational orientation, and finally moving to a global orientation that sees the whole world as a potential market. Organizations typically use an export department, then use an international department, and eventually develop into a worldwide geographical or product structure. Geographical structures are most effective for organizations that can benefit from a multidomestic strategy, meaning that products and services will do best if tailored to local needs and cultures. A product structure supports a globalization strategy, which means that products and services can be standardized and sold worldwide. Huge global firms might use a matrix structure to respond to both local and global forces simultaneously. Many firms use hybrid structures by combining elements of two or more different structures to meet the dynamic conditions of the global environment.

Succeeding on a global scale is not easy. Three aspects of the global organizational challenge are addressing environmental complexity through greater organizational complexity and differentiation, achieving integration and coordination among the highly differentiated units, and implementing mechanisms for the transfer of knowledge and innovations. Common ways to address the problem of integration and knowledge transfer are through global teams, stronger headquarters planning and control, and specific coordination roles. Managers also recognize that diverse national and cultural values influence the organization's approach to coordination and control. Three varied national approaches are the centralized coordination and control typically found in many Japanese-based firms, a decentralized approach common among European firms, and the formalization approach often used by North America–based international firms. Most companies, however, no matter their home country, use a combination of elements from each of these approaches.

Many companies are also finding a need to broaden their coordination methods and are moving toward the transnational model of organization. The transnational model is based on a philosophy of interdependence. It is highly differentiated yet offers very high levels of coordination, learning, and transfer of knowledge across far-flung divisions. The transnational model represents the ultimate global design in terms of both organizational complexity and organizational integration. Each part of the transnational organization is aware of and closely integrated with the organization as a whole so that local actions complement and enhance other company parts.

Key Concepts

consortia, p. 200
domestic stage, p. 198
economies of scale, p. 197
economies of scope, p. 197
factors of production, p. 197
global companies, p. 199
global geographical structure, p. 205
global matrix structure, p. 207
global product structure, p. 204
global stage, p. 199
global teams, p. 212
globalization strategy, p. 201
international division, p. 203
international stage, p. 198
joint venture, p. 200
multidomestic, p. 198
multidomestic strategy, p. 202
multinational stage, p. 199
power distance, p. 214
standardization, p. 201
transnational model, p. 218
uncertainty avoidance, p. 214

Discussion Questions

1. Under what conditions should a company consider adopting a global geographical structure as opposed to a global product structure?
2. Name some companies that you think could succeed today with a globalization strategy and explain why you selected those companies. How does the globalization strategy differ from a multidomestic strategy?
3. Why would a company want to join a strategic alliance rather than go it alone in international operations? What do you see as the potential advantages and disadvantages of international alliances?
4. Why is knowledge sharing so important to a global organization?
5. What are some of the primary reasons a company decides to expand internationally? Identify a company in the news that has recently built a new overseas facility. Which of the three motivations for global expansion described in the chapter do you think best explains the company's decision? Discuss.
6. When would an organization consider using a matrix structure? How does the global matrix differ from the domestic matrix structure described in Chapter 3?
7. Name some of the elements that contribute to greater complexity for international organizations. How do organizations address this complexity? Do you think these elements apply to an online company such as eBay that wants to grow internationally? Discuss.
8. Traditional values in Mexico support high power distance and a low tolerance for uncertainty. What would you predict about a company that opens a division in Mexico and tries to implement global teams characterized by shared power and authority and a lack of formal guidelines, rules, and structure?
9. Do you believe it is possible for a global company to simultaneously achieve the goals of global efficiency and integration, national responsiveness and flexibility, and the worldwide transfer of knowledge and innovation? Discuss.
10. Compare the description of the transnational model in this chapter to the elements of the learning organization described in Chapter 1. Do you think the transnational model seems workable for a huge global firm? Discuss.
11. What does it mean to say that the transnational model is based on a philosophy of interdependence?

Chapter 6 Workbook: Appreciating Cultural Differences

Go the Hofstede's website at http://www.geert-hofstede.com, and look up scores for his five dimensions for Canada and two other countries. Record them here.

Power Distance	Individualism	Masculinity	Uncertainty Avoidance	Long-Term Orientation
1. Canada				
2.				
3.				

Questions

1. What similarities and differences did you observe?
2. How can managers use Hofstede's dimensions when working internationally?

Case for Analysis: Ivanhoe Mines

Mining magnate Robert Friedland has made a career of dancing on the knife's edge. His Ivanhoe Mines Ltd., for example, operates in Mongolia, Myanmar and Kazakhstan—countries where, to varying degrees, governments can be oppressive and unstable, civil unrest can break out without warning, contracts can be abandoned with impunity, corruption may run rampant, or all of the above. Friedland's appetite for risk is not unique: surging metals prices have renewed interest for mining in unstable countries with promising ore bodies. Recent turmoil at Ivanhoe's property in Myanmar, however, provides a sobering reminder of what can go wrong. Which, in this case, includes pretty much everything.

While other foreign investors fled Myanmar (commonly known by its former name, Burma) because of its unfriendly business climate and opposition from shareholders and consumers, Vancouver-based Ivanhoe charged headlong into the Southeast Asian country during the 1990s. The fruit of its efforts is the Monywa Copper Project, an open-pit mine located on the lowland plains west of Mandalay. Ivanhoe owns half of the joint venture company; its partner is No. 1 Mining Enterprise, which is controlled by the State Peace and Development Council (SPDC). The mine has become mired in international sanctions and disputes over taxation and permits. Ivanhoe is now in talks to sell a significant portion of its interest in the project to Asian buyers.

Much of Monywa's problems stem from Friedland's choice of business partners. The SPDC is a military junta that seized control of Burma in 1988 and held onto power despite democratic opposition and its loss of an election in 1990. Its international image is poor. According to the U.S. State Department, the SPDC maintains its control by censoring information, suppressing ethnic minorities and repressing the rights of its people. Amnesty International accuses it of restricting freedom of movement, employing forced labour and keeping more than 1,300 political prisoners in custody. And Human Rights Watch, a nongovernmental organization, claims that "the junta's pledges of democratic reform and respect for human rights continue to be empty rhetoric." Assuming that the SPDC earns the same amount of income from the mine as Ivanhoe, Monywa provided the junta with nearly US$23 million last year. Given the SPDC's international unpopularity, one might think that windfall would give the regime ample reason to keep Ivanhoe happy. In fact, relations between the two parties have evidently soured.

One threat commonly faced by mining companies abroad is called tax risk. "The rates of import duties, royalties, withholding taxes and corporate income taxes can have a big effect on the profitability of a project," explained Nabil Khodadad, a London-based partner with international law firm Chadbourne & Parke LLP, in a 2005 paper about mining risks. "The local regime can break a project by making it unprofitable." Ivanhoe became embroiled in a dispute when the Myanmar government imposed a commercial tax on copper exported from Monywa, applied retroactively from the beginning of 2003. This would amount to US$11 million from Ivanhoe's pockets, the company claims, plus the increased ongoing costs. As far as Ivanhoe is concerned, its joint-venture agreement precludes such a tax, and it has sought a written legal opinion from the attorney general of Myanmar to that effect. Even if Ivanhoe's interpretation is correct, however, it is dealing with an authoritarian government with little respect for the rule of law.

When operating in developing countries, mining firms also must worry about whether the government will expropriate a property, revoke licences or otherwise interfere with their ability to operate—which is known as political risk. Monywa includes the Sabetaung and Kyisintaung "S&K" deposits and the much larger Letpadaung ore body. The grade of ore extracted at S&K deteriorated significantly last year, and Ivanhoe announced plans to increase capacity. It then ordered the necessary mining equipment. But the SPDC has so far not issued the required import permits, so the equipment sits offshore, idle and depreciating. This year, Ivanhoe predicts that copper production from S&K will drop by more than half.

As for Letpadaung, Ivanhoe has long planned to develop it. But the Canadian company has so far not been able to obtain the necessary approvals from the SPDC, for unspecified reasons. These are serious problems. "Without a substantial increase in mining capacity, these two deposits cannot be economically developed," the company's recently released 2005 annual report warned. Mines that cannot be economically developed are effectively worthless and must be shut down.

International politics create more challenges. In 1997, the U.S. government prohibited its citizens and U.S. companies from making new investments in Myanmar. In 2003, it added a ban on imports and the export of financial services to the country following an attack on the convoy of the National League for Democracy's Aung San Suu Kyi, the prominent opposition leader. (The European Union, Australia, Canada, Japan and Korea have applied their own sanctions.) As a result of the U.S. sanctions, both Monywa's insurance broker and its offshore bank terminated their relationship with Ivanhoe last year. As Ivanhoe explained candidly in its annual report, the sanctions "have started to seriously impact the mine's ability to function in a normal way." And Ivanhoe doesn't have anything to fall back on: the company isn't insured for political or environmental risks.

These difficulties could have profound financial consequences. Ivanhoe currently estimates its stake in Monywa to be worth nearly US$140 million, or roughly 35% of total assets on its balance sheet. Ivanhoe has said that if it cannot resolve problems there, it may be forced to write-down that value significantly. Meanwhile, Monywa also accounts for the lion's share of Ivanhoe's income; the company has recorded 26 consecutive quarters of negative free cash flow.

It would seem, though, that shareholders are taking it all in stride: Ivanhoe's stock (TSX: IVN) has risen in the months since Monywa's troubles were revealed. The reason is that Monywa is not their focus. Ivanhoe's appeal to investors has largely been rooted in its Oyu Tolgoi property in Mongolia's Gobi Desert, where the company says it is focused on exploring and developing "a major discovery of copper and gold." As such, Ivanhoe is widely seen as an exploration firm, and such companies are expected to burn cash. The cash flow generated by Monywa pales in comparison to the outside investment Ivanhoe relies on to fund its operations. In late April, the company closed a $189-million bought-deal financing without any apparent difficulty.

Ivanhoe's predicament at Monywa could become more acute should it erode confidence in the company's ability to manage government relations in Mongolia and bring Oyu Tolgoi into production. (Ivanhoe recently announced that John Macken, the president and COO, will become CEO "to assemble and guide the team that will build a world-class copper and gold mine at Oyu Tolgoi.") Ivanhoe has been negotiating with the Mongolian government to reach a formal agreement on how to develop Oyu Tolgoi since 2003, and those discussions recently sparked protests in the capital, Ulan Bator, by critics who want more mineral-generated wealth to stay in the country. The protests apparently worked: on May 12, the Mongolian parliament approved a surprise windfall-profits tax on foreign miners. The move helped to send Ivanhoe stock into a tailspin; it fell nearly 22% in one day of trading.

But there's another problem. Such is Oyu Tolgoi's importance—Ivanhoe estimates the project could produce an annual average of more than one billion pounds of copper and 330,000 ounces of gold for at least 35 years—that the Canadian company is considering the sale of "non-core assets" to fund it. This apparently includes Monywa. Ivanhoe's annual report claimed that the company signed a memorandum of understanding with "an established large Korean corporation" to sell a significant portion of its interest in Monywa. More recently, in mid-April, The Korea Herald reported that a consortium of three South Korean companies had signed a preliminary agreement with Ivanhoe to jointly develop Monywa, and pay US$120 million to buy half of Ivanhoe's stake. One of the consortium's members, Korea Resources Corp., said the deal is subject to due diligence; even if prospective buyers are comfortable with having the SPDC as a business partner, Monywa's misfortunes can only reduce Friedland's bargaining position in getting the best value for shareholders. Moreover, the non-binding agreement with the Koreans is subject to regulatory approval from the SPDC. And Myanmar's generals, it seems, have not been in an accommodating mood of late.

Source: M. McClearn, "Mine Games: Ivanhoe Mines," Canadian Business (May 22–June 4, 2006) at http://www.canadianbusiness.com/shared/print.jsp?content=20060522_77851_77851 (accessed July 16, 2008). Used with permission.

Case for Analysis: TopDog Software

At the age of 39, after working for nearly 15 years at a leading software company on the West Coast, Ari Weiner and his fiancee, Mary Carpenter, had cashed in their stock options, withdrawn all their savings, maxed out their credit cards, and started their own business, naming it TopDog Software after their beloved Alaskan malamute. The two had developed a new software package for customer relationship management (CRM) applications and they were certain far superior to anything on the market at that time. TopDog's software was particularly effective for use in call centres because it provided a highly efficient way to integrate massive amounts of customer data and make it almost immediately accessible to call centre representatives as they worked the phones. The software, which could be used as a stand-alone product or easily integrated with other major CRM software packages, dramatically expedited customer identification and verification, rapidly selected pertinent bits of data, and provided them in an easily interpreted format so that call centre or customer service reps could provide fast, friendly, and customized service.

The timing proved to be right on target. CRM was just getting hot, and TopDog was poised to take advantage of the trend as a niche player in a growing market. Weiner and Carpenter brought in two former colleagues as partners and were soon able to catch the attention of a venture capitalist firm to gain additional funding. Within a couple of years, TopDog had 28 employees and sales had reached nearly four million dollars.

Now, though, the partners are facing the company's first major problem. TopDog's head of sales, Samantha Jenkins, has learned of a new company based in London,

U.K. that is beta-testing a new CRM package that promises to outpace TopDog's—and the London-based company, FastData, has been talking up its global aspirations in the press. "If we stay focused on local markets and they start out as a global player, they'll kill us within months!" Sam moaned. "We've got to come up with an international strategy to deal with this kind of competition."

In a series of group meetings, off-site retreats, and one-on-one conversations, Weiner and Carpenter have gathered opinions and ideas from their partners, employees, advisors, and friends. Now they have to make a decision—should TopDog go global? And if so, what approach would be most effective? There's a growing market for CRM software overseas, and new companies such as FastData will soon be cutting into TopDog's local market share as well. Samantha Jenkins isn't alone in her belief that TopDog has no choice but to enter new international markets or get eaten alive. Others, however, are concerned that TopDog isn't ready for that step. The company's resources are already stretched to the limit, and some advisors have warned that rapid global expansion could spell disaster. TopDog isn't even well established at home, they argue, and expanding internationally could strain the company's capabilities and resources. Others have pointed out that none of the managers has any international experience and the company would have to hire someone with significant global exposure even to think about entering new markets.

Although Mary tends to agree that TopDog for the time being should stay focused on building its business in the United States, Ari has come to believe that global expansion of some type is a necessity. But if TopDog does eventually decide on global expansion, he wonders how on earth they should proceed in such a huge, complex environment. Sam, the sales manager, is arguing that the company should set up its own small foreign offices from scratch and staff them primarily with local people. Building a U.K. office and an Asian office, she asserts, would give TopDog an ideal base for penetrating markets around the world. However, it would be quite expensive, not to mention the complexities of dealing with language and cultural differences, legal and government regulations, and other matters. Another option would be to establish alliances or joint ventures with small European and Asian companies that could benefit from adding CRM applications to their suite of products. The companies could share expenses in setting up foreign production facilities and a global sales and distribution network. This would be a much less costly operation and would give TopDog the benefit of the expertise of the foreign partners. However, it might also require lengthy negotiations and would certainly mean giving up some control to the partner companies.

One of TopDog's partners is urging still a third, even lower-cost approach—that of licensing TopDog's software to foreign distributors as a route to international expansion. By giving foreign software companies rights to produce, market, and distribute its CRM software, TopDog could build brand identity and customer awareness while keeping a tight rein on expenses. Ari likes the low-cost approach, but he wonders if licensing would give TopDog enough participation and control to successfully develop its international presence. As another day winds down, Weiner and Carpenter are no closer to a decision about global expansion than they were when the sun came up.

Source: Reprinted by permission of *Harvard Business Review,* based on "Go Global—Or No?" by Walter Kuemmerle, (June 2001), 37–49.

Chapter 6 Workshop: Working Abroad

Working in your class teams, identify the country of origin of each team member. After each member provides some information about his/her country, select one country that you are all interested in learning more about. Collect information on that country's (1) social practices, (2) cultural mores, (3) religious and other belief systems, (4) politics, and (5) business and professional practices.[93]

The research is to be done in class, so ensure that at least one team member has his/her laptop. Once the information has been identified and classified under the five topics, discuss how best to present the material to the whole class during the following session. The presentation should be an informational one that helps employees who are about to go on a two-year international posting. The employees need to know how to behave—and how *not* to behave—in the country.

At the next session, two teams will present for seven to ten minutes and will be expected to answer questions. This process will continue during the term until all teams have presented.

The order of the presentations will be random and the instructor will ensure at the first session that each team is researching a different country.

Questions

1. As you worked on your team's country, what was the most significant thing you learned? Why?
2. Now that you have heard all the presentations, what do you think are the main considerations to ensure a good international work assignment?

PART 4

Internal Design Elements

7 Manufacturing and Service Technologies

JIM R. BOUNDS/Bloomberg News/Landov

A Look Inside

General Electric at Bromont, Québec (Bromont)

The Bromont plant (see photo) began operations in 1983; it manufactures compressor airfoils for aircraft engines, led by the CFM56, the most widely used commercial jet engine. The plant's mandates are to (1) use innovative technologies and manufacturing processes; (2) achieve cost superiority, (3) maintain optimum quality, and (4) optimize both its technical and social systems. Its mission statement states, "Manufacture Six Sigma quality blades at lowest cost."[1]

Bromont's manufacturing process of more than 100 steps involves precision forging, grinding, and turning, up to tolerances of one 1/1000th of an inch. The process is a very technical one. Once the product is manufactured, it is shipped to a plant in the United States where the jet engines are assembled. Bromont uses a variety of automated systems in the manufacture of the compressor airfoils. They include robots, robotic vision systems, programmable controllers, five axis CNC (computer numerical control) milling machines, and updated quality and maintenance information online.

The plant's design was based on core values that focus on participation, personal development, social climate and structure, justice, family and community involvement, and organizational renewal. The plant was structured around five production businesses, each of which represents one of the technologies used in the manufacturing process. They are forging, pinch and roll, vanes, small rotors, and large rotors. The first two involve forming the product and the latter three involve machining the product.

Bromont has three levels of hierarchy: production teams of operators in each business; supervisory teams for each business; and support teams for the plant as a whole and the senior management team. The plant has various standing committees to manage plant-wide issues. They include committees to manage the gain-sharing system, social activities, safety procedures, and communications. Bromont is guided by a steering committee, which comprises senior representatives from operations.

The plant has been seen as a model plant as it has had stellar productivity rates and has been a high–net income producer for GE. In 2005, GE invested further in Bromont, creating 100 more jobs to bring the total number of employees to more than 700. According to Philippe Simonato, Bromont's plant manager, "[this] new production mandate for more than 200,000 airfoils a year is an acknowledgement of the exceptional quality of the work done in Bromont."[2]

Manufacturing plants in North America are being threatened as never before. Many companies have found it more advantageous to outsource manufacturing to contractors in other countries that can do the work less expensively, as we discussed in Chapter 3. Overall, manufacturing has been on the decline in Canada and other developed countries for years, with services becoming an increasingly greater part of the economy. However, some manufacturing organizations, like Bromont, are applying new technology to gain a new competitive edge.

This chapter explores both service and manufacturing technologies, and how technology is related to organizational structure. Technology is a broad concept as it refers to the work processes, techniques, machines, and actions used to transform organizational inputs (materials, information, ideas) into outputs (products and services).[3] **Technology** is an organization's production process and includes work procedures as well as machinery.

An organization's **core technology** is the work process that is directly related to the organization's mission, such as teaching in a university, medical services in a health clinic, or manufacturing at Bromont. For example, at Bromont, the core technology begins with raw materials (e.g., steel, aluminium, and composite metals). Employees take action on the raw material to make a change in it (they cut and forge metals), thus transforming the raw material into the output of the organization (vanes and blades). For a service organization like Purolator Courier, the core technology includes the production equipment (e.g., sorting machines, package-handling equipment, trucks, airplanes), and procedures for delivering packages and overnight mail. In addition, as at companies like Purolator and Bromont, computers and new information technology have revolutionized work processes in both manufacturing and service organizations. The specific impact of new information technology on organizations will be described in Chapter 8.

Exhibit 7.1 features an example of core technology for a manufacturing plant. Note how the core technology consists of raw material inputs, a transformation work process (materials handling, milling, inspection, assembly) that changes and adds value to the raw material and produces the ultimate product or service output that is sold to consumers in the environment. In today's large, complex organizations, core work processes vary widely and sometimes can be hard to pinpoint. A core technology can be partly understood by examining the raw materials flowing into the organization,[4] the variability of work activities,[5] the degree to which the production process is mechanized,[6] the extent to which one task depends on another in the workflow,[7] or the number of new product or service outputs.[8]

An important theme in this chapter is how core technology influences organizational structure. Thus, understanding core technology provides insight into how an organization can be structured for efficient performance.[9]

Organizations are made up of many departments, each of which may use a different work process (technology) to provide a good or service within the organization. A noncore technology is a department work process that is important to the organization

EXHIBIT 7.1
Core Transformation Process for a Manufacturing Company

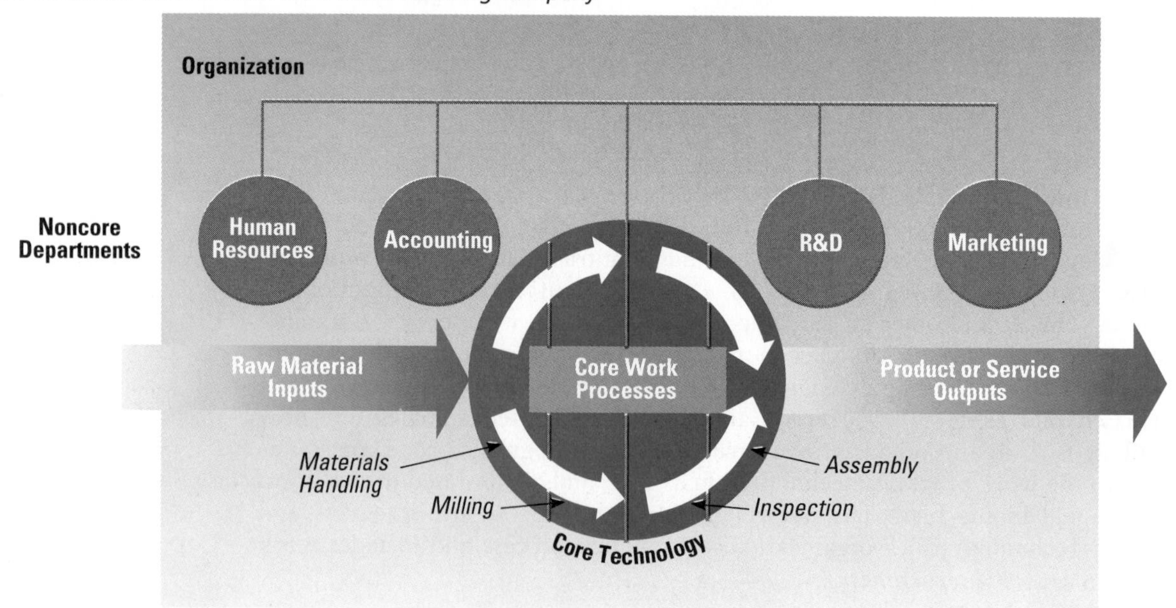

but is not directly related to its primary mission. In Exhibit 7.1, noncore work processes are illustrated by the departments of human resources (HR), accounting, research and development (R&D), and marketing. Thus, R&D transforms ideas into new products, and marketing transforms inventory into sales, each using a somewhat different work process. The output of the HR department is people to work in the organization, and accounting produces accurate statements about the organization's financial condition.

Purpose of This Chapter

In this chapter, we will discuss both core and noncore work processes and their relationship to designing organizational structure. The optimal organizational design is based on a variety of elements. Exhibit 7.2 illustrates that forces affecting organizational design come from both outside and inside the organization. External strategic needs, such as environmental conditions, strategic direction, and **organizational goals,** create top-down pressure for designing the organization in such a way as to fit the environment and accomplish goals. These pressures on design have been discussed in previous chapters. However, decisions about design should also take into consideration pressures from the bottom up—from the work processes that are performed to produce the organization's products or services. The operational work processes will influence the structural design associated with both the core technology and noncore departments. Thus, the subject with which this chapter is concerned is, "How should the organization be designed to accommodate and facilitate its operational work processes?"

The remainder of the chapter will unfold as follows. First, we examine how the technology for the organization as a whole influences organizational structure and design. This discussion includes both manufacturing and service technologies. Next, we examine differences in departmental technologies and how the technologies influence the design and management of organizational subunits. Third, we explore how interdependence—flow of materials and information—among departments affects structure.

EXHIBIT 7.2
Pressures Affecting Organizational Design

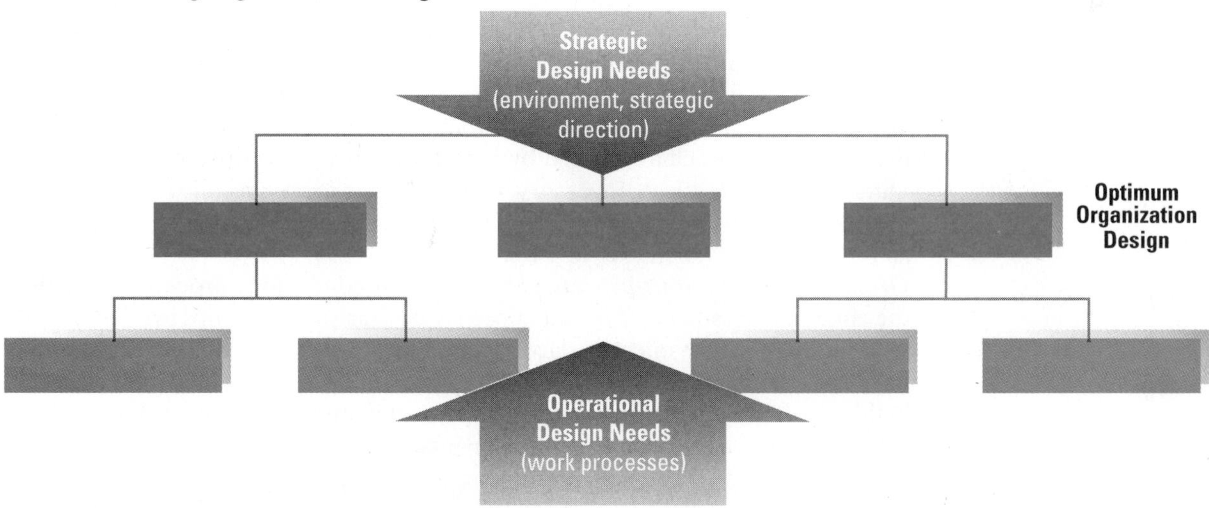

Source: Based on David A. Nadler and Michael L. Tushman, with Mark B. Nadler, *Competing by Design: The Power of Organizational Architecture* (New York: Oxford University Press, 1997), 54. By permission of Oxford University Press, Inc.

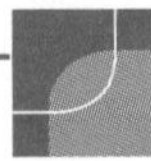

Core Organization Manufacturing Technology

Manufacturing technologies include traditional manufacturing processes and contemporary applications, such as flexible manufacturing and lean manufacturing.

Manufacturing Firms

The first and most influential study of manufacturing technology was conducted by Joan Woodward, a British industrial sociologist. Her research began as a field study of management principles in south Essex, England. The prevailing management wisdom at the time (1950s) was contained in what were known as universal principles of management. These principles were "one best way" prescriptions that effective organizations were expected to adopt. Woodward surveyed 100 manufacturing firms firsthand to learn how they were organized.[10] She and her research team visited each firm, interviewed managers, examined company records, and observed the manufacturing operations. Her data included a wide range of structural characteristics (span of control, levels of management), dimensions of management style (written versus oral communications, use of rewards), and types of manufacturing process. Data were also obtained that reflected commercial success of the firms.

PDA Remember...

Use the categories developed by Woodward to diagnose whether the production technology in a manufacturing firm is small batch, mass production, or continuous process. Use a more organic structure with small-batch or continuous-process technologies and with new flexible manufacturing systems. Use a mechanistic structure with mass-production technologies.

Woodward developed a scale and organized the firms according to technical complexity of the manufacturing process. **Technical complexity** represents the extent of mechanization of the manufacturing process. High technical complexity means most of the work is performed by machines. Low technical complexity means workers play a larger role in the production process. Woodward's scale of technical complexity originally had ten categories, as summarized in Exhibit 7.3. These categories were further consolidated into three basic technology groups:

- *Group I: Small-batch and unit production.* **Small-batch production** firms tend to be job shop operations that manufacture and assemble small orders to meet specific needs of customers. Custom work is the norm. Small-batch production relies heavily on the human operator; it is thus not highly mechanized. Schleese Saddlery Service, in Holland Landing, Ontario, makes customized saddles that are designed to fit a particular rider and horse.[11] Similarly, Kiln Art in Chester Basin, Nova Scotia, makes small batches of fused glass plates and bowls.[12] Both organizations and their founders have been recognized for the quality of their customized products.
- *Group II: Large-batch and mass production.* **Large-batch production** is a manufacturing process characterized by long production runs of standardized parts. Output often goes into inventory from which orders are filled, because customers do not have special needs. Examples include most assembly lines, such as for cars, trucks or trailer homes.
- *Group III: Continuous-process production.* In **continuous-process production,** the entire process is mechanized. There is no starting and stopping. This represents mechanization and standardization one step beyond those in an assembly line. Automated machines control the continuous process, and outcomes are highly predictable. Examples include chemical plants, oil refineries, beer makers, pharmaceuticals, and nuclear power plants.

Using this classification of technology, Woodward's data made sense. The number of management levels and the manager-to-total-personnel ratio, for example,

EXHIBIT 7.3
Woodward's Classification of 100 British Firms According to Their Systems of Production

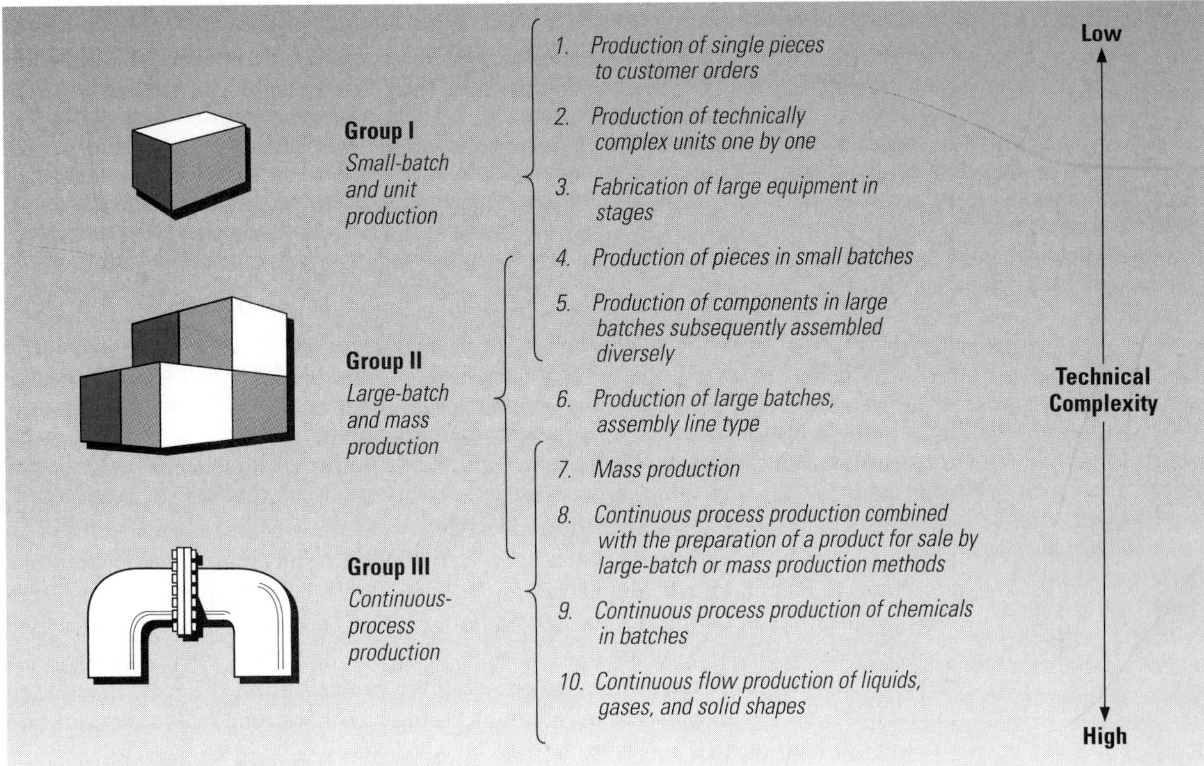

Source: Adapted from Joan Woodward, *Management and Technology* (London: Her Majesty's Stationery Office, 1958). Used with permission of Her Britannic Majesty's Stationery Office.

show definite increases as technical complexity increases from unit production to continuous process. This indicates that greater management intensity is needed to manage complex technology. The direct-to-indirect labour ratio decreases with technical complexity because more indirect workers are required to support and maintain complex machinery. Other characteristics, such as span of control, formalized procedures, and centralization, are high for mass-production technology because the work is standardized, but low for other technologies. Unit-production and continuous-process technologies require highly skilled workers to run the machines and verbal communication to adapt to changing conditions. Mass production is standardized and routinized, so few exceptions occur, little oral communication is needed, and employees are less skilled.

Overall, the management systems in both unit-production and continuous-process technology are characterized as organic, as defined in Chapter 4. They are more free-flowing and adaptive, with fewer procedures and less standardization. Mass production, however, is mechanistic, with standardized jobs and formalized procedures. Woodward's discovery about technology thus provided substantial new insight into the causes of organizational structure. In Woodward's own words, "[d]ifferent technologies impose different kinds of demands on individuals and organizations, and those demands had to be met through an appropriate structure."[13]

PDA
Remember...

When adopting a new technology, realign strategy, structure, and management processes to achieve top performance.

Strategy, Technology, and Performance

Another portion of Woodward's study examined the success of the firms along dimensions such as profitability, market share, stock price, and reputation. As indicated in Chapter 2, the measurement of effectiveness is neither simple nor precise, but Woodward was able to rank firms on a scale of commercial success according to whether they displayed above-average, average, or below-average performance on strategic objectives.

Woodward compared the structure–technology relationship against commercial success and discovered that successful firms tended to be those that had complementary structures and technologies. Many of the organizational characteristics of the successful firms were near the average of their technology category. Below-average firms tended to depart from the structural characteristics for their technology type. Another conclusion was that structural characteristics could be interpreted as clustering into organic and mechanistic management systems. Successful small-batch and continuous-process organizations had organic structures, and successful mass-production organizations had mechanistic structures. Subsequent research has replicated Woodward's findings.[14]

This illustrates for today's companies that strategy, structure, and technology need to be aligned, especially when competitive conditions change.[15] For example, computer makers had to realign strategy, structure, and technology to compete with Dell in the personal computer market. Manufacturers such as IBM, which once tried to differentiate their products and charge a premium price, switched to a low-cost strategy, adopted new technology to enable them to customize PCs, revamped supply chains, and began outsourcing manufacturing to other companies that could do the job more efficiently.

Today, many North American manufacturers farm out production to other companies. Doepker Industries of Annaheim, Saskatchewan, however, has gone in the opposite direction and achieved success by carefully aligning technology, structure, and management processes to achieve strategic objectives.

In Practice

Doepker Industries (Doepker)

Six Doepker brothers started the family business as a repair shop in 1948. They then ventured into farm equipment manufacturing, and, in 1972, they produced their first grain trailer. Doepker now manufactures trailers for a number of industries, including agriculture, commercial, industrial/construction, and forestry. Doepker has expanded but kept its head office in Annaheim, a town of 220. Doepker has 75,300 square feet of production and office space in Annaheim, 24,400 square feet in Moose Jaw, 28,800 square feet of production space and 8,600 square feet of office space in Humboldt, and 23,000 square feet in Salmon Arm, B.C. The plants employ 500 people, use modern equipment such as a state-of-the-industry paint department, 3-D solids modelling engineering and design software, robotics, and CNC equipment technology.

The location of each of the plants was chosen strategically to be close to the Doepker's largest markets in Western Canada. Doepker is looking at realigning its dealer network in Eastern Canada to create a strong distribution network there. Doepker is expanding into the U.S. market where it already has a few outlets selling its specialized trailers.

In 2005, Dave Doepker, executive chairman of the board of Doepker Industries announced the appointment of Gurcan Kocdag to the position of President. Kocdag is the first non-family member named to the position of president in the company's 57-year history. Part of his mandate is to continue to operate the company as a family business.[16]

Today's increased global competition means more volatile markets, shorter product life cycles, and more sophisticated and knowledgeable consumers; and flexibility to meet these new demands has become a strategic imperative for many companies.[17] Manufacturing companies can adopt new technologies to support the strategy of flexibility. However, organizational structures and management processes must also be realigned, as a highly mechanistic structure hampers flexibility and prevents the company from reaping the benefits of the new technology.[18] Managers

Book Mark 7.0 (HAVE YOU READ THIS BOOK?)

Inviting Disaster: Lessons from the Edge of Technology

By James R. Chiles

Dateline: Paris, France, July 25, 2000. Less than two minutes after Air France Concorde Flight 4590 departs Charles DeGaulle Airport, something goes horribly wrong. Trailing fire and billowing black smoke, the huge plane rolls left and crashes into a hotel, killing all 109 people aboard and 4 more on the ground. It's just one of the technological disasters James R. Chiles describes in his book, *Inviting Disaster: Lessons from the Edge of Technology.* One of Chiles's main points is that advancing technology makes possible the creation of machines that strain the human ability to understand and safely operate them. Moreover, he asserts, the margins of safety are thinner as the energies we harness become more powerful and the time between invention and use grows shorter. Chiles believes that today, "for every twenty books on the pursuit of success, we need a book on how things fly into tiny pieces despite enormous effort and the very highest ideals." All complex systems, he reminds us, are destined to fail at some point.

HOW THINGS FLY INTO PIECES: EXAMPLES OF SYSTEM FRACTURES

Chiles uses historical calamities such as the sinking of the *Titanic* and modern disasters such as the explosion of the space shuttle *Challenger* (the book was published before the 2003 crash of the *Columbia* shuttle) to illustrate the dangers of system fracture, a chain of events that involves human error in response to malfunctions in complex machinery. Disaster begins when one weak point links up with others.

- *Sultana* (American steamboat on the Mississippi River near Memphis, Tennessee), April 25, 1865. The boat, designed to carry a maximum of 460 people, was carrying more than 2,000 Union ex-prisoners north—as well as 200 additional crew and passengers—when three of the four boilers exploded, killing 1,800 people. One of the boilers had been temporarily patched to cover a crack, but the patch was too thin. Operators failed to compensate by resetting the safety valve.
- Piper Alpha (offshore drilling rig in the North Sea), July 6, 1988. The offshore platform processed large volumes of natural gas from other rigs via pipe. A daytime work crew that didn't complete a repair of a gas-condensate pump relayed a verbal message to the next shift, but workers turned the pump on anyway. When the temporary seal on the pump failed, a fire trapped crewmen with no escape route, killing 167 crew and rescue workers.
- Union Carbide (India) (release of highly toxic chemicals into a community), Bhopal, Mahdya Pradesh, India, December 3, 1984. There are three competing theories for how water got into a storage tank, creating a violent reaction that sent highly toxic methyl isocyanate for herbicides into the environment, causing an estimated 7,000 deaths: (1) poor safety maintenance, (2) sabotage, or (3) worker error.

WHAT CAUSES SYSTEM FRACTURES?

There is a veritable catalogue of causes that lead to such disasters, from design errors, insufficient operator training, and poor planning, to greed and mismanagement. Chiles wrote this book as a reminder that technology takes us into risky locales, whether into outer space, up a 2,000-foot tower, or into a chemical processing plant. Chiles also cites examples of potential disasters that were averted by quick thinking and appropriate response. To help prevent system fractures, managers can create organizations in which people throughout the company are expert at picking out the subtle signals of real problems—and where they are empowered to report them and take prompt action.

Inviting Disaster: Lessons from the Edge of Technology, by James R. Chiles, is published by HarperBusiness.

should always remember that the technological and human systems of an organization are intertwined. This chapter's Book Mark provides a different perspective on technology by looking at the dangers of failing to understand the human role in managing technological advances.

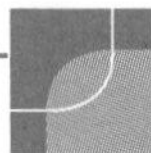

Contemporary Applications

In the years since Woodward's research, new developments have occurred in manufacturing technology. Despite the decline in Canadian manufacturing, in 2007, it represented 24 percent of all employment in Canada.[19] However, the factory of today is far different from the industrial firms Woodward studied in the 1950s. In particular, computers have revolutionized all types of manufacturing—small batch, large batch, and continuous process. Oil and gas companies, as well as chemical and mining and power companies have used electronic technology "to drive significant improvements in their operating results . . . while reducing their costs and meeting regulatory compliance and safety standards."[20] An example in continuous-process manufacturing comes from Shell's unionized petrochemical plant in Sarnia, Ontario. Technicians who would have once manually monitored hundreds of complex processes now focus their energy on surveying long-term production trends. Controlling the continuous production of petrochemicals today is handled faster, smarter, more precisely, and more economically by computer. The Sarnia plant was one of Shell's most productive plants.

Mass production manufacturing has seen similar transformations. Two significant contemporary applications of manufacturing technology are flexible manufacturing systems and lean manufacturing.

Flexible Manufacturing Systems

Most of today's factories use a variety of new manufacturing technologies, including robots, numerically controlled machine tools, radio-frequency identification (RFID), wireless technology, and computerized software for product design, engineering analysis, and remote control of machinery. The ultimate automated factories are referred to as **flexible manufacturing systems** (FMS).[21] Also called computer-integrated manufacturing, smart factories, advanced manufacturing technology, agile manufacturing, or the factory of the future, FMS links manufacturing components that previously stood alone. Thus, robots, machines, product design, and engineering analysis are coordinated by a single computer.

The result has already revolutionized the shop floor, enabling large factories to deliver a wide range of custom-made products at low mass-production costs.[22] Flexible manufacturing also enables small companies to go toe to toe with larger factories and lower-cost competitors. The manufacturing process at Weyerhaeuser Company's Chemainus Sawmill on Vancouver Island, while similar to traditional sawmilling in that it uses hydraulic and pneumatic technology, also uses computerized precision scanning technology to get value out of the logs for different orders. The sawmill was the company's first manufacturing facility to achieve ISO 14001 registration.[23]

Flexible manufacturing is typically the result of three subcomponents:

- *Computer-aided design (CAD).* Computers are used to assist in the drafting, design, and engineering of new parts. Designers guide their computers to draw specified configurations on the screen, including dimensions and component details. Hundreds of design alternatives can be explored, as can scaled-up or scaled-down versions of the original.[24]
- *Computer-aided manufacturing (CAM).* Computer-controlled machines in materials handling, fabrication, production, and assembly greatly increase the speed at which items can be manufactured. CAM also permits a production line to shift rapidly from producing one product to any variety of other products by changing the instruction tapes or software codes in the computer. CAM enables the production line to quickly honour customer requests for changes in product design and product mix.[25]
- *Integrated information network.* A computerized system links all aspects of the firm—including accounting, purchasing, marketing, inventory control, design, production, and so forth. This system, based on a common data and information base, enables managers to make decisions and direct the manufacturing process in a truly integrated fashion.

The combination of CAD, CAM, and integrated information systems means that a new product can be designed on the computer and a prototype can be produced untouched by human hands. The ideal factory can switch quickly from one product to another, working quickly and with precision, without paperwork or recordkeeping to bog down the system.[26] CAD/CAM can be used for a variety of products. For example, Montréal's Foot Crafters makes personalized insoles and foot orthoses. Using a computer and a graphic interface, it visualizes in real time a foot's pressure distribution and enables two- or three-dimensional shape analysis. The data are then sent internally or online to its manufacturing site. The manufacturing process of the orthesis is completely computer assisted. A numerically controlled milling machine then creates the orthesis. The time from order to manufacture has decreased considerably.[27]

Designersilversmiths.com, located in Devon, England, uses CAD/CAM software to design jewellery. According to Hillary Corney, owner of Designersilversmiths, "[projects] that would have taken months can now be completed in weeks. [Another] advantage is that any duplicated elements can be reproduced almost instantly."[28]

Some advanced factories have moved to a system called product life-cycle management (PLM). PLM software can manage a product from idea through development, manufacturing, testing, and even maintenance in the field. The PLM software provides three primary advantages for product innovation. PLM (1) stores data on ideas and products from all parts of the company; (2) links product design to all departments (and even outside suppliers) involved in new product development; and (3) provides three-dimensional images of new products for testing and maintenance. PLM has been used to coordinate people, tools, and facilities around the world for the design, development, and manufacture of products as diverse as product packaging for Procter & Gamble consumer products and Boeing's 7E7 Dreamliner passenger jet.[29]

Lean Manufacturing

Flexible manufacturing reaches its ultimate level to improve quality, customer service, and cost cutting when all parts are used interdependently and combined with flexible management processes in a system referred to as lean manufacturing. **Lean manufacturing** uses highly trained employees at every stage of the production process, who take a painstaking approach to details and problem solving to cut waste and improve quality. It incorporates technological elements, such as CAD/CAM and PLM, but the heart of lean manufacturing is not machines or software, but people. Lean manufacturing requires changes in organizational systems, such as decision-making processes and management processes, as well as an organizational culture that supports active employee participation. Employees are trained to "think lean," which means attacking waste and striving for continuous improvement in all areas.[30] Canada Post, for example, adopted a lean manufacturing approach when it eliminated a large automated sorting machine and replaced it with a much smaller manual cell. "I used to think that we weren't a manufacturing company; we didn't produce anything," said Don McLellan, director, Mail Operations, at the Calgary facility, "but you can lean out mail operations. What we're looking for is flow; in one door and out another."[31]

Japan's Toyota Motor Corporation, which pioneered lean manufacturing, is often considered the premier manufacturing organization in the world. The famed Toyota Production System combines techniques such as just-in-time inventory, product life-cycle management, continuous-flow production, quick changeover of assembly lines, continuous improvement, and preventive maintenance with a management system that encourages employee involvement and problem solving. Any employee can stop the production line at any time to solve a problem. In addition, designing equipment to stop automatically so that a defect can be fixed is a key element of the system.[32] The cartoon in Exhibit 7.4 shows us how important it is to fix a defect before shipping a product!

EXHIBIT 7.4
The Challenge of Quality Control

Many North American organizations have studied the Toyota Production System and seen dramatic improvements in productivity, inventory reduction, and quality. Garrison Guitars of St. John's, Newfoundland and Labrador, used Toyota's ideas to create some of the world's best acoustic guitars.

In Practice

Garrison Guitars (Garrison)

Chris Griffiths started Garrison when he was 19. Garrison guitars are now used by such performers as Alanis Morrisette, Stompin' Tom Connors, Tom Cochrane, and The Tragically Hip. Garrison guitars are sold in 35 countries through a dealer network of more than 450 music retailers worldwide. The guitars retail from $400 to more than $3000. In 2007, the company had annual sales of $5 million.

Garrison started off as a one-person guitar repair shop but has grown into a manufacturer of specially designed guitars. Griffiths had an epiphany in 1995 after visiting some guitar manufacturers. He wondered "[wouldn't] it be more efficient if we could make all the braces out of one piece?" Griffiths was the first person to make the guitar's bracing system out of artificial materials while the rest of the guitar was made of wood. In 2000, Griffiths got the patents for the design and then raised $3.5 million to build a 20,000 square-foot production facility that uses robotics and laser technology.

At Garrison, it takes 45 seconds to complete a guitar frame rather than the two hours it takes to machine and to assemble 30 wooden pieces using the traditional approach to manufacturing guitars. The Garrison system uses injection moulding to build a single-piece guitar frame that is 40 percent glass. The remainder of the moulding is Griffiths's "secret sauce."[33] Garrison is able to sell its guitars for 25 percent less than its competitors. "The [manufacturing] system also makes the guitar sound better—an unexpected side effect caused by reducing the number of parts and their vibrations—and last longer as there's less wood to be affected by humidity and temperature changes."[34] Garrison also applied the Toyota Production System to the plant to maximize its efficiency.

Eleven years later the St. John's company was bought by the Gibson Guitar of Nashville, Tennessee. Griffiths is not concerned, however, about any hollowing out of the Canadian guitar industry. As Griffiths says, "I just don't see how we could have grown as exponentially as we're about to grow by just continuing on in our current path" as he plans to quintuple production, in 12 months, so that the Garrison Guitar produces 60 guitars a day.[35]

Lean manufacturing and flexible manufacturing systems have paved the way for **mass customization,** which refers to using mass-production technology to quickly and cost-effectively assemble goods that are uniquely designed to fit the demands of individual customers.[36] Mass customization first took hold when Dell Computer Corporation began building computers to order, and has since expanded to products as diverse as farm machinery, water heaters, clothing, and industrial detergents. Today, you can buy jeans customized for your body, glasses moulded to precisely fit and flatter your face, windows in the exact shape and size you want for your new home, and pills with the specific combination of vitamins and minerals you need.[37] Dell, described in the Leading by Design box, still provides an excellent example of the flexible manufacturing needed to make mass customization work.

Auto manufacturers, too, are moving toward mass customization. Sixty percent of the cars BMW sells in Europe are built to order.[38] North American manufacturers are building and remodelling plants to catch up with Japanese manufacturers such as Nissan and Honda in the ability to offer customers personalized products. For example, Ford's Kansas City, Missouri, plant, one of the largest manufacturing facilities in the world, produces around 490,000 F-150s, Ford Escapes, and Mazda Tributes a year. With just a little tweaking, the assembly lines in Kansas City can be

Leading *by Design*

Dell Computer

It's a tough time in the computer industry, but Dell Computer, like the Energizer bunny, just keeps going and going and going. Even competitors agree that there is just no better way to make, sell, and deliver personal computers (PCs) than the way Dell does it. Dell PCs are made to order and are delivered directly to the consumer. Each customer gets exactly the machine he or she wants—and gets it faster and cheaper than Dell's competitors could provide it.

Dell's speedy, flexible, cost-efficient system is illustrated by the company's newest factory, the Topfer Manufacturing facility near Dell headquarters in Round Rock, Texas, where Dell created a new way of making PCs that helped spur the company from number three to number one in PC sales. The process combines just-in-time delivery of parts from suppliers with a complicated, integrated computer manufacturing system that practically hands a worker the right part—whether it be any of a dozen different microprocessors or a specific combination of software—at just the right moment. The goal is to not only slash costs but also save time by reducing the number of worker-touches per machine. Dell used to build computers in progressive assembly-line fashion, with up to 25 different people building one machine. Now, teams of three to seven workers build a complete computer from start to finish by following precise guidelines and using the components that arrive in carefully indicated racks in front of them. The combination of baskets, racks, and traffic signals that keeps the whole operation moving is called the Pick-to-Light system. Pick-to-Light is based on an up-to-the-minute database and software tying it to a stockroom system. That means the system can make sure teams have everything they need to complete an order, whether it be for one PC or 200. The system keeps track of which materials need replenishing and makes sure the racks and baskets are supplied with the proper components. Precise coordination, aided by sophisticated supply-chain software, means that Dell can keep just two hours' worth of parts inventory and replenish only what it needs throughout the day. The flexible system works so well that 85 percent of orders are built, customized, and shipped within eight hours.

Dell's new system has dramatically improved productivity, increasing manufacturing speed and throughput of custom-made computers by 150 percent. Employees are happier too because they now use more skills and build a complete machine within the team rather than performing the same boring, repetitive task on an assembly line. The system that began at one cutting-edge factory has been adopted at all of the company's manufacturing plants. With this kind of flexibility, no wonder Dell was number one.[39]

programmed to manufacture any kind of car or truck Ford makes. The new F-150 has so many options that there are more than 1 million possible configurations of that model alone. Robots in wire cages do most of the work, while people act as assistants, taking measurements, refilling parts, and altering the system if something goes wrong. Assembly is synchronized by computers, right down to the last rearview mirror. Ford's flexible manufacturing system is projected to save the company $2 billion over the next 10 years.[40] Plant efficiency experts believe the trend toward mass customization will grow as flexible manufacturing systems become even more sophisticated and adaptive.

Performance and Structural Implications

The advantage of flexible manufacturing is that products of different sizes, types, and customer requirements freely intermingle on the assembly line. Bar codes imprinted on a part enable machines to make instantaneous changes—such as putting a larger screw in a different location—without slowing the production line. A manufacturer can turn out an infinite variety of products in unlimited batch sizes, as illustrated in Exhibit 7.5. In traditional manufacturing systems studied by Woodward, choices

EXHIBIT 7.5
Relationship of Flexible Manufacturing Technology to Traditional Technologies

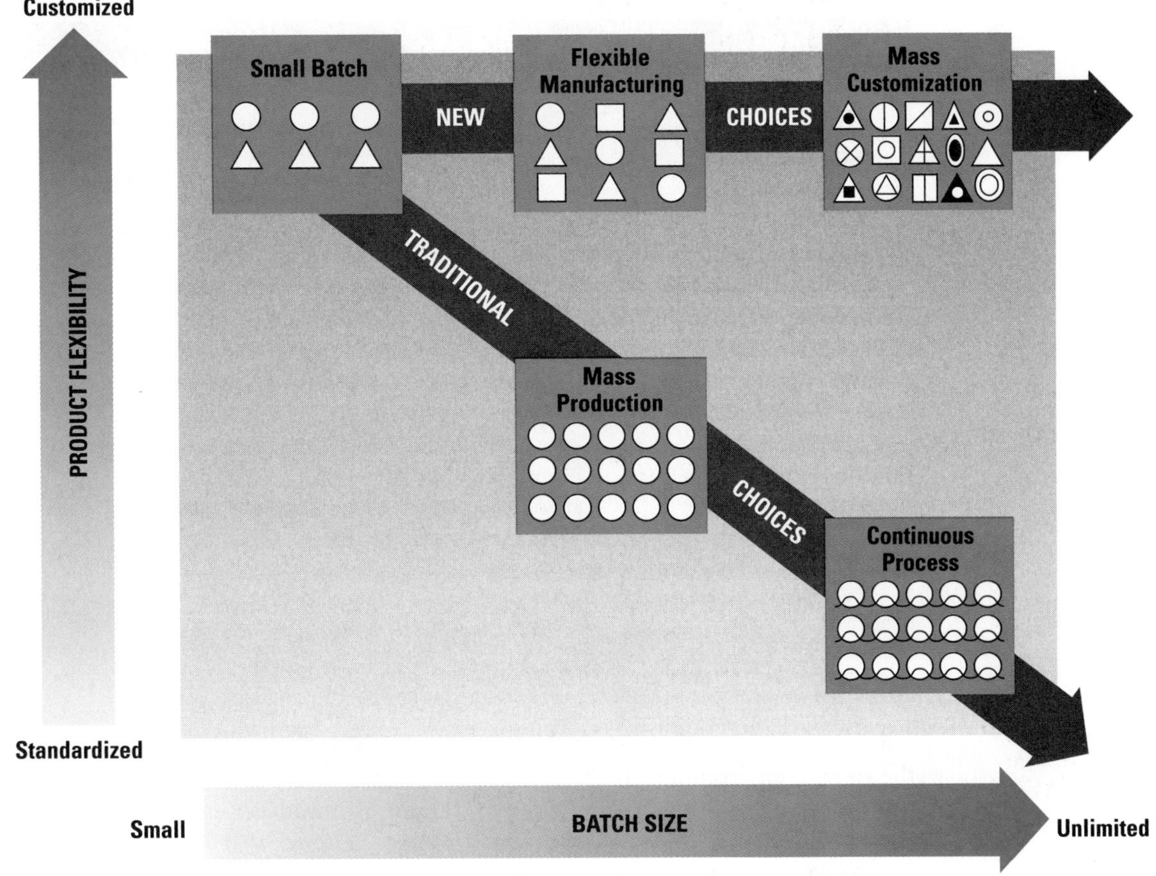

Source: Based on Jack Meredith, "The Strategic Advantages of New Manufacturing Technologies for Small Firms," *Strategic Management Journal* 8 (1987), 249–258; Paul Adler, "Managing Flexible Automation," *California Management Review* (Spring 1988), 34–56; and Otis Port, "Custom-made Direct from the Plant," *BusinessWeek/21st Century Capitalism* (November 18, 1994), 158–159.

were limited to the diagonal. Small batch allowed for high product flexibility and custom orders, but because of the "craftsmanship" involved in custom-making products, batch size was necessarily small. Mass production could have large batch size, but offered limited product flexibility. Continuous process could produce a single standard product in unlimited quantities. Flexible manufacturing systems (FMS) allow plants to break free of this diagonal and to increase both batch size and product flexibility at the same time. When taken to its ultimate level, FMS allows for mass customization, with each specific product tailored to customer specification. This high-level use of FMS has been referred to as computer-aided craftsmanship.[41]

Studies suggest that with FMS, machine utilization is more efficient, labour productivity increases, scrap rates decrease, and product variety and customer satisfaction increase.[42] Some North American manufacturing companies are reinventing the factory using FMS and lean manufacturing systems to increase productivity.

Research into the relationship between FMS and organizational characteristics is beginning to emerge, and the patterns are summarized in Exhibit 7.6. Compared with traditional mass-production technologies, FMS has a narrow span of control,

EXHIBIT 7.6
Comparison of Organizational Characteristics Associated with Mass Production and Flexible Manufacturing Systems

Characteristic	Mass Production	FMS
Structure		
Span of control	Wide	Narrow
Hierarchical levels	Many	Few
Tasks	Routine, repetitive	Adaptive, craft-like
Specialization	High	Low
Decision making	Centralized	Decentralized
Overall	Bureaucratic, mechanistic	Organic, self-regulating
Human Resources		
Interactions	Standalone	Teamwork
Training	Narrow, one time	Broad, frequent
Expertise	Manual, technical	Cognitive, social Solve problems
Interorganizational		
Customer demand	Stable	Changing
Suppliers	Many, arm's length	Few, close relationships

Source: Based on Patricia L. Nemetz and Louis W. Fry, "Flexible Manufacturing Organizations: Implications for Strategy Formulation and Organization Design," *Academy of Management Review* 13 (1988), 627–638; Paul S. Adler, "Managing Flexible Automation," *California Management Review* (Spring 1988), 34–56; and Jeremy Main, "Manufacturing the Right Way," *Fortune* (May 21, 1990) 54–64.

few hierarchical levels, adaptive tasks, low specialization, and decentralization, and the overall environment is characterized as organic and self-regulative. Employees need the skills to participate in teams; training is broad (so workers are not overly specialized) and frequent (so workers are up to date). Expertise tends to be cognitive so workers can process abstract ideas and solve problems. Interorganizational relationships in FMS firms are characterized by changing demand from customers—which is easily handled with the new technology—and close relationships with a few suppliers that provide top-quality raw materials.[43]

Technology alone cannot give organizations the benefits of flexibility, quality, increased production, and greater customer satisfaction. Research suggests that FMS can become a competitive burden rather than a competitive advantage unless organizational structures and management processes are redesigned to exploit the new technology.[44] However, when top managers make a commitment to implement new structures and processes that empower workers and support a learning and knowledge-creating environment, FMS can help companies be more competitive.[45]

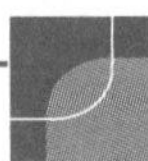

Core Organization Service Technology

Another big change occurring in the technology of organizations is the growing service sector. The percentage of the workforce employed in manufacturing continues to decline, not only in Canada, but also in the United States, France, Germany, the United Kingdom, and Sweden.[46] The service sector has increased three times as quickly as the manufacturing sector in the North American economy. Service technologies are different from manufacturing technologies and, in turn, require a specific organizational structure.

Service Firms

Definition. Whereas manufacturing organizations achieve their primary purpose through the production of products, service organizations accomplish their primary purpose through the production and provision of services, such as education, health care, transportation, banking, and hospitality. Studies of service organizations have focused on the unique dimensions of service technologies. The characteristics of service technology are compared to those of manufacturing technology in Exhibit 7.7.

The most obvious difference is that **service technology** produces an intangible output, rather than a tangible product, such as a refrigerator produced by a manufacturing firm. A service is abstract and often consists of knowledge and ideas rather than a physical product. Thus, whereas manufacturers' products can be inventoried for later sale, services are characterized by simultaneous production and consumption. A client meets with a doctor or lawyer, for example, and students and teachers come together in the classroom or over the Internet. A service is an intangible product that does not exist until it is requested by the customer. It cannot be stored, inventoried, or viewed as a finished good. If a service is not consumed immediately upon production, it disappears.[47] This typically means that service firms are labour- and knowledge-intensive, with many employees needed to meet the needs of customers, whereas manufacturing firms tend to be capital-intensive, relying on mass production, continuous process, and flexible manufacturing technologies.[48]

Direct interaction between customer and employee is generally very high with services, while there is little direct interaction between customers and employees in the technical core of a manufacturing firm. This direct interaction means that the human

PDA
Remember...

Use the concept of service technology to evaluate the production process in nonmanufacturing firms. Service technologies are intangible and are usually located close to the customer. Hence, service organizations may have an organizational structure with fewer boundary roles, greater geographical dispersion, decentralization, highly skilled employees in the technical core, and generally less control than in manufacturing organizations.

EXHIBIT 7.7
Differences between Manufacturing and Service Technologies

Service Technology
1. *Intangible output*
2. *Production and consumption take place simultaneously*
3. *Labor- and knowledge-intensive*
4. *Customer interaction generally high*
5. *Human element very important*
6. *Quality is perceived and difficult to measure*
7. *Rapid response time is usually necessary*
8. *Site of facility is extremely important*

Manufacturing Technology
1. *Tangible product*
2. *Products can be inventoried for later consumption*
3. *Capital asset-intensive*
4. *Little direct customer interaction*
5. *Human element may be less important*
6. *Quality is directly measured*
7. *Longer response time is acceptable*
8. *Site of facility is moderately important*

Service	Product and Service	Product
Airlines	*Fast-food outlets*	*Soft drink companies*
Hotels	*Cosmetics*	*Steel companies*
Consultants	*Real estate*	*Automobile manufacturers*
Health care	*Stockbrokers*	*Mining corporations*
Law firms	*Retail stores*	*Food processing plants*

Source: Based on F. F. Reichheld and W. E. Sasser, Jr., "Zero Defections: Quality Comes to Services," Harvard Business Review 68 (September–October 1990), 105–111; and David E. Bowen, Caren Siehl, and Benjamin Schneider, "A Framework for Analyzing Customer Service Orientations in Manufacturing," Academy of Management Review 14 (1989), 75–95.

element (employees) becomes extremely important in service firms. While most people never meet the workers who manufactured their cars, they interact directly with the salesperson who sold them their Honda Element or Toyota Prius. The treatment received from the salesperson—or from a doctor, lawyer, or hairstylist—affects the perception of the service received and the customer's level of satisfaction. The quality of a service is perceived, and cannot be directly measured and compared in the same way that the quality of a tangible product can. Another characteristic that affects customer satisfaction and perception of quality service is rapid response time. A service must be provided when the customer wants and needs it. When you take a friend to dinner, you want to be seated and served in a timely manner; you would not be very satisfied if the host or manager told you to come back tomorrow when there would be more tables or servers available to accommodate you.

The final defining characteristic of service technology is that site selection is often much more important than with manufacturing. Because services are intangible, they have to be located where the customer wants to be served. For example, fast-food franchises usually disperse their facilities into local stores. Most towns of even moderate size today have two or more McDonald's restaurants rather than one large one in order to provide service where customers want it.

In reality, it is difficult to find organizations that reflect 100 percent service or 100 percent manufacturing characteristics. Some service firms take on characteristics of manufacturers, and vice versa. Many manufacturing firms are placing a greater emphasis on customer service to differentiate themselves and be more competitive. In addition, manufacturing organizations have departments such as purchasing, HR, and marketing that are based on service technology. For example, Lo-Pel Manufacturing, a family-owned company founded in 2001, located in Rosenort, Manitoba, not only manufactures earthmoving scrapers but also provides service support for its customers. According to Ken Rempel, designer of the scraper, "[if] anyone has a problem, we address it quickly and efficiently to reach a solution; that has built a lot of faith in our company."[49] On the other hand, organizations such as gas stations, stockbrokers, retail stores, and restaurants belong to the service sector, but the provision of a product is a significant part of the transaction. The vast majority of organizations involve some combination of products and services. The important point is that all organizations can be classified along a continuum that includes both manufacturing and service characteristics, as illustrated in Exhibit 7.7.

New Directions in Services. Service firms have always tended toward providing customized output—that is, providing exactly the service each customer wants and needs. When you visit a hairstylist, you don't automatically get the same cut the stylist gave the three previous clients. The stylist cuts your hair the way you request it. However, the trend toward mass customization that is revolutionizing manufacturing has had a significant impact on the service sector as well. Customer expectations of what constitutes good service are rising.[50] Service companies such as the Ritz-Carlton Hotels and Bell Canada use new technology to keep customers coming back. All Ritz-Carlton hotels are linked to a database filled with the preferences of half a million guests, allowing any desk clerk or bellhop to find out what your favourite wine is, whether you're allergic to feather pillows, and how many extra towels you want in your room.[51] At Bell Canada, much of its customer service is performed online but there are customer service representatives available as well.

The expectation for better service is also pushing service firms in industries from package delivery to banking to take a lesson from manufacturing. Japan Post, under

EXHIBIT 7.8
Configuration and Structural Characteristics of Service Organizations versus Product Organizations

Structural Characteristic	Service	Product
1. Separate boundary roles	Few	Many
2. Geographical dispersion	Much	Little
3. Decision making	Decentralized	Centralized
4. Formalization	Lower	Higher
Human Resources		
1. Employee skill level	Higher	Lower
2. Skill emphasis	Interpersonal	Technical

pressure to cut a $191 million loss on operations, hired Toyota's Toshihiro Takahashi to help apply the Toyota Production System to the collection, sorting, and delivery of mail. In all, Takahashi's team came up with 370 improvements and reduced the post office's person-hours by 20 percent. The waste reduction is expected to cut costs by around $350 million a year.[52]

Designing the Service Organization

The feature of service technologies with a distinct influence on organizational structure and control systems is the need for technical core employees to be close to the customer.[53] The differences between service and product organizations necessitated by customer contact are summarized in Exhibit 7.8.

The impact of customer contact on organizational structure is reflected in the use of boundary roles and structural disaggregation.[54] Boundary roles are used extensively in manufacturing firms to handle customers and to reduce disruptions for the technical core. They are used less in service firms because a service is intangible and cannot be passed along by boundary spanners, so service customers must interact directly with technical employees, such as doctors or brokers.

A service firm deals in information and intangible outputs and does not need to be large. Its greatest economies are achieved through disaggregation into small units that may be located close to customers. Stockbrokers, doctors' clinics, consulting firms, and banks disperse their facilities into regional and local offices. Some quick service chains, such as Tim Hortons, are taking this a step further, selling coffee, muffins, and sandwiches anywhere people gather—war zones, airports, gas stations, college or university campuses, or street corners.

Manufacturing firms, on the other hand, tend to aggregate operations in a single area that has raw materials and an available workforce. A large manufacturing firm can take advantage of economies derived from expensive machinery and long production runs.

Service technology also influences internal organization characteristics used to direct and control the organization. For one thing, the skills of technical core employees typically need to be higher. These employees need enough knowledge and awareness to handle customer problems rather than just enough to perform mechanical tasks. Employees need social and interpersonal skills as well as technical skills.[55] Because of higher skills and structural dispersion, decision making often tends to be decentralized in service firms, and formalization tends to be low. In general, employees in service organizations have more freedom and discretion on the job. However, some service organizations, such as many fast-food chains, have set rules and procedures for customer service. The U.K. chain Pret a Manger hopes to differentiate itself in the fast-food market by taking a different approach.

In Practice

Pret a Manger (Pret)

"Would you like fries with that?" The standard line is rattled off by fast-food workers who have been taught to follow a script in serving customers. But at Pret, a fast-growing chain based in London, you won't hear any standard lines. Employees aren't given scripts for serving customers or pigeonholed into performing the same repetitious tasks all day long. Managers want people to let their own personalities come through in offering each customer the best service possible. "Our customers say, 'I like to be served by human beings,'" explains Ewan Stickley, head of employee training. London's *Sunday Times* recently ranked Pret as one of the top 50 companies to work for in Britain—the only restaurant to make the cut. Pret turns over roughly £150 million a year and is working to make a 9 percent profit.

"Pret opened in London in 1986. College friends, Sinclair and Julian, made proper sandwiches using natural, preservative-free ingredients. The two of them had woefully little experience in the world of business. They created the sort of food they craved but couldn't find anywhere else."[56]

Pret a Manger (faux French for "ready to eat") operates 150 outlets in the United Kingdom and is expanding into the United States. "Nobody has ever gone to America, the home of fast food, with a concept that turned out to be a successful national chain. We think we can do that," says chairman and CEO Andrew Rolfe. Translating that confidence into success in the United States has been a struggle. To help make the transition, Pret has allied itself with a powerful partner—McDonald's. Some worry that McDonald's might corrupt the company's values and emphasis on fresh, healthy food and individualized service, but Rolfe believes he and his employees are up to the challenge.

Pret's concept is based on organizing a mass-market service business around innovation rather than standardization. The menu is based on salads, fresh-made sandwiches, hot soups, sushi, and a variety of yogurt parfaits and blended juices. Menu items are constantly changing, based on what sells and what customers want. Pret has built in a number of mechanisms for getting fast feedback. The CEO reviews customer and employee comments every Friday. Employees who send in the best ideas for changes to products or procedures can win up to $1,500. Managers spend one day each quarter working in a store to keep in touch with customers and see how their policies affect employees. As well, "[whenever] a customer calls or writes to congratulate a member of our staff for being helpful, professional or simply great, off goes a [solid silver custom-designed] Tiffany Star to the staff member. We are thrilled to have awarded hundreds and hundreds over the years."[57]

In its native England, Pret has been a huge hit. Pret supports dozens of charities helping the homeless by offering unsold sandwiches to them at the end of each day. The Pret Charity Run collects and distributes over 12,000 meals to the homeless every week of the year. Many charities collect directly from the Pret shops at the end of each day too.[58]

Understanding the nature of its service technology helps managers at Pret a Manger align strategy, structure, and management processes that are quite different from those for a product-based or traditional manufacturing technology. For example, the concept of separating complex tasks into a series of small jobs and exploiting economies of scale is a cornerstone of traditional manufacturing, but researchers have found that applying it to service organizations often does not work so well.[59] Some service firms have redesigned jobs to separate low- and high-customer contact activities, with more rules and standardization in the low-contact jobs. High-touch service jobs, like those at Pret a Manger, need more freedom and less control to satisfy customers.

Understanding service technology is important for manufacturing firms, too, especially as they put greater emphasis on customer service. Managers can use these concepts and ideas to strengthen their company's service orientation.

Now let's turn to another perspective on technology, that of production activities within specific organizational departments. Departments often have characteristics similar to those of service technology, providing services to other departments within the organization.

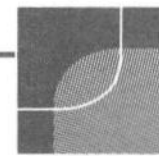

Noncore Departmental Technology

This section shifts to the department level of analysis for departments not necessarily within the technical core. Each department in an organization has a production process that consists of a distinct technology. General Motors has departments for engineering, R&D, HR, advertising, quality control, finance, and dozens of other functions. This section analyzes the nature of **noncore departmental technology** and its relationship with departmental structure.

The framework that has had the greatest impact on the understanding of departmental technologies was developed by Charles Perrow.[60] Perrow's model has been useful for a broad range of technologies, which made it ideal for research into departmental activities.

Variety

Perrow specified two dimensions of departmental activities that were relevant to organizational structure and process. The first is the number of exceptions in the work. This refers to task variety, which is the frequency of unexpected and novel events that occur in the conversion process. **Task variety** concerns whether work processes are performed the same way every time or differ from time to time as employees transform the organization's inputs into outputs.[61] When individuals encounter a large number of unexpected situations, with frequent problems, variety is considered high. When there are few problems, and when day-to-day job requirements are repetitious, technology contains little variety. Variety in departments can range from repeating a single act, such as on a traditional assembly line, to working on a series of unrelated problems or projects.

Analyzability

The second dimension of technology concerns the **analyzability** of work activities. When the conversion process is analyzable, the work can be reduced to mechanical steps and participants can follow an objective, computational procedure to solve problems. Problem solution may involve the use of standard procedures, such as instructions and manuals, or technical knowledge, such as that in a textbook. On the other hand, some work is not analyzable; when problems arise, it is difficult to identify the correct solution. There is no store of techniques or procedures to tell a person exactly what to do. The cause of or solution to a problem is not clear, so employees rely on accumulated experience, intuition, and judgment. Philippos Poulos, a tone regulator at Steinway & Sons, has an unanalyzable technology. Tone regulators carefully check each piano's hammers to ensure they produce the proper Steinway sound.[62] These quality-control tasks require years of experience and practice; standard procedures will not tell a person how to do such tasks.

Framework

The two dimensions of technology and examples of departmental activities on Perrow's framework are shown in Exhibit 7.9. The dimensions of variety and analyzability form the basis for four major categories of technology: routine, craft, engineering, and nonroutine.

Routine technologies are characterized by little task variety and the use of objective, computational procedures. The tasks are formalized and standardized. Examples include an automobile assembly line and a bank teller department.

Craft technologies are characterized by a fairly stable stream of activities, but the conversion process is not analyzable or well understood. Tasks require extensive training and experience because employees respond to intangible factors on the basis of wisdom, intuition, and experience. Although advances in machine technologies seem to have reduced the number of craft technologies in organizations, craft technologies are still important. For example, steel furnace engineers continue to mix steel based on intuition and experience, pattern makers at apparel firms convert rough designers' sketches into saleable garments, and teams of writers for

EXHIBIT 7.9
Framework for Department Technologies

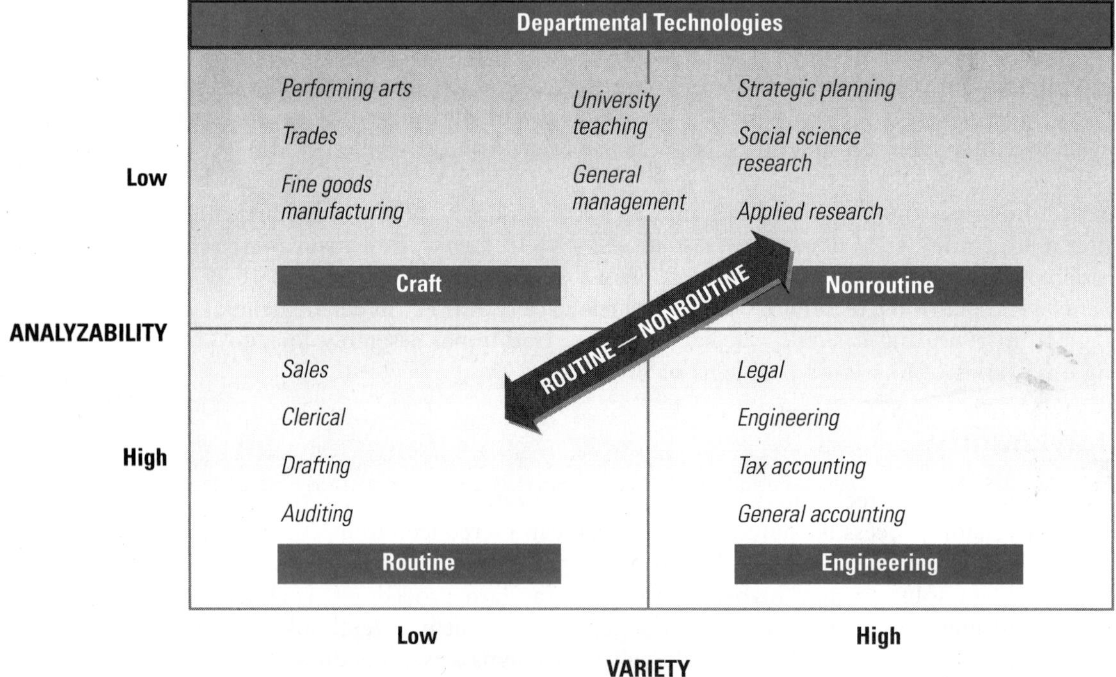

Source: Adapted with permission from Richard Daft and Norman Macintosh, "A New Approach to Design and Use of Management Information," *California Management Review* 21 (1978), 82–92. Copyright © 1978 by the Regents of the University of California. Reprinted by permission of the Regents.

television series such as *CSI* or *Little Mosque on the Prairie* convert ideas into story lines.

Engineering technologies tend to be complex because there is substantial variety in the tasks performed. However, the various activities are usually handled on the basis of established formulas, procedures, and techniques. Employees normally refer to a well-developed body of knowledge to handle problems. Engineering and accounting tasks usually fall in this category.

Nonroutine technologies have high task variety, and the conversion process is not analyzable or well understood. In nonroutine technology, a great deal of effort is devoted to analyzing problems and activities. Several equally acceptable options typically can be found. Experience and technical knowledge are used to solve problems and perform the work. Basic research, strategic planning, and other work that involves new projects and unexpected problems are nonroutine. The blossoming biotechnology industry also represents a nonroutine technology. Breakthroughs in understanding metabolism and physiology at a cellular level depend on highly trained employees who use their experience and intuition as well as scientific knowledge. A scientist manipulating the chemical rungs on a DNA molecule has been compared to a musician playing variations on a theme.[63]

Routine versus Nonroutine. Exhibit 7.9 also illustrates that variety and analyzability can be combined into a single dimension of technology. This dimension is called routine versus nonroutine technology, and it is the diagonal line in Exhibit 7.9. The analyzability and variety dimensions are often correlated in departments, meaning that technologies high in variety tend to be low in analyzability, and technologies low in variety tend to be analyzable. Departments can be evaluated along a single dimension of routine versus nonroutine that combines both analyzability and variety, which is a useful shorthand measure for analyzing departmental technology.

The following questions show how departmental technology can be analyzed for determining its placement on Perrow's technology framework in Exhibit 7.9.[64] Employees normally circle a number from 1 to 7 in response to each question.

Variety:

1. To what extent would you say your work is routine?
2. Do most people in this unit do about the same job in the same way most of the time?
3. Do you think unit members perform repetitive activities when doing their jobs?

Analyzability:

1. To what extent is there a clearly known way to do the major types of work you normally encounter?
2. To what extent is there an understandable sequence of steps that can be followed in doing your work?
3. To do your work, to what extent can you actually rely on established procedures and practices?

If answers to the above questions indicate high scores for analyzability and low scores for variety, the department would have a routine technology. If the opposite occurs, the technology would be nonroutine. Low variety and low analyzability indicate a craft technology, and high variety and high analyzability indicate an engineering technology. As a practical matter, most departments fit somewhere along the diagonal and can be most easily characterized as routine or nonroutine.

Department Design

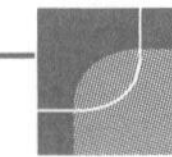

PDA Remember...

Use the two dimensions of variety and analyzability to discover whether the work in a department is routine or nonroutine. If the work in a department is routine, use a mechanistic structure and process. If the work in a department is nonroutine, use an organic management process.

Once the nature of a department's technology has been identified, the appropriate structure can be determined. Department technology tends to be associated with a cluster of departmental characteristics, such as the skill level of employees, formalization, and pattern of communication. Definite patterns exist in the relationship between work-unit technology and structural characteristics, which are associated with departmental performance.[65] Key relationships between technology and other dimensions of departments are described in this section and are summarized in Exhibit 7.10.

The overall structure of departments may be characterized as either organic or mechanistic. Routine technologies are associated with a mechanistic structure and processes, with formal rules and rigid management processes. Nonroutine technologies are associated with an organic structure, and department management is more

EXHIBIT 7.10
Relationship of Department Technology to Structural and Management Characteristics

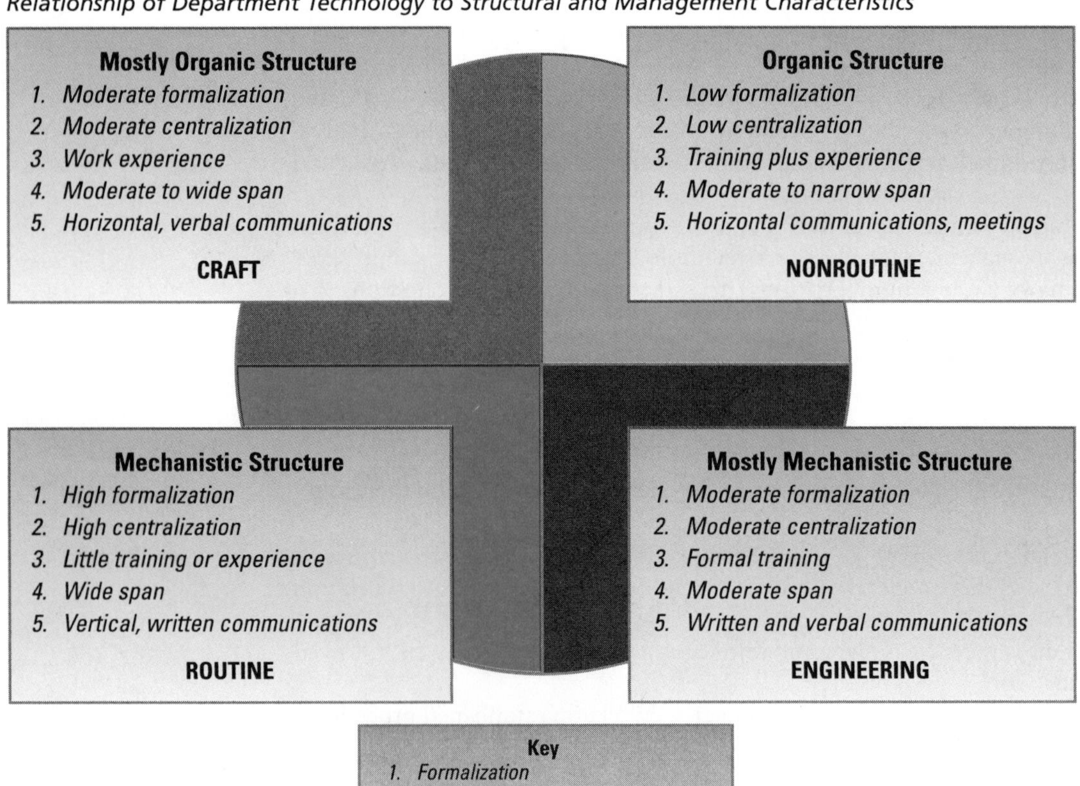

flexible and free-flowing. The specific design characteristics of formalization, decentralization, worker skill level, span of control, and communication and coordination vary, depending on work-unit technology.

1. *Formalization.* Routine technology is characterized by standardization and division of labour into small tasks that are governed by formal rules and procedures. For nonroutine tasks, the structure is less formal and less standardized. When variety is high, as in a research department, fewer activities are covered by formal procedures.[66]
2. *Decentralization.* In routine technologies, most decision making about task activities is centralized to management.[67] In engineering technologies, employees with technical training tend to acquire moderate decision authority because technical knowledge is important to task accomplishment. Production employees who have long experience obtain decision authority in craft technologies because they know how to respond to problems. Decentralization to employees is greatest in nonroutine settings, where many decisions are made by employees.
3. *Worker skill level.* Work staff in routine technologies typically require little education or experience, which is congruent with repetitious work activities. In work units with greater variety, staff are more skilled and often have formal training in technical schools or universities. Training for craft activities, which are less analyzable, is more likely to be through job experience. Nonroutine activities require both formal education and job experience.[68]
4. *Span of control.* Span of control is the number of employees who report to a single manager or supervisor. This characteristic is normally influenced by departmental technology. The more complex and nonroutine the task, the more problems arise in which the supervisor becomes involved. Although the span of control may be influenced by other factors, such as skill level of employees, it typically should be smaller for complex tasks because on such tasks the supervisor and subordinate must interact frequently.[69]
5. *Communication and coordination.* Communication activity and frequency increase as task variety increases.[70] Frequent problems require more information sharing to solve problems and ensure proper completion of activities. The direction of communication is typically horizontal in nonroutine work units and vertical in routine work units.[71] The form of communication varies by task analyzability.[72] When tasks are highly analyzable, statistical and written forms of communication (memos, reports, rules, and procedures) are frequent. When tasks are less analyzable, information typically is conveyed face to face, over the telephone, or in group meetings.

Two important points are reflected in Exhibit 7.10. First, departments differ from one another and can be categorized according to their workflow technology.[73] Second, structural and management processes differ based on departmental technology. Managers should design their departments so that requirements based on technology can be met. Design problems are most visible when the design is clearly inconsistent with technology. Studies have found that when structure and communication characteristics did not reflect technology, departments tended to be less effective.[74] Employees could not communicate with the frequency needed to solve problems. Consider how the design characteristics of Aravind Eye Hospital contribute to a smoothly functioning department.

In Practice

Aravind Eye Hospital (Aravind)

In 1976, Dr. Govindappa Venkataswamy founded a 12-bed eye hospital in Madurai, India. Now, he and his siblings run five hospitals that perform more than 180,000 operations annually. Seventy percent of the patients cannot pay while the remainder seek Dr. Venkataswamy's services as he was a cataract surgeon of international renown.

When Dr. Venkataswamy started the hospital, there were about eight ophthalmologists in India and 20 million people with cataracts. Now, Aravind is the world's largest single provider of eye surgery in the world. In 1998, the Aravind hospitals saw 1.2 million outpatients and performed 183,000 cataract operations. In 2005, the five hospitals performed 200,000 surgeries and treated 2 million people. While Dr. Venkataswamy died in 2006, his work continues.[75]

In addition to the hospitals, Aravind has its own laboratory, Aurolab, which pioneered the development of high-quality, low-cost intraocular lenses. Aurolab produces 750,000 lenses annually for Aravind and other organizations.

Seeing 400 patients is a slow day at Aravind. The hospital grounds are full with the families and friends of the patients. " . . . [A] slow day at Aravind would drive most [North] American hospital officials mad."[76] It costs Aravind $10 for one cataract surgery. Two or more patients are put in the same operating theatre so that the surgeon can go easily from patient to patient. Each patient in the theatre is prepped and ready for the surgery. Avarind's surgeons have created equipment that allows them to swivel around to work on the next patient as soon as they have performed the ten-minute surgery on their first patient. Post-op patients are wheeled out and new patients are wheeled in. There have been no problems with infections.

No one at Aravind uses the term *the poor*. According to Dr. Venkataswamy, "[to] think of certain people as 'the poor' puts you in a superior position, blinds you to the ways in which you are poor—and in the West there are many such ways: emotionally and spiritually, for example. You have comforts in [North] America, but are afraid of each other."[77]

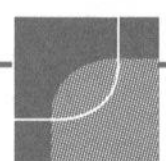

Workflow Interdependence among Departments

So far, this chapter has explored how organization and department technologies influence structural design. The final characteristic of technology that influences structure is called interdependence. **Interdependence** means the extent to which departments depend on each other for resources or materials to accomplish their tasks. Low interdependence means that departments can do their work independently of each other and have little need for interaction, consultation, or exchange of materials. High interdependence means departments must constantly exchange resources.

Types

James Thompson defined three types of interdependence that influence organizational structure.[78] These interdependencies are illustrated in Exhibit 7.11 and are discussed in the following sections.

Pooled. **Pooled interdependence** is the lowest form of interdependence among departments. In this form, work does not flow between units. Each department is part of the organization and contributes to the common good of the organization, but works independently. Subway restaurants or branch banks are examples of pooled interdependence. An outlet in Kelowna need not interact with an outlet in Peterborough. Pooled interdependence may be associated with the relationships within a divisional structure, defined in Chapter 3. Divisions or branches share

Form of Interdependence	Demands on Horizontal Communication, Decision Making	Type of Coordination Required	Priority for Locating Units Close Together
Pooled (bank) Clients	Low communication	Standardization, rules, procedures Divisional structure	Low
Sequential (assembly line) Client	Medium communication	Plans, schedules, feedback Task forces	Medium
Reciprocal (hospital) Client	High communication	Mutual adjustment, cross-departmental meetings, teamwork Horizontal structure	High

EXHIBIT 7.11
Thompson's Classification of Interdependence and Management Implications

financial resources from a common pool, and the success of each division contributes to the success of the overall organization.

Thompson proposed that pooled interdependence would exist in firms with what he called a mediating technology. A **mediating technology** provides products or services that mediate or link clients from the external environment and, in so doing, allows each department to work independently. Banks, brokerage firms, and real estate offices all mediate between buyers and sellers, but the offices work independently within the organization.

The management implications associated with pooled interdependence are quite simple. Thompson argued that managers should use rules and procedures to standardize activities across departments. Each department should use the same procedures and financial statements so the outcomes of all departments can be measured and pooled. Very little day-to-day coordination is required among units.

PDA Remember...

Evaluate the interdependencies among organizational departments. Use the general rule that, as interdependencies increase, mechanisms for coordination must also increase. Consider a divisional structure for pooled interdependence. For sequential interdependence, use task forces and integrators for greater horizontal coordination. At the highest level of interdependence (reciprocal interdependence), a horizontal structure may be appropriate.

Sequential. When interdependence is of serial form, with parts produced in one department becoming inputs to another department, it is called **sequential interdependence.** The first department must perform correctly for the second department to perform correctly. This is a higher level of interdependence than pooled interdependence, because departments exchange resources and depend on others to perform well. Sequential interdependence creates a greater need for horizontal mechanisms such as integrators or task forces.

Sequential interdependence occurs in what Thompson called **long-linked technology,** which "refers to the combination in one organization of successive stages of production; each stage of production uses as its inputs the production of the preceding stage and produces inputs for the following stage."[79] An example of sequential interdependence comes from the shipbuilding industry. Until recently, ship designers made patterns and moulds out of paper and plywood, which were passed on to assembly. Mistakes in measurements or pattern mix-ups, though, often caused errors in the cutting and assembly process, leading to delays and increased costs. Naval architect Filippo Cali created a complex software program that serves as a bridge between design and assembly. The software eliminates the need for paper and plywood moulds by putting that crucial part of the design process in a computer program.[80] Another example of sequential interdependence would be an automobile assembly line, which must have all the parts it needs, such as engines, steering mechanisms, and tires, to keep production rolling.

The management requirements for sequential interdependence are more demanding than those for pooled interdependence. Coordination among the linked plants or departments is required. Since the interdependence implies a one-way flow of materials, extensive planning and scheduling are generally needed. Department B needs to know what to expect from Department A so both can perform effectively. Some day-to-day communication among plants or departments is also needed to handle unexpected problems and exceptions that arise.

Reciprocal. The highest level of interdependence is **reciprocal interdependence**. This exists when the output of operation A is the input to operation B, and the output of operation B is the input back again to operation A. The outputs of departments influence those departments in reciprocal fashion.

Reciprocal interdependence tends to occur in organizations with what Thompson called **intensive technologies**, which provide a variety of products or services in combination to a client. Hospitals, such as Aravind, are an excellent example because they provide coordinated services to patients. A patient may move back and forth between x-ray, surgery, and physical therapy as needed to be cured. A firm developing new products is another example. Intense coordination is needed between design, engineering, manufacturing, and marketing to combine all their resources to suit the customer's product need.

Management requirements are greatest in the case of reciprocal interdependence. Because reciprocal interdependence requires that departments work together intimately and be closely coordinated, a horizontal structure may be appropriate. The structure must allow for frequent horizontal communication and adjustment. Extensive planning is required, but plans will not anticipate or solve all problems. Daily interaction and mutual adjustment among departments are required. Managers from several departments are jointly involved in face-to-face coordination, teamwork, and decision making. Reciprocal interdependence is the most complex interdependence for organizations to handle.

Structural Priority

As indicated in Exhibit 7.11, because decision making, communication, and coordination problems are greatest for reciprocal interdependence, reciprocal interdependence should receive first priority in organizational structure. New product development is one area of reciprocal interdependence that is of growing concern to managers as companies face increasing pressure to get new products to market quickly. Many firms are revamping the design–manufacturing relationship by closely integrating CAD and CAM technologies discussed earlier in this chapter.[81]

Activities that are reciprocally interdependent should be grouped close together in the organization so managers have easy access to one another for mutual adjustment. These units should report to the same person on the organizational chart and should be physically close so the time and effort for coordination can be minimized. A horizontal structure, with linked sets of teams working on core processes, can provide the close coordination needed to support reciprocal interdependence. Poor coordination will result in poor performance for the organization. If reciprocally interdependent units are not located close together, the organization should design mechanisms for coordination, such as daily meetings between departments or an intranet to facilitate communication. The next priority is given to sequential interdependencies, and finally to pooled interdependencies.

This strategy of organizing keeps the communication channels short where coordination is most critical to organizational success. For example, the Toronto facility of Celestica underwent a significant organizational redesign with the objective of reducing costs, accelerating the rate of new product introduction and increasing response timeliness and capability. As a result of the redesign, there have been considerable performance improvements; productivity has doubled, manufacturing cycle times were reduced, and quality has improved.[82]

Structural Implications

Most organizations experience various levels of interdependence, and structure can be designed to fit these needs.[83] In a manufacturing firm, new product development entails reciprocal interdependence among the design, engineering, purchasing, manufacturing, and sales departments. Perhaps a horizontal structure or cross-functional teams could be used to handle the back-and-forth flow of information and resources. Once a product is designed, its actual manufacture would be sequential interdependence, with a flow of goods from one department to another, such as among purchasing, inventory, production control, manufacturing, and assembly. The actual ordering and delivery of products is pooled interdependence, with warehouses working independently. Customers could place an order with the nearest facility, which would not require coordination among warehouses, except in unusual cases such as a stock outage.

The three levels of interdependence are illustrated by a study of athletic teams that examined interdependency among players and how it influences other aspects of baseball, football, and basketball teams.

In Practice
Sports Teams

A major difference between baseball, football, and basketball is the interdependence among players. Baseball is low in interdependence, football is medium, and basketball represents the highest player interdependence. The relationships among interdependence and other characteristics of team play are illustrated in Exhibit 7.12.

In baseball, interdependence among team players is low and can be defined as pooled. Each member acts independently, taking a turn at bat and playing his or her own position. When interaction does occur, it is between only two or three players, as in a double play. Players are physically dispersed, and the rules of the game are the primary means of coordinating players. Players practise and develop their skills individually, such as by taking batting practice and undergoing physical conditioning. Management's job is to select good players. If each player is successful as an individual, the team should win.

In football, interdependence among players is higher and tends to be sequential. The line first blocks the opponents to enable the backs to run or pass. Plays are performed sequentially from first

EXHIBIT 7.12
Relationships among Interdependence and Other Characteristics of Team Play

	Baseball	Football	Basketball
Interdependence	Pooled	Sequential	Reciprocal
Physical Dispersion of Players	High	Medium	Low
Coordination	Rules that govern the sport	Game plan and position roles	Mutual adjustment and shared responsibility
Key Management Roles	Select players and develop their skills	Prepare and execute game	Influence flow of game

Source: Based on William Pasmore, Carol E. Francis, and Jeffrey Haldeman, "Sociotechnical Systems: A North American Reflection on the Empirical Studies of the 70s," *Human Relations* 35 (1982): 1179–1204.

down to fourth down. Physical dispersion is medium, which allows players to operate as a coordinated unit. The primary mechanism for coordinating players is developing a game plan along with rules that govern the behaviour of team members. Each player has an assignment that fits with other assignments, and management designs the game plan to achieve victory.

In basketball, interdependence tends to be reciprocal. The game is free-flowing, and the division of labour is less precise than in other sports. Each player is involved in both offence and defence, handles the ball, and attempts to score. The ball flows back and forth among players. Team members interact in a dynamic flow to achieve victory. Management skills involve the ability to influence this dynamic process, either by substituting players or by working the ball into certain areas. Players must learn to adapt to the flow of the game and to one another as events unfold.

Interdependence among players is a primary factor explaining the difference among the three sports. Baseball is organized around an autonomous individual, football around groups that are sequentially interdependent, and basketball around the free flow of reciprocal players.[84]

Impact of Technology on Job Design

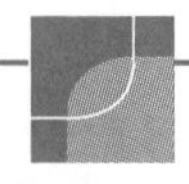

PDA Remember...

The introduction of a new technology has significant impact on job design. Consider using the sociotechnical systems approach to balance the needs of workers with the requirements of the new technological system.

So far, this chapter has described models for analyzing how manufacturing, service, and department technologies influence structure and management processes. The relationship between a new technology and organization seems to follow a pattern, beginning with immediate effects on the content of jobs followed (after a longer period) by impact on design of the organization. The ultimate impact of technology on employees can be partially understood through the concepts of job design and sociotechnical systems.

Job Design

Job design includes the assignment of goals and tasks to be accomplished by employees. Managers may consciously change job design to improve productivity or worker motivation. For example, when workers are involved in performing boring, repetitive tasks, managers may introduce **job rotation**, which means moving employees from job to job to give them a greater variety of tasks. However, managers may also unconsciously influence job design through the introduction of new technologies, which can change how jobs are done and the very nature of jobs.[85] Managers should understand how the introduction of a new technology may affect employees' jobs. The common theme of new technologies in the workplace is that they in some way substitute machinery for human labour in transforming inputs into outputs. Automated teller machines (ATMs) have replaced thousands of human bank tellers, for example. IBM has even built a plant in Austin, Texas, that can produce laptop computers without the help of a single worker.[86]

In addition to actually replacing human workers, technology may have several different effects on the human jobs that remain. Research has indicated that mass-production technologies tend to produce **job simplification**, which means that the variety and difficulty of tasks performed by a single person are reduced. The consequence is boring, repetitive jobs that generally provide little satisfaction. More advanced technology, on the other hand, tends to cause **job enrichment**, meaning that the job provides greater responsibility, recognition, and opportunities for growth and development. These technologies create a greater need for employee training and education because workers need higher-level skills and greater competence to master their tasks. For example, ATMs took most of the routine tasks (deposits and withdrawals) away from bank tellers and left them with the more complex tasks that require higher-level skills. Studies of flexible manufacturing found that it produces three noticeable results for employees: more opportunities for intellectual mastery and enhanced cognitive skills for workers; more worker responsibility for results; and greater interdependence among workers, enabling more social interaction and the development of teamwork and coordination skills.[87] Flexible manufacturing technology may also contribute to **job enlargement**, which is an expansion of the number of different tasks performed by an employee. Fewer workers are needed with the new technology, and each employee has to be able to perform a greater number and variety of tasks.

With advanced technology, workers have to keep learning new skills because technology is changing so rapidly. Advances in information technology, to be discussed in detail in the next chapter, are having a significant effect on jobs in the service industry, including doctors' offices and medical clinics, law firms, financial planners, and libraries. Workers may find that their jobs change almost daily because of new software programs, increased use of the Internet, and other advances in information technology.

Advanced technology does not always have a positive effect on employees, but research findings in general are encouraging, suggesting that jobs for workers are enriched rather than simplified, engaging their higher mental capacities, offering opportunities for learning and growth, and providing greater job satisfaction.

Sociotechnical Systems

The **sociotechnical systems approach** recognizes the interaction of technical and human needs in effective job design, combining the needs of people with the organization's need for technical efficiency. The *socio* portion of the approach refers to the people and groups that work in organizations and how work is organized and

EXHIBIT 7.13
Sociotechnical Systems Model

Source: Based on T. Cummings, "Self-Regulating Work Groups: A Socio-Technical Synthesis," *Academy of Management Review* 3 (1978): 625–634; Don Hellriegel, John W. Slocum, and Richard W. Woodman, Organizational Behavior, 8th ed. (Cincinnati, Ohio: South-Western, 1998), 492; and Gregory B. Northcraft and Margaret A. Neale, *Organizational Behavior: A Management Challenge,* 2nd ed. (Fort Worth, Tex.: The Dryden Press, 1994), 551.

coordinated. The *technical* portion refers to the materials, tools, machines, and processes used to transform organizational inputs into outputs.

Exhibit 7.13 illustrates the three primary components of the sociotechnical systems model.[88] The social system includes all human elements—such as individual and team behaviours, organizational culture, management practices, and degree of communication openness—that can influence the performance of work. The technical system refers to the type of production technology, the level of interdependence, the complexity of tasks, and so forth. The goal of the sociotechnical systems approach is to design the organization for **joint optimization**, which means that an organization functions best only when the social and technical systems are designed to fit the needs of one another. Designing the organization to meet human needs while ignoring the technical systems, or changing technology to improve efficiency while ignoring human needs, may inadvertently cause performance problems. The sociotechnical systems approach attempts to find a balance between what workers want and need and the technical requirements of the organization's production system.[89]

One example comes from a museum that installed a closed-circuit TV system. Rather than having several guards patrolling the museum and grounds, the television could easily be monitored by a single guard. Although the technology saved money because only one guard was needed per shift, it led to unexpected performance problems. Guards had previously enjoyed the social interaction provided by patrolling; monitoring a closed-circuit television led to alienation and boredom. When a federal agency did an 18-month test of the system, only 5 percent of several thousand experimental covert intrusions were detected by the guard.[90] The system was inadequate because human needs were not taken into account.

Sociotechnical principles evolved from the work of the Tavistock Institute, a research organization in England, during the 1950s and 1960s.[91] There are 11 core principles that underlie sociotechnical systems thinking and design. They are:

1. Compatibility—the process used to redesign must be compatible with its objectives.
2. Minimum critical specification—design should specify no more than is necessary.

3. Variance control—control variances not removed through technology at the point closest to their origin.
4. Boundary location—locate boundaries so that a team can regulate itself.
5. Information flow—have information go first to the point of action.
6. Power and authority—empower employees.
7. Multifunctional/multiskills—each team and each person should have more than one function.
8. Support congruence—design systems of social support to reinforce the behaviours that the organizational structure is designed to elicit.
9. Design and human values—design the organization to achieve a high quality of working life.
10. Bridging the transition—minimize stressors during redesign.
11. Incompletion—design is an iterative process.[92]

The GE plant at Bromont, described in this chapter's A Look Inside section, is one of the world's best examples of the sociotechnical systems principles in practice.

Examples of organizational change using sociotechnical systems principles have occurred in numerous organizations, including General Motors, Volvo, Celestica, and Procter & Gamble.[93] Although there have been failures, in many of these applications the joint optimization of changes in technology and structure to meet the needs of people as well as efficiency improved performance, safety, quality, absenteeism, and turnover. In some cases, work design was not the most efficient based on technical and scientific principles, but worker involvement and commitment more than made up for the difference. Thus, once again research shows that new technologies need not have a negative impact on workers, because the technology often requires higher-level mental and social skills and can be organized to encourage the involvement and commitment of employees, thereby benefiting both the employee and the organization.

The sociotechnical systems principle that people should be viewed as resources with much potential and provided with appropriate skills, meaningful work, and suitable rewards becomes even more important in today's world of growing technological complexity.[94] One study of paper manufacturers found that organizations that put too much faith in machines and technology and pay little attention to the appropriate management of people do not achieve advances in productivity and flexibility. Today's most successful companies strive to find the right mix of machines, computer systems, and people, and the most effective way to coordinate them.[95]

Although many principles of sociotechnical systems theory are still valid, current scholars and researchers are also arguing for an expansion of the approach to capture the dynamic nature of today's organizations, the chaotic environment, and the shift from routine to nonroutine jobs brought about by advances in technology.[96]

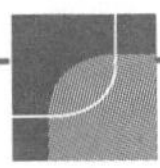

Summary and Interpretation

This chapter reviewed several frameworks and key research findings on the topic of organizational technology. The potential importance of technology as a factor in organizational structure was discovered during the 1960s. Since then, a flurry of research activity has been undertaken to understand more precisely the relationship of technology to other characteristics of organizations.

Five ideas in the technology literature stand out. The first is Woodward's research into manufacturing technology. Woodward went into organizations and collected practical data on technology characteristics, organizational structure, and management systems. She found clear relationships between technology and structure in high-performing organizations. Her findings are so clear that managers can analyze their own organizations on the same dimensions of technology and structure. In addition, technology and structure can be co-aligned with organizational strategy to meet changing needs and provide new competitive advantages.

The second important idea is that service technologies differ in a systematic way from manufacturing technologies. Service technologies are characterized by intangible outcomes and direct client involvement in the production process. Service firms do not have the fixed, machine-based technologies that appear in manufacturing organizations; hence, organizational design often differs as well.

The third significant idea is Perrow's framework applied to department technologies. Understanding the variety and analyzability of a technology tells one about the management style, structure, and process that should characterize that department. Routine technologies are characterized by mechanistic structure and nonroutine technologies by organic structure. Applying the wrong management system to a department will result in dissatisfaction and reduced efficiency.

The fourth important idea is interdependence among departments. The extent to which departments depend on each other for materials, information, or other resources determines the amount of coordination required between them. As interdependence increases, demands on the organization for coordination increase. Organizational design must allow for the correct amount of communication and coordination to handle interdependence across departments.

The fifth important idea is that new flexible manufacturing systems are being adopted by organizations and affecting organizational design. For the most part, the impact is positive, with shifts toward more organic structures both on the shop floor and in the management hierarchy. These technologies replace routine jobs, give employees more autonomy, produce more challenging jobs, encourage teamwork, and let the organization be more flexible and responsive. The new technologies are enriching jobs to the point where organizations are happier places to work.

Several principles of sociotechnical systems theory, which attempts to design the technical and human aspects of an organization to fit one another, are increasingly important as advances in technology alter the nature of jobs and social interaction in today's companies.

Key Concepts

analyzability, p. 247
continuous process production, p. 232
core technology, p. 230
craft technologies, p. 248
engineering technologies, p. 249
flexible manufacturing systems, p. 236
intensive technologies, p. 254
interdependence, p. 252
job design, p. 256
job enlargement, p. 257
job enrichment, p. 257
job rotation, p. 257
job simplification, p. 257
joint optimization, p. 258

large-batch production, p. 232
lean manufacturing, p. 238
long-linked technology, p. 253
mass customization, p. 239
mediating technology, p. 253
noncore technology, p. 247
nonroutine technologies, p. 249
organizational goals, p. 231
pooled interdependence, p. 252
reciprocal interdependence, p. 254
routine technologies, p. 248
sequential interdependence, p. 253
service technology, p. 243
small-batch production, p. 232
sociotechnical systems approach, p. 257
task variety, p. 247
technical complexity, p. 232
technology, p. 229

Discussion Questions

1. Where would your university or college department be located on Perrow's technology framework? Look for the underlying variety and analyzability characteristics when making your assessment. Would a department devoted exclusively to teaching be put in a different quadrant from a department devoted exclusively to research?
2. Explain Thompson's levels of interdependence. Identify an example of each level of interdependence in the university or college setting. What kinds of coordination mechanisms should an administration develop to handle each level of interdependence?
3. Describe Woodward's classification of organizational technologies. Explain why each of the three technology groups is related differently to organizational structure and management processes.
4. What relationships did Woodward discover between supervisor span of control and technological complexity?
5. How do flexible manufacturing and lean manufacturing differ from other manufacturing technologies? Why are these new approaches needed in today's environment?
6. What is a service technology? Are different types of service technologies likely to be associated with different structures? Explain.
7. Mass customization of products has become a common approach in manufacturing organizations. Discuss ways in which mass customization can be applied to service firms as well.
8. In what primary ways does the design of service firms typically differ from that of product firms? Why?
9. A top executive claimed that top-level management is a craft technology because the work contains intangibles, such as handling personnel, interpreting the environment, and coping with unusual situations that have to be learned through experience. If this is true, is it appropriate to teach management in a business school? Does teaching management from a textbook assume that the manager's job is analyzable, and hence that formal training rather than experience is most important?
10. In which quadrant of Perrow's framework would a mass-production technology be placed? Where would small-batch and continuous process technologies be placed? Why? Would Perrow's framework lead to the same recommendation about organic versus mechanistic structures that Woodward made? Why?
11. To what extent does the development of new technologies simplify and routinize the jobs of employees? How can new technology lead to job enlargement? Discuss.
12. Describe the sociotechnical systems model. Why might some managers oppose a sociotechnical systems approach?

Chapter 7 Workbook: Bistro Technology*

You will be analyzing the technology used in three different restaurants—McDonald's, Subway, and a typical family-owned restaurant. Your instructor will tell you whether to do this assignment as individuals or in a group.

You must visit all three restaurants and infer how the work is done, according to the following criteria. You are not allowed to interview any employees, but instead you will be an observer. Take lots of notes when you are there.

	McDonald's	Subway	Family-owned Restaurant
Organization goals: Speed, service, atmosphere, etc.			
Authority structure			
Type of technology using Woodward's model			
Organizational structure: Mechanistic or organic?			
Team versus individual: Do people work together or alone?			
Interdependence: How do employees depend on each other?			
Tasks: Routine versus Nonroutine			
Specialization of tasks by employees			
Standardization: How varied are tasks and products?			
Expertise required: Technical versus social			
Decision making: Centralized versus Decentralized			

Questions

1. Is the technology used the best one for each restaurant, considering its goals and environment?
2. From the preceding data, determine if the structure and other characteristics fit the technology.
3. If you were part of a consulting team assigned to improve the operations of each organization, what recommendations would you make and why?

*Adapted loosely by Dorothy Marcic from "Hamburger Technology," in Douglas T. Hall et al., *Experiences in Management and Organizational Behavior*, 2nd ed. (New York: Wiley, 1982), 244–247, as well as "Behavior, Technology, and Work Design" in A. B. Shani and James B. Lau, *Behavior in Organizations* (Chicago: Irwin, 1996), M16–23 to M16–26.

Case for Analysis: Improving Production at Beothic Fish Processors*

Improving Production at Beothic Fish Processors Ltd.

"The Pelagic processing area at the plant in Valleyfield, Newfoundland, has not worked out as well as we had hoped for processing capelin," identified the General Manager of Beothic Fish Processors Ltd. "Although the company continues to be very successful, if we are to offer competitive prices and still earn a profit we must keep our production costs as low as possible, and given that production costs are a function of production efficiency, it is imperative that we improve our present production system. It appears to me that we must look carefully at our existing plant layout to accomplish this."

Company Background

Beothic Fish Processors Ltd. (Beothic) was one of the largest processors of pelagic (capelin, mackerel and herring) fish species in Newfoundland and Labrador, with capelin being, by far, the primary species. Although the company began in 1967, it was not until 1979, when a modern cold storage facility was constructed at Valleyfield, and new blast freezers were installed, that the company was able to handle capelin. By 1989, capelin was a major contributor to Beothic's overall profitability.

By Newfoundland standards, capelin processing was a relatively new fishery, having been developed about thirty years ago. Originally, capelin were sorted by hand; however, it proved impossible to handle the enormous quantities demanded by the market in this manner. The industry soon turned to the use of mechanical sorters which, although not perfect, were able to process large quantities quickly and at relatively low cost.

The Present Production System

The capelin processing facilities at Beothic are illustrated in Exhibit 1. Capelin entered the system via a water-filled infeed hopper, labelled as 1 on the exhibit. At this point, the insulated containers used for transport were simply

EXHIBIT 1
Existing Layout of Processing Area

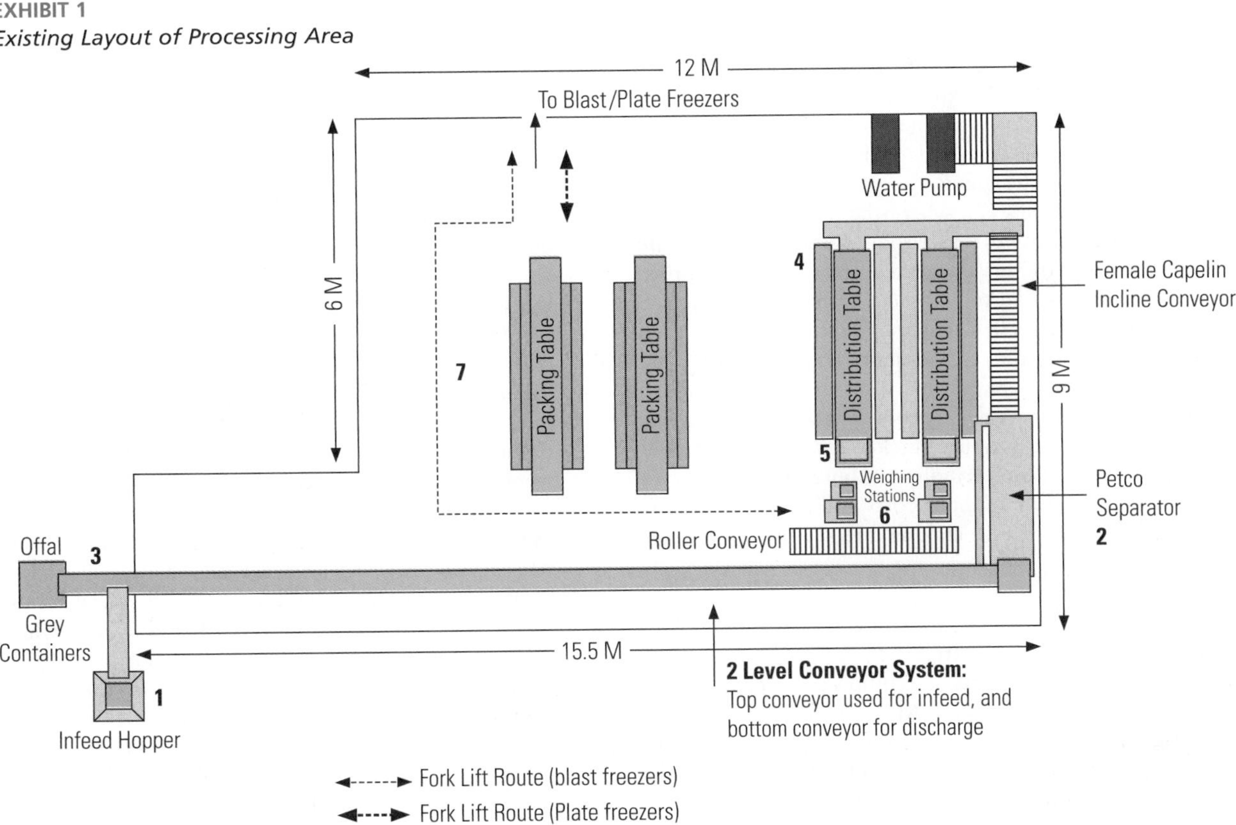

emptied into the hopper. They then proceeded along a conveyor belt to the mechanical separator—a Petco 3500 (2). The separator consisted of a series of ribbed slots, which gradually increased in size, that the capelin were shaken across. The very small capelin fell out first, and were conveyed back to the offal area where the unusable portion of the raw material was collected (3). The intermediate sized capelin, which were the marketable females, fell through next, and were conveyed to the distribution tables (4). The capelin, which were primarily male, proceeded to the end of the separator and joined the small females on the conveyor as offal. At each distribution table, which was actually a conveyor, approximately 18 workers removed by hand and discarded any unsuitable product that was not eliminated mechanically. At the end of each table (5), the capelin fell into boxes, which were hand-carried to the weighing stations (6). At this point, the boxes were checked to ensure that predetermined weights were contained in each. Boxes were then placed on a metal roller conveyor where they were closed and strapped. They were then placed on pallets, brought by forklift to the blast freezing area, and frozen to a temperature of −21°C, a process that normally took 12 to 16 hours. Pelagic species such as capelin were generally blast frozen unless these freezers were already filled to capacity.

As a variation on the blast freezing system, which would normally only occur when the blast freezers were completely full, plate freezing may be used. The capelin falling off the distribution tables (5) were caught in plastic pans, which were carried by hand to the weighing stations (6). After weighing, the pans were hand-carried to the packing tables (7), where they were emptied into cartons designed for plate freezing. Because in the plate freezing process the plates exerted pressure on the product, these cartons had to be placed in metal pans, which helped them retain their shape. The capelin were then transported by forklift to the main plant area for plate freezing. The metal pans were then manually removed from each frozen carton of product (the "knocking out process"), and the product stacked on pallets for cold storage. The additional handling required by this type of freezing increased unit labour costs and could potentially damage the product, thus making it relatively unattractive to the processor.

Problems of the Present System

Shortly after preparing this description of his capelin processing facility, the General Manager held a planning meeting with the plant manager and three production supervisors. The purpose of the meeting was to review the pelagic production plan for the upcoming year, particularly with respect to capelin.

"As you probably know," he began, "the single most profitable species processed here at the plant is capelin. Because the season is so short, only three weeks at best, it is vital that production be maximized in that period. We have three blast freezers and several plate freezers. It is absolutely vital that these freezers be kept full. Too often last year, we were not at capacity during this period. I'd like to take each aspect of our capelin processing system and examine it for problems."

When the meeting had ended, the following list of problem areas were identified by the management group:

1. *Space:* All of the group agreed that the production area was extremely crowded with, as one of the supervisors stated, "people tripping over each other." Suggested solutions to this problem ranged from expanding the building to provide more space, to reorganizing the equipment in the present building to provide better working areas. The General Manager felt the equipment was poorly organized and that there were too many places on the line where the product had to be handled by people, thus increasing labour costs. He felt that if the equipment could be laid out in a straighter line many of these extra people could be eliminated and production could proceed more smoothly.
2. *The infeed system:* The supervisors were critical of the amount of wasted raw material caused by capelin falling off the beginning of the infeed conveyor to the offal conveyor below. A possible solution would be to simply move the hopper closer to the separator and to remove the conveyor completely.
3. *The distribution tables:* All three of the supervisors commented on the way that the distribution tables were organized. The inclined conveyor leading from the separator deposited the female capelin at one end of a table. They then had to be pushed manually to the ends of the distribution tables.
4. *The weighing system:* Another problem area identified during the meeting concerned the weighing system. Capelin arriving at the end of the distribution tables were caught in either blast freezer boxes or in plate freezer pans, depending on the freezing method to be used. They were then moved to the weighing stations, where sufficient capelin were added or removed to bring the package to the desired weight. Blast freezer boxes were then placed on the roller conveyor, where they were closed in preparation for transport by forklift to the freezers. In order to do this, the forklift operator had to manoeuvre around the packing tables. Although this was not a problem for a skilled forklift operator, it created a potential safety risk to those working in that area of the plant. As the plant manager put it, "they often worked with one eye on the job

and the other on the forklift." When the product was to be plate frozen, the plastic freezer pans had to be carried from the weigh stations to the packing tables. There, the capelin were transferred from the pans to cardboard boxes, which, in turn, were placed into the metal freezer pans for plate freezing.

Conclusion

After reviewing his notes, the General Manager realized that his entire capelin production system needed to be reorganized. In general, there were two key items to be addressed. First, the movement of capelin through the plant from the raw material stage to finished product was generally inefficient. Secondly, he considered the critical problem of the plant to be an inability to keep its freezers working at full capacity. He knew that he needed to look at the overall plant layout to make appropriate changes to improve production at the plant.

*This case was adapted from a case prepared by Professors Wayne King and Donna Stapleton as a basis for classroom discussion, and is not meant to illustrate either effective or ineffective management.

8 Information Technology and Control

Photo by Bill Sandford - used with permission.

Information Technology Evolution

Information for Decision Making and Control

Organizational Decision-Making Systems • Feedback Control Model • Management Control Systems • The Balanced Scorecard

Adding Strategic Value: Strengthening Internal Coordination

Intranets • Enterprise Resource Planning • Knowledge Management

Adding Strategic Value: Strengthening External Relationships

The Integrated Enterprise • Customer Relationship Management • E-Business Organizational Design

IT Impact on Organizational Design

Summary and Interpretation

A Look Inside

"Mr. Fix-it"

Edward Melcarek (see photo), an electromechanical engineer from Barrie, Ontario, was looking for possible money-making opportunities on the Internet when he stumbled on InnoCentive.com, a website that posts research challenges by organizations willing to pay for answers. Melcarek took on various puzzles that the organizations' R&D departments had not been able to solve. By 2007, he had won three awards totalling $50,000—a record among the North American solvers on the site. He had come up with ways to purify silicone-based solvents, to add fluoride powder to toothpaste tubes and to control dust in the packaging of drywall powder. As Melcarek says, "[not] bad for a few minutes' work . . ."[1]

InnoCentive.com is one of several online forums that link scientists with for-profit and nonprofit organizations that have some sort of conundrum that they themselves have not been able to solve. Founded in 2001 by Eli Lilly, it now brings together more than 125,000 of the world's brightest minds "to create breakthrough solutions that touch every human life."[2] According to InnoCentive.com's CEO, Dwayne Spradlin, "[we] can structurally change the way innovation works. . . . Dollars clearly help to focus the masses on solving problems, to go outside the four walls of monolithic organizations and get to a new level of R&D."[3] One current InnoCentive.com challenge, from a nonprofit organization, Prize4Life, offers $1 million for finding the biomarker for measuring the progression of Amyotrophic Lateral Sclerosis, more commonly known as Lou Gehrig's disease. InnoCentive.com brings together solvers and seekers in what it calls its open innovation marketplace. Among the seekers are well-known organizations such as Procter & Gamble, Boeing and the Rockefeller Foundation.

Open innovation is very useful in fast-paced industries such T-shirt makers and sports equipment manufacturers. Researchers from the open innovation program at Massachusetts Institute of Technology have found that more than half the ideas for new skateboards, mountain bikes, and folding scooters have come from committed customers.[4]

Effectively using information technologies and processes in knowledge-based firms such as the accounting and consulting firm KPMG; the National Aboriginal Health Organization, created "to improve and promote . . . the health of Aboriginal Peoples and communities"[5]; and Business Wire, which provides business and corporate information, has long been fundamental to the business. Today, information technology (IT) has become a crucial factor helping companies in all industries maintain a competitive edge in the face of growing global competition and rising customer demands for speed, convenience, quality, and value. Oliver Bonacini Restaurants, a small gourmet restaurant chain, uses computerized systems to measure and control everything from bathroom cleanliness to food preparation time. The physical and technological upgrades at Brampton (Ontario) Civic Hospital include an integrated communications network and patient information system that lets hospital staff measure performance and gauge effectiveness using a variety of metrics.[6] See the next In Practice for more detail on the planned use of IT at Brampton Civic Hospital.

Yet, the rapidly growing use of IT and the Internet presents not only new opportunities, but also new challenges for managers. Most importantly, the balance of power has shifted to the customer or the consumer. With unlimited access to information on the Internet, customers are much better informed and much more demanding, making customer loyalty harder to build.[7] In addition, the concept of electronically linking suppliers, partners, and customers is forcing companies to rethink their strategies, organizational design, and business processes. The pace of business is moving at "warp speed,"[8] and the Internet's ongoing development has had a significant impact on organizational practices. Planning horizons are shorter, expectations of customers change rapidly, and new competitors spring up almost overnight. All this means managers, as well as employees throughout the organization, need accurate and timely information at their fingertips. It is noteworthy that *Time* magazine named the Internet as its 2006 *person* of the year. While the choice was mocked by some pundits, "... the choice may ultimately be viewed as the tipping point when the remarkable outbreak of Internet participation that encompasses millions of bloggers, music remixers, amateur video creators, citizen journalists, wikipedians, and Flickr photographers broke into the mainstream."[9]

Highly successful organizations today are typically those that most effectively collect, store, distribute, and use information. More than facilities, equipment, or even products, it is the information a company has and how it uses it that defines organization success—some would say even organization survival.[10] Top managers look for ways to manage, lever, and protect what is rapidly becoming the most valuable asset of any organization: information and knowledge.

Purpose of This Chapter

IT is an essential component of successful organizations. Managers spend a significant majority of their time actively exchanging information. They need this information to hold the organization together. For example, the vertical and horizontal information linkages described in Chapter 3 are designed to provide managers with relevant information for decision making, evaluation, and control. This chapter examines the evolution of IT. The chapter begins by looking at IT systems applied to organizational operations and then examines how IT is used for decision making and control of the organization. The next sections consider how IT can add strategic value through the use of internal coordination applications such as intranets, enterprise resource planning, and knowledge management systems, as well as applications for external collaboration, such as extranets, customer-relationship management systems, e-business, and the integrated enterprise. The final section of the chapter presents an overview of how IT affects interorganizational relationships and organizational design.

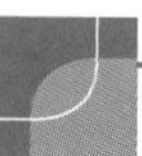

Information Technology Evolution

The evolution of IT is illustrated in Exhibit 8.1. First-line management is typically concerned with well-defined problems about operational issues and past events. Top management, by contrast, deals mostly with uncertain, ambiguous issues, such as strategy and planning. As the complexity of computer-based IT systems has increased, applications have grown to support effective top management control and decision making about complex and uncertain problems.

Initially, IT systems in organizations were applied to operations. These initial applications were based on the notion of machine-room efficiency—that is, current operations could be performed more efficiently with the use of computer technology. The goal was to reduce labour costs by having computers take over some tasks. These systems became known as **transaction processing systems** (TPS), which automate the

EXHIBIT 8.1
Evolution of Organizational Applications of IT

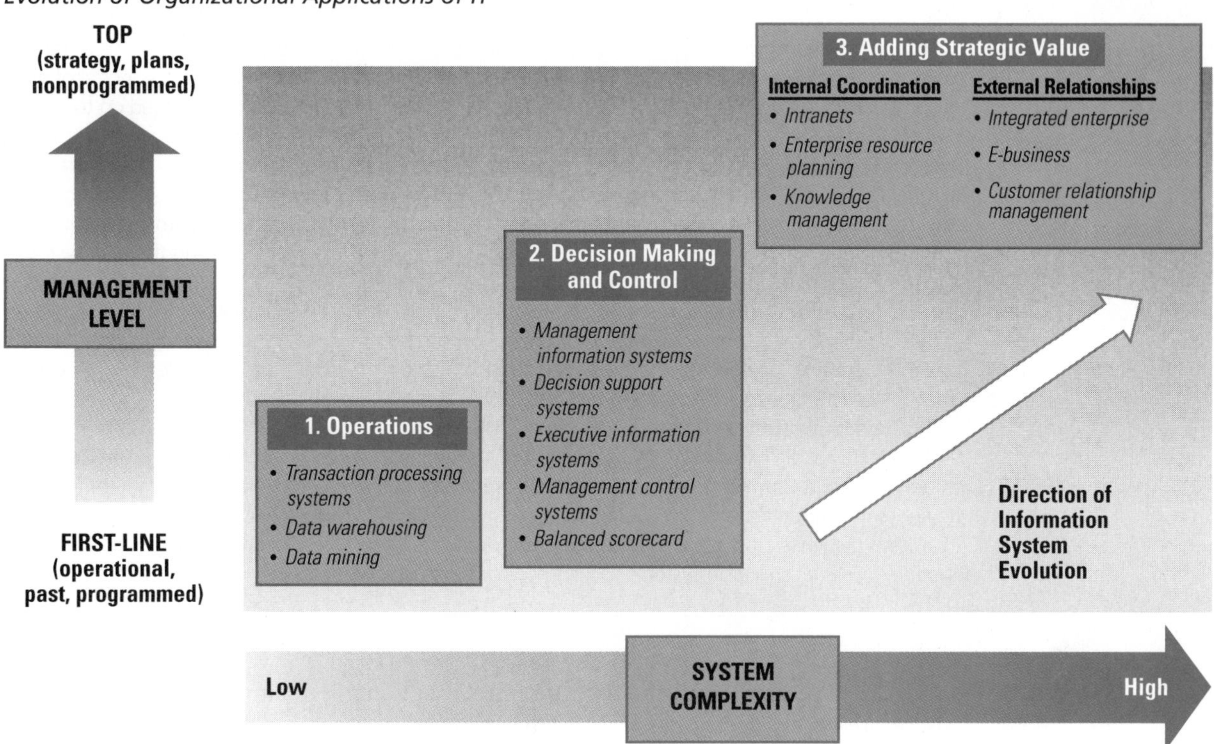

organization's routine, day-to-day business transactions. A TPS collects data from transactions such as sales, purchases from suppliers, and inventory changes, and stores them in a database. For example, at Enterprise Rent-a-Car, a computerized system keeps track of the 1.4 million transactions the company logs every hour. The system can provide front-line employees with up-to-the-minute information on car availability and other data, enabling them to provide exceptional customer service.[11]

In recent years, the use of data warehousing and business intelligence software has expanded the usefulness of these accumulated data. **Data warehousing** is the use of huge databases that combine all of an organization's data to allow users to access the data directly, create reports, and obtain responses to what-if questions. Building a database at large organizations is a huge undertaking that includes defining hundreds of gigabytes of data from many existing systems, providing a means of continually updating the data, making it all compatible, and linking it to other software that makes it possible for users to search and analyze the data and produce helpful reports. Software for business intelligence helps users make sense of all these data. **Business intelligence** refers to the high-tech analysis of a company's data in order to make better strategic decisions.[12] Sometimes referred to as **data mining**, business intelligence means searching out and analyzing data from multiple sources across the enterprise, and sometimes from outside sources as well, to identify patterns and relationships that might be significant.

Organizations spent $4 billion on business intelligence software in 2003, and the amount was expected to double by 2006.[13] Consider how Brampton Civic Hospital is planning to use its data warehousing capabilities.

In Practice
Brampton Civic Hospital (BCH)

BCH, a 479-bed hospital, opened in late 2007 and implemented some of the most advanced information technologies as part of its $500 million redesign. BCH has been heralded as a model of electronic health, known as e-health. There are no paper records—all information is logged on to a computer. The hospital is entirely wireless—computerized monitors record patients' vital signs and treatment information that can then be accessed through hand-held devices. Prescriptions are filled by drug robot called PillPick.[14] According to BCH's chief information officer, Judy Middleton, "[all] the technology installed has benefits realization factored into our approach, both qualitative and quantitative."[15] BCH will assess its operational efficiency every three months, using the new systems' built-in performance measurement capabilities.

Inside the front lobby of the large hospital, patients will check themselves in by swiping their health cards. Their information will be displayed on a screen and maps will direct patients further. Then the patients will go the Fast Lane Registrar to pick up their bar-coded bracelets. BCH believes that the self-service check-in system will reduce wait times and will increase safety.

BCH is implementing CareSuite, a system designed to track emergency room patients throughout their stay at the hospital. "We'll always know where everybody is all the time."[16] The CareSuite system will also help with triage. As well, the hospital will use a fingerprint biometric system for identifying and authenticating all hospital staff and health care providers. For example, the automated medicine dispensers, located throughout the hospital, can be opened only through the biometric system. BCH's information systems focus, therefore, on not only efficiency but also patient safety.

BCH expects that all the data it collects will enable managers to make smarter and more timely decisions. Thus, IT has evolved to more complex systems for managerial decision making and control of the organization, the second stage illustrated in Exhibit 8.1. Further advancements have led to the use of IT to add strategic value, the highest level of application. The remainder of this chapter will focus on these two stages in the evolution of IT.

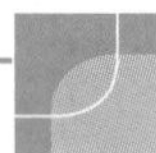

Information for Decision Making and Control

Through the application of more sophisticated computer-based systems, managers have tools to improve the performance of departments and the organization as a whole. These applications use information stored in corporate databases to help managers control the organization and make important decisions. Exhibit 8.2 illustrates the various elements of information systems used for decision making and control. Management information systems—including information reporting systems, decision support systems, and executive information systems—facilitate rapid and effective decision making. Feedback control systems include management control systems and a procedure known as the balanced scorecard. In an organization, these systems are interconnected, as illustrated by the dashed lines in Exhibit 8.2. The systems for decision making and control often share the same basic data, but the data and reports are designed and used for a primary purpose of decision making versus control.

Organizational Decision-Making Systems

A **management information system** (MIS) is a computer-based system that provides information and support for managerial decision making. The MIS is supported by

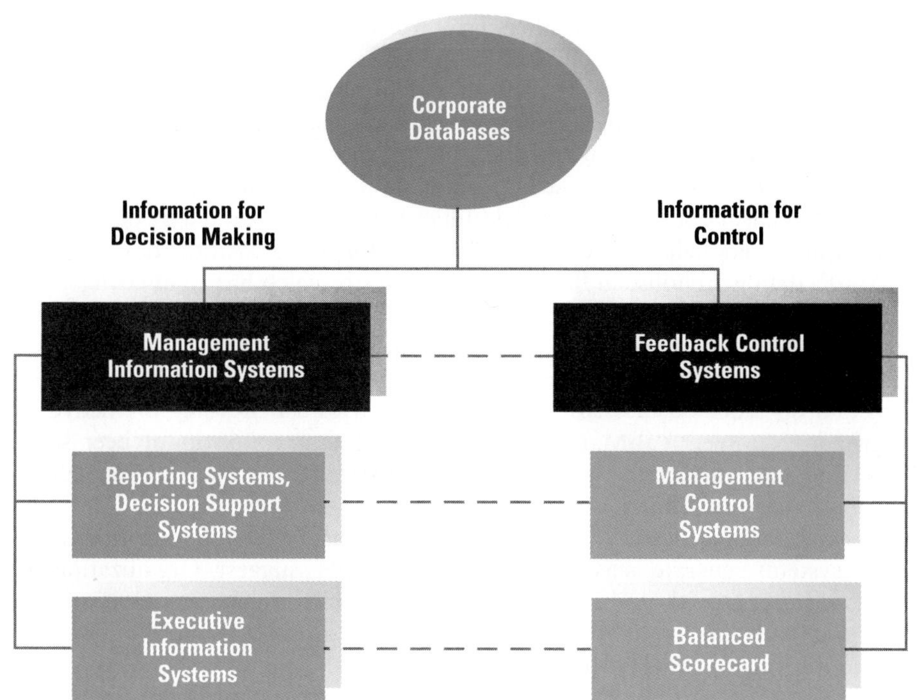

EXHIBIT 8.2
Information Systems for Managerial Control and Decision Making

the organization's transaction processing systems and by organizational and external databases. The **information reporting system**, the most common form of MIS, provides mid-level managers with reports that summarize data and support day-to-day decision making. For example, when managers need to make decisions about production scheduling, they can review the data on the anticipated number of orders within the next month, inventory levels, and availability of human resources.

Canadian National (CN) piloted SmartYard, an information system at its MacMillan Yard, CN's largest freight-car classification yard north of Toronto. The system takes data from various CN systems, combines the data and then models the best sequence for cars in the yard's inventory. According to CN's assistant vice president, Network Optimization, Mack Barker, the SmartYard system is not just about technology, "[it's] about orchestrated process management."[17] He comments further that "SmartYard produced a six-hour reduction in the average time a train is in MacMillan Yard, and produced [a] 300 percent improvement in a train's dwell time in the receiving track."[18]

An **executive information system** (EIS) is a higher-level application that facilitates decision making at the highest levels of management. These systems are typically based on software that can convert large amounts of complex data into pertinent information and provide that information to top managers in a timely fashion. A **decision support system** (DSS) provides specific benefits to managers at all levels of the organization. These interactive, computer-based systems rely on decision models and integrated databases. Using decision support software, users can pose a series of what-if questions to test possible alternatives. Based on assumptions used in the software or specified by the user, managers can explore various alternatives and receive information to help them choose the alternative that will likely have the best

PDA Remember...

Improve the performance of the organization by using IT for better decision making. Implement management information systems, decision support systems, and information reporting systems to provide lower- and middle-level managers with reports and information that support day-to-day decision making. Use executive information systems to facilitate better decision making at the highest levels of the organization.

outcome. For example, Longo Brothers Fruit Markets designed a system called Market PO Application to enable Joey and Mike Longo, the company's owners, to transmit data to their stores about what they buy daily at the Ontario Food Terminal.[19]

Wal-Mart uses an EIS and a DSS that rely on a massive database to make decisions about what to stock, how to price and promote, and when to reorder. Information about what products are selling and what items are often purchased together is obtained at checkout scanners. Wireless handheld units operated by clerks and department managers help keep close tabs on inventory levels. All the data are sent to Wal-Mart's data warehouse in Bentonville, Arkansas, which has an amazing 460 terabytes of data, according to company representatives. (A terabyte is equivalent to equal to 1,000 gigabytes or 10^{12}, i.e., 1,000,000,000,000 bytes.)[20] Wal-Mart uses its mountain of data to push for greater efficiency at all levels, as well as to forecast trends and do more business. By analyzing data with a DSS using predictive technology, for example, Wal-Mart managers learned that six-packs of beer sell out quickly and sales of strawberry Pop-Tarts zoom seven times their normal sales rate in the days ahead of a hurricane.[21]

However, organizations need to be careful to ensure that the information that their IT systems generate is as useful as these examples suggest. Organizations now face exponential growth in the volume of information they generate. One study estimates that each person in the world, on average, produces 800 megabytes of recorded information each year. It would take about 10 metres of books to store the 800 megabytes on paper![22] As a result, more and more organizations are adopting some form of archiving technology; 36 percent of organizations in Canada had archiving systems in 2007, and 18 percent reported that they would implement a system in 2008.[23] Exhibit 8.3 highlights one of the pitfalls of having the wrong kind of IT systems!

EXHIBIT 8.3
Information Technology versus Information

"We have lots of information technology. We just don't have any information."

Feedback Control Model

Another primary use of information in organizations is for control. Effective control systems involve the use of feedback to determine whether organizational performance meets established standards to help the organization attain its goals. Managers set up systems for organizational control that consist of the four key steps in the **feedback control model.** The cycle of control includes setting strategic goals for departments or the organization as a whole, establishing metrics and standards of performance, comparing metrics of actual performance to standards, and correcting or changing activities as needed. Feedback control helps managers make needed adjustments in work activities, standards of performance, or goals to help the organization be successful. For example, by evaluating sales performance, customer ratings, and other feedback, managers at McDonald's saw a need to adjust the fast-food chain's menu to include healthier options such as salads, a choice of apple slices and milk instead of fries and soft drinks in Happy Meals, and all-white-meat Chicken McNuggets.[24] In the following sections, we will discuss two commonly used methods that operate as feedback control systems: management control systems and the balanced scorecard.

PDA
Remember...

Devise control systems that consist of the four essential steps of the feedback control model: set goals, establish standards of performance, measure actual performance and compare to standards, and correct or change activities as needed.

Management Control Systems

Management control systems are broadly defined as the formal routines, reports, and procedures that use information to maintain or alter patterns in organization activities.[25] These control systems include the formalized information-based activities for planning, budgeting, performance evaluation, resource allocation, and employee rewards. Targets are set in advance, outcomes compared to targets, and variance reported to managers for corrective action. Advances in IT have dramatically improved the efficiency and effectiveness of these systems. For example, many organizations use *executive dashboards*, which enable managers to see at a glance key control indicators such as sales in relation to targets, number of products on back-order, or percentage of customer service calls resolved within a specified time period.[26] Dashboard systems coordinate, organize, and display the metrics that managers consider most important to monitor on a regular basis, with software automatically updating the figures. For example, the Trillium Health Centre, one of Canada's largest community hospitals serving more than one million patients, designed and redesigned its dashboard system. Its system, called THINK (or Transforming Healthcare into Integrated Networks of Knowledge), aims to simplify information access and exchange.[27] Trillium Health Centre also uses the balanced scorecard approach, which is described later in the chapter.

Exhibit 8.4 lists four control system elements that are often considered the core of management control systems: the budget and financial reports; statistical reports; reward systems; and quality-control systems.[28]

The *budget* is typically used to set targets for the organization's expenditures for the year and then report actual costs on a monthly or quarterly basis. As a means of control, budgets report actual as well as planned expenditures for cash, assets, raw materials, salaries, and other resources so that managers can take action to correct variances. Sometimes the variance between budgeted and actual amounts for each line item is listed as a part of the budget. Managers also rely on a variety of other financial reports. The *balance sheet* shows a firm's financial position with respect to assets and liabilities at a specific point in time. An *income statement*, sometimes called a

EXHIBIT 8.4
Management Control Systems

Subsystem	Content and Frequency
Budget, financial reports	Financial, resource expenditures, profit and loss; monthly, usually computer-based
Statistical reports	Nonfinancial outputs; weekly or monthly, usually computer-based
Reward systems	Evaluation of managers based on department goals and performance, set rewards; yearly
Quality-control systems	Participation, benchmarking guidelines, Six Sigma goals; continuous

Source: Based on Richard L. Daft and Norman B. Macintosh, "The Nature and Use of Formal Control Systems for Management Control and Strategy Implementation," *Journal of Management* 10 (1984): 43–66.

profit and loss statement (P&L), summarizes the company's financial performance for a given time interval, such as for the week, month, or year. This statement shows revenues coming into the organization from all sources and subtracts all expenses, such as cost of goods sold, interest, taxes, and depreciation. The *bottom line* indicates the net income—profit or loss—for the given time period.

Managers use periodic statistical reports to evaluate and monitor nonfinancial performance, such as customer satisfaction, employee performance, or rate of staff turnover. For e-commerce organizations, important measurements of nonfinancial performance include metrics such as *stickiness* (how much attention a site gets over time), the *conversion rate*, the ratio of buyers to site visitors, and *site performance data*, such as how long it takes to load a page or how long it takes to place an order.[29] E-commerce managers regularly review reports on conversion rates, customer dropoff, and other metrics to identify problems and improve their business. For all organizations, nonfinancial reports typically are computer based and may be available daily, weekly, or monthly. The online auction company eBay provides a good illustration of using both financial and nonfinancial statistical reports for feedback control.

In Practice
eBay

Meg Whitman, CEO of eBay, has a guiding mantra: "If you can't measure it, you can't control it." Whitman runs a company that is obsessed with performance measurement. She personally monitors performance metrics such as number of site visitors, percentage of new users, and time spent on the site, as well as profit and loss statements and the ratio of eBay's revenues to the value of goods traded. Managers throughout the company also monitor performance regularly. Category managers, for example, have clear standards of performance for their auction categories (such as sports memorabilia, jewellery and watches, health and beauty, etc.). They continuously measure, tweak, and promote their categories to meet or outperform their targets.

Whitman believes that getting a firm grip on performance measurement is essential for a company to know where to spend money, where to assign more personnel, and which projects to promote or abandon. The more statistics available, the more early warnings managers have about problems and opportunities. But performance isn't just about numbers at eBay. Measuring customer (user) satisfaction requires a mix of methods, such as surveys, monitoring eBay discussion boards, and personal contact with customers at regular live conferences.

By defining standards and effectively using financial and statistical reports, eBay managers can identify trouble spots and move quickly to take corrective action when and where it is needed.[30]

In addition to performance measurement, eBay also effectively uses the other control system elements listed in Exhibit 8.4—reward systems and quality-control systems. Reward systems offer incentives for managers and employees to improve performance and meet departmental goals. Managers and employees evaluate how well previous goals were met, set new goals, and establish rewards for meeting the new targets. Rewards are often tied to the annual performance appraisal process, during which managers assess employee performance and provide feedback to help the employee improve performance and obtain rewards.

The final control element listed in Exhibit 8.4 is quality-control systems, which managers use to train employees in quality-control methods, set targets for employee participation, establish benchmarking guidelines, and assign and measure Six Sigma goals. For example, at eBay, Whitman uses benchmarking to measure how the company's website performs compared to its peers. She found eBay's site weak in the area of adding new features, so managers have taken action to improve the site's performance in that area. The first end-of-chapter case details the particular performance challenges eBay Canada faced in implementing a site for its Québec market. **Benchmarking** means the process of continually measuring products, services, and practices against tough competitors or other organizations recognized as industry leaders.[31] **Six Sigma**, originally conceived by Motorola, is a highly ambitious quality standard that specifies a goal of no more than 3.4 defects per million parts.[32]

However, Six Sigma has deviated from its precise definition to become a generic term for a whole set of control procedures that emphasize a relentless pursuit of higher quality and lower costs. The discipline is based on a methodology referred to as DMAIC (Define, Measure, Analyze, Improve, and Control, pronounced *de-MAY-ick*, for short), which provides a structured way for organizations to approach and solve problems.[33] Organizations such as Air Canada, Ontario Lottery and Gaming Corporation, Rogers Communications, Dow Chemical, and 3M have saved millions of dollars by rooting out inefficiencies and waste through Six Sigma processes.[34]

PDA

Remember...

Establish management control systems that use budgets and financial reports, statistical reports, reward systems, and quality-control systems. Use a balanced scorecard to integrate various control dimensions and get a more complete picture of organizational performance. Select indicators in the areas of financial performance, customer service, internal processes, and learning and growth.

One finding from research into management control systems is that each of the four control systems focuses on a different aspect of the production process. These four systems thus form an overall management control system that provides middle managers with control information about resource inputs, process efficiency, and outputs.[35] Moreover, the use of and reliance on control systems depends on the strategic targets set by top management.

The budget is used primarily to allocate resource inputs. Managers use the budget for planning the future and reducing uncertainty about the availability of human and material resources needed to perform department tasks. Computer-based statistical reports are used to control outputs. These reports contain data about output volume and quality and other indicators that provide feedback to middle management about departmental results. The reward system and quality-control systems are directed at the production process. Quality-control systems specify standards for employee participation, teamwork, and problem solving. Reward systems provide incentives to meet goals and can help guide and correct employee behaviour. Managers also use direct supervision to keep departmental work activities within desired limits.

The Balanced Scorecard

In the past, most organizations relied largely on financial accounting measures as the primary basis for measuring organizational performance, but today, they realize that a balanced view of both financial and operational measures is needed for successful organizational control.

The four control elements listed in Exhibit 8.4 help provide managers with a balanced view. In addition, a recent innovation is to integrate internal financial measurements and statistical reports with a concern for markets and customers as well as employees. The **balanced scorecard** is a comprehensive management control system that balances traditional financial measures with operational measures relating to an organization's critical success factors.[36] A balanced scorecard contains four major perspectives, as illustrated in Exhibit 8.5: financial performance, customer service indicators, internal business process indicators, and the organization's potential for learning and growth.[37] Within these four areas, managers identify key performance indicators the organization will track. The *financial performance* reflects a concern that the organization's activities contribute to improving short- and long-term financial performance. It includes traditional measures such as net income and return on investment. *Customer service indicators* measure such things as how customers view the organization, as well as customer retention and satisfaction. *Internal business process indicators* focus on production and operating statistics, such as order fulfillment or cost per order. The final component looks at the organization's *potential for learning and growth*, focusing on how well resources and human capital are being managed for the company's future. Measurements include such things as employee retention, business process improvements, and the introduction of new products. The components of the scorecard are designed in an integrative manner so that they reinforce one another and link short-term actions with long-term strategic goals, as illustrated in Exhibit 8.5. Managers can use the scorecard to set goals, allocate resources, plan budgets, and determine rewards.[38]

The balanced scorecard helps managers focus on the key strategic measures that define the success of a particular organization over time and communicate them clearly throughout the organization. The scorecard has become the core management control system for many organizations today, including Hilton Hotels, Bell Emergis (a division of Bell Canada), and British Airways. British Airways clearly ties its use of the balanced scorecard to the feedback control model. Scorecards serve as the agenda for monthly management meetings, where managers evaluate performance, discuss what corrective actions need to be taken, and set new targets for the various elements.[39] EISs facilitate use of the balanced scorecard by enabling top managers to easily track measurements in multiple areas, rapidly analyze the data, and convert huge amounts of data into clear information reports. The scorecard is not necessarily the best for all situations, and small organizations seem to have been less effective in implementing a balanced-scorecard approach. One study, for example, found that, although many small manufacturing firms measure a wide variety of nonfinancial factors, most did not integrate the data with other performance measures, a key feature of the balanced scorecard.[40]

EXHIBIT 8.5
Major Perspectives of the Balanced Scorecard

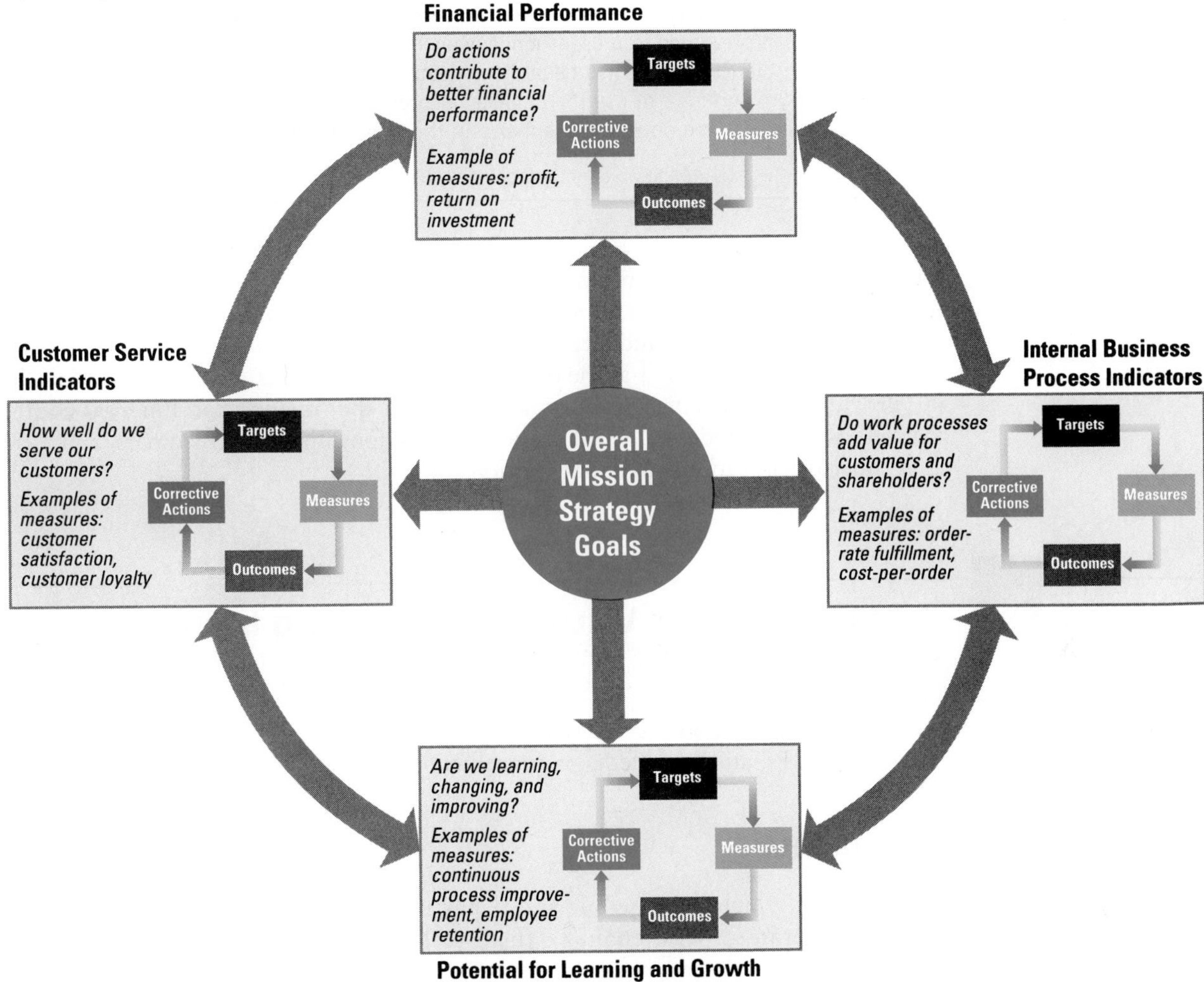

Source: Based on Robert S. Kaplan and David P. Norton, "Using the Balanced Scorecard as a Strategic Management System," *Harvard Business Review* (January–February 1996), 75–85; Chee W. Chow, Kamal M. Haddad, and James E. Williamson, "Applying the Balanced Scorecard to Small Companies," *Management Accounting* 79, no. 2 (August 1997): 21–27; and Cathy Lazere, "All Together Now," CFO (February 1998), 28–36.

In Practice
Ontario Hospital Association (OHA)

In the late 1990s, the OHA evaluated 89 hospitals using the balance-scorecard approach. According to Sandra Conley of the OHA, "[it] was certainly one of the largest Balanced Scorecard efforts ever in North America, in terms of its scope, that has ever been made public."[41] The OHA sent a patient survey to 55,000 people who had received acute care at one of its member hospitals. More than 26,000 patients responded. The scorecard evaluations focused on four areas: (1) how well staff handled acute patient care needs such as responding to heart attacks, strokes, and pneumonia; (2) financial conditions and performance of the hospital (metrics included such factors such as liquidity, human resources, and amount of patient care performed for total staff hours); (3) patient satisfaction, and (4) how the hospital was investing in the future. Of the 81 hospitals for which the OHA was able to collect data, 61 were rated as average, 11 were rated as above average, and the remaining nine were rated as below average.

One of the problems with the process and outcome of the OHA's balanced scorecard was that findings were not presented in a user-friendly way. However, Conley maintains that " . . . [our] research shows that the public has been craving this type of publicly available information."[42] The OHA plans to continue to use the balanced-scorecard approach to collect data from other types of patients with the objective of enhancing the effectiveness and efficiency of its member hospitals.

Following the use of information systems for managerial decision making and control, IT has evolved further as a strategic tool for organizations such as Wal-Mart, Harrah's Entertainment, and General Electric. This is the highest level of application, as illustrated in Exhibit 8.1 at the beginning of the chapter. IT can add strategic value by providing better data and information within the organization (internal coordination) as well as redefining and supporting relationships with customers, suppliers, and other organizations (external relationships).

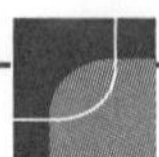

Adding Strategic Value: Strengthening Internal Coordination

Three primary IT tools for internal coordination are intranets, enterprise resource planning (ERP), and knowledge-management systems.

Intranets

Networking, which links people and departments within a particular building or across corporate offices, enabling them to share information and cooperate on projects, has become an important strategic tool for many companies. Networks may take many forms, but the fastest-growing form of corporate networking is the **intranet**, a private, organization-wide information system that uses the communications protocols and standards of the Internet and the World Wide Web but is accessible only to people within the organization. To view files and information, users simply navigate the site with a standard web browser, clicking on links.[43] Because intranets are web-based, they can be accessed from any type of computer or workstation.

Today, most organization with intranets have moved their MISs, EISs, and so forth over to the intranet so they are accessible to anyone who needs them. In addition, having these systems as part of the intranet means new features and applications can easily be added and accessed through a standard browser.

Intranets can improve internal communications and unlock hidden information. They enable employees to keep in touch with what's going on around the organization, quickly and easily find information they need, share ideas, and work on projects collaboratively. The most advanced intranets, such as those at Ford Motor Company, Nike, and Weyerhaeuser, are linked into the proprietary systems that govern a company's business functions. Ford's global intranet connects more than

100,000 workstations to thousands of sites offering proprietary information such as market research, analyses of competitors' components, and product development.[44] The National Research Council of Canada's Industrial Research Assistance Program (NRC-IRAP) has an intranet that has been recognized for its usability.[45] NRC-IRAP's mandate is to stimulate wealth creation for Canada through technological innovation by providing technology assistance to small and medium-sized organizations at all stages of the innovation process, to build their innovation capacity. One of NRC-IRAP's many successful clients, Winnipeg-based ClearOption Technologies, designed a custom intranet file system that has morphed into a shared virtual office system, complete with secure online storage and file manipulation. The system, named DataVault, has been gaining market share in Manitoba and beyond.[46]

Enterprise Resource Planning

Another recent approach to information management helps pull together various types of information to see how decisions and actions in one part of the organization affect other parts of the firm. A growing number of companies are setting up broad-scale information systems that take a comprehensive view of the organization's activities. These **enterprise resource planning** (ERP) systems collect, process, and provide information about a company's entire enterprise, including order processing, product design, purchasing, inventory, manufacturing, distribution, human resources, receipt of payments, and forecasting of future demand.[47] An ERP system can serve as the backbone for an entire organization by integrating and optimizing all the various business processes across the entire firm.[48] To illustrate, when a salesperson takes an order, the ERP system checks to see how the order affects inventory levels, scheduling, HR, purchasing, and distribution. The system replicates organizational processes in software, guides employees through the processes step by step, and automates as many of them as possible. ERP software can automatically cut an accounts payable cheque as soon as a clerk confirms that goods have been received in inventory, send an online purchase order immediately after a manager has authorized a purchase, or schedule production at the most appropriate plant after an order is received.[49]

In addition, because the system integrates data about all aspects of operations, managers and employees at all levels can see how decisions and actions in one part of the organization affect other parts, using this information to make better decisions. ERP can provide the kind of information furnished by transaction processing systems, as well as that provided by information reporting systems, DSSs, or EISs. The key is that ERP weaves all of these systems together so people can see the big picture and act quickly, helping the organization be smarter and more effective. Médecins du Monde, an international aid organization, uses an ERP system to keep precise track of expenses, supplies, and needs to enable doctors and volunteers in the field to see what resources are available and where they're most urgently needed.[50]

Knowledge Management

A primary goal for IT systems today is to support efforts to manage and leverage organizational knowledge. Increasingly, intellectual capital is the primary way in which businesses measure their value.[51] Therefore, managers see knowledge as an important resource to manage, just as they manage cash flow, raw materials, or other resources. A survey of CEOs attending the World Economic Forum's annual meeting found that 97 percent of senior executives see knowledge management as a critical issue for their organizations.[52] To learn and change, organizations must effectively acquire, create, and transfer knowledge across the organization and modify their activities to reflect new knowledge and insight.[53] Organizations as diverse as Hewlett-Packard, the World Health Organization, the World Bank, Case Corporation and CIDA (Canadian International Development Agency), to name a few, use some sort of knowledge management system to capture and to share their employees' knowledge.[54]

Knowledge management is a new way to think about organizing and sharing an organization's intellectual and creative resources. It refers to the efforts to systematically find, organize, and make available a company's intellectual capital and to foster a culture of continuous learning and knowledge sharing so that organizational activities build on what is already known.[55] The company's **intellectual capital** is the sum of its knowledge, experience, understanding, relationships, processes, innovations, and discoveries. Although most of an organization's knowledge is within the formal boundaries of the organization, tapping into the knowledge of outside experts is also important because it brings new knowledge into the organization that can be combined with existing knowledge to highlight problems or opportunities and make the organization more competitive.[56] More and more organizations are recognizing the value of knowledge management; 25 percent of Fortune 500 companies, for example, now have chief knowledge officers. However, many Canadian firms have not made knowledge management a priority. According to Nick Bontis, director of the Institute for Intellectual Capital Research at McMaster University, "[by] 2010, the world's accumulated information base will double every 11 hours. . . . We're going to be bombarded. So you have to come up with skills and tools to protect your company."[57] On the other hand, some practitioners are questioning the value of knowledge management systems. In a recent posting on http://www.communicatorsnetwork.com, one blogger commented that "[knowledge management] was a theory . . . supported by dysfunctional technology, while social computing is increasingly functional technology without any clear theory or way of looking at the world."[58]

A variety of new software tools for social computing supports collaboration and knowledge sharing through services such as web conferencing, knowledge portals, content management, and the use of wikis, a web 2.0 collaboration tool. The word *wiki* comes from the Hawaiian word *wikiwiki* which means *quick*.[59] **Wikis** are an extension of the concept of blogs (web logs); rather than simply allowing an individual to broadcast his or her views to an online audience, as blogs do, wikis let people edit and add content to the running log.[60] "Working together on [a wiki] is like being in the same room together using a whiteboard."[61] A 2006 Jupiter Research survey of companies with at least $50 million in revenues found that 30 percent of executives report that their organizations are using wikis and 40 percent are using RSS (Really Simple Syndication) feeds.[62] Calgary-based Black & McDonald, a construction and maintenance contractor, for example, uses its wiki primarily to store knowledge such as safety information that is needed by more than one person. According to Vice President Tom Wilkinson, "what would have taken an hour to find before takes 20 seconds now."[63] As well, it took Black & McDonald's technology team less than two hours to set up the wiki. As discussed in the chapter's Book Mark, new social computing processes are transforming how we create and share knowledge in and beyond organizations.

Book Mark 8.0 (HAVE YOU READ THIS BOOK?)

Wikinomics: How Mass Collaboration Changes Everything
By Don Tapscott and Anthony D. Williams

Don Tapscott is an internationally acclaimed guru on the digital economy; he is chief executive of New Paradigm, a technology and business think tank, and the author of 11 books including *Paradigm Shift, The Digital Economy,* and *Growing Up Digital*. Wikinomics is his most recent book and it was nominated in 2007 as one of six finalists for the prestigious Financial Times and Goldman Sachs Business Book of the Year Award. Anthony Williams is vice president and executive editor at nGenera Insight where he leads a global investigation into the impact of web 2.0 and wikinomics on the future of government and democracy.[64]

The authors argue that "[smart] companies are encouraging, rather than fighting, the heaving growth of massive online communities—many of which emerged from the fringes of the Web . . . "[65] They provide many fascinating examples of peer production. Rob McEwen, CEO of Goldcorp, had an epiphany and decided to open source all the firm's geological data and share it globally. Mining is an extremely secretive industry and geological data are closely guarded. McEwen's epiphany was not well received even by his own geologists! In March 2000, McEwen created the Goldcorp Challenge—the company provided $575,000 in prize money for participants who provided the best estimates and methods for finding gold in Red Lake Mine in Northern Ontario. All the information that Goldcorp had about the mining site was posted on the company's website. The response was quick and considerable; all sorts of virtual prospectors—from geologists to graduate students to mathematicians to military officers—identified 100 targets at the mine site, half of which had not been previously identified. McEwen's contest "[not] only . . . [yielded] copious quantities of gold, it catapulted his underperforming $100 million company into a $9 billion juggernaut . . . "[66]

In their penultimate chapter, the authors describe eight wikinomic design principles. They are (1) take your cue from your lead users as Flickr has done; (2) build critical mass as the co-developers of Linux have done; (3) supply an infrastructure for collaboration to support innovation; (4) take the time necessary to get the correct structures and governance processes; (5) ensure all participants can get some sort of benefit from the collaboration; (6) abide by the written and unwritten rules of the wiki community; (7) let the process evolve; and (8) develop a more collaborative, i.e., less controlling, mindset. Their last chapter, entitled "The Wikinomics Playbook," has only one sentence: "Join us in peer producing the definitive guide to twenty-first-century strategy at www.wikinomics.com."[67]

Wikinomics: How Mass Collaboration Changes Everything, by Don Tapscott and Anthony D. Williams, is published by the Penguin Group.

What Is Knowledge? Knowledge is not the same thing as data or information, although it uses both. **Data** are simple, absolute facts and figures that, in and of themselves, may be of little use. A company might have data that show 30 percent of a particular product is sold to customers in Prince Edward Island (PEI). To be useful to the organization, the data are processed into finished *information* by connecting them with other data—for example, nine out of ten of the products sold in PEI are bought by people over the age of 60. **Information** is data that have been linked with other data and converted into a useful context for specific use. Knowledge goes a step further; it is a conclusion drawn from the information after it is linked to other information and compared to what is already known. Knowledge, as opposed to information and data, always has a human factor. Books can contain information, but the information becomes knowledge only when a person absorbs it and puts it to use.[68]

PDA
Remember...

Improve internal coordination, integration, and information sharing with intranets, ERP systems, and knowledge management systems. Use ERP systems to integrate and optimize business processes across the entire firm.

Organizations deal with both explicit knowledge and implicit, or tacit, knowledge.[69] **Explicit knowledge** is formal, systematic knowledge that can be codified, written down, and passed on to others in documents or general instructions. Tacit knowledge, on the other hand, is often difficult to put into words. **Tacit knowledge** is based on personal experience, rules of thumb, intuition, and judgment. It includes professional know-how and expertise, individual insight and experience, and creative solutions that are difficult to communicate and pass on to others. Explicit knowledge may be equated with *knowing about*; tacit knowledge is equated with *knowing how*.[70]

Finding ways to transfer both explicit and tacit knowledge—the knowing about and the knowing how—across the organization is critical.[71] Although explicit knowledge can easily be captured and shared in documents and through IT systems, as much as 80 percent of an organization's valuable knowledge may be tacit knowledge that is not easily captured and transferred.[72]

Approaches to Knowledge Management. Two distinct approaches to knowledge management are outlined in Exhibit 8.6. The first approach outlined in Exhibit 8.6 deals primarily with the collection and sharing of explicit knowledge, largely through the use of sophisticated IT systems.[73] Explicit knowledge may include intellectual properties such as patents and licences; work processes such as policies and procedures; specific information on customers, markets, suppliers, or competitors; competitive intelligence reports; benchmark data; and so forth. When an organization uses this approach, the focus is on collecting and codifying knowledge and storing it in databases where it can easily be accessed and reused by anyone in the organization. With this "people-to-documents" approach, knowledge is gathered from the individuals who possess it and is organized into documents that others can access and reuse. When Environment Canada faced delays in finding internal expertise, it created a knowledge management system that had a simple search/browse function so that its staff could get timely information.[74]

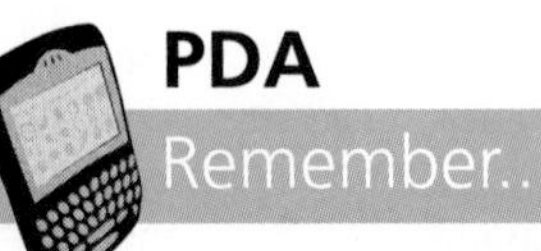

Establish systems to facilitate both explicit and tacit knowledge sharing to help the organization learn and improve.

EXHIBIT 8.6
Two Approaches to Knowledge Management

Explicit		Tacit
Provide high-quality, reliable, and fast information systems for access of codified, reusable knowledge		Channel individual expertise to provide creative advice on strategic problems
People-to-documents approach *Develop an electronic document system that codifies, stores, disseminates, and allows reuse of knowledge*	**Knowledge Management Strategy**	**Person-to-person approach** *Develop networks for linking people so that tacit knowledge can be shared*
Invest heavily in information technology, with a goal of connecting people with reusable, codified knowledge	**Information Technology Approach**	*Invest moderately in information technology, with a goal of facilitating conversations and the personal exchange of tacit knowledge*

Source: Based on Morten T. Hansen, Nitin Nohria, and Thomas Tierney, "What's Your Strategy for Managing Knowledge?" *Harvard Business Review* (March–April 1999), 106–116.

Although IT plays an important role in knowledge management by enabling the storage and dissemination of data and information across the organization, IT is only one piece of a larger puzzle.[75] A complete knowledge management system includes not only processes for capturing and storing knowledge and organizing it for easy access, but also ways to generate new knowledge through learning and to share knowledge throughout the organization.

The second approach focuses on levering individual expertise and know-how—tacit knowledge—by connecting people face-to-face or through interactive media. Tacit knowledge includes professional know-how, individual insights and creativity, and personal experience and intuition. With this approach, managers concentrate on developing personal networks that link people for the sharing of tacit knowledge. The organization uses IT systems primarily for facilitating conversation and person-to-person sharing of experience, insight, and ideas. For example, intranets are important for helping employees, especially those who are geographically dispersed, share ideas and tap into expert knowledge throughout the organization.

Organizations typically combine several methods and technologies to facilitate the sharing and transfer of both explicit and tacit knowledge. Consider the example of Montgomery-Watson Harza (MWH), one of the world's leading experts on power, water, and wastewater issues.

In Practice

Montgomery-Watson Harza (MWH)

Headquartered in Broomfield, Colorado, MWH is a private, employee-owned firm with approximately 6,000 employees worldwide. MWH designs, builds, finances, and manages some of the largest and most technologically advanced water distribution, drainage, flood control, wastewater treatment, water remediation, and power plant projects in the world. Recent projects, for example, include a $700 million contract for treating wastewater from an Intel facility in China and a complex project with the New Zealand Department of Conservation to solve sewerage problems in Abel Tasman National Park.

Innovation is an MWH hallmark, and it isn't limited to serving clients. The firm has implemented sophisticated collaborative systems that enable project teams to share knowledge and manage client work more effectively, giving MWH a competitive edge. Consider the work of design teams, which once had to meet face to face on site for development, design, and project management work. On average, teams spent three weeks researching a project proposal by searching out documents in various MWH libraries. Getting feedback and comments took more time, and design changes often occurred at the last minute. Project designs typically took months to complete.

Now teams can access a database that enables them to find out how other projects have handled specific issues and done things better, more efficiently, faster, or more safely (explicit knowledge). In addition, team members can share information and tacit knowledge online and tap into the expertise of anyone who might be able to facilitate or strengthen the project.

The use of knowledge management systems has shortened the design-to-delivery cycle, improved the quality of designs, and increased efficiency for MWH projects.[76] In 2003, MWH won the annual DM Review 2003 World Class Solutions Award competition for its implementation of MWH's KnowledgeNet/KNet project. "MWH vied for top honours in the Knowledge Management category against over one hundred submittals from global companies including fellow finalists, Ford Motor Company and Factiva. Each applicant submitted comprehensive project summaries and participated in one-on-one interviews with judges explaining program philosophy and system capabilities. According to the judges, the KnowledgeNet/KNet project [represents] world-class excellence and innovation."[77]

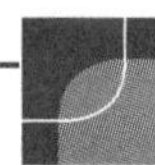

Adding Strategic Value: Strengthening External Relationships

External applications of IT for strengthening relationships with customers, suppliers, and partners include systems for supply chain management and the integrated enterprise, customer relationship management systems, and e-business organizational design. The extension of corporate intranets to include customers and partners has expanded the potential for external collaboration. An **extranet** is an external communications system that uses the Internet and is shared by two or more organizations. Each organization moves certain data outside its private intranet, but makes the data available only to the other companies sharing the extranet. For example, Pitney Bowes's extranet might enable a small supplier of wood pallets to use an extranet to see how many of its products Pitney Bowes has on hand and how many it will need in the next few days.

PDA Remember...

Use IT applications such as extranets, systems for supply chain management and enterprise integration, and e-business systems to strengthen relationships with customers, suppliers, and business partners.

The Integrated Enterprise

Extranets play a critical role in today's integrated enterprise. The **integrated enterprise** is an organization that uses advanced IT to enable close coordination within the company as well as with suppliers, customers, and partners. An important aspect of the integrated enterprise is *supply-chain management*, which means managing the sequence of suppliers and purchasers covering all stages of processing from obtaining

Leading *by Design*

Best Buy Company (Best Buy)

Best Buy had modest beginnings—it started in 1966 as Sound of Music in St. Paul, Minnesota. It is now North America's largest consumer electronics retailer and continues to grow rapidly. It sells consumer electronics, home-office products, entertainment software, appliances and related services through more than 1,150 retail stores in the United States, Canada, and China. Its holdings include Best Buy (BestBuy.com, BestBuy.ca, and BestBuy.com.cn), Future Shop (FutureShop.ca), Geek Squad (GeekSquad.com and GeekSquad.ca), Pacific Sales Kitchen and Bath Centers (PacificSales.com), Magnolia Audio Video (Magnoliaav.com), Speakeasy (Speakeasy.net) and Jiangsu Five Star Appliance Co. (Five-Star.cn).[78]

CEO Brad Anderson's strategy for growth rests on his vision of unleashing "the power of human capital"[79] by relying on the knowledge of Best Buy's store managers and frontline employees who are in the best position to understand their consumers. In 2007, Best Buy announced several executive changes, all designed, "[to] strengthen the company's ability to draw insights from employees, customers and partners in order to provide excellent customer experiences and solutions; provide clear accountability for each element of the enterprise's growth strategy; and place leaders with strong points of view on how to generate growth in roles where they can bring those ideas to life."[80]

Best Buy is switching from relying on market researchers to looking for innovation from the store-level managers. "To stimulate their thinking, store managers go online to brainstorm and swap experiences with one another. In the retail realm, this is radical."[81] Best Buy is becoming a wiki-based organization.

Best Buy's success with wikis rests, in part, on the commitment and support from its CEO and other senior executives. Strong leadership is particularly important for the implementation of collaborative tools as they "need to acquire a critical mass of users and content before they become valuable."[82]

raw materials to distributing finished goods to consumers.[83] For organizations to operate efficiently and provide high-quality items that meet customer needs, the company must have reliable deliveries of high-quality, reasonably priced supplies and materials. It also requires an efficient and reliable system for distributing finished products, making them readily accessible to customers.

Information Linkages. The most recent advances involve the use of computer networks or extranets to achieve the right balance of low inventory levels and customer responsiveness. By establishing electronic linkages between the organization and key partners for the sharing and exchange of data, the integrated enterprise creates a seamless, integrated line stretching from end consumers to raw materials suppliers.[84] For example, as consumers purchase products in retail stores, the data are automatically fed into the retail chain's information system. In turn, the chain gives access to these constantly updated data to the manufacturing company through a secure extranet. With knowledge of the demand data, the manufacturer can produce and ship products when needed. As products are made by the manufacturer, data about raw materials used in the production process, updated inventory information, and updated forecasted demand are electronically provided to the manufacturer's suppliers, and the suppliers automatically replenish the manufacturer's raw materials inventory as needed.

PDA Remember...

Transform your organization into an integrated enterprise by establishing horizontal information linkages between the organization and key outsiders. Create a seamless, integrated line stretching from end consumers to raw materials suppliers that will meet customers' product and time demands.

Horizontal Relationships. The purpose of integrating the supply chain is for everyone to work closely together, moving in lockstep to meet customers' product and time demands. Service organizations also use extranets. For example, Hill and Knowlton Canada, a strategic communications consultancy, with 69 offices in 34 countries, developed an extranet to share information with its clients as well as its employees.[85]

As with the newer organizational designs described in Chapter 3, for the integrated enterprise to work, horizontal relationships get more emphasis than vertical relationships. Enterprise integration can create a level of cooperation not previously imaginable if managers approach the practice with an attitude of trust and partnership, as in the interorganizational relationships described in Chapter 5. For example, Wal-Mart and Procter & Gamble (P&G) started simply by sharing sales data so P&G goods could be automatically replaced as they were sold off Wal-Mart's shelves. However, this computer-to-computer exchange evolved into a horizontal relationship that has the two firms sharing customer information, shopper loyalty information, and other data that provides strategic advantages for both sides of the trading partnership.[86]

Customer Relationship Management

Another approach to strengthening external relationships is through the use of **customer relationship management**(CRM) systems. These systems help companies track customers' interactions with the firm and allow employees to call up a customer's past sales and service records, outstanding orders, or unresolved problems.[87] CRM stashes in a database all the customer information that a small-town store owner would keep in his or her head—the names of customers, what they bought, what problems they've had with purchases, and so forth. The system helps coordinate sales, marketing, and customer service departments so that all are smoothly working together.

E-Business Organizational Design

CRM and the integrated enterprise are both components of e-business, a new approach to how organizations conduct their business activities. **E-business** can be defined as any business that takes place by digital processes over a computer network rather than in physical space. Most commonly, it refers to electronic linkages over the Internet with customers, partners, suppliers, employees, or other key constituents. Despite the dot-com crash of the early 2000s, the Internet continues to transform traditional ways of doing business, helping companies in industries from banking to manufacturing to music retailing cut costs, speed innovation, and enhance relationships with customers.[88] There are now many organizations that exist only online. The next In Practice describes an e-business that is based on wiki principles.

In Practice

Northern Blue Publishing (Northern Blue)

Northern Blue provides digital publishing and creates collaborative learning portals for schools and libraries. "Northern Blue's mission is to help schools make the best of digital learning opportunities, to enable schools to adopt research-based practices to thrill, to inspire, and to capture the imagination of our students, to create environments for deeper cognitive development through inquiry, real and relevant project-based learning, and differentiated instruction, to help students communicate, collaborate, conceptualize, research, solve real-world problems, produce artifacts, and engage in drill and practice or tutorial support, to help schools adopt new models of teaching, learning, and meaningful assessment and to help provincial bodies and local districts justify spending to implement technology-supported learning opportunities, by offering low-cost, high quality content services and e-learning platforms."[89]

It produced Canada's first multimedia CD-ROM, *Canadisk,* in 1989 in partnership with Britannica Learning Materials. It has worked with Apple and Microsoft Encarta. Northern Blue's products include *The History of Canada Online,* a digital textbook and knowledge portal that allows comment, contribution, and collaboration by users and *Canada's First People,* Canada's first Aboriginal and Native Studies textbook and resource centre.[90]

It makes its products available through a licensing service for schools and school districts. The schools then receive secure Internet access to the digital texts and portals they have chosen. The schools can enable access from home as well as use CD or print versions of the products. Licensees can share web links and resources, and contribute to the content. Northern Blue can provide content management and social networking tools too. In addition, Northern Blue staff and authors provide consultation and custom publishing services. While Northern Blue is one of four divisions of http://www.northernblue.ca, based in Waterloo, Ontario, it operates as an e-business.

Many traditional organizations have set up Internet operations to strengthen and improve these external relationships, but managers have to make a decision about how best to integrate *bricks and clicks*—that is, how to blend their traditional operations with an Internet initiative. In the early days of e-business, many organizations set up dot-com initiatives with little understanding of how those activities could and should be integrated with their overall business. As the reality of e-business has evolved, companies have gained valuable lessons in how to merge online and offline activities.[91]

The range of basic strategies for setting up an Internet operation is illustrated in Exhibit 8.7. At one end of the spectrum, companies can set up an in-house division that is closely integrated with the traditional business. The opposite approach is to

EXHIBIT 8.7
The Range of Strategies for Integrating Bricks and Clicks

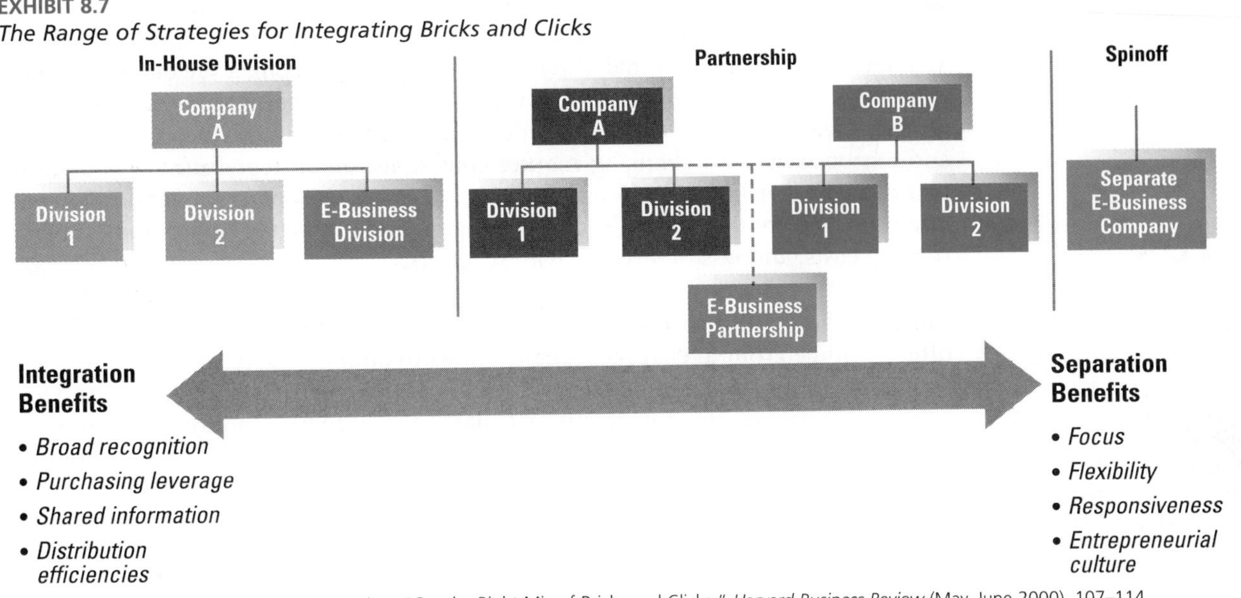

Source: Based on Ranjay Gulati and Jason Garino, "Get the Right Mix of Bricks and Clicks," *Harvard Business Review* (May–June 2000), 107–114.

create a spinoff company that is totally separate from the traditional organization. Many companies take a middle road by forging strategic partnerships with other organizations for their Internet initiative. Each of these options presents distinct advantages and disadvantages.[92]

In-House Division. An in-house division offers tight integration between the Internet operation and the organization's traditional operation. The organization creates a separate unit within the company that functions within the structure and guidance of the traditional organization. This approach gives the new division several advantages by piggybacking on the established company. These include brand recognition, purchasing leverage with suppliers, shared customer information and marketing opportunities, and distribution efficiencies.

Tesco, Britain's largest supermarket chain, for example, achieved success in online grocery delivery by keeping Tesco.com closely integrated with the existing grocery chain. By being part of the greater Tesco enterprise, Tesco.com was able to ride on the back of the parent company, leveraging its brand, suppliers, advertising, and customer database. By integrating the new operation with the traditional stores, Tesco didn't have to build new warehouses; the Internet division simply used the established warehouses and distribution systems of the chain and picked goods off supermarket shelves to fill customer orders. Using the store-based picking approach kept start-up costs low. Tesco spent only $58 million on its Internet operation during the first four years, and the operation was profitable from the beginning. By mid-2004, Tesco.com had grown to cover 95 percent of the United Kingdom and was receiving 70,000 orders per week.[93]

Tesco's success illustrates many of the advantages of the in-house approach. A potential problem with an in-house division, however, is that the new operation doesn't have the flexibility and autonomy needed to move quickly in the Internet world.

PDA Remember...

- Use an in-house e-business division to provide tight integration between the Internet operation and the traditional operation, and leverage the brand name, customer information, suppliers, and marketing muscle of the parent company.
- Create a spinoff company if the e-business unit needs greater autonomy and flexibility to adapt to rapidly changing market conditions.
- Consider a strategic partnership as a middle ground, but remember that partnerships involve dependency on other firms and require greater time spent managing relationships and resolving potential conflicts.

Spinoff. To give the Internet operation greater organizational autonomy, flexibility, and focus, some organizations choose to create a separate spinoff company. For example, Whirlpool Corporation created a spinoff called Brandwise.com, a site designed to help consumers find the best products and value—even if that means from other manufacturers. Advantages of a spinoff include faster decision making, increased flexibility and responsiveness to changing market conditions, an entrepreneurial culture, and management that is totally focused on the success of the online operation. Potential disadvantages are the loss of brand recognition and marketing opportunities, higher start-up costs, and loss of leverage with suppliers.

PDA Remember...

With greater use of IT, consider smaller organizational units, decentralized structures, improved internal coordination, and greater interorganizational collaboration, including the possibility of outsourcing or a network structure.

Strategic Partnership. Partnerships, whether through joint ventures or alliances, offer a middle ground, enabling organizations to attain some of the advantages and overcome some of the disadvantages of the purely in-house or spinoff options. Drew Sharma, managing director of Internet marketing agency Mindfire Interactive, advises smaller companies going online to partner: "If you can stand on the shoulders of giants, then why not?"[94] A primary disadvantage of partnerships is time spent managing relationships, potential conflicts between partners, and a possibility that one company will fail to deliver as promised or go out of business.

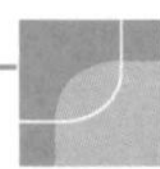

IT Impact on Organizational Design

Not every bricks-and-mortar organization will become involved in e-business. However, advances in IT and the Internet are having a tremendous impact on all organizations in every industry. Some specific implications of these advances for organizational design are smaller organizations, decentralized structures, improved horizontal coordination, improved interorganizational relationships, and enhanced network structures.

1. *Smaller organizations.* Some Internet-based businesses exist almost entirely in cyberspace; there is no formal organization in terms of a building with offices, desks, and so forth. One or a few people may maintain the site from their homes or a rented workspace. Even for traditional businesses, new IT enables the organization to do more work with fewer people. Companies can also outsource many functions and thus use fewer in-house resources.
2. *Decentralized organizational structures.* IT enables organizations to reduce layers of management and decentralize decision making. Information that may have previously been available only to top managers at headquarters can be quickly and easily shared throughout the organization, even across great geographical distances. Managers in varied business divisions or offices have the information they need to make important decisions quickly rather than waiting for decisions from headquarters. Technologies that enable people to meet and coordinate online can facilitate communication and decision making among distributed, autonomous groups of workers. In addition, technology allows for telecommuting, whereby individual workers can perform work that was once done in the office from their computers at home or other remote locations. People and groups no longer have to be located under one roof to collaborate and share information. An organization might be made up of numerous small teams or even individuals who work autonomously but coordinate electronically. Although management philosophy and organizational culture have a substantial impact on whether IT is used to

decentralize information and authority or to reinforce a centralized authority structure,[95] most organizations today use technology to further decentralization.

3. *Improved horizontal coordination.* Perhaps one of the greatest outcomes of IT is its potential to improve coordination and communication within the firm. Intranets and other networks can connect people even when their offices, factories, or stores are scattered around the world. For example, General Motors' intranet, dubbed Socrates on the basis that the Greek philosopher's name would be recognizable worldwide, connects some 100,000 staff members around the globe. Managers use the intranet to communicate with one another and to stay aware of organizational activities and outcomes.[96] They can also provide key information to employees throughout the organization with just a few keystrokes.
4. *Improved interorganizational relationships.* IT can also improve horizontal coordination and collaboration with external parties such as suppliers, customers, and partners. Extranets are increasingly important for linking companies with contract manufacturers and outsourcers, as well as for supporting the integrated enterprise, as described earlier. Exhibit 8.8 shows differences between traditional interorganizational relationship characteristics and emerging relationship characteristics. Traditionally, organizations had an arm's-length relationship with suppliers. However, as we discussed in Chapter 5, suppliers are becoming closer partners, tied electronically to the organization for orders, invoices, and payments. In addition, new IT has increased the power of consumers by giving them electronic access to a wealth of information from thousands of companies just by clicking a mouse. Consumers also have direct access to manufacturers, altering their perceptions and expectations regarding convenience, speed, and service. They also have access to consumer ratings, which may well influence their decisions.

Studies have shown that interorganizational information networks tend to heighten integration, blur organizational boundaries, and create shared strategic contingencies among firms.[97]

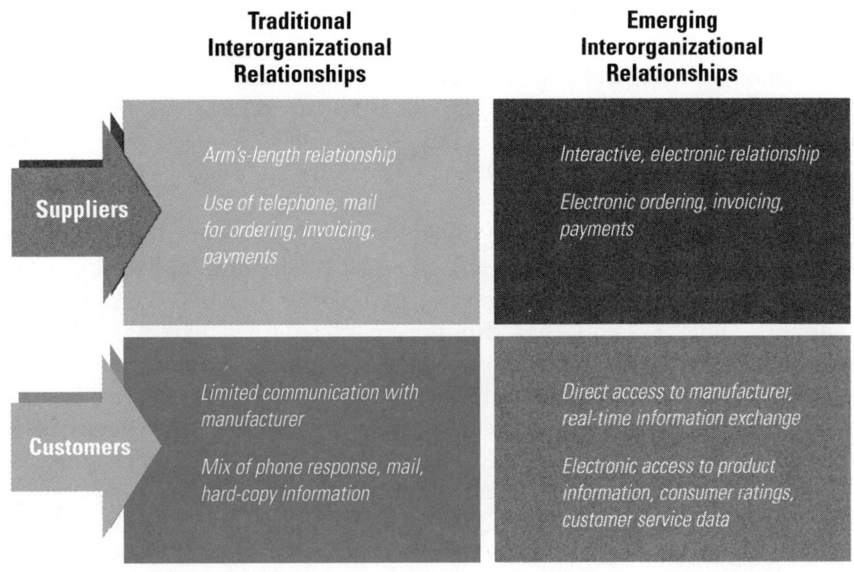

EXHIBIT 8.8
Key Characteristics of Traditional versus Emerging Interorganizational Relationships
Source: Based on Charles V. Callahan and Bruce A. Pasternack, "Corporate Strategy in the Digital Age," *Strategy & Business,* 15 (Second Quarter 1999): 10–14.

5. *Enhanced network structures.* The high level of interorganizational collaboration needed in a virtual network organization structure, described in Chapter 3, would not be possible without the use of advanced IT. In the business world, these are also sometimes called *modular structures* or *virtual organizations*. Outsourcing has become a major trend, thanks to computer technology that can tie companies together into a seamless information flow. For example, Hong Kong's Li & Fung is one of the biggest providers of clothing for retailers such as Abercrombie & Fitch, Guess, Ann Taylor, The Limited, and Disney, but the company doesn't own any factories, machines, or fabrics. Li & Fung specializes in managing information, relying on an electronically connected web of 7,500 partners in 37 countries to provide raw materials and assemble the clothes. Using an extranet allows Li & Fung to stay in touch with worldwide partners and move items quickly from factories to retailers. It also lets retailers track orders as they move through production and make last-minute changes and additions.[98] With a network structure, most activities are outsourced, so that different companies perform the various functions needed by the organization. The speed and ease of electronic communication makes the network structure a viable option for companies that want to keep costs low but expand activities or market presence.

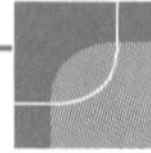

Summary and Interpretation

This chapter covered a number of important topics related to IT. The information revolution has had a tremendous impact on organizations in all industries. Highly successful organizations today are generally those that most effectively collect, store, distribute, and use information. IT systems have evolved to a variety of applications to meet organizations' information needs. Operations applications are applied to well-defined tasks at lower organization levels and help to improve efficiency. These include transaction processing systems, data warehousing, and data mining. Advanced computer-based systems are also used for better decision making and control of the organization. Decision-making systems include MISs, reporting systems, DSSs, and EISs, which are typically used at middle and upper levels of the organization. Management control systems include budgets and financial reports, periodic statistical reports, reward systems, and quality-control systems. An innovation called the *balanced scorecard* provides managers with a balanced view of the organization by integrating traditional financial measurements and statistical reports with a concern for markets, customers, and employees.

Today, all the various computer-based systems have begun to merge into an overall IT system that can be used to add strategic value. Intranets, ERP, and knowledge management systems are used primarily to support greater internal coordination and flexibility. Systems that support and strengthen external relationships include extranets and the integrated enterprise, customer relationship management, and e-business. The integrated enterprise uses advanced IT to enable close coordination among a company and its suppliers, partners, and customers. Customer relationship management systems help companies track their customers' interactions with the organization and provide better service. To establish an e-business, companies can choose among an in-house division, a spinoff, or a strategic partnership. Each has strengths and weaknesses.

Advanced IT and social computing are having a significant impact on organizational design. Technology has enabled creation of the network organization structure, in which a company subcontracts most of its major functions to separate companies that are connected electronically to the headquarters organization. Even organizations that do not use a network structure are rapidly evolving toward greater interorganizational collaboration. Other specific implications of advances in technology for organizational design include smaller organizations, decentralized organization structures, and improved internal and external coordination.

Key Concepts

balanced scorecard, p. 276
benchmarking, p. 275
business intelligence, p. 269
customer relationship management, p. 285
data, p. 281
data mining, p. 269
data warehousing, p. 269
decision support system, p. 271
e-business, p. 286
enterprise resource planning, p. 279
executive information system, p. 271
explicit knowledge, p. 281
extranet, p. 284
feedback control model, p. 273
information, p. 281
information reporting system, p. 271
integrated enterprise, p. 284
intellectual capital, p. 280
intranet, p. 278
knowledge, p. 281
knowledge management, p. 280
management control systems, p. 273
management information system, p. 270
networking, p. 278
Six Sigma, p. 275
tacit knowledge, p. 282
transaction processing systems, p. 268
wiki, p. 280

Discussion Questions

1. Do you think technology will eventually enable top managers to do their jobs with little face-to-face communication? Discuss.
2. Why might an organization consider using an intranet rather than traditional management and executive information systems?
3. How might an ERP system be used to improve strategic management of a manufacturing organization?
4. Discuss some ways a large insurance company might use MISs to improve decision making.
5. Describe how the four management control system elements discussed in the chapter might be used for feedback control within organizations. Compare and contrast this four-part system with use of the balanced scorecard.
6. Describe your use of explicit knowledge when you research and write a term paper. Do you also use tacit knowledge regarding this activity? Discuss.
7. Why is knowledge management particularly important to a company that wants to become a learning organization?
8. What is meant by the term *integrated enterprise*? Describe how organizations can use extranets to extend and enhance horizontal relationships required for enterprise integration.
9. What are some competitive issues that might lead a company to take a partnership approach to e-business rather than setting up an in-house Internet division? What are the advantages and disadvantages of each approach?
10. How might the adoption of IT affect how an organization is designed?

Chapter 8 Workbook: Are You Fast Enough to Succeed in Internet Time?*

Does your business have what it takes to move at Internet speed?

What is an Internet year? It's the time in which an e-company needs to accomplish the kind of business goals that once took a year. Conventional wisdom puts an Internet year at anywhere from 60 to 90 days. Regardless, few will argue that companies need to move faster now than ever imagined.

Can you afford the luxury of in-depth analysis, full due diligence, building consensus, test marketing—all the cornerstones of responsible corporate management? Does their value change when you weigh it against the cost to your company's scarcest commodity—time? Kelsey Biggers, executive vice president of Micro Modeling Associates (MMA), offers the following scenarios to help determine whether you are capable of operating at Internet speed. Choose the best course of action from the choices given (answers below):

1. You have met a company that can be a potential strategic partner for marketing your service to a new industry online. The vibes are good, and you want to map out the potential relationship, but to do so you need to share client and billing information. A nondisclosure agreement (NDA) is necessary, and the company hands you its standard agreement. What do you do?
   a. Get a copy of your company's standard nondisclosure agreement and submit it to your potential partner as an alternative to its NDA.
   b. Fax the agreement to your lawyer and ask him or her to get back to you ASAP with any amendments so you can continue the conversation.
   c. Look over the agreement and sign it right away.
2. You're looking for a creative director for your Web site, and you know the position will be critical to your whole look and feel online. You hope to have three or four excellent candidates to choose from and have considered doing a retained search for the position. Out of nowhere your old college roommate, whom you respect enormously, refers you to an associate for the position. You meet the candidate for breakfast and you are blown away by the person's credentials and personality. You have three choices:
   a. Offer the candidate the job before the check arrives.
   b. Give the candidate a strong "warm and fuzzy" about the job while you initiate a quick search for a couple of alternative candidates.
   c. Schedule a round of interviews with your senior colleagues back in the office to confirm your positive instincts, while also identifying one or two alternative candidates for comparison.
3. Your online strategy calls for targeting two vertical markets for your service in the next 9 months. Your service can be tailored to meet the buying needs of companies in several industries, so it's a matter of picking the right industries to target. High-growth, dynamic industries are obviously preferred. Which approach would you select?
   a. Hire an MBA with expertise in finance and marketing to create high-level screening criteria for target industries and identify the five best fits for your services.
   b. Hire your neighbor, who happens to be a doctor, knows the healthcare industry, and can make several introductions to HMOs (Health Maintenance Organization) and pharmaceutical companies.
   c. Ask an intern to research publicly available information from Gartner Group, Forrester Research, and other industry analyst organizations for online spending habits in different industries and make recommendations.
4. Your company has been looking to merge with a strategic partner for some time. You have identified three companies that would be good fits, but each has its advantages and disadvantages. Which would you choose?
   a. Company A offers a service that is perfectly complementary to your own, and the price is right. However, the company has indicated that it doesn't think it has enough scale to do a merger now and would rather wait 9 months until after the holiday selling season to complete the transaction.
   b. Company B is smaller and dynamic, but has grown too fast and has a bad balance sheet. It could be picked up immediately, but your company would have to assume some unwanted debt along with the merger.
   c. Company C has a great offline presence in its space, but has not yet executed its e-commerce plan. The two companies might be a great fit once Company C has established its online presence by midsummer.
5. Your e-commerce strategy requires a real-time fulfillment system that can process orders straight through and provide data on client buying patterns. You have looked outside your firm for technology support to help bring this capability online and have been presented with three alternatives:
   a. A senior programmer from your prior firm is now a freelance consultant. He can get started immediately and hire a dozen coders who promise to get a capability up and running in 60 days and grow out the functionality.

b. Your internal technology group can staff a team of a dozen people to build out the system in a year and will then have the ability to support and grow the service when it goes live.
c. An e-solutions consultancy can project manage and build the entire system, but would want to take 60 days to design the technical architecture before starting development. The consultancy insists this time is necessary to ensure a scalable service.

Answers (Each correct answer is worth one point.)

Question 1

c. The objective is to make a decision quickly and to move the process forward without a great deal of red tape and delay. The legal process can oftentimes slow decision making—whether by 3 weeks or 3 months—and time is of the essence in the online world. Moreover, when was the last time an NDA about client information materially affected your business? Better to spend your time building trust than protecting against an unlikely downside.

Question 2

a. Offer the candidate the job while waiting for the check. If this person has been vouched for by someone you trust and you love the person's work, grab the candidate while he or she is available and put that person to work. If you think the candidate is a great hire, chances are, so will your competitors.

Question 3

b. Hire your neighbor. Any list of dynamic industries you put together is bound to include healthcare, and your biggest challenge is to find a credible person with industry know-how and contacts who can take you into the industry. Your neighbor can do that. Now start looking for the other industries you want to focus on.

Question 4

b. Buy Company B. Company B has proven itself fast-moving and dynamic, and its balance sheet issues makes it open to a favorable price. Companies A and C are both tying their success to future events—a strong holiday selling season or a successful online launch—either of which might not happen and both of which are in the distant Internet future.

Question 5

c. The one area a company cannot afford to get wrong is its technical architecture. It must scale and be reliable, or your whole business will be at risk. Programmers without a blueprint cannot ensure a successful online environment, and staffing internally is time-consuming and uncertain. Better to outsource the project immediately while building an internal team to take it over after its launch.

* "Are You Fast Enough to Succeed in Internet Time? Does Your Business Have What It Takes to Move at Internet Speed?" Reprinted with permission from *Entrepreneur Magazine*, September 1999, http://www.entrepreneur.com.

Case for Analysis: eBay Canada

Putting up websites in French as well as English has become standard practice for Canadian businesses—a simple matter of posting the same information in both languages.

For e-commerce sites, where virtually all business is conducted online, it's not so easy, and for an auction site like eBay Canada it was a monstrous undertaking.

eBay operates tens of millions of individual Web pages that change constantly and connect buyers and sellers around the world. Getting a "français" toggle switch at the top of its Canadian pages took the work of 200 people and almost a year of development.

When Jordan Banks joined eBay Canada in 2000, the company was already mulling over ways of boosting its presence in French Canada. "In Québec, we were grossly under-penetrated, versus the penetration we had in every other region of Canada," Mr. Banks said. That left the door open for a potential competitor, like a specialized local French-language auction site, to gain a foothold in the province.

After becoming eBay Canada's managing director in the summer of 2005, Mr. Banks made it his top priority to tackle the company's Québec problem.

eBay Canada boasts a visitor penetration of about 50 percent for the country, meaning half of Canada's online population of 24 million users visits the site in any given month. In Québec, however, visitor penetration was around 25 to 30 per cent.

Mr. Banks felt that many French users, while capable of navigating the Internet in English, were unwilling to conduct transactions in a second language. "We asked ourselves: 'How many people are not using eBay now because they are not comfortable in English?' And there were more than you think," Mr. Banks said.

The easiest, quickest and cheapest way for eBay Canada to access the Québec market would have been to launch a so-called mini site, which makes a few key options and features available in a second language. Mini sites operating in Vietnam, the Philippines, Ireland, Malaysia, Singapore, Hong Kong and Switzerland have limited translated content.

But when he learned that 20 per cent of computer browsers in Canada are set to French as the default language, Mr. Banks became convinced of Québec's massive untapped potential.

So he opted instead for the complicated, long, expensive option: Building eBay's first dual-language site. His idea was to treat Québec almost as its own country with a fully translated site along the lines of those operating in countries such as France, Germany, and Italy, but integrated within eBay Canada. First, however, he had to persuade eBay's senior executives in San Jose, [California], to go ahead with the Canadian division's most expensive single project since launching in 2000.

Soon after taking the Canadian reins, Mr. Banks went to San Jose armed with what he says was a strong business model based on long-term growth projections of new visitors and registered users in Québec. His biggest hurdle was the sticker shock of developing a new site and the manual translation required to create a parity of experience for French users. "If there's not an incredibly compelling reason not to do it, we need to have it," Mr. Banks said.

But there was one such compelling reason standing between Mr. Banks and his goal of absolute parity. A parallel French site could not include translated product details in eBay listings. That information, including anything a seller wants to say about a product, is controlled by each individual seller when putting an item on the auction block. When placing a bid, product details, as well as the user feedback posted that evaluates each merchant, can only be seen in English. Only eBay-controlled content, like standard options, menus and buttons, and anything related to the bidding and payment process, would appear in French on any of the 50 million listings available to Canadians.

"We audited a bunch of translation services, and we just didn't find one we thought was so incredibly accurate that it wouldn't compromise the integrity of the listing," Mr. Banks said. That setback strengthened the case for a simple mini site that would have been up and running much sooner, and with higher returns, at least over the medium term.

On the upside, Mr. Banks had the stellar performance of eBay Canada to back his argument. eBay transactions account for one-quarter of the roughly $5 billion (U.S.) spent by Canadians in online purchases each year, excluding groceries and travel. That ranks the Canadian site in the top three in the eBay universe, which now spans 38 markets.

In December 2005, eBay's executives agreed that the auction site needed to speak French in order to get more Québeckers buying and selling. "It was undoubtedly the right thing to do," Mr. Banks said. "The Québec market is a very distinct market, and there was no way we could continue doing what we were doing in English Canada, if we wanted to attract new French users."

The massive development and translation effort would take the better part of the following year. eBay is designed on a hub-and-spoke model, in which each country's spoke site travels through the main platform, thereby allowing a rancher in Alberta to bid on a Texan's spurs, for example. Integrating the French into the matrix required the development of a brand new spoke, and many millions of new Web pages, all of which had to be translated.

Ten months after launch, Mr. Banks said the move has paid off, even if the eBay Canada in French is still operating at a loss. In June, visitors to the French site jumped 45 per cent year over year, and the growth in registered users now doubles that of the rest of Canada. Profits will come, Mr. Banks said, over the long term.

Québec is also well represented among the 33,000 Canadians making a primary or secondary living on eBay, selling everything from speakers to marmalade. Poring over the wares of French Canadians has become one of his favourite eBay pastimes, Mr. Banks said. "They're unbelievable. In the DNA of a lot of French Canadians is this scrappy entrepreneurial nature."

While the numbers are encouraging, Mr. Banks said the job is not yet finished. "I would love one day to get to the point where all across eBay, you can translate either eBay text, or buyer and seller text, into the language of your choice in real time. That's an ideal we will continue to strive for."

Source: T. Shufelt, "Jordan Banks: Distinctly Translating Commerce for the Masses," *The Globe and Mail* (August 24, 2007).

Case for Analysis: Product X*

Several years ago the top management of a multibillion-dollar corporation decided that Product X was a failure and should be disbanded. The losses involved exceeded $100 million. At least five people knew that Product X was a failure six years before the decision was made to stop producing it. Three of those people were plant managers who lived daily with the production problems. The other two were marketing officials who realized that the manufacturing problems were not solvable without expenditures that would raise the price of the product to the point where it would no longer be competitive in the market.

There are several reasons why this information did not get to the top sooner. At first, the subordinates believed that with exceptionally hard work they might turn the errors into successes. But the more they struggled, the more they realized the massiveness of the original error. The next task was to communicate the bad news upward so that it would be heard. They knew that in their company bad news would not be well received at the upper levels if it was not accompanied with suggestions for positive action. They also knew that the top management was enthusiastically describing Product X as a new leader in its field. Therefore, they spent much time composing memos that would communicate the realities without shocking top management.

Middle management read the memos and found them too open and forthright. Since they had done the production and marketing studies that resulted in the decision to produce X, the memos from lower-level management questioned the validity of their analysis. They wanted time to really check these gloomy predictions and, if they were accurate, to design alternative corrective strategies. If the pessimistic information was to be sent upward, middle management wanted it accompanied with optimistic action alternatives. Hence further delay.

Once middle management was convinced that the gloomy predictions were valid, they began to release some of the bad news to the top—but in carefully measured doses. They managed the releases carefully to make certain they were covered if top management became upset. The tactic they used was to cut the memos drastically and summarize the findings. They argued that the cuts were necessary because top management was always complaining about receiving long memos; indeed, some top executives had let it be known that good memos were memos of one page or less. The result was that top management received fragmented information underplaying the intensity of the problem (not the problem itself) and overplaying the degree to which middle management and the technicians were in control of the problem.

Top management therefore continued to speak glowingly about the product, partially to ensure that it would get the financial backing it needed from within the company. Lower-level management became confused and eventually depressed because they could not understand this continued top management support, nor why studies were ordered to evaluate the production and marketing difficulties that they had already identified. Their reaction was to reduce the frequency of their memos and the intensity of their alarm, while simultaneously turning over the responsibility for dealing with the problem to middle-management people. When local plant managers, in turn, were asked by their foremen and employees what was happening, the only response they gave was that the company was studying the situation and continuing its support. This information bewildered the foremen and led them to reduce their own concern.

*Excerpted from C. Argyris and D. Schon, *Organizational Learning: A Theory of Action Perspective.* Argyris/Schon, Organizational Learning, © 1978, Addison–Wesley Publishing Co., Inc., Reading, Massachusetts. Pages 1–2. Reprinted with permission. Case appeared in Gareth Morgan, *Creative Organization Theory* (1989), Sage Publications.

9 Organization Size, Life Cycle, and Decline

AFP/Getty Images/JOSEPH BARRAK

A Look Inside

Interpol

Interpol was created in 1923 and is the world's largest police organization. Interpol has a membership from 184 countries and 11 territories; its permanent headquarters is in Lyon, France. Interpol has to work with countries from every corner of the globe, fostering cooperation among people with different cultural values, languages, and legal and political systems. Interpol operates through National Central Bureaus in its member countries. Canada joined Interpol in 1949, and the RCMP was delegated the responsibility for Interpol in Canada.[1] In 2005, the Secretary General of Interpol, Ronald Noble (see photo), visited Canada. "In a world where the law enforcement community faces increasing and changing threats from criminals and terrorists, the need for international police co-operation and communication has never been greater," he said. "Canada, through the RCMP, has recognized the need for increased integration and co-ordination, and continues to play an important role in supporting Interpol and the world's police."[2]

When Interpol works, it works very well, leading to the quick capture of international terrorists, murderers, and other fugitives. But when Noble took over the international police organization in 2000, it wasn't working very well. Rather than a fast-moving, crime-fighting organization, Noble found at Interpol a clumsy, slow-moving, bureaucratic agency that was ill equipped to respond to the massive challenges of a world increasingly reliant on worldwide coordinated law enforcement to prevent tragedies such as the World Trade Center attacks of September 2001. If a request for assistance and information on Mohammed Atta, one of the terrorist leaders, for example, came into Interpol on a weekend, too bad—the agency was closed until Monday morning. Interpol "Red Notices" (urgent, global wanted-persons alerts) took up to six months to process and were sent out by third-class mail to save postage costs.

Noble knew that kind of slow response had to change. Since taking over as head of Interpol, he has moved the organization forward by leaps and bounds, reducing bureaucracy and transforming Interpol into a modern, fast-moving organization. Keeping Interpol open 24 hours a day, seven days a week, was one of his first changes. A policy of issuing red alerts for terrorists within 24 hours and notices for less-threatening criminals within 72 hours went into effect immediately after the U.S. attacks on September 11, 2001. Noble has reorganized Interpol to increase speed and flexibility and to focus on the "customer" (law enforcement groups in its member countries). Today, the most critical notices are translated immediately, posted online, and sent by express-delivery service.

The reorganization also includes mechanisms for better coordination and information gathering. Noble's goal is for Interpol to become the number-one global police agency, one that coordinates and leads a multidimensional crime-fighting approach. Combating terrorism and organized crime, Noble knows, requires that everyone have the information they need when they need it and that local police, judicial, intelligence, diplomatic, and military services all work together. A major step toward a more coordinated worldwide effort came when Interpol recently appointed its first-ever representative to the United Nations.[3]

As organizations grow large and complex, they need more complex systems and procedures for guiding and controlling the organization. Unfortunately, these characteristics can also cause problems of inefficiency, rigidity, and slow response time. Every organization—from international agencies to locally owned restaurants and auto body shops—wrestles with questions about organizational size, bureaucracy, and control. Most entrepreneurs who start a business want their organization to grow. Yet, as organizations become larger, they often find it difficult to respond quickly to changes in the environment. Today's organizations are looking for ways to be more flexible and responsive to a rapidly changing environment while continuing to grow.

During the 20th century, large organizations became widespread, and bureaucracy has become a major topic of study in organizational theory.[4] Most large organizations have bureaucratic characteristics, which can be very effective. These organizations provide us with abundant goods and services and accomplish astonishing feats—explorations of Mars, overnight delivery of packages to any location in the world, scheduling and coordination of thousands of airline flights a day—that are testimony to their effectiveness. On the other hand, bureaucracy is also accused of creating inefficiency, rigidity, and demeaning routinized work that alienates both employees and the customers an organization is trying to serve.

Purpose of This Chapter

In this chapter, we explore the question of large versus small organizations and how size relates to structure and control. Organization size is a contextual variable that influences organizational design and functioning just as do the contextual variables—technology, environment, goals—discussed in previous chapters. In the first section, we look at the advantages of large versus small size. Then, we explore an organization's life cycle and the structural characteristics at each stage. Next, we examine the historical need for bureaucracy as a means to control large organizations and compare bureaucratic control to various other control strategies. Finally, the chapter looks at the causes of organizational decline and discusses some methods for dealing with downsizing. By the end of this chapter, you should be able to recognize when bureaucratic control can make an organization effective and when other types of control are more appropriate.

Organization Size: Is Bigger Better?

The question of big versus small begins with the notion of growth and the reasons so many organizations feel the need to grow large.

Pressures for Growth

The vision of practically every businessperson is to have his or her company become a member of the Fortune 500 list—to grow fast and to grow large.[5] Sometimes this goal is more urgent than to make the best products or show the greatest profits. A decade ago, analysts and management scholars were heralding a shift away from "bigness" toward small, nimble companies that could quickly respond in a fast-changing environment. Yet, despite the proliferation of new, small organizations, the giants such as Procter & Gamble, Toyota, and Wal-Mart and General Electric (GE) continue to grow. GE, for example, founded in 1878, now has 319,000 employees in 100 countries and competes in a variety of industries such as energy, transportation, finance, and television.[6] Similarly, Canadian Pacific Railway Ltd. is growing through acquisition; it bought Dakota Minnesota & Eastern Railroad for $1.48 billion as its first step in its multibillion-dollar plan to haul U.S. coal.[7]

Today, the business world has entered an era of the mega-corporation. Merger mania has given rise to behemoths such as DaimlerChrysler AG and Citigroup.[8] The advertising industry is controlled by four giant agencies—the Omnicom Group and the Interpublic Group of Companies, both with headquarters in New York; London's WPP Group; and Publicis Groupe, based in Paris.[9] These huge conglomerates own scores of companies that soak up more than half the ad industry's revenues and reach into the advertising, direct-mail marketing, and public relations of every region on the planet. Moreover, these agencies grew primarily to better serve their clients, which were themselves growing larger and more global. Companies in all industries, from aerospace to consumer products to media, strive for growth to acquire the size and resources needed to compete on a global scale, to invest in new technology, and to control distribution channels and guarantee access to markets.[10]

There are other pressures for organizations to grow. Many executives have found that firms must grow to stay economically healthy and believe that to stop growing is to stagnate. To be stable means that customers may not have their demands fully met or that competitors will increase market share at the expense of your organization. For example, Digital Extremes, a London, Ontario–based computer games creator, has the goal of creating at least one new product each year. Digital Extremes was founded in 1994 and now has 63 employees and generates about $8 million a year in revenues. According to the company's chief financial officer (and brother of the founder), Michael Schmalz, "[what] you need to survive, much less prosper today, are blockbuster releases, . . . [better] yet what you want to do is to create a new game that will become a franchise, with each release breaking ground for the next."[11] Even so, growth alone is insufficient for success as companies such as The Loewen Group, Cinar Films, and 724 Solutions illustrate—their global promise fizzled out.[12]

Scale is crucial to economic success in marketing-intensive companies such as Coca-Cola, Procter & Gamble, and Molson-Coors. Greater size gives these companies power in the marketplace and thus increases revenues.[13] In addition, growing organizations can be vibrant, exciting places to work, which enables these companies to attract and keep quality employees. When the number of employees is expanding, an organization can offer many challenges and opportunities for advancement.

PDA Remember...

Decide whether your organization should act like a large or small organization. To the extent that economies of scale, global reach, and complexity are important, introduce greater bureaucratization as the organization increases in size. As it becomes necessary, add rules and regulations, written documentation, job specialization, technical competence in hiring and promotion, and decentralization.

Dilemmas of Large Size

Organizations feel compelled to grow, but how much and how large? What size organization is better poised to compete in a global environment? The arguments are summarized in Exhibit 9.1.

Large. Huge resources and economies of scale are needed for many organizations to compete globally. Only large organizations can build a massive pipeline in the North. Only a large corporation like Airbus Industrie can afford to build the A380, the world's first double-deck passenger airline, and only a large Virgin Atlantic Airways can buy it. Only a large Johnson & Johnson can invest hundreds of millions in new products such as bifocal contact lenses and a patch that delivers contraceptives through the skin. In addition, large organizations have the resources to be a supportive economic and social force in difficult times. In 2006, the Canadian Government undertook the largest evacuation in our country's history. Over 14,000 citizens were evacuated from Lebanon to Cyprus and Turkey in ships and airplanes chartered by the government. While there was considerable criticism of the evacuation, only a large organization like the federal government would have been able to mobilize the

EXHIBIT 9.1
Differences between Large and Small Organizations
Source: Based on John A. Byrne, "Is Your Company Too Big?" *BusinessWeek* (March 27, 1989), 84–94, and E.E. Lawler, III "Rethinking Organization Size," *Organizational Dynamics,* 26, 2 (1997): 24–35.

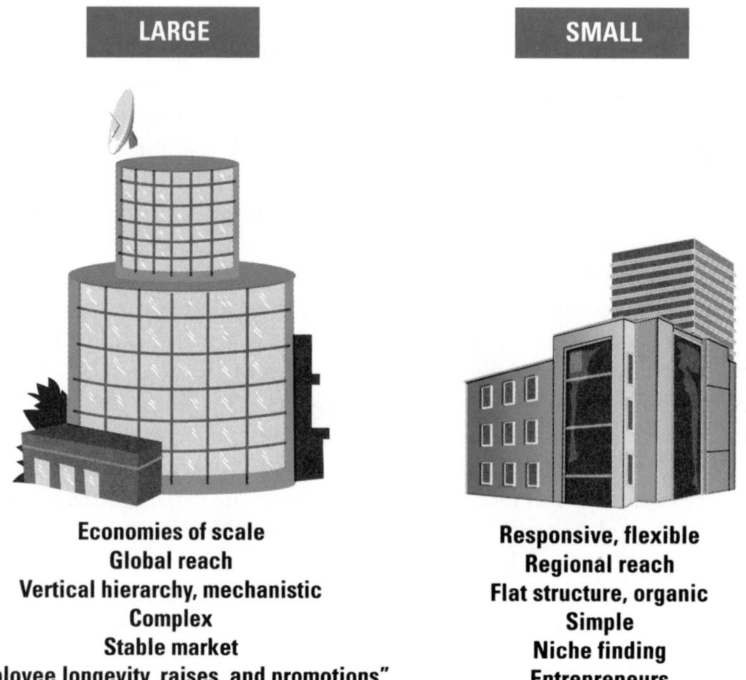

necessary resources to conduct the rescue. Large organizations also are able to get back to business more quickly following a disaster, giving employees a sense of security and belonging during an uncertain time.

Large companies are standardized, often mechanistically run, and complex. The complexity offers hundreds of functional specialties within the organization to perform multifaceted tasks and to produce varied and complicated products. Moreover, large organizations, once established, can be a presence that stabilizes a market for years and at which managers can work for many years. The organization can provide longevity, raises, and promotions.

Small. The competing argument says small is beautiful because the crucial requirements for success in a global economy are responsiveness and flexibility in fast-changing markets. Small scale can provide significant advantages in terms of quick reaction to changing customer needs or shifting environmental and market conditions.[14]

Small organizations have a flat structure and an organic, free-flowing management style that encourages entrepreneurship and innovation. Today's leading biotechnological drugs, for example, were all discovered by small, young firms, such as Montréal's Theratechnologies, which is developing a compound to treat HIV lipodystrophy, rather than by huge pharmaceutical companies.[15] Moreover, the personal involvement of employees in small firms encourages entrepreneurial motivation and commitment, because employees personally identify with the company's mission.

Although the North American economy contains many large and successful organizations, research shows that as global trade has accelerated, smaller organizations have become the norm. Since the mid-1960s, most of the then-existing large businesses have lost market share worldwide.[16] Many large companies have grown even larger through merger or acquisition in recent years, yet research indicates that few of these mergers live up to their expected performance levels.[17] A study of ten of the largest mergers of all time, including AOL/Time Warner, Glaxo/SmithKline, and Daimler/Chrysler, showed a significant decline in shareholder value for eight of the ten combined companies. Only two, Exxon/Mobil and Travelers/Citicorp, actually increased in value.[18] Although there are numerous factors involved in the decline in value, many researchers and analysts agree that frequently, bigness just does not add up to better performance.[19] This chapter's Book Mark argues that one reason large companies sometimes fail is that top leaders get too far away from the nuts and bolts of running the business. Any major strategic initiative, such as a merger, falters without proper execution.

Despite the increasing size of many companies, the economic vitality of Canada, as well as most of the world, is tied to small and mid-sized businesses. In 2001, there were more than 1.5 million small and medium-sized businesses in Canada. Fifty-eight percent of the businesses are in Ontario and Québec.[20] By 2004, small and medium-sized firms accounted for 87 and 11 percent, respectively, of the firms in the private sector.[21] The growth of the Internet and other information technologies is making it easier for small companies to act big, as described in Chapter 8. The growing service sector also contributes to a decrease in average organization size, as many service companies remain small to better serve customers.

Big-Organization/Small-Organization Hybrid. The paradox is that the advantages of small organizations sometimes enable them to succeed and, hence, grow large. Most of the 100 firms on *Fortune* magazine's list of the fastest-growing companies are small firms characterized by an emphasis on being fast and flexible in responding to the environment.[22] Small companies, however, can become victims of their own success as they grow large, shifting to a mechanistic structure emphasizing vertical hierarchies and spawning "corporate drones" rather than entrepreneurs. Giant companies are "built for optimization, not innovation."[23] Big companies may become committed to their existing products and technologies, and have a hard time supporting innovation for the future.

PDA
Remember...

If responsiveness, flexibility, simplicity, and niche finding are important, subdivide the organization into simple, autonomous divisions that have freedom and a small-organization approach.

The solution is what Jack Welch, retired chairman of GE, called the "big-company/small-company hybrid" that combines a large corporation's resources and reach with a small company's simplicity and flexibility. Full-service global firms need a strong resource base and sufficient complexity and hierarchy to serve clients around the world. Size is not necessarily at odds with speed and flexibility, as evidenced by large companies such as GE, Wal-Mart, and eBay, which continue to try new things and move quickly to change the rules of business. The divisional structure, described in Chapter 3, is one way some large organizations attain a big/small design. By reorganizing into groups of small companies, huge corporations such as Johnson & Johnson capture the mindset and advantages of smallness. Johnson & Johnson is actually a group of 204 separate companies. When a new product is created in one of Johnson & Johnson's 56 labs, a new company is created along with it.[24]

The development of new organizational forms, with an emphasis on decentralizing authority and cutting out layers of the hierarchy, combined with the increasing use of information technology described in Chapter 8, is making it easier than ever for organizations to be simultaneously large and small, thus capturing the advantages of each. Big companies also find a variety of ways to act both large and small. Retail giants Home Depot and Wal-Mart, for example, use the advantage of size in areas such as advertising, purchasing, and raising capital; however, they also give each individual store the autonomy needed to serve customers as if it were a small, hometown shop.[25] To encourage innovation, the giant corporation Royal

Book Mark 9.0 (HAVE YOU READ THIS BOOK?)

Execution: The Discipline of Getting Things Done

By Larry Bossidy and Ram Charan, with Charles Burke

Why do so many grand strategies fail and so many large companies go wrong? This is the central question addressed by Larry Bossidy, chairman and former CEO of Allied Signal, and management consultant Ram Charan in their book, *Execution: The Discipline of Getting Things Done*. Success for any organization, large or small, is found in the details. *Execution* offers a practical guide for translating great ideas into successful action. Companies that deliver on their promises year after year are those whose CEOs are skilled in the discipline of execution.

BASIC BUILDING BLOCKS

The discipline of execution is based on the following three basic building blocks:

- *Essential leadership behaviours.* The authors emphasize that execution is the primary job of a leader. This doesn't mean leaders should micromanage, but they must be actively and passionately involved, putting in place a culture, structure, and the right people to make things happen. Seven essential leader behaviours form the first basic building block of execution: (1) know your people and your business, (2) insist on realism and confronting problems head-on, (3) set clear goals and priorities, (4) follow through, (5) reward the "doers," (6) expand people's capabilities, and (7) know yourself.
- *An organizational culture that reinforces a discipline of execution.* Leaders focus on changing people's beliefs and behaviours so that they produce *results*, not just ideas, plans, and strategies. To shift toward a results-oriented culture, leaders make clear the results they want, coach people on how to achieve them, and reward them for doing so. When people consistently fail to achieve results, leaders need the courage to give them other jobs or let them go. Consistently acting in this manner produces a culture of getting things done.
- *The right people in the right place.* One job no leader should delegate, the authors insist, is recruiting, hiring, promoting, and developing the right people. Even though most leaders claim that "people are our most important asset," they pay very little attention to this aspect of their business, choosing instead to pass it off to the human resources department. Having the right people in the right place, particularly those in the leadership pool, is a key element of successful companies, and one leaders can directly control. As CEO of Allied Signal, Larry Bossidy devoted as much as 40 percent of his day to hiring and developing leaders throughout the company!

THE IMPORTANCE OF EXECUTION

Execution is not simply getting things done; it means understanding the elements that have to be in place in order to get things done. As the authors put it, "Execution is a systematic process of rigorously discussing hows and whats, questioning, tenaciously following through, and ensuring accountability." By having the right people—individually and collectively—focusing on the right details at the right time, organizations can effectively execute and accomplish amazing results.

Execution: The Discipline of Getting Things Done, by Larry Bossidy and Ram Charan, with Charles Burke, is published by Crown Business.

Dutch/Shell created a strategy in its exploration-and-production division to set aside 10 percent of the division's research budget for so-called outlandish ideas. Anyone can apply for the funds, and decisions are made not by managers but by a small group of nonconformist employees.[26] Small organizations that are growing can also use these ideas to help them retain the flexibility and customer focus that fuelled their growth.

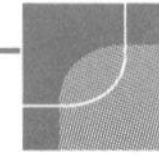

Organizational Life Cycle

A useful way to think about organizational growth and change is the concept of an organizational **life cycle**,[27] which suggests that organizations are born, grow older, and eventually die. Organization structure, leadership style, and administrative systems follow a fairly predictable pattern through stages in the life cycle. Stages are sequential and follow a natural progression.

Stages of Life-Cycle Development

Research on organizational life cycle suggests that four major stages characterize organizational development.[28] These stages are illustrated in Exhibit 9.2, along with the problems associated with transition to each stage. Growth is not easy. Each time an organization enters a new stage in the life cycle, it enters a whole new arena with a new set of rules for how the organization functions internally and how it relates to the external environment.[29] For technology companies today, life cycles are getting shorter; to stay competitive, companies like eBay and Google have to successfully progress through stages of the cycle faster.

PDA

Remember...

Grow when possible. With growth, you can provide opportunities for employee advancement and greater profitability and effectiveness. Apply new management systems and structural configurations at each stage of an organization's development. Interpret the needs of the growing organization and respond with the management and internal systems that will carry the organization through to the next stage of development.

1. *Entrepreneurial stage.* When an organization is born, the emphasis is on creating a product or service and surviving in the marketplace. The founders are entrepreneurs, and they devote their full energies to the technical activities of production

EXHIBIT 9.2
Organizational Life Cycle

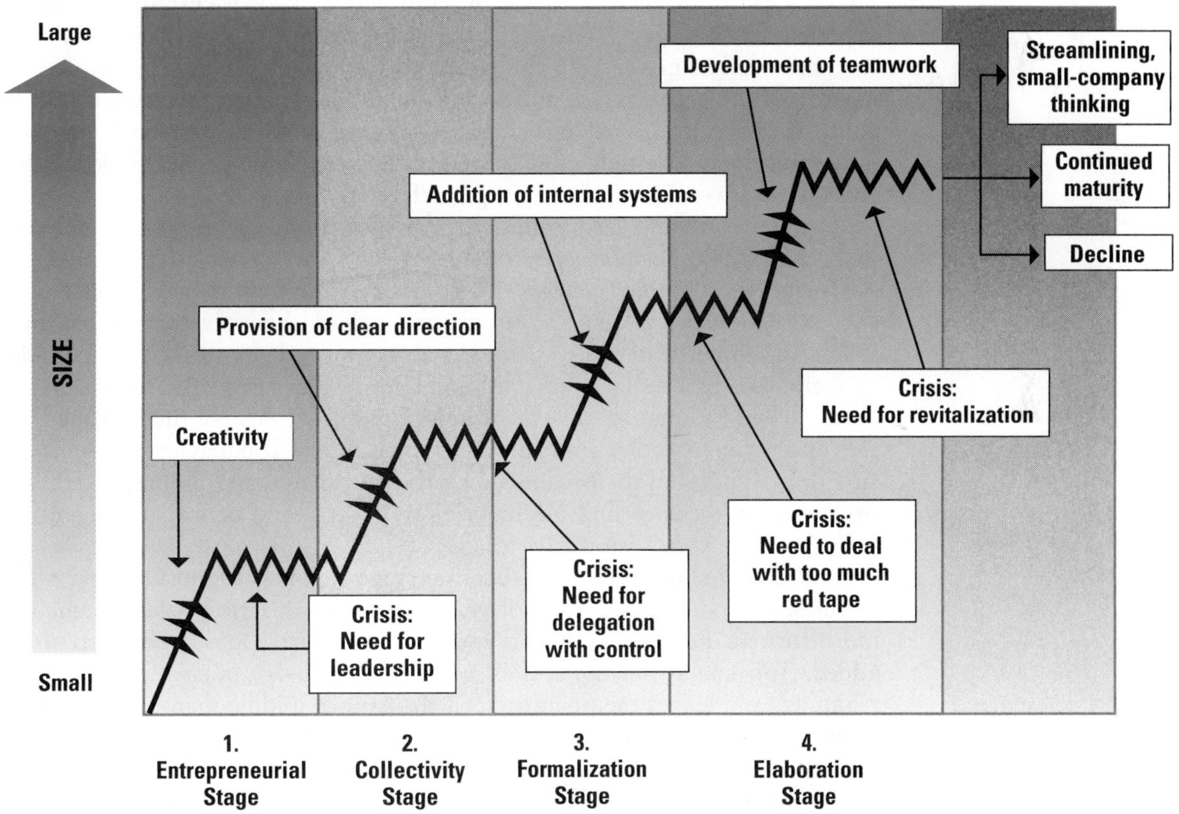

Source: Adapted from Robert E. Quinn and Kim Cameron, "Organizational Life Cycles and Shifting Criteria of Effectiveness: Some Preliminary Evidence," *Management Science* 29 (1983): 33–51; and Larry E. Greiner, "Evolution and Revolution as Organizations Grow," *Harvard Business Review* 50 (July–August 1972): 37–46.

and marketing. The organization is informal and nimble. The hours of work are long. Control is based on the owners' personal supervision. Growth is from a creative new product or service. Apple was in the **entrepreneurial stage** when it was created by Steve Jobs and Stephen Wozniak in Wozniak's parents' garage.

Crisis: Need for leadership. As the organization starts to grow, the larger number of employees causes problems. The creative and technically oriented owners are confronted with management issues, but they may prefer to focus their energies on making and selling the product or inventing new products and services. At this time of crisis, entrepreneurs must either adjust the structure of the organization to accommodate continued growth or else bring in strong managers who can do so. When Apple began a period of rapid growth, A.C. Markkula was brought in as a leader because neither Jobs nor Wozniak was qualified or cared to manage the expanding company.

2. *Collectivity stage.* If the leadership crisis is resolved, strong leadership is obtained and the organization begins to develop clear goals and direction. Departments are established along with a hierarchy of authority, job assignments, and a beginning division of labour. Web search engine Google has quickly moved from the entrepreneurial to the collectivity stage. Founders Larry Page and Sergey Brin devoted their full energy to making sure Google is the most powerful, fastest, and simplest search engine available, then brought in a skilled manager, former Novell CEO Eric Schmidt, to run the company. Google is currently hiring other experienced executives to manage various functional areas and business units as the organization grows.[30] In the **collectivity stage**, employees identify with the mission of the organization and spend long hours helping the organization succeed. Members feel part of a collective, and communication and control are mostly informal although a few formal systems begin to appear. Apple was in the collectivity stage during the rapid growth years from 1978 to 1981. Employees threw themselves into the business as the major product line was established and more than 2,000 dealers signed on.

   Crisis: Need for delegation with control. If the new management has been successful, lower-level employees gradually find themselves restricted by the strong top-down leadership. Lower-level managers begin to acquire confidence in their own functional areas and want more discretion. An autonomy crisis occurs when top managers, who were successful because of their strong leadership and vision, do not want to give up responsibility. Top managers want to make sure that all parts of the organization are coordinated and pulling together. The organization needs to find mechanisms to control and coordinate departments without direct supervision from the top.

3. *Formalization stage.* The **formalization stage** involves the installation and use of rules, procedures, and control systems. Communication is less frequent and more formal. Engineers, human resource specialists, and other staff may be added. Top management becomes concerned with issues such as strategy and planning, and leaves the operations of the firm to middle management. Product groups or other decentralized units may be formed to improve coordination. Incentive systems based on profits may be implemented to ensure that managers work toward what is best for the overall company. When effective, the new coordination and control systems enable the organization to continue growing by establishing linkage mechanisms between top management and field units. Apple was in the formalization stage in the mid-to-late 1980s.

Crisis: Need to deal with too much red tape. At this point in the organization's development, the proliferation of systems and programs may begin to strangle middle-level executives. The organization seems bureaucratized. Middle management may resent the intrusion of staff. Innovation may be restricted. The organization seems too large and complex to be managed through formal programs. It was at this stage of Apple's growth that Jobs resigned from the company and a new CEO took control to face his own management challenges.

4. *Elaboration stage.* The solution to the red-tape crisis is a new sense of collaboration and teamwork. Throughout the organization, managers develop skills for confronting problems and working together. Bureaucracy may have reached its limit. Social control and self-discipline reduce the need for additional formal controls. Managers learn to work within the bureaucracy without adding to it. Formal systems may be simplified and replaced by manager teams and task forces. To achieve collaboration, teams are often formed across functions or divisions of the company. The organization may also be split into multiple divisions to maintain a small-company philosophy. Apple is currently in the **elaboration stage** of the life cycle. Apple is looking at ways to increase its 3 percent market share in the computer industry. The Macintosh had limited retail presence, so Apple ran a pilot project in 2006 with Best Buy to get shelf space for Macs. By the end of 2007, there should be Macs in 300 Best Buy stores; however, Best Buy has not agreed to place Macs in all its stores.[31]

   Crisis: Need for revitalization. After the organization reaches maturity, it may enter periods of temporary decline.[32] A need for renewal may occur every ten to 20 years. The organization shifts out of alignment with the environment or perhaps becomes slow moving and over-bureaucratized and must go through a stage of streamlining and innovation. Top managers are often replaced during this period. At Apple, the top spot has changed hands a number of times as the company struggled to revitalize. CEOs John Sculley, Michael Spindler, and Gilbert Amelio were each ousted by the board as Apple's problems worsened. Steve Jobs returned in mid-1997 to run the company he had founded nearly 25 years earlier. During those 25 years, Jobs had gained management skills and experience he needed to help Apple through its problems. An older and smarter Jobs quickly reorganized the company, weeded out inefficiencies, and refocused Apple on innovative products for the consumer market, introducing a sleek new iMac in one of the hottest new product launches ever. Even more important, Jobs brought the entrepreneurial spirit back to Apple by moving the company into a whole new direction with the iPod music system. The iPod jump-started growth at Apple as the personal computer market continued to decline. Sales and profits are zooming at Apple thanks to the iPod and an expanding line of innovative consumer electronics products.[33] All mature organizations have to go through periods of revitalization or they will decline, as shown in the last stage of Exhibit 9.2.

Summary. Eighty-four percent of organizations that make it past the first year still fail within five years because they can't make the transition from the entrepreneurial stage.[34] The transitions become even more difficult as organizations progress through future stages of the life cycle. Organizations that do not successfully resolve the problems associated with these transitions are restricted in their growth and may even fail. From within an organization, the life cycle crises are very real. For example, Sam the Record Man was not able to survive the significant decline in CD sales as consumers shifted to digital downloading as their preferred method for buying music. In the first quarter of 2007, CD sales dropped 35 percent in Canada! According to Bobby Sniderman, son of the founder, "[we] are making a responsible decision [to close on June 30, 2007] in recognizing the status of the record industry and the increasing impact of technology."[35]

In Practice

Nike

Nike has always been sort of the "bad boy" of sports marketing. Phil Knight and his college track coach, Bill Bowerman, started the company with $500 each and got the inspiration for their first training shoe from a waffle iron (the shoe was named the Waffle Trainer because of its unique treads). Nike reveres creativity above all; leaders have supported a free-wheeling culture and seemed to almost scoff at the business side of things. Until recently, the company had been run largely on instinct and bravado.

But Nike began to suffer from its antiestablishment attitude, and Phil Knight recently made some major changes to move the company out of its lingering adolescence into a new stage of the life cycle. After hitting the $9.6 billion mark in 1998, sales stagnated. The company's previous approach of guessing how many shoes to manufacture and then flooding the market with them backfired when Nikes were left gathering dust on store shelves. A series of poorly conceived acquisitions and accusations that workers were being exploited in Nike's Asian factories didn't help matters. Nike didn't have the discipline and the formal systems it needed to cope with these kinds of problems. Consider that for a couple of years in the 1990s, the huge company didn't even have a chief financial officer. When Nike's French division went millions over budget in a promotional effort, Wall Street started asking if anyone was in charge at the company.

Although the Nike culture was powerful in terms of design and marketing, Knight realized the company could no longer operate like it was a young, small, entrepreneurial firm. Getting the basic pieces of the business side right—operating principles, financial management, supply chain and inventory management, and so forth—became a priority. He started by putting together a new team of experienced managers, including some Nike veterans but also some outsiders, such as CFO Donald Blair, who was lured from Pepsi. These managers, in turn, have brought the discipline Nike needs, such as establishing clear lines of authority, setting up top-flight systems for inventory and supply-chain management, and creating a department to deal with labour issues.

Nike seems to have successfully moved into the formalization stage, and the newfound discipline is paying off. After four years under the new management team, Nike's sales climbed 15 percent and the company earned almost $1 billion.[36]

Phil Knight's management overhaul didn't stop until it reached the top. In early 2005, Knight retired as CEO of the company and picked Bill Perez, former CEO of S.C. Johnson Company, as his successor. Some observers worry that without Knight, Nike will again founder. However, Knight believes Perez is the right leader for the organization's current stage of the life cycle. He continues to provide vision and guidance in his role as chairman, but the day-to-day running of the company is now in the hands of others.[37]

Nike has had to deal with significant criticism about the working conditions of its factories. The global anti-sweatshop movement has been targeting Nike since 1996 as it is the world's largest shoe supplier.[38] Nike responded by setting up an inspection system whereby its staff inspects several hundred factories a year, grades them on labour standards, and works with managers to improve problems. Nike also allows random factory inspections by the Fair Labour Association.[39]

Organizational Characteristics during the Life Cycle

As organizations evolve through the four stages of the life cycle, changes take place in structure, control systems, innovation, and goals. The organizational characteristics associated with each stage are summarized in Exhibit 9.3.

EXHIBIT 9.3
Organization Characteristics during Four Stages of Life Cycle

Characteristic	1. Entrepreneurial Nonbureaucratic	2. Collectivity Bureaucratic	3. Formalization Bureaucratic	4. Elaboration Very Bureaucratic
Structure	Informal, one-person show	Mostly informal, some procedures	Formal procedures, division of labour, new specialties added	Teamwork within bureaucracy, small-company thinking
Products or services	Single product or service	Major product or service, with variations	Line of products or services	Multiple product or service lines
Reward and control systems	Personal, paternalistic	Personal, contribution to success	Impersonal, formalized systems	Extensive, tailored to product and department
Innovation	By owner-manager	By employees and managers	By separate innovation group	By institutionalized R&D department
Goal	Survival	Growth	Internal stability, market expansion	Reputation, complete organization
Top management style	Individualistic, entrepreneurial	Charismatic, direction-giving	Delegation with control	Team approach, attack bureaucracy

Source: Adapted from Larry E. Greiner, "Evolution and Revolution as Organizations Grow," *Harvard Business Review* 50 (July–August 1972): 37–46; G. L. Lippitt and W. H. Schmidt, "Crises in a Developing Organization," *Harvard Business Review* 45 (November–December 1967): 102–112; B. R. Scott, "The Industrial State: Old Myths and New Realities," *Harvard Business Review* 51 (March–April 1973): 133–148; Robert E. Quinn and Kim Cameron, "Organizational Life Cycles and Shifting Criteria of Effectiveness," *Management Science* 29 (1983): 33–51.

Entrepreneurial. Initially, the organization is small, nonbureaucratic, and a one-person show. The top manager provides the structure and control system. Organizational energy is devoted to survival and the production of a single product or service. For example, Michael Cowpland, founder of Corel Corporation and co-founder of Mittel, took over the tiny ZIM Technologies International in 2001 so he could "get his hands dirty and work with start-up companies [again]."[40]

Collectivity. This is the organization's youth. Growth is rapid, and employees are excited and committed to the organization's mission. The structure is still mostly informal, although some procedures are emerging. Strong charismatic leaders like Steve Jobs of Apple or Phil Knight at Nike provide direction and goals for the organization. Continued growth is a major goal.

Formalization. At this point, the organization is entering midlife. Bureaucratic characteristics emerge. The organization adds staff support groups, formalizes procedures, and establishes a clear hierarchy and division of labour. At the formalization stage, organizations may also develop complementary products to offer a complete product line. Innovation may be achieved by establishing a separate innovation department. Major goals are internal stability and market expansion. Top management delegates, but it also implements formal control systems.

EXHIBIT 9.4
Life Cycle!

At this stage, for example, Microsoft founder Bill Gates turned the daily management of the company over to Steven Ballmer, who developed and implemented formal planning, management, and financial systems throughout the company. Gates wanted someone who could manage daily business operations so that he could focus his energies on technological innovation.[41]

Elaboration. The mature organization is large and bureaucratic, with extensive reward and control systems, rules, and procedures. Top managers attempt to develop a team orientation within the bureaucracy to prevent further bureaucratization. Their goal is to establish a complete organization that provides multiple product or service lines well. Innovation is institutionalized through an R&D department. Management may attack the bureaucracy and streamline it.

Summary. Growing organizations move through stages of a life cycle, and each stage is associated with specific characteristics of structure, control systems, goals, and innovation. The life-cycle phenomenon is a powerful concept used for understanding problems facing organizations and how managers can respond in a positive way to move an organization to the next stage.

Exhibit 9.4 presents another way to look at the organizational life cycle!

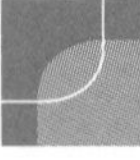

Organizational Bureaucracy and Control

As organizations progress through the life cycle, they usually take on bureaucratic characteristics as they grow larger and more complex. The systematic study of bureaucracy was launched by Max Weber, a sociologist who studied government organizations in Europe and developed a framework of administrative characteristics that would make large organizations rational and efficient.[42] Weber wanted to understand how organizations could be designed to play a positive role in the larger society.

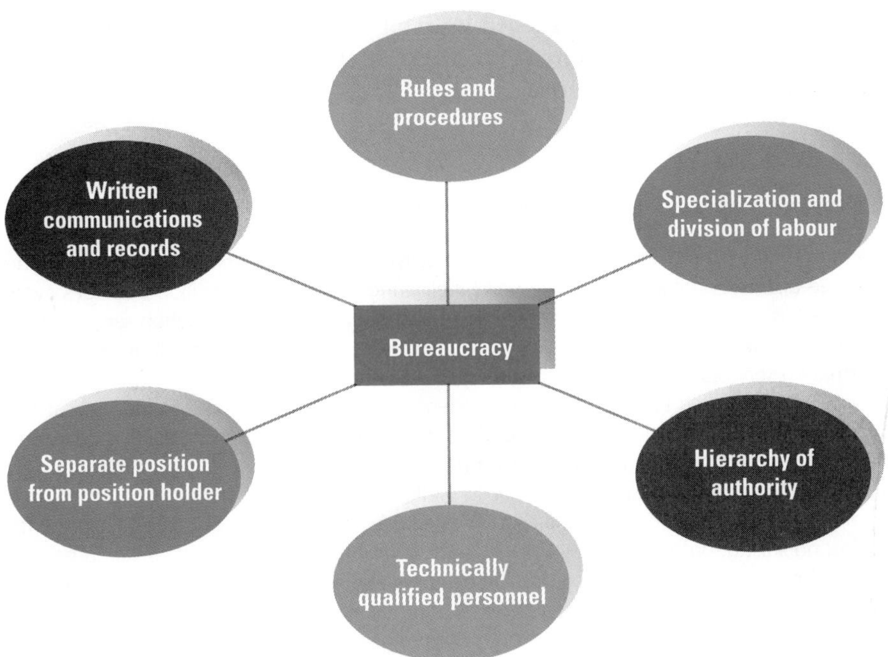

EXHIBIT 9.5
Weber's Dimensions of Bureaucracy

What Is Bureaucracy?

Although Weber perceived **bureaucracy** as a threat to basic personal liberties, he also recognized it as the most efficient possible system of organizing. He predicted the triumph of bureaucracy because of its ability to ensure more efficient functioning of organizations in both business and government settings. Weber identified a set of organizational characteristics, listed in Exhibit 9.5, that could be found in successful bureaucratic organizations.

Rules and standard procedures enabled organizational activities to be performed in a predictable, routine manner. Specialized duties meant that each employee had a clear task to perform. Hierarchy of authority provided a sensible mechanism for supervision and control. Technical competence was the basis by which people were hired rather than friendship, family ties, and favouritism, which dramatically increased work performance. The separation of the position from the position holder meant that individuals did not own or have an inherent right to the job, which promoted efficiency. Written records provided an organizational memory and continuity over time.

Although bureaucratic characteristics carried to an extreme are widely criticized today, the rational control introduced by Weber was a significant idea and a new form of organization. Bureaucracy provided many advantages over organization forms based on favouritism, social status, family connections, or graft. For example, when he was appointed as commissioner of internal revenue in the Philippines some 30 years ago, Efren Plana found massive corruption, including officials hiring their relatives for high-ranking jobs and tax assessors winning promotions by bribing their superiors.[43] In Mexico, an American lawyer had to pay a $500 bribe to get a telephone. The tradition of giving government posts to relatives is widespread in places such as China; however, China's emerging class of educated people does not like seeing the best jobs going to children and other relatives of officials.[44] By comparison, the logical and rational form of organization described by Weber allows work to be conducted efficiently and according to established rules.

The bureaucratic characteristics listed in Exhibit 9.5 can have a positive impact on many large firms. Consider United Parcel Service (UPS), one of the most efficient large organizations in North America.

In Practice

United Parcel Service (UPS)

UPS, sometimes called *Big Brown* for the colour of its delivery trucks and employee uniforms, is the largest package-distribution company in the world, delivering more than 13 million packages every business day. UPS is also gaining market share in air service, logistics, and information services. Television commercials ask, "What can Brown do for you today?" signifying the company's expanding global information services.

How did UPS become so successful? Many efficiencies were realized through adoption of the bureaucratic model of organization. UPS is bound up in rules and regulations. It teaches drivers an astounding 340 precise steps to correctly deliver a package. For example, it tells them how to load their trucks, how to fasten their seat belts, how to walk, and how to carry their keys. Strict dress codes are enforced—clean uniforms (called *browns*) every day, black or brown polished shoes with non-slip soles, no shirt unbuttoned below the first button, no hair below the shirt collar, no beards, no smoking in front of customers, and so on. The company conducts three-minute physical inspections of its drivers each day, a practice begun by the founder in the early 1900s. There are safety rules for drivers, loaders, clerks, and managers. Employees are asked to clean off their desks at the end of each day so they can start fresh the next morning. Managers are given copies of policy books with the expectation that they will use them regularly, and memos on various policies and rules circulate by the hundreds every day.

Despite the strict rules, employees are satisfied and UPS has a retention rate of more than 90 percent. Employees are treated well and paid well, and the company has maintained a sense of equality and fairness. Everyone is on a first-name basis. The policy book states, "A leader does not have to remind others of his authority by use of a title. Knowledge, performance, and capacity should be adequate evidence of position and leadership." Technical qualification, not favouritism, is the criterion for hiring and promotion. Top executives started at the bottom—the current chief executive, James Kelly, for example, began as a temporary holiday-rush driver. The emphasis on equality, fairness, and a promote-from-within mentality inspires loyalty and commitment throughout the ranks.

UPS has also been a leader in using new technology to enhance reliability and efficiency. Drivers use a computerized clipboard, called DIAD (Delivery Information Acquisition Device), to record everything from driver's miles per gallon to data on parcel delivery. Technology is enabling UPS to expand its services and become a global mover of knowledge and information as well as packages. Top managers know the new technology means some of UPS's rigid procedures may have to bend. However, it's likely they won't bend too far. When you're moving more than 13 million items a day, predictability and stability are the watchwords, whether you're using the company's first Model T Ford or its latest technological wizardry.[45]

UPS illustrates how bureaucratic characteristics increase with large size. UPS is so productive and dependable that it dominates the small package–delivery market. As it expands and transitions into a global, knowledge-based logistics business, UPS managers may need to find effective ways to reduce bureaucracy. The new technology and new services place more demands on workers, who may need more flexibility and autonomy to perform well. Now, let's look at some specific ways size affects organizational structure and control.

Size and Structural Control

In the field of organizational theory, organization size has been described as an important variable that influences structural design and methods of control. Should an organization become more bureaucratic as it grows larger? In what size organizations are bureaucratic characteristics most appropriate? More than 100 studies have attempted to answer these questions.[46] Most of these studies indicate that large organizations are different from small organizations along several dimensions of bureaucratic structure, including formalization, centralization, and personnel ratios.

PDA Remember...

As the organization grows, design greater formalization to achieve standardization and control. Guard against excessive overhead by keeping administrative, clerical, and support staff costs low.

Formalization and Centralization. **Formalization**, as described in Chapter 1, refers to rules, procedures, and written documentation, such as policy manuals and job descriptions, that prescribe the rights and duties of employees.[47] The evidence supports the conclusion that large organizations are more formalized, as at UPS. The reason is that large organizations rely on rules, procedures, and paperwork to achieve standardization and control across their large numbers of employees and departments, whereas top managers can use personal observation to control a small organization.[48]

Centralization refers to the level of hierarchy with authority to make decisions. In centralized organizations, decisions tend to be made at the top. In decentralized organizations, similar decisions would be made at a lower level.

Decentralization represents a paradox because, in the perfect bureaucracy, all decisions would be made by the top administrator, who would have perfect control. However, as an organization grows larger and has more people and departments, decisions cannot be passed to the top because senior managers would be overloaded. Thus, the research on organization size indicates that larger organizations permit greater decentralization.[49] Consider Microsoft, where CEO Steven Ballmer and Chairman Bill Gates used to make every important decision. In a company with 50,000 employees and multiple product lines, however, the traditional structure was too top heavy. Decision making had slowed to a snail's pace. Ballmer reorganized the 50,000-employee firm into seven divisions and gave division heads greater decision-making authority.[50] In small start-up organizations, on the other hand, the founder or top executive can effectively be involved in every decision, large and small.

Personnel Ratios. Another characteristic of bureaucracy relates to **personnel ratios** for administrative, clerical, and professional support staff. The most frequently studied ratio is the administrative ratio.[51] Two patterns have emerged. The first is that the ratio of top administration to total employees is actually smaller in large organizations,[52] indicating that organizations experience administrative economies as they grow larger. The second pattern concerns clerical and professional support staff ratios.[53] These groups tend to *increase* in proportion to organization size. The clerical ratio increases because of the greater communication and reporting requirements needed as organizations grow larger. The professional staff ratio increases because of the greater need for specialized skills in larger, complex organizations.[54]

The net effect for direct workers is that they decline as a percentage of total employees. In summary, whereas top administrators do not make up a disproportionate number of employees in large organizations, the idea that proportionately greater overhead is required in large organizations is supported. Although large organizations reduced overhead during the difficult economic years of the 1980s, overhead costs for many North American corporations began creeping back up again as revenues soared during the late-1990s.[55] With the declining North American economy following the crash of the technology sector, threats of war and terrorism, and general feelings of uncertainty, many companies have again been struggling to cut overhead costs. Keeping costs for administrative, clerical, and professional support staff low represents an ongoing challenge for large organizations.[56]

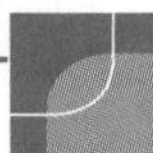

Bureaucracy in a Changing World

Weber's prediction of the triumph of bureaucracy proved accurate. Bureaucratic characteristics have many advantages and have worked extremely well for many of the needs of the industrial age.[57] By establishing a hierarchy of authority and specific rules and procedures, bureaucracy provided an effective way to bring order to large groups of people and prevent abuses of power. Impersonal relationships based on roles rather than people reduced the favouritism and nepotism characteristic of many pre-industrial organizations. Bureaucracy also provided for systematic and rational ways to organize and manage tasks too complex to be understood and handled by a few individuals, thus greatly improving the efficiency and effectiveness of large organizations.

The world is rapidly changing, however, and the machinelike bureaucratic system of the industrial age no longer works so well as organizations face new challenges. With global competition and uncertain environments, many organizations are fighting against increasing formalization and professional staff ratios. The problems caused by over-bureaucratization are evident in the inefficiencies of some government organizations. Some agencies have so many clerical staff members and confusing job titles that no one is really sure who does what. Some confusing titles include initiative officer, under-secretary to the sub-committee, and associate vice-president![58]

Some critics have blamed government bureaucracy for intelligence, communication, and accountability failures related to the September 11, 2001, terrorist attacks, the space shuttle disasters, and the December 26, 2004 tsunami. "Every time you add a layer of bureaucracy, you delay the movement of information up the chain of command . . . And you dilute the information because at each step some details are taken out."[59] Many business organizations, too, need to reduce formalization and bureaucracy. Narrowly defined job descriptions, for example, tend to limit the creativity, flexibility, and rapid response needed in today's knowledge-based organizations.

Organizing Temporary Systems for Flexibility and Innovation

How can organizations overcome the problems of bureaucracy in rapidly changing environments? Some are implementing innovative structural solutions. One structural concept, called the *incident command system* (ICS), is commonly used by organizations, such as police and fire departments or other emergency management agencies, that have to respond rapidly to emergency or crisis situations. The **incident command system** was developed to maintain the efficiency and control benefits of bureaucracy yet prevent the problem of slow response to crises.[60] The approach is being adapted by other types of organizations to help them respond quickly to new opportunities, unforeseen competitive threats, or organizational crises.

The basic idea behind the ICS is that the organization can glide smoothly between a highly formalized, hierarchical structure that is effective during times of stability and a more flexible, loosely structured one needed to respond well to unexpected and demanding environmental conditions. The hierarchical side with its rules, procedures, and chain of command helps maintain control and ensure adherence to rules that have been developed and tested over many years to cope with well-understood problems and situations. However, during times of high uncertainty, the most effective structure is one that loosens the lines of command and enables people to work across departmental and hierarchical lines to anticipate, avoid, and solve unanticipated problems within the context of a clearly understood mission and guidelines.

The approach can be seen on the deck of a nuclear aircraft carrier, where there is a rigid chain of command and people are expected to follow orders promptly and without question.[61] Formalization is high, with manuals detailing proper procedures for every known situation. However, at times of high uncertainty, such as the launching and recovery of planes during real or simulated warfare, an important shift occurs. The rigid hierarchy seems to dissolve, and a loosely organized, collaborative structure in which sailors and officers work together as colleagues takes its place. People discuss the best procedures to use, and everyone typically follows the lead of whoever has the most experience and knowledge in a particular area. During this time, no one is thinking about job titles, authority, or chain of command; they are just thinking about the best way to accomplish the mission safely.

A variety of mechanisms ensure smooth functioning of the ICS.[62] For example, despite the free-flowing and flexible nature of crisis response, someone is always in charge. The *incident commander* is ultimately responsible for all activities that occur, and everyone knows clearly who is in charge of what aspect of the situation. This helps maintain order in a chaotic environment. The key is that, whereas formal authority relationships are fixed, decision-making authority is dispersed to individuals who best understand the particular situation. The system is based on trust that lower-level workers have a clear understanding of the mission and make decisions and take actions within guidelines that support the organization's goals. Developing an ICS requires a significant commitment of time and resources, but it offers great potential for organizations that require extremely high reliability, flexibility, and innovation. One organization that effectively uses the incident command model is the Salvation Army, as described in this chapter's Leading by Design box.

PDA Remember...

Consider using the incident command system to maintain the efficiency and control benefits of bureaucracy but prevent the problem of slow response to rapid environmental change. Enable the organization to glide smoothly from a formalized system during times of stability to a more flexible, loosely structured one when facing threats, crises, or unexpected environmental changes.

Other Approaches to Reducing Bureaucracy

Organizations are taking a number of other, less-dramatic steps to reduce bureaucracy. Many are cutting layers of the hierarchy, keeping headquarters staff small, and giving lower-level workers greater freedom to make decisions rather than burdening them with excessive rules and regulations. The point is ensure that organizations are not top heavy with lawyers, accountants, and financial analysts who inhibit the flexibility and autonomy of divisions. The rise in the Canadian dollar has challenged the manufacturing sector to become lean and flexible so that it can better compete globally. Manufacturers such as Edson and Elettra Technologies in Hamilton, Ontario, have responded by streamlining their internal processes and organizational designs.[63]

Of course, many companies must be large to have sufficient resources and complexity to produce products for a global environment, but companies such as 3M, Coca-Cola, Weyerhaeuser, and Heinz are striving toward greater decentralization and leanness. They are giving frontline workers more authority and responsibility to define and direct their own jobs, often by creating self-directed teams that find ways to coordinate work, improve productivity, and better serve customers.

Another attack on bureaucracy is from the increasing professionalism of employees. Professionalism is defined as the length of formal training and experience of employees. More employees need college or university degrees, MBAs, and other professional degrees to work as lawyers, researchers, or doctors at large organizations. Internet-based companies may be staffed entirely by well-educated knowledge workers. Studies of professionals show that formalization is not needed because professional training regularizes a high standard of behaviour for employees that acts as a substitute for bureaucracy.[64] Organizations also enhance this trend when they provide ongoing training for *all* employees, from the front office to the shop floor, in a push for continuous individual and organizational learning. Increased training substitutes for bureaucratic rules and procedures that can constrain the creativity of employees in solving problems and increases organizational capability.

Leading *by Design*

The Salvation Army

The Salvation Army has been called "the most effective organization in the world" by leading management scholar, the late Peter Drucker. One reason the organization is so effective and powerful is its approach to organizing, which makes use of the incident command system to provide the right amount of structure, control, and flexibility to meet the requirements of each situation. The Salvation Army refers to its approach as "organizing to improvise."

The Salvation Army provides day-to-day assistance to the homeless and economically disadvantaged. In addition, the organization rushes in whenever there is a major disaster—whether a tornado, flood, hurricane, airplane crash, or terrorist attack—to network with other agencies to provide disaster relief. Long after the most desperate moments of the initial crisis have passed, the Salvation Army continues helping people rebuild their lives and communities—offering financial assistance; meeting physical needs for food, clothing, and housing; and providing emotional and spiritual support to inspire hope and help people build a foundation for the future. The Army's management realizes that emergencies demand high flexibility. At the same time, the organization must have a high level of control and accountability to ensure its continued existence and meet its day-to-day responsibilities. As a former national commander puts it, "We have to have it both ways. We can't choose to be flexible and reckless or to be accountable and responsive . . . We have to be several different kinds of organizations at the same time."

In the early emergency moments of a crisis, the Salvation Army deploys a temporary organization that has its own command structure. People need to have a clear sense of who's in charge to prevent the rapid response demands from degenerating into chaos. For example, when the Army responds a crisis, manuals clearly specify in advance who is responsible for talking to the media, who is in charge of supply inventories, who liaises duties with other agencies, and so forth. This model for the temporary organization keeps the Salvation Army responsive and consistent. In the later recovery and rebuilding phases of a crisis, supervisors frequently give people general guidelines and allow them to improvise the best solutions. There isn't time for supervisors to review and sign off on every decision that needs to be made to get families and communities re-established. On September 11, 2001, the Salvation Army in Corner Brook, Newfoundland and Labrador, had to support 150 people whose flight had been diverted to Stephenville. According to Major Ross Bungay, "[it] was an operation of mercy in a crisis environment, and even in situations we had not been specifically trained for ... the cumulative talent and expertise served us all well."[65]

The Salvation Army actually has people simultaneously working in all different types of organization structures, from traditional vertical command structures, to horizontal teams, to a sort of network form that relies on collaboration with other agencies. Operating in such a fluid way enables the organization to accomplish amazing results. It has been recognized as a leader in putting money to maximal use, meaning donors are willing to give because they trust the organization to be responsible and accountable at the same time it is flexible and innovative in meeting human needs.[66]

A form of organization called professional partnership has emerged that is made up completely of professionals.[67] These organizations include medical practices, law firms, and consulting firms, such as McKinsey & Company and Managerial Design. The general finding concerning professional partnerships is that branches have substantial autonomy and decentralized authority to make necessary decisions. They work with a consensus orientation rather than the top-down direction typical of traditional business and government organizations. Thus, the trend of increasing professionalism, combined with rapidly changing environments, is leading to less bureaucracy in North America.

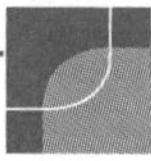

Organizational Control Strategies

Even though many organizations are trying to decrease bureaucracy and reduce rules and procedures that constrain employees, every organization needs systems for guiding and controlling the organization. Employees may have more freedom in today's companies, but control is still a major responsibility of management.

Managers at the top and middle levels of an organization can choose among three overall control strategies. These strategies come from a framework for organizational control proposed by William Ouchi. Ouchi suggested three control strategies that organizations could adopt—bureaucratic, market, and clan.[68] Each form of control uses different types of information. However, all three types may appear simultaneously in an organization. The requirements for each control strategy are given in Exhibit 9.6.

Bureaucratic Control

Bureaucratic control is the use of rules, policies, hierarchy of authority, written documentation, standardization, and other bureaucratic mechanisms to standardize behaviour and assess performance. Bureaucratic control uses the bureaucratic characteristics defined by Weber and illustrated in the UPS case. The primary purpose of bureaucratic rules and procedures is to standardize and control employee behaviour.

Recall that as organizations progress through the life cycle and grow larger, they become more formalized and standardized. Within a large organization, thousands of work behaviours and information exchanges take place both vertically and horizontally. Rules and policies evolve through a process of trial and error to regulate these behaviours. Some degree of bureaucratic control is used in virtually every organization. Rules, regulations, and directives contain information about a range of behaviours.

EXHIBIT 9.6
Three Organizational Control Strategies

Type	Requirements
Bureaucracy	Rules, standards, hierarchy, legitimate authority
Market	Prices, competition, exchange relationship
Clan	Tradition, shared values and beliefs, trust

Source: Based on William G. Ouchi, "A Conceptual Framework for the Design of Organizational Control Mechanisms," *Management Science* 25 (1979): 833–848.

To make bureaucratic control work, managers must have the authority to maintain control over the organization. Weber argued that legitimate, rational authority granted to managers was preferred over other types of control (e.g., favouritism or payoffs) as the basis for organizational decisions and activities. Within the larger society, however, Weber identified three types of authority that could explain the creation and control of a large organization.[69]

Rational-legal authority is based on employees' belief in the legality of rules and the right of those elevated to positions of authority to issue commands. Rational-legal authority is the basis for both creation and control of most government organizations and is the most common base of control in organizations worldwide. **Traditional authority** is the belief in traditions and in the legitimacy of the status of people exercising authority through those traditions. Traditional authority is the basis for control for monarchies, churches, and some organizations in Latin America and the Middle East. **Charismatic authority** is based on devotion to the exemplary character or to the heroism of an individual person and the order defined by him or her. Revolutionary military organizations are often based on the leader's charisma, as are North American organizations led by charismatic individuals such as Steve Jobs. The organization reflects the personality and values of the leader.

More than one type of authority—such as long tradition and the leader's special charisma—may exist in organizations, but rational-legal authority is the most widely used form to govern internal work activities and decision making, particularly in large organizations.

Market Control

Market control occurs when price competition is used to evaluate the output and productivity of an organization. The idea of market control originated in economics.[70] A dollar price is an efficient form of control, because managers can compare prices and profits to evaluate the efficiency of their corporation. Top managers nearly always use the price mechanism to evaluate performance in organizations. Corporate sales and costs are summarized in a profit-and-loss statement that can be compared against performance in previous years or with that of other corporations.

The use of market control requires that outputs be sufficiently explicit for a price to be assigned and competition exist. Without competition, the price does not accurately reflect internal efficiency. Increasingly, governments and nonprofit organizations are turning to market control. Market control was once used primarily at the level of the entire organization, but it is increasingly used in product divisions. Profit centres are self-contained product divisions, such as those described in Chapter 3. Each division contains resource inputs needed to produce a product. Each division can be evaluated on the basis of profit or loss compared with other divisions. Asea Brown Boveri (ABB), a multinational electrical contractor and manufacturer of electrical equipment, includes three different types of profit centres, all operating according to their own bottom line and all interacting through buying and selling with one another and with outside customers.[71] The network organization, also described in Chapter 3, illustrates market control as well. Different companies compete on price to provide the functions and services required by the hub organization. The organization typically contracts with the company that offers the best price and value.

Some firms require that individual departments interact with one another at market prices—buying and selling products or services among themselves at prices equivalent to those quoted outside the firm. To make the market control system work, internal units also have the option to buy and sell with outside companies. Imperial Oil Limited of Canada (formerly Esso) transformed its R&D department into a semiautonomous profit centre several years ago.

In Practice

Imperial Oil Limited

In the early 1990s, Imperial Oil's R&D was a monopoly service provider allocated an annual budget of about $45 million. However, Imperial Oil felt that this method of operating gave the 200 scientists and staff little incentive to control costs or advance quality.

Today, R&D receives a much smaller budget and essentially supports itself through applied research and lab-services contracts negotiated with internal and external customers. Contracts spell out the costs of each program, analysis, or other service, and cost-conscious Imperial Oil managers can shop for lower prices among external labs.

R&D has even introduced competition within its own small unit. For example, research teams are free to buy some lab services outside the company if they feel their own laboratories are overpriced or inefficient. However, quality and efficiency have dramatically improved at Imperial Oil's R&D, and the unit's high-quality, low-cost services are attracting a great deal of business from outside the company. Canadian companies routinely send samples of used motor oil to the R&D labs for analysis, manufacturers use R&D to autopsy equipment failures, and vehicle makers like General Motors and Ford test new engines at Imperial Oil's R&D's chassis dynamometer lab. According to John Charlton, Imperial Oil's corporate strategic planning manager, applying market control to R&D has led to an increase in the amount of work the unit does, as well as a 12 percent reduction in internal costs.[72]

Market control can be used only when the output of an organization, division, or department can be assigned a dollar price and when there is competition. Organizations are finding that they can apply the market control concept to internal departments such as accounting, data processing, legal, and information services.

Clan Control

Clan control is the use of social characteristics, such as organizational culture, shared values, commitment, traditions, and beliefs, to control behaviour. Organizations that use clan control require shared values and trust among employees.[73] Clan control is important when ambiguity and uncertainty are high. High uncertainty means the organization cannot put a price on its services, and things change so quickly that rules and regulations are not able to specify every correct behaviour. Under clan control, people may be hired because they are committed to the organization's purpose, such as in a religious organization. New employees may be subjected to a long period of socialization to gain acceptance by colleagues. Clan control is most often used in small, informal organizations or in organizations with a strong culture, because of personal involvement in and commitment to the organization's purpose. For example, St. Luke's Communications Ltd., a London, U.K. advertising firm committed to equal employee ownership, is especially careful to bring in only new employees who believe in the agency's philosophy and mission. The company even turned down a $90 million contract because it meant rapidly recruiting new employees who might not fit with St. Luke's distinctive culture. Clan control works for St. Luke's; the agency is highly respected and its revenues continue to grow.[74]

Traditional control mechanisms based on strict rules and close supervision are ineffective for controlling behaviour in conditions of high uncertainty and rapid change.[75] In addition, the growing use of computer networks and the Internet, which often leads to a democratic spread of information throughout the organization, may force many companies to depend less on bureaucratic control and more on shared values that guide individual actions for the corporate good.[76] Labatt Brewing Company Limited represents a good example of clan control.

In Practice

Labatt Brewing Company Limited (Labatts)

"Don't expect working life [at Labatts] to be like one continuous beer commercial."[77] New employees learn immediately that they need to fit into the organization's culture or leave. They are told, on their first day at work, that those who cannot or will not embrace the InBev Way are in the wrong organization. (InBev SA is the Belgium-based company that owns Labatts.) According to John Stacey, vice president, People Matters, it is not enough to deliver results but that people must fit into Labatts or leave. He says, "You may think that it's a harsh comment but we want both [fit and performance]."[78] He goes on to say that there's zero tolerance for complacency at Labatts and describes Labatts as a hard-driving environment.

John Stacey's principal role at Labatts is to ensure that the InBev Way—the values—permeate the organization. InBev has a global training program so that it can develop its own leadership from within the organization. Management trainees spend ten months learning all aspects of the business and then they are assigned junior management positions. The trainees are selected through a rigorous process—only 14 of more than 3,000 are hired.

Labatts has been through several organizational changes and now brews more than 60 brands of beer worldwide. The InBev Way is designed to inspire and to control behaviour among the 3,200 Canadian employees.

Labatts is successfully using clan control, but this story illustrates that large size increases the demands on managers to maintain strong cultural values that support this type of control. Today's companies that are trying to become learning organizations often use clan control or self-control rather than relying on rules and regulations. Self-control is similar to clan control, but whereas clan control is a function of being socialized into a group, self-control stems from the values, goals, and standards of individuals. The organization attempts to induce a change such that individual employees' own internal values and work preferences are brought in line with the organization's values and goals.[79] With self-control, employees generally set their own goals and monitor their own performance, yet companies relying on self-control need strong leaders who can clarify boundaries within which employees exercise their own knowledge and discretion.

PDA Remember...

Implement one of the three basic choices—bureaucratic, clan, market—as the primary means of organizational control. Use bureaucratic control when organizations are large, have a stable environment, and use routine technology. Use clan control in small, uncertain departments. Use market control when outputs can be priced and when competitive bidding is available.

Clan control or self-control may also be used in some departments, such as strategic planning, where uncertainty is high and performance is difficult to measure. Managers of departments that rely on these informal control mechanisms must not assume that the absence of written, bureaucratic control means no control is present. Clan control is invisible yet very powerful. One study found that the actions of employees were controlled even more powerfully and completely with clan control than with a bureaucratic hierarchy.[80] When clan control works, bureaucratic control is not needed.

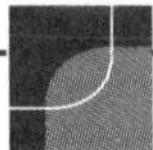

Organizational Decline and Downsizing

Earlier in the chapter, we discussed the organizational life cycle, which suggests that organizations are born, grow older, and eventually die. Every organization goes through periods of temporary decline. In addition, a reality in today's environment is that for some organizations, continual growth and expansion may not be possible.

All around, we see evidence that some organizations have stopped growing, and many are declining. Huge organizations such as Enron, WorldCom, and Arthur Andersen have collapsed partly as a result of rapid growth and ineffective control. The Catholic Church continues to lose membership following reports of child molestation by priests and the failure in higher levels of the organization to remove molesters and prevent further abuse. Municipalities have been forced to close schools and lay off teachers as tax revenues have declined. Many big companies, including DaimlerChrysler, Nortel Networks, General Motors, and General Electric, have had significant job cuts in recent years, and hundreds of Internet companies that once looked poised for rapid growth have gone out of business.

In this section, we examine the causes and stages of organizational decline and then discuss how leaders can effectively manage the downsizing that is a reality in today's companies.

Definition and Causes

The term **organizational decline** is used to define a condition in which a substantial, absolute decrease in an organization's resource base occurs over a period.[81] Organizational decline is often associated with environmental decline in the sense that an organizational domain experiences either a reduction in size (such as shrinkage in customer demand or erosion of a city's tax base) or a reduction in shape (such as a shift in customer demand). In general, three factors are considered to cause organizational decline.

1. *Organizational atrophy.* Atrophy occurs when organizations grow older and become inefficient and overly bureaucratized. The organization's ability to adapt to its environment deteriorates. Often, atrophy follows a long period of success, because an organization takes success for granted, becomes attached to practices and structures that worked in the past, and fails to adapt to changes in the environment.[82] For example, Blockbuster, which was king of the video-store industry in the 1980s and 1990s, has had trouble adapting to the new world of video-on-demand (VOD) and digital downloading. Blockbuster is way behind upstarts like the United States' Netflix in pay VOD delivery because managers had trouble giving up the traditional successful approach of renting out videos in stores and online. Experts warn that companies risk becoming obsolete by sticking to patterns that were successful in the past but might no longer be effective.[83] Some warning signals for organizational atrophy include excess administrative and support staff, cumbersome administrative procedures, lack of effective communication and coordination, and outdated organizational structure.[84]
2. *Vulnerability.* Vulnerability reflects an organization's strategic inability to prosper in its environment. This often happens to small organizations that are not

yet fully established. They are vulnerable to shifts in consumer tastes or in the economic health of the larger community. Small e-commerce companies that had not yet become established were the first to go out of business when the technology sector began to decline. Some organizations are vulnerable because they are unable to define the correct strategy to fit the environment. Vulnerable organizations typically need to redefine their environmental domain to enter new industries or markets.

3. *Environmental decline or competition.* Environmental decline refers to reduced energy and resources available to support an organization. When the environment has less capacity to support organizations, the organization has to either scale down operations or shift to another domain.[85] New competition increases the problem, especially for small organizations. Consider what's happening to North American toolmakers, the companies that make the dies, moulds, jigs, fixtures, and gauges used on factory floors to manufacture everything from car doors to laser-guided bombs. Many have gone out of business in recent years, unable to compete with the super-low prices their counterparts in China are offering. As a result, there has been a decrease of 8 percent, between 1997 and 2004, in the number of workers employed in the toolmaker sector.[86]

PDA Remember...

Understand the causes and stages of decline. Be vigilant to detect signs of decline in the organization and take action as quickly as possible to reverse course. Quick action in the early stages prevents the organization from deteriorating to a stage-4 crisis, when a turnaround becomes much more difficult.

A Model of Decline Stages

Based on an extensive review of organizational decline research, a model of decline stages has been proposed and is summarized in Exhibit 9.7. This model suggests

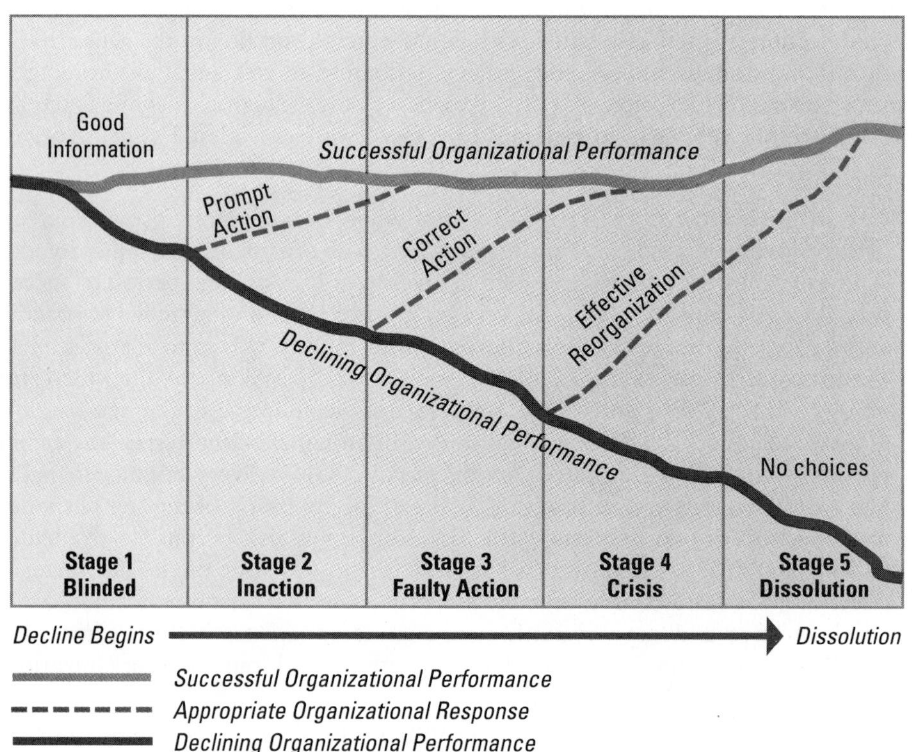

EXHIBIT 9.7
Stages of Decline and the Widening Performance Gap
Source: Reprinted from "Decline in Organizations: A Literature Integration and Extension," by William Weitzel and Ellen Jonsson, published in *Administrative Science Quarterly,* 34, no. 1 (March 1989), by permission of Administrative Science Quarterly. © Johnson Graduate School of Management, Cornell University.

that decline, if not managed properly, can move through five stages resulting in organizational dissolution.[87]

1. *Blinded stage.* The first stage of decline is the internal and external change that threatens long-term survival and may require the organization to tighten up. The organization may have excess personnel, cumbersome procedures, or lack of harmony with customers. Leaders often miss the signals of decline at this point, and the solution is to develop effective scanning and control systems that indicate when something is wrong. With timely information, alert executives can bring the organization back to top performance.
2. *Inaction stage.* The second stage of decline is called inaction in which denial occurs despite signs of deteriorating performance. Leaders may try to persuade employees that all is well. "Creative accounting" may make things look fine during this period. The solution is for leaders to acknowledge decline and take prompt action to realign the organization with the environment. Leadership actions may include new problem-solving approaches, increasing decision-making participation, and encouraging expression of dissatisfaction to learn what is wrong.
3. *Faulty action stage.* In the third stage, the organization is facing serious problems, and indicators of poor performance cannot be ignored. Failure to adjust to the declining spiral at this point can lead to organizational failure. Leaders are forced by severe circumstances to consider major changes. Actions may involve retrenchment, including downsizing personnel. Leaders should reduce employee uncertainty by clarifying values and providing information. A major mistake at this stage decreases the organization's chance for a turnaround.
4. *Crisis stage.* In the fourth stage, the organization still has not been able to deal with decline effectively and is facing a panic. The organization may experience chaos, efforts to go back to basics, sharp changes, and anger. It is best for managers to prevent a stage-4 crisis, and the only solution is major reorganization. The social fabric of the organization is eroding, and dramatic actions, such as replacing top administrators and revolutionary changes in structure, strategy, and culture, are necessary. Workforce downsizing may be severe.
5. *Dissolution stage.* This stage of decline is irreversible. The organization is suffering loss of markets and reputation, the loss of its best personnel, and capital depletion. The only available strategy is to close down the organization in an orderly fashion and reduce the separation trauma of employees.

The following example of a once-respected Canadian retailer shows how failure to respond appropriately to signs of decline can lead to disaster.

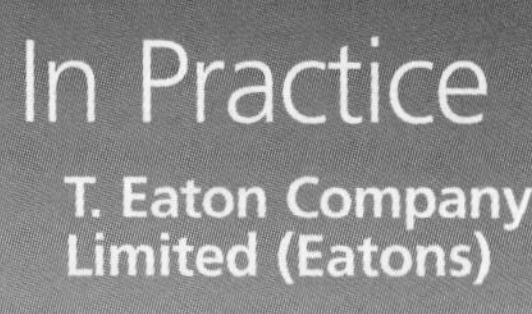

Eatons was founded by Timothy Eaton in 1869 on Yonge Street in downtown Toronto. His first venture, a bakery in St, Marys, Ontario, failed but he successfully changed the shop from a bakery to a dry goods store. He worked very hard and took the view that " . . . we never close the store in the evening while there is anybody on the street."[88] Timothy Eaton was an innovator—he pioneered "sales in cash only" and "satisfaction guaranteed or money refunded" approaches to retail. By the mid-1880s, Eatons had electric lights and a sprinkler system and, in 1884, Eatons distributed its first mail-order catalogue. The Eaton family ran the company without interruption for many years. During World War II, Eatons had a staff of 30,000. Eatons had a strong culture—employees referred to themselves proudly as Eatonians. Eatonians received lavish presents from the family considered by many to be royalty. Even so, workers tried, unsuccessfully, to unionize Eatons in 1952 in response to the long hours and low wages that they endured. In 1984, they tried again and failed again to unionize the chain.[89]

From the 1960s onward, Eatons faced increasing competition from Simpson-Sears and boutiques across the country. In 1997, the Eaton family, who owned all the shares in Eatons, sought bankruptcy protection. At the time, Eatons had 90 stores and 24,500 employees. In 1998, Eatons went public and reduced the number of its stores to 64. Even so, Eatons suffered a net loss of $72 million and in 1999, it closed more stores and restructured. In August 1999, after its share price had plummeted from a June 1998 high of $16 to 71¢, Eatons went bankrupt.[90] The restructuring effort had failed and what was once the largest privately held department chain in the world became not much more than a real estate play. The Royal Canadian Air Farce gave Eatons a funeral and noted that Eatons was Wal-Marted![91]

While there are many possible explanations for Eaton's demise, one important factor was Timothy Eaton's children and grandchildren's lack of interest in the business. "Fundamentally, it appears that the problem-sensing ability of management was missing at the troubled Eaton's."[92] Sears Canada bought the rights to the Eaton name but, on February 26, 2002, conceded defeat in its efforts to relaunch Eatons as an upscale retailer.

As this example shows, properly managing organizational decline is necessary if an organization is to avoid dissolution. Leaders have a responsibility to detect the signs of decline, acknowledge them, implement necessary action, and reverse course. Some of the most difficult decisions pertain to downsizing, which refers to intentionally reducing the size of a company's workforce.

Downsizing Implementation

PDA Remember...

When layoffs are necessary, handle them with great care. Treat departing employees humanely, communicate with employees and provide as much information as possible, provide assistance to displaced workers, and remember the emotional needs of survivors.

The economic downturn that began in 2000 has made **downsizing** a common practice in North American corporations. In addition, downsizing is a part of many change initiatives in today's organizations.[93] Reengineering projects, mergers and acquisitions, global competition, and the trend toward outsourcing have all led to job reductions.[94]

Some researchers have found that massive downsizing has often not achieved the intended benefits and in some cases has significantly harmed the organization.[95] Nevertheless, there are times when downsizing is a necessary part of managing organizational decline. A number of techniques can help smooth the downsizing process and ease tensions for employees who leave and for those who remain.[96]

1. *Communicate more, not less.* Some organizations seem to think the less that's said about a pending layoff, the better. Not so. Organizational managers should provide advance notice with as much information as possible. At 3Com Corporation, managers drew up a three-stage plan as they prepared for layoffs. First, they warned employees several months ahead that layoffs were inevitable. Soon thereafter, they held on-site presentations at all locations to explain to employees why the layoffs were needed and to provide as much information as they could about what employees should expect. Employees being cut

were given the required full 60 days' notice.[97] Managers should remember that it is impossible to over-communicate during turbulent times. Remaining employees need to know what is expected of them, whether future layoffs are a possibility, and what the organization is doing to help co-workers who have lost their jobs.

2. *Provide assistance to displaced workers.* The organization has a responsibility to help displaced workers cope with the loss of their jobs and get re-established in the job market. The organization can provide training, severance packages, extended benefits, and outplacement assistance. In addition, counselling services for both employees and their families can ease the trauma associated with a job loss. Another key step is to allow employees to leave with dignity, giving them an opportunity to say goodbye to colleagues and meet with leaders to express their hurt and anger.
3. *Help the survivors thrive.* Leaders should remember the emotional needs of survivors as well. Many people experience survivor guilt, anger, confusion, and sadness after the loss of colleagues, and these feelings should be acknowledged. Survivors might also be concerned about their own jobs and have difficulty adapting to the changes in job duties, responsibilities, and so forth.

Even the best-managed organizations may sometimes need to lay off employees in a turbulent environment or to revitalize the organization and reverse decline. Leaders can attain positive results if they handle downsizing in a way that lets departing employees leave with dignity and enables remaining organization members to be motivated, productive, and committed to a better future.

In Practice
Dofasco

C.W. Sherman created the Dominion Steel Casting Company in 1912 to make steel castings for Canadian railways. It was not until 1918 that its name was changed to Dofasco. In 1938, Dofasco became the first Canadian manufacturer to introduce profit sharing. "[World War II] put added pressure on Canada's heavy industries. In 1941, production started at Dofasco's armour plate shop. Every inch of armour plate used to protect Canadian soldiers was manufactured by Dofasco."[98]

In the 1970s, the North American steel industry shrank considerably—32 percent of its steel-making capacity disappeared. Dofasco, however, survived by improving customer service and by automating many of its processes. A 1985 article in *The Globe and Mail* reported that "steel industry watchers are beginning to run out of superlatives to describe the continued robust performance of Dofasco."[99] However, in the late 1980s and early 1990s, Dofasco downsized considerably. The number of employees dropped from 12,800 to 7,000 through attrition and voluntary early retirements.

In April 1994, when 650 employees were laid off, their layoffs were handled through the Canadian Steel Trade and Employment Congress, a joint venture between Canadian steel companies and the United Steelworkers of America. The Congress provides various services to steel industry workers such as worker adjustment services, helping workers affected by layoff and/or shutdowns, as well as training services for the workforce.[100] Dofasco created an action committee from all its stakeholders and 14 people were assigned to develop a program to assist employees to adjust to the layoffs. The resulting program was called the Dofasco Transition Assistance Program. The laid-off workers received new skills training, career counselling, and job placement. At the same time,

Dofasco introduced a program called Play-to-Win designed to reduce the negative impact of the layoffs on those who were not laid off. The program consisted of a three-day experiential session that focused on such topics as coping with change, rebuilding trust and working together in a team environment.[101]

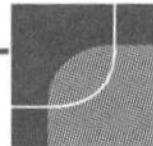

Summary and Interpretation

The material covered in this chapter contains several important ideas about organizations. Organizations evolve through distinct life cycle stages as they grow and mature. Organization structure, internal systems, and management issues are different for each stage of development. Growth creates crises and revolutions along the way toward large size. A major task of managers is to guide the organization through the entrepreneurial, collectivity, formalization, and elaboration stages of development. As organizations progress through the life cycle and grow larger and more complex, they generally take on bureaucratic characteristics, such as rules, division of labour, written records, hierarchy of authority, and impersonal procedures. Bureaucracy is a logical form of organizing that lets firms use resources efficiently. However, in many large corporate and government organizations, bureaucracy has come under attack with attempts to decentralize authority, flatten organization structure, reduce rules and written records, and create a small-company mindset. These companies are willing to trade economies of scale for responsive, adaptive organizations. Many companies are subdividing to gain small-company advantages. Another approach to overcoming the problems of bureaucracy is to use a structural concept called the incident command system, which enables the organization to glide smoothly between a highly formalized, hierarchical style that is effective during times of stability and a more flexible, loosely structured one needed to respond to unexpected or volatile environmental conditions.

In large organizations, greater support is required from clerical and professional staff specialists. This is a logical outcome of employee specialization and the division of labour. By dividing an organization's tasks and having specialists perform each part, the organization can become more efficient.

All organizations, large and small, need systems for control. Managers can choose among three overall control strategies: bureaucratic, market, and clan. Bureaucratic control relies on standard rules and the rational-legal authority of managers. Market control is used where product or service outputs can be priced and competition exists. Clan control and, more recently, self-control are associated with uncertain and rapidly changing organization processes. They rely on commitment, tradition, and shared values for control. Managers may use a combination of control approaches to meet the organization's needs.

Many organizations have stopped growing, and some are declining. Organizations go through stages of decline, and it is the responsibility of managers to detect the signs of decline, implement necessary action, and reverse course. One of the most difficult decisions is downsizing the workforce. To smooth the downsizing process, managers should communicate with employees and provide as much information as possible, provide assistance to displaced workers, and remember to address the emotional needs of those who remain with the organization.

Key Concepts

bureaucracy, p. 309
bureaucratic control, p. 315
centralization, p. 311
charismatic authority, p. 316
clan control, p. 317
collectivity stage, p. 304
downsizing, p. 322
elaboration stage, p. 305
entrepreneurial stage, p. 304
formalization, p. 311
formalization stage, p. 304
incident command system, p. 312
life cycle, p. 302
market control, p. 316
organizational decline, p. 319
personnel ratios, p. 311
rational-legal authority, p. 316
traditional authority, p. 316

Discussion Questions

1. Discuss the key differences between large and small organizations. Which kinds of organizations would be better off acting as large organizations, and which are best trying to act as big-company/small-company hybrids?
2. Why do large organizations tend to be more formalized?
3. If you were managing a department of college professors, how might you structure the department differently than if you were managing a department of bookkeepers? Why?
4. Apply the concept of life cycle to an organization with which you are familiar, such as a university or a local business. What stage is the organization in now? How did the organization handle or pass through its life cycle crises?
5. Describe the three bases of authority identified by Weber. Is it possible for each of these types of authority to function at the same time within an organization?
6. In writing about types of control, William Ouchi said, "The Market is like the trout and the Clan like the salmon, each a beautiful highly specialized species which requires uncommon conditions for its survival. In comparison, the bureaucratic method of control is the Catfish—clumsy, ugly, but able to live in the widest range of environments and ultimately, the dominant species." Discuss what Ouchi meant by that analogy.
7. Government organizations often seem more bureaucratic than for-profit organizations. Could this partly be the result of the type of control used in government organizations? Explain.
8. The incident command system has been used primarily by organizations that regularly deal with crisis situations. Discuss whether this approach seems workable for a large media company that wants to reduce bureaucracy. How about for a manufacturer of cell phones?
9. Refer to the Air Canada case at the beginning of Chapter 1 and discuss how Air Canada illustrates the various stages of the organizational life cycle. In what stage of the life cycle does Air Canada seem to be?
10. Do you think a "no growth" philosophy of management should be taught in business schools? Discuss.

Chapter 9 Workbook: Control Mechanisms*

Think of two situations in your life: your school and your work experiences. How is control exerted? Fill out the tables.

On the Job

Your job responsibilities	How your boss controls	Positives of this control	Negatives of this control	How you would improve control
1.				
2.				
3.				
4.				

At the University

Items	How professor A (small class) controls	How professor B (large class) controls	How these controls influence you	What you think is a better control
1. Exams				
2. Assignments/papers				
3. Class participation				
4. Attendance				
5. Other				

Questions

1. What are the advantages and disadvantages of the various controls?
2. What happens when there is too much control? too little?
3. Does the type of control depend on the situation and the number of people involved?
4. *Optional:* How do the control mechanisms in your tables compare to those of other students?

Case for Analysis: Sleeman Breweries (Sleeman)

I didn't grow up drinking beer. It's not like I fell in love with it. I wasn't a brewer making beer in a plastic pail in the basement.

My parents to this day don't drink alcohol. They weren't involved in the alcohol business. We didn't sit around the dining room Sunday nights talking about the good old days at the Sleeman Brewery.

I really wasn't aware of the Sleeman history and background. It was my aunt who came along and said, "It's probably about time you found out about your family heritage. You're in the beer business anyway. Here's the recipe book, and here's an old bottle."

It is a rather strange coincidence that I ended up starting a pub, getting into the imported beer business, all about the same time it made sense to start up a brewery, and about the same time my aunt showed up and said, "Well, the liquor board said no one with the name Sleeman would get a liquor licence for 50 years and now it's 51 years—here ya go." Looking back, it's rather coincidental that all the signs in the universe lined up at the right time.

We haven't hid the fact that my grandfather and his brothers got caught smuggling. The family's not particularly proud of it.

I never wanted to be the radio voice. We had a marketing guy named Kevin Meens, and he played a bit of a trick on me and got me into the studio when I thought somebody else was going to do the commercials. I ended up being the voice because we couldn't afford anybody anyway, and I work for free. It was a point of difference. Beer business advertising was glitzy commercials, great soundtracks and babes in bikinis.

You either take risks and you're entrepreneurial, or you're a fake. I personally believe it's in your genetic code. There's nothing wrong with those people, because you need them to help businesses be successful. A place can't run if it's populated solely by entrepreneurs.

I'm a leader, not a follower. I want to take risks. If we all sit around, hold hands and decide this is too much risk, we're not going to do it, eventually the enterprise is going to fail.

Doug Berchtold [one-time Sleeman president] said, "Let me ask you a very simple question: do you want to own 100% of a bankrupt company, or do you want to own 10% of a $100-million or $200-million company?" For entrepreneurs, that puts things in focus.

If I listened to everybody who said I was going to be an abject failure, we wouldn't be having this conversation.

People assume they are destined for greatness. I'm not sure I believe in any of that. I believe in getting up every day, looking at opportunities, and picking and choosing.

One thing my mum drilled into me is that pride comes before a fall. You get on an Air Canada flight, and people say, "This is great beer, we can't seem to keep enough on the flight." It's not long before your head is so big you can't get off the plane. Then my mum's saying comes back to me.

I may be the quarterback, but the team runs because people are catching the ball, running the ball, blocking. That's why this company continues to be prosperous. If I start thinking it's because of me, something's going to come along and take the wind out of my sails.

I didn't get into the beer business because I love beer. I happen to love scotch, wine, beer and Diet Coke. I got into the beer business because I was motivated by a business idea that I thought would be successful. I'm also very motivated by growth. It excites me.

I'm not a brewmaster, so all I can do is sit down with those in our company who are and say, "Here's my grandfather's recipe book," or, "Here's a new idea, how do we make it come to life?" And I'm excited by the success of that new product.

People who are so fixated on—in our case—the liquid, to the exclusion of growing their business are missing fabulous opportunities. You need to rise above it and have a look at what you're doing.

The reasons the businesses I've started have been successful have more to do with the management people who have helped me run the businesses. It's one thing to have the idea, and have the drive so that, when people say no, you don't give up. But it's another prospect to take a business idea and develop it, have it managed properly, and grow.

Maybe the only thing I do well is pick good people. One of things I seem to be able to do is figure out when people are genuine and when they're not.

I quit school, but I'm not a quitter.

What I lacked in education, perhaps I made up in sheer bullheaded desire to get out there and prove to all the people who said I was going to be a failure that there was a chance that wasn't going to happen.

I have no interest in going back [to school]. I would never want to have the entrepreneurial, risk-taking spirit drilled out of me by going through MBA school, where they tell you to avoid risk. I surround myself with those guys.

What can a parent give their kids other than an education? A reasonably good background, where they know they're loved and supported. But I don't believe in giving my kids all kinds of money. I want them to get out there and make a life of their own.

I genuinely believe—and this is something my parents instilled in me and was actually reinforced by my management training at McDonald's—that you should treat people the way you want to be treated yourself.

I credit McDonald's with giving me a sense of responsibility. You're handling cash, you're dealing with customers, some of them irate. At the age of 16 or 17, you've got people reporting to you, and you have to learn how to be a manager.

There is this folly in Canada that if we can make it here, we can make it everywhere, especially in the States. That just isn't the case. Look at our steel industry, our lumber industry; there are tariffs if you start to get successful. The American government supports its own industries and hurts importers. It's not always the Promised Land.

Advice? Do your homework and don't give up. Believe in yourself and your idea. You also have to be rational in what your ideas are. Your ideas have to have some credence.

I have my name on the door, but I'd like to be remembered as somebody who didn't give up in the face of overwhelming odds.

When you really love what you're doing, it's hard not to just spend another five minutes and get this done, or 10 minutes to make this phone call or meet with this guy. I'm not at all good at balancing. My wife and kids will be the first to admit that I'm not.

Could I quit tomorrow? Financially, I guess I could. It just doesn't appeal to me. The age on my birth certificate belies how old I feel mentally.

When I turned 50, I said to my wife, "I'm working harder now than when I was at 30. I thought it was supposed to be the reverse."

My ego is most comfortably satisfied by walking anonymously into a bar or restaurant and seeing people drinking Sleeman.

Source: A. Holloway "Live and Learn: John Sleeman," *Canadian Business Magazine*, (May 10, 2004).

Case for Analysis: I Love Rewards Inc.

Razor Suleman started out creating T-shirts and other inexpensive items while he was a university student. He has turned that fledgling business into a growing player in the consumer reward/incentive industry with a strong footing in Canada and a toehold in the massive U.S. market.

Razor Suleman has a plan. Over the next five years, he wants to build I Love Rewards Inc., the company he started in his dorm room at Waterloo, Ont.'s Wilfrid Laurier University, into a $1-billion, online powerhouse. He can see the company, which today generates less than $10-million in sales, becoming to loyalty rewards what Google is to search engines.

"I think it is supremely doable," he says. "Loyalty rewards programs are enormously popular across North America and we have found a business model that will extend them to the Internet, which is wide open territory right now."

Loyalty rewards are simple programs where merchants give customers points with each purchase. Those points can be redeemed for a range of goods and services. Think Aeroplan, Air Miles, Amex Membership Rewards and even Petro-points.

I Love Rewards recently moved into the consumer rewards field. It won its spurs creating employee incentive programs for clients such as ING, KPMG and Rogers Communications. The expansion into the consumer field seemed a natural move, Mr. Suleman says.

"Our first client was a large packaged food company that made those corndogs on a stick," he explains. "We created a program where consumers would buy the product and look for a code on the package. They could then go to a dedicated Web site, enter the code and receive rewards points.

"When they amassed enough points they could trade them for electronics from Sony, things like MP3 players. It worked well and that led to other, similar promotions."

But as he was turning out online incentive programs for others, an idea struck him. Why not do it for himself? Why not create RazorPoints and enlist online merchants without incentive programs to sign up as clients? For them, it would be an administrative no brainer. All they had to do was decide what level of RazorPoints to offer per $1 spent; I LoveRewards would handle the rest.

Razorpoints.com becomes a reality this fall. In March, Mr. Suleman began testing a version among employees, friends and the employees of clients. Membership is by invitation only. How it works is simple.

Visitors go to the site, become members of the program and create a home page, which effectively becomes their personal launching point for all the sites they visit on the Internet. Each time they take an online shopping spree that starts from the Razorpoints.com site, participating merchants award a fixed number of RazorPoints based on a percentage of the sale before taxes. Some might offer 5% while others may offer up to 10%, he says.

Each RazorPoint will be worth 1¢. Collectors can cash them in for a variety of merchandise, travel-related and service rewards such as Apple iPods and BestBuy Gift Cards, up to golf holidays with Tiger Woods. RazorPoints makes its money by cashing in the dollar value of those points with merchants and on the spread between what it pays for its rewards and what it redeems them for.

"The idea is to get teenagers in the habit of using the site as their home base," he says. "Loyalty programs rely on habit. If you get teens engaged, then the chances are you will have them as collectors for life."

He can also see an enormous appeal for his program among small merchants who cannot afford to create their own loyalty program and larger ones who have been shut out of programs such as Air Miles because those programs offer exclusivity within certain categories to participating merchants.

"We have added to our management team to tackle this project. We hired a new marketing vice-president formerly with the Disney organization. This is a whole new business and its future is terribly exciting," he says.

Mr. Suleman's enthusiasm has carried him a long way since he started the predecessor to I Love Rewards in his second year of university. The idea was to create T-shirts, sweatshirts, mugs and other items that the student union could sell to undergraduates.

"It made me enough that I graduated without any debt," he says.

After graduation, the idea of working for anyone else had little appeal. He thought there might be a market for employee incentive programs based on his T-shirts in the corporate world. As it turned out, he was right, but not in the way he was moving.

His first client was ING, the Dutch virtual bank. ING wanted T-shirts to motivate its call centre staff and to create a sort of team spirit as they sold GICs, mortgages and such. "They came to us and said: 'This is not as effective as we would like. Can you create a more results-oriented incentive program?'"

Mr. Suleman devised an incentive program based on point rewards. Sell a mortgage or a GIC and earn a corresponding number of rewards. For rewards, he used the catalogue of items I Love Rewards was selling to clients and expanded it to include hot, low-cost electronics such as iPods, and the program took off.

"ING found it was indeed a profound motivational tool," he says. "Sales took off."

Rogers Communications became his next major client, starting with a trial program covering one division and now expanded to include the entire company. KPMG is using one of the company's incentive programs to reward employees who show they adhere to and practise the company's core values.

Two years ago, I Love Rewards entered the consumer space with its Pogo Points program. Today, corporate programs generate 70% of the revenues while consumer programs account for the balance.

To crack the vast U.S. market, Mr. Suleman opened an office in New York City. "U.S. companies want to do business with U.S. companies," he says. "If we wanted to crack the U.S. market, we had to put a U.S. face on the company."

So far, that strategy is successful, he says. I Love Rewards is picking up U.S. clients.

The company has also won a reputation for its employment policies. It has been named one of the 100 best employers in Canada and one of the top 50 in Toronto. It gives staff time off for charitable and community involvement and, this fall, it will introduce an employment share ownership plan.

"We have grown 5,000% in the past five years," Mr. Suleman says. "And I think that is just the beginning. As I say, we have the potential to be a billion-dollar company in five to 10 years."

I Love Rewards Inc.

Head office Toronto, Ont.
Business sector Incentive Rewards and loyalty programs
Market North America
Number of Employees 44
Number of Employees $10-million
Web site www.iloverewards.com

Source: "Entrepreneur," Special Feature to *The National Post*, (June 18, 2007), FP8.

PART 5

Managing Dynamic Processes

10 Organizational Culture and Ethical Values

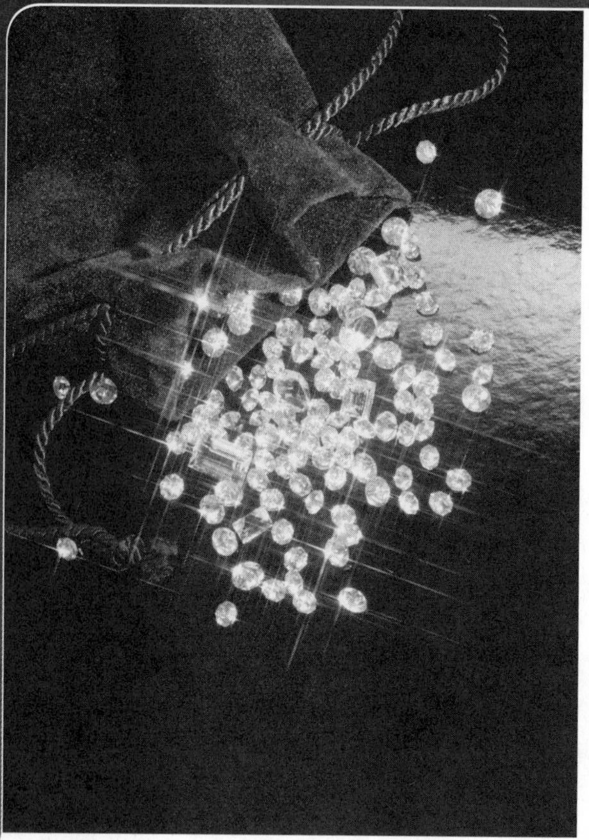

Photos.com/Jupiter Images

Organizational Culture

What Is Culture? • Emergence and Purpose of Culture • Interpreting Culture

Organizational Design and Culture

The Adaptability Culture • The Mission Culture • The Clan Culture • The Bureaucratic Culture • A Culture of Discipline • Culture Strength and Organizational Subcultures

Organizational Culture, Learning, and Performance

Ethical Values and Social Responsibility

Sources of Individual Ethical Principles • Managerial Ethics and Social Responsibility • Does It Pay to Be Good?

Sources of Ethical Values in Organizations

Personal Ethics • Organizational Culture • Organizational Systems • External Stakeholders

How Leaders Shape Culture and Ethics

Values-Based Leadership • Formal Structure and Systems

Organizational Culture and Ethics in a Global Environment

Summary and Interpretation

A Look Inside

Birks & Mayors Inc. (Birks)

In 1879, Henry Birks founded Henry Birks & Sons, an exclusive jewellery store (see photo) that emphasized quality and service. It dominated Canada's market for many years and has been recognized internationally for its innovative designs in diamond jewellery. In 1993, Regaluxe Investment bought Birks and, in 2002, Birks acquired a controlling interest in Mayors Jewelers Inc.[1] In 2007, Birks was selected as the official jeweller for the Vancouver 2010 Winter Olympic Games.

The 2006 film, *Blood Diamond* starring Leonardo DiCaprio, raised global awareness about the horrors of blood (or conflict) diamonds. Blood diamonds are those diamonds that are mined, often by children, in war zones and sold to finance armed conflicts and civil wars.

Partnership Africa Canada in Sierra Leone reports that more than 50,000 people have been killed, many more displaced, and much of the country's infrastructure ruined. Meanwhile, the underground trade of illicit diamonds is booming. Conflict diamonds are valued between 4 percent and 15 percent of the world total and generate annual trade revenues of $7.5 billion.[2]

In response to the advocacy of the United Nations and many nonprofit organizations around the world, the Kimberley Process Certification Scheme was created in 2003. The Kimberley Process requires that signatory countries certify that all rough-diamond exports are conflict-free and that the country will allow importation of diamonds only from participating countries.

Birks has implemented measures to comply with the Kimberley Process and notifies its vendors of the requirement to comply with the Kimberley Process Certification Scheme. It sources diamonds only from cutters who declare on their invoices that the diamonds have been obtained in compliance with the Kimberley Process.[3]

However, in a new initiative, Birks has gone beyond compliance to the Kimberley Process. Birks is launching a new line of jewellery using diamonds from Botswana. The line will be sourced exclusively through Diamond Trade Company Botswana, which is part of DeBeers. According to John Orrico, Birks' senior vice president, as the diamonds will be cut and polished in Botswana, "[you] can feel good that it's giving back to the people from whose country it was originally mined."[4]

Purpose of This Chapter

This chapter explores ideas about organizational culture and associated ethical values, and how these are influenced by organizations. The first section describes the nature of organizational culture, its origins and purpose, and how to identify and interpret culture through ceremonies, stories, and symbols. We then examine how culture reinforces the strategy and structural design the organization needs to be effective in its environment and discuss the important role of culture in organizational learning and high performance. Next, the chapter turns to ethical values and social responsibility. We consider how managers implement the structures and systems that influence ethical and socially responsible behaviour. The chapter also discusses how leaders shape culture and ethical values in a direction suitable for strategy and performance outcomes. The chapter closes with a brief overview of the complex cultural and ethical issues managers face in an international environment.

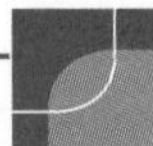

Organizational Culture

Every organization, like Birks, has a set of values that characterize how people behave and how the organization carries out everyday business. Sometimes, these values get out of alignment with the environment and cause problems for the organization. One of the most important jobs organizational leaders do is instill and support the kind of values needed for the company to thrive.

Strong cultures can have a profound impact on a company, which can be either positive or negative for the organization. For example, Teva Neuroscience in Montréal, which was selected in 2007 as the best small company to work for, based on a survey of 120 organizations, "borders on the obsessive to living its values."[5] It works to hire the right people, to keep staff well informed and to collect feedback from its employees. According to Jon Congleton, "[we] focus on three clarities: clarity of structure: Where do I fit in with this company? Clarity of direction: Where am I going? And clarity of measurement: How do I know I did a good job?"[6] Negative cultural norms, however, can damage a company just as powerfully as positive ones can strengthen it. Consider the case of Enron, where the organizational culture supported pushing everything to the limits: business practices, rules, personal behaviour, and laws. Executives drove expensive cars, challenged employees to participate in risky competitive behaviour, and often celebrated big deals by heading off to a bar or dance club.[7]

A related concept concerning the influence of norms and values on how people work together and how they treat one another and customers is called *social capital.* **Social capital** refers to the quality of interactions among people and whether they share a common perspective. In organizations with a high degree of social capital, for example, relationships are based on trust, mutual understandings, and shared norms and values that enable people to cooperate and coordinate their activities to achieve organizational goals.[8] An organization can have either a high or a low level of social capital. One way to think of social capital is as *goodwill.* When relationships both within the organization and with customers, suppliers, and partners are based on honesty, trust, and respect, a spirit of goodwill exists and people willingly cooperate to achieve mutual benefits. A high level of social capital enables frictionless social interactions and exchanges that help to facilitate smooth organizational functioning.

Think of eBay, which relies largely on social capital to bring millions of buyers and sellers together on its website. In 2006, it earned $1.13 billion, up 4 percent from 2005.[9] The company builds goodwill through such mechanisms as a feedback system that enables buyers and sellers to rate one another, discussion boards that build a sense of community among site users, and regular all-day focus groups with representative buyers and sellers. Another example of a company with high social capital is Deloitte & Touche, LLP, Calgary, According to Esher Colwill, who has worked at the firm for six years, the firm recognizes everyone as individuals. She recounts what happened when she shared her goal of scaling the Seven Summits—the highest mountain in each continent. "[The organization] gave her a satellite phone and asked her to leave messages now and then. The firm also gave her tens of thousands of dollars in sponsorship money and accommodated the six months off she needed over five years to complete her goal, including her three-month Everest expedition in 2005 that gave her 15 cold, dizzying minutes at the top of the world. 'I joined Deloitte . . . wondering if at some point I would have to leave,' says Colwill. 'I really had no idea how open they would be, but they were amazing.'"[10]

Other organizations also build social capital by being open and honest and cultivating positive social relationships among employees and with outsiders. Relationships based on cutthroat competition, self-interest, and subterfuge, such as those at Enron, can be devastating to a company. Social capital relates to both organizational culture and ethics, which is the focus of this chapter.

The popularity of the organizational culture topic raises a number of questions. Can we identify cultures? Can culture be aligned with strategy? How can cultures be managed or changed? The best place to start is by defining culture and explaining how it can be identified in organizations.

What Is Culture?

Culture is the set of values, norms, guiding beliefs, and understandings that is shared by members of an organization and is taught to new members.[11] It represents the unwritten, feeling part of the organization. Everyone participates in culture, but culture generally goes unnoticed. It is only when organizations try to implement new strategies or programs that go against basic cultural norms and values that they come face to face with the power of culture.

Organizational culture exists at two levels, as illustrated in Exhibit 10.1. On the surface are visible artifacts and observable behaviours—the ways people dress and

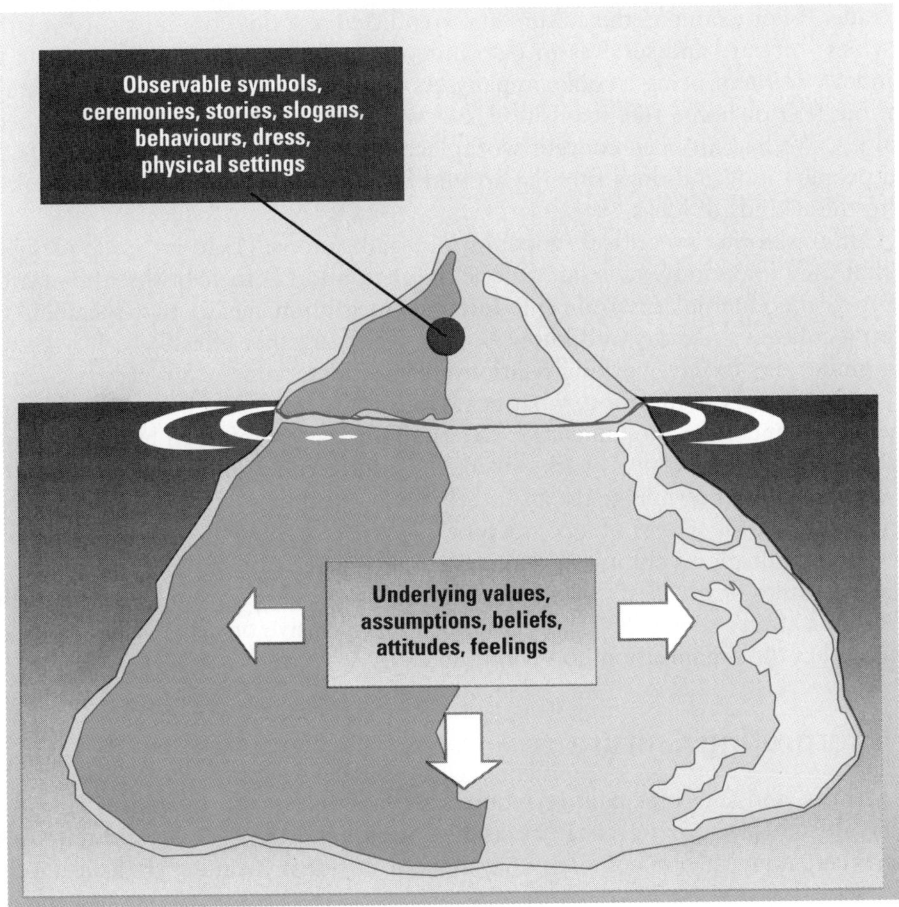

EXHIBIT 10.1
Levels of Organizational Culture

act, and the symbols, stories, and ceremonies organization members share. The visible elements of culture, however, reflect deeper values in the minds of organization members. These underlying values, assumptions, beliefs, and thought processes are the true culture.[12] For example, The Body Shop incorporated an on-site biological sewage treatment system in a greenhouse near its Toronto headquarters. "Beauty and function combine in the botanical and biological workings of the system, [enabling] the company to show off its corporate philosophy, [a commitment to sustainability]. Every drop reused is a drop of municipal water saved and a drop less discharged."[13] The attributes of culture display themselves in many ways but typically evolve into a patterned set of activities carried out through social interactions.[14] Those patterns can be used to interpret culture.

Emergence and Purpose of Culture

Culture provides members with a sense of organizational identity and generates in them a commitment to beliefs and values that are larger than themselves. Though ideas that become part of culture can come from anywhere within the organization, an organization's culture generally begins with a founder or early leader who articulates and implements particular ideas and values as a vision, philosophy, or business strategy.

When these ideas and values lead to success, they become institutionalized, and an organizational culture emerges that reflects the vision and strategy of the founder or leader.[15] For example, the culture at ExtendMedia, a dot-com-bust survivor that provides software and services to distribute content through the Web, reflects the founder's vision of being a cool company. As Keith Kocho puts it "There was never that big IPO or home run acquisition, but we've always been in advance of being cool . . . We had an open concept workplace with stock options and a beer fridge and people's kids and dogs running around before Silicon Valley was even waking up to these kinds of ideas."[16]

Cultures serve two critical functions in organizations: (1) to integrate members so that they know how to relate to one another, and (2) to help the organization adapt to the external environment. **Internal integration** means that members develop a collective identity and know how to work together effectively. It is culture that guides day-to-day working relationships and determines how people communicate within the organization, what behaviour is acceptable or not acceptable, and how power and status are allocated. **External adaptation** refers to how the organization meets goals and deals with outsiders. Culture helps guide the daily activities of workers to meet certain goals. It can help the organization respond rapidly to customer needs or the moves of a competitor.

The organization's culture also guides employee decision making in the absence of written rules or policies.[17] Thus, both functions of culture are related to building the organization's social capital, by forging either positive or negative relationships both within the organization and with outsiders.

Interpreting Culture

To identify and interpret culture requires that people make inferences based on observable artifacts. Artifacts can be studied but are hard to decipher accurately. An award ceremony in one company may have a different meaning than in another

EXHIBIT 10.2
A Typology of Organization Rites and Their Social Consequences

Type of Rite	Example	Social Consequences
Passage	Induction and basic training, Canadian military	Facilitate transition of persons into social roles and statuses that are new for them
Enhancement	Annual awards night	Enhance social identities and increase status of employees
Renewal	Organization development activities	Refurbish social structures and improve organization functioning
Integration	Office holiday party	Encourage and revive common feelings that bind members together and commit them to the organization

Source: Adapted from Harrison M. Trice and Janice M. Beyer, "Studying Organizational Cultures through Rites and Ceremonials," *Academy of Management Review* 9 (1984), 653–659. Used with permission.

company. To decipher what is really going on in an organization requires detective work and probably some experience as an insider. Some of the typical and important observable aspects of culture are rites and ceremonies, stories, symbols, and language.[18]

PDA Remember...

Pay a lot of attention to organizational culture. Understand the underlying values, assumptions, and beliefs on which culture is based as well as its observable manifestations. Evaluate organizational culture based on rites and ceremonies, stories and heroes, symbols, and language.

Rites and Ceremonies. Important artifacts for culture are **rites and ceremonies**, the elaborate, planned activities that make up a special event and are often conducted for the benefit of an audience. Managers can hold rites and ceremonies to provide dramatic examples of what a company values. These are special occasions that reinforce specific values, create a bond among people for sharing an important understanding, and anoint and celebrate heroes and heroines who symbolize important beliefs and activities.[19]

Four types of rites that appear in organizations are summarized in Exhibit 10.2. Rites of passage facilitate the transition of employees into new social roles. Rites of enhancement create stronger social identities and increase the status of employees. Rites of renewal reflect training and development activities that improve organization functioning. Rites of integration create common bonds and good feelings among employees and increase commitment to the organization. The following examples illustrate how these rites and ceremonies are used by top managers to reinforce important cultural values.

- In a major bank, election as an officer was seen as the key event in a successful career. A series of activities accompanied every promotion to bank officer, including a special method of notification, taking the new officer to the officers' dining room for the first time, and the new officer buying drinks on the Friday after his or her notification.[20] This is a rite of passage.
- Mary Kay Cosmetics Company holds elaborate awards ceremonies, presenting gold and diamond pins, furs, and luxury cars to high-achieving sales consultants. The most successful consultants are introduced by film clips, such as the kind used to introduce award nominees in the entertainment industry. This is a rite of enhancement.

- An important event at Walt Disney Company is the "Gong Show." Three times a year, executives hold events around America at which any employee, down to the level of secretaries, janitors, and mailroom personnel, can pitch movie ideas to top executives. The fun event is a way to symbolize and support the company's commitment to employee involvement and innovation.[21] This is a rite of renewal.
- Whenever a Wal-Mart executive visits one of the stores, he or she leads employees in the Wal-Mart cheer: "Give me a W! Give me an A! Give me an L! Give me a squiggly! (All do a version of the twist.) Give me an M! Give me an A! Give me an R! Give me a T! What's that spell? Wal-Mart! What's that spell? Wal-Mart! Who's No. 1? THE CUSTOMER!" The cheer strengthens bonds among employees and reinforces their commitment to common goals.[22] This is a rite of integration.

Stories. **Stories** are narratives based on true events that are frequently shared among organizational employees and told to new employees to inform them about an organization. Many stories are about company **heroes** who serve as models or ideals for serving cultural norms and values. Some stories are considered **legends** because the events are historic and may have been embellished with fictional details. Other stories are **myths**, which are consistent with the values and beliefs of the organization but are not supported by facts.[23] Stories keep alive the primary values of the organization and provide a shared understanding among all employees. Examples of how stories shape culture are as follows:

- At 3M, the story is told of a vice president who was fired early in his career for persisting with a new product even after his boss had told him to stop because the boss thought it was a stupid idea. After the worker was fired, he stayed in an unused office, working without a salary on the new product idea. Eventually he was rehired, the product was a success, and he was promoted to vice president. The story symbolizes the 3M value of persisting in what you believe in.[24]
- In the Canadian Pacific Railway (CPR) hotels, now operating under the Fairmont banner, William Cornelius Van Horne's statement that "If we can't export the scenery, we'll import the tourists!"[25] is still repeated as part of the lore about the creation of the chain of grand hotels across Canada.

Symbols. Another tool for interpreting culture is the **symbol**. A symbol is something that represents another thing. In one sense, ceremonies, stories, slogans, and rites are all symbols. They symbolize deeper values of an organization. Another symbol is a physical artifact of the organization. Physical symbols are powerful because they focus attention on a specific item. Symbols can also represent negative elements of organizational culture. At Enron, premium parking spots were symbols of power, wealth, and winning at any cost. At the company's London (U.K.) office, executives submitted blind e-mail bids for the limited spaces. One top manager paid more than $6,000 to use a well-placed company spot for a year.[26]

On a light-hearted note, see Exhibit 10.3, which shows the power of symbols in organizations! They are often organizational practices that employees follow unthinkingly.

EXHIBIT 10.3
The Power of Organizational Culture

"I don't know how it started, either. All I know is that it's part of our corporate culture."

Language. The final technique for influencing culture is **language**. Many companies use a specific saying, slogan, metaphor, or other form of language to convey special meaning to employees. Slogans can be readily picked up and repeated by employees as well as customers of the company. Hudson's Bay Company's motto "We are Canada's merchants" applies to employees and customers but has become an ironic motto as the company is now American-owned. Averitt Express, a trucking company, uses the slogan "Our driving force is people" to emphasize the importance of treating employees as well as they are expected to treat customers. Drivers and customers, not top executives, are seen as the power that fuels a company's success. Other significant uses of language to shape culture are as follows:

- At Environics Communications, the ESRA (arse spelled backwards!) awards are designed to get staff laughing at their embarrassing moments and the Five for Five program allows employees to go to other countries; in their fifth year of employment, they are given $5000, an extra week of holiday and encouraged to go anywhere.[27]
- Tourism British Columbia holds monthly CEO mouth-abouts to update staff on decisions made by a rotating employee committee whose mandate is to make organizational values go beyond words on a page.[28]

Recall that culture exists at two levels—the underlying values and assumptions and the visible artifacts and observable behaviours. The slogans, symbols, and ceremonies just described are artifacts that reflect underlying company values. These visible artifacts and behaviours can be used by managers to shape company values and to strengthen organizational culture.

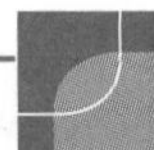

Organizational Design and Culture

Organizational culture should reinforce the strategy and structural design that the organization needs to be effective within its environment. For example, if the external environment requires flexibility and responsiveness, such as the environment for Internet-based companies like eBay, the culture should encourage adaptability. The correct relationship among cultural values, organizational strategy and structure, and the environment can enhance organizational performance.[29]

Culture can be assessed along many dimensions, such as the extent of collaboration versus isolation among people and departments, the importance of control and where control is concentrated, or whether the organization's time orientation is short range or long range.[30] Here, we will focus on two specific dimensions: (1) the extent to which the competitive environment requires flexibility or stability; and (2) the extent to which the organization's strategic focus and strength are internal or external. Four categories of culture associated with these differences, as illustrated in Exhibit 10.4, are adaptability, mission, clan, and bureaucratic.[31] These four categories relate to the fit among cultural values, strategy, structure, and the environment. Each can be successful, depending on the needs of the external environment and the organization's strategic focus.

The Adaptability Culture

The **adaptability culture** is characterized by strategic focus on the external environment through flexibility and change to meet customer needs. The culture encourages entrepreneurial values, norms, and beliefs that support the capacity of the organization to detect, interpret, and translate signals from the environment into new

EXHIBIT 10.4
Relationship of Environment and Strategy to Organizational Culture
Source: Based on Daniel R. Denison and Aneil K. Mishra, "Toward a Theory of Organizational Culture and Effectiveness," *Organization Science* 6, no. 2 (March–April 1995): 204–223; R. Hooijberg and F. Petrock, "On Cultural Change: Using the Competing Values Framework to Help Leaders Execute a Transformational Strategy," *Human Resource Management* 32 (1993): 29–50; and R. E. Quinn, *Beyond Rational Management: Mastering the Paradoxes and Competing Demands of High Performance* (San Francisco: Jossey-Bass, 1988).

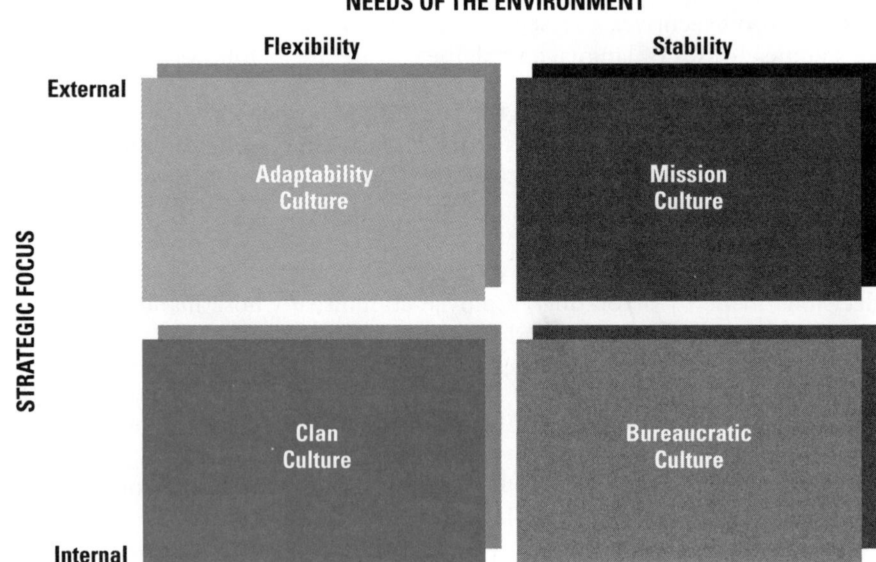

behaviour responses. This type of company, however, doesn't just react quickly to environmental changes—it actively creates change. Innovation, creativity, and risk taking are valued and rewarded.

An example of the adaptability culture is 3M, a company whose values promote individual initiative and entrepreneurship. All new employees attend a class on risk taking, where they are told to pursue their ideas even if it means defying their supervisors. IBM has been shifting to an adaptability culture to support a new strategy that requires flexibility, speed, and innovation. IBM has implemented practices and procedures that support teamwork, egalitarianism, and creativity, such as dismantling the 92-year-old executive committee that previously ruled the company and replacing it with three cross-functional and cross-hierarchical teams for strategy, operations, and technology, and a clear external focus.[32] Most e-commerce companies, such as eBay, Amazon, and Google, as well as companies in the marketing, electronics, and cosmetics industries, use this type of culture because they must move quickly to satisfy customers.

An example of an adaptability culture is Sandvine, a tech start-up founded in 2001 in the Kitchener-Waterloo region, which provides networking equipment. In 2007, it was named one of Canada's best places to work.[33] It is listed on the Toronto and London Stock Exchanges and, in 2007, had a market cap of about $600 million.

In Practice
Sandvine

Sandvine was founded from the ashes of telecom industry's meltdown. David Caputo, the current President of Sandvine, learned that Cisco Systems was closing down the organization that it had bought from him. In response, Caputo told his 30 engineers to think about the future of the Internet while he raised some capital to create a new company. As Caputo puts it, "It was like we had gone from the best of times to the worst of time almost overnight . . . But we also saw that the tech crash had created a huge pool of talented people that all of a sudden had some time on their hands."[34]

On August 31, 2001, Sandvine was born. At the all-employee meeting, Caputo revealed the Sandvine Way, an eight-point statement that is on every employee's ID.[35] The eight points are (1) customer first, (2) showcase flexibility, (3) underpromise and overdeliver, (4) amazing tool utilization, (5) team work, (6) knowledge sharing, (7) zero politics, and (8) risk taking. The Sandvine culture, according to Caputo, was engineered "[as] we're a bunch of engineers."[36] In Caputo's view, an organization's culture is of such importance that he designed the Sandvine Way even before he knew what Sandvine was going to produce.

Sandvine's leaders are required to follow the *Leaders 10 Commandments* to ensure that the culture of Sandvine is reinforced. The Commandments state (1) Treat your team with respect. Have fun. (2) Disagree and then commit to new company strategies. (3) Make decisions, communicate decisions. (4) Always explain "why" something needs to be done. (5) Never complain downward in the organization. (6) Openly praise, privately criticize. (7) Coach—don't fix. (8) Meet with your team as a team regularly. (9) Meet your team members individually regularly. (10) Encourage each team member to have/own a minimum of three objectives.[37]

The Mission Culture

An organization concerned with serving specific customers in the external environment, but without the need for rapid change, is suited to the mission culture. The **mission culture** is characterized by emphasis on a clear vision of the organization's purpose and on the achievement of goals, such as sales growth, profitability, or market share, to help achieve the purpose. Individual employees may be responsible for a specified level of performance, and the organization promises specified rewards in return. Managers shape behaviour by envisioning and communicating a desired future state for the organization. Because the environment is stable, they can translate the vision into measurable goals and evaluate employee performance for meeting them. In some cases, mission cultures reflect a high level of competitiveness and a profit-making orientation.

The Clan Culture

The **clan culture** has a primary focus on the involvement and participation of the organization's members and on rapidly changing expectations from the external environment. This culture is similar to the clan form of control described in Chapter 9. More than any other, this culture focuses on the needs of employees as the route to high performance. Involvement and participation create a sense of responsibility and ownership and, hence, greater commitment to the organization.

In a clan culture, an important value is taking care of employees and making sure they have whatever they need to help them be satisfied as well as productive. Companies in the fashion and retail industries often adopt this culture because it releases the creativity of employees to respond to rapidly changing tastes. Mountain Equipment Co-op is an example of an organization that combines attributes of the clan and mission cultures; for example, it looks for "... people who share our passion for wild spaces, outdoor activities, and great gear. If you think a job should be more than a paycheque, check out our current postings."[38]

In Practice
Mountain Equipment Co-op (MEC)

MEC was started in 1971 by a group of students at the University of British Columbia. It sold sporting equipment not otherwise available in Canada such as avalanche beacons, climbing rope, and ice crampons. The students charged a one-time membership fee of five dollars. The founders insisted that MEC should never make a profit and did no advertising.

Since then, MEC has become a large "anti-retailer"[39] with stores across Canada and a website that both educates as well as sells. Its 2007 sales were approximately $200 million. MEC's Vancouver head office is housed in a converted building formerly used as an auto parts warehouse, and many of the fixtures were salvaged from other buildings. MEC's buildings are award winning—the Ottawa and Winnipeg stores were the first and second retail buildings in Canada to comply with Canada's C2000 Green Building Standard—a Natural Resources Canada program that acknowledges buildings that achieve a 50 percent reduction in energy consumption over conventional structures. As well, in 1998, it was one of the first Canadian retailers to have rooftop gardens on its stores.

The green building program rests on four principles: (1) Reduce—Avoid using unnecessary materials, (2) Reuse—Incorporate existing materials, (3) Recycle—Incorporate existing materials in new ways, and (4) Rethink—Look for new and better building solutions.

MEC reinforces its commitment to sustainability in various ways. It has recycle bins in its stores for used polyester clothing, which it turns into new clothing and resells. It uses environmentally responsible paper made with a minimum of 30 percent post-consumer waste. In 2007, MEC announced that it had joined the One Percent for the Planet, an alliance of 500 companies in more than 20 countries that pledge to give one percent of their revenue to environmental causes. It is estimated that MEC will donate $2.25 million in 2007.

MEC's core values of ethical conduct and respect for others and the environment are enshrined in its logo, two mountain peaks and the name of the co-op, as it is seen as a declaration of social responsibility. In 2006, MEC released its first annual accountability report and was the only Canadian retailer to make the top ten companies to report their labour practices transparently.[40] The Conference Board of Canada recognized MEC for incorporating sustainability in all aspects of its strategy. MEC received the prestigious Conference Board of Canada/Spencer Stuart 2008 national awards in governance in two categories—nonprofit organizations and all organizations.[41]

The Bureaucratic Culture

The **bureaucratic culture** has an internal focus and a consistency orientation for a stable environment. This organization has a culture that supports a methodical approach to doing business. Symbols, heroes, and ceremonies support cooperation, tradition, and following established policies and practices as ways to achieve goals. Personal involvement is somewhat lower here, but that is outweighed by a high level of consistency, conformity, and collaboration among members. This organization succeeds by being highly integrated and efficient.

Today, most managers are shifting away from bureaucratic cultures because of a need for greater flexibility. However, one thriving new company, Pacific Edge Software, has successfully implemented some elements of a bureaucratic culture, ensuring that all its projects are on time and on budget. The co-founders implanted a culture of order, discipline, and control from the moment they founded the company. The emphasis on order and focus means employees can generally go home by 6:00 p.m. rather than working all night to finish an important project. The co-founders insist that the company's culture isn't rigid or uptight, just *careful*. Although sometimes being careful means being slow, so far Pacific Edge has managed to keep pace with the demands of the external environment.[42]

PDA

Remember...

Ensure that organizational culture is consistent with strategy and the environment. Culture can be shaped to fit the needs of both. Four types of culture are adaptability culture, mission culture, clan culture, and bureaucratic culture.

A Culture of Discipline

Collins identifies a number of characteristics that define truly great companies. One aspect is a culture of discipline, in which everyone in the organization is focused on doing whatever is needed to keep the company successful.[43] How is a culture of discipline built? Here are some of the key factors:

- *Level 5 leadership.* All good-to-great companies begin with a top leader who exemplifies what Collins calls level 5 leadership. Level 5 leaders are characterized by an almost complete lack of personal ego, coupled with a strong will and ambition for the success of the organization. They develop a strong corps of leaders throughout the organization so that when they leave, the company can grow even more successful. Values of selfishness, greed, and arrogance have no place in a great company.
- *The right values.* Leaders build a culture based on values of individual freedom and responsibility, but within a framework of organizational purpose, goals, and systems. People have the autonomy to do whatever it takes—within well-defined boundaries and clear, consistent guidelines—to move the organization toward achieving its goals and vision.
- *The right people in the right jobs.* Leaders of good-to-great organizations look for self-disciplined people who embody values that fit the culture. These people are described using terms such as *determined*, *diligent*, *precise*, *systematic*,

consistent, *focused*, *accountable*, and *responsible*. They are willing to go the extra mile to become the best they can be and help the organization continuously improve.
- *Knowing where to go*. Good-to-great companies base their success on a deep understanding throughout the organization of three essential ideas, conceptualized as three intersecting circles: what they can be the best in the world at, what they are deeply passionate about, and what makes economic sense for the organization. This understanding is translated into a vision and strategy that guides all actions.

No company makes the leap from good to great in one fell swoop. The process is one of buildup followed by breakthrough, similar to pushing a giant flywheel in one direction, turn after turn, building momentum until a breakthrough is reached. Once leaders get the right people in the right jobs, support the right values, and focus on activities that fit within the three intersecting circles, people begin to see positive results, which pushes the flywheel to full momentum. As success builds on success, the organization makes the move from good to great.

Culture Strength and Organizational Subcultures

A strong organizational culture can have a powerful impact on company performance. **Culture strength** refers to the degree of agreement among members of an organization about the importance of specific values. If widespread consensus exists about the importance of those values, the culture is cohesive and strong; if little agreement exists, the culture is weak.[44]

A strong culture is typically associated with the frequent use of ceremonies, symbols, stories, heroes, and slogans. These elements increase employee commitment to the values and strategy of a company. In addition, managers who want to create and maintain strong organizational cultures often emphasize the selection and socialization of employees.[45,46] At the Lannick Group of Companies, potential employees can participate in a one-day job shadow and meet employees from across the organization. Once they are hired, they receive orientation and training.[47]

However, culture is not always uniform throughout the organization, particularly in large companies. Even in organizations that have strong cultures, there may be several sets of subcultures. **Subcultures** develop to reflect the common problems, goals, and experiences that members of a team, department, or other unit share. An office, branch, or unit of a company that is physically separated from the company's main operations may also take on a distinctive subculture. Sometimes, subcultures are so different in an organization that employees feel cultural anxieties when they have to move to other units or when their organizations are taken over by merger or acquisitions.[48]

For example, although the dominant culture of an organization may be a mission culture, various departments may also reflect characteristics of adaptability, clan, or bureaucratic cultures. The manufacturing department of a large organization may thrive in an environment that emphasizes order, efficiency, and obedience to rules, whereas the research and development (R&D) department may be characterized by employee empowerment, flexibility, and customer focus. This is similar to the concept of differentiation described in Chapter 4, where employees in manufacturing, sales, and research departments studied by Paul Lawrence and Jay Lorsch[49] developed different values with respect to time horizon, interpersonal relationships, and formality in order to perform the job of each particular department most effectively. The credit division of Pitney Bowes, a huge corporation that manufactures postage meters, copiers, and other office equipment, developed a distinctive subculture to encourage innovation and risk taking. Pitney Bowes has long thrived in an environment of order and predictability. Its headquarters reflects a typical corporate environment and an orderly culture with its blank walls and bland carpeting. But step onto the third floor of the Pitney Bowes building in Shelton, Connecticut, and you might think you're at a different company. The domain of Pitney Bowes Credit Corporation looks more like an indoor theme park, featuring cobblestone-patterned carpets, faux gas lamps, and an ornate town square-style clock. It also has a French-style café, a 1950s-style diner, and the "Cranial Kitchen," where employees sit in cozy booths to surf the Internet or watch training videos. The friendly hallways encourage impromptu conversations, where people can exchange information and share ideas they would not otherwise share.[50]

Subcultures typically include the basic values of the dominant organizational culture plus additional values unique to members of the subculture. However, subcultural differences can sometimes lead to conflicts between departments, especially in organizations that do not have strong overall organizational cultures. When subcultural values become too strong and outweigh the corporate cultural values, conflicts may emerge and hurt organizational performance. Conflict will be discussed in detail in Chapter 13.

PDA Remember...

Consciously manage culture to shift values toward high performance and goal accomplishment.

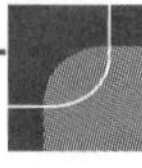

Organizational Culture, Learning, and Performance

Culture can play an important role in creating an organizational climate that enables learning and innovative response to challenges, competitive threats, or new opportunities. A strong culture that encourages adaptation and change enhances organizational performance by energizing and motivating employees, unifying people around shared goals and a higher mission, and shaping and guiding employee behaviour so that everyone's actions are aligned with strategic priorities. Thus, creating and influencing an adaptive culture is one of the most important jobs for organizational leaders. The right culture can drive high performance.[51]

A number of studies have found a positive relationship between culture and performance.[52] In *Corporate Culture and Performance*, Kotter and Heskett provided evidence that companies that intentionally managed cultural values outperformed similar companies that did not. Some companies have developed systematic ways to measure and manage the impact of culture on organizational performance. At Home Depot, leaders identified key aspects of the culture that needed to be changed to meet more demanding performance goals. They use various tools to strengthen the business and to modify its culture. They use tools such as strategic operating and resource planning, disciplined talent reviews, store manager learning forums, Monday morning conference calls of the organization's top 15 executives, employee task forces, as well an array of leadership and employee development programs.[53]

PDA Remember...

To support a learning orientation, emphasize cultural values of openness and collaboration, equality and trust, continuous improvement, and risk taking. Build a strong internal culture that encourages adaptation to changing environmental conditions.

Strong cultures that don't encourage adaptation, however, can hurt the organization. A danger for many successful organizations is that the culture becomes set and the company fails to adapt as the environment changes. When organizations are

Leading *by Design*

WestJet Airlines Ltd (WestJet)

I am convinced now that THE COMPETITIVE ISSUE OF OUR TIME IS CULTURE AS EXPRESSED IN VOICE. Firms that use voice and an adult culture of genuine care will destroy those that use scripts and efficiency.

What on Earth do I mean by that? Let me illustrate by offering up a few things that happened to me while flying WestJet last week.

1. We land at Pearson. The FA comes on and says. "Please be careful and stay buckled up as there is always a chance that we may have to stop suddenly if we get caught in traffic" Wow—someone did not give us orders but gave us context for remaining buckled up. On Air Canada, everyone is fiddling with their stuff well before the ramp. Why—because of the tone of voice—On most airlines we are lectured to.
2. We have 2 unaccompanied minors on the return flight. Members of the crew played cards, chatted and generally fooled around with them the entire trip. They were really well looked after—not just the mundane look after—but genuinely cared for as people. Caring is not the same as service. There was no script. Children have great bullshit detectors and these men passed. By the way it was the male FA's who were front and centre with the kids.
3. On our approach into Moncton. we suddenly hit very bad turbulence—amongst the worst in 50 years of flying. We were suddenly being tossed all over the sky. The First Officer came on immediately—Flight Attendants grab a seat! Now folks we are entering the jet-stream at 29,000 and we will come out the other side at 23,000. Just hang on a few minutes and it will be smooth again". Well we all looked at each other and gasped. Someone had told us what was really happening. With context and [an adult peer-to-peer tone] we were all calm. At AC the seat belt sign would have come on. If we were lucky this Test Pilot Voice would tell us to buckle up as we were having some turbulence. At WestJet, the FA safety was dealt with immediately and we were all taken in to the confidence as adults by the flight deck.

What we all experienced was that the real service issue is not doing things—there are no meals on WestJet. It is how you are and how you related to each other and then with the customer. At WestJet we are all called "Guests". Words mean something. A Guest is someone you legitimately care for. A passenger or a customer is someone you are paid to do things for.

So what is wrong with most organizations today? They use the voice of the grumpy teacher. [They] confuse doing things with love and with care. When confronted with a culture of care, they look and feel terrible.

The blog, "WestJet—The Difference that Culture makes," was posted by Robert Paterson on June 29, 2004 at 04:45 PM in Organizations and Culture. Robert Paterson is the president of The Renewal Consulting Group Inc. which was founded in 1994.[54]

successful, the values, ideas, and practices that helped attain success become institutionalized. As the environment changes, these values may become detrimental to future performance. Many organizations become victims of their own success, clinging to outmoded and even destructive values and behaviours. Thus, the impact of a strong culture is not necessarily positive. Typically, healthy cultures not only provide for smooth internal integration but also encourage adaptation to the external environment. Nonadaptive cultures encourage rigidity and stability. Strong adaptive cultures often incorporate the following values:

1. *The whole is more important than the parts, and boundaries between parts are minimized.* People are aware of the whole system, how everything fits together, and the relationships among various organizational parts. All members consider how their actions affect other parts and the total organization. This emphasis on the whole reduces boundaries both within the organization and with other companies. Although subcultures may form, everyone's primary attitudes and behaviours reflect the organization's dominant culture. The free flow of people, ideas, and information allows coordinated action and continuous learning.

EXHIBIT 10.5
Adaptive versus Maladaptive Organizational Cultures

	Adaptive Cultures	Maladaptive Cultures
Core Values	Managers care deeply about customers, stockholders, and employees. They value processes that can create useful change.	Managers care about themselves and their immediate work group, and value orderly and risk-reducing processes. They value short-term gains.
Common Behaviours	Managers pay attention to their stakeholders and initiate change to serve their interests. They create an organizational climate that is supportive of employee participation, development, and creativity.	Managers tend to be somewhat isolated, political, and bureaucratic. They tend to resist change and when they must change, they tend push ideas down the hierarchy and restrict employee creativity.

Source: J.P. Kotter and J. Heskett, *Corporate Culture and Performance* (New York: The Free Press, 1992); and J. Cangemi and R. Miller, Breaking-out-of-the-box in Organizations, *Journal of Management Development,* 26, 5 (2007): 401–410.

2. *Equality and trust are primary values.* The culture creates a sense of community and caring for one another. The organization is a place for creating a web of relationships that allows people to take risks and develop to their full potential. The emphasis on treating everyone with care and respect creates a climate of safety and trust that allows experimentation, frequent mistakes, and learning. Managers emphasize honest and open communications as a way to build trust.
3. *The culture encourages risk taking, change, and improvement.* A basic value is to question the status quo. Constant questioning of assumptions opens the gates to creativity and improvement. The culture rewards and celebrates the creators of new ideas, products, and work processes. To symbolize the importance of taking risks, an adaptive culture may also reward those who fail in order to learn and grow.

As illustrated in Exhibit 10.5, adaptive organizational cultures have different values and behaviour patterns than maladaptive cultures.[55] In adaptive cultures, managers are concerned with customers and employees as well as with the internal processes and procedures that bring about useful change. Behaviour is flexible and managers initiate change when needed, even if it involves risk. In maladaptive cultures, managers are more concerned about themselves or their own special projects, and their values discourage risk taking and change. Thus, strong, healthy cultures, such as those in learning companies, help organizations adapt to the external environment, whereas strong, unhealthy cultures can encourage an organization to march resolutely in the wrong direction.

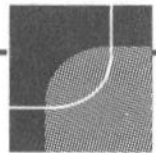

Ethical Values and Social Responsibility

Of the values that make up an organization's culture, ethical values are now considered among the most important. Widespread corporate accounting scandals, allegations that top managers of some organizations made personal use of company funds, and charges of insider trading have blanketed the newspapers and airwaves in recent years. Top corporate managers are under scrutiny from the public as never before, and even small companies are finding a need to put more emphasis on ethics to restore trust among their customers and the community. As the University of Calgary's Gregory Daneke notes "[in] the aftermath of major corporate scandals, such as Enron and Hollinger, it is high time that ethics and economics become reacquainted."[56]

Sources of Individual Ethical Principles

Ethics is the code of moral principles and values that governs the behaviours of a person or group with respect to what is right or wrong. An individual manager's values can be shaped by his/her background and experiences. Ethical values set standards as to what is good or bad in conduct and decision making.[57] Ethics are personal and unique to each individual, although in any given group, organization, or society there are many areas of consensus about what constitutes ethical behaviour.[58] Exhibit 10.6 illustrates the varied sources of individual ethical principles. Each person is a creation of his or her time and place in history. National culture, religious heritage, historical background, and so forth lead to the development of societal morality, or society's view of what is right and wrong. Societal morality is often reflected in norms of behaviour and values about what makes sense for an orderly society. Some principles are codified into laws and regulations, such as laws against drunk driving, robbery, or murder.

These laws, as well as unwritten societal norms and values, shape the local environment within which each individual acts, such as a person's community, family, and place of work. Individuals absorb the beliefs and values of their family, community,

EXHIBIT 10.6
Sources of Individual Ethical Principles and Actions
Source: Thanks to Susan H. Taft and Judith White for providing this exhibit.

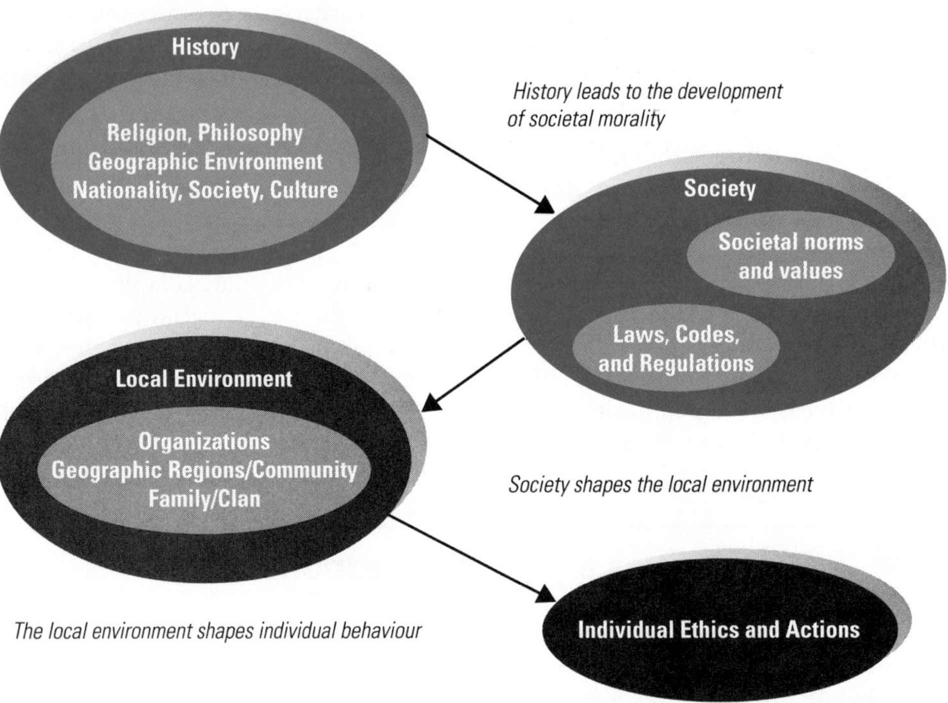

culture, society, religious community, and geographic environment, typically discarding some and incorporating others into their own personal ethical standards. Each person's ethical stance is thus a blending of his or her historical, cultural, societal, and family backgrounds and influences.

It is important to look at individual ethics because ethics always involve an individual action, whether it be a decision to act or the failure to take action against wrongdoing by others. In organizations, an individual's ethical stance may be affected by peers, subordinates, and supervisors, as well as by the organizational culture. Organizational culture often has a profound influence on individual choices and can support and encourage ethical actions or promote unethical and socially irresponsible behaviour.

PDA

Remember...

Take control of ethical values in the organization. Ethics is not the same as following the law. Ethical decisions are influenced by management's personal background, by organizational culture, and by organizational systems.

Managerial Ethics and Social Responsibility

Recent events have demonstrated the powerful influence of organizational standards on ethical behaviour. Strict ethical standards are becoming part of the formal policies and informal cultures of many organizations, and courses in ethics are taught in many business schools. Many of the recent scandals in the news have dealt with people and corporations that broke the law. But it is important to remember that ethics goes far beyond behaviours governed by law.[59] The **rule of law** arises from a

Book Mark 10.0 (HAVE YOU READ THIS BOOK?)

The Corporation: The Pathological Pursuit of Profit and Power
By Joel Bakan

The Corporation, written by Joel Bakan, a professor at the University of British Columbia's Law School, is both controversial and uplifting. Bakan argues that corporations are rapacious entities interested only in power and profits. Bakan goes on to show some parallels in the behaviours of corporations and psychopaths. He writes that "as a psychopathic creature, the corporation can neither recognize nor act upon moral reasons to refrain from harming others. Nothing in its legal makeup limits what it can do to others in pursuit of its selfish ends, and it is compelled to cause harm when the benefits of doing so outweigh the costs."[60]

Bakan suggests that corporations pursue socially and environmentally responsible actions, not for altruistic reasons, but for strategic reasons designed to enhance their own performance. He acknowledges that corporate social responsibility initiatives can and do good, although he believes that often they are token responses. While his is a depressing account of the ruthless power of the corporation, Bakan remains an optimist. He believes that it is vital that the regulatory systems affecting corporations are reconceived and legitimated "as the principal means for bringing corporations under democratic control and ensuring that they respect the interests of citizens, communities, and the environment."[61] He also believes that there should be tighter restrictions on lobbying and that we need to create a stronger social sphere where fundamental social services are offered by organizations other than corporations.

The film, of the same name, has received critical acclaim and received eight audience choice awards, including one from the Sundance Film Festival. Noam Chomsky of the Massachusetts Institute of Technology comments that "[this] vivid and often mesmerizing film lifts the veil from one of the most important and least understood features of modern age: the extraordinary powers that have been bestowed on virtually unaccountable private tyrannies, required by law to act in ways that severely undermine democracy and the most elementary human rights, and that pose a serious threat even to survival."[62]

The Corporation: The Pathological Pursuit of Profit and Power by Joel Bakan, is published by Penguin.

set of codified principles and regulations that describe how people are required to act, that are generally accepted in society, and that are enforceable in the courts.[63]

Ethical standards for the most part apply to behaviour not covered by the law, and the rule of law applies to behaviours not necessarily covered by ethical standards. Our laws often reflect combined moral judgments, but not all moral judgments are codified into law. The morality of aiding a drowning person, for example, is not specified by law, and driving on the right-hand side of the road has no moral basis; but in acts such as robbery or murder, rules and moral standards overlap.

Unethical conduct in organizations is surprisingly widespread. More than 54 percent of human resource (HR) professionals polled by the Society for Human Resource Management and the Ethics Resource Center reported observing employees lying to supervisors or coworkers, falsifying reports or records, or abusing drugs or alcohol while on the job.[64] Many people believe that if you are not breaking the law, then you are behaving in an ethical manner, but this is not necessarily true. Many behaviours have not been codified, and managers must be very sensitive to emerging norms and values. Increasingly, a stellar track record does not protect a CEO from scrutiny; for example, (former) Boeing CEO Harry Stonecipher was fired in 2005 over a romance with an employee. "It used to be that as long as an executive performed well on the job, no one much cared about what they were doing in their free time—or even behind closed doors in the office . . . But a sea change has occurred, with every aspect of managers' conduct being scrutinized—and ever more closely the higher up one goes."[65]

Managerial ethics are principles that guide the decisions and behaviours of managers with regard to whether they are right or wrong. The notion of **social responsibility** is an extension of this idea and refers to management's obligation to make choices and take action so that the organization contributes to the welfare and interest of all organizational stakeholders, such as employees, customers, shareholders, the community, and the broader society.[66]

Examples of the need for managerial ethics are as follows:[67]

- Top executives are considering promoting a rising sales manager who consistently brings in $70 million a year and has cracked open new markets in places like Brazil and Turkey that are important to the organization's international growth. However, female employees have been complaining for years that the manager is verbally abusive to them, tells offensive jokes, and throws temper tantrums if female employees don't do exactly as he says.
- The manager of a beauty supply store is told that she and her salespeople can receive large bonuses for selling a specified number of boxes of a new product, a permanent-wave solution that costs nearly twice as much as what most of her salon customers typically use. She orders the salespeople to store the old product in the back and tell customers there's been a delay in delivery.
- The project manager for a construction planning project wondered whether some facts should be left out of a report because the community where the facility would be built might object if they discovered certain environmental aspects of the project.
- A North American manufacturer operating abroad was asked to make cash payments (a bribe) to government officials and was told it was consistent with local customs, despite being illegal in North America.

As these examples illustrate, ethics and social responsibility are about making decisions. Managers make choices every day about whether to be honest or deceitful with suppliers, treat employees with respect or disdain, and be a good or a harmful corporate citizen. Some issues are exceedingly difficult to resolve and often represent ethical dilemmas. An **ethical dilemma** arises in a situation concerning right and wrong in which values are in conflict.[68] Right or wrong cannot be clearly identified in such situations. For example, for a salesperson at the beauty supply store, the value conflict is between being honest with customers and adhering to the boss's expectations. The manufacturing manager may feel torn between respecting and following local customs in a foreign country or adhering to domestic laws concerning bribes. Sometimes, each alternative choice or behaviour seems undesirable.

Ethical dilemmas are not easy to resolve, but top executives can aid the process by establishing organizational values that provide people with guidelines for making the best decision from a moral standpoint.

Does It Pay to Be Good?

The relationship of an organization's ethics and social responsibility to its performance concerns both organizational managers and organization scholars. Studies have provided varying results but generally have found that there is a small positive relationship between ethical and socially responsible behaviour and financial results.[69] For example, a recent study of the financial performance of large U.S. corporations considered "best corporate citizens" found that they have both superior reputations and superior financial performance.[70] Similarly, Governance Metrics International, an independent corporate governance ratings agency, found that the stocks of companies run on more selfless principles perform better than those run in a self-serving manner. According to another study, corporate philanthropy adds to shareholder wealth: "businesses that have earned a reputation for being generous through acts of philanthropy are given the benefit of the doubt when negative events occur.[71] Of course, philanthropy is not confined to corporations; for example, members of the Union of Food and Commercial Workers of Canada raised about $1.5 million in 2007 for the Leukemia & Lymphoma Society and have raised $10,805,000 since 1985.[72]

As discussed earlier in the chapter, long-term organizational success relies largely on social capital, which means companies need to build a reputation for honesty, fairness, and doing the right thing. Researchers have found that people prefer to work for companies that demonstrate a high level of ethics and social responsibility, so these companies can attract and retain high-quality employees.[73] Timberland, for example, which gives employees 40 hours of unpaid leave annually to do community volunteer work and supports a number of charitable causes, is consistently ranked on *Fortune*'s list of the 100 best companies to work for. One vice president says she has turned down lucrative offers from other companies because she prefers to work at a company that puts ethics and social responsibility ahead of just making a profit.[74]

Customers pay attention, too. A study by Walker Research indicates that, price and quality being equal, two-thirds of people say they would switch brands to do business with a company that makes a high commitment to ethics.[75]

Companies that put ethics on the back burner in favour of fast growth and short-term profits ultimately suffer. To gain and keep the trust of employees, customers, investors, and the general public, organizations must put ethics first. "Just saying you're ethical isn't very useful," says Charles O. Holliday, Jr., chairman and CEO of DuPont Co. "You have to earn trust by what you do every day."

Bruce Poon Tip, founder and CEO of GAP Adventures says "[it] is my duty as the founder and CEO . . . to help preserve our planet, her people and to make sure her treasures are around for the next generation of eager travellers and wide-eyed explorers."[76] Through his Planeterra Foundation, he has supported community projects around the world by matching individual donations and paying administration costs so that all the monies go to support the projects.

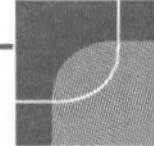

Sources of Ethical Values in Organizations

Ethics in organizations is both an individual and an organizational matter. The standards for ethical or socially responsible conduct are embodied within each employee as well as within the organization itself. In addition, external stakeholders can influence standards of what is ethical and socially responsible. The immediate forces that impinge on ethical decisions in organizations are summarized in Exhibit 10.7. Individual beliefs and values, a person's ethical decision framework, and moral development influence personal ethics. Organizational culture, as we have already discussed, shapes the overall framework of values within the organization. Moreover, formal organizational systems influence values and behaviours according to the organization's policy framework and reward systems. Companies also respond to numerous stakeholders in determining what is right. They consider how their actions may be viewed by customers, government agencies, shareholders, and the general community, as well as the impact each alternative course of action may have on various stakeholders. All of these factors can be explored to understand ethical and socially responsible decisions in organizations.[77]

EXHIBIT 10.7
Forces That Shape Managerial Ethics

Personal Ethics
Beliefs and values
Moral development
Ethical framework

Organizational Culture
Rituals, ceremonies
Stories, heroes
Language, slogans
Symbols
Founder, history

Is Decision or Behaviour Ethical and Socially Responsible?

Organizational Systems
Structure
Policies, rules
Code of ethics
Reward system
Selection, training

External Stakeholders
Government regulations
Customers
Special-interest groups
Global market forces

Personal Ethics

Every individual brings a set of personal beliefs and values into the workplace. Personal values and the moral reasoning that translates these values into behaviour are an important aspect of ethical decision making in organizations.[78]

As we discussed earlier, the historical, cultural, family, religious, and community backgrounds of managers shape their personal values and provide principles by which they carry out business. In addition, people go through stages of moral development that affect their ability to translate values into behaviour. For example, children have a low level of moral development, making decisions and behaving to obtain rewards and avoid physical punishment. At an intermediate level of development, people learn to conform to expectations of good behaviour as defined by colleagues and society. Most managers are at this level, willingly upholding the law and responding to societal expectations. At the highest level of moral development are people who develop an internal set of standards. These are self-chosen ethical principles that are more important to decisions than external expectations. Only a few people reach this high level, which can mean breaking laws if necessary to sustain higher moral principles.[79]

The other personal factor is whether managers have developed an *ethical framework* that guides their decisions. *Utilitarian theory*, for example, argues that ethical decisions should be made to generate the greatest benefits for the largest number of people. This framework is often consistent with business decisions because costs and benefits can be calculated in dollars. The *personal liberty* framework argues that decisions should be made to ensure the greatest possible freedom of choice and liberty for individuals. Liberties include the freedom to act on one's conscience, freedom of speech, due process of law, and the right to privacy. The *distributive justice* framework holds that moral decisions are those that promote equity, fairness, and impartiality with respect to the distribution of rewards and the administration of rules, which are essential for social cooperation.[80]

One promising tool to give guidance to CEOs of corporations has been developed by Roger Martin, dean of the Rotman School of Management, in Toronto. Martin developed a conceptual framework for addressing critical questions about responsibility such as (1) What drives the market for responsible corporate behaviour? (2) What creates the public demand for greater responsibility? (3) Why does globalization raise concerns about corporate responsibility? (4) What are the barriers to increasing responsible behaviours? and (5) What forces can add to the supply of corporate responsibility?[81] The virtue matrix itself shows the forces that generate corporate social responsibility. The bottom two quadrants are the civil foundation, which consists of norms, customs, and laws that govern corporate behaviours. Corporations either choose to comply with the requirements of the civil foundation or are mandated to do so. The upper two quadrants of the matrix are the frontier where innovations in socially responsible behaviour occur either for the benefit of the shareholders and society or for society alone. Each quadrant raises questions that need to be answered before developing a corporate social responsibility strategy. (The Workshop at the end of this chapter has the questions to use in identifying socially responsible activities for an organization.)

Organizational Culture

Rarely can ethical or unethical business practices be attributed entirely to the personal ethics of a single individual. Business practices also reflect the values, attitudes, and behaviour patterns of an organization's culture. To promote ethical behaviour in the workplace, companies should make ethics an integral part of the organization's culture. Raymond Royer, president and CEO of Domtar Corporation, came to the realization that Domtar and environmental groups shared the same goals, i.e., to have sustainability in the forest. He comments that "[you] have to put yourself in the position of whoever does business with you ... [at] the end of the day, we are taking fibre, so like it or not, we have to be involved with the environment."[82]

Organizational culture has a powerful impact on individual ethics because it helps to guide employees in making daily decisions. When the culture supports wrongdoing, it is easier for individual employees to go along. One young Enron employee explained how he slid into unethical decisions and practices in his job: "It was easy to get into, 'Well, everybody else is doing it, so maybe it isn't so bad.'"[83]

Organizational Systems

The third category of influences that shape managerial ethics is formal organizational systems. This includes the basic architecture of the organization, such as whether ethical values are incorporated in policies and rules; whether an explicit code of ethics is available and issued to members; whether organizational rewards, including praise, attention, and promotions, are linked to ethical behaviour; and whether ethics is a consideration in the selection and training of employees. These formal efforts can reinforce ethical values that exist in the informal culture.

Many companies have established formal ethics programs. For example, Alcan Inc has a 32-page Worldwide Code of Employee and Business Conduct that codifies its values of integrity, accountability, teamwork, trust, and transparency.[84] Alcan ranks eighth on the 2007 Global 100 Most Sustainable Corporations in the World and is the highest-ranked Canadian organization.[85]

External Stakeholders

Managerial ethics and social responsibility are also influenced by a variety of external stakeholders, groups outside the organization that have a stake in the organization's performance. Ethical and socially responsible decision making recognizes that the organization is part of a larger community and considers the impact of a decision or action on all stakeholders.[86] Important external stakeholders are government agencies, customers, and special-interest groups such as those concerned with the natural environment.

Companies must operate within the limits of certain government regulations, such as safety laws, environmental protection requirements, and many other laws and regulations. Numerous companies, including Hollinger, WorldCom, Merrill Lynch, and Xerox, have come under investigation by the U.S. Securities and Exchange Commission for alleged violations of laws related to financial controls and accounting practices. Companies in the health care industry have to respond to numerous laws and regulations, as do organizations such as schools and day care centres. Customers are another important stakeholder group. Customers are primarily concerned about the quality, safety, and availability of goods and services. For example, McDonald's has reduced trans–fatty acids in its fried foods in response to growing customer concerns about possible health risks associated with a fast-food diet.[87]

Special-interest groups continue to be one of the largest stakeholder concerns that companies face. Today, those concerned with corporate responsibility to the natural environment are particularly vocal. Thus, environmentalism is becoming an integral part of organizational planning and decision making for leading companies. The concept of *sustainable development*, a dual concern for economic growth and environmental sustainability, has been gaining ground among many business leaders. The public is no longer comfortable with organizations focusing solely on profit at the expense of the natural environment. For example, Ron Dembo, founder of Algorithmics, has started Zerofootprint, an Internet hub providing information, products, and services to help organizations and individuals reduce their environmental impact.[88] Environmental sustainability—meaning that what is taken out of the environmental system for food, shelter, clothing, energy, and other human uses is restored to the system in waste that can be reused—is a part of strategy for companies like IKEA, Electrolux, Scandic Hotels, MacMillan-Bloedel, and Interface. Interface, a $1 billion leader in the floor-covering industry, is instituting changes that will allow the company to manufacture without pollution, waste, or fossil fuels. From the factory floor to the R&D lab, sustainability is as important a consideration at Interface as profitability. The emphasis on environmentalism hasn't hurt Interface. Over a one-year period, sales increased from $800 million to $1 billion. During that time, the amount of raw materials used by the company dropped almost 20 percent per dollar of sales.[89]

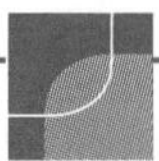

How Leaders Shape Culture and Ethics

In a study of ethics policy and practice in successful, ethical companies such as Johnson & Johnson and General Mills, no point emerged more clearly than the role of top management in providing commitment, leadership, and examples for ethical behaviour.[90] The CEO and other top managers must be committed to specific values and provide constant leadership in tending and renewing the values. Values can be communicated in a number of ways—speeches, company publications, policy statements, and, especially, personal actions. Top leaders are responsible for creating and sustaining a culture that emphasizes the importance of ethical behaviour for all employees every day. When the CEO engages in unethical practices or fails to take firm and decisive action in response to the unethical practices of others, this attitude filters down through the organization. Formal ethics codes and training programs are worthless if leaders do not set and live up to high standards of ethical conduct.[91]

The following sections examine how managers signal and implement values through leadership as well as through the formal systems of the organization.

PDA Remember...

Act as a leader for the internal culture and ethical values that are important to the organization. Influence the value system through values-based leadership, including the use of ceremonies, slogans, symbols, and stories. Communicate important values to employees to enhance organizational effectiveness, and remember that actions speak louder than words.

Values-Based Leadership

The underlying value system of an organization cannot be managed in the traditional way. Issuing an authoritative directive, for example, has little or no impact on an organization's value system. Organizational values are developed and strengthened primarily through **values-based leadership**, a relationship between a leader and followers that is based on shared, strongly internalized values that are advocated and acted upon by the leader.[92]

Leaders influence cultural and ethical values by clearly articulating a vision for organizational values that employees can believe in, communicating the vision throughout the organization, and institutionalizing the vision through everyday behaviour, rituals, ceremonies, and symbols, as well as through organizational systems and policies. The Vancouver 2010 Winter Olympic Games is using environmentally friendly construction and operation of all events in Whistler. The Games will showcase its use of alternative energy sources; it is working with wind-generation companies and expects to have a wind-monitoring station in the mountain in time for the Games.[93]

Managers should remember that every statement and action has an impact on culture and values. For example, a survey of readers of the magazine *The Secretary* found that employees are acutely aware of their bosses' ethical lapses. Something as simple as having a secretary notarize a document without witnessing the signature may seem insignificant, but it communicates that the manager doesn't value honesty.[94] Employees learn about values, beliefs, and goals from watching managers, just as students learn which topics are important for an exam, what professors like, and how to get a good grade from watching professors. To be effective values-based leaders, executives often use symbols, ceremonies, speeches, and slogans that match the values. Citigroup's CEO, Charles Prince, devoted a tremendous amount of time to talking about values with both employees and customers. Prince knew that for a company the size of Citigroup, just strengthening rules and systems isn't enough. To get the company to "internalize" a strong code of ethics around the globe, Prince was making a visible commitment to values through speeches, video addresses, and regular communication.[95] Prince also said he will be "ruthless" with managers and employees who don't follow the rules. Actions speak louder than words, so values-based leaders "walk their talk."[96] In late 2007, Prince himself faced a crisis, and he resigned from Citigroup. As he put it, "[it] is my judgment that given the size of the recent losses in our mortgage-backed securities business, the only honourable course for me to take as chief executive officer is to step down."[97]

Values-based leaders engender a high level of trust and respect from employees, based not only on their stated values but also on the courage, determination, and self-sacrifice they demonstrate in upholding them. Leaders can use this respect and trust to motivate employees toward high-level performance and a sense of purpose in achieving the organizational vision. When leaders are willing to make personal sacrifices for the sake of values, employees also become more willing to do so. This element of self-sacrifice puts a somewhat spiritual connotation on the process of leadership. Indeed, one writer in organizational theory, Karl Weick, has said that "managerial work can be viewed as managing myth, symbols, and labels . . . ; because managers traffic so often in images, the appropriate role for the manager may be evangelist rather than accountant."[98]

John Tu and David Sun, cofounders of Kingston Technology Co., headquartered in the United States, provide an example of values-based leadership. "Business is not about money," says David Sun, vice president and CEO of Kingston Technology Co., which manufactures memory products for personal computers, laser printers, digital cameras, and other products, "It's about relationships." Sun and his president John Tu, strive to develop deep, caring, trusting relationships with employees. "They are part of the team," says one employee of the partnership that workers feel with leaders at Kingston. "They are not owners; they are employees. And that . . . value system is passed on." Sun and Tu believe everyone in the company is a leader, so they share the wealth with employees. When the two sold 80 percent of Kingston to Softbank of Japan for $1.5 billion, they set aside $100 million of the proceeds for employee bonuses. The initial distribution of $38 million went to about 550 employees who were with the company at the time of its sale. Another $40 million has since been divvied up among the company's current 1,500 workers. Sun and

Tu seem genuinely puzzled by people's astonishment that they would give $100 million to employees. It seems only right to them.[99]

Formal Structure and Systems

Another set of tools leaders can use to shape cultural and ethical values is the formal structure and systems of the organization. These systems have been especially effective in recent years for influencing managerial ethics.

Structure. Managers can assign responsibility for ethical values to a specific position. This not only allocates organization time and energy to the problem but symbolizes to everyone the importance of ethics. One example is an **ethics committee**, which is a cross-functional group of executives who oversee company ethics. The committee provides rulings on questionable ethical issues and assumes responsibility for disciplining wrongdoers. By appointing top-level executives to serve on the committee, the organization signals the importance of ethics.

Today, many organizations are setting up ethics departments that manage and coordinate all corporate ethics activities. These departments are headed by a **chief ethics officer**, a high-level company executive who oversees all aspects of ethics, including establishing and broadly communicating ethical standards, setting up ethics training programs, supervising the investigation of ethical problems, and advising managers on the ethical aspects of corporate decisions.[100] The title of chief ethics officer was almost unheard of a decade ago, but recent ethical and legal problems have created a growing demand for these specialists. Between 1992 and early 2005, membership in the Ethics Officer Association, a trade group, soared from only 12 companies to more than 1,000.[101]

Ethics offices sometimes also work as counselling centres to help employees resolve difficult ethical dilemmas. The focus is as much on helping employees make the right decisions as on disciplining wrongdoers. Most ethics offices have confidential **ethics hotlines** that employees can use to seek guidance as well as report questionable behaviour. One organization calls its hotline a "Guide Line" to emphasize its use as a tool for making ethical decisions as well as reporting lapses.[102] Holding organizations accountable depends to some degree on individuals who are willing to speak up if they suspect illegal, dangerous, or unethical activities. According to Gary Edwards, president of the Ethics Resource Center, between 65 and 85 percent of calls to hotlines in the organizations he advises are calls for counsel on ethical issues. Randstad Canada, a placement agency, encourages honesty and integrity through its 1-800-INTEGRITY phone line where employees can report misconduct anonymously.[103]

PDA Remember...

Use the formal systems of the organization to implement desired cultural and ethical values. These systems include an ethics committee, a chief ethics officer, disclosure mechanisms, a code of ethics, a mission statement, and training in ethical decision-making frameworks.

Disclosure Mechanisms. Organizations can establish policies and procedures to support and protect whistle-blowers. **Whistle-blowing** is employee disclosure of illegal, immoral, or illegitimate practices on the part of the organization.[104] One value of corporate policy is to protect whistle-blowers so they will not be transferred to lower-level positions or fired because of their ethical concerns. A policy can also encourage whistle-blowers to stay within the organization—for instance, to quietly blow the whistle to responsible managers.[105] Whistle-blowers have the option to stop organizational activities by going to newspaper or television reporters, but as a last resort. As ethical problems in the corporate world increase, many companies are looking for ways to protect whistle-blowers. In addition, calls are increasing for stronger legal protection for those who report illegal or unethical business activities.[106]

When there are no protective measures, whistle-blowers suffer, and the company may continue its unethical or illegal practices.

Many whistle-blowers suffer financial and personal loss to maintain their personal ethical standards. In 1992, Joanna Gualtieri, then a young lawyer working for the Canadian government, wrote some reports critical of the residences and offices of Canadian diplomats overseas. According to Gualtieri, her efforts were thwarted by her bosses for two years. Then, as a way to go public with her claims, she sued her former bosses at the Department of Foreign Affairs and International Trade. She argues that "[it] is just so simple. If there is respect for the truth, . . . let your people speak."[107] Similarly, when five RCMP officers and staff exposed a scandal about the force's pension plan, their claims were met with three years of inertia, denials, and career reprisals. According to the special investigator looking into their claims, "[it] was their perseverance in tracking misdeeds in the force's pension fund that revealed a horribly broken management culture out of step with the RCMP's own values of honesty and accountability."[108] The five whistle-blowers received the force's highest honour, the Commissioner's Commendation in June 2007. Even so, when the whistle-blowers were asked if it was worth it, " . . . each, in separate interviews, [paused] long and hard."[109]

A recent study of Canadian organizations found that less than half of the firms had any guidelines to support whistle-blowers. As well, the same study found that only half of the responding firms had created an ombudsperson role or department, a mechanism vital for fostering ethical behaviours.[110] Enlightened organizations, however, strive to create a climate and a culture in which employees feel free to point out problems, and managers take swift action to address concerns about unethical or illegal activities. Organizations can view whistle-blowing as a benefit to the company, helping to prevent the kind of disasters that have hit companies such as Enron, Arthur Andersen, and WorldCom, and make dedicated efforts to encourage and protect whistle-blowers.

Code of Ethics. A survey of *Fortune* 1,000 companies found that 98 percent address issues of ethics and business conduct in formal corporate policies, and 78 percent have separate codes of ethics that are widely distributed to employees.[111] A **code of ethics** is a formal statement of the company's values concerning ethics and social responsibility; it clarifies to employees what the company stands for and its expectations for employee conduct. Codes of ethics may cover a broad range of issues, including statements of the company's guiding values; guidelines related to issues such as workplace safety, the security of proprietary information, or employee privacy; and commitments to environmental responsibility, product safety, and other matters of concern to stakeholders.

Some companies use broader values statements within which ethics is a part. These statements define ethical values as well as organizational culture and contain language about company responsibility, quality of product, and treatment of employees. A formal statement of values can serve as a fundamental organizational document that defines what the organization stands for, and legitimizes value choices for employees.[112] For example, Citigroup is implementing a new statement of cultural and ethical values after being stung by a series of scandals in the United States, Japan, and Europe. Charles Prince, former CEO, explains: "Our goal is to make explicit what is implicit. Every employee, starting with me, has the ability to refocus our reputation and our integrity."[113]

Written codes of ethics are important because they clarify and formally state the company's values and expected ethical behaviours. However, it is essential that top managers support and reinforce the codes through their actions, including rewards for compliance and discipline for violations. Otherwise, a code of ethics is nothing more than a piece of paper. Indeed, one study found that companies with a written code of ethics are just as likely as those without a code to be found guilty of illegal activities.[114]

Training Programs. To ensure that ethical issues are considered in daily decision making, companies can supplement a written code of ethics with employee training programs.[115] At Citigroup, a new online ethics training program is mandatory for all 300,000 employees worldwide.[116] All Texas Instruments (TI) employees go through an eight-hour ethics training course that includes case examples giving people a chance to wrestle with ethical dilemmas. In addition, TI incorporates an ethics component into every training course it offers.[117] All Telus employees are required to take an e-learning ethics course.[118]

In an important step, ethics programs also include frameworks for ethical decision making, such as the utilitarian approach described earlier in this chapter. Learning these frameworks helps managers act autonomously and still think their way through a difficult decision. In a few companies, managers are also taught about the stages of moral development, which helps to bring them to a high level of ethical decision making. This training has been an important catalyst for establishing ethical behaviour and integrity as critical components of strategic competitiveness.[119]

These formal systems and structures can be highly effective. However, they alone are not sufficient to build and sustain an ethical company. Leaders should integrate ethics into the organizational culture and support and renew ethical values through their words and actions. For example, since 1995, Telus has been an Imagine Caring Company, a designation by Imagine Canada (formerly the Canadian Centre for Philanthropy). Caring companies donate more than one percent of their pre-tax profits to charitable purposes each year. Telus has contributed over $76 million of financial and in-kind assistance to charitable organizations across Canada in the past six years. As part of its corporate social responsibility initiatives, Telus has created community boards across Canada to more effectively allocate $3.5 million annually to local communities.

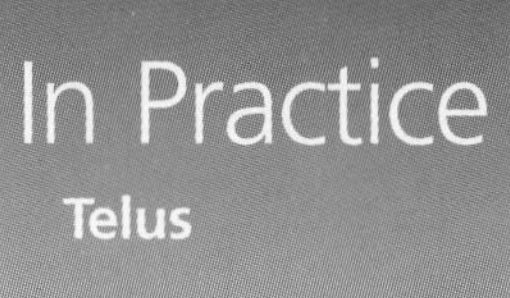

Community boards have been established in Vancouver, Edmonton, Calgary, Toronto, Ottawa, Montreal, and Rimouski. Prominent community representatives and senior Telus team members make up the community boards, which are designed to support and expand Telus's investment in smaller grassroots efforts. Selection of community board members is based on the needs of each community, usually focusing on one of Telus's key areas of investment: arts and culture, education and sports, and health and well-being.

The Telus community boards have five principal goals: (1) to determine where and how to invest resources to optimize the benefits that accrue to the community; (2) to determine whether or not the benefits envisioned mutually were successfully created; (3) to identify opportunities that may have been overlooked; (4) to secure additional partners in order to optimize the good to be achieved; and (5) to identify where best to deploy human capital—Telus executives who are willing to lend their time to serve communities.

In May 2006, Telus launched the Telus Toronto Community Board as part of its national philanthropic program. As a result, Toronto community initiatives will receive an increase of $500,000 annually from Telus. According to President and CEO Darren Entwistle, "[members of] the Telus Toronto Community Board will help provide the local insight, knowledge and inspiration to determine where and how we can donate funds to maximize the benefits that accrue to the community. They will also play key roles in helping Telus identify where best to deploy our executives who are excited to lend their time to serve the Toronto community and business organizations. At Telus, we are deeply committed to supporting the communities where we live, work and serve."[120]

Darren Entwistle is striving to integrate ethical and socially responsible values into the very core of Telus. By integrating ethics and corporate social responsibility into the core of the organization, Entwistle is making organizational integrity and community engagement a part of day-to-day business. Only when employees are convinced that ethical values play a key role in all management decisions and actions can they become committed to making them a part of their everyday behaviour. Organizations that operate on a global scale also face challenges related to culture and ethics.

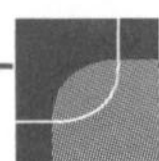

Organizational Culture and Ethics in a Global Environment

A Hudson Institute report, *Workforce 2020*, states, "The rest of the world matters to a degree that it never did in the past."[121] Managers are finding this to be true not only in terms of economics or HR issues, but also in terms of cultural and ethical values. Organizations operating in many different areas of the world have a tough time because of the various cultural and market factors they must deal with. The greater complexity of the environment and organizational domain create a greater potential for ethical problems or misunderstandings.[122] Consider that in Europe, privacy has been defined as a basic human right and there are laws limiting the amount and kind of information companies can collect and governing how they use it. How do managers translate the ideas for developing strong organizational cultures to a complex global environment? How do they develop ethics codes or other ethical structures and systems that address the complex issues associated with doing business on a global scale?

Organizational culture and national culture are often intertwined, and the global diversity of many of today's companies presents a challenge to managers trying to build a strong organizational culture. Employees who come from different countries often have varied attitudes and beliefs that make it difficult to establish a sense of community and cohesiveness based on the organizational culture. In fact, research has indicated that national culture has a greater impact on employees than does organizational culture.[123] For example, a study of effectiveness and cultural values in Russia found that flexibility and collectivism (working together in groups), which are key values in the national culture, are considerably more important to organizational effectiveness than they are for most U.S.–based companies.[124] When these values are not incorporated into the organizational culture, employees do not perform as well. Another recent study found that differences in national cultural values and preferences also create significant variance in ethical attitudes among people from different countries.[125]

Some companies have been successful in developing a broad global perspective that permeates the entire organizational culture. For example, Omron, a global company with headquarters in Kyoto, Japan, has offices on six continents. However, until a few years ago, Omron had always assigned Japanese managers to head them. Today, it relies on local expertise in each geographical area and blends the insights and perspectives of local managers into a global whole. Global planning meetings are held in offices around the world. In addition, Omron established a global database and standardized its software to ensure a smooth exchange of information among its offices worldwide. It takes time to develop a broad cultural mind-set and spread it throughout the company, but firms such as Omron try to bring a multicultural approach to every business issue.[126]

Vijay Govindarajan, a Dartmouth College professor of international business, offers some guidance for managers trying to build a global culture. His research indicates that, even though organizational cultures may vary widely, specific components characterize a global culture. These include an emphasis on multicultural rather than national values, basing status on merit rather than nationality, being open to new ideas from other cultures, showing excitement rather than trepidation when entering new cultural environments, and being sensitive to cultural differences without being limited by them.[127]

Global ethics is also challenging today's organizations to think more broadly. Many are using a wide variety of mechanisms to support and reinforce their ethics initiatives on a global scale. One of the most useful mechanisms for building global ethics is the **social audit**, which measures and reports the ethical, social, and environmental impact of a company's operations.[128] Concerns about the labour practices and working conditions of many major U.S. corporations' overseas suppliers originally spurred the Council on Economic Priorities Accreditation Agency to propose a set of global social standards to deal with issues such as child labour, low wages, and unsafe working conditions. Today, the Social Accountability 8000, or SA 8000, is the only auditable social standard in the world. The system is designed to work like the ISO 9000 quality-auditing system of the International Standards Organization.

Many companies, such as Avon Products, Nike, and Toys "R" Us, are taking steps to ensure that their factories and suppliers meet SA 8000 standards. Organizations can also ask an outside company to perform an independent social audit to measure how well the company is living up to its ethical and social values, and how it is perceived by different stakeholder groups. An interesting Canadian experiment is Me to We [Responsible Design]. It is social enterprise that provides ethically manufactured apparel for the socially conscious consumer. The product line is domestically produced, sweatshop-free, and made using certified organic cotton and bamboo. Fifty percent of the profit goes to Free the Children, to support development projects in rural and impoverished areas across the world.[129]

In the coming years, organizations will continue to evolve in their ability to work with varied cultures, combine them into a cohesive whole, live up to high social and ethical standards worldwide, and cope with the conflicts that may arise when working in a multicultural environment.

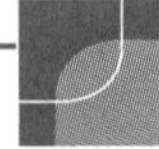

Summary and Interpretation

This chapter covered a range of material on organizational culture, the importance of cultural and ethical values, and techniques managers can use to influence these values. Cultural and ethical values help determine the organization's social capital, and the right values can contribute to organizational success.

Culture is the set of key values, beliefs, and norms shared by members of an organization. Organizational cultures serve two critically important functions—to integrate members so that they know how to relate to one another and to help the organization adapt to the external environment. Culture can be observed and interpreted through rites and ceremonies, stories and heroes, symbols, and language.

Organizational culture should reinforce the strategy and structure that the organization needs to be successful in its environment. Four types of culture that may exist in organizations are adaptability culture, mission culture, clan culture, and bureaucratic culture. When widespread consensus exists about the importance of specific values, the organizational culture is strong and cohesive. However, even in organizations with strong cultures, several sets of subcultures may emerge, particularly in large organizations. Strong cultures can be either adaptive or maladaptive. Adaptive cultures have different values and different behaviour patterns than maladaptive cultures. Strong but unhealthy cultures can be detrimental to a company's chances for success. On the other hand, strong adaptive cultures can play an important role in creating high performance and innovative response to challenges, competitive threats, or new opportunities.

An important aspect of organizational values is managerial ethics, which is the set of values governing behaviour with respect to what is right or wrong. Ethical decision making in organizations is shaped by many factors: personal characteristics, which include personal beliefs, moral development, and the adoption of ethical frameworks for decision making; organizational culture, which is the extent to which values, heroes, traditions, and symbols reinforce ethical decision making; organizational systems, which pertain to the formal structure, policies, codes of ethics, and reward systems that reinforce ethical or unethical choices; and the interests and concerns of external stakeholders, which include government agencies, customers, and special-interest groups.

The chapter also discussed how leaders can shape culture and ethics. One important idea is values-based leadership, which means leaders define a vision of proper values, communicate it throughout the organization, and institutionalize it through everyday behaviour, rituals, ceremonies, and symbols. We also discussed formal systems that are important for shaping ethical values. Formal systems include an ethics committee, an ethics department, disclosure mechanisms for whistle-blowing, ethics training programs, and a code of ethics or values statement that specifies ethical values. As business increasingly crosses geographical and cultural boundaries, leaders face difficult challenges in establishing strong cultural and ethical values with which all employees can identify and agree. Companies that develop global cultures emphasize multicultural values, base status on merit rather than nationality, are excited about new cultural environments, remain open to ideas from other cultures, and are sensitive to different cultural values without being limited by them. Social audits are important tools for organizations trying to maintain high ethical standards on a global basis.

Key Concepts

adaptability culture, p. 340
bureaucratic culture, p. 343
chief ethics officer, p. 357
clan culture, p. 342
code of ethics, p. 358
culture, p. 335
culture strength, p. 344
ethical dilemma, p. 351
ethics, p. 348
ethics committee, p. 357
ethics hotlines, p. 357
external adaptation, p. 336
heroes, p. 338
internal integration, p. 336
language, p. 339
legends, p. 338
managerial ethics, p. 350
mission culture, p. 341
myths, p. 338
rites and ceremonies, p. 337
rule of law, p. 349
social audit, p. 361
social capital, p. 334
social responsibility, p. 350
stories, p. 338
subcultures, p. 344
symbol, p. 338
values-based leadership, p. 355
whistle-blowing, p. 357

Discussion Questions

1. Describe observable symbols, ceremonies, dress, or other aspects of culture and the underlying values they represent for an organization where you have worked.
2. What might be some of the advantages of having several subcultures within an organization? the disadvantages?
3. Explain the concept of social capital. Name an organization currently in the business news that seems to have a high degree of social capital and one that seems to have a low degree.
4. Do you think a bureaucratic culture would be less employee oriented than a clan culture? Discuss.
5. Why is values-based leadership so important to the influence of culture? Does a symbolic act communicate more about company values than an explicit statement? Discuss.
6. Are you aware of a situation in which either you or someone you know was confronted by an ethical dilemma, such as being encouraged to inflate an expense account? Do you think the person's decision was affected by individual moral development or by the accepted values within the company? Explain.
7. Why is equality an important value to support learning and innovation? Discuss.
8. What importance would you attribute to leadership statements and actions for influencing ethical values and decision making in an organization?
9. How do external stakeholders influence ethical decision making in an organization? Discuss why globalization has contributed to more complex ethical issues related to external stakeholders.
10. Codes of ethics have been criticized for transferring responsibility for ethical behaviour from the organization to the individual employee. Do you agree? Do you think a code of ethics is valuable for an organization?
11. Top executives at numerous technology companies, including AOL/Time Warner, Gateway, Sun Microsystems, and Cisco, made millions of dollars from the sale of stock during the "bubble years" of 1999–2001. When the bubble burst, ordinary investors lost 70 to 90 percent of their holdings. Do you see anything wrong with this from an ethical standpoint? How do you think this affects the social capital of these organizations?

Chapter 10 Workbook: Shop' til You Drop: Organizational Culture in the Retail World*

To understand more about organizational culture, visit two retail stores and compare them according to various factors. Go to one discount or low-end store, such as Wal-Mart or Zellers and to one high-end store, such as Holt Renfrew or Simons. Do not interview any employees, but instead be an observer or a shopper. After your visits, fill out the following table for each store. Spend at least two hours in each store on a busy day and be very observant.

Culture Item	Discount Store	High-End Store
1. Mission of store: What is it, and is it clear to employees?		
2. Individual initiative: Is it encouraged?		
3. Reward system: What are employees rewarded for?		
4. Teamwork: Do people within one department or across departments work together or talk with each other?		
5. Company loyalty: Is there evidence of loyalty or of enthusiasm to be working there?		
6. Dress: Are there uniforms? Is there a dress code? How strong is it? How do you rate employees' personal appearance in general?		
7. Diversity or commonality of employees: Is there diversity or commonality in age, education, race, personality, and so on?		
8. Service orientation: Is the customer valued or tolerated?		
9. Human resource development: Is there opportunity for growth and advancement?		

Questions

1. How does the culture seem to influence employee behaviour in each store?
2. What effect does employees' behaviour have on customers?
3. Which store was more pleasant to be in? How does that relate to the mission of the store?

Case for Analysis: Queen's Returns Radler Gift*

Queen's Board of Trustees has decided to return all monies received in relation to a gift pledge from David Radler and remove the Radler name from a wing of its School of Business and from Queen's Benefactor Wall.

"This was not an easy decision. However, we were guided by the simple principle of what is the right thing to do in this particular situation," says Vice-Principal (Advancement) George Hood.

Mr. Radler entered a plea of guilty to fraud in a U.S. federal court last Tuesday. The following day, the board made its decision, which was communicated in a public statement by the university on Thursday.

The gift pledge of $1 million (of which $915,180 has been received by the university) was to Goodes Hall building fund. It involved donations from Mr. Radler and from a number of corporate newspaper organizations with which he has been associated. The university plans to take immediate steps to return all monies to these donors. "This gift was given and received in good faith by the university and in accordance with approved parameters of its Gift Acceptance Policy and used according to the intended philanthropic purpose," the statement says.

"The quality of Queen's learning and research environment depends heavily on the generosity and support of our alumni and other supporters. We feel in this case, however, that the integrity of this gift to the university has been compromised."

"These actions by the university are in keeping with our policies and with our primary commitment to act in the best interest of our students, our alumni, other members of the Queen's community, our donors, and the general public."

"Ethics and corporate social responsibility are a cornerstone of good business practice, and we take them very seriously at Queen's," says School of Business Dean David Saunders. "Our decision to return Mr. Radler's gift is consistent with what we teach our students, and I have received nothing but supportive comments from alumni, students, faculty and others. It is unfortunate we were faced with this decision but we made the right one."

A number of post-secondary institutions have faced similar issues with respect to gift acceptance and donor recognition. While there doesn't appear to be a comparable Canadian precedent, the Washington-based Council for the Advancement and Support of Education (CASE) cites a number of U.S. schools which have encountered similar issues, including the universities of Harvard, Princeton, Brown, Cornell, Michigan, and North Carolina at Chapel Hill.

There don't appear, however, to be any consistent guidelines or policies within the higher education philanthropic sector for dealing with such donor matters. Responses in these U.S. cases have ranged broadly from no action or maintaining status quo to the removal of named recognition only or removal of naming coupled with return of funds. "It appears that each situation has been handled through case-by-case review and relied ultimately upon the judgement of the university's administrators, staff, trustees, and faculty in examining their particular circumstance," says Mr. Hood. The two main university policies that informed the board's decision are the Queen's University Naming Policy and the Gift Acceptance Policy.

The naming policy notes that "ultimate authority to discontinue the designated name of a building, room, or area, or to transfer the name to another building room or area" at Queen's rests with the Board of Trustees. It goes on to say that "no naming will be approved or (once approved) continued that will call into serious question the public respect of the university."

A recent *Globe and Mail* editorial suggested that charities should not return donations. "Clearly, there will be many different opinions on this," says George Hood. "Queen's thoroughly discussed all the ramifications of this matter and decided what it felt was the best course of action."

*Kershaw, A. (2006) Queen's returns Radler Gift, alumni.queensu.ca/enewsletter/articles/gazette/10_Oct/radler_gift.htm.

Case for Analysis Best Workplaces 2006: Lessons from Some of the Best*

Urban Systems Ltd.

Kamloops, BC | consulting in engineering, planning and landscape architecture | 227 employees

In March, the 40 partners who together own consulting firm Urban Systems gathered for their annual general meeting. One agenda item was to affirm formally a long-standing principle: the company is not for sale, at any price.

It's a message that employees hear often—and warmly receive. Management's message is clear: we're not out to use your hard work to line someone else's pockets; we see you as future owners. "There is certainly stability in knowing that this is not a short-term thing," says Samantha Ward, a consultant who joined Urban Systems in 2001, one year after graduating from Queen's University with a civil engineering degree. "If you're here and enjoy what you do, you could feasibly spend the rest of your career at this company and not feel limited in any sense."

What makes such enthusiasm possible is a supportive and collaborative atmosphere, where responsibilities and rewards are shared. Knowledge transfer is emphasized through internal training sessions that bring together staff from the company's six offices in British Columbia and Alberta, and "novice consultants" (who have two to five years' experience) [who] pick personal coaches who offer career advice and mentoring. "It's very informal and interactive," says Ward. "It's not like you sit down once a year and go through your goals and walk away."

Founded 31 years ago by eight equal partners, Urban Systems prides itself on a flat management structure, rejects authority based on seniority, and has an actively designed and managed corporate culture. But the firm has grown quickly in the past five years—and preserving and revitalizing that culture is a top priority.

Each year, for example, principals take employee suggestions and select an annual theme based on a timely or important aspect of Urban Systems' culture, such as "generosity," or this year's theme, "commitment to excellence." The managing partner at each office then asks one employee—usually a relatively newer staff member—to build a volunteer team to devise and plan a series of events that advance that concept throughout the year. Ward was part of a team that organized a "generosity" event in 2004 that got small teams at each of the firm's offices to compete in small groups building children's bikes—surprise gifts for needy children who were invited to come and receive them. "It was certainly a sense of pride for the whole office to be able to contribute to the community in that way," says Ward.

Cameron Gatey, a 14-year veteran and a partner who in December succeeded co-founder Gordon Petersen as CEO, says Urban Systems is very much like a family. "When people feel that connection," he says, "they are more inclined to think their contribution actually has meaning. I think they feel that their contribution helps to ensure the longevity of the organization." A.W.

Trico Homes Inc.

Calgary | construction and real estate | 76 employees

The way Trico Homes CEO Wayne Chiu sees it, a work environment that encourages the Calgary home builder's employees to participate in the charitable and cultural life of the city pays back in spades. "I want to create a culture where we work as a team—where each person covers the other's butts," says Chiu, a Hong Kong native who started up Trico in 1993. Helping the wider community by organizing or taking part in events, like Kids Cancer Care Foundation of Alberta, Hong Kong Days or Paint the Town Red (when staff descend on a low-income senior's home for a "Trico Extreme Makeover"), he adds, is "great for the company, great for morale, great for the team." A high participation rate in non-work events (in some cases more than 80%) is important, Chiu emphasizes, when you're a fast-growing company. Trico is now the eighth-largest builder in Calgary, compared to 15th five years ago, and has almost quadrupled its number of employees in the same period.

The community spirit has had a huge impact on how employees work together to handle the challenges of being part of the red-hot Calgary real estate market. Trico may have many of the same organizational features that other companies use—weekly executive, marketing, sales and operational meetings and biannual company-wide gatherings more focused on strategic planning—but bonding outside the office makes its long-term planning and development that much more successful, according to Chiu. He cites the example of how Trico came up with a five-year strategic plan in an all-staff "bottom up" process that outlined expectations for the future. Says Chiu: "The five-year plan is owned by the people who work for Trico, not by senior management, not by me."

Another important aspect of Trico's work culture is promoting multiculturalism. As the booming Alberta economy and high oil prices attract people from all over Canada—and, indeed, the world—Calgary is becoming more culturally diverse. A good number of Trico's staff members—about 15%—are visible minorities, but involvement with Calgary's Dragon Boat Festival, the Calgary Immigrant Aid Society and English as a second language programs also gives the firm a good "in" when it comes to figuring out the housing needs of people from other cultures, one that can be used in marketing its homes. "Ethnic buyers are probably going to be one of the more significant growth markets we'll see," says Richard Gotfried, vice-president of marketing.

Another pillar of Trico's culture is diversity of experience and background. "We like to bring people with different skills to the company," says Norm Mross, vice-president of operations, adding that "aptitude and attitude" are often more important than experience. "I can teach people the skills they will need for a particular job. I can't teach attitude." Z.O.

Sapient

Toronto | information-technology consulting firm | 117 employees

Openness. It's a word that comes up a lot at many of Canada's best workplaces. But consulting firm Sapient Canada takes the concept rather literally. "Some people claim their doors are always open," president Hank Summy jokes, "but I don't even have a door."

Neither does anyone else at the company. Far from being chained to their cubicles, the 100-plus people who work at Sapient's bright offices on the edge of Toronto's financial district sit with co-workers in wall-less pods, arranged according to the projects they are undertaking at any given time. That an open office environment can make a real difference may sound a little hokey, Summy acknowledges, as he walks past his own wall-less workstation, but managers at Sapient have learned that the simple act of being able to see the people who work with you can indirectly go a long way toward creating happy employees and healthy profits.

Whether it's small gestures like creating a more collegial work environment, or larger perks, like $6,000 in tuition reimbursement and negotiable 12-month sabbaticals after only six months' employment, Sapient takes the concept of investing in its people to new levels.

Of course, in the knowledge-based consulting industry, it makes sense to focus on your workers, so perhaps it's no wonder Sapient invests in human capital. If the company's financial performance is any indication, it's getting a pretty fair return on investment—revenues at U.S. parent Sapient Corp. jumped 26%, to US$319 million, in 2005. Clearly, Sapient's people-first strategy is paying off. And even when there are short-term costs to incur, the company doesn't let a focus on the bottom line trump strategic investment in staff, senior manager of technology Michael Tayag points out.

A few years ago, when Sapient decided it would open an office in India, it filled the facility with expatriates from western offices, at western salaries, eschewing the obvious cost benefits that drew other North American companies to the subcontinent. "There were around 30 or 40 of us, so it was a significant hit," Tayag says. "But they saw the long-term gain of installing that Sapient strategy, so they took the short-term pain for long-term gain."

Indeed, far from costing money, the Sapient example proves how having a great workplace can boost morale, decrease turnover, increase productivity and pad your bottom line. As Tayag puts it, "People don't realize that the benefits outweigh the costs. If you're going to claim something is a core value, you have to be willing to make concessions to adhere to it, and I see that every day here." P.E.

TD Bank Financial Group

Toronto | financial services | 54,995 employees

Size can be a great tool for taking advantage of economies of scale. But when it comes to effectively managing office culture, it can be both a blessing and a curse. That's why it's important for large organizations to put a high priority on monitoring workplace culture. To that end, TD Bank Financial Group checks in twice a year with employees via a survey, says Teri Currie, executive vice-president of human resources.

Like many financial institutions, TD has an attractive compensation package, with competitive base salaries and a popular employee stock-purchase plan that 75% of its staff signs up for. But creating contented workers isn't all about cash. "We've found that it's really about pride," Currie says. "Making that goodwill sustainable means helping your people achieve their own definition of success. They stay because they're proud to be here."

One of the best ways that TD has found to instil that sense of pride, Currie says, is by actively supporting volunteerism. And here again, it's not just about the money: not only did the bank give $27.5 million to charities in 2005, but it encourages employees to get involved by allowing paid time off—over and above vacation days—for volunteer activities. Though the bank works with countless organizations, some of the major beneficiaries in 2005 were the Children's Miracle Network, the Juvenile Diabetes Research Foundation, the United Way and Habitat for Humanity. TD employees can also apply for a grant for charities they support, after accruing at least 40 hours per year volunteering with the organization. "Our program allows them the flexibility in their schedule to be out in the community donating their time, and backing that activity up with corporate funding," Currie says. At the end of the day, giving back to employees and their community pays for itself in spades. "Employees like to work for winning organizations," Currie argues, "and winning organizations tend to create engaged employees, which produces results, which enhances shareholder value. Our internal research shows that's clearly the case at TD."

Though Currie says TD has a long track record in employee relations, the tipping point might have been the bank's acquisition of Canada Trust in 2000. "Both organizations had a strong history of listening to employees and acting on suggestions. But post-integration, it became important to define the culture because the road map had changed." Employees needed to know what the new corporate focus was. So Currie says that making the corporate values clear and displaying them in a practical way that resonated with all staff members was vitally important—and benefited everyone in the long run, because they knew what they had to do to get ahead. The TD-Canada Trust union wasn't just the largest bank merger in Canadian history; it was a blending of two successful corporate cultures, Currie adds. And it's worth noting that the new bank's CEO, Ed Clark, came not from the original TD, but from Canada Trust, the acquired company. It just goes to show: at TD, even a small fish can one day find himself the biggest fish in an even bigger pond. P.E.

Hilti (Canada) Corp.

Mississauga, ON | construction equipment | 274 employees

For 10 years, Hilti developed a can-do attitude using Gung Ho!—the title of a book by Escondido, Calif.-based international management training and consulting guru Ken Blanchard—as its mantra. The slogan appeared on internal communications. Employees even used it as a salute. But Gung Ho! was also a training program—complete with a sometimes unintentionally hilarious video—designed to introduce employees to the construction-equipment manufacturer, whose products range from handheld drilling tools to demolition equipment.

Hilti takes its culture very seriously. So seriously, in fact, that new recruits get two days of "culture training" before they begin four weeks of product and sales training. That's after four weeks of pre-training.

Last year, though, Gung Ho! was transformed into a new program called Culture Journey. It's not as catchy, certainly, so don't expect employees to use it as a salutation. But Gareth Lewis, vice-president of human resources for Hilti in North America, says it's kind of like Gung Ho! all grown up. Over the past year, nearly every Hilti employee has gone through a mandatory two-day Culture Journey that not only reintroduces the company's culture, but also examines how it is using employee and customer feedback surveys. "Team camps" are broken down into workshops that focus on three specific principles: we do worthwhile work; we take self-responsibility to achieve our goals; and, we encourage each other and recognize results. "At the Culture Journey we sit down and take a critical look at ourselves and say, 'This is where we are not so strong, this is where we need to improve,'" says Lewis. "Because if you don't know where you are and where your problems are, how can you set a direction for the future?"

High-brow ideals aside, the Culture Journey makes sure every employee knows what Hilti stands for and expects. That's especially important given the parent company is a US$3-billion worldwide behemoth based in Liechtenstein that deals directly with its customers through account managers and its retail outlets Hilti Centers and Hilti Pro Shops. While neither the company's framework ideals of integrity, courage, teamwork and commitment, nor its underlying business philosophy have changed, Culture Journey is meant to be interpreted locally, says Lewis, giving employees a say in how they deal with their customers. That means an account manager in northern British Columbia doesn't have to call head office over every little detail.

Perhaps the most important aspect of Culture Journey is that it's a process that never ends. Preparations are underway for Team Camp 2 this August. A.H.

SaskTel

Regina | telecommunications | 4,146 employees

The first time Lena Tanner invited her SaskTel colleagues to participate in a traditional sweat-lodge ceremony to learn more about her Aboriginal heritage, she was understandably nervous. "I don't think a lot of people understand Indian culture," says Tanner, 50, who helps develop new products and services for the Regina-based telecom. She needn't have worried—the ceremony, held in October 2004, was a resounding success for all the participants, both Aboriginal and not. "When a corporation is prepared to invest in initiatives like these, it's because it cares about its people," says Tanner, who also organized a "medicine walk" on the Piapot First Nation reserve to educate coworkers on the healing powers of indigenous plants and flowers. In both cases, SaskTel senior management threw its full support behind each event. "Where else could you work that gives you that?"

Caring about its Aboriginal employees is a strategic goal for this 98-year-old Crown corporation, which provides cellular, phone, Internet, and multimedia services to 13 cities and more than 500 remote communities in Saskatchewan, many of them inhabited by First Nations and Métis people. Those groups currently make up almost 8% of SaskTel's workforce, a number company president and CEO Robert Watson is hoping will one day mirror the provincial population of 13.5%. But what makes SaskTel different, says diversity manager Terry Bird, is that the $1.2-billion company does more than pay lip service to its representative workforce strategy. By valuing Aboriginal participation and supporting the goal of self-determination for Saskatchewan's 130,000 Aboriginal people, SaskTel also encourages its employees to think of new ways of doing business that will directly benefit First Nations and Métis people.

Case in point: For the past seven years SaskTel has contracted a call centre to service its customers in three different First Nations languages. In 2004, the company also set up a high-tech, interactive drop-in centre at its Regina headquarters to encourage Aboriginal youth to consider careers in Saskatchewan's growing telecom industry.

SaskTel says such moves have helped position it as an employer-of-choice in a province where a rapidly aging workforce threatens to create skilled-worker shortages. "Making the workplace more inclusive benefits everyone," says Carolynne Warner, human-resources diversity manager. "This is not just about engaging our employees within the workplace, it's about creating opportunities for them outside these walls too. Saskatchewan's youth are our future employee base—and our future customer base." E.P.

S. C. Johnson and Son Ltd.

Brantford, ON | manufacturing, personal and household goods | 463 employees

S. C. Johnson is a family company. No, really, it's right there next to its name: S. C. Johnson, A Family Company. Yes, it's true that the 119-year-old manufacturer of household goods with international headquarters in Racine, Wis., has been run for five generations by the Johnson clan. But the company—whose products include such well-known brands as Edge, Pledge and Windex—also treats its employees like kin. From an on-site massage therapist and recreation complex to local day care and a cottage resort on ritzy Lake Joseph in Ontario's Muskoka region, S. C. Johnson offers the kind of perks you'd want your relatives to have. Not to mention an excellent bonus system that includes extremely generous profit-sharing, something the company offers to each and every employee. Perhaps that's why more than one-quarter of its workforce has been with Johnson for more than 15 years, and the company has never had to lay off a single employee. Ever.

Drew Franklin, president of S. C. Johnson's Canadian division, says that while those benefits certainly stand out, it's the company's flexibility and informal culture that attract and keep people working in Brantford, a 90-minute drive southwest of Toronto that is a little off the beaten track for most consumer packaged-goods businesses. For example, S. C. Johnson allows employees to telecommute or work flexible hours to meet the needs of their families and do their jobs. "More students and new recruits are looking for some of those intangibles," says Franklin. The organization also lets workers recover from illness or family emergencies at their own pace by offering two weeks of sick leave at full pay and 24 weeks at two-thirds pay after just one year's service. After five years, employees get 10 weeks of sick leave at full pay, and 16 weeks at two-thirds pay.

One Canadian-only program is the company's Kid's Camps, which operate on days such as Easter Monday and school breaks when day care is closed. Instead of forcing employees to choose between finding alternative child care or taking vacation time, they can, for a nominal fee, bring their children into work, where they are taken care of by YMCA staff, says Shirley Harries-Langley, vice-president of human resources. The company will also hand out pagers for a period of time if employees need to be instantly reachable by their families. Harries-Langley says the idea started for expectant parents, but has evolved to cover many other scenarios. "We allow our employees to have a relationship with us that provides them with a situation where there are fewer work/life trade-offs," she says.

Although S. C. Johnson has sales offices in Calgary and Montreal, and a small manufacturing plant in Varennes, Que., most employees work in the Brantford facility, where there is a full-sized gym—which doubles as an assembly room for semi-annual full-employee meetings—a squash court and a weight room that spouses and children can also use free of charge. Two or three times a week, a ball-hockey game will break out during lunch. After all, the family that plays together, stays together. A.H.

Keller Williams Ottawa Realty

Ottawa | real estate | 175 employees

No matter how great a workplace is, it won't be a perfect fit for everyone. A successful company must attract and nurture the right mix of people. Case in point: the real-estate franchise Keller Williams, which has more than 380 branches in the U.S. and Canada. Its values statement gives "spirituality, family and then business" top priority. At the Ottawa office—quite a culturally diverse agency—some 20 co-workers gather over lunch every Tuesday to discuss the Bible. That's not a common practice in your typical secular workplace in Canada, but Keller Williams promotes such soulful pursuits, even urging individuals to adopt a "personal mission." For some, it may sound strange. "Oftentimes, we're called an airy-fairy company, or we're called a cult," says CEO Mo Anderson on a recruiting DVD. "And I just say to people who just get so worried about that, 'Oh honey, don't worry about it. They're just ignorant.' They don't know the difference between the words "cult"—that's where you drink the Kool-Aid—and "culture," which is simply a belief system or a value system that you have clearly defined and you attempt to follow."

Keller Williams' pay structure encourages teamwork—quite uncommon in the ultra-competitive real-estate world—because profit-sharing is based on the commissions of recruits agents refer to the company and, in turn, those people's referrals. Each year, agents give up 30% of their first $50,000 in commissions to the agency (about 10 house sales), but keep 100% over and above that. And unlike most real-estate brokerages, if they fall short of target, they don't have to top up the difference. The result? A positive atmosphere that supports new recruits. "There is a learning environment that I've never seen at any other real estate office, and this is my third," says Lori Briard, director of agent services. In less than five years, Keller Williams' Ottawa office has become one of the largest agencies in the city. That's good for more than just the soul. A.W.

*Wahl, A., Z. Olijnyk, P. Evans, A. Holloway & E. Pooley (2006) Best workplaces 2006: Lessons from some of the best, Canadian Business, April 10, www.canadianbusiness.com/managing/employees/article.jsp?content=20060410_76257_76257.

Chapter 10 Workshop: Where to Begin—A Framework for Developing Your CSR Strategy*

Using an organization you know well, answer the questions for each of the quadrants in the virtue matrix. What ideas do you have for improving the social responsibility of the organization?

Civil Foundation—Compliance Quadrant Questions

1. To what extent do we seek to be in full compliance with the key laws and regulations to which we are subject?
2. And if so, how do we ensure, demonstrate and communicate that we meet all laws and regulations?
3. What are the two or three priorities, if any, for overcoming compliance issues?

Civil Foundation—Choice Quadrant Questions

1. What are the key norms and customs in the industry?
2. To what extent are we currently a leader or a laggard in adopting the norms?
3. What are our aspirations for leading in adherence to customs and norms?
4. What two or three initiatives would be most important to improve adherence to customs and norms?

Strategic Frontier Quadrant Questions

1. What are activities that your corporation's customers, employees, shareholders, or suppliers want that you could provide if you chose?
2. How could we develop a business case to overcome the impediment to undertaking such new practices?
3. What two or three initiatives would be of the highest priority?

Structural Frontier Quadrant Questions

1. What practices that are desired by customers/employees/shareholders/stakeholders would require collective action among firms in the industry to make them happen?
2. How would a coalition of interested forms be pulled together for each potential practice?
3. What governmental/non-governmental organizations might your corporation include in a coalition?
4. What two or three new initiatives would be of the highest priority?

*Martin, R. (nd) Where to Begin—A Framework for Developing your CSR Strategy, Microsoft Social Responsibility Series Part 2, *Canadian Business*, Summer 2005.

11

Innovation and Change

NORM BETTS/Bloomberg News/Landov

A Look Inside

Toyota Motor Corporation

In auto manufacturing, Japanese companies rule, and one manufacturer outshines them all. Toyota increasingly dominates the global auto market, pushing ever closer to its goal of overtaking General Motors (GM) as the world's number one automaker. The basis of Toyota's supremacy lies primarily in its steady stream of technological and product innovation. Toyota executives created the doctrine of *kaizen*, or continuous improvement, and the company applies it relentlessly. Toyota hands the responsibility for continuous improvement to every employee. People on the shop floor can get cash rewards for searching out production glitches and finding ways to solve them.

Although thinking big can be important, Toyota knows that sweating the details is just as critical for driving innovation. Consider this: Several years ago, Toyota made a small change to its production lines (see photo) by using a single master brace to hold automobile frames in place as they were welded, instead of the dozens of braces used in a standard auto factory. It seemed almost insignificant in the context of the company's complex manufacturing system, yet it was a radical manufacturing innovation. That one change, referred to now as the Global Body Line system, slashed 75 percent from the cost of retrofitting a production line and made it possible for Toyota to produce different car and truck models on a single line. The result has been billions of dollars in annual cost savings.

For developing new models, Toyota applies the concept of *obeya*, which literally means "big room." To make sure all the critical factors are considered from the beginning, product development teams made up of manufacturing and product engineers, designers, marketers, and suppliers hold regular face-to-face brainstorming sessions. New software programs, including product life cycle management software, also make it possible for these cross-functional teams to collaborate digitally, viewing product design changes and associated costs. That way, if a designer makes a change that conflicts with manufacturing's needs or a supplier's capability, it can be noted and adjusted immediately. This collaborative process created Toyota's sturdy small truck, the Hilux, which is sold mostly in developing countries and is favoured by oil companies and other organizations working in areas where a pickup breakdown can mean life or death. A new version of the Hilux is key to Toyota's strategy of overtaking GM by capturing 15 percent of the world auto market by 2010.[1] In the first quarter of 2007, Toyota passed GM as the world's number-one automaker.[2]

Canada has had a long and interesting history of innovation and invention. Pablum cereal, kerosene, and the electron microscope were invented in Canada. In 1927, the Creed telegraph system was designed; it was the first teleprinter that combined transmitting and receiving. This innovation resulted in the expansion of news wire services and increased the amount of news available to newspapers. In 1937, the self-propelled combine harvester, built by Thomas Carroll, transformed agriculture by rolling all the stages of wheat harvesting into one operation. The innovation has benefited farmers all across North America. As well, the first North American commercial jet was built in Toronto.[3]

Today, every company, whether Canadian or global, must change and innovate to survive. New discoveries and inventions quickly replace standard ways of doing things. Organizations like Toyota, Microsoft, Apple, and Research in Motion are searching for any innovation edge they can find. Some companies, like 3M, the maker of Post-it Notes, Thinsulate insulation, Scotch-Brite scouring pads, and thousands of other products, are known for innovation. 3M's culture supports a risk-taking and entrepreneurial spirit that keeps it bubbling over with new ideas and new products. However, many large, established companies have a hard time being entrepreneurial and continually look for ways to encourage change and innovation to keep pace with changes in the external environment.

The pace of change is revealed in the fact that the parents of today's post-secondary-age students grew up without debit cards, video on demand, iPods, laser checkout systems, cellular phones, instant messaging, and the Internet. The idea of communicating instantly with people around the world was unimaginable to many people as recently as a decade ago.

Purpose of This Chapter

This chapter will explore how organizations change and how managers direct the innovation and change process. We discuss the difference between incremental and radical change, the four types of change—technology, product, structure, people—occurring in organizations, and how to manage change successfully. The organizational structure and management approach for facilitating each type of change is then discussed. Management techniques for influencing both the creation and implementation of change are also covered.

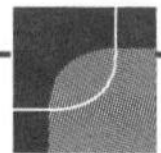

Innovate or Perish: The Strategic Role of Change

If there is one theme or lesson that emerges from previous chapters, it is that organizations must run quickly to keep up with changes taking place all around them. Large organizations must find ways to act like small, nimble organizations. Manufacturing firms need to reach out for new, flexible manufacturing technology and service firms for new information technology (IT). Today's organizations must poise themselves to innovate and change, not only to prosper but also to survive in a world of increased competition.[4] As illustrated in Exhibit 11.1, a number of environmental forces drive this need for major organizational change. Powerful forces associated with advancing technology, international economic integration, the maturing of domestic markets, and the shift to capitalism in formerly communist regions have brought about a globalized economy that affects every business, from the largest to the smallest, creating more threats as well as more opportunities. To recognize and manage the threats and take advantage of the opportunities, today's organizations are undergoing dramatic changes in all areas of their operations.

As we have seen in previous chapters, many organizations are responding to global forces by adopting self-directed teams and horizontal structures that enhance communication and collaboration, streamlining supply and distribution channels, and overcoming barriers of time and place through IT and e-business. Others become involved in joint ventures or consortia to exploit opportunities and extend operations or markets internationally. Some adopt structural innovations such as the virtual network approach to focus on their core competencies while outside specialists handle other activities. In addition, today's organizations face a need for dramatic strategic and cultural change and for rapid and continuous innovations in technology, services, products, and processes. A key element of the success of companies such as 3M

EXHIBIT 11.1
Forces Driving the Need for Major Organizational Change
Source: Based on John P. Kotter, *The New Rules: How to Succeed in Today's Post-Corporate World* (New York: The Free Press, 1995).

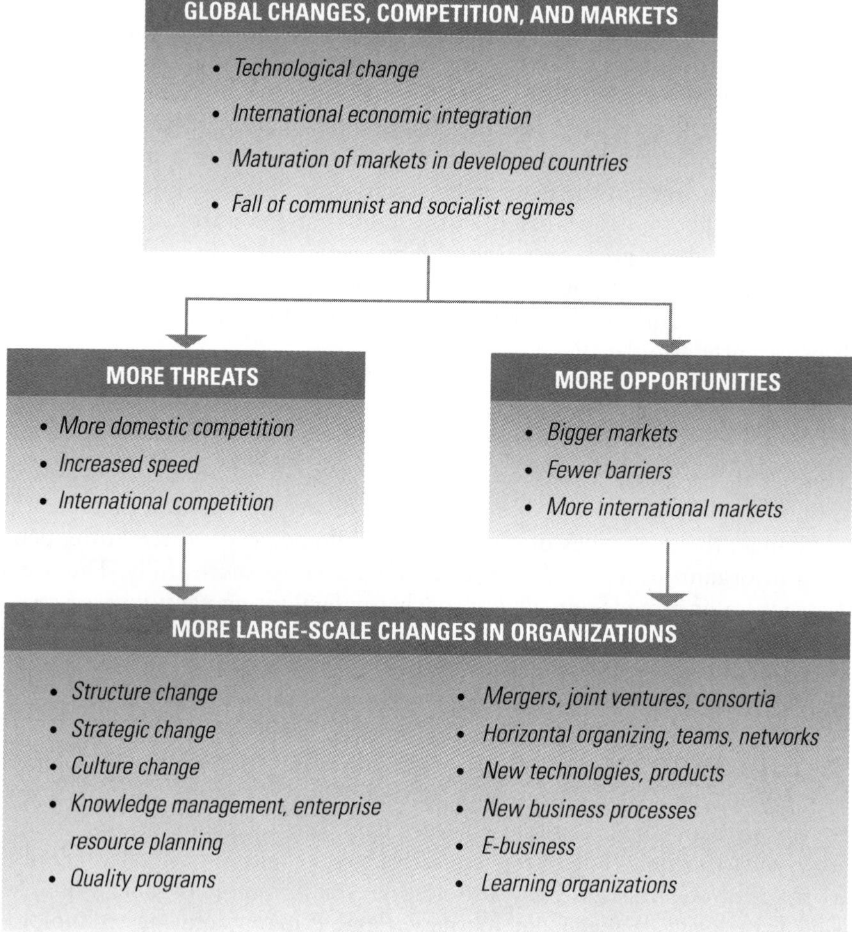

Corporation, Research in Motion, and eBay has been their passion for creating and sustaining change.

Change, rather than stability, is the norm today. Whereas change once occurred incrementally and infrequently, today it is often dramatic and constant. Exhibit 11.2 shows the impact of change that many organizations have experienced and continue to experience!

Incremental versus Radical Change

The changes used to adapt to the environment can be evaluated according to scope—that is, the extent to which changes are incremental or radical for the organization.[5] As summarized in Exhibit 11.3, **incremental change** represents a series of continual progressions that maintain the organization's general equilibrium and often affect only one organizational part. **Radical change,** by contrast, breaks the frame of reference for the organization, often transforming the entire organization. For example, an incremental change is the implementation of sales teams in the marketing department, whereas a radical change is shifting the entire organization from a vertical to a horizontal structure, with all employees who work on specific core

EXHIBIT 11.2
When Change Occurs at Dramatic Speed . . .

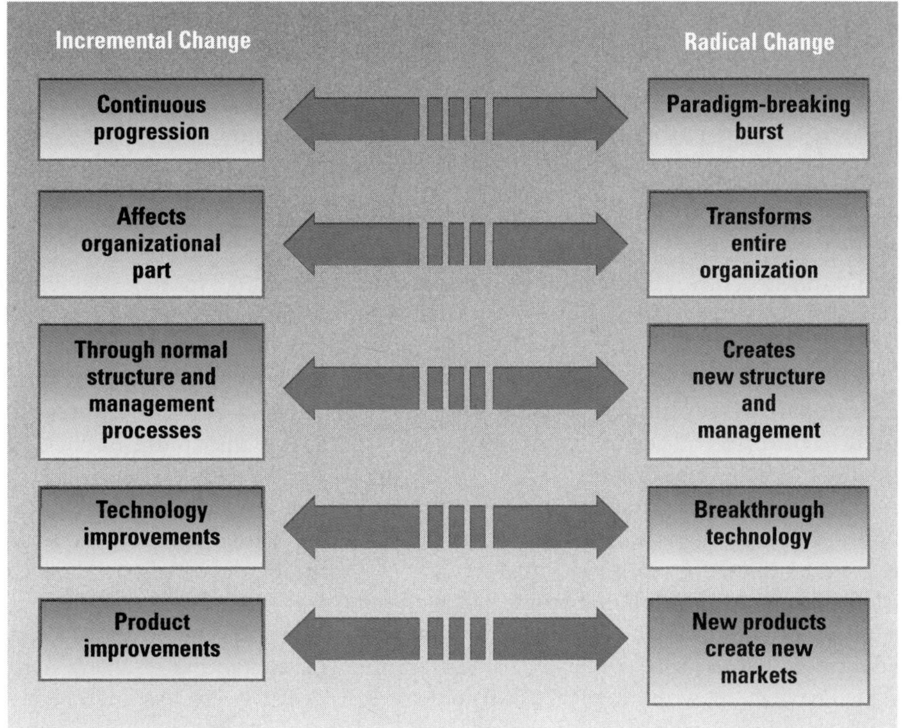

EXHIBIT 11.3
Incremental versus Radical Change
Source: Based on Alan D. Meyer, James B. Goes, and Geoffrey R. Brooks, "Organizations in Disequilibrium: Environmental Jolts and Industry Revolutions," in George Huber and William H. Glick, eds., *Organizational Change and Redesign* (New York: Oxford University Press, 1992), 66–111; and Harry S. Dent, Jr., "Growth through New Product Development," *Small Business Reports* (November 1990), 30–40.

processes brought together in teams rather than being separated into functional departments such as marketing, finance, production, and so forth. Although bold, transforming change gets a lot of attention and can be powerful for an organization, recent research indicates that incremental change—the constant implementation of small ideas, such as at Toyota—more often results in a sustainable competitive advantage. At the two Honda plants in Alliston, Ontario, for example, New Honda (NH) quality circles try to find cost-cutting or efficiency improvements through teamwork. One NH circle modified the way the stamping press line could be changed so that the hood and frame could be stamped from one metal sheet, which resulted in an annual saving of $500,000.[6] The search engine company Google, based in Mountain View, California, also thrives on a culture that encourages continuous incremental change, as described in the Leading by Design box.

For the most part, incremental change occurs through the established structure and management processes, and it may include technology improvements—such as the introduction of flexible manufacturing systems—or product improvements—such as Procter & Gamble's addition to Tide detergent of cleaning agents that protect colours and fabrics. Radical change involves the creation of a new structure and new management processes. The technology is likely to be breakthrough, and new products thereby created will establish new markets.

As we have just discussed, there is a growing emphasis on the need for radical change because of today's turbulent, unpredictable environment.[7] One example of radical change is Apple, which has transformed itself from a personal computer (PC) manufacturer to a dominant force in the digital entertainment business. By creating the iPod and iTunes online store, giving people easy, legal access to lots of songs, Apple has changed the rules of the game in consumer electronics, entertainment, and software.[8] Corporate transformations and turnarounds, such as Mike Zafirovski's ongoing work to turn around Nortel Networks or Lou Gerstner's transformation of IBM, are also considered radical change. Major turnarounds involve changes in all areas of the organization, including structure, management systems, culture, technology, and products or services.

Strategic Types of Change

Managers can focus on four types of change within organizations to achieve strategic advantage. These four types of change are changes of products and services, strategy and structure, culture, and technology. We touched on overall leadership and organizational strategy in Chapter 2 and on organizational culture in Chapter 10. These factors provide an overall context within which the four types of change serve as a competitive wedge to achieve an advantage in the international environment. Each company has a unique configuration of products and services, strategy and structure, culture, and technology that can be focused for maximum impact upon the company's chosen markets.[9]

PDA Remember...

Recognize that the four types of change are interdependent and therefore changes in one area often require changes in others.

Product and service changes pertain to the product or service outputs of an organization. New products include small adaptations of existing products or entirely new product lines. New products and services are normally designed to increase the market share or to develop new markets, customers, or clients. Toyota's Hilux truck is a new product designed to increase market share, whereas Apple's iPod is a new product that created a new market for the company. An example of a new service designed to reach new markets and customers is IKEA's entry into low-income housing, which is being piloted in Gateshead, U.K.[10]

Leading *by Design*

Google

Google quickly became the most popular search engine on the Internet with its smarter, faster approach to providing users with what they are looking for. But to maintain that success, managers knew the company needed to continuously innovate.

Product manager Marissa Mayer suggested that the company come up with new ideas the same way its search engine scours the Web. To provide users with the best Web search experience possible, Google searches far and wide, combing through billions of documents. Then it ranks the search results by relevance and zaps them to the user quickly. The idea search process works much the same way by casting a wide net across the organization. The process begins with an easy-to-use intranet. Even employees with limited technology expertise can quickly set up a page of ideas. "We never say, 'This group should innovate and the rest should just do their jobs,'" says Jonathan Rosenberg, vice president of product management. "Everyone spends a fraction of [the] day on R&D." The intranet has also tapped into more ideas from technologically savvy Google employees who may not be very vocal or assertive in meetings. Mayer says some engineers had lots of good ideas but were shy about putting them forth in open meetings. Now, employees can post their ideas on the intranet and see what kind of response they get.

Mayer searches the site each day to see which ideas are generating the most excitement and comments. Once a week, she sits down with a team to hash out the ideas and flesh out at least six or seven that can be fast-tracked into development. In addition to the internal search process, users continue to play a key role in innovation. Ten full-time employees read and respond to user e-mails and pass along ideas to project teams, who are constantly tweaking Google's service. Engineers work in teams of three and have the authority to make any changes that improve the quality of the user experience and get rid of anything that gets in the way. Moreover, Google allows all software developers to integrate its search engine into their own applications. The download is easy and the licence is free. It sounds crazy to some businesses, but Google says it "turns the world into Google's development team."

Google's organic approach to innovation has been highly successful. Indeed, the company is no longer just a hugely successful search engine. Google has evolved into a software company that is emerging as a major threat to Microsoft's dominance. While Microsoft has been struggling to catch up in the game of search, Google has quietly been launching products such as desktop search; Gmail; software to manage, edit, and send digital photos; and programs for creating, editing, and posting documents. The idea that Google could one day marginalize Microsoft's operating system and bypass Windows applications is being taken seriously by Microsoft managers. Microsoft is ten times the size of Google and has plenty of cash with which to compete. But Microsoft leaders know that, for now, Google's innovation process gives it an edge. "Here Microsoft was spending $600 million a year in R&D for MSN [Microsoft Networks], $1 billion a year for Office, and $1 billion a year for Windows, and Google [got] desktop search out before us," said a Microsoft executive. "It was a real wake-up call."[11]

Strategy and structure changes pertain to the administrative domain in an organization. The administrative domain involves the supervision and management of the organization. These changes include changes in organizational structure, strategic management, policies, reward systems, labour relations, coordination devices, management information and control systems, and accounting and budgeting systems. Structure and system changes are usually top-down, that is, mandated by top management, whereas product and technology changes may often come from the bottom up. A system change instituted by management in a university might be a new merit-pay plan. Corporate downsizing and the shift to horizontal teams are other examples of top-down structure change.

Culture changes refer to changes in the values, attitudes, expectations, beliefs, abilities, and behaviour of employees. Culture changes pertain to changes in how employees think; these are changes in mind-set rather than technology, structure, or products.

Technology changes are changes in an organization's production process, including its knowledge and skill base, that enable distinctive competence. These changes are designed to make production more efficient or to produce greater volume. Changes in technology involve the techniques for making products or services. They include work methods, equipment, and workflow. For example, a technology change at UPS was the implementation of the DIAD (Delivery Information Acquisition Device). When a customer signs for a package on a computerized clipboard, the device automatically transmits the information to the website, where the sender can verify that the package has been delivered before the driver even gets back to the truck.[12]

PDA Remember...

Make sure every change undertaken has a definite need, idea, adoption decision, implementation strategy, and resources. Avoid failure by not proceeding until each element is accounted for.

The four types of change are interdependent—a change in one often means a change in another. A new product may require changes in the production technology, or a change in structure may require new employee skills. For example, during the 1999 merger of TD and Canada Trust, the largest merger in the history of Canadian financial services, much attention was directed at getting the most efficient technological solutions by drawing on the expertise in both organizations. The merger required significant structural and technological changes. Organizations are interdependent systems, and changing one part often has implications for other organization elements.

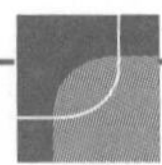

Elements for Successful Change

Regardless of the type or scope of change, there are identifiable stages of innovation, which generally occur as a sequence of events, though innovation stages may overlap.[13] In the research literature on innovation, **organizational change** is considered the adoption of a new idea or behaviour by an organization.[14] **Organizational innovation,** in contrast, is the adoption of an idea or behaviour that is new to the organization's industry, market, or general environment.[15] The first organization to introduce a new product is considered the innovator, and organizations that copy are considered to adopt changes. Innovations typically are assimilated into an organization through a series of steps or elements. Organization members first become aware of a possible innovation, evaluate its appropriateness, and then evaluate and choose the idea.[16] Tom Kelley, general manager of IDEO, the internationally renowned design firm, has identified the ten "faces" of innovation.[17] The ten faces provide insight into the many stages and components of innovation. Exhibit 11.4 highlights the ten and their principal characteristics.

EXHIBIT 11.4
The Ten Faces of Innovation

Learning Faces	1. Anthropologist—looks at human interactions 2. Experimenter—prototypes new ideas 3. Cross-Pollinator—explores other industries and cultures
Organizing Faces	4. Hurdler—develops ways to deal with roadblocks 5. Collaborator—brings together an eclectic group 6. Director—sparks creative talents
Building Faces	7. Experience Architect—creates experiences that go beyond product/service's functionality 8. Set Designer—creates the right space 9. Caregiver—delivers special service 10. Storyteller—builds internal morale and external awareness

Source: Based on Tom Kelley, *The Ten Faces of Innovation* (New York: Currency Doubleday, 2005), 8–12.

EXHIBIT 11.5
Sequence of Elements for Successful Change

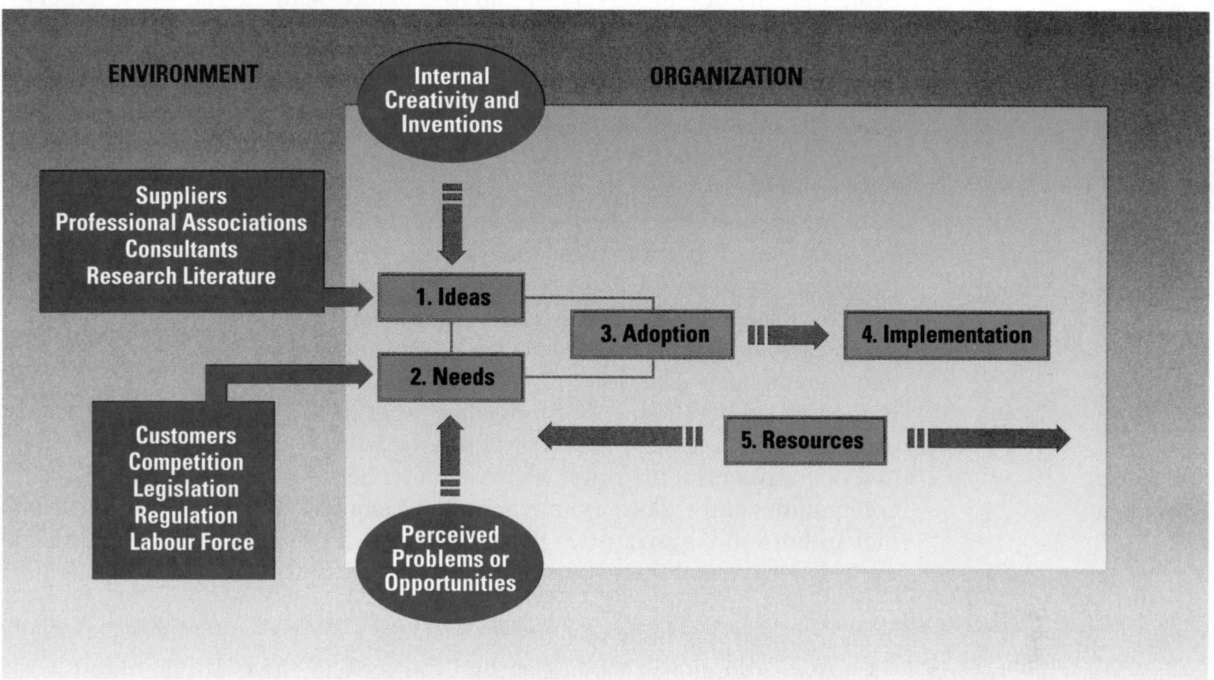

The required elements of successful change are summarized in Exhibit 11.5. For a change to be successfully implemented, managers must ensure each element occurs in the organization. If one of the elements is missing, the change process will fail. For purposes of managing change, however, the terms *innovation* and *change* will be used interchangeably because the **change process** within organizations tends to be identical whether a change is early or late with respect to other organizations in the environment.

1. *Ideas.* No company can remain competitive without new ideas; change is the outward expression of those ideas.[18] An idea is a new way of doing things. It may be a new product or service, a new management concept, or a new procedure for working together in the organization. Ideas can come from within or from outside the organization. Internal creativity is a dramatic element of organizational change. **Creativity** is the generation of novel ideas that may meet perceived needs or respond to opportunities. Umbra, for example, has brought high design to everyday objects while making them affordable. One of its signature objects, the Garbino wastepaper basket with its tulip shape, its opalescent glow, and its handles, is on permanent display New York's Museum of Modern Art. "Applying innovative designs to standard products and seeing the potential in new technology are hallmarks of Umbra's work."[19] In 2007, Umbra opened its first retail store in Toronto to make its designs more accessible still.

   Some techniques for spurring internal creativity are to increase the diversity within the organization, make sure employees have plenty of opportunities to interact with people different from themselves, give employees time and freedom for experimentation, and support risk taking and making mistakes.[20] At IDEO, prototypes are developed rapidly and then shared with the end users. IDEO first proposed a pop-on, pop-off cap for Procter & Gamble's Crest toothpaste to alleviate the problem of the screw-on cap filling up with paste. However, the designers noticed that the users continued to try unscrew the cap even when told about the new design. So the designers came up with a hybrid—a twist-off cap with a short thread that would be easy to clean.[21]

2. *Needs.* Ideas are generally not seriously considered unless there is a perceived need for change. A perceived need for change occurs when managers see a gap between actual performance and desired performance in the organization. Managers try to establish a sense of urgency so that others will understand the need for change. Sometimes a crisis provides an undoubted sense of urgency. In many cases, however, there is no crisis, so managers have to recognize a need and communicate it to others.[22] Over the last 20 years, Nortext of Nunavut has pioneered the development of fonts and programs to publish in approximately 40 Aboriginal languages in both syllabic and Roman orthographies. It organizes "co-operative printing runs" sharing materials and costs among Aboriginal communities and regions as an efficient and innovative way to promote Aboriginal authors and illustrators.[23] A study of innovativeness in industrial firms, for example, suggests that organizations that encourage close attention to customers and market conditions and support for entrepreneurial activity produce more ideas and are more innovative.[24]
3. *Adoption.* Adoption occurs when decision makers choose to go ahead with a proposed idea. Key managers and employees need to be in agreement to support the change. For a major organizational change, the decision might require the signing of a legal document by the board of directors. For a small change, adoption might occur with informal approval by a middle manager.
4. *Implementation.* Implementation occurs when organization members actually use a new idea, technique, or behaviour. Materials and equipment may have to be acquired, and workers may have to be trained to use the new idea. Implementation is a very important step because without it, previous steps are to no avail. Implementation of change is often the most difficult part of the change process. Until people use the new idea, no change has actually taken place.
5. *Resources.* Human energy and activity are required to bring about change. Change does not happen on its own; it requires time and resources, for both creating and implementing a new idea. Employees have to provide energy to see both the need and the idea to meet that need. Someone must develop a proposal and provide the time and effort to implement it. 3M has an unwritten but widely understood rule that its 8,300 researchers can spend up to 15 percent of their time working on any idea of their choosing, without management approval. Most innovations go beyond ordinary budget allocations and require special funding. At 3M, exceptionally promising ideas become "pacing programs" and receive high levels of funding for further development.[25] As well, 3M's CEO boosted research and development (R&D) funding to $1.5 billion in 2007 and directed much of the funding to 3M's core product lines of abrasives, flexible electronics, and nanotechnology.[26] Some companies use task forces, as described in Chapter 3, to focus resources on a change. Others set up seed funds or venture funds that employees with promising ideas can access.

One point about Exhibit 11.5 is especially important. Needs and ideas are listed simultaneously at the beginning of the change sequence. Either may occur first. Many organizations adopted the computer, for example, because it seemed a promising way to improve efficiency. The search for a vaccine against the AIDS virus, on the other hand, was stimulated by a severe need. Whether the need or the idea occurs first, for the change to be accomplished, each of the steps in Exhibit 11.5 must be completed.

In Practice
Cirque du Soleil

Cirque du Soleil was cofounded by Guy Laliberté and Daniel Gauthier in Montréal, and has grown from a band of street performers to a large innovative organization that has transformed the essence of a circus. Cirque's primary audience is adults, not children, and it does not use any animals in its shows. It offers a combination of feats of aerobatics with theatre, opera, and original music—it has created a new art form. It has its own record label, a retail operation and a deal with Carnival Cruise Lines. As well, it has six touring shows and permanent facilities at Disneyworld in Orlando, Florida, and Las Vegas, Nevada. Cirque du Soleil sells about seven million tickets a year and has an estimated annual revenue of $500–$600 million.

According to Mario D'Amico, chief marketing officer for Cirque du Soleil, the organization invented a new market by inventing a new brand of circus by using a "blue ocean" strategy. Cirque aims to maintain a constant delicate tension between art and commerce. D'Amico also emphasizes the importance of building failure into the creative process, noting that Cirque routinely spends time and money developing acts that never make it into a performance. "Any time spent pursuing an idea is time well spent."[27]

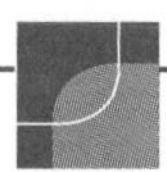

Technology Change

In today's business world, any company that isn't continually developing, acquiring, or adapting new technology will likely be out of business in a few years. However, organizations face a contradiction when it comes to technology change, because the conditions that promote new ideas are not generally the best for implementing those ideas for routine production. An innovative organization is characterized by flexibility and empowered employees and the absence of rigid work rules.[28] As discussed earlier in this book, an organic, free-flowing organization is typically associated with change and is considered the best organization form for adapting to a chaotic environment.

The flexibility of an organic organization contributes to people's freedom to be creative and introduce new ideas. Organic organizations encourage a bottom-up innovation process. Ideas bubble up from middle- and lower-level employees because they have the freedom to propose ideas and to experiment. A mechanistic structure, in contrast, stifles innovation with its emphasis on rules and regulations, but it is often the best structure for efficiently producing routine products. The challenge for managers is to create both organic and mechanistic conditions within the organization to achieve both innovation and efficiency. To attain both aspects of technological change, many organizations use the ambidextrous approach.

PDA
Remember...

Facilitate frequent changes in internal process and technology by adopting an organic organizational structure. Give technical personnel freedom to analyze problems and develop solutions, or create a separate, organically structured department or venture group to conceive and propose new ideas.

The Ambidextrous Approach

Recent thinking has refined the idea of organic versus mechanistic structures with respect to innovation creation versus innovation utilization. For example, sometimes an organic structure generates innovative ideas but is not the best structure for using those ideas.[29] In other words, the initiation and the utilization of change are two distinct processes. Organic characteristics such as decentralization and employee freedom are excellent for initiating ideas; but these same conditions often make it hard to implement a change because employees are less likely to comply. Employees can ignore the innovation because of decentralization and a generally loose structure.

How does an organization solve this dilemma? One remedy is for the organization to use an **ambidextrous approach**—to incorporate structures and management processes that are appropriate to both the creation and the implementation of innovation.[30] Another way to think of the ambidextrous approach is to look at the organizational design elements that are important for *exploring* new ideas versus the design elements that are most suitable for *exploiting* current capabilities. Exploration means encouraging creativity and developing new ideas, whereas exploitation means implementing those ideas to produce routine products. The organization can be designed to behave in an organic way for exploring new ideas and in a mechanistic way to exploit and use the ideas. Exhibit 11.6 illustrates how one department is structured organically to explore and develop new ideas, and another department is structured mechanistically for routine implementation of innovations. Research has shown that organizations that use an ambidextrous approach by designing for both exploration and exploitation are significantly more successful in launching innovative new products or services.[31]

For example, a study of long-established Japanese companies such as Honda and Canon that have succeeded in breakthrough innovations found that these companies use an ambidextrous approach.[32] To develop ideas related to a new technology, the companies assign teams of young staff members who are not entrenched in the "old way of doing things" to work on the project. The teams are headed by an esteemed elder and are charged with doing whatever is needed to develop new ideas and products, even if it means breaking rules that are important in the larger organization.

EXHIBIT 11.6
Division of Labour in the Ambidextrous Organization

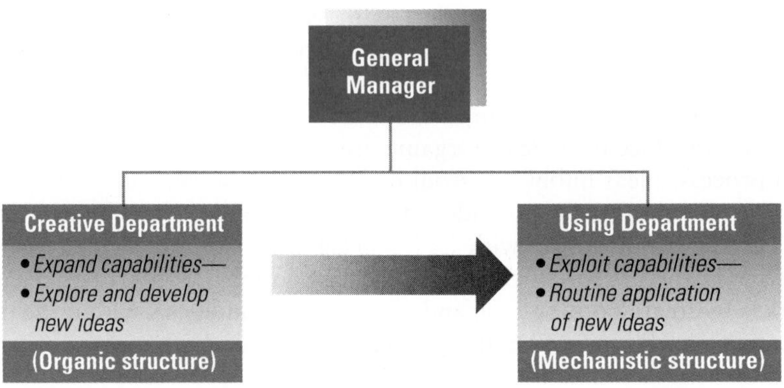

Techniques for Encouraging Technology Change

Some of the techniques used by companies to maintain an ambidextrous approach are switching structures, separate creative departments, venture teams, and corporate entrepreneurship.

Switching Structures. Switching **structures** means an organization creates an organic structure when such a structure is needed for the initiation of new ideas.[33] Some of the ways organizations have switched structures to achieve the ambidextrous approach are as follows:

- For example, Tesco of the United Kingdom experiments with new store formats and non-food offerings while achieving record profits in its core business.[34]
- Corus Entertainment is creating an ambidextrous organization that is adept at managing core business activities while encouraging innovation and exploring new business models. Corus Entertainment maintains a fund to support employee innovations, which has resulted in 15 new projects as of 2007.[35]
- The NUMMI plant, a Toyota subsidiary located in Fremont, California, creates a separate, organically organized, cross-functional subunit, called the Pilot Team, to design production processes for new car and truck models. When the model they are preparing moves into production, workers return to their regular jobs on the shop floor.[36]

Each of these organizations found creative ways to be ambidextrous, establishing organic conditions for developing new ideas in the midst of more mechanistic conditions for implementing and using those ideas.

Separate Creative Departments. In many large organizations the initiation of innovation is assigned to separate **creative departments.**[37] Staff departments, such as research and development, engineering, design, and systems analysis, create changes for adoption in other departments. Departments that initiate change are organically structured to facilitate the generation of new ideas and techniques. Departments that use those innovations tend to have a mechanistic structure more suitable for efficient production.

One example of a creative department is the research lab at Oksuka Pharmaceutical Company. Although most large North American drug firms have switched to using robots and other high-tech tools to perform large-scale drug experiments, Japanese companies such as Oksuka are achieving success by continuing to emphasize human creativity. To get the kind of creative spirit that is willing to try new things and look for the unexpected, Oksuka's president Tatsuo Higuchi says its research labs "put a high value on weird people."[38] However, in the department that manufactures drugs, where routine and precision is important, a pharmaceutical company would prefer to have less unusual people who are comfortable following rules and standard procedures.

Another type of creative department is the **idea incubator,** an increasingly popular way to facilitate the development of new ideas within the organization. An idea incubator provides a safe harbour where ideas from employees throughout the organization can be developed without interference from company bureaucracy or politics.[39] The incubator gives people throughout the organization a place to go rather than having to shop a new idea all over the company and hope someone will pay attention. In 2003, the Sudbury Centre of Innovation and Technology was created as a business incubator for the community. According to its founder, Mark Charbonneau, "[the] idea is more inventions are hatched over a cup of coffee than anything else."[40] Similarly, in 2007, the Government of Alberta created Canada's first idea incubator for agri-food entrepreneurs, to bring together up to eight organizations at a time to support the development of creative ideas.[41]

Venture Teams. **Venture teams** are a technique used to give free rein to creativity within organizations. Venture teams are often given a separate location and facilities so they are not constrained by organizational procedures. A venture team is like a small company within a large company. Numerous organizations have used the venture team concept to free creative people from the bureaucracy of a large corporation. At 3M, a program called *3M Acceleration* allows an employee with a promising idea for a new technology or product to recruit people from around the company to serve on a new venture team. 3M provides the space, funding, and freedom the team needs to fast-track the idea into a marketable product.[42] Many established companies that have successful Internet-based operations have set them up as venture teams so they have the freedom and authority to explore and develop the new technology. To create the Macintosh, for example, Steve Jobs created a separate physical space to let the engineers and designers do their innovative work.

One type of venture team is called a *skunkworks*.[43] A **skunkworks** is a separate, small, informal, highly autonomous, and often secretive group that focuses on breakthrough ideas for the business. The original skunkworks was created by Lockheed Martin in the United States more than 50 years ago and is still in operation. The essence of a skunkworks is that highly talented people are given the time and freedom to let creativity reign. Much of the design work on the Razr cell phone was done at Moto City, a Chicago innovation lab decorated in stylish colours rather than at Motorola's traditional research and development facility outside Chicago, Illinois. Care is taken to design open team-based facilities to encourage communication. Skunkworks are also known as mosh pits of creativity![44] A variation of the venture team concept is the **new-venture fund**, which provides financial resources for employees to develop new ideas, products, or businesses.

Corporate Entrepreneurship. Corporate entrepreneurship attempts to develop an internal entrepreneurial spirit, philosophy, and structure that will produce a higher-than-average number of innovations. Corporate entrepreneurship may involve the use of creative departments and new venture teams, but it also attempts to release the creative energy of all employees in the organization. Managers can create systems and structures that encourage entrepreneurship. The MaRS Venture Group, for example, focuses on supporting Canadian organizations by securing investment from the seed stage onward from Canadian and international venture capitalists. The MaRS Discovery Centre opened in 2005 to improve Canada's ability to innovate and to commercialize its innovations.[45] One of MaRS's tenants, Skymeter , has developed a black box to be attached to the windshield of a car. The box contains a GPS receiver, some memory, a processor and a telecommunications chip. The satellite beams down to the earth, and the GPS receiver computes where it is and uploads its history to a data centre to generate the bill. The vehicle measures its own use and a bill is itemized like a cell phone bill.[46] It can used for such services as pay-as-you-drive insurance.

An important outcome of corporate entrepreneurship is to facilitate **idea champions.** These go by a variety of names, including *advocate, intrapreneur,* or *change agent.* Idea champions provide the time and energy to make things happen.

They fight to overcome natural resistance to change and to convince others of the merit of a new idea.[47] Idea champions need not be within the organization. Some companies have found that fostering idea champions among regular customers can be a highly successful approach.[48] The importance of the idea champion is illustrated by a fascinating fact discovered by Texas Instruments (TI): when TI reviewed 50 successful and unsuccessful technical projects, it discovered that every failure was characterized by the absence of a volunteer champion. There was no one who passionately believed in the idea, who pushed the idea through every obstacle to make it work. TI took this finding so seriously that now its number-one criterion for approving new technical projects is the presence of a zealous champion.[49]

Idea champions usually come in two types. The **technical champion,** or *product champion,* is the person who generates or adopts and develops an idea for a technological innovation and is devoted to it, even to the extent of risking position or prestige. The **management champion** acts as a supporter and sponsor to shield and promote an idea within the organization.[50] The management champion sees the potential application, and has the prestige and authority to get the idea a fair hearing and to allocate resources to it. Technical and management champions often work together because a technical idea will have a greater chance of success if a manager can be found to sponsor it. Numerous studies have identified the importance of idea champions as a factor in the success of new products.[51]

Companies encourage idea champions by providing freedom and slack time to creative people. Companies such as IBM, General Electric, and 3M allow employees to develop new technologies without company approval. Known as *bootlegging,* the unauthorized research often pays big dividends. As one IBM executive said, "We wink at it. It pays off. It's just amazing what a handful of dedicated people can do when they are really turned on."[52]

In Practice
Pratt & Whitney Canada (P&WC)

Pratt & Whitney Canada (P&WC), whose head office is in Longueuil, Québec, designs, develops, manufactures, and markets turboprop, turbofan, and turboshaft engines. It also provides support and maintenance services, which account for half its revenues. P&WC has customers in over 180 countries, more than a dozen domestic plants, and a network of service centres around the world.

Its competitors include General Electric, Honeywell, and Rolls Royce-Allison. In 1999, P&WC controlled about 24 percent of the increasingly fragmented and global market that was moving toward a mass customization approach. As a response to the difficult competitive environment, P&WC increased its engine models and cut production times so that it could deliver customized orders in a timely way. Between June 1996 and January 1999, P&WC implemented an ERP system as one way to deal with the changing demands of its environment. (ERP, or enterprise resource planning, is a software system designed to assist in managing all aspects of manufacturing from product planning and inventory management to order tracking. It is uses relational database systems to integrate the information necessary for effective manufacturing processes.)

The implementation is considered a particularly successful one. There are three key reasons for its success. First, at the strategic level, senior managers created a clear vision of the role of the ERP project, created a sense of urgency around the project, and supported the change with sufficient resources. Second, at the tactical level, PW&C redesigned its organization, took on technological partners, and used an established methodology and process. The company also used clear metrics to gauge progress. At the operational level, change leadership and knowledge-transfer teams were used to be sensitive to employee needs throughout the change. Employees were involved in the training, which helped both the transfer of knowledge and the acceptance of the implementation.[53]

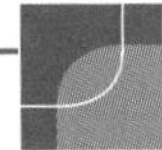

New Products and Services

Although the ideas just discussed are important to product and service as well as technology changes, other factors also need to be considered. In many ways, new products and services are a special case of innovation because they are used by customers outside the organization. Since new products are designed for sale in the environment, uncertainty about the suitability and success of an innovation is very high.

New Product Success Rate

Research has explored the enormous uncertainty associated with the development and sale of new products.[54] To understand what this uncertainty can mean to organizations, just consider such flops as the Bricklin car with its distinctive gull-wing design. American promoter Malcolm Bricklin wanted to build his own U.S.–designed sports car, and, enticed by loan guarantees and other investments, he set up shop in Saint John and Minto, New Brunswick, where the fibreglass bodies were made. Production was delayed as both the gull wings and the fibreglass body were difficult to build. The company owed $23 million to the provincial government, at which point the government refused to grant more aid unless the private sector provided 50 percent of the financing. The private sector would not, and Bricklin fell into receivership. During 1974 and 1975, only 2,857 cars were made and sent to the United States.[55]

The Avro Arrow (CF-105) is another spectacular failure. The Arrow was a supersonic interceptor jet developed in the 1950s to counter the perceived threat to the Canadian North from Soviet bombers. The costs for building the plane skyrocketed to $12.5 million per aircraft. In 1959, the government cancelled the project, which had already cost $400 million. As a result, 14,000 employees were fired, and all plans and prototypes were ordered destroyed. Many of the research scientists and engineers left Canada to work in the aircraft industry in the United States.[56] The Avro Arrow story is one of failure but also of mystery as speculation continues about the reasons for destroying the plans and the prototypes.

Experts estimate that about 80 percent of new products fail upon introduction and another 10 percent disappear within five years. Considering that it can cost $50 million or more to successfully launch a new product, new product development is a risky, high-stakes game for organizations. Nevertheless, more than 25,000 new products appeared in one year alone, including more than 5,000 new toys.[57] A survey some years ago examined 200 projects in 19 chemical, drug, electronics, and petroleum laboratories to learn about success rates.[58] To be successful, the new product had to pass three stages of development: technical completion, commercialization, and market success. On the average, only 57 percent of all projects undertaken in the R&D laboratories achieved technical objectives, which means all technical problems were solved and the projects moved on to production. Of all projects that were started, less than one-third (31 percent) were fully marketed and commercialized. Several projects failed at this stage because production estimates or test market results were unfavourable. Finally, only 12 percent of all projects originally undertaken achieved economic success. Most of the commercialized products did not earn sufficient returns to cover the cost of development and production. This means that only about one project in eight returned a profit to the company.

Reasons for New Product Success

The next question to be answered by research was why some products are more successful than others. Other studies indicated that innovation success is related to collaboration between technical and marketing departments. Successful new products and services seem to be technologically sound and also carefully tailored to customer needs.[59] A study called Project SAPPHO examined 17 pairs of new product innovations, with one success and one failure in each pair, and concluded the following:

1. Successful innovating companies had a much better understanding of customer needs and paid much more attention to marketing.
2. Successful innovating companies made more effective use of outside technology and outside advice, even though they did more work in-house.
3. Top management support in the successful innovating companies was from people who were more senior and had greater authority.

Thus there is a distinct pattern of tailoring innovations to customer needs, making effective use of technology, and having influential top managers support the project. These ideas taken together indicate that the effective design for new product innovation is associated with horizontal coordination across departments.

PDA Remember...

Encourage marketing, research, and production departments to develop linkages to each other and to their environments when new products or services are needed.

Horizontal Coordination Model

The organizational design for achieving new product innovation involves three components—departmental specialization, boundary spanning, and horizontal coordination. These components are similar to the horizontal coordination mechanisms discussed in Chapter 3, such as teams, task forces, and project managers, and the differentiation and integration ideas discussed in Chapter 4. Exhibit 11.7 illustrates these components in the **horizontal coordination model.**

EXHIBIT 11.7
Horizontal Coordination Model for New Product Innovations

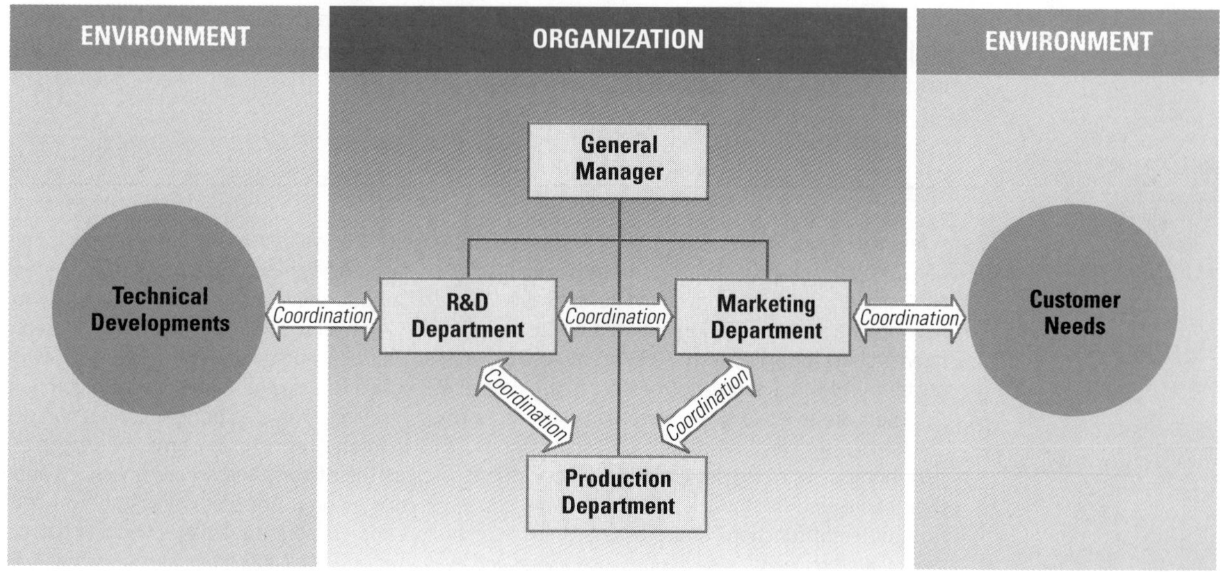

Specialization. The key departments in new product development are R&D, marketing, and production. The specialization component means that the personnel in all three of these departments are highly competent at their own tasks. The three departments are differentiated from each other and have skills, goals, and attitudes appropriate for their specialized functions.

Boundary Spanning. This component means each department involved with new products has excellent linkage with relevant sectors in the external environment. R&D personnel are linked to professional associations and to colleagues in other R&D departments. They are aware of recent scientific developments. Marketers need to be closely linked to customer needs. They listen to what customers have to say, and they analyze competitor products and suggestions from distributors. For example, Puretracks listened to its customers and started selling some songs online without copy protection in early 2007. The unprotected catalogue includes music from The Barenaked Ladies and Sarah McLachlan. As well, the songs will be playable on devices that they did not work on previously such as the iPod.[60]

Horizontal Coordination. This component means that technical, marketing, and production people share ideas and information. Research people inform marketing of new technical developments to learn whether the developments are applicable to customers. Marketing people provide customer complaints and information to R&D to use in the design of new products. People from both R&D and marketing coordinate with production because new products have to fit within production capabilities so costs are not exorbitant. The decision to launch a new product is ultimately a joint decision among all three departments. Horizontal coordination, using mechanisms such as cross-functional teams, increases both the amount and the variety of information for new product development, enabling the design of products that meet customer needs and circumventing manufacturing and marketing problems.[61]

Recall the chapter-opening example of Toyota, which uses a product development technique called *obeya*. The idea behind *obeya* is to change the way people think about product innovation and development by changing how they share information. "There are no taboos in obeya," explains Takeshi Yoshida, chief engineer for the 2003 Corolla. "Everyone in that room is an expert. They all have a part to play in building the car."[62] Consumer products firm Procter & Gamble is also taking a bold new approach to innovation.

In Practice

Procter & Gamble (P&G)

A few years ago, Procter & Gamble (P&G) was a stodgy (over 160-year-old) consumer products company selling successful but tired brands such as Tide, Crest, and Pampers. Today, the 169-year-old company has re-emerged as a master brand-builder and a hot growth company, thanks largely to a new approach to innovation initiated by CEO A. G. Lafley. Between 2002 and 2004, P&G raised its new product hit rate from 70 percent to 90 percent. Products such as Olay Regenerist, Swiffer dusters, and Mr. Clean AutoDry have made Procter & Gamble look like a nimble start-up company.

There are several key elements to Lafley's innovation machine. One is a stronger connection with consumers. Rather than relying on focus groups, P&G marketers now spend time with people in their homes, watching how they wash their dishes or clean their floors, and asking questions about their habits and frustrations with household chores or child rearing. Another key is getting people from different functions and divisions to exchange ideas and collaborate. Lafley conducts half-day "innovation reviews" in each unit once a year and evaluates how well marketers and researchers are sharing ideas. Besides opportunities for face-to-face meetings and internal trade shows, an internal website called InnovationNet connects employees from all divisions and departments worldwide. R&D people located in twenty technical facilities in nine countries can post a question such as "How can you clean without rinsing?" and get suggestions from employees across the company and around the world. The technologies that enable Mr. Clean AutoDry, a power gun that sprays your car clean and dry, came from P&G's Cascade division, which knew how to reduce water spots on dishes, and the PuR water filter unit, which had a technology for reducing minerals in water.

The most revolutionary part of Lafley's approach is encouraging collaboration with outside people and other firms, even competitors. "The idea, since dubbed 'connect and develop,' was a radical departure from P&G's invent-it-ourselves culture, which relied mostly on 7,500 company scientists to churn out new products."[63] For example, Glad Press 'n Seal was developed collaboratively with Clorox, which competes fiercely with P&G in floor mops and water purification products. Lafley is pushing for half of P&G's innovations to be derived from outside sources. "Inventors are evenly distributed in the population," he says, "and we're as likely to find invention in a garage as in our labs."[64]

Research findings show that collaboration with other firms and with customers can be a significant source of product innovation, and can even stimulate stronger internal coordination. Cooperating with external parties requires the involvement of people from different areas of the company, which in turn necessitates that organizations set up stronger internal coordination mechanisms.[65] Companies such as Procter & Gamble and Corel routinely turn to customers and other organizations for advice.

Such companies use the concept of horizontal coordination to achieve competitive advantage. Famous innovation failures—such as McDonald's Arch Deluxe or the baby-food company Gerber's Singles for Adults—usually violate the horizontal linkage model. Employees fail to connect with customer needs and market forces or internal departments fail to adequately share needs and coordinate with one another. Recent research has confirmed a connection between effective boundary spanning that keeps the organization in touch with market forces, smooth coordination among departments, and successful product development.[66]

■ Achieving Competitive Advantage: The Need for Speed

The rapid development of new products is becoming a major strategic weapon in the shifting international marketplace.[67] To remain competitive, companies are learning to develop ideas into new products and services incredibly quickly. Whether the approach is called the *horizontal linkage model, concurrent engineering, companies without walls, the parallel approach,* or *simultaneous coupling of departments*, the point is the same—get people working together simultaneously on a project rather than in sequence. Many companies are learning to sprint to market with new products.

Time-based competition means delivering products and services faster than competitors, giving companies a competitive edge. Some companies use what are called *fast cycle teams* as a way to support highly important projects and deliver products and services faster than competitors. A fast cycle team is a multifunctional, and sometimes multinational, team that works under stringent timelines and is provided with high levels of company resources and empowerment to accomplish an accelerated product development project.[68] Using virtual reality, collaborative software, and a horizontal, integrated design process, GM has cut its time from concept to production on a new vehicle model to a mere 18 months. Not so long ago, it took GM an astounding four years to complete that process. The new approach to product development has given GM a speed advantage over competitors in the design and production of hot new car models that capitalize on fashion trends and capture the market for younger car buyers.[69]

Another critical issue is designing products that can compete on a global scale and successfully marketing those products internationally. Companies such as Quaker Oats, Häagen Dazs, and Levi's are trying to improve horizontal communication and collaboration across geographical regions, recognizing that they can pick up winning product ideas from customers in other countries. Many new product development teams today are global teams because organizations have to develop products that will meet diverse needs of consumers all over the world.[70] GM's collaborative, computer-based product development system enables engineers and suppliers from all over the world to work together on a project. Ford Motor Company also uses an intranet and global teleconferencing to link car design teams around the world into a single unified group.[71] When companies enter the arena of intense international competition, horizontal coordination across countries is essential to new product development.

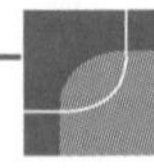

Strategy and Structure Change

The preceding discussion focused on new production processes and products, which are based in the technology of an organization. The expertise for such innovation lies within the technical core and professional staff groups, such as research and engineering. This section turns to an examination of strategy and structure changes.

All organizations need to make changes in their strategies, structures, and administrative procedures from time to time. In the past, when the environment was relatively stable, most organizations focused on small, incremental changes to solve immediate problems or take advantage of new opportunities. However, over the past decade, companies throughout the world have faced the need to make radical changes in strategy, structure, and management processes to adapt to new competitive demands.[72] Many organizations are cutting out layers of management and decentralizing decision making. There is a strong shift toward more horizontal structures, with teams of front-line workers empowered to make decisions and solve problems on their own. Some companies are breaking totally away from traditional organization forms and shifting toward virtual network strategies and structures. Numerous companies are reorganizing and shifting their strategies as the expansion of e-business changes the rules. Global competition and rapid technological change will likely lead to even greater strategy-structure realignments over the next decade.

These types of changes are the responsibility of the organization's top managers, and the overall process of change is typically different from the process for innovation in technology or new products.

PDA Remember...

Facilitate changes in strategy and structure by adopting a top-down approach. Use a mechanistic structure when the organization needs to adopt frequent administrative changes in a top-down fashion.

The Dual-Core Approach

The **dual-core approach** to organizational change compares administrative and technical changes. Administrative changes pertain to the design and structure of the organization itself, including restructuring, downsizing, teams, control systems, information systems, and departmental grouping. Research into administrative change suggests two things. First, administrative changes occur less frequently than do technical changes. Second, administrative changes occur in response to different environmental sectors and follow a different internal process than do technology-based changes.[73] The dual-core approach to organizational change identifies the unique processes associated with administrative change.[74]

Organizations—schools, hospitals, municipal governments, welfare agencies, government bureaucracies, and many business firms—can be conceptualized as having two cores: a *technical core* and an *administrative core*. Each core has its own employees, tasks, and environmental domain. Innovation can originate in either core.

The administrative core is above the technical core in the hierarchy. The responsibility of the administrative core includes the structure, control, and coordination of the organization itself and concerns the environmental sectors of government, financial resources, economic conditions, human resources, and competitors. The technical core is concerned with the transformation of raw materials into organizational products and services, and involves the environmental sectors of customers and technology.[75]

The point of the dual-core approach is that many organizations—especially not-for-profit and government organizations—must adopt frequent administrative changes and need to be structured differently from organizations that rely on frequent technical and product changes for competitive advantage.

Organizational Design for Implementing Administrative Change

The findings from research comparing administrative and technical change suggest that a mechanistic organizational structure is appropriate for frequent administrative changes, including changes in goals, strategy, structure, control systems, and personnel.[76] Administrative changes in policy, regulations, or control systems are more critical than technical changes in many government organizations that are bureaucratically structured. Organizations that successfully adopt many administrative changes often have a larger administrative ratio, are larger in size, and are centralized and formalized compared with organizations that adopt many technical changes.[77] The reason is the top-down implementation of changes in response to changes in the government, financial, or legal sectors of the environment. If an organization has an organic structure, lower-level employees have more freedom and autonomy and, hence, may resist top-down initiatives.

The innovation approaches associated with administrative versus technical change are summarized in Exhibit 11.8. Technical change, such as changes in production techniques and innovation technology for new products, is facilitated by an organic structure, which allows ideas to bubble upward from lower- and middle-level employees. Organizations that must adopt frequent administrative changes, in contrast, tend to use a top-down process and a mechanistic structure. For example, policy changes, such as the adoption of no-smoking policies, sexual harassment policies, or new safety procedures, are facilitated by a top-down approach. Downsizing and significant restructuring are nearly always managed top down. When Bobby Genovese took over the moribund Clearly Canadian Beverage Corp in 2006, he installed a new management team, which has developed a new strategy of new products, celebrity-filled marketing and the company's own reality-TV series.[78]

Research into civil service reform found that the implementation of administrative innovation was extremely difficult in organizations that had an organic technical core. The professional employees in a decentralized agency could resist civil service changes.

EXHIBIT 11.8
Dual-Core Approach to Organizational Change

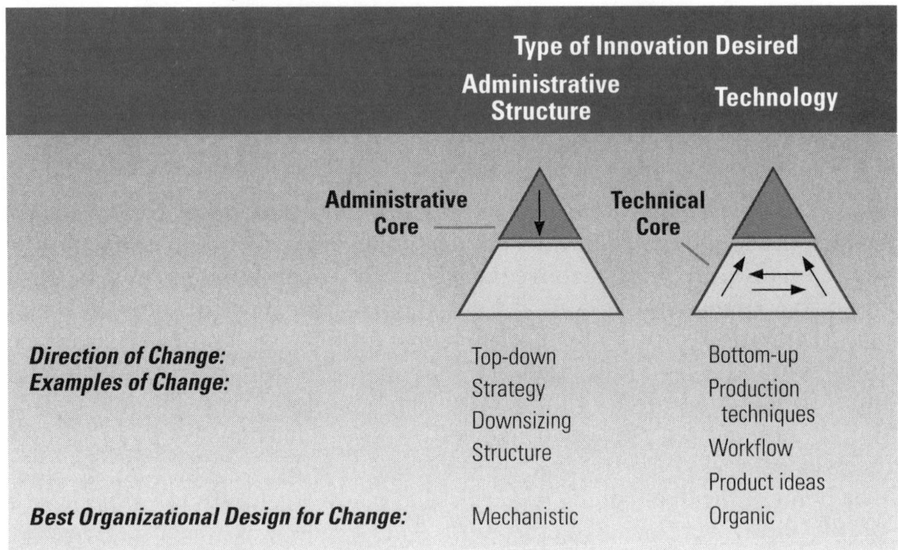

By contrast, organizations that were considered more bureaucratic in the sense of high formalization and centralization adopted administrative changes readily.[79]

What about business organizations that are normally technologically innovative in bottom-up fashion but suddenly face a crisis and need to reorganize? Or a technically innovative, high-tech firm that must reorganize frequently to accommodate changes in production technology or the environment? Technically innovative firms may suddenly have to restructure, reduce the number of employees, alter pay systems, disband teams, or form a new division.[80] The answer is to use a top-down change process. The authority for strategy and structure change lies with top management, who should initiate and implement the new strategy and structure to meet environmental circumstances. Employee input may be sought, but top managers have the responsibility to direct the change.

Some top-down changes, particularly those related to restructuring and downsizing, can be very painful for employees, so top managers should move quickly and authoritatively to make them as humane as possible.[81] A study of successful corporate transformations, which frequently involve painful changes, found that managers followed a fast, focused approach. When top managers spread difficult changes such as downsizing over a long time period, employee morale suffers and the change is much less likely to lead to positive outcomes.[82] Top managers should also remember that top-down change means initiation of the idea occurs at upper levels and is implemented downward. It does not mean that lower-level employees are not educated about the change or allowed to participate in it.

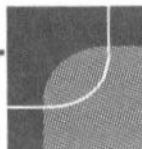

Culture Change

Organizations are made up of people and their relationships with one another. Changes in strategy, structure, technologies, and products do not happen on their own, and changes in any of these areas involve changes in people as well. Employees must learn how to use new technologies, or market new products, or work effectively in a team-based structure. Sometimes achieving a new way of thinking requires a focused change in the underlying cultural values and norms. Changing organizational culture fundamentally shifts how work is done in an organization and generally leads to renewed commitment and empowerment of employees and a stronger bond between the company and its customers.[83]

Forces for Culture Change

A number of recent trends have contributed to a need for cultural makeovers at companies such as the merged Canada Trust and Toronto Dominion Bank, IBM, and Canada Revenue Agency.[84] Some of the primary changes requiring a shift in culture and employee mind-set are re-engineering and the move toward horizontal forms of organizing, greater employee and customer diversity, and the shift to the learning organization.

Re-Engineering and Horizontal Organizing. As described in Chapter 3, re-engineering involves redesigning a vertical organization along its horizontal workflows. This changes the way managers and employees need to think about how work is done and requires greater focus on employee empowerment, collaboration, information sharing, and meeting customer needs. In his book *The Reengineering Revolution*, Michael Hammer refers to people change as "the most perplexing, annoying, distressing, and confusing part" of re-engineering.[85] Managers may confront powerful emotions as employees react to rapid, massive change with fear or anger.

In the horizontal organization, managers and front-line workers need to understand and embrace the concepts of teamwork, empowerment, and cooperation. Managers shift their thinking to view workers as colleagues rather than cogs in a wheel; and workers learn to accept not only greater freedom and power, but also the higher level of responsibility that comes with them. Mutual trust, risk taking, and tolerance for mistakes become key cultural values in the horizontal organization.

Diversity. Diversity is a fact of life for today's organizations, and many are implementing new recruiting, mentoring, and promotion methods; diversity training programs; tough policies regarding sexual harassment and racial discrimination; and new benefits programs that respond to a more diverse workforce. However, if the underlying culture of an organization does not change, all other efforts to support diversity will fail. Managers at Mitsubishi are still struggling with this reality. Even though the company settled a sexual harassment lawsuit filed by women at its Normal, Illinois, plant; established a zero-tolerance policy; and fired workers who were guilty of blatant sexual or racial harassment, employees said the work environment at the plant remained deeply hostile to women and minorities. Incidents of blatant harassment declined, but women and various minority workers still felt threatened and powerless because the culture that allowed the harassment to occur had not changed.

The Learning Organization. The learning organization involves breaking down boundaries both within and between organizations to create companies that are focused on knowledge sharing and continuous learning. Recall from Chapter 1 that shifting to a learning organization involves changes in a number of areas. For example, structures become horizontal and involve empowered teams working directly with customers. There are few rules and procedures for performing tasks, and knowledge and control of tasks are located with employees rather than supervisors. Information is broadly shared rather than being concentrated with top managers. In addition, employees, customers, suppliers, and partners all play a role in determining the organization's strategic direction. Clearly, all of these changes require new values, new attitudes, and new ways of thinking and working together. A learning organization cannot exist without a culture that supports openness, equality, adaptability, and employee participation. WestJet Airlines Ltd. has tried, from its founding, to create a culture of openness and employee participation.

In Practice

WestJet Airlines Ltd.

WestJet sees itself as part of the hospitality industry rather than the airline industry. From the outset, it wanted a culture that encouraged innovation and a passion to succeed. WestJet's co-founder, Don Bell, is considered its culture guru, its spiritual leader who championed teamwork and rewarded innovation. According to Bell, the culture of WestJet is its greatest strategic advantage. He notes that "[everyone] is unique, and if you embrace people's personalities rather than turn them into robots, and give them the guidelines and the working environment to blossom, it creates something that's very hard to reckon with."[86]

It is a youthful and fun culture. There is a committee of flight attendants called WestJesters whose job is to write comedy for the end of flights. There is a demonstrated commitment to minimize status differences. Everyone, including President Clive Beddoes, helps pick up garbage at the end of a flight. As Bell comments, "I always say [a great culture] starts by the actions of the leaders." As Sherril Hatch, a call centre attendant put it, "Everyone here is first-class."[87]

At least once a year, employees attend small chat sessions with management to raise concerns, ask questions, and make suggestions. An employee-based Pro-Active Communication System provides one way to deal with issues before they become a problem. Employees participate in a profit-sharing system and can have some of their pay in the form of WestJet stock.

In a 2005 survey of senior managers at 107 companies, WestJet was chosen as having the most admired organizational culture in Canada. It was admired for its entrepreneurial spirit, its winning attitude, and for living up to its commitments.

Organization Development Culture Change Interventions

PDA

Remember...

Work with organization development consultants for large-scale changes in the attitudes, values, or skills of employees, and when shifting to a learning organization culture.

Managers use a variety of approaches and techniques for changing organizational culture, some of which we discussed in Chapter 10. One method of quickly bringing about culture change is known as **organization development** (OD), which focuses on the human and social aspects of the organization as a way to improve the organization's ability to adapt and solve problems. OD emphasizes the values of human development, fairness, openness, freedom from coercion, and individual autonomy, which allow workers to perform the job as they see fit, within reasonable organizational constraints.[88] In the 1970s, OD evolved as a separate field that applied the behavioural sciences in a process of planned organization-wide change, with the goal of increasing organizational effectiveness. Today the concept has been enlarged to examine how people and groups can change to a learning organization culture in a complex and turbulent environment. Organization development is not a step-by-step procedure to solve a specific problem but a process of fundamental change in the human and social systems of the organization, including organizational culture.[89]

OD uses knowledge and techniques from the behavioural sciences to create a learning environment through increased trust, open confrontation of problems, employee empowerment and participation, knowledge and information sharing, the design of meaningful work, cooperation and collaboration between groups, and the full use of human potential.

OD interventions involve training specific groups or everyone in the organization. For OD interventions to be successful, senior management in the organization must see the need for OD and provide enthusiastic support for the change. Techniques used by many organizations for improving people skills through OD include the following.

Large Group Intervention. Most early OD activities involved small groups and focused on incremental change. However, in recent years, there has been growing interest in the application of OD techniques to large group settings, which are more attuned to bringing about radical or transformational change in organizations operating in complex environments.[90] The **large group intervention** approach[91] brings together participants from all parts of the organization—often including key stakeholders from outside the organization as well—in an off-site setting to discuss problems or opportunities and plan for change. A large group intervention might involve 50 to 500 people and last for several days. The off-site setting limits interference and distractions, enabling participants to focus on new ways of doing things. General Electric's "Work Out" program, an ongoing process of solving problems, learning, and improving, begins with large-scale off-site meetings that get people talking across functional, hierarchical, and organizational boundaries. Hourly and salaried workers come together from many different parts of the organization and join with customers and suppliers to discuss and solve specific problems.[92] The process forces a rapid analysis of ideas, the creation of solutions, and the development of a plan for implementation. Over time, Work Out creates a culture where ideas are rapidly translated into action and positive business results.[93]

Team Building. Team building promotes the idea that people who work together can work as a team. A work team can be brought together to discuss conflicts, goals, the decision-making process, communication, creativity, and leadership. The team can then plan to overcome problems and improve results. Team-building activities are also used in many companies to train task forces, committees, and new product development groups. These activities enhance communication and collaboration and strengthen the cohesiveness of organizational groups and teams.

Interdepartmental Activities. Representatives from different departments are brought together in a mutual location to expose problems or conflicts, diagnose the causes, and plan improvements in communication and coordination. This type of intervention has been applied to union–management conflict, headquarters–field office conflict, interdepartmental conflict, and mergers.[94] A box-storage business, which stores archived records for other companies, found interdepartmental meetings to be a key means of building a culture based on team spirit and customer focus. People from different departments met for hour-long sessions every two weeks and shared their problems, told stories about their successes, and talked about things they'd observed in the company. The meetings helped people understand the problems faced in other departments and see how everyone depended on each other to do their jobs successfully.[95]

One current area in which OD can provide significant value is in spurring culture change toward valuing diversity.[96] In addition, today's organizations are continuously adapting to environmental uncertainty and increasing global competition, and OD interventions can respond to these new realities as companies strive to create greater capability for learning and growth.[97]

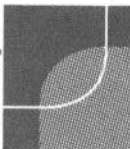

Strategies for Implementing Change

Managers and employees can think of inventive ways to improve the organization's technology, creative ideas for new products and services, fresh approaches to strategies and structures, or ideas for fostering adaptive cultural values, but until the ideas are put into action, they are worthless to the organization. Implementation is the most crucial part of the change process, but it is also the most difficult. Change is frequently disruptive and uncomfortable for managers as well as employees. This chapter's Book Mark explores how managers can improve change implementation by understanding the emotional aspects of the change process. Change is complex,

Book Mark 11.0 (HAVE YOU READ THIS BOOK?)

The Change Monster: The Human Forces That Fuel or Foil Corporate Transformation and Change

By Jeanie Daniel Duck

The change monster is lurking in every organization, just waiting to gobble up unsuspecting managers who are striving to implement new strategies, accomplish reorganizations, or complete mergers. Jeanie Daniel Duck uses the term *change monster* in her book by the same name to refer to all the complex human emotions and social dynamics that emerge during major change efforts. Many managers, she says, simplify or ignore the people issues of change, a sure prescription for failure.

MASTERING THE CHANGE CURVE

Duck says that major organizational change typically follows a change curve—a roller-coaster ride that brings out myriad unexpected and conflicting emotions.

- *Stagnation*. This is the period during which the organization has lost direction or is moving in the wrong direction. The change monster is generally quiet—people feel comfortable and safe. However, it is the job of managers to recognize stagnation and create a sense of urgency for change.
- *Preparation*. In this stage, Duck says, "the change monster is rudely awakened from its hibernating slumber and stretches itself, causing all kinds of emotional tremors." This is the period during which change leaders define and refine their vision for change and begin to involve others in the change process. Emotions range from excitement and hopefulness to anxiety and betrayal. Everyone is jittery and distracted.
- *Implementation*. This phase is the actual tactical start of the change journey, and as such is the longest and typically the most painful. There is an explosion of emotions, both positive and negative, in the organization. During this phase, employees often feel in limbo. Everything has changed, and yet the changes haven't been solidified. Many people feel uncertain about their ability to function in the new environment.
- *Determination*. During this period, Duck says, the change monster is roaming the hallways, ready to do its worst damage. Many managers think the change has been accomplished and turn their attention elsewhere right at the time when reinforcement is most needed. People often exhibit *retroactive resistance*, a sort of change fatigue and a desire to revert to the old familiar patterns.
- *Fruition*. Ahhhh . . . the time when all the hard work pays off at last. In this phase, the changes have become a part of the accepted way of doing things. The whole organization may feel new and different. Employees have gained confidence and are optimistic and energized. The change monster has been corralled.

COMING FULL CIRCLE

It is the goal of every change initiative to reach fruition. But Duck cautions that a new period of stagnation is just around the corner. When an organization accomplishes a major change, people need to take time to bask in the success. But managers must be on guard that basking doesn't turn to napping. Managers can teach their organizations how to perpetually adapt and help them muster the will to do so. "When an organization sees itself as a hearty band of monster slayers, change becomes a challenge they're ready to meet rather than a threat that signals retreat."

The Change Monster: The Human Forces That Fuel or Foil Corporate Transformation and Change, by Jeanie Daniel Duck, is published by Crown Business.

dynamic, and messy, and implementation requires strong and persistent leadership. In this final section, we briefly discuss the role of leadership for change, some reasons for resistance to change, and techniques that managers can use to overcome resistance and successfully implement change.

Leadership for Change

The pressures on organizations to change will probably increase over the next few decades. Leaders must develop the personal qualities, skills, and methods needed to help their companies remain competitive. Indeed, some management experts argue that to survive the upheaval of the early 21st century, managers must turn their organizations into *change leaders* by using the present to actually create the future—breaking industry rules, creating new market space, and routinely abandoning outmoded products, services, and processes to free up resources to build the future.[98]

The need for change within organizations and the need for leaders who can successfully manage change continue to grow. The leadership style of the top executive sets the tone for how effective the organization is at continuous adaptation and innovation. One style of leadership, referred to as *transformational leadership*, is particularly suited for bringing about change. Top leaders who use a transformational leadership style enhance organizational innovation both directly, by creating a compelling vision, and indirectly, by creating an environment that supports exploration, experimentation, risk taking, and sharing of ideas.[99]

Successful change can happen only when employees are willing to devote the time and energy needed to reach new goals, as well as endure possible stress and hardship. Having a clearly communicated vision that embodies flexibility and openness to new ideas, methods, and styles sets the stage for a change-oriented organization and helps employees cope with the chaos and tension associated with change.[100] Leaders also build organization-wide commitment by taking employees through three stages of the change commitment process, illustrated in Exhibit 11.9.[101] In the first stage,

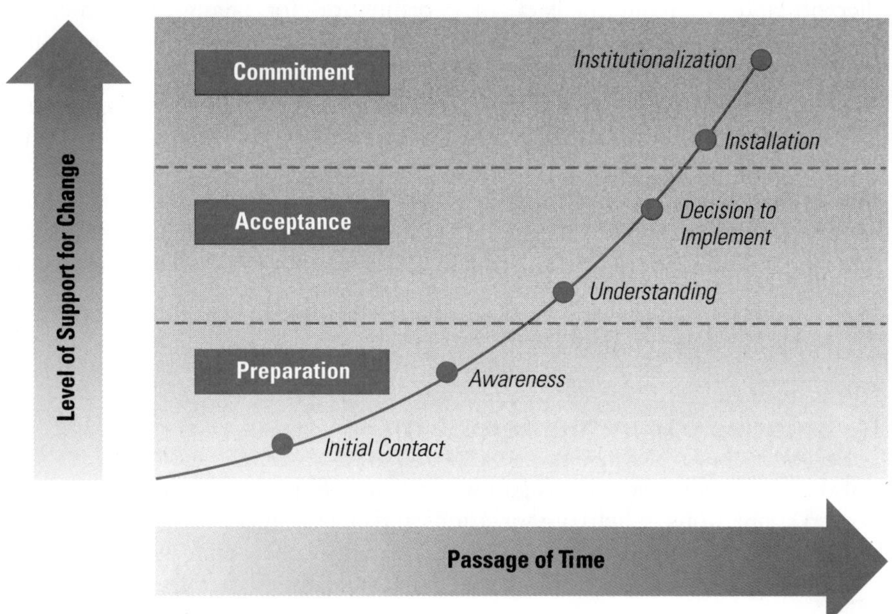

EXHIBIT 11.9
Stages of Commitment to Change
Source: Adapted from Daryl R. Conner, *Managing at the Speed of Change* (New York: Villard Books, 1992), 148. Used with permission.

preparation, employees hear about the change through memos, meetings, speeches, or personal contact, and become aware that the change will directly affect their work. In the second stage, *acceptance,* leaders should help employees develop an understanding of the full impact of the change and the positive outcomes of making the change. When employees perceive the change as positive, the decision to implement is made. In the third stage, the true *commitment* process begins. The commitment stage involves the steps of installation and institutionalization. Installation is a trial process for the change, which gives leaders an opportunity to discuss problems and employee concerns, and build commitment to action. In the final step, *institutionalization,* employees view the change not as something new but as a normal and integral part of organizational operations.

Barriers to Change

Visionary leadership is crucial for change; however, leaders should expect to encounter resistance as they attempt to take the organization through the three stages of the change commitment process. It is natural for people to resist change, and many barriers to change exist at the individual and organizational levels.[102]

1. *Excessive focus on costs.* Management may possess the mind-set that costs are all-important and may fail to appreciate the importance of a change that is not focused on costs—for example, a change to increase employee motivation or customer satisfaction.
2. *Failure to perceive benefits.* Any significant change will produce both positive and negative reactions. Education may be needed to help managers and employees perceive more positive than negative aspects of the change. In addition, if the organization's reward system discourages risk taking, a change process might falter because employees think that the risk of making the change is too high.
3. *Lack of coordination and cooperation.* Organizational fragmentation and conflict often result from the lack of coordination for change implementation. Moreover, in the case of new technology, the old and new systems must be compatible.
4. *Uncertainty avoidance.* At the individual level, many employees fear the uncertainty associated with change. Constant communication is needed so that employees know what is going on and understand how it affects their jobs.
5. *Fear of loss.* Managers and employees may fear the loss of power and status—or even their jobs. In these cases, implementation should be careful and incremental, and all employees should be involved as closely as possible in the change process.

Implementation can typically be designed to overcome many of the organizational and individual barriers to change.

Techniques for Implementation

One of the pioneers in the serious-gaming industry, ExperiencePoint, has developed web-based simulations to help organizations and change agents to practise both their diagnostic and implementation skills before actually proceeding with change. That way, organizations can learn about the many challenges of effectively managing change.[103] Top leaders articulate the vision and set the tone, but managers and employees throughout the organization are involved in the process of change. A number of techniques can be used to successfully implement change.[104]

1. *Establish a sense of urgency for change.* Once managers identify a true need for change, they need to thaw resistance by creating a sense of urgency that change is really needed. Organizational crises can help unfreeze employees and make them willing to invest the time and energy needed to adopt new techniques or procedures. However, in many cases, there is no public crisis and managers have to make others aware of the need for change.
2. *Establish a coalition to guide the change.* Change managers have to build a coalition of people throughout the organization who have enough power and influence to steer the change process. For implementation to be successful, there must be a shared commitment to the need and possibilities for change. Top management support is crucial for any major change project, and lack of top management support is one of the most frequent causes of implementation failure.[105] In addition, the coalition should involve lower-level supervisors and middle managers from across the organization. For smaller changes, the support of influential managers in the affected departments is important.
3. *Create a vision and strategy for change.* Leaders who have taken their organizations through major successful transformations often have one thing in common: They focus on formulating and articulating a compelling vision and strategy that will guide the change process. Even for a small change, a vision of how the future can be better and strategies to get there are important motivations for change.
4. *Find an idea that fits the need.* Finding the right idea often involves search procedures—talking with other managers, assigning a task force to investigate the problem, sending out a request to suppliers, or asking creative people within the organization to develop a solution. The creation of a new idea requires organic conditions. This is a good opportunity to encourage employee participation, because employees need the freedom to think about and explore new options.[106] Toyota's suggestion system has generated an estimated 20 million suggestions over 40 years and the average number of suggestions per employees is estimated at 50.[107]
5. *Develop plans to overcome resistance to change.* Many good ideas are never used because managers failed to anticipate or prepare for resistance to change by consumers, employees, or other managers. No matter how impressive the performance characteristics of an innovation, its implementation will conflict with some interests and jeopardize some alliances in the organization. To increase the chance of successful implementation, management must acknowledge the conflict, threats, and potential losses perceived by employees. Several strategies can be used by managers to overcome the resistance problem:
    - *Alignment with needs and goals of users.* The best strategy for overcoming resistance is to make sure change meets a real need. Employees in R&D often come up with great ideas that solve nonexistent problems. This happens because initiators fail to consult with the intended users. Resistance can be frustrating for managers, but moderate resistance to change is good for an organization. Resistance provides a barrier to frivolous changes and to change for the sake of change. The process of overcoming resistance to change normally requires that the change be good for its users.

- *Communication and training.* Communication means informing users about the need for change and the consequences of a proposed change, preventing rumours, misunderstanding, and resentment. In one study of change efforts, the most commonly cited reason for failure was that employees learned of the change from outsiders. Top managers concentrated on communicating with the public and shareholders but failed to communicate with the people who would be most intimately involved with and most affected by the change—their own employees.[108] Open communication often gives management an opportunity to explain what steps will be taken to ensure that the change will have no adverse consequences for employees. Training is also needed to help employees understand and cope with their role in the change process.
- *An environment that affords psychological safety.* Psychological safety means that people feel a sense of confidence that they will not be embarrassed or rejected by others in the organization. People need to feel secure and capable of making the changes that are asked of them.[109] Change requires that people be willing to take risks and do things differently, but many people are fearful of trying something new if they think they might be embarrassed by mistakes or failure. Managers support psychological safety by creating a climate of trust and mutual respect in the organization. "Not being afraid someone is laughing at you helps you take genuine risks," says Andy Law, one of the founders of St. Luke's, an advertising agency based in London, England.[110]
- *Participation and involvement.* Early and extensive participation in a change should be part of implementation. Participation gives those involved a sense of control over the change activity. They understand it better, and they become committed to successful implementation. One study of the implementation and adoption of technology systems at two companies showed a much smoother implementation process at the company that introduced the new technology using a participatory approach.[111] The team-building and large group intervention activities described earlier can be effective ways to involve employees in a change process.
- *Forcing and coercion.* As a last resort, managers may overcome resistance by threatening employees with the loss of jobs or promotions or by firing or transferring them. In other words, management power is used to overwhelm resistance. In most cases, this approach is not advisable because it leaves people angry at change managers, and the change may be sabotaged. However, this technique may be needed when speed is essential, such as when the organization faces a crisis. It may also be required for needed administrative changes that flow from the top down, such as downsizing the workforce.[112]

6. *Create change teams.* Throughout this chapter the need for resources and energy to make change happen has been discussed. Separate creative departments, new-venture groups, and ad hoc teams or task forces are ways to focus energy on both creation and implementation. A separate department has the freedom to create a new technology that fits a genuine need. A task force can be created to see that implementation is completed. The task force can be responsible for communication, involvement of users, training, and other activities needed for change.

PDA

Remember...

Lead employees through the three stages of commitment to change—preparation, acceptance, and commitment—and use techniques to achieve successful implementation. These include obtaining top management support, implementing the change in a series of steps, assigning change teams or idea champions, and overcoming resistance by actively communicating with workers and encouraging their participation in the change process.

7. *Foster idea champions.* One of the most effective weapons in the battle for change is the idea champion. The most effective champion is a volunteer champion who is deeply committed to a new idea. The idea champion sees that all technical activities are correct and complete. An additional champion, such as a manager sponsor, may also be needed to persuade people about implementation, even using coercion if necessary.

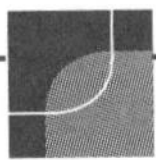

Summary and Interpretation

Organizations face a dilemma. Managers prefer to organize day-to-day activities in a predictable, routine manner. However, change—not stability—is the natural order of things in today's global environment. Thus, organizations need to build in change as well as stability, to facilitate innovation as well as efficiency.

Most change in organizations is incremental, but there is a growing emphasis on the need for radical change. Four types of change—technology, products and services, strategy and structure, and culture—may give an organization a competitive edge, and managers can make certain each of the necessary ingredients for change is present.

For technical innovation, which is of concern to most organizations, an organic structure that encourages employee autonomy works best because it encourages a bottom-up flow of ideas. Other approaches are to establish a separate department charged with creating new technical ideas, establish venture teams or idea incubators, and encourage idea champions. New products and services generally require cooperation among several departments, so horizontal linkage is an essential part of the innovation process.

For changes in strategy and structure, a top-down approach is typically best. These innovations are in the domain of top administrators who take responsibility for restructuring, for downsizing, and for changes in policies, goals, and control systems.

Culture changes are also generally the responsibility of top management. Some recent trends that may create a need for broad-scale culture change in the organization are re-engineering, the shift to horizontal forms of organizing, greater organizational diversity, and the learning organization. All of these changes require significant shifts in employee and manager attitudes and ways of working together. One method for bringing about this level of culture change is organization development (OD). OD focuses on the human and social aspects of the organization and uses behavioural science knowledge to bring about changes in attitudes and relationships.

Finally, the implementation of change can be difficult. Strong leadership is needed to guide employees through the turbulence and uncertainty and build organization-wide commitment to change. A number of barriers to change exist, including excessive focus on cost, failure to perceive benefits, lack of coordination and cooperation, individual uncertainty avoidance, and fear of loss. Managers can thoughtfully plan how to deal with resistance to increase the likelihood of success. Techniques that will facilitate implementation are to establish a sense or urgency for change; establish a coalition to guide the change; create a vision and strategy for change; develop plans to overcome resistance by aligning with the needs and goals of users, creating communication and training, providing psychological safety, encouraging participation and involvement, and, in rare cases, forcing the innovation if necessary; create change teams; and foster idea champions.

Key Concepts

ambidextrous approach, p. 382
change process, p. 379
creative departments, p. 383
creativity, p. 379
culture changes, p. 377
dual-core approach, p. 390
horizontal coordination model, p. 387
idea champion, p. 384
idea incubator, p. 383
incremental change, p. 374
large group intervention, p. 395
management champion, p. 385
new-venture fund, p. 384
organization development, p. 394
organizational change, p. 378
organizational innovation, p. 378
product and service changes, p. 376
radical change, p. 374
skunkworks, p. 384
strategy and structure changes, p. 377
switching structures, p. 383
team building, p. 395
technical champion, p. 385
technology changes, p. 377
time-based competition, p. 389
venture teams, p. 384

Discussion Questions

1. How is the management of radical change likely to differ from the management of incremental change?
2. How are organic characteristics related to changes in technology? to administrative changes?
3. Describe the dual-core approach. How does administrative change normally differ from technology change? Discuss.
4. How might organizations manage the dilemma of needing both stability and change? Discuss.
5. Why do organizations experience resistance to change? What steps can managers take to overcome this resistance?
6. "Bureaucracies are not innovative." Discuss.
7. A noted organization theorist said, "Pressure for change originates in the environment; pressure for stability originates within the organization." Do you agree? Discuss.
8. Of the seven elements required for successful change, which element do you think managers are most likely to overlook? Discuss.
9. How do the underlying values of organization development compare to the values underlying other types of change? Why do the values underlying OD make it particularly useful in shifting to a learning organization?
10. The manager of R&D for a drug company said that only 5 percent of the company's new products ever achieve market success. He also said the industry average is 10 percent and wondered how his organization might increase its success rate. If you were acting as a consultant, what advice would you give him concerning organizational structure?
11. Review the stages of commitment to change illustrated in Exhibit 11.9 and the seven techniques for implementing change discussed on page 398. At which stage of change commitment would each of the seven techniques most likely be used?

Chapter 11 Workbook: Innovation Climate*

In order to examine differences in the level of innovation encouragement in organizations, you will be asked to rate two organizations. The first should be an organization in which you have worked, or the college or university. The second should be someone else's workplace, that of a family member, a friend, or an acquaintance. You will have to interview that person to answer the questions below. You should put your own answers in column A, your interviewee's answers in column B, and what you think would be the ideal in column C.

Innovation Measures

Item of Measure	A Your Organization	B Other Organization	C Your Ideal
Score items 1–5 on this scale: *1 = disagree completely to 5 = agree completely*			
1. Creativity is encouraged here.*			
2. People are allowed to solve the same problems in different ways.*			
3. I get to pursue creative ideas.**			
4. The organization publicly recognizes and also rewards those who are innovative.**			
5. Our organization is flexible and always open to change.*			
Score items 6–10 on the opposite scale: *1 = agree completely to 5 = don't agree at all*			
6. The primary job of people here is to follow orders that come from the top.*			
7. The best way to get along here is to think and act like the others.*			
8. This place seems to be more concerned with the status quo than with change.*			
9. People are rewarded more if they don't rock the boat.**			
10. New ideas are great, but we don't have enough people or money to carry them out.**			

*These items indicate the organization's innovation climate.

**These items show resource support.

Questions

1. What comparisons in terms of innovation climates can you make between these two organizations?
2. How might productivity differ between a climate that supports innovation and a climate that does not?
3. Where would you rather work? Why?

*Adapted by Dorothy Marcic from Susanne G. Scott and Reginald A. Bruce, "Determinants of Innovative Behavior: A Path Model of Individual Innovation in the Workplace," *Academy of Management Journal* 37, no. 3 (1994), 580–607.

Case for Analysis: The Delta Change Process at the Mutual Group*

The Delta Change Process at the Mutual Group

Linda Padfield paused at the antiquated vault which stood at the centre of the atrium in the "old section" of The Mutual Group building. The vault's sheer size was impressive. Its heavy steel structure and capable locks offered a kind of security that most took for granted a few years ago at this large, Waterloo, Ontario-based insurance company. But even brass and thick stainless steel could not fend off changes in the industry itself. She continued back to her desk, an open concept location at one end of the old section.

On the way, she thought back to the slide show she had presented a few hours earlier. The presentation detailed the sweeping process of change which The Mutual Group [TMG] had undergone in the past two years. Each time she presented it, she felt as though she understood the process better, yet inevitably, as many questions as answers resulted from these presentations. This time she had taken notes on several emerging issues that she wanted to consider more closely.

Linda was the Project Manager of what had been dubbed the "Delta" change process. Her current role of Training and Quality Service Consulting Officer put her in a position to recognize and help deal with the outcomes of this process, what she often referred to as "the Daughters of Delta". Today, with a sheet of unanswered questions looming in front of her, she was inclined to think of these outcomes as the "Prodigal Sons". Intuitively, she knew that the change had to happen, they did what had to be done; the staid old world that the insurance industry had enjoyed so long had fallen to the forces of increased competition. And the change process they had employed, focusing on guiding principles and not knowing the answers before they began, although more ambiguous than striving for targets, certainly had more integrity, and appeared to have been successful.

Still, there were no solid measures as to whether what they had achieved was the right thing. Time would tell, but for right now, glancing down the list of questions, she struggled for answers.

Notes from Presentation, September 1, 1996

- How would they keep the process of change going?
- Was the organization restructuring successful?
- Had they moved from a culture of entitlement to one of self-sufficiency?
- Were the levels of service chosen in the process appropriate?
- How could The Mutual Group maintain Truly Corporate services & at the same time increase the autonomy of the business units?
- Was the move toward decentralization the best one in all cases?

The ambiguity that now characterized The Mutual Group culture was a startling contrast to the certainty embodied in the vault. But she was more intrigued than unsettled by these questions about the outcomes of Delta. She didn't have immediate answers, but felt confident they were on the right track.

The Insurance Industry: External Pressures for Change

The Canadian life and health insurance industry provides financial security products to more than 20 million Canadians. A 1996 independent rating agency report stated that the earnings outlook for the industry was the best in three years and Canadian companies were among the strongest in the world.

While the outlook was good, the nature of the industry was changing. The marketplace was dramatically shifting, and through the 1990s the insurance industry was faced with rapid and increasingly intense competition. In particular, the banks posed a formidable challenge to the other players in the industry. The Canadian Imperial Bank of Commerce had stated publicly that it would be able to take away business from organizations such as The Mutual Group, and the industry anticipated head-to-head bank competition by the year 1997. The life insurance industry had appealed to the Federal Department of Finance, concerned about the regulatory advantages enjoyed by the banks, the concentration of power, and issues of privacy. While current regulations did not allow it, the banks' insurance operations might ultimately have access to the customer data bases of the financial operations, which would give them a distinct marketing advantage. As well, banks have highly developed information systems which would minimize their cost of administering policies. Bank branches, with their large menu of services, are a more efficient and less expensive method of sales compared to independent agents. However, the Consumers Association of Canada (CAC) stated to the Department of Finance that:

> *... many Canadian consumers would respond less favourably to the concept of bank retailing if they were aware of some of the potential drawbacks. CAC fears that bank retailing of insurance will provide more opportunity for oligopolistic behaviour in the marketplace, which will mean less price competition and less consumer choice. (Del Piero 1995: 5)*

The Mutual Group had joined the industry in its opposition to the extension of insurance powers to the banks. While uncertain about the impact of these new entrants upon the industry, they were preparing to face increased competition in the near future.

The market was also changing, as consumer attitudes shifted away from savings-type products with low margins.

Customer demands had increased with a growing emphasis placed on service and access to top quality products at lower prices. With the issue of quality coming centre-stage, consumers were relying more on rating agencies to assess the stability of financial institutions. As a result of pressure on margins and devalued investments in real estate ratings, companies such as Royal Trustco experienced poor profitability and a rapid downgrading in ratings. Confederation Life, a company with the same longevity as The Mutual Group and some of the same traditions, was also downgraded as a consequence of poor real estate investments. In fact, it was downgraded four times in just over two years and finally went bankrupt. The collapse of insurers began to question the credibility of those who remained, and the rating agencies were demanding a lot more from companies such as The Mutual Group to retain their top rating.

The Mutual Group: Internal Considerations

Pressures from the external environment meant The Mutual Group had to be increasingly concerned with developing a long-term strategy. The strategy would have to balance resource allocation to align with business needs and focus on results. A blanket reduction in costs was attempted the year before, under the assumption that resources were allocated in the optimal arrangement. Many employees were frustrated by this approach, which focused simply on setting a target for cutting costs. In order to balance cost-cutting and quality, a better re-allocaton of resources to various services and activities was needed.

It was essential to maintain this balance of quality and cost-cutting in order to improve margins, increase competitiveness, and ultimately make The Mutual Group a better place to work, providing rewarding careers for everyone.

Corporate Services

The Corporate Services Division has approximately 800 employees who provide services to other business units within The Mutual Group. Corporate Services includes Information Systems, Finance and Corporate Actuarial, Strategy Development and Corporate Planning, Corporate Affairs, Legal Services and Human Resources.

Prior to 1993, the organization was structured with some internal service departments reporting to the CEO and some reporting to operating units. These operating units in turn would report to the President (Exhibit 1).

In early 1993, Jack Masterman, then CEO, retired and became Chairman of the Board. Robert Astely took over duties as President and Chief Executive Officer of the Mutual Group. With this change in leadership came a change in the organization structure. Operating and Internal Service functions now both reported to the same person. The internal service function became a separate division headed by a Senior VP of Corporate Services (Exhibit 2).

In March of 1993, Mary Anne Elliot was hired as the Senior VP of Corporate Services. Mary Anne came from an HR position at GE where she had worked for 14 years. One of Mary Anne's strengths was her change management skills, and one of her mandates was to help bring these skills into the organization. She was in favour of a collaborative management style. Communication was of key importance to her, and she made herself available to all employees.

In meetings with business unit managers, Mary Anne became aware that the high cost of internal services was a serious concern to them. In fact, it was often difficult for those working within Corporate Services to see their contribution to the corporate bottom line. They were removed from the external client, and so it was difficult to align themselves with what was important. Others within the company were also not clear on the value added by Corporate Services.

Recognizing the need to address this concern, Mary Anne proposed a new strategy team consisting of the seven V.P.'s of the new Corporate Services division. These V.P.'s had developed the existing organziation and had large personal investments in it. However, they had not worked together in the past and were initially cool to the idea. As a result, Mary Anne conducted some research to identify people within Corporate Services who shared her concern for change. This team consisted of herself and three others: an internal consultant, a planner, and the Director of Finance. This group met through the summer and developed a plan for Corporate Services. In the fall of 1993, Mary Anne asked that each V.P. nominate the person who they believed could best represent their department on a "Vision Team". These people were then asked if they would dedicate half of their time over the next six months to work on the Vision Team project. This was just the beginning of the Mutual Group's serious commitment of resources to the change process.

Their goal was to develop a vision and direction for Corporate Services. After talks with some 80 managers for the four different business units, this group came to an initial diagnosis of the Mutual Group's situation. They described Corporate Services as having a "civil service" attitude with a lack of accountability for costs and a low concern for quality of service. Within Corporate Services, a "culture of entitlement" existed. Many were not aware of the external competitive environment. They had been in a sheltered and paternalistic culture for a very long time, a tradition of no layoffs or firings, and didn't see or feel the need for change.

The Delta Team Forms

In January of 1994 the Vision Team moved to the next step of getting the V.P.s involved. A consultant was hired to engage the V.P.s in a team building process.

After this training took place the nine members of the Vision Team combined with the 7 person V.P. team to form the "Delta Team". The 16 person Delta Team's mandate was to facilitate the development of a long-term strategy for Corporate Services and oversee the implementation of that strategy. The purpose of the strategy was to reduce costs and to improve services by re-engineering Corporate Services' activities and organization, as well as Corporate Services relationships with other divisions of the company.

The Delta Way: A Principled Approach to Change

From January to June of 1994, the Delta team was dedicated to the development of the Corporate Services Long-Term Strategy.

One of the first operating principles of the team was that of engagement. Engagement meant involving those who would be affected by the changes in the development of the strategy (Exhibit 3 is how engagement was explained to Corporate Services staff). Meetings with hundreds of Corporate Services staff took place at the individual and small-group level. In this way, the Delta Team's ideas could be discussed and amended based on feedback received before the ideas were fixed in place.

The Delta Team based their strategy on five guiding principles, rather than strict rules or targets. The intent of this was to allow for innovative solutions to be reached on how to allocate resources in a way that was aligned with the needs of the business and was focused on results.

These five guiding principles were:

- Competitive Advantage
- Cost/Value Equation
- Relationships
- Diversity
- Urgency and Accountability

Competitive Advantage meant that The Mutual Group would be adopting a new approach for making decisions about resource allocation. The degree of competitive advantage a service would provide would be crucial in determining the amount of resources that would be devoted to any service. The Mutual Group would invest in services that offered competitive advantage. In addition they would shrink the cost and use of essential services that didn't provide competitive advantage, and would continuously look for less expensive options. Essential services were defined as something that TMG had to do at least some of in order to remain in business. The Mutual Group would stop providing non-essential services both internally and externally that did not provide competitive advantage.

The degree of competitive advantage a service provided would be measured in each of five levels of a pyramid. To provide competitive advantage, a service would

lead to long-term financial & organizational strengthenhance the ability to innovatefacilitate increased revenue reduce the unit cost reduction of TMG's products deliver required level of services at lowest sustainable cost (must exist in all services)

Moving from bottom to top in the competitive advantage pyramid meant increasing in the level of long-term impact a service would have. Competitive advantage would be defined by the external market place; the degree to which Corporate Services contributed to the competitive advantage of The Mutual Group's products in the marketplace would have to be measured. The more levels a service provided, the more likely it would be to yield a high degree of competitive advantage.

Cost/Value Equation meant that Corporate Services and business services must make decisions based on the cost and value of services. To do this, the costs must be visible and competitive. Both current costs and future costs must be considered. The level of acceptable costs would be defined by the marketplace.

Delta defined the ***Relationships*** between users and providers of services *within* the Mutual Group as different from external suppliers who are motivated by increasing their own income and increasing reliance on their service. Internal service providers should work to decrease reliance on their services and maximize the client's revenue. Since both the users and providers of the services within The Mutual Group are in the same business, they should have aligned goals; they share the rewards of success and the costs of failure. This principle in the Long-Term Strategy was intended to assist the providers in understanding the user's needs, negotiate the terms of their relationships, and negotiate conflicts with respect to the best interests of TMG.

The principle of ***Diversity*** acknowledged that different business units have different needs. For this reason, a lesser emphasis was placed on consistency, and there was a greater acceptance of the diversity of the business units and their identity as a "federation of businesses". This would mean increased decision-making autonomy, as each unit made more informed, more competitive decisions in its operating marketplace. As of June 1994, many of these business units were paying for the same level of service, regardless of their specific needs as defined by the market. This would be expected to change, with each business paying for its particular service requirement.

Urgency and Accountability meant that fundamental changes would need to take place in the attitudes, values, and beliefs of the Mutual Group's traditional culture. A sense of urgency was necessary to respond rapidly to changing market conditions. A sense that one was in partnership with clients, and accountable for decisions made was also necessary to support the new culture. This culture would encourage innovation, learning, and decision-making closest to the client, and discourage decision-making that operated solely via the reporting hierarchy.

Roll-out of the Long-Term Strategy

On June 30 of 1994, the Corporate Services Long-Term Strategy was presented to the 800 employees in the division in groups of 50. Many were still unsure of this consultative approach to management. In the past, orders always came top-down and the roles of both management and the employees were very well-defined; management knew the answers and the employees followed their direction. The Long-Term Strategy challenged these familiar roles, and was met with a mixture of interest, suspicion and anxiety, depending on each person's inclination. Those who had been at the Mutual Group for a number of years, and were most familiar with the longstanding paternalistic approach to management found it especially difficult to accept what they were hearing.

Mary Anne started the Rollout with these words;

How many of you think that I am here to downsize the organization? Come on? Is that all? Ok, then, how many of you have heard a rumour that the reason I came to The Mutual Group was to eliminate as many jobs as I could?

With the extra encouragement, Mary Anne was now facing a sea of reluctantly offered hands. It confirmed what she knew was true: a high level of suspicion still surrounded this change process. This was understandable, as it really wasn't the way which the Mutual Group was known to do business. She silently renewed her commitment to do anything and everything to continuously communicate throughout the change effort, an essential element to building trust throughout this new way of doing business.

Mary Anne continued;

Well, that's not why I'm here. You can trust me now or later, but I'll tell you what the Long-Term Strategy is all about. The objectives are really two-fold. First, we want to provide information to the business areas about the services which our department provides, and their costs, so that together we can determine what value each service has to them. Second, by doing this we can determine which activities Corporate Services should invest in, which to shrink, and which to stop altogether.

The way that this will be done is by following a set of guiding principles. We do not have targets. We do not have answers. We aren't looking just to cut jobs, or to cut services. We will follow this process, and by using the guiding principles, together we will learn what the face of the new organization will look like.

Mary Anne then went on to explain what the guiding principles were and the role which they would play in the evaluation of services.

I must repeat: we don't know how the new organization will look. Based on the guiding principles, these are our expected outcomes:

- *We want to have real sustainable cost savings in 1995 and beyond.*
- *We need to build a model of what we are doing that is both usable and flexible. Change will have to be an ongoing process here at The Mutual Group if we want to remain competitive with the rest of the industry. We don't want to just use this approach once and put it on the shelf. It's a new way of doing business.*
- *We want a flexible structure to be able to react quickly to market forces.*
- *We need the business units to work with us to define needs and service levels.*
- *We want business units to be able to tailor services based on market requirements.*
- *Truly Corporate services should be minimized, explicit, and widely understood. These are services performed for the sole purpose of the Corporation. That is, things required by law, and those designated to be of strategic importance. You might consider these activities "the price of admission" to The Mutual Group. We want to minimize the Truly Corporate and emphasize a diversity of needs.*
- *We want to enhance our partnership between Corporate Services and the business units. We envision working together to assess options and needs as the only way to provide quality services.*
- *If a different organizational structure is required to administer these outcomes, we will deal with that once the process has been followed. But whether a service should be centralized or decentralized is not the main issue. What is important is the relationship and method of delivering the service, the rest will follow. In general, Truly Corporate activities would naturally be centralized while those which the business units should manage will most likely be decentralized. Those services which fall in between will require the organization's structure to be negotiated. We will do this by taking into account managing costs, technical expertise, accountability, responsibilities, and risk management.*

Overall, we want costs to be visible and understood. This is the key principle we are operating on, and the key outcome desired from the change process.

Mary Anne paused to answer some questions. She could tell by some of the looks she was getting that there were those who were interested in the process, and others, perhaps the majority, who looked uncomfortable and were turning to their neighbours to make comments. Not discouraged by this, and realizing it would take months of committed actions to win many employees over to this participative strategy, she continued to describe the decision-making model.

There is going to be an issue of resourcing. Because we are engaging you in this process your time will be divided between your everyday responsibilities and the Long-Term Strategy. Some will have more demands on their time than others but everyone is asked to be involved in the decision-making in some capacity.

The decision-making model will be quite different than anything you have experienced so far at The Mutual

Group. Instead of decisions being made by management and passed along to the employees as orders to follow, you will all be involved in this procedure. The model may intimidate some of you because there are no clear-cut rules, only guidelines. There is a series of steps to be followed to evaluate the services and to make choices, but the model is based on the guiding principles and as such, requires judgement. By following these principles, your judgement should be consistent with the objectives of the change process we discussed earlier.

I can appreciate that for many of you this is may be a complex and unsettling new way of operating. But we hope that through the Delta change process both The Mutual Group and its employees will benefit, and that while your work may be more difficult at first it will also be more rewarding.

With those words Mary Anne finished the presentation. She took time to answer questions from the group, and then the employees returned back to their work.

A great deal of discussion and differences in opinions were aired after the roll-out:

"How are we going to have Truly Corporate activities if everyone is in it for themselves?" remarked one employee to another as they were walking out.

"What do you mean everyone is 'in it for themselves'", her counterpart responded. "We are doing what is best for The Mutual Group and that's good for all of us".

"Sounds like legislated anarchy to me" remarked a manager.

"Well, it's either that or we go down with a sinking ship", offered another manager.

"The world outside of Waterloo isn't standing still and we can't either if we want to have a company to work for."

The buzz in the organization for the next few months was about what services would be cut and which ones would survive. Even services like the cafeteria and the daycare program, once strong institutions in the paternalistic culture, were unlikely to continue, based on the Guiding Principles. Many employees still believed that The Mutual Group could not cut such services; it was unimaginable.

The Change Procedure Begins

By July 1, 1994 a report including a draft list of processes had been completed. Linda Padfield was selected as the Project Manager for the Delta change effort and her role would be to ensure the integrity of the evaluation procedure and to coordinate training throughout Delta. Each of the steps in the Delta change effort was worked on in partnership between service users and providers. The first stage was to identify processes, purposes, client needs and activities.

Processes

All of Corporate Service's activities were to be represented by approximately 50 processes (which were later reduced to 25 processes). Processes included such items as compensating employees, corporate communications and maintaining head office/branch office buildings and grounds, among others. Exhibit 7a illustrates one such process.

Purposes/Client Needs

Purposes and/or Client Needs would be identified for each process. Purposes/Client Needs can be understood as the goals of each of the processes. Purposes were to be documented by identifying those which had legal requirements, those which were business unit supported and those which were Truly Corporate.

Activities

Each of these processes would consist of a number of activities. The size of the activities was to be around $250 000 to $1 million or 5 to 20 FTEs (full time equivalents, since there were many part-time employees at The Mutual Group); any more than this and people were not breaking it down far enough and any less and they were breaking it down too much. The number of activities would vary with each process. For example, the process "Maintaining Head Office/Branch Office Buildings and Grounds", would consist of activities such as "Building Operations—External" and "Building Operations—Internal".

Sub-Activities

These activities would then be broken down further into "sub-activities". To continue with the above example, the activity of "Building Operations—External" would have sub-activities such as Lawn Maintenance, Exterior Gardening and Landscaping, Snow Removal, and External Building Maintenance (see Exhibit 4). Levels of service would then be determined for each of these sub-activities.

By Aug 1 a list of processes, 23 in all (Exhibit 5), had been confirmed. The senior leadership team assigned a Process Team Leader for each process, drawing them from the ranks of middle managers. As the Delta Project unfolded, the Process Team Leader role was to become one of the most stressful roles in the change project (the different roles of those involved in the Delta change project are list in Exhibit 6). Each Process Team Leader was requested to select a service provider team for his or her process and to attempt to ensure balanced representation from all parts of the process. Some did so. Others traded off on the issue of balance and placed more emphasis on selecting people they believed could contribute most effectively to their service provider term. The service provider teams for each process numbered between 8 and 12 people. In total, about 250 people were involved in the Delta project. The people who would fill these roles were identified and their training undertaken.

Senior managers of the four business units (Individual, U.S., Group, and Investment business units) were then assigned to meet with the 23 service provider teams and implementation began with the service providers and business unit managers working in partnership to determine the impact of the Long-Term Strategy on each of the processes. Service providers were not legislated any numerical goals. However, if they could not present a level of service starting at 50% they were required to explain why.

Communication teams were developed to promote a greater understanding concerning the transition among the employees. They were to receive information and feedback information. These teams were led by those who did not normally supervise people in that team. All Corporate and Senior Officers in the Corporate Services Division were assigned the task of leading a communication team. Teams were to comprise about 25 people each, with everyone in Corporate Services represented. They were required to conduct team meetings every two weeks and other meetings, large and small, were called when the need was identified by members of these teams. About 35 communication teams were formed. They were deliberately cross-functional and cross-level and involved everyone in the Corporate Services Division. These teams were required to meet beginning in July 1994 and would continue meeting until early 1995.

Some employees felt that the Communication Teams were not very well equipped. They had varying degrees of knowledge and skill; team leaders were randomly picked and were exclusively from senior management. Although there were only supposed to be 25 people in each team, groups of about 35 emerged. Some felt these groups were too large, and that the meetings were inconsistent. Because this was an important venue to share information and voice concerns with the communication leader, several employees expressed the opinion that it would have been better to have leaders from all levels and to have smaller groups. As well, this was an avant-garde approach to communication for The Mutual Group; some were not ready for it and did not attend meetings. They believed more traditional methods of communication such as a newsletter should have been used in conjunction with the meetings. Those who did not attend the meetings were often perceived as being more cynical than others.

The Principle of Engagement

The implementation of the Strategy involved increased "engagement" of the members of the Corporate Services division. Engagement was one of the first operating principles the Delta Team developed (Exhibit 3). Engagement meant:

- Being participative and actively seeking input from as many people as possible, but particularly directly involving the people who needed to be involved.
- As the Delta's Teams thinking emerged, exposing it to others in Corporate Services and the business units for feedback.
- Laying the foundation for ideas by talking about them widely before they were set in stone, and amending the ideas based on feedback received.

Introducing engagement was a challenge for the Delta Team. People were accustomed to receiving concrete direction. What Delta was initially delivering was often vague, general and intangible, sometimes leading to frustration and rumours. Linda Padfield, Delta Team Project Manager commented:

Engagement is time consuming and has meant meetings with literally hundreds of people. We'd have liked to have engaged more people more often in the development of the strategy than we ended up doing. We have learned a lot about engagement, and how we can do better at it. We'll be trying to apply those learnings as we continue this engagement process through implementation of the strategy.

Engagement was an important element in the next step, which was to determine the levels of service for the activities within the process. While everyone did not have direct involvement in determining levels of service, each person was given avenues for their ideas and concerns to be heard. This was a challenging aspect to the engagement process which could not be successful without individual commitment.

Some areas used the principle of engagement more effectively than others. Some managers were uncomfortable with the consultative approach and struggled with their new role. There was difficulty which emerged in certain cases where employees wanted not only to be heard but to see that they had been heard. While some said this was not always realistic, others felt certain leaders were simply paying lip-service to the engagement process. In many cases the process of engagement generated frustation and opportunity to be directly involved and people at all levels seemed to feel that it contributed a great deal to the process, both in enhancing its integrity and in generating creative ideas.

Determining Levels of Service Through the Decision-Making Model

The decision-making model used in determining the levels of service was a business-process based approach. It was supported by the Guiding Principles and was built around the processes which the Mutual Group engaged in. It questioned why the Mutual Group needed to perform certain activities and what contribution these processes offered.

Because the decision-making model was built on the concept of levels of service around which decisions may be made, it required breaking down activities into levels (Exhibit 4 illustrates how an activity—*Building Operations-External*—within the process "*Head Office and Branch Office Buildings and Grounds*", is broken down into different levels of service). The levels of service were thought of as blocks which could be stacked or ranked. Blocks at the bottom were those which provided the most benefit relative to cost with boxes higher up the stack providing incremental benefit for incremental cost. If an activity had an essential level of service then it would be the first block in the stack.

Exhibits 7A-7E are drawn from a document that was distributed to all Corporate Services employees to illustrate the approach to be used to re-examine each Corporate Services process. "*Communicating with employees*", is an example of a typical, though fictitious, Corporate Services process. Exhibit 7A identifies the process, its purpose or client needs, and the activities it comprises. Each service provider team, working with representatives of each of the four business units simultaneously, develops blocks of subactivities and creates stacks of the blocks in ascending order of essential to less essential levels of service. Exhibit 7B illustrates the process for one typical activity called *Mutual Express* which supports the purpose of "*aligning employees with The Mutual Group's vision*"). Stacks of blocks for "like" activities are then compared and merged to form a common stack (Exhibit 7C). Then stacks of "unlike" activities are compared and merged to form a single stack for all the Corporate Services associated with that particular process (Exhibit 7D). There could be very many blocks in a stack. For example, one of the largest of the Corporate Services processes developed a completed stack of 297 blocks.

After the first part of the decision-making was completed, all processes were then prioritized with the value of the service determined by the degree of competitive advantage it conferred. A line was drawn by the business units based on their strategy and needs (Exhibit 7E), and also with input from senior management. This line delineated between services that would receive resources, and those that would not. These levels of service were to be revisited every two years. (In the example of the Corporates Services processes with 297 blocks, the first 144 blocks were considered essential services, the next 62 blocks were incremental levels of service that were retained. Ninety-one blocks were above the line and were no longer eligible for resources, which meant elimination.)

Outsourcing was suggested to both business unit partners and service providers as an option but core competencies (those things that must be kept within the company even at a higher cost) had to be defined. For this purpose, a "Best Practices" comparison was undertaken. Costs were to be compared outside of The Mutual Group to see if they were providing services as effectively as possible. Other companies were consulted which specialized in the service, both within and outside of the financial services industry.

While employees were encouraged not to be inhibited by the organization's current structure, some had more difficulty than others thinking "outside of the box". It seemed that if you had a dynamic team who were very driven to take the initiative you could be creative and generate quality solutions. Employees felt that a diverse enough group allowed them to be innovative and others believed that the level of innovation depended on how entrenched you were in a department. Some employees thought their group did not do the benchmarking well. They were concerned that there were no checks in place to push the employees to be innovative and nothing to ensure the quality of decisions that were being made.

Ambiguity and Change

Most employees felt that the Guiding Principles, which were oriented to the external environment and represented in the decision-making model, helped them to make sound decisions and value-added changes that were consistent with the needs of the Mutual Group. For many it helped to take the emotion out of the analysis. However, this was the first major change the organization had gone through and some were not comfortable with the ambiguity associated with the Delta Project and the decision-making model. It was tough for them not to think in targets. Employees who were very analytical had trouble with the ambiguity. Certain groups handled this better than others.

The Mutual Group had a reputation as an organization that was uncomfortable with uncertainty, by nature of the very business they were in. It was difficult for people to hear "I don't know" and just as trying for managers to deliver the phrase. The manager's role had changed, away from directing, toward facilitating and mobilizing; however, some couldn't change as fast as their roles. This created a significant amount of stress for those leading, and those led. At the same time, it also provided a vehicle for innovation and change. Things emerged through the indefinite approach which people wouldn't have imagined changing had they been locked into a more traditional strategy. It helped many to dig deeper and be more resourceful. Mary Anne maintained that it allowed the Mutual Group to develop a strategy that was not just an operating plan. The approach which was taken relied upon a great deal of immediate trust from employees. It was a struggle for some, especially at the beginning; people felt they could not spend the time or were doubtful that it would work. But as time went on, and people witnessed the events, many developed faith in the approach and in management.

While it was an ambitious time line, starting in July 1994 with a target date of all the changes being identified by December of 1994 and implementation completed by March 1995, people were eager to work through the Delta process quickly because of the ambiguity involved. In order to maintain the energy level necessary to have a quality project, employees were committed to the time line which had been outlined for them, even though it would mean that serious issues around resourcing might emerge.

The process was very complex and time consuming. An issue of resourcing did surface and was exacerbated by some unfortunate timing. Implementation was scheduled to begin December 5th, while a major acquisition of the

Canadian operations of the Prudential Insurancy Company took effect on December 6th. The stress mounted as employees struggled with how they could keep the business operating while going through the change. Through Delta they had a minimum level of staffing and tight time lines and pressure meant that communication and engagement had to happen quickly. Some employees felt that they missed a lot where attention to detail was concerned. While this happened so quickly, the culture did not evolve at the same pace. Many people did not buy into the fact that change would be an ongoing process and while Delta took place at a rapid rate, the psychological change was still an issue for them.

One of the outcomes of employing the decision-making model meant that the daycare facilities would be cut. Many of the employees were shocked, although they knew the move was driven by the Guiding Principles. Still, it was a symbol to many that this change was real and permanent, and the Mutual Group would never be the same.

Changes After Delta

Many things stopped working after Delta. Because of this, it became obvious that the Mutual Group was no longer organized properly. A transformation in the organization's structure became a necessary outcome, rather than a cause of the change. After all of the steps were completed then the best structure to manage these processes was determined. Management knew this would result in outcomes such as centralizing a service or decentralizing others.

Some of the smaller departments changed dramatically, both in numbers and functioning ability, as compared to larger departments. Because they were no longer allowed the luxury of a department of specialists, certain areas needed more of a team structure with no one person working alone on projects. Initially, departments conducted their own reorganization. However, an off-site job redesign was undertaken by senior management which resulted in further restructuring.

This restructuring was traumatic for many employees, especially those who had worked at the Mutual Group for many years. Even though the rationale was very well explained, a lot of emotional issues emerged for both management and employees.

Issues of governance surfaced through the Delta process which generated some conflict. While it made sense for certain things to be centralized, with diverse and more autonomous business units, a centralized service would have to produce a diverse level of service.

At the end of the Delta process, Human Resources was still a centralized function. In the subsequent organization redesign by Senior Management, Human Resources was decentralized to be more in tune with business unit needs. Some employees questioned the wisdom of this move, arguing that what Delta had achieved was a shifting of costs and responsibilities rather than streamlining, or eliminating services. They saw the decentralization of Human Resources as more expensive because they would now be designing competencies for divisions independently. While this was the trade-off, the immediacy and alignment which this structure facilitated was, arguably, of greater value. Employees questioned why the Delta change process did not account for these emergent issues with the Human Resource Department.

The new organization structure (Exhibit 8) presented a number of issues which still had to be addressed. While the Delta Project initially resulted in an increase in the autonomy of the business units, subsequently different areas seem to be moving back to more commonality within their autonomy. There is a recognition that there needs to be enough commonality to allow for standardized decision making frameworks. Even the change in reporting relationships has had a negative psychological effect, as some are now reporting to an employee who would have been considered a "subordinate" in the old structure.

Reassessing Levels of Service

Levels of service which were defined during Delta have now proved insufficient in many cases. Many business units are realizing that they need more or less of certain levels of service; while they bought X amount they are demanding Y. Some employees believe this happened because there was not enough engagement in the decision-making model and that this scenario could have been avoided or minimized with a more diverse group choosing the levels of service. In many cases, senior managers said "We don't need these services" but they were not in touch with what was necessary for the day-to-day operation of the business. Employees felt that some of them did not realize the value of the services they were choosing. The levels of service now have to be renegotiated in many cases. Employees were concerned that there was nothing to ensure the quality of the decisions that were being made.

Determining the Outcomes of Delta

Linda shut off her computer and moved some papers from her desk to a file drawer. A copy of the Mutual Group's Annual Report for 1995 fell out of the stack. She picked it up and leafed through, observing the values of trust, partnership, knowledge, relationships, integrity, flexibility and confidence which were listed throughout the slender volume. She felt good that many of these values were part of the new culture at the Mutual Group. Delta had certainly played a role in introducing employees to their worth and their necessity for the organization to prosper and for employees to be satisfied.

She read further, trying to clarify for herself the intuitive feeling that Delta had been, and was still, a positive driver in the Mutual Group's success. The report listed several items she could trace to Delta:

- lower unit costs which were a result of time spent re-engineering processes and reconsidering levels of service in the business units
- development of leading edge strategies on capital management, HR practices, organizational design, use of technology, and activity-based management and costing which made costs more visible and better-understood
- significant contribution to the acquisition, amalgamation and integration of the Prudential operations
- development of an integrated North American information technology strategy with a commitment to invest in resulting key initiatives to position the company to deliver effectively to clients in the future

The report further detailed that the Mutual Group had achieved strong financial results in 1995, earning $192 million, a 24% increase over 1994 (Exhibits 8 and 9). This achievement was partly a result of the Prudential acquisition which contributed to growth in premium and net income. However, Linda felt that Delta had also contributed to the bottom line.

She thought about other projects which had emerged so naturally after Delta. There was a distinction between the Delta "events" of the past two years and the Delta "process" which was ongoing. Delta taught people how to approach problems in a new way and how to think in terms of external conditions of the market place as well as considerations internal to the firm. A lot of recent projects had started because of this new way of thinking and were now operating using the Guiding Principles of Delta.

There were many outcomes of the Delta process that were less tangible than the projects but no less real. A high awareness of change developed in most employees. People spoke of the level of passion and enthusiasm as one result of Delta. In many groups there persisted an urgency to get better quicker which was in tune with the nature of the product market.

The Guiding Principles had helped to reshape the organization's culture. Delta had enhanced communication, encouraging a movement toward face to face interaction, getting closer to business partners to improve quality of services. This meant thinking of services, not just as overhead, but as an integral part of getting business done in conjunction with the business plan. The change in the organization structure meant that where, previously, Corporate Services did not exist as a coherent whole, now it does. Line partners now truly seem to appreciate the services which they receive. There is a higher level of trust in the organization as management built-up credibility through the process. When they said they did not have the answers, they did not and employees learned to have faith in this as Delta progressed.

The principle of engagement brought a level of integrity to the process. People appreciated being involved and innovative solutions emerged as employees took ownership of the project. Engagement widened the perspective of many of the employees and helped to facilitate the culture change which is just beginning.

Other outcomes, as Linda had either witnessed or heard from employees, were not so positive. The issues surrounding increased autonomy of the business units, resistance of rapid change, levels of service purchased, resourcing, and communication problems certainly had emerged. But she believed that the benefits far outweighed the problems. Delta had driven the stakes in the ground which allowed them to go forward. It helped them develop the ability to model things as they were doing them in order to pass those learnings on to the next effort. Still, where is the proof? It is difficult to evaluate any organizational change. Is a change that focuses on the process rather than the targets impossible to evaluate?

Linda glanced at the clock and was surprised to see that it was already 6:30. She packed the rest of her things and put on her coat. Change was an ongoing process and Delta was just the beginning, with Guiding Principles that would keep them in touch with the competitive environment. As she walked through the old section of The Mutual Group into the new she noticed that there were still lights on in several of the offices. The days were long but rewarding.

References

Del Piero, Kenton J.

1995 "An Application of Change Implementation Models". Unpublished Paper.

The Mutual Group

1994 Corporate Services Long-Term Strategy—Implementation Guide"

1994 "Corporate Services Long-Term Strategy—User's Guide"

1995 "Annual Report"

1995 "Corporate Services Long-Term Strategy—Slide Show Notes"

*Prepared for Professor Harvey Kolodny, Joseph L. Rotman School of Management, University of Toronto by Elizabeth C. Kurucz, Centre for Industrial Relations, University of Toronto. March 1997 (revised May 1998).

EXHIBIT 1
Corporate Structure Pre-1993

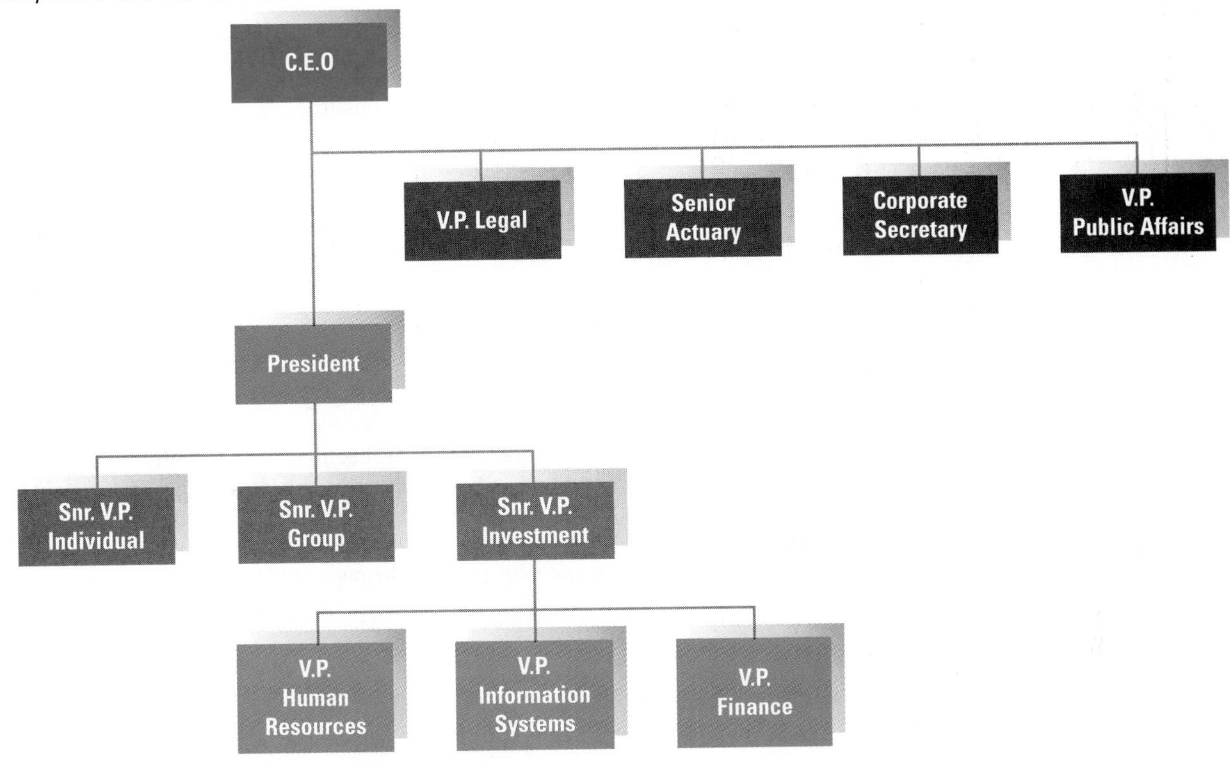

EXHIBIT 2
Corporate Structure with Consolidated Corporate Services

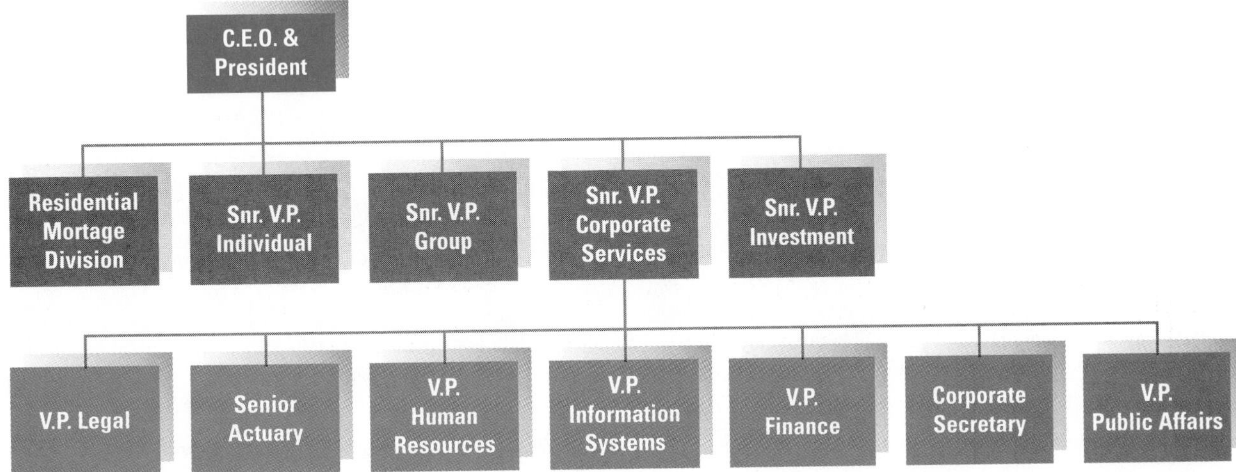

EXHIBIT 3
Engagement

- One of the first operating principles the Delta Team developed was something that became known as "engagement". Engagement means:
  - Actively seeking input from as many people as possible
  - Exposing the Delta Team's current thinking to others in Corporate Services and the business units for feedback as it emerges
  - Laying the foundation for ideas by talking about them widely before they are set in stone, and amending the ideas based on feedback received

Engagement has had its challenges:

- People are accustomed to receiving concrete direction—what Delta has been delivering so far has often been vague, general and intangible—sometimes leading to frustration and rumours
- Engagement is time consuming and has meant meetings with literally hundreds of people. We'd have liked to have engaged more people more often in the development of the strategy than we ended up doing. We have learned a lot about engagement, and how we can do better at it. We'll be trying to apply those learnings as we continue the engagement process through implementation of the strategy

Engagement has its rewards:

- Engagement is participatory
- Engagement directly involves the people who need to be involved

The implementation of the Strategy will involve increased engagement of the members of the Corporate Services division.

EXHIBIT 4
Levels of Service Worksheet
(optional for working out different service level packages)

PROCESS NAME: HO & BO Building and Grounds
ACTIVITY: Building Operations—External

Service Levels / Sub-Activities	Essential	Level 1 (max. of 50% of current)	Level 2 (increments of 15–20%)	Level 3
Lawn Maintenance	cut lawn twice/month remove noxious weeds →	spot spray lawn every 3 yrs. cut lawn once per week →	spray lawn annually →	
Exterior Gardening and Landscaping	trim trees once/year →	maintain garden court entrance flower beds →	limited external gardens →	provide display plants water office plants ~~limited external gardens~~
Snow Removal	within 24 hours of snowfall	sidewalks-immediate parking lot within 24 hours	sidewalks and parking lots immediate →	
External Building Maintenance		annual inspection →		

EXHIBIT 5
Corporate Services Processes

- Compensating employees
- Training, counselling, consulting, quality and education
- Wellness and staff services
- Hiring, induction, orienting and terminating employees
- Creative services
- Corporate communications
- Corporate image and reputation
- Governance
- Providing legal services
- Strategic planning
- Decision support for financial services
- Cost and risk management
- Financial transaction processing
- Head and branch office buildings and grounds
- Graphic services
- Purchasing
- Records management, archives and library
- Serving Québec with corporate services
- Translation
- Providing internal and external communication services
- Delivering and maintaining computer business system applications
- Providing education and consulting to users of information technology in the business units
- Providing technical support for users of information technology in all areas of the company

EXHIBIT 6
Roles in the Delta Change Project

1. Corporate Services Strategy Team (DELTA)
    - maintain integrity of strategy
    - engagement of all corporate service staff
    - ensure process stays on track
2. Resource Team (DIRT)
    - act as resource/facilitator/trainer for process teams
3. Process Team Leaders (PTL)
    - lead process teams to identify purposes, activities and service level packages
    - responsible for achieving all deadlines
4. Line Partners
    - assist process team leaders in definition of purposes and level of service packages
    - draw the line of need and affordability for truly corporate and line services
    - line partners for truly corporate are Bob and the SPG
5. Cost Advisory Team (CAT)
    - Providing cost model for use by process teams
    - available for consulting for costing of current activities and service level packages
6. Strategic Planning Group (SPG)
    - Clearing barriers and ensuring resources
    - determine level of need and affordability for truly corporate and line services
    - accountability for line services decision-making in process teams
7. Communication Teams
    - communication to and from all Corporate Services staff
8. Transition Support
    - creating transition support plan
    - provide support through EAAP

EXHIBIT 7A

Process, Purpose and Activities Example

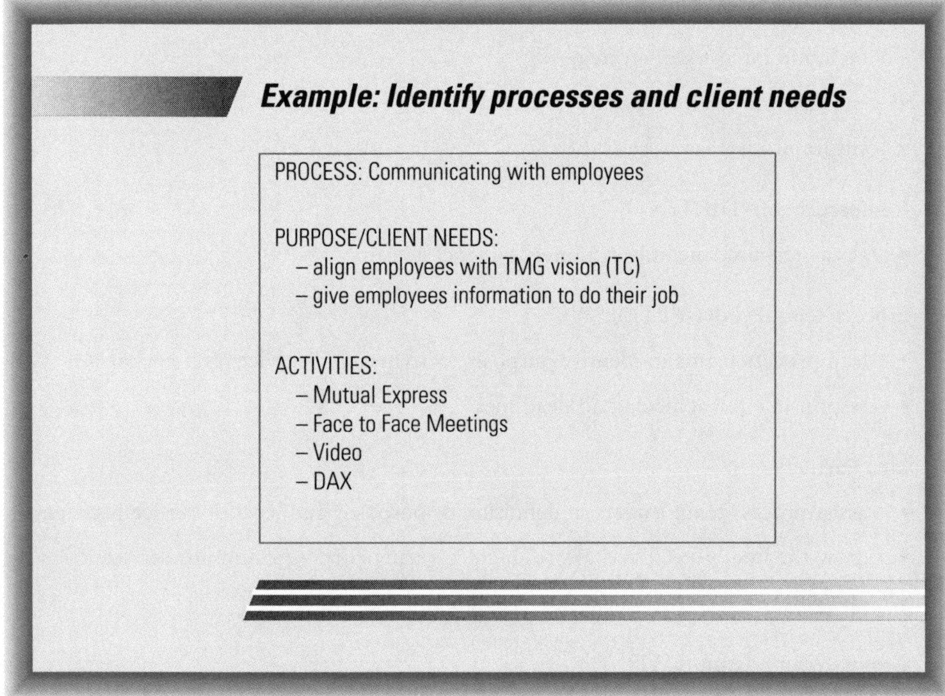

- Assume that all the processes have been identified. One of the ones identified is "communicating with employees".
- The purposes/needs identified around that process are listed out, and the activities we do (or could do) toward those goal are enumerated.
- Determine which goals are corporately oriented, and which are business unit oriented. The first one is truly corporate (TC), the second is not.
- Who does this step? Corporate services will develop a draft and review and flesh it out by meeting with our partners.
- We are developing guide-lines to help analyze processes and activities.
    - We want to keep processes at a high level. All Corporate Services activities will be represented by approximately 50 processes.
    - Activities should be analyzed at a level that represents the work of 5–20 people.

EXHIBIT 7B
Different Levels of Service Example

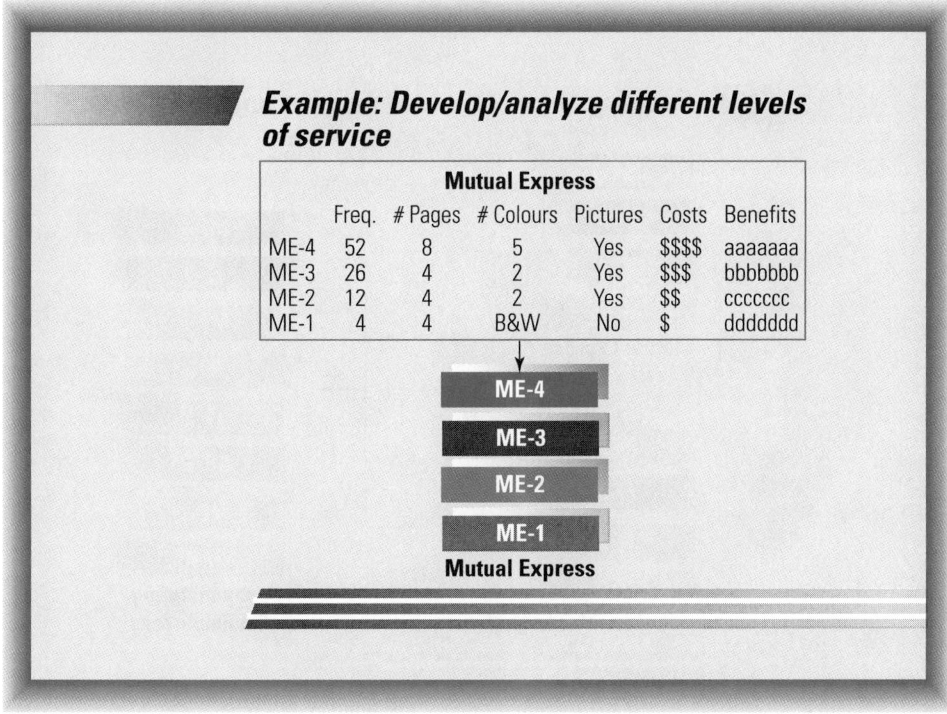

- The next step is to separate the "Truly Corporate" goals from the business goals, and to work through the truly corporate ones (starting down the left side of the diagram from a few minutes ago).
- Building on our example of Communication with employees, one of the goals was to align people with the vision, a Truly Corporate goal.
- We'll look now at how the activities do that. Using Mutual Express as an example of one way we align employees with the vision. There are different service levels for Mutual Express to align employees, each with associated costs and benefits (describing both tangible and intangible benefits). This step involves determining those levels, and understanding how additional service adds to the goal.
- For example, Mutual Express could be produced with different frequencies (4 times a year to weekly), and other features like colour or pictures.
- We can think of these levels as blocks which can be stacked, with an ordering as indicated at the bottom.
- Blocks at the bottom are those that provide the most benefit relative to cost, with higher boxes providing incremental benefit for incremental cost.
- If the activity has an essential level of service, that is the first block in the stack.
- Guide-lines are being developed for breaking activities down in to these blocks:
    - We need enough blocks to allow decision making on the service levels.
    - We want large enough blocks to avoid micro-management.
    - 3 or 4 blocks per activity is probably in the right range.

EXHIBIT 7C
Ranking "like" Levels of Service Example

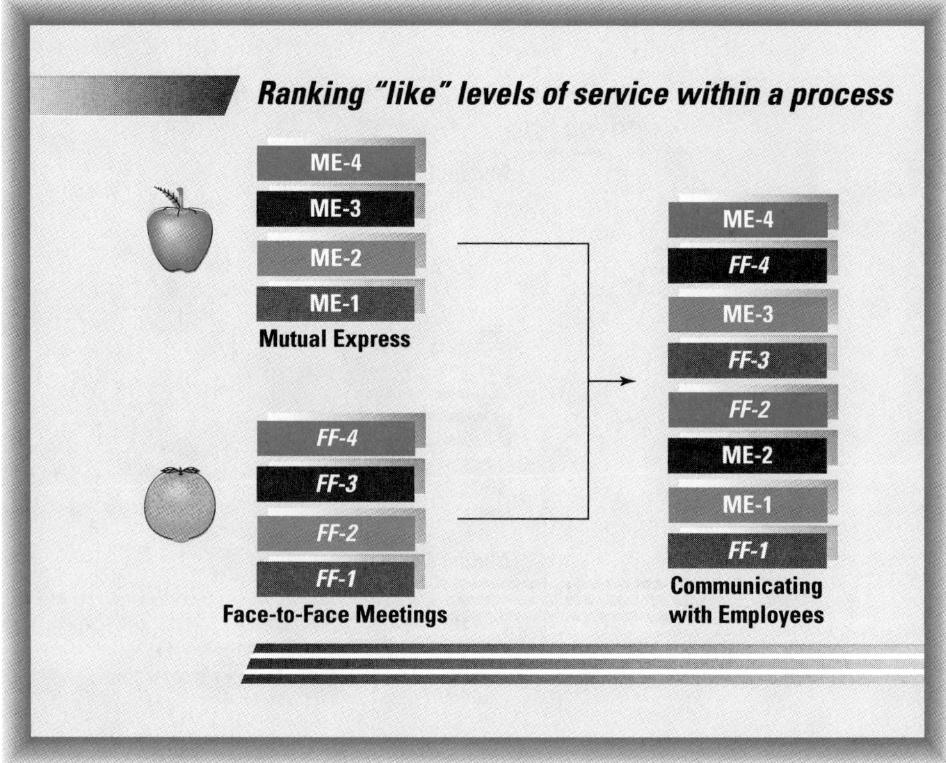

- Stacks of blocks will be developed for all the current activities, as well as for any new activities that are viable options for meeting the purpose/needs.
- The next step is to take these stacks of boxes for all activities which accomplish this purpose, and merge them together.
- Will require an apples to oranges comparison.
- For this example, we're taking our stack from Mutual Express, and a similar stack for Face to Face meetings.
- The stacks are merged according to the degree in which they accomplish the purpose relative to cost.
    - Essential levels of service (if there are any) are put at the bottom of the stack. In this example, there is no "essential" service level.
    - The bottom level of face-to-face meetings is deemed to provide the best value relative to cost, so it is ranked at the bottom of the resulting stack.
    - Then the ME-1 option is ranked next, followed by ME-2
    - The second and third face-to-face boxes are ranked next.
    - and so on . . .
- Again, the boxes near the bottom of the big stack provide the most value relative to cost, with higher boxes providing incremental value for incremental cost.
- Who does this? The service provider and our partners.

EXHIBIT 7D
Ranking/Prioritizing Levels of Service for Different Processes Example

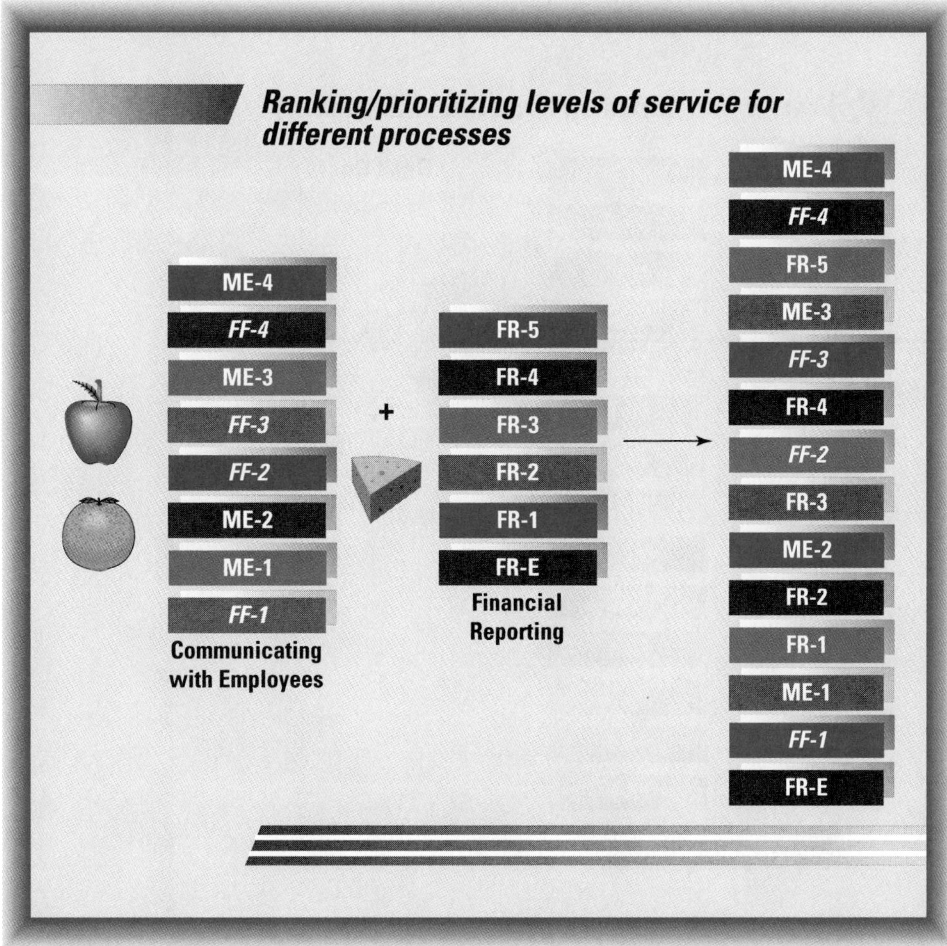

- The next step is to combine the stacks for all processes with truly corporate purposes to produce a single stack. This is the middle box on the left leg of our diagram.
- In this example, we see the stack we just produced for communicating with employees, merged with the stack for another process, financial reporting. The bottom block in the financial reporting stack, denoted "FR-E" is essential. That means it is the least amount of financial reporting we must do to be in the business we are in.
- This is comparing unlike stacks—similar to comparing apples and oranges to wedges of cheese!
- Essential services are ranked first. In this example, "FR-E" is an essential service level, and it appears at the bottom of the resulting stack. Then, the other (unlike) services are ranked based on the amount of competitive advantage produced by those services. We'd rank those which provide more competitive advantage ahead of those which provide less.
- This is a high level activity, done in partnership with senior providers and senior users. For truly corporate, it would be the Strategic Planning Group.

EXHIBIT 7E
Determining Need and Affordability Example

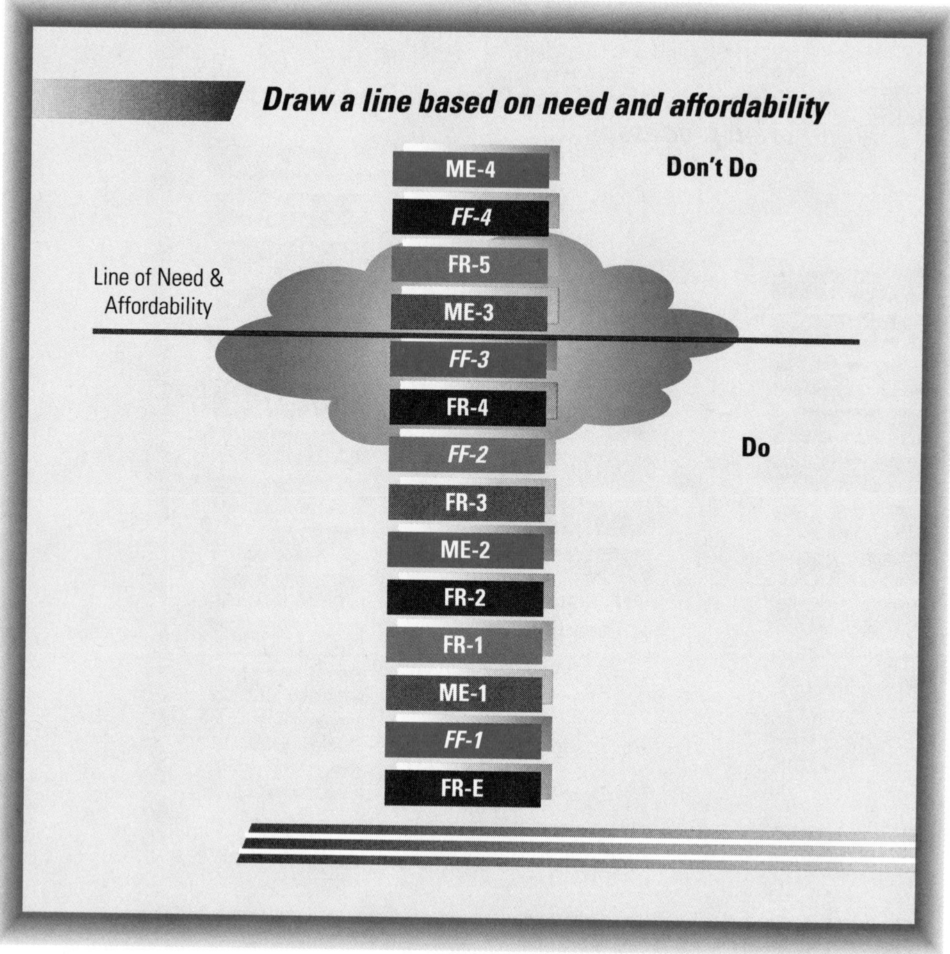

- At this point we know the values produced by each box, the costs associated with each, and we also have them ranked against each other.
- The next step involves drawing a line based on business needs and affordability. This is the last box in the left leg of the diagram.
- Things below the line get resources, and things above the line do not. It is important to consider those levels of service which are close to either side of the line—the area covered by the cloud in the picture. The goal in doing this is to ensure the line is appropriately placed, and that there are no items above the line that we cannot live without.
- The line has to be drawn to include at least the essential blocks.
- The process as illustrated so far in this example has dealt with truly corporate services. Then the 3 steps are re-done down the right side of the diagram with each business unit for their needs. This will yield different stacks (and lines) for each business unit.
- At this point we will deal with any problems created by services being on different sides of the lines for the different business units. Some reconsideration/redrawing may be required.
- In the last step of the process (at the bottom of the diagram) decisions are driven forward based on the activities we are going to resource. The "Do's".
- We recognize that we need to develop a full plan for dealing with the redeployment of people for those activities or levels or service which fall above the line. This plan will be developed over the summer months as part of the implementation phase.
- This is where questions around structure, organization, and management of these services are addressed.

EXHIBIT 8
Corporate Services—Organization Structure

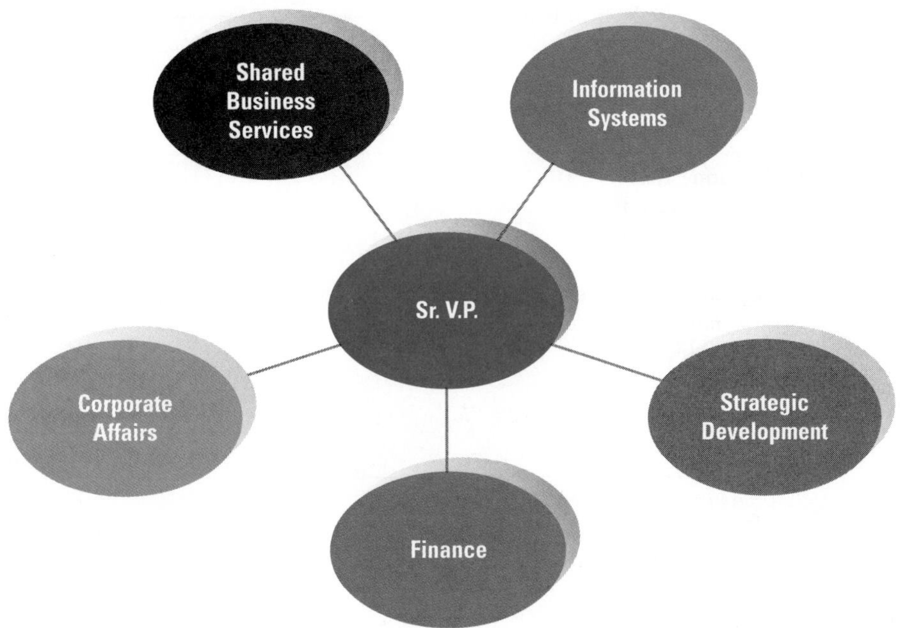

EXHIBIT 9
The Mutual Group—1995 Financial Results

The Year in Brief

	in millions		
	1995	1994	% Change
Operating Results			
Premium income	$ 2,576	$ 2,239	15.1
Investment income	$ 1,727	$ 1,419	21.7
Benefits paid and provided for	$ 3,425	$ 2,912	17.6
Policyholder experience dividends *(included in benefits paid and provided for)*	$ 239	$ 201	18.9
Net income	$ 192	$ 155	23.9
Return on assets (%)	0.83	0.87	(4.6)
Return on equity (%)	11.0	9.8	12.2
Policyholders' equity	**$ 1,839**	**$ 1,653**	**11.3**
Assets under management			
Total company assets	$ 24,402	$ 18,907	29.1
Segregated fund investments	2,697	2,490	8.3
Other assets under management	5,611	5,216	7.6
Total	$ 32,710	$ 26,613	22.9
Life insurance in force			
Canadian individual	$ 74,533	$ 57,692	29.2
Canadian group	37,575	35,266	6.5
United States	32,775	28,990	13.1
Total	$ 144,883	$ 121,948	18.8
Annuities in force (liability)			
Canadian individual	$ 5,828	$ 4,974	17.2
Canadian group	6,580	4,993	31.8
United States	432	484	(10.7)
Total	$ 12,840	$ 10,451	22.9
Health insurance in force			
Canadian premiums plus administrative services only equivalent	$ 903	$ 866	4.3
United States premiums	302	301	0.3
Total	$ 1,205	$ 1,167	3.3

EXHIBIT 10

The Mutual Group

Five Year Financial Performance: 1991–1995

5 Year Performance at a Glance

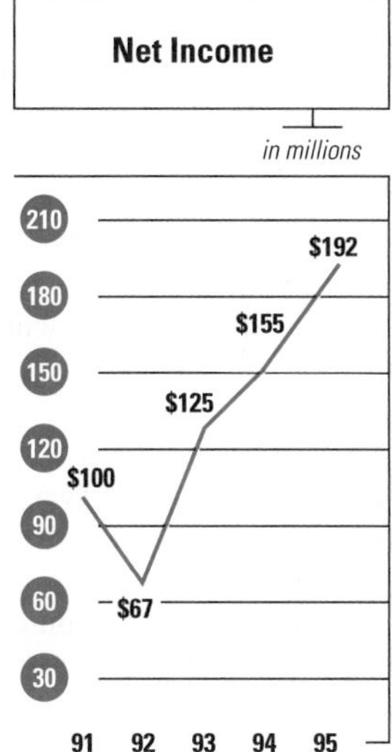

- business volume growth and recent acquisitions key factors
- outstanding results in Canadian operations
- excellent expense management

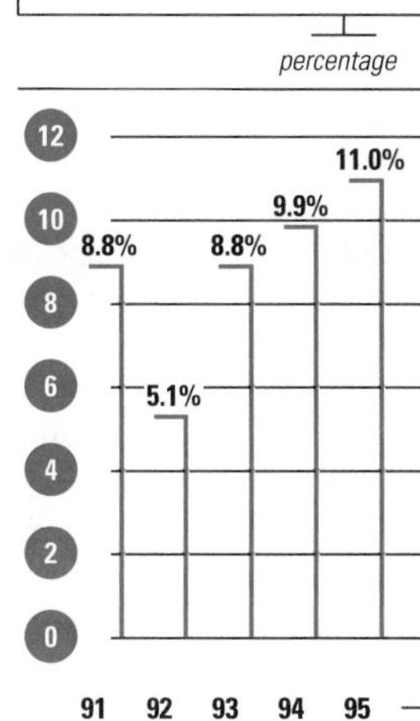

- equity growth averaging above 10%
- strong earnings from volumes and growth

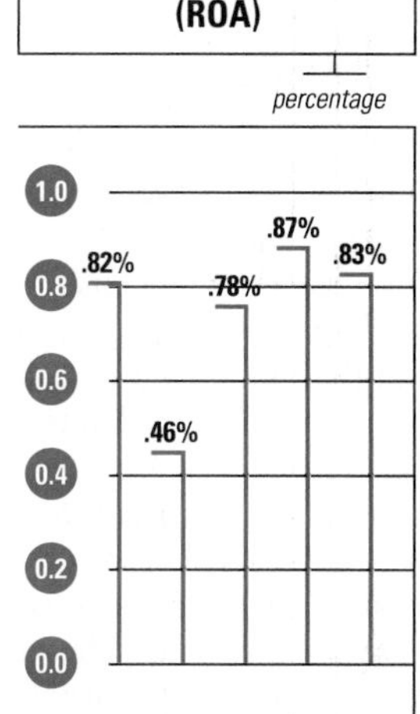

- asset growth from acquisitions
- net income growth above 20% in 1995

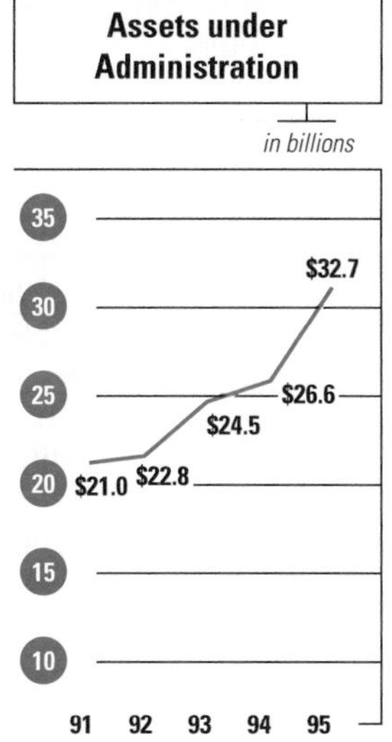

- recent acquisitions have added $3 billion to asset base
- large asset base of financial products operations

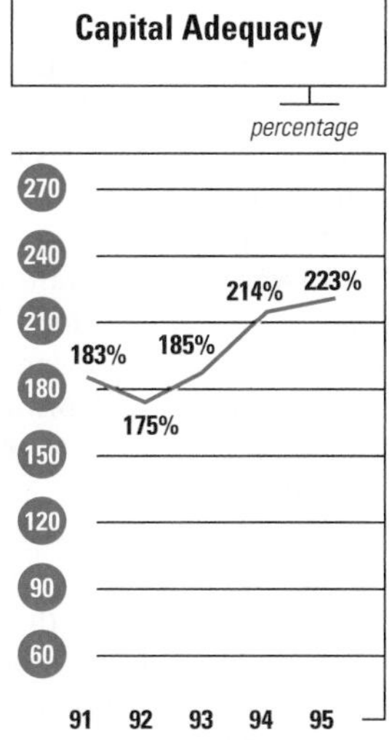

- well capitalized
- prudent approach to risk management

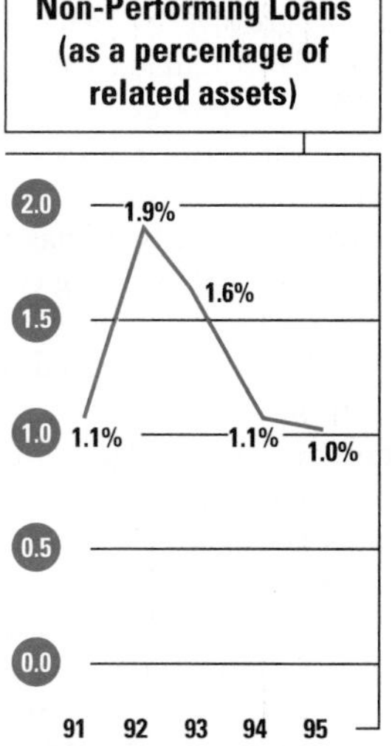

- addition of $3 billion high quality assets
- continued weakness in Canadian commercial real estate market

Case for Analysis: Osoyoos Band*

Over the last decade, British Columbia's Osoyoos Band has been on an economic tear. With nine businesses—including the year-old Desert Cultural Centre—going strong, and an entrepreneurial chief unafraid to shun tradition, it's no wonder there are more jobs than band members. A case study in self-sustainability.

Evening light pours across the land like a thick golden liquid and the shadows grow long. Waves of bunch grass morph between yellow, saffron and deep magenta as the sun dips towards Kobau Mountain across the valley.

In the softening light, tiny yellow flowers become visible on the twisted branches of antelope brush, a stoic desert plant that sends deep tap roots into the seared earth of the south Okanagan in search of moisture. Lofty Ponderosa pines, with their fire-protective skins of thick bark, gather in shallow draws like old men stopping to chat about the weather.

Moments ago on this pleasant May evening, I was relaxing with my feet up in a plush spa resort condo. Now I walk gingerly amongst the antelope brush, alert for clumps of prickly pear cactus or perhaps the venomous Western rattlesnake coiled and concealed somewhere underfoot.

If you could project the cartoon setting of the Road Runner and Wile E. Coyote into some kind of three-dimensional, metaphysical reality, it might resemble this extraordinary landscape, right here in Canada's desert country in the south Okanagan. Home to myriad fascinating rare plant and animal species, this is also the traditional territory of the Osoyoos people, an upstart Native band that is striking an enterprising balance between their traditional roots and a progressive approach to economic development that is the talk of Canada's aboriginal community and the tourism industry at large.

Admittedly, vineyards, golf courses, spa hotels and RV parks aren't exactly hallmarks of traditional Native culture, but the Osoyoos Indian Band has no problem keeping one foot in the past while striding confidently forward with the other.

One year ago, the band celebrated the opening of the deluxe Nk'Mip (pronounced "ink-a-meep") Desert Cultural Centre, showcasing both the flora and fauna of the region and the ingenuity of an ancient culture that flourished here for millennia. With a $9-million price tag mostly paid for with government grants, this 12,000-square-foot facility houses interpretive displays, a theatre and a rattlesnake research program, forming the cultural cornerstone of an extensive tourist development that includes a golf course, the award-winning Nk'Mip Wine Cellars and the Spirit Ridge Resort and Spa, my home for the past several days.

"We're not perfect. This centre has been talked about since the early '90s and a lot of debate went into this, but we're proud of the result," explains Clarence Louie, the tough-talking entrepreneurial chief of the Osoyoos Indian Band. "It was worth the time and effort to advance and preserve our heritage and culture."

Though the Osoyoos are proud of their past, they're not content to be simply a museum culture. They're growing a business empire. By striving for economic self-sufficiency, the 450-strong band is slowly overcoming some of the social ills of drug and alcohol abuse, unemployment and the crippling dependence fostered over years on spoon-fed, ill-conceived government handouts and programs. Capitalizing on its south Okanagan location, the Osoyoos Indian Band is setting a high benchmark for Native entrepreneurship in the local economy. The band owns nine businesses with annual revenues of $14.5 million, marking significant growth from 1997 when revenues were a mere $1.45 million.

Last year, Chief Louie and his economic team penned a unique agreement with the Province of British Columbia that will accommodate the development of nearby Mount Baldy—located on traditional band land—into a destination resort by its owners, Idaho-based Winter Recreation ULC. The band also has a small 2.5 per cent equity in the Mt. Baldy Ski Corporation and is close to inking a deal with Bellstar Resorts and Hotels Inc. to buy a 25 per cent share in its Spirit Ridge development. With all its business holdings, the band creates more jobs than it has working-age band members, a fact Chief Louie is fond of trumpeting during speeches to other Native bands, government bureaucrats and business leaders.

Four years ago, Alberta-based Bellstar decided to seriously consider a desert country investment after witnessing the Osoyoos Indian Band's efforts to balance economic development with cultural and ecological conservation. Last fall, Bellstar completed the $23-million first phase of its Spirit Ridge Spa and Resort complex, all on leased band land. The next phase, worth roughly $50 million, will bring the total number of resort suites and villas to 226, complete with conference facilities and a business centre.

"We liked how the chief spoke about business. The band council was willing to listen but they never strayed from their vision of economic development," says Ed Romanewski, president and CEO of Bellstar, over the phone from his Calgary office.

"Frankly, in our previous experience with Indian bands, we didn't see that kind of focus. We saw this as a great investment in a truly unique part of Canada."

To understand where the Osoyoos people are today, you need to dust off the history books and gaze into their past—and at the landscape that has defined them.

Their tenacity and pride has roots that date back to well before the tourist town of Osoyoos sprang up on the shores of its namesake lake, now buzzing with powerboats and Jet Skis. In 1915, when aboriginal culture was being torn asunder by the residential school and reservation system, then-Osoyoos chief Baptiste George stood firm. With uncanny foresight, he persuaded the federal government of the day to allow the band to build and manage its own school. Seven months later, the Nk'Mip Day School welcomed its first students. In the early years, the school struggled to retain teachers, opening and closing its doors as overwhelmed instructors came and went. Then in 1932, a visionary young man named Anthony Walsh arrived at the school. It was a fortuitous meeting.

Given the troubled times of white-Native politics, Walsh had unusual empathy towards indigenous culture. Rather than suppress the Native language and traditional values of his young pupils, he encouraged them. Subsequently, Osoyoos culture flowered during Walsh's tenure. This unique synergy between student and teacher reached far beyond the sleepy backwater of the south Okanagan. Thanks to Walsh's knack for promotion, in 1936 a Nativity scene painted on buckskin by young Francis Baptiste was singled out for distinction at the Royal Drawing Society's Annual Exhibition at London's Guildhall Gallery. The following year, a portfolio of drawings and sketches by Osoyoos youth depicting ancient and modern Osoyoos life was shown at the Cizek Juvenile Art Centre in Vienna. Then, in 1938, Walsh toured Europe, exhibiting the children's work in Dublin, London, Glasgow and Paris.

Today the legacy of these precocious Osoyoos youngsters lives on in a new exhibit at the Nk'Mip Centre, where visitors get a taste of the south Okanagan beyond beach blankets and wine tours.

"The centre is here to serve the community, but also to share in the rich living culture of the Okanagan people," says manager Charlotte Sanders, adding that it exceeded first-year expectations by welcoming more than 12,750 visitors last season.

There's no question, scientists across Canada recognize traditional Osoyoos land as a threatened biological treasure, home to more at-risk species than any other ecosystem in British Columbia. Not surprisingly, people are naturally drawn to the pleasant Okanagan climate and its proximity to lakes and beaches. Golf courses, vineyards, resorts and urban development sprawl across a landscape once blanketed in sage and antelope brush. The Osoyoos Natives have also seen fit to bulldoze sections of the desert to make way for vineyards, fairways and condos. Chief Louie doesn't apologize.

"Conservation of the desert is important but we also need to develop land, create jobs and generate revenue for our people. If this land wasn't in Osoyoos band hands, I bet every square inch of this desert would be developed," Chief Louie says with characteristic candor.

In what's left of the desert, like the land adjacent to the Nk'Mip Centre, extreme temperatures and severe aridity combine to create one of the country's most unusual and rich ecosystems. There is nothing frivolous or extravagant about life here. It lacks the exuberance and fecundity of a West Coast rainforest, yet its riches and subtleties are revealed upon closer inspection. Like, for example, the curious tapestry of lichens and mosses underfoot, known in scientific circles as the sci-fi-sounding "cryptogamic crust." Essential for maintaining sensitive soil structures and preserving moisture, this crust is so sensitive that it can be destroyed by an afternoon of grazing Herefords, rendering this biological marvel irreparable. At-risk species like the Western rattlesnake, the spadefoot toad, the burrowing owl and even the antelope brush also cling to a precarious existence.

"There are so many species here that are at the margins of their habitat," says Bob Lincoln, retired wildlife branch manager for the B.C. Environment Ministry's Okanagan Region and a full-time conservation activist. "It's also one of the richest areas because you can go from aquatic to riparian to desert to cliffs in a span of a few kilometres."

As I hike through this surreal landscape of cactus, snakes and sagebrush next to the Nk'Mip Centre, I ponder life in an environment like this. It's spring and a recent rainfall has infused the land with a freshness that could be misleading. During summer, temperatures frequently soar into the punishing mid-40°C range; enough to wilt even the hardiest desert traveller. Just as the stubborn flora and fauna of the south Okanagan persevere in the extremes, the Osoyoos people have survived and are now making their distinct mark on the future of Canada's aboriginal peoples.

*Source: A. Findlay, High and Dry—How the Okanagan's Osoyoos Band Turned Aboriginal Tourism on its Head, Up! (May 2007), 51–59.

12 Decision-Making Processes

The Canadian Press/Thunder Bay Chronicle/BRENT LINTON

A Look Inside

Anishinabek Nation

In March 2007, Grand Council Chief John Beaucage pledged to do more to preserve the water of the Great Lakes and to take better care of the environment. He created the Anishinabek Women's Water Commission to advise the Union of Ontario Indians; the Commission provides advice on all aspects of the management of the Great Lakes. According to the Chief, "[we] need to ensure that First Nations, especially our women, maintain their role as stewards of the water and give a voice to our most precious resource."[1] The founding Chief Commissioner is Josephine Mandamin (see photo), an elder from Wikwemikong Unceded Nation. She notes that "[water] is a great uniter . . . Hearing Mother Earth cry about how ill she is and how she is having a hard time feeding her children is a reminder to us all that our women feel the same way. We must unite in this momentous task."[2] Mandamin created the Mother Earth Water Walk and leads walks around each of the Great Lakes.

Chief Beaucage notes that The First Nations are dedicated to the principles of co-management—"[we] acknowledge Ontario's jurisdiction in managing the Great Lakes on behalf of their citizens, while we [are] asserting traditional management principles on behalf of our citizens.[3] The Anishinabek Nation signed a memorandum of understanding with the Ministry of Natural Resources that strengthens the relationship between them. The memorandum commits the Government of Ontario and the Anishinabek Nation (1) to hold an annual meeting between the Anishinabek Grand Council Chief and the Minister of Natural Resources, (2) to establish a joint Great Lakes Charter Annex Agreement Implementation Committee, and (3) to help build Anishinabek Nation advisory and technical capacity through the Union of Ontario Indians by retaining a technical advisor, as well as other measures.

Every organization grows, prospers, or fails as a result of decisions by its managers, and decisions can be risky and uncertain, without any guarantee of success. Sometimes, decision making is a trial-and-error process, in which top managers continue to search for appropriate ways to solve complex problems. Decision making is done amid constantly changing factors, unclear information, and conflicting points of view. The 2002 decision to merge Hewlett-Packard (H-P) and Compaq, for example, was highly controversial. Former H-P CEO Carly Fiorina and her supporters believed it was essential for H-P's future success, but other managers and board members argued that it was ill-advised to risk H-P's printer business and move the company more deeply into the highly competitive computer world. Fiorina's side ultimately won out, but results of the merger have been disappointing. Hewlett-Packard's board ousted Fiorina in early 2005, partly due to issues related to the Compaq merger.[4] Similarly, Canada Tire Corporation's 1982 purchase of White Stores, a money-losing Texas-based chain of automotive parts, furniture, and appliance stores cost the CEO, Dean Muncaster, his job. The decision to buy White Stores cost Canadian Tire \$300 million in three years.[5]

Many organizational decisions are complete failures. A classic example is the 1985 introduction of New Coke, which Coca-Cola executives were sure was the company's answer to winning back market share from Pepsi. Within three months, the company had gotten more than 400,000 angry letters and phone calls, and New Coke quietly faded from store shelves.[6] Even the most successful companies sometimes make big blunders. DreamWorks, the studio that made *Shrek 2*, the biggest box-office hit of 2004, poured tens of millions into marketing for the DVD release of the monster hit. Sales during the initial release period boomed, so DreamWorks flooded the market. Managers got a shock when retailers began returning millions of unsold copies. Based on patterns in the past, DreamWorks wrongly assumed the strong early sales would continue and perhaps even grow.[7]

Yet managers also make many successful decisions every day. Meg Whitman made eBay today's model of what an Internet company should be by steering clear of get-rich-quick schemes and keeping the company focused on nurturing its community of buyers and sellers. Cadillac managers' decision to ditch stuffy golf and yachting sponsorships in favour of tying in with popular Hollywood movies has boosted sales and revived Cadillac's image. And Carlos Ghosn implemented structural, management, and product changes that transformed Nissan from a directionless, debt-ridden company into one of the more dynamic and profitable automakers in the world.[8]

Purpose of This Chapter

At any time, an organization may be identifying problems and implementing alternatives for hundreds of decisions. Managers and organizations somehow muddle through these processes.[9] The purpose here is to analyze these processes to learn what decision making is actually like in organizational settings. Decision-making processes can be thought of as the brain and nervous system of an organization. Decision making is the end use of the information and control systems described in Chapter 8. Decisions are made about organization strategy, structure, innovation, and acquisitions. This chapter explores how organizations can and should make decisions about these issues.

The first section defines decision making. The next section examines how individual managers make decisions. Then several models of organizational decision making are explored. Each model is used in a different organizational situation. The final section in this chapter combines the models into a single framework that describes when and how they should be used, and discusses special issues, such as decision mistakes.

Definitions

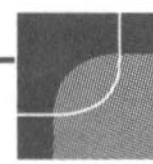

PDA

Remember...

Adapt decision processes to fit the organizational situation. Understand how processes differ for programmed and nonprogrammed decisions.

Organizational decision making is formally defined as the process of identifying and solving problems. The process has two major stages. In the **problem identification** stage, information about environmental and organizational conditions is monitored to determine if performance is satisfactory and to diagnose the cause of shortcomings. The **problem solution** stage is when alternative courses of action are considered and one alternative is selected and implemented.

Organizational decisions vary in complexity and can be categorized as programmed or nonprogrammed.[10] **Programmed decisions** are repetitive and well defined, and procedures exist for resolving the problem. They are well structured because criteria of performance are normally clear, good information is available about current performance, alternatives are easily specified, and there is relative certainty that the chosen alternative will be successful. Examples of programmed decisions include decision rules, such as when to replace an office copy machine, when to reimburse managers for travel expenses, or whether an applicant has sufficient qualifications for an assembly-line job. Many companies adopt rules based on experience with programmed decisions. For example, a rule for large hotels staffing banquets is to allow one server per 30 guests for a sit-down function and one server per 40 guests for a buffet.[11]

Nonprogrammed decisions are novel, ill-structured, and poorly defined, and no procedure exists for solving the problem. They are used when an organization has not seen a problem before and may not know how to respond. Clear-cut decision criteria do not exist. Alternatives are fuzzy. There is uncertainty about whether a proposed solution will solve the problem. Typically, few alternatives can be developed for a nonprogrammed decision, so a single solution is custom-tailored to the problem.

Many nonprogrammed decisions involve strategic planning, because uncertainty is significant and decisions are complex. One recent example of a nonprogrammed decision comes from Tupperware, the maker of food storage products and kitchen gadgets traditionally sold at home Tupperware parties. Managers hit a home run with the decision to set up booths in shopping malls and push sales over the Internet. Thus, a further push into retail sales by placing Tupperware in a U.S. retail chain in the United States, with volunteer salespeople to demonstrate the products, seemed destined for success. But moving into Target turned out to be one of the biggest disasters in Tupperware's history. Some Target stores and shoppers didn't know how to deal with the influx of Tupperware salespeople, who ended up feeling slighted and stopped volunteering for store duty. Sales were slow. At the same time, the availability of Tupperware in the retail stores decreased the interest in home parties, further hurting sales and alienating independent sales representatives. Although overseas sales remained strong, sales of Tupperware in North America fell to a three-year low and profits plummeted nearly 50 percent. Managers are currently considering new decisions about how to turn things around.[12]

Particularly complex nonprogrammed decisions have been referred to as "wicked" decisions, because simply defining the problem can turn into a major task. Wicked problems are associated with manager conflicts over objectives and alternatives, rapidly changing circumstances, and unclear linkages among decision elements. Managers dealing with a wicked decision may hit on a solution that merely proves they failed to correctly define the problem to begin with.[13]

Today's managers and organizations are dealing with a higher percentage of nonprogrammed decisions because of the rapidly changing business environment. As outlined in Exhibit 12.1, today's environment has increased both the number and complexity of decisions that have to be made and has created a need for new decision-making processes. Managers in rapidly changing e-business departments, for example, often have to make quick decisions based on very limited information. Another example is globalization. The trend toward moving production to low-wage countries has managers all over North America struggling with ethical decisions concerning working conditions in the developing world and the loss of manufacturing jobs in North America.

EXHIBIT 12.1
Decision Making in Today's Environment
Source: Reprinted by permission of Harvard Business School Press. From *Leading Change* by John P. Kotter. Boston, MA, 1996, p. 56. Copyright © 1996 by the Harvard Business School Publishing Corporation, all rights reserved.

Today's Business Environment

- *Demands more large-scale change via new strategies, reengineering, restructuring, mergers, acquisitions, downsizing, new product or market development, and so on*

Decisions Made Inside the Organization

- *Are based on bigger, more complex, more emotionally charged issues*
- *Are made more quickly*
- *Are made in a less certain environment, with less clarity about means and outcomes*
- *Require more cooperation from more people involved in making and implementing decisions*

A New Decision-Making Process

- *Is required because no one individual has the information needed to make all major decisions*
- *Is required because no one individual has the time and credibility needed to convince lots of people to implement the decision*
- *Relies less on hard data as a basis for good decisions*
- *Is guided by a powerful coalition that can act as a team*
- *Permits decisions to evolve through trial and error and incremental steps as needed*

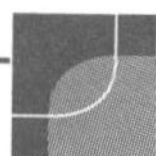

Individual Decision Making

Individual decision making by managers can be described in two ways. First is the **rational approach**, which suggests how managers should try to make decisions. Second is the **bounded rationality perspective**, which describes how decisions actually have to be made under severe time and resource constraints. The rational approach is an ideal that managers may work toward but never reach.

Rational Approach

The rational approach to individual decision making stresses the need for systematic analysis of a problem followed by choice and implementation in a logical, step-by-step sequence. The rational approach was developed to guide individual decision making because many managers were observed to be unsystematic and arbitrary in their approach to organizational decisions.

Although the rational model is an ideal not fully achievable in the real world of uncertainty, complexity, and rapid change highlighted in Exhibit 12.1, the model does help managers think about decisions more clearly and rationally. Managers should use systematic procedures to make decisions whenever possible. When managers have a deep understanding of the rational decision-making process, it can help them make better decisions even when there is a lack of clear information. According to the rational approach, decision making can be broken down into eight steps.

The eight steps are demonstrated by a retail sector example. (A recent Statistics Canada survey revealed that two million people work in retail across Canada, making them the country's second-largest workforce. The sector had sales of $350 billion in 2004.)[14]

1. *Monitor the decision environment.* In the first step, a manager monitors internal and external information that will indicate deviations from planned or acceptable behaviour. She talks to colleagues and reviews financial statements, performance evaluations, industry indices, competitors' activities, and so forth. For example, during the pressure-packed five-week winter holiday season, the general manager of a retail store checks out competitors around the mall, eyeing whether they are marking down merchandise. She also scans printouts of her store's previous day's sales to learn what is or is not moving.[15]
2. *Define the decision problem.* The manager responds to deviations by identifying essential details of the problem: where, when, who was involved, who was affected, and how current activities are influenced. The general manager needs to determine if store profits are low because overall sales are less than expected or because certain lines of merchandise are not moving as expected.
3. *Specify decision objectives.* The manager determines what performance outcomes should be achieved by a decision.
4. *Diagnose the problem.* In this step, the manager digs below the surface to analyze the cause of the problem. Additional data might be gathered to facilitate this diagnosis. Understanding the cause enables appropriate treatment—the cause of slow sales, for example, might be competitors' marking down of merchandise or the store's failure to display hot-selling items in a visible location.
5. *Develop alternative solutions.* Before a manager can move ahead with a decisive action plan, he or she must have a clear understanding of the various options available to achieve desired objectives. The manager may seek ideas and suggestions from other people. The general manager's alternatives for increasing profits could include buying fresh merchandise, running a sale, or reducing the number of employees.
6. *Evaluate alternatives.* This step may involve the use of statistical techniques or personal experience to gauge the probability of success. The merits of each alternative are assessed, as well as the probability that it will reach the desired objectives.
7. *Choose the best alternative.* This step is the core of the decision process. The manager uses her analysis of the problem, objectives, and alternatives to select a single alternative that has the best chance for success. The general manager may choose to reduce the number of staff as a way to meet the profit goals rather than increase advertising or markdowns.
8. *Implement the chosen alternative.* Finally, the manager uses managerial, administrative, and persuasive abilities and gives directions to ensure that the decision is carried out. The monitoring activity (step 1) begins again as soon as the solution is implemented. The decision cycle should be a continuous process, with new decisions made daily based on monitoring her environment for problems and opportunities.

The first four steps in this sequence are the problem identification stage, and the next four steps are the problem solution stage of decision making. A manager normally goes through all eight steps in making a decision, although each step may not be a distinct element. Managers may know from experience exactly what to do in a situation, so one or more steps will be minimized. The following In Practice illustrates how the rational approach can be used to make a decision about a human resource problem.

In Practice

Alberta Consulting

1. *Monitor the decision environment.* It is Monday morning, and Joe DeFoe, Alberta's accounts receivable supervisor, is absent again.
2. *Define the decision problem.* This is the fourth consecutive Monday DeFoe has been absent. Company policy forbids unexcused absenteeism, and DeFoe has been warned about his excessive absenteeism on the last two occasions. A final warning is in order but can be delayed, if warranted.
3. *Specify decision objectives.* DeFoe should attend work regularly and establish the invoice collection levels of which he is capable. The time period for solving the problem is two weeks.
4. *Diagnose the problem.* Discreet discussions with DeFoe's co-workers and information gleaned from DeFoe indicate that DeFoe has a drinking problem. He apparently uses Mondays to dry out from weekend binges. Discussion with other company sources confirms that DeFoe is a problem drinker.
5. *Develop alternative solutions.* (1) Fire DeFoe. (2) Issue a final warning without comment. (3) Issue a warning and accuse DeFoe of being an alcoholic to let him know you are aware of his problem. (4) Talk with DeFoe to see if he will discuss his drinking. If he admits he has a drinking problem, delay the final warning and suggest that he enrol in the company's new employee assistance program for help with personal problems, including alcoholism. (5) Talk with DeFoe to see if he will discuss his drinking. If he does not admit he has a drinking problem, let him know that the next absence will cost him his job.
6. *Evaluate alternatives.* The cost of training a replacement is the same for each alternative. Alternative 1 ignores cost and other criteria. Alternatives 2 and 3 do not adhere to company policy, which advocates counselling where appropriate. Alternative 4 is designed for the benefit of both DeFoe and the company. It might save a good employee if DeFoe is willing to seek assistance. Alternative 5 is primarily for the benefit of the company. A final warning might provide some incentive for DeFoe to admit he has a drinking problem. If so, dismissal might be avoided, but further absences will no longer be tolerated.
7. *Choose the best alternative.* DeFoe does not admit that he has a drinking problem. Choose alternative 5.
8. *Implement the chosen alternative.* Write up the situation and issue the final warning.

In the preceding example, issuing the final warning to Joe DeFoe was a programmed decision. The standard of expected behaviour was clearly defined, information on the frequency and cause of DeFoe's absence was readily available, and acceptable alternatives and procedures were described. The rational procedure works best in such cases, when the decision maker has sufficient time for an orderly, thoughtful process. Moreover, Alberta Consulting had mechanisms in place to implement the decision, once made.

When decisions are nonprogrammed, ill-defined, and piling on top of one another, the individual manager should still try to use the steps in the rational approach, but he or she often will have to take shortcuts by relying on intuition and experience. Deviations from the rational approach are explained by the bounded rationality perspective.

Bounded Rationality Perspective

The point of the rational approach is that managers should try to use systematic procedures to arrive at good decisions. When organizations are facing little competition and are dealing with well-understood issues, managers generally use rational procedures to make decisions.[16] Yet research into managerial decision making shows that often managers are *unable* to follow an ideal procedure. Many decisions must be made very quickly. Time pressure, a large number of internal and external factors affecting a decision, and the ill-defined nature of many problems make systematic analysis virtually impossible. Managers have only so much time and mental capacity and, hence, cannot evaluate every goal, problem, and alternative. Mintzberg's research in the 1970s found that managerial work is demanding, open-ended, fragmented, and full of brevity, variety and interruption.[17] The attempt to be rational is bounded (limited) by the enormous complexity of many problems. There is a limit to how rational managers can be. For example, an executive in a hurry may have a choice of 20 shirts but will take the first or second one that matches his/her suit. The executive doesn't carefully weigh all 20 alternatives because the short amount of time and the large number of plausible alternatives would be overwhelming. The manager simply selects the first solution that addresses the problem and moves on quickly to the next task.

PDA Remember...

Use rational decision processes when possible, but recognize that many constraints may impinge on decision makers and prevent a perfectly rational decision. Apply the bounded rationality perspective and use intuition when confronting ill-defined, nonprogrammed decisions.

Constraints and Tradeoffs. Not only are large organizational decisions too complex to fully comprehend, but several other constraints impinge on the decision maker, as illustrated in Exhibit 12.2. For many decisions, the circumstances are ambiguous, requiring social support, a shared perspective on what happens, and acceptance and agreement. In the SARS outbreak in Toronto in 2003, for example, many complex decisions needed to be made in trying circumstances by many different health care practitioners. Setting the correct priorities was vital in responding to the many demands of the crisis. According to a recent study, "[in] the midst of a crisis such as SARS where guidance is incomplete, consequences uncertain, and information constantly changing, where hour-by-hour decisions involve life and death, fairness is more important rather than less."[18]

EXHIBIT 12.2
Constraints and Tradeoffs during Nonprogrammed Decision Making

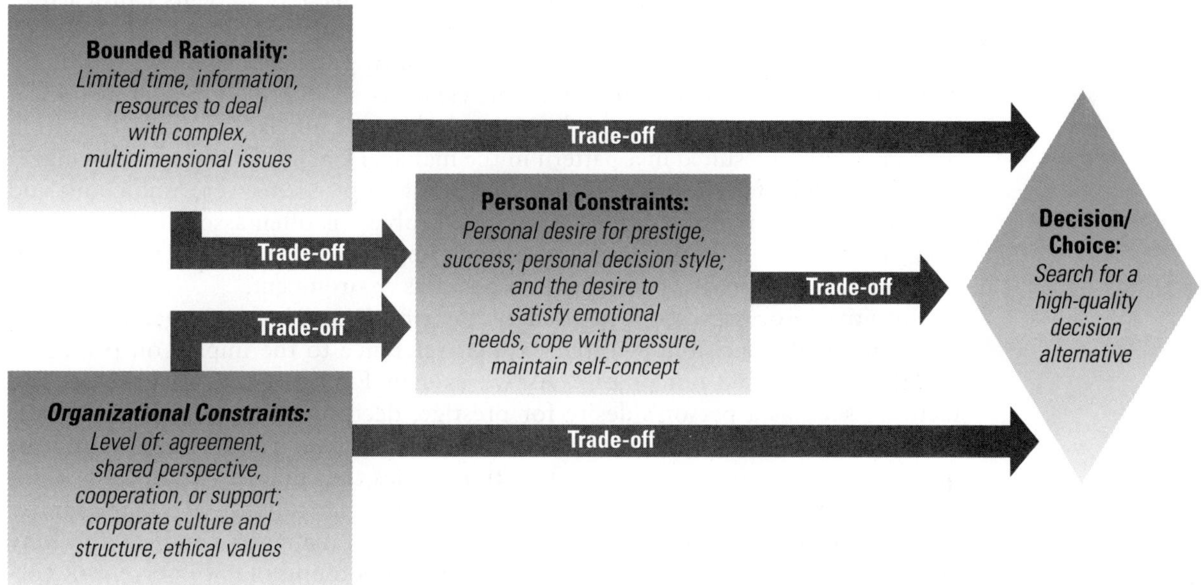

Source: Adapted from Irving L. Janis, *Crucial Decisions* (New York: Free Press, 1989); and A. L. George, *Presidential Decision Making in Foreign Policy: The Effective Use of Information and Advice* (Boulder, Colo.: Westview Press, 1980).

29 Organizational culture and ethical values also influence decision making, as discussed in Chapter 10. This chapter's Leading by Design box describes how Ricardo Semler, CEO of Brazil's Semco, has created a culture where decisions are made based on a primary goal of improving the lives of employees and customers. Managers also often make decisions within a context of trying to please upper managers, people who are perceived to have power within the organization, or others they respect and want to emulate.[19]

Personal constraints—such as decision style, work pressure, desire for prestige, or simple feelings of insecurity—may constrain either the search for alternatives or the acceptability of an alternative. All of these factors constrain a perfectly rational approach that should lead to an obviously ideal choice.[20] Even seemingly straightforward decisions, such as selecting a job on graduation from university, can quickly become so complex that a bounded rationality approach is used. Graduating students have been known to search for a job until they have two or three acceptable job offers, at which point their search activity rapidly diminishes. Many firms may be available for interviews, and two or three job offers fall short of the maximum number that would be possible if students made the decision based on perfect rationality.

The Role of Intuition. The bounded rationality perspective is often associated with intuitive decision processes. In **intuitive decision making**, experience and judgment rather than sequential logic or explicit reasoning are used to make decisions.[21] Intuition is not arbitrary or irrational because it is based on years of practice and hands-on experience, often stored in the subconscious. When managers use their intuition based on long experience with organizational issues, they more rapidly perceive and understand problems, and they develop a gut feeling or hunch about which alternative will solve a problem, speeding the decision-making process.[22] The value of intuition for effective decision making is supported by a growing body of research from psychology, organizational science, and other disciplines.[23] Indeed, many universities are offering courses in creativity and intuition so business students can learn to understand and use these processes.

In a situation of great complexity or ambiguity, previous experience and judgment are needed to incorporate intangible elements at both the problem identification and problem solution stages.[24] Bits and pieces of unrelated information from informal sources resulted in a pattern in the manager's mind. One study of manager problem finding, for example, showed that 30 of 33 problems were ambiguous and ill-defined.[25] A simplistic view of a complex problem is often associated with decision failure.[26] Intuition plays an increasingly important role in problem identification in today's fast-paced and uncertain business environment.

Intuitive processes are also used in the problem solution stage. Executives frequently make decisions without explicit reference to the impact on profits or to other measurable outcomes.[27] As we saw in Exhibit 12.2, many intangible factors—such as a person's desire for prestige, decision style, and ability to deal with pressure—influence selection of the best alternative. These factors cannot be quantified in a systematic way, so intuition guides the choice of a solution. Managers may make a decision based on what they sense to be right rather than on what they can document with hard data. A survey of managers conducted in May 2002 by executive search firm Christian & Timbers found that 45 percent of corporate executives say they rely more on instinct than on facts and figures to make business decisions.[28]

Leading *by Design*

Semco

Ricardo Semler graduated from the Harvard Business School with an MBA at age 20, and took over Semco from his father in 1984. Semco started off manufacturing pumps and propellers but has become a large diversified company providing environmental consulting, inventory services, mobile maintenance services, industrial equipment, and postal and document management services. Semler has been named the Global Leader of Tomorrow by the World Economic Form, twice as Brazil's Business Leader of the Year, and Latin American Businessman of the year by *The Wall Street Journal's* América Economia magazine.[29] Semler is also the author of two books, *Maverick: The Success Story Behind the World's Most Unusual Workplace* and *The Seven Day Weekend*. He is founder of the Lumiar School in Sao Paulo, which provides an unstructured education without classrooms, homework, or prescribed playtime for children aged two to six.

On his first day as CEO, Semler renamed the company Semco, fired two-thirds of the management staff, and eliminated all secretarial positions. He dismantled the managerial structure to eliminate what he considered to be corporate oppression and to encourage the core business values of employee participation, profit sharing, and open information flows. Semler had an epiphany after he collapsed from overwork and decided that everyone at Semco would enjoy a proper work–life balance. Semler observes that "[people] who have learned to answer email on Sunday evenings also need to learn how to go to the movies on Monday afternoons. By redesigning the architecture of time, we can make room for work, leisure, and idleness."[30] He started with flextime and then did away with dedicated receptionists, organizational charts, and the central office. Semler "encouraged employees to suggest what they should be paid, to evaluate their bosses, to learn each other's jobs, and to tolerate dissent—even when divisive."[31]

According to Semco, its way is "A company full of crazy people? A Group of nutters? If you think that Semco is something along these lines, you're not entirely wrong. However, it is not by chance that unconventional ideas are created at this company. They are created and managed within an open management model, different from conventional models and this is exactly what we want."[32] Semler comments that it's hard to describe Semco but has attempted to in the following way.

Semco has no official structure. It has no organizational chart. There's no business plan or company strategy, no two-year or five-year plan, no goal or mission statement, no long-term budget. The company often does not have a fixed CEO. There are no vice presidents or chief officers for information technology or operations. There are no standards or practices. There's no human resources department. There are no career plans, no job descriptions or employee contracts. No one approves reports or expense accounts. Supervision or monitoring of workers is rare indeed.

Most important, success is not measured only in profit and growth.

Strange, eh? My summary may make Semco sound like a company with an offbeat management style that wouldn't succeed anywhere else. Nevertheless, hundreds of corporate leaders from around the world have visited Sao Paulo to find out what makes us tick. The visitors are curious about Semco because they want what we have—huge growth in spite of a fluctuating economy, unique market niches, rising profits, highly motivated employees, low turnover, diverse products, and service areas.

Our visitors want to understand how Semco has increased its annual revenue between 1994 and 2003 from $35 million a year to $212 million when I—the company's largest shareholder—rarely attend meetings and almost never make decisions. They want to know how my employees, with a show of hands, can veto new product ideas or scrap whole business ventures.

It's our lack of formal structure, our willingness to let workers follow their interests and their instincts when choosing jobs or projects.

It's our insistence that workers seek personal challenges and satisfaction before trying to meet the company's goals.

It's our commitment to encouraging employees to ramble through their day or week so that they will meander into new ideas and new business opportunities.

It's our philosophy of embracing democracy and open communication, and inciting questions and dissent in the workplace.[33]

Howard Schultz turned Starbucks into a household name by pursuing his intuition that the leisurely caffeine-and-conversation *caffe* model he observed in Italy would work in the United States, despite market research that indicated Americans would never pay $3 for a cup of coffee. Jerry Jones based his decision to buy the losing Dallas Cowboys on intuition, then made a series of further intuitive decisions that turned the team back into a winner. Similarly, the vice president for talent development and casting at MTV relied on intuition to create the show *The Osbournes.* "We never tested the show," he says. "We just knew it would make great TV."[34]

However, there are also many examples of intuitive decisions that turned out to be complete failures.[35] This chapter's Book Mark discusses how managers can give their intuition a better chance of leading to successful decisions.

Managers may walk a fine line between two extremes: on the one hand, making arbitrary decisions without careful study, and on the other, relying obsessively on numbers and rational analysis.[36] Remember that the bounded rationality perspective

Book Mark 12.0 (HAVE YOU READ THIS BOOK?)

Blink: The Power of Thinking without Thinking
By Malcolm Gladwell

Snap decisions can be just as good as—and sometimes better than—decisions that are made cautiously and deliberately. Yet they can also be seriously flawed or even dangerously wrong. That's the premise of Malcolm Gladwell's *Blink: The Power of Thinking without Thinking*. Gladwell, a Canadian working in New York City, explores how our "adaptive unconscious" arrives at complex, important decisions in an instant—and how we can train it to make those decisions good ones.

SHARPENING YOUR INTUITION

Even when we think our decision making is the result of careful analysis and rational consideration, Gladwell says, most of it actually happens subconsciously in a split second. This process, which he refers to as "rapid cognition," provides room for both amazing insight and grave error. Here are some tips for improving rapid cognition:

- *Remember that more is not better.* Gladwell argues that giving people too much data and information hampers their ability to make good decisions. He cites a study showing that emergency room doctors who are best at diagnosing heart attacks gather less information from their patients than other doctors do. Rather than overloading on information, search out the most meaningful parts.
- *Practice thin-slicing*. The process Gladwell refers to as *thin-slicing* is what harnesses the power of the adaptive unconscious and enables us to make smart decisions with minimal time and information. Thin-slicing means focusing on a thin slice of pertinent data or information and allowing your intuition to do the work for you. Gladwell cites the example of a Pentagon war game, in which an enemy team of commodities traders defeated a U.S. Army that had "an unprecedented amount of information and intelligence" and "did a thoroughly rational and rigorous analysis that covered every conceivable contingency." The commodities traders were used to making thousands of instant decisions an hour based on limited information. Managers can practise spontaneous decision making until it becomes second nature.
- *Know Your Limits*. Not every decision should be based on intuition. When you have a depth of knowledge and experience in an area, you can put more trust in your gut feelings. Gladwell also cautions to beware of biases that interfere with good decision making. *Blink* suggests that we can teach ourselves to sort through first impressions and figure out which are important and which are based on subconscious biases such as stereotypes or emotional baggage.

CONCLUSION

Blink is filled with lively and interesting anecdotes, such as how firefighters can "slow down a moment" and create an environment where spontaneous decision making can take place. Gladwell asserts that a better understanding of the process of split-second decision making can help people make better decisions in all areas of their lives, as well as help them anticipate and avoid miscalculations.

Blink: The Power of Thinking without Thinking, by Malcolm Gladwell, is published by Little, Brown.

and the use of intuition apply mostly to nonprogrammed decisions. The novel, unclear, complex aspects of nonprogrammed decisions mean hard data and logical procedures are not available. One study of executive decision making found that managers simply could not use the rational approach for nonprogrammed decisions, such as when to buy a CT (computed tomography) scanner for an osteopathic hospital or whether a city had a need for and could reasonably adopt an enterprise resource planning system.[37] In those cases, managers had limited time and resources, and some factors simply couldn't be measured and analyzed. Trying to quantify such information may cause mistakes because it may oversimplify decision criteria. Intuition can also balance and supplement rational analysis to help organization leaders make better decisions. At Paramount Pictures, a top management team combined intuition and analysis to keep the studio consistently profitable.

In Practice

Paramount Pictures (Paramount)

When she was head of Paramount Pictures, Sherry Lansing and her boss, Jonathan Dolgen, head of Viacom Entertainment Group, made a powerful team. Unlike many studios, which lose money despite successful box-office films, Paramount has consistently turned a profit every year since Lansing and Dolgen were put in charge.

As a former independent producer, Lansing relied on her experience and intuition to pick good scripts and the right actors to make them work. Consider 1994's *Forrest Gump*. "It was a film about a guy on a bench," said Lansing. "It was one of the riskiest films ever made." But Lansing's intuition told her that Tom Hanks sitting on a bench talking about life being "like a box of chocolates" would work, and the film reaped $329 million at the box office. More recent successes under the leadership of Lansing and Dolgen include *Along Came a Spider*, *Vanilla Sky*, and *Lara Croft: Tomb Raider*. Dolgen, a former lawyer, provided the analytical side of the partnership. Dolgen's intelligence and careful attention to detail helped Paramount generate consistently good returns. Sometimes, his analysis would suggest that a risk was just not worth taking, even though it meant the studio turned down a potential blockbuster.

Lansing and Dolgen were considered one of the most effective management teams in Hollywood. They combined their natural strengths—one intuitive, the other analytical—to make good decisions that kept Paramount consistently profitable in a difficult, high-risk, unpredictable business. Although Paramount has turned out a string of well-planned, reliable movies, top executives at Viacom are pushing the studio to take bigger risks and come up with some box-office blockbusters. Lansing recently left Paramount and a new leader will try his hand at the business of picking successful movies. Like Lansing, though, he will likely rely largely on intuition. There's no formula for accurately predicting which stories will resonate with today's fickle movie-going audience.[38]

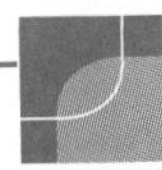

Organizational Decision Making

Organizations are composed of managers who make decisions using both rational and intuitive processes; but organization-level decisions are not usually made by a single manager. Many organizational decisions involve several managers. Problem identification and problem solution involve many departments, multiple viewpoints, and even other organizations, which are beyond the scope of an individual manager.

PDA

Remember...

Use a rational decision approach—computation, management science—when a problem situation is well understood.

The processes by which decisions are made in organizations are influenced by a number of factors, particularly the organization's own internal structures and the degree of stability or instability of the external environment.[39] Research into organization-level decision making has identified four primary types of organizational decision-making processes: the management science approach, the Carnegie model, the incremental decision process model, and the garbage can model.

Management Science Approach

The **management science approach** to organizational decision making is the analog to the rational approach by individual managers. Management science came into being during World War II.[40] At that time, mathematical and statistical techniques were applied to urgent, large-scale military problems that were beyond the ability of individual decision makers.

Mathematicians, physicists, and operations researchers used systems analysis to develop artillery trajectories, antisubmarine strategies, and bombing strategies such as salvoing (discharging multiple shells simultaneously). Consider the problem of a battleship trying to sink an enemy ship several miles away. The calculation for aiming the battleship's guns should consider distance, wind speed, shell size, speed and direction of both ships, pitch and roll of the firing ship, and curvature of the earth. Methods for performing such calculations using trial and error and intuition are not accurate, take far too long, and may never achieve success.

This is where management science came in. Analysts were able to identify the relevant variables involved in aiming a ship's guns and could model them with the use of mathematical equations. Distance, speed, pitch, roll, shell size, and so on could be calculated and entered into the equations. The answer was immediate, and the guns could begin firing. Factors such as pitch and roll were soon measured mechanically and fed directly into the targeting mechanism. Today, the human element is completely removed from the targeting process. Radar picks up the target, and the entire sequence is computed automatically.

Management science yielded astonishing success for many military problems. This approach to decision making diffused into corporations and business schools, where techniques were studied and elaborated. Today, many corporations have assigned departments to use these techniques. The computer department develops quantitative data for analysis. Operations research departments use mathematical models to quantify relevant variables and develop a quantitative representation of alternative solutions and the probability of each one solving the problem. These departments also use such devices as linear programming, Bayesian statistics, PERT charts, and computer simulations. As you can see from Exhibit 12.3, organizations need computers to deal with organizational complexity!

Management science is an excellent device for organizational decision making when problems are analyzable and when the variables can be identified and measured. Mathematical models can contain a thousand or more variables, each one relevant in some way to the ultimate outcome. Management science techniques have been used to correctly solve problems as diverse as finding the right spot for a church camp, test-marketing the first of a new family of products, drilling for oil, and radically altering the distribution of telecommunications services.[41] Other problems amenable to management science techniques are the scheduling of ambulance technicians, telephone operators, and toll collectors.[42]

EXHIBIT 12.3
"And That's Why We Need a Computer."

In Practice
Algorithms Rule!

Three professors at the Rotman School of Management, Opher Baron, Oded Berman, and Dimitry Krass, have developed a complex algorithm that reduces waiting times for many services from lining up to get a cup of coffee to waiting times for hospital services. The three researchers used a three-pronged approach to the waiting problem by accounting for the regulation of demand, capacity versus waiting time, and the cost versus the number and location of a facility. The algorithm is dynamic so it can account for such variables as politics.[43]

"Algorithms, they say, are taking over the world. They hold the answers to everything from designing better cars to finding the perfect mate. . . . "[44] While the trio has not commercialized their algorithm, according to Dr. Berman "that is part of the research game . . . We may work at a business school but in truth we are researchers and scientists, not business people."[45] Even so, the type of research they do in advanced mathematics is being used in a partnership between McMaster University in Hamilton, Ontario, and the world-renowned Princess Margaret Hospital in Toronto to determine the optimal level of radiation for cancer patients.[46]

"Mathematical models are bound to play a greater role in business and even personal decision making," Dr. Baron predicts.[47] For example, MapQuest uses algorithms to work out optimal routes for drivers.

Management science can accurately and quickly solve problems that have too many explicit variables for human processing. This system is at its best when applied to problems that are analyzable, are measurable, and can be structured in a logical way. Increasingly sophisticated computer technology and software programs are allowing the expansion of management science to cover a broader range of problems than ever before. For example, some retailers, including Home Depot, Hudson Bay Company, and Club Monaco, now use software to analyze current and historical sales data and determine when, where, and how much to mark down prices. Managers at Harrah's Entertainment have turned the company into one of the hottest operators of casinos by amassing plenty of data about customers and using sophisticated computer systems to make decisions about everything from casino layout to hotel room pricing. Prices quoted for rooms, for instance, are based on a complex mathematical formula that takes into account how long the customers typically stay, what games they play and how often, and other details.[48]

Management science has also produced many failures.[49] In recent years, many banks have begun using computerized scoring systems to rate those applying for credit, but some argue that human judgment is needed to account for extenuating circumstances.

PDA Remember...

Use a coalition-building approach when organizational goals and problem priorities are in conflict. When managers disagree about priorities or the true nature of the problem, they should discuss and seek agreement about priorities.

One problem with the management science approach is that quantitative data are not rich and do not convey tacit knowledge, as described in Chapter 8. Informal cues that indicate the existence of problems have to be sensed on a more personal basis by managers.[50] The most sophisticated mathematical analyses are of no value if the important factors cannot be quantified and included in the model. Such things as competitor reactions, consumer tastes, and product warmth are qualitative dimensions. In these situations, the role of management science is to supplement manager decision making. Quantitative results can be given to managers for discussion and interpretation along with their informal opinions, judgment, and intuition. The final decision can include both qualitative factors and quantitative calculations.

Carnegie Model

The **Carnegie model** of organizational decision making is based on the work of Richard Cyert, James March, and Herbert Simon, who were all associated with Carnegie-Mellon University.[51] Their research helped formulate the bounded rationality approach to individual decision making, as well as provide new insights about organizational decisions.

Until their work, research in economics assumed that business firms made decisions as a single entity, as if all relevant information were funnelled to the top decision maker for a choice. Research by the Carnegie group indicated that organization-level decisions involved many managers and that a final choice was based on a coalition among those managers. A **coalition** is an alliance among several managers who agree about organizational goals and problem priorities.[52] It could include managers from line departments, staff specialists, and even external groups, such as powerful customers, bankers, or union representatives.

Management coalitions are needed during decision making for two reasons. First, organizational goals are often ambiguous, and operative goals of departments are often inconsistent. When goals are ambiguous and inconsistent, managers disagree about problem priorities. They must bargain about problems and build a coalition around the question of which problems to solve.

The second reason for coalitions is that individual managers intend to be rational but function with human cognitive limitations and other constraints, as described earlier. Managers do not have the time, resources, or mental capacity to identify all dimensions and to process all information relevant to a decision. These limitations lead to coalition-building behaviour. Managers talk to each other and exchange points of view to gather information and reduce ambiguity. People who have relevant information or a stake in a decision outcome are consulted. Building a coalition will lead to a decision that is supported by interested parties.

The process of coalition formation has several implications for organizational decision behaviour. First, decisions are made to *satisfice* rather than to optimize problem solutions. **Satisficing** means organizations accept a satisfactory rather than a maximum level of performance, enabling them to achieve several goals simultaneously. In decision making, the coalition will accept a solution that is perceived as satisfactory to all coalition members. Second, managers are concerned with immediate problems and short-run solutions. They engage in what Cyert and March called *problemistic search*.[53]

Problemistic search means managers look around in the immediate environment for a solution to quickly resolve a problem. Managers don't expect a perfect solution when the situation is ill defined and conflict-laden. This contrasts with the management science approach, which assumes that analysis can uncover every reasonable alternative. The Carnegie model says that search behaviour is sufficient to produce a satisfactory solution and that managers typically adopt the first satisfactory solution that emerges.

Third, discussion and bargaining are especially important in the problem identification stage of decision making. Unless coalition members perceive a problem, action will not be taken.

The decision process described in the Carnegie model is summarized in Exhibit 12.4. The Carnegie model points out that building agreement through a managerial coalition is a major part of organizational decision making. This is especially true at upper management levels. Discussion and bargaining are time consuming, so search procedures are usually simple and the selected alternative satisfices rather than optimizes problem solution. When problems are programmed—are clear and have been seen before—the organization will rely on previous procedures and routines. Rules and procedures prevent the need for renewed coalition formation and political bargaining. Nonprogrammed decisions, however, require bargaining and conflict resolution.

Organizations suffer when managers are unable to build a coalition around goals and problem priorities, as illustrated by the case of Encyclopaedia Britannica.

EXHIBIT 12.4
Choice Processes in the Carnegie Model

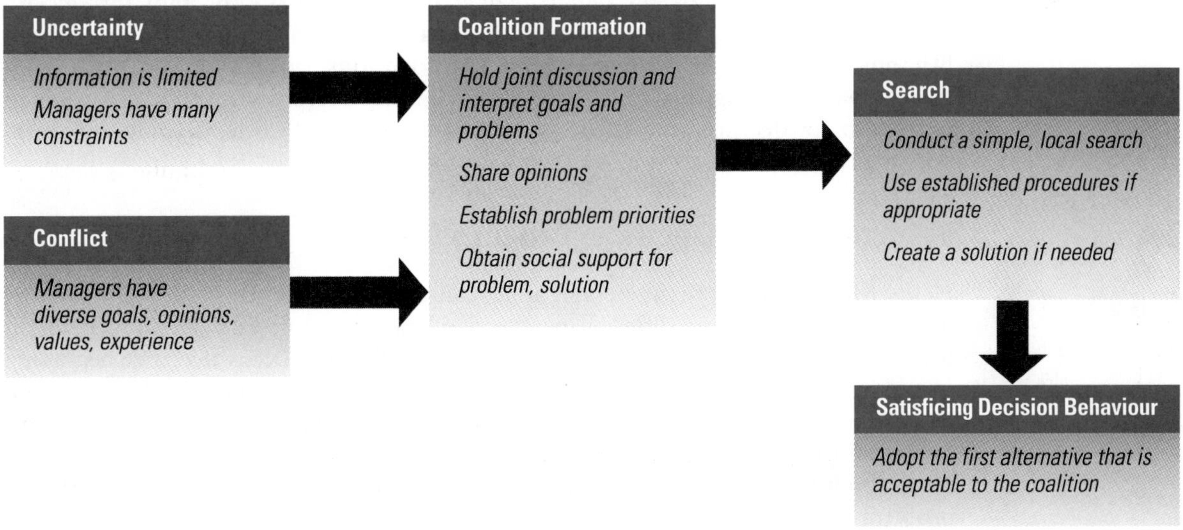

Uncertainty
Information is limited
Managers have many constraints

Conflict
Managers have diverse goals, opinions, values, experience

Coalition Formation
Hold joint discussion and interpret goals and problems
Share opinions
Establish problem priorities
Obtain social support for problem, solution

Search
Conduct a simple, local search
Use established procedures if appropriate
Create a solution if needed

Satisficing Decision Behaviour
Adopt the first alternative that is acceptable to the coalition

In Practice
Encyclopaedia Britannica

For most of its 231-year history, the *Encyclopaedia Britannica* had been viewed as an illustrious repository of cultural and historical knowledge—almost a national treasure. Generations of students and librarians relied on the *Britannica*—but that was before CD-ROMs and the Internet became the study tools of choice. Suddenly, the 32-volume collection of encyclopedias, stretching four feet on a bookshelf and costing as much as a personal computer (PC), seemed destined to fade into history.

When Swiss-based financier Joseph Safra bought Britannica, he discovered one of the reasons. For nearly a decade, managers had bickered over goals and priorities. Some top executives believed the company needed to invest more in electronic media, but others supported Britannica's traditional direct-to-home sales force. Eventually, the company's Compton unit, a CD-ROM pioneer now being used by millions of consumers, was sold, leaving Britannica without any presence in the new market. In the 1980s, Microsoft had approached Britannica to develop a CD-ROM encyclopedia; when it didn't work out, Microsoft went with Funk & Wagnalls and developed Encarta. Microsoft arranged to have Encarta preinstalled on PCs, so the CD-ROM was essentially free to new PC buyers. When Britannica finally came out with its CD-ROM version, however, it was priced at a staggering $1,200. The squabbling among managers, owners, and editors about product development, pricing, distribution, and other important decisions contributed to the company's decline.

The first step in Safra's turnaround strategy was to install a new top management team, led by one of his long-time advisers. The team immediately coalesced around the important problem of establishing a presence in the world of electronic media. With this goal, the company rushed out a revamped, lower-cost CD-ROM package and launched the Britannica.com website, which allows users to call up encyclopedia entries online as well as get a list of links to related websites. The team also created a separate digital media division to focus on new product development, such as for wireless Web technology. Managers are looking toward the wireless Web as the best route to a successful future and have teamed up with numerous wireless carriers and licensed Britannica's content to other web sites.

Building a coalition focused on common goals rather than having managers pushing and pulling in different directions got Britannica off the critical list by helping it cross the bridge to the digital era. Now, managers are in the process of evaluation to see what new decisions need to be made to help the company thrive in the digital world.[54]

The Carnegie model is particularly useful at the problem identification stage. However, a coalition of key department managers is also important for smooth implementation of a decision, particularly a major reorganization. Top executives at Britannica realize the importance of building coalitions for decision making to keep the company moving forward. When top managers perceive a problem or want to make a major decision, they need to reach agreement with other managers to support the decision.[55]

PDA Remember...

Take risks and move the company ahead by increments when a problem is defined but solutions are uncertain. Try solutions step by step to learn whether they work.

Incremental Decision Process Model

Henry Mintzberg and his associates at McGill University approached organizational decision making from a different perspective. They identified 25 decisions made in organizations and traced the events associated with these decisions from beginning to end.[56] Their research identified each step in the decision sequence. This approach to decision making, called the **incremental decision process model**, places less emphasis on the political and social factors described in the Carnegie model, but tells more about the structured sequence of activities undertaken from the discovery of a problem to its solution.[57]

Sample decisions in Mintzberg's research included choosing which jet aircraft to acquire for a regional airline, developing a new supper club, developing a new container terminal in a harbour, identifying a new market for a deodorant, installing a controversial new medical treatment in a hospital, and firing a star radio announcer.[58] The scope and importance of these decisions are revealed in the length of time taken to complete them. Most of these decisions took more than a year, and one-third of them took more than two years. Most of these decisions were nonprogrammed and required custom-designed solutions.

One discovery from this research is that major organization choices are usually a series of small choices that combine to produce the major decision. Thus, many organizational decisions are a series of nibbles rather than a big bite. Organizations move through several decision points and may hit barriers along the way. Mintzberg called these barriers *decision interrupts*. An interrupt may mean an organization has to cycle back through a previous decision and try something new. Decision loops or cycles are one way the organization learns which alternatives will work. The ultimate solution may be very different from what was initially anticipated.

The pattern of decision stages discovered by Mintzberg and his associates is shown in Exhibit 12.5. Each box indicates a possible step in the decision sequence. The steps take place in three major decision phases: identification, development, and selection.

Identification Phase. The identification phase begins with *recognition*. Recognition means one or more managers become aware of a problem and the need to make a decision. Recognition is usually stimulated by a problem or an opportunity. A problem exists when elements in the external environment change or when internal performance is perceived to be below standard. In the case of firing a radio announcer, comments about the announcer came from listeners, other announcers, and advertisers. Managers interpreted these cues until a pattern emerged that indicated a problem had to be addressed.

The second step is *diagnosis*, in which more information is gathered if needed to define the problem situation. Diagnosis may be systematic or informal, depending upon the severity of the problem. Severe problems do not allow time for extensive diagnosis; the response must be immediate. Mild problems are usually diagnosed in a more systematic manner.

Development Phase. In the development phase, a solution is shaped to solve the problem defined in the identification phase. The development of a solution takes one of two directions. First, *search* procedures may be used to seek out alternatives within the organization's repertoire of solutions. For example, in the case of firing a star announcer, managers asked what the radio station had done the last time an announcer had to be let go. To conduct the search, organization participants may look into their own memories, talk to other managers, or examine the formal procedures of the organization.

The second direction of development is to *design* a custom solution. This happens when the problem is novel so that previous experience has no value. Mintzberg found that in these cases, key decision makers have only a vague idea of the ideal solution. Gradually, through a trial-and-error screening process, a custom-designed alternative will emerge. Development of the solution is a groping, incremental procedure, building a solution brick by brick.

Selection Phase. The selection phase is when the solution is chosen. This phase is not always a matter of making a clear choice among alternatives. In the case of

EXHIBIT 12.5
The Incremental Decision Process Model

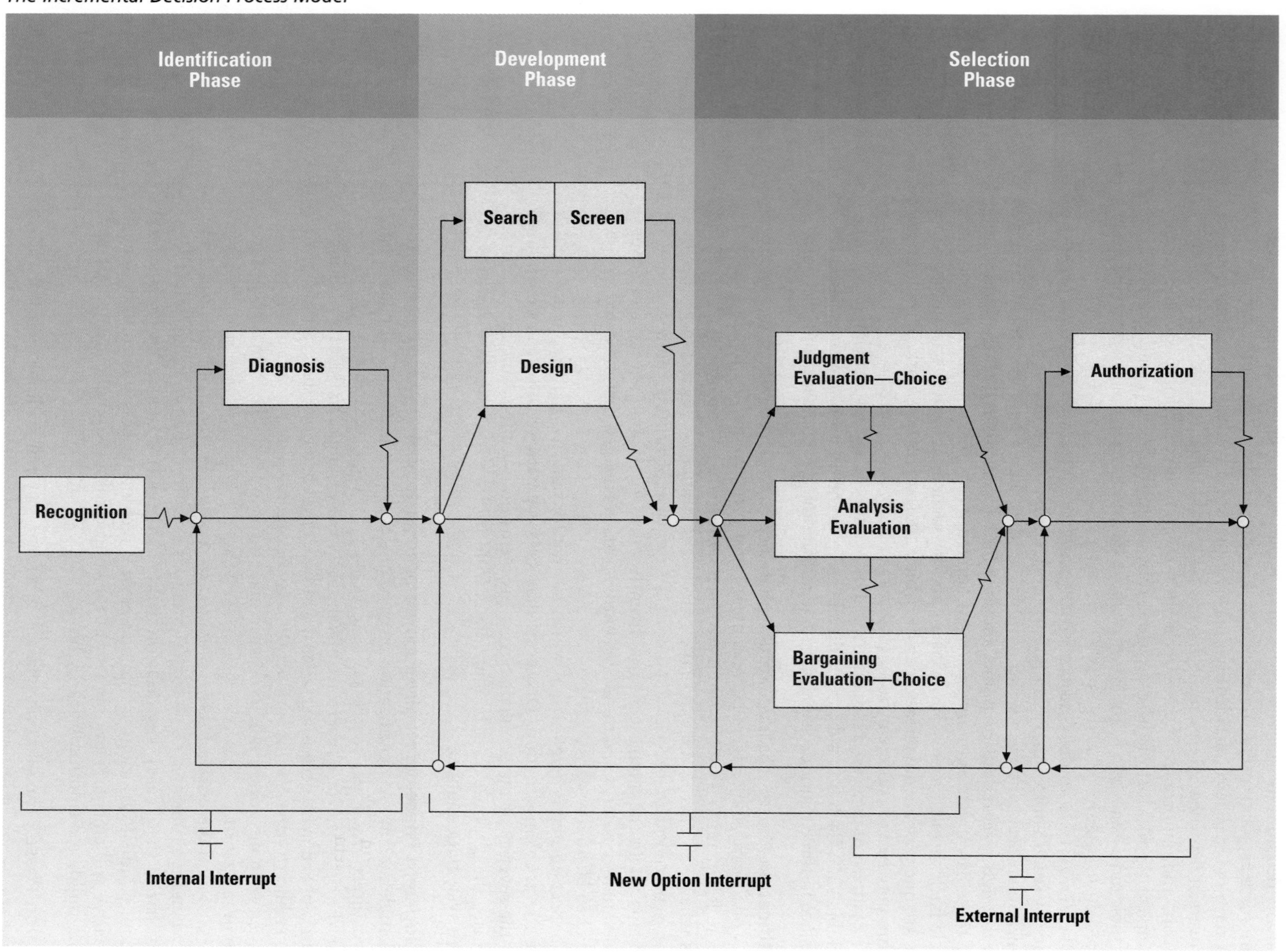

Source: Adapted and reprinted from "The Structure of Unstructured Decision Processes" by Henry Mintzberg, Duru Raisinghani, and André Théorêt, published in *Administrative Science Quarterly* 21, no. 2 (1976): 266, by permission of *The Administrative Science Quarterly*. Copyright © 1976 Cornell University.

custom-made solutions, selection is more an evaluation of the single alternative that seems feasible.

Evaluation and choice may be accomplished in three ways. The *judgment* form of selection is used when a final choice falls upon a single decision maker, and the choice involves judgment based upon experience. In analysis, alternatives are evaluated on a more systematic basis, such as with management science techniques. Mintzberg found that most decisions did not involve systematic analysis and evaluation of alternatives. *Bargaining* occurs when selection involves a group of decision makers. Each decision maker may have a different stake in the outcome, so conflict emerges. Discussion and bargaining occur until a coalition is formed, as in the Carnegie model described earlier.

When a decision is formally accepted by the organization, *authorization* takes place. The decision may be passed up the hierarchy to the responsible hierarchical level. Authorization is often routine because the expertise and knowledge rest with the lower-level decision makers who identified the problem and developed the solution. A few decisions are rejected because of implications not anticipated by lower-level managers.

Dynamic Factors. The lower part of the chart in Exhibit 12.5 shows lines running back toward the beginning of the decision process. These lines represent loops or cycles that take place in the decision process. Organizational decisions do not follow an orderly progression from recognition through authorization. Minor problems arise that force a loop back to an earlier stage. These are decision interrupts. If a custom-designed solution is perceived as unsatisfactory, the organization may have to go back to the very beginning and reconsider whether the problem is truly worth solving. Feedback loops can be caused by problems of timing, politics, disagreement among managers, inability to identify a feasible solution, turnover of managers, or the sudden appearance of a new alternative. For example, when a small local airline made the decision to acquire jet aircraft, the board authorized the decision, but shortly after, a new chief executive was brought in who cancelled the contract, recycling the decision back to the identification phase. He accepted the diagnosis of the problem but insisted upon a new search for alternatives. Then a foreign airline went out of business and two used aircraft became available at a bargain price. This presented an unexpected option, and the chief executive used his own judgment to authorize the purchase of the aircraft.[59]

Because most decisions take place over an extended period of time, circumstances change. Decision making is a dynamic process that may require a number of cycles before a problem is solved. An example of the incremental process and cycling that can take place is illustrated in Gillette's decision to create a new razor.

The Gillette Company uses incremental decision making to perfect the design of razors such as the Sensor, the Mach3, and the vibrating M3Power. Consider the development of the Mach3. While searching for a new idea to increase sales in Gillette's mature shaving market, researchers at the company's British research lab came up with a bright idea to create a razor with three blades to produce a closer, smoother, more comfortable shave (recognition and diagnosis). Ten years later, the Mach3 reached the market, after thousands of shaving tests, numerous design modifications, and a development and tooling cost of $750 million, roughly the amount a pharmaceutical firm invests in developing a blockbuster drug.

The technical demands of building a razor with three blades that would follow a man's face and also be easy to clean had several blind alleys. Engineers first tried to find established techniques (search, screen), but none fit the bill. Eventually a prototype called Manx was built (design), and in shaving tests it "beat the pants off" Gillette's Sensor Excel, the company's best-selling razor at the time. However, Gillette's CEO insisted that the razor had to have a radically new blade edge so the razor could use thinner blades (internal interrupt), so engineers began looking for new technology that could produce a stronger blade (search, screen). Eventually, the new edge, known as DLC for diamond-like carbon coating, would be applied atom by atom with chip-making technology (design).

The next problem was manufacturing (diagnosis), which required an entirely new process to handle the complexity of the triple-bladed razor (design). Although the board gave the go-ahead to develop manufacturing equipment (judgment, authorization), some members became concerned because the new blades, which are three times stronger than stainless steel, would last longer and cause Gillette to sell fewer cartridges (internal interrupt). The board eventually made the decision to continue with the new blades, which have a blue indicator strip that fades to white and signals when it's time for a new cartridge.

The board gave final approval for production of the Mach3 to begin in the fall of 1997. The new razor was introduced in the summer of 1998 and began smoothly sliding off shelves. Gillette recovered its huge investment in record time. Gillette then started the process of searching for the next shaving breakthrough all over again, using new technology that can examine a razor blade at the atomic level and high-speed video that can capture the act of cutting a single whisker. The company has moved ahead in increments; in 2006, Gillette launched its Fusion Power line of razors, which took eight years of innovation to develop. The line has 20 patented features.[60]

At Gillette, the identification phase occurred because executives were aware of the need for a new razor and became alert to the idea of using three blades to produce a closer shave. The development phase was characterized by the trial-and-error custom design leading to the Mach3. During the selection phase, certain approaches were found to be unacceptable, causing Gillette to cycle back and redesign the razor, including using thinner, stronger blades. Advancing once again to the selection phase, the Mach3 passed the judgment of top executives and board members, and manufacturing and marketing budgets were quickly authorized. This decision took more than a decade, finally reaching completion in the summer of 1998.

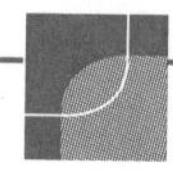

The Learning Organization

PDA

Remember...

Apply both the Carnegie model and the incremental process model in situations with high uncertainty about both problems and solutions. Decision making may also employ garbage can procedures. Move the organization toward better performance by proposing new ideas, spending time working in important areas, and persisting with potential solutions.

At the beginning of this chapter, we discussed how the rapidly changing external business environment is creating greater uncertainty for decision makers. Some organizations that are particularly affected by this trend are shifting to the learning organization concept. These organizations are marked by a tremendous amount of uncertainty at both the problem identification and problem solution stages. Two approaches to decision making have evolved to help managers cope with this uncertainty and complexity. One approach is to combine the Carnegie and incremental process models just described. The second is a unique approach called the garbage can model.

Combining the Incremental Process and Carnegie Models

The Carnegie description of coalition building is especially relevant for the problem identification stage. When issues are ambiguous, or if managers disagree about problem severity, discussion, negotiation, and coalition building are needed. Once agreement is reached about the problem to be tackled, the organization can move toward a solution.

The incremental process model tends to emphasize the steps used to reach a solution. After managers agree on a problem, the step-by-step process is a way of trying various solutions to see what will work. When problem solution is unclear, a trial-and-error solution may be designed. For example, in 1999, executives from three of the world's largest music companies formed a coalition to provide online consumers with a legal alternative to the digital piracy of Internet song-swapping services. However, making the joint venture MusicNet an appealing choice was a challenge. As originally conceived, the service didn't provide music lovers with the features they wanted, so managers took an incremental approach to try to make MusicNet more user-friendly by enabling customized downloads and subscription services distributed through providers such as Yahoo!, AOL, and Virgin Digital. Managers have continued to use an incremental approach as the industry evolves with the introduction of Apple's iTunes and other new distribution channels. In 2007, MusicNet expanded its content and changed its name to MediaNet Digital. As one executive put it, "This is a business of trial and error."[61]

The two models do not disagree with one another. They describe how organizations make decisions when either problem identification or solution is uncertain. The application of these two models to the stages in the decision process is illustrated in Exhibit 12.6. When both parts of the decision process are simultaneously highly uncertain, which is often the case in learning organizations, the organization is in an extremely difficult position. Decision processes in that situation may be a combination of Carnegie and incremental process models, and this combination may evolve into a situation described in the garbage can model.

Garbage Can Model

The **garbage can model** is one of the interesting descriptions of organizational decision processes. It is not directly comparable to the earlier models, because the garbage can model deals with the pattern or flow of multiple decisions within organizations, whereas the incremental and Carnegie models focus on how a single decision is made. The garbage can model helps managers think of the whole organization and the frequent decisions being made by managers throughout.

Organized Anarchy. The garbage can model was developed to explain the pattern of decision making in organizations that experience extremely high uncertainty,

EXHIBIT 12.6
Decision Process When Problem Identification and Problem Solution Are Uncertain

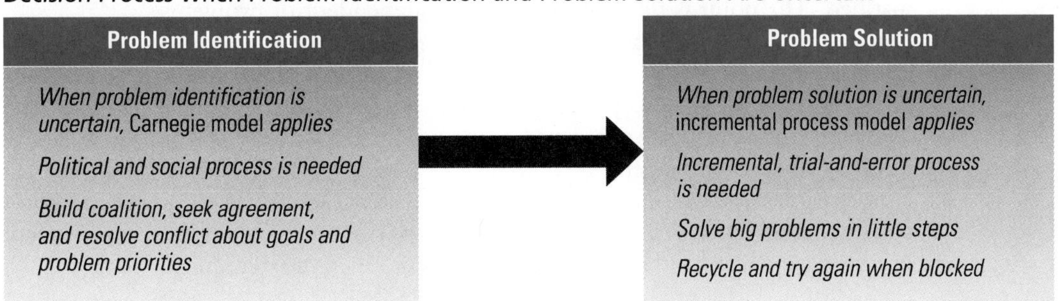

such as the growth and change required in a learning organization. Michael Cohen, James March, and Johan Olsen, the originators of the model, called the highly uncertain conditions an **organized anarchy**, which describes an extremely organic organization.[62] Organized anarchies do not rely on the normal vertical hierarchy of authority and bureaucratic decision rules. They result from three characteristics:

1. *Problematic preferences.* Goals, problems, alternatives, and solutions are ill defined. Ambiguity characterizes each step of a decision process.
2. *Unclear, poorly understood technology.* Cause-and-effect relationships within the organization are difficult to identify. An explicit database that applies to decisions is not available.
3. *Turnover.* Organizational positions experience turnover of participants. In addition, employees are busy and have only limited time to allocate to any one problem or decision. Participation in any given decision will be fluid and limited.

An organized anarchy is characterized by rapid change and a collegial, nonbureaucratic environment. No organization fits this extremely organic circumstance all the time, although learning organizations and today's Internet-based companies may experience it much of the time. Many organizations will occasionally find themselves in positions of making decisions under unclear, problematic circumstances. The garbage can model is very useful for understanding the pattern of these decisions.

Streams of Events. The unique characteristic of the garbage can model is that the decision process is not seen as a sequence of steps that begins with a problem and ends with a solution. Indeed, problem identification and problem solution may not be connected to each other. An idea may be proposed as a solution when no problem is specified. A problem may exist and never generate a solution. Decisions are the outcome of independent streams of events within the organization. The four streams relevant to organizational decision making are as follows:

1. *Problems.* Problems are points of dissatisfaction with current activities and performance. They represent a gap between desired performance and current activities. Problems are perceived to require attention. However, they are distinct from solutions and choices. A problem may lead to a proposed solution or it may not. Problems may not be solved when solutions are adopted.
2. *Potential solutions.* A solution is an idea somebody proposes for adoption. Such ideas form a flow of alternative solutions through the organization. Ideas may be brought into the organization by new personnel or may be invented by existing personnel. Participants may simply be attracted to certain ideas and push them as logical choices regardless of problems. Attraction to an idea may cause an employee to look for a problem to which the idea can be attached and, hence, justified. The point is that solutions exist independent of problems.
3. *Participants.* Organization participants are employees who come and go throughout the organization. People are hired, reassigned, and fired. Participants vary widely in their ideas, perception of problems, experience, values, and training. The problems and solutions recognized by one manager will differ from those recognized by another manager.
4. *Choice opportunities.* Choice opportunities are occasions when an organization usually makes a decision. They occur when contracts are signed, people are hired, or a new product is authorized. They also occur when the right mix of participants,

solutions, and problems exists. Thus, a manager who happened to learn of a good idea may suddenly become aware of a problem to which it applies and, hence, can provide the organization with a choice opportunity. Match-ups of problems and solutions often result in decisions.

With the concept of four streams, the overall pattern of organizational decision making takes on a random quality. Problems, solutions, participants, and choices all flow through the organization. In one sense, the organization is a large garbage can in which these streams are being stirred, as illustrated in Exhibit 12.7. When a problem, solution, and participant happen to connect at one point, a decision may be made and the problem may be solved; but if the solution does not fit the problem, the problem may not be solved.

Thus, when viewing the organization as a whole and considering its high level of uncertainty, one sees problems arise that are not solved and solutions tried that do not work. Organization decisions are disorderly and not the result of a logical, step-by-step sequence. Events may be so ill defined and complex that decisions, problems, and solutions act as independent events. When they connect, some problems are solved, but many are not.[63] One study of 2,476 white collar workers in 21 Japanese companies, using a computer simulation, found some support for the garbage can model and underscored the usefulness of the model in saving time in decision making.[64]

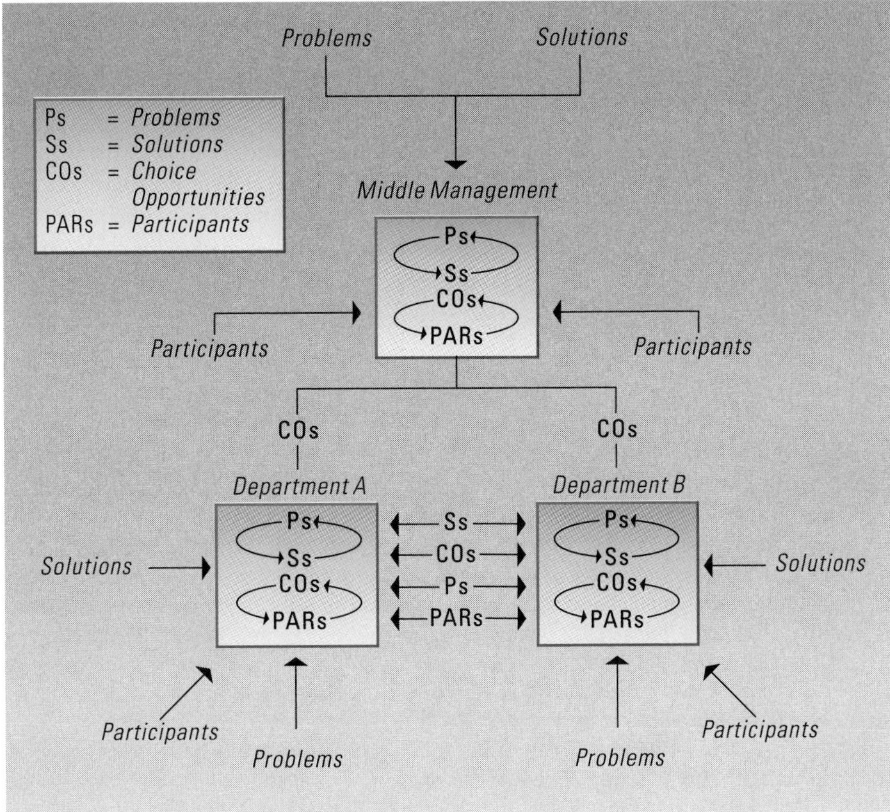

EXHIBIT 12.7
Illustration of Independent Streams of Events in the Garbage Can Model of Decision Making

Consequences. There are four specific consequences of the garbage can decision process for organizational decision making:

1. *Solutions may be proposed even when problems do not exist.* An employee might be sold on an idea and might try to sell it to the rest of the organization. An example was the adoption of computers by many organizations during the 1970s. The computer was an exciting solution and was pushed by both computer manufacturers and systems analysts within organizations. The computer did not solve any problems in those initial applications. Indeed, some computers caused more problems than they solved.
2. *Choices are made without solving problems.* A choice such as creating a new department may be made with the intention of solving a problem; but, under conditions of high uncertainty, the choice may be incorrect. Moreover, many choices just seem to happen. People decide to quit, the organization's budget is cut, or a new policy bulletin is issued. These choices may be oriented toward problems but do not necessarily solve them.
3. *Problems may persist without being solved.* Organization participants get used to certain problems and give up trying to solve them; or participants may not know how to solve certain problems because the technology is unclear. For example, a university was placed on probation by the American Association of University Professors because a professor had been denied tenure without due process. The probation was a nagging annoyance that the administrators wanted to remove. Fifteen years later, the nontenured professor died. The probation continues because the university did not acquiesce to the demands of the heirs of the association to re-evaluate the case. The university would like to solve the problem, but administrators are not sure how, and they do not have the resources to allocate to it. The probation problem persists without a solution.
4. *A few problems are solved.* The decision process does work in the aggregate. In computer simulation models of the garbage can model, important problems were often resolved. Solutions do connect with appropriate problems and participants so that a good choice is made. Of course, not all problems are resolved when choices are made, but the organization does move in the direction of problem reduction.

The effects of independent streams and the rather chaotic decision processes of the garbage can model can be seen in the production of David O. Russell's movie *I ♥ Huckabees,* which has been called an "existential comedy."

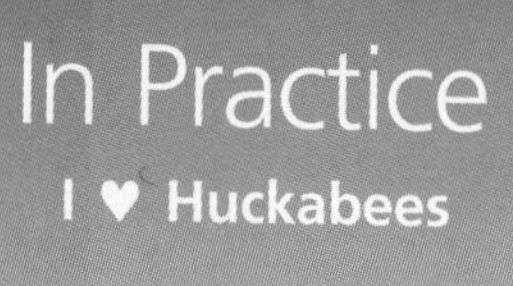

In Practice
I ♥ Huckabees

Screenwriter and director David O. Russell has become known for creating intelligent, original movies such as *Flirting with Disaster* and *Three Kings*. His 2004 film *I ♥ Huckabees* might be the most original—or some would say just plain weird—so far. *The New York Times* noted that the film "will probably drive some audiences bonkers. Loud, messy, aggressively in your face and generally played for the back row in the theater, the film doesn't offer up solutions, tender any comfort or rejoice in the triumph of the human spirit." Yet the movie got decent critical reviews and was picked by the *Village Voice* as one of the best films of 2004.[65]

Russell had a vision of what he wanted the movie to be from the beginning, but few others could grasp what that was. Most of the actors who signed on to star in *I ♥ Huckabees* admit that they didn't really understand the script, but trusted Russell's vision and imagination. Two of the biggest actors in Hollywood, Jude Law and Gwyneth Paltrow, signed on to play employees at a department store chain called Huckabees. But Paltrow backed out before filming ever started. Nicole Kidman was interested but had a conflict. Jennifer Aniston became—and as quickly unbecame—a possibility. Finally, Naomi Watts, who had been Russell's original choice for the role, was able to free herself from scheduling conflicts to take the part. The casting wasn't quite set though. Jude Law dropped out for unknown reasons—but just as quickly dropped back in.

Filming was chaotic. As the actors were on camera saying the lines they'd memorized, Russell was a few feet away continually calling out new lines to them. In one scene, Law became so exhausted and frustrated that he started pounding his fists in the grass and shouting expletives. Russell loved the improvisation and kept the cameras rolling. Actors were unsure of how to develop their characterizations, so they just did whatever seemed right at the time, often based on Russell's efforts to keep them off balance. Scenes were often filmed blindly with no idea of how they were supposed to fit in the overall story.

After Russell's hours in the editing room, the final film turned out to be quite different from what the actors thought they'd shot. Some major scenes, including one that was supposed to articulate the film's theme that everything is connected, were cut entirely.

Amazingly, considering the chaos on the set, the film was completed on schedule and on budget. Although *I ♥ Huckabees* is emotionally and intellectually dense, and not the kind of movie that reaps big bucks, the haphazard process worked to create the movie David O. Russell wanted to make.[66]

The production of *I ♥ Huckabees* was not a rational process that started with a clear problem and ended with a logical solution. Many events occurred by chance and were intertwined, which characterizes the garbage can model. Everyone from the director to the actors continuously added to the stream of new ideas for the story. Some solutions were connected to emerging problems: Naomi Watts cleared her schedule just in time to take the role after Gwyneth Paltrow dropped out, for example. The actors (participants) daily made personal choices regarding characterization that proved to be right for the story line. The garbage can model, however, doesn't always work—in the movies or in organizations. A similar haphazard process during the filming of *Waterworld* led to the most expensive film in Hollywood history and a decided box-office flop for Universal Pictures.[67]

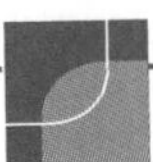

Contingency Decision-Making Framework

This chapter has covered several approaches to organizational decision making, including management science, the Carnegie model, the incremental decision process model, and the garbage can model. It has also discussed rational and intuitive decision processes used by individual managers. Each decision approach is a relatively accurate description of the actual decision process, yet all differ from each other. Management science, for example, reflects a different set of decision assumptions and procedures than does the garbage can model.

One reason for having different approaches is that they appear in different organizational situations. The use of an approach is contingent on the organization setting. Two characteristics of organizations that determine the use of decision approaches are (1) problem consensus and (2) technical knowledge about the means to solve those problems.[68] Analyzing organizations along these two dimensions suggests which approach will be used to make decisions.

Problem Consensus

Problem consensus refers to the agreement among managers about the nature of a problem or opportunity and about which goals and outcomes to pursue. This variable ranges from complete agreement to complete disagreement. When managers agree, there is little uncertainty—the problems and goals of the organization are clear, and so are standards of performance. When managers disagree, organization direction and performance expectations are in dispute, creating a situation of high uncertainty. One example of problem uncertainty occurred at Wal-Mart stores regarding the use of parking lot patrols. Some managers presented evidence that golf-cart patrols significantly reduced auto theft, assault, and other crimes in the stores' lots and increased business because they encouraged more shopping at night. These managers argued that the patrols should be used, but others believed the patrols were not needed and were too expensive, emphasizing that parking lot crime was a society problem rather than a store problem.[69]

Problem consensus tends to be low when organizations are differentiated, as described in Chapter 4. Recall that uncertain environments cause organizational departments to differentiate from one another in goals and attitudes to specialize in specific environmental sectors. This differentiation leads to disagreement and conflict, so managers must make a special effort to build coalitions during decision making. For example, NASA has been criticized for failing to identify problems with the *Columbia* space shuttle that might have prevented the February 2003 disaster. Part of the reason was high differentiation and conflicting opinions between safety managers and scheduling managers, in which pressure to launch on time overrode safety concerns. In addition, after the launch, engineers three times requested—and were denied—better photos to assess the damage from a piece of foam debris that struck the shuttle's left wing just seconds after launch. Investigations now indicate that the damage caused by the debris may have been the primary physical cause of the explosion. Mechanisms for hearing dissenting opinions and building coalitions can improve decision making at NASA and other organizations dealing with complex problems.[70]

Problem consensus is especially important for the problem identification stage of decision making. When problems are clear and agreed on, they provide clear standards and expectations for performance. When problems are not agreed on, problem identification is uncertain and management attention must be focused on gaining agreement about goals and priorities.

Technical Knowledge about Solutions

Technical knowledge refers to understanding and agreement about how to solve problems and reach organizational goals. This variable can range from complete agreement and certainty to complete disagreement and uncertainty about cause–effect relationships leading to problem solution. One example of low technical knowledge occurred at PepsiCo's 7Up division. Managers agreed on the problem to be solved—they wanted to increase market share from 6 to 7 percent. However, the means for achieving this increase in market share were not known or agreed on. A few managers wanted to use discount pricing in supermarkets. Other managers believed they should increase the number of soda fountain outlets in restaurants and fast-food chains. A few other managers insisted that the best approach was to increase advertising through radio and television. Managers did not know what would cause an increase in market share. Eventually, the advertising judgment prevailed at 7Up, but it did not work very well. The failure of its decision reflected the managers low technical knowledge about how to solve the problem.

When means (methods) are well understood, the appropriate alternatives can be identified and calculated with some degree of certainty. When means are poorly understood, potential solutions are ill defined and uncertain. Intuition, judgment, and trial and error become the basis for decisions.

Contingency Framework

Exhibit 12.8 describes the **contingency decision-making framework**, which brings together the two dimensions of problem consensus and technical knowledge about solutions. Each cell represents an organizational situation that is appropriate for the decision-making approaches described in this chapter.

Cell 1. In cell 1 of Exhibit 12.8, rational decision procedures are used because problems are agreed on and cause–effect relationships are well understood, so there is little uncertainty. Decisions can be made in a computational manner. Alternatives can be identified and the best solution adopted through analysis and calculations. The rational models described earlier in this chapter, both for individuals and for the organization, are appropriate when problems and the means for solving them are well defined.

Cell 2. In cell 2, there is high uncertainty about problems and priorities, so bargaining and compromise are used to reach consensus. Tackling one problem might mean the organization must postpone action on other issues. The priorities given to respective problems are decided through discussion, debate, and coalition building.

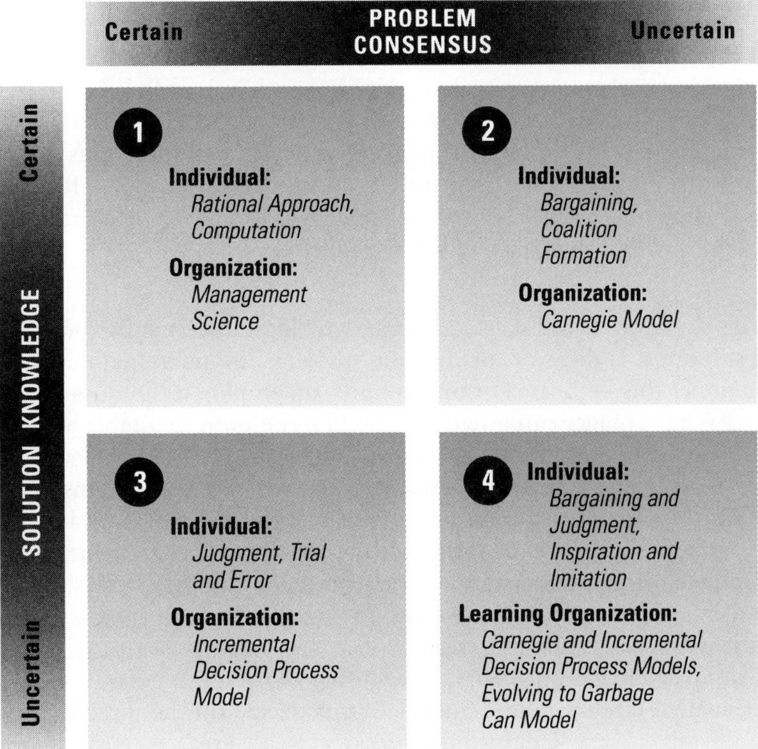

EXHIBIT 12.8
Contingency Framework for Using Decision Models

Managers in this situation should use broad participation to achieve consensus in the decision process. Opinions should be surfaced and discussed until compromise is reached. The organization will not otherwise move forward as an integrated unit. In the case of Wal-Mart, managers will discuss conflicting opinions about the benefits and costs of parking lot patrols.

The Carnegie model applies when there is dissension about organizational problems. When groups within the organization disagree, or when the organization is in conflict with constituencies (government regulators, suppliers, unions), bargaining and negotiation are required. The bargaining strategy is especially relevant to the problem identification stage of the decision process. Once bargaining and negotiation are completed, the organization will have support for one direction.

Cell 3. In a cell 3 situation, problems and standards of performance are certain, but alternative technical solutions are vague and uncertain. Techniques to solve a problem are ill defined and poorly understood. When an individual manager faces this situation, intuition will be the decision guideline. The manager will rely on past experience and judgment to make a decision. Rational, analytical approaches are not effective because the alternatives cannot be identified and calculated. Hard facts and accurate information are not available.

The incremental decision process model reflects trial and error on the part of the organization. Once a problem is identified, a sequence of small steps enables the organization to learn a solution. As new problems arise, the organization may recycle back to an earlier point and start over. Eventually, over a period of months or years, the organization will acquire sufficient experience to solve the problem in a satisfactory way.

McDonald's provides an example of a cell 3 situation. Managers are searching for ways to revive flagging sales at the fast-food chain's North American restaurants. They are using trial and error to come up with the right combination of management changes, new menu items such as the Fruit and Walnut Salad, and fresh advertising approaches that will rekindle sales and recharge McDonald's image.

The situation in cell 3, of senior managers agreeing about problems but not knowing how to solve them, occurs frequently in business organizations. If managers use incremental decisions in such situations, they will eventually acquire the technical knowledge to accomplish goals and solve problems.

Cell 4. The situation in cell 4, characterized by high uncertainty about both problems and solutions, is difficult for decision making. An individual manager making a decision under this high level of uncertainty can employ techniques from both cell 2 and cell 3. The manager can attempt to build a coalition to establish goals and priorities and use judgment, intuition, or trial and error to solve problems. Additional techniques, such as inspiration and imitation, also may be required. **Inspiration** refers to an innovative, creative solution that is not reached by logical means. Inspiration sometimes comes like a flash of insight, but—similar to intuition—it is often based on deep knowledge and understanding of a problem that the unconscious mind has had time to mull over.[71] **Imitation** means adopting a decision tried elsewhere in the hope that it will work in this situation.

For example, in one university, accounting department faculty were unhappy with their current circumstances but could not decide on the direction the department should take. Some faculty members wanted a greater research orientation, whereas others wanted greater orientation toward business firms and accounting applications. The disagreement about goals was compounded because neither group was sure about the best technique for achieving its goals. The ultimate solution was inspirational on the part of the dean. An accounting research centre was established with funding from major accounting firms. The funding was used to finance research activities for faculty interested in basic research and to provide contact with business firms for other faculty. The solution provided a common goal and unified people within the department to work toward that goal.

When an entire organization is characterized by high uncertainty regarding both problems and solutions, as in learning organizations, elements of the garbage can model will appear. Managers may first try techniques from both cells 2 and 3, but logical decision sequences starting with problem identification and ending with problem solution will not occur. Potential solutions will precede problems as often as problems precede solutions. In this situation, managers should encourage widespread discussion of problems and idea proposals to facilitate the opportunity to make choices. Eventually, through trial and error, the organization will solve some problems.

Research has found that decisions made following the prescriptions of the contingency decision-making framework tend to be more successful; the study noted that nearly six of ten strategic management decisions failed to follow the framework, leading to a situation in which misleading or missing information decreased the chance of an effective decision choice.[72]

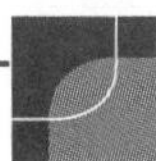

Special Decision Circumstances

In a highly competitive world beset by global competition and rapid change, decision making seldom fits the traditional rational, analytical model. Today's managers have to make high-stakes decisions more often and more quickly than ever before in an environment that is increasingly less predictable. For example, interviews with CEOs in high-tech industries found that they strive to use some type of rational process, but the uncertainty and change in the industry often make that approach unsuccessful. These managers actually reach decisions through a complex process of interacting with other managers, subordinates, environmental factors, and organizational events.[73]

Three issues of particular concern for today's decision makers are coping with high-velocity environments, learning from decision mistakes, and avoiding escalating commitment.

PDA Remember...

Track real-time information, build multiple alternatives simultaneously, and try to involve everyone—but move ahead anyway when making decisions in a high-velocity environment.

High-Velocity Environments

In some industries today, the rate of competitive and technological change is so extreme that market data are either unavailable or obsolete; strategic windows open and shut quickly, perhaps within a few months; and the cost of poor decisions is company failure. Research has examined how successful companies make decisions in these **high-velocity environments**, especially to understand whether organizations abandon rational approaches or have time for incremental implementation.[74]

A comparison of successful with unsuccessful decisions in high-velocity environments found the following patterns:

- Successful decision makers tracked information in real time to develop a deep and intuitive grasp of the business. Two to three intense meetings per week with all key players were usual. Decision makers tracked operating statistics about cash, scrap, backlog, work in process, and shipments to constantly feel the pulse of what was happening. Unsuccessful firms were more concerned with future planning and forward-looking information, with only a loose grip on immediate happenings.
- During a major decision, successful companies began immediately to build multiple alternatives. Implementation of alternatives sometimes ran in parallel before management finally settled on a final choice. Companies that made decisions slowly developed just one alternative, moving to another only after the first one failed.
- Fast, successful decision makers sought advice from everyone and depended heavily on one or two savvy, trusted colleagues as counsellors. Slow companies were unable to build trust and agreement among the best people.
- Fast companies involved everyone in the decision and tried for consensus; but if consensus did not emerge, the top manager made the choice and moved ahead. Waiting for everyone to be on board created more delays than was warranted. Slow companies delayed decisions to achieve a uniform consensus.
- Fast, successful choices were well integrated with other decisions and the overall strategic direction of the company. Less successful choices considered the decision in isolation from other decisions; the decision was made in the abstract.[75]

When speed matters, a slow decision is as ineffective as the wrong decision. As we discussed in Chapter 11, speed is a crucial competitive weapon in a growing number of industries, and companies can learn to make decisions quickly. To improve the chances of a good decision under high-velocity conditions, some organizations stimulate constructive conflict through a technique called **point–counterpoint**, which divides decision makers into two groups and assigns them different, often competing responsibilities.[76] The groups develop and exchange proposals and debate options until they arrive at a common set of understandings and recommendations. Groups can often make better decisions because multiple and diverse opinions are considered. In the face of complexity and uncertainty, the more people who have a say in the decision making, the better. At Intel, the decision-making process typically involves people from several different areas and levels of hierarchy, "jousting with one another about the pros and cons of this or that," says CEO Craig Barrett.[77]

In group decision making, a consensus may not always be reached, but the exercise gives everyone a chance to consider options and state their opinions, and it gives top managers a broader understanding. Typically, those involved support the final choice. However, if a very speedy decision is required, top managers are willing to make the decision and move forward. Once a decision has been made at Intel, for example, it is everyone's responsibility to be involved and commit, even if they disagree. As Barrett says, "No backbiting, no second-guessing. We make a decision, we charge ahead."[78]

Decision Mistakes and Learning

Organizational decisions result in many errors, especially when made in conditions of great uncertainty. Managers simply cannot determine or predict which alternative will solve a problem. In these cases, the organization must make the decision—and take the risk—often in the spirit of trial and error. If an alternative fails, the organization can learn from it and try another alternative that better fits the situation. Each failure provides new information and insight. The point for managers is to move ahead with the decision process despite the potential for mistakes. "Chaotic action is preferable to orderly inaction."[79]

In some organizations, managers are encouraged to instill a climate of experimentation to facilitate creative decision making. If one idea fails, another idea should be tried. Failure often lays the groundwork for success, such as when technicians at 3M developed Post-it Notes based on a failed product—a not-very-sticky glue. Companies such as PepsiCo believe that if all their new products succeed, they're doing something wrong, not taking the necessary risks to develop new markets.[80]

Only by making mistakes can managers and organizations go through the process of **decision learning** and acquire sufficient experience and knowledge to perform more effectively in the future. Robert Townsend, who was president at Avis Corporation, gives the following advice:

Admit your mistakes openly, maybe even joyfully. Encourage your associates to do likewise by commiserating with them. Never castigate. Babies learn to walk by falling down. If you beat a baby every time he falls down, he'll never care much for walking.

My batting average on decisions at Avis was no better than a .333. Two out of every three decisions I made were wrong. But my mistakes were discussed openly and most of them corrected with a little help from my friends.[81]

PDA
Remember...

Do not persist in a course of action that is failing. Some actions will not work if uncertainty is high, so encourage organizational learning by readily trying new alternatives. Seek information and evidence that indicate when a course of action is failing, and allocate resources to new choices rather than to unsuccessful ventures.

Escalating Commitment

A much more dangerous mistake is to persist in a course of action when it is failing, a tendency referred to as **escalating commitment**. Research suggests that organizations often continue to invest time and money in a solution despite strong evidence that it is not working. Two explanations are given for why managers escalate commitment to a failing decision. The first is that managers block or distort negative information when they are personally responsible for a negative decision. They simply don't know when to pull the plug. In some cases, they continue to throw good money after bad even when a strategy seems incorrect and goals are not being met.[82]

A second explanation is that consistency and persistence are valued in contemporary society. Consistent managers are considered better leaders than those who switch from one course of action to another. Even though organizations learn through trial and error, organizational norms value consistency. These norms may result in a course of action being maintained, resources being squandered, and learning being inhibited. Senior managers, however, seem less likely to engage in escalating commitment.[83] For example, Ballard Power Systems had maintained its automotive division by pouring millions of dollars into developing a hydrogen-powered car. It claimed that the division was a key component of its business. Developing a hydrogen car was "the holy grail Ballard has chased for two and half decades."[84] In 2007, Ballard Power Systems announced that it was "reviewing strategic alternatives" with Daimler AG and the Ford Motor Company in what analysts described as an admission that the holy grail was unattainable. The automotive division was sold in November 2007. Twenty percent of Ballard's R&D employees were transferred to a newly created private company, managed and funded by Daimler AG and the Ford Motor Company, which "will be positioned for success in automotive fuel cell technology over the longer term . . . "[85]

Failure to admit a mistake and adopt a new course of action should be replaced by an attitude that tolerates mistakes to encourage learning. Based on what has been said about decision making in this chapter, one can expect companies to be ultimately successful in their decision making by adopting a learning approach toward solutions. They will make mistakes along the way, but they will resolve uncertainty through the trial-and-error process.

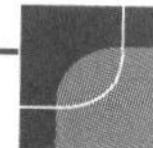

Summary and Interpretation

The most important idea in this chapter is that most organizational decisions are not made in a logical, rational manner. Most decisions do not begin with the careful analysis of a problem, followed by systematic analysis of alternatives, and finally implementation of a solution. On the contrary, decision processes are characterized by conflict, coalition building, trial and error, speed, and mistakes. Managers operate under many constraints that limit rationality; hence, intuition and hunch often are the criteria for choice.

Another important idea is that individuals make decisions, but organizational decisions are not made by a single individual. Organizational decision making is a social process. Only in rare circumstances do managers analyze problems and find solutions by themselves. Many problems are not clear, so widespread discussion and coalition building take place. Once goals and priorities are set, alternatives to achieve those goals can be tried. When a manager does make an individual decision, it is often a small part of a larger decision process. Organizations solve big problems through a series of small steps. A single manager may initiate one step but should be aware of the larger decision process to which it belongs.

The greatest amount of conflict and coalition building occurs when problems are not agreed on. Priorities must be established to indicate which goals are important and what problems should be solved first. If a manager attacks a problem other people do not agree with, the manager will lose support for the solution to be implemented. Thus, as the Carnegie model suggests, time and activity should be spent building a coalition in the problem identification stage of decision making. Then the organization can move toward solutions. Under conditions of low technical knowledge, the solution unfolds through an incremental decision process that will gradually lead to an overall solution. In contrast, the management science approach works well when problems are analyzable.

The most novel description of decision making is the garbage can model. This model describes how decision processes can seem almost random in highly organic organizations such as learning organizations. Decisions, problems, ideas, and people flow through these organizations and mix together in various combinations. Through this process, the organization gradually learns. Some problems may never be solved, but many are, and the organization will move toward maintaining and improving its level of performance.

Finally, many organizations must make decisions with speed, which means staying in immediate touch with operations and the environment. Moreover, in an uncertain world, organizations will make mistakes, and mistakes made through trial and error should be encouraged to facilitate organizational learning. On the other hand, an unwillingness to change from a failing course of action can have serious negative consequences for an organization. Norms for consistency and the desire to prove one's decision correct can lead to continued investment in a useless course of action.

Key Concepts

bounded rationality perspective, p. 432
Carnegie model, p. 442
coalition, p. 442
contingency decision-making framework, p. 455
decision learning, p. 459
escalating commitment, p. 459
garbage can model, p. 449
high-velocity environments, p. 457
imitation, p. 456
incremental decision process model, p. 444
inspiration, p. 456
intuitive decision making, p. 436
management science approach, p. 440
nonprogrammed decisions, p. 431
organizational decision making, p. 430
organized anarchy, p. 450
point–counterpoint, p. 458
problem consensus, p. 454
problem identification, p. 430
problem solution, p. 430
problemistic search, p. 443
programmed decisions, p. 430
rational approach, p. 432
satisficing, p. 443
technical knowledge, p. 454

Discussion Questions

1. When you are faced with choosing between several valid options, how do you typically make your decision? How do you think managers typically choose between several options? What are the similarities between your decision process and what you think managers do?
2. A professional economist once told her class, "An individual decision maker should process all relevant information and select the economically rational alternative." Do you agree? Why or why not?
3. Do you think intuition is a valid way to make important business decisions? Why or why not? Can you think of a time when you used intuition to make a decision?
4. The Carnegie model emphasizes the need for a political coalition in the decision-making process. When and why are coalitions necessary?
5. What are the three major phases in Mintzberg's incremental decision process model? Why might an organization recycle through one or more phases of the model?
6. An organization theorist once told his class, "Organizations never make big decisions. They make small decisions that eventually add up to a big decision." Explain the logic behind this statement.
7. How would you make a decision to select a building site for a new waste-treatment plant in South Africa? Where would you start with this complex decision, and what steps would you take? Explain which decision model in the chapter best describes your approach.
8. Why would managers in high-velocity environments worry more about the present than the future? Discuss.
9. Describe the four streams of events in the garbage can model of decision making. Do you think those streams are independent of each other? Why?
10. Why are decision mistakes usually accepted in organizations penalized in university courses and exams that are designed to train managers?

Chapter 12 Workbook: Decision Styles*

Think of some recent decisions that have influenced your life. Choose two significant decisions that you made and two decisions that other people made. Fill out the following table, using Exhibit 12.8 to determine decision styles.

Your decisions	Approach used	Advantages and disadvantages	Your recommended decision style
1.			
2.			
Decisions by others			
1.			
2.			

*Adapted by Dorothy Marcic from "Action Assignment" in Jennifer M. Howard and Lawrence M. Miller, *Team Management* (Miller Consulting Group, 1994), 205.

Questions

1. How can a decision approach influence the outcome of the decision? What happens when the approach fits the decision? When it doesn't fit?
2. How can you know which approach is best?

Case for Analysis: Decision Making in Command and Control

Throughout history, military commanders have been confronted with the problem of planning and controlling operations amid the confusion and constant change of the battlefield. Modern technology has not changed this,[1] as uncertainty remains an inevitable feature of command. Yet, decisiveness is an essential requirement of effective command, especially as the tempo of warfare has increased. The changing global political situation is forcing military organizations, including the Canadian Forces (CF), to expand and change the ways they conduct operations. Thus, there is a continued need for the study of decision making in the military context, ranging from basic research on how people make decisions and solve complex problems to applied work on the development of training and support systems to aid commanders' decision making in the field. This sort of research is especially important today because military operations are becoming increasingly demanding, fast-paced, and risk-filled.[2]

Two Approaches of Decision Making

The purpose of this paper is to contrast two general but highly influential approaches to understanding decision making. These approaches differ in a number of key respects, but each has been applied, in some form, to the study of military Command and Control (C2). Classically, theories within the first approach of decision making are based on the premise that human decision making can be modelled in terms of formal processes predicted by normative theories of probability and logic.[3] These theories have been popular in the development, by researchers, of support for military decision makers, perhaps because there is often an assumption that good decision making follows a rational approach in which decisions are based on expected outcomes and there is an attempt to select a course of action that will bring the optimal outcome.[4]

Within that last 15 years, however, there has been recognition that the nature of the real-world battlefield limits a human decision maker's ability to implement truly analytic processes.[5] This has led to the development of another approach that comprises what are called naturalistic or intuitive theories of decision making. This approach is based on the premise that people use informal procedures or heuristics to make decisions within the restrictions of available time, limited information, and limited cognitive processing capacity. Intuitive decision making, as we will see, offers a clearly different way to think about decision making than the analytic approach. We will later argue, however, that these diverging approaches can nevertheless be synthesized into an effective framework for understanding military decision making in its broadest sense.

The Analytic Approach

In taking normative theories as bases for developing descriptive models of decision making, researchers in the analytic tradition have emphasized explicitly computable processes to take in information, code it symbolically, manipulate these symbolic representations, and generate some output.[6] Analytic theories require some kind of formal comparison among decision alternatives using deliberate and procedural rules that quantify those alternatives.[7] This assumes that all pertinent factors can be both identified and quantified in terms of their absolute or relative impact. Methods of comparison are based on various kinds of sequential or distributed, logical and/or mathematical algorithms,[8] so that there is a direct link between facts and conclusions. Numerous specific procedures for comparing alternatives are known, most of which can be computationally modelled by production systems operating on a representation of the problem space.[9] Many, for example, are based on Bayesian statistics and evaluate options in terms of base rates for different hypotheses and probabilities of the accuracy of different observations.[10] Other analytic strategies include subjective expected utility analysis, single feature difference, and elimination by aspects.[11]

To select a decision alternative, the decision maker needs to specify one or more dimensions along which to compare the alternatives. Typically, researchers propose that these computations are based on compensatory algorithms in which information types are weighted and values of one type can compensate for the absence of other types.[12] A popular general form of analytic theory is the linear compensatory model, which involves the computation of an overall score for each decision alternative based on the sum of relevant dimension values for each alternative, weighted by each dimension's importance.[13] Because the score of each alternative is based on all known dimensions, effects of large and small dimension values can compensate one another in determining the overall desirability of the alternative.[14]

A core assumption of analytic theories is that the goal of decision making is to reach an optimal decision as assessed along some criterion dimension.[15] Optimality is a difficult concept to operationalize in the military (or any other) context, but it is generally defined in terms of maximizing benefits, such as enemy units destroyed and friendly units preserved in tactical situations, while minimizing costs.[16] A premise related to achieving optimality is that all possible hypotheses must be analyzed because there is no *a priori* means of knowing what alternative will be optimal.[17] As a consequence, analytic decision making entails extensive computations, except for very simple problems.

Although analytic theories have been tested with great experimental rigor, there are a number of conceptual problems with this approach. Analytic theories generally assume some form of exhaustive option generation and evaluation, implying that people either have access to all possible options or are somehow able to generate a complete set. Such a comprehensive search, however, would be extremely time consuming, if not impossible, in real-world problems, given limitations on human knowledge and cognitive capacity. In fact, studies have found that expert decision makers tend to generate only a few potential solutions when solving complex real world problems.[18] Moreover, it may not be possible to construct a complete representation of the problem space, including their goals, the values of potential outcomes, and the probabilities of certain actions producing certain outcomes.[19] This is especially true for a complex military problem. Decision makers may lack access to knowledge that would allow them to determine potential outcomes and their probabilities. In cases where the problem is not simple, the number of parameters and potential courses of action may make the process of just describing the problem space so complex that one would have to assume near-omniscient capabilities to process the data in real-time.

Tests of analytic theories have generally been conducted in the context of relatively simple problems, such as inferences with binary choices or problems with small amounts of data, and situations in which decision makers have sufficient time and access to all relevant knowledge and information.[20] Such situations bear little similarity to the fast paced, high risk environment of military operations, thus raising questions regarding the applicability of analytic theories to this domain.[21] In real-world domains, people are likely to deal with multiple pieces of information that may be ambiguous, highly inter-related, and potentially obscured or missing. Such limitations can make analytical theories intractable and highly implausible as descriptive models of human decision making.[22]

The Intuitive Approach

Over the past 10 to 12 years, intuitive theories of decision making have become influential in explaining decision making in C2 and other complex, real-world domains. Intuitive theories, or Natural Decision Making (NDM) theories as they are most often called,[23] are based on descriptive, rather than normative, models of the strategies employed by experienced decision makers in coping with real problems.[24] Lipshitz, Klein, Orasanu, and Salas,[25] for example, base assessments of the quality of decision making on the behaviours exhibited by experts rather than some formal model. In particular, intuitive theories dispense with the concept of normative choice and assume that human decision makers use much less formal but much faster strategies.

Three basic principles underlie intuitive theories.[26] The first is that decisions are made by sequential, *holistic evaluation* of potential courses of action against some criterion of acceptability rather than by feature-by-feature comparison of multiple alternatives along multiple dimensions. The second principle is that the decision maker relies primarily on *recognition-based processes* to generate options and compare them to previous experiences (including actual on-the-job and training experiences). Thus, there is no exhaustive generation and comparison of alternatives.

Instead, the decision maker identifies potential courses of action by first assessing the situation then recognizing past situations that are similar. Based on past experience, the decision maker can recall previously taken courses of action and determine their acceptability to the current situation. The third principle is that decision makers adopt a satisficing criterion, stopping the search when an acceptable course of action is identified, rather than searching for an optimal solution.[27] Real world situations often demand very rapid responses and decision makers may have to accept a solution that merely works without considering whether a better solution exists.

An influential example of the intuitive approach to decision making is Klein's[28] Recognition-Primed Decision (RPD) model.[29] Like all intuitive models, it eschews formal, logical processes and instead emphasizes pattern matching processes, in which the decision maker first appraises the situation to classify it as familiar or not, based on experience. The RPD model incorporates additional processes meant to complement recognition in cases where the decision maker is unable to recognize the current situation.[30] A typical reaction is to seek more information and this sort of on-going situation assessment is a crucial component of decision making in the RPD model.[31] In addition, diagnostic processes such as story building can resolve ambiguous situations. In this case, the decision maker deliberately notes features of the situation and attempts to create a detailed hypothesis, or story, that could explain that configuration of features, even in cases in which the availability of information is limited. Once the decision maker has diagnosed the situation, he or she can use mental simulation to form expectations about future events that serve to test the working hypothesis. If there are too many inconsistencies between the hypothesis and the situation, the decision maker must revise his or her hypothesis.

The major problem for research with the intuitive approach to decision making has been the generally vague level at which models have been formulated. Indeed, Todd and Gigerenzer[32] have argued that researchers have deliberately avoided detailed theorization in the mistaken belief that decision making processes actually used in real-world environments cannot be formally modeled. Certainly, researchers in the behavioural sciences have traditionally sought general models of cognitive functioning, but this does not preclude in-depth modeling of specific cognitive operations in specific decision making settings. Without more detailed models, it will be difficult to develop meaningfully specific hypotheses to test intuitive models of decision making.

Decision Making in the Military Context

Both classes of theory have received empirical support in various contexts,[33] and this precludes a simple conclusion that one is an inherently better theory than the other. The best that can be done is to consider the question of the particular military situations and conditions under which one type of theory might serve as a better model of human decision making than the other.

Although analytic models generally do a poor job of describing how people actually make decisions, they are highly explainable and prescriptive. The steps and processes involved in decision making are clearly specified and can usually be implemented as computer programmes. Consequently, these models are excellent tools for predicting and exploring military decision making performance. In addition, the focus of analytic models is on obtaining the optimal solution to a problem, which is, of course, highly desirable in any domain as long as it can reasonably be achieved. This suggests that analytic models might apply in situations in which there are well-defined goals and in which factors and options can be explicitly defined.

Intuitive theories have the advantages of being closely linked to what expert decision makers actually do in real-world situations and of being applicable to dynamic, uncertain, and high risk environments, as demonstrated in numerous empirical studies.[34] Intuitive approaches certainly are better suited to situations where time and data are limited.[35] Their usefulness as models of decision making, however, can be limited by their informal nature, which makes it difficult to develop specific, testable hypotheses for research.[36] Also, intuitive theories are, by their nature, more descriptive than prescriptive, making them effective for understanding human decision making but less so for developing systems to aid/support actual decision making performance.[37]

In all likelihood, no single decision making approach can be considered best for explaining how people make decisions in all situations. Certain phases of a military operation, such as planning and preparation, afford more time, more complete data, and greater access to computing resources than do other phases, such as activities related to surveillance, threat detection, and threat response. Thus, what should be considered an appropriate approach to modelling decision making will depend on the particular operational context. In this case, we can perhaps see analytic and intuitive decision making not as competing classes of theories but as different kinds of decision making *strategies*. By strategy, we mean a specific mental procedure by which the decision maker computes or infers his/her choice of a course of action. Analytic strategies would represent an ideal set of procedures that can be used to approach optimality, whereas intuitive strategies would represent a more practical set of procedures suited to situations of limited time, information, and computational power. We assume that people have access to both types of decision making approaches, depending on their needs and the nature of the situation. Perhaps the key factor for choosing between analytic and intuitive strategies (i.e., a specific procedure to be applied to a specific problem) is whether one can accept a merely workable solution or whether one requires an optimal solution. It may be under only some circumstances in military command, such as planning and preparation, that decision makers have the time and high quality data needed to engage in truly analytic processing.

The idea that people have access to many different decision making strategies/procedures is not new, as others have distinguished 'strong' (formal) from 'weak' (heuristic or intuitive) methods of reasoning.[38] We likewise believe that analytic and intuitive decision making theories actually represent distinct strategies or methods of decision making. Moreover, these methods fall at opposing ends of a continuum of possible decision making procedures, as illustrated in Figure 1. This continuum is based on the formalism of the decision making method, which is defined by how exhaustive, quantitative, and compensatory the procedure is, and by how many options are evaluated, and whether the options are considered sequentially against a criterion or concurrently through feature-by-feature evaluation. Analytic methods are those in which multiple options are evaluated through an exhaustive, quantitative, and compensatory feature-based analysis. Intuitive methods are those in which alternatives are evaluated holistically through a sequential comparison process that is generally qualitative, noncompensatory and not exhaustive. Thus, there are many kinds of analytic procedures and many kinds of intuitive procedures, all varying in their degree of formalism.[39]

Both analytic and intuitive methods seem to be valid, as empirical evidence suggests that people have access to at least these two broad classes of decision making processes. A particular decision making procedure can be selected as needed, depending on the problem and situation.[40] Although truly analytic processing is difficult to apply, except to simple problems, the constraints of knowledge and time vary in real-world problems, allowing applied decision making strategies to vary in terms of their analytic formalism. Because military planning typically takes place under (relatively) light time pressure and sometimes (if not always) with relatively large amounts of high quality data (especially if various decision and computation tools are available for use over extended periods of time), analytic strategies may be better suited to this stage of operations. When planning, decision makers are more likely to have the time and access to resources needed to clearly define the problem and consider multiple courses of action. Also, there is greater emphasis on determining the best possible solutions rather than merely satisfactory ones because the goal is to develop the best possible plans and procedures to achieve mission objectives. When the enemy is engaged, however, commanders may be forced to rely on intuitive methods because their time and knowledge are limited. The reliance on intuitive decision making strategies would not be surprising in tactical situations, given the advantages of speed and information processing efficiency conveyed by these strategies.

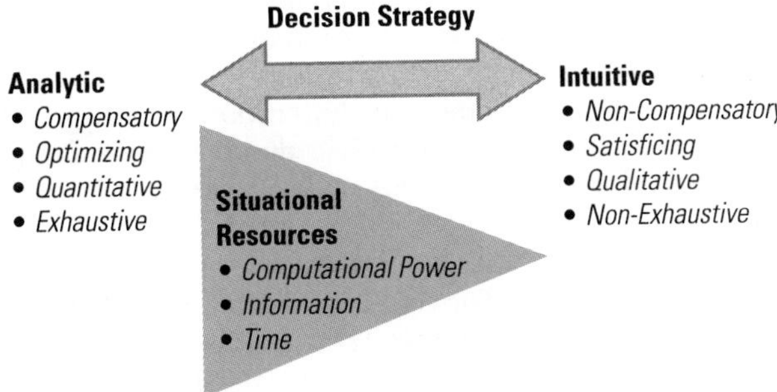

FIGURE 1
Proposed Continuum of Decision Making Strategies and Its Relation to the Amount of Resources Available in the Situation.

Some studies suggest that analytic and intuitive decision making strategies interact in complex problem domains.[41] Roth,[42] for example, found that nuclear power station crews exhibited both situation assessment activities, consistent with intuitive decision making, and procedural activity in which crews attempted to apply pre-planned responses when responding to simulated emergencies. This is, in a sense, an intuitive strategy but it relies on analytic approaches having been performed in a preparatory phase; that is, operators developed links between anticipated events and the responses that would be appropriate. In this case, crews spent time before confronting the emergency developing procedures to deal with a range of potential events and situations. Intuitive strategies, in contrast, seem better suited to dealing with fast paced, evolving problems or events in the field. Here, there is greater time pressure and the goal is focused on accomplishing the mission in an effective manner more than finding the optimal way to accomplish the mission.

The Roth study highlights the importance of not focusing only on crisis situations when studying decision making, but also considering the decision making done during planning prior to entering specific situations that require action. Mission planning and preparation is a distinct phase of operations that is defined by the need to acquire information about expected threats. The plans developed prepare the force to meet anticipated threats by providing detailed analyses of enemy and friendly force capabilities, the political and civil situations, neutral forces, and parameters of the mission (rules of engagement, political resolve, etc.). The key point to make is that plans serve as bases for intuitive decision making. When time is available individuals can study potential events and conditions to make them easier to recognize during more time-stressed situations. In addition, they can develop pre-planned courses of action to aid in the generation of acceptable responses. To date, there is no clear indication of the extent to which people employ analytic strategies in planning. It is likely that here, too, there are certain constraints that limit the comprehensive analysis of a problem and alternate solutions. Nevertheless, it seems fruitful to consider analytic and intuitive decision making as synergistic styles that together can greatly enhance decision making.

A potential problem, however, is that planned responses are not helpful unless the decision maker on the spot recognizes the relation of the current situation to the planned contingency. Decision makers in the field are likely to rely on intuitive, recognition-based strategies to retrieve suitable course of actions during time-stressed events. If they have not themselves participated in generating pre-planned responses, it will likely be much harder for them to match the situation to planned contingencies and retrieve the pre-planned response. Because intuitive decision making procedures often do not generalize widely across different decision problems,[43] a decision maker may fail to see the connection between the current situation and previously planned responses, including the degree of modification required. This failure occurs when the situation is not exactly the same as the situation anticipated in planning—even if the planned contingencies are similar to or even formally equivalent to the current situation.

A discrepancy between decision strategies used in planning and in the field is not, in and of itself, a bad thing. But we must recognize the synergy between analytic and intuitive strategies to enhance overall decision making success. Specifically, analytic strategies could be used in planning to generate high quality courses of action to anticipated problems so that these courses of action can be rapidly selected and implemented by intuitive, recognition-based decision making during critical events. In this way, the benefits of analytic decision making can be indirectly imported to intuitive decision making under stress and time pressure. Thus, a major area of opportunity for the design of decision support is improving the connection between planning and action.

Conclusion

Traditionally viewed as competitors, the analytic and intuitive approaches differ in many respects and have distinct strengths and weaknesses. It seems unlikely that an entirely analytic approach or an entirely intuitive approach will serve as a useful model for every aspect of military decision making. Consequently, effort should be directed at employing the advantageous aspects of each approach.

In practical terms, the most immediate use for our knowledge of decision making is to guide research into the development of decision support through the provision of tools, information systems, computers, displays, etc. Specifically, the CF should work towards identifying the demands and constraints (lack of information, lack of time) placed on decision making in different aspects of military operations, then determine specific decision making strategies best suited to these conditions. Tools and procedures that clarify the link between analytic and intuitive decision strategies have the potential to enhance both plans and decisions made in the field. With such an analysis, the CF would be better placed to support, through training and technology, the employment of effective decision making procedures in appropriate situations.

The CF will likely be called upon to serve in non-traditional environments and perform a wider range of missions in the future. This will create a large number of problems for effective C2 (e.g., greater uncertainty, greater constraints on movement and action). Thus, it makes sense to pursue research into ways of supporting decision making in this environment. Recognition of the continuum of decision making strategies will be crucial to asking the right questions—questions concerning how to make planning and the communication of plans more effective, how to build common intent within units and teams,[44] and how to design effective decision support at all levels of command.

Notes

1. J. F. Schmitt and G. Klein, "Fighting in the fog: Dealing with battlefield uncertainty." *Human Performance in Extreme Environments* 3 (1998), pp. 57–63.
2. J. O'Neill, "The Role of Problem-Solving in C3I Systems." *Proceedings of Second International Symposium on Command and Control Research and Technology*. (Market Bosworth, Warwickshire, UK, 1996), pp. 348–355.
3. G. Gigerenzer, "Bounded rationality: Models of fast and frugal inference." *Swiss Journal of Economics and Statistics* 133 (1997), pp. 201–218.
4. A. B. Dahl, "Command dysfunction: Minding the cognitive war." (Unpublished thesis. School of Advanced Airpower Studies, Air University. Maxwell Air Force Base, AL, 1996).
5. Ibid.
6. J. R. Anderson, *The Adaptive Character of Thought*. (Hillsdale, NJ: Lawrence Erlbaum Associates, 1990). See also K. R. Hammond, "Functionalism and Illusionalism: Can integration be usefully achieved?" In R. M. Horgarth, eds., *Insights in decision making* (Chicago, IL: University of Chicago Press, 1990), pp. 227–261.

7. Anderson, 1990; G. Klein, "An Overview of Naturalistic Decision Making Applications" in G. Klein and C. E. Zsambok, eds., *Naturalistic Decision Making* (Lawrence Erlbaum Associates Inc, Mahwah, NJ, 1997), pp. 49–59; and A. Newell, *Unified Theories of Cognition*. (Cambridge, MA: Harvard University Press, 1990).
8. J. St.B. Evans, D. E. Over and K. I. Manktelow, "Reasoning, Decision Making and Rationality." *Cognition* 49 (1993), pp. 165–187; J. W. Leland, "Informal reasoning in decision theory" in J. F. Voss, D. N. Perkins, et al. (Eds.), *Informal Reasoning and Education* (Hillsdale, NJ: Lawrence Erlbaum Associates,1991), pp. 209–223; and R. M. Roe, J. R. Busemeyer and J. T. Townsend, "Multialternative Decision Field Theory: A dynamic connectionist model of decision making." *Psychological Review* 108 (2001), pp. 370–392.
9. Anderson, 1990; K. J. Holyoak, "Problem solving" in D. N. Osherson and E. E. Smith (Eds.), *Thinking: An Invitation to Cognitive Science,* Vol. 3 (Cambridge, MA: The MIT Press, 1990), pp. 117–146; and H. J. M. Tabachneck-Schijf, A. M. Leonardo and H. A. Simon, "CaMeRa: A computational model of multiple representations." *Cognitive Science* 21 (1997), pp. 305–350.
10. G. Klein, *Decision Making in Complex Military Environments*. (Klein Associates, Fairborn, OH: Final Contract Summary Report, prepared for Naval Command, Control and Ocean Surveillance Center, San Diego, CA, 1992).
11. J. F. Yates, *Judgment and Decision Making*. (Englewood Cliffs, NJ: Prentice Hall, 1990).
12. Anderson, 1990; E. Hunt, "Problem solving" in R. J. Sternberg (Ed.), *Thinking and Problem Solving*. (San Diego, CA: Academic Press, 1994), pp. 215–232.
13. R. M. Hogarth, *Judgment and Choice: The psychology of decision*. (New York: John Wiley, 1980); See also Yates, 1990.
14. H. Ben-Zur, "Dimensions and patterns in decision-making models and the controlled/automatic distinction in human information processing." *European Journal of Cognitive Psychology* 10 (1998), pp. 171–189.
15. P. C. Fishburn, "Normative theories of decision making under risk and under uncertainty" in D. E. Bell, H. Raiffa et al. (Eds.), *Decision Making: Descriptive, normative, and prescriptive interactions* (New York: Cambridge University Press, 1988), pp. 78–98. See also D. R. Luce and H. Raiffa, "Utility Theory" in P. K. Moser (Ed.), *Rationality in Action: Contemporary approaches* (New York: Cambridge University Press, 1990), pp. 19–40.
16. Ibid.
17. S. G. Hutchins, *Principles for Intelligent Decision Aiding*. (Naval Command, Control and Ocean Surveillance Center, 1996).
18. G. Klein, S. Wolf, L. Militello, C. Zsambok, "Characteristics of Skilled Option Generation in Chess." *Organizational Behavior and Human Decision Processes* 62 (1995), pp. 63–69.
19. P. M. Todd and G. Gigerenzer, "Precis of Simple heuristics that make us smart." *Behavioral and Brain Sciences* 23 (2000), pp. 727–780.
20. G. Gigerenzer, & D. G. Goldstein, "Reasoning the fast and frugal way: Models of bounded rationality." *Psychological Review* 103 (1996), pp. 650–669.
21. Klein, 1992; Klein, 1997 and Hutchins, 1996.
22. Gigerenzer & Goldstein, 1996.
23. Although the term "Naturalistic Decision Making" (NDM) has achieved widespread acceptance, we prefer the term "intuitive decision making" because it more clearly distinguishes the assumed processes underlying this kind of model from those proposed by analytic theories.
24. Klein, 1997.
25. R. Lipshitz, G. Klein, J. Orasanu and E. Salas, "Taking Stock of Naturalistic Decision Making." *Journal of Behavioral Decision Making* 14 (2001), pp. 331–352.
26. Klein, 1997; and D. K. Leedom, L. Adelman and J. Murphy, "Critical Indicators in Naturalistic Decision Making." *Fourth Conference on Naturalistic Decision Making*. (Warrenton, VA: Klein Associates, 1998).
27. Klein, 1992 and Klein et al., 1995.
28. Klein, 1997.
29. Klein et al., 1995; and Leedom et al., 1998.
30. Klein, 1997.
31. Klein et al., 1995.
32. P. M. Todd and G. Gigerenzer, "Putting naturalistic decision making into the Adaptive Toolbox." *Journal of Behavioral Decision Making*, 14 (2001), pp. 353–384.
33. L. Adelman, *Evaluating Decision Support and Expert Systems*. (New York: John Wiley & Sons, 1992); G. L. Kaempf, G. Klein, M. L. Thordsen and S. Wolf, "Decision making in complex naval command-and-control environments." *Human Factors* 38 (1996), pp. 220–231; Leedom et al., 1998; Newell, 1990; and Yates, 1990.
34. J. A. Cannon-Bowers and H. H. Bell, "Training Decision Makers for Complex Environments: Implications of the Naturalistic Decision Making Perspective" in G. Klein & C. E. Zsambok (Eds.) *Naturalistic Decision Making*. (Lawrence Erlbaum Associates, Inc, Mahwah, NJ, 1997), pp. 99–110; Kaempf et al., 1996; Leedom et al., 1998; and R. Pascual &

S. Henderson, "Evidence of Naturalistic Decision Making in Military Command and Control" in Klein and Zsambok (Eds.) Naturalistic Decision Making, pp. 217–226.
35. Lt Col. J. J. McMenamin, *Operational Decision Making: The Impact of Time and Information.* (Naval War College, Newport, RI, 1992).
36. Todd & Gigerenzer, 2001.
37. Lipshitz et al., 2001.
38. A. B. Markman and D. Gentner, "Thinking." *Annual Review of Psychology* 52 (2001), pp. 223–247.
39. It may be difficult to clearly distinguish where one class of decision making strategy ends and the other begins because the separation along the continuum becomes somewhat arbitrary.
40. Gigerenzer, 1997; and Todd and Gigerenzer, 2000.
41. Y. Xiao, P. Milgram and D. J. Doyle, "Capturing and Modelling Planning Expertise in Anesthesiology: Results of a Field Study" in Klein and Zsambok (Eds.) Naturalistic Decision Making, pp. 197–205.
42. E. M. Roth, "Analysis of Decision Making in Nuclear Power Plant Emergencies: An Investigation of Aided Decision Making" in Klein and Zsambok (Eds.) Naturalistic Decision Making, pp. 175–182.
43. M. L. Gick and K. J. Holyoak, "Schema Induction Analogical Transfer." *Cognitive Psychology* 15 (1983), pp. 1–38; and Klein, 1997.
44. See C. McCann and R., Pigeau, *The Human in Command: Exploring the modern military experience.* (New York, NY: Kluwar Academic/Plenum Publishers, 2000).

Source: David J. Bryant, Robert D.G. Webb, and Carol McCann "Synthesizing Two Approaches to Decision Making in Command and Control," *Canadian Military Journal* (Spring 2003), 29–34. Dr. David Bryant is a Defence Scientist with Defence R&D Canada, Toronto, where he is pursuing research on inferential processes involved in situation assessment and tactical picture compilation. Dr. Robert Webb is Principal Consultant of Humansystems Incorporated, where his recent military work includes analyses of cognitive and information flow issues in a naval frigate operations room. Carol McCann heads the Leadership and Trust Group in the Command Effectiveness Section at DRDC Toronto, where she has been involved in extensive investigations of human factor aspects of command and control.

Case for Analysis: Nackawic Community Story

Nackawic, New Brunswick, is the home of the world's largest axe and is also New Brunswick's newest town. It is situated in the Saint John River Valley where the Nackawic stream meets the Saint John River. Nackawic gets its name from the Maliseet word meaning 'straight' or 'not in the direction it seems to be'. The town was designated Canada's forestry capital in 1991. Forestry has been the primary industry in the area for many generations.

The town's mission's statement reads "[by] committing ourselves to necessary change and improved quality, we are dedicated to providing cost effective and reliable municipal services for the long term benefit of the residents of the Town . . . and, where mutually agreed upon, to the communities surrounding the Town."[1] The town's population is 1,100 and the population in the surrounding area is 7,000.

In September 2004, 400 mill workers were locked out of the St. Anne Pulp and Paper Mill. As well, the woods workers, construction workers, contractors, truck drivers and suppliers lost work. "One by one, small business owners in the town and surrounding villages closed up shop and a pall of loss and grief settled over the area."[2] In response, the town council hired a consultant to hold strategic planning sessions and created a committee called the Nackawic Regional Economic Development Team. The work of the committee resulted in the sale of the Mill to an Indian company and the mill was re-opened in 2006 as AV Nackawic. The re-opening, however, was not without its problems. While some of the locked out workers were rehired, the company also hired new workers from the surrounding communities. Further, as the pension fund had been under-funded, pensioners lost about 35 per cent of their retirement funds as the limited funds had to be shared among all the pensioners. The re-opening pitted family members against one another and local communities against one another. There was a fear that the Mill would not last as there was a downturn in the market trend for forestry. Area residents were anxious.

A local non-profit organization, the Neighbourhood Alliance of North York (NANY), decided that action was necessary to deal with the negative attitudes in and of the town of Nackawic and the surrounding communities. "[NANY] felt it was time to take stock of what [existed] and to scrutinize the potential for growth and development in the area."[3] NANY decided to use a decision-making tool called Asset Mapping. Asset Mapping is a method used both to collect information on the positive attributes of a community and to discover why people value them. It produces a common view of what is considered important in a community. It provides a useful starting point, potentially leading to a strategic planning process and/or community/organizational development. There are three approaches to Asset Mapping: Storytelling, Heritage, and Whole Assets. NANY used the Whole Assets approach that involves the following eight steps.

1. First, each participant is encouraged to identify the top six assets in their community, and they record these assets on three separate cards;
2. The participants post their cards under asset categories on a wall. Examples of asset categories include Built, Social, Service, Natural and Economic;
3. The group is encouraged to discuss why these assets are important. Possible questions to ask include 'Were there any surprises?' and 'What do those surprises mean?';
4. Afterwards, each participant identifies the most important asset in each category by posting a dot beside that item. The item containing the most dots becomes the most important asset for the group;
5. The participants are divided into smaller groups of five to seven people. Each group selects the asset category with which they would like to work;
6. Each small group discusses asset supports and threats, and identifies ways in which the asset can be preserved or strengthened;
7. The small groups present a summary of their thoughts to all participants; and
8. Finally, the larger group is encouraged to determine next steps.[4]

Over ten weeks, NANY held five formal meetings and conducted numerous telephone interviews/conversations. In total, 300 people participated. The Whole Assets approach yielded many insights. The people of Nankawic identified the natural beauty of the Saint John River Valley as its most valuable asset. Participants felt that the protection of the river was critical as there are many threats to the river. Secondly, the participants noted that Nackawic, although a rural area, has the infrastructure more typical of urban areas. Its education system has been recognized all over the world for its inclusive curriculum. Educators from Sweden, China, Iceland, Spain, Mexico and other countries have visited Nackawic. The participants also identified various economic assets including a well-trained (if ageing) work force and a variety of potential employers such as an expanding call centre, a trucking company, a log home manufacturer and a poker chip plant.

Many asked if there was going to be any follow-up to the process. Focus groups have been formed to address opportunities for riverfront development, small business, youth, promotion, community linkages and seniors. The town and the community are now galvanized—"[we] must get out there and sell ourselves. It is not wrong to promote what we hold as valuable."[5]

Notes

1. www.nackawic.com/about-us/.
2. rural.gc.ca/decision/nackawic/nackawic_e.phtml.
3. Ibid.
4. rural.gc.ca/decision/tools_e.phtml#ASSET%20 MAPPING.
5. rural.gc.ca/decision/nackawic/nackawic_e.phtml.

Source: Ann Armstrong. This case references the report prepared by J.A. Stone, "Nackawic Community Story: Asset Mapping Project" posted at HYPERLINK "http://www.rural.gc.ca/decision/nackawic/nackawic_e.phtml"\l"1"www.rural.gc.ca/decision/nackawic/nackawic_e.phtml#1 (accessed Sept. 29, 2008).

Chapter 12 Workshop: Mist Ridge

It is approximately 9 a.m. on August 23, and you and four friends are about to set off on an all day hike in the mountains of Southwestern Alberta. Having driven southwest from Calgary, Alberta, you have arrived at Kananaskis Provincial Park, located on the boundary between British Columbia and Alberta. Just off Highway 40, you turn into the Mist Creek day use area and have just parked the car. You can see a sign indicating the beginning of the Mist Ridge trail, which you have selected for your hike, but you know that from there on, the trail proceeds along unmarked paths and logging roads. You can also see another sign that allows campfires only in designated rest areas.

Since it is mid-week, few others should be on the Mist Ridge trail. You and your friends are looking forward to an enjoyable day walking the long grass and rock ridge as it is usually dry and sunny at this time of the year, when a mere few kilometres away across the valley Mist Mountain can be covered in rain clouds. Hiking from the parking lot to the ridge, then along the whole top of the ridge to Rickert's Pass, then returning at ground level alongside the Mist Creek is, at minimum, an eight hour trip. In guidebooks it is classified as a long day hike covering a distance of 23 kilometres with a height gain of 808 metres and a maximum elevation of 2515 metres.

The weather at the moment is cool but not cold, and the sun is beaming down, beginning to heat the air. In general, the climate of Southwestern Alberta is cold continental, having long cold winters and cool summers, though summers do have brief hot spells. Annual precipitation peaks in the summer and thunderstorms occur regularly. Hikers at this time of year must be prepared for rain or cold weather. Snow has been known to fall by the middle of August in this area, with accumulations on the ground of up to 20 centimetres. Also, the weather can be somewhat changeable and unpredictable. What starts out as a warm, sunny morning could easily change into a cold, snowy afternoon. Therefore, experienced hikers will make sure that they have adequate reserve clothing for the rain or snow that could develop. It is also known that temperatures are expected to be cooler at the top of the ridge, as temperatures decrease, in general, 2 degrees Celsius for every 300 metres of altitude.

There are a few dangers to watch out for during your hike. If you get soaked crossing a river, loss of body heat may result in hypothermia, even when temperatures are above freezing. Death from hypothermia is quite possible within a few hours of the first symptoms if proper care is not taken. On the other hand, the exertions of walking and climbing will probably cause you to sweat. Dehydration can increase your chance of sunstroke and hypothermia. In terms of animals, you may encounter a bear looking for berries. While bear attacks on humans are not common, they are not unusual either. It is also possible that elk or moose may be encountered. These large plant eaters are not usually dangerous to humans, but should be avoided during the mating season. There are also some insects to be considered. Ticks can carry Rocky Mountain Spotted Fever, which can be fatal if left untreated. Bees can also be dangerous if the person stung has a strong allergic reaction.

You are all currently dressed in warm clothes including wool socks and sturdy hiking boots, and each person has a day pack in which to carry those items that you deem necessary.

Part I: Individual Decision

There are 15 items listed below. Before you set out on your hike your task is to rank these items according to their general importance for a hiker, not for you specifically. Rank the items from 1, the most important, to 15, the least important. No ties are allowed. You might want to consider "If a hiker was allowed to take only one item, what would it be?" That item would be ranked number 1. Then, "If a hiker was allowed only one more item, what would it be?" That item would rank number 2. Write your rankings in the column below titled "Your Ranking." It is important to remember that the decisions that you are making are for your group as a whole and should not be influenced by factors affecting you as an individual.

Items	Your Ranking	Group Ranking	Expert Ranking	Your Score	Group Score
Canteen with water	______	______	______	______	______
Matches	______	______	______	______	______
Compass	______	______	______	______	______
Hat	______	______	______	______	______
Repair kit (includes short length of cord, string, duct tape, and shoelaces)	______	______	______	______	______
First aid kit (includes blister protection and aspirin)	______	______	______	______	______
Five sleeping bags	______	______	______	______	______
Sunglasses	______	______	______	______	______
Flashlight	______	______	______	______	______
Topographic map and Kananaskis Country Trail guide book	______	______	______	______	______

Items	Your Ranking	Group Ranking	Expert Ranking	Your Score	Group Score
Food	______	______	______	______	______
5-person tent with waterproof fly	______	______	______	______	______
Sunscreen	______	______	______	______	______
Rain gear	______	______	______	______	______
Insect repellent	______	______	______	______	______

Part II: Group Decision

Now form into groups. Take a few minutes to examine and discuss your individual assumptions before you begin to discuss how to rank specific items. Use constructive controversy decision rules to guide your decision method and rank the 15 items again. To refresh our memory, they are: (1) be critical of ideas, not people; (2) focus on making the best possible decision, not on winning; (3) encourage everyone to participate in the discussion; (4) listen to everyone's ideas, even if you do not agree; (5) restate what someone has said if their point is not clear to you; (6) bring out the ideas and facts supporting both sides of the argument and then try to integrate them; (7) try to understand both sides of the issue under discussion; and (8) change your mind if the evidence clearly indicates that you should do so (from Johnson, D.W. & R.T. Johnson [1992] *Cooperation and Competition: Intellectual Challenge in the Classroom,* Edina, MN: Interaction Book.)

Write your group's answers in the "Group Ranking" column.

Part III: Scoring

Your instructor will inform you of how experts have ranked these 15 items. Write these rankings into the column titled "Expert Ranking." To calculate your personal score, calculate for each of the 15 items the absolute difference between your ranking and the expert's ranking, then sum these 15 absolute value differences. Determine your group's score in the same manner. Write these scores and summary statistics into the spaces below.

Your total score ______

Average of the individual scores in your group ______

Your group's total score ______

Number of individuals in our group having a lower score than your group's total score ______

 Based on information in Joseph Graham Ambrosi, *Hiking Alberta's Southwest* (Vancouver, BC: Douglas & McIntyre, 1984); Gillean Daffern, *Kananaskis Country: A Guide to Hiking, Skiing, Equestrian & Bike Trails,* 2nd edition (Calgary, AB: Rocky Mountain Books, 1985); and Patricia E. Kariel *Hiking Alberta's David Thompson Country* (Edmonton, AB: Lone Pine Publishing, 1987).

13 Conflict, Power, and Politics

The Canadian Press/FRANK GUNN

A Look Inside

Harold Ballard and the Toronto Maple Leafs

Harold Ballard was—and remains—arguably the most reviled team owner in the history of the National Hockey League. In 1961, Ballard, along with John Bassett and Conn Smythe's son, bought Smythe's controlling interest in the Toronto Maple Leafs (see photo). In 1971, Ballard took control of Maple Leaf Gardens as well. "He quickly developed a reputation for only thinking of the bottom line, and letting players and fans suffer for it."[1] For example, Ballard refused to have the players' names sewn on to the back of their jerseys as he thought that having the players easily identifiable would hurt program sales. After being fined $2000 a day by the League, he had the names sewn on in the same colour as the jerseys so that they would be difficult to read.

In 1972, Ballard was found guilty on 48 of 50 charges of theft and fraud. According to the judge, Ballard had demonstrated "a clear pattern of fraud" including using monies that belonged to Maple Leaf Gardens to renovate his house.[2] Ballard was sentenced to three consecutive one-year terms. He spent one year in Millhaven penitentiary, which he compared to a motel, complete with such luxuries such as golf, beer, and steak.

The Toronto Maple Leafs last won the Stanley Cup in 1967. The 1970s were marred by Ballard's tyrannical rule: "[his] antics included firing Red Kelley, hiring Roger Nielson, firing him and hiring him back, and once again firing him along with Bob Davidson—all in the span of weeks."[3] He is reputed to have told Nielson that he had to wear a bag over his head when he was rehired; Nielson refused.

In 1981, Ballard was in conflict with his oldest son, Bill Ballard, and bought shares owned by his son Harold Ballard, Jr. for $25 million to prevent the possibility of a takeover of the team and the Gardens. According to Harold Ballard, "Bill and Molson [Breweries] were trying to get control of the place . . . It would have given them control. But I've pretty much got all of it now, and I'm going to make a private company to buy up the public's stock too. I told Molson that if they ever set foot into the building, I'll have them thrown out."[4] When Ballard died in 1990, the Toronto Maple Leafs were struggling both on and off the ice.

According to *Toronto Star* columnist Damien Cox, the Toronto Maple Leafs' bumbling history continues today. "In all, it's as big of a tangled web of intrigue now as it was during the days of Smythe-Bassett-Ballard, or when Fletcher was fighting Stavro, or when Dryden and Smith were trying to get each other fired. It's the Leaf way."[5]

Although the conflicts at the Toronto Maple Leafs Organization are an extreme example, all organizations are a complex mix of individuals and groups pursuing various goals and interests. Conflict is a natural and inevitable outcome of the close interaction of people who may have diverse opinions and values, pursue different objectives, and have differential access to information and resources within the organization. Individuals and groups will use power and political activity to handle their differences and manage conflict.[6]

Too much conflict can be harmful to an organization, as was the case during Harold Ballard's reign. However, conflict can also be a positive force because it challenges the status quo, encourages new ideas and approaches, and leads to change.[7] Some degree of conflict occurs in all human relationships—between friends, romantic partners, and teammates, as well as between parents and children, teachers and students, and bosses and employees. Conflict results from the normal interaction of varying human interests. Within organizations, individuals and groups frequently have different interests and goals they wish to achieve through the organization. In learning organizations, which encourage a democratic push and pull of ideas, the forces of conflict, power, and politics may be particularly evident. Managers in all organizations regularly deal with conflict and struggle with decisions about how to get the most out of employees, enhance job satisfaction and team identification, and realize high organizational performance.

Purpose of This Chapter

In this chapter we discuss the nature of conflict and the use of power and political tactics to manage and reduce conflict among individuals and groups. The notion of conflict has appeared in previous chapters. In Chapter 3, we talked about horizontal linkages such as task forces and teams that encourage collaboration among functional departments. Chapter 4 introduced the concept of differentiation, which means that different departments pursue different goals and may have different attitudes and values. Chapter 10 discussed the emergence of subcultures, and in Chapter 12, coalition building was proposed as one way to resolve disagreements among departments.

The first sections of this chapter explore the nature of intergroup conflict, characteristics of organizations that contribute to conflict, and the use of a political versus a rational model of organization to manage conflicting interests. Subsequent sections examine individual and organizational power, the vertical and horizontal sources of power for managers and other employees, and how power is used to attain organizational goals. The latter part of the chapter looks at politics, which is the application of power and authority to achieve desired outcomes. We also discuss some tactics managers can use to enhance collaboration among people and departments.

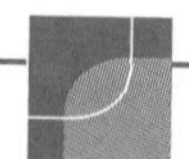

Intergroup Conflict in Organizations

Intergroup conflict requires three ingredients: group identification, observable group differences, and frustration. First, employees have to perceive themselves as part of an identifiable group or department.[8] Second, there has to be an observable group difference of some form. Groups may be located on different floors of the building, members may have different social or educational backgrounds, or members may work in different departments. The ability to identify oneself as a part of one group and to observe differences in comparison with other groups is necessary for conflict.[9]

The third ingredient is frustration. Frustration means that if one group achieves its goal, the other will not; it will be blocked. Frustration need not be severe and needs only to be anticipated to set off intergroup conflict. Intergroup conflict will appear when one group tries to advance its position in relation to other groups. **Intergroup conflict** can be defined as the behaviour that occurs among organizational groups when participants identify with one group and perceive that other groups may block their group's goal achievement or expectations.[10] Conflict means that groups clash directly, that they are in fundamental opposition. Conflict is similar to competition but more severe. **Competition** is rivalry among groups in the pursuit of a common prize, whereas conflict presumes direct interference with goal achievement.

Intergroup conflict within organizations can occur horizontally across departments or vertically between different levels of the organization.[11] The production department of a manufacturing company may have a dispute with quality control because new quality procedures reduce production efficiency. Teammates may argue about the best way to accomplish tasks and achieve goals. Workers may clash with bosses about new work methods, reward systems, or job assignments. Another typical area of conflict is between groups such as unions and management or franchise owners and headquarters. For example, there have been many conflicts between the Canadian Auto Workers (CAW), the country's largest private-sector union and General Motors, the Ford Motor Company, and Daimler-Chrysler. The founding of the CAW in 1985 was itself fraught with conflict. "The decision of the Canadian section of the United Auto Workers (UAW) to form its own Canadian union was rooted in the different responses of unionists in . . . Canada and the United States to an increasing belligerence on the part of the corporations. While this break from an 'international' union was not the first such action within the Canadian labour movement, it was perhaps the most dramatic and certainly the most significant."[12] Similarly, franchise owners for McDonald's, Taco Bell, Burger King, and KFC have clashed with headquarters because of the increase of company-owned stores in neighbourhoods that compete directly with franchisees.[13]

Conflict can also occur between different divisions or business units within an organization, such as between the auditing and consulting units of big firms such as PricewaterhouseCoopers and Deloitte Touche Tohmatsu.[14] In global organizations, conflicts between regional managers and business division managers, among different divisions, or between divisions and headquarters are common because of the complexities of international business, as described in Chapter 6. Conflicts often occur after a merger or acquisition; for example, Porsche's takeover of the Volkswagen (VW) Group has brought together two different organizational cultures and, as a result, a power struggle has emerged. The conflict began when "Porsche CEO Wendelin Wiedeking, alarmed about the considerable influence of the VW's labour representatives . . . said that nothing could be considered sacred. According to Wiedeking, all things should be questioned to determine whether they are still timely and in keeping with corporate strategy."[15]

PDA
Remember...

Recognize that some interdepartmental conflict is natural and can benefit the organization. Associate the organizational design characteristics of goal incompatibility, differentiation, task interdependence, and resource scarcity with greater conflict among groups. Expect to devote more time and energy to resolving conflict in these situations.

Sources of Conflict

Some specific organizational characteristics can generate conflict. These **sources of intergroup conflict** are goal incompatibility, differentiation, task interdependence, and limited resources. These characteristics of organizational relationships are determined by the contextual factors of environment, size, technology, strategy and goals, and organizational structure, which have been discussed in previous chapters. These characteristics, in turn, help shape the extent to which a rational model of behaviour versus a political model of behaviour is used to accomplish objectives.

Goal Incompatibility. Goal incompatibility is probably the greatest cause of intergroup conflict in organizations.[16] The goals of each department reflect the specific objectives members are trying to achieve. The achievement of one department's goals often interferes with another department's goals. University police, for example, have a goal of providing a safe and secure campus. They can achieve their goal by locking all buildings on evenings and weekends and not distributing keys. Without easy access to buildings, however, progress toward the science department's research

EXHIBIT 13.1
Marketing–Manufacturing Areas of Potential Goal Conflict

	Marketing versus	Manufacturing
Goal Conflict	**Operative Goal is Customer Satisfaction**	**Operative Goal is Production Efficiency**
Conflict Area	**Typical Comment**	**Typical Comment**
1. Breadth of product line	"Our customers demand variety."	"The product line is too broad—all we get are short, uneconomical runs."
2. New product introduction	"New products are our lifeblood."	"Unnecessary design changes are prohibitively expensive."
3. Product scheduling	"We need faster response. Our customer lead times are too long."	"We need realistic commitments that don't change like wind direction."
4. Physical distribution	"Why don't we ever have the right merchandise in inventory?"	"We can't afford to keep huge inventories."
5. Quality	"Why can't we have reasonable quality at lower cost?"	"Why must we always offer options that are too expensive and offer little customer utility?"

Source: Based on Benson S. Shapiro, "Can Marketing and Manufacturing Coexist?" *Harvard Business Review* 55 (September–October 1977): 104–114; and Victoria L. Crittenden, Lorraine R. Gardiner, and Antonie Stam, "Reducing Conflict between Marketing and Manufacturing," *Industrial Marketing Management* 22 (1993): 299–309.

goals will proceed slowly. On the other hand, if scientists come and go at all hours and security is ignored, police goals for security will not be met. Goal incompatibility throws the departments into conflict with each other.

The potential for conflict is perhaps greater between marketing and manufacturing than between other departments because the goals of these two departments are frequently at odds. Exhibit 13.1 shows examples of goal conflict between typical marketing and manufacturing departments. Marketing strives to increase the breadth of the product line to meet customer tastes for variety. A broad product line means short production runs, so manufacturing has to bear higher costs.[17] Other areas of goal conflict are quality, cost control, and new products or services. For example, when a human resources (HR) department wants to implement a new self-service benefits system that would let employees manage their benefits from their home computers, the high price of the software licenses conflicts with the finance department's goal of controlling costs.[18] Goal incompatibility exists among departments in most organizations.

Differentiation. *Differentiation* was defined in Chapter 4 as "the differences in cognitive and emotional orientations among managers in different functional departments." Functional specialization requires people with specific education, skills, attitudes, and time horizons. For example, people may join a sales department because they have ability and aptitude consistent with sales work. After becoming members of the sales department, they are influenced by departmental norms and values. Departments or divisions within an organization often differ in values, attitudes, and standards of behaviour, and these subcultural differences lead to conflicts.[19] Exhibit 13.2 shows another view of the conflict between manufacturing and marketing!

"I wouldn't worry about it—this is marketing's headache."

EXHIBIT 13.2
Manufacturing versus Marketing

Leading *by Design*

Bennett Jones LLP

Bennett Jones LLP was founded in 1922 in Calgary, Alberta, and began as Bennett, Hannah & Sanford. It has had many name changes as partners came and went. In the 1980s, the firm felt that it was time to have a name that would be institutionalized. It took the last name of the founding partner, R.B. Bennett, our Prime Minister from 1930–1935, and the last name of the most senior living partner, Mac Jones.

Bennett Jones has expanded rapidly from its Alberta base. It followed a go-east strategy and now has 120 partners and associates in its Toronto office alone, up from 76 in 2005. The growth in the Toronto office has been extraordinary. "What makes this situation unique, says [Hugh] MacKinnon [Chair and CEO], is that . . . senior lawyers chose to decamp from long-time partnerships at prestigious, well-regarded Toronto firms, opting to join the Bennett Jones fold."[20]

According to MacKinnon, Bennett Jones has an egalitarian culture, functioning as a meritocracy. Bennett Jones has appeared on the Top 50 Employers in Canada list every year since 2003 and ranked fourth in 2006. It is the only law firm to have been on the Top 50 list. Bennett Jones states that it has three core values: "to be the law firm of choice having earned a reputation as being one of the very best providers of legal services in all areas in which we practice, to provide individuals in the firm with an opportunity to perform stimulating, interesting, and rewarding work in a collegial team environment, and to promote an atmosphere of excellence through strong personal commitment and the encouragement of a balanced life.[21]

Professional firms, like law firms, are often fraught with conflict. Sources of conflict in law firms include divergent goals, differences in individual style, status conflicts, value differences, role pressures, dysfunctional organizational structures, limited resources and unsatisfactory communications.[22] Bennett Jones seems to be the exception. As MacKinnon puts it, "[the] difference between Bennett Jones and other firms is in the execution, internally and externally the way our law firm interacts with our lawyers and with our clients."[23]

Task Interdependence. Task interdependence refers to the dependence of one unit on another for materials, resources, or information. As described in Chapter 7, *pooled interdependence* means there is little interaction; *sequential interdependence* means the output of one department goes to the next department; and *reciprocal interdependence* means that departments mutually exchange materials and information.[24]

PDA Remember...

Use the rational model of organization when alternatives are clear, when goals are defined, and when managers can estimate the outcomes accurately. In these circumstances, coalition building, cooptation, or other political tactics are not needed and will not lead to effective decisions.

Generally, as interdependence increases, the potential for conflict increases.[25] In the case of pooled interdependence, units have little need to interact. Conflict is at a minimum. Sequential and reciprocal interdependence require employees to spend time coordinating and sharing information. Employees must communicate frequently, and differences in goals or attitudes will surface. Conflict is especially likely to occur when agreement is not reached about the coordination of services to each other. Greater interdependence means departments often exert pressure for a fast response because departmental work has to wait on other departments.[26]

Limited Resources. Another major source of conflict involves competition between groups for what members perceive as limited resources.[27] Organizations have limited money, physical facilities, staff resources, and human resources to share among departments. In their desire to achieve goals, groups want to increase their resources. This throws them into conflict. Managers may develop strategies, such as inflating budget requirements or working behind the scenes, to obtain a desired level of resources.

Resources also symbolize power and influence within an organization. The ability to obtain resources enhances prestige. Departments typically believe they have a legitimate claim on additional resources. However, exercising that claim results in conflict. For example, in almost every organization, conflict occurs during the annual budget exercise, often creating political activity.

Rational versus Political Model

The sources of intergroup conflict are listed in Exhibit 13.3. The degree of goal incompatibility, differentiation, interdependence, and conflict over limited resources determines whether a rational or political model of behaviour is used within the organization to accomplish goals.

When goals are in alignment, there is little differentiation, departments are characterized by pooled interdependence, and resources seem abundant, managers can use a **rational model** of organization, as outlined in Exhibit 13.3. As with the rational approach to decision making described in Chapter 12, the rational model of organization is an ideal that is not fully achievable in the real world, though managers strive to use rational processes whenever possible. In the rational organization, behaviour is not random or accidental. Goals are clear and choices are made in a logical way. When a decision is needed, the goal is defined, alternatives are identified, and the choice with the highest probability of success is selected. The rational model is also characterized by centralized power and control, extensive information systems, and an efficiency orientation.[28] The opposite view of organizational processes is the **political model**, also described in Exhibit 13.3. When differences are great, organization groups have separate interests, goals, and values. Disagreement and conflict are normal, so power and influence are needed to reach decisions. Groups will engage in the push and pull of debate to decide goals and reach decisions. Information is ambiguous and incomplete. The political model particularly describes organizations that strive for democracy and participation in decision making by empowering workers. Purely rational procedures do not work in democratic organizations, such as learning organizations.

Both rational and political processes are normally used in organizations. In most organizations, neither the rational model nor the political model characterizes things fully, but each will be used some of the time. At Amazon.com, founder and

EXHIBIT 13.3
Sources of Conflict and Use of Rational versus Political Model

Sources of Potential Intergroup Conflict

- *Goal incompatibility*
- *Differentiation*
- *Task interdependence*
- *Limited resources*

When Conflict Is Low, Rational Model Describes Organization		When Conflict Is High, Political Model Describes Organization
Consistent across participants	*Goals*	*Inconsistent, pluralistic within the organization*
Centralized	*Power and control*	*Decentralized, shifting coalitions and interest groups*
Orderly, logical, rational	*Decision process*	*Disorderly, result of bargaining and interplay among interests*
Norm of efficiency	*Rules and norms*	*Free play of market forces; conflict is legitimate and expected*
Extensive, systematic, accurate	*Information*	*Ambiguous; information used and withheld strategically*

CEO Jeff Bezos emphasizes a rational approach to planning and decision making whenever possible. "The great thing about fact-based decisions," he says, "is that they overrule the hierarchy. The most junior person in the company can win an argument with the most senior person with a fact-based decision." For decisions and situations that are complex, ill-defined, and controversial, however, Bezos uses a political model, discussing the issues with people, building agreement among senior executives, and then relies on his own judgment.[29]

Managers may strive to adopt rational procedures but will find that politics is needed to accomplish objectives. The political model means managers learn to acquire, develop, and use power to accomplish objectives.

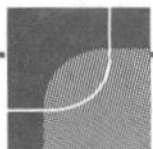

Power and Organizations

Power is an intangible force in organizations. It cannot be seen, but its effect can be felt. *Power* is often defined as the potential ability of one person (or department) to influence other people (or departments) to carry out orders[30] or to do something they would not otherwise have done.[31] Other definitions stress that power is the ability to achieve goals or outcomes that power holders desire.[32] The achievement of desired outcomes is the basis of the definition used here: **power** is the ability of one person or department in an organization to influence other people to bring about desired outcomes. It is the potential to influence others within the organization with the goal of attaining desired outcomes for power holders.

Power exists only in a relationship between two or more people, and it can be exercised in either vertical or horizontal directions. The source of power often derives from an exchange relationship in which one position or department provides scarce or valued resources to other departments. When one person is dependent on another person, a power relationship emerges in which the person with the resources has greater power.[33] Sometimes power is described as a relationship of asymmetric or unequal dependence between two or more individuals in a department.[34]

When power exists in a relationship, the power holders can achieve compliance with their requests. Powerful individuals are often able to get bigger budgets for their departments, more favourable production schedules, and more control over the organization's agenda.[35]

As an illustration, consider how power is shifting in the game of baseball. Seasoned team managers, who typically base their decisions on instinct and experience, are losing power to general managers using business theories and new analytical tools to come up with statistical benchmarks and operational standards that are believed to improve performance. As a result of their increased power, some general managers are now suggesting player lineups, handpicking members of the coaching staff, and generally telling team managers how to run the team.[36]

Individual versus Organizational Power

In popular literature, power is often described as a personal characteristic, and a frequent topic is how one person can influence or dominate another person.[37] You probably recall from an earlier management or organizational behaviour course that managers have five sources of personal power.[38] *Legitimate power* is the authority granted by the organization to the formal management position a manager holds. *Reward power* stems from the ability to bestow rewards—a promotion, raise, or pat on the back—to other people. The authority to punish or recommend punishment is called *coercive power*. *Expert power* derives from a person's greater skill or knowledge about the tasks being performed. The last, *referent power,* is derived from personal characteristics: people admire the manager and want to be like or identify with the manager out of respect and admiration. Each of these sources may be used by individuals within organizations.

Power in organizations, however, is often the result of *structural* characteristics.[39] Organizations are large, complex systems that contain hundreds, even thousands, of people. These systems have a formal hierarchy in which some tasks are more important regardless of who performs them. In addition, some positions have access to greater resources, or their contribution to the organization is more critical. Thus, the important power processes in organizations reflect larger organizational relationships, both horizontal and vertical.

Power versus Authority

Anyone in an organization can exercise power to achieve desired outcomes. When the Discovery Channel wanted to extend its brand beyond cable television, Tom Hicks began pushing for a focus on the Internet. Even though Discovery's CEO favoured exploring interactive television, Hicks organized a grassroots campaign that eventually persuaded the CEO to focus instead on Web publishing, indicating that Hicks had power within the organization. Today, Hicks runs Discovery Channel Online.[40]

The concept of formal authority is related to power but is narrower in scope. **Authority** is also a force for achieving desired outcomes, but only as prescribed by the formal hierarchy and reporting relationships. Three properties identify authority:

1. *Authority is vested in organizational positions.* People have authority because of the positions they hold, not because of personal characteristics or resources.
2. *Authority is accepted by subordinates.* Subordinates comply because they believe position holders have a legitimate right to exercise authority.[41] In most North American organizations, employees accept that supervisors can legitimately tell them what time to arrive at work, the tasks to perform while they're there, and what time they can go home.
3. *Authority flows down the vertical hierarchy.*[42] Authority exists along the formal chain of command, and positions at the top of the hierarchy are vested with more formal authority than are positions at the bottom.

Organizational power can be exercised upward, downward, and horizontally in organizations. Formal authority is exercised downward along the hierarchy and is the same as legitimate power. In the following sections, we will examine vertical and horizontal sources of power for employees throughout the organization.

Vertical Sources of Power

PDA

Understand and use the vertical sources of power in organizations, including formal position, resources, control of decision premises and information, and network centrality.

All employees along the vertical hierarchy have access to some sources of power. Although a large amount of power is typically allocated to top managers by the organizational structure, employees throughout the organization often obtain power disproportionate to their formal positions and can exert influence in an upward direction, as Tom Hicks did at the Discovery Channel. There are four major sources of vertical power: formal position, resources, control of decision premises and information, and network centrality.[43]

Formal Position. Certain rights, responsibilities, and prerogatives accrue to top positions. People throughout the organization accept the legitimate right of top managers to set goals, make decisions, and direct activities. Thus, the power from formal position is sometimes called *legitimate power*.[44] Senior managers often use symbols and language to perpetuate their legitimate power, both in the workplace and their homes. For example, an intriguing economic study shows a negative correlation between CEOs buying lavish houses and the price of their organizations' shares. "It gives you some insight into the CEO's mindset . . . entrenched [CEOs perceive themselves] as immune from discipline by [their] board and [are] uninterested in maintaining or improving [their] performance to attract outside offers."[45]

The amount of power provided to middle managers and lower-level participants can be built into the organization's structural design. The allocation of power to middle managers and staff is important because power enables employees to be productive. When job tasks are nonroutine, and when employees participate in self-directed teams and problem-solving task forces, employees are encouraged to be flexible and creative and to use their own discretion. Allowing people to make their own decisions increases their power.

Power is also increased when a position encourages contact with high-level people. Access to powerful people and the development of a relationship with them provide a strong base of influence.[46] For example, in some organizations an administrative assistant to the president might have more power than a department head because the assistant has access to the senior executive on a daily basis.

The logic of designing positions with more power assumes that an organization does not have a limited amount of power to be allocated among high-level and low-level employees. The total amount of power in an organization can be increased by designing tasks and interactions along the hierarchy so everyone can exert more influence. eBay CEO Meg Whitman, for example, tops *Fortune*'s list of the most powerful women in American business. Yet Whitman believes that to have power, you have to give it away. She makes sure executives and employees at eBay have the power and authority they need to contribute to the company's astounding success.[47] Similarly, Sylvia Vogel, founder and CEO of Québec's Canderm Pharmacal, and one of the most powerful women entrepreneurs in Canada,[48] believes that "[the] company . . . is like my home." For example, Vogel enforces her approach to organizational values by decreeing that no personal assistant or secretary is allowed to serve coffee in the office. "People are people and they have to be respected," she insists.[49] Both CEOs recognize that if the distribution of power is skewed too heavily toward the top, the organization will be less effective.[50]

Resources. Organizations allocate huge amounts of resources. Buildings are constructed, salaries are paid, and equipment and supplies are purchased. Each year, new resources are allocated in the form of budgets. These resources are allocated downward from top managers. Top managers often own stock, which gives them property rights over resource allocation. However, in some of today's organizations, employees throughout the organization also share in ownership, which increases their power.

In most cases, top managers control the resources and, hence, can determine their distribution. Resources can be used as rewards and punishments, which are additional sources of power. Resource allocation also creates a dependency relationship. Lower-level participants depend on top managers for the financial and physical resources needed to perform their tasks. Top management can exchange resources in the form of salaries and bonuses, stock options, personnel, promotions, and physical facilities for compliance with the outcomes they desire.

Control of Decision Premises and Information. Control of **decision premises** means that top managers place constraints on decisions made at lower levels by specifying a decision frame of reference and guidelines. In one sense, top managers make big decisions, whereas lower-level participants make small decisions. Top management decides which goal an organization will try to achieve, such as increased market share. Lower-level participants then decide how the goal is to be reached. In one company, top management appointed a committee to select a new marketing vice president. The CEO provided the committee with detailed qualifications that the new vice president should have. He also selected people to serve on the committee. In this way, the CEO shaped the decision premises within which the marketing vice president would be chosen. Top manager actions and decisions such as these place limits on the decisions of lower-level managers and thereby influence the outcome of their decisions.[51]

The control of information can also be a source of power. Managers in today's organizations recognize that information is a primary business resource and that by controlling what information is collected, how it is interpreted, and how it is shared, they can influence how decisions are made.[52] In some of today's companies, especially in learning organizations, information is openly and broadly shared, which increases the power of people throughout the organization. However, top managers generally have access to more information than do other employees. This information can be released as needed to shape the decision outcomes of other people.

Control of information can also be used to shape decisions for self-serving, unethical, and even illegal purposes. For example, at Hollinger International, which owns newspapers including the *Chicago Sun-Times* and *Jerusalem Post,* the board approved a series of transactions that allowed then CEO Lord Conrad Black and his colleagues to improperly draw off millions of dollars from the company for personal gain. Although the board has been criticized for its lax governance, several directors insist that their decisions were based on false, skewed, or misleading information provided by Lord Black.[53] On July 13, 2007, Conrad Black was found guilty of three counts of mail fraud and one count of obstruction of justice. His three co-defendants were convicted of three counts each of mail fraud.[54]

Middle managers and lower-level employees may also have access to information that can increase their power. A secretary to a senior executive can often control information that other people want and will thus be able to influence those people. Top executives depend on people throughout the organization for information about problems or opportunities. Middle managers or lower-level employees may manipulate the information they provide to top managers in order to influence decision outcomes.

Network Centrality. **Network centrality** means being centrally located in the organization and having access to information and people that are critical to the company's success. Top executives are more successful when they put themselves at the centre of a communication network, building connections with people throughout the company. Sir Howard Stringer, the new CEO of Sony, is known as a skilled corporate politician who builds trust and alliances across different divisions and hierarchical levels. Stringer has been praised for his ability to network with almost everyone. He will need those political skills to gain an understanding of the sprawling Sony empire and get the various divisions working together. "He's the only one I know who can manage the Japanese [electronics side] and the show-bizzers [entertainment side]," said a former head of Sony Pictures Entertainment.[55] Stringer continues with his ambitious vision for Sony—in 2008, he announced that "[we] want to restore the TV to the center of the home."[56]

Middle managers and lower-level employees can also use the ideas of network centrality. For example, several years ago at PricewaterhouseCoopers (PwC), two trainees, Amy Middelburg and James Shaw, were asked to write a proposal about what values should shape the merging firm. They proposed that PwC measure its business success not only by financial goals but also by global social impact. The recommendation was a radical one in a culture that was very focussed on a single financial bottom line. The two passed their proposal to a partner who passed it on to another. Even so, the proposal went nowhere. Middelburg and Shaw then started to network, talking with PwC's global managing partner at a conference; recruiting a friend, Fabio Sparagli, to help; and tailoring their message carefully to different members of their networks. The three became lead members of a team looking at ways that might revolutionize the way PwC does business. "We've had an impact on the firm because we're starting conversations," Sgaragli says. "I'm absolutely convinced that we've already planted some seeds."[57] He also was quoted as saying, "Few industries in the world are as innately conservative as the accountancy profession, yet the multi-million dollar initiatives spawned by this group were part of a major industry rethink about how to measure value."[58]

Employees also have more power when their jobs are related to current areas of concern or opportunity. When a job pertains to pressing organizational problems, power is more easily accumulated. For example, managers at all levels who possess crisis leadership skills have gained power in today's world of terror alerts, major natural disasters, and general uncertainty. A communications manager at the U.S. company Empire Blue Cross and Blue Shield, for instance, gained power following the September 11, 2001, terrorist attacks in New York because he acted on his own and worked around the clock to get phone lines and voice mail restored.[59]

Employees increase their network centrality by becoming knowledgeable and expert about certain activities or by taking on difficult tasks and acquiring specialized knowledge that makes them indispensable to managers above them. People who show initiative, work beyond what is expected, take on undesirable but important projects, and show interest in learning about the company and industry often find themselves with influence. Physical location also helps because some locations are in the centre of things. Central location lets a person be visible to key people and become part of important interaction networks.

People. Top leaders often increase their power by surrounding themselves with a group of loyal executives.[60] Loyal managers keep the top leader informed and in touch with events, and report possible disobedience or troublemaking in the organization. Top executives can use their central positions to build alliances and exercise substantial power when they have a management team that is fully in support of their decisions and actions.

This works in the opposite direction too. Lower-level people have greater power when they have positive relationships and connections with higher-ups. By being loyal and supportive of their bosses, employees sometimes gain favourable status and exert greater influence.

It is not uncommon for CEOs to surround themselves with their loyal allies as one way to reinforce their power base. According to Richard Breeden's report on Conrad Black, Hollinger Inc was "a corporate kleptocracy" and "unfortunately, most members of the Board also saw Hollinger as Black's Company. They weren't selected by institutional shareholders for board seats, they were selected by Black."[61] Similarly, according to a senior banker from a rival firm, in describing the situation after the merger between Morgan Stanley and Dean Witter Discover & Co., "What do you really have here? A CEO who isn't terribly popular, who gets rid of any executive who isn't loyal to him. He packs the board with his pals, and the company's stock performance is mediocre. So what? That's like most companies on the S&P 500." Indeed, many top executives strive to build a cadre of loyal and supportive executives to help them achieve their goals for the organization. The U.S. government, for example, hand picked the advisers and committee members who would influence decisions made by the interim Iraqi government.[62]

Horizontal Sources of Power

Horizontal power pertains to relationships across departments or divisions. All vice presidents are usually at the same level on the organizational chart. Does this mean each department has the same amount of power? No. Horizontal power is not defined by the formal hierarchy or the organizational chart. Each department makes a unique contribution to organizational success. Some departments will have greater say and

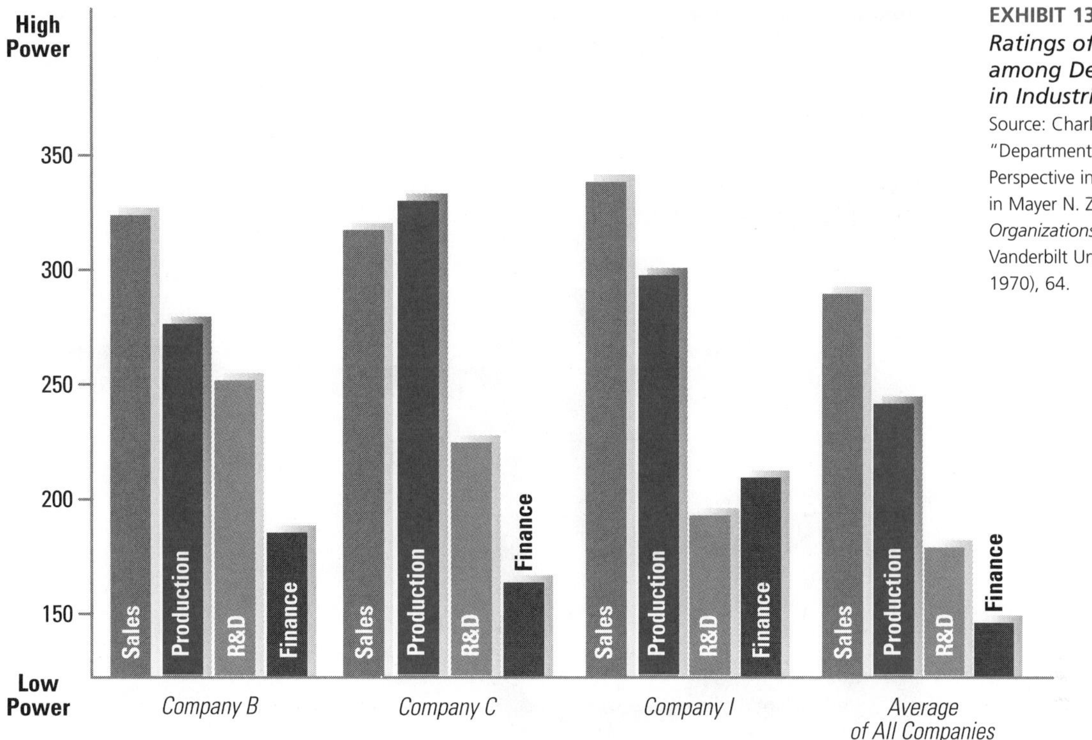

EXHIBIT 13.4
Ratings of Power among Departments in Industrial Firms
Source: Charles Perrow, "Departmental Power and Perspective in Industrial Firms," in Mayer N. Zald, ed., *Power in Organizations* (Nashville, Tenn.: Vanderbilt University Press, 1970), 64.

will achieve their desired outcomes, whereas others will not. For example, Charles Perrow surveyed managers in several industrial firms.[63] He bluntly asked, "Which department has the most power?" among four major departments: production, sales and marketing, R&D, and finance and accounting. Partial survey results are given in Exhibit 13.4.

In most firms, sales had the greatest power. In a few firms, production was also quite powerful. On average, the sales and production departments were more powerful than R&D and finance, although substantial variation existed. Differences in the amount of horizontal power clearly occurred in those firms. Today, IT departments have growing power in many organizations.

Horizontal power is difficult to measure because power differences are not defined on the organizational chart. However, some initial explanations for departmental power differences, such as those shown in Exhibit 13.4, have been found. The theoretical concept that explains relative power is called strategic contingencies.[64]

Strategic Contingencies. **Strategic contingencies** are events and activities both inside and outside an organization that are essential for attaining organizational goals. Departments involved with strategic contingencies for the organization tend to have greater power. Departmental activities are important when they provide strategic value by solving problems or crises for the organization. For example, if an organization faces an intense threat from lawsuits and regulations, the legal department will gain power and influence over organizational decisions because it copes with such a threat. If product innovation is the key strategic issue, the power of R&D can be expected to be high.

EXHIBIT 13.5
Strategic Contingencies That Influence Horizontal Power among Departments

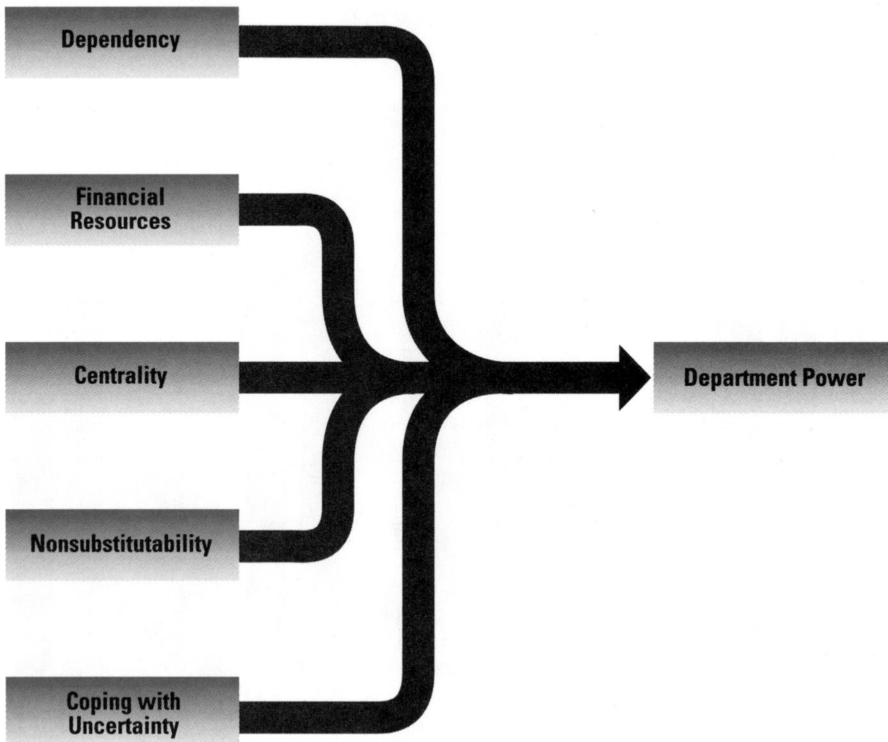

The strategic contingency approach to power is similar to the resource dependence model described in Chapters 4 and 5. Recall that organizations try to reduce dependency on the external environment. The strategic contingency approach to power suggests that the departments most responsible for dealing with key resource issues and dependencies in the environment will become most powerful.

Power Sources. Jeffrey Pfeffer and Gerald Salancik, among others, have been instrumental in conducting research on the strategic contingency theory.[65] Their findings indicate that a department rated as powerful may possess one or more of the characteristics illustrated in Exhibit 13.5.[66] In some organizations these five **power sources** overlap, but each provides a useful way to evaluate sources of horizontal power.

1. **Dependency.** Interdepartmental dependency is a key element underlying relative power. Power is derived from having something someone else wants. The power of department A over department B is greater when department B depends on department A.[67] Materials, information, and resources may flow between departments in one direction, such as in the case of sequential task interdependence (see Chapter 7). In such cases, the department receiving resources is in a lower power position than the department providing them. The number and strength of dependencies are also important. When seven or eight departments must come for help to the engineering department, for example, engineering is in a strong power position. In contrast, a department that depends on many other departments is in a low power position. Likewise, a department in an otherwise low power position might gain power through dependencies. If a factory cannot

produce without the expertise of maintenance workers to keep the machines working, the maintenance department is in a strong power position because it has control over a strategic contingency.

2. **Financial resources.** There's a so-called golden rule in the business world: "The person with the gold makes the rules."[68] Control over resources is an important source of power in organizations. Money can be converted into other kinds of resources that are needed by other departments. Money generates dependency; departments that provide financial resources have something other departments want. Departments that generate income for an organization have greater power. Exhibit 13.4 showed sales as the most powerful unit in most industrial firms. This is because salespeople find customers and bring in money, thereby removing an important problem for the organization. An ability to provide financial resources also explains why certain departments are powerful. For example, fundraising departments in universities are often powerful as they bring in the funds necessary for research.

In Practice

Dr. Nancy Olivieri and Apotex

In 1996, Dr. Olivieri discovered an unexpected risk during her clinical trials of one of Apotex's drugs for the treatment of thalassemia, a potentially fatal blood disorder. When she tried to inform her patients of the risk, Apotex ended the trials early and warned her of legal action should she disclose the risk to anyone. Some time later, Olivieri found another, more significant risk and was warned again of possible legal action. Even so, Olivieri informed her patients and published her research in 1998 in a leading scientific journal. At the same time, the University of Toronto had reached an agreement in principle with Apotex to receive what would have been the largest donation ever received by the University.

The Canadian Association of University Teachers, in its review of the case, found that "[from] 1996 onward, Dr. Olivieri was subjected to a series of strongly adverse actions, by senior staff [at the Hospital for Sick Children], the Hospital Board of Trustees, officers at Apotex and others, some of them highly public."[69]

When the Report of the Committee of Inquiry on the Case Involving Dr. Nancy Olivieri, the Hospital for Sick Children, the University of Toronto, and Apotex was released, Dr. Olivieri noted that the report vindicated her position and had found that some of the administrators at the Hospital for Sick Children had tried to discredit her and her work.

PDA

Remember...

Be aware of the important horizontal power relationships that come from the ability of a department to deal with strategic contingencies that confront the organization. Increase the horizontal power of a department by increasing involvement in strategic contingencies.

This much-layered conflict was a catalyst for positive change in the University's policies on industry-sponsored research. The current policy states that scientists can no longer be prevented from disclosing risks to patients.[70]

Power accrues to departments that bring in or provide resources that are highly valued by an organization. Power enables those departments to obtain more of the scarce resources allocated within the organization.[71] "Power derived from acquiring resources is used to obtain more resources, which in turn can be employed to produce more power—the rich get richer."[72]

3. **Centrality.** Centrality reflects a department's role in the primary activity of an organization.[73] One measure of centrality is the extent to which the work of the department affects the final output of the organization. For example, the production

department is more central and usually has more power than staff groups (assuming no other critical contingencies). Centrality is associated with power because it reflects the contribution made to the organization. The corporate finance department of an investment bank generally has more power than the stock research department. By contrast, in the manufacturing firms described in Exhibit 13.4, finance tends to be low in power. When the finance department has the limited task of recording money and expenditures, it is not responsible for obtaining critical resources or for producing the products of the organization. Today, however, finance departments have greater power in many organizations because of the greater need for controlling costs.

4. **Nonsubstitutability.** Power is also determined by *nonsubstitutability,* which means that a department's function cannot be performed by other readily available resources. Similiarly, if an employee cannot be easily replaced, his or her power is greater. If an organization has no alternative sources of skill and information, a department's power will be greater. This can be the case when management uses outside consultants. Consultants might be used as substitutes for staff people to reduce the power of staff groups.

   The impact of substitutability on power was studied for programmers in computer departments.[74] When computers were first introduced, programming was a rare and specialized occupation. Programmers controlled the use of organizational computers because they alone possessed the knowledge to program them. Over a period of about ten years, computer programming became a more common activity. People could be substituted easily, and the power of programming departments dropped.

5. **Coping with uncertainty.** Elements in the environment can change swiftly and can be unpredictable and complex. In the face of uncertainty, little information is available to managers on appropriate courses of action. Departments that reduce this uncertainty for the organization will increase their power.[75] When market research personnel accurately predict changes in demand for new products, they gain power and prestige because they have reduced a critical uncertainty. But forecasting is only one technique. Sometimes uncertainty can be reduced by taking quick and appropriate action after an unpredictable event occurs.

   Departments can cope with critical uncertainties by (1) obtaining prior information, (2) prevention, and (3) absorption.[76] Obtaining prior information means a department can reduce an organization's uncertainty by forecasting an event. Departments increase their power through prevention by predicting and forestalling negative events. Absorption occurs when a department takes action after an event to reduce its negative consequences.

Horizontal power relationships in organizations change as strategic contingencies change. In a hospital dealing with a major health crisis, the public relations department might gain power, for example, by soothing public fears and keeping people informed about the hospital's efforts to control the spread of disease. As another example, large retailers such as Wal-Mart and Home Depot attempting to build new stores often face challenges from community activists fighting urban sprawl. The public relations department can gain power by helping the organization present a positive side to the story and counteract the arguments of protestors. Departments that help organizations cope with new strategic issues will have greater power.

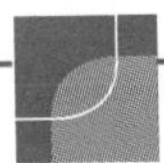

Political Processes in Organizations

Politics, like power, is intangible and difficult to measure. It is hidden from view and is hard to observe in a systematic way. Two surveys uncovered the following reactions of managers toward political behaviour.[77]

1. Most managers have a negative view toward politics and believe that politics will more often hurt than help an organization in achieving its goals.
2. Most managers believe that political behaviour is common in all organizations.
3. Most managers think that political behaviour occurs more often at upper rather than lower levels in organizations.
4. Most managers believe that political behaviour arises in certain decision domains, such as structural change, but is absent from other decisions, such as handling employee grievances.

Based on these surveys, politics seems more likely to occur at the top levels of an organization and around certain issues and decisions. Moreover, managers do not approve of political behaviour. The remainder of this chapter explores more fully what political behaviour is, when it should be used, the type of issues and decisions most likely to be associated with politics, and some political tactics that may be effective.

Definition

Power has been described as the available force or potential for achieving desired outcomes. *Politics* is the use of power to influence decisions in order to achieve those outcomes. The exercise of power and influence has led to two ways to define politics—as self-serving behaviour or as a natural organizational decision process. The first definition emphasizes that politics is self-serving and involves activities that are not sanctioned by the organization.[78]

In this view, politics involves deception and dishonesty for purposes of individual self-interest and leads to conflict and disharmony within the work environment. This dark view of politics is widely held by laypeople, and political activity certainly can be used in this way. Recent studies have shown that workers who perceive this kind of political activity within their companies often have related feelings of anxiety and job dissatisfaction. Studies also support the belief that inappropriate use of politics is related to low employee morale, inferior organizational performance, and poor decision making.[79] This view of politics explains why managers in the aforementioned surveys did not approve of political behaviour.

Although politics can be used in a negative, self-serving way, the appropriate use of political behaviour can serve organizational goals.[80] The second view sees politics as a natural organizational process for resolving differences among organizational interest groups.[81] Politics is the process of bargaining and negotiation that is used to overcome conflicts and differences of opinion. In this view, politics is similar to the coalition-building decision processes defined in Chapter 12.

The organizational theory perspective views politics as described in the second definition—as a normal decision-making process. Politics is simply the activity through which power is exercised in the resolution of conflicts and uncertainty. Politics is neutral and is not necessarily harmful to the organization. The formal definition of organizational politics is as follows: **Organizational politics** involves

PDA
Remember...

Expect and allow for political behaviour in organizations. Politics provides the discussion and clash of interests needed to crystallize points of view and to reach a decision. Build coalitions, expand networks, control decision premises, enhance legitimacy, and make a direct appeal to attain desired outcomes.

activities to acquire, develop, and use power and other resources to obtain the outcome when there is uncertainty or disagreement about choices.[82]

Political behaviour can be either a positive or a negative force. Uncertainty and conflict are natural and inevitable, and politics is the mechanism for reaching agreement. Politics includes informal discussions that enable participants to arrive at consensus and make decisions that otherwise might be stalemated or unsolvable.

When Is Political Activity Used?

Politics is a mechanism for arriving at consensus when uncertainty is high and there is disagreement over goals or problem priorities. Recall the rational versus political models described in Exhibit 13.3. The political model is associated with conflict over goals, shifting coalitions and interest groups, ambiguous information, and uncertainty. Thus, political activity tends to be most visible when managers confront nonprogrammed decisions, as discussed in Chapter 12, and is related to the Carnegie model of decision making. Because managers at the top of an organization generally deal with more nonprogrammed decisions than do managers at lower levels, more political activity will appear at higher levels. Moreover, some issues are associated with inherent disagreement. Resources, for example, are critical for the survival and effectiveness of departments, so resource allocation often becomes a political issue. Rational methods of allocation do not satisfy participants. Three **domains of political activity** (areas in which politics plays a role) in most organizations are structural change, management succession, and resource allocation.

Structural reorganizations strike at the heart of power and authority relationships. Reorganizations such as those discussed in Chapter 3 change responsibilities and tasks, which also affects the underlying power base from strategic contingencies. For these reasons, a major reorganization can lead to an explosion of political activity.[83] Managers may actively bargain and negotiate to maintain the responsibilities and power bases they have. Mergers and acquisitions also frequently create tremendous political activity, as we saw with the Porsche-VW example.

Organizational changes such as hiring new executives, promotions, and transfers have great political significance, particularly at top organizational levels where uncertainty is high and networks of trust, cooperation, and communication among executives are important.[84] Hiring decisions can generate uncertainty, discussion, and disagreement. Managers can use hiring and promotion to strengthen network alliances and coalitions by putting their own people in prominent positions.

The third area of political activity is resource allocation. Resource allocation decisions encompass all resources required for organizational performance, including salaries, operating budgets, employees, office facilities, equipment, use of the company airplane, and so forth. Resources are so vital that disagreement about priorities exists, and political processes help resolve the dilemmas.

In Practice

Liberal Party of Canada

On June 2, 2002, Jean Chrétien fired Paul Martin, Jr. as his finance minister. Martin had served for nearly a decade in the position. According Chrétien, he had replaced Martin for nongovernment reasons: "[we] agreed that for the good of the governance of the country . . . it was better that he [Paul Martin] was not to be the minister of finance."[85] Martin claimed, however, that the differences were related to differences in government policy. Chrétien and Martin had had a professional working relationship until March 2000 when Chrétien heard that a "pro-Martin cabal was plotting his overthrow . . . "[86]As well, the prime minister's supporters were well aware of the power brokers behind the so-called PM-in-waiting. "A relatively small but well-connected lobbying and consulting firm, Earnscliffe, had been dubbed the shadow PMO."[87]

As a result, there was a public division between Chrétien's supporters and Martin's supporters. Martin charged that Chrétien had punished Liberals who were working against Chrétien. Chrétien responded by saying that he had never acted against those who had financially supported his political opponents. Some of Chrétien's cabinet ministers called Martin's allegations unfair and insisted that Chrétien would be supported by a majority of Liberals at the February 2003 leadership review.[88] After Chrétien resigned, Paul Martin became leader of the Liberal Party. "The Liberal gathering at Toronto's Air Canada Centre [was] more of a coronation than a convention. Martin [had] rock stars singing his praises and, more importantly, the vote of almost every single delegate in the building."[89] In Martin's first election as prime minister, the Liberal government was reduced to a minority government and, in the 2006 election, the Liberal Party was defeated by the Conservative Party. When Martin then announced that he would not continue as Liberal leader, "[not] even Liberals shed many tears for the departure of Paul Martin."[90] In 2008, Stéphane Dion, Martin's successor, faces questions about his leadership and his future.

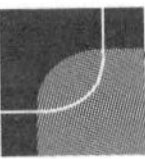

Using Power, Politics, and Collaboration

One theme in this chapter has been that power in organizations is not primarily a phenomenon of the individual. It is related to the resources departments command, the role departments play in an organization, and the environmental contingencies with which departments cope. Position and responsibility, more than personality and style, determine a manager's influence on outcomes in the organization.

Power is used through individual political behaviour, however. Individual managers seek agreement about a strategy to achieve their departments' desired outcomes. Individual managers negotiate decisions and adopt tactics that enable them to acquire and use power. In addition, managers develop ways to increase cooperation and collaboration within the organization to reduce damaging conflicts.

To fully understand the use of power within organizations, it is important to look at both structural components and individual behaviour.[91] Although the power comes from larger organizational forms and processes, the political use of power involves individual-level activities. For instance, all managers use tactics to exert influence, but research indicates that managers in HR departments may use softer, more subtle approaches than do managers in more powerful finance departments. In one study, HR executives, who were not seen as having centrality to the firm's mission, took a low-key approach to try to influence others, whereas finance executives, who had a more central and powerful position, used harder, more direct influence tactics.[92] The following sections briefly summarize various tactics that managers can use to increase the power base of their departments, political tactics they can use to achieve desired outcomes, and tactics for increasing collaboration. These tactics are summarized in Exhibit 13.6.

Tactics for Increasing Power

Four **tactics for increasing power** for the organization are as follows:

1. *Enter areas of high uncertainty*. One source of departmental power involves coping with critical uncertainties.[93] If department managers can identify key

EXHIBIT 13.6
Power and Political Tactics in Organizations

Tactics for Increasing the Power Base	Political Tactics for Using Power	Tactics for Enhancing Collaboration
1. Enter areas of high uncertainty. 2. Create dependencies. 3. Provide scarce resources. 4. Satisfy strategic contingencies.	1. Build coalitions and expand networks. 2. Assign loyal people to key positions. 3. Control decision premises. 4. Enhance legitimacy and expertise. 5. Make a direct appeal.	1. Create integration devices. 2. Use confrontation and negotiation. 3. Schedule intergroup consultation. 4. Practice member rotation. 5. Create shared mission and superordinate goals.

uncertainties and take steps to remove those uncertainties, the department's power base will be enhanced. Uncertainties could arise from stoppages on an assembly line, from the quality demanded of a new product, or from the inability to predict a demand for new services. Once an uncertainty is identified, the department can take action to cope with it. By their very nature, uncertain tasks will not be solved immediately. Trial and error will be needed, which is to the advantage of the department. The trial-and-error process provides experience and expertise that cannot easily be duplicated by other departments.

2. *Create dependencies*. Dependencies are another source of power.[94] When the organization depends on a department for information, materials, knowledge, or skills, that department will hold power over others. This power can be increased by incurring obligations. Doing additional work that helps out other departments will obligate the other departments to respond at a future date. The power accumulated by creating a dependency can be used to resolve future disagreements in the department's favour. An equally effective and related strategy is to reduce dependency on other departments by acquiring necessary information or skills. IT departments have created dependencies in many organizations because of the rapid changes in this area. Employees in other departments depend on the IT unit to master complex software programs, changing use of the Internet, and other advances so that they will have the information they need to perform effectively.
3. *Provide scarce resources*. Resources are always important to organizational survival. Departments that accumulate resources and provide them to an organization in the form of money, information, or facilities will be powerful. For example, sales departments are powerful in industrial firms because they bring in financial resources.
4. *Satisfy strategic contingencies*. The theory of strategic contingencies says that some elements in the external environment and within the organization are especially important for organizational success. A contingency could be a critical event, a task for which there are no substitutes, or a central task that is interdependent with many others in the organization. An analysis of the organization and its changing environment will reveal strategic contingencies. To the extent that contingencies are new or are not being satisfied, there is room for a department to move into those critical areas and increase its importance and power.

In summary, the allocation of power in an organization is not random. Power is the result of organizational processes that can be understood and predicted. The abilities to reduce uncertainty, increase dependency on one's own department, obtain resources, and cope with strategic contingencies all enhance a department's power. Once power is available, the next challenge is to use it to attain helpful outcomes.

Political Tactics for Using Power

The use of power in organizations requires both skill and willingness. Many decisions are made through political processes because rational decision processes do not fit; uncertainty or disagreement is too high. **Political tactics for using power** to influence decision outcomes include the following:

1. *Build coalitions and expand networks.* Coalition building means taking the time to talk with other managers to persuade them to a point of view.[95] Most important decisions are made outside formal meetings; managers discuss issues with each other and reach agreement. Effective managers are those who huddle, meeting in groups of twos and threes to resolve key issues.[96] Effective managers also build networks of relationships across hierarchical and functional boundaries. Networks can be expanded by (1) reaching out to establish contact with additional managers and (2) coopting dissenters. A recent research project found that the ability to build networks has a positive impact on both employees' perception of a manager's effectiveness and the ability of the manager to influence performance.[97] Establishing contact with additional managers means building good interpersonal relationships based on liking, trust, and respect. Reliability and the motivation to work with rather than exploit others are part of both networking and coalition building.[98] The second approach to expanding networks, cooptation, is the act of bringing a dissenter into one's network. One example of cooptation involved a university committee whose membership was based on promotion and tenure. Several professors who were critical of the tenure and promotion process were appointed to the committee. Once a part of the administrative process, they could see the administrative point of view. Cooptation effectively brought them into the administrative network.[99]
2. *Assign loyal people to key positions.* Another political tactic is to assign trusted and loyal people to key positions in the organization or department. Top managers as well as department heads often use the hiring, transfer, and promotion processes to place in key positions people who are sympathetic to the outcomes of the department, thus helping to achieve departmental goals.[100] Top leaders frequently use this tactic, as we discussed earlier. For example, since he became CEO at Merrill Lynch & Co., Stan O'Neal removed a whole generation of top talent and moved in other managers who support his vision and goals for the organization. He then brought back a popular retired executive, countering charges that he was stacking the management ranks only with people who wouldn't challenge his power and authority.[101]
3. *Control decision premises.* To control decision premises means to constrain the boundaries of a decision. One technique is to choose or limit information provided to other managers. A common method is simply to put the department's

best foot forward, such as selectively presenting favourable criteria. A variety of statistics can be assembled to support the departmental point of view. A university department that is growing rapidly and has a large number of students can make claims for additional resources by emphasizing its growth and large size. Such objective criteria do not always work, but they are a valuable step.

Decision premises can be further influenced by limiting the decision process. Decisions can be influenced by the items put on an agenda for an important meeting or even by the sequence in which items are discussed.[102] Items discussed last, when time is short and people want to leave, receive less attention than those discussed earlier. Calling attention to specific problems and suggesting alternatives also will affect outcomes. Stressing a specific problem to get it—rather than problems not relevant to one's department—on the agenda is an example of agenda setting.

4. *Enhance legitimacy and expertise.* Managers can exert the greatest influence in areas in which they have recognized legitimacy and expertise. If a request is within the task domain of a department and is consistent with the department's vested interest, other departments will tend to comply. Members can also identify external consultants or other experts within the organization to support their cause.[103] For example, a financial vice president in a large retail firm wanted to fire the director of HR management. She hired a consultant to evaluate the HR projects undertaken to date. A negative report from the consultant provided sufficient legitimacy to fire the director, who was replaced with a director loyal to the financial vice president.
5. *Make a direct appeal.* If managers do not ask, they seldom receive. Political activity is effective only when goals and needs are made explicit so the organization can respond. Managers should bargain aggressively and be persuasive. An assertive proposal may be accepted because other managers have no better alternatives. Moreover, an explicit proposal will often receive favourable treatment because other alternatives are ambiguous and less well defined. Effective political behaviour requires sufficient forcefulness and risk taking to at least ask for what is needed to achieve desired outcomes.

The use of power, however, should not be obvious.[104] If managers formally draw on their power base in a meeting by saying, "My department has more power, so the rest of you have to do it my way," their power will be diminished. Power works best when it is used quietly. To call attention to power is to lose it. People know who has power. Explicit claims to power are not necessary and can even harm the department's cause.

When using any of the preceding tactics, recall that most people think self-serving behaviour hurts rather than helps an organization. If managers are perceived to be throwing their weight around or pursuing goals that are self-serving rather than beneficial to the organization, they will lose respect. On the other hand, managers must recognize the relational and political aspect of their work. It is not sufficient to be rational and technically competent. Politics is a way to reach agreement. This chapter's Book Mark describes some basic psychological principles that underlie successful political influence tactics. Managers can use this understanding to assert influence and get things done within the organization. When managers ignore political tactics, they may find themselves failing without understanding why. This is partly the reason Tim Koogle failed to accomplish a key acquisition at Yahoo!, described in the next In Practice.

Book Mark 13.0 (HAVE YOU READ THIS BOOK?)

Influence: Science and Practice
By Robert B. Cialdini

Managers use a variety of political tactics to influence others and bring about desired outcomes. In his book *Influence: Science and Practice*, Robert Cialdini examines the social and psychological pressures that cause people to respond favourably to these various tactics. Over years of study, Cialdini, Regents' Professor of Psychology at Arizona State University, has identified some basic *influence principles*, "those that work in a variety of situations, for a variety of practitioners, on a variety of topics, for a variety of prospects."

INFLUENCE PRINCIPLES

Having a working knowledge of the basic set of persuasion tools can help managers predict and influence human behaviour, which is valuable for interacting with colleagues, employees, customers, partners, and even friends. Some basic psychological principles that govern successful influence tactics are as follows:

- *Reciprocity*. The principle of reciprocity refers to the sense of obligation people feel to give back in kind what they have received. For example, a manager who does favours for others creates in them a sense of obligation to return the favours in the future. Smart managers find ways to be helpful to others, whether it be helping a colleague finish an unpleasant job or offering compassion and concern for a subordinate's personal problems.
- *Liking*. People say yes more often to those they like. Companies such as Tupperware have long understood that familiar faces and congenial characteristics sell products. In-home Tupperware parties allow customers to buy from a friend instead of an unknown salesperson. Salespeople in all kinds of companies often try to capitalize on this principle by finding interests they share with customers as a way to establish rapport. In general, managers who are pleasant, generous with praise, cooperative, and considerate of others' feelings find that they have greater influence.
- *Credible authority*. Legitimate authorities are particularly influential sources. However, research has discovered that the key to successful use of authority is to be knowledgeable, credible, and trustworthy. Managers who become known for their expertise, who are honest and straightforward with others, and who inspire trust can exert greater influence than those who rely on formal position alone.
- *Social validation*. One of the primary ways people decide what to do in any given situation is to consider what others are doing. That is, people examine the actions of others to validate correct choices. For instance, when homeowners were shown a list of neighbours who had donated to a local charity during a fundraiser, the frequency of contributions increased dramatically. By demonstrating, or even implying, that others have already complied with a request, managers gain greater cooperation.

THE PROCESS OF SOCIAL INFLUENCE

Because life as a manager is all about influencing others, learning to be genuinely persuasive is a valuable management skill. Cialdini's book helps managers understand the basic psychological rules of persuasion—how and why people are motivated to change their attitudes and behaviours. When managers use this understanding in an honest and ethical manner, they improve their effectiveness and the success of their organizations.

Influence: Science and Practice (4th edition), by Robert B. Cialdini, is published by Allyn & Bacon.

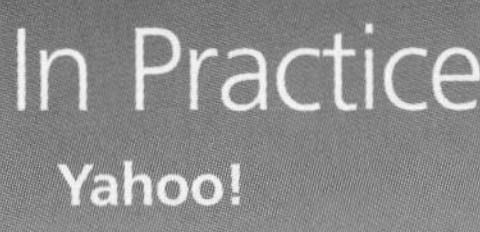

In Practice
Yahoo!

In late March 2000, Yahoo! began negotiating to buy online auction leader eBay. Tim Koogle, Yahoo!'s CEO at the time, was fully in support of the deal, believing it would enable the company to beef up its e-commerce revenues and bring needed new blood to the increasingly insular Yahoo! culture. But the deal never happened, and while Yahoo!'s fortunes flagged, eBay's revenues and net income continue to climb.

What happened? Jeffrey Mallett, Yahoo!'s president, opposed the acquisition of eBay, and he used political tactics to quash it. Koogle had always been a consensus-style manager. He believed the top leaders would debate the pros and cons of the acquisition and arrive at the best decision.

PDA Remember...

If conflict becomes too strong, use tactics for enhancing collaboration, including integration devices, confrontation and negotiation, intergroup consultation, member rotation, and superordinate goals. Select the technique that fits the organization and the conflict.

In addition, he felt sure the merits of the eBay deal would ultimately win the day. But Mallett, who insiders say was already angling to take over the CEO job, began courting co-founders Jerry Yang and David Filo. Eventually, he convinced them that the eBay culture was a poor fit with Yahoo!. With Koogle outnumbered, the deal fell apart. A former Yahoo! manager called it management by persuasion.

By failing to build a coalition, Koogle allowed Mallett to control this important decision. It's only one example of several that ultimately led to Koogle being pushed out as CEO. Despite Mallett's political moves, he was passed over for the top job in favour of an outsider who board members felt could turn the struggling company around. Koogle took the decision to seek a new CEO calmly and blamed himself for not keeping a closer eye on Mallett.[105]

Tactics for Enhancing Collaboration

Power and political tactics are important means for getting things done within organizations. Most organizations today have at least moderate interunit conflict. An additional approach in many organizations is to overcome conflict by stimulating cooperation and collaboration among departments to support the attainment of organizational goals. **Tactics for enhancing collaboration** include the following:

1. *Create integration devices.* As described in Chapter 3, teams, task forces, and project managers who span the boundaries between departments can be used as integration devices. Bringing together representatives from conflicting departments in joint problem-solving teams is an effective way to enhance collaboration because representatives learn to understand each other's point of view.[106] Sometimes a full-time integrator is assigned to achieve cooperation and collaboration by meeting with members of the respective departments and exchanging information. The integrator has to understand each group's problems and must be able to move both groups toward a solution that is mutually acceptable.[107]

   Teams and task forces reduce conflict and enhance cooperation because they integrate people from different departments. Integration devices can also be used to enhance cooperation between labour and management, as the example of the Brotherhood of Locomotive Engineers, the United Transportation Union, and the Canadian Pacific Railway shows.

In Practice

Brotherhood of Locomotive Engineers, United Transportation Union and Canadian Pacific Railway (CPR)

"Canadian Pacific Railway was founded in 1881 to link Canada's populated centres with the vast potential of its relatively unpopulated West. This incredible engineering feat was completed on [November] 7, 1885—six years ahead of schedule—when the last spike was driven at Craigellachie, B.C. . . . Canadian Pacific Railway was formed to physically unite Canada and Canadians from coast to coast."[108] It now provides freight transportation services over a 22,400 kilometre network in Canada and the United States.

In the 1980–1990s, railroad companies in North America were selling or abandoning branch lines that they considered peripheral to their core routes. Union leaders from the Brotherhood of Locomotive Engineers and the United Transportation Union approached both CPR and Canadian National to join them to study what could be done instead of selling or abandoning the lines. The four organizations began their study in 1994. In order to reduce labour costs by 30 percent and to maintain the levels of employee wages and benefits, the study committee recommended "revolutionary changes to turn two branch lines into . . . internal short-line operations."[109] Employees would jointly manage the lines through a process of co-determination. Co-determination entailed (1) senior labour–management participation on an oversight advisory board, (2) self-managed work groups, (3) minimally specified work rules, (4) multitasking, and (5) a new pay plan made up of salary and profit-sharing components.

As a result of the joint study committee's work, union workers were able to keep their jobs and CPR was able to keep two lines that would have been lost. "Based on the generally positive results of the two short-line railways, CPR has developed five criteria to judge potential, additional short-line railways [for] CPR: (1) the potential for the property to be self-managed, (2) the ratio of capital investment to potential revenue, (3) the degree of self-containment of the property, (4) the profits from the property must be low enough to make it desirable to convert to a short line and potential profits must be high enough to make it viable on its own, and (5) the interests of the unions and the company must be in alignment."[110]

Labour–management teams, which are designed to increase worker participation and provide a cooperative model for solving union–management problems, are increasingly being used at companies such as Goodyear, Ford Motor Company, and Xerox. In the steel industry, American companies such as USX and Wheeling-Pittsburgh Steel have signed pacts that give union representatives seats on the board.[111] Although unions continue to battle over traditional issues such as wages, these integration devices are creating a level of cooperation that many managers would not have believed possible just a few years ago.

2. *Use confrontation and negotiation.* **Confrontation** occurs when parties in conflict directly engage one another and try to work out their differences. **Negotiation** is the bargaining process that often occurs during confrontation and that enables the parties to systematically reach a solution. These techniques bring appointed representatives from the departments together to work out a serious dispute. Confrontation and negotiation involve some risk. There is no guarantee that discussions will focus on a conflict or that emotions will not get out of hand. However, if members are able to resolve the conflict on the basis of face-to-face discussions, they will find new respect for each other, and future collaboration becomes easier. The beginnings of relatively permanent attitude change are possible through direct negotiation.

   Confrontation and negotiation are successful when managers engage in a *win–win strategy*. Win–win means both sides adopt a positive attitude and strive to resolve the conflict in a way that will benefit each other.[112] If the negotiations deteriorate into a strictly win–lose strategy (each group wants to defeat the other), the confrontation will be ineffective. The differences between win–win and win–lose strategies of negotiation are shown in Exhibit 13.7. With a win–win strategy—which includes defining the problem as mutual, communicating openly, and avoiding threats—understanding can be changed while the dispute is resolved.

   One type of negotiation, used to resolve a disagreement between workers and management, is referred to as **collective bargaining.** The bargaining process is usually accomplished through a union and results in an agreement that specifies each party's responsibilities for the next two to three years. For example, Teamsters Canada and Molson Coors negotiated a team design for some warehouse, shipping and garage operations as well as multi-skill premiums for client service activities and for brewing operations.[113]

EXHIBIT 13.7
Negotiating Strategies

Win–Win Strategy	Win–Lose Strategy
1. Define the conflict as a mutual problem.	1. Define the problem as a win–lose situation.
2. Pursue joint outcomes.	2. Pursue own group's outcomes.
3. Find creative agreements that satisfy both groups.	3. Force the other group into submission.
4. Be open, honest, and accurate in communicating the group's needs, goals, and proposals.	4. Be deceitful, inaccurate, and misleading in communicating the group's needs, goals, and proposals.
5. Avoid threats (to reduce the other's defensiveness).	5. Use threats (to force submission).
6. Communicate flexibility of position.	6. Communicate strong commitment (rigidity) regarding one's position.

Source: Adapted from David W. Johnson and Frank P. Johnson, *Joining Together: Group Theory and Group Skills* (Englewood Cliffs, N.J.: Prentice-Hall, 1975), 182–183.

3. *Schedule intergroup consultation.* When conflict is intense and enduring, and department members are suspicious and uncooperative, top managers may intervene as third parties to help resolve the conflict or bring in third-party consultants from outside the organization.[114] This process, sometimes called *workplace mediation*, is a strong intervention to reduce conflict because it involves bringing the disputing parties together and allowing each side to present its version of the situation. The technique has been developed by such psychologists as Robert Blake, Jane Mouton, and Richard Walton.[115]

   Department members attend a workshop, which may last for several days, away from day-to-day work problems. This approach is similar to the organization development (OD) approach described in Chapter 11. The conflicting groups are separated, and each group is invited to discuss and make a list of its perceptions of itself and the other group. Group representatives publicly share these perceptions, and together the groups discuss the results.

   Intergroup consultation can be quite demanding for everyone involved. Although it is fairly easy to have conflicting groups list perceptions and identify discrepancies, exploring their differences face to face and agreeing to change is more difficult. If handled correctly, these sessions can help department employees understand each other much better and lead to improved attitudes and better working relationships for years to come.
4. *Practise member rotation.* Rotation means that individuals from one department can be asked to work in another department on a temporary or permanent basis. The advantage is that individuals become submerged in the values, attitudes, problems, and goals of the other department. In addition, individuals can explain the problems and goals of their original departments to their new colleagues. This enables a frank, accurate exchange of views and information. Rotation works slowly to reduce conflict but is very effective for changing the underlying attitudes and perceptions that promote conflict.[116]
5. *Create shared mission and superordinate goals.* Another strategy is for top management to create a shared mission and establish superordinate goals that require

cooperation among departments.[117] As discussed in Chapter 10, organizations with strong, adaptive cultures, where employees share a larger vision for their company, are more likely to have a united, cooperative workforce. Studies have shown that when employees from different departments see that their goals are linked together, they will openly share resources and information.[118] To be effective, superordinate goals must be substantial, and employees must be granted the time and incentives to work cooperatively in pursuit of the superordinate goals rather than departmental subgoals.

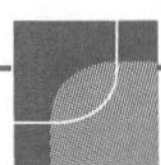

Summary and Interpretation

The central message of this chapter is that conflict, power, and politics are natural outcomes of organizing. Differences in goals, backgrounds, and tasks are necessary for organizational excellence, but these differences can throw groups into conflict. Managers use power and politics to manage and resolve conflict. Two views of organization were presented. The rational model of organization assumes that organizations have specific goals and that problems can be logically solved. The other view, the political model of organization, is the basis for this chapter. This view assumes that the goals of an organization are not specific or agreed upon. Departments have different values and interests, so managers come into conflict. Decisions are made on the basis of power and political influence. Bargaining, negotiation, persuasion, and coalition building decide outcomes.

The chapter also discussed the vertical and horizontal sources of power. Vertical sources of power include formal position, resources, control of decision premises and information, and network centrality. In general, managers at the top of the organizational hierarchy have more power than people at lower levels. However, positions all along the hierarchy can be designed to increase the power of employees. As organizations face increased competition and environmental uncertainty, top executives are finding that increasing the power of middle managers and lower-level employees can help the organization be more competitive. Research into horizontal power processes has revealed that certain characteristics make some departments more powerful than others. Such factors as dependency, resources, centrality, nonsubstitutability, and coping with uncertainty determine the influence of departments.

Managers can use political tactics such as building coalitions and expanding networks, assigning loyal people to key positions, controlling decision premises, enhancing legitimacy and expertise, and making a direct appeal to help departments achieve desired outcomes. Many people distrust political behaviour, fearing that it will be used for selfish ends that benefit the individual but not the organization. However, politics is often needed to achieve the legitimate goals of a department or organization. Three areas in which politics often plays a role are structural change, management succession, and resource allocation because these are areas of high uncertainty. Although conflict and political behaviour are natural and can be used for beneficial purposes, managers also strive to enhance collaboration so that conflict between groups does not become too strong. Tactics for enhancing collaboration include integration devices, confrontation and negotiation, intergroup consultation, member rotation, and shared mission and superordinate goals.

Key Concepts

authority, p. 481
centrality, p. 487
collective bargaining, p. 497
competition, p. 474
confrontation, p. 497
coping with uncertainty, p. 488
decision premises, p. 482
dependency, p. 486
domains of political activity, p. 490
financial resources, p. 487
intergroup conflict, p. 474
labour–management teams, p. 497
negotiation, p. 497
network centrality, p. 483
nonsubstitutability, p. 488
organizational politics, p. 489
political model, p. 478
political tactics for using power, p. 493
power sources, p. 486
power, p. 479
rational model, p. 478
sources of intergroup conflict, p. 475
strategic contingencies, p. 485
tactics for enhancing collaboration, p. 496
tactics for increasing power, p. 491

Discussion Questions

1. Give an example from your personal experience of how differences in tasks, personal background, and training lead to conflict among groups. How might task interdependence have influenced that conflict?
2. A noted expert on organizations said that some conflict is beneficial to organizations. Discuss.
3. In a rapidly changing organization, are decisions more likely to be made using the rational or political model of organization? Discuss.
4. What is the difference between power and authority? Is it possible for a person to have formal authority but no real power? Discuss.
5. Discuss ways in which a department in a hospital could help the CEO respond to changes in provincial health care policies.
6. In Exhibit 13.4, R&D has greater power in company B than in the other firms. Discuss possible strategic contingencies that give R&D greater power in this firm.
7. What are some sources of power for university or college students? What are some sources of power for university professors and administrators? How might students increase their power?
8. A bookkeeper tried for several years to expose fraud in an organization's accounting department, but couldn't get anyone to pay attention to his claims. How would you evaluate this employee's power? What might he have done to increase his power and call notice to the ethical and legal problems at the organization?
9. The engineering school at a major university brings in three times as many government research dollars as does the rest of the university combined. Engineering appears wealthy and has many professors on full-time research status. Yet, when internal research funds are allocated, engineering gets a larger share of the money, even though it already has substantial external research funds. Why would this happen?
10. Which do you believe would have a greater long-term impact on changing employee attitudes toward increased collaboration—intergroup consultation or confrontation and negotiation? Discuss.

Chapter 13 Workbook: How Do You Handle Conflict?*

Think of some disagreements you have had with a friend, relative, manager, or co-worker. Then indicate how frequently you engage in each of the following behaviours. There are no right or wrong answers, so answer the items honestly. Respond to all items using the following scale from 1 to 7.

Scale

Always	Very often	Often	Sometimes	Seldom	Very seldom	Never
1	2	3	4	5	6	7

_______ 1. I blend my ideas to create new alternatives for resolving a disagreement.
_______ 2. I shy away from topics that are sources of disputes.
_______ 3. I make my opinion known in a disagreement.
_______ 4. I suggest solutions that combine a variety of viewpoints.
_______ 5. I steer clear of disagreeable situations.
_______ 6. I give in a little on my ideas when the other person also gives in.
_______ 7. I avoid the other person when I suspect that he or she wants to discuss a disagreement.
_______ 8. I integrate arguments into a new solution from the issues raised in a dispute.
_______ 9. I will go 50–50 to reach a settlement.
_______ 10. I raise my voice when I'm trying to get the other person to accept my position.
_______ 11. I offer creative solutions in discussions of disagreements.
_______ 12. I keep quiet about my views in order to avoid disagreements.
_______ 13. I give in if the other person will meet me halfway.
_______ 14. I downplay the importance of a disagreement.
_______ 15. I reduce disagreements by making them seem insignificant.
_______ 16. I meet the other person at a midpoint in our differences.
_______ 17. I assert my opinion forcefully.
_______ 18. I dominate arguments until the other person understands my position.
_______ 19. I suggest we work together to create solutions to disagreements.
_______ 20. I try to use the other person's ideas to generate solutions to problems.
_______ 21. I offer tradeoffs to reach solutions in disagreements.
_______ 22. I argue insistently for my stance.
_______ 23. I withdraw when the other person confronts me about a controversial issue.
_______ 24. I sidestep disagreements when they arise.
_______ 25. I try to smooth over disagreements by making them appear unimportant.
_______ 26. I insist my position be accepted during a disagreement with the other person.
_______ 27. I make our differences seem less serious.
_______ 28. I hold my tongue rather than argue with the other person.
_______ 29. I ease conflict by claiming our differences are trivial.
_______ 30. I stand firm in expressing my viewpoints during a disagreement.

Scoring and interpretation: Three categories of conflict-handling strategies are measured in this instrument: solution oriented, nonconfrontational, and control. By comparing your scores on the following three scales, you can see which of the three is your preferred conflict-handling strategy.

To calculate your three scores, add the individual scores for the items and divide by the number of items measuring the strategy. Then subtract each of the three mean scores from seven.

Solution oriented: Items 1, 4, 6, 8, 9, 11, 13, 16, 19, 20, 21 (total = 11)

Nonconfrontational: Items 2, 5, 7, 12, 14, 15, 23, 24, 25, 27, 28, 29 (total = 12)

Control: Items 3, 10, 17, 18, 22, 26, 30 (total = 7)

Solution-oriented strategies tend to focus on the problem rather than on the individuals involved. Solutions reached are often mutually beneficial, with neither party defining himself or herself as the winner and the other party as the loser.

Nonconfrontational strategies tend to focus on avoiding the conflict by either avoiding the other party or by simply allowing the other party to have his or her way. These strategies are used when there is more concern with avoiding a confrontation than with the actual outcome of the problem situation.

Control strategies tend to focus on winning or achieving an individual's goals without regard for the other party's needs or desires. Individuals using these strategies often rely on rules and regulations in order to win the battle.

Questions

1. Which strategy do you find easiest to use? Most difficult? Which do you use more often?
2. How would your answers have differed if the other person was a friend, family member, or co-worker?
3. What is it about the conflict situation or strategy that tells you which strategy to use in dealing with a conflict situation?

*From "How Do You Handle Conflict?" in Robert E. Quinn et al., *Becoming a Master Manager* (New York: Wiley, 1990), 221–223.

Case for Analysis: The Irving Dynasty to End?

In November 2007, there were media reports that the three Irving brothers, J.K., Arthur and Jack, were going to break up their 125-year-old family business. "The reason, as in most family splits, is a succession impasse . . . "[1] While the three brothers had been able to make decisions collegially, their five children have not been able to do so. J.K.'s two sons run J.D. Irving Limited, the forestry side of the business. Arthur's two sons run the refinery side of the business and Jack's son, who has a Harvard MBA, "is a bit of an enigma."[2]

As the tensions between the cousins escalated, the three brothers were afraid of having the sort of internecine clashes that the McCain family had endured. As part of a planned restructuring, the family members will be offered the choice of cash or business interests. No assets will be sold to outsiders.

J.D. Irving established a sawmill in the late 1800s and K.C. Irving founded Irving Oil, both in Boutouche, New Brunswick. In 2008, the town was selected as the only finalist from Canada for the global Tourism for Tomorrow awards. Boutouche, located near Moncton, has a long Acadian history as well as being the original home of the Irving empire.[3]

K.C. Irving's first business was a small service station; he lived in the apartment above the station. In just over 80 years, it has grown into a $6 billion regional energy processing, transportation, retail, media, and marketing company headquartered in Saint John. It is privately owned and has 7,000 employees, 800 retail sites, operations from 13 marine terminals, and a fleet of tractor-trailers. It operates Canada's largest refinery and produces over 300,000 barrels of finished energy products daily.[4] It also has operations in Eastern Canada, Québec, and New England. According to the *Canadian Business* 2007 list of the richest Canadians, the Irvings are the fifth richest family in Canada, after the Thomsons, Edward (Ted) Rogers, the Westons, and Paul Desmarais, Sr.[5]

In 2006, Irving Oil announced that it was planning to build a second refinery in Saint John so that it could double its capacity. While the provincial government has responded positively to the proposed refinery, environmentalists are suing the federal government; they allege that federal government ignored its own laws by restricting the environmental assessment of the proposed refinery.[6] The lawsuit was launched by Ecojustice for the Conservation Council of New Brunswick, the Fundy Baykeeper, and the Friends of the Earth Canada.

Both Irving Oil and the Irvings themselves are part of the lore of New Brunswick. Much of the Irving mythology revolves around the life and times of K.C. Irving:

> *[He is seen] as [a] powerful tycoon, a work-obsessed, hard-nosed dealmaker who took no prisoners, who crushed unions and competitors without pity, who would sue anyone who dared touch an errant Irving-branded log, and who used vertical integration as if it were an evil conspiracy. He is seen by some as a man with too much power, a man who couldn't give a square damn about the environment, who owned rather than employed people, and who took his fortune and hoarded it in a Caribbean tax haven.*[7]

There is even a web site—http://www.irvingsucks.com—which provides a mixture of news and criticism of Irving Oil. To counter its reputation for secrecy about its human resource policies, the company sends its leaders on executive development programs. Kenneth Irving, Arthur Irving's eldest son, was one of the first people to take the course and has emphasized the value of such courses for helping managers to address issues as varied as refinery operations to email overload.[8]

The future of the Irving family and its empire remains uncertain. There are 24 grandchildren who may want to work in the various businesses. What is certain is that "[the] ownership structure [created by K.C. Irving] can't survive."[9]

Notes

1. G. Pitts, and J. McNish, "Irving Brothers Look to Break up Empire," *The Globe and Mail* (November 21, 2007).
2. G. Pitts. and J. McNish, "The Irvings: Shaking the Family Tree," *The Globe and Mail* (November 22, 2007), B1.
3. C. Alphonso, "Historic Boutouche Wins a Tourism Boost," *The Globe and Mail* (February 7, 2007), A10.
4. Irving Oil, "About Us" (2008) at http://www.irvingoil.com/company (accessed June 27, 2008).
5. J. Gray, M. Harman, L. McKeon, Z. Olijnyk, and R. Ray, "The Rich 100: Canada's Wealthiest People," (November 30, 2007) at http://www.canadianbusiness.com/after_hours/article.jsp?content=20071131_198701_198701 (accessed July 13, 2008).
6. "Lawsuit Challenges Ottawa over Irving Oil Refinery" (January 14, 2008) at http://www.cbc.ca/canada/new-brunswick/story/2008/01/14/nb-environmentalists.html?ref=rss (accessed July 13, 2008).
7. H. Sawler, *Twenty-first Century Irvings* (Halifax: Nimbus Publishing, 2007), xiii.
8. K. Cox, "Irving Oil Fuels its Leaders," *The Globe and Mail*, April 21, 2004).
9. G. Pitts, and J. McNish (2007) Irving Brothers Look to Break up Empire.

Source: Ann Armstrong.

Chapter 13 Workshop: Understanding Conflict in Your Teams*

You need to do this workshop activity with your teammates.

1. Describe a recent conflict that your team has experienced.
2. Discuss what caused the conflict.
3. How did you resolve the conflict? If you did not resolve the conflict, what should you have done differently and why?
4. What have you learned about conflict and power dynamics in your team?

*By Ann Armstrong

Integrative Cases

Integrative Case 1.0

Tim Hortons: A Taste of Home

Introduction
Tim Hortons and the Canadian Military
Tim Hortons' Mission
Tim Hortons as a Part of Canadian Culture
Tim Hortons' Organizational Structure
Employee Reward Philosophy
Tim Hortons' Expansion Experience

Integrative Case 2.0

The Hospital for Sick Children (SickKids®)

Background
Current Strategy
Emergency Department
One Emergency Room Story—Caitlin
Emergency Department Reorganization
Haj-Assaad's Reflections on the Design

Integrative Case 3.0

Rogers' Chocolates

The Premium Chocolate Market
Competitors
Rogers' Company History
Current Operations
Production
Markets
Marketing
Financials
Leadership
Growth Opportunities

Integrative Case 4.0

Institutionalizing People Change Management

The People Change Management (PCM) Process
Early Change Management at CIBC
People Change Management Gains Organizational Recognition
The CIBC Culture
PCM Gains a Significant Foothold in Retail Markets Technology
Project Management Within Retail Markets Technology
Technology Solutions
Integrating People Change Management and Project Management
Developing Effective Project Sponsorship
PCM Gains a Second Foothold: Retail Markets Process Engineering Group
PCM Gains a Third Foothold: The Human Resources Function
PCM Gains a Fourth Foothold: The New Initiatives Approval Process
Sustaining People Change Management in CIBC
Appendix 1: The People Change Management (PCM) Process
Appendix 2: Project Managers as Change Agents
Appendix 3: The Business/Technology Process

Integrative Case 5.0

Solomon Business School: Implementing the New Strategy

Background
Solomon Business School
The Strategic Task Force
The Task Force Process

Integrative Case 6.0

Workbrain Corporation

Introduction
Eric Green
Workbrain
The Challenge

Integrative Case 1.0

Tim Hortons: A Taste of Home*

1.0

Introduction

On June 29, 2006, a couple of days before Canada Day, Tim Donuts Limited (TDL) opened a new Tim Hortons location at the military base in Kandahar, Afghanistan. It was opened at the request of the former Canadian Chief of the Defence Staff, General Rick Hillier. While Tim Hortons had experience with serving military bases in Canada, this particular location was definitely a departure from Tim Hortons' cautious franchise-based expansion strategy through Canada and, more recently, the United States.

The Tim Hortons' location in Kandahar, Afghanistan, poses a number of unique organizational challenges. For example, the location is Tim Hortons' furthest venture outside the North American continent. There are numerous operational issues to be resolved for a company that promotes its products and services with the slogan "Always Fresh."

The staffing issues at Kandahar are compounded by the wider context of employment in Canada. First, the number of younger workers in the food and beverage service industry in Canada is expected to fall short of long-term projected requirements. Second, the booming oil industry in Western Canada has created a current shortage of employees and wage inflation pressures on a low-margin food industry. Third, Tim Hortons at Kandahar will not be able to provide the benefits of flexible work schedules, community involvement, and organizational growth opportunities that are highly valued by Tim Hortons employees in Canada. The location itself restricts freedom of movement and family involvement for employees. Employees are recruited through the Canadian Forces Personnel Support Agency (CFPSA) and receive training on such matters as how to handle a potential nuclear or biological attack before working at the military base.[1]

Tim Hortons and the Canadian Military

Just as there is a Tim Hortons available within a short distance of most Canadians' homes, there are Tim Hortons franchises located near or often within Canadian Forces Bases in Canada. Therefore, the armed forces personnel living and working on Canadian Forces Bases are accustomed to having a Tim Hortons coffee, donut, or sandwich on a regular basis. Tim Hortons' employees working at Canadian Forces Bases have access to standard Tim Hortons' training and benefits.

Tim Hortons employees at Kandahar have to go through a rigorous training process, including learning about the danger of landmines, gas mask training for nuclear and biological attacks, medicine in developing countries, and learning how to handle themselves in a hostage situation. According to Jennifer Jones, a Kandahar employee,

We're prone to rocket attacks. Of course, we're the only Tim Hortons where the majority of customers come in fully armed. But by now I'm used to the sight of a soldier with a rifle in one hand and a coffee in the other. We're also prone to rocket attacks on the base, and when the alarm sounds, we have to get all the customers out of the store and sit in the back until the all clear sounds. There's a heavy thud, a feeling of impact and then the eerie wail of an old air-raid siren. That's the signal to get to a bunker, or to the back of the store, if I'm working.[2]

The Tim Hortons operation in Kandahar has been reported to be heavily subsidized by the federal government. According to Global Media, it will cost the Canadian taxpayer $4 million to subsidize the Tim Hortons in Kandahar. In early 2008, Tim Hortons legally challenged the Global Media claim. For the company, the Kandahar operation is about reputation, and the daily lineups and hundreds of people applying for a few dozen positions in Afghanistan are an encouraging sign for the company.

Retired Major-General Cam Ross told the Spectator that he believes the opening of a Tim Hortons will boost the troop's spirits. Ross is speaking from experience. He spent two years as UN force commander in the Middle East and frequently used Tim Hortons' goodies to make people feel at home. "I can definitely tell you Tim Hortons does influence positively [the] morale of deployed troops," he said. "It connects with Canada. How much more Canadian can you get than roll up the rim or Tim Hortons?" Ross added, "And I don't get paid by Tim Hortons for saying so."[3]

*Written by Ushnish Sengupta, for the First Canadian Edition, 2008.

[1]"Hopefuls for Tim Hortons Kandahar outlet get survival training" (May 5, 2006) at http://www.cbc.ca/canada/story/2006/05/05/timhortons-afghan060505.html (accessed July 18, 2008).

[2]J. Jones, "Tim Hortons in Kandahar, Afghanistan: An Insider's View," *Canadian Living* (November 2007), at http://www.canadianliving.com/life/community/tim_hortons_in_kandahar_afghanistan_an_insiders_view.php

[3]"Troops in Kandahar to Get a Tim Hortons Shop," CTV.ca News Staff, (March 7, 2006), at http://www.ctv.ca/servlet/ArticleNews/story/CTVNews/20060306/afghan_timhortons_06030y/20060307? hub=Canada (accessed July 20, 2008).

Tim Hortons' Mission

Tim Hortons was founded by Tim Horton, a professional hockey player, and eventually taken over by Ron Joyce, a savvy businessman from Tatamagouche, Nova Scotia. As Ron Joyce explains in his book, *Always Fresh*,[4] Tim Hortons has always relied on high quality and customer service as the foundation of its successful business. "Our mission, in partnership with every storeowner and employee, is to be the industry leader through commitment to excellence in people, product quality, value, cleanliness, customer service, and community leadership."[5]

Tim Hortons ensures consistently high quality by maintaining an efficient distribution network, which distributes semi-processed food to be quickly prepared and served. Tim Hortons also maintains a high level of customer service by selecting suitable franchise candidates and providing continuous support and training for staff. Standards are also checked through unannounced inspections, which include passing food quality, customer service, and cleanliness criteria in order to maintain the franchise license.

The Tim Hortons location in Kandahar is housed in a trailer truck. It relies on the military cargo delivery system for supplies, and occasionally runs out of popular items. The location in Kandahar is also dependent on the personnel who apply through the Canadian Forces Personnel Support Agency.

Tim Hortons as a Part of Canadian Culture

Tim Hortons is one of the most recognized brands in Canada. Canadians habitually visit Tim Hortons for its fresh coffee and donuts the same way Americans flock to Krispy Kreme when the red "Hot Now" light goes on. (Krispy Kreme's foray into Canada was unsuccessful, in part due to Tim Hortons' established brand. After opening its first store outside the United States in Mississauga, Ontario, in 2001, Krispy Kreme Canada expanded to 32 stores, but was put under bankruptcy protection in 2005.)

Tim Hortons was rated as one of Canada's best-managed brands by *Canadian Business* magazine in 2006. Historian Pierre Berton wrote, "[in] so many ways the story of Tim Hortons is the essential Canadian story. It is a story of success and tragedy, of big dreams and small towns, of old-fashioned values and tough-fisted business, of hard work and of hockey."[6]

Tim Hortons operates almost 3,000 restaurants in Canada, and a "Tim's" can always be found a short distance away home for most Canadians. The brand familiarity and convenience of location were developed through strategic franchise-based expansion by Tim Hortons management. In 2005, Tim Hortons' market share was 76 percent of the Canadian market for baked goods (based on the number of customers served) and 62 percent of the Canadian coffee market (compared to Starbucks, in the number-two position, at 7 percent).[7]

Tim Hortons is an important part of Canada, and Canada is responsible for the company's success. A Canadian term made popular by Tim Hortons is "double-double," indicating a coffee with two creams and two sugars. The term was added to the second edition of the *Canadian Oxford Dictionary* on August 10, 2004.[8] Canadian Tim Hortons employees in Kandahar are amused and entertained by the orders placed by British, Dutch, and American troops at the military base. Taylor boasts that she can tell a soldier's nationality at the base, even if they speak perfect English and are not wearing a uniform, simply by what they order. "The British and the Dutch mostly will order Boston creams and Canadian maples . . . and the Americans will probably order five dozen donuts at a time. And the British and the Dutch always order the very sweet cappuccinos," Taylor explained. "Canadians order bagels and coffee."[9] Although Tim Hortons is welcomed in most places in Canada, sometimes its expansion plans are challenged. For example, a small Tim Hortons store has existed for a number of years in the University of Toronto's Sidney Smith Hall, a popular student hangout for lunch. Tim Hortons' expansion was strongly challenged by the University of Toronto student union, which staged an "eat-in" protest at the location, protesting that the expansion would take up valuable student social space.[10]

[4]Ron Joyce with Robert Thompson, *Always Fresh, The Untold Story of Tim Hortons by the Man who created a Canadian Empire*, Toronto: HarperCollins Publishers, 2006.

[5]Ibid.

[6]Doug Fischer, "Investing in an Icon: Why Everyone Wants a Piece of Tim Hortons," (March 24, 2006) at http://www.canada.com/ottawacitizen/news/story.html?id=f695c530-37cd-4b7f-988c-d7c1ab7f964a&k=89369 (accessed July 20, 2008).

[7]Josh Fineman and David Scanlan, "Tim Hortons Raises C$783 Million in Initial Offering," (March 23, 2006) at http://www.bloomberg.com/apps/news?pid=10000103&sid=aVbau_WUTixk&refer=news_index (accessed July 20, 2008). http://www.bloomberg.com/apps/news?pid=10000103&sid=aVbau_WUTixk&refer=news_index

[8]"'Double-double'? Now You Can Look It Up" (July 5, 2004) at http://www.cbc.ca/arts/story/2004/06/30/doubledouble040630.html (accessed July 16, 2008).

[9]"Tim Hortons Coffee Popular in Afghanistan, But Lingo Still Hard for Some to Master" (November 28, 2006) at http://feedfury.com/content/537693-tim_hortons_coffee_popular_in_afghanistan_but_lingo_still_hard_for_some_to_master.html (accessed July 20, 2008).

[10]André Bovee-Begun "Tim Hortons' Sid Smith Scheme Rolls Out Discontent," (February 25, 2008) at http://www.thevarsity.ca/article/2087 (accessed July 20, 2008).

Tim Hortons' Organizational Structure

Tim Hortons' organization consists of a head office (including human resources, corporate, real estate and franchise law, property management, purchasing, customer service, corporate communications, construction and store design, distribution, finance and taxation, information technology, marketing and corporate affairs, operations, real estate, and research and development), regional offices, distribution centers, a national training centre, and franchises. Tim Hortons is a franchise-based organization, with more than 95 percent of restaurants being operated by franchisees.

1.0

The Tim Hortons location in Kandahar, however, is not a franchise, and is, of course, considered a nonstandard restaurant. Tim Hortons' other nonstandard restaurants include counters in educational settings, health care locations, retail, offices, and gas stations and other travel-oriented locations. The company has a long-term partnership with Imperial Oil, with almost half of nonstandard restaurants located in Esso convenience stores.

A standard Tim Hortons' restaurant organizational structure consists of six levels: (1) storefront employee, (2) production employee, (3) designated trainer, (4) team supervisor, (5) assistant manager, and (6) store manager. A storefront employee is the first point of contact with customers and, therefore, a plays a significant part in maintaining a high standard of customer service.[11] Production staff, such as bakers, produce baked goods requiring some specialized training and skills. A designated trainer trains and coaches new and existing employees to maintain a consistently high quality of product and customer service. Team supervisors lead by example as model employees, and are empowered to find opportunities for improvement in the business. An assistant manager at Tim Hortons typically has considerable experience in the food service industry and supports the store manager and owner with day-to day operations of the business. A store manager provides expertise in recruiting, training, and coaching Tim Hortons' franchise staff to achieve and maintain high standards of operation. Store managers plan and execute methods of increasing sales and achieving targeted costs.

Employee Reward Philosophy

As of 2006, Tim Hortons had approximately 1,665 employees in its principal offices, regional offices, and distribution centres. Tim Hortons directly operated 34 restaurants in Canada and 61 restaurants in the United States. The number of full-time employees working in these corporate restaurants in 2006 was approximately 500, with another approximately 1,600 employees working part-time. At franchised store locations, employees are hired and governed by the franchisees and not the company. Tim Hortons' franchise stores employ over 100,000 people in Canada and the United States.[12]

Tim Hortons offers store employees flexible schedules, advancement opportunities, computer-based and on-the-job training, incentive and recognition programs that recognize staff for excellence in customer service and teamwork.[13] The Tim Hortons' scholarship program provides store employees who have demonstrated leadership in community and volunteer activities the opportunity to receive funding for postsecondary education.[14] Tim Horton's stores actively participate in local community and volunteer activities, providing employees with additional opportunities to develop leadership and teamwork skills. Tim Hortons proudly exhibits its local community involvement through pictures, plaques, and certificates prominently displayed on restaurant walls.

Head office employees at Tim Hortons are offered additional benefits: (1) pension plan, employee assistance plan, wellness programs; (2) learning and development programs including performance management, leadership skills development, tuition reimbursement, and career development; and (3) company-sponsored events such as annual staff celebrations, golf tournaments, and barbeques, opportunities to participate in the Tim Horton Children's Foundation, and membership at the Tim Fit fitness centre.[15]

Tim Hortons proudly provides text and video testimonial from employees on its website, in order to attract new employees. However, not all employees at Tim Hortons stores are entirely pleased with their jobs. Social networking sites such as Facebook host hundreds of Tim Hortons–related groups, including those listing employee complaints about company management.[16]

The opportunities for flexible schedules, convenient locations, career advancement, access to training and head office staff, and community involvement are severely limited for the staff in Kandahar, Afghanistan. At the same time, wages are competitive, and employees are provided with a tax-free spending allowance by the CFPSA. CFPSA positions in Afghanistan are in demand; approximately 1,200 people applied every six months for 63 CFPSA positions in

[11]"Continue to Learn and Grow" at http://www.timhortons.com/en/join/team-4.html (accessed July 20, 2008).

[12]Benefits and Rewards at www.timhortons.com (accessed July 18, 2008).

[13]Ibid.

[14]Ibid.

[15]Ibid.

[16]Marianne White, "Rants fuel Tim Hortons Facebook Groups," (January 11, 2008) at http://www.canada.com/topics/technology/story.html?id=db414da4-c72a-4409-b5e6-5a5bfd1875d3 (accessed July 20, 2008).

Kandahar, including 21 positions at the Tim Hortons donut shop.[17]

Tim Hortons' Expansion Experience

In the United States, Tim Hortons has a regional presence with 336 restaurants in ten states as of 2006, concentrated in the Northeast in New York, Connecticut, Rhode Island, and Maine, and in the Midwest in Michigan and Ohio. Tim Hortons' entry strategy into the U.S. market has focused on gradual expansion through standard stores to enable the company to develop brand awareness with American customers. At the same time, Tim Hortons' expansion strategy in the United States has encountered some cultural barriers and lagged behind investors' expectations. Wendy Evans, a Toronto retail consultant who specializes in cross-border expansion, said that:

In Canada companies have tended to exist side by side with their competitors, whereas in the United States companies are out to annihilate each other . . . There's just no room for nice guys down there.[18]

Expansion outside North America has not been part of Tim Hortons' main corporate strategy. (One of the company's forays into the electronic frontier involved setting up a storefront on Second Life, a virtual reality-based application on the Internet.)[19]

1.0

Tim Hortons' greatest human resource issues in the year 2008 stem from the booming natural resource–based economy of Alberta. Employees require wages that compete with oil patch jobs; Tim Hortons' employees are mostly migratory workers, resulting in high turnover issues. Tim Hortons is also subject to national demographic trends, facing a shortage of front-line employees for expansion. A report by the Canadian Restaurant and Food Services Association in 2006, *Help Wanted: The Labour Shortage Crisis and Canada's Foodservice Industry*, indicates a growing demographic issue for fast-food restaurants, with a growing base of baby boomer customers, and a shrinking group of young workers.[20] These factors make Tim Horton's organizational design strategy a critical component of its long-term expansion strategy.

[17]Matthew Fisher, "Tim Hortons Franchise in Afghanistan a Raging Success," (March 27, 2008) at http://www.canada.com/ch/cheknews/news/story.html?id=238252a5-2fb3-47ed-9d93-543625fd1d83&k=77256 (accessed July 20, 2008).

[18]Jason Kirby, "Tim's Takes on America," *Maclean's* (March 24, 2008), 32–33.

[19]Akela Talamasca, "Tim Hortons Needs Timbits" (May 27, 2007) at http://www.secondlifeinsider.com/2007/05/27/tim-hortons-needs-timbits/(accessed July 20, 2008).

[20]Canadian Restaurant and Food Services Association, Help Wanted: The Labour Shortage Crisis and Canada's Foodservice Industry, June 2006.

Integrative Case 2.0

The Hospital for Sick Children (SickKids®)*

2.0

The Hospital for Sick Children, commonly and affectionately known as SickKids, is located in hospital row in Toronto. SickKids is a world-renowned teaching and research hospital and is one of Toronto's best-known and much-loved Toronto landmarks.

Background

In 1875, Elizabeth McMaster led a group of determined socially prominent women to found the hospital. The Ladies Committee ran the hospital for 17 years. McMaster was actively involved in the management of the hospital; in 1891, motivated by a spiritual commitment to social action, she became a trained nurse and served as lady superintendent.[1] When the hospital started to expand, its governance was transferred to a board of trustees, an organizational design that continues today.

Throughout its history SickKids has had many accomplishments: (1) in 1908, the hospital installed the first milk pasteurization plant in Canada, 30 years before it was legally mandated; (2) it pioneered renowned surgical developments such as the Salter operation to repair the dislocation of a hip and the Mustard operation to correct an often-fatal heart defect; (3) in the 1960s, it opened one of the first intensive care units in North America devoted exclusively to the care of critically ill newborn and premature babies; and (4) its researchers determined that humidity is an ineffective therapy for the common childhood ailment croup.[2]

SickKids has also piloted the use of PEBBLES (Providing Education By Bringing Learning Environments to Students). PEBBLES allows students to maintain a connection to their regular educational environment from an isolated and unusual setting, such as a hospital. PEBBLES is a joint undertaking between the Centre for Learning Technologies at Ryerson University, the Adaptive Technology Resource Centre at the University of Toronto, and Telebotics.[3]

In 2006, SickKids launched the SickKids Learning Institute whose purpose is to enhance training and education by coordinating activities across professions and specialties. According to Dr. Susan Tallett, director of the institute, "[by] making SickKids' expertise more accessible, we will build local, national, and international networks of educators and learners that can work together on key child care issues."[4] (To see many more milestones at SickKids, visit http://www.sickkids.ca/AboutHSC/section.asp?s=History+and+Milestones&sID=11889&ss=Milestones&ssID=488).

Current Strategy

SickKids has a clear and compelling vision—*Healthier children. A better world.*™ SickKids is guided by five strategic directions: (1) to lead nationally and internationally; (2) to enhance system capabilities by partnering with other organizations so that children have equitable access to health care; (3) to integrate further its activities of care, education, and research; (4) to establish its own focus areas in care, education, and research; and (5) to achieve operational excellence so that evidence-based decision making, accountability, information management, and accountability are institutionalized in the SickKids' culture.[5]

Emergency Department

For many Ontario residents, the Emergency Department is the first and only contact they have with SickKids. It is a time of acute anxiety for both children and parents. The triage nurse is first person that the children and parents meet. She/He must determine the severity of the child's condition to ensure that those children who have acute conditions receive treatment first. The child is then seen by a nurse, followed by one or more physicians. The Emergency Department pediatrician has final responsibility for the child's care. Specialists may be called for consultation.[6]

One Emergency Room Story—Caitlin

Caitlin had just turned two and she appeared to be the picture of health. But her mother Natalie was concerned about

*Written by Ann Armstrong, 2008 for the first Canadian edition. The author is most grateful to Lutfi Haj-Assaad, Director of Emergency Medicine, Poison Information Centre, Motherisk Program, Division of Infectious Diseases, Pediatric Medicine and Respiratory Medicine for his insights and support.

[1] J. Young, "A Divine Mission: Elizabeth McMaster and the Hospital for Sick Children, 1875–92, *CBMH/BCHM,* 11 (1994), 71–90.

[2] "SickKids History" (December 15, 2005) at http://www.sickkids.ca/AboutHSC/section.asp?s=History+and+Milestones&sID=11889&ss=SickKids+History&ssID=211 (accessed July 11, 2008).

[3] "Pebbles" at http://www.ryerson.ca/pebbles (accessed July 12, 2008); and A. Blackburn-Evans, "Connecting Sick Kids to the Classroom," Edge, 4 (2003), 1.

[4] *The Hospital for Sick Children 2006–07 Annual Report,* 13.

[5] Ibid.

[6] "Welcome to Emergency" (September 7, 2007) at http://www.sickkids.ca/FamilyInformation/section.asp?s=Emergency&sID=7388&ss=Welcome+to+Emergency&ssID=7389 (accessed July 12, 2008).

her stomach, which seemed to be distended. She took Caitlin to their family doctor, who sent them to a local hospital for blood tests. Doctors there knew something wasn't right and immediately transferred her to SickKids for further examination.

In the Emergency Department, doctors re-ran all the blood tests to confirm the diagnosis. Caitlin was admitted to the Hematology/Oncology inpatient unit, where she had to endure even more tests. Doctors discovered that many of her organs were enlarged from the disease, and started her on chemotherapy immediately.

Caitlin was initially at SickKids for over seven weeks. Although she responded well to treatment, she had her ups and downs. When she first started chemotherapy, there were numerous complications, including several bouts of bowel inflammation. Since many of the chemotherapy drugs she was taking can result in pneumatosis, her treatment had to be delayed until she recovered. She was so ill at one point that the Critical Care team at SickKids was on standby in case she had to be transferred to the Critical Care Unit.

She received chemotherapy as an outpatient at her local hospital, which was set up as one of the satellite oncology centres. There, pediatricians and nurses trained at SickKids administered chemotherapy and took care of central lines. Though she was treated at a satellite local hospital, she still came to SickKids every 12 weeks for checkups, blood tests, and lumbar punctures.

Caitlin recently celebrated a big milestone—she finished her chemotherapy treatment for the leukemia she's fought for two-and-a-half years.[7]

[7] "Meet Caitlin" (2007) at http://www.sickkidsfoundation.com/believe/caitlin.asp# (accessed July 12, 2008).

Emergency Department Reorganization

In 2002, approximately 50 members of the Emergency Department team participated in a facilitated strategic retreat. Lutfi Haj-Assaad, the director of the department, asked participants to work on the following three assignments: (1) what we want the Emergency Department to be—for patients, the department, and ourselves: Creating a vision for the Emergency Department; (2) how we need to function to make the vision happen: The vision starts with us; and (c) how we will improve Emergency Department decision making: The proposed departmental structure. At the retreat, Haj-Assaad shared a possible structure, a shared governance model. Participants were divided into six working groups for the day. Following each assignment, each working group presented the results of their work to the larger group. The detailed results are presented in Exhibit 1 on the next page.

2.0

Forty-seven participants evaluated the retreat and forty-three gave a positive assessment of the retreat. See Table 1 for their responses.

The retreat resulted in five immediate action steps: (1) circulating the facilitator's notes to all staff and physicians of the department; (2) inviting staff feedback and questions regarding the draft vision created during the strategic retreat and proposed organizational structure within two weeks; (3) asking Emergency Department staff to sign up to participate on one of the decision-making councils, (4) assigning Haj-Assaad to chair the first meeting of each decision-making council to help facilitate the development of council ground rules and terms of references, and to help select a chairperson; and (5) scheduling the governance council's first meeting in April 2002.

TABLE 1
Retreat Evaluation Data

What was good about the day? (percentage of participants)	What could have been better? (percentage of participants)
Constructive discussion and brainstorming, 34%	More concrete solutions/direction, 23%
Team and multidisciplinary participation, 28%	More information about shared governance, 17%
Worked like a team/worked in teams, 19%	More planning of committees and shared governance, 13%
Solution/positive focused, 17%	More of the Emergency Department doctors present, 4%
Got to know/meet members of team, 13%	Agenda in advance, 4%
Feeling there's hope, 9%	Talk about conflict resolution re: staff who won't "play ball," 4%
Feeling there's leadership, 9%	More staff participation, 2%
Lunch, 6%	Discussion geared to medical stakeholders, 2%
shared governance model, 4%	More staff present, 2%
We have a common vision, 2%	
Structure of the day/we were on time, 2%	

EXHIBIT 1
Detailed Findings from Retreat

2.0

A. What we want Emergency Department to be—for patients, the department, and ourselves: Creating a vision for the Emergency Department.

Background

- The Emergency Department has been operating in a crisis management mode.
- There is a lot of energy within the department—lots of people doing lots of things—but this activity could be more focused.
- Decisions are not being made, accepted, and/or implemented.
- Resources are strained and the scarcity is fragmenting the team.
- The Emergency Department has no guiding vision or directing principles to help focus activity, energy, and decision making.

The Assignment

- Form six groups and write a great vision statement that clearly communicates your aspirations for the Emergency Department—what *you* want it to be—in the future.
- Include in your vision statement your aspirations of how the Emergency Department will be for patients, the staff who work there, and the hospital.

Results

- The six groups presented their vision statements to the entire group.
- During the break, participants voted for the **two** vision statements that best captured their aspirations for the department.
- Each participant has two votes, but could not vote for the vision statement created by his own group.

  There was a clear favorite among the 6 vision statements, with a total of 27 votes.

  The Emergency Department will deliver family-centred patient care through dedicated, skilled professionals.

  We will create a supportive environment of mutual respect and responsiveness to the individual needs of all families and staff.

  We will foster partnerships to develop innovative therapies to set the gold standard for children's care.

- There was a high degree of overlap or commonality between the six vision statements. Some of the common themes included aspirations about:
  - **Being the best**—"exceptional," "gold standard," "leader in delivery," and "world-class."
  - **How team members would treat each other (and patients/families)**—words such as "mutually supportive, morale-enhancing academic environment," "supportive environment of mutual respect," "tolerance and respect for all," "respecting cultural and religious diversity," and "great place to work and learn."
  - **Being responsive to patients' needs (and staff needs)**—"timely accessible family-centred care," "timely evidence-based holistic," and "responsive to the needs of families and ourselves."
  - **Continuous learning and improvement**—"outcome-based, quality-based," "innovative ideas," "continuously re-evaluated," and "innovative therapies."

- **Collaboration**—"community involvement and collaboration with agencies and intra-hospital services" and "foster partnerships."
- **The team**—"committed staff' and "dedicated, skilled professionals.'

B. How we need to function to make the vision happen: The vision starts with us.

Background

- The visions created in the previous exercise are not apparent in the Emergency Department today.
- There are plenty of issues outside the Emergency Department that need to be resolved before the Department's vision can be realized.
- There are also plenty of things we can do that will make a substantial difference inside the Emergency Department to move toward the vision.
- We need to change within the Emergency Department, before we can change the Emergency Department.

The Assignment

- Form six groups and identify how we need to operate or function within the Emergency Department to start making the vision real—what can we do as individuals and as a group to change the Emergency Department?
  - State clearly what needs to change inside the Emergency Department that is related to how we behave (e.g., what we do and how we do it).
  - Briefly explain why this is a potential roadblock to realizing the vision.
  - Propose at least one solution.
- "Thought-starters" for the assignment: orientation, professionalism, standards, training, education, morale, disagreement, quality work-life, teamwork, communication, decision making, attitude, feedback, conflict, measurement, management leadership decisions.
- Each team will present its findings to the large group.

Results

- The six groups presented the issues they identified to the larger group, along with some of their solutions.
- There was a high degree of overlap between the issues identified by groups, and a high degree of consensus among participants that these issues are important.
- The key issues are listed below:
  - Patient flow
  - Physical resource allocation and use
  - Staff resource allocation and use (including skill mix versus need)
  - Communication between team members and teams
  - Quality assurance and measurement
  - Protocols, guidelines, and standards being met/followed
  - Mutual respect/morale/how we treat each other
  - Education, orientation, and mentoring
- In the discussion following the presentation of the Emergency Department internal issues, three issues surfaced:
  - It was noted that the tension and pressure inherent in an Emergency Department often result in people treating each other in ways they otherwise wouldn't. Under stress, respect, courtesy, and dignity are often compromised.

(Continued)

2.0

- There is a high degree of frustration inside the Emergency Department that was fuelling this stress; frustration at the lack of progress and change, and a feeling of powerlessness to effect change.
- While the morning exercises were valuable, the group *had* created a vision and identified a similar list of issues confronting the Division four years ago. Nothing had changed in the interim.

- The ensuing discussion focused on accountability, summarized by the following questions:
  1. Is each of us accountable for how we treat others—for what we say and how we behave? What are we saying about ourselves when we say the stress and tension of the Emergency Department make us behave in ways we're not accountable for? Are we or are we not accountable for our own actions?
  2. Nothing has changed in four years since these issues were first identified—who is accountable for allowing this to continue? Who are we now holding accountable for making the necessary changes we've discussed today? Who will we point the finger at if the changes don't happen over the next four years: ourselves or someone else?
  3. Does each of us feel *personally* accountable for moving the Emergency Department toward the vision?

C. How we'll improve Emergency Department decision making: The proposed departmental structure.

Background

- There is frustration within the Emergency Department at the lack of positive meaningful change and decision making.
- People feel powerless to effect change.
- We each need to be more accountable for moving the Emergency Department in the direction of the vision.
- Shared governance was introduced as a means of putting decision making and accountability in the hands of the Emergency Department team.
- Six decision-making groups were described: education, research, human resources and scheduling, social, quality and ethics, and policy and practice. The seventh group, the governance council, was introduced as the link between the six groups as well as providing direction and counsel.
- Group decision-making processes need to be decided and worked out by the team.
- Group composition, membership, and rules of conduct need to be established.
- When asked for comments or questions, there was mostly silence from participants. A couple of people in the team remarked that the concept sounded positive.
- Mostly people seemed either shocked by the idea or puzzled as to what it really meant and how it would affect them and the Emergency Department.

The Assignment

- The Challenge: Again, form six groups. Each will be assigned to one of the six councils. Pick one of the high-priority issues from the list that you think is most closely related to your council's mandate. Decide (1) what to do about the issue and (2) the best process for deciding what to do about it.

2.0

Results

- The six groups wrestled with their issues. Some had heated discussions.
  - The groups presented their findings to the entire group.
  - Some presented lists of ideas and potential solutions, but little in the way of decisions.
  - Others presented decisions, and processes for making future decisions.
  - In this exercise, participants experienced a little of what shared governance is about.
  - Participants were asked, in the context of shared governance, what they wanted from their leadership. Here's what they said:
    1. Trust our decisions.
    2. Support our decisions and, when you can't, give us direction.
    3. Be visible in the department.
    4. Take an interest in what we're doing and what we're confronting.
    5. Be responsive with feedback: if it can't be done, tell us why not, and if it can, tell us when.
    6. Keep us on track and focused on the vision in shared governance groups.
    7. Help us deal with conflict and group impasse in our shared governance decision making.
    8. Give us more information about shared governance (e.g., how it works, history, philosophy, principles, and examples).

The shared governance model splits decision making into six councils: policy and practice, education, research, human resource and scheduling, social, and quality and ethics. The governance council is charged with strategic planning, goal setting, and performance monitoring. It is the formal link between the six councils and deals with any issues that are not within the councils' purview. (See Figure 1.)

The Policy and Practice Council has three mandates: (1) to review, promote and evaluate professional and clinical practice, (2) to develop, review and approve policies and procedures within the department, and (3) to foster continuous patient care improvement. The Education Council has four mandates: (1) to provide a forum for education that enhances professional practice, (2) to identify staff learning needs, (3) to develop plans to meet staff educational needs, and (4) to develop an equitable system to reimburse staff educational expenses. The HR and Scheduling Council's mandate spans the range of human resource activities from work assignment to employee selection to skills assessment to developing rules for schedule changes. The Ethics and Quality Management Council has four mandates: (1) to provide a forum for discussion of ethical situations, (2) to monitor risk and quality management issues, (3) to develop audit tools and to conduct audits, and (4) to recommend change, as necessary. The Social Council is to develop tactics to boost morale and to plan activities based on staff interest. Lastly, the Research Council is responsible for approving any studies conducted in the department and ensuring that all research follows appropriate ethics protocols.

Emergency Department Structure, October 2007

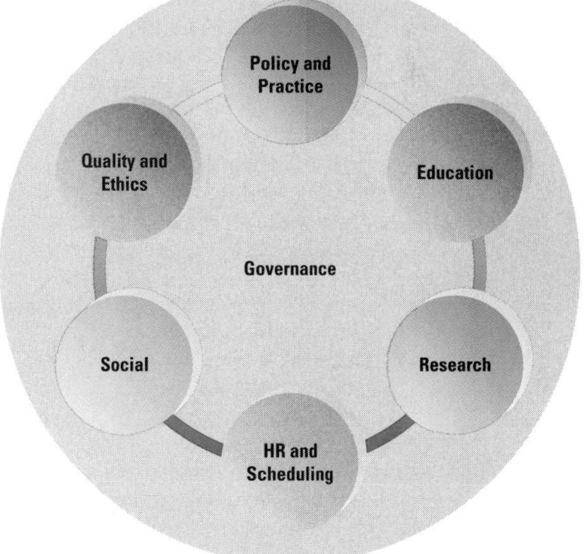

FIGURE 1

Each council has a chair—he/she works on the frontline in the department. In late 2007, three were chaired by physicians, two by nurses and one co-chaired by a volunteer and an employee of the Child Life Specialist. Haj-Assaad chairs the governance council. All the councils are open to all the Emergency Department staff. However, only the permanent members of a particular council can vote on the council's decisions. Membership on a council is attained by being an active participant in the council's work. Councils make many difficult and sometimes contentious decisions. In the five years of the shared governance model experience, Haj-Assaad has not had to veto any council decisions.

2.0

The shared governance model was a radical departure from the previous departmental structure. As well, it is a structure that is not used in other hospitals' emergency rooms in the way it is implemented at SickKids. The structure is guided by three core principles—the structure must be first in the best interests of the patients, then the department as a whole, and, lastly, the different disciplines. The structure allows for decisions to be made as close as possible to point of service and, as a result, is empowering. It also requires accountability and "there's no place for non-participation or non-ownership of the process."[8]

[8]Personal communication with Lutfi Haj-Assaad, February 10, 2008.

Haj-Assaad's Reflections on the Design

Staff engagement in the operation of the department is extremely powerful and important to the success of our work. The integrity and sincerity of the department's leadership in supporting the shared governance structure is paramount. The understanding of the staff members of what the structure is and/or is not make implementing and living it much easier. The design was meant to increase the department effectiveness and provide a context for partnership, equity, accountability, and ownership. On many occasions, the staff needed to be reminded that this design is not democratic-based as much as it's accountability-based. Any time new staff is hired, the structure is explained to them with the expectation that every employee of the department plays a role in decision making either through councils' representation or decision implementation.

Often the staff will go to the managers with an issue and it's always tempting to make a decision and solve the problem. However, the manager has to be conscious of not doing so and must direct the employee to take his/her issue with potential solutions to the appropriate council.

Having used this design for over five years, I can't imagine the Emergency Department staff accepting any . . . alternative decision-making structure.

Integrative Case 3.0

Rogers' Chocolates*

Steve Parkhill was thinking about his options for growing Rogers' Chocolates (Rogers'). It was March 2007, and he had just started his new job as president of the company, after training with the former president for two months. The board of directors had asked him to double or triple the size of the company within 10 years. Each board member of the privately held company, and each member of the management team (most of whom also held shares), had a different idea about what Rogers' needed to do to achieve that growth. Parkhill needed to devise a strategy that would fit the company's culture, and then gain the support of the board, the management team and the employees.

The Premium Chocolate Market

The Canadian market size for chocolates was US$167 million in 2006 and it was projected to grow at 2 per cent annually.[1] The growth rate in the chocolate industry as a whole had been falling, however, so traditional manufacturers such as Hershey's and Cadburys were moving into the premium chocolate market through acquisitions or upmarket launches. The premium chocolate market was growing at 20 per cent annually,[2] as aging baby boomers purchased more chocolate and emphasized quality and brand in their purchases.

About one quarter of chocolate sales typically occur in the eight weeks prior to Christmas. Twenty per cent of "heavy users" accounted for 54 per cent of these pre-Christmas sales in 2006. These heavy users tended to be established families, middle aged childless couples and empty nesters with high incomes, and they tended to purchase more high quality boxed chocolate than bars or lower quality chocolate.[3] The margins in premium chocolate were much better than those in lower quality segments.

[1]P. M. Parker, The World Outlook for Chocolate and Chocolate Type Confectionery, INSEAD, http://www.marketresearch.com/, February 20, 2007.

[2]S. David. Sprinkle, The U.S. Chocolate Market, Packaged Facts. New Orleans: MarketResearch.com, 2005.

[3]Company insider citing a presentation by Neilson at the Confectionary Manufacturer's Association of Canada conference, 2007.

Purchasers were also demanding more from chocolate than taste. In line with a broad social trend for healthier diets, the demand for organic products, including organic chocolates was growing. Consumers looked for products with no trans fats.[4] Demand for dark chocolate, traditionally less popular than milk chocolate in North America, was growing in part because of its heart-healthy anti-oxidant properties. At the same time, however, larger chocolate manufacturers were seeking a redefinition of the term "chocolate" under USFDA guidelines, so that they could produce cheaper versions of the product and still call it chocolate.

Consumers and employees were also demanding that chocolate companies (like other companies) followed good corporate social responsibility practices. Environmental concerns, which were very strong in Victoria, influenced packaging, procurement and operational decisions. Human rights concerns were also high on the list for consumer expectations of chocolate companies, as forced labour and child labour was still used in some of the production of cocoa beans in West Africa. One customer email received by Rogers' read as follows:

I am drawing the conclusion that Rogers' buys their raw product from West Africa. Rogers' is uninterested in making a real effort to eradicate this crisis. Furthermore, Rogers' is making contributions to the unethical side of the conflict and in so doing is endorsing the vile acts that continue to occur in West Africa. If any of my conclusions are incorrect, please let me know. I would appreciate it if you kept my email address on file and notified me if Rogers' begins to value the lives of people even though they are not potential consumers.

Competitors

Chocolate competitors in the premium chocolate segment in Canada featured strong regional brands plus a few larger players. Godiva, backed by Nestle, had taken the business by storm with glitzy packaging, high price points, and widespread distribution among retailers of gift items. Godiva's

[4]Rogers' was one of the first chocolate companies to announce a trans-fat free product line.

*Charlene Zietsma wrote this case solely to provide material for class discussion. The author does not intend to illustrate either effective or ineffective handling of a managerial situation. The author may have disguised certain names and other identifying information to protect confidentiality.

quality was not as high as Rogers' but it was able to obtain about 15 per cent higher price points for standard products on the strength of its packaging, advertising and distribution. For truffle only collections and seasonal collections, the price points were often two to three times the price of Rogers' chocolates, though these featured exceptionally sleek and modern packaging, significant variations in chocolate molding, and chocolates of various colours.

3.0

Bernard Callebaut[5] was a premium chocolate producer out of Calgary that had begun to grow in similar locations to Rogers (tourist and downtown retail), though it also had mall locations. There were 32 stores, mostly across the West, but with four in the United States and two in Ontario. The company's quality was good and it excelled in new flavour introductions, with an often seasonal influence. Callebaut's packaging was also superior with copper and gold boxes that could be customized for the consumer at the store, and great seasonal displays. Bernard Callebaut attracted similar price points to Godiva, but emphasized a retail strategy instead of a wholesale strategy, though bars for immediate consumption could be found in grocery outlets and other retailers.

Lindt was a large and well established Swiss chocolate producer that offered a large variety of chocolates and distributed them broadly in mass merchandisers, drug and grocery retailers. The product quality and packaging was mid-range and their pricing was about 90 per cent of Rogers' pricing. They emphasized bars and small bags of truffles for immediate consumption though they also produced gift boxes. They also produced the Ghirardelli brand, which was of higher quality but focused on pure chocolate squares.

Purdy's was a Vancouver based company that was 120 years old, and had been very successful with a variety of products, particularly its hedgehogs. Purdy's had over 50 locations, nearly all of which were based in malls. While they had stores nationally, their biggest and most successful presence was in British Columbia. Purdy's had tried to launch its products in Seattle, but had not done well there. Purdy's price point was significantly lower than Rogers' (about 35 per cent lower), and product quality level was also lower than Rogers', though still high. Their packaging and store displays were very good. Purdy's did a strong business in corporate gifts and group purchases, offering 20 per cent to 25 per cent discounts for high volume orders.

Other premium chocolate companies ranged from the extremely high end custom chocolatiers that carried a very small line of chocolates in exclusive packaging, and often produced custom orders, to Belgian producers that sold in Canada through established retailers or online, to niche players in single varietal bean chocolates or organic chocolates carried only at high end grocery or retail stores.

[5]Note that Bernard Callebaut was not the same as the international chocolatier, Callebaut.

There were also companies that commanded price premiums over their quality level because of their distribution and/or store concept. For example, Laura Secord, which emphasized mall stores, and Rocky Mountain Chocolate Company, which sold more candy than chocolate and used a franchise model, had higher price points than Purdy's but lesser quality. Laura Secord had had several ownership changes over the last decade.

Rogers' Company History

Founded by Charles "Candy" Rogers in 1885, Rogers' Chocolates, based in Victoria, British Columbia (BC), was Canada's oldest chocolate company and British Columbia's second oldest company. After Charles's death, his wife ran the company until the late 1920s, when she sold the firm to a customer. Since then the company has changed hands three times. For the last two decades (during which time the company had grown sales by more than 900 per cent), the company had been owned by a private group comprised principally of two financial executives and partners with Connor, Clark & Lunn, a Vancouver-based investment firm; an art dealer and private investor; and a former owner of Pacific Coach Lines, a Victoria-based bus company. These four plus a past president of Rogers' comprised the board of directors.

Current Operations

Rogers' head office was located above its flagship store in the Inner Harbour area of Victoria, near the world famous Empress Hotel. The head office consisted of a board room and offices for the management team. Those involved in production worked out of the factory about eight kilometres away, and the national wholesale sales manager worked in Kitchener, Ontario.

Rogers' main products were high-quality, hand-wrapped chocolates including its premiere line, the Victoria Creams, along with truffles, nuts and chews, almond bark, nutcorn and various assortments. In addition to pure milk chocolate, dark chocolate and white chocolate bars, and baking/fondue chocolate blocks, Rogers' also produced specialty items, such as chocolate-covered ginger, truffles, caramels, brittles and orange peel. Rogers' also produced no-sugar-added chocolates. Select Rogers' products are shown in Exhibit 1. The company also produced and sold a line of premium ice cream novelty items through its retail stores. Rogers' chocolates were of the highest quality, and the company had many loyal customers around the world. In 2006, the company won a prestigious 2006 Superior Taste Award from the International Taste & Quality Institute (ITQI), an independent organization of leading sommeliers, beverage experts and gourmet chefs, based in Brussels, Belgium. A company press release stated:

"Classy, refined and elegant," were just a few of the words used to describe the 120-year-old company's chocolate line. The discerning panel of European chefs also identified

EXHIBIT 1
Rogers' Products

Empress Squares | Dark Chocolate Almond Brittle | Marquis Assortment

Collectible Gift Tins | Fruit & Nut Collection | Ice Cream and Ice Cream Bars

3.0

EXHIBIT 2
Retail Stores Sales in Fiscal 2007

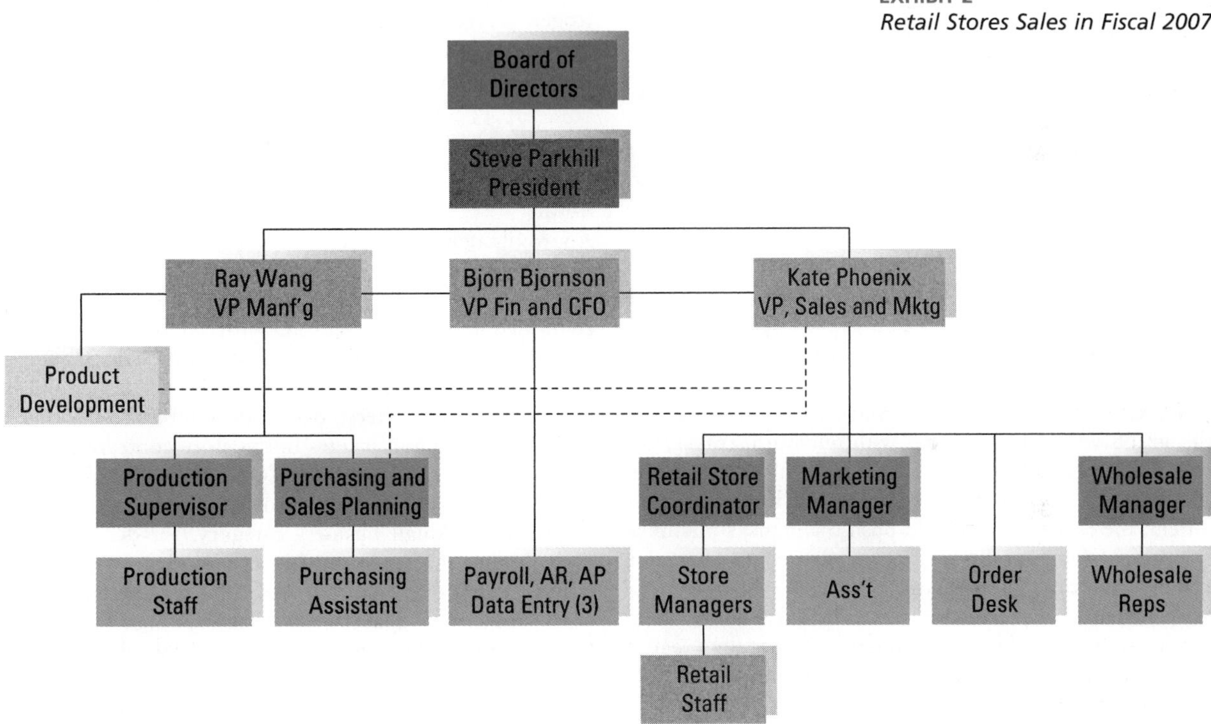

the Rogers' assortment as a "top-of-the-range-product," filled with "abundant and rich chocolate aromas."[6]

Production

Rogers' chocolates were produced in a 24,000-square-foot manufacturing facility on the outskirts of Victoria. There were about 110 non-unionized retail and production employees, with about 35 in production and the remainder in retail. Twenty employees worked seasonally in the two departments for the Christmas season. An additional 20 employees worked in management, administration and sales, as shown in the organization chart in Exhibit 2. Production, which took place on a one-shift operation (day shift), was labor-intensive, since most chocolates were handmade then hand-packed. Since there were so many different product offerings, most production consisted of batch processing, utilizing technology that had been used in the chocolate business

[6]"Canadian Chocolate Legend Receives Taste Award from Top European Chefs," Press Release, May 9, 2006, available at www.rogerschocolates.com/archives, accessed December 21, 2006.

for decades. Set-up times and equipment cleaning times were a significant component of costs, especially since they were required at the beginning and end of each eight-hour shift. To date, there had been no meaningful measures of productivity or efficiency in the plant, and thus no way of telling on a day to day basis if the plant was doing a good job.

3.0

Demand forecasting was difficult due to the seasonality of sales, but a long product shelf life (approximately six months) and a monthly sales forecast allowed Rogers' to deal with the ups and downs of sales patterns through healthy inventories kept on site. Nevertheless, the complicated nature of seasonal production created problems with out-of-stocks: souvenir items and ice cream were required in the spring and summer, then core Rogers' products and seasonal items were required for the fall and Christmas. The Christmas season was particularly chaotic, with 24 per cent of annual sales occurring in the eight week run up to Christmas. Valentines and spring items were required for early January, which overlapped with the end of Christmas production. The wholesale business required early production for seasonal needs, whereas the online and retail business required late production. Art tins used for chocolate assortments came from China, and some were season-specific. The Chinese supplier was sometimes unable to produce tins in a timely way due to lack of electricity. As soon as there were out-of-stocks for one product, the back order production of that product would throw the schedule off for the next product.

Production planning was made even more complicated by the impact of out-of-stocks on the historical information that was used to plan the following year's sales. For example, when an item was out of stock for a month, and the back orders were filled in a short period of time, the sales graph would be distorted with unnatural spikes; yet these spikes would be used for production planning for the following year. When there were over-stock problems on an item, the retail stores would push the items, sometimes discounting them, again creating distortions in the sales data, which would be replicated over time since that data would be used for production planning. Because the same process recurred for hundreds of items, these issues created significant havoc for production planning and inventory management. Ice cream presented a problem in that it was a new item (two years old), and it was difficult to predict sales volume accurately.

The out-of-stock issue was a major one for the company. Each week, numerous products were shorted. Because out-of-stocks in the wholesale channel created problems with customers, and because the previous president had favoured the wholesale channel, short supplies were diverted from the company's own stores and delivered to wholesalers. Furthermore, when a special order arrived in wholesale, it was not uncommon for the president to tell the plant to put production plans on hold to focus on the special order.

The plant was non-union, which was a direct reflection of the company's long history and strong family values. Some production workers were third-generation Rogers' employees. Employees were quite proud of the Rogers' heritage and commitment to quality and were quite passionate about the company. This passion sometimes created resistance to change: anything new caused concern that the company was compromising its values and its heritage. Employees learned multiple job functions and enjoyed a variety of work and tasks. Employees took great care in hand wrapping chocolates, folding the traditional gingham packaging "just so", and hand ribboning boxes, tins and bags. Several disabled people were employed in the plant, and Rogers' supported a local social service agency by allowing a group of brain-damaged individuals in every Friday to help with production. Turnover was low, and wages were competitive. Permanent employees were on a first-name basis with all of the senior leaders, including the president.

Markets

Rogers' currently earned revenues in four major areas: retailing chocolate products through company-owned stores, wholesaling chocolate products, online/mail order sales of chocolate products and sales from Sam's Deli, a well-known eatery in Victoria, which Rogers' had purchased in 2004.

Retail

Approximately 50 per cent of the company's sales came from Rogers' 11 retail stores. The stores featured Rogers' many products displayed attractively in glass cases, merchandised to suit the season, with an overall Victorian theme. Rogers' flagship store on Government Street had been designated a Heritage Site by Parks Canada. Uniformed sales staff offered chocolate samples to customers, and the aromas and images in the store contributed to an excellent retail experience. In 2000, Rogers' had won the Retail Council of Canada's Innovative Retailer of the Year award in the small business category, for demonstrating "outstanding market leadership and innovative approaches to customer and employee relations. Through creative ideas and strong delivery, the winning retailer has taken their brand to the top of their class."[7] Each of Rogers' retail stores, other than the factory store itself, was located in a tourist area, such as Whistler, Granville Island and Gastown, or at BC Ferry locations.[8]

Each store was wholly owned by Rogers'. Most were leased, with a minimum of a 10-year lease. The factory store and the downtown Victoria store were owned. The stores were typically about 500 square feet in size, with the exception of the ferry terminal locations, which were booths or catering wagons open on a seasonal basis and selling primarily ice cream. The ferry terminal locations

[7]From www.retailcouncil.org/awards/rcc/innovative, accessed December 7, 2006.

[8]The Whistler store was at the world-class Whistler ski area. Gastown and Granville Island were tourist attractions in Vancouver.

EXHIBIT 3
Retail Stores sales in fiscal 2007 (rounded to nearest thousand)

Store	Date Acquired	Approximate Annual Sales	Contribution Margin
Downtown Victoria	1885	$2,775,000	45.3%
Sam's Deli	2004	$1,598,000	8.9%*
Factory	1985	$726,000	36.7%
Granville Island	Dec. 2005	$686,000	(11.5%)
Whistler	1995	$639,000	8.2%
Tudor Sweet Shoppe	1983	$517,000	22.86%
Sidney	2003	$401,000	29.1%
Gastown	April 2006	$138,000	(22.3%)
Swartz Bay—BC Ferries	2000	$60,000 (Mostly ice cream)	15.5%
Departure Bay—BC Ferries	2006	$42,000 (All ice cream; summer only)	18.2%
Duke Point—BC Ferries	2005	$35,000 (All ice cream; summer only)	21.1%

*Reflects full cost of expenses to refurbish the store.

3.0

were leased on an annual agreement basis, and rents were fixed as a percentage of sales. Although other retailers sold Rogers' Chocolates, they purchased the products wholesale through direct sales from Rogers'. Exhibit 3 shows the store locations and their approximate annual sales.

The Victoria stores could sell almost anything because of Rogers' positive brand image on the Island. They were often used to clear inventory problems. The two newest stores, Gastown and Granville Island in Vancouver, were showing steady sales growth in their first two years of operations, but significantly shy of expectations. The Granville Island store was located next to the popular Arts Club Theatre, but it was, unfortunately, also behind several large metal refuse bins. Rogers' had waited a number of years for a location to open up on Granville Island, so although the present location wasn't perfect, it was the best that could be obtained. The Gastown store was in a good location, likely to attract considerable cruise ship business.

Wholesale

Approximately 30 per cent of sales came from wholesale accounts in five categories: 1) independent gift/souvenir shops, 2) large retail chains, 3) tourist retailers, such as duty-free stores, airport or train station stores and hotel gift shops, 4) corporate accounts that purchased Rogers' products for gifts for customers or employees and 5) a new segment, specialty high-end food retailers, such as Thrifty Foods on Vancouver Island, Sobeys in Western Canada, Sunterra in Alberta and Whole Foods in Toronto, Oakville and Vancouver. Some large accounts, such as the Bay, Crabtree & Evelyn and Second Cup, had been significant Rogers' customers, but had recently changed their purchasing to focus either on their own products or on less expensive lines. As a result, Rogers' wholesale sales had dropped over the last two years. Sales were strongest in BC, followed by Ontario. Sales in Alberta, Manitoba and Saskatchewan had increased very recently due to the Sobeys roll-out, but sales were weak in Quebec and the Maritimes.

The wholesale business was supported by a sales structure that included a salaried national sales manager based in Ontario, who had been with the company for eight years, and nine sales reps across Canada, of which eight were sales agents. The one salaried rep, who had been with the company for 10 years, was located on Vancouver Island. Currently, sales agents were in place in the following territories: Vancouver/Lower Mainland; Interior BC and Alberta; Saskatchewan and Manitoba; Northern Ontario; Niagara Falls and Metro Toronto; east of Toronto to Ottawa area; Quebec and the Maritimes.

Sales agents maintained independent businesses but made agreements with Rogers' to have exclusive rights to sell Rogers' products within a certain geographical territory. These agreements were not contracted, and thus they were open to review at any time. Generally, terminations were given 90 days' notice by either party. Many had been with the company as long as the previous president, who had established the wholesale division nearly two decades earlier. Rogers' sales agents typically carried several non-competing lines, such as maple syrup, gourmet condiments, plush toys, smoked salmon and kitchenware. A couple of sales agents were also customers as they also operated independent retail outlets that carried Rogers' Chocolates. Marketing Vice-President Kate Phoenix had the following to say about sales agents and the sales rep on Vancouver Island:

Some perform very well. They cite many challenges with our brand—niche market, high prices, inadequate shelf life, old fashioned ("not glitzy or fashionable enough") packaging, and an unknown brand in many areas of Canada. We intend to introduce a "Tastes of Canada" product this year that we hope will play well to our wholesale and souvenir buyers.

Some reps have other much stronger lines and just carry Rogers' as an add-on to their existing accounts, which can be effective as their existing relationships with buyers gives us an "in" that a new salesperson would not have. The salaried rep on Vancouver Island receives a constant series of requests for our products, as it is our "home turf" and we do extensive advertising in our local market for our own stores. The brand is very well established and seen as a desirable product. In the Victoria area, some accounts will say they are honored to carry Rogers'. In other parts of Canada they have not heard of us and are dismissive of the products and their price points as they do not understand the brand and the value of the product. If the remote reps are not well trained, they just cannot present the brand adequately and sell it.

Similar to most gift products, retailers typically marked items up by about 100 per cent. Rogers' earned about half the gross margins on wholesale sales as it did on retail and online sales and the company paid its sales agents approximately 10 per cent commission. The salaried sales rep on the island earned a 1 per cent commission on sales above her salary, but benefited significantly from Rogers' high profile in Victoria, and the extensive advertising the company did there.

There were 585 active wholesale customers in 2006. Of those, 346 purchased less than $2000 per year. Of the 346, 221 purchased less than $1000 per year. Rogers' provided these smaller customers with the same level of service as other retailers, sometimes crediting them for stale stock, and paying the shipping expenses on orders of more than $350. There had been problems in the past with smaller accounts selling stock past its expiration date.

Some of the wholesale accounts ordered custom products, such as logo bars for special events. Rogers' would custom-produce molds, then chocolate bars for the customers featuring their logos. In the past, some regular customers had created problems by ordering with too little lead time, so the plant typically kept some logo bars in inventory for customers in anticipation of their orders.

Online, Phone and Mail Orders

A further 10 per cent of sales came from the company's online (approximately four per cent) and mail order (approximately 6 per cent) business. Sixty per cent of all orders were from regular customers. The average sale per phone or mail order was $138, while the average sale per website order was $91. Parkhill felt that online orders could be increased, since 30 per cent of men, and 18 per cent of women in Canada were shopping online in 2006—these tended to be people in the 18-34 age group (44 per cent), while only 20 per cent of online purchasers were in the 35-54 age group.

Orders received by phone, mail or online were generally processed within three to four days, wrapped in attractive packaging, then shipped via FedEx in a sturdy outer box. In addition to the order, a separate thank you and confirmation letter from Rogers' was sent with a catalogue. In the summer, orders were shipped in insulated containers and packed with frozen ice packs. Shipping charges ranged from $10 for three- to five-day delivery within Canada and $15 to the United States for five-day shipping, to $42 for international air shipping, on products up to a $27 value. As the value of the product increased, shipping charges also increased: with product approaching $500, the costs were $18.50 within Canada for three- to five-day shipping, $37.50 to the United States and $122 internationally. For orders over $500, Rogers' paid the shipping charges.

Approximately 60 per cent of phone, mail and online sales were shipped to Canadian destinations, while 35 per cent went to the United States and five per cent shipped to 50 countries internationally. Many of the mail-order sales came from rural locations in Canada, where the mail-order tradition was strong. Rogers' chocolates were delivered to the far North, sometimes via dogsled, and were shipped to lighthouses on both coasts. Many of the rural mail-order customers placed very large orders.

Products ordered through the online and mail-order business were given priority for inventory allocation, and thus could usually be shipped within one or two working days. If there was a shortage of a particular product, its stock would be transferred back to the factory from the retail stores to meet mail-order commitments. The next priority for shipping was wholesale accounts, since wholesale back orders had to be shipped at Rogers' expense, and many accounts would not accept back orders. Yet, given that Rogers' margins on wholesale sales were much lower than in the retail business, this policy meant that sometimes a high-margin retail sale would be foregone for the much lower margins at wholesale.

Sam's Deli

The remaining sales were generated from Sam's Deli, a cafeteria-style restaurant on the Inner Harbour in Victoria, between the Rogers' head office store and the Empress Hotel. Sam's Deli featured made-to-order sandwiches, soups and salads, desserts (many featuring Rogers' chocolate) baked on the premises or at the Rogers' chocolate factory, and wine and beer. Sam's had strong sales of ice cream as well. At lunchtime in the summer, the lineup regularly extended out the door.

Sam's Deli had been a Victoria institution for many years. Since Rogers' purchased it, most of the long term staff had turned over, and recruiting new employees was difficult in Victoria's tight labour market. Sam's had had to curtail its evening hours of operations due to staff recruiting problems. Although Sam's had a liquor license, the volume of alcohol sold was very small. Parkhill felt that Sam's wasn't living up to its potential.

Marketing

Target Market

Since Rogers' chocolates were fairly expensive relative to others in the market (due to their quality ingredients and their hand packaging processes), the company targeted affluent customers looking for a luxury experience with a superior taste, or an elegant, prestigious and uncommon gift item. Many were cruise ship visitors and general tourists, though many locals were frequent visitors to the store and loyal to the brand. Some were huge spenders. Many local businesses also saw Rogers' as their corporate gift of choice. According to Phoenix:

Our best and most loyal client base comes from customers (in all three sales channels) that have an emotional connection to Rogers'. For example, they were in the Victoria store on a holiday or a honeymoon, etc., or it was a traditional gift in their family. By tending this market carefully, it has grown. Many of those people then give Rogers' as a corporate gift or a personal gift to a substantial list and some of those recipients then become loyal customers. It's classic viral marketing.

Other customers are affluent people who want to give something unique. They've found us on the Internet or in their travels and see us as an obscure but classic gift. What do rich people give each other as a present in this society of indulgence and privilege? Unique wines, flowers, a handmade cake or cookies from a remote little shop, or Rogers'!

But how do you reach these people to promote to them? Advertising to this target is so expensive and they are scattered across Canada and USA predominantly and of course they are courted by every advertiser around so are ceasing to respond to advertising. The best way in our experience to sell to them is not to make mistakes or disappoint them in any way. If you do, apologize and replace the product immediately—good old-fashioned service. This segment continues to grow for us.

Tourists often became mail-order or online customers—especially American tourists, since there were no American resellers. Happy customers from resellers often became mail-order or online customers as well since information about Web and mail-order sales was available in all packaging. Rogers' also had an easy-to-navigate website and a superior search engine ranking that attracted Web shoppers.

Brand

The Rogers' brand had both significant strengths and some weaknesses. The brand was established around Rogers' long history, with traditional packaging, including pink or brown gingham-wrapped Victoria Creams, Chocolate Almond Brittle and Empress Squares. Chocolates were packed in Rogers' traditional burgundy box, a new gold box, or tins. Some tins featured old-fashioned scenes such as English roses, cornucopias or floral arrangements, while others featured Canadian art, particularly from the west coast. Chocolate and candy bars were also available, with a mixed variety of packaging. In the retail stores, individual chocolates could be purchased for immediate consumption or custom-packed into gift boxes to suit the buyers' tastes. Rogers' was a classic premium brand, Canadian and of high perceived value. Ingredients were mostly natural.

The brand had a very loyal following, particularly in the Victoria area. Parkhill described the brand perception:

When I first began investigating Rogers', I asked everyone I knew what they thought of the brand. I received one of two reactions. People either said, "I've never heard of it", or they said "Oooooh, Rogers'. That is the best chocolate I've ever tasted". People would tell me stories about what Rogers' meant to them.

It's become clear to me that the retail experience is key in creating the memories that lead to repeat sales. Through our store décor, sampling, aromas, taste and service, I think we are delivering "chocolate orgasms" to our customers.

If the company wanted to grow, it needed to become known more broadly. The challenge would be to increase awareness without diluting the brand with weak messaging or presentation to wholesale accounts, or without cheapening the product. The premium price scared some consumers and wholesale accounts away. Although those who knew the brand were willing to pay for the product, those who didn't know the brand were often unwilling to try it. Discounting the product, or developing cheaper products to piggyback on the brand, would risk destroying brand integrity.

An additional problem was associated with the traditional image of the brand. As Rogers' loyal customers aged, who would take their place? Younger buyers were less likely to be attracted by the traditional image of Rogers' brand. Developing an organic or fair trade product might be a possibility, but Rogers' chocolate supplier did not yet have organic or fair trade capabilities, and Rogers' was not large enough to pressure its supplier to change. Rogers' would also have to source organic versions of all the other ingredients. Phoenix identified with brands such as Chanel and Lancome, which had developed classic images and refused to compromise the brand, and brands such as Jaguar, Cadillac, BMW and Volvo, which had developed a younger, sexier image while maintaining core design elements to keep the integrity of the brand.

Advertising

Rogers' used several types of advertising. To reach tourists, the company advertised in guide magazines, such as *WHERE*; in flyers available on the ferry boat brochure rack;

in hotel magazines and in the *Enroute* magazine available on Air Canada flights. Seasonal print advertising, radio spots and a small amount of TV advertising (in Victoria only) were also used. Rogers' also donated product extensively to charitable events in its markets, and participated in promotional events; for example, Rogers' was the headline sponsor for the Arts Club Theatre, next door to the Granville Island store. Rogers' had also purchased a delivery truck for Victoria last year and covered it with advertising. Rogers' preferred to use advertising that served each of the three major channels; for example, the *Enroute* magazine advertisements promoted Rogers' stores, its wholesale accounts and its website to Air Canada flyers, a demographic with a large number of online shoppers. Direct mail and solid search engine rankings promoted the online business.

3.0

Website

Rogers' website was the key point of contact for the online business. It featured beauty shots of the different chocolate assortments, an easy ordering facility, a reminder service that emailed customers when a special occasion they had entered was upcoming, frequently updated online links and optimized search engine placement. The website also had links to resellers, which provided added value to those retailers and helped customers find the nearest location that carried Rogers' chocolates. However, the sales agents had not been prompt about responding to requests to provide links for their top accounts, as they did not seem to understand the value provided by such links.

Financials[9]

Rogers' was in a strong financial position. As a privately held firm, Rogers' was under less pressure than a public firm to manage shareholders' expectations. Therefore, many of its financial strategies were designed to minimize taxable earnings. Assets were depreciated as quickly as possible under the Canada Revenue Agency's guidelines.

Although Rogers' had gone through a period of significant growth just after the current shareholders acquired the company, growth had slowed considerably in the past few years. In part, this decline had resulted from the slowdown in tourism from the United States since September 11, 2001, and the subsequent decline in the U.S. dollar. In fact, chocolate sales had declined since 2004, though the company's revenues had grown slightly, due to the contributions of Sam's Deli. Margins remained strong, however, at about 50 per cent of sales on average. Financial statements are shown in Exhibits 4 to 7.

[9]Since Rogers' is a privately held company, all financial figures in the case are disguised.

Leadership

Jim Ralph had been president and general manager of Rogers' from 1989 until 2007. It was his impending retirement that had launched the search for a new president. Ralph had been a well-networked sales manager in the gift business prior to his appointment as president, and as a result, he had grown Rogers' wholesale business during his tenure. Ralph arrived every morning at 5 a.m. and oversaw Rogers' operations closely.

When Ralph announced his intention to retire in 2005, the controlling shareholders (and board of directors) considered selling Rogers'. It was a healthy company with significant assets, great cash flow and good margins. Yet the board felt that Rogers' had significant potential to grow even more. They decided to hold onto the company and seek a leader who could take the company to the next level. They retained an executive recruitment firm, and the job ad shown in Exhibit 8 was posted on www.workopolis.com. In the two years during the search, managers were aware that Ralph was retiring, and significant decisions were put off until a new leader could be found.

A friend of Steve Parkhill saw the ad and thought it fitted Parkhill perfectly. Parkhill agreed. At the time, he was vice-president of operations for Maple Leaf Foods, in charge of six plants and approximately 2,300 employees. Previously, Parkhill had been president of a seafood company and general manager of a meat processing subsidiary. His career had involved stints in marketing and sales in addition to operations, and he had an MBA from the Richard Ivey School of Business. Parkhill was known as an exceptional leader with an empowering style and significant personal integrity. He missed the strategy involved in his general management days and was looking for a smaller company to settle into: the west coast was very appealing. After several rounds of interviews, Parkhill was offered the position, and he accepted with excitement. Both Parkhill and the board of directors agreed that the position was intended to be a long-term one—10 years or more. To that end, the offer had a provision requiring Parkhill to purchase a significant number of shares in the company each year for the first three years, with an option to increase his holdings further after that.

The senior management team included three others. Kate Phoenix, vice-president of Sales and Marketing, a Rogers' employee since 1994, managed the retail outlets, developed marketing plans and oversaw the online and wholesale businesses, as well as Sam's Deli. She was also responsible for the ice cream business. She supervised the wholesale sales manager, the retail operations manager, a communications manager and the order desk staff. The product development person and purchasing and sales planning person also reported indirectly to Phoenix, though they worked more directly with Ray Wong. Phoenix worked long hours at the office, had regularly helped out at Sam's Deli during short staff situations, and often drove product around to stores on the weekends when they ran out or were short-shipped by the factory. Before coming to Rogers', Phoenix had been an independent systems consultant, and had served as director, information systems and distribution, and assistant divisional manager, retail operations for Gidden Industries. Phoenix was a shareholder in the company.

Ray Wong, vice-president of production, oversaw production and worked at the factory. Wong completed a Bachelor of Food Science from the University of Alberta in 1978, and later took courses in material requirements planning, candy-making, ice-cream making and management. He had worked in progressively responsible operations positions in a variety of food and beverage companies prior to joining Rogers' in 1990. Wong did not own shares in the company. Wong was especially interested in computer programming, and he had developed all of Rogers' internal production planning systems himself.

Bjorn Bjornson, vice-president of Finance and chief financial officer, had retired as chief financial officer of Pacific Coach Lines in 1991, but joined Rogers' in 1997 at the urging of his former partner, who was on Rogers' board. Previously, Bjornson had worked in financial management in manufacturing and retail after articling as a chartered accountant with Price Waterhouse. Bjornson's expertise was in reorganizations, acquisitions and dispositions. He maintained Rogers' books by hand, as he had never learned accounting or spreadsheet software programs. Bjornson owned shares in the company.

Phoenix and Bjornson were a cohesive team. In the past, there had been conflict between marketing and production, as marketing sought to reduce out of stocks and launch new products, while production sought to retain control of its own scheduling and production processes. Conflict between Phoenix and Wong had escalated to the board level during the past two years of uncertainty. Furthermore, because the wholesale division was favoured by the past president, the wholesale manager in Kitchener had regularly gone over Phoenix's head to have the president overturn her decisions. Phoenix had indicated significant frustration with her job.

Growth Opportunities

During the recruitment process, and in his first few months on the job, Parkhill had been probing the managers and board members to get their perspectives on growth options. There was a dizzying array of options. One board member, who was very well connected in the tourism business in Victoria, had said Rogers' approach to cruise ship traffic needed to be reconsidered. Although for years Rogers' had counted on cruise ship passengers for business, representatives from Victoria's Butchart Gardens now boarded the cruise ships in San Francisco, and promoted bus tours from the ship north to Butchart Gardens in Victoria. Many of the passengers were thus no longer going downtown.

The idea of franchising Rogers' outlets had been discussed but not truly investigated, because the board was concerned about giving up control of the brand and pricing. Parkhill had visited a store in Banff that had a Rogers' chocolate store attached to a larger gift store. Yet the store was not owned or franchised by Rogers': the gift store had merely displayed the Rogers' chocolates in a separate area for their own purposes. Others who purchased Rogers' chocolates wholesale merely displayed Rogers' merchandise along with their regular merchandise. For example, the Kingsmill's department store in London, Ontario, carried Rogers' chocolates in its food section. Of course, it might also be possible to franchise Sam's Deli.

The online business also appeared exciting. With low costs of sales and no intermediaries, the profits on the online business were exceptional. With such a high reorder rate, the chance to build a loyal following of online customers seemed like a sure winner.

The corporate gift market also seemed promising. Offering discounts of 25 per cent to corporate purchasers enabled Rogers' to still earn stronger margins than wholesale, without the costs of retail. Furthermore, corporate gifting expanded trial of the product.

There were many other possibilities for growth. The Olympics were coming to Vancouver and Whistler in 2010, promising a huge boon for BC tourism. Although Rogers' wasn't big enough to gain official Olympic status, it needed a strategy to take advantage of the crowds. With two stores in Vancouver, and one in Whistler, Rogers' should be able to generate increased sales. Should Rogers' obtain more stores in Vancouver? Or should Rogers' extend its product line to take advantage of its strong franchise in British Columbia? Although ice cream had not been the runaway success the company had hoped, its sales were still building. Rogers' had a sugar-free chocolate line that served a small but growing market.

Another option might be for Rogers' to concentrate its efforts outside of BC. If American tourists had stopped coming to Victoria, due to the decline in the American dollar, should Rogers' go to them? Should Rogers' attempt to increase its penetration in Ontario or other parts of Canada? Should Rogers' attempt to extend its wholesale distribution outside of British Columbia? Would the current sales agency structure be appropriate for increased penetration? Should Rogers' consider an acquisition of another niche chocolate company or a joint venture with another firm to increase its geographical reach? Were there opportunities to pair Rogers' chocolates with other high end products or brands for mutual benefit?

There was also the issue of the brand image. While Rogers' traditional image was treasured by loyal customers and employees alike, it didn't seem to play as well outside of Victoria. The packaging had been described as homey or dowdy by some, yet others were adamant that it should not be changed. Parkhill had spoken to a brand image consultant that had won numerous awards in the wine industry for the spunky brands he had designed. The consultant had suggested that the only dangerous thing in today's market was to play it safe—consumers loved edgy brands. Should Rogers' throw off tradition and try to reinvent itself?

3.0

Of course, if sales were to be increased, Rogers' would need more internal capacity to produce products and fill orders. Should more capacity be added in Victoria, with its expensive real estate and significant shipping costs to get product off the island, or should it be placed somewhere with lower costs and easier access to markets?

As Parkhill pondered all these options, he also knew that he had to take into consideration the culture of the organization and the desires of the board of directors and owners. Would the current managers and employees be willing and able to grow the organization? Would the board endorse a growth strategy that would increase the risk profile of the company? And with all these options, what should Rogers' do first?

EXHIBIT 4
Rogers' Chocolates Ltd. Consolidated Statement of Earnings and Retained Earnings

Year Ended March 31	2006	2005
Sales	$11,850,480	$11,991,558
Cost of sales		
Amortization of property and equipment	135,385	108,759
Direct labour	1,545,794	1,677,247
Direct materials	1,770,603	2,745,995
Overhead	1,933,306	846,186
	5,385,088	5,378,187
Gross profit	6,465,392	6,613,371
Interest income	664	1,610
	6,466,056	6,614,981
Expenses		
Interest on long term debt	91,465	86,943
Selling and administrative	5,221,520	5,007,145
	5,312,985	5,094,088
Earnings before income taxes	1,153,071	1,520,893
Income taxes	261,989	451,567
Net earnings	$891,082	$1,069,326
Retained earnings, beginning of year	$4,748,611	4,381,155
Net earnings	891,081	1,069,326
Dividends	-	(701,870)
Retained earnings, end of year	$ 5,639,692	$4,748,611

EXHIBIT 5
Rogers' Chocolates Ltd.—Schedule of Selling and Administrative Expenses

3.0

Year ended March 31		2006	2005
Selling	Advertising & Promotion	$489,345	$536,886
	Bad debts	23,000	12,796
	Credit card charges	125,198	125,544
	Mail order	118,606	133,081
	Office & Telephone	29,975	27,274
	Postage and freight	483,003	476,724
Stores:	Factory Store	112,885	122,897
	Sam's Deli	572,495	323,995
	Sidney	75,854	84,047
	Swartz Bay	42,709	38,592
	The Bay Vancouver (closed in 2006)	3,938	4,058
	The Bay Victoria (closed in 2006)	4,236	2,759
	Tsawwassen	—	24,179
	Tudor Sweet Shoppe	87,103	119,058
	Whistler	168,157	182,939
	Royalties	29,862	31,099
	Salaries & benefits	812,269	715,325
	Travel	68,364	46,830
	Total	3,246,999	3,013,658
	Less: postage and freight recoveries	343,116	369,823
		2,903,883	2,638,260
Admin	Amortization	196,970	135,267
	Automotive	28,658	24,404
	Bank charges and interest	22,533	20,882
	Consulting	102,241	107,379
	Foreign exchange	–6,272	
	Insurance	80,704	78,777
	Management fees	191,226	183,627
	Office supplies and postage	134,159	118,582
	Professional fees	42,872	67,952
	Rent, property taxes and utilities	61,211	56,815
	Repairs and maintenance	18,378	21,105
Stores:	Sam's Deli	326,901	179,834
	Sidney	26,559	28,159
	Swartz Bay	22,038	26,927
	The Bay Vancouver	10,082	18,251
	The Bay Victoria	32,123	37,939
	Tsawwassen		14,647
	Tudor Sweet Shoppe	49,849	45,002
	Whistler	112,450	105,720
	Salaries and benefits	810,049	1,030,336
	Telecommunications	27,824	32,588
	Travel and promotion	27,082	34,692
Total Admin Expenses		$2,317,637	$2,368,885
TOTAL S, G & A Expenses		$5,221,520	$5,007,145

EXHIBIT 6
Rogers' Chocolates Ltd.—Consolidated Balance Sheet

3.0

March 31	2006	2005
Assets		
Current		
Cash	$ 112,185	$ 750,948
Receivables	358,969	461,874
Inventories		
Packaging materials	620,452	576,287
Raw materials	169,235	179,119
Work in progress	89,146	66,467
Manufactured finished goods	643,105	692,517
Finished goods for resale	21,878	36,241
	1,543,816	1,550,631
Investments	103,136	76,822
Income taxes receivable	127,515	–
Prepaids	84,620	56,566
	2,330,241	2,896,842
Property and equipment (see Note 1)	4,364,527	3,922,183
Intangible assets		
Goodwill	916,999	916,999
Trademarks	783,596	783,596
Total Intangible Assets	1,700,595	1,700,595
TOTAL ASSETS	$ 8,395,363	$ 8,519,620
Liabilities		
Current		
Bank indebtedness	$ 186,929	$ 599,146
Payables and accruals	1,098,232	1,226,570
Income taxes payable	-	127,845
Current portion of long term debt	419,971	373,405
	1,705,132	2,326,966
Long term debt	1,017,679	1,411,184
TOTAL LIABILITIES	2,722,811	3,738,150
Shareholders' Equity		
Capital stock	32,860	32,860
Retained earnings	5,639,691	4,748,611
TOTAL EQUITY	5,672,551	4,781,471
TOTAL LIABILITIES & EQUITY	$ 8,395,362	$ 8,519,621

Note 1

Property and equipment			2006	2005
	Cost	**Accumulated Amortization**	**Net Book Value**	**Net Book Value**
Land	1,219,819.20	–	1,219,819.20	1,219,819.20
Buildings	2,799,181.35	1,099,926.90	1,699,254.45	1,770,056.19
Manufacturing equipment	1,693,140.69	1,375,596.00	317,544.69	231,858.99
Furniture and fixtures	749,496.78	385,684.35	363,812.43	249,376.83
Office equipment	108,352.86	90,299.22	18,053.64	24,020.76
Computer equipment	250,683.90	225,157.26	25,526.64	53,214.81
Leasehold improvements	914,332.83	193,817.19	720,515.64	373,836.12
	7,735,007.61	3,370,480.92	4,364,526.69	3,922,182.90

EXHIBIT 7
Rogers' Chocolates Ltd.—Consolidated Statements of Cash Flows

Year Ended March 31	2006	2005
Increase (decrease) in cash and cash equivalents		
Operating		
Net earnings	**$ 891,081**	$ 1,069,326
Amortization	**332,355**	244,026
	1,223,436	1,313,352
Change in non-cash oper. working capital	**(328,344)**	350,045
	895,092	1,663,397
Financing		
(Repayments of) advances from LT debt	**(349,168)**	661,806
Dividends paid	–	(701,870)
	(349,168)	(40,064)
Investing		
Purchase of assets of Sam's Deli	–	(1,198,500)
Purchase of property and equipment	**(772,470)**	(419,307)
	(772,470)	(1,617,807)
Net (decrease) increase in cash and cash equivalents	**(226,546)**	5,526
Cash and cash equivalents, beginning of year	**151,802**	146,276
Cash and cash equivalents, end of year	**$ 74,744**	$ 151,802
Comprising:		
Cash	**$ 112,185**	$ 750,948
Bank indebtedness	**(186,929)**	(599,146)
	$ 74,744	$ 151,802

3.0

EXHIBIT 8
Workopolis Job Ad

A unique company........ a unique location........... a unique opportunity.

Our client, one of Canada's oldest and respected confectionery companies, is seeking a PRESIDENT to oversee the entire business on a day-to-day basis, and provide the vision and guidance for long-term success and profitable growth.

Reporting to the Board of Directors, the President will:

- Deliver superior results and guide the organization to improve.
- Develop formal planning systems and ongoing personnel development.
- Oversee the development of business and marketing strategies to maintain market leadership.
- Provide the necessary leadership to motivate and transform the organization to meet growth expectations.
- Leads, protects and reinforces the positive corporate culture, and is the overseer of the ethics and values in the organization.

An executive level compensation plan commensurate with the importance of this role is offered. An opportunity that blends an executive level position with the lifestyle only Victoria can offer.

(Continued)

3.0

CANDIDATE PROFILE:

Given the high levels of autonomy and accountability, the President must display considerable maturity and business experience.

From a personal perspective, the ideal candidate will be:

- A strong non-authoritative team builder.
- A highly motivated and results oriented self-starter.
- Extremely customer, quality and safety oriented.
- People oriented with the innate ability to establish a high degree of credibility.
- Capable of providing objective insight in a non-confrontational manner.

The successful candidate will likely be or have been in one of the following positions in a manufacturing environment:

- President or General Manager
- At a VP level in operations/finance/marketing looking to rise to the next level

While food manufacturing experience would be a clear asset, it is not a pre-requisite.

Integrative Case 4.0

Institutionalizing People Change Management*

By 2004, People Change Management (PCM) was becoming an important process for identifying the people risks associated with the implementation of significant initiatives or business changes at CIBC. Retail Markets, one of CIBC's three major business lines, was committed to seeing the PCM process used on most of its major technology projects. Retail Markets had worked closely with the Retail Markets Technology group which provided them with project management support to make PCM an integral part of project management practice. The PCM process was also being adopted in other parts of the Bank: in another business line, in a support department and within a central operations process. Unlike other managerial innovations that were implemented within CIBC but were not sustained over the long term, PCM appeared to have a good chance of being institutionalized into its change management practice and subsequently incorporated into CIBC's culture for implementing business change. But the jury was still out.

The People Change Management (PCM) Process

CIBC recognized that without paying attention to the impact of a change on either the people who have to implement it or those who will be affected by it, implementation was often less than optimal. Business leaders lost twice: they ran the risk of ending up with only superficial adoption of the change and few or none of the intended benefits, and their credibility was undermined as employees become increasingly skeptical, indeed cynical about the organization's ability to implement and sustain change.

Therefore, the focus of PCM is to develop appropriate mitigation plans to manage the people related risks which may hinder the effective implementation of any new initiative or business change.

The PCM process begins with an initial assessment of the degree of people impact and risk at the outset of an initiative or business change. (See Appendix 1 for a description of the People Change Management Process.) The extent to which the PCM process is required is dependent upon the nature and degree of human impact. If a sufficient people impact is identified, project managers are required to fully engage the PCM process and maintain it throughout the project life cycle.

As part of the process, all stakeholders who are impacted in any way by the project are identified and mapped on a Stakeholder Role Map. Key sponsors are identified and sponsorship risk is evaluated. Depending upon the nature and degree of risk identified, mitigating strategies are developed and implemented. The success of the strategies is tracked and revised to ensure that there is a sufficient level of effective sponsorship in the right places at the right times. Resistance is also initially assessed and mitigating strategies developed and implemented so that stakeholders can begin early on to engage in the behaviours required for successful implementation. An important aspect of effective implementation is ensuring that sustaining mechanisms such as new performance targets, on-going learning and coaching programs, organizational structures and functions are being considered as part of project implementation.

Early Change Management at CIBC

At CIBC, the change management practice evolved over a number of years. Recognition of the need to address the people issues associated with implementing change emerged in 1988 when it was anticipated that new technology solutions would in some cases create job redundancy and in others, new work methods, both of which would have a huge impact on people. Early education through workshops was designed to help managers throughout the organization begin to appreciate the process of change, its impact on people, on work quality and productivity, and begin to develop some behavioural skills to more comfortably address the people issues and concerns with which they were confronted.

During the mid-1990s, a curriculum of programs was developed to shift the culture of the organization through a deliberate introduction of a number of leadership concepts. Built into some of these programs was the leader's role in managing change. CIBC began to adopt many of the concepts, principles and tools developed by Conner Partners (formerly ODR), a change management consulting firm, and offered training on change management to a number of people in the HR community. Sheila Legon and Brian Morris, two internal OD consultants associated with the Leadership Centre, were applying change management processes and tools to various projects in the organization. However, as change management was not an organizationally

*Sheila Legon, Organization Initiatives, CIBC Human Resources, Toronto, Ontario, Canada, and Harvey Kolodny, Joseph L. Rotman School of Management, University of Toronto, Toronto, Ontario, Canada. Sheila Legon and Harvey Kolodny prepared this case as a basis for class discussion. The case study was developed for the exclusive purpose of providing material for training seminar discussions. It is not intended to illustrate either effective or ineffective handling of a managerial situation. Any reproduction, in any form, of the material is prohibited except with the written consent of the Joseph L. Rotman School of Management, University of Toronto or for use within CIBC. (Revised April 15, 2005)

endorsed process, it was used only where business leaders were receptive or where projects ran into trouble with implementation and called for help. Sheila described the prevailing perspective of project managers:

> *Project Managers viewed their role as developing and implementing the technical aspects of a change initiative, in other words, installing a technical solution. They did not perceive themselves as being responsible for getting people to change their behaviour so that the benefits could be realized over the long term.*

People Change Management Gains Organizational Recognition

In the spring of 2000, CIBC undertook a large-scale program of change, the Brand Promise initiative, to revitalize and differentiate the corporate brand within the Retail division of the bank. A project team was established to conduct a thorough analysis of what it would take to accomplish a revitalization of this nature. During implementation of this initiative, it became increasingly evident that not only was there a deficit in project management skill across the Retail and Technology areas, but project managers also each used very different approaches and methodologies to manage their respective projects. The Project Office, which had been established to monitor and track the entire portfolio of projects found it extremely difficult to develop consolidated and accurate reporting when each of the projects used different processes and tools.

With this initiative, CIBC engaged ODR to assist in developing a basic change management process that could be adopted by all the projects including work at the overall program level to ensure that people issues were identified and mitigated prior to and during implementation. ODR principles, processes and practices were slowly introduced into the organization through application on specific projects.

Over the next few years, understanding of change management continued to develop in pockets of the organization as well as within Human Resources. A common language was beginning to take hold as well as a much deeper intellectual understanding of the need to address people issues. Also, some project managers were beginning to appreciate that the projects they managed were all introducing change to the organization and began to see themselves as "agents of change".

The CIBC Culture

CIBC is well recognized in the industry for its forward thinking and innovative approach to business strategy. The banking culture within CIBC is an entrepreneurial one, attracting people with big ideas and new or different approaches to doing things, and the organization gives people a lot of freedom to explore ideas. Although business proposals with sufficient sponsorship are implemented, sponsorship attention is often diverted to other new initiatives, sometimes compromising the ability to fully realize the intended business benefits. Joyce Philips, Executive Vice-President for Human Resources, put it succinctly:

> *My concern with how projects are implemented here, from an HR perspective within CIBC, is that we are very good at coming up with ideas, we are very good in implementing it—that is in getting it done, but we are also very good at washing our hands of it and saying, "OK, now it is done. Let's move on to the next thing." My concern is making sure that change is more than just doing the act itself, but when it is an important project or initiative, that we are actually changing behaviours, and that it is not just surface stuff, but that we are actually getting into the fabric of the organization and moving away from the tactical nature of just implementing.*

With the organizational investment in change each year continuing to increase, it was becoming more critical that CIBC achieve not only the business benefits but also the return on investment.

PCM Gains a Significant Foothold in Retail Markets Technology

PCM is a component of CIBC's project management practice within Retail Markets Technology, a practice that is formally called the Methodology for Project Management. MPM was developed to standardize and improve the quality of project management approaches. MPM was, in turn, the major component of the Project Management Centre of Excellence (PMCOE) that had been created in 2002. Sheila Legon, Senior Director of Organizational Effectiveness within the Organizational Initiatives group of Human Resources, had been one of the champions of PCM and one of the proponents of its widespread adoption within the Bank through its integration with project management practice. Now that PCM was, in fact, an integral part of project management practice within Retail Markets Technology, Sheila Legon was looking forward to promoting PCM more widely across the Bank. She commented:

> *Having PCM become part of an organization's fabric is an evolving journey. Over time, as the level of awareness and understanding around PCM increases, as projects experience modest to significant success in applying PCM and achieving project objectives and as project leaders and sponsors commit to benefit realization rather than installation, the seeds of institutionalization will begin to take hold within the world of project management.*

A wide variety of project management practices still existed within the Bank and although most project managers agreed that greater standardization was needed across the hundreds of projects taking place simultaneously within the Bank, PMCOE's efforts to promote standardization had created resentment among some of the project managers. As a result, the long-term sustainability of PMCOE and MPM were not assured and that, in turn, raised serious concerns about the sustainability of PCM.

Project Management Within Retail Markets Technology

Retail Markets is one of three business lines within CIBC that reports directly to the CEO (the other two are Wealth Management and World Markets—see Exhibit 1). Seven portfolio groups, each headed by an Executive Vice President or a Senior Vice President, report into the Senior Executive Vice President of Retail Markets, (two such portfolio groups are shown in Exhibit 1). A Project Management Office (RM-PPMO) that keeps track of the many projects taking place in the seven portfolio groups resides within the Retail Markets business line. The RM-PPMO also provides project management advice and guidance to individuals within Retail Markets involved in project management undertakings.

Technology Solutions comprises three technology areas that align with each of the business lines of the Bank as well as a Business Management Office. The technology area that aligns with Retail Markets is called Retail Markets Technology. Reporting to the SVP-CIO (Senior Vice President and Chief Information Officer) of Retail Markets Technology are seven VP-CIO executives whose technology portfolios co-align with each of the seven Retail Markets portfolio groups (two such portfolios are shown in Exhibit 1). A Project Management Office (PMO) headed by a Project Director exists within each technology portfolio. These technology portfolio PMOs serve as functional homes both for the project managers who report to that Project Director as well as for project team members. There are approximately 160 project managers within Retail Markets Technology.

In a typical Retail Markets technology project, an initiative would arise from the business side, which would then approach Retail Markets Technology for technical help in developing and delivering a solution. Since interdependencies on retail products is high, the business executive who initiates the request expects the project director or project manager on the technology side to interface with all other areas that would be affected or whose

EXHIBIT 1
Retail Markets and Technology Solutions

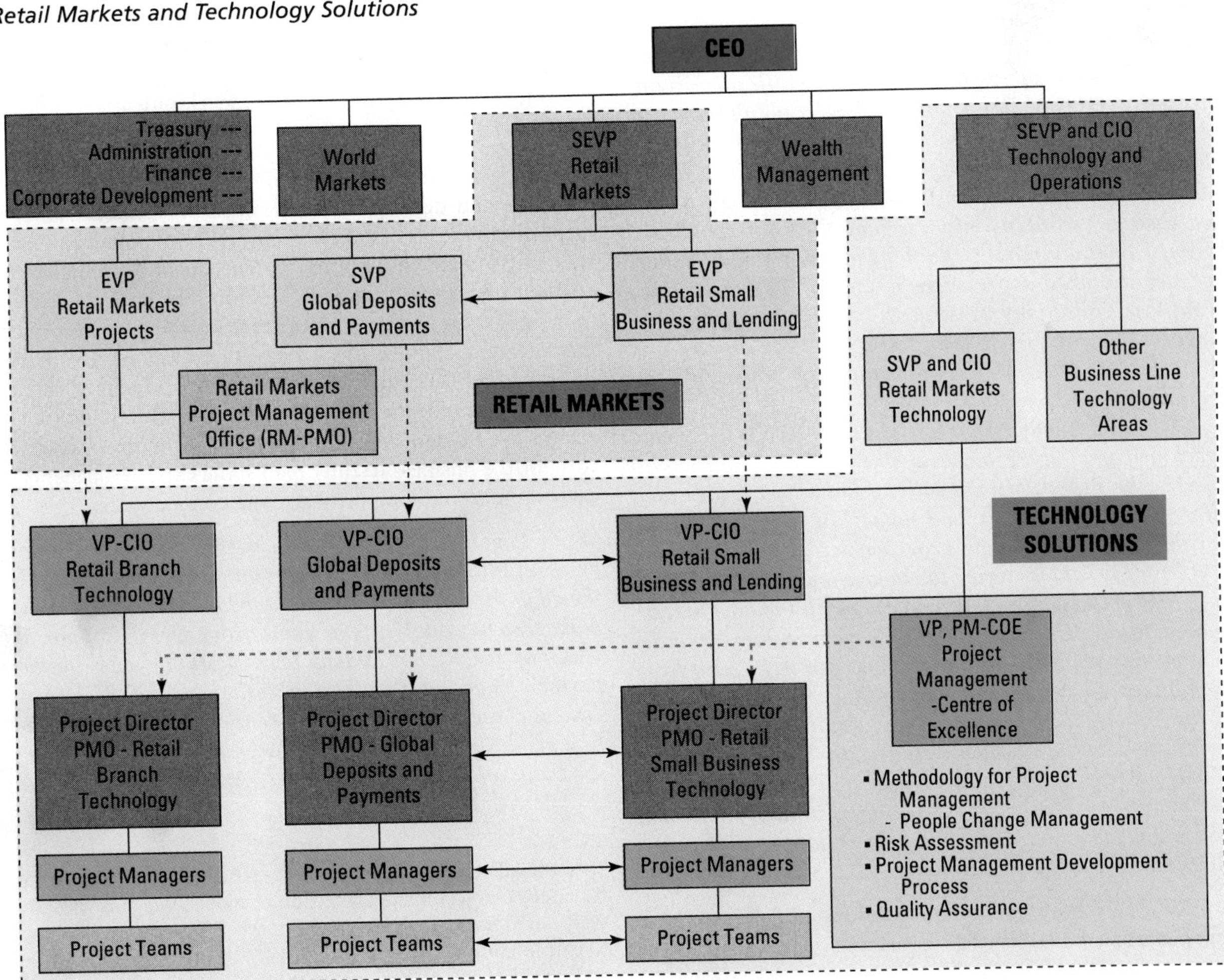

cooperation was required to advance the solution. (Appendix 2 describes a typical project management interaction between the business and technology organizations.)

Technology Solutions

4.0

Technology Solutions is responsible for implementing all the technology projects across the entire organization. Yearly, this organization implements hundreds of projects worth hundreds of millions of dollars, many of which are infrastructure projects and key to the success of the bank.

Lynda Bell headed up the Project Management Centre of Excellence in Retail Markets Technology before her retirement from the Bank at the end of 2003. She described the situation in the technology group when the Brand Promise was taking place:

Our business partners were trying to transform the retail business with the Brand Promise initiative, but to implement the business strategy that appeared to be so simple and straightforward was in fact complex, from both a process and technology perspective. There was a lot of frustration on the part of the lines of business because the changes they wanted to make were time-consuming, expensive, and highly dependent on technology. But even when they were successful in getting significant funding to start making major changes, they couldn't ramp up enough project management resources to spend what they had negotiated so hard to get approved. Complaints began to surface from the businesses about having to sacrifice their own line of business initiatives for the Brand Promise ones, and that technology was not able to deliver because it lacked appropriate resources. The technology groups were equally frustrated because their business partners did not always seem to be practical, and did not appreciate the technical implications of some of their requirements.

A Project Management Office (RM-PPMO) was being developed out of the business side in Retail Markets to oversee the Brand Promise suite of initiatives, understand all its interdependencies, and manage it from a portfolio perspective. So while the program was driven from the RM-PPMO that was trying to manage the portfolio of projects at a very high level, it didn't have all the information needed to do proper portfolio management (e.g., interdependencies, etc.). This information needed to be built from the bottom up by project managers in technology, but most of the projects were in the initial phases and could provide very little detail. Both sides were feeling the lack of project management processes and the dearth of experienced project managers. There was a sense of frustration all round, and it was inevitable that some friction developed between the business PMO and technology.

Although both the Retail Markets and Technology organizations had identified a need for stronger project management capability, it was decided that it would be Retail Markets Technology that would take responsibility for the development of a professional project management environment and discipline within the technology organization. In the fall of 2000, Retail Markets Technology assembled a strategy team to develop recommendations for an organization that would establish standard project management practices, including processes, tools, and templates. The strategy team's report recommended the creation of a Project Management Centre of Excellence (PMCOE) for the CIBC Technology Group.[1]

In October of 2001, PMCOE was established under the sponsorship of the SVP & CIO of Retail Markets Technology (see Exhibit 1), the technology group responsible for implementing technology projects for the Retail Markets business. The mandate of PMCOE was twofold: to implement consistent methodologies and processes that met industry standards of best practice and to sustain continuous improvement through services and ongoing support to project managers and PMOs throughout the Technology Group. PMCOE initially comprised four separate functions:

- Methodology for Project Management;
- Risk Assessment;
- Project Manager Training and Development;
- Quality Assurance.

While the Technology organization had responsibility to define and develop a single consistent project management discipline across Technology, it was recognized that it was being done in response to the business demand for efficient project delivery and therefore, the business needed to be engaged in the development of the overall project management framework. Lynda Bell explained that the business had one other requirement—to integrate change management into the project management methodology to ensure the human issues would be dealt with, paving the way for the business to fully realize the expected benefits of each of its technology projects. She commented:

Sheila Legon had been introducing People Change Management into the Brand Promise initiative. It was based on the all work she had done in that field as well as the change management concepts that came from Daryl Connor, the CEO of ODR. Sheila had been working with business partners in getting their buy-in to the idea that PCM was a critical success factor in implementing major change, and as a result the Retail Markets PMO had come to believe in the value of the PCM processes. After some negotiating,

[1]The recommended framework was based on the ESI's *Project-FLAGSHIP©* project management office model, which is consistent with the Project Management Institute's "A Guide to the Project Management Body of Knowledge".

the senior executives of the RM-PPMO and the newly formed technology PMCOE agreed in January of 2002 that PCM would be included in the scope of developing the project management methodology. PMCOE required PCM expertise to assist with this, and so the business PMO agreed that we could use Sheila Legon as a resource to support us.

Integrating People Change Management and Project Management

Project management has always incorporated change management. However, the interpretation of change management in the project community is related to change control and effectively managing changes in project scope. The organizational mindset is to install change rather than realize change. Sheila Legon emphasized the distinction:

A critical issue in reaping the full benefits of technological or business solutions is in understanding the distinction between installation and realization. Successful project change management is about assessing the people impact of the change; it is about recognizing and dealing with resistance to the change; and it is about ensuring effective sponsorship to support the change through to benefit realization and to maintain it over time. CIBC has equated installation, which is "putting something in place" with successful implementation. The propensity to take on more and more change and to simply install it, without attending to all the people issues surrounding the change, in large part accounts for the failure to achieve the expected business benefits and the return on investment. Effective implementation requires that not only must people change their behaviours, sponsors must see the change through to full benefit realization.

In the minds of project mangers, the accountability for behavioural change rested with the business. Therefore, it was a major mindset shift for them to take on responsibility for creating the organizational environment that would allow for behaviour change, the necessary precursor for benefit realization. Project managers needed to understand that failure to attend to the people issues of sponsorship and resistance was a major risk to project success.

PMCOE developed a standard, disciplined project management methodology, following the principles and practices of PMBOK and PMI.[2] People change management was positioned as a risk category to be managed throughout the project life cycle in the same manner as any other technical, financial or operational risk. Project Managers are attuned to managing risk and so positioning PCM as human risk was fundamental to its being understood, accepted and integrated into the project management discipline. The benefits of incorporating PCM meant that people issues related to sponsorship, resistance, cultural alignment and user capacity to assimilate the change were surfaced and dealt with from the onset of a project.

However, Lynda Bell felt that PCM was being accepted by project managers with some difficulty:

PCM is experiential. Like many other things, it is difficult to acquire by taking a course. There are ones who "get it" and who use it and use it to their advantage. In fact, one of the exercises we do is to ask project managers to give us three examples of where a project was successful and three examples of where it wasn't and it [is] so easy to see. Everyone realizes where it was successful that it is about people and about communications. So if these things are so important, then let's put a process in place to make sure these things happen. We say, "You, project managers, are accountable for PCM. However, you don't have to do it yourself. You can use a PCM person." Then it is our challenge to find the kind of support that these project managers need. We are developing that capability within PMCOE.

Teresa Caine is a Project Director within PMCOE with direct responsibility for the Methodology for Project Management. She had come to a similar conclusion about the receptivity of project managers to PCM:

It is somewhat mixed. It is like quality and quality management. People don't understand it. We are still challenged with People Change Management as well. There are some pockets where: "Oh I really get it. I know what this means." And some where: "I don't know what this means. It looks like a lot more work to do on my projects, so I am going to see if I can ignore it."

Mark McMaster, a Project Director in the Global Deposits and Payments Technology Group, referred to his experience with People Change Management and the possibility of having someone else do the PCM part on behalf of the project manager:

For a lot of People Change Management, if you are going to build support for your product ideas, then you need to invest in doing that work. A lot of it comes back to funding. If there were acceptance that People Change Management is one of the critical success factors of the project, then you would have people who could do that role, whether they were sitting on the Business side or wherever; people you could draw on. One person could handle two or three projects. Then you would have them assigned to your project rather than have the project manager saying "I want to cover this off" and then have a challenge finding someone to do it.

Developing Effective Project Sponsorship

In mapping the relevant stakeholders involved in a change project, CIBC distinguishes between initiating sponsors and sustaining sponsors. Initiating sponsors are individuals

[2]PMBOK is "A Guide to the Project Management Body of Knowledge" published by the Project Management Institute (PMI).

with significant authority within the bank who are called upon to support a major project. They are the only ones empowered to stop such a project. It is to the initiating sponsor that the project turns to when a significant intervention is required to move it along or to change its scope. A sustaining sponsor for a project usually will be organizationally within the chain of command of the initiating sponsor but situated more locally to the project or sub-project. There may be more than one sustaining sponsor for a project.

When sponsors initiate change, they do so in order to achieve specific benefits for the organization, such as cost reduction, increased customer loyalty or improved productivity. The change project that is initiated is a proposed solution to deliver those particular benefits. Too often, though, time and effort is dominantly expended on developing and implementing the technical aspects of the solution, in other words, in *installing* the change rather than *realizing* the intended benefits. Benefit realization only occurs when those impacted by the change actually adopt the new attitudes and behaviours that will ultimately deliver reduced costs, increased productivity or enhanced customer relationships.

Active sponsorship is critical for successful change implementation. Sponsors must not only endorse the change for their direct reports, they must demonstrate through their behaviour the importance of the change and ensure that both positive reinforcing consequences are in place for those who adopt the change and negative sanctions are applied to those who do not.

Jim Breen, Vice President for Business Management Operations within Technology Solutions, had assumed responsibility for PMCOE. He commented on the sponsor role:

There is not a strong articulation of the project sponsor role. It is not being played well. In Technology Solutions there is not a strong enough recognition that project sponsors are necessary for success.

Technology and Operations take risks for the businesses. Who should take the risks? We have to send a very strong message to all our senior people. We are not here just to take orders. We have stewardship for the investment in technology. We have to take a stand for our role. My message is that they will get support for doing that. Sponsorship needs to become more of a regular discipline.

Shelley Kirkbride, a Vice President of Product Development within Global Deposits and Payments, discussed her role as a Sustaining Sponsor:

My role is to clear roadblocks. If they can't find a solution to this, and they have tried their best effort, then I need to escalate it to my peer level to see if I can solve it and get things prioritized in a different way or prioritize my project differently. If there are communications where we have changed fundamentally the product or some features or enhancement around it from management, then I need to sit down with the team and explain why that's happening in a way that they understand. Things change and I need to be able to explain that to them and support them.

Mark McMaster described the sponsor role for a situation in which he was the Project Director on a project for which Shelley Kirkbride was the Sustaining Sponsor:

The Project Sponsor role is critical. The Sponsor has a legitimate authority. They have the money to support the decision of whether we start or stop. The key work package leaders have a link to the sponsor through the Project Steering Committee. For example, for a phase transfer where we confirm we are "OK to go" for a launch, I had the Work Package Leaders report on their deliverables to the Sponsor. Part of the value is that it gives the Sponsor the chance to ask questions before giving me the authority to execute or to install to be sure they are really confident. To me it is like, "Here's your last chance. Don't just go because I say we are ready. If you have questions, you need to get them answered." The other side of it is that it gives the Work Package Leaders a chance to talk about their work and get some recognition from the executive.

Sheila Legon commented on the importance of sponsors understanding their role:

Frequently, people in sponsoring roles who fail to demonstrate their commitment do not know what is expected and needed from them, nor are they aware of the impact of their behaviour. However, when they are not actively engaged as effective sponsors, the change effort is put at risk. When sponsorship commitment is not evident, people tend not to take the change seriously. As a result, the change may be only superficially adopted over the short-term or adopted with inconsistency and distortion. Sometimes, it is not adopted at all. Any of these outcomes are dangerous for leaders. People lose confidence in leaders who fail to fulfill the promise of their announced intentions, resulting in skepticism and cynicism with respect to organizational change. People learn to ignore management directives, which increases the organizational response time to change. As a consequence, the probability of achieving changes on time and within budget is compromised and the prospect of achieving the expected business benefits may be lost entirely.

When sponsors do not actively and effectively play their role, not only are project managers often tempted to step in on their behalf, but sponsors are more than willing to delegate this role. This is a recipe for failure . . . only sponsors can make the change real and tangible for those affected.

Teresa Caine discussed the role of project sponsors from a PMCOE perspective:

Project sponsorship is essential to make this place work. If you don't have that, there is not much you can do. There really isn't. It is absolutely key. People get some of it. The most successful piece of this is Risk Assessment. We have a tool and a methodology. So people can figure out, "What are my project risks? What are my technical risks? What are my organization risks?" And then, "What are my people risks?" We have a way and a method for people to figure out for their project whether it is high risk or low risk or medium risk. From a project management perspective, people can understand that, because project managers understand risk. Not so for the softer things around the cultural changes, or "I have identified that my sponsor for this project isn't there for me and isn't supporting the project and isn't doing what they need to do." Then you get into the whole hierarchy of this organization, which is very hierarchical, as well as the fear that "If I raise that, what's going to happen to me and my job?" That big culture change where it is okay to do this is yet to come.

PCM Gains a Second Foothold: Retail Markets Process Engineering Group

In parallel with her involvement with MPM and PMCOE, Sheila Legon was also working to extend PCM adoption in the bank through the support she was providing to the Process Engineering (PE) group in Retail Markets. This group had developed a process engineering process that incorporated Six Sigma and Lean Thinking to re-engineer key processes within Retail Markets such as the Personal Deposit Account Open Process. Process Engineering had adopted MPM as their methodology for managing their projects and as such, PCM became an integral part of the Process Engineering Process. PCM was identified as a crucial element to building a more comprehensive methodology that would allow the group to deliver changes to the frontline. Steve Tyers, a Senior Director in the Process Engineering Group was tasked with building the key concepts and tools into the PE methodology. This included concepts such as sponsorship, the sponsorship backbone and the identification of blackholes in the sponsorship cascade, as well as a thorough analysis of the extent of the required behaviour change through a comprehensive gap analysis. The exact templates and terms were modified to integrate with the lexicon of the existing process engineering methodology, while maintaining the principles of PCM. Steve Tyers noted:

Process Engineering quickly learned the value of PCM in its early days. While the combination of Six Sigma and Lean Thinking in its methodology allowed the group to design technically flawless processes, they gave little guidance on how to implement the change. With the focus of PE's work on the 15,000 frontline employees and the processes they conduct day in and day out, PCM became a necessary part of the methodology.

PE developed tools specific to process engineering which complemented the PCM tool set within MPM. Five key Process Engineering tools from the methodology (which has over 200) were identified as crucial to the success and mandated for all funded projects in Retail Markets in order to drive better results on all projects. Two of the tools are directly linked to PCM tools, although all are associated as PE tools.

4.0

The extent of integration led to a blurring of PCM concepts, whereby department members are not even aware they are using it. A Process Engineering VP asked, "Do we use change management?" The changes to business processes were adopted so flawlessly that many could barely recall the changes. In fact, the existing PE support desk called the project after delivery wondering what was going on and why they weren't getting any "noise" and complaints.

Steve Tyers and several other consultants in the process engineering group attended a PCM Certification Program which was offered to areas within the bank that were interested in incorporating PCM into their existing processes. Through his involvement in developing and delivering the training in the PE methodology, Steve Tyers became a strong advocate and supporter of PCM. He commented:

When major change projects were being delivered flawlessly to the field our department was receiving accolades on how well received it was by the change targets. PE instead of PCM was getting the credit. But did it matter? The methodology was clearly driving results, and the executives were beginning to take notice. PCM plays a fundamental role in everything PE does, and is gaining broader acceptance and acknowledgement across Retail Markets, even if under a different banner.

PCM Gains a Third Foothold: The Human Resources Function

Joyce Phillips, Executive Vice President for Human Resources, is the Initiating Sponsor for People Change Management within CIBC Human Resources. She described the development of PCM:

A couple of our internal OD consultants have been working with different parts of the business on specific projects or change initiatives for a number of years providing change management consulting and expertise. Those people now work in a group in Human Resources called Organizational Initiatives. And that group in Human Resources looks at different types of organizational behaviours that are going on. We started on a much more disciplined approach about three years ago. There was a process started in the organization that my group was involved with that had to do with culture. "What kind of branding do we want?" which relates to culture. We had read a lot of books on this whole idea of how you engage and excite a population around branding, changing the culture around branding, etc. From there, there are a lot of materials that we created for the organization on People Change Management skills, People Change Management processes, what is the best of the best? i.e., what kinds of organizations have been successful in doing it? what do they do? That is how it all started. There was a need being expressed within the organization and people in my function were asked to participate in that. Through a lot of dialogue, a team of business people and human resources looked at how people had to change their behaviours in order to accept the new brand from a culture perspective. It was my group who read the best of the best in the books, got feedback from the businesses and put it together in a process for People Change Management at CIBC.

Human Resources also adopted MPM, the organizational methodology for project management, and was developing the governance structures to ensure that HR projects were effectively monitored and tracked, with all project risks, be they technical, operational, financial or people, being raised and mitigated appropriately. Joyce Phillips explained the role of PCM in helping HR play out its role as an agent of change:

As employees in Human Resources are in the people business, whether they are in recruiting, learning or consulting to the business, each person is in effect, helping the organization effectively manage change. With that in mind, HR has undertaken a program to transfer foundational People Change Management capability to every employee within HR, so that they employ PCM principles and processes in their work with business clients and employees and, as such, transfer PCM knowledge and understanding more broadly. PCM is becoming a core competency for HR professionals. We believe in it. We believe that if it is done properly and correctly, it is the way to make things stick in the organization.

However, integrating change management with project management was not only accomplished through movement on the part of project managers. It required movement from the business side as well. Joyce Phillips commented:

People Change Management doesn't necessarily give people "business speak". PCM has a very fluffy HR subjectivity to it. So for the businesses to really take it seriously, to recognize it as an important new initiative that they needed to be concerned about it, you had to add "business speak" to it. You had to put it in their language, to let them see how important it was from their perspective for running a business as well as the business attributes and profits that can be derived from it. By bringing PCM together with project management you can have a defensible, articulated plan that is more meaningful, meaty, quantifiable, and measurable that the businesses really can touch and feel. That is what happened when we turned PCM into that process—it added more concrete substance to what was considered HR fluff, i.e., People Change Management. So we put it together and we had a solid process.

PCM Gains a Fourth Foothold: The New Initiatives Approval Process

Joyce Phillips was instrumental in influencing the adoption of PCM into a high leverage business process.

We are also building it into other process that we have here at CIBC. We have, for instance, a New Initiatives Approval Process (NIAP). Any new business initiative has to go through a process where they have to identify that initiative and get all the stakeholders that are involved in it to become familiar with the initiative and therefore sign off on it from an operational risk standpoint and an approval standpoint. The risk categories include Strategic Risk, Credit Risk, Market Risk, Operational Risk[,] and, most recently, People Change Management Risk has been incorporated into the overall risk profile. The process is designed to ensure all risks are identified early in the project process and that appropriate strategies are developed and effectively implemented to mitigate those risks prior to the launch of the initiative. NIAP is run through Audit and Compliance and we have actually built this PCM process into that. So not only do you look at the dollars and cents and the regulatory and compliance issues, but you are also looking at People Change Management.

In 2000, CIBC decided to integrate two large but separate human resource information systems and business processes into one common platform and one operating model. Peoplesoft was selected as the common enterprise resource planning system with its implementation outsourced to a provider. People Change Management was integrated into Peoplesoft through NIAP. Every new product/system had to have a risk assessment done and if the PCM risk assessment resulted in a score above a predetermined threshold, then human resource practices related to change management were called upon to mitigate the risk. Before NIAP, there was no way to capture the change management risk. Once NIAP was in place, then change management could be examined by business unit and Human Resources could then bring a standard tool kit to bear against any identified change management risks.

Kevin Patterson, Senior Vice President, Internal Audit and Corporate Security, assumed responsibility for NIAP in the Fall of 2002. Peoplesoft went through NIAP in February 2003 and went live on Labour Day 2003. Kevin Patterson reinforced Joyce Phillips' comments:

Peoplesoft went in smoothly because all the pieces were there. Acceptance was easier having PCM as part of the implementation process. Without NIAP to legitimize PCM, its implementation would have been more adversarial. The PCM processes were a by-product of the success. We don't look for PCM when we are auditing. We look for it as part of NIAP, for such things as: How were management people brought to bear on the process? Was there a stakeholder analysis? Have change management risks been identified? If the risks were identified properly up front, then we audit that actions were taken to manage the risks.

Sustaining People Change Management in CIBC

Joyce Phillips viewed the process of institutionalizing PCM as a process that had to be managed thoughtfully:

We are on a journey. We still have a long way to go. Where we are today is not where we will end up in a year from now. It is something that we will get better at. We will keep on improving, evolving as we go. For a function, what is important for us is to get the knowledge out to the businesses when the need arises. We are going to depend on word of mouth. We are going to depend on success stories so that we can actually show where this has been of value and has been well received and let the feedback speak for itself. I have to make sure I keep training my people in the function so that it is not just left to the Organizational Initiatives group but is part of my HR function that is out there with the businesses day in and day out. When a need arises in the businesses, to make sure we implement this kind of a process, it is going to be critical that everyone who is trained in Human Resources at least know enough about PCM. We will need to determine which of the initiatives we will say that we will work with you on using this process. Still, I am picking and choosing. I don't want to over sell it so much that it is going to lose its value until I make sure I have enough success stories so you can actually see what you can get from this process. I have built it to where I think I can get to critical leverage for it and then continue to keep nurturing it.

What we have to do is pick and choose initially where to sell it and to brand it by word of mouth and then success will speak for itself.

Appendix 1
The People Change Management (PCM) Process

What is PCM? People Change Management is a process to identify people risks that may have an impact on the effective implementation of any new initiative or business change. The focus of PCM is to develop appropriate mitigation plans to manage the people risk; these plans are integrated into the overall project plan.

Why is PCM important? Failure to pay sufficient attention to the impact of a change on the people who have to either implement it or who will be affected by it results in implementation that is less than optimal. Business leaders run the risk of ending up with only superficial adoption of the change and few or none of the intended benefits.

How is PCM implemented?

- Identify and graphically map all the key stakeholders who will be involved with or impacted by the change.
- Identify the goals (i.e., human objectives) for the people directly affected.
  - To ensure that the benefits of the change can be fully realized, what new or different attitudes or mindsets will people need to adopt; what new or different behaviours and activities will people need to engage in.
- Determine how successful adoption of the change will be measured.
- Conduct an Impact Assessment
  - To determine the nature, degree and timing of impact on affected stakeholders
  - To identify their change role(s) as sponsor, agent, target or a combination of roles
  - To determine how critical they are to the success of the change
- Complete a stakeholder risk assessment for all key sponsors, change agents and targets of the change against five targeted risk factors:
  - Sponsor commitment
  - Target resistance
  - Change Agent capability
  - Cultural alignment
  - Organizational capacity
- Assess the level of identified risk; develop and implement strategies and action plans to mitigate significant stakeholder risk; all actions plans are incorporated into the overall project plan.
- Monitor and track progress; revise strategies and action plans as required.
- Report on the issues and risks so they can be monitored, tracked and escalated for resolution as appropriate.

4.0

Appendix 2
Project Managers as Change Agents

As change agents, project managers have an important role in ensuring that the sponsors they work with are fully engaged in their sponsorship role. This may mean that they need to spend time educating their sponsors on what they need them to do and when and how they need them to do it. People in sponsoring roles have many other managerial roles to fulfill at any given time, so it is helpful if the project managers are somewhat prescriptive in advising their sponsors about what needs to be done. For instance, they will ensure that the right speeches are developed for the right audiences. They will set up meetings with individuals or groups as required. They will make sure all the work is done to ensure the sponsor is successful in his or her role . . . and they will provide sponsors with feedback. Therefore, it is beneficial for the sponsor and the project manager to establish an effective working relationship where feedback on actions by either party can be readily discussed.

4.0 Although delivery of the solution is an important and critical aspect, it is a means to an end and not the end itself. Therefore, it is not enough for project sponsors and project managers to concern themselves only with the technical solution. Project managers must go beyond just deploying the change and involve both the project and the business in creating the business environment in which the change can thrive and be sustained over time. This means that all the sustaining mechanisms must be identified and established as part of the project. For instance, while the project may identify at the outset the need for training of new skills, they need also to concern themselves with ensuring that the new skills are adopted over time. This may mean developing performance measures and having them become part of the performance management process; it may mean developing a coaching program which the business agrees to maintain; it may mean having these new skills become part of an on-going training curriculum; it may mean developing sustaining organizational structures or functions that will assume on-going responsibilities. Any number of strategies may be proposed and developed to ensure that the business benefits will be achieved after the project has formally closed. When the project manager formally closes the project, having met time, cost and quality measures, they will also have established and gained business agreement to fulfill the commitments required to achieve the intended business benefits.

Appendix 3
The Business/Technology Process

Shelley Kirkbride is Vice President of Product Development within Global Deposits and Payments, a portfolio of products and services, and one of the seven portfolio groups within the Retail Markets business line (see Exhibit 1). GDP houses a Product Development Group and a Product Management Group (see Exhibit 2). Shelley Kirkbride explained the terminology:

Project Management and Product Management are different. Project Management means being able to deliver and execute on products and services while the Product Management Team are the individuals who manage our deposits products, such as checking and savings products. The Product Development Group develops those products and services. For example, my team will come up with products and services such as a new High Interest Rate Savings product that we just launched. I would have a Project Manager or Project Director who is in the Technology Solutions area work with my team to execute that project within the organization. They would work on the project and my team would act as the business account manager.

EXHIBIT 2
GDP and Technology Solutions: Partial Organization Chart

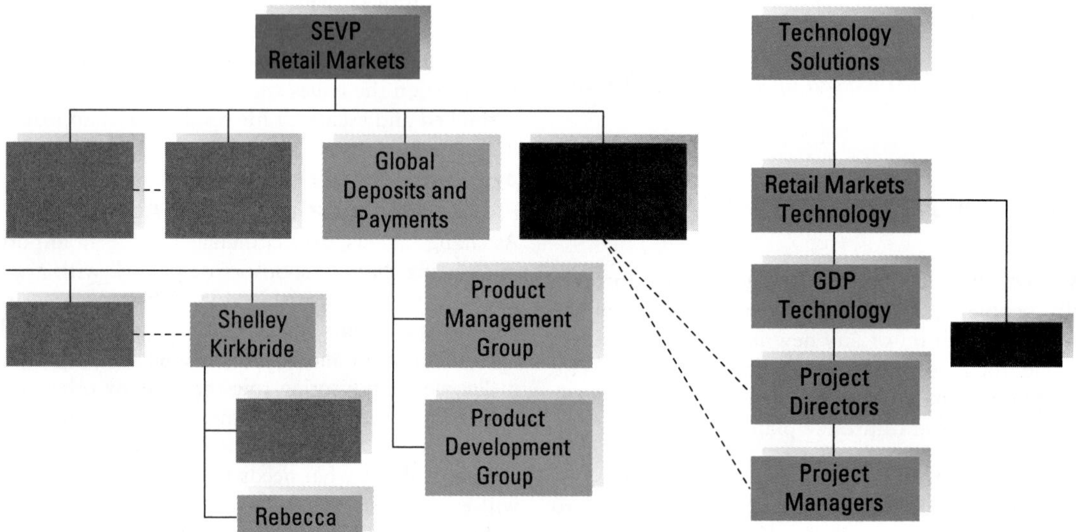

EXHIBIT 3
Methodology for Project Management

Phase 0	Phase 1	Phase 2	Phase 3	Phase 4	Phase 5
Basic Idea Business Responsibility	Initiate & Plan PM-COE Responsibility	Requirements & Design PM-COE Responsibility	Construction PM-COE Responsibility	Test & Launch PM-COE Responsibility	Benefits Realization Business Responsibility

Retail Markets had its own Project Management Office which is at the peer level of GDP (see Exhibits 1 and 2). The RM-PMO provides support and tracking from a dollar perspective. They also provide guidance around business cases and some of the other early, phase 0, stages of project management as well as support on the financial side (see Exhibit 3). From a reporting perspective, they have a dotted line relationship with project directors and project managers who work on different GDP projects (Exhibit 2). The VP-CIO for Global Products Technology, within Technology Solutions, oversees all GDP projects to ensure that interdependencies between GDP projects and between GDP and other portfolios within Retail Markets are managed from a portfolio perspective.

Shelley explained some of the reporting relationships:

Refer to Exhibit 2. In GDP we have a Product Development Group. I have a couple of people from this group on my team. We have a matrix organization. So there is a matrixed Technology Solutions Group that we work with. They have a group that are project directors or project managers. They follow what we call, internally, our PMCOE (Project Management Centre of Excellence) process, which is our project management process. If I am creating a bonus hiring product, I would have Rebecca (see Exhibit 2) phone up somebody in the GDP Project Management office and say, "I need a project manager. Ask them to come over here. I want to create this type of product. How do I deliver it? What do I need to do? What makes sense? Here's what the product looks like. I will give you the specs." They will then go away and develop it.

This Project Director will actually create a team of individuals. We then sit as a participant on this team with our person on this team referred to as the "Technology Lead". One of the work packages might be led by one of my team members. We have overarching responsibility for delivery of the product but these individuals help us deliver it through the project management cycle (Exhibit 3). Once it is developed and put in place, then a team from the Product Management Group takes over and they manage it on a day to day basis. The project management people are pretty much out of it by then.

Integrative Case 5.0

Solomon Business School: Implementing the New Strategy*

5.0

It was July 2005, and the strategic task force of the Solomon Business School of Northcote University had just finished meeting with one of their colleagues, Professor Abramowitz, who was a recognized academic and professional commentator and authority on leading change. Professor Abramowitz had presented the key issues on change to the members of the task force, and they now realized the enormity of the task they faced in repositioning the Solomon Business School to be successful in a rapidly changing environment. Faced with a deadline less than 60 days away, in order to start the recruitment of students for the next academic year, they also realized that many of the issues raised by Abramowitz could not be managed well within that time frame. But postponement of the change was not, in the task force's view, a feasible alternative.

Background

The Solomon Business School had been in existence as part of Northcote University for 102 years. Northcote University had been founded as a private university in Northcote City, in the state of Illinois in 1863, 50 miles from the city of Chicago. The founders of the university, a group of businessmen with strong support from the Presbyterian Church had envisaged a university dedicated to the pursuit of knowledge in both science and the humanities, as well as a College of Divinity. The university had prospered, although during the depression of the 1930s, many faculty (including those with tenure) and staff had been let go for financial exigencies.

After the Second World War, the university had grown and added a College of Medicine, a College of Engineering and a College of Art and Design. The university as a whole had grown to 20,000 students, with about 5,000 graduate students. Solomon had some 800 undergraduate (BBA) students and some 300 graduate (MBA) students, was the second largest behind Engineering, 2000 students and Medicine with 600 students in its MD program. (Fellows were not included in the student count in Medicine of Northcote University as they were in one of nine teaching hospitals in Chicago.)

Solomon Business School

In 1998, Ezekiel Solomon had donated $20 million to the university to rename the College of Business the Solomon Business School. The $20 million had been used to: endow four professorships, fund several student scholarships, allow building expansion, branding, and operations. Solomon was a local businessman who had graduated from Northcote University with a BBA and who had made his fortune (estimated at $350 million) in property development in New York City, Miami and Atlanta. Solomon wanted the school to become a top 15 business school in both the *BusinessWeek* and *Financial Times* rankings. He wished to see real innovation on the part of the school.

The years between the gift and 2004 had been both the best of times and the worst of times for Solomon. The school had grown its undergraduate program by 130 students per year. (Students at Solomon are admitted into the program at the end of first year based on academic grades, evidence of extracurricular activities and interviews.) Successful applicants were assigned to a section of some 65 students for the first two years of their BBA program. They took elective courses in the senior year. Prior to 1998, most undergraduate students at Solomon had come from Illinois, Ohio, Wisconsin and Michigan. However, the program growth had meant that the undergraduate program had received national attention, the culmination of which was an article in the *New York Times* about the Midwestern business school that provided a great education, real value and was providing the New York investment banks and the national consumer packaged goods companies with outstanding graduates.

Another development during this period was the retirement of many older faculty members and the recruitment of many outstanding junior faculty members from top-tier business schools. These new recruits were attracted to Northcote because of its espoused collegiality, its commitment to outstanding teaching and its desire to become a first-class

Richard Ivey School of Business
The University of Western Ontario

*Professor Murray J. Bryant prepared this case solely to provide material for class discussion. The author does not intend to illustrate either effective or ineffective handling of a managerial situation. The author may have disguised certain names and other identifying information to protect confidentiality.

business school, recognized by its academic peers. The faculty growth was roughly 15 per cent, and the net impact on the faculty profile of this dramatic hiring was that the average age of faculty went down from 54 years to 41 years.

The dramatic growth of faculty was not without difficulties. The new faculty members were keen to establish themselves as researchers, many with little business background, and thus, special teaching arrangements (e.g. reduced teaching, buying out of teaching) were required. As well, additional space had to be made available for behavioral laboratory space, additional research staff and so on, and ongoing demands for more space continued to be felt by the administration.

The new faculty had also demanded that the PhD program be expanded from 12 students per year to 24 students. The benefit of this expansion was to increase faculty research productivity; the costs included additional funds for entrance, financial support for up to five years, space and competing teaching demands on faculty.

The bad news on the horizon was the realization that the flagship MBA program of the school was in trouble. Traditionally, Northcote graduates had been sought after by major national recruiters: investment banking in New York and Chicago, financial services in Chicago, management consulting nationally and internationally, and packaged goods firms nationally. A major recruiter was 3M in Minneapolis. However, the downturn in the employment market in the past three to five years had meant that not all MBAs seeking employment had received job offers. In fact, in 2002/3, the graduates of 2002 were competing for jobs with graduates of 2003.

Analysis indicated that the top of the class was good, but the tail was too long and not very good. The effects of this phenomenon were that: morale among students was low; rankings in *BusinessWeek*, as it was heavily weighted towards employment statistics, dropped quite dramatically; anecdotally, recruiters were saying that the current group of graduating students were not as prepared as they should have been. Many faculty had dismissed these concerns even though application numbers had dropped by some 30 per cent. Other peer schools had dropped by 10 per cent to 40 per cent. Rankings depended also on student satisfaction so a potential downward slide was inevitable; morale drops, rankings drop, and then applications drop.

In 2003 a new dean, Professor Grover, had been appointed. Professor Grover had been a faculty member at Yale Business School but had left to become an economic advisor to the Clinton Administration in the Department of Labor. Professor Grover was appointed by Northcote search committee with the following mandate: make Solomon a great business school with a national and international reputation. Professor Grover had strong links to the Solomon family and was also a director of 3M so the search committee felt he had the right capabilities and competencies to lead the school.

During 2004, Professor Grover spent most of his time on the road talking to alumni, corporations and foundations, assessing whether the time was appropriate to start a $250 million campaign. The campaign would be focused on a new building (Solomon had committed an additional $25 million towards this, provided that he had design input on the choice of an architect) and an endowment to provide additional operating funds of $8 million to $10 million per annum.

5.0

At the end of 2004, Professor Grover came back to his management team of Professor Angela Hause, Associate Dean Research and Faculty; Professor Thomas J. Burns, Associate Dean Programs; Professor Carol Epping, BBA Program Director; Professor Peter Blank, MBA Program Director; Clyde Wells, Chief Financial Officer (CFO), and Ryan Thomas, Director of Development, with two key ideas: the positioning and strategic direction of the school had to be in place before the capital campaign, and the MBA program needed real attention to restore the school's competitive position.

In January 2005, Professor Grover hired CD&H, an international consulting firm, to help the faculty in terms of the strategic formulation process. In March 2005, the firm presented its findings to an open forum of staff, faculty and an advisory board. Their findings were:

The MBA has become a commodity. Your competitors have grown stronger, you are not attracting the "best and brightest" of students in the MBA, the BBA is an outstanding product, and the faculty are not viewed even in Illinois as opinion leaders with a few exceptions.

The reaction at the open forum was one of disbelief and denial. Many of the established faculty were outraged at the report. Those who seemed to accept it put all the blame on the newer faculty who had been engaged during the last 10 years and who now constituted more than one-third of the total faculty complement. These newer faculty blamed the older faculty for having held back the School and refusing change.

The Strategic Task Force

In March 2005, after the open forum, the dean appointed a strategic task force. The task force included: the management team; the director of career management, Brian Thomas; a professor of Strategy, Professor James Hathaway; a professor of marketing, Professor Leo Chang; and a professor of finance, governance and risk, Professor Ivor Lukowitz.

The task force's mandate was to prepare a visioning document, a strategy and an implementation plan in time for the annual recruiting season, which started in October of each year.

The members of the team had not previously worked closely with each other before, but they had much in common. Professors Hause, Epping, Hathaway and Blank as well as Brian Thomas were all graduates of the school and thus knew well the values and culture of the school. Interestingly enough, the task force did not include any individuals, apart from the dean, who had been hired in the recent past. This was partly due to the fact that most of the group members were in the early stages of their careers and had not yet been tenured. (Tenure at Northcote was made in the eighth year of appointment, and traditionally about 60 per cent of those candidates who stayed seven years were tenured.)

At the onset of their deliberations in March, after digesting the implications of the CD&H report, the task force deliberated on the question of how to do their work.

Previous change attempts at Solomon (i.e. a new undergraduate curriculum, a new MBA program, the growth of the BBA program) had been extremely difficult. The collegial culture that was imbedded at Solomon meant that the change process had been, in the words of Thomas Burns, captured by the various departments or functional areas within the Solomon school. The effects of this capture were that the design of the new MBA program, instead of being a tightly integrated program, was:

> Bitty—bits of this and bits of that. *It was hard to determine the logical progression of the students' learning process, everyone "owned" the program, but no one was really accountable for it, and student assessment had become a lot more problematic. The latter point was quite critical as many employers used the grades in January of the first year as the filter to identify which students to interview for summer employment. Student satisfaction was a critical part of rankings. As this data was lagged, any decline in rankings would last several years and directly impact admissions. Professor Epping was a lot more harsh: "We set out to design a racehorse and we finished up with a donkey with strong legs."*

The collegial atmosphere had worked well in the distant past due to several factors. First, the faculty was smaller. Second, as all the faculty prior to joining Solomon had relevant professional and managerial experience, the faculty bias towards managerial relevance was clear. Third, negotiation took place between departments, but it was with a clear understanding of the role of the program in educating its target market, whether BBA or MBA. Fourth, the faculty were relatively homogeneous as most tended to be middle-aged U.S.-trained and educated males.

Professors Epping and Hause were strongly of the view that the strategic task force could not be as collegial as in the past as the school was in a crisis situation and that real, substantive change through a democratic process would not be possible in the time period allowed. Further, the faculty would preserve too many sacred cows if a full open collegial process were adopted.

Professor Grover had other views. He did not know all the past history that his colleagues were aware of, and his experience in the Clinton administration had been one of open dialogue, full discussion of competing views. Often in cabinet discussions, the views of State were at odds with Treasury, and Labor was often at odds with Treasury and Defense. Each cabinet minister, prior to sessions with the president, had often role-played with his/her staff the likely reaction from other affected stakeholders so that the process of both policy formulation and policy implementation was enhanced. In fact, Professor Grover had been personally involved in the debates on policy and implementation with respect to textiles, affecting several critical politically sensitive/at-risk states. He felt the need for openness, but even though he was Dean, he was unable to persuade his colleagues of the need for openness.

The Task Force Process

During the months of April, May, June, July and even August, the task force met frequently. Some meetings lasted an entire week, and the committee felt that progress was being made.

At the end of May, the group tested its vision statement: "to be the school producing graduates, both BBA and MBA, that are viewed by our recruiters as the most prepared for long-term careers." The major test of the vision was with the top 20 recruiters who had recruited from Solomon in the past five years. In addition, a selection of a few similar firms that did not recruit at Solomon were contacted regarding the resonance of the vision. One of the latter firms felt that it would now recruit at Solomon. The top 20 recruiter firms felt that Solomon's approach of excellence through customer intimacy was a good one. However, one of the major investment banks commented that although Solomon was in the top 25 schools from whom it recruited, in a down-market, the bank would reduce this number to only five schools. When questioned by the task force, the bank commented in the following vein: "No one makes a mistake at their firm by hiring a Chicago, Tuck, Wharton, Columbia or Harvard graduate, and in a down-market that is where we will look."

Several in the task force wondered whether this information was indicative that the customer intimacy strategy was perhaps a difficult one for Solomon but, in contrast, in their view, perhaps appropriate for Tuck and the so-called Tuck "mafia" who had a strong position in both investment banking and management consulting. It seemed to the group that customer intimacy required not only understanding the customer's needs today but required an ability to anticipate the customer's needs tomorrow and alter admissions requirements and applicant profiles as well as program activities, both inside and outside the classroom, in order to ensure that their graduates had the "right stuff" to succeed at those firms.

Professor Cheng said that customer intimacy characterized some great companies, such as General Electric and some parts of the chemical business, ICI PLC, with respect to customers in food processing and manufacturers of automobile airbags.

At this point, the task force turned to the representatives from CD&H in terms of information about their direct and indirect competitors. One thing that surprised Professor Glover in this discussion was how little direct knowledge the task force had regarding competitive intelligence. There were lots of anecdotal data, but apart from a perusal of application and promotional material coupled with comparison of GMAT scores, work experience and average undergraduate grades, little seemed to be known by the task force. This dearth of good information was in contrast to Grover's experience at Labor, when the issue was not a lack of good information but often too much analysis of that information so that policy alternatives were not delineated clearly enough.

The members of the task force then thought a little more deeply about their ability to produce a strategy that could differentiate the school and bring it into the top 15 business schools on the two rankings, deemed so critical by Ezekiel Solomon.

Professor Hause suggested that perhaps the approach to differentiation should focus on faculty research. Innovation would count if it appealed both to the "academic academy" as well as practice. She felt this was the mark of a great business school—able to bridge the apparent divide between theory (creation of new knowledge) and practice (application of that knowledge). Hause then reflected on the existing faculty complement and felt that there was a potential disconnect between aspirations and realizations. Others on the task force challenged her, but discussion had to be highly diplomatic as the group was assessing research qualities and impact of their colleagues, many of whom had both personal and professional links to those individuals. Faculty were often reluctant to confront performance management issues with colleagues as many of these individuals were often friends as well.

Professor Cheng used the industry analogy of Microsoft, Sony, Hewlett Packard, Goldman and Sachs, and the major pharmaceutical companies as evidence of how some firms outside business schools choose to compete. Others around the table said that, overall, this strategy required high investment in innovation and in research and development in order to make this a viable approach for Solomon. The question was posed to the chief financial officer (CFO): "Could we afford it?" The answer: "Perhaps," but it was a "bet the farm" approach to strategy formulation.

The CD&H advisors brought the task force back down to earth.

In the past you were good because (i) you had a clear market niche, (ii) your competitors were all over the map, (iii) you exploited that niche, and (iv) you had a group of faculty who agreed on the what but who disagreed only at the margin on the how, and (v) your alumni were your greatest unexploited asset.

The group then spent some time thinking about what it was that had made them so successful in the past but was not working well today. The group quickly came to a consensus: the arrogance of being good in the past had blinded them to the competitive moves of new and existing competitors. It was not just the fact that they had slipped; almost unnoticed competitors had made quite dramatic, exciting moves that Solomon and its faculty had ignored. The question was, could they simply execute more effectively than their competitors? To achieve this type of strategy meant that they needed to move the organization from a complacent one to a high-performing, driven organization. Could this change come about without totally altering the organization? Much would have to change:

5.0

1. admissions, scholarships, career management on the student side;
2. faculty: how to achieve research impact with a total budget of $80 million (largely for faculty salaries) on both the research academy and practicing management;
3. hiring, promotion and reward systems for both faculty and staff;
4. performance management, including setting standards of performance that were consistent with the strategy;
5. communication to all stakeholders;
6. organizational structures: was the departmental structure the appropriate one?
7. the organizational culture: in the past, conflict was avoided to the extent that if a senior faculty member disagreed, complete reversals were not uncommon;
8. how to deal with the average performers while retaining high performance individuals, often performance issues had been ignored in the past;
9. how to achieve focus and concerted effort while preserving academic independence?

The task force reflected on the leading planned change model presented by Professor Abramowitz and thought about the likely reaction of their colleagues to the change. Would they be supported? Would they be trusted? What was negotiable? What was non-negotiable? How could they set up all the required processes in 60 days? It seemed impossible. If they could not, what could they do? What should they do?

It seemed to the task force that there was an obvious strategy: a shortened MBA with a heavy integrative focus. What was less obvious was the setting up of alignment of structures, people, policies and rewards. And yet the strategy would fail if the group did not get these parts right. How could they achieve high performance *and* achieve buy-in by all the key stakeholders at Solomon?

Integrative Case 6.0

Workbrain Corporation*[1]

6.0

It's almost as if I had another eye added to my head. This person would give me insight to see different perspectives, yet at the same time be part of the company. I don't like the term "outsider" but, really, it's like adding a new function to the business that allowed me to think in new directions.

DAVID OSSIP, PRESIDENT AND CEO OF WORKBRAIN CORPORATION

Introduction

Eric Green, the newly hired vice-president, Corporate Development at Workbrain Corporation, looked at his offer letter (which was one half page long) and wondered how his role would evolve. There was no job description in the letter, and the president of the firm had given him some far-reaching and abstract goals. The position had been described to him as one that would mainly involve developing external partnerships with some emphasis on the internal development of the firm. However, from Green's perspective, there were many issues that needed to be handled both on the internal and external sides of the business. At the time, the Workbrain sales team was in the process of securing a major client, there were some growth goals that needed to be achieved and there were no organizational protocols for making a sale in place. There was little time to organize his new office.

Eric Green

Eric Green had recently graduated from an MBA program in Fontainebleau, France. Having both practised corporate law and been a management consultant, he had several years of corporate experience behind him, yet when he graduated he had entrepreneurial aspirations. It was through the process of trying to start his own business that he was made aware of Workbrain.

A couple of my friends and I had worked together in cyber-entrepreneurship class and we had put together a business plan that we were quite excited about. After school, we came back thinking we would shop it around to see what we would find.

In the course of doing that I called a friend of mine who had been involved in the Internet for five years in Toronto who I figured would be a good person to run it by. He referred me to David Ossip saying that David was a strong technology guy and could probably shed some light on the industry. He also suggested that David was starting a company and that I might want to look at it.

I went to the (old) Workbrain website and it didn't look that interesting. My friend called me later and said that David wanted me to call him and he felt I would be a good fit with his company. I thought he would want me to be an implementation consultant and that was not what I was looking to do. I was looking for business development, with a more strategic focus. When I finally met with David we didn't talk about my business plan at all because what he told me about the company was a very powerful and compelling story. It was almost too good to be true; he was looking for somebody to do exactly what I wanted to do, and it was in a company at the exact stage of development that I wanted, in the industry I wanted.

Green's role was very loosely defined and there were high expectations of him. He was given a lot of responsibility but also a lot of autonomy to make the decisions he needed to make and David Ossip was completely on his side. Ossip described the role and the type of person he wanted to fill it:

The individual I was looking for was someone who was very bright, who was a quick thinker, someone who could push the organization and really push me into growing it and who would be able to communicate the vision to the other people in the organization.

[1]Some of the information in this case is taken from internal Workbrain documents authored by Daniel Debow, Matt Chapman, Eric Green and other members of the Workbrain management team.

Richard Ivey School of Business
The University of Western Ontario

*Trevor Hunter prepared this case under the supervision of Professor Mary Crossan solely to provide material for class discussion. The authors do not intend to illustrate either effective or ineffective handling of a managerial situation. The authors may have disguised certain names and other identifying information to protect confidentiality.

I also wanted someone who could function as a recruiter to get other very bright people into the company. I needed a person who would be able to work out how we were going to get the right people we needed into the corporation, and how we were going to come up with an environment to keep them.

Also, we had to define what these people would be doing. Because we were a new company, a lot of the time we would have to hire people before we had active projects and we had to make sure that they would be busy and productive even though they might be (in consultants' terms) on the beach.

I wanted someone who could come in and think in almost textbook terms of how we could scale the business up and build an infrastructure while the rest of us were focused on more operational kinds of functions. It was right up front that I thought about this position.

Ossip did not have to sell Green on the job. Green knew Ossip's track record and was confident in his abilities. Although the job was not well defined, Green felt that the way it was presented to him, this job would offer him the challenges he wanted:

He described the role as both external development and internal development. I knew coming in that I would be wearing many different hats. On the external side I would be helping with the strategy, the marketing side and forming alliances. Since we knew that we wanted to partner with consulting firms, my background made me a good fit. On the internal side, I would be managing the strategic growth of the company, which was of interest to me since some of my experience was applicable to that as well.

When I first joined the company we were in the middle of an RFP (request for proposal) development for a large client that we were pitching and it was a good opportunity to get involved right away. I was helping to draft documents about a system that I didn't really know. At the time I was the only person in the company who didn't have a technical background.

Workbrain

Workbrain was founded in 1999 by a group of former employees of a leading supplier of client-server labor management systems, headed by president and CEO David Ossip. Years earlier, Ossip had founded this previously very successful company that had specialized in time and attendance management.

Ossip possessed a combination of technical, industry and management experience that he turned into a successful business that was eventually purchased by a larger firm. When he sold the firm and began thinking about starting a new company, he was able to gather together a trusted group of former colleagues to form the management team out of which the concept for Workbrain was born.

The members of the Workbrain management team all had extensive contacts in various industries and were recognized for their firm's expertise. At the time of Green's arrival, Workbrain was not very large. Table 1 presents a list of all the employees and their roles. As can be seen, at the time, every employee was also a senior executive.

6.0

The firm had secured US$5.5 million in start-up capital from investors. The main activities in the small offices they rented were either the preparation of the RFP or the development and testing of the system.

From his knowledge of the industry, Ossip recognized that an opportunity existed in the form of the millions of routine employee transactions that took place to track and manage hourly or "blue-collar" workforces (e.g., time-clock entries, employee scheduling, overtime allocation, etc.). Exhibit 1 presents the competitive position of Workbrain in relation to its indirect competitors. Several firms had developed automated systems to manage the activities of so-called "white-collared" or professional workers (e.g., expense reports, travel schedules, etc.); however, there were no firms that focused directly on the "blue-collar" workforce. Considering that in the United States alone, it was estimated that there were 64 million "blue-collar" workers,[2] there was clearly an opportunity. The market was generally broken out on a "per seat" basis, which referred to a per employee calculation. Therefore, the market size calculation was found by taking the number of employees in target companies multiplied by the dollar value per seat. The enterprise software industry generally priced its software between US$100 to US$300 per seat.

Workbrain's main product was an e-business application suite that combined workforce management, workplace administration and workplace community process automation.

The market in which Workbrain operated was highly competitive, yet the other firms all could be described as indirect competitors. There were no other firms that had

[2]U.S. Bureau of Statistics.

TABLE 1

Name	Role
David Ossip	President and CEO
Martin Ossip	Executive Director
Ezra Kiser	VP and GM, US Operations
Scott Morrell	VP Technology
Raymond Nunn	VP Operations
David Stein	VP Sales
Eric Green	VP Corporate Development

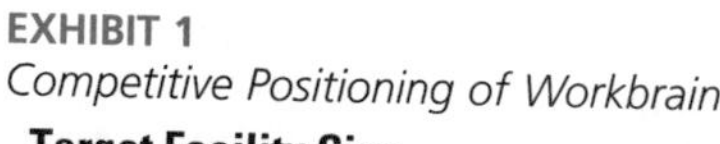

EXHIBIT 1
Competitive Positioning of Workbrain

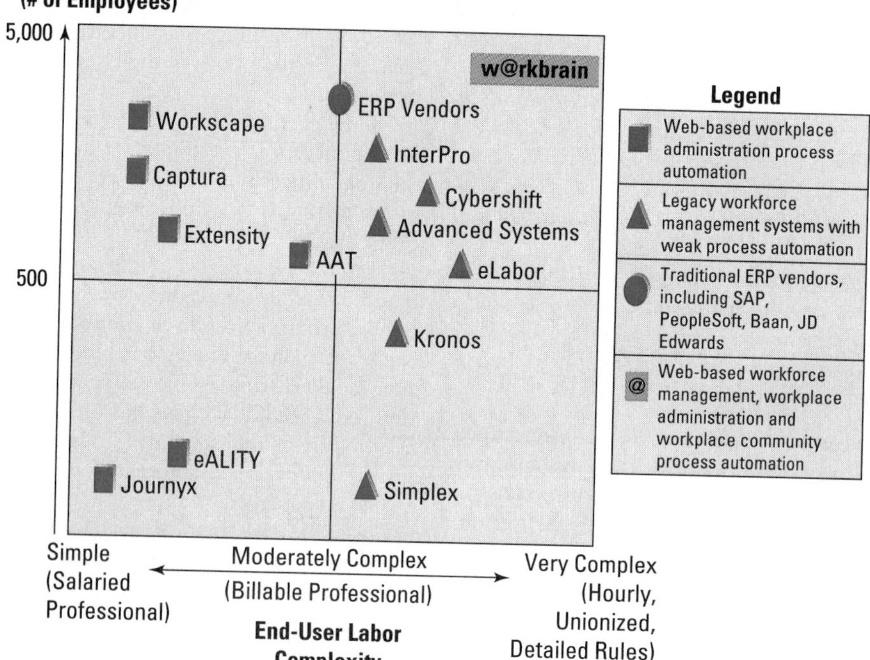

Source: Company reports and Web sites; Workbrain Analysis, 2000

workforce management products specifically designed for the large "blue-collar" workforce. Those "blue-collar" workforce management systems that were available were either "shrink-wrapped systems" that were "optimized for smaller organizations with less complex hourly labor rules," or were "based on older client-server technologies" that were more difficult and costly to deploy.

A direct comparison with the workforce management industry leader, Kronos Inc. (which had an estimated 50 per cent of the market), revealed that more than 75 per cent of the company's installed base used UNIX and DOS-based applications that meant they had limited Internet functionality.[3] Internet functionality was the basis of Workbrain's product and was in line with industry analysts who predicted that much of the workforce management would soon be web-based. The low implementation cost, flexible architecture and web-based ease of operation gave Workbrain a strong competitive advantage.

Once the product was installed, managers of Workbrain's clients could more effectively automate hourly employee processes such as time and attendance tracking, activity-based costing and employee scheduling. At the same time their clients' employees could, in turn, request shift changes, vacations, and overtime, administer their benefits claims and carry out a host of other value-added, third-party transactions. In short, the product allowed Workbrain's clients to better manage their workforce through real time information transfer and analysis, while also providing the hourly employees more control over their activities and access to information that they needed to better perform their jobs and make their lives away from work easier, all through web-based technology.

There were clear benefits to the clients in that the system would significantly reduce a number of administrative costs and payroll charges. It was estimated that form-processing costs ranged between \$36 and \$175 per submitted form[4] when one included the time spent filling in, submitting, approving and auditing employee-related forms. For a facility employing 500 or more employees these costs would add up quickly. In addition, automated time and attendance systems reduced input errors and misrepresented working times that, on average, resulted in a loss equivalent to one per cent to six per cent of total payroll costs.[5] Improved labor analytics allowed managers to perform robust scenario analyses to determine impacts of potential labor policy changes and union contract terms on their firm's financials.

[3]Hambrecht & Quist, 1999

[4]American Express & AMR Research, 1997

[5]American Payroll Association

EXHIBIT 2
Screen Shot of the Workbrain System

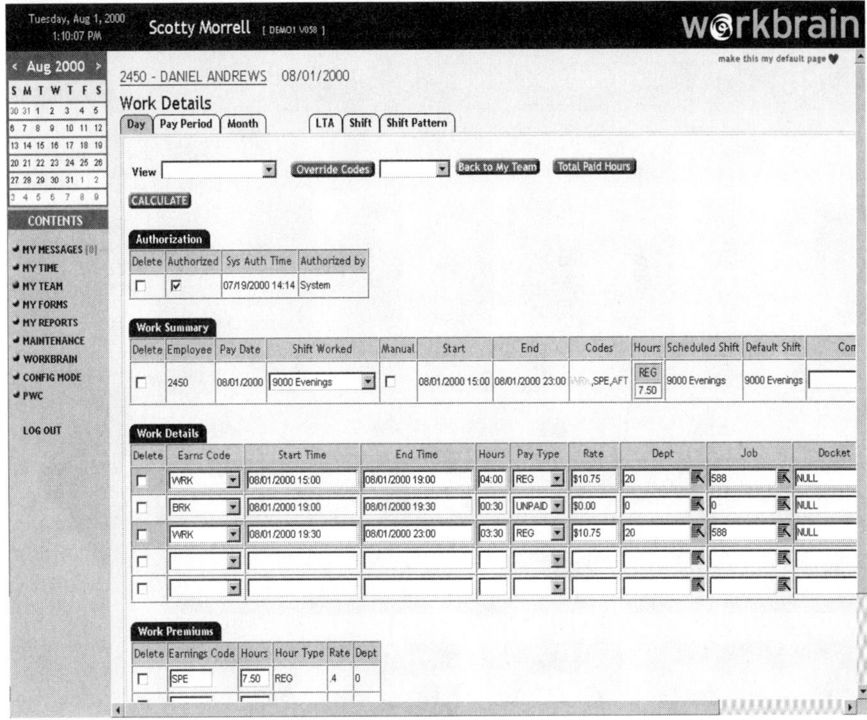

Source: Workbrain Corporation, 2000

Ossip discussed one of the many examples of how a client could decrease costs by using Workbrain's product:

Forms for any type of business process can be created and defined in real-time. This is just one of the many business objects embedded in our system. For example, if a company wanted to create something like a new safety glove requisition form project from scratch, that required access passwords and security for every employee, the cost could easily reach $100 000 to get it started. When our system is installed, it would be a five-minute job. To send out a new type of process form, the new form is created first. Since everyone has a mailbox with complete messaging service built in, the new report is just a business object that is then messaged out to everyone. Our system allows companies to create a data store that can be uploaded (things like procedure manuals, ISO check-lists, etc. can be accessed). We make it more convenient for the employees to access the information they need to do their jobs.

Employees were presented with a number of services and functions designed to enhance their work and personal lives through a web-based interface allowing them to contact their managers through any Internet access portal. Beyond directly work-related functions, a worker would be presented with email, and a business-to-employee "concierge" service through which they could take salary cash advances, make travel arrangements, and take advantage of e-procurement systems. These employee services would be provided through various alliances with partner firms who would gain direct access to many regular users with each additional contract. David Ossip described the product as follows (Exhibit 2 presents a screen shot of one of the Workbrain web pages):

The first level of contact is the employee self-service access, through kiosks onsite or from other Internet portals. Below that are the workforce management systems, which are our expertise—time and attendance plus labor analytics, shop floor data capture, attendance control, scheduling, etc. (Exhibit 3 presents a graphic of the concept.) We believe that provides the client with an information layer that benefits them. In between the Workbrain transaction servers we can design different types of business objects that can either be provided by us or by other companies.

If an employee wants to see her/his pay, there is a pay stub viewer. The employee can see the pay stub before it's printed. For benefit administration an employee can change the benefit plan to see different scenarios (this could be provided by a partner like Wattson Wyatt or Mercer Consulting

6.0

EXHIBIT 3
Graphic of the Workbrain Concept

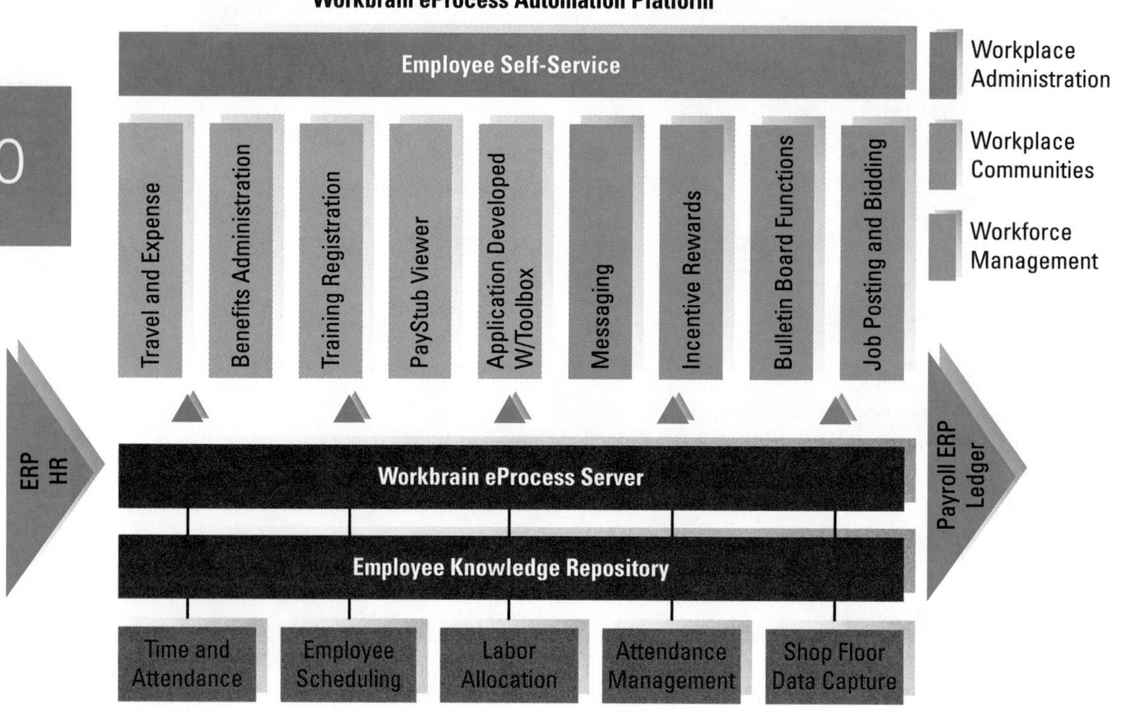

Source: Workbrain Corporation, 2000

in the form of additional modules). Another module might be incentive calculators, where an employee gets points based on things that are accomplished which can then be used to purchase things.

The vision is the end-to-end total solution. We want to own the "blue-collar desktop." It is completely web-based so it can be accessed from any web portal. They can log-on, check their time, do their schedule and at the same time they can use these other business objects that we have provided for them.

Our advantage is that our competitors only do one facet of the solution (i.e., the workflow automation or the workforce management) but they can't do the full end-to-end solution. We provide a very different view point because all we are trying to do is make it friendlier. We believe that in the long run, in order for companies to retain people, they have to make the workplace more friendly or less frustrating to do things. That is what we are selling. That is the vision. It is not just our time and attendance management expertise that gives us our advantage. Our comprehensive approach (we view ourselves as consultants), the thoroughness of our proposals, and the quality of our work is what sets us apart.

It was clear that Ossip placed a high level of importance on the recruitment of alliance partners. Exhibit 3 presents Workbrain's strategy for alliances. The product was seen as a "win-win-win" situation for the client, their employees and the partners since it brought everyone together in a virtual marketplace where job-shifts, benefits, processes, products and services were exchanged in one arena.

Along with cutting-edge technology, there were two other keys to success that Ossip recognized: alliances and people, both of which fell under Green's responsibility. Exhibit 4 presents the firm's strategies for ensuring that these keys were in place. Distribution and content were the two important components to their strategy that alliances gave Workbrain.

The Challenge

Workbrain was armed with what seemed like an industry-leading product, and highly skilled people to implement and service the systems and able salespeople to find clients. The key now was to develop an organization that would allow Ossip to bring his vision to reality and that job fell to Eric Green.

EXHIBIT 4
Workbrain's Alliance and Recruiting Strategy

6.0

Alliance Strategy

Workbrain recognizes that strategic alliances and partnerships are critical to the company's success, enabling the company to scale revenues quickly, leverage its resources and focus on software development. Accordingly, Workbrain will partner with best-in-class companies to establish and enhance its market position.

Partnership opportunities fall into four categories:

- *Sales and Marketing Partners*. Channel partners who will sell and co-market Workbrain solutions. The value to Workbrain would include expanded distribution and business scalability. As well, the value-added sales approach taken by some of these partners will position Workbrain as part of a broader business process redesign solution, potentially leading to higher prices and faster sales cycles. Value to partners would include a percentage of product sales and the ability to offer a broader set of solutions to clients. Such partners would include:
  - Systems consultants and management consultants with strong technology capabilities (e.g., PriceWaterhouseCoopers, Andersen Consulting, A.T. Kearney/EDS, Origin, Cambridge Technology Partners)
  - HR consultants with technology practices (e.g., Watson Wyatt, AON)
  - Enterprise software vendors (e.g., PeopleSoft, JD Edwards, SAP)
  - Application Service Providers (e.g., Corio, US Internetworking)
- *Implementation Partners*. Systems integrators and consultants who will lead and support the implementation of Workbrain solutions. As in the case of sales and marketing partnerships, implementation partners will help increase the scalability of Workbrain by not limiting the company's execution capacity. These partners will derive value by earning software configuration fees, systems integration fees, software development fees (e.g., designing additional modules to leverage the system's workflow infrastructure), and training fees. It is expected that in most cases, these partners will also have sold the Workbrain solution to the client. This group would, therefore, include the systems integration firms and the ASPs outlined above.
- *Solution Partners*. Hardware and software vendors whose products will be bundled with Workbrain to offer a more complete solution to clients. The benefits to Workbrain would include an enhanced value proposition and expanded solution portfolio, as well as a co-marketing channel. Solution Partners would derive value through hardware and software sales, as well as new and/or strengthened customer relationships. This group would include:
  - OEMs, including makers of PCs and servers (e.g., Dell, Compaq), Internet appliances (e.g., Netpliance), wireless devices (e.g., Palm, Research in Motion), and data capture devices (e.g., Synel Industries)
  - Enterprise software vendors (e.g., PeopleSoft, JD Edwards, SAP)
  - E-business software vendors and service providers (e.g., Ariba, Icarian, Healtheon/WebMD, RewardsPlus)
- *Commerce Partners*. Providers of goods and services who will enhance the value of the workplace community aspect of the Workbrain solution. These partnerships are fundamental to Workbrain to execute its vision to be the gateway for hourly employees to the outside world. By providing the 'sticky' content for hourly workers (e.g., payment and schedule information), Workbrain can build a large user base that would be attractive to other companies seeking to acquire customers. Transaction fees would be shared between the client, Workbrain, and the Commerce Partner. This group of partners would include:
  - Incentive management administrators (e.g., Maritz)
  - B2E aggregators (e.g., Perksatwork.com, employeesavings.com)
  - B2C vendors (e.g., Expedia.com, Citibank, E-trade, Paymybills.com, Amazon.com)

(Continued)

6.0

Workbrain is currently developing training and alliance programs to ensure that partners work effectively with Workbrain in executing all aspects of its strategy.

Rapid market penetration is key to Workbrain's long-term success. Although it is anticipated that in the longer term, the majority of software sales will be derived from channel partners, Workbrain is committed to building a strong direct sales force that will build market presence and complement our Sales and Marketing Partners.

Human Resources Strategy

Workbrain management recognizes that in today's competitive labor market, the ability to attract, develop, retain and inspire exceptional people is the single most important key success factor in building a great company. Workbrain's growth philosophy, therefore, focuses on excellence in recruiting, workplace environment and compensation policies.

- *Recruiting*. Workbrain is growing rapidly in Toronto and Atlanta by aggressively recruiting both experienced industry professionals and new graduates. Workbrain is looking primarily for results-oriented employees who understand the implementation needs of complex projects. Accordingly, the company's recruiting resources are focused on attracting experienced project managers from the industry segments that Workbrain serves. Workbrain management is leveraging their industry relationships to identify, recruit and train these sales and technology leaders with strong client contacts. Undergraduate, MBA, and IT recruiting is being conducted in conjunction with innovative human resources firms. Incentive compensation for *all* Workbrain employees recognizes their contribution to the firm's recruiting strategy.
- *Workplace Environment*. Workbrain management is intensely focused on creating an inspiring place to work, where risk-taking, results, creativity, and fun are all valued and rewarded. Responsibility is distributed to allow employees to make a real impact and to create uniquely stretching jobs. Cutting-edge productivity technologies and workplace amenities (including on-site health club memberships), flexible work hours, a relaxed workplace, and a genuine respect for work/life balance are all part of Workbrain's work environment.
- *Compensation*. All Workbrain employees receive highly competitive cash and equity-based compensation and best-in-class benefits, including health and dental insurance, continuing education, and a broad variety of employee perquisites.

Source: Workbrain Corporation, 2000

One of the first things I did was to put together an organizational chart that described who did what. It only had about five boxes. I tried to get an idea of all the internal activities that went on in the company such as legal, accounting, operations, technology, and who owned what. There seemed to be no real definition of roles. It seemed as though everyone was just working on this RFP and everything was directed towards a client focus at that point.

David didn't necessarily think in terms of organizational structure. I don't think that was really his interest. I think he was very much product-driven. He really loved the technology. He loved playing around with the coding. I guess I was the one who was supposed to be focusing on the internal growth and managing that growth.

One of the major things I did was really push the recruiting forward. More than once I was referred to as the "fluffy" guy; it became a bit of a joke where people would say that if it was not selling or coding, then it was fluffy. For example, on my first day they were interviewing a candidate for the position of Director of Human Relations. I met with him and we really didn't click. At the end of the day we met to discuss whether we should make him an offer. Everyone was very nonchalant about it and David liked him because he saw an immediate need to hire someone for the HR position—which is a credit to David because a lot of entrepreneurs just don't think HR is important. I didn't want to talk out of turn but I really didn't feel he was right for the job for a few reasons. I left that day afraid that I had insulted some people, but we couldn't afford to make hiring mistakes, especially at that stage in the company's life. On the one hand there was a sense of urgency that we needed to fill roles and get people doing things, but if we made mistakes, it would have been a lot harder to correct them.

One of the things that seemed to be like a black hole was the whole selling process because David Stein, VP Sales, was used to doing almost everything. He is technical. He's a great salesman. He's very smart. He can do the documentation. He can do everything. He felt that all he needed to do was hire people like himself, but people like him were impossible to find. He had a very unique skill set. I put together charts and documents to visually communicate what it was that I wanted to get across. It helped David Stein separate some of the issues that he may have been co-mingling. I wanted him to create an organizational structure to allow him to understand the type of people he needed to hire and what skills they needed to possess. It put some clarity around what his organization needed to look like.

I was stressing recruiting, but it was really more strategic thinking. I was getting them (the senior managers) to realize that there were a lot of complementary skill sets out there. They didn't have to find every skill resident in one person. I think that since these guys worked in small companies where a few people did a lot of different things, especially in an industry where a person's experience is very industry-related, some people had to take a leap of faith that we could hire someone with general skills rather than industry-specific knowledge.

Another thing that was a bit concerning was that compensation seemed to be somewhat ad hoc. Salary levels and difficult compensation packages that included options were not really well thought out. I had to determine how much a VP or an analyst should be paid. I felt that we couldn't hire anyone until we really understood or knew what we were going to offer them in compensation.

Another important task was to develop job descriptions. We had to ask a lot of questions. What would this person be doing? What skills were we looking for and where could we find them? We needed to build processes to answer these questions. To do this we needed to start from the job descriptions and really think about what needed to get done and what each department was responsible for and who was going to do what.

There was one watershed moment where it seemed to me that it all became clear to everyone. I had been under the assumption that everyone had been working with the same vision and the same growth plan, that to me was represented by the business plan that was put together before I was hired. To me, the business plan was the company. What I later learned was that due to time constraints, some of the technical and implementation team had not been as involved in the planning process as they should have. There was some resentment that they had not been a part of it because some of them were founders of the firm. There was a disconnect about where they thought the company was going that had manifested itself in the way they were thinking about hiring.

At a meeting of the senior managers, which David Ossip could not attend, the department heads were discussing projects on the horizon, the expected value, and how many people they felt were needed for each project. I felt that we needed to hire about ten implementation people. They came out with numbers like 2.3 people for a project. I felt this was wrong and that it indicated that there was an assumption that we would grow using internally generated cash—I felt that we needed to get big fast. I suggested that the business would come but we needed to build up the infrastructure, which to me was the people.

6.0

There was definitely a lot of cynicism from the guys who came from a different environment who were not in this new economy, dot.com kind of thinking. To them it seemed ridiculous to hire people with nothing to do right now. I thought we had a lot to do. There was a lot of infrastructure to be developed for every group. All the materials and processes had to be developed because we were starting from scratch. We needed to get up to speed before we could take on another project and to me that seemed like a lot of work. People needed to be convinced that there was work to do that was not immediately realizing value or revenue.

At the conclusion of that meeting I think a lot of us were quite frustrated and I realized that a lot of those guys had never even seen the business plan. They weren't really quite sure what the vision was.

When David came back he saw that I was really frustrated. He called everyone into a meeting and walked everyone through the vision as he saw it and how the company should grow. This wasn't going to be a company that would grow using internally generated cash; we needed to build quickly. This is what we were promising investors. We were supposed to be 170 people by September 2001 and we had clear revenue targets. We couldn't do that by building incrementally. When David heard about the 2.3 people thing, he reiterated that we should not be thinking that way. We needed to get everyone on the same page and he said specifically that I was here to do that. Because I came from a big company, I thought like a big company and that's what we needed to be and, although I was pulling people in a different direction, that was the way we had to go.

That stands out in my mind as a real turning point in the company. It's not as if it changed overnight, but that started the sequence of events that started to get everyone on the same page. What was encouraging the whole time was that David had taken the step to hire someone like me in the first place because his last company didn't have anyone like me. To me that meant that as tough as this stuff might be to sell internally to get people thinking a certain way, I had his buy in.

It wasn't my vision. These guys had it before I got here. It disappeared for a little while under the bulk of the work that we had. I think that for the guys that came from the previous company it was a bit of a mind shift on a couple of fronts. On the product front, they had to stop thinking only in terms of time and attendance functionality and think more broadly, remembering that this was just one process within the system, and what we were building was a platform for all sorts of processes. Secondly, they had to stop thinking in terms of incremental growth and think more big bang. We were going to be up to 60 people after only eight months in business; that meant that we needed to think big. We needed big company processes. We needed to hire people dedicated to hiring and we needed to act like a big company. We needed to develop our infrastructure to support what we thought we were going to be. The people who came from the last company just had to get their heads around it.

In its first months of existence, Workbrain was on pace to exceed its revenue goals. However, the firm still needed to develop the crucial partnerships and client relationships that were required to secure investors in its next round of funding. With this success came more challenges in maintaining the vision, cementing and creating new processes and mental models within the firm. As divisions grew, the roles of the managers would have to be altered and new divisions would need to be created. As the firm grew, how could the culture Ossip espoused be maintained? The firm was staffed with and pursued highly talented, and thus much sought-after, people. How could they be retained? The task of answering these questions lay on the shoulders of Eric Green.

References

Chapter 1

1. Much of the description of Air Canada comes from CBC News Indepth: Air Canada at http://www.cbc.ca/news/background/aircanada/index.html and much of the information on WestJet comes from http://www.flightnetwork.com/airlines/westjet (both accessed May 30, 2008) as well as from each airline's website.
2. "WestJet's CEO Named One of Canada's Most Respected (January 2005) at http://findarticles.com/p/articles/mi_hb5559/is_200501/ai_n23470045 (accessed July 15, 2008).
3. C. Sorenson, "WestJet Apologizes to Air Canada for Snooping," *Financial Post* (May 30, 2006) at http://www.canada.com/nationalpost/financialpost/story.html?id=6ca8461a-fb61-4bcc-be49-002f092c337f&k=61096 (accessed May 30, 2008).
4. Transcript: Robert Milton, Chairman & CEO, ACE Aviation at edition.cnn.com/2006/BUSINESS/10/06/boardroom.milton (accessed May 30, 2008).
5. G. Pitts, "Ganong Finds Its Profits Are Not as Sweet," *The Globe and Mail* (March 23, 2007), B3.
6. Harry G. Barkema, Joel A. C. Baum, and Elizabeth A. Mannix, "Management Challenges in a New Time," *Academy of Management Journal* 45, no. 5 (2002), 916–930; Eileen Davis, "What's on American Managers' Minds?" *Management Review* (April 1995), 14–20.
7. Barkema et al., "Management Challenges."
8. Keith H. Hammonds, "Smart, Determined, Ambitious, Cheap: The New Face of Global Competition," *Fast Company* (February 2003), 91–97; William J. Holstein, "Samsung's Golden Touch," *Fortune* (April 1, 2002), 89–94; Pete Engardio, Aaron Bernstein, and Manjeet Kripalani, "Is Your Job Next?" *BusinessWeek* (February 3, 2003), 50–60.
9. Andy Serwer, "Inside the Rolling Stones Inc.," *Fortune* (September 30, 2002), 58–72; and William J. Holstein, "Innovation, Leadership, and Still No Satisfaction," *The New York Times* (December 19, 2004), Section 3, 11.
10. Rebecca Smith and Jonathan Weil, "Ex-Enron Directors Reach Settlement," *The Wall Street Journal* (January 10, 2005), C3; Kara Scannell and Jonathan Weil, "Supreme Court to Hear Andersen's Appeal of Conviction," *The Wall Street Journal* (January 10, 2005), C1; "ImClone to Pay $75 Million to Settle 2002 Suit," *The New York Times* (January 25, 2005), C3; Joann S. Lublin, "Travel Expenses Prompt Yale to Force Out Institute Chief," *The Wall Street Journal* (January 10, 2005), B1.
11. David Wessel, "Venal Sins: Why the Bad Guys of the Boardroom Emerged en Masse," *The Wall Street Journal* (June 20, 2002), A1, A6.
12. Bernard Wysocki Jr., "Corporate Caveat: Dell or Be Delled," *The Wall Street Journal* (May 10, 1999), A1.
13. Andy Reinhardt, "From Gearhead to Grand High Pooh-Bah," *BusinessWeek* (August 28, 2000), 129–130.
14. G. Pascal Zachary, "Mighty Is the Mongrel," (June 2000) at http://www.fastcompany.com/magazine/36/mongrel.html (accessed June 28, 2008).
15. Canadian Heritage, "Annual Report on the Operation of the *Canadian Multiculturalism Act*, 2005–2006," (2007) at http://www.multiculturalism.pch.gc.ca (accessed May 30, 2008).
16. Capitalizing on Canada's Diversity Is Key to Nation's Future Prosperity, *RBC Financial Group Special Reports*, at http://www.rbc.com/newstoom/20051020diversity.html (accessed April 1, 2007).
17. Debra E. Meyerson and Joyce K. Fletcher, "A Modest Manifesto for Shattering the Glass Ceiling," *Harvard Business Review* (January–February 2000), 127–136; Annie Finnigan, "Different Strokes," *Working Woman* (April 2001), 42–48; Joline Godfrey, "Been There, Doing That," *Inc.* (March 1996), 21–22; Paula Dwyer, Marsha Johnston, and Karen Lowry Miller, "Out of the Typing Pool, into Career Limbo," *BusinessWeek* (April 15, 1996), 92–94.
18. Howard Aldrich, *Organizations and Environments* (Englewood Cliffs, N.J.: Prentice-Hall, 1979), 3.
19. This section is based largely on Peter F. Drucker, *Managing the Non-Profit Organization: Principles and Practices* (New York: HarperBusiness, 1992); and Thomas Wolf, *Managing a Nonprofit Organization* (New York: Fireside/Simon & Schuster, 1990).
20. Christine W. Letts, William Ryan, and Allen Grossman, *High Performance Nonprofit Organizations* (New York: John Wiley & Sons, 1999), 30–35.

21. J. Foley, "Joining of Big Brothers & Big Sisters Organizations Signals Trend Towards Alliances" (2001) at http://www.charityvillage.com/cv/archive/acov/acov01/acov0145.hmtl (accessed April 8, 2007).
22. Robert N. Stern and Stephen R. Barley, "Organizations and Social Systems: Organization Theory's Neglected Mandate," *Administrative Science Quarterly* 41 (1996): 146–162.
23. Brent Schlender, "The New Soul of a Wealth Machine," *Fortune* (April 5, 2004), 102–110.
24. Schlender, "The New Soul of a Wealth Machine," and Keith H. Hammonds, "Growth Search," *Fast Company* (April 2003), 75–80.
25. James D. Thompson, *Organizations in Action* (New York: McGraw-Hill, 1967), 4–13.
26. Henry Mintzberg, *The Structuring of Organizations* (Englewood Cliffs, N.J.: Prentice-Hall, 1979), 215–297; and Henry Mintzberg, "Organization Design: Fashion or Fit?" *Harvard Business Review* 59 (January–February 1981), 103–116.
27. The following discussion was heavily influenced by Richard H. Hall, *Organizations: Structures, Processes, and Outcomes* (Englewood Cliffs, N.J.: Prentice-Hall, 1991); D. S. Pugh, "The Measurement of Organization Structures: Does Context Determine Form?" *Organizational Dynamics* 1 (Spring 1973), 19–34; and D. S. Pugh, D. J. Hickson, C. R. Hinings, and C. Turner, "Dimensions of Organization Structure," *Administrative Science Quarterly* 13 (1968), 65–91.
28. Both quotes from http://www.ellisdon.com/ed/about (accessed April 8, 2007).
29. http://www.mocca.toronto.on.ca and personal communication.
30. T. Donaldson and L. E. Preston, "The Stakeholder Theory of the Corporation: Concepts, Evidence, and Implications," *Academy of Management Review* 20 (1995), 65–91; Anne S. Tusi, "A Multiple-Constituency Model of Effectiveness: An Empirical Examination at the Human Resource Subunit Level," *Administrative Science Quarterly* 35 (1990), 458–483; Charles Fombrun and Mark Shanley, "What's in a Name? Reputation Building and Corporate Strategy," *Academy of Management Journal* 33 (1990), 233–258; Terry Connolly, Edward J. Conlon, and Stuart Jay Deutsch, "Organizational Effectiveness: A Multiple-Constituency Approach," *Academy of Management Review* 5 (1980), 211–217.
31. Charles Fishman, "The Wal-Mart You Don't Know—Why Low Prices Have a High Cost," *Fast Company* (December 2003), 68–80.
32. Connolly, Conlon, and Deusch, "Organizational Effectiveness: A Multiple-Constituency Approach."
33. Fombrun and Shanley, "What's in a Name?"
34. Information from http://www.mackenziegasproject.com/theProject; Article 13—CSR best practice cases studies—Mackenzie Valley Pipeline, http://www.article13.com/A13_ContentList.asp?strAction+GetPublication&PNID=1162 and K. Hoggan (2003) Mackenzie Valley Gas Controversy May Put $5 Billion Project on Hold, *Aboriginal Times* at http://www.aboriginaltimes.com/economic-development/oil%20pipeline/view (accessed April 9, 2007).
35. Ibid.
36. Joint Review Panel Hearing Phase Concludes, *The MGP Exchange*, 14, 1, February 2008.
37. Ann Harrington, "The Big Ideas," *Fortune* (November 22, 1999), 152–154; Robert Kanigel, *The One Best Way: Frederick Winslow Taylor and the Enigma of Efficiency* (New York: Viking, 1997); and Alan Farnham, "The Man Who Changed Work Forever," *Fortune* (July 21, 1997), 114. For a discussion of the impact of scientific management on American industry, government, and nonprofit organizations, also see Mauro F. Guillén, "Scientific Management's Lost Aesthetic: Architecture, Organization, and the Taylorized Beauty of the Mechanical," *Administrative Science Quarterly* 42 (1997), 682–715.
38. Amanda Bennett, *The Death of the Organization Man* (New York: William Morrow, 1990).
39. Johannes M. Pennings, "Structural Contingency Theory: A Reappraisal," *Research in Organizational Behavior* 14 (1992), 267–309.
40. This discussion is based in part on Toby J. Tetenbaum, "Shifting Paradigms: From Newton to Chaos," *Organizational Dynamics* (Spring 1998), 21–32.
41. William Bergquist, *The Postmodern Organization* (San Francisco: Jossey-Bass, 1993).
42. Based on Tetenbaum, "Shifting Paradigms: From Newton to Chaos," and Richard T. Pascale, "Surfing the Edge of Chaos," *Sloan Management Review* (Spring 1999), 83–94.
43. C. White, *Seismic Shifts—Leading in Times of Change* (Toronto: United Church Publishing House, 2006) 3.
44. Information from http://www.kairos.org and http://www.united-church.ca.
45. Organizational Chart of the United Church of Canada, (January 2007) at http://www.united-church.ca.
46. Polly LaBarre, "This Organization Is Disorganization," *Fast Company* (June–July 1996), 77–81.
47. "Conversations on Work and Well-Being—Response-Ability and Power to Please—Delta Hotels," at http://www.vifamily.ca.
48. David K. Hurst, *Crisis and Renewal: Meeting the Challenge of Organizational Change* (Boston, Mass.: Harvard Business School Press, 1995), 32–52.
49. Information from http://www.magna.com.
50. Information from http://archives.cbc.ca/300c.asp??id=1-69-377 and J.P. Sheppard and S.D. Chowdhury, "Riding the Wrong Wave: Organizational Failure as a Failed Turnaround," *Long Range Planning*, 38 (2005), 250.
51. Information from http://www.bostonpizza.com/?q=bostonpizza_aboutus_history (accessed May 30, 2008).
52. Thomas Petzinger, *The New Pioneers: The Men and Women Who Are Transforming the Workplace and Marketplace* (New York: Simon & Schuster, 1999), 91–93; and "In

Search of the New World of Work," *Fast Company* (April 1999), 214–220; Peter Katel, "Bordering on Chaos," *Wired* (July 1997), 98–107; Oren Harari, "The Concrete Intangibles," *Management Review* (May 1999), 30–33; and "Mexican Cement Maker on Verge of a Deal," *The New York Times* (September 27, 2004), A8

53. Robert House, Denise M. Rousseau, and Melissa Thomas-Hunt, "The Meso Paradigm: A Framework for the Integration of Micro and Macro Organizational Behavior," *Research in Organizational Behavior* 17 (1995): 71–114.

Chapter 2

1. "Double, Double? Now You Can Look It Up" (July 5, 2004) at http://www.cbc.ca/arts/story/2004/06/30/doubledouble040630.html (accessed June 1, 2008).
2. As of this writing, there are more than 2,723 stores across Canada, and over 339 locations in the United States.
3. "Tim Hortons Touches Down in Kandahar (June 12, 2006) at http://www.cbc.ca/world/story/2006/06/12/tim-hortons-kandahar.html (accessed June 1, 2008).
4. "Media Kit" (2008) at http://www.timhortons.com/en/about/media_kit.html (accessed June 3, 2008).
5. "Canadian Donut War: Krispy Kreme vs. Tim Hortons," July 13, 2002, News and Media Center, NACS Online.
6. "Tim Hortons Raises C$783 Million in Initial Offering" (March 23, 2006) at http://quote.bloomberg.com/apps/news?pid=10000103&sid=aVbau_WUTixk&refer=news_index (accessed June 3, 2008).
7. John Grey, "Staying Power: Strong Brands" *Canadian Business* (November 6–19, 2006) at http://www.canadianbusiness.com/managing/strategy/article.jsp?content=20061106_82398_82398 (accessed June 3, 2008).
8. CNW Group, "Canada's Top Performing Brands Valued by Interbrand" at http://www.newswire.ca/en/releases/archive/July2006/24/c8737.html (accessed June 3, 2008).
9. "Timmies: An Iconic Canadian Brand" (2005) http://www.wendys-invest.com/fin/annual/2005/wen05ar_th.pdf (accessed June 3, 2008).
10. Amitai Etzioni, *Modern Organizations* (Englewood Cliffs, N.J.: Prentice-Hall, 1964), 6.
11. John P. Kotter, "What Effective General Managers Really Do," *Harvard Business Review* (November–December 1982), 156–167; Henry Mintzberg, *The Nature of Managerial Work* (New York: Harper & Row, 1973).
12. Building on Strength: Improving Governance and Accountability in Canada's Voluntary Sector. Panel on Accountability and Governance in the Voluntary Sector. Final Report, February 1999, at http://www.voluntary-sector.ca/eng/publications/1999/building_strength.pdf (accessed June 3, 2008).
13. Charles C. Snow and Lawrence G. Hrebiniak, "Strategy, Distinctive Competence, and Organizational Performance," *Administrative Science Quarterly* 25 (1980), 317–335.
14. Amy Barrett, "Staying on Top," *BusinessWeek* (May 5, 2003), 60–68.
15. T. Ready, "Can CEOs Cure Cancer?" Fast Company Issue 117 (July 2007), 35.
16. Forest R. David and Fred R. David, "It's Time to Redraft Your Mission Statement," *Journal of Business Strategy* (January–February 2003), 11–14; John Pearce and Fred David, "Corporate Mission Statements: The Bottom Line," *Academy of Management Executive* 1, no. 2 (May 1987), 109–116; and Christopher Bart and Mark Baetz, "The Relationship Between Mission Statements and Firm Performance: An Exploratory Study," *Journal of Management Studies* 35 (1998).
17. Barbara Bartkus, Myron Glassman, and R. Bruce McAfee, "Mission Statements: Are They Smoke and Mirrors?" *Business Horizons* (November–December 2000), 23–28.
18. Mark C. Suchman, "Managing Legitimacy: Strategic and Institutional Approaches," *Academy of Management Review* 20, no. 3 (1995), 571–610.
19. Kurt Eichenwald, "Miscues, Missteps, and the Fall of Andersen," *The New York Times* (May 8, 2002), C1, C4; Ian Wilson, "The Agenda for Redefining Corporate Purpose: Five Key Executive Actions," *Strategy & Leadership* 32, no. 1 (2004), 21–26.
20. Bill George, "The Company's Mission is the Message," *Strategy & Business*, Issue 33 (Winter 2003), 13–14; Jim Collins and Jerry Porras, *Built to Last: Successful Habits of Visionary Companies* (New York: HarperBusiness, 1994).
21. Charles Perrow, "The Analysis of Goals in Complex Organizations," *American Sociological Review* 26 (1961), 854–866.
22. Johannes U. Stoelwinder and Martin P. Charns, "The Task Field Model of Organization Analysis and Design," *Human Relations* 34 (1981), 743–762; Anthony Raia, *Managing by Objectives* (Glenview, Ill.: Scott, Foresman, 1974).
23. "Update 1—Audi vehicle sales hit record," Reuters (July 5, 2007) at http://www.reuters.com/article/tnBasicIndustries-SP/idUSL0519702220070705 (accessed June 3, 2008); "Audi Bids to be Market Leader," (August 3, 2007), *Business Monitor International*, Document ENDN000020070804e3830000h.
24. Government of British Columbia, "September Update, Budget 2005" at http://www.bcbudget.gov.bc.ca/2005_Sept_Update/sp/cfd/Goals,Objectives,StrategiesandResults6.htm (accessed June 3, 2008).
25. Service Measurement Framework Report, submitted to Treasury Board of Canada, Secretariat, (March 1, 2005) at http://www.tbs-sct.gc.ca/si-as/initiative/2004/smfr-rcms/smfr-rcms00-eng.asp (accessed July 3, 2008).
26. "United Way Reaches Record-Breaking Heights" (January 17, 2008) at http://www.uwgt.org/media/mediareleases/2008/pr_20080117.php (accessed July 3, 2008).
27. Alex Taylor III, "Honda Goes Its Own Way," Fortune (July 22, 2002), 148–152; Joseph Pereira and Christopher J. Chipello, "Battle of the Block Makers," The Wall Street Journal (February 4, 2004), B1.

28. "50 Best Employers in Canada," The Globe and Mail, December 20, 2005, at http://www.theglobeandmail.com/servlet/story/RTGAM.20051220.rm50best1223/BNStory/specialROBmagazine (accessed June 3, 2008).
29. Michael Arndt, "3M: A Lab for Growth?" BusinessWeek (January 21, 2002), 50–51.
30. Kim Cross, "Does Your Team Measure Up?" *Business2.com* (June 12, 2001), 22–28; J. Lynn Lunsford, "Lean Times: With Airbus on Its Tail, Boeing is Rethinking How It Builds Planes," The Wall Street Journal (September 5, 2001), A11.
31. Wiedmann, T. and M. Lenzen (2006) Triple-Bottom-Line Accounting of Social, Economic and Environmental Indicators—A New Life-Cycle Software Tool for UK Businesses, Third Annual International Sustainable Development Conference,15–16 November 2006, Perth, Scotland.
32. P.T. Lee and N. Krause, "The Impact of a Worker Health Study on Working Conditions," Journal of Public Health Policy, 23, 3 (2002), 268–285.
33. Unite Here, "Our History" (2006) at http://www.unitehere.org/about/history.php (accessed June 3, 2008).
34. Andrea C. Poe, "Keeping Hotel Workers: It Takes More Than Money to Retain Lower-Paid Employees—Employment & Staffing Agenda" *HR Magazine* (February 2003).
35. Ibid.
36. Alex Markels, "Dishing It Out in Style," U.S. News and World Report (April 15, 2007).
37. The Honourable Dennis R. O'Connor, Report of the Walkerton Inquiry: The Events of May 2000 and Related Issues Ontario. Part One: A Summary. Ministry of the Attorney General, Queen's Printer for Ontario 2002.
38. James D. Thompson, Organizations in Action (New York: McGraw-Hill, 1967), 83–98.
39. Michael E. Porter, "What Is Strategy?" Harvard Business Review (November–December 1996), 61–78.
40. Michael E. Porter, Competitive Strategy: Techniques for Analyzing Industries and Competitors (New York: Free Press, 1980).
41. Zena Olijnyk, "Beat China on Quality: Cervélo Bets on Premium Design to Win," Canadian Business (November 7–20, 2005).
42. http://c5dsp.westjet.com/guest/media/investorMedia.jsp;jsessionid=1c28Lp9LjT44ZTk4XqtCqn93nYVBSDrXKvpJdD5y8JQj5k2D1KJS!280111429?id=Facts# (accessed June 30, 2008) and Williams, N. (2005) Why it's (still) good to be WestJet, Strategy Magazine, November at http://www.strategymag.com/articles/magazine/20051101/westjet.html (accessed June 30, 2008).
43. Richard Teitelbaum, "The Wal-Mart of Wall Street," *Fortune* (October 13, 1997), 128–130.
44. Kevin J. O'Brien, "Focusing on Armchair Athletes, Puma Becomes a Leader," *The New York Times* (March 12, 2004), W1.
45. Michael E. Porter, "Strategy and the Internet," *Harvard Business Review* (March 2001), 63–78; and John Magretta, "Why Business Models Matter," *Harvard Business Review* (May 2002), 86.
46. Raymond E. Miles and Charles C. Snow, *Organizational Strategy, Structure, and Process* (New York: McGraw-Hill, 1978).
47. "Miles and Snow: Enduring Insights for Managers: Academic Commentary by Sumantra Ghoshal," *Academy of Management Executive* 17, no. 4 (2003), 109–114.
48. Pallavi Gogoi and Michael Arndt, "Hamburger Hell," *BusinessWeek* (March 3, 2003), 104–108; and Michael Arndt, "McDonald's: Fries with That Salad?" *BusinessWeek* (July 5, 2004), 82–84.
49. "On the Staying Power of Defenders, Analyzers, and Prospectors: Academic Commentary by Donald C. Hambrick," *Academy of Management Executive* 17, no. 4 (2003), 115–118.
50. Etzioni, *Modern Organizations*, 8.
51. Etzioni, *Modern Organizations*, 8; and Gary D. Sandefur, "Efficiency in Social Service Organizations," *Administration and Society* 14 (1983), 449–468.
52. Richard M. Steers, *Organizational Effectiveness: A Behavioral View* (Santa Monica, Calif.: Goodyear, 1977), 51.
53. Karl E. Weick and Richard L. Daft, "The Effectiveness of Interpretation Systems," in Kim S. Cameron and David A. Whetten, eds., *Organizational Effectiveness: A Comparison of Multiple Models* (New York: Academic Press, 1982).
54. David L. Blenkhorn and Brian Gaber, "The Use of 'Warm Fuzzies' to Assess Organizational Effectiveness," *Journal of General Management*, 21, no. 2 (Winter 1995), 40–51.
55. Steven Strasser, J. D. Eveland, Gaylord Cummins, O. Lynn Deniston, and John H. Romani, "Conceptualizing the Goal and Systems Models of Organizational Effectiveness—Implications for Comparative Evaluation Research," *Journal of Management Studies* 18 (1981), 321–340.
56. The discussion of the resource-based approach is based in part on Michael V. Russo and Paul A. Fouts, "A Resource-Based Perspective on Corporate Environmental Performance and Profitability," *Academy of Management Journal* 40, no. 3 (June 1997), 534–559; and Jay B. Barney, J. L. "Larry" Stempert, Loren T. Gustafson, and Yolanda Sarason, "Organizational Identity within the Strategic Management Conversation: Contributions and Assumptions," in *Identity in Organizations: Building Theory through Conversations*, David A. Whetten and Paul C. Godfrey, eds. (Thousand Oaks, Calif.: Sage Publications, 1998), 83–98.
57. Lucy Mccauley, "Unit of One: Measure What Matters," *Fast Company* (May 1999), 97.
58. Richard I. Priem, "Is the Resource-Based 'View' a Useful Perspective for Strategic Management Research?" *Academy of Management Review* 26, no. 1 (2001), 22–40.
59. Chris Argyris, *Integrating the Individual and the Organization* (New York: Wiley, 1964); Warren G. Bennis, *Changing Organizations* (New York: McGraw-Hill, 1966); Rensis Likert, *The Human Organization* (New York: McGraw-Hill, 1967); and Richard Beckhard, *Organization Development Strategies and Models* (Reading, Mass.: Addison-Wesley, 1969).

60. Cheri Ostroff and Neal Schmitt, "Configurations of Organizational Effectiveness and Efficiency," *Academy of Management Journal* 36 (1993), 1345–1361; Peter J. Frost, Larry F. Moore, Meryl Reise Louis, Craig C. Lundburg, and Joanne Martin, *Organizational Culture* (Beverly Hills, Calif.: Sage, 1985).
61. J. Barton Cunningham, "Approaches to the Evaluation of Organizational Effectiveness," *Academy of Management Review* 2 (1977), 463–474; Beckhard, *Organization Development.*
62. "Living on the Edge at American Apparel," at http://www.businessweek.com/magazine/content/05_26/b3939108_mz017.htm?chan=search (accessed June 30, 2008).
63. Stanley Holmes, "A New Black Eye for Boeing?" *BusinessWeek* (April 26, 2004), 90–92; Robert Levering and Milton Moskowitz, "The 100 Best Companies to Work For," *Fortune* (January 24, 2005), 72–90.
64. James L. Price, "The Study of Organizational Effectiveness," Sociological Quarterly 13 (1972), 3–15.
65. "Ridership Growth Strategy" (March 2003) at http://www.toronto.ca/ttc/textonly/textonly%20-%20ridership%20growth%20strategy.htm (accessed June 3, 2008).
66. Ibid.
67. "City Council Builds a Cleaner, Greener and More Transit-friendly Toronto with an Approved Five-Year Capital Plan" (March 7, 2007) at http://wx.toronto.ca/inter/it/newsrel.nsf/9da959222128b9e885256618006646d3/340c0d4612969fe485257297007f7b4c?OpenDocument (accessed June 3, 2008).
68. CBC News.ca "TTC Faces Driver Dilemma as Ridership Rockets" (January 8, 2007) at http://www.cbc.ca/canada/toronto/story/2007/01/08/ttc-ridership.html (accessed June 3, 2008).
69. Richard H. Hall and John P. Clark, "An Ineffective Effectiveness Study and Some Suggestions for Future Research," Sociological Quarterly 21 (1980), 119–134; Price, "The Study of Organizational Effectiveness"; and Perrow, "Analysis of Goals."
70. Diavik Diamond Mines, "Vision," at http://www.diavik.ca/vs.htm (accessed June 3, 2008).
71. GlobeAdvisor.com, "A Simple Loblaw Equation" (July 10, 2007) at https://secure.globeadvisor.com/servlet/ArticleNews/story/RTGAM/20070710/wrdecloet10 (accessed June 3, 2008).
72. Eric J. Walton and Sarah Dawson, "Managers' Perceptions of Criteria of Organizational Effectiveness," *Journal of Management Studies* 38, no. 2 (2001), 173–199.
73. Beth Dickey, "NASA's Next Step," *Government Executive* (April 15, 2004), 341.
74. Robert E. Quinn and John Rohrbaugh, "A Spatial Model of Effectiveness Criteria: Toward a Competing Values Approach to Organizational Analysis," *Management Science* 29 (1983), 363–377.
75. Regina M. O'Neill and Robert E. Quinn, "Editor's Note: Applications of the Competing Values Framework," *Human Resource Management* 32 (Spring 1993), 1–7.
76. Robert E. Quinn and Kim Cameron, "Organizational Life Cycles and Shifting Criteria of Effectiveness: Some Preliminary Evidence," *Management Science* 29 (1983), 33–51.

Chapter 3

1. Ontario Co-operative Association, "The Co-op Sector," at http://www.ontario.coop/pages/index.php?main_id=312 (accessed June 4, 2008).
2. Desjardins Group, "2007 Social Responsibility and Cooperative Report," at http://www.desjardins.com (accessed June 4, 2008).
3. Desjardins Group, "2007 Annual Report," http://www.desjardins.com (accessed June 4, 2008).
4. Daniel J. Wakin, "Following a Shifting Flock: As Some Churches Falter and Others Grow, Catholic Church Plans Overhaul," (October 26, 2003) at http://query.nytimes.com/gst/fullpage.html?res=9c00e2dd1031f935a15753c1a9659c8b63&sec=&spon=&pagewanted=print *The New York Times* (accessed July 4, 2008).
5. John Child, *Organization* (New York: Harper & Row, 1984).
6. Stuart Ranson, Bob Hinings, and Royston Greenwood, "The Structuring of Organizational Structures," *Administrative Science Quarterly* 25 (1980), 1–17; and Hugh Willmott, "The Structuring of Organizational Structure: A Note," *Administrative Science Quarterly* 26 (1981), 470–474.
7. This section is based on Frank Ostroff, *The Horizontal Organization: What the Organization of the Future Looks Like and How It Delivers Value to Customers* (New York: Oxford University Press, 1999).
8. David Nadler and Michael Tushman, *Strategic Organization Design* (Glenview, Ill.: Scott Foresman, 1988).
9. William C. Ouchi, "The Implementation of a Decentralized Organization Design in Three Large Public School Districts: Edmonton, Seattle, and Houston" (unpublished manuscript, Anderson School of Management, University of California–Los Angeles, 2004).
10. "Country Managers: From Baron to Hotelier," *The Economist* (May 11, 2002), 55–56.
11. Based on Jay R. Galbraith, *Designing Complex Organizations* (Reading, Mass.: Addison-Wesley, 1973), and *Organization Design* (Reading, Mass.: Addison-Wesley, 1977), 81–127.
12. Rochelle Garner and Barbara Darrow, "Oracle Plots Course," *CRN* (January 24, 2005), 3; and Anthony Hilton, "Dangers behind Oracle's Dream," *Evening Standard* (February 11, 2005), 45.
13. Lee Iacocca with William Novak, *Iacocca: An Autobiography* (New York: Phantom Books, 1984), 152–153.
14. Based on Galbraith, *Designing Complex Organizations.*
15. "Mandate 2003: Be Agile and Efficient," *Microsoft Executive Circle* (Spring 2003), 46–48.
16. Jay Galbraith, Diane Downey, and Amy Kates, "How Networks Undergird the Lateral Capability of

an Organization—Where the Work Gets Done," *Journal of Organizational Excellence* (Spring 2002), 67–78.

17. Amy Barrett, "Staying on Top," *BusinessWeek* (May 5, 2003), 60–68.
18. Walter Kiechel III, "The Art of the Corporate Task Force," *Fortune* (January 28, 1991), 104–105; and William J. Altier, "Task Forces: An Effective Management Tool," *Management Review* (February 1987), 52–57.
19. Neal E. Boudette, "Marriage Counseling; At Daimler-Chrysler, A New Push to Make Its Units Work Together," *The Wall Street Journal* (March 12, 2003), A1, A15.
20. "Daimler A.G." at http://topics.nytimes.com/top/news/business/companies/daimler_ag/index.html (accessed June 30, 2008).
21. Keith Naughton and Kathleen Kerwin, "At GM, Two Heads May Be Worse Than One," *BusinessWeek* (August 14, 1995), 46.
22. Paul R. Lawrence and Jay W. Lorsch, "New Managerial Job: The Integrator," *Harvard Business Review* (November–December 1967), 142–151.
23. Imagination, "Our Company" (2007) at http://www.imagination.com/our_company (accessed June 4, 2008).
24. C. Fishman, Total Teamwork—Imagination Ltd., *Fast Company* 33 (2000), 156.
25. Charles Fishman, "Total Teamwork: Imagination Ltd.," *Fast Company* (April 2000), 156–168; Thomas L. Legare, "How Hewlett-Packard Used Virtual Cross-Functional Teams to Deliver Healthcare Industry Solutions," *Journal of Organizational Excellence* (Autumn 2001), 29–37.
26. "The Stalling of Motor City," *BusinessWeek* (November 1, 2004), 128.
27. "Ford Unveils a New Plug-in Hybrid" (December 3, 2007) at http://www.greenlivingonline.com/gettingaround/ford-unveils-a-new-plug-in-hybrid (accessed June 30, 2008).
28. S. Duffy, "Hybrid Car Global Sales Set to Explode to 7.8 Million Units By 2020" at http://www.hybridcar.com (accessed April 15, 2007).
29. Chuck Salter, "Ford's Escape Route," *Fast Company* (October 2004), 106–110; "Ford Escape Hybrid Named Best Truck on Detroit," *The Jakarta Post* (January 27, 2005), 18; and Bernard Simon, "Ford Aims To Build On Escape Hybrid's Success," *National Post* (January 26, 2005), FP–10.
30. Henry Mintzberg, *The Structuring of Organizations* (Englewood Cliffs, N.J.: Prentice-Hall, 1979).
31. Based on Robert Duncan, "What Is the Right Organization Structure?" *Organizational Dynamics* (Winter 1979), 59–80; and W. Alan Randolph and Gregory G. Dess, "The Congruence Perspective of Organization Design: A Conceptual Model and Multivariate Research Approach," *Academy of Management Review* 9 (1984), 114–127.
32. Rahul Jacob, "The Struggle to Create an Organization for the 21st Century," *Fortune* (April 3, 1995), 90–99.
33. Amy Barrett, "Staying On Top"; Joseph Weber, "A Big Company That Works," *BusinessWeek* (May 4, 1992), 124–132; and Elyse Tanouye, "Johnson & Johnson Stays Fit by Shuffling Its Mix of Businesses," *The Wall Street Journal* (December 22, 1992), A1, A4.
34. Robert A. Guth, "Midlife Correction; Inside Microsoft, Financial Managers Winning New Clout," *The Wall Street Journal* (July 23, 2003), A1, A6; and Michael Moeller, with Steve Hamm and Timothy J. Mullaney, "Remaking Microsoft," *BusinessWeek* (May 17, 1999), 106–114.
35. Based on Duncan, "What Is the Right Organization Structure?"
36. Weber, "A Big Company That Works."
37. Phred Dvorak and Merissa Marr, "Stung by iPod, Sony Addresses a Digital Lag," *The Wall Street Journal* (December 30, 2004), B1.
38. Maisie O'Flanagan and Lynn K. Taliento, "Nonprofits: Ensuring That Bigger Is Better," *McKinsey Quarterly*, Issue 2 (2004), 112ff.
39. "MSF Charter" at http://www.msf.ca/about/msf-charter (accessed June 30, 2008).
40. "What we do" at http://www.msf.ca/about/what-we-do (accessed June 30, 2008).
41. "40 Degrees in the Sudanese Shade," (October 30) at http://www.msf.ca/blogs/mikew.php (accessed June 4, 2008).
42. Stanley M. Davis and Paul R. Lawrence, *Matrix* (Reading, Mass.: Addison-Wesley, 1977), 11–24.
43. Erik W. Larson and David H. Gobeli, "Matrix Management: Contradictions and Insight," *California Management Review* 29 (Summer 1987), 126–138.
44. Davis and Lawrence, *Matrix*, 155–180.
45. Defence Research and Development Canada, "Delivering Science and Technology for Impact," at http://www.drdc-rddc.gc.ca/ststrategy/delivering1_e.asp (accessed June 4, 2008).
46. Robert C. Ford and W. Alan Randolph, "Cross-Functional Structures: A Review and Integration of Matrix Organizations and Project Management," *Journal of Management* 18 (June 1992), 267–294; and Duncan, "What Is the Right Organization Structure?".
47. Lawton R. Burns, "Matrix Management in Hospitals: Testing Theories of Matrix Structure and Development," *Administrative Science Quarterly* 34 (1989), 349–368.
48. Carol Hymowitz, "Managers Suddenly Have to Answer to a Crowd of Bosses" (In the Lead column), *The Wall Street Journal* (August 12, 2003), B1; and Michael Goold and Andrew Campbell, "Making Matrix Structures Work: Creating Clarity on Unit Roles and Responsibilities," *European Management Journal* 21, no. 3 (June 2003), 351–363.
49. Christopher A. Bartlett and Sumantra Ghoshal, "Matrix Management: Not a Structure, a Frame of Mind," *Harvard Business Review* (July–August 1990), 138–145.
50. This case was inspired by John E. Fogerty, "Integrative Management at Standard Steel" (unpublished manuscript, Latrobe, Pennsylvania, 1980); Stanley Reed with Adam Aston, "Steel: The Mergers Aren't Over Yet," *Business-Week* (February 21, 2005), 6; Michael Amdt, "Melting

Away Steel's Costs," *BusinessWeek* (November 8, 2004), 48; and "Steeling for a Fight," *The Economist* (June 4, 1994), 63.

51. Michael Hammer, "Process Management and the Future of Six Sigma," *Sloan Management Review* (Winter 2002), 26–32; and Michael Hammer and Steve Stanton, "How Process Enterprises *Really* Work," *Harvard Business Review* 77 (November–December 1999), 108–118.
52. Hammer, "Process Management and the Future of Six Sigma."
53. Based on Ostroff, *The Horizontal Organization*, and Richard L. Daft, *Organization Theory and Design*, 6th ed. (Cincinnati, Ohio: South-Western, 1998), 250–253.
54. Ann Armstrong, "Pay for Knowledge and Skill Systems: A Multilevel Exploratory Investigation," (1993) unpublished University of Toronto Ph.D. Dissertation, 201.
55. Melissa A. Schilling and H. Kevin Steensma, "The Use of Modular Organizational Forms: An Industry-Level Analysis," *Academy of Management Journal* 44, no. 6 (2001), 1149–1168; Jane C. Linder, "Transformational Outsourcing," *MIT Sloan Management Review* (Winter 2004), 52–58; and Denis Chamberland, "Is It Core or Strategic? Outsourcing as a Strategic Management Tool," *Ivey Business Journal* (July–August 2003), 1–5.
56. Denis Chamberland, "Is It Core or Strategic?"; Philip Siekman, "The Snap-Together Business Jet," *Fortune* (January 21, 2002), 104[A]–104[H]; Keith H. Hammonds, "Smart, Determined, Ambitious, Cheap: The New Face of Global Competition," *Fast Company* (February 2003), 91–97; Kathleen Kerwin, "GM: Modular Plants Won't Be a Snap," *BusinessWeek* (November 9, 1998), 168–172; and Giuseppe Bonazzi and Cristiano Antonelli, "To Make or To Sell? The Case of In-House Outsourcing at Fiat Auto," *Organization Studies* 24, no. 4 (2003), 575–594.
57. Schilling and Steensma, "The Use of Modular Organizational Forms"; Raymond E. Miles and Charles C. Snow, "The New Network Firm: A Spherical Structure Built on a Human Investment Philosophy," *Organizational Dynamics* (Spring 1995), 5–18; and R. E. Miles, C. C. Snow, J. A. Matthews, G. Miles, and H. J. Coleman Jr., "Organizing in the Knowledge Age: Anticipating the Cellular Form," *Academy of Management Executive* 11, no. 4 (1997), 7–24.
58. Paul Engle, "You *Can* Outsource Strategic Processes," *Industrial Management* (January–February 2002), 13–18.
59. Don Tapscott, "Rethinking Strategy in a Networked World," *Strategy & Business* 24 (Third Quarter, 2001), 34–41.
60. Miles and Snow, "The New Network Firm"; Gregory G. Dess, Abdul M. A. Rasheed, Kevin J. McLaughlin, and Richard L. Priem, "The New Corporate Architecture," *Academy of Management Executive* 9, no. 2 (1995), 7–20; and Engle, "You *Can* Outsource Strategic Processes."
61. The discussion of weaknesses is based on Engle, "You *Can* Outsource Strategic Processes"; Henry W. Chesbrough, and David J. Teece, "Organizing for Innovation: When Is Virtual Virtuous?" *Harvard Business Review* (August 2002), 127–134; Dess et al., "The New Corporate Architecture"; and N. Anand, "Modular, Virtual, and Hollow Forms of Organization Design," working paper, London Business School, 2000.
62. Based on Ostroff, *The Horizontal Organization*, 29–44.
63. S. Helgesen, *The Web Of Inclusion: Architecture For Building Great Organizations* (New York: Beard Books, 2005).
64. "The Canadian Inquisition" at http://torquiz.freeshell.org/about/about.html (accessed June 4, 2008).
65. L. Mann, Personal Communication, September 13, 2007.
66. Based on Child, *Organization*, Ch. 1; and Jonathan D. Day, Emily Lawson, and Keith Leslie, "When Reorganization Works," *The McKinsey Quarterly*, 2003 Special Edition: The Value in Organization, 21–29.
67. G. Morgan, "Images of Organization" (Updated Edition) (Thousand Oaks, Calif.: Sage Publications, 2006), 4.
68. Ibid., 366.

Chapter 4

1. David Pringle, "Wrong Number; How Nokia Chased Top End of Market, Got Hit in Middle," *The Wall Street Journal* (June 1, 2004), A1; and Andy Reinhardt with Moon Ihlwan, "Will Rewiring Nokia Spark Growth?" *BusinessWeek* (February 14, 2005), 46ff.
2. Andrew Yeh, "China Set To Be Nokia's Top Market," *Financial Times* (February 24, 2005), 24; and Reinhardt and Ihlwan, "Will Rewiring Nokia Spark Growth?".
3. "Cellphone Maker Nokia Sees High Market Share in 2008," (December 4, 2007) at http://www.cbc.ca/technology/story/2007/12/04/nokiaoutlook.html (accessed July 2, 2008).
4. Paul Keegan, "Is the Music Store Over?" *Business 2.0* (March 2004), 115–118; Tom Hansson, Jürgen Ringbeck, and Markus Franke, "Fight for Survival: A New Business Model for the Airline Industry," *Strategy 1 Business*, Issue 31 (Summer 2003), 78–85.
5. P. Shrivastava, CASTRATED Environment: GREENING Organizational Studies, *Organization Studies*, (1994) 15, 5, 705–726.
6. "The NHLPA and the David Suzuki Foundation Announce 'Green' Partnership," (December 7, 2007) at http://www.davidsuzuki.org/latestnews/dsfnews12070702.asp (accessed June 5, 2008).
7. Dana Milbank, "Aluminum Producers, Aggressive and Agile, Outfight Steelmakers," *The Wall Street Journal* (July 1, 1992), A1.
8. Sarah Ellison, "Eating Up; As Shoppers Grow Finicky, Big Food Has Big Problems," *The Wall Street Journal* (May 21, 2004), A1.
9. "The Skills Gap in Canada: The Knowledge Intensity of Canadians' Jobs is Growing Rapidly," (December 21, 2006) at http://www.ccl-cca.ca/CCL/Reports/

LessonsInLearning/LinL20061220SkillsGap.htm (accessed June 6, 2008).

10. Douglas, M.J. (n.d.) "The Challenges of a Canadian Workforce," http://content.monster.ca/7249_en-CA_p1.asp (accessed June 6, 2008).
11. Andrew Pollack, "Yet Another Sector Embraces Outsourcing to Asia: Life Sciences," *International Herald Tribune* (February 25, 2005), 17.
12. Samuel Loewenberg, "Europe Gets Tougher on U.S. Companies," *The New York Times* (April 20, 2003), Section 3, 6.
13. V. Galt, "Diversity at Work: 77 People, 27 Languages," *The Globe and Mail* (December 5, 2007), C1–2.
14. Mark Landler, "Woes at Two Pillars of German Journalism," *The New York Times* (January 19, 2004), C8.
15. David Kirkpatrick and Daniel Roth, "Why There's No Escaping the Blog," *Fortune* (January 10, 2005), 44–50.
16. International Telecommunication Union, "Estimated 100 Million Blogs Worldwide in Early 2006" at http://www.itu.int/osg/spu/newslog/Estimated+100+Million+Blogs+Worldwide+In+Early+2006.aspx (accessed June 6, 2008).
17. Robert Frank, "Silver Lining; How Terror Fears Brought Tiny Firm to Brink of Success," *The Wall Street Journal* (May 8, 2003), A1, A14.
18. Andrew Kupfer, "How American Industry Stacks Up," *Fortune* (March 9, 1992), 36–46.
19. "Sapporo Acquisition of Sleeman on Tap," (August 11, 2006) at http://www.cbc.ca/money/story/2006/08/11/sapporo-sleeman.html (accessed July 2, 2008).
20. "Methane to Markets" (n.d.) at http://www.methanetomarkets.org (accessed June 5, 2008).
21. R. Harris, "Ogilvy & Mather," *Marketing* (November 12, 2007).
22. Devin Leonard, "Nightmare on Madison Avenue," *Fortune* (June 28, 2004), 93–108; and Brian Steinberg, "Agency Cost-Accounting Is under Trial," *The Wall Street Journal* (January 28, 2005), B2.
23. Randall D. Harris, "Organizational Task Environments: An Evaluation of Convergent and Discriminant Validity," *Journal of Management Studies* 41, no. 5 (July 2004), 857–882; Allen C. Bluedorn, "Pilgrim's Progress: Trends and Convergence in Research on Organizational Size and Environment," *Journal of Management* 19 (1993), 163–191; Howard E. Aldrich, *Organizations and Environments* (Englewood Cliffs, N.J.: Prentice-Hall, 1979); and Fred E. Emery and Eric L. Trist, "The Casual Texture of Organizational Environments," *Human Relations* 18 (1965), 21–32.
24. Gregory G. Dess and Donald W. Beard, "Dimensions of Organizational Task Environments," *Administrative Science Quarterly* 29 (1984), 52–73; Ray Jurkovich, "A Core Typology of Organizational Environments," *Administrative Science Quarterly* 19 (1974), 380–394; Robert B. Duncan, "Characteristics of Organizational Environment and Perceived Environmental Uncertainty," *Administrative Science Quarterly* 17 (1972), 313–327.
25. Christine S. Koberg and Gerardo R. Ungson, "The Effects of Environmental Uncertainty and Dependence on Organizational Structure and Performance: A Comparative Study," *Journal of Management* 13 (1987), 725–737; and Frances J. Milliken, "Three Types of Perceived Uncertainty about the Environment: State, Effect, and Response Uncertainty," *Academy of Management Review* 12 (1987), 133–143.
26. Mike France with Joann Muller, "A Site for Soreheads," *BusinessWeek* (April 12, 1999), 86–90; Kirkpatrick and Roth, "Why There's No Escaping the Blog."
27. J. A. Litterer, *The Analysis of Organizations,* 2d ed. (New York: Wiley, 1973), 335.
28. Constance L. Hays, "More Gloom on the Island of Lost Toy Makers," *The New York Times* (February 23, 2005) at http://www.nytimes.com (accessed June 9, 2008).
29. "Mattel CEO: 'Rigorous Standards' after Massive Toy Recall" (November 15, 2007) at http://www.cnn.com/2007/US/08/14/recall (accessed June 9, 2008).
30. Rosalie L. Tung, "Dimensions of Organizational Environments: An Exploratory Study of Their Impact on Organizational Structure," *Academy of Management Journal* 22 (1979), 672–693.
31. Joseph E. McCann and John Selsky, "Hyper-turbulence and the Emergence of Type 5 Environments," *Academy of Management Review* 9 (1984), 460–470.
32. Annual Statistical Bulletin, 2006, Brewers Association of Canada.
33. Vera Ovanin, "Former WestJetters Look at New Airline" (October 22, 2007) at http://calsun.canoe.ca/News/Alberta/2007/10/22/pf-4596698.html (accessed June 9, 2008).
34. James D. Thompson, *Organizations in Action* (New York: McGraw-Hill, 1967), 20–21.
35. Sally Solo, "Whirlpool: How to Listen to Consumers," *Fortune* (January 11, 1993), 77–79.
36. David B. Jemison, "The Importance of Boundary Spanning Roles in Strategic Decision-Making," *Journal of Management Studies* 21 (1984), 131–152; and Mohamed Ibrahim Ahmad At-Twaijri and John R. Montanari, "The Impact of Context and Choice on the Boundary-Spanning Process: An Empirical Extension," *Human Relations* 40 (1987), 783–798.
37. Michelle Cook, "The Intelligentsia," *Business 2.0* (July 1999), 135–136.
38. Robert C. Schwab, Gerardo R. Ungson, and Warren B. Brown, "Redefining the Boundary-Spanning Environment Relationship," *Journal of Management* 11 (1985), 75–86.
39. Innovation in Canada (October 28, 2005) at http://www.innovationstrategy.gc.ca/gol/innovation/site.nsf/en/in03621.html (accessed June 5, 2008).
40. Steve Mossop, "Companies not Spending Enough on Business Intelligence Activities" (November 24, 2005) at http://www.ipsos-na.com/news/pressrelease.cfm?id=2874# (accessed June 9, 2008).
41. Pia Nordlinger, "Know Your Enemy," *Working Woman* (May 2001), 16.

42. Ken Western, "Ethical Spying," *Business Ethics* (September/October 1995), 22–23; Stan Crock, Geoffrey Smith, Joseph Weber, Richard A. Melcher, and Linda Himelstein, "They Snoop to Conquer," *BusinessWeek* (October 28, 1996), 172–176; and Kenneth A. Sawka, "Demystifying Business Intelligence," *Management Review* (October 1996), 47–51.
43. Edwin M. Epstein, "How to Learn from the Environment about the Environment—A Prerequisite for Organizational Well-Being," *Journal of General Management* 29, no. 1 (Autumn 2003), 68–80.
44. "Snooping on a Shoestring," *Business 2.0* (May 2003), 64–66.
45. Mike France with Joann Muller, "A Site for Soreheads," *BusinessWeek* (April 12, 1999), 86–90.
46. Emily Wexler, "Not Your Average Joe," (2005) at http://www.citylifemagazine.ca/sucessstory_joe.php (accessed June 9, 2008).
47. Ibid.
48. "Joe Fresh Style Launched in Toronto," Fashion Monitor Toronto at http://toronto.fashion-monitor.com/news.php/fashion/2006031307fresh-fashion-launch (accessed June 18, 2008).
49. Jay W. Lorsch, "Introduction to the Structural Design of Organizations," in Gene W. Dalton, Paul R. Lawrence, and Jay W. Lorsch, eds., *Organizational Structure and Design* (Homewood, Ill.: Irwin and Dorsey, 1970), 5.
50. Paul R. Lawrence and Jay W. Lorsch, *Organization and Environment* (Homewood, Ill.: Irwin, 1969).
51. Lorsch, "Introduction to the Structural Design of Organizations," 7.
52. Jay W. Lorsch and Paul R. Lawrence, "Environmental Factors and Organizational Integration," in J. W. Lorsch and Paul R. Lawrence, eds., *Organizational Planning: Cases and Concepts* (Homewood, Ill.: Irwin and Dorsey, 1972), 45.
53. Tom Burns and G. M. Stalker, *The Management of Innovation* (London: Tavistock, 1961).
54. John A. Courtright, Gail T. Fairhurst, and L. Edna Rogers, "Interaction Patterns in Organic and Mechanistic Systems," *Academy of Management Journal* 32 (1989), 773–802.
55. Dennis K. Berman, "Crunch Time," *BusinessWeek Frontier* (April 24, 2000), F28–F38.
56. Robert A. Guth, "Eroding Empires: Electronics Giants of Japan Undergo Wrenching Change," *The Wall Street Journal* (June 20, 2002), A1, A9.
57. Thomas C. Powell, "Organizational Alignment as Competitive Advantage," *Strategic Management Journal* 13 (1992), 119–134; Mansour Javidan, "The Impact of Environmental Uncertainty on Long-Range Planning Practices of the U.S. Savings and Loan Industry," *Strategic Management Journal* 5 (1984), 381–392; Tung, "Dimensions of Organizational Environments," 672–693; and Thompson, *Organizations in Action*.
58. Ian Wylie, "There Is No Alternative To . . . ," *Fast Company* (July 2002), 106–110.
59. "Manitoba Telcom Services, Inc." (n.d) at http://www.referenceforbusiness.com/history2/76/Manitoba-Telecom-Services-Inc.html (accessed July 7, 2008) and at http://www.mts.ca/portal/site/mts/menuitem.e21815bb3f30fc8e7ee558c3408021a0/?vgnextoid=13ef82cd24bf1110VgnVCM1000000408120aRCRD&vgnextfmt=print General (accessed July 7, 2008).
60. Ibid.
61. J. Swayze and A. Bromilow, *"Not Just an Operator"—How the Manitoba Telephone System (MTS) & Communication, Energy & Paperworkers Union (CEP) Jointly Implemented Work Redesign* (1993).
62. Ibid.
63. David Ulrich and Jay B. Barney, "Perspectives in Organizations: Resource Dependence, Efficiency, and Population," *Academy of Management Review* 9 (1984), 471–481; and Jeffrey Pfeffer and Gerald Salancik, *The External Control of Organizations: A Resource Dependent Perspective* (New York: Harper & Row, 1978).
64. Andrew H. Van de Ven and Gordon Walker, "The Dynamics of Interorganizational Coordination," *Administrative Science Quarterly* (1984), 598–621; and Huseyin Leblebici and Gerald R. Salancik, "Stability in Interorganizational Exchanges: Rulemaking Processes of the Chicago Board of Trade," *Administrative Science Quarterly* 27 (1982), 227–242.
65. Kevin Kelly and Zachary Schiller with James B. Treece, "Cut Costs or Else: Companies Lay Down the Law to Suppliers," *BusinessWeek* (March 22, 1993), 28–29.
66. G. Pascal Zachary, "Many Journalists See a Growing Reluctance to Criticize Advertisers," *The Wall Street Journal* (February 6, 1992), A1, A9.
67. Judith A. Babcock, *Organizational Responses to Resource Scarcity and Munificence: Adaptation and Modification in Colleges within a University* (Ph.D. diss., Pennsylvania State University, 1981).
68. Peter Smith Ring and Andrew H. Van de Ven, "Developmental Processes of Corporative Interorganizational Relationships," *Academy of Management Review* 19 (1994), 90–118; Jeffrey Pfeffer, "Beyond Management and the Worker: The Institutional Function of Management," *Academy of Management Review* 1 (April 1976), 36–46; and John P. Kotter, "Managing External Dependence," *Academy of Management Review* 4 (1979), 87–92.
69. Bryan Borys and David B. Jemison, "Hybrid Arrangements as Strategic Alliances: Theoretical Issues in Organizational Combinations," *Academy of Management Review* 14 (1989), 234–249.
70. McMillan Binch Mendelsohn, "M&A Developments in Canada," *Securities Bulletin* (February 2007), 2.
71. B. Marotte, B. Erman, and J. Parttridge, "TMX Group Formed as Toronto, Montréal Exchanges Merge," *The Globe and Mail* (December 10, 2007), A1.
72. Ibid.
73. R. Trichur, "Toronto, Montreal Exchanges Tie the Knot," Toronto Star (December 10, 2007) at http://www

.thestar.com/Business/article/284166 (accessed July 15, 2008).

74. Julie Cohen Mason, "Strategic Alliances: Partnering for Success," *Management Review* (May 1993), 10–15.
75. Teri Agins and Alessandra Galloni, "After Gianni; Facing a Squeeze, Versace Struggles to Trim the Fat," *The Wall Street Journal* (September 30, 2003), A1, A10; John F. Love, *McDonald's: Behind the Arches* (New York: Bantam Books, 1986).
76. Zachary Schiller and Wendy Zellner with Ron Stodghill II and Mark Maremont, "Clout! More and More, Retail Giants Rule the Marketplace," *BusinessWeek* (December 21, 1992), 66–73.
77. Borys and Jemison, "Hybrid Arrangements as Strategic Alliances."
78. "Joint venture with Canada to Expand Nickel production to 49,000 Tons," (April 19, 2006) at http://granmai.cubasi.cu/ingles/2006/abril/mier19/17niquel.html, (accessed July 2, 2008).
79. Donald Palmer, "Broken Ties: Interlocking Directorates and Intercorporate Coordination," *Administrative Science Quarterly* 28 (1983), 40–55; F. David Shoorman, Max H. Bazerman, and Robert S. Atkin, "Interlocking Directorates: A Strategy for Reducing Environmental Uncertainty," *Academy of Management Review* 6 (1981), 243–251; and Ronald S. Burt, *Toward a Structural Theory of Action* (New York: Academic Press, 1982).
80. James R. Lang and Daniel E. Lockhart, "Increased Environmental Uncertainty and Changes in Board Linkage Patterns," *Academy of Management Journal* 33 (1990), 106–128; and Mark S. Mizruchi and Linda Brewster Stearns, "A Longitudinal Study of the Formation of Interlocking Directorates," *Administrative Science Quarterly* 33 (1988), 194–210.
81. Kotter, "Managing External Dependence."
82. William C. Symonds, with Farah Nayeri, Geri Smith, and Ted Plafker, "Bombardier's Blitz," *BusinessWeek* (February 6, 1995), 62–66; and Joseph Weber, with Wendy Zellner and Geri Smith, "Loud Noises at Bombardier," *BusinessWeek* (January 26, 1998), 94–95.
83. "Canadian Companies Lobby for Missile Shield Contracts" (March 17, 2004) at http://www.cbc.ca/canada/story/2004/03/16/missileshield040316.html (accessed June 9, 2008).
84. Jeanne Cummings, "Joining the PAC; Wal-Mart Opens for Business in a Tough Market: Washington," *The Wall Street Journal* (March 24, 2004), A1.
85. "Quebec Court of Appeal Declines to Hear Wal-Mart Case" (May 16, 2006) at http://www.nupge.ca/news_2006/n16my06a.htm (accessed July 7, 2008); "Wal-Mart Store Closing Chills Union Drive in 25 Canada Outlets" (April 29, 2005) at http://www.bloomberg.com/apps/news?pid=71000001&refer=canada&sid=alpljhOyZjW4 (accessed July 2, 2008).
86. David B. Yoffie, "How an Industry Builds Political Advantage," *Harvard Business Review* (May–June 1988), 82–89; and Jeffrey H. Birnbaum, "Chief Executives Head to Washington to Ply the Lobbyist's Trade," *The Wall Street Journal* (March 19, 1990), A1, A16.
87. Anthony J. Daboub, Abdul M. A. Rasheed, Richard L. Priem, and David A. Gray, "Top Management Team Characteristics and Corporate Illegal Activity," *Academy of Management Review* 20, no. 1 (1995), 138–170.
88. I. Austen, "WestJet Settles Spy Case with Rival Air Canada" (May 31, 2006) at http://www.iht.com/articles/2006/05/30/business/canair.php (accessed July 2, 2008).
89. Barry M. Staw and Eugene Szwajkowski, "The Scarcity-Munificence Component of Organizational Environments and the Commission of Illegal Acts," *Administrative Science Quarterly* 20 (1975), 345–354; and Kimberly D. Elsbach and Robert I. Sutton, "Acquiring Organizational Legitimacy through Illegitimate Actions: A Marriage of Institutional and Impression Management Theories," *Academy of Management Journal* 35 (1992), 699–738.
90. K. Donovan, "Toronto Charity ICAN Suspended by Federal Regulator," *Toronto Star*, (November 30, 2007), A10.

Chapter 5

1. "14 Management Principles from the World's Greatest Manufacturer" (February 1, 2006) at http://www.industryweek.com/PrintArticle.aspx?ArticleID=11303 (accessed June 10, 2008).
2. N. Kehler, "Interorganizational Relationships and Learning; Deep Supplier Relationships Drive Automakers' Success" (July 6, 2005) at http://Knowledge.wpcarey.asu.edu/index.cfm?fa=viewfeature&id=1061 (accessed June 10, 2008); and J. Teresko "Learning from ToyotaAgain" (February 1, 2006) at http://www.industryweek.com/PrintArticle.aspx?ArticleID=11301 (accessed June 10, 2008).
3. Christine Oliver, "Determinants of Interorganizational Relationships: Integration and Future Directions," Academy of Management Review 15 (1990), 241–265.
4. James Moore, The Death of Competition: Leadership and Strategy in the Age of Business Ecosystems (New York: HarperCollins, 1996); Brent Schlender, "How Big Can Apple Get?" Fortune (February 21, 2005), 66–76.
5. D. George-Cosh, "Hello, Magna: Apples's iPhone Contains Surprise Component" (July 4, 2007) The Globe and Mail, B3.
6. Howard Muson, "Friend? Foe? Both? The Confusing World of Corporate Alliances," Across the Board (March–April 2002), 19–25; and Devi R. Gnyawali and Ravindranath Madhavan, "Cooperative Networks and Competitive Dynamics: A Structural Embeddedness Perspective," Academy of Management Review 26, no. 3 (2001), 431–445.
7. Thomas Petzinger, Jr., The New Pioneers: The Men and Women Who Are Transforming the Workplace and Marketplace (New York: Simon & Schuster, 1999), 53–54.
8. James Moore, "The Death of Competition," Fortune (April 15, 1996), 142–144.
9. "Indigo Improves Supplier Relationships Using Electronic Data Interchange," Microsoft Windows Server System

Customer Solution Case Study, 2004; "Indigo, Chapters and Coles Partner with iUniverse," (November 17, 2006) at http://www.expertclick.com/NewsReleaseWire/default.cfm?Action=ReleaseDetail&ID=14512 (accessed June 10, 2008); and "Blue Nile Launches Canadian Website and partners with Leading Canadian Ecommerce Destination chapters.indigo.ca" (January 21. 2005) at http://www.internetretailer.com/internet/marketing-conference/54840-blue-nile-launches-canadian-website-partners-leading-canadian-ecommerce-destination-chaptersindigoca.html (accessed June 10, 2008).

10. Brian Goodwin, How the Leopard Changed Its Spots: The Evolution of Complexity (New York: Touchstone, 1994), 181, quoted in Petzinger, The New Pioneers, 53.
11. J. Markoff. "Intel, in Shift, Joins Project on Education," The New York Times, July 14, 2007.
12. T. Wong, "Rivals Unite to Build Film Studio," Toronto Star (July 5. 2007), B1, B4.
13. Ibid., B4.
14. Sumantra Ghoshal and Christopher A. Bartlett, "Changing the Role of Top Management: Beyond Structure and Process," Harvard Business Review (January–February 1995), 86–96.
15. "GBC History," at http://www.gbcimpact.org/live/about/history.php (accessed July 7, 2009).
16. J. Pfeffer and G. R. Salancik, The External Control of Organizations: A Resource Dependence Perspective (New York: Harper & Row, 1978).
17. Derek S. Pugh and David J. Hickson, Writers on Organizations, 5th ed. (Thousand Oaks, Calif.: Sage, 1996).
18. A.J. Armstrong-Doherty, "Resource Dependence-based Perceived Control: An Examination of Canadian Interuniversity Athletics," Journal of Sports Management (1996) 10, 1, 49–64.
19. L. Thibault and J. Harvey, "Fostering Interorganizational Linkages in the Canadian Sport Delivery System," Journal of Sports Management (1997) 11, 1, 45–68 and K. Babiak, "Determinants of Interorganizational Relationships: The Case of a Canadian Nonprofit Sport Organizations," Journal of Sports Management (2007) 21, 3, 3.
20. "Canadian National Swim Team Helps Red Cross Kick off Water Safety Week with a Splash," Canada Newswire, June 1, 2006.
21. This discussion is based on Matthew Schifrin, "The Big Squeeze," Forbes (March 11, 1996), 45–46; Wendy Zellner with Marti Benedetti, "CLOUT!" BusinessWeek (December 21, 1992), 62–73; Kevin Kelly and Zachary Schiller with James B. Treece, "Cut Costs or Else," BusinessWeek (March 22, 1993), 28–29; and Lee Berton, "Push from Above," *The Wall Street Journal* (May 23, 1996), R24.
22. "Fitting In; In Bow to Retailers' New Clout, Levi Strauss Makes Alterations," The Wall Street Journal (June 17, 2004), A1.
23. Robert A. Guth and Don Clark, "Peace Program; Behind Secret Settlement Talks: New Power of Tech Customers," The Wall Street Journal (April 5, 2004), A1.
24. M.K. Foster and A. Meinhard, "Women's Voluntary Organizations in Canada: Bridgers, Bonders or Both?" Voluntas: International Journal of Voluntary and Nonprofit Organizations, 16, 2 (2005), 143–159.
25. Mitchell P. Koza and Arie Y. Lewin, "The Co-Evolution of Network Alliances: A Longitudinal Analysis of an International Professional Service Network," Center for Research on New Organizational Forms, Working Paper 98–09–02; and Kathy Rebello with Richard Brandt, Peter Coy, and Mark Lewyn, "Your Digital Future," BusinessWeek (September 7, 1992), 56–64.
26. Christine Oliver, "Determinants of Inter-organizational Relationships: Integration and Future Directions," Academy of Management Review, 15 (1990), 241–265; Ken G. Smith, Stephen J. Carroll, and Susan Ashford, "Intra- and Interorganizational Cooperation: Toward a Research Agenda," Academy of Management Journal, 38 (1995), 7–23; and Ken G. Smith, Stephen J. Carroll, and Susan Ashford, "Intra- and Interorganizational Cooperation: Toward a Research Agenda," Academy of Management Journal 38 (1995), 7–23.
27. Timothy M. Stearns, Alan N. Hoffman, and Jan B. Heide, "Performance of Commercial Television Stations as an Outcome of Interorganizational Linkages and Environmental Conditions," Academy of Management Journal 30 (1987), 71–90; and David A. Whetten and Thomas K. Kueng, "The Instrumental Value of Interorganizational Relations: Antecedents and Consequences of Linkage Formation," Academy of Management Journal 22 (1979), 325–344.
28. Angiotech's Corporate Partner, Boston Scientific, Announces Japanese Launch of TAXUS Express2 Coronary Stent System (May 2007) at http://www.medicalnewstoday.com/articles/70342.php (accessed June 10, 2008).
29. Muson, "Friend? Foe? Both?"
30. "Leave No Trace" (n.d.) at http://www.leavenotrace.ca/about/founding.html (accessed June 10, 2008).
31. Ontario Craft Brewers, "News on Tap" (June 2005) at http://www.ontariocraftbrewers.com/content2.php?nextpage=ocb_press_release_june3 (accessed June 10, 2008).
32. Keith G. Provan and H. Brinton Milward, "A Preliminary Theory of Interorganizational Network Effectiveness: A Comparative of Four Community Mental Health Systems," Administrative Science Quarterly 40 (1995), 1–33.
33. Myron Magnet, "The New Golden Rule of Business," Fortune (February 21, 1994), 60–64; Grittner, "Four Elements of Successful Sourcing Strategies"; and Jeffrey H. Dyer and Nile W. Hatch, "Using Supplier Networks to Learn Faster," MIT Sloan Management Review (Spring 2004), 57–63.
34. Peter Smith Ring and Andrew H. Van de Ven, "Developmental Processes of Corporate Interorganizational Relationships," Academy of Management Review 19 (1994), 90–118; Jeffrey H. Dyer, "How Chrysler Created an American Keiretsu," Harvard Business Review (July–August 1996), 42–56; Grittner, "Four Elements of

Successful Sourcing Strategies"; Magnet, "The New Golden Rule of Business"; and Mick Marchington and Steven Vincent, "Analysing the Influence of Institutional, Organizational and Interpersonal Forces in Shaping Inter-Organizational Relationships," Journal of Management Studies 41, no. 6 (September 2004), 1029–1056.

35. Pete Engardio, "The Barons of Outsourcing," BusinessWeek (August 28, 2000), 177–178.
36. Andrew Raskin, "Who's Minding the Store?" Business 2.0 (February 2003), 70–74.
37. Marchington and Vincent, "Analysing the Influence of Institutional, Organizational and Interpersonal Forces in Shaping Inter-Organizational Relationships."
38. Fred R. Blekley, "Some Companies Let Suppliers Work on Site and Even Place Orders," The Wall Street Journal (January 13, 1995), A1, A6.
39. Philip Siekman, "The Snap-Together Business Jet," Fortune (January 21, 2002), 104[A]–104[H].
40. Ibid.
41. This section draws from Joel A. C. Baum, "Organizational Ecology," in Stewart R. Clegg, Cynthia Hardy, and Walter R. Nord, eds., Handbook of Organization Studies (Thousand Oaks, Calif.: Sage, 1996); Jitendra V. Singh, Organizational Evolution: New Directions (Newbury Park, Calif.: Sage, 1990); Howard Aldrich, Bill McKelvey, and Dave Ulrich, "Design Strategy from the Population Perspective," Journal of Management 10 (1984), 67–86; Howard E. Aldrich, Organizations and Environments (Englewood Cliffs, N.J.: Prentice Hall, 1979); Michael Hannan and John Freeman, "The Population Ecology of Organizations," American Journal of Sociology 82 (1977), 929–964; Dave Ulrich, "The Population Perspective: Review, Critique, and Relevance," Human Relations 40 (1987), 137–152; Jitendra V. Singh and Charles J. Lumsden, "Theory and Research in Organizational Ecology," Annual Review of Sociology 16 (1990), 161–195; Howard E. Aldrich, "Understanding, Not Integration: Vital Signs from Three Perspectives on Organizations," in Michael Reed and Michael D. Hughes, eds., Rethinking Organizations: New Directions in Organizational Theory and Analysis (London: Sage, 1992); Jitendra V. Singh, David J. Tucker, and Robert J. House, "Organizational Legitimacy and the Liability of Newness," Administrative Science Quarterly 31 (1986), 171–193; and Douglas R. Wholey and Jack W. Brittain, "Organizational Ecology: Findings and Implications," Academy of Management Review 11 (1986), 513–533.
42. Pugh and Hickson, Writers on Organizations; and Lex Donaldson, American Anti-Management Theories of Organization (New York: Cambridge University Press, 1995).
43. Bullfrog Power (n.d). at http://www.bullfrogpower.com/about/about.cfm (accessed June 10, 2008).
44. Thomas Moore, "The Corporate University: Transforming Management Education" (presentation in August 1996; Thomas Moore is the Dean of the Arthur D. Little University).
45. Peter Newcomb, "No One is Safe," Forbes (July 13, 1987), 121; "It's Tough Up There," Forbes (July 13, 1987), 145–160.
46. D. Crane, "Striking a Balance on Foreign Ownership," Toronto Star (July 23, 2007), B5.
47. "Canadian National RF to Buy Most of EJ&E from US Steel Subsidiary" (September 27, 2007) at http://chestertontribune.com/business/9273%20canadian_national_rr_to_buy_most.htm (accessed July 8, 2008).
48. David Stires, "Fallen Arches," *Fortune* (April 29, 2002), 74–76.
49. "SDC Partners with Shazam to Create Simple, Secure Music Download," *M2Presswire* (February 14, 2005), 1; Steve McClure, "Shazam Works Its Magic," *Billboard* (August 21, 2004), 60; Adam Jolly, "Going for a Song and Growth," *Sunday Times* (June 13, 2004), 17; Michael Parsons, "I Got Music, I Got Algorithm," *Red Herring* (May 2002), 54–57; and "MTV and Shazam Lead Japanese Market Extending Music Recognition Offering to KDDI Subscribers and Expanding Local Music Database," *M2Presswire* (February 16, 2005), 1.
50. "McDonald's Canada Announces Next Phase of Balanced Lifestyles Initiative," (2005) at http://www.crfa.ca/research/resources/foodandfitnessfacts/news/mcdonalds_announces_next_phase_of_initiative.asp (accessed July 7, 2008).
51. T. Watson "A State of Bliss in Steeltown," Canadian Business "June 18, 2007).
52. David J. Tucker, Jitendra V. Singh, and Agnes G. Meinhard, "Organizational Form, Population Dynamics, and Institutional Change: The Founding Patterns of Voluntary Organizations," Academy of Management Journal 33 (1990), 151–178; Glenn R. Carroll and Michael T. Hannan, "Density Delay in the Evolution of Organizational Populations: A Model and Five Empirical Tests," Administrative Science Quarterly 34 (1989), 411–430; Jacques Delacroix and Glenn R. Carroll, "Organizational Foundings: An Ecological Study of the Newspaper Industries of Argentina and Ireland," Administrative Science Quarterly 28 (1983), 274–291; Johannes M. Pennings, "Organizational Birth Frequencies: An Empirical Investigation," Administrative Science Quarterly 27 (1982), 120–144; David Marple, "Technological Innovation and Organizational Survival: A Population Ecology Study of Nineteenth-Century American Railroads," Sociological Quarterly 23 (1982), 107–116; and Thomas G. Rundall and John O. McClain, "Environmental Selection and Physician Supply," American Journal of Sociology 87 (1982), 1090–1112.
53. Robert D. Hof and Linda Himelstein, "eBay vs. Amazon.com," BusinessWeek (May 31, 1999), 128–132; and Maria Mallory with Stephanie Anderson Forest, "Waking Up to a Major Market," BusinessWeek (March 23, 1992), 70–73.
54. Arthur G. Bedeian and Raymond F. Zammuto, Organizations: Theory and Design (Orlando, Fla.: Dryden Press, 1991); and Richard L. Hall, Organizations: Structure, Process and Outcomes (Englewood Cliffs, N.J.: Prentice-Hall, 1991).

55. The Rich 100: 11, www.canadianbusiness.com/article.jsp?content=23143, July 30, 1999.
56. P. Waldie, "Apotex Founder Hits Hard in Legal Family Feud," October 26, 2007) at http://www.theglobeandmail.com/servlet/story/LAC.20071026.RSHERMAN26/PPVStory?URL_Article_ID=LAC.20071026.RSHERMAN26&DENIED=1 (accessed July 8, 2008).
57. "Corporate Overview" at http://www.apotex.com/ca/en/aboutapotex/corporate.asp (accessed July 8, 2008).
58. "Rwanda to Override Patents and Import Cheaper Generic AIDS Drugs," International Herald Tribune (July 20, 2007); E. Pooley, "Pandemic Polemics," Canadian Business, September 11–24, 2006).
59. M. Tina Dacin, Jerry Goodstein, and W. Richard Scott, "Institutional Theory and Institutional Change: Introduction to the Special Research Forum," Academy of Management Journal 45, no. 1 (2002), 45–47. Thanks to Tina Dacin for her material and suggestions for this section of the chapter.
60. J. Meyer and B. Rowan, "Institutionalized Organizations: Formal Structure as Myth and Ceremony," American Journal of Sociology 83 (1990), 340–363.
61. Mark C. Suchman, "Managing Legitimacy: Strategic and Institutional Approaches," Academy of Management Review 20 (1995), 571–610.
62. "Best 50 Corporate Citizens 2007" at http://static.corporateknights.ca/Best50_2007.pdf (accessed July 8, 2008).
63. "World's Biggest Retailer Wal-Mart Closes Up Shop in Germany" (July 28, 006) at http://www.dw-world.de/dw/article/0,2144,2112746,00.html (accessed July 7, 2008).
64. M. Lander, "Wal-Mart Gives up Germany" (July 29, 2006) at http://www.iht.com/articles/2006/07/28/business/walmart.php (accessed July 7, 2008).
65. "Wal-Mart Is Canada's Largest Purchaser of Green Power" (June 8, 2007) at Execdigital June News at http://www.canada-digital.com/wal-mart-is-canada-s-largest-purchaser-of-green-power-_514.aspx (accessed July 7, 2008).
66. Jerry Useem, "Should We Admire Wal-Mart?" Fortune (March 8, 2004), 118–120; Charles Fishman, "The Wal-Mart You Don't Know: Why Low Prices Have a High Cost," Fast Company (December 2003), 68–80; Ronald Alsop, "In Business Ranking, Some Icons Lose Luster," The Wall Street Journal (November 15, 2004), B1; and Ronald Alsop, "Corporate Scandals Hit Home," The Wall Street Journal (February 19, 2004), B1.
67. "Ten Steps to Turn Around Wal-Mart" at http://blog.fastcompany.com/archives/2005/12/02/ten_steps_to_turn_around_walmart.html#more (accessed July 8, 2008).
68. Richard J. Martinez and Patricia M. Norman, "Whither Reputation? The Effects of Different Stakeholders," Business Horizons 47, no. 5 (September–October 2004), 25–32.
69. Pamela S. Tolbert and Lynne G. Zucker, "The Institutionalization of Institutional Theory," in Stewart R. Clegg, Cynthia Hardy, and Walter R. Nord, eds., Handbook of Organization Studies (Thousand Oaks, Calif.: Sage, 1996).
70. Pugh and Hickson, Writers on Organizations; and Paul J. DiMaggio and Walter W. Powell, "The Iron Cage Revisited: Institutional Isomorphism and Collective Rationality in Organizational Fields," American Sociological Review 48 (1983), 147–160.
71. This section is based largely on DiMaggio and Powell, "The Iron Cage Revisited"; Pugh and Hickson, Writers on Organizations; and W. Richard Scott, Institutions and Organizations (Thousand Oaks, Calif.: Sage, 1995).
72. Ellen R. Auster and Mark L. Sirower, "The Dynamics of Merger and Acquisition Waves," The Journal of Applied Behavioral Science 38, no. 2 (June 2002), 216–244.
73. William McKinley, Jun Zhao, and Kathleen Garrett Rust, "A Sociocognitive Interpretation of Organizational Downsizing," Academy of Management Review 25, no. 1 (2000), 227–243.
74. Barry M. Staw and Lisa D. Epstein, "What Bandwagons Bring: Effects of Popular Management Techniques on Corporate Performance, Reputation, and CEO Pay," Administrative Science Quarterly 45, no. 3 (September 2000), 523–560.
75. Jeremy Kahn, "Deloitte Restates Its Case," Fortune (April 29, 2002), 64–72.

Chapter 6

1. A. Hoffman, "Not in My Backfjord, Icelanders Tell Alcan," *The Globe and Mail* (April 3, 2007) B11.
2. Ibid., B1, B11.
3. T. Watson, "Beat China in Asia: Magna Faces a New World Order," (November 7–20, 2005) at http://www.canadianbusiness.com/managing/strategy/article.jsp?content=20060109_155853_4528 (accessed July 8, 2008).
4. The Wired 40 (March 2007) at http://www.wired.com/wired/archive/15.04/wired40_list.html (accessed June 13, 2008).
5. Sony, "Financial Highlights" (2008) at http://www.sony.net/SonyInfo/IR/financial/highlight/index.html (accessed June 13, 2008).
6. TescoShopping, "Lavinia Olde English Gourmet Plum Pudding and Rum Sauce" at http://www.tesco-shopping.com/Lavinia_2.htm (accessed June 13, 2008).
7. Paola Hject, "The Fortune Global 500," *Fortune* (July 26, 2004), 159–180.
8. "Fortune Global 500" (July 23, 2007) at http://money.cnn.com/magazines/fortune/global500/2007 (accessed July 8, 2008).
9. This discussion is based heavily on Christopher A. Bartlett and Sumantra Ghoshal, *Transnational Management: Text, Cases, and Readings in Cross-Border Management*, 3rd ed. (Boston: Irwin McGraw-Hill, 2000), 94–96; and Anil K. Gupta and Vijay Govindarajan, "Converting Global Presence into Global Competitive Advantage," *Academy of Management Executive* 15, no. 2 (2001), 45–56.
10. J. McIntosh, "The Marathon Man," *Macleans* (August 6, 2007), 44.
11. Ibid.

12. B. Marotte, "First la Belle Province, then the World," *The Globe and Mail* (July 7, 2007), B3.
13. Jim Carlton, "Branching Out; New Zealanders Now Shear Trees Instead of Sheep," *The Wall Street Journal* (May 29, 2003), A1, A10.
14. "Little Trouble in Big China," *FSB* (March 2004), 56–61; "Trade Gap," sidebar in *Fast Company* (June 2004), 42.
15. R. Luciw, "Gildan Activewear Profits with Offshore Moves," (February 8, 2007) at http://www.reportonbusiness.com/servlet/story/RTGAM.20070802.wgildan0802/BNStory/robNEWS/home (accessed July 2, 2008).
16. R R. Luciw, "Gildan Takes $21.5-million (U.S.) Charge to Shutter Plants," at http://www.theglobeandmail.com.com/servlet/story/RTGAM.20070327.wgildanstaff0327/BNStory/Business/home (accessed March 27, 2007).
17. Todd Zaun, Gregory L. White, Norihiko Shirouzu, and Scott Miller, "More Mileage: Auto Makers Look for Another Edge Farther from Home," *The Wall Street Journal* (July 31, 2002), A1, A8.
18. Ken Belson, "Outsourcing, Turned Inside Out," *The New York Times* (April 11, 2004), Section 3, 1.
19. Based on Nancy J. Adler, *International Dimensions of Organizational Behavior*, 4th ed. (Cincinnati, Ohio: South-Western, 2002); Theodore T. Herbert, "Strategy and Multinational Organizational Structure: An Interorganizational Relationships Perspective," *Academy of Management Review* 9 (1984), 259–271; and Laura K. Rickey, "International Expansion—U.S. Corporations: Strategy, Stages of Development, and Structure" (unpublished manuscript, Vanderbilt University, 1991).
20. S. Prashad, "Couple Bake their Way to Business Perfection," *Toronto Star* (January 27, 2007), D1, D20.
21. Michael E. Porter, "Changing Patterns of International Competition," *California Management Review* 28 (Winter 1986), 9–40.
22. William J. Holstein, "The Stateless Corporation," *BusinessWeek* (May 14, 1990), 98–115.
23. Debra Sparks, "Partners," *BusinessWeek*, Special Report: Corporate Finance (October 25, 1999), 106–112.
24. "QLT Inc." at http://www.qltinc.com/Qlinc/main/mainpages.cfm?InternetPageID=194 (accessed July 23, 2007).
25. David Lei and John W. Slocum, Jr., "Global Strategic Alliances: Payoffs and Pitfalls," *Organizational Dynamics* (Winter 1991), 17–29.
26. Joseph Weber with Amy Barrett, "Volatile Combos," *BusinessWeek*, Special Report: Corporate Finance (October 25, 1999), 122; and Lei and Slocum, "Global Strategic Alliances."
27. Stratford Sherman, "Are Strategic Alliances Working?" *Fortune* (September 21, 1992), 77–78; and David Lei, "Strategies for Global Competition," *Long-Range Planning* 22 (1989), 102–109.
28. J. McDonald, "Chinese Car Companies in Tie-up," *Toronto Star* (July 31, 2007), B3.
29. Carol Matlack, "Nestlé Is Starting to Slim Down at Last; But Can the World's No. 1 Food Colossus Fatten Up Its Profits As It Slashes Costs?" *BusinessWeek* (October 27, 2003), 56ff.
30. Ron Grover and Richard Siklos, "When Old Foes Need Each Other," *BusinessWeek,* Special Report: Corporate Finance (October 25, 1999), 114, 118.
31. K. Fitchard, "Nortel Used Joint Ventures to Advance in Asian Market," *Telephony*, January 31, 2005), 16–17.
32. "Joint Venture Agreement and Resource Acquisition by Robex," *PR Newswire* (March 8, 2005), 1
33. "ICICI Announces General Insurance Foray with Lombard of Canada." (October 1, 2000) at http://www.icicibank.com/pfsuser/aboutus/investorelations/pressrelease/oct04-2000.htm (accessed June 14, 2008).
34. Sparks, "Partners."
35. Sparks, "Partners."
36. Kevin Kelly and Otis Port, with James Treece, Gail DeGeorge, and Zachary Schiller, "Learning from Japan," *BusinessWeek* (January 27, 1992), 52–60; and Gregory G. Dess, Abdul M. A. Rasheed, Kevin J. McLaughlin, and Richard L. Priem, "The New Corporate Architecture," *Academy of Management Executive* 9, no. 3 (1995), 7–20.
37. Kenichi Ohmae, "Managing in a Borderless World," *Harvard Business Review* (May–June 1989), 152–161.
38. Constance L. Hays, "From Bentonville to Beijing and Beyond," at http://www.nytimes.com/2004/12/06/business/businessspecial2/06walmart.html?_r=1&scp=1&sq=bentonville+beijing+hays&st=nyt&oref=slogin (accessed July 8, 2008).
39. N. Buck, "Tapping into 'a very lucrative market,'" *The Globe and Mail* (June 13, 2007), B6.
40. Conrad de Aenlle, "Famous Brands Can Bring Benefit, or a Backlash," *The New York Times* (October 19, 2003), Section 3, 7.
41. Cesare R. Mainardi, Martin Salva, and Muir Sanderson, "Label of Origin: Made on Earth," *Strategy & Business* 15 (Second Quarter 1999), 42–53; and Joann S. Lublin, "Place vs. Product: It's Tough to Choose a Management Model," *The Wall Street Journal* (June 27, 2001), A1, A4.
42. N. Shirouzu and J. McCracken, "Toyota, Ford Signalling Possible Tie-up," *The Globe and Mail*, (January 22, 2007), B4.
43. Gupta and Govindarajan, "Converting Global Presence into Global Competitive Advantage."
44. José Pla-Barber, "From Stopford and Wells's Model to Bartlett and Ghoshal's Typology: New Empirical Evidence," *Management International Review* 42, no. 2 (2002), 141–156.
45. Sumantra Ghoshal and Nitin Nohria, "Horses for Courses: Organizational Forms for Multinational Corporations," *Sloan Management Review* (Winter 1993), 23–35; and Roderick E. White and Thomas A. Poynter, "Organizing for Worldwide Advantage," *Business Quarterly* (Summer 1989), 84–89.

46. Robert J. Kramer, Organizing for Global Competitiveness: The Country Subsidiary Design (New York: The Conference Board, 1997), 12.
47. Laura B. Pincus and James A. Belohlav, "Legal Issues in Multinational Business: To Play the Game, You Have to Know the Rules," *Academy of Management Executive* 10, no. 3 (1996), 52–61.
48. John D. Daniels, Robert A. Pitts, and Marietta J. Tretter, "Strategy and Structure of U.S. Multinationals: An Exploratory Study," *Academy of Management Journal* 27 (1984), 292–307.
49. Robert J. Kramer, *Organizing for Global Competitiveness: The Product Design* (New York: The Conference Board, 1994).
50. Robert J. Kramer, *Organizing for Global Competitiveness: The Business Unit Design* (New York: The Conference Board, 1995), 18–19.
51. Carol Matlack, "Nestlé is Starting to Slim Down."
52. Based on Robert J. Kramer, *Organizing for Global Competitiveness: The Geographic Design* (New York: The Conference Board, 1993).
53. Carol Matlack, "Nestlé is Starting to Slim Down."
54. "McCain Foods" at http://www.mccain.com/mc_home.htm (accessed August 3, 2007) and D. McMurdy (2001) "Frying the Competition," at http://www.canadianbusiness.com/shared/print.jsp?content=41265 (accessed July 30, 2007).
55. D. McMurdy, "Frying the Competition," at http://www.canadianbusiness.com/shared/print.jsp?content=41265 (accessed July 30, 2007).
56. Ibid.
57. "McCain Business Empire has Deep Roots," (March 19, 2004) at http://www.cbc.ca/money/story/2004/03/19/mccainbiz_040319.html, accessed June 14, 2008.
58. William Taylor, "The Logic of Global Business: An Interview with ABB's Percy Barnevik," *Harvard Business Review* (March–April 1991), 91–105; Carla Rappaport, "A Tough Swede Invades the U.S.," *Fortune* (January 29, 1992), 76–79; Raymond E. Miles and Charles C. Snow, "The New Network Firm: A Spherical Structure Built on a Human Investment Philosophy," *Organizational Dynamics* (Spring 1995), 5–18; and Manfred F. R. Kets de Vries, "Making a Giant Dance," *Across the Board* (October 1994), 27–32.
59. Matthew Karnitschnig, "Identity Question; For Siemens, Move into U.S. Causes Waves Back Home."
60. Gupta and Govindarajan, "Converting Global Presence into Global Competitive Advantage."
61. Robert Frank, "Withdrawal Pains: In Paddies of Vietnam, Americans Once Again Land in a Quagmire," *The Wall Street Journal* (April 21, 2000), A1, A6.
62. "InoWeb" at http://www.inowebinc.com/#home (accessed July 8, 2008).
63. The discussion of these challenges is based on Bartlett and Ghoshal, *Transnational Management*.
64. Paul De Grauwe and F. Camerman *How Big are the Big Multinational Companies?* (2002) Working paper.
65. Ian Katz and Elisabeth Malkin, "Battle for the Latin American Net," *BusinessWeek* (November 1, 1999), 194–200; and Pamela Drukerman and Nick Wingfield, "Lost in Translation: AOL's Big Assault in Latin America Hits Snags in Brazil," *The Wall Street Journal* (July 11, 2000), A1.
66. Neil King Jr., "Competition from China and India Is Changing the Way Businesses Operate" and "Little Trouble in Big China."
67. Shirley Leung, "McHaute Cuisine: Armchairs, TVs, and Espresso—Is It McDonald's?" *The Wall Street Journal* (August 30, 2002), A1, A6.
68. Adam Lashinsky, "Saving Face at Sony," *Fortune* (February 21, 2005), 79–86; Phred Dvorak and Merissa Marr, "Stung by iPod, Sony Addresses a Digital Lag," *The Wall Street Journal* (December 30, 2004), A1; Ken Belson, "An Executive Who Could Not Bring the Company into Focus with His Vision," *The New York Times* (March 8, 2005); Randall Stross, "How the iPod Ran Circles around the Walkman," *The New York Times* (March 13, 2005), Business Section, 5; Brian Bremner with Cliff Edwards, Ronald Grover, Tom Lowry, and Emily Thornton, "Sony's Sudden Samurai," *BusinessWeek* (March 21, 2005), 28ff; and Lorne Manly and Andrew Ross Sorkin, "At Sony, Diplomacy Trumps Technology," *The New York Times* (March 8, 2005).
69. "Apple Releases Q2006 Second Quarter Results, Wildly Exceeds Expectations Again," at http://www.arstechnica.com/journals/apple.ars/2006/4/19/3665 (accessed June 14, 2008).
70. P. Ingrassia, "Industry Is Shopping Abroad for Good Ideas to Apply to Products," *The Wall Street Journal* (April 29, 1985), A1.
71. Based on Gupta and Govindarajan, "Converting Global Presence into Global Competitive Advantage."
72. Vijay Govindarajan and Anil K. Gupta, "Building an Effective Global Business Team," *MIT Sloan Management Review* 42, no. 4 (Summer 2001), 63–71.
73. Charlene Marmer Solomon, "Building Teams across Borders," *Global Workforce* (November 1998), 12–17.
74. Charles C. Snow, Scott A. Snell, Sue Canney Davison, and Donald C. Hambrick, "Use Transnational Teams to Globalize Your Company," *Organizational Dynamics* 24, no. 4 (Spring 1996), 50–67.
75. Jane Pickard, "Control Freaks Need Not Apply," *People Management* (February 5, 1998), 49.
76. Snow et al., "Use Transnational Teams to Globalize Your Company."
77. Robert J. Kramer, Organizing for Global Competitiveness: The Corporate Headquarters Design (New York: The Conference Board, 1999).
78. Manly and Sorkin, "At Sony, Diplomacy Trumps Technology."
79. These roles are based on Christopher A. Bartlett and Sumantra Ghoshal, *Managing across Borders: The Transnational Solution*, 2nd ed. (Boston: Harvard Business School Press, 1998), Chapter 11, 231–249.

80. See Jay Galbraith, "Building Organizations around the Global Customer," *Ivey Business Journal* (September–October 2001), 17–24, for a discussion of both formal and informal lateral networks used in multinational companies.
81. This section is based on Morten T. Hansen and Nitin Nohria, "How to Build Collaborative Advantage," *MIT Sloan Management Review* (Fall 2004), 22ff.
82. Geert Hofstede, "The Interaction between National and Organizational Value Systems," *Journal of Management Studies* 22 (1985), 347–357; and Geert Hofstede, *Cultures and Organizations: Software of the Mind* (London: McGraw-Hill, 1991).
83. Geert Hofstede "Cultural Dimensions" at http://www.geert-hofstede.com (accessed July 8, 2008).
84. See Mansour Javidan and Robert J. House, "Cultural Acumen for the Global Manager: Lessons from Project GLOBE," *Organizational Dynamics* 29, no. 4 (2001), 289–305; and R. J. House, M. Javidan, Paul Hanges, and Peter Dorfman, "Understanding Cultures and Implicit Leadership Theories across the Globe: An Introduction to Project GLOBE," *Journal of World Business* 37 (2002), 3–10.
85. This discussion is based on "Culture and Organization," Reading 2-2 in Christopher A. Bartlett and Sumantra Ghoshal, *Transnational Management*, 3rd ed. (Boston: Irwin McGraw-Hill, 2000), 191–216, excerpted from Susan Schneider and Jean-Louis Barsoux, *Managing across Cultures* (London: Prentice-Hall, 1997).
86. Gesteland, R. R. (1997) *Cross-Cultural Business Behaviur* (Copenhagen: Handelshojskolens Forlag).
87. Based on Bartlett and Ghoshal, *Managing across Borders*, 181–201.
88. Martin Hemmert, "International Organization of R&D and Technology Acquisition Performance of High-Tech Business Units," *Management International Review* 43, no. 4 (2003), 361–382.
89. Jean Lee, "Culture and Management—A Study of a Small Chinese Family Business in Singapore," *Journal of Small Business Management* 34, no. 3 (July 1996), 63ff; "Olivier Blanchard and Andrei Shleifer, "Federalism with and without Political Centralization: China versus Russia," *IMF Staff Papers* 48 (2001), 171ff.
90. Nailin Bu, Timothy J. Craig, and T. K. Peng, "Reactions to Authority," *Thunderbird International Business. Review* 43, no. 6 (November–December 2001), 773–795.
91. Sumantra Ghoshal and Christopher Bartlett, "The Multinational Corporation as an Inter-organizational Network," *Academy of Management Review* 15 (1990), 603–625.
92. The description of the transnational organization is based on Bartlett and Ghoshal, *Transnational Management* and *Managing across Borders*.
93. The Workshop was inspired by Tovey, J. (1997) Addressing Issues of Cultural Diversity in Business Communication, *Business Communication Quarterly*, 60, 1,19.

Chapter 7

1. Ann Armstrong, Pay for Knowledge and Skill Systems: A Multilevel Exploratory Investigation, Doctoral Dissertation (1993), University of Toronto; Normand Charron, HR Manager, GE Aviation, Bromont, Personal Communication (April 17, 2008).
2. A. Bruns, "Something in the Air," *Site Selection* (September, 2005).
3. Charles Perrow, "A Framework for the Comparative Analysis of Organizations," *American Sociological Review* 32 (1967), 194–208; and R. J. Schonberger, *World Class Manufacturing: The Next Decade* (New York: The Free Press, 1996).
4. Linda Argote, "Input Uncertainty and Organizational Coordination in Hospital Emergency Units," *Administrative Science Quarterly* 27 (1982), 420–434; Charles Perrow, *Organizational Analysis: A Sociological Approach* (Belmont, Calif.: Wadsworth, 1970); and William Rushing, "Hardness of Material as Related to the Division of Labor in Manufacturing Industries," *Administrative Science Quarterly* 13 (1968), 229–245.
5. Lawrence B. Mohr, "Organizational Technology and Organization Structure," *Administrative Science Quarterly* 16 (1971), 444–459; and David Hickson, Derek Pugh, and Diana Pheysey, "Operations Technology and Organization Structure: An Empirical Reappraisal," *Administrative Science Quarterly* 14 (1969), 378–397.
6. Joan Woodward, *Industrial Organization: Theory and Practice* (London: Oxford University Press, 1965); and Joan Woodward, *Management and Technology* (London: Her Majesty's Stationery Office, 1958).
7. Hickson, Pugh, and Pheysey, "Operations Technology and Organization Structure"; and James D. Thompson, *Organizations in Action* (New York: McGraw-Hill, 1967).
8. Edward Harvey, "Technology and the Structure of Organizations," *American Sociological Review* 33 (1968), 241–259.
9. Wanda J. Orlikowski, "The Duality of Technology: Rethinking the Concept of Technology in Organizations," *Organization Science* 3 (1992), 398–427.
10. Based on Woodward, *Industrial Organization and Management and Technology.*
11. Diane McCurdy "You, Inc.," (September 2007) at http://www.chatelaine.com/english/moneymavens/article.jsp?content=20070607_155708_4940 (accessed June 16, 2008).
12. Kiln Art, "About Us," at http://www.kilnart.ca/aboutus.php (accessed July 10, 2008).
13. Woodward, *Industrial Organization*, vi.
14. William L. Zwerman, New Perspectives on *Organizational Theory* (Westport, Conn.: Greenwood, 1970); and Harvey, "Technology and the Structure of Organizations."
15. Dean M. Schroeder, Steven W. Congden, and C. Gopinath, "Linking Competitive Strategy and Manufacturing Process Technology," *Journal of Management Studies* 32, no. 2 (March 1995), 163–189.

16. "What's New" at http://www.doepker.com/what'snew.html (accessed June 16, 2008).
17. Fernando F. Suarez, Michael A. Cusumano, and Charles H. Fine, "An Empirical Study of Flexibility in Manufacturing," *Sloan Management Review* (Fall 1995), 25–32.
18. Raymond F. Zammuto and Edward J. O'Connor, "Gaining Advanced Manufacturing Technologies' Benefits: The Roles of Organization Design and Culture," *Academy of Management Review* 17, no. 4 (1992), 701–728; and Schroeder, Congden, and Gopinath, "Linking Competitive Strategy and Manufacturing Process Technology."
19. Statistics Canada, "Employment by Major Industry Groups, Seasonally Adjusted, By Province (Monthly)," CANSIM table 282-0088 at http://www40.statcan.ca/l01/cst01/labr67a.htm (accessed July 10, 2008).
20. C. Rogers, "Pacesetting Strategies for the Paper Industry," *Pulp & Paper Canada*, 107, 1 (2006), 30.
21. Jack R. Meredith, "The Strategic Advantages of the Factory of the Future," *California Management Review* 29 (Spring 1987), 27–41; Jack Meredith, "The Strategic Advantages of the New Manufacturing Technologies for Small Firms," *Strategic Management Journal* 8 (1987), 249–258; and Althea Jones and Terry Webb, "Introducing Computer Integrated Manufacturing," *Journal of General Management* 12 (Summer 1987), 60–74.
22. Raymond F. Zammuto and Edward J. O'Connor, "Gaining Advanced Manufacturing Technologies' Benefits: The Roles of Organization Design and Culture," *Academy of Management Review* 17 (1992), 701–728.
23. "Weyerhaeuser's BC Coastal Group Units Achieve New Certifications," (December 5, 2000) at http://forests.org/archive/Canada/weybccgr.htm (accessed June 16, 2008); Ann Armstrong, "Chemainus Sawmill Division of MacMillan Bloedel: Its Pay for Knowledge and Skill System," *ASTD Casebook Volume II* (1999).
24. Paul S. Adler, "Managing Flexible Automation," *California Management Review* (Spring 1988), 34–56.
25. Bela Gold, "Computerization in Domestic and International Manufacturing," *California Management Review (*Winter 1989), 129–143.
26. Graham Dudley and John Hassard, "Design Issues in the Development of Computer Integrated Manufacturing (CIM)," *Journal of General Management* 16 (1990), 43–53.
27. ShoeInfoNet at http://www.shoeinfonet.com/technology/cad%20cam/NA/cadcam_ca.htm (accessed June 16, 2008).
28. *news.delcam*, Issue 1 (2007),12.
29. Ibid; and Tom Massung, "Manufacturing Efficiency," *Microsoft Executive Circle* (Winter 2004), 28–29.
30. Brian Heymans, "Leading the Lean Enterprise," *Industrial Management* (September–October 2002), 28–33; and Fara Warner, "Think Lean," *Fast Company* (February 2002), 40, 42.
31. "New LEI Case Study—Canada Post" (August 26, 2005) at http://www.leanblog.org/2005/08/new-lei-case-study-canada-post.html (accessed June 16, 2008).
32. Peter Strozniak, "Toyota Alters Face of Production," *IndustryWeek* (August 13, 2001), 46–48.
33. T. Shufelt, "Gibson Grooves on Garrison's Guitars," *The Globe and Mail* (July 5, 2007), B5.
34. A. Holloway, "Between the Rock and a Hard Place," *Canadian Business* (December 2004).
35. T. Shufelt, "Gibson Grooves on Garrison's Guitars."
36. B. Joseph Pine II, *Mass Customization: The New Frontier in Business* Competition (Boston: Harvard Business School Press, 1999).
37. Barry Berman, "Should Your Firm Adopt a Mass Customization Strategy?" *Business Horizons* (July–August 2002), 51–60.
38. Erick Schonfeld, "The Customized, Digitized, Have-It-Your- Way Economy," *Fortune* (September 28, 1998), 115–124.
39. Kathryn Jones, "The Dell Way," *Business 2.0* (February 2003), 61–66; Stewart Deck, "Fine Line," CIO (February 1, 2000), 88–92; Andy Serwer, "Dell Does Domination," *Fortune* (January 21, 2002), 71–75; and Betsy Morris, "Can Michael Dell Escape the Box?" *Fortune* (October 16, 2000), 93–110.
40. Grainger David, "One Truck a Minute," and Scott McMurray, "Ford F-150: Have It Your Way," *Business* 2.0 (March 2004), 53–55.
41. Joel D. Goldhar and David Lei, "Variety Is Free: Manufacturing in the Twenty-First Century," *Academy of Management Executive* no. 4 (1995), 73–86.
42. Meredith, "The Strategic Advantages of the Factory of the Future."
43. Patricia L. Nemetz and Louis W. Fry, "Flexible Manufacturing Organizations: Implementations for Strategy Formulation and Organization Design," *Academy of Management Review* 13 (1988), 627–638; Paul S. Adler, "Managing Flexible Automation," *California Management Review* (Spring 1988), 34–56; Jeremy Main, "Manufacturing the Right Way," *Fortune* (May 21, 1990), 54–64; and Frank M. Hull and Paul D. Collins, "High-Technology Batch Production Systems: Woodward's Missing Type," *Academy of Management Journal* 30 (1987), 786–797.
44. Goldhar and Lei, "Variety Is Free: Manufacturing in the Twenty-First Century"; P. Robert Duimering, Frank Safayeni, and Lyn Purdy, "Integrated Manufacturing: Redesign the Organization before Implementing Flexible Technology," *Sloan Management Review* (Summer 1993), 47–56; Zammuto and O'Connor, "Gaining Advanced Manufacturing Technologies' Benefits."
45. Goldhar and Lei, "Variety Is Free: Manufacturing in the Twenty-First Century."
46. "Manufacturing's Decline," *Johnson City Press* (July 17, 1999), 9; Ronald Henkoff, "Service Is Everybody's Business," *Fortune* (June 27, 1994), 48–60; Ronald Henkoff, "Finding, Training, and Keeping the Best Service Workers," *Fortune* (October 3, 1994), 110–122.
47. Byron J. Finch and Richard L. Luebbe, *Operations Management: Competing in a Changing Environment* (Fort Worth, Tex.: The Dryden Press, 1995), 51.

48. David E. Bowen, Caren Siehl, and Benjamin Schneider, "A Framework for Analyzing Customer Service Orientations in Manufacturing," *Academy of Management Review* 14 (1989), 79–95; Peter K. Mills and Newton Margulies, "Toward a Core Typology of Service Organizations," *Academy of Management Review* 5 (1980), 255–265; Peter K. Mills and Dennis J. Moberg, "Perspectives on the Technology of Service Operations," *Academy of Management Review* 7 (1982), 467–478; and G. Lynn Shostack, "Breaking Free from Product Marketing," *Journal of Marketing* (April 1977), 73–80.
49. "*Ken, Greta and Phyllis Rempel Win BDC's Young Entrepreneur Award for Manitoba*" (October 18, 2005) at http://www.bdc.ca/en/about/mediaroom/news_releases/2005/2005101810.htm (accessed June 16, 2008).
50. Ron Zemke, "The Service Revolution: Who Won?" *Management Review* (March 1997), 10–15; and Wayne Wilhelm and Bill Rossello, "The Care and Feeding of Customers," *Management Review* (March 1997), 19–23.
51. Schonfeld, "The Customized, Digitized, Have-It-Your-Way Economy."
52. Paul Migliorato, "Toyota Retools Japan," *Business* 2.0 (August 2004), 39–41.
53. Richard B. Chase and David A. Tansik, "The Customer Contact Model for Organization Design," *Management Science* 29 (1983), 1037–1050.
54. Ibid.
55. David E. Bowen and Edward E. Lawler III, "The Empowerment of Service Workers: What, Why, How, and When," *Sloan Management Review* (Spring 1992), 31–39: Gregory B. Northcraft and Richard B. Chase, "Managing Service Demand at the Point of Delivery," *Academy of Management Review* 10 (1985), 66–75; and Roger W. Schmenner, "How Can Service Businesses Survive and Prosper?" *Sloan Management Review* 27 (Spring 1986), 21–32.
56. "About Our Company," at http://www.pret.com/about (accessed June 16, 2008).
57. "Our Customers," at http://www.pret.com/about/customers.htm (accessed June 16, 2008).
58. Scott Kirsner, "Recipe for Reinvention," *Fast Company* (April 2002), 38–42.
59. Richard Metters and Vincente Vargas, "Organizing Work in Service Firms," *Business Horizons* (July–August 2000), 23–32.
60. Perrow, "A Framework for Comparative Analysis" and *Organizational Analysis*.
61. Brian T. Pentland, "Sequential Variety in Work Processes," *Organization Science* 14, no. 5 (September–October 2003), 528–540.
62. Jim Morrison, "Grand Tour. Making Music: The Craft of the Steinway Piano," *Spirit* (February 1997), 42–49, 100.
63. Stuart F. Brown, "Biotech Gets Productive," *Fortune*, special section, "Industrial Management and Technology" (January 20, 2003), 170[A]–170[H].
64. Michael Withey, Richard L. Daft, and William C. Cooper, "Measures of Perrow's Work Unit Technology: An Empirical Assessment and a New Scale," *Academy of Management Journal* 25 (1983), 45–63.
65. Christopher Gresov, "Exploring Fit and Misfit with Multiple Contingencies," *Administrative Science Quarterly* 34 (1989), 431–453; and Dale L. Goodhue and Ronald L. Thompson, "Task-Technology Fit and Individual Performance," *MIS Quarterly* (June 1995), 213–236.
66. Gresov, "Exploring Fit and Misfit with Multiple Contingencies"; Charles A. Glisson, "Dependence of Technological Routinization on Structural Variables in Human Service Organizations," *Administrative Science Quarterly* 23 (1978), 383–395; and Jerald Hage and Michael Aiken, "Routine Technology, Social Structure and Organizational Goals," *Administrative Science Quarterly* 14 (1969), 368–379.
67. Gresov, "Exploring Fit and Misfit with Multiple Contingencies"; A. J. Grimes and S. M. Kline, "The Technological Imperative: The Relative Impact of Task Unit, Modal Technology, and Hierarchy on Structure," *Academy of Management Journal* 16 (1973), 583–597; Lawrence G. Hrebiniak, "Job Technologies, Supervision and Work Group Structure," Administrative Science Quarterly 19 (1974), 395–410; and Jeffrey Pfeffer, *Organizational Design* (Arlington Heights, Ill.: AHM, 1978), Chapter 1.
68. Patrick E. Connor, *Organizations: Theory and Design* (Chicago: Science Research Associates, 1980); Richard L. Daft and Norman B. Macintosh, "A Tentative Exploration into Amount and Equivocality of Information Processing in Organizational Work Units," *Administrative Science Quarterly* 26 (1981), 207–224.
69. Paul D. Collins and Frank Hull, "Technology and Span of Control: Woodward Revisited," *Journal of Management Studies* 23 (1986), 143–164; Gerald D. Bell, "The Influence of Technological Components of Work upon Management Control," *Academy of Management Journal* 8 (1965), 127–132; and Peter M. Blau and Richard A. Schoenherr, *The Structure of Organizations* (New York: Basic Books, 1971).
70. W. Alan Randolph, "Matching Technology and the Design of Organization Units," *California Management Review* 22–23 (1980–81), 39–48; Daft and Macintosh, "Tentative Exploration into Amount and Equivocality of Information Processing"; and Michael L. Tushman, "Work Characteristics and Subunit Communication Structure: A Contingency Analysis," *Administrative Science Quarterly* 24 (1979), 82–98.
71. Andrew H. Van de Ven and Diane L. Ferry, *Measuring and Assessing Organizations* (New York: Wiley, 1980); and Randolph, "Matching Technology and the Design of Organization Units."
72. Richard L. Daft and Robert H. Lengel, "Information Richness: A New Approach to Managerial Behavior and Organization Design," in Barry Staw and Larry L. Cummings, eds., *Research in Organizational Behavior,* vol. 6 (Greenwich, Conn.: JAI Press, 1984), 191–233; Richard L. Daft and Norman B. Macintosh, "A New Approach into Design and Use of Management Information," *California*

Management Review 21 (1978), 82–92; Daft and Macintosh, "A Tentative Exploration into Amount and Equivocality of Information Processing"; W. Alan Randolph, "Organizational Technology and the Media and Purpose Dimensions of Organizational Communication," *Journal of Business Research* 6 (1978), 237–259; Linda Argote, "Input Uncertainty and Organizational Coordination in Hospital Emergency Units," *Administrative Science Quarterly* 27 (1982), 420–434; and Andrew H. Van de Ven and Andre Delbecq, "A Task Contingent Model of Work Unit Structure," *Administrative Science Quarterly* 19 (1974), 183–197.

73. Peggy Leatt and Rodney Schneck, "Criteria for Grouping Nursing Subunits in Hospitals," *Academy of Management Journal* 27 (1984), 150–165; and Robert T. Keller, "Technology-Information Processing," *Academy of Management Journal* 37, no. 1 (1994), 167–179.
74. Gresov, "Exploring Fit and Misfit with Multiple Contingencies"; Michael L. Tushman, "Technological Communication in R&D Laboratories: The Impact of Project Work Characteristics," *Academy of Management Journal* 21 (1978), 624–645; and Robert T. Keller, "Technology-Information Processing Fit and the Performance of R&D Project Groups: A Test of Contingency Theory," *Academy of Management Journal* 37, no. 1 (1994), 167–179.
75. Richard l. Litwin, "Govindappa Venkataswamy, MD: 1918 to 2006," Cataract & Refractive Surgery Today (September 2006), 1.
76. R. Rubin, "The Perfect Vision of Dr. V.," *Fast Company*, January, 43 (2001), 146.
77. Ibid.
78. James Thompson, *Organizations in Action* (New York: McGraw-Hill, 1967).
79. Ibid., 40.
80. Gene Bylinsky, "Shipmaking Gets Modern," *Fortune*, special section, "Industrial Management and Technology" (January 20, 2003), 170[K]–170[L].
81. Paul S. Adler, "Interdepartmental Interdependence and Coordination: The Case of the Design/Manufacturing Interface," *Organization Science* 6, no. 2 (March–April 1995), 147–167.
82. R. Dyck, "Team-based Organization at Celestica," *Journal for Quality and Participation*, (September–October 1999).
83. Christopher Gresov, "Effects of Dependence and Tasks on Unit Design and Efficiency," *Organization Studies* 11 (1990), 503–529; Andrew H. Van de Ven, Andre Delbecq, and Richard Koenig, "Determinants of Coordination Modes within Organizations," *American Sociological Review* 41 (1976), 322–338; Linda Argote, "Input Uncertainty and Organizational Coordination in Hospital Emergency Units"; Jack K. Ito and Richard B. Peterson, "Effects of Task Difficulty and Interdependence on Information Processing Systems," *Academy of Management Journal* 29 (1986), 139–149; and Joseph L. C. Cheng, "Interdependence and Coordination in Organizations: A Role-System Analysis," *Academy of Management Journal* 26 (1983), 156–162.
84. Robert W. Keidel, "Team Sports Models as a Generic Organizational Framework," *Human Relations* 40 (1987), 591–612; Robert W. Keidel, "Baseball, Football, and Basketball: Models for Business," *Organizational Dynamics* (Winter 1984), 5–18; and Nancy Katz, "Sports Teams as a Model for Workplace Teams: Lessons and Liabilities," *Academy of Management Executive* 15, no. 3 (2001), 56–67.
85. Michele Liu, Hélène Denis, Harvey Kolodny, and Benjt Stymne, "Organization Design for Technological Change," *Human Relations* 43 (January 1990), 7–22.
86. Stephen P. Robbins, *Organizational Behavior* (Upper Saddle River, N.J.: Prentice-Hall, 1998), 521.
87. Gerald I. Susman and Richard B. Chase, "A Sociotechnical Analysis of the Integrated Factory," *Journal of Applied Behavioral Science* 22 (1986), 257–270; and Paul Adler, "New Technologies, New Skills," *California Management Review* 29 (Fall 1986), 9–28.
88. Based on Don Hellriegel, John W. Slocum, Jr., and Richard W. Woodman, *Organizational Behavior,* 8th ed. (Cincinnati, Ohio: South-Western, 1998), 491–495; and Gregory B. Northcraft and Margaret A. Neale, *Organizational Behavior: A Management Challenge*, 2nd ed. (Fort Worth, Tex.: The Dryden Press, 1994), 550–553.
89. F. Emery, "Characteristics of Sociotechnical Systems," Tavistock Institute of Human Relations, document 527, 1959; William Pasmore, Carol Francis, and Jeffrey Haldeman, "Sociotechnical Systems: A North American Reflection on Empirical Studies of the 70s," *Human Relations* 35 (1982), 1179–1204; and William M. Fox, "Sociotechnical System Principles and Guidelines: Past and Present," *Journal of Applied Behavioral Science* 31, no. 1 (March 1995), 91–105.
90. W. S. Cascio, *Managing Human Resources* (New York: McGraw-Hill, 1986), 19.
91. Eric Trist and Hugh Murray, eds., *The Social Engagement of Social Science: A Tavistock Anthology*, vol. II (Philadelphia: University of Pennsylvania Press, 1993); and William A. Pasmore, "Social Science Transformed: The Socio-Technical Perspective," *Human Relations* 48, no. 1 (1995), 1–21.
92. Taylor, J.C. & D.F. Felten, *Performance by Design: Sociotechnical Systems in North America* (Upper Saddle River, NJ: Prentice Hall, 1993).
93. R. E. Walton, "From Control to Commitment in the Workplace," *Harvard Business Review* 63, no. 2 (1985), 76–84; E. W. Lawler, III, High Involvement Management (London: Jossey-Bass, 1986), 84; and Hellriegel, Slocum, and Woodman, *Organizational Behavior*, 491.
94. William A. Pasmore, "Social Science Transformed: The Socio-Technical Perspective," *Human Relations* 48, no. 1 (1995), 1–21.
95. David M. Upton, "What Really Makes Factories Flexible?" *Harvard Business Review* (July–August 1995), 74–84.

96. Pasmore, "Social Science Transformed: The Socio-Technical Perspective"; H. Scarbrough, "Review Article: *The Social Engagement of Social Science: A Tavistock Anthology, Vol. II*," *Human Relations* 48, no. 1 (1995), 23–33.

Chapter 8

1. M. Gooderham, "Who Needs R&D—Just Email Mr. Fix-It," *The Globe and Mail* (April 24, 2007).
2. Innocentive, "Awarded Challenges" at http://www.innocentive.com/servlets/project/ProjectInfo.po?s=AW (accessed July 10, 2008.
3. M. Gooderham, "Who Needs R&D—Just Email Mr. Fix-It."
4. H. Schmundt, "Using the Internet to Solve R&D Problems," (December 19, 2005) at http://www.spiegel.de/international/spiegel/0,1518,392055,00.html (accessed July 10, 2008.
5. *Establishing a Leading Knowledge-based Organization*, National Aboriginal Health Organization, March 2001.
6. M-L. Guzman, "Brampton Gets $550M Health Care Facelift," (October 15, 2007) at http://www.itworldcanada.com/Pages/Docbase/ViewArticle.aspx?id=idgml-98ed1a50-83c3-4aae-b181-58e5dafed118 (accessed July 10, 2008).
7. Charles V. Callahan and Bruce A. Pasternack, "Corporate Strategy in the Digital Age," *Strategy & Business*, Issue 15 (Second Quarter 1999), 10–14.
8. Ibid.
9. Michael Geist, "*Time*'s Choice Could Prove Inspired," (January 8, 2007) at http://www.thestar.com/printArticle/168762 (accessed June 17, 2008).
10. Bill Richards, "A Total Overhaul," *The Wall Street Journal* (December 7, 1998), R30.
11. Erik Berkman, "How to Stay Ahead of the Curve," *CIO* (February 1, 2002), 72–80; and Heather Harreld, "Pick-Up Artists," *CIO* (November 1, 2000), 148–154.
12. "Business Intelligence," special advertising section, *Business 2.0* (February 2003), S1–S4; and Alice Dragoon, "Business Intelligence Gets Smart," *CIO* (September 15, 2003), 84–91.
13. Julie Schlosser, "Looking for Intelligence in Ice Cream," *Fortune* (March 17, 2003), 114–120.
14. S. Ubelacker, "New Hospital a Model of Electronic Health," *The Globe and Mail* (October 16, 2007), L4.
15. M-L. Guzman, "Brampton Gets $550M Health Care Facelift."
16. Ibid.
17. New Technologies Address Challenges, *The Globe and Mail*, A Special Information Supplement (October 15, 2007), RAC4.
18. Ibid.
19. J.P. Menezes, "Longo's Takes a Fresh Approach to Business," (October 15, 2007) at http://www.itworldcanada.com//Pages/Docbase/ViewArticle.aspx?ID=idgml-e1433b72-e2d3-4774-9e42-4630d27e9c60 (accessed July 10, 2008).
20. "Terabyte" at http://www.thefreedictionary.com/terabyte (accessed June 17, 2008).
21. Constance L. Hays, "What They Know About You; Wal-Mart—An Obsessive Monitor of Customer Behavior," *The New York Times* (November 14, 2004), Section 3, 1.
22. "How Much Information? 2003," at http://www2.sims.berkeley.edu/research/projects/how-much-info-2003 (accessed June 17, 2008).
23. K. Lau, "'Intelligent Apps' Handle Information Avalanche," at http://www.ITWorldCanada.com (accessed February 16, 2007 at http://www.itworldcanada.com/a/search/a28acb21-1c64-4d27-bffc-638aaf5ade33.html (accessed July 10, 2008).
24. Michael Arndt, "McDonald's: Fries with That Salad?" *BusinessWeek* (July 5, 2004), 82–84.
25. Robert Simons, "Strategic Organizations and Top Management Attention to Control Systems," *Strategic Management Journal* 12 (1991), 49–62.
26. Kevin Ferguson, "Mission Control," *Inc. Magazine* (November 2003), 27–28; and Russ Banham, "Seeing the Big Picture: New Data Tools Are Enabling CEOs to Get a Better Handle on Performance Across Their Organizations," *Chief Executive* (November 2003), 46ff.
27. Trillium Health Centre at http://www.cognos.com.
28. Richard L. Daft and Norman B. Macintosh, "The Nature and Use of Formal Control Systems for Management Control and Strategy Implementation," *Journal of Management* 10 (1984), 43–66.
29. Susannah Patton, "Web Metrics That Matter," *CIO* (November 14, 2002), 84–88; and Ramin Jaleshgari, "The End of the Hit Parade," *CIO* (May 14, 2000), 183–190.
30. Adam Lashinsky, "Meg and the Machine," *Fortune* (September 1, 2003), 68–78.
31. Howard Rothman, "You Need Not Be Big to Benchmark," *Nation's Business* (December 1992), 64–65.
32. Tom Rancour and Mike McCracken, "Applying 6 Sigma Methods for Breakthrough Safety Performance," *Professional Safety* 45, no. 10 (October 2000), 29–32; Lee Clifford, "Why You Can Safely Ignore Six Sigma," *Fortune* (January 22, 2001), 140.
33. Michael Hammer and Jeff Goding, "Putting Six Sigma in Perspective," *Quality* (October 2001), 58–62; Michael Hammer, "Process Management and the Future of Six Sigma," *Sloan Management Review* (Winter 2002), 26–32.
34. Michael Arndt, "Quality Isn't Just for Widgets," BusinessWeek (July 22, 2002), 72–73 and http://www.sixsigmacanada.net/about (accessed July 10, 2008.
35. Daft and Macintosh, "The Nature and Use of Formal Control Systems for Management Control and Strategy Implementation"; Scott S. Cowen and J. Kendall Middaugh II, "Matching an Organization's Planning and Control System to Its Environment," *Journal of General Management* 16 (1990), 69–84.
36. "On Balance," a CFO Interview with Robert Kaplan and David Norton, *CFO* (February 2001), 73–78; Chee W. Chow, Kamal M. Haddad, and James E. Williamson, "Applying the Balanced Scorecard to Small Companies,"

Management Accounting 79, No. 2 (August 1997), 21–27; and Robert Kaplan and David Norton, "The Balanced Scorecard: Measures That Drive Performance," *Harvard Business Review* (January–February 1992), 71–79.

37. Based on Kaplan and Norton, "The Balanced Scorecard"; Chow, Haddad, and Williamson, "Applying the Balanced Scorecard"; Cathy Lazere, "All Together Now," *CFO* (February 1998), 28–36.
38. Debby Young, "Score It a Hit," *CIO Enterprise*, Section 2 (November 15, 1998), 27ff.
39. Nils–Göran Olve, Carl-Johan Petri, Jan Roy, and Sofie Roy, "Twelve Years Later: Understanding and Realizing the Value of Balanced Scorecards," *Ivey Business Journal* (May–June 2004), 1–7.
40. William Davig, Norb Elbert, and Steve Brown, "Implementing a Strategic Planning Model for Small Manufacturing Firms: An Adaptation of the Balanced Scorecard," *SAM Advanced Management Journal* (Winter 2004), 18–24.
41. T. Leahy, "Tailoring the Balanced Scorecard" (August 1, 2000) at http://businessfinancemag.com/article/tailoring-balanced-scorecard-0801 (accessed July 10, 2008.
42. Ibid.
43. Wayne Kawamoto, "Click Here for Efficiency," *BusinessWeek Enterprise* (December 7, 1998), Ent. 12–Ent. 14.
44. Mary J. Cronin, "Ford's Intranet Success," *Fortune* (March 30, 1998), 158; Eryn Brown, "9 Ways to Win on the Web," *Fortune* (May 24, 1999), 112–125.
45. Jacob Nielsen's Alertbox: Ten Best Government Intranets (June 21, 2004) at http://www.useit.com/alertbox/20040621.html (accessed June 17, 2008).
46. National Research Council Canada, "ClearOption Technologies Inc., Winnipeg, Manitoba: Finessing the Online File," (January 24, 2005) at http://irap-pari.nrc-cnrc.gc.ca/success/clearoption-print_e.html (accessed June 17, 2008).
47. Derek Slater, "What Is ERP?" *CIO Enterprise*, Section 2 (May 15, 1999), 86; and Jeffrey Zygmont, "The Ties That Bind," *Inc. Tech* no. 3 (1998), 70–84.
48. Vincent A. Mabert, Ashok Soni, and M. A. Venkataramanan, "Enterprise Resource Planning: Common Myths versus Evolving Reality," *Business Horizons* (May–June 2001), 69–76.
49. Slater, "What Is ERP?"
50. Susannah Patton, "Doctors' Group Profits from ERP," *CIO* (September 1, 2003), 32.
51. Research reported in Eric Seubert, Y. Balaji, and Mahesh Makhija, "The Knowledge Imperative," *CIO Advertising Supplement* (March 15, 2000), S1–S4.
52. Andrew Mayo, "Memory Bankers," *People Management* (January 22, 1998), 34–38; Gary Abramson, "On the KM Midway," *CIO Enterprise*, Section 2 (May 15, 1999), 63–70.
53. David A. Garvin, "Building a Learning Organization," in *Harvard Business Review on Knowledge Management* (Boston, Mass.: President and Fellows of Harvard College, 1998), 47–80.
54. F. Bouthillier and K. Shearer, "Understanding Knowledge Management and Information Management: The Need for an Empirical Perspective," *Information Research*, 8, 1 (October 2002).
55. Based on Mayo, "Memory Bankers"; William Miller, "Building the Ultimate Resource," *Management Review* (January 1999), 42–45; and Todd Datz, "How to Speak Geek," *CIO Enterprise*, Section 2 (April 15, 1999), 46–52.
56. Vikas Anand, William H. Glick, and Charles C. Manz, "Thriving on the Knowledge of Outsiders: Tapping Organizational Social Capital," *Academy of Management Executive* 16, no. 1 (2002), 87–101.
57. D. Cawfield, "Hands On; Use It or Lose It," *Profit* (May 2005).
58. "Is KM Dead and Are Social Computing Tools Providing a Better Alternative?" *Knowledge Management Review*, 10, 3 (July/August 2007), 3.
59. "Wiki" at http://www.webopedia.com/TERM/w/wiki.htm (accessed June 17, 2008).
60. Tony Kontzer, "Kitchen Sink: Many Collaborative Options," *Information Week* (May 5, 2003), 35; sidebar in Tony Kontzer, "Learning to Share," *Information Week* (May 5, 2003), 29–37.
61. J. Rivkin, "Hands On: Why You Need a Wiki," *Profit* (March 2006).
62. S. Bowness, "Sneaking Up on the Enterprise," *Canadian Business* (December 5, 2006).
63. J. Rivkin, "Hands On: Why You Need a Wiki."
64. Wikinomics, "About the Authors," at http://www.wikinomics.com/book/authors.php (accessed July 10, 2008).
65. D. Tapscott, D. and A.D. Williams, *Wikinomics—How Mass Collaboration Changes Everything* (Toronto: Portfolio, 2006), 1.
66. Ibid., 9.
67. Ibid., 291.
68. Richard McDermott, "Why Information Technology Inspired but Cannot Deliver Knowledge Management," *California Management Review* 41, no. 4 (Summer 1999), 103–117.
69. Based on Ikujiro Nonaka and Hirotaka Takeuchi, *The Knowledge-Creating Company: How Japanese Companies Create the Dynamics of Innovation* (New York: Oxford University Press, 1995), 8–9; and Robert M. Grant, "Toward a Knowledge-Based Theory of the Firm," *Strategic Management Journal* 17 (Winter 1996), 109–122.
70. Grant, "Toward a Knowledge-Based Theory of the Firm."
71. Martin Schulz, "The Uncertain Relevance of Newness: Organizational Learning and Knowledge Flows," *Academy of Management Journal* 44, no. 4 (2001), 661–681.
72. C. Jackson Grayson, Jr., and Carla S. O'Dell, "Mining Your Hidden Resources," *Across the Board* (April 1998), 23–28.

73. Based on Morten T. Hansen, Nitin Nohria, and Thomas Tierney, "What's Your Strategy for Managing Knowledge?" *Harvard Business Review* (March–April 1999), 106–116.
74. "Neo Insight Case Studies—Environment Canada," at http://www.neoinsight.com/caseStudies/caseStudy7.html (accessed June 17, 2008).
75. Louisa Wah, "Behind the Buzz," *Management Review* (April 1999), 17–26.
76. Michael A. Fontaine, Salvatore Parise, and David Miller, "Collaborative Environments: An Effective Tool for Transforming Business Processes," *Ivey Business Journal* (May–June 2004); Mary Flood, "Hawk Vote for California Firm Unanimous," *Houston Chronicle* (May 15, 2001), 15; and "Firm Finalist for Innovation," *The Nelson Mail* (May 23, 2003), 4.
77. DM Review's "2003 World Class Solution Award" (February 6, 2002) at http://www.mwhglobal.com/press_template.asp?pressURL=press_2003_6_2.asp (accessed June 17, 2008).
78. "Best Buy Acquires Pacific Sales Kitchen and Bath Centers, Inc.; California Retailer Caters to Upscale Remodelers; Extends Best Buy's Reach With High-End Home Improvement Products" (December 22, 2005) at http://findarticles.com/p/articles/mi_m0EIN/is_2005_Dec_22/ai_n15967958 (accessed July 10, 2008); "Jiangsu Five Star Appliance Co., Ltd." at http://investing.businessweek.com/research/stocks/private/snapshot.asp?privcapId=26338879 (accessed July 10, 2008); "Best Buy Acquires Speakeasy" (March 27, 2007) at http://www.speakeasy.net/press/pr/pr032707.php (accessed July 10, 2008); "Best Buy Co., Inc." at http://www.fundinguniverse.com/company-histories/Best-Buy-Co-Inc-Company-History.html (accessed July 10, 2008).
79. D. Tapscott, and A.D. Williams, "Building a Wiki Workplace," (May 1, 2007) at http://www.backbonemag.com/Magazine/CoverStory_05010701.asp (accessed June 17, 2008).
80. "Best Buy Appoints New Chief Information Officer for North America," (October 1, 2007) at http://www.internetretailer.com/dailyNews.asp?id=23938 (accessed June 17, 2008).
81. D. Tapscott, and A.D. Williams, "Building a Wiki Workplace."
82. Ibid.
83. Steven A. Melnyk and David R. Denzler, *Operations Management: A Value-Driven Approach* (Burr Ridge, Ill.: Richard D. Irwin, 1996), 613.
84. Jim Turcotte, Bob Silveri, and Tom Jobson, "Are You Ready for the E-Supply Chain?" *APICS—The Performance Advantage* (August 1998), 56–59.
85. Case Studies: Hill and Knowlton Canada Limited (March 3, 2002) at http://www.microsoft.com/canada/casestudies/handk.mspx (accessed June 17, 2008).
86. Christopher Koch, "It All Began with Drayer," *CIO* (August 1, 2002), 56–60.
87. Brian Caulfield, "Facing Up to CRM," *Business 2.0* (August–September 2001), 149–150; and "Customer Relationship Management: The Good, The Bad, The Future," special advertising section, *BusinessWeek* (April 28, 2003), 53–64.
88. Timothy J. Mullaney, "E-Biz Strikes Again," *BusinessWeek* (May 10, 2004), 80–90.
89. Northern Blue Technology, "Twentieth Century Education with Northern Blue Technology," at http://www.northernblue.ca/products/index.php/21st_Century_Education_with_Northern_Blue_Technology (accessed June 17, 2008).
90. Northern Blue Technology, "Products and Portals," at http://www.northernblue.ca/products/index.php/Products_and_Portals (accessed June 17, 2008).
91. Christopher Barnatt, "Embracing E-Business," *Journal of General Management* 30, no. 1 (Autumn 2004), 79–96.
92. This discussion is based on Ranjay Gulati and Jason Garino, "Get the Right Mix of Bricks and Clicks," *Harvard Business Review* (May–June 2000), 107–114.
93. Andy Reinhardt, "Tesco Bets Small—and Wins Big," *BusinessWeek E.Biz* (October 1, 2001), EB26–EB32; and Patrick Barwise and Sean Meehan, "The Benefits of Getting the Basics Right," *Financial Times* (October 8, 2004), 4.
94. Andrew Blackman, "A Strong Net Game," *The Wall Street Journal* (October 25, 2004), R1, R11.
95. Siobhan O'Mahony and Stephen R. Barley, "Do Digital Telecommunications Affect Work and Organization? The State of Our Knowledge," *Research in Organizational Behavior* 21 (1999), 125–161.
96. Sari Kalin, "Overdrive," *CIO Web Business*, Section 2 (July 2, 1999), 36–40.
97. O'Mahony and Barley, "Do Digital Telecommunications Affect Work and Organization?"
98. Joanne Lee-Young and Megan Barnett, "Furiously Fast Fashions," *The Industry Standard* (June 11, 2001), 72–79.

Chapter 9

1. RCMP Interpol Ottawa, (February 2, 2007) at http://www.rcmp-grc.gc.ca/intpolicing/interpol_e.htm (accessed June 18, 2008).
2. "Secretary General of Interpol to Visit Canada from March 29–31," (March 23, 2005) at http://www.rcmp-grc.gc.ca/news/2005/adv_0504_e.htm (accessed September 21, 2007).
3. Chuck Salter, "Terrorists Strike Fast . . . Interpol Has to Move Faster . . . Ron Noble Is on the Case," *Fast Company* (October 2002), 96–104; and "Interpol Pushing to Be UN Globocop," *The New American* (November 1, 2004), 8.
4. James Q. Wilson, *Bureaucracy* (New York: Basic Books, 1989); and Charles Perrow, *Complex Organizations: A Critical Essay* (Glenview, Ill.: Scott, Foresman, 1979), 4.
5. Tom Peters, "Rethinking Scale," *California Management Review* (Fall 1992), 7–29.

6. Fortune Global 500, "General Electric" at http://money.cnn.com/magazines/fortune/global500/2007/snapshots/170.html (accessed July 11, 2008); http://www.careerbuilder.com/Jobs/Company/C37M9740Z3XVVPSBPJ/General-Electric-Corporate/ (accessed July 11, 2008).
7. B. Jang, "CPR Eyes Big League of U.S. Carriers," *The Globe and Mail* (September 6, 2007), B1.
8. Matt Murray, "Critical Mass: As Huge Companies Keep Growing, CEOs Struggle to Keep Pace," *The Wall Street Journal* (February 8, 2001), A1, A6.
9. Stuart Elliott, "Advertising's Big Four: It's Their World Now," *The New York Times* (March 31, 2002), Section 3, 1, 10.
10. Donald V. Potter, "Scale Matters," *Across the Board* (July–August 2000), 36–39.
11. Entrepreneur, *National Post*, January 29, 2007, FP14.
12. D. Calleja, "Get Big—or Die Tryin'," *The Globe and Mail*, June 22, 2007).
13. James B. Treece, "Sometimes, You've Still Gotta Have Size," *BusinessWeek/Enterprise* (1993), 200–201 (April, 2003), 66ff.
14. Frits K. Pil and Matthias Holweg, "Exploring Scale: The Advantages of Thinking Small," *MIT Sloan Management Review* (Winter 2003), 33–39.
15. F. Taylor, "Theratech Drug Gets Encouraging Word," *The Globe and Mail* (September 21, 2007) B15.
16. David Friedman, "Is Big Back? Or Is Small Still Beautiful?" *Inc.* (April 1998), 23–28.
17. David Henry, "Mergers: Why Most Big Deals Don't Pay Off," *BusinessWeek* (October 14, 2002), 60–70.
18. Keith H. Hammonds, "Size Is Not a Strategy," *Fast Company* (September 2002), 78–86.
19. See Hammonds, "Size Is Not a Strategy," Henry, "Mergers: Why Most Big Deals Don't Pay Off," and Tom Brown, "How Big Is Too Big?" *Across the Board* (July–August 1999), 15–20, for a discussion.
20. "Key Small Business Financing Statistics" at http://sme-fdi.gc.ca/epic/site/sme_fdi-prf_pme.nsf/en/01259e.html (accessed on September 17, 2007).
21. L. Earl, *Are Small Businesses Positioning Themselves for Growth? A Comparative Look at the Use of Selected Management Practices by Firm Size*, Statistics Canada, 2006.
22. "The Hot 100," *Fortune* (September 5, 2005), 75–80.
23. Gary Hamel, quoted in Hammonds, "Size Is Not a Strategy."
24. Richard A. Melcher, "How Goliaths Can Act Like Davids," *BusinessWeek/Enterprise* (1993), 192–201.
25. Ibid.
26. Hammonds, "Size Is Not a Strategy."
27. John R. Kimberly, Robert H. Miles, and associates, *The Organizational Life Cycle* (San Francisco: Jossey-Bass, 1980); Ichak Adices, "Organizational Passages—Diagnosing and Treating Lifecycle Problems of Organizations," *Organizational Dynamics* (Summer 1979), 3–25; Danny Miller and Peter H. Friesen, "A Longitudinal Study of the Corporate Life Cycle," *Management Science* 30 (October 1984), 1161–1183; and Neil C. Churchill and Virginia L. Lewis, "The Five Stages of Small Business Growth," *Harvard Business Review* 61 (May–June 1983), 30–50.
28. Larry E. Greiner, "Evolution and Revolution as Organizations Grow," *Harvard Business Review* 50 (July–August 1972), 37–46; and Robert E. Quinn and Kim Cameron, "Organizational Life Cycles and Shifting Criteria of Effectiveness: Some Preliminary Evidence," *Management Science* 29 (1983), 33–51.
29. George Land and Beth Jarman, "Moving beyond Breakpoint," in Michael Ray and Alan Rinzler, eds., *The New Paradigm* (New York: Jeremy P. Tarcher/Perigee Books, 1993), 250–266; and Michael L. Tushman, William H. Newman, and Elaine Romanelli, "Convergence and Upheaval: Managing the Unsteady Pace of Organizational Evolution," *California Management Review* 29 (1987), 1–16.
30. Adam Lashinsky, "Google Hires a Grown-up," *Business 2.0* (February 2002), 22.
31. R. Stross, "A Window of Opportunity for Macs, Soon to Close," (September 16, 2007) at http://www.nytimes.com/2007/09/16/technology/16digi.html?_r=1&sq=window%20opportunity%20macs%20soon%20to%20close&st=nyt&oref=slogin&scp=1&pagewanted=print (accessed September 16, 2007).
32. David A. Whetten, "Sources, Responses, and Effects of Organizational Decline," in John R. Kimberly, Robert H. Miles, and associates, *The Organizational Life Cycle*, 342–374.
33. Brent Schlender, "How Big Can Apple Get?" *Fortune* (February 21, 2005), 67–76; and Josh Quittner with Rebecca Winters, "Apple's New Core—Exclusive: How Steve Jobs Made a Sleek Machine That Could Be the Home-Digital Hub of the Future," *Time* (January 14, 2002), 46.
34. Land and Jarman, "Moving beyond Breakpoint."
35. D. Black, "Sam the Record Man Finally Signs Off," (May 30, 2007) at http://www.thestar.com/printArticle/219252 (accessed September 21, 2007).
36. Stanley Holmes, "The New Nike," *BusinessWeek* (September 20, 2004), 78–86.
37. Daniel Roth, "Can Nike Still Do It without Phil Knight?" *Fortune* (April 4, 2005), 58–68.
38. Global Exchange, "Sweatfree Communities," (October 28, 2007) at http://www.globalexchange.org/campaigns/sweatshops/nike/faq.html (accessed July 11, 2008).
39. A. Bernstein "Online Extra: Nike's New game Plan for Sweatshops," (September 20, 2004) at http://www.businessweek.com/magazine/content/04_38/b3900011_mz001.htm (accessed July 11, 2008).
40. Corel Founder Cowpland Resurfaces at Tiny Zim Technologies, *CRN* (February 6, 2001) at http://www.crn.com/it-channel/18835301 (accessed June 19, 2008).
41. Jay Greene, "Microsoft's Midlife Crisis," *BusinessWeek* (April 19, 2004), 88–98.

42. Max Weber, *The Theory of Social and Economic Organizations*, translated by A.M. Henderson and T. Parsons (New York: Free Press, 1947).
43. Tina Rosenberg, "The Taint of the Greased Palm," *The New York Times Magazine* (August 10, 2003), 28.
44. John Crewdson, "Corruption Viewed as a Way of Life," *Bryan-College Station Eagle* (November 28, 1982), 13A; Barry Kramer, "Chinese Officials Still Give Preference to Kin, Despite Peking Policies," *The Wall Street Journal* (October 29, 1985), 1, 21.
45. Kelly Barron, "Logistics in Brown," *Forbes* (January 10, 2000), 78–83; Scott Kirsner, "Venture Vérité: United Parcel Service," *Wired* (September 1999), 83–96; and Kathy Goode, Betty Hahn, and Cindy Seibert, *United Parcel Service: The Brown Giant* (unpublished manuscript, Texas A&M University, 1981).
46. Allen C. Bluedorn, "Pilgrim's Progress: Trends and Convergence in Research on Organizational Size and Environment," *Journal of Management Studies* 19 (Summer 1993), 163–191; John R. Kimberly, "Organizational Size and the Structuralist Perspective: A Review, Critique, and Proposal," *Administrative Science Quarterly* (1976), 571–597; Richard L. Daft and Selwyn W. Becker, "Managerial, Institutional, and Technical Influences on Administration: A Longitudinal Analysis," *Social Forces* 59 (1980), 392–413.
47. James P. Walsh and Robert D. Dewar, "Formalization and the Organizational Life Cycle," *Journal of Management Studies* 24 (May 1987), 215–231.
48. Nancy M. Carter and Thomas L. Keon, "Specialization as a Multidimensional Construct," *Journal of Management Studies* 26 (1989), 11–28; Cheng-Kuang Hsu, Robert M. March, and Hiroshi Mannari, "An Examination of the Determinants of Organizational Structure," *American Journal of Sociology* 88 (1983), 975–996; Guy Geeraerts, "The Effect of Ownership on the Organization Structure in Small Firms," *Administrative Science Quarterly* 29 (1984), 232–237; Bernard Reimann, "On the Dimensions of Bureaucratic Structure: An Empirical Reappraisal," *Administrative Science Quarterly* 18 (1973), 462–476; Richard H. Hall, "The Concept of Bureaucracy: An Empirical Assessment," *American Journal of Sociology* 69 (1963), 32–40; and William A. Rushing, "Organizational Rules and Surveillance: A Proposition in Comparative Organizational Analysis," *Administrative Science Quarterly* 10 (1966), 423–443.
49. Jerald Hage and Michael Aiken, "Relationship of Centralization to Other Structural Properties," *Administrative Science Quarterly* 12 (1967), 72–91.
50. Steve Lohr and John Markoff, "You Call This a Midlife Crisis?" *The New York Times* (August 31, 2003), Section 3, 1.
51. Peter Brimelow, "How Do You Cure Injelitance?" *Forbes* (August 7, 1989), 42–44; Jeffrey D. Ford and John W. Slocum, Jr., "Size, Technology, Environment and the Structure of Organizations," *Academy of Management Review* 2 (1977), 561–575; and John D. Kasarda, "The Structural Implications of Social System Size: A Three-Level Analysis," *American Sociological Review* 39 (1974), 19–28.
52. Graham Astley, "Organizational Size and Bureaucratic Structure," *Organization Studies* 6 (1985), 201–228; Spyros K. Lioukas and Demitris A. Xerokostas, "Size and Administrative Intensity in Organizational Divisions," *Management Science* 28 (1982), 854–868; Peter M. Blau, "Interdependence and Hierarchy in Organizations," *Social Science Research* 1 (1972), 1–24; Peter M. Blau and R. A. Schoenherr, *The Structure of Organizations* (New York: Basic Books, 1971); A. Hawley, W. Boland, and M. Boland, "Population Size and Administration in Institutions of Higher Education," *American Sociological Review* 30 (1965), 252–255; Richard L. Daft, "System Influence on Organization Decision-Making: The Case of Resource Allocation," *Academy of Management Journal* 21 (1978), 6–22; and B. P. Indik, "The Relationship between Organization Size and the Supervisory Ratio," *Administrative Science Quarterly* 9 (1964), 301–312.
53. T. F. James, "The Administrative Component in Complex Organizations," *Sociological Quarterly* 13 (1972), 533–539; Daft, "System Influence on Organization Decision-Making"; E. A. Holdaway and E. A. Blowers, "Administrative Ratios and Organization Size: A Longitudinal Examination," *American Sociological Review* 36 (1971), 278–286; and John Child, "Parkinson's Progress: Accounting for the Number of Specialists in Organizations," *Administrative Science Quarterly* 18 (1973), 328–348.
54. Richard L. Daft and Selwyn Becker, "School District Size and the Development of Personnel Resources," *Alberta Journal of Educational Research* 24 (1978), 173–187.
55. Thomas A. Stewart, "Yikes! Deadwood Is Creeping Back," *Fortune* (August 18, 1997), 221–222.
56. Cathy Lazere, "Resisting Temptation: The Fourth Annual SG&A Survey," *CFO* (December 1997), 64–70.
57. Based on Gifford and Elizabeth Pinchot, *The End of Bureaucracy and the Rise of the Intelligent Organization* (San Francisco: Berrett-Koehler Publishers, 1993), 21–29.
58. Listoff, "Confusing Job Titles" (June 26, 2007) at http://listoff.blogspot.com/2007/06/confusing-job-titles.html (accessed July 11, 2008).
59. Scott Shane, "The Beast That Feeds on Boxes: Bureaucracy," (April 10, 2005) at http://www.nytimes.com/2005/04/10/weekinreview/10shane.html?sq=The%20Beast%20That%20Feeds%20on%20Boxes:%20Bureaucracy&st=cse&scp=1&pagewanted=print&position (accessed July, 11, 2008).
60. Gregory A. Bigley and Karlene H. Roberts, "The Incident Command System: High-Reliability Organizing for Complex and Volatile Task Environments," *Academy of Management Journal* 44, no. 6 (2001), 1281–1299.
61. Robert Pool, "In the Zero Luck Zone," *Forbes ASAP* (November 27, 2000), 85.
62. Based on Bigley and Roberts, "The Incident Command System."

63. L.G. Marr, Lean and Mean, *The Hamilton Spectator* (January 2005).
64. Philip M. Padsakoff, Larry J. Williams, and William D. Todor, "Effects of Organizational Formalization on Alienation among Professionals and Nonprofessionals," *Academy of Management Journal* 29 (1986), 820–831.
65. "Local Salvation Army Response to 9-11 Happenings Recalled by Mayor" (September 14, 2006) at http://www.salvationarmy.ca/2006/09/14/local-salvation-army-response-to-9-11-happenings-recalled-by-major/ (accessed June 19, 2008).
66. This *In Practice* box is based, in large part, on information from Robert A. Watson and Ben Brown, *The Most Effective Organization in the U.S.: Leadership Secrets of the Salvation Army* (New York: Crown Business, 2001), 159–181.
67. Royston Greenwood, C. R. Hinings, and John Brown, "'P2-Form' Strategic Management: Corporate Practices in Professional Partnerships," *Academy of Management Journal* 33 (1990), 725–755; Royston Greenwood and C. R. Hinings, "Understanding Strategic Change: The Contribution of Archetypes," *Academy of Management Journal* 36 (1993), 1052–1081.
68. William G. Ouchi, "Markets, Bureaucracies, and Clans," *Administrative Science Quarterly* 25 (1980), 129–141; idem, "A Conceptual Framework for the Design of Organizational Control Mechanisms," *Management Science* 25 (1979), 833–848.
69. Weber, *The Theory of Social and Economic Organizations*, 328–340.
70. Oliver A. Williamson, *Markets and Hierarchies: Analyses and Antitrust Implications* (New York: Free Press, 1975).
71. Raymond E. Miles, Henry J. Coleman, Jr., and W. E. Douglas Creed, "Keys to Success in Corporate Redesign," *California Management Review* 37, no. 3 (Spring 1995), 128–145.
72. Micossi, "Creating Internal Markets."
73. Ouchi, "Markets, Bureaucracies, and Clans."
74. Anna Muoio, ed., "Growing Smart," *Fast Company* (August 1998), 73–83.
75. Richard Leifer and Peter K. Mills, "An Information Processing Approach for Deciding upon Control Strategies and Reducing Control Loss in Emerging Organizations," *Journal of Management* 22, no. 1 (1996), 113–137.
76. Stratford Sherman, "The New Computer Revolution," *Fortune* (June 14, 1993), 56–80.
77. V. Galt, "Don't Like it Here? Don't Bother Crying in Your Beer," *The Globe and Mail*, (September 8, 2007), B18.
78. Ibid.
79. Leifer and Mills, "An Information Processing Approach for Deciding upon Control Strategies"; and Laurie J. Kirsch, "The Management of Complex Tasks in Organizations: Controlling the Systems Development Process," *Organization Science* 7, no. 1 (January–February 1996), 1–21.
80. James R. Barker, "Tightening the Iron Cage: Concertive Control in Self-Managing Teams," *Administrative Science Quarterly* 38 (1993), 408–437.
81. Kim S. Cameron, Myung Kim, and David A. Whetten, "Organizational Effects of Decline and Turbulence," *Administrative Science Quarterly* 32 (1987), 222–240.
82. Danny Miller, "What Happens after Success: The Perils of Excellence," *Journal of Management Studies* 31, no. 3 (May 1994), 325–358.
83. Kris Frieswick, "The Turning Point: What Options Do Companies Have When Their Industries Are Dying?" (April 1, 2005) at http://www.cfo.com/printable/article.cfm/3786531/c_3805512?f=options (accessed July 11, 2008).
84. Leonard Greenhalgh, "Organizational Decline," in Samuel B. Bacharach, ed., *Research in the Sociology of Organizations* 2 (Greenwich, Conn.: JAI Press, 1983), 231–276; and Peter Lorange and Robert T. Nelson, "How to Recognize—and Avoid—Organizational Decline," *Sloan Management Review* (Spring 1987), 41–48.
85. Kim S. Cameron and Raymond Zammuto, "Matching Managerial Strategies to Conditions of Decline," *Human Resources Management* 22 (1983), 359–375; and Leonard Greenhalgh, Anne T. Lawrence, and Robert I. Sutton, "Determinants of Workforce Reduction Strategies in Organizations," *Academy of Management Review* 13 (1988), 241–254.
86. Service Canada, "Tool and Die Makers" (March 31, 2007) at http://www.jobfutures.ca/noc/7232p4.shtml (accessed June 19, 2008).
87. William Weitzel and Ellen Jonsson, "Reversing the Downward Spiral: Lessons from W. T. Grant and Sears Roebuck," *Academy of Management Executive* 5 (1991), 7–21; William Weitzel and Ellen Jonsson, "Decline in Organizations: A Literature Integration and Extension," *Administrative Science Quarterly* 34 (1989), 91–109.
88. R. Corelli, "Eaton's: A Dynasty in Decline," (March 10, 1997) at http://www.thecanadianencyclopedia.com/index.cfm?PgNm=TCE&Params=M1ARTM0011178 (accessed July 11, 2008).
89. "Eaton's: A Canadian Institution, December 8, 1869–February 18, 2002," at http://archives.cbc.ca/300i.asp?id=1-69-377 (accessed September 23, 2007).
90. K. Noble, "Eaton's Goes Bankrupt," (August 30, 1999) at http://www.thecanadianencyclopedia.com/index.cfm?PgNm=TCE&Params=M1ARTM0012007 (accessed July 11, 2008).
91. "Eaton's: A Canadian Institution, December 8, 1869–February 18, 2002).
92. J.P. Sheppard and S.D. Chowdhury, "Riding the Wrong Wave: Organizational Failure as a Failed Turnaround," *Long Range Planning*, 38 (2005), 256.
93. William McKinley, Carol M. Sanchez, and Allen G. Schick, "Organizational Downsizing: Constraining, Cloning, Learning," *Academy of Management Executive* 9, no. 3 (1995), 32–42.
94. Gregory B. Northcraft and Margaret A. Neale, *Organizational Behavior: A Management Challenge*, 2nd ed. (Fort Worth, Tex: The Dryden Press, 1994), 626; and A. Catherine Higgs, "Executive Commentary" on McKinley, Sanchez,

and Schick, "Organizational Downsizing: Constraining, Cloning, Learning," 43–44.

95. Wayne Cascio, "Strategies for Responsible Restructuring," *Academy of Management Executive* 16, no. 3 (2002), 80–91; James R. Morris, Wayne F. Cascio, and Clifford E. Young, "Downsizing after All These Years: Questions and Answers about Who Did It, How Many Did It, and Who Benefited from It," *Organizational Dynamics* (Winter 1999), 78–86; Stephen Doerflein and James Atsaides, "Corporate Psychology: Making Downsizing Work," *Electrical World* (September–October 1999), 41–43; and Brett C. Luthans and Steven M. Sommer, "The Impact of Downsizing on Workplace Attitudes," *Group and Organization Management* 2, no. 1 (1999), 46–70.
96. These techniques are based on Bob Nelson, "The Care of the Un-Downsized," *Training and Development* (April 1997), 40–43; Shari Caudron, "Teach Downsizing Survivors How to Thrive," *Personnel Journal* (January 1996), 38; Joel Brockner, "Managing the Effects of Layoffs on Survivors," *California Management Review* (Winter 1992), 9–28; Ronald Henkoff, "Getting beyond Downsizing," *Fortune* (January 10, 1994), 58–64; Kim S. Cameron, "Strategies for Successful Organizational Downsizing," *Human Resource Management* 33, no. 2 (Summer 1994), 189–211; and Doerflein and Atsaides, "Corporate Psychology: Making Downsizing Work."
97. Matt Murray, "Stress Mounts as More Firms Announce Large Layoffs, But Don't Say Who or When" (Your Career Matters column), *The Wall Street Journal* (March 13, 2001), B1, B12.
98. Dofasco, "1940–1960" at http://www.dofasco.ca/bins/content_page.asp?cid=339-9516-9556-9650 (accessed June 19, 2008).
99. Ibid.
100. *Canadian Case Study: Steel Industry Worker Adjustment Program*, Asia-Pacific Economic Co-operation, 2001.
101. Ibid.

Chapter 10

1. "A Journey Milestone," at http://www.birksandmayors.com/index.asp?cs=386&css=390 (accessed July 9. 2008); and "Stronger Together," at http://www.birksandmayors.com/index.asp?cs=386&css=391 (accessed July 9. 2008).
2. P.P. Brown, "Blood Diamonds," (December 13, 2005) at http://www.worldpress.org/africa/2193.cfm (accessed July 11, 2008).
3. "Birks FAQ," at http://www.birks.com/index.asp?cFlag=content&incFile=faq&langid=1 (accessed July 9, 2008).
4. R. Mendleson, "Your Bling Can Save the World," (June 11, 2008) at http://www.macleans.ca/business/companies/article.jsp?content=20080611_45238_45237 (accessed July 9, 2008).
5. C. Silverman, "How One Firm Saw the Light on Hiring," *The Globe and Mail* (January 31, 2007), C1, C3.
6. Ibid.
7. Anita Raghavan, Kathryn Kranhold, and Alexei Barrionuevo, "Full Speed Ahead: How Enron Bosses Created a Culture of Pushing Limits," *The Wall Street Journal* (August 26, 2002), A1, A7.
8. Mark C. Bolino, William H. Turnley, and James M. Bloodgood, "Citizenship Behavior and the Creation of Social Capital in Organizations," *Academy of Management Review* 27, no. 4 (2002), 505–522; and Don Cohen and Laurence Prusak, *In Good Company: How Social Capital Makes Organizations Work* (Boston, Mass.: Harvard Business School Press, 2001), 3–4.
9. "EBay Profit Increases 24 per cent," (January 24, 2007) at http://www.theglobeandmail.com/servlet/story/RTGAM.20070124.gtebay0124/BNStory/Technology/einsider (accessed June 23, 2008).
10. Esther Colwill, Best Workplaces at a Glance (April 23, 2007) at http://www.canadianbusiness.com/managing/career/article.jsp?content=20070425_85422_85422 (accessed June 24, 2008).
11. W. Jack Duncan, "Organizational Culture: 'Getting a Fix' on an Elusive Concept," *Academy of Management Executive* 3 (1989), 229–236; Linda Smircich, "Concepts of Culture and Organizational Analysis," *Administrative Science Quarterly* 28 (1983), 339–358; and Andrew D. Brown and Ken Starkey, "The Effect of Organizational Culture on Communication and Information," *Journal of Management Studies* 31, no. 6 (November 1994), 807–828.
12. Edgar H. Schein, "Organizational Culture," *American Psychologist* 45 (February 1990), 109–119.
13. "The Body Shop Canada Living Machine Effluent Reuse" (2001) at http://www.ecowerks.ca/clients.htm (accessed July 12, 2008).
14. Harrison M. Trice and Janice M. Beyer, "Studying Organizational Cultures through Rites and Ceremonials," *Academy of Management Review* 9 (1984), 653–669; Janice M. Beyer and Harrison M. Trice, "How an Organization's Rites Reveal Its Culture," *Organizational Dynamics* 15 (Spring 1987), 5–24; Steven P. Feldman, "Management in Context: An Essay on the Relevance of Culture to the Understanding of Organizational Change," *Journal of Management Studies* 23 (1986), 589–607; and Mary Jo Hatch, "The Dynamics of Organizational Culture," *Academy of Management Review* 18 (1993), 657–693.
15. This discussion is based on Edgar H. Schein, *Organizational Culture and Leadership*, 2d ed. (Homewood, Ill.: Richard D. Irwin, 1992); and John P. Kotter and James L. Heskett, *Corporate Culture and Performance* (New York: Free Press, 1992).
16. S. Valentine, "ExtendMedia—Courting Jane Q. Public," (May 27, 2007) at http://www.redcanary.ca/view/extendmedia-courting (accessed July 12, 2008).
17. Larry Mallak, "Understanding and Changing Your Organization's Culture," *Industrial Management* (March–April 2001), 18–24.

18. For a list of various elements that can be used to assess or interpret corporate culture, see "10 Key Cultural Elements," sidebar in Micah R. Kee, "Corporate Culture Makes a Fiscal Difference," *Industrial Management* (November–December 2003), 16–20.
19. Charlotte B. Sutton, "Richness Hierarchy of the Cultural Network: The Communication of Corporate Values" (unpublished manuscript, Texas A&M University, 1985); and Terrence E. Deal and Allan A. Kennedy, "Culture: A New Look through Old Lenses," *Journal of Applied Behavioral Science* 19 (1983), 498–505.
20. Thomas C. Dandridge, "Symbols at Work" (working paper, School of Business, State University of New York at Albany, 1978), 1.
21. Jennifer A. Chatman and Sandra Eunyoung Cha, "Leading by Leveraging Culture," *California Management Review* 45, no. 4 (Summer 2003), 20–34.
22. Don Hellriegel and John W. Slocum, Jr., *Management*, 7th ed. (Cincinnati, Ohio: South-Western, 1996), 537.
23. Trice and Beyer, "Studying Organizational Cultures through Rites and Ceremonials."
24. Sutton, "Richness Hierarchy of the Cultural Network"; and Terrence E. Deal and Allan A. Kennedy, *Corporate Cultures: The Rites and Rituals of Corporate Life* (Reading, Mass.: Addison-Wesley, 1982).
25. S. Foster, "Our Love Affair with Trains," at http://www.crossculturedtraveler.com/Archives/Nov2003/Canada.htm (accessed July 12, 2008).
26. Raghavan, Kranhold, and Barrionuevo, "Full Speed Ahead."
27. A. Wahl, J. Castaldo, Z. Olijnyk, E. Pooley and A. Jezovit Best Workplaces '07, (April 25, 2007) at http://www.canadianbusiness.com/managing/career/article.jsp?content=20070425_133041_5516 (accessed July 12, 2008).
28. Ibid.
29. Jennifer A. Chatman and Sandra Eunyoung Cha, "Leading by Leveraging Culture," *California Management Review* 45, no. 4 (Summer 2003), 20–34; and Abby Ghobadian and Nicholas O'Regan, "The Link between Culture, Strategy, and Performance in Manufacturing SMEs," *Journal of General Management* 28, no. 1 (Autumn 2002), 16–34.
30. James R. Detert, Roger G. Schroeder, and John J. Mauriel, "A Framework for Linking Culture and Improvement Initiatives in Organizations," *Academy of Management Review* 25, no. 4 (2000), 850–863.
31. Based on Daniel R. Denison, *Corporate Culture and Organizational Effectiveness* (New York: Wiley, 1990), 11–15; Daniel R. Denison and Aneil K. Mishra, "Toward a Theory of Organizational Culture and Effectiveness," *Organization Science* 6, no. 2 (March–April 1995), 204–223; R. Hooijberg and F. Petrock, "On Cultural Change: Using the Competing Values Framework to Help Leaders Execute a Transformational Strategy," *Human Resource Management* 32 (1993), 29–50; and R. E. Quinn, *Beyond Rational Management: Mastering the Paradoxes and Competing Demands of High Performance* (San Francisco: Jossey-Bass, 1988).
32. Steve Lohr, "Big Blue's Big Bet: Less Tech, More Touch," *The New York Times* (January 25, 2004), Sec. 3, 1.
33. A. Wahl,"Canada's Best Workplaces: Overview," *Canadian Business* (April 26, 2007).
34. S. Valentine, "The Sandvine Way," (2006) at http://www.theredcanary.com/print?articleID=130 (accessed June 24, 2008).
35. "Best Workplaces in Canada 2007" at http://www.greatplacetowork.ca/best/list-ca-2007.htm (accessed July 12, 2008).
36. Ibid.
37. The Leaders 10 Commandments (and the Eight Points) provided by Sandvine Public Affairs, June 2007.
38. "Jobs at MEC" at http://www.mec.ca/Main/content_text.jsp;jsessionid=L5TrWB4sVyyNvntKVhVMpdfJHhp0QJffsLvLX6FGWG3BMGK22qZD!-1599383407?FOLDER%3C%3Efolder_id=1408474396038661&FOLDER%3C%3EbrowsePath=1408474396038661&bmUID=1215909419636 (accessed July 14, 2008).
39. G. Harris cited in Mountain Equipment Co-op (profile) in http://thecanadianencyclopedia.com/PrinterFriendly.cfm?Params=M1ARTM0012398 (accessed June 24, 2008).
40. "Mountain Equipment Co-op" at http://dotherightthing.com/companies/mountain-equipment-co-op (accessed July 12, 2008); A. Holloway, "It's All in the Details," Canadian Business (December 25–January 14, 2006); "Mountain Equipment Co-op (profile)" at http://thecanadianencyclopedia.com/PrinterFriendly.cfm?Params=M1ARTM0012398 (accessed June 24, 2008); R. de Lazzer, "Clothing Retailer Pledges 1 percent of Revenue to Planet," The Globe and Mail (April 5, 2007), Q12; S. Prashad, "Good Green Goals," Toronto Star (April 22, 2007), A12; and "Ethical Sourcing: What it Means to Us" at http://www.mec.ca/Main/content_text.jsp?FOLDER%3C%3Efolder_id=1408474396038947&FOLDER%3C%3EbrowsePath=1408474396038947&bmUID=1203874207701 (accessed July 12, 2008).
41. "MEC Wins Canada's Governance Award" (February 2, 2008) at http://www.8264.net/article.php?id=881 (accessed July 12, 2008).
42. Rekha Balu, "Pacific Edge Projects Itself," *Fast Company* (October 2000), 371–381.
43. Jim Collins, *Good to Great: Why Some Companies Make the Leap . . . and Others Don't* (New York: HarperCollins, 2001), 120–133.
44. Bernard Arogyaswamy and Charles M. Byles, "Organizational Culture: Internal and External Fits," *Journal of Management* 13 (1987), 647–659.
45. Chatman and Cha, "Leading by Leveraging Culture."
46. J. Collins, "From Good to Great" (New York: HarperCollins, 2001).
47. "Best Workplaces in Canada 2006" at http://www.greatplacetowork.ca/best/list-ca-2006.htm (accessed July 12, 2008).

48. A. Styhre, S. Börjesson, and J. Wickenberg, "Managed by the Other: Cultural Anxieties in Two Anglo-Americanized Swedish Firms," *International Journal of Human Resource Management*, 17, 7 (2006), 1293–1306.
49. Paul R. Lawrence and Jay W. Lorsch, *Organization and Environment* (Homewood, Ill.: Irwin, 1969).
50. Scott Kirsner, "Designed for Innovation," *Fast Company* (November 1998), 54, 56.
51. Chatman and Cha, "Leading by Leveraging Culture"; Jeff Rosenthal and Mary Ann Masarech, "High-Performance Cultures: How Values Can Drive Business Results," *Journal of Organizational Excellence* (Spring 2003), 3–18.
52. Ghobadian and O'Regan, "The Link between Culture, Strategy and Performance"; G. G. Gordon and N. DiTomaso, "Predicting Corporate Performance from Organisational Culture," *Journal of Management Studies* 29, no. 6 (1992), 783–798; and G. A. Marcoulides and R. H. Heck, "Organizational Culture and Performance: Proposing and Testing a Model," *Organization Science* 4 (1993), 209–225.
53. R. Charan, "Home Depot's Blueprint for Culture Change," *Harvard Business Review* (April 2006), 4.
54. Robert Paterson, "WestJet—The Difference that Culture Makes," (June 29, 2004) at smartpei.typepad.com/robert_patersons_weblog/2004/06/westjet_the_dif.html (accessed June 25, 2008).
55. John P. Kotter and James L. Heskett, *Corporate Culture and Performance* (New York: The Free Press, 1992).
56. G. Danake, cited in D. Haskayne, *Northern Tigers—Building Ethical Canadian Corporate Champions, A Memoir and a Manifesto* (Toronto: Key Porter Books, 2007), 284.
57. Gordon F. Shea, *Practical Ethics* (New York: American Management Association, 1988); Linda K. Treviño, "Ethical Decision Making in Organizations: A Person–Situation Interactionist Model," *Academy of Management Review* 11 (1986), 601–617; and Linda Klebe Treviño and Katherine A. Nelson, *Managing Business Ethics: Straight Talk about How to Do It Right*, 2nd ed. (New York: John Wiley & Sons, Inc., 1999).
58. Thanks to Susan H. Taft, Kent State University, and Judith White, University of Redlands, for this overview of the sources of individual ethics.
59. Dawn-Marie Driscoll, "Don't Confuse Legal and Ethical Standards," *Business Ethics* (July–August 1996), 44.
60. J. Bakan, *The Corporation: The Pathological Pursuit of Profit and Power* (Toronto: Penguin, 2004), 60.
61. Ibid., 161.
62. Noam Chomsky (n.d.) at http://www.thecorporation.com/index.cfm?page_id=7 (accessed June 25, 2008).
63. LaRue Tone Hosmer, *The Ethics of Management*, 2d ed. (Homewood, Ill.: Irwin, 1991).
64. Geanne Rosenberg, "Truth and Consequences," *Working Woman* (July–August 1998), 79–80.
65. D. Schwarz in C. Hymowitz, "Ain't Misbehavin'—Increasingly, That's What Firms Are Demandin'" *The Globe and Mail* (June 20, 2007), C8.
66. N. Craig Smith, "Corporate Social Responsibility: Whether or How?" *California Management Review* 45, no. 4 (Summer 2003), 52–76; and Eugene W. Szwajkowski, "The Myths and Realities of Research on Organizational Misconduct," in James E. Post, ed., *Research in Corporate Social Performance and Policy*, vol. 9 (Greenwich, Conn.: JAI Press, 1986), 103–122.
67. Some of these incidents are from Hosmer, *The Ethics of Management*.
68. Linda K. Treviño and Katherine A. Nelson, *Managing Business Ethics: Straight Talk about How to Do It Right* (New York: John Wiley & Sons, 1995), 4.
69. Curtis C. Verschoor and Elizabeth A. Murphy, "The Financial Performance of Large U.S. Firms and Those with Global Prominence: How Do the Best Corporate Citizens Rate?" *Business and Society Review* 107, no. 2 (Fall 2002), 371–381; Homer H. Johnson, "Does It Pay to Be Good? Social Responsibility and Financial Performance," *Business Horizons* (November–December 2003), 34–40; Quentin R. Skrabec, "Playing By the Rules: Why Ethics Are Profitable," *Business Horizons* (September–October 2003), 15–18; Marc Gunther, "Tree Huggers, Soy Lovers, and Profits," *Fortune* (June 23, 2003), 98–104; Dale Kurschner, "5 Ways Ethical Business Creates Fatter Profits," *Business Ethics* (March–April 1996), 20–23. Also see various studies reported in Lori Ioannou, "Corporate America's Social Conscience," *Fortune,* special advertising section (May 26, 2003), S1–S10.
70. Verschoor and Murphy, "The Financial Performance of Large U.S. Firms."
71. P. Godfrey, "Corporate Philanthropy Adds to Shareholder Wealth, says BYU Study," (October 28, 2005) at http://www.csrwire.com/print.cgi?sfArticleId=4620 (accessed June 25, 2008).
72. "UFCW Canada Members Raise Record $1.424 Million for Leukemia Charity" (June 16, 2007) at http://new.marketwire.com/2.0/release.do?id=742969 (accessed June 25, 2008).
73. Daniel W. Greening and Daniel B. Turban, "Corporate Social Performance as a Competitive Advantage in Attracting a Quality Workforce," *Business and Society* 39, no. 3 (September 2000), 254.
74. Christopher Marquis, "Doing Well and Doing Good," *The New York Times* (July 13, 2003), Section 3, 2; and Joseph Pereira, "Career Journal: Doing Good and Doing Well at Timberland," *The Wall Street Journal* (September 9, 2003), B1.
75. "The Socially Correct Corporate Business," in Leslie Holstrom and Simon Brady, "The Changing Face of Global Business," *Fortune*, special advertising section (July 24, 2000), S1–S38.
76. *Planeterra Annual Report*, 2006–2007.
77. Linda Klebe Treviño, "A Cultural Perspective on Changing and Developing Organizational Ethics," in Richard Woodman and William Pasmore, eds., *Research and*

Organizational Change and Development, vol. 4 (Greenwich, Conn.: JAI Press, 1990); and Lynn Sharp Paine, "Managing for Organizational Integrity," *Harvard Business Review* (March/April 1994), 106–117.

78. James Weber, "Exploring the Relationship between Personal Values and Moral Reasoning," *Human Relations* 46 (1993), 435–463.
79. L. Kohlberg, "Moral Stages and Moralization: The Cognitive-Developmental Approach," in T. Likona, ed., *Moral Development and Behavior: Theory, Research, and Social Issues* (New York: Holt, Rinehart & Winston, 1976).
80. Hosmer, *The Ethics of Management.*
81. R. Martin, "The Virtue Matrix: Calculating the Return on Corporate Responsibility," *Harvard Business Review* (March 2002), 68.
82. G. Pitts, "Feisty Forest Guy Royer Unafraid to Go Green," *The Globe and Mail* (May 7, 2007), B10.
83. John A. Byrne with Mike France and Wendy Zellner, "The Environment Was Ripe for Abuse," *BusinessWeek* (February 25, 2002), 118–120.
84. Alcan, "Our Values" (2008) at http://www.alcan.com/web/publishing.nsf/content/About+Alcan+-+Our+Values (accessed June 25, 2008).
85. Global 100, "The 2007 List," at http://www.global100.org/2007/index.asp (accessed June 25, 2008).
86. David M. Messick and Max H. Bazerman, "Ethical Leadership and the Psychology of Decision Making," *Sloan Management Review* (Winter 1996), 9–22; Dawn-Marie Driscoll, "Don't Confuse Legal and Ethical Standards," *Business Ethics* (July–August 1996), 44; and Max B. E. Clarkson, "A Stakeholder Framework for Analyzing and Evaluating Corporate Social Performance," *Academy of Management Review* 20, no. 1 (1995), 92–117.
87. Roger Parloff, "Is Fat the Next Tobacco?" *Fortune* (February 3, 2003), 51–54.
88. Cristina Howorun, "PEOPLE: Ron Dembo and Zerofootprint" (August 31, 2007) at http://www.redcanary.ca/view/people-ron-dembo-and (accessed July 12, 2008).
89. Gwen Kinkead, "In the Future, People Like Me Will Go to Jail," Fortune (May 24, 1999) , 190–200; "Sustainability Overview" at http://www.interfaceinc.com/goals/sustainability_overview.html (accessed July 12, 2008); and "Recycled and Bio-based Content in Products" at http://www.interfacesustainability.com/metrics.html (accessed July 13, 2008).
90. *Corporate Ethics: A Prime Business Asset* (New York: The Business Round Table, February 1988).
91. Andrew W. Singer, "The Ultimate Ethics Test," *Across the Board* (March 1992), 19–22; Ronald B. Morgan, "Self and Co-Worker Perceptions of Ethics and Their Relationships to Leadership and Salary," *Academy of Management Journal* 36, no. 1 (February 1993), 200–214; and Joseph L. Badaracco, Jr., and Allen P. Webb, "Business Ethics: A View from the Trenches," *California Management Review* 37, no. 2 (Winter 1995), 8–28.
92. This discussion is based on Robert J. House, Andre Delbecq, and Toon W. Taris, "Value Based Leadership: An Integrated Theory and an Empirical Test" (working paper, 1998).
93. Tamara Schweitzer, "Skiing Green," (February 2007) at http://www.fastcompany.com/articles/2007/02/green-ski-resorts.html?page=0%2C1 (accessed July 12, 2008).
94. Michael Barrier, "Doing the Right Thing," *Nation's Business* (March 1998), 33–38.
95. Mitchell Pacelle, "Citigroup CEO Makes 'Value' a Key Focus," *The Wall Street Journal* (October 1, 2004), C1.
96. Thomas J. Peters and Robert H. Waterman, Jr., *In Search of Excellence* (New York: Harper & Row, 1982).
97. "Citigroup's Day of Reckoning" (November 4 2007) at http://money.cnn.com/2007/11/04/news/companies/citigroup_prince/index.htm (accessed July 12, 2008).
98. Karl E. Weick, "Cognitive Processes in Organizations," in B. M. Staw, ed., *Research in Organizations*, vol. 1 (Greenwich, Conn.: JAI Press, 1979), 42.
99. Richard Osborne, "Kingston's Family Values," *IndustryWeek* (August 13, 2001), 51–54.
100. Alan Yuspeh, "Do the Right Thing," *CIO* (August 1, 2000), 56–58.
101. Amy Zipkin, "Getting Religion on Corporate Ethics," The New York Times (October 18, 2000), C1, C10; and "The Standards of Conduct Business Ethics and Compliance Professionals" at http://www.theecoa.org/AM/Template.cfm?Section=Professional_Standards (accessed July 12, 2008).
102. Treviño and Nelson, Managing Business Ethics, 212.
103. A. Wahl, J. Castaldo, Z. Olijnyk, E. Pooley and A. Jezovit,"Best Workplaces '07" (April 25, 2007) at http://www.canadianbusiness.com/managing/career/article.jsp?content=20070425_133041_5516 (accessed July 12, 2008).
104. Janet P. Near and Marcia P. Miceli, "Effective Whistle-Blowing," *Academy of Management Review* 20, no. 3 (1995), 679–708.
105. Richard P. Nielsen, "Changing Unethical Organizational Behavior," *Academy of Management Executive* 3 (1989), 123–130.
106. Jene G. James, "Whistle-Blowing: Its Moral Justification," in Peter Madsen and Jay M. Shafritz, eds., *Essentials of Business Ethics* (New York: Meridian Books, 1990), 160–190; and Janet P. Near, Terry Morehead Dworkin, and Marcia P. Miceli, "Explaining the Whistle-Blowing Process: Suggestions from Power Theory and Justice Theory," *Organization Science* 4 (1993), 393–411.
107. D. Jacobs, "Whistleblower Awaits Justice after 14 Years, *Ottawa Citizen* (May 15, 2006), 2.
108. T. MacCharles, "High Cost of Whistleblowing," *Toronto Star* (June 30, 2007), A15.
109. Ibid.
110. J. B. Singh, "Ethics Programs in Canada's Largest Corporations," *Business and Society Review*, 111:2 (2006), 119–136.

111. Linda Klebe Treviño, Gary R. Weaver, David G. Gibson, and Barbara Ley Toffler, "Managing Ethics and Legal Compliance: What Works and What Hurts?" *California Management Review* 41, no. 2 (Winter 1999), 131–151.
112. Carl Anderson, "Values-Based Management," *Academy of Management Executive* 11, no. 4 (1997), 25–46.
113. "Citigroup Begins Implementing 5-Point Ethics Program," *Dow Jones Newswires*, March 1, 2005, at http://online.wsj.com.
114. Ronald E. Berenbeim, *Corporate Ethics Practices* (New York: The Conference Board, 1992).
115. James Weber, "Institutionalizing Ethics into Business Organizations: A Model and Research Agenda," *Business Ethics Quarterly* 3 (1993), 419–436.
116. Landon Thomas Jr. "On Wall Street, a Rise in Dismissals over Ethics," (March 25, 2005) at http://www.nytimes.com/2005/03/29/business/29wall.html?_r=1&scp=1&sq=On+Wall+Street%2C+a+Rise+in+Dismissals+over+ (accessed July 12, 2008).
117. Mark Henricks, "Ethics in Action," *Management Review* (January 1995), 53–55; Dorothy Marcic, *Management and the Wisdom of Love* (San Francisco: Jossey-Bass, 1997); and Beverly Geber, "The Right and Wrong of Ethics Offices," *Training* (October 1995), 102–118.
118. Elearning, "Case Study" (Winter 2005) at http://elearning.b2bmediaco.com/issues/winter05/casestudy01_0205.html (accessed June 25, 2008).
119. Susan J. Harrington, "What Corporate America Is Teaching about Ethics," *Academy of Management Executive* 5 (1991), 21–30.
120. Telus, "We're Committed to Developing Athletes" (n.d.) at http://about.telus.com/community/community_boards/index.html (accessed June 25, 2008).
121. Richard W. Judy and Carol D'Amico, *Workforce 2020: Work and Workers in the 21st Century* (Indianapolis, Ind.: Hudson Institute, 1997).
122. Jerry G. Kreuze, Zahida Luqmani, and Mushtaq Luqmani, "Shades of Gray," *Internal Auditor* (April 2001), 48.
123. S. C. Schneider, "National vs. Corporate Culture: Implications for Human Resource Management," *Human Resource Management* (Summer 1988), 239.
124. Carl F. Fey and Daniel R. Denison, "Organizational Culture and Effectiveness: Can American Theory Be Applied in Russia?" *Organization Science* 14, no. 6 (November–December 2003), 686–706.
125. Terence Jackson, "Cultural Values and Management Ethics: A 10-Nation Study," *Human Relations* 54, no. 10 (2001), 1267–1302.
126. Gail Dutton, "Building a Global Brain," *Management Review* (May 1999), 34–38.
127. Ibid.
128. Homer H. Johnson, "Corporate Social Audits—This Time Around," *Business Horizons* (May–June 2001), 29–36.
129. "Me to We, Our Story" at http://www.metowestyle.com/ourstory_aboutus_s/134.htm (accessed July 12, 2008).

Chapter 11

1. Robert D. Hof, "Building an Idea Factory," *BusinessWeek* (October 11, 2004), 194–200; Brian Bremner and Chester Dawson, "Can Anything Stop Toyota?" *BusinessWeek* (November 17, 2003), 114–122; and Norihiko Shirouzu and Jathon Sapsford, "Heavy Load; For Toyota, a New Small Truck Carries Hopes for Topping GM," *The Wall Street Journal* (May 12, 2005), A1, A6.
2. "Toyota Passes GM as World's Number One Automaker," WDET News, (April 24, 2007) at http://www.wdetfm.org/article.php?id=1620 (accessed June 24, 2008).
3. "Innovation in Canada" (n.d). at http://www.mta.ca/faculty/arts/canadian_studies/english/about/innovation/index.htm (accessed June 24, 2008).
4. Based on John P. Kotter, *Leading Change* (Boston, Mass.: Harvard Business School Press, 1996), 18–20.
5. David A. Nadler and Michael L. Tushman, "Organizational Frame Bending: Principles for Managing Reorientation," *Academy of Management Executive* 3 (1989), 194–204; and Michael L. Tushman and Charles A. O'Reilly III, "Ambidextrous Organizations: Managing Evolutionary and Revolutionary Change," *California Management Review* 38, no. 4 (Summer 1996), 8–30.
6. R. Colman, "Shifting into High Gear—Honda Canada Drives Process Innovation with Its Employees," (October 1, 2002) at http://www.allbusiness.com/automotive/motor-vehicle-models-motorcycles/10602037-1.html (accessed July 13, 2008).
7. William A. Davidow and Michael S. Malone, *The Virtual Corporation* (New York: HarperBusiness, 1992); and Gregory G. Dess, Abdul M. A. Rasheed, Kevin J. McLaughlin, and Richard L. Priem, "The New Corporate Architecture," *Academy of Management Executive* 9, no. 3 (1995), 7–20.
8. Brent Schlender, "How Big Can Apple Get?" *Fortune* (February 21, 2005), 66–76.
9. Joseph E. McCann, "Design Principles for an Innovating Company," *Academy of Management Executive* 5 (May 1991), 76–93.
10. HØme Swede HØme, *Wired* (April 2007), 94.
11. Fara Warner, "How Google Searches Itself," *Fast Company* (July 2002), 50–52; Fred Vogelstein, "Search and Destroy," *Fortune* (May 2, 2005), 72–82; and Keith H. Hammonds, "How Google Grows . . . and Grows . . . and Grows," *Fast Company* (April 2003), 74.
12. Kelly Barron, "Logistics in Brown," *Forbes* (January 10, 2000), 78–83; and Scott Kirsner, "Venture Vérité: United Parcel Service," *Wired* (September 1999), 83–96.
13. Richard A. Wolfe, "Organizational Innovation: Review, Critique and Suggested Research Directions," *Journal of Management Studies* 31, no. 3 (May 1994), 405–431.
14. John L. Pierce and Andre L. Delbecq, "Organization Structure, Individual Attitudes and Innovation," *Academy of Management Review* 2 (1977), 27–37; and Michael Aiken and Jerald Hage, "The Organic

Organization and Innovation," *Sociology* 5 (1971), 63–82.

15. Richard L. Daft, "Bureaucratic versus Non-bureaucratic Structure in the Process of Innovation and Change," in Samuel B. Bacharach, ed., *Perspectives in Organizational Sociology: Theory and Research* (Greenwich, Conn.: JAI Press, 1982), 129–166.
16. Alan D. Meyer and James B. Goes, "Organizational Assimilation of Innovations: A Multilevel Contextual Analysis," *Academy of Management Journal* 31 (1988), 897–923.
17. T. Kelley, *The Ten Faces of Innovation* (New York: Currency Doubleday, 2005).
18. Richard W. Woodman, John E. Sawyer, and Ricky W. Griffin, "Toward a Theory of Organizational Creativity," *Academy of Management Review* 18 (1993), 293–321; and Alan Farnham, "How to Nurture Creative Sparks," *Fortune* (January 10, 1994), 94–100.
19. D. Flavelle, "Where Design Meets Function," *Toronto Star* (April 1, 2007), A12.
20. Robert I. Sutton, "Weird Ideas That Spark Innovation," *MIT Sloan Management Review* (Winter 2002), 83–87; Robert Barker, "The Art of Brainstorming," *BusinessWeek* (August 26, 2002), 168–169; Gary A. Steiner, ed., *The Creative Organization* (Chicago, Ill.: University of Chicago Press, 1965), 16–18; and James Brian Quinn, "Managing Innovation: Controlled Chaos," *Harvard Business Review* (May–June 1985), 73–84.
21. J.M. Pethokousis, "The Design of Design—From the Computer Mouse to the Newest Swiffer, IDEO Is the Firm Behind the Scenes," *U.S. News and World Report* (September 24, 2006) at http://www.usnews.com/usnews/biztech/articles/060924/2best_print.htm (accessed June 24, 2008).
22. J. Kotter, *Leading Change*, 20–25; and John P. Kotter, "Leading Change," *Harvard Business Review* (March–April 1995), 59–67.
23. J. Nortext, "First Language Schoolbooks" (n.d.) at http://www.nortext.com/schoolbooks.htm (accessed June 24, 2008).
24. J. G. Tomas M. Hult, Robert F. Hurley, and Gary A. Knight, "Innovativeness: Its Antecedents and Impact on Business Performance," *Industrial Marketing Management* 33 (2004), 429–438.
25. J. L. D. DiSimone, comments about 3M in "How Can Big Companies Keep the Entrepreneurial Spirit Alive?" *Harvard Business Review* (November–December 1995), 184–185; and Thomas A. Stewart, "3M Fights Back," *Fortune* (February 1996), 94–99.
26. J. B. Hindo, "At 3M, A Struggle between Efficiency and Creativity," (June 11, 2007) at http://www.businessweek.com/magazine/content/07_24/b4038406.htm (accessed July 13, 2008).
27. J. L. Tischler, "Join the Circus," *Fast Company*, 96 (2005), 53; and John Gustavson, "Meeting the Green Challenge (February 2007) at http://www.the-cma.org/?WCE=C=47%7CK=226716 (accessed June 24, 2008).
28. J. D. Bruce Merrifield, "Intrapreneurial Corporate Renewal," *Journal of Business Venturing* 8 (September 1993), 383–389; Linsu Kim, "Organizational Innovation and Structure," *Journal of Business Research* 8 (1980), 225–245; and Tom Burns and G. M. Stalker, *The Management of Innovation* (London: Tavistock Publications, 1961).
29. J. James Q. Wilson, "Innovation in Organization: Notes toward a Theory," in James D. Thompson, ed., *Approaches to Organizational Design* (Pittsburgh, Penn.: University of Pittsburgh Press, 1966), 193–218.
30. Charles A. O'Reilly III and Michael L. Tushman, "The Ambidextrous Organization," *Harvard Business Review* (April 2004), 74–81; M. L. Tushman and C. A. O'Reilly III, "Building an Ambidextrous Organization: Forming Your Own 'Skunk Works,'" *Health Forum Journal* 42, no. 2 (March–April 1999), 20–23; J. C. Spender and Eric H. Kessler, "Managing the Uncertainties of Innovation: Extending Thompson (1967)," *Human Relations* 48, no. 1 (1995), 35–56; and Robert B. Duncan, "The Ambidextrous Organization: Designing Dual Structures for Innovation," in Ralph H. Killman, Louis R. Pondy, and Dennis Slevin, eds., *The Management of Organization*, vol. 1 (New York: North-Holland, 1976), 167–188.
31. C. A. O'Reilly III and M. L. Tushman, "The Ambidextrous Organization."
32. Tushman and O'Reilly, "Building an Ambidextrous Organization."
33. Edward F. McDonough III and Richard Leifer, "Using Simultaneous Structures to Cope with Uncertainty," *Academy of Management Journal* 26 (1983), 727–735.
34. J. Birkinshaw, "The Ambidextrous Organization—Driving Leadership," (2006) at http://www.mannaz.com/Mail.asp?MailID=102&TopicID=1160 (accessed July 13, 2008).
35. John Gustavson, "Meeting the Green Challenge."
36. Paul S. Adler, Barbara Goldoftas, and David I. Levine, "Ergonomics, Employee Involvement, and the Toyota Production System: A Case Study of NUMMI's 1993 Model Introduction," *Industrial and Labor Relations Review* 50, no. 3 (April 1997), 416–437.
37. Judith R. Blau and William McKinley, "Ideas, Complexity, and Innovation," *Administrative Science Quarterly* 24 (1979), 200–219.
38. Peter Landers, "Back to Basics; With Dry Pipelines, Big Drug Makers Stock Up in Japan," *The Wall Street Journal* (November 24, 2003), A1, A7.
39. Sherri Eng, "Hatching Schemes," *The Industry Standard* (November 27–December 4, 2000), 174–175.
40. I. Ross, "Making His Mark," *Northern Ontario Business* (March 2004), 1.
41. "Alberta Opens First Canadian Incubator for Food Processors," (May 16, 2007) at http://www.gov.ab.ca/home/NewsFrame.cfm?ReleaseID=/acn/200705/2146695822D72-0272-3519-73F8E08198276853.html (accessed July 13, 2008).

42. Christine Canabou, "Fast Ideas for Slow Times," *Fast Company* (May 2003), 52.
43. Christopher Hoenig, "Skunk Works Secrets," *CIO* (July 1, 2000), 74–76.
44. J. Weber, "'Mosh Pits' of Creativity" (November 7, 2005) at http://www.businessweek.com/magazine/content/05_45/b3958078.htm (accessed July 13, 2008).
45. "MaRS Services" (2007) at http://www.marsdd.com/mars/MaRS-Services.html (accessed July 13, 2008).
46. J. Steed, "Kicking out the Jams," (February 19, 2007) at http://www.thestar.com/article/183136 (accessed July 13, 2008).
47. Jane M. Howell and Christopher A. Higgins, "Champions of Technology Innovation," *Administrative Science Quarterly* 35 (1990), 317–341; and Jane M. Howell and Christopher A. Higgins, "Champions of Change: Identifying, Understanding, and Supporting Champions of Technology Innovations," *Organizational Dynamics* (Summer 1990), 40–55.
48. Peter F. Drucker, "Change Leaders," *Inc.* (June 1999), 65–72; and Peter F. Drucker, *Management Challenges for the 21st Century* (New York: HarperBusiness, 1999).
49. Thomas J. Peters and Robert H. Waterman, Jr., *In Search of Excellence* (New York: Harper & Row, 1982).
50. Peter J. Frost and Carolyn P. Egri, "The Political Process of Innovation," in L. L. Cummings and Barry M. Staw, eds., *Research in Organizational Behavior*, vol. 13 (New York: JAI Press, 1991), 229–295; Jay R. Galbraith, "Designing the Innovating Organization," *Organizational Dynamics* (Winter 1982), 5–25; and Marsha Sinatar, "Entrepreneurs, Chaos, and Creativity—Can Creative People Really Survive Large Company Structure?" *Sloan Management Review* (Winter 1985), 57–62.
51. See Lionel Roure, "Product Champion Characteristics in France and Germany," *Human Relations* 54, no. 5 (2001), 663–682 for a recent review of the literature related to product champions.
52. Ibid., 205.
53. A. Tchokogué, C. Bareil, and C.R. Duguay, "Key Lessons from the Implementation of an ERP at Pratt & Whitney Canada," *International Journal of Production Economics*, 95 (2005), 151–163.
54. Christopher Power with Kathleen Kerwin, Ronald Grover, Keith Alexander, and Robert D. Hof, "Flops," *BusinessWeek* (August 16, 1993), 76–82; Modesto A. Maidique and Billie Jo Zirger, "A Study of Success and Failure in Product Innovation: The Case of the U.S. Electronics Industry," *IEEE Transactions in Engineering Management* 31 (November 1984), 192–203.
55. "Bricklin" at http://www.thecanadianencyclopedia.com/index.cfm?PgNm=TCE&Params=A1ARTA0000983 (accessed June 24, 2008).
56. Avro Arrow at http://www.thecanadianencyclopedia.com/index.cfm?PgNm=TCE&Params=A1ARTA0000425 (accessed July 13, 2008).
57. Cliff Edwards, "Many Products Have Gone Way of the Edsel," *Johnson City Press* (May 23, 1999), 28, 30; Paul Lukas, "The Ghastliest Product Launches," *Fortune* (March 16, 1998), 44; Robert McMath, *What Were They Thinking? Marketing Lessons I've Learned from Over 80,000 New-Product Innovations and Idiocies* (New York: Times Business, 1998).
58. Edwin Mansfield, J. Rapaport, J. Schnee, S. Wagner, and M. Hamburger, *Research and Innovation in Modern Corporations* (New York: Norton, 1971); and Antonio J. Bailetti and Paul F. Litva, "Integrating Customer Requirements into Product Designs," *Journal of Product Innovation Management* 12 (1995), 3–15.
59. Shona L. Brown and Kathleen M. Eisenhardt, "Product Development: Past Research, Present Findings, and Future Directions," *Academy of Management Review* 20, no. 2 (1995), 343–378; F. Axel Johne and Patricia A. Snelson, "Success Factors in Product Innovation: A Selective Review of the Literature," *Journal of Product Innovation Management* 5 (1988), 114–128; and Science Policy Research Unit, University of Sussex, *Success and Failure in Industrial Innovation* (London: Centre for the Study of Industrial Innovation, 1972).
60. P. Nowak, "Puretracks Takes Lead in Rights Fight," (February 22, 2007) at http://www.financialpost.com/story.html?id=c4fe4fe1-bd7c-489b-bfdf-54991a0587be (accessed July 13, 2008).
61. Brown and Eisenhardt, "Product Development"; Dan Dimancescu and Kemp Dwenger, "Smoothing the Product Development Path," *Management Review* (January 1996), 36–41.
62. Fara Warner, "In a Word, Toyota Drives for Innovation," *Fast Company* (August 2002), 36–38.
63. Alex Markels, "Turning the Tide at P&G," (October 22, 2006) at http://www.usnews.com/usnews/news/articles/061022/30lafley_2.htm (accessed July 12, 2008).
64. Patricia Sellers, "P&G: Teaching an Old Dog New Tricks," *Fortune* (May 31, 2004), 167–180; Robert D. Hof, "Building an Idea Factory"; and Bettina von Stamm, "Collaboration with Other Firms and Customers: Innovation's Secret Weapon," *Strategy & Leadership* 32, no. 3 (2004), 16–20.
65. Bettina von Stamm, "Collaboration with Other Firms and Customers"; Bas Hillebrand and Wim G. Biemans, "Links between Internal and External Cooperation in Product Development: An Exploratory Study," *The Journal of Product Innovation Management* 21 (2004), 110–122.
66. Kenneth B. Kahn, "Market Orientation, Interdepartmental Integration, and Product Development Performance," *The Journal of Product Innovation Management* 18 (2001), 314–323; and Ali E. Akgün, Gary S. Lynn, and John C. Byrne, "Taking the Guesswork Out of New Product Development: How Successful High-Tech Companies Get That Way," *Journal of Business Strategy* 25, no. 4 (2004), 41–46.
67. John A. Pearce II, "Speed Merchants," *Organizational Dynamics* 30, no. 3 (2002), 191–205; Kathleen M. Eisenhardt and Behnam N. Tabrizi, "Accelerating Adaptive Processes: Product Innovation in the Global Computer Industry," *Administrative Science Quarterly*

40 (1995), 84–110; Dougherty and Hardy, "Sustained Product Innovation in Large, Mature Organizations"; and Karne Bronikowski, "Speeding New Products to Market," *Journal of Business Strategy* (September–October 1990), 34–37.

68. V. K. Narayanan, Frank L. Douglas, Brock Guernsey, and John Charnes, "How Top Management Steers Fast Cycle Teams to Success," *Strategy & Leadership* 30, no. 3 (2002), 19–27.

69. Steve Konicki, "Time Trials," *Information Week* (June 3, 2002), 36–44.

70. Edward F. McDonough III, Kenneth B. Kahn, and Gloria Barczak, "An Investigation of the Use of Global, Virtual, and Colocated New Product Development Teams," *The Journal of Product Innovation Management* 18 (2001), 110–120.

71. Dimancescu and Dwenger, "Smoothing the Product Development Path."

72. Raymond E. Miles, Henry J. Coleman, Jr., and W. E. Douglas Creed, "Keys to Success in Corporate Redesign," *California Management Review* 37, no. 3 (Spring 1995), 128–145.

73. Fariborz Damanpour and William M. Evan, "Organizational Innovation and Performance: The Problem of 'Organizational Lag,'" *Administrative Science Quarterly* 29 (1984), 392–409; David J. Teece, "The Diffusion of an Administrative Innovation," *Management Science* 26 (1980), 464–470; John R. Kimberly and Michael J. Evaniski, "Organizational Innovation: The Influence of Individual, Organizational and Contextual Factors on Hospital Adoption of Technological and Administrative Innovation," *Academy of Management Journal* 24 (1981), 689–713; Michael K. Moch and Edward V. Morse, "Size, Centralization, and Organizational Adoption of Innovations," *American Sociological Review* 42 (1977), 716–725; and Mary L. Fennell, "Synergy, Influence, and Information in the Adoption of Administrative Innovation," *Academy of Management Journal* 27 (1984), 113–129.

74. Richard L. Daft, "A Dual-Core Model of Organizational Innovation," *Academy of Management Journal* 21 (1978), 193–210.

75. Daft, "Bureaucratic versus Nonbureaucratic Structure"; Robert W. Zmud, "Diffusion of Modern Software Practices: Influence of Centralization and Formalization," *Management Science* 28 (1982), 1421–1431.

76. Daft, "A Dual-Core Model of Organizational Innovation"; Zmud, "Diffusion of Modern Software Practices."

77. Fariborz Damanpour, "The Adoption of Technological, Administrative, and Ancillary Innovations: Impact of Organizational Factors," *Journal of Management* 13 (1987), 675–688.

78. J. Castaldo, "Refreshing! A Clearly Canadian Comeback," (September 11, 2006) at http://www.canadianbusiness.com/managing/strategy/article.jsp?content=20060911_80201_80201 (accessed July 13, 2008).

79. Gregory H. Gaertner, Karen N. Gaertner, and David M. Akinnusi, "Environment, Strategy, and the Implementation of Administrative Change: The Case of Civil Service Reform," *Academy of Management Journal* 27 (1984), 525–543.

80. Claudia Bird Schoonhoven and Mariann Jelinek, "Dynamic Tension in Innovative, High Technology Firms: Managing Rapid Technology Change through Organization Structure," in Mary Ann Von Glinow and Susan Albers Mohrman, eds., *Managing Complexity in High Technology Organizations* (New York: Oxford University Press, 1990), 90–118.

81. David Ulm and James K. Hickel, "What Happens after Restructuring?" *Journal of Business Strategy* (July–August 1990), 37–41; and John L. Sprague, "Restructuring and Corporate Renewal: A Manager's Guide," *Management Review* (March 1989), 34–36.

82. Stan Pace, "Rip the Band-Aid Off Quickly," *Strategy & Leadership* 30, no. 1 (2002), 4–9.

83. Benson L. Porter and Warrington S. Parker, Jr., "Culture Change," *Human Resource Management* 31 (Spring–Summer 1992), 45–67.

84. H. Kolodny, (n.d.) *Culture Change at Canada Revenue Agency: Implementing Alternate Dispute Resolution.*

85. Quoted in Anne B. Fisher, "Making Change Stick," *Fortune* (April 17, 1995), 122.

86. A. Wahl, "Culture Shock: A survey of Canadian executives reveals that corporate culture is in need of improvement," (October 10–23, 2005) at http://www.canadianbusiness.com/managing/employees/article.jsp?content=20060106_160426_5512 (accessed July 13, 2008); and G. Seijts, WestJet Airlines (A): the Culture that Breeds a Passion to Succeed (Ivey Management Services, 2001).

87. M. Magnan, "People Power," (October 10, 2005) at http://www.canadianbusiness.com/managing/strategy/article.jsp?content=20051010_71478_71478 (accessed July 13, 2008).

88. W. Warner Burke, "The New Agenda for Organization Development," in Wendell L. French, Cecil H. Bell, Jr., and Robert A. Zawacki, *Organization Development and Transformation: Managing Effective Change* (Burr Ridge, Ill.: Irwin McGraw-Hill, 2000), 523–535.

89. W. Warner Burke, *Organization Development: A Process of Learning and Changing*, 2nd ed. (Reading, Mass.: Addison-Wesley, 1994); and Wendell L. French and Cecil H. Bell, Jr., "A History of Organization Development," in French, Bell, and Zawacki, *Organization Development and Transformation*, 20–42.

90. French and Bell, "A History of Organization Development."

91. The information on large group intervention is based on Kathleen D. Dannemiller and Robert W. Jacobs, "Changing the Way Organizations Change: A Revolution of Common Sense," *The Journal of Applied Behavioral Science* 28, no. 4 (December 1992), 480–498; Barbara B. Bunker and Billie T. Alban, "Conclusion: What Makes Large Group Interventions Effective?" *The Journal of Applied Behavioral Science* 28, no. 4 (December 1992), 570–591;

and Marvin R. Weisbord, "Inventing the Future: Search Strategies for Whole System Improvements," in French, Bell, and Zawacki, *Organization Development and Transformation*, 242–250.

92. J. Quinn, "What a Workout!" *Performance* (November 1994), 58–63; and Bunker and Alban, "Conclusion: What Makes Large Group Interventions Effective?"
93. Dave Ulrich, Steve Kerr, and Ron Ashkenas, with Debbie Burke and Patrice Murphy, *The GE Work Out: How to Implement GE's Revolutionary Method for Busting Bureaucracy and Attacking Organizational Problems—Fast!* (New York: McGraw-Hill, 2002).
94. Paul F. Buller, "For Successful Strategic Change: Blend OD Practices with Strategic Management," *Organizational Dynamics* (Winter 1988), 42–55.
95. Norm Brodsky, "Everybody Sells," (Street Smarts column), *Inc. Magazine* (June 2004), 53–54.
96. Richard S. Allen and Kendyl A. Montgomery, "Applying an Organizational Development Approach to Creating Diversity," *Organizational Dynamics* 30, no. 2 (2001), 149–161.
97. Jyotsna Sanzgiri and Jonathan Z. Gottlieb, "Philosophic and Pragmatic Influences on the Practice of Organization Development, 1950–2000," *Organizational Dynamics* (Autumn 1992), 57–69.
98. Bernard M. Bass, "Theory of Transformational Leadership Redux," *Leadership Quarterly* 6, no. 4 (1995), 463–478; and Dong I. Jung, Chee Chow, and Anne Wu, "The Role of Transformational Leadership in Enhancing Organizational Innovation: Hypotheses and Some Preliminary Findings," *The Leadership Quarterly* 14 (2003), 525–544.
99. Ronald Recardo, Kathleen Molloy, and James Pellegrino, "How the Learning Organization Manages Change," *National Productivity Review* (Winter 1995/96), 7–13.
100. Based on Daryl R. Conner, *Managing at the Speed of Change* (New York: Villard Books, 1992), 146–160.
101. Drucker, *Management Challenges for the 21st Century*; Tushman and O'Reilly, "Ambidextrous Organizations"; Gary Hamel and C. K. Prahalad, "Seeing the Future First," *Fortune* (September 4, 1994), 64–70; and Linda Yates and Peter Skarzynski, "How Do Companies Get to the Future First?" *Management Review* (January 1999), 16–22.
102. Based on Carol A. Beatty and John R. M. Gordon, "Barriers to the Implementation of CAD/CAM Systems," *Sloan Management Review* (Summer 1988), 25–33.
103. G. Scott, "Games Get Down to Business," *The Globe and Mail* (May 3, 2007).
104. These techniques are based partly on John P. Kotter's eight-stage model of planned organizational change, Kotter, *Leading Change*, 20–25.
105. Everett M. Rogers and Floyd Shoemaker, *Communication of Innovations: A Cross Cultural Approach*, 2d ed. (New York: Free Press, 1971); Stratford P. Sherman, "Eight Big Masters of Innovation," *Fortune* (October 15, 1984), 66–84.
106. Richard L. Daft and Selwyn W. Becker, *Innovation in Organizations* (New York: Elsevier, 1978); and John P. Kotter and Leonard A. Schlesinger, "Choosing Strategies for Change," *Harvard Business Review* 57 (1979), 106–114.
107. "Employee Suggestion Systems" (September 19, 2001) at http://www.hi.is/~joner/eaps/ds_esug.htm (accessed June 25, 2008).
108. Peter Richardson and D. Keith Denton, "Communicating Change," *Human Resource Management* 35, no. 2 (Summer 1996), 203–216.
109. Edgar H. Schein and Warren Bennis, *Personal and Organizational Change via Group Methods* (New York: Wiley, 1965); and Amy Edmondson, "Psychological Safety and Learning Behavior in Work Teams," *Administrative Science Quarterly* 44 (1999), 350–383.
110. Diane L. Coutu, "Creating the Most Frightening Company on Earth; An Interview with Andy Law of St. Luke's," *Harvard Business Review* (September–October 2000), 143–150.
111. Philip H. Mirvis, Amy L. Sales, and Edward J. Hackett, "The Implementation and Adoption of New Technology in Organizations: The Impact on Work, People, and Culture," *Human Resource Management* 30 (Spring 1991), 113–139; Arthur E. Wallach, "System Changes Begin in the Training Department," *Personnel Journal* 58 (1979), 846–848, 872; and Paul R. Lawrence, "How to Deal with Resistance to Change," *Harvard Business Review* 47 (January–February 1969), 4–12, 166–176.
112. Dexter C. Dunphy and Doug A. Stace, "Transformational and Coercive Strategies for Planned Organizational Change: Beyond the O.D. Model," *Organizational Studies* 9 (1988), 317–334; and Kotter and Schlesinger, "Choosing Strategies for Change."

Chapter 12

1. "Anishinabek Nation Appoints Women's Water Commission," (March 27, 2007) http://www.anishinabek.ca/index.php?option=com_content&task=view&id=167&Itemid=47 (accessed June 27, 2008) 2007.
2. Ibid.
3. Anishinabek/Ontario Agreements Pledge Cooperation, http://www.anishinabek.ca/index.php?option=com_content&task=view&id=162&Itemid=2.
4. Carol J. Loomis, "Why Carly's Big Bet Is Failing," *Fortune* (February 7, 2005), 50–64; David Bank and Joann S. Lublin, "For H-P, No Shortage of Ideas; Turnaround Experts Offer Wide Range of Conflicting Strategies," *Asian Wall Street Journal* (February 14, 2005), M5; and James B. Stewart, "Common Sense: Finding a New CEO Won't Help Unless H-P Finds New Products," *The Wall Street Journal* (February 23, 2005), D3.
5. C. Boyd, *Canadian Tire (A)*, College of Commerce, University of Saskatchewan, 1989).

6. Alex Markels, "10 Biggest Business Blunders," *U.S. News & World Report* (November 8, 2004), EE2–EE8.
7. Merissa Marr, "Return of the Ogre; How DreamWorks Misjudged DVD Sales of Its Monster Hit," *The Wall Street Journal* (May 31, 2005), A1, A9.
8. Saul Hansell, "Meg Whitman and eBay, Net Survivors," *The New York Times* (May 5, 2002), 17; Michael V. Copeland and Owen Thomas, "Hits (& Misses)," *Business 2.0* (January–February 2004), 126; Carlos Ghosn, "Saving the Business without Losing the Company," *Harvard Business Review* (January 2002), 37–45.
9. Charles Lindblom, "The Science of 'Muddling Through,'" *Public Administration Review* 29 (1954), 79–88.
10. Herbert A. Simon, *The New Science of Management Decision* (Englewood Cliffs, N.J.: Prentice-Hall, 1960), 1–8.
11. Paul J. H. Schoemaker and J. Edward Russo, "A Pyramid of Decision Approaches," *California Management Review* (Fall 1993), 9–31.
12. Rick Brooks, "Sealing Their Fate; A Deal with Target Put Lid on Revival at Tupperware," *The Wall Street Journal* (February 18, 2004), A1, A9.
13. Michael Pacanowsky, "Team Tools for Wicked Problems," *Organizational Dynamics* 23, no. 3 (Winter 1995), 36–51.
14. Retail Council of Canada, "Retail Reaches Major Milestone" (March 1, 2005) at http://www.retailcouncil.org/education/career_resources/pr20050301.asp (accessed June 27, 2008).
15. Based on Francine Schwadel, "Christmas Sales' Lack of Momentum Test Store Managers' Mettle," *The Wall Street Journal* (December 16, 1987), 1.
16. James W. Dean, Jr., and Mark P. Sharfman, "Procedural Rationality in the Strategic Decision-Making Process," *Journal of Management Studies* 30 (1993), 587–610.
17. H. Mintzberg, *The Nature of Managerial Work* (New York: Harper & Row, 1993).
18. J.A.H. Bell, S. Hyland, T. DePellegrin, R.E.G. Upshur, M. Bernstein, and D.K. Martin, "SARS and Hospital Priority Setting: A Qualitative Case Study and Evaluation," *BMC Health Services Research*, 4 (2004), 36.
19. Art Kleiner, "Core Group Therapy," *Strategy & Business*, 27 (Second Quarter, 2002), 26–31.
20. Irving L. Janis, *Crucial Decisions: Leadership in Policymaking and Crisis Management* and (New York: The Free Press, 1989); and Paul C. Nutt, "Flexible Decision Styles and the Choices of Top Executives," *Journal of Management Studies* 30 (1993), 695–721.
21. Herbert A. Simon, "Making Management Decisions: The Role of Intuition and Emotion," *Academy of Management Executive* 1 (February 1987), 57–64; and Daniel J. Eisenberg, "How Senior Managers Think," *Harvard Business Review* 62 (November–December 1984), 80–90.
22. Stefan Wally and J. Robert Baum, "Personal and Structural Determinants of the Pace of Strategic Decision Making," *Academy of Management Journal* 37, no. 4 (1994), 932–956; and Orlando Behling and Norman L. Eckel, "Making Sense Out of Intuition," *Academy of Management Executive* 5, no. 1 (1991), 46–54.
23. Gary Klein, Intuition at Work: Why Developing Your Gut Instincts Will Make You Better at What You Do (New York: Doubleday, 2002); Milorad M. Novicevic, Thomas J. Hench, and Daniel A. Wren, "'Playing By Ear . . . In an Incessant Din of Reasons': Chester Barnard and the History of Intuition in Management Thought," Management Decision 40, no. 10 (2002), 992–1002; Alden M. Hayashi, "When to Trust Your Gut," Harvard Business Review (February 2001), 59–65; Brian R. Reinwald, "Tactical Intuition," Military Review 80, no. 5 (September–October 2000), 78–88; Thomas A. Stewart, "How to Think with Your Gut," Business 2.0 (November 2002) at http://www.manyworlds.com/exploreco.aspx?coid=CO11120210263240 (accessed July, 13, 2008); Bill Breen, "What's Your Intuition?" Fast Company (September 2000), 290–300; and Henry Mintzberg and Frances Westley, "Decision Making: It's Not What You Think," MIT Sloan Management Review (Spring 2001), 89–93.
24. Thomas F. Issack, "Intuition: An Ignored Dimension of Management," *Academy of Management Review* 3 (1978), 917–922.
25. Marjorie A. Lyles, "Defining Strategic Problems: Subjective Criteria of Executives," *Organizational Studies* 8 (1987), 263–280; and Marjorie A. Lyles and Ian I. Mitroff, "Organizational Problem Formulation: An Empirical Study," *Administrative Science Quarterly* 25 (1980), 102–119.
26. Marjorie A. Lyles and Howard Thomas, "Strategic Problem Formulation: Biases and Assumptions Embedded in Alternative Decision-Making Models," *Journal of Management Studies* 25 (1988), 131–145.
27. Ross Stagner, "Corporate Decision-Making: An Empirical Study," *Journal of Applied Psychology* 53 (1969), 1–13.
28. Reported in Eric Bonabeau, "Don't Trust Your Gut," *Harvard Business Review* (May 2003), 116ff.
29. Ricardo Semler, "Semco SA," (October 7, 2004) at http://edition.cnn.com/2004/BUSINESS/06/29/semler.profile/ (accessed July 13, 2008).
30. Balancing Time, (February 23, 2006) at http://blog.fastcompany.com/archives/2006/02/ (accessed July 13, 2008).
31. B. Wieners, "Ricardo Semler: Set Them Free," (April 1, 2004) at http://www.cioinsight.com/c/a/Expert-Voices/Ricardo-Semler-Set-Them-Free (accessed July 13, 2008).
32. Survival Manual at semco.locaweb.com.br/en/content.asp?content=3&contentID=567 (accessed November 15, 2007).
33. "The Seven-Day Weekend: Changing the Way Work Works," at http://www.fastcompany.com/bookclub/excerpts/1591840260.html (accessed June 27, 2008).

34. Thomas George, "Head Cowboy Gets Off His High Horse," *The New York Times* (December 21, 2003), Section 8, 1; Stewart, "How to Think with Your Gut."
35. Bonabeau, "Don't Trust Your Gut."
36. Ann Langley, "Between 'Paralysis by Analysis' and 'Extinction by Instinct,'" *Sloan Management Review* (Spring 1995), 63–76.
37. Paul C. Nutt, "Types of Organizational Decision Processes," *Administrative Science Quarterly* 29 (1984), 414–450.
38. Geraldine Fabrikant, "The Paramount Team Puts Profit Over Splash," *The New York Times* (June 30, 2002), 1, 15.
39. Nandini Rajagopalan, Abdul M. A. Rasheed, and Deepak K. Datta, "Strategic Decision Processes: Critical Review and Future Decisions," *Journal of Management* 19 (1993), 349–384; Paul J. H. Schoemaker, "Strategic Decisions in Organizations: Rational and Behavioral Views," *Journal of Management Studies* 30 (1993), 107–129; Charles J. McMillan, "Qualitative Models of Organizational Decision Making," *Journal of Management Studies* 5 (1980), 22–39; and Paul C. Nutt, "Models for Decision Making in Organizations and Some Contextual Variables Which Stimulate Optimal Use," *Academy of Management Review* 1 (1976), 84–98.
40. Hugh J. Miser, "Operations Analysis in the Army Air Forces in World War II: Some Reminiscences," *Interfaces* 23 (September–October 1993), 47–49; Harold J. Leavitt, William R. Dill, and Henry B. Eyring, *The Organizational World* (New York: Harcourt Brace Jovanovich, 1973), chap. 6.
41. Stephen J. Huxley, "Finding the Right Spot for a Church Camp in Spain," *Interfaces* 12 (October 1982), 108–114; James E. Hodder and Henry E. Riggs, "Pitfalls in Evaluating Risky Projects," *Harvard Business Review* (January–February 1985), 128–135.
42. Edward Baker and Michael Fisher, "Computational Results for Very Large Air Crew Scheduling Problems," *Omega* 9 (1981), 613–618; Jean Aubin, "Scheduling Ambulances," *Interfaces* 22 (March–April, 1992), 1–10.
43. Di Meglio, F. (2007) B-Schools Profs Want to Know, *BusinessWeek*, October 7.
44. Terrence Belford, "Where Best to Set up Shop? Do the Math," (November 13, 2007) at http://www.theglobeandmail.com/servlet/story/RTGAM.20071113.winnomath13/BNStory/Technology (accessed June 27, 2008).
45. Ibid.
46. Ibid.
47. Ibid.
48. Julie Schlosser, Markdown Lowdown," *Fortune* (January 12, 2004), 40; Christina Binkley, "Numbers Game; Taking Retailers' Cues, Harrah's Taps Into Science of Gambling," *The Wall Street Journal* (November 22, 2004), A1, A8.
49. Harold J. Leavitt, "Beyond the Analytic Manager," *California Management Review* 17 (1975), 5–12; and C. Jackson Grayson, Jr., "Management Science and Business Practice," *Harvard Business Review* 51 (July–August 1973), 41–48.
50. Richard L. Daft and John C. Wiginton, "Language and Organization," *Academy of Management Review* (1979), 179–191.
51. Based on Richard M. Cyert and James G. March, *A Behavioral Theory of the Firm* (Englewood Cliffs, N.J.: Prentice-Hall, 1963); and James G. March and Herbert A. Simon, *Organizations* (New York: Wiley, 1958).
52. William B. Stevenson, Joan L. Pearce, and Lyman W. Porter, "The Concept of 'Coalition' in Organization Theory and Research," *Academy of Management Review* 10 (1985), 256–268.
53. Cyert and March, *A Behavioral Theory of the Firm*, 120–222.
54. Pui-Wing Tam, "One for the History Books: The Tale of How Britannica Is Trying to Leap from the Old Economy Into the New One," *The Wall Street Journal* (December 11, 2000), R32; and Richard A. Melcher, "Dusting Off the *Britannica*," *BusinessWeek* (October 20, 1997), 143–146.
55. Lawrence G. Hrebiniak, "Top-Management Agreement and Organizational Performance," *Human Relations* 35 (1982), 1139–1158; and Richard P. Nielsen, "Toward a Method for Building Consensus during Strategic Planning," *Sloan Management Review* (Summer 1981), 29–40.
56. Based on Henry Mintzberg, Duru Raisinghani, and André Théorêt, "The Structure of 'Unstructured' Decision Processes," *Administrative Science Quarterly* 21 (1976), 246–275.
57. Lawrence T. Pinfield, "A Field Evaluation of Perspectives on Organizational Decision Making," *Administrative Science Quarterly* 31 (1986), 365–388.
58. Mintzberg et al., "The Structure of 'Unstructured' Decision Processes."
59. Ibid., 270.
60. William C. Symonds with Carol Matlack, "Gillette's Edge," *BusinessWeek* (January 19, 1998), 70–77; William C. Symonds, "Would You Spend $1.50 for a Razor Blade?" BusinessWeek (April 27, 1998), 46; Peter J. Howe, "Innovative; For the Past Half Century, 'Cutting Edge' Has Meant More at Gillette Co. Than a Sharp Blade," Boston Globe (January 30, 2005), D1; and FAQ at http://www.gillettefusion.com/us/custom/en_US/ (accessed July 13, 2008).
61. Anna Wilde Mathews, Martin Peers, and Nick Wingfield, "Off-Key: The Music Industry Is Finally Online, but Few Listen," The Wall Street Journal (May 7, 2002), A1, A20; and "Medianet Overview" at http://www.musicnet.com/about/overview.html (accessed July 13, 2008).
62. Michael D. Cohen, James G. March, and Johan P. Olsen, "A Garbage Can Model of Organizational Choice," Administrative Science Quarterly 17 (March 1972), 1–25; and Michael D. Cohen and James G. March, Leadership and Ambiguity: The American College President (New York: McGraw-Hill, 1974).
63. Michael Masuch and Perry LaPotin, "Beyond Garbage Cans: An AI Model of Organizational Choice," Administrative Science Quarterly 34 (1989), 38–67.

64. N. Takahashi, "A Single Garbage Can Model and the Degree of Anarchy in Japanese Firms, Human Relations, 50, 1 (1997), 91–109.
65. Manohla Dargis "On a Stroll in Angstville With Dots Disconnected." (October 1, 2004) at http://movies.nytimes.com/2004/10/01/movies/01HUCK.html (accessed July 13, 2008).
66. Sharon Waxman, "The Nudist Buddhist Borderline-Abusive Love-In," The New York Times (September 19, 2004), Section 2, 1; and V. A. Musetto, "Crix Pick Best Pix," The New York Post (May 29, 2005), 93.
67. Thomas R. King, "Why 'Waterworld,' with Costner in Fins, Is Costliest Film Ever," The Wall Street Journal (January 31, 1995), A1.
68. Adapted from James D. Thompson, Organizations in Action (New York: McGraw-Hill, 1967), chap. 10; and McMillan, "Qualitative Models of Organizational Decision Making," 25.
69. Louise Lee, "Courts Begin to Award Damages to Victims of Parking-Area Crime," The Wall Street Journal (April 23, 1997), A1, A8.
70. Beth Dickey, "NASA's Next Step," Government Executive (April 15, 2004), 34ff; and Jena McGregor, "Gospels of Failure," Fast Company (February 2005), 61–67.
71. Mintzberg and Wheatley, "Decision Making: It's Not What You Think."
72. Paul C. Nutt, "Selecting Decision Rules for Crucial Choices: An Investigation of the Thompson Framework," The Journal of Applied Behavioral Science 38, no. 1 (March 2002), 99–131; and Paul C. Nutt, "Making Strategic Choices," Journal of Management Studies 39, no. 1 (January 2002), 67–95.
73. George T. Doran and Jack Gunn, "Decision Making in High-Tech Firms: Perspectives of Three Executives," Business Horizons (November–December 2002), 7–16.
74. L. J. Bourgeois III and Kathleen M. Eisenhardt, "Strategic Decision Processes in High Velocity Environments: Four Cases in the Microcomputer Industry," Management Science 34 (1988), 816–835.
75. Kathleen M. Eisenhardt, "Speed and Strategic Course: How Managers Accelerate Decision Making," California Management Review (Spring 1990), 39–54.
76. David A. Garvin and Michael A. Roberto, "What You Don't Know about Making Decisions," *Harvard Business Review* (September 2001), 108–116.
77. James Surowiecki, *The Wisdom of Crowds: Why the Many Are Smarter Than the Few and How Collective Wisdom Shapes Business, Economies, Societies, and Nations* (New York: Doubleday, 2004); Doran and Gunn, "Decision Making in High-Tech Firms."
78. Doran and Gunn, "Decision Making in High-Tech Firms."
79. Karl Weick, *The Social Psychology of Organizing*, 2d ed. (Reading, Mass.: Addison-Wesley, 1979), 243.
80. Christopher Power with Kathleen Kerwin, Ronald Grover, Keith Alexander, and Robert D. Hof, "Flops," *BusinessWeek* (August 16, 1993), 76–82.
81. Robert Townsend, *Up the Organization* (New York: Knopf, 1974), 115.
82. Helga Drummond, "Too Little Too Late: A Case Study of Escalation in Decision Making," *Organization Studies* 15, no. 4 (1994), 591–607; Joel Brockner, "The Escalation of Commitment to a Failing Course of Action: Toward Theoretical Progress," *Academy of Management Review* 17 (1992), 39–61; Barry M. Staw and Jerry Ross, "Knowing When to Pull the Plug," *Harvard Business Review* 65 (March–April 1987), 68–74; and Barry M. Staw, "The Escalation of Commitment to a Course of Action," *Academy of Management Review* 6 (1981), 577–587.
83. S. B. Salter, and D. Sharp, "Agency Effects and Escalation of Commitment: Do Small National Culture Differences Matter?" *The International Journal of Accounting*, 36, 1 (2001), 33–45.
84. N. VanderKlippe, "Hydrogen Highway Hits Dead End, (November 5, 2007) at http://www.financialpost.com/story.html?id=356bed57-656b-4ffd-b3b0-f7f5a96ace29&k=80493 (accessed July 13, 2008).
85. "Ballard Power to Sell Auto Fuel Cell Assets to Ford, Daimler," (November 8, 2007) at http://www.theglobeandmail.com/servlet/story/RTGAM.20071108.wballard1108/BNStory/Business/ (accessed July 13, 2008).

Chapter 13

1. "Harold Ballard Convicted of Fraud," archives.cbc.ca/IDC-1-41-252-1290/sports/ballard_fraud/clip1.
2. Ibid.
3. Hockey Fans, "Toronto Maple Leafs," at http://www.hockey-fans.com/northeast/mapleleafs (accessed June 27, 2008).
4. "Leafs' President Averts Possibility of Takeover," (June 22, 1989) at http://query.nytimes.com/gst/fullpage.html?res=950DEFD91538F931A15755C0A96F948260&scp=1&sq=Leafs%92+President+Averts+Possibility+of+Takeover&st=nyt (accessed July 13, 2008).
5. "The Leaf Way" (March 2006) at http://mirtle.blogspot.com/2006_03_01_archive.html (accessed June 27, 2008).
6. Lee G. Bolman and Terrence E. Deal, *Reframing Organizations: Artistry, Choice, and Leadership* (San Francisco: Jossey-Bass, 1991).
7. Paul M. Terry, "Conflict Management," *The Journal of Leadership Studies* 3, no. 2 (1996), 3–21; and Kathleen M. Eisenhardt, Jean L. Kahwajy, and L. J. Bourgeois III, "How Management Teams Can Have a Good Fight," *Harvard Business Review* (July–August 1997), 77–85.
8. Clayton T. Alderfer and Ken K. Smith, "Studying Intergroup Relations Imbedded in Organizations," *Administrative Science Quarterly* 27 (1982), 35–65.
9. Muzafer Sherif, "Experiments in Group Conflict," *Scientific American* 195 (1956), 54–58; and Edgar H. Schein, *Organizational Psychology*, 3d ed. (Englewood Cliffs, N.J.: Prentice-Hall, 1980).

10. M. Afzalur Rahim, "A Strategy for Managing Conflict in Complex Organizations," *Human Relations* 38 (1985), 81–89; Kenneth Thomas, "Conflict and Conflict Management," in M.D. Dunnette, ed., *Handbook of Industrial and Organizational Psychology* (Chicago, Ill.: Rand McNally, 1976); and Stuart M. Schmidt and Thomas A. Kochan, "Conflict: Toward Conceptual Clarity," *Administrative Science Quarterly* 13 (1972), 359–370.
11. L. David Brown, "Managing Conflict among Groups," in David A. Kolb, Irwin M. Rubin, and James M. McIntyre, eds., *Organizational Psychology: A Book of Readings* (Englewood Cliffs, N.J.: Prentice-Hall, 1979), 377–389; and Robert W. Ruekert and Orville C. Walker, Jr., "Interactions between Marketing and R&D Departments in Implementing Different Business Strategies," *Strategic Management Journal* 8 (1987), 233–248.
12. S. Ginden," Breaking Away: The Formation of the Canadian Auto Workers," at http://www.caw.ca/whoweare/ourhistory/gindin_index.asp (accessed June 27, 2008).
13. Joseph B. White, Lee Hawkins, Jr., and Karen Lundegaard, "UAW Is Facing Biggest Battles in Two Decades," *The Wall Street Journal* (June 10, 2005), B1; Amy Barrett, "Indigestion at Taco Bell," *BusinessWeek* (December 14, 1994), 66–67; Greg Burns, "Fast-Food Fight," *BusinessWeek* (June 2, 1997), 34–36.
14. Nanette Byrnes, with Mike McNamee, Ronald Grover, Joann Muller, and Andrew Park, "Auditing Here, Consulting Over There," *BusinessWeek* (April 8, 2002), 34–36.
15. D. Hawranek, "Porsche and VW Battle it Out," (September 19, 2007) at http://www.businessweek.com/globalbiz/content/sep2007/gb20070919_640245_page_3.htm (accessed September 28, 2007).
16. Thomas A. Kochan, George P. Huber, and L. L. Cummings, "Determinants of Intraorganizational Conflict in Collective Bargaining in the Public Sector," *Administrative Science Quarterly* 20 (1975), 10–23.
17. Victoria L. Crittenden, Lorraine R. Gardiner, and Antonie Stam, "Reducing Conflict between Marketing and Manufacturing," *Industrial Marketing Management* 22 (1993), 299–309; and Benson S. Shapiro, "Can Marketing and Manufacturing Coexist?" *Harvard Business Review* 55 (September–October 1977), 104–114.
18. Ben Worthen, "Cost-Cutting versus Innovation: Reconcilable Differences," *CIO* (October 1, 2004), 89–94.
19. Eric H. Neilsen, "Understanding and Managing Intergroup Conflict," in Jay W. Lorsch and Paul R. Lawrence, eds., *Managing Group and Intergroup Relations* (Homewood, Ill.: Irwin and Dorsey, 1972), 329–343; and Richard E. Walton and John M. Dutton, "The Management of Interdepartmental Conflict: A Model and Review," *Administrative Science Quarterly* 14 (1969), 73–84.
20. W. Cline, "Hugh MacKinnon: The Managing Partner behind Bennett Jones' Rapid Expansion," *Lawyers Weekly*, 27 (2007), 20.
21. Values at http://www.bennettjones.ca/about_values.aspx (accessed on October 1, 2007).
22. J.W. Zinober, "Resolving Conflict in the Firm," *Law Practice Management*, 16, 6 (1990), 20.
23. W. Cline, "Hugh MacKinnon: The Managing Partner behind Bennett Jones' Rapid Expansion."
24. James D. Thompson, *Organizations in Action* (New York: McGraw-Hill, 1967), 54–56.
25. Walton and Dutton, "The Management of Interdepartmental Conflict."
26. Joseph McCann and Jay R. Galbraith, "Interdepartmental Relations," in Paul C. Nystrom and William H. Starbuck, eds., *Handbook of Organizational Design*, vol. 2 (New York: Oxford University Press, 1981), 60–84.
27. Roderick M. Cramer, "Intergroup Relations and Organizational Dilemmas: The Role of Categorization Processes," in L. L. Cummings and Barry M. Staw, eds., *Research in Organizational Behavior*, vol. 13 (New York: JAI Press, 1991), 191–228; Neilsen, "Understanding and Managing Intergroup Conflict"; and Louis R. Pondy, "Organizational Conflict: Concepts and Models," *Administrative Science Quarterly* 12 (1968), 296–320.
28. Jeffrey Pfeffer, *Power in Organizations* (Marshfield, Mass.: Pitman, 1981).
29. Alan Deutschman, "The Mind of Jeff Bezos," *Fast Company* (August 2004), 53–58.
30. Robert A. Dahl, "The Concept of Power," *Behavioral Science* 2 (1957), 201–215.
31. W. Graham Astley and Paramijit S. Sachdeva, "Structural Sources of Intraorganizational Power: A Theoretical Synthesis," *Academy of Management Review* 9 (1984), 104–113; Abraham Kaplan, "Power in Perspective," in Robert L. Kahn and Elise Boulding, eds., *Power and Conflict in Organizations* (London: Tavistock, 1964), 11–32.
32. Gerald R. Salancik and Jeffrey Pfeffer, "The Bases and Use of Power in Organizational Decision-Making: The Case of the University," *Administrative Science Quarterly* 19 (1974), 453–473.
33. Richard M. Emerson, "Power-Dependence Relations," *American Sociological Review* 27 (1962), 31–41.
34. D. Mechanic, "Sources of Power of Lower Participants in Complex Organizations," *Administrative Science Quarterly*, 7, 3 (1962), 349–364.
35. Rosabeth Moss Kanter, "Power Failure in Management Circuits," *Harvard Business Review* (July–August 1979), 65–75.
36. Sam Walker, "On Sports: Meet the Micro Manager," *The Wall Street Journal* (July 11, 2003), W12.
37. Examples are Robert Greene and Joost Elffers, *The 48 Laws of Power* (New York: Viking, 1999); Jeffrey J. Fox, *How to Become CEO* (New York: Hyperion, 1999).
38. John R. P. French, Jr., and Bertram Raven, "The Bases of Social Power," in *Group Dynamics*, D. Cartwright and A. F. Zander, eds. (Evanston, Ill.: Row Peterson, 1960), 607–623.
39. Ran Lachman, "Power from What? A Reexamination of Its Relationships with Structural Conditions," *Administrative Science Quarterly* 34 (1989), 231–251; and Daniel J. Brass,

"Being in the Right Place: A Structural Analysis of Individual Influence in an Organization," *Administrative Science Quarterly* 29 (1984), 518–539.
40. Michael Warshaw, "The Good Guy's Guide to Office Politics," *Fast Company* (April–May 1998), 157–178.
41. A. J. Grimes, "Authority, Power, Influence, and Social Control: A Theoretical Synthesis," *Academy of Management Review* 3 (1978), 724–735.
42. Astley and Sachdeva, "Structural Sources of Intraorganizational Power."
43. Jeffrey Pfeffer, *Managing with Power: Politics and Influence in Organizations* (Boston, Mass.: Harvard Business School Press, 1992).
44. Robert L. Peabody, "Perceptions of Organizational Authority," *Administrative Science Quarterly* 6 (1962), 479.
45. M. Brush, "CEO Mansions: A Stock Indicator?" (April 11, 2007) at articles.moneycentral.msn.com/Investing/CompanyFocus/CEOMansionsAStockIndicator.aspx (accessed June 27, 2008).
46. Richard S. Blackburn, "Lower Participant Power: Toward a Conceptual Integration," *Academy of Management Review* 6 (1981), 127–131.
47. Patricia Sellers, "eBay's Secret," *Fortune* (October 18, 2004), 161–178.
48. Women's Executive Network at http://www.wxnetwork.com/top100.html (accessed June 27, 2008).
49. "Sylvia Vogel" at http://www.chronicle.ca/vogel_eng.html (accessed June 27, 2008).
50. Kanter, "Power Failure in Management Circuits," 70.
51. Pfeffer, *Power in Organizations.*
52. Erik W. Larson and Jonathan B. King, "The Systemic Distortion of Information: An Ongoing Challenge to Management," *Organizational Dynamics* 24, no. 3 (Winter 1996), 49–61; and Thomas H. Davenport, Robert G. Eccles, and Laurence Prusak, "Information Politics," *Sloan Management Review* (Fall 1992), 53–65.
53. Robert Frank and Elena Cherney, "Paper Tigers; Lord Black's Board: A-List Cast Played Acquiescent Role," *The Wall Street Journal* (September 27, 2004), A1.
54. "Black Found Guilty of Obstruction, Mail Fraud" (July 13, 2007) at http://www.cbc.ca/money/story/2007/07/13/black-verdict.html (accessed on June 27, 2008).
55. Lorne Manly and Andrew Ross Sorkin, "At Sony, Diplomacy Trumps Technology," (March 8, 2005) at http://www.nytimes.com/2005/03/08/business/worldbusiness/08reconstruct.html?scp=1&sq=At+Sony%2C+Diplomacy+Trumps+Technology&st=nyt (accessed July 13, 2008).
56. Kenji Hall "Stringer, Sony Step On the Gas," (June 26, 2008) at http://www.businessweek.com/globalbiz/content/jun2008/gb20080626_493388.htm?campaign_id=rss_tech (accessed July 13, 2008).
57. B. Breen, and C. Dahle, "Fire Starters," *Fast Company*, 30 (1999), 386.
58. Paul Gibbons, "From Managing to Leading: Making the Leap," *Academy of Management MSR Newsletter*, Winter 2003, 4–7.
59. Carol Hymowitz, "Companies Experience Major Power Shifts as Crises Continue" (In the Lead column), *The Wall Street Journal* (October 9, 2001), B1.
60. Astley and Sachdeva, "Structural Sources of Intraorganizational Power"; and Noel M. Tichy and Charles Fombrun, "Network Analysis in Organizational Settings," *Human Relations* 32 (1979), 923–965.
61. Report of Investigation by the Special Committee of the Board of Directors pf Hollinger International Inc. at http://www.sec.gov/Archives/edgar/data/868512/000095012304010413/y01437exv99w2.htm, (accessed July 13, 2008), 4.
62. Greg Ip, Kate Kelly, Susanne Craig, and Ianthe Jeanne Dugan, "A Bull's Market; Dick Grasso's NYSE Legacy: Buffed Image, Shaky Foundation," *The Wall Street Journal* (December 30, 2003), A1, A6; Yochi J. Dreazen and Christopher Cooper, "Lingering Presence; Behind the Scenes, U.S. Tightens Grip on Iraq's Future," *The Wall Street Journal* (May 13, 2004), A1.
63. Charles Perrow, "Departmental Power and Perspective in Industrial Firms," in Mayer N. Zald, ed., *Power in Organizations* (Nashville, Tenn.: Vanderbilt University Press, 1970), 59–89.
64. D. J. Hickson, C. R. Hinings, C. A. Lee, R. E. Schneck, and J. M. Pennings, "A Strategic Contingencies Theory of Intraorganizational Power," *Administrative Science Quarterly* 16 (1971), 216–229; and Gerald R. Salancik and Jeffrey Pfeffer, "Who Gets Power—and How They Hold onto It: A Strategic-Contingency Model of Power," *Organizational Dynamics* (Winter 1977), 3–21.
65. Pfeffer, *Managing with Power*; Salancik and Pfeffer, "Who Gets Power"; C. R. Hinings, D. J. Hickson, J. M. Pennings, and R. E. Schneck, "Structural Conditions of Intraorganizational Power," *Administrative Science Quarterly* 19 (1974), 22–44.
66. Carol Stoak Saunders, "The Strategic Contingencies Theory of Power: Multiple Perspectives," *Journal of Management Studies* 27 (1990), 1–18; Warren Boeker, "The Development and Institutionalization of Sub-Unit Power in Organizations," *Administrative Science Quarterly* 34 (1989), 388–510; and Irit Cohen and Ran Lachman, "The Generality of the Strategic Contingencies Approach to Sub-Unit Power," *Organizational Studies* 9 (1988), 371–391.
67. Emerson, "Power-Dependence Relations."
68. Pfeffer, *Managing with Power.*
69. J. Thompson, P.A. Baird, and J. Downie, "The Olivieri Case: Context and Significance," (December 2005) at http://www.ecclectica.ca/issues/2005/3/index.asp?Article=2 (accessed June 27, 2008).
70. J. Thompson, P.A. Baird, and J. Downie, "The Olivieri Case: Context and Significance,"
71. Jeffrey Pfeffer and Gerald Salancik, "Organizational Decision-Making as a Political Process: The Case of a University Budget," *Administrative Science Quarterly* (1974), 135–151.

72. Salancik and Pfeffer, "Bases and Use of Power in Organizational Decision-Making," 470.
73. Hickson et al., "A Strategic Contingencies Theory."
74. Pettigrew, *The Politics of Organizational Decision-Making.*
75. Hickson et al., "A Strategic Contingencies Theory."
76. Ibid.
77. Jeffrey Gantz and Victor V. Murray, "Experience of Workplace Politics," *Academy of Management Journal* 23 (1980), 237–251; and Dan L. Madison, Robert W. Allen, Lyman W. Porter, Patricia A. Renwick, and Bronston T. Mayes, "Organizational Politics: An Exploration of Managers' Perception," *Human Relations* 33 (1980), 79–100.
78. Gerald R. Ferris and K. Michele Kacmar, "Perceptions of Organizational Politics," *Journal of Management* 18 (1992), 93–116; Parmod Kumar and Rehana Ghadially, "Organizational Politics and Its Effects on Members of Organizations," *Human Relations* 42 (1989), 305–314; Donald J. Vredenburgh and John G. Maurer, "A Process Framework of Organizational Politics," *Human Relations* 37 (1984), 47–66; and Gerald R. Ferris, Dwight D. Frink, Maria Carmen Galang, Jing Zhou, Michele Kacmar, and Jack L. Howard, "Perceptions of Organizational Politics: Prediction, Stress-Related Implications, and Outcomes," *Human Relations* 49, no. 2 (1996), 233–266.
79. Ferris et al., "Perceptions of Organizational Politics: Prediction, Stress-Related Implications, and Outcomes"; John J. Voyer, "Coercive Organizational Politics and Organizational Outcomes: An Interpretive Study," *Organization Science* 5, no. 1 (February 1994), 72–85; and James W. Dean, Jr., and Mark P. Sharfman, "Does Decision Process Matter? A Study of Strategic Decision-Making Effectiveness," *Academy of Management Journal* 39, no. 2 (1996), 368–396.
80. Jeffrey Pfeffer, *Managing with Power: Politics and Influence in Organizations* (Boston, Mass.: Harvard Business School Press, 1992).
81. Amos Drory and Tsilia Romm, "The Definition of Organizational Politics: A Review," *Human Relations* 43 (1990), 1133–1154; and Vredenburgh and Maurer, "A Process Framework of Organizational Politics"; and Lafe Low, "It's Politics, As Usual," *CIO* (April 1, 2004), 87–90.
82. Pfeffer, *Power in Organizations*, 70.
83. Madison et al., "Organizational Politics"; Jay R. Galbraith, *Organizational Design* (Reading, Mass.: Addison-Wesley, 1977).
84. Gantz and Murray, "Experience of Workplace Politics"; Pfeffer, *Power in Organizations.*
85. "Prime Minister Chrétien Fires Paul Martin," at http://www.mapleleafweb.com/old/education/spotlight/issue_16/?q=education/spotlight/issue_16 (accessed October 7, 2007).
86. CBC.ca, "The Feud Boils Over," (June 2, 2004) at http://archives.cbc.ca/IDC-1-73-2148-13114/politics_economy/paul_martin/clip1 (accessed June 27, 2008).
87. S. Anderson, "Martin's Shadow PMO," *NOW Magazine Online Edition*, 21 (2002), 52.
88. "PM Says He Never Punished Liberals who Supported Paul Martin," (July 17, 2002) at http://www.cbc.ca/canada/story/2002/07/16liberals0 . . . (accessed October 7, 2007).
89. CBC.ca, "The Paul Martin Era Begins," (November 14, 2003) at http://archives.cbc.ca/IDC-1-73-2148-13115/politics_economy/paul_martin/clip1 (accessed June 27, 2008).
90. John Gray, "Whatever Became of Paul Martin?" (January 24, 2006) at http://www.cbc.ca/canadavotes/realitycheck/martin.html (accessed July 13, 2008).
91. Daniel J. Brass and Marlene E. Burkhardt, "Potential Power and Power Use: An Investigation of Structure and Behavior," *Academy of Management Journal* 38 (1993), 441–470.
92. Harvey G. Enns and Dean B. McFarlin, "When Executives Influence Peers, Does Function Matter?" *Human Resource Management* 4, no. 2 (Summer 2003), 125–142.
93. Hickson et al., "A Strategic Contingencies Theory."
94. Pfeffer, *Power in Organizations.*
95. Ibid.
96. V. Dallas Merrell, *Huddling: The Informal Way to Management Success* (New York: AMACON, 1979).
97. Ceasar Douglas and Anthony P. Ammeter, "An Examination of Leader Political Skill and Its Effect on Ratings of Leader Effectiveness," *The Leadership Quarterly* 15 (2004), 537–550.
98. Vredenburgh and Maurer, "A Process Framework of Organizational Politics."
99. Pfeffer, *Power in Organizations.*
100. Ibid.
101. Ann Davis and Randall Smith, "Merrill Switch: Popular Veteran Is In, Not Out," *The Wall Street Journal* (August 13, 2003), C1.
102. Pfeffer, *Power in Organizations.*
103. Ibid.
104. Kanter, "Power Failure in Management Circuits"; Pfeffer, *Power in Organizations.*
105. Ben Elgin, "Inside Yahoo!" *BusinessWeek* (May 21, 2001), 114–122.
106. Robert R. Blake and Jane S. Mouton, "Overcoming Group Warfare," *Harvard Business Review* (November–December 1984), 98–108.
107. Blake and Mouton, "Overcoming Group Warfare"; Paul R. Lawrence and Jay W. Lorsch, "New Management Job: The Integrator," *Harvard Business Review* 45 (November–December 1967), 142–151.
108. Canadian Pacific, "A Brief History," (n.d.) at http://www8.cpr.ca/cms/English/General+Public/Heritage/A+Brief+History.htm (accessed June 27, 2008).
109. D. Shenfield, A. Ponak, and B. Painter, "Beyond Collision: High Integrity Labour Relations—CPR Short-line Railway Case Study" (June 1, 2007) at http://www

.hrsdc.gc.ca/en/lp/wid/articles/article6.shtml (accessed June 27, 2008).

110. Ibid.

111. Aaron Bernstein, "Look Who's Pushing Productivity," *BusinessWeek* (April 7, 1997), 72–75.

112. Robert R. Blake, Herbert A. Shepard, and Jane S. Mouton, *Managing Intergroup Conflict in Industry* (Houston: Gulf Publishing, 1964); Doug Stewart, "Expand the Pie before You Divvy It Up," *Smithsonian* (November 1997), 78–90.

113. Suzanne Payette, "Innovative Practices in Collective Agreements" (Summer 2005) at http://www.hrsdc.gc.ca/en/lp/wid/win/presentation_2005.shtml (accessed June 27, 2008).

114. Patrick S. Nugent, "Managing Conflict: Third-Party Interventions for Managers," *Academy of Management Executive* 16, no. 1 (2002), 139–155.

115. Blake and Mouton, "Overcoming Group Warfare"; Schein, *Organizational Psychology*; Blake, Shepard, and Mouton, *Managing Intergroup Conflict in Industry*; and Richard E. Walton, *Interpersonal Peacemaking: Confrontation and Third-Party Consultations* (Reading, Mass.: Addison-Wesley, 1969).

116. Neilsen, "Understanding and Managing Intergroup Conflict"; McCann and Galbraith, "Interdepartmental Relations."

117. Neilsen, "Understanding and Managing Intergroup Conflict"; McCann and Galbraith, "Interdepartmental Relations"; Sherif et al., *Intergroup Conflict and Cooperation.*

118. Dean Tjosvold, Valerie Dann, and Choy Wong, "Managing Conflict between Departments to Serve Customers," *Human Relations* 45 (1992), 1035–1054.

Glossary

A

adaptability culture a culture characterized by strategic focus on the external environment through flexibility and change to meet customer needs (p. 340).

administrative principles a closed systems management perspective that focuses on the total organization and grows from the insights of practitioners (p. 25).

ambidextrous approach a characteristic of an organization that can behave in both an organic and a mechanistic way (p. 382).

analyzability a dimension of technology in which work activities can be reduced to mechanical steps and participants can follow an objective, computational procedure to solve problems (p. 247).

analyzer a business strategy that seeks to maintain a stable business while innovating on the periphery (p. 60).

authority a force for achieving desired outcomes that is prescribed by the formal hierarchy and reporting relationships (p. 481).

B

balanced scorecard a comprehensive management control system that balances traditional financial measures with operational measures relating to an organization's critical success factors (p. 276).

benchmarking process whereby companies find out how others do something better than they do and then try to imitate or improve on it (p. 275).

boundary spanning roles activities that link and coordinate an organization with key elements in the external environment (p. 142).

bounded rationality perspective how decisions are made when time is limited, a large number of internal and external factors affect a decision, and the problem is ill defined (p. 432).

buffering roles activities that absorb uncertainty from the environment (p. 142).

bureaucracy an organizational framework marked by rules and procedures, specialization and division of labour, hierarchy of authority, technically qualified personnel, separation of position and person, and written communications and records (p. 309).

bureaucratic control the use of rules, policies, hierarchy of authority, written documentation, standardization, and other bureaucratic mechanisms to standardize behaviour and assess performance (p. 315).

bureaucratic culture a culture that has an internal focus and a consistency orientation for a stable environment (p. 343).

bureaucratic organization a perspective that emphasizes management on an impersonal, rational basis through such elements as clearly defined authority and responsibility, formal recordkeeping, and uniform application of standard rules (p. 25).

business intelligence high-tech analysis of large amounts of internal and external data to identify patterns and relationships (p. 269).

C

Carnegie model organizational decision making involving many managers and a final choice based on a coalition among those managers (p. 442).

centrality a trait of a department whose role is in the primary activity of an organization (p. 487).

centralization to the level of hierarchy with authority to make decisions (p. 311).

centralized decision making is limited to higher authority (p. 87).

change process the way in which changes occur in an organization (p. 95).

change strategy a plan to guide an organizational change (p. 5).

chaos theory a scientific theory that suggests that relationships in complex, adaptive systems are made up of numerous interconnections that create unintended effects and render the environment unpredictable (p. 26).

charismatic authority based in devotion to the exemplary character or heroism of an individual and the order defined by him or her (p. 316).

chief ethics officer high-level company executive who oversees all aspects of ethics, including establishing and broadly communicating ethical standards, setting up ethics training programs, supervising the investigation of ethical problems, and advising managers in the ethical aspects of corporate decisions (p. 357).

clan control the use of social characteristics, such as corporate culture, shared values, commitments, traditions, and beliefs, to control behaviour (p. 317).

clan culture a culture that focuses primarily on the involvement and participation of the organization's members and on rapidly changing expectations from the external environment (p. 342).

closed system a system that is autonomous, enclosed, and not dependent on its environment (p. 13).

coalition an alliance among several managers who agree through bargaining about organizational goals and problem priorities (p. 442).

code of ethics a formal statement of the company's values concerning ethics and social responsibility (p. 358).

coercive forces external pressures such as legal requirements exerted on an organization to adopt structures, techniques, or behaviours similar to other organizations (p. 183).

collaborative network an emerging perspective whereby organizations allow themselves to become dependent on other organizations to increase value and productivity for all (p. 170).

collective bargaining the negotiation of an agreement between management and workers (p. 497).

collectivity stage the life-cycle phase in which an organization has strong leadership and begins to develop clear goals and direction (p. 304).

competing values approach a perspective on organizational effectiveness that combines diverse indicators of performance that represent competing management values (p. 69).

competition rivalry between groups in the pursuit of a common prize (p. 474).

confrontation a situation in which parties in conflict directly engage one another and try to work out their differences (p. 497).

consortia groups of firms that venture into new products and technologies (p. 200).

contextual dimensions traits that characterize the whole organization, including its size, technology, environment, and goals (p. 17).

contingency a theory meaning one thing depends on other things; the organization's situation dictates the correct management approach (p. 26).

contingency decision-making framework a perspective that brings together the two organizational dimensions of problem consensus and technical knowledge about solutions (p. 455).

continuous process production a completely mechanized manufacturing process in which there is no starting or stopping (p. 232).

cooptation when leaders from important sectors in the environment are made part of an organization (p. 152).

coping with uncertainty a source of power for a department that reduces uncertainty for other departments by obtaining prior information, prevention, and absorption (p. 488).

core technology the work process that is directly related to the organization's mission (p. 230).

craft technology technology characterized by a fairly stable stream of activities but in which the conversion process is not analyzable or well understood (p. 248)

creative departments organizational departments that initiate change, such as research and development, engineering, design, and systems analysis (p. 383).

creativity the generation of novel ideas that may meet perceived needs or respond to opportunities (p. 379).

culture the set of values, guiding beliefs, understandings, and ways of thinking that are shared by members of an organization and are taught to new members as correct (p. 335).

culture changes changes in the values, attitudes, expectations, beliefs, abilities, and behaviour of employees (p. 377).

culture strength the degree of agreement among members of an organization about the importance of specific values (p. 344).

customer relationship management systems that help companies track customer interactions with the firm and allow employees to call up a customer's past sales and service records, outstanding orders, or unresolved problems (p. 285).

D

data the input of a communication channel (p. 281).

data mining software that uses sophisticated decision-making processes to search raw data for patterns and relationships that may be significant (p. 269).

data warehousing the use of a huge database that combines all of an organization's data and allows users to access the data directly, create reports, and obtain answers to "what-if" questions (p. 269).

decentralized decision making and communication are spread out across the company (p. 87).

decision learning a process of recognizing and admitting mistakes that allows managers and organizations to acquire the experience and knowledge to perform more effectively in the future (p. 459).

decision premises constraining frames of reference and guidelines placed by top managers on decisions made at lower levels (p. 482).

decision support system a system that enables managers at all levels of the organization to retrieve, manipulate, and display information from integrated databases for making specific decisions (p. 271).

defender a business strategy that seeks stability or even retrenchment rather than innovation or growth (p. 60).

departmental grouping a structure in which employees share a common supervisor and resources, are jointly responsible for performance, and tend to identify and collaborate with each other (p. 95).

dependency one aspect of horizontal power: when one department is dependent on another, the latter is in a position of greater power (p. 486).

differentiation the cognitive and emotional differences among managers in various functional departments of an organization and formal structure differences among these departments (p. 144).

direct interlock a situation that occurs when a member of the board of directors of one company sits on the board of another (p. 152).

divisional grouping a grouping in which people are organized according to what the organization produces (p. 97).

divisional structure the structuring of the organization according to individual products, services, product groups, major projects, or profit centres; also called *product structure* or *strategic business units* (p. 99).

domain an organization's chosen environmental field of activity (p. 133).

domains of political activity areas in which politics plays a role. Three domains in organizations are structural change, management succession, and resource allocation (p. 490).

domestic stage the first stage of international development in which a company is domestically oriented while managers are aware of the global environment (p. 198).

downsizing intentionally reducing the size of a company's workforce by laying off employees (p. 322).

dual-core approach an organizational change perspective that identifies the unique processes associated with administrative change compared to those associated with technical change (p. 390).

E

e-business any business that takes place by digital processes over a computer network rather than in physical space (p. 286).

economies of scale achieving lower costs through large volume production; often made possible by global expansion (p. 197).

economies of scope achieving economies by having a presence in many product lines, technologies, or geographic areas (p. 197).

effectiveness the degree to which an organization achieves its goals (p. 21).

efficiency the amount of resources used to produce a unit of output (p. 21).

elaboration stage the organizational life cycle phase in which the red-tape crisis is resolved through the development of a new sense of teamwork and collaboration (p. 305).

engineering technology technology in which there is substantial variety in the tasks performed, but activities are usually handled on the basis of established formulas, procedures, and techniques (p. 249).

enterprise resource planning (ERP) sophisticated computerized systems that collect, process, and provide information about a company's entire enterprise, including order processing, product design, purchasing, inventory, manufacturing, distribution, human resources, receipt of payments, and forecasting of future demand (p. 279).

entrepreneurial stage the life-cycle phase in which an organization is born and its emphasis is on creating a product and surviving in the marketplace (p. 304).

escalating commitment persisting in a course of action when it is failing; occurs because managers block or distort negative information and because consistency and persistence are valued in contemporary society (p. 459).

ethical dilemma when each alternative choice or behaviour seems undesirable because of a potentially negative ethical consequence (p. 351).

ethics the code of moral principles and values that governs the behaviour of a person or group with respect to what is right or wrong (p. 348).

ethics committee a group of executives appointed to oversee company ethics (p. 357).

ethics hotline a telephone number that employees can call to seek guidance and to report questionable behaviour (p. 357).

executive information system (EIS) interactive systems that help top managers monitor and control organizational operations by processing and presenting data in usable form (p. 271).

explicit knowledge formal, systematic knowledge that can be codified, written down, and passed on to others in documents or general instructions (p. 281).

external adaptation the manner in which an organization meets goals and deals with outsiders (p. 336).

extranet private information network (p. 284).

F

factors of production supplies necessary for production, such as land, raw materials, and labour (p. 197).

feedback control model a control cycle that involves setting goals, establishing standards of performance, measuring actual performance and comparing it to standards, and changing activities as needed based on the feedback (p. 273).

financial resources control over money is an important source of power within an organization (p. 487).

flexible manufacturing systems (FMS) using computers to link manufacturing components such as robots, machines, product design, and engineering analysis to enable fast switching from one product to another (p. 236).

focus an organization's dominant perspective value, which may be internal or external (p. 70).

focus strategy a strategy in which an organization concentrates on a specific regional market or buyer group (p. 59).

formalization the degree to which an organization has rules, procedures, and written documentation (p. 311).

formalization stage the phase in an organization's life cycle involving the installation and use of rules, procedures, and control systems (p. 304).

functional grouping the placing together of employees who perform similar functions or work processes or who bring similar knowledge and skills to bear on a task (p. 97).

functional matrix a structure in which functional bosses have primary authority, and product or project managers simply coordinate product activities (p. 107).

functional structure the grouping of activities by common function (p. 97).

G

garbage can model model that describes the pattern or flow of multiple decisions within an organization (p. 449).

general environment includes those sectors that may not directly affect the daily operations of a firm but will indirectly influence it (p. 135).

generalist an organization that offers a broad range of products or services and serves a broad market (p. 178).

global company a company that no longer thinks of itself as having a home country (p. 199).

global geographical structure a form in which an organization divides its operations into world regions, each of which reports to the CEO (p. 205).

global matrix structure a form of horizontal linkage in an international organization in which both product and geographical structures are implemented simultaneously to achieve a balance between standardization and globalization (p. 207).

global product structure a form in which product divisions take responsibility for global operations in their specific product areas (p. 204).

global stage the stage of international development in which the company transcends any one country (p. 199).

global teams work groups comprising multinational members whose activities span multiple countries; also called *transnational teams* (p. 212).

globalization strategy the standardization of product design and advertising strategy throughout the world (p. 201).

goal approach an approach to organizational effectiveness that is concerned with output and whether the organization achieves its output goals (p. 65).

green environment our natural environment (p. 132).

H

Hawthorne Studies a series of experiments on worker productivity begun in 1924 at the Hawthorne plant of Western Electric Company in Illinois; attributed employees' increased output to managers' better treatment of them during the study (p. 25).

heroes organizational members who serve as models or ideals for serving cultural norms and values (p. 338).

high-velocity environments industries in which competitive and technological change is so extreme that market data are either unavailable or obsolete, strategic windows open and shut quickly, and the cost of a decision error is company failure (p. 457).

horizontal coordination model a model of the three components of organizational design needed to achieve new product innovation: departmental specialization, boundary spanning, and horizontal linkages (p. 387).

horizontal grouping the organizing of employees around core work processes rather than by function, product, or geography (p. 97).

horizontal linkage the amount of communication and coordination that occurs horizontally across organizational departments (p. 90).

horizontal structure a structure that virtually eliminates both the vertical hierarchy and departmental boundaries by organizing teams of employees around core work processes; the end-to-end work, information, and material flows that provide value directly to customers (p. 109).

human relations model emphasis on an aspect of the competing values model that incorporates the values of an internal focus and a flexible structure (p. 71).

hybrid structure a structure that combines characteristics of various structural approaches (functional, divisional, geographical, horizontal) tailored to specific strategic needs (p. 116).

I

idea champions organizational members who provide the time and energy to make things happen; sometimes called *advocates, intrapreneurs,* and *change agents* (p. 384).

idea incubator safe harbour where ideas from employees throughout the organization can be developed without interference from company bureaucracy or politics (p. 383).

imitation the adoption of a decision tried elsewhere in the hope that it will work in the present situation (p. 456).

incident command system developed to maintain the efficiency and control benefits of bureaucracy yet prevent the problems of slow response to crises (p. 312).

incremental change a series of continual progressions that maintain an organization's general equilibrium and often affects only one organizational part (p. 374).

incremental decision process model a model that describes the structured sequence of activities undertaken from the discovery of a problem to its solution (p. 444).

indirect interlock a situation that occurs when a director of one company and a director of another are both directors of a third company (p. 152).

information that which alters or reinforces understanding (p. 281).

information reporting systems the most common form of management information system, these computerized systems provide managers with reports that summarize data and support day-to-day decision making (p. 271).

inspiration an innovative, creative solution that is not reached by logical means (p. 456).

institutional environment norms and values from stakeholders (customers, investors, boards, government, etc.) that organizations try to follow in order to please stakeholders (p. 179).

institutional perspective an emerging view that holds that, under high uncertainty, organizations imitate others in the same institutional environment (p. 179).

institutional similarity the emergence of common structures, management approaches, and behaviours among organizations in the same field (p. 182).

integrated enterprise an organization that uses advanced information technology to enable close coordination within the company as well as with suppliers, customers, and partners (p. 284).

integration the quality of collaboration between departments of an organization (p. 145).

integrator a position or department created solely to coordinate several departments (p. 91).

intellectual capital the sum of an organization's knowledge, experience, understanding, processes, innovations, and discoveries (p. 280).

intensive technologies a variety of products or services provided in combination to a client (p. 254).

interdependence the extent to which departments depend on each other for resources or materials to accomplish their tasks (p. 252).

intergroup conflict behaviour that occurs between organizational groups when participants identify with one group and perceive that other groups may block their group's goal achievements or expectations (p. 474).

interlocking directorate a formal linkage that occurs when a member of the board of directors of one company sits on the board of another company (p. 152).

internal integration a state in which organization members develop a collective identity and know how to work together effectively (p. 336).

internal process approach an approach that looks at internal activities and assesses effectiveness by indicators of internal health and efficiency (p. 66).

internal process emphasis an aspect of the competing values model that reflects the values of internal focus and structural control (p. 71).

international division a division that is equal in status to other major departments within a company and has its own hierarchy to handle business in various countries (p. 203).

international stage the second stage of international development, in which the company takes exports seriously and begins to think multidomestically (p. 198).

interorganizational relationships the relatively enduring resource transactions, flows, and linkages that occur among two or more organizations (p. 165).

intranet a private, company-wide information network that uses the communications protocols and standards of the Internet but is accessible only to people within the company (p. 278).

intuitive decision making the use of experience and judgment rather than sequential logic or explicit reasoning to solve a problem (p. 436).

J

job design the assignment of goals and tasks to be accomplished by employees (p. 256).

job enlargement the designing of jobs to expand the number of different tasks performed by an employee (p. 257).

job enrichment the designing of jobs to increase responsibility, recognition, and opportunities for growth and achievement (p. 257).

job rotation moving employees from job to job to give them a greater variety of tasks and alleviate boredom (p. 257).

job simplification the reduction of the number and difficulty of tasks performed by a single person (p. 257).

joint optimization the goal of the sociotechnical systems approach, which states that an organization will function best only if its social and technical systems are designed to fit the needs of one another (p. 258).

joint venture a separate entity for sharing development and production costs and penetrating new markets that is created with two or more active firms as sponsors (p. 200).

K

knowledge a conclusion drawn from information that has been linked to other information and compared to what is already known (p. 281).

knowledge management the efforts to systematically find, organize, and make available a company's intellectual capital and to foster a culture of continuous learning and knowledge sharing so that organizational activities build on existing knowledge (p. 280).

L

labour-management teams teams designed to increase worker participation and to provide a cooperative model for addressing union-management issues (p. 497).

language slogans, sayings, metaphors, or other expressions that convey a special meaning to employees (p. 339).

large-batch production a manufacturing process characterized by long production runs of standardized parts (p. 232).

large-group intervention an approach that brings together participants from all parts of the organization (and may include outside stakeholders as well) to discuss problems or opportunities and plan for change (p. 395).

lean manufacturing uses highly trained employees at every stage of the production process who take a painstaking approach to details and continuous problem solving to cut waste and improve quality (p. 238).

learning organization an organization in which everyone is engaged in identifying and solving problems, enabling the organization to continuously experiment, improve, and increase its capability (p. 27).

legends stories of events based in history that may have been embellished with fictional details (p. 338).

legitimacy the general perspective that an organization's actions are desirable, proper, and appropriate within the environment's system of norms, values, and beliefs (p. 179).

level of analysis in systems theory, the subsystem on which the primary focus is placed; four levels of analysis normally characterize organizations (p. 31).

liaison role the function of a person located in one department who is responsible for communicating and achieving coordination with another department (p. 91).

life cycle a perspective on organizational growth and change that suggests that organizations are born, grow older, and eventually die (p. 302).

long-linked technology the combination within one organization of successive stages of production, with each stage using as its inputs the production of the preceding stage (p. 253).

low-cost leadership a strategy that tries to increase market share by emphasizing low cost when compared with competitors' products (p. 58).

M

management champion a manager who acts as a supporter and sponsor of a technical champion to shield and promote an idea within the organization (p. 385).

management control systems the formalized routines, reports, and procedures that use information to maintain or alter patterns in organizational activity (p. 273).

management information system a comprehensive, computerized system that provides information and supports day-to-day decision making (p. 270).

management science approach organizational decision making that is the analog to the rational approach by individual managers (p. 440).

managerial ethics principles that guide the decisions and behaviours of managers with regard to whether they are morally right or wrong (p. 350).

market control a situation that occurs when price competition is used to evaluate the output and productivity of an organization (p. 316).

mass customization the use of computer-integrated systems and flexible work processes to enable companies to mass produce a variety of products or services designed to exact customer specification (p. 239).

matrix structure a strong form of horizontal linkage in which both product and functional structures (horizontal and vertical) are implemented simultaneously (p. 104).

mechanistic an organization system marked by rules, procedures, a clear hierarchy of authority, and centralized decision making (p. 146).

mediating technology the provision of products or services that mediate or link clients from the external environment and allow each department to work independently (p. 253).

meso theory a new approach to organization studies that integrates both micro and macro levels of analysis (p. 32).

mimetic forces under conditions of uncertainty, the pressure to copy or model other organizations that appear to be successful in the environment (p. 182).

mission the organization's reason for its existence (p. 52).

mission culture a culture that places emphasis on a clear vision of the organization's purpose and on the achievement of specific goals (p. 341).

multidomestic company a company that deals with competitive issues in each country independent of other countries (p. 198).

multidomestic strategy competition in each country is handled independently of competition in other countries (p. 202).

multifocused grouping a structure in which an organization embraces structural grouping alternatives simultaneously (p. 97).

multinational stage the stage of international development in which a company has marketing and production facilities in many countries and more than one-third of its sales outside its home country (p. 199).

myths stories that are consistent with the values and beliefs of the organization but are not supported by facts (p. 338).

N

negotiation the bargaining process that often occurs during confrontation and enables the parties to systematically reach a solution (p. 497).

network centrality top managers increase their power by locating themselves centrally in an organization and surrounding themselves with loyal subordinates (p. 483).

networking linking computers within or between organizations (p. 278).

new-venture fund a fund that provides financial resources to employees to develop new ideas, products, or businesses (p. 384).

niche a domain of unique environmental resources and needs (p. 175).

non-core technology a department work process that is important to the organization but is not directly related to its central mission (p. 247).

nonprogrammed decisions novel and poorly defined, these are used when no procedure exists for solving the problem (p. 431).

nonroutine technology technology in which there is high task variety and the conversion process is not analyzable or well understood (p. 249).

nonsubstitutability a trait of a department whose function cannot be performed by other readily available resources (p. 488).

normative forces pressures to adopt structures, techniques, or management processes because they are considered by the community to be up to date and effective (p. 183).

O

official goals the formally stated definition of business scope and outcomes the organization is trying to achieve; another term for *mission* (p. 53).

open system a system that must interact with the environment to survive (p. 13).

open systems emphasis an aspect of the competing values model that reflects a combination of external focus and flexible structure (p. 71).

operative goals descriptions of the ends sought through the actual operating procedures of the organization; these explain what the organization is trying to accomplish (p. 54).

organic an organization system marked by free-flowing, adaptive processes, an unclear hierarchy of authority, and decentralized decision making (p. 146).

organization development a behavioural science field devoted to improving performance through trust, open confrontation of problems, employee empowerment and participation, the design of meaningful work, cooperation between groups, and the full use of human potential (p. 394).

organization structure designates formal reporting relationships, including the number of levels in the hierarchy and the span of control of managers and supervisors; identifies the grouping together of individuals into departments and of departments into the total organization; and includes the design of systems to ensure effective communication, coordination, and integration of efforts across departments (p. 86).

organization theory a macro approach to organizations that analyzes the whole organization as a unit (p. 32).

organizational behaviour a micro approach to organizations that focuses on the individuals within organizations as the relevant units for analysis (p. 32).

organizational change the adoption of a new idea or behaviour by an organization (p. 378).

organizational decision making the organizational process of identifying and solving problems (p. 430).

organizational decline a condition in which a substantial, absolute decrease in an organization's resource base occurs over a period of time (p. 319).

organizational ecosystem a system formed by the interaction of a community of organizations and their environment, usually cutting across traditional industry lines (p. 165).

organizational environment all elements that exist outside the boundary of the organization and have the potential to affect all or part of the organization (p. 132).

organizational form an organization's specific technology, structure, products, goals, and personnel (p. 175).

organizational goal a desired state of affairs that the organization attempts to reach (p. 50).

organizational innovation the adoption of an idea or behaviour that is new to an organization's industry, market, or general environment (p. 378).

organizational politics activities to acquire, develop, and use power and other resources to obtain one's preferred outcome when there is uncertainty or disagreement about choices (p. 489).

organizations social entities that are goal-directed, deliberately structured activity systems linked to the external environment (p. 9).

organized anarchy extremely organic organizations characterized by highly uncertain conditions (p. 450).

outsourcing contracting out certain corporate functions, such as manufacturing, information technology, or credit processing, to other companies (p. 114).

P

personnel ratios the proportions of administrative, clerical, and professional support staff (p. 311).

point–counterpoint a decision-making technique that divides decision makers into two groups and assigns them different, often competing responsibilities (p. 458).

political model a definition of an organization as being made up of groups that have separate interests, goals, and values in which power and influence are needed to reach decisions (p. 478).

political tactics for using power these include building coalitions, expanding networks, controlling decision premises, enhancing legitimacy and expertise, and making a direct appeal (p. 493).

pooled interdependence the lowest form of interdependence among departments, in which work does not flow between units (p. 252).

population a set of organizations engaged in similar activities with similar patterns of resource utilization and outcomes (p. 174).

population ecology perspective a perspective in which the focus is on organizational diversity and adaptation within a community or population or organizations (p. 174).

power the ability of one person or department in an organization to influence others to bring about desired outcomes (p. 479).

power distance the level of inequality people are willing to accept within an organization (p. 214).

power sources there are five sources of horizontal power in organizations: dependency, financial resources, centrality, nonsubstitutability, and the ability to cope with uncertainty (p. 486).

problem consensus the agreement among managers about the nature of problems or opportunities and about which goals and outcomes to pursue (p. 454).

problem identification the decision-making stage in which information about environmental and organizational conditions is monitored to determine if performance is satisfactory and to diagnose the cause of shortcomings (p. 430).

problem solution the decision-making stage in which alternative courses of action are considered and one alternative is selected and implemented (p. 430).

problemistic search when managers look around in the immediate environment for a solution to resolve a problem quickly (p. 443).

process organized group of related tasks and activities that work together to transform inputs into outputs that create value for customers (p. 109).

product and service changes changes in an organization's product or service outputs (p. 376).

product matrix a variation of the matrix structure in which project or product managers have primary authority, and functional managers simply assign technical personnel to projects and provide advisory expertise (p. 107).

programmed decisions repetitive and well-defined procedures that exist for resolving problems (p. 430).

prospector a business strategy characterized by innovation, risk taking, seeking out new opportunities, and growth (p. 60).

R

radical change a breaking of the frame of reference for an organization, often creating a new equilibrium because the entire organization is transformed (p. 374).

rational approach a process of decision making that stresses the need for systematic analysis of a problem followed by choice and implementation in a logical sequence (p. 432).

rational goal emphasis an aspect of the competing-values model that reflects values of structural control and external focus (p. 478).

rational-legal authority based on employees' belief in the legality of rules and the right of those in authority to issue commands (p. 71).

rational model a description of an organization characterized by a rational approach to decision making, extensive and reliable information systems, central power, a norm of optimization, uniform values across groups, little conflict, and an efficiency orientation (p. 316).

reactor a business strategy in which environmental threats and opportunities are responded to in an ad hoc fashion (p. 60).

reciprocal interdependence the highest level of interdependence, in which the output of one operation is the input of a second, and the output of the second operation is the input of the first (for example, a hospital) (p. 254).

re-engineering redesigning a vertical organization along its horizontal workflows and processes (p. 109).

resource dependence a situation in which organizations depend on the environment but strive to acquire control over resources to minimize their dependence (p. 149).

resource-based approach an organizational perspective that assesses effectiveness by observing how successfully the organization obtains, integrates, and manages valued resources (p. 66).

retention the preservation and institutionalization of selected organizational forms (p. 176).

rites and ceremonies the elaborate, planned activities that make up a special event and often are conducted for the benefit of an audience (p. 337).

role a part in a dynamic social system that allows an employee to use his or her discretion and ability to achieve outcomes and meet goals (p. 28).

routine technologies technologies characterized by little task variety and the use of objective, computational procedures (p. 248).

rule of law that which arises from a set of codified principles and regulations that describe how people are required to act, are generally accepted in society, and are enforceable in the courts (p. 349).

S

satisficing the acceptance by organizations of a satisfactory rather than a maximum level of performance (p. 443).

scientific management a classical approach that claims decisions about organization and job design should be based on precise, scientific procedures (p. 24).

sectors subdivisions of the external environment that contain similar elements (p. 133).

selection the process by which organizational variations are determined to fit the external environment; variations that fail to fit the needs of the environment are "selected out" and fail (p. 176).

sequential interdependence a serial form of interdependence in which the output of one operation becomes the input to another operation (p. 253).

service technology technology characterized by simultaneous production and consumption, customized output, customer participation, intangible output, and being labour intensive (p. 243).

simple-complex dimension the number and dissimilarity of external elements relevant to an organization's operation (p. 138).

Six Sigma quality standard that specifies a goal of no more than 3.4 defects per million parts; expanded to refer to a set of control procedures that emphasize the relentless pursuit of higher quality and lower costs (p. 275).

skunkworks separate, small, informal, highly autonomous, and often secretive group that focuses on breakthrough ideas for the business (p. 384).

small-batch production a manufacturing process, often custom work, that is not highly mechanized and relies heavily on the human operator (p. 232).

social audit measures and reports the ethical, social, and environmental impact of a company's operations (p. 361).

social capital the quality of interactions among people, affected by whether they share a common perspective (p. 334).

social responsibility management's obligation to make choices and take action so that the organization contributes to the welfare and interest of society as well as itself (p. 350).

sociotechnical systems approach an approach that combines the needs of people with the needs of technical efficiency (p. 257).

sources of intergroup conflict factors that generate conflict, including goal incompatibility, differentiation, task interdependence, and limited resources (p. 475).

specialist an organization that has a narrow range of goods or services or serves a narrow market (p. 178).

stable-unstable dimension the state of an organization's environmental elements (p. 138).

stakeholder any group within or outside an organization that has a stake in the organization's performance (p. 22).

stakeholder approach also called the *constituency approach,* this perspective assesses the satisfaction of stakeholders as an indicator of the organization's performance (p. 22).

standardization a policy that ensures all branches of the company at all locations operate in the same way (p. 201).

stories narratives based on true events that are frequently shared among organizational employees and told to new employees to inform them about an organization (p. 338).

strategic contingencies events and activities inside and outside an organization that are essential for attaining organizational goals (p. 485).

strategy the current set of plans, decisions, and objectives that have been adopted to achieve the organization's goals (p. 57).

strategy and structure changes changes in the administrative domain of an organization, including structure, policies, reward systems, labour relations, coordination devices, management information control systems, and accounting and budgeting (p. 377).

structural dimensions descriptions of the internal characteristics of an organization (p. 17).

structure the formal reporting relationships, groupings, and systems of an organization (p. 51).

struggle for existence a principle of the population ecology model that holds that organizations are engaged in a competitive struggle for resources and fighting to survive (p. 178).

subcultures cultures that develop within an organization to reflect the common problems, goals, and experiences that members of a team, department, or other unit share (p. 344).

subsystems divisions of an organization that perform specific functions for the organization's survival; organizational subsystems perform the essential functions of boundary spanning, production, maintenance, adaptation, and management (p. 14).

switching structures an organization creates an organic structure when such a structure is needed for the initiation of new ideas (p. 383).

symbol something that represents another thing (p. 338).

symptoms of structural deficiency signs of the organization structure being out of alignment, including delayed or poor-quality decision making, failure to respond innovatively to environmental changes, and too much conflict (p. 119).

system a set of interacting elements that acquires inputs from the environment, transforms them, and discharges outputs to the external environment (p. 14).

T

tacit knowledge knowledge that is based on personal experience, intuition, rules of thumb, and judgment, and cannot be easily codified and passed on to others in written form (p. 282).

tactics for enhancing collaboration techniques such as integration devices, confrontation and negotiation, intergroup consultation, member rotation, and shared mission and superordinate goals that enable groups to overcome differences and work together (p. 496).

tactics for increasing power these include entering areas of high uncertainty, creating dependencies, providing resources, and satisfying strategic contingencies (p. 491).

task a narrowly defined piece of work assigned to a person (p. 28).

task environment sectors with which the organization interacts directly and that have a direct effect on the organization's ability to achieve its goals (p. 133).

task force a temporary committee composed of representatives from each department affected by a problem (p. 91).

team building activities that promote the idea that people who work together can work together as a team (p. 395).

teams permanent task forces often used in conjunction with a full-time integrator (p. 93).

technical champion a person who generates or adopts and develops an idea for a technological innovation and is devoted to it, even to the extent of risking position or prestige; also called *product champion* (p. 385).

technical complexity the extent of mechanization in the manufacturing process (p. 232).

technical knowledge understanding and agreement about how to solve problems and reach organizational goals (p. 454).

technology the tools, techniques, and actions used to transform organizational inputs into outputs (p. 229).

technology changes changes in an organization's production process, including its knowledge and skills base, that enable distinctive competence (p. 377).

time-based competition delivering products and services faster than competitors, giving companies a competitive edge (p. 389).

traditional authority based in the belief in traditions and the legitimacy of the status of people exercising authority through those traditions (p. 316).

transaction processing systems (TPS) automation of the organization's routine, day-to-day business transactions (p. 268).

transnational model a form of horizontal organization that has multiple centres, subsidiary managers who initiate strategy and innovations for the company as a whole, and unity and coordination achieved through corporate culture and shared vision and values (p. 218).

U

uncertainty occurs when decision makers do not have sufficient information about environmental factors and have a difficult time predicting external changes (p. 138).

uncertainty avoidance the level of tolerance for and comfort with uncertainty and individualism within a culture (p. 214).

V

values-based leadership a relationship between a leader and followers that is based on strongly shared values that are advocated and acted upon by the leader (p. 355).

variation appearance of new organizational forms in response to the needs of the external environment; analogous to mutations in biology (p. 176).

variety in terms of tasks, the frequency of unexpected and novel events that occur in the conversion process (p. 247).

venture teams a technique to foster creativity within organizations in which a small team is set up as its own company to pursue innovations (p. 384).

vertical information system the periodic reports, written information, and computer-based communications distributed to managers (p. 89).

vertical linkages communication and coordination activities connecting the top and bottom of an organization (p. 89).

virtual cross-functional teams teams comprised of individuals from different functions who are separated in space and time as well (p. 93)

virtual network grouping organization that is a loosely connected cluster of separate components (p. 97).

virtual network structure the firm subcontracts many or most of its major processes to separate companies and coordinates their activities from a small headquarters organization (p. 114).

virtual team made up of organizationally or geographically dispersed members who are linked through advanced information and communications technologies. Members frequently use the Internet and collaborative software to work together, rather than meeting face to face (p. 93).

W

whistle-blowing employee disclosure of illegal, immoral, or illegitimate practices on the part of the organization (p. 357).

wiki web page that can be modified by readers (p. 280).

Name Index

Page numbers followed by the letter n indicate the note in which the entry is located.

L

M

N

O

P

Q

R

S

T

Organization Name Index

D

E

F

G

X

Y

Z

Subject Index

D

E

P

Q

R

S